iGAAP 2014

A guide to IFRS reporting

Seventh edition

VOLUME A
PART 1

Principal authors

Norma Hall
Phil Barden
Veronica Poole

Deloitte.

Deloitte refers to one or more of Deloitte Touche Tohmatsu Limited ("DTTL"), a UK private company limited by guarantee, and its network of member firms, each of which is a legally separate and independent entity. Please see www.deloitte.co.uk/about for a detailed description of the legal structure of DTTL and its member firms.

© 2013 Deloitte Touche Tohmatsu Limited

International Accounting Standards Board Material:
Extracts from International Financial Reporting Standards, International Accounting Standards and Exposure Drafts are reproduced with the permission of the IFRS Foundation.

Published by LexisNexis, a Division of Reed Elsevier (UK) Ltd, Lexis House, 30 Farringdon Street, London EC4A 4HH, and London House, 20–22 East London Street, Edinburgh EH7 4BQ

ISBN 978 0 7545 4784 6

This publication contains general information only and is not intended to be comprehensive nor to provide specific accounting, business, financial, investment, legal, tax or other professional advice or services. This publication is not a substitute for such professional advice or services, and it should not be acted on or relied upon or used as a basis for any decision or action that may affect you or your business. Before making any decision or taking any action that may affect you or your business, you should consult a qualified professional advisor.

Whilst every effort has been made to ensure the accuracy of the information contained in this publication, this cannot be guaranteed, and neither Deloitte Touche Tohmatsu Limited nor any related entity shall have any liability to any person or entity that relies on the information contained in this publication. Any such reliance is solely at the user's risk.

Views expressed in this publication are the authors' and are not necessarily those of their firm.

No responsibility for loss occasioned to any person acting or refraining from action as a result of any material in this publication can be accepted by the authors or publisher.

British Library Cataloguing-in-Publication Data

A catalogue record of this book is available from the British Library.

Typeset by Letterpart Limited, Caterham on the Hill, Surrey CR3 5XL

Printed and bound by CPI Group (UK) Ltd, Croydon, CR0 4YY

Foreword by Veronica Poole

Looking back at 2013, entities were focused on implementing several new and significantly amended IFRSs, each of which presented unique challenges. Most notable were the issues raised by IFRS 13 *Fair Value Measurement*, especially when measuring illiquid investments and identifying the unit of account, and the considerable acumen required to apply IFRS 10 *Consolidated Financial Statements* in complex scenarios. The challenge that caught many entities unaware was the transition from IAS 31 to IFRS 11 *Joint Arrangements*, which proved to be more problematic than first expected; 'joint venture' versus 'joint operation' is a distinction that we will be grappling with for some time.

2013 also saw the IASB continue its work on four major projects although, regrettably, none of these has yet been finalised. In the area of financial instruments, the complexities of loan impairment refused to yield to the efforts of the IASB and FASB to develop an operational Standard that also achieved convergence. Despite their sustained endeavours, significant differences remain, and the boards are now doubtful that complete convergence can be achieved. The response to exposure drafts on Leases and Insurance Contracts has demonstrated that these proposals remain controversial and we are not yet in a position to predict the final outcome of these projects with any accuracy. Closest to completion is the new IFRS on Revenue. This Standard will govern the 'top line' of every income statement and, for some entities, will result in significant changes to that key area of investor focus. The good news is that it will be fully converged with US GAAP and will increase substantially the guidance on revenue recognition in IFRSs.

Looking ahead to 2014, the IASB will be able to concentrate on areas identified as a result of its Agenda Consultation in 2011. Indeed, it has already begun to do so by opening discussions on its Conceptual Framework and on the effects of rate regulation.

The Board has also started work on a disclosure framework. Its disclosure forum in early 2013 brought together preparers, users, auditors and regulators to discuss the problems of disclosure overload and suggest possible actions. The IASB's work on disclosure aims to cut clutter and boilerplate and enable entities to identify clearly, and users to find more easily, the information most critical to the assessment of the financial condition, performance and cash flows of the entity.

A significant development in the IASB's consultative procedures during 2013 was the establishment of the Accounting Standards Advisory Forum, bringing together eight national standard-setters and four regional bodies from around the world. It is hoped that the Forum will assist the IASB to identify operational challenges early and improve Standards before they are issued.

Away from standard-setting, the focus has been on the role of financial statements in the wider context of how entities can communicate more effectively with shareholders and other stakeholders. In particular, the draft Framework published by the International Integrated Reporting Council (IIRC) proposed how an entity might bring together its financial information with information already produced on topics as diverse as environmental impact and social responsibility to show how the entity creates value and the resources it uses in the process.

Financial accounting and reporting remain at the heart of entities' communication with stakeholders, and particularly investors. The developments we have seen in 2013, from the IASB, the IIRC and regulators, as well as the work planned for 2014 and beyond, should help to improve the clarity of that communication. The core objective is simple – entities need to be able to explain their financial results in a coherent way and link the primary financial statements, relevant detail in the notes and the management commentary as a single continuous narrative. Clear, concise, high-quality financial reporting is what we aim to encourage as we share our knowledge and experience in this book.

Veronica Poole

Global IFRS Leader
Deloitte Touche Tohmatsu Limited

October 2013

Acknowledgements

Our thanks to the members of the UK technical department and Deloitte's Global IFRS Leadership Team for their assistance in writing, reviewing and otherwise contributing to this book.

Glossary of terms and abbreviations

AC	Acquiring company
AFS	Available-for-sale
ARC	The Accounting Regulatory Committee which advises the European Commission on endorsement of IFRSs
ASC	Accounting Standards Codification, issued by the FASB
BAC	Japan's Business Accounting Council
CESR	The former Committee of European Securities Regulators (replaced by ESMA from 1 January 2011)
CGU	Cash-generating unit
Commission	European Commission
CU	Currency Unit
EBT	Employee benefit trust
EC	European Commission
ED	Exposure draft
EEA	European Economic Area (i.e. the EU plus Norway, Iceland and Liechtenstein)
EFRAG	The European Financial Reporting Advisory Group, a private sector body which makes recommendations to the European Commission's Accounting Regulatory Committee
EIR	Effective interest rate
EPS	Earnings per share
ESOP	Employee share ownership plan
ESMA	European Securities and Markets Authority
EU	European Union
FASB	Financial Accounting Standards Board (USA)
FIFO	First in, first out
FSA	Financial Services Agency (Japan)
FTSE 100	Financial Times Stock Exchange top 100 companies (share index)
FVTOCI	Fair value through other comprehensive income
FVTPL	Fair value through profit or loss
GAAP	Generally accepted accounting practice

Glossary of terms and abbreviations

HTM	Held-to-maturity
IAS	International Accounting Standard
IASB	International Accounting Standards Board
IASC	International Accounting Standards Committee, predecessor to the IASB
IFRIC	The former International Financial Reporting Interpretations Committee of the IASB, now renamed the IFRS Interpretations Committee (also refers to individual interpretations issued by the Committee)
IFRS	International Financial Reporting Standard
Individual financial statements	See the guidance at **2.2** in **chapter A4**
IOSCO	International Organization of Securities Commissions
IRR	Internal rate of return
JCE	Jointly controlled entity
JV	Joint venture
LIBOR	London Inter-Bank Offer Rate
LIFO	Last in, first out
LTIP	Long-term incentive plan
MFR	Minimum funding requirement
MOU	Memorandum of Understanding
NASDAQ	National Association of Securities Dealers Automated Quotation System (a US securities market)
NCI	Non-controlling interest
NRV	Net realisable value
OCI	Other comprehensive income
ROI	Return on investment
RPI	Retail price index
SAC	Standards Advisory Council
SARG	Standards Advisory Review Group, established by the European Commission to review endorsement advice from EFRAG
SAYE	Save as you earn
SEC	Securities and Exchange Commission (USA)
Separate financial statements	See the definition and explanations in **section 3** of **chapter A29** or in **section 6** of **appendix A1**
SFAS	Statement of Financial Accounting Standards, issued by the FASB, now codified (see ASC above)

SIC	Standing Interpretations Committee, predecessor to IFRIC (also refers to individual interpretations issued by SIC)
SME(s)	Small and medium-sized entity(ies)
SPE	Special purpose entity
TC	Target company
TSR	Total shareholder return
VAT	Value added tax
WEEE	Waste electrical and electronic equipment
WE&EE Directive	The European Union's Directive on Waste Electrical and Electronic Equipment

Table of Contents

Introduction

1 Scope and objectives of this manual

The objective of this manual is to introduce and explain the financial reporting requirements under International Financial Reporting Standards (IFRSs). As explained in **section 3** below, IFRSs are defined to include the numbered IFRSs issued by the International Accounting Standards Board (IASB), International Accounting Standards (IASs) originally issued by its predecessor body (as amended) and approved Interpretations of these Standards. The expression is used in this broad sense in this manual unless the context requires otherwise.

2 Structure of this manual

The structure of this manual is as follows:

- **chapter A1** provides background information on the IASB and on the application of IFRSs globally;

- **chapters A2** to **A41** and **appendices A1** to **A3** deal with the framework and Standards issued by the IASB and Interpretations of those Standards, and **appendix A4** deals with the International Financial Reporting Standard for Small and Medium-sized Entities (IFRS for SMEs);

- **Volume B** deals with accounting for financial instruments for entities that have adopted IFRS 9 *Financial Instruments*. It covers IAS 32 *Financial Instruments: Presentation*, IAS 39 *Financial Instruments: Recognition and Measurement* (as amended by IFRS 9), IFRS 7 *Financial Instruments: Disclosures* and IFRS 9; and

- **Volume C** deals with accounting for financial instruments for entities that have not yet adopted IFRS 9. It covers IAS 32, IAS 39 (prior to amendment by IFRS 9) and IFRS 7.

Transition requirements are discussed for Standards that have become effective for periods beginning on or after 1 January 2012. In addition, when IFRS 1 *First-time Adoption of International Financial Reporting Standards* requires compliance with the transition requirements in Standards, the relevant requirements are explained.

The format of the manual has been devised to give guidance on reporting and accounting matters as clearly as possible. Text is highlighted differently to reflect whether it represents official or interpretative material. Accordingly:

- requirements drawn from official IASB material are shown in unshaded text; and

- interpretative material supplementing the IASB guidance is highlighted by grey shading.

Except when the context requires otherwise, interpretative examples follow the convention often adopted by the IASB of referring to years as 20X1, 20X2 etc. rather than specifying real calendar years. In such examples, although 20X3 follows 20X2, no further significance attaches to the final digit. Thus, subject to context, 20X1 might represent 2013 or any other relevant year.

3 References and abbreviations used

International Financial Reporting Standards are defined in IAS 1 *Presentation of Financial Statements* as Standards and Interpretations adopted by the IASB. They comprise:

- International Financial Reporting Standards;

- International Accounting Standards;

- IFRIC Interpretations; and

- SIC Interpretations.

These are referred to collectively in this manual as 'IFRSs'.

References to International Financial Reporting Standards, International Accounting Standards, IFRIC Interpretations and SIC Interpretations are indicated as follows:

IFRS 2:19	Paragraph 19 of IFRS 2
IFRS 9(2010):5.4.3	Paragraph 5.4.3 of IFRS 9 (as issued in 2010)
IAS 19(2011):13	Paragraph 13 of IAS 19 (as revised in 2011)
IFRIC 1:2	Paragraph 2 of IFRIC Interpretation 1
SIC-27:3	Paragraph 3 of SIC Interpretation 27

Unless otherwise stated, all references to 'IFRS 9' are to IFRS 9 as issued in 2010.

References to material accompanying International Financial Reporting Standards, International Accounting Standards, IFRIC Interpretations and SIC Interpretations are indicated as follows:

IAS 39:AG4	Paragraph AG4 of the application guidance to IAS 39
IFRS 2:B18	Paragraph B18 of Appendix B to IFRS 2
IFRIC 13:BC21	Paragraph BC21 of the Basis for Conclusions on IFRIC 13
IFRS 4:IG3	Paragraph IG3 of the guidance on implementing IFRS 4
IAS 32:IE32	Paragraph IE32 of the illustrative examples accompanying IAS 32
CF:OB10	Paragraph OB10 of the *Conceptual Framework for Financial Reporting*
MC:13	Paragraph 13 of the IFRS Practice Statement *Management Commentary*

A glossary of abbreviations used in the text is presented at the front of this manual.

4   Contents of this edition

This edition of the manual includes the reporting and accounting requirements contained in:

- IFRSs 1 to 13;

- IASs 1, 2, 7, 8, 10 to 12, 16 to 21, 23, 24, 26 to 29, 31 to 34 and 36 to 41;

- SIC Interpretations 7, 10, 12, 13, 15, 21, 25, 27, 29, 31 and 32; and

- IFRIC Interpretations 1 to 21 (excluding 3 which was withdrawn, and 8 and 11 which have been superseded).

4.1   Specialised industries

This manual does not deal with certain requirements and issues that will affect entities in specialised industries, particularly banking and insurance. In particular, although **Volumes B** and **C** provide an overview of the requirements of IAS 32 *Financial Instruments: Presentation*, IAS 39 *Financial Instruments: Recognition and Measurement*, IFRS 7 *Financial Instruments: Disclosures* and IFRS 9 *Financial Instruments*, they do not address some of the more complex issues (particularly in the area of hedging) that may affect banks and similar financial institutions.

Introduction

The specialised issues facing insurance companies are beyond the scope of this manual but the requirements of IFRS 4 *Insurance Contracts* are discussed in **chapter A39**. Those requirements are of wider application, because they specify how all entities should determine whether certain arrangements are within the scope of IFRS 4 or of other Standards such as IAS 39 or IFRS 9.

A1 About International Financial Reporting Standards

Contents

1   Introduction

This chapter provides a brief introduction to the IFRS reporting regime.

2   History

2.1   IASC (1973 – 2000)

The International Accounting Standards Committee (IASC) was established in 1973, through an agreement made by professional accountancy bodies from Australia, Canada, France, Germany, Japan, Mexico, the Netherlands, the United Kingdom and Ireland, and the United States of America. Its goal was to develop, in the public interest, accounting standards that would be accepted all over the world to improve financial reporting. By 2000, sponsorship of the IASC had grown to include all of the professional accountancy bodies that were members of the International Federation of Accountants (IFAC) – 152 organisations from 112 countries. However, even after nearly 30 years of effort, few countries had actually adopted the IASC's standards even for listed companies.

Until 2001, accounting standards were set by a part-time, volunteer IASC Board that, in its later years, had 13 country members and three additional organisational members. The individuals came from a wide range of backgrounds – accounting practice, business (particularly multinational businesses), financial analysis, accounting education and national accounting standard-setting. The Board also had a number of observer members (including representatives of the International Organization of Securities Commissions (IOSCO), the US Financial Accounting Standards Board and the European Commission) who participated in the debate but did not vote.

From 1997, the IASC also had an interpretative body, the Standing Interpretations Committee (SIC), formed for the purpose of developing interpretations of International Accounting Standards (IASs) for final approval by the IASC.

2.2   IASB

In 1997, the IASC concluded that, to continue to perform its role effectively, it should find a way to bring about convergence between national accounting standards and practices and to develop high quality global accounting standards. To achieve that objective, the organisation was restructured, replacing the part-time IASC with a full-time International

Accounting Standards Board (IASB), with strengthened due process, greater resources, complete independence and other structural changes.

The IASC Foundation constitution took effect on 1 July 2000. On 1 April 2001, the IASB assumed accounting standard-setting responsibilities. On 1 July 2010, the IASC Foundation was re-named the IFRS Foundation.

3   IASB structure

The principal body within the IFRS Foundation is the IASB (the Board), which has sole responsibility for establishing International Financial Reporting Standards (IFRSs). Other components of the structure are the Trustees of the IFRS Foundation, a Monitoring Board of capital market regulatory authorities that oversees the Foundation, the IFRS Interpretations Committee (the Interpretations Committee) and the IFRS Advisory Council (the Advisory Council).

The overall structure is illustrated below.

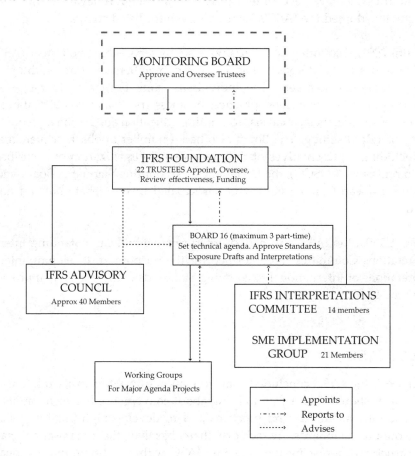

3.1 Monitoring Board

The Monitoring Board provides a mechanism for formal interaction between capital markets authorities responsible for the form and content of financial reporting and the IFRS Foundation. In particular, it assures public accountability of the IFRS Foundation through a formal reporting line from the IFRS Foundation Trustees to the Monitoring Board.

The responsibilities of the Monitoring Board include:

- participating in the process for appointing Trustees and approving the appointment of Trustees according to the guidelines set out in the IFRS Foundation constitution;

- reviewing the adequacy and appropriateness of Trustee arrangements for financing the IASB;

- reviewing the Trustees' oversight of the IASB's standard-setting process, in particular with respect to its due process arrangements;

- conferring with the Trustees regarding their responsibilities, particularly in relation to the regulatory, legal and policy developments that are pertinent to the IFRS Foundation's oversight of the IASB; and

- referring matters of broad public interest related to financial reporting to the IASB through the IFRS Foundation.

As at 30 June 2013, the Monitoring Board comprised the relevant Member of the European Commission, and the chairs of the Financial Services Agency of Japan, the US Securities and Exchange Commission (SEC), the Emerging Markets Committee of IOSCO, and the Chair of the IOSCO Board. The Basel Committee on Banking Supervision is a non-voting observer.

In May 2013, the Monitoring Board commenced a process to appoint up to a further four members. Prospective members must be a capital markets authority responsible for setting the form and content of financial reporting in its jurisdiction, and meet specified requirements about the use of IFRSs in that jurisdiction and continuing participation in the IFRS Foundation's funding arrangements.

3.2 IFRS Foundation

The governance of the IFRS Foundation rests with its 22 Trustees. Their geographical mix is six Trustees from the Asia/Oceania region, six from Europe, six from North America, and four from any area (subject to

maintaining overall geographical balance). The IFRS Foundation's constitution requires an appropriate balance of professional backgrounds,
including auditors, preparers, users, academics, and other officials serving
the public interest.

Between 2008 and 2012, the Trustees undertook a series of reviews of the
structure, constitution and governance of the IFRS Foundation. Changes
have been made with a view to strengthening all aspects of the IFRS
Foundation's institutional structures to ensure that it acts as a truly global
accounting standard setter, independent yet accountable to public authorities (via the Monitoring Board).

3.3   International Accounting Standards Board

The IASB is the body responsible for establishing IFRSs.

The Board has 16 members (of whom up to three may serve 'part-time'
although, at the time of writing, all members serve on a full-time basis).
The Board's principal responsibilities are to:

- develop and issue IFRSs in accordance with its established due
  process; and

- approve Interpretations developed by the IFRS Interpretations Committee (the Interpretations Committee).

The key qualification for Board membership is professional competence
and practical experience. The group is required to represent the best
available combination of technical expertise and diversity of international
business and market experience. To achieve a balance of perspectives and
experience, Board members are required to have an appropriate mix of
recent practical experience among auditors, preparers, users and academics.

The Board is required to be internationally diverse: there will normally be
four members from the Asia/Oceania region; four from Europe; four from
North America; one each from Africa and South America; and two
appointed from any area, subject to maintaining overall geographical
balance.

3.4   IFRS Advisory Council

The Advisory Council is the formal advisory body to the IASB and the
IFRS Foundation Trustees, and it provides a forum for a wide range of
representatives from user groups, preparers, financial analysts, academics,

auditors, regulators, professional accounting bodies and investor groups that are affected by and interested in the IASB's work. The Advisory Council provides advice on a wide range of issues, including:

- input on the IASB's agenda;

- input on the IASB's work programme including project priorities, and consultation on any changes in agenda and priorities; and

- advice on projects, with particular emphasis on practical application and implementation issues, including matters relating to existing Standards that may warrant consideration by the Interpretations Committee.

3.5   IFRS Interpretations Committee

The Interpretations Committee (previously referred to as the 'IFRIC') has 14 voting members appointed by the Trustees for terms of three years. Like the IASB, the Interpretations Committee comprises the best available combination of technical expertise and diversity of international business and market experience, but with the added requirement that they be experienced in the practical application of IFRSs and analysis of financial statements prepared in accordance with IFRSs. The Interpretations Committee assists the IASB in improving financial reporting through timely identification, discussion and resolution of financial reporting issues within the IFRS framework. The Interpretations Committee's responsibilities are to:

- interpret the application of IFRSs and provide timely guidance on financial reporting issues not specifically addressed in IFRSs in the context of the IASB's *Conceptual Framework for Financial Reporting* in accordance with established due process, and to undertake other tasks at the request of the Board (including responsibility for the Annual Improvements process); and

- report to the Board and obtain Board approval for final Interpretations.

Following completion in 2012 of a review of the efficiency and effectiveness of the Interpretations Committee undertaken by the IFRS Foundation, the Committee has available to it a wider range of possible actions to respond to issues referred to it:

- enhancing mandatory requirements (new or revised requirements within IFRSs); and

- providing non-mandatory guidance.

The mandatory requirements can include:

- IFRIC Interpretations; and

- amendments to Standards through:

  - the Annual Improvements process; or

  - proposals to the IASB for targeted, narrow-scope amendments that are beyond the scope of the Annual Improvements process. These might include proposals for additional application guidance.

Non-mandatory solutions that the Interpretations Committee can use to address issues include:

- proposals for additional illustrative examples;

- explanations via rejection notices; and

- referral to the IFRS Education Initiative.

4   Use of IFRSs around the world

The following sections provide a brief review of IFRS application on a regional basis. IFRSs are used by listed entities in over 120 countries, and by unlisted entities in over 90 countries. The IFRS Foundation has compiled detailed information on the use of IFRSs around the world. Information on over 60 countries is available at *www.ifrs.org*. In addition, a detailed country-by-country list of the status of adoption of IFRSs for most countries is available at *www.iasplus.com*.

4.1   Use of IFRSs in Europe

Since 2005, European Union (EU) and European Economic Area (EEA) companies listed on a regulated market have been required to follow IFRSs in their consolidated financial statements.

The IFRS requirement applies not only in the 28 EU countries but also in the three EEA countries. Most large companies in Switzerland (not an EU or EEA member) already used IFRSs prior to 2005.

For the purpose of filings by non-EU companies listed on an EU-regulated market, the European Commission (EC) has designated the GAAPs of the United States, Japan, China, South Korea and India to be equivalent to IFRSs as adopted by the EU. Companies from other countries must use either IFRSs as adopted by the EU or IFRSs as adopted by the IASB.

EU Member States may also extend the IFRS requirement to non-listed companies and to separate (i.e. 'company-only') financial statements. Nearly all Member States permit some or all non-listed companies to use IFRSs in their consolidated statements and the majority permit it in separate financial statements.

4.1.1   Endorsement of IFRSs for use in Europe

IFRSs must be individually endorsed for use in Europe because the IASB has no legislative powers within the EU. The endorsement process involves the following steps:

- the EU translates the IFRSs into all European languages;

- the private-sector European Financial Reporting Advisory Group (EFRAG) gives its endorsement advice to the EC;

- the EC's Accounting Regulatory Committee makes an endorsement recommendation; and

- the EC submits the endorsement proposal to the European Parliament and to the 28-member Council of the EU. Both must not oppose (or, in specified circumstances, approve) endorsement within three months, otherwise the proposal is sent back to the EC for further consideration.

The process also allows for amending the IASB version of IFRSs. Currently, only one such amendment ('carve-out') exists, which allows the use of fair value hedge accounting for interest rate hedges of banks' core deposits on a portfolio basis.

4.2   Use of IFRSs in the Americas

4.2.1   Use of IFRSs in the United States

4.2.1.1   IFRS-US GAAP convergence

For the past several years, the IASB and the US Financial Accounting Standards Board (FASB) have been working together to achieve convergence of IFRSs and US GAAP. In 2002, as part of the Norwalk agreement, the boards issued a Memorandum of Understanding (MOU) formalising their commitment to:

- making their existing financial reporting standards fully compatible as soon as practicable; and

- co-ordinating their future work programmes to ensure that, once achieved, compatibility is maintained.

In September 2008, an updated MOU was published, which set out priorities and milestones to be achieved on major joint projects. The final milestones for most of these projects are expected to be achieved by the end of 2013 (see *www.iasplus.com* for more detail, including the most up-to-date programme).

4.2.1.2   SEC recognition of IFRSs

Of the approximately 12,000 companies whose securities are registered with the US Securities and Exchange Commission (SEC), about 950 are non-US companies. Prior to November 2007, if these foreign private issuers submitted IFRS or local GAAP financial statements rather than US GAAP, a reconciliation of net income and net assets to US GAAP was required.

Since November 2007, the SEC has permitted foreign private issuers to submit financial statements using IFRSs as issued by the IASB without having to include a reconciliation to US GAAP.

4.2.1.3   Recent regulatory developments

The SEC has been exploring whether and, if so, how to incorporate IFRSs into the financial reporting system for US domestic issuers. The SEC issued several consultation documents, including a *Concept Release* (August 2007), and a proposed IFRS 'roadmap' (November 2008). In February 2010, the SEC published a *Statement in Support of Convergence and Global Accounting Standards* in which it directed its staff to develop and execute a 'Work Plan' with a view to enabling the SEC to make a decision regarding incorporating IFRSs into the financial reporting system for US issuers. As part of that Work Plan, the SEC issued further staff papers: *A Possible Method of Incorporation* (May 2011); *Comparison of US GAAP and IFRS*; and *An analysis of IFRS Practice* (both November 2011).

In July 2012, the SEC issued their final staff report *Work Plan for the Consideration of Incorporating International Financial Reporting Standards into the Financial Reporting System for U.S. Issuers*. The final report did not include a recommendation to the Commission. At the time of writing, the SEC has not signalled when it might make a policy decision about whether (and, if so, when and how) IFRSs should be incorporated into the US financial reporting system.

4.2.2   Use of IFRSs in Canada

Canada adopted IFRSs for most 'publicly accountable enterprises' for financial years beginning on or after 1 January 2011.

Publicly accountable enterprises are entities, other than not-for-profit organisations, that have issued, or are in the process of issuing, debt or equity instruments that are, or will be, outstanding and traded in a public market or hold assets in a fiduciary capacity for a broad group of outsiders as one of their primary businesses.

Mandatory adoption of IFRSs has been deferred for investment companies and segregated accounts of life insurance enterprises until 2014 and for entities with rate-regulated activities until 2015. Those deferrals were provided to give time for the IASB to complete projects affecting those entities.

4.2.3   Use of IFRSs elsewhere in the Americas

Nearly all countries in South America require or permit IFRSs as the basis for preparing financial statements (or are in the process of introducing such requirements). Argentina adopted IFRSs for all companies from 2012 (except banks and insurance companies which continue to apply domestic requirements). Brazil adopted IFRSs for all listed companies and banks effective 2010. Chile adopted IFRSs for all public interest companies in 2012, completing a phased adoption of IFRSs that began in 2009. Mexico has adopted IFRSs for all listed entities other than banks and insurance companies which apply Mexican Financial Reporting Standards (MFRSs). A convergence project is underway to eliminate differences between MFRSs and IFRSs. IFRSs are already required in a number of other Latin American and Caribbean countries.

4.3   Use of IFRSs in Asia-Pacific

4.3.1   Use of IFRSs in Japan

Under Cabinet Office Ordinances published by the Financial Services Agency of Japan (FSA) in December 2009 and effective for fiscal years ending on or after 31 March 2010, listed companies whose financial or operational activities are conducted internationally are permitted to pre-pare their consolidated financial statements using IFRSs.

The FSA operates a process called 'designation' to endorse IFRSs for use in Japan. At the time of writing, all IFRSs issued by the IASB up to June 2013 (including IFRIC Interpretations) have been designated for use in Japan. Accordingly, designated IFRSs in Japan are identical to IFRSs as issued by the IASB.

At the time of writing (July 2013), there are draft proposals that would permit considerable expansion of the use of IFRSs by Japanese listed

companies and groups, such that by 2016 at least 300 Japanese international companies would use IFRSs. Such a move would, it is argued,
demonstrate a tangible step towards the G20's ambition of developing a
"single set of high quality global accounting standards". In addition, it
would permit Japan to claim "prominent application of IFRSs" in Japan
which is one of the membership criteria for the Monitoring Board.

In 2012, the IFRS Foundation opened a satellite office in Tokyo for
enhanced liaison in the Asia-Oceania region. The establishment of the
Tokyo office allows for expanded opportunities for direct contact for the
Foundation and its stakeholders in the region. It is anticipated that the
Foundation and IASB resources will be deployed in Tokyo to assist in
ongoing consultations and to provide assistance to those countries using
or planning to adopt IFRSs.

4.3.2   Use of IFRSs elsewhere in Asia-Pacific

Other Asia-Pacific jurisdictions are taking a variety of approaches toward
convergence of GAAP for domestic companies with IFRSs.

Australia, Hong Kong, Korea, New Zealand and Sri Lanka are taking the
approach that their national standards are virtually word-for-word IFRSs.
However, effective dates and transitions may differ from IFRSs. New
Zealand has eliminated some accounting policy options and added some
disclosures and guidance.

The Philippines and Singapore have adopted most IFRSs word-for-word,
but have made some significant modifications. In 2009, the Singapore
Accounting Standards Council (ASC) announced a plan to achieve full
convergence by 2012 of Singapore Financial Reporting Standards for
Singapore listed companies with IFRSs. This timetable has now been
delayed because the ASC has identified a few key outstanding issues that
need to be resolved before full convergence can be implemented.
Although no deadline for convergence has been announced, it is not
expected to be achieved before 2015.

Plans have been announced to adopt IFRSs in full as national GAAP for
listed companies in Pakistan, Malaysia and India (IFRS converged Indian
Accounting Standards have been issued but the effective application date
of these standards has been deferred without any new date being notified).

IFRSs are looked to in developing national GAAP to varying degrees in
China, Indonesia, Thailand and Vietnam, but significant differences exist.

4.4 Use of IFRSs in other parts of the world

Many countries in the rest of the world are either already requiring or permitting IFRSs or are in the process of moving to IFRSs. South African listed companies must use IFRSs, and many of the former Soviet Union countries have adopted (in part or comprehensively) IFRSs as their primary accounting framework. For a detailed country-by-country list of the status of adoption of IFRSs, see *www.iasplus.com*.

5 IFRS for Small and Medium-sized Entities

In July 2009, the IASB issued the IFRS for Small and Medium-sized Entities (SMEs). It is a self-contained Standard of about 230 pages tailored for the needs and capabilities of smaller businesses. Many of the principles in full IFRSs for recognising and measuring assets, liabilities, income and expenses have been simplified; topics not relevant to SMEs have been omitted; and the number of required disclosures has been significantly reduced. To lessen the reporting burden for SMEs further, revisions to the IFRS for SMEs will be limited to once every three years (the first such review commenced in June 2012). The Standard was effective immediately on issue.

The IFRS for SMEs is separate from full IFRSs and is therefore available for any jurisdiction to adopt whether or not it has adopted full IFRSs. It is also for each jurisdiction to determine which entities should use the Standard.

See **appendix A4** for an overview of the IFRS for SMEs.

A2 Conceptual framework for financial reporting

Contents

1   Introduction

For several years, the IASB and the FASB worked together on a joint project to develop an improved and converged conceptual framework for IFRSs and US GAAP. This project was being carried out in phases with the objective that, as each phase was finalised, the relevant paragraphs in the *Framework for the Preparation and Presentation of Financial Statements* (the IASB's predecessor framework) would be replaced.

The boards completed the first phase of their project in September 2010, when they issued two chapters of the *Conceptual Framework for Financial Reporting* (the Conceptual Framework) – Chapter 1 *The objective of general purpose financial reporting* and Chapter 3 *Qualitative characteristics of useful financial information*. After that first phase was complete, the IASB deferred further work on the joint project until after other more urgent convergence projects were finalised. In 2012, the project was reactivated as an IASB-only project, with a further discussion paper issued in July 2013 (see **section 9**).

This chapter follows the text of the *Conceptual Framework for Financial Reporting* in the IASB's 2013 Bound Volume. It incorporates the two chapters of the Conceptual Framework completed in September 2010, with the remaining text (**sections 6** to **8** below) carried forward from the predecessor framework pending completion of the remaining phases.

The Conceptual Framework sets out the concepts underlying the preparation and presentation of financial statements for external users. A comprehensive discussion of each of the topics covered in the Conceptual Framework is beyond the scope of this text. The following sections therefore provide a very brief summary of the matters discussed therein.

1.1   Terminology

When the IASB revised IAS 1 *Presentation of Financial Statements* in 2007, it did not amend the terminology used in the *Framework for the Preparation and Presentation of Financial Statements*, and this pre-2007 terminology is carried forward to the Conceptual Framework. Accordingly, the Conceptual Framework still refers, for example, to the 'balance sheet' rather than to the 'statement of financial position'.

2   Purpose and status of the Conceptual Framework

The purpose of the Conceptual Framework is:

- to assist the IASB in the development of future IFRSs and in its review of existing IFRSs;

- to assist the IASB in promoting harmonisation of regulations, accounting standards and procedures relating to the presentation of financial statements by providing a basis for reducing the number of alternative accounting treatments permitted by IFRSs;

- to assist national standard-setting bodies in developing national standards;

- to assist preparers of financial statements in applying IFRSs and in dealing with topics that have yet to form the subject of an IFRS;

- to assist auditors in forming an opinion as to whether financial statements comply with IFRSs;

- to assist users of financial statements in interpreting the information contained in financial statements prepared in conformity with IFRSs; and

- to provide those who are interested in the work of the IASB with information about its approach to the formulation of IFRSs.

The Conceptual Framework is not itself an International Financial Reporting Standard and, therefore, it does not define standards for particular recognition, measurement, presentation or disclosure issues. There may be conflicts between the Conceptual Framework and individual Standards or Interpretations, which are being addressed by the IASB over time. When such a conflict arises, the Standard or Interpretation takes precedence. This is a key point in that it clarifies that the principles of the Conceptual Framework cannot be used to justify a treatment that contravenes an extant IFRS.

In the absence of a Standard or an Interpretation that specifically applies to a transaction or event, IAS 8 *Accounting Policies, Changes in Accounting Estimates and Errors* requires that management should use its judgement in developing and applying an accounting policy that results in information that is relevant and reliable. In making that judgement, IAS 8:11 requires management to consider first the requirements and guidance in Standards and Interpretations dealing with similar and related issues, and second the definitions, recognition criteria and measurement concepts for assets, liabilities, income and expenses in the Conceptual Framework (see **section 3.1** of **chapter A5**).

3   Scope

The Conceptual Framework deals specifically with:

- the objective of general purpose financial reporting (see **section 4** below);

- the qualitative characteristics of useful financial information (see **section 5** below);

- the definition, recognition and measurement of the elements from which financial statements are constructed (see **sections 6** and **7** below); and

- concepts of capital and capital maintenance (see **section 8** below).

> The Conceptual Framework is not directly relevant for entities applying the *IFRS for SMEs*, which includes a section setting out its underlying concepts and pervasive principles.

4   The objective of general purpose financial reporting

Chapter 1 of the Conceptual Framework addresses the objective of general purpose financial reporting (hereafter, just 'financial reporting') – which is considered to be the foundation of the Conceptual Framework from which the other aspects flow logically.

The objective of financial reporting is identified as being "to provide financial information about the reporting entity that is useful to existing and potential investors, lenders and other creditors in making decisions about providing resources to the entity. Those decisions involve buying, selling or holding equity and debt instruments, and providing or settling loans and other forms of credit". [CF:OB2]

The primary users of general purpose financial reports are identified as existing and potential investors, lenders and other creditors who cannot require the entity to provide information directly to them and who, consequently, rely on general purpose financial reports for much (but not all) of the financial information they need. [CF:OB5] Other parties (e.g.

regulators and members of the public) may make use of general purpose financial reports but the information included therein is not primarily directed to such parties. [CF:OB10]

The needs of all of the primary users are not the same – and the Conceptual Framework establishes the principle that, in developing IFRSs, the IASB "will seek to provide the information set that will meet the needs of the maximum number of primary users". [CF:OB8]

Information is considered to be 'useful' if it helps the primary users of general purpose financial reports to assess the prospects for future net cash inflows to an entity; such an assessment enables the primary users to estimate the return that they can expect from transacting with the entity. [CF:OB3]

To assess an entity's prospects for future net cash inflows, the primary users need information regarding (1) the resources of the entity and claims against the entity, and (2) how efficiently and effectively the entity's management has discharged its responsibilities. [CF:OB4]

> The responsibilities referred to in CF:OB4 are generally referred to as management's 'stewardship' responsibilities. Examples of such responsibilities include protecting the entity's resources from unfavourable effects of economic factors such as price and technological changes and ensuring that the entity complies with applicable laws, regulations and contractual provisions.
>
> This subject sparked considerable debate during the development of Chapter 1 of the Conceptual Framework. While 'stewardship' is not a separate objective of financial reporting in the final chapter as some had requested, the IASB has acknowledged that evaluating past performance of an entity is as important as predicting future cash flows.

4.1   Information about the resources of the entity and claims against the entity

General purpose financial reports provide information about: [CF:OB12 & OB15]

- the financial position of an entity (i.e. information about its economic resources and claims against it);

- the financial performance of an entity; and

- the effects of other events and transactions that affect the entity's economic resources and claims against it (e.g. issuing debt or equity securities).

> Although the Conceptual Framework refers to financial performance, it does not define it. However, it appears clear that financial performance does not reflect all changes in the financial position of an entity in that it excludes changes that relate to contributions from and distributions to equity participants (see the discussion in **section 7** below).

Information about the nature and amounts of an entity's economic resources and claims against it is useful for assessing its financial strengths and weaknesses, such as the liquidity of the entity and its financing needs. Information about priorities and payment requirements of existing claims helps users to predict how future cash flows will be distributed among those with a claim against the entity. [CF:OB13]

Information about the performance of an entity helps users to understand the return that the entity has produced from its economic resources (which is an indication of how well management has discharged its stewardship responsibilities). Information regarding the performance of an entity is prepared using the accrual basis of accounting (i.e. focusing on the effects of events and transactions when they occur and not necessarily when cash is received or paid), which is considered to provide a better basis for assessing the entity's past and future performance than information solely about cash receipt and payments. [CF:OB16 & 17]

Information about an entity's cash flows during a period is also considered to be useful in the assessment of the entity's ability to generate future net cash inflows; it helps users to understand an entity's operations, evaluate its financing and investing activities, assess its liquidity or solvency, and interpret other information about financial performance. [CF:OB20]

Finally, information regarding changes in the entity's resources and claims against it for reasons other than financial performance (e.g. the issue of additional ownership shares) is needed to provide users of general purpose financial reports with a complete understanding of why the entity's economic resources and claims against it have changed and the implications of those changes for its future financial performance. [CF:OB21]

5   Qualitative characteristics of useful financial statements

Chapter 3 of the Conceptual Framework considers the qualitative characteristics of decision-useful financial information, and constraints on the information that can be provided by financial reporting, so as to identify the types of information that are likely to be most useful to the primary users of general purpose financial reports.

The Conceptual Framework states that if financial information is to be useful, it must be relevant and faithfully represent what it purports to represent; these are the two fundamental qualitative characteristics of useful financial information – 'relevance' and 'faithful representation'. [CF:QC4 & 5] Information must be both relevant and faithfully represented if it is to be useful. Neither a faithful representation of an irrelevant phenomenon nor an unfaithful representation of a relevant phenomenon helps users make good decisions. [CF:QC17]

The usefulness of financial information is considered to be enhanced if it is comparable, verifiable, timely and understandable. [CF:QC4] 'Comparability', 'verifiability', 'timeliness' and 'understandability' are therefore described as enhancing qualitative characteristics. [CF:QC19] The Conceptual Framework notes that such enhancement should be maximised to the extent possible. However, these qualitative characteristics cannot make information useful if the information is irrelevant or not faithfully represented. [CF:QC33]

Notably, the Conceptual Framework does not include any discussion of 'substance over form' or 'prudence'. These omissions are discussed in the Basis for Conclusions on the Conceptual Framework.

The Board determined that 'substance over form' should not be presented as a separate component of faithful representation because it would be redundant. Faithful representation means that financial information presents the substance of events and transactions rather than merely their legal form. Representing a legal form that differs from the economic substance of the underlying economic event or transaction could not result in a faithful representation. [CF:BC3.26] Therefore, although not specifically referred to in the Conceptual Framework, the concept of 'substance over form' continues to be relevant (see **section 3.1** of **chapter A4** for further discussion).

No reference is made to prudence (or conservatism) as an aspect of faithful representation because the Board considered that including either would be inconsistent with neutrality. The Board concluded that, even with the prohibitions against deliberate misstatement that appear elsewhere, an admonition to be prudent would be likely to lead to a bias. [CF:BC3.27 – BC3.29]

5.1   Fundamental qualitative characteristics

5.1.1   Relevance

Financial information is relevant when it is "capable of making a difference in the decisions made by users". [CF:QC6] Information is capable of making a difference in a decision-making process if it has predictive value (i.e. it can be used as an input to predict future outcomes), confirmatory value (i.e. it provides feedback about previous evaluations), or both.

In determining whether or not information is relevant to the needs of users, preparers of financial information need to take account of the nature and materiality of the information. Information is considered to be material if omitting it or misstating it could influence the decisions of users taken on the basis of the financial information. Because materiality is an entity-specific characteristic to be determined in the context of an individual entity's financial report, the IASB has concluded that it cannot specify a uniform quantitative threshold for materiality or predetermine what could be material in a particular situation. [CF:QC11]

5.1.2   Faithful representation

Relevant financial information must also be faithfully represented to be useful. A faithful representation is one that is "complete, neutral, and free from error" to the extent possible.
[CF:QC12 – QC15]

- A depiction is 'complete' if it includes all of the information that a user needs to understand what is being reported, including all necessary descriptions and explanations.

- A depiction is 'neutral' if it is without bias in the selection or presentation of financial information (i.e. it is not slanted, weighted, emphasised, de-emphasised or otherwise manipulated to increase the probability that financial information will be received favourably or unfavourably by users).

- A depiction is 'free from error' if there are no errors or omissions in the information provided and the process used to produce the reported information has been selected and applied with no errors in the process. In this context, free from error does not mean perfectly accurate in all respects.

5.2   Enhancing qualitative characteristics

Comparability, verifiability, timeliness and understandability are qualitative characteristics that enhance the usefulness of information that is relevant and faithfully represented. The enhancing qualitative characteristics may also help determine which of two ways should be used to depict an event or transaction if both are considered equally relevant and faithfully represented. [CF:QC19]

5.2.1   Comparability

Information about an entity is considered to be more useful if it can be compared with similar information about other entities and with similar information about the same entity for another period or another date. Comparability is the qualitative characteristic that enables users to identify and understand similarities in, and differences among, items. [CF:QC20 & 21]

Using the same methods for the same items, either from period to period within an entity or in a single period across entities (i.e. consistency), helps to achieve comparability. [CF:QC22]. Although an economic event or transaction can sometimes be faithfully represented in multiple ways, permitting alternative accounting methods for the same economic phenomenon diminishes comparability. [CF:QC25]

5.2.2   Verifiability

Verifiability means that different knowledgeable and independent observers could reach consensus, although not necessarily complete agreement, that a particular depiction is a faithful representation. Quantified information need not be a single point estimate to be verifiable – a range of possible amounts and the related probabilities can also be verified. Verifiability helps assure users that information faithfully represents the events or transactions it purports to represent. [CF:QC26]

Verification can be direct or indirect. Direct verification means verifying an amount or other representation through direct observation (e.g. by counting cash). Indirect verification means checking the inputs to a model, formula or other technique and recalculating the outputs using the same methodology. [CF:QC27]

It may not be possible to verify some explanations and forward-looking financial information until a future period, if at all. To help users decide whether they want to use that information, it would normally be necessary to disclose the underlying assumptions, the methods of compiling the information, and other factors and circumstances that support the information. [CF:QC28]

5.2.3   Timeliness

Timeliness means having information available to decision-makers in time to be capable of influencing their decisions. Generally, the older the information is the less useful it is. However, some information may continue to be timely long after the end of a reporting period because, for example, some users may need to identify and assess trends. [CF:QC29]

5.2.4   Understandability

Classifying, characterising and presenting information clearly and concisely makes it understandable. [CF:QC30]

The Conceptual Framework allows a preparer to assume that users have a reasonable knowledge of business and economic activities, and that users review and analyse the information diligently. Complex financial information should not be excluded from financial reports in order to make those financial reports easier to understand, because the resulting information would be incomplete and, therefore, potentially misleading. [CF:QC31 & 32]

5.3   The cost constraint on financial reporting

The Conceptual Framework acknowledges that cost is a pervasive constraint on the information that can be provided by financial reporting. Reporting financial information imposes costs, and it is important that those costs are justified by the benefits of reporting that information. [CF:QC35]

Costs are incurred by providers of financial information in collecting, processing, verifying and disseminating financial information; users of financial information also incur costs when analysing and interpreting the information provided. If needed information is not provided, users incur additional costs to obtain that information elsewhere or to estimate it. [CF:QC36]

In applying the cost constraint when developing IFRSs, the IASB assesses whether the benefits of reporting particular information are likely to justify the costs incurred to provide and use that information. The Board seeks to consider costs and benefits in relation to financial reporting generally and not just in relation to individual reporting entities. That does not mean that assessments of costs and benefits always justify the same reporting requirements for all entities. Differences may be appropriate because of different sizes of entities, different ways of raising capital (publicly or privately), different users' needs, or other factors. [CF:QC38 & 39]

6   Assumptions underlying the preparation of financial statements

Chapter 4 of the Conceptual Framework identifies 'going concern' as one assumption underlying the preparation of financial statements. This assumption (together with a number of other general features of financial statements introduced in IAS 1 *Presentation of Financial Statements*) is discussed in **chapter A4.**

7   The elements of financial statements

Chapter 4 of the Conceptual Framework (carried forward from the IASB's predecessor framework) provides definitions for the elements of financial statements, as well as principles for the recognition and measurement of those elements.

7.1   Assets

7.1.1   *Definition*

The Conceptual Framework defines an asset as a resource controlled by the entity as a result of past events and from which future economic benefits are expected to flow to the entity. [CF:4.4(a)]

The future economic benefit embodied in an asset is the potential to contribute, directly or indirectly, to the flow of cash and cash equivalents. [CF:4.8] Such benefits may flow to the entity in a number of ways – e.g. by use in the production process, by exchange for other assets, as settlement of a liability, or by distribution to the owners of the entity.

Many assets have physical form – but that is not essential to the existence of an asset. For example, intangibles such as patents and copyrights are assets if future economic benefits are expected to flow from them to the entity and if they are controlled by the entity. [CF:4.11]

The entity's control over those future economic benefits will most commonly be evidenced by legal ownership, but that is not essential. For example, property held on lease is an asset if the entity controls the benefits that are expected to flow from it. [CF:4.12]

The entity will usually have legal rights over an asset – but not necessarily so. For example, know-how obtained from a development activity may meet the definition of an asset when, by keeping the know-how secret, an entity controls the benefits that are expected to flow from it. [CF:4.12]

The assets of an entity must result from a past transaction or event. Assets are most usually acquired by purchasing or producing them – but this will not always be the case (e.g. when assets may be received by way of government grant or contributions from equity participants). [CF:4.13]

There is a 'close association' between incurring expenditure and generating assets, but the two do not necessarily coincide. An entity may incur expenditure with a view to obtaining future economic benefits, but the expenditure may not result in an item satisfying the definition of an asset. Equally, an item may satisfy the definition of an asset without any expenditure having been incurred (e.g. a donated asset). [CF:4.14]

7.1.2   Recognition

An asset should be recognised in the balance sheet when:
[CF:4.44]

- it is probable that the future economic benefits will flow to the entity; and

- the asset has a cost or value that can be measured reliably.

The assessment of the degree of uncertainty attaching to the flow of future economic benefits is made on the basis of the evidence available when the financial statements are prepared. An asset is not recognised in the balance sheet when expenditure has been incurred from which it is considered improbable that economic benefits will flow to the entity beyond the current accounting period. Instead, such a transaction is dealt with as an expense in the income statement.

7.1.3   Measurement

The determination of the monetary amount at which an asset is to be recognised in the balance sheet involves the selection of a particular basis of measurement.

The most common bases of measurement for assets are:
[CF:4.55]

- historical cost – assets are recorded at the amount of cash or cash equivalents paid or the fair value of the consideration given to acquire them at the time of their acquisition;

- current cost – assets are carried at the amount of cash or cash equivalents that would have to be paid if the same or an equivalent asset was acquired currently;

- realisable value – assets are carried at the amount of cash or cash equivalents that could currently be obtained by selling the asset in an orderly disposal; and

- present value – assets are carried at the present discounted value of the future net cash inflows that the item is expected to generate in the normal course of business.

The Conceptual Framework does not indicate a preference for any of these measurement bases. It points out that the measurement basis most commonly adopted is historical cost – often combined with other bases. For example, inventories are usually carried at the lower of cost and net realisable value. [CF:4.56]

7.2   Liabilities

7.2.1   Definition

The Conceptual Framework defines a liability as a present obligation of the entity arising from past events, the settlement of which is expected to result in an outflow from the entity of resources embodying economic benefits. [CF:4.4(b)]

An essential characteristic of a liability is that the entity has a present obligation. An obligation is a duty or responsibility to act or perform in a certain way. Obligations may be legally enforceable (e.g. a binding contract or a statutory requirement). Obligations also arise, however, from normal business practice, custom and a desire to maintain good business relations or to act in an equitable manner. For example, an entity may decide as a matter of policy to rectify faults in its products after the warranty period has expired, even though it has no legal obligation to do so, with the objective of maintaining its reputation with customers. [CF:4.15]

The Conceptual Framework draws a distinction between a present obligation and a future commitment. A decision by management to acquire an asset or to incur expenditure in the future does not, of itself, create a present obligation. An obligation normally arises only when the goods are delivered or an irrevocable agreement is entered into. [CF:4.16]

The settlement of a liability usually involves the entity giving up resources embodying economic benefits – whether by payment of cash, transfer of other assets, provision of services, replacement of the obligation by another obligation, or conversion of the obligation to equity. [CF:4.17]

7.2.2   Recognition

A liability should be recognised in the balance sheet when: [CF:4.46]

- it is probable that an outflow of resources embodying economic benefits will result from the settlement of a present obligation; and

- the amount at which the settlement will take place can be measured reliably.

In practice, obligations under contracts that are equally proportionately unperformed (e.g. liabilities for inventories ordered but not yet received) are generally not recognised as liabilities in the financial statements (see **chapter A12** for a discussion of executory contracts).

7.2.3   Measurement

The determination of the monetary amount at which a liability is to be recognised in the balance sheet involves the selection of a particular basis of measurement.

The most common bases of measurement for liabilities are: [CF:4.55]

- historical cost – liabilities are recorded at the amount of the proceeds received in exchange for the obligation or at the amounts of cash or cash equivalents expected to be paid to satisfy the liability in the normal course of business;

- current cost – liabilities are carried at the undiscounted amount of cash or cash equivalents that would be required to settle the obligation currently;

- settlement value – liabilities are carried at their settlement values, i.e. at the undiscounted amounts of cash or cash equivalents expected to be paid to satisfy the liabilities in the normal course of business; and

- present value – liabilities are carried at the present discounted value of the future net cash outflows that are expected to be required to settle the liabilities in the normal course of business.

The Conceptual Framework does not indicate a preference for any of these measurement bases.

7.3   Equity

The Conceptual Framework defines equity as the residual interest in the assets of the entity after deducting all of its liabilities. [CF:4.4(c)]

Equity may be sub-classified in the balance sheet. For example, funds contributed by shareholders, retained earnings and capital reserves may be shown separately. Such classifications can be relevant to the decision needs of users of the financial statements when they indicate legal or other restrictions on the ability of the entity to distribute or otherwise apply its equity. They may also reflect the fact that parties with ownership interests in an entity have differing rights in relation to the receipt of dividends and the repayment of capital. [CF:4.20]

7.4   Income

7.4.1   Definition

Income is defined as increases in economic benefits during the accounting period in the form of inflows or enhancements of assets, or decreases of liabilities, that result in increases in equity, other than those relating to contributions from equity participants. [CF:4.25(a)]

Income can be subdivided into:

- revenue – which arises in the course of the ordinary activities of the entity and is referred to by a variety of different names including sales, fees, interest, dividends, royalties and rent; and

- gains – which represent other items that meet the definition of income. They include, for example, gains arising on the disposal of non-current assets, and unrealised gains arising on the revaluation of financial instruments or non-current assets.

7.4.2   Recognition

Income is recognised when an increase in future economic benefits related to an increase in an asset or a decrease in a liability has arisen that can be measured reliably. [CF:4.47] This means that recognition of income occurs simultaneously with the recognition of increases in assets or decreases in liabilities. Generally, such recognition will occur when the movements in assets/liabilities can be measured reliably and have a sufficient degree of certainty.

The amount at which income is recognised will be determined by the movements in assets/liabilities as discussed in the previous sections.

Specific criteria for the recognition of particular types of revenue are set out in IAS 18 *Revenue* (see **chapter A14**).

7.5   Expenses

7.5.1   Definition

Expenses are defined as decreases in economic benefits during the accounting period in the form of outflows or depletions of assets, or incurrences of liabilities, that result in decreases in equity, other than those relating to distributions to equity participants. [CF:4.25(b)]

7.5.2   Recognition

Expenses are recognised in the income statement when a decrease in future economic benefits related to a decrease in an asset or an increase in a liability has arisen that can be measured reliably. [CF:4.49] This means that recognition of expenses occurs simultaneously with the recognition of decreases in assets or increases in liabilities.

The amount at which expenses are recognised will be determined by the movements in assets/liabilities as discussed in the previous sections.

The recognition of expenses in the income statement will be affected by any direct association between the costs incurred and the earning of specific items of income (i.e. matching). However, the application of the matching concept does not allow the recognition of items in the balance sheet that do not meet the definition of assets or liabilities. [CF:4.50]

When economic benefits are expected to arise over several accounting periods, and the association with income can only be broadly or indirectly determined, expenses are recognised in the income statement on the basis of systematic and rational allocation procedures (e.g. depreciation or amortisation of non-current assets). These allocation procedures are intended to recognise expenses in the accounting periods in which the associated economic benefits are consumed or expire. [CF:4.51]

An expense is recognised immediately in the income statement in those cases when the expenditure produces no future economic benefits, or when future economic benefits do not qualify, or cease to qualify, for recognition in the balance sheet as an asset. [CF:4.52]

An expense is also recognised in the income statement when a liability is incurred without the recognition of an asset (e.g. when a liability arises under a product warranty). [CF:4.53]

7.6   Transactions with equity participants

The definitions of both income and expenses set out in the previous sections exclude contributions from and distributions to equity participants. These exclusions are based on the principle that profit or loss of the entity cannot be created simply by transferring resources to or from the owners of the entity.

8   Concepts of capital and capital maintenance

The Conceptual Framework identifies two concepts of capital maintenance:
[CF:4.59]

- financial capital maintenance – under which profit is earned only if the financial (or money) amount of the net assets at the end of the reporting period exceeds the financial (or money) amount of net assets at the beginning of the reporting period, after excluding any distributions to, and contributions from, owners during the period; and

- physical capital maintenance – under which a profit is earned only if the physical productive capacity (or operating capability) of the entity (or the resources or funds needed to achieve that capacity) at the end of the period exceeds the physical productive capacity at the beginning of the period, after excluding any distributions to, and contributions from, owners during the period.

The Conceptual Framework does not indicate a preference for either of these concepts of capital maintenance.

The selection of a concept of capital maintenance (and of the measurement basis to be used) determines the accounting model used in preparation of the financial statements. The Conceptual Framework acknowledges that different accounting models exhibit different degrees of relevance and reliability, and that preparers of financial statements should seek a balance between those characteristics.

9   Future developments

The joint IASB/FASB project on developing a common conceptual framework was effectively abandoned in September 2010 following completion of only one phase (see **section 1**). As an outcome of its Agenda Consultation project, the IASB decided in September 2012 to reactivate the Conceptual Framework project as an IASB-only comprehensive project.

A discussion paper titled *A Review of the Conceptual Framework for Financial Reporting* was issued in July 2013. The discussion paper suggests the following significant changes to the existing Conceptual Framework:

- a revised statement of the primary purpose of the Conceptual Framework;

- revised definitions of assets and liabilities;

- additional guidance on applying the definitions of assets and liabilities;

- revised guidance on when assets and liabilities should be recognised;

- new guidance on when assets and liabilities should be derecognised;

- a new way to present information about equity claims against the reporting entity;

- a new section on the concepts that should guide the IASB when it selects measurements in a new or revised Standard or Interpretation;

- a new section on presentation and disclosure; and

- principles for distinguishing profit or loss from other comprehensive income.

Comments on the discussion paper are requested by 14 January 2014.

A3   First-time adoption of IFRSs

Contents

1   Introduction

IFRS 1 *First-time Adoption of International Reporting Standards* establishes the requirements for an entity's first financial statements prepared in accordance with IFRSs, particularly regarding the transition from the accounting principles previously applied by the entity (previous GAAP). The objective of IFRS 1 is to ensure that an entity's first-time IFRS financial statements (and interim financial reports for part of the period covered by those financial statements) contain high quality information that: [IFRS 1:1]

- is transparent for users and comparable over all periods presented;

- provides a suitable starting point for accounting under IFRSs; and

- can be generated at a cost that does not exceed the benefits to users.

IFRS 1 was most recently amended in October 2012 by consequential amendments arising from amendments to IFRS 10 *Consolidated Financial Statements* (the *Investment Entities* amendments) which introduce an exception to IFRS 10's general consolidation requirements when the reporting entity is an 'investment entity' as defined (see **section 15** of **chapter A24** for detailed discussion). The consequential amendments to IFRS 1 address the application of certain of IFRS 1's optional exemptions in circumstances affected by the exception from consolidation (see **7.9.1** and **7.9.2** below). The consequential amendments also introduce an additional short-term exemption allowing first-time adopters to apply some of the transition reliefs in the *Investment Entities* amendments for a limited period (see **7.21.2** below).

2   Overview of the Standard

The general principle underlying IFRS 1 is that IFRSs effective at the date of an entity's first IFRS financial statements should be applied retrospectively in the opening IFRS statement of financial position, the comparative period and the first IFRS reporting period. In practical terms, this means that if an entity adopts IFRSs for the year ended 31 December 2013, it must apply all IFRSs effective at that date retrospectively to the 2013 and 2012 reporting periods, and to the opening statement of financial position on 1 January 2012 (assuming that only one year of comparative information is presented). Effectively, this general principle would result in full retrospective application of IFRSs as if they had been the framework for an entity's accounting since its inception. However, IFRS 1 adapts this general principle of retrospective application by adding a limited number of 'exceptions' and 'exemptions'.

The 'exceptions' to retrospective application (of which there are seven) are mandatory (see **section 6**). The 'exemptions' (20 in total) are optional – a first-time adopter may choose whether and which exemptions to apply (see **section 7**).

From time to time, the IASB also adds short-term exemptions from IFRSs (see **section 7**).

Careful analysis is required to understand fully the nature and impact of both the exceptions and the exemptions when applying IFRS 1.

An entity is only permitted to apply IFRS 1 in its first IFRS financial statements (a term tightly defined to mean the first annual financial statements in which the entity adopts IFRSs by an explicit and unreserved statement of compliance with IFRSs). The Standard provides specific examples of what might or might not qualify as an entity's first IFRS financial statements (see **section 4**).

The following summarises the steps required in preparing an entity's first IFRS financial statements.

1.   An opening IFRS statement of financial position is prepared at the 'date of transition'. This is the starting point for an entity's accounting in accordance with IFRSs. The date of transition is the beginning of the first period for which an entity presents full comparative information under IFRSs in its first IFRS financial statements. For entities that present one year of comparative information in their financial reports, the date of transition is the first day of the comparative period.

2.   In its first IFRS financial statements, an entity applies the version of IFRSs effective at the end of its first IFRS reporting period. As a general principle, all IFRSs effective at that date are applied retrospectively, subject to certain exceptions and exemptions set out in IFRS 1 (discussed in detail in **sections 6 and 7**, respectively). The exceptions and exemptions are very specific, and may not be applied by analogy to other items.

3.   The entity recognises all assets and liabilities in accordance with the requirements of IFRSs, and derecognises assets and liabilities that do not qualify for recognition under IFRSs.

4.   All adjustments resulting from the application of IFRSs to the opening IFRS statement of financial position are recognised in

retained earnings (or, if appropriate, another category of equity) at the date of transition, except for reclassifications between goodwill and intangible assets.

5.   With limited exceptions, estimates in accordance with IFRSs at the date of transition must be consistent with estimates made for the same date under previous GAAP.

6.   An entity's first IFRS financial statements include at least three statements of financial position (including one at the date of transition, i.e. at the beginning of the comparative period), two statements of profit or loss and other comprehensive income, two statements of cash flows and two statements of changes in equity. All of these statements must be in compliance with IFRSs.

7.   Entities are permitted to present historical summaries of certain data for periods before the date of transition which do not comply with IFRSs, as long as the information is prominently labelled as not being prepared in accordance with IFRSs. When such information is presented, the entity must also explain the nature of the main adjustments that would be required to render the information compliant with IFRSs.

8.   IFRS 1 requires compliance with all of the presentation and disclosure requirements of other Standards and Interpretations, and imposes additional disclosure requirements specific to the first IFRS financial statements. In particular, a first-time adopter is required to provide reconciliations between amounts reported under previous GAAP and the equivalent measures under IFRSs. These reconciliations must clearly identify the correction of any errors in relation to an entity's previous GAAP financial statements.

3   Definitions

Appendix A to IFRS 1, which is an integral part of the IFRS, provides definitions for terms that are used in the Standard. This section sets out those definitions with additional explanation as necessary.

3.1   Date of transition to IFRSs

The date of transition to IFRSs is defined as follows.
[IFRS 1:Appendix A]

> "The beginning of the earliest period for which an entity presents full comparative information under IFRSs in its first IFRS financial statements."

This date is of particular significance because it is the date at which an entity prepares its opening IFRS statement of financial position.

3.2   Deemed cost

Deemed cost is defined as follows.
[IFRS 1:Appendix A]

> "An amount used as a surrogate for cost or depreciated cost at a given date. Subsequent depreciation or amortisation assumes that the entity had initially recognised the asset or liability at the given date and that its cost was equal to the deemed cost."

The use of fair value or a previous revaluation as deemed cost on transition to IFRSs is considered at **7.4** below.

3.3   Fair value

The definition of fair value is amended for entities that adopt IFRS 13 *Fair Value Measurement* in their first IFRS financial statements (see **3.3.1** below). IFRS 13 establishes a single framework for measuring fair value when that is required by other Standards. It replaces the guidance regarding the measurement of fair value previously included in other Standards (including IFRS 1).

IFRS 13 is effective for annual periods beginning on or after 1 January 2013, with earlier adoption permitted. Although the general transition provisions of IFRS 13 require that it be applied prospectively, this requirement does not apply for first-time adopters. Therefore, a first-time adopter that applies IFRS 13 in its first IFRS financial statements should apply IFRS 13's measurement requirements in its opening statement of financial position and throughout all periods presented in its first IFRS financial statements (see **5.2** below).

3.3.1   Entities that adopt IFRS 13

Fair value is defined as follows.
[IFRS 1:Appendix A]

> "The price that would be received to sell an asset or paid to transfer a liability in an orderly transaction between market participants at the measurement date."

3.3.2   Entities that do not adopt IFRS 13

Fair value is defined as follows.
[IFRS 1:Appendix A]

> "The amount for which an asset could be exchanged, or a liability settled, between knowledgeable, willing parties in an arm's length transaction."

An entity also applies any more specific guidance in other IFRSs on the determination of fair value when applying IFRS 1. [IFRS 1:19]

3.4   First IFRS financial statements

The first IFRS financial statements are defined as follows.
[IFRS 1:Appendix A]

> "The first annual financial statements in which an entity adopts International Financial Reporting Standards (IFRSs), by an explicit and unreserved statement of compliance with IFRSs."

The meaning of an 'explicit and unreserved statement of compliance with IFRSs' is considered in **section 4** below.

3.5   First IFRS reporting period

The first IFRS reporting period is defined as follows.
[IFRS 1:Appendix A]

> "The latest reporting period covered by an entity's first IFRS financial statements."

3.6   First-time adopter

A first-time adopter is defined as follows.
[IFRS 1:Appendix A]

> "An entity that presents its first IFRS financial statements."

A newly incorporated company presenting its first financial statements under IFRSs is not generally viewed as a 'first-time adopter' for the purposes of IFRS 1 – there are no 'past transactions' to restate. This is also the case when a newly incorporated company establishes a business and subsequently acquires another entity in a transaction that is accounted for using the acquisition method in accordance with IFRS 3 *Business Combinations*. In this situation, it is irrelevant for the purposes of the consolidated financial statements of the acquiring company whether the acquired entity previously reported under IFRSs and, if so, its date of transition.

However, a newly incorporated company may be a continuation of an existing operating entity. This may be the case, for example, when a business is transferred to the company in a common control transaction or as a result of the acquisition of another company (which becomes a 'legal subsidiary') in circumstances which require reverse-acquisition accounting (i.e. for financial reporting purposes, the 'legal subsidiary' is portrayed as acquiring the newly incorporated 'legal parent'). The position may be different in these cases.

For example, consider the circumstances in which a new parent is added at the top of a group by way of a share-for-share exchange and this is accounted for in the same way as a reverse acquisition in accordance with IFRS 3. If the existing group already reports under IFRSs, the new parent 'inherits' the date of transition of the existing group for the purposes of its consolidated financial statements. The new parent should not apply IFRS 1 because reverse-acquisition accounting assumes the continuity of the 'acquired' business and that business is already applying IFRSs.

In contrast, in the case of a reverse acquisition when the 'continuing entity' (i.e. the financial reporting acquirer) did not previously report under IFRSs, the new parent is a first-time adopter for the purposes of IFRS 1 and the Standard is applied in the usual way.

Similar considerations may apply to a combination of businesses under common control that is accounted for as a continuation of an existing business.

3.7   International Financial Reporting Standards (IFRSs)

International Financial Reporting Standards are defined as follows.
[IFRS 1:Appendix A]

"Standards and Interpretations adopted by the International Accounting Standards Board (IASB). They comprise:

- International Financial Reporting Standards;

- International Accounting Standards;

- IFRS Interpretations; and

- SIC Interpretations."

3.8   Opening IFRS statement of financial position

An opening IFRS statement of financial position is defined as follows.
[IFRS 1:Appendix A]

> "An entity's statement of financial position at the date of transition to IFRSs."

3.9   Previous GAAP

Previous GAAP is defined as follows.
[IFRS 1:Appendix A]

> "The basis of accounting that a first-time adopter used immediately before adopting IFRSs."

An entity may have previously prepared two complete sets of financial statements under different GAAPs. For example, a company may have prepared its statutory financial statements under local GAAP and, in addition, prepared a complete set of US GAAP financial statements because it is listed on a US stock exchange.

In such cases, it is for management to determine, in accordance with its regulatory environment, whether to transition from the statutory financial statements (under local GAAP) or from the other set of financial statements it has presented. The determination of which GAAP is 'previous GAAP' is subject to the following:

- an entity cannot have more than one set of IFRS financial statements. Therefore, it must have only one starting point for transition to IFRSs (albeit that it may choose to reconcile between this starting point and another previously used accounting framework);

- under IFRSs, management has a free choice in identifying its previous GAAP. However, such a free choice may be eliminated by the regulatory regime(s) within which the entity operates; and

- the choice of previous GAAP must be a reasonable one (e.g. previous financial statements prepared for a specific purpose with limited circulation would not be an appropriate starting point when compared with the financial statements prepared for circulation to the entity's main user groups).

4   Scope

An entity should apply IFRS 1 in:
[IFRS 1:2]

- its first IFRS financial statements; and

- each interim financial report, if any, that it presents under IAS 34 *Interim Financial Reporting* for part of the period covered by its first IFRS financial statements.

As noted at **3.4**, an entity's first IFRS financial statements are the first annual financial statements in which the entity adopts IFRSs, by an explicit and unreserved statement in those financial statements of compliance with IFRSs. [IFRS 1:3]

IFRS 1 indicates that financial statements under IFRSs are an entity's first IFRS financial statements if, for example, the entity presented its most recent previous financial statements:
[IFRS 1:3(a)]

- in accordance with national requirements that are not consistent with IFRSs in all respects;

- in conformity with IFRSs in all respects, except that the financial statements did not contain an explicit and unreserved statement that they complied with IFRSs;

- containing an explicit statement of compliance with some, but not all, IFRSs;

- in accordance with national requirements inconsistent with IFRSs, using some individual IFRSs to account for items for which national requirements did not exist; or

- in accordance with national requirements, with a reconciliation of some amounts to the amounts determined under IFRSs.

Further examples of situations in which IFRS financial statements would be considered an entity's first IFRS financial statements for the purposes of IFRS 1 include situations in which an entity previously:
[IFRS 1:3(b) – (d)]

- prepared financial statements under IFRSs for internal use only, without making them available to the entity's owners or any other external users;

- prepared a reporting package under IFRSs for consolidation purposes without preparing a complete set of financial statements as defined in IAS 1; or

- did not present financial statements for previous periods.

It is not appropriate to apply IFRS 1 when an entity:
[IFRS 1:4]

- stops presenting financial statements in accordance with national requirements, having previously presented them as well as another set of financial statements that contained an explicit and unreserved statement of compliance with IFRSs;

- presented financial statements in the previous year under national requirements and those financial statements contained an explicit and unreserved statement of compliance with IFRSs; or

- presented financial statements in the previous year that contained an explicit and unreserved statement of compliance with IFRSs, even if the auditors qualified their audit report on those financial statements.

Some commentators on the exposure draft (ED) preceding IFRS 1 suggested that the test imposed in the ED was too rigid and that an entity should not be regarded as a first-time adopter if its previous financial statements contained a statement of compliance with IFRSs except for some specified and explicit departures. This argument might be particularly strong if the departures related to disclosure only. The IASB considered this and noted that to implement such an approach, it would be necessary to establish how many departures are needed, and how serious they must be, before an entity would conclude that it had not adopted IFRSs. Therefore, the IASB decided that the Standard should contain a simple test that gives an unambiguous answer. [IFRS 1:BC5]

IFRS 1 does not apply to changes in accounting policies made by an entity that already applies IFRSs. Such changes are subject to the requirements of IAS 8 *Accounting Policies, Changes in Accounting Estimates and Errors* (see **chapter A5**) and specific transition requirements in other IFRSs. [IFRS 1:5]

The following examples illustrate some of the situations described in the previous paragraphs.

Example 4A

Compliance with IFRSs claimed in the previous year but subsequently discovered that financial statements were not IFRS-compliant

In 20X1, Company A issued financial statements stating compliance with all IFRSs, and with an unqualified audit opinion. In 20X2, Company A's auditors note that certain disclosure requirements of IAS 1 *Presentation of Financial Statements* were omitted, in error, from the 20X1 financial statements.

For the purposes of its 20X2 financial statements, is Company A within the scope of IFRS 1?

No. In the circumstances described, the 20X1 financial statements were stated to be IFRS-compliant. While Company A should not have claimed unreserved compliance with IFRSs in its 20X1 financial statements, those financial statements have already been considered IFRS-compliant and relied upon as such. Therefore, any errors are accounted for in accordance with IAS 8.

Example 4B

Reserved statement of compliance with IFRSs in previous year

An entity included a reserved statement of compliance with IFRSs (i.e. a statement of compliance with some, but not all, IFRSs) in its 20X1 financial statements.

Can the entity be a first-time adopter in 20X2?

Yes. An entity that included a reserved statement of compliance with IFRSs in its most recent previous financial statements is not excluded from the scope of IFRS 1 for the current year. The entity becomes a first-time adopter when its financial statements first contain an explicit and *unreserved* statement of compliance with IFRSs.

The following would not be considered unreserved statements of compliance:

- a statement of compliance with local GAAP that is 'consistent with' or 'similar to' IFRSs; or

- a statement of compliance with IFRSs, except for certain Standards or disclosure requirements.

Example 4C

Supplementary IFRS financial statements distributed to external users

In 20X1, Company B prepared and presented its statutory financial statements in accordance with local GAAP. It also prepared a supplementary set of financial statements stating compliance with IFRSs and distributed those supplementary financial statements to a select group of users (financial institutions). In 20X2, Company B intends to prepare its statutory financial statements in accordance with IFRSs.

Will Company B be considered a first-time adopter of IFRSs in 20X2?

No. If financial statements stating compliance with IFRSs have been issued externally, regardless of the extent of distribution, those financial statements prevent the entity from being regarded as a first-time adopter. The same principle would apply if an entity had previously issued a set of IFRS financial statements to the counterparties in a specific commercial transaction.

Example 4D

Listing documents as the first IFRS financial statements

Company C prepared and published its financial statements for the year ended 31 December 20X7 under national GAAP. During 20X8, in connection with an Initial Public Offering (IPO), it published listing documents containing IFRS financial information for the three years ended 31 December 20X7. The 20X7 statutory financial statements were not amended or reissued.

During 20X9, Company C published IFRS financial statements for the year ended 31 December 20X8 with one year of comparative information and an unreserved statement of compliance with IFRSs.

What is Company C's date of transition to IFRSs?

If the listing documents contained an unreserved statement of compliance with IFRSs, then those listing documents will be the entity's first IFRS financial statements. Consequently, the date of transition to IFRSs will be the beginning of the earliest comparative period for which full IFRS information was provided (i.e. 1 January 20X5).

If the listing documents did not contain an unreserved statement of compliance with IFRSs (e.g. because certain disclosure requirements were omitted as permitted by the local regulator), they cannot be the entity's first IFRS financial statements. In such circumstances, the entity's first IFRS financial statements are those for the year ended 31 December 20X8 and the date of transition to IFRSs is 1 January 20X7.

4.1   Repeated application of IFRS 1

As part of *Annual Improvements to IFRSs: 2009-2011 Cycle* (the 2009–2011 Improvements), issued in May 2012, IFRS 1 was amended to provide specific guidance for an entity that has applied IFRSs in past years but not in its most recent annual financial statements. One example of such circumstances cited in IFRS 1:BC6A is an entity that prepared IFRS financial statements in a previous reporting period to meet the listing requirements in a foreign jurisdiction, subsequently delisted and ceased preparing IFRS financial statements, and is facing a requirement to prepare IFRS financial statements in the current period because the reporting requirements in its local jurisdiction have changed.

An entity that has applied IFRS 1 in a previous accounting period, but whose most recent previous annual financial statements did not contain an explicit and unreserved statement of compliance with IFRSs, can choose either:
[IFRS 1:4A]

- to apply IFRS 1 (i.e. the entity is treated as a 'first-time' adopter of IFRSs notwithstanding that it has prepared IFRS financial statements in past years but not the most recent previous year); or

- to apply IFRSs retrospectively in accordance with IAS 8 as if the entity had never stopped applying IFRSs.

The exposure draft preceding the 2009–2011 Improvements proposed to *require* an entity to apply IFRS 1 in the circumstances described. However, the Board was persuaded by respondents' comments on that exposure draft to allow as an alternative full retrospective application of IFRSs. This alternative has been permitted because the Board believes that an entity returning to IFRSs might determine that the benefits of applying IFRSs as if it had continued to do so without interruption would exceed the costs of preparing such information, and that an entity should not be prohibited from following that approach. [IFRS 1:BC6C]

Whichever option is taken:

- hindsight should not be applied in preparing IFRS financial statements (see IFRS 1:BC6C); and

- additional disclosure requirements apply (see **9.2.1**).

Example 4.1

Repeated application of IFRS 1

Company B issued financial statements in 20X1 and 20X2 with an explicit and unreserved statement of compliance with IFRSs. In 20X3, Company B stated compliance with local GAAP only.

If Company B wishes to prepare IFRS-compliant financial statements in 20X4, on what basis should those financial statements be prepared?

In 20X4, Company B can choose either:

- to apply IFRS 1; or

- to apply IFRSs retrospectively as if it had never stopped applying IFRSs.

If Company B elects not to apply IFRS 1 in 20X4, it will in effect need to recreate the IFRS accounting that would have been required if it had prepared financial statements in accordance with IFRSs in 20X3.

The requirements of IFRS 1:4A are effective for annual periods beginning on or after 1 January 2013, with earlier application permitted.

Prior to the May 2012 amendments, it was generally agreed that an entity returning to IFRSs in the circumstances described was required to comply with IFRS 1 (see the agenda decision published by the IFRS Interpretations Committee in the September 2010 *IFRIC Update*); the option of applying IFRSs as if the entity had continued to do so without interruption was not available. Consequently, if an entity is 're-adopting' IFRSs for a period beginning before 1 January 2013 and it wishes to apply IFRSs retrospectively as if it had never stopped applying IFRSs, the entity is required to state explicitly that it is applying the May 2012 amendments in advance of their effective date and comply with the additional disclosure requirements in IFRS 1:23A and 23B (see **9.2.1**).

5   Recognition and measurement – general principle

The general principle underlying IFRS 1 is that a first-time adopter should apply the version of each IFRS effective at the end of its first IFRS reporting period retrospectively. Therefore, the first IFRS financial statements are presented as if the entity had always applied IFRSs, subject to the exceptions and exemptions discussed later in this chapter.

5.1   Opening IFRS statement of financial position

A first-time adopter is required to prepare and present an opening IFRS statement of financial position (see **3.8** above) at the date of transition to IFRSs (see **3.1** above). This is the starting point for its accounting under IFRSs. [IFRS 1:6]

As discussed in **5.2** below, an entity is required to apply the same accounting policies in its opening IFRS statement of financial position and throughout all periods presented in its first IFRS financial statements. These policies are based on IFRSs effective at the end of the first IFRS reporting period, which is at least two years after the date of transition to IFRSs (i.e. the 'as at' date for the opening IFRS statement of financial position). Therefore, it will not be possible to finalise the opening IFRS statement of financial position until it is known that no new or amended IFRSs will be effective for the entity's first IFRS reporting period. If an entity publishes an opening IFRS statement of financial position before this is known (e.g. if the entity is required by the local regulator to disclose information to the market regarding its opening IFRS position but the IASB is still considering amendments which may be effective for the entity's first IFRS financial statements), the entity should state that the amounts disclosed may need to be revised if there are subsequent pronouncements by the IASB that affect the period(s) presented.

The following timeline summarises these requirements and illustrates key dates for a first-time adopter with a calendar year end that presents comparative information for one year.

IFRS adoption timeline

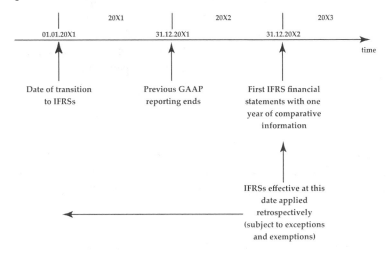

Subject to the exceptions and exemptions discussed in **sections 6** and **7**, respectively, in its opening IFRS statement of financial position an entity should:
[IFRS 1:10]

- recognise all assets and liabilities whose recognition is required by IFRSs;

- not recognise items as assets or liabilities if IFRSs do not permit such recognition;

- reclassify items that it recognised under previous GAAP as one type of asset, liability or component of equity, but are a different asset, liability or component of equity under IFRSs; and

- apply IFRSs in measuring all recognised assets and liabilities.

5.2   Accounting policies

IFRS 1 requires an entity to use the same accounting policies in its opening IFRS statement of financial position and throughout all periods presented in its first IFRS financial statements. Those accounting policies must comply with each IFRS effective at the end of its first IFRS reporting period, subject to exceptions and exemptions that are explained in **sections 6** and **7** below. [IFRS 1:7]

The selection of accounting policies under IFRSs is considered in **section 3** of **chapter A5**. An entity is not bound by the accounting policy choices it made under previous GAAP when adopting IFRSs, even if the previous GAAP treatment is consistent with IFRSs. In particular, in circumstances in which IFRSs permit an explicit choice, that choice is not constrained by the policy adopted under previous GAAP (e.g. whether to use the revaluation basis for a class of property, plant and equipment). However, in other cases (e.g. when there is no specific guidance in IFRSs), the factors that were relevant in selecting an appropriate policy under previous GAAP should be considered when applying IAS 8.

An entity may not, therefore, apply different versions of IFRSs that were effective at earlier dates. However, new IFRSs that are not yet mandatory may be applied if they permit early adoption. [IFRS 1:8]

In May 2012, the IFRS Interpretations Committee confirmed that if application of a new IFRS is not yet mandatory at the end of an entity's first IFRS reporting period, but the IFRS permits early application, the entity is permitted, but not required, to apply the IFRS in its first IFRS financial statements provided that the IFRS is applied throughout all periods presented. Although the requirements of IFRS 1 are considered to be clear in this regard, at the time of writing it is proposed to amend IFRS 1:BC11 (which refers to 'current' versions of IFRSs) as part of *Annual Improvements to IFRSs: 2011–2013 Cycle*, so as to avoid any potential for misunderstanding (see **section 10** below).

Example 5.2

First-time adopter applying IFRS 9 in advance of its effective date – which version of IFRS 9 should be applied?

Entity A is a first-time adopter of IFRSs. Its date of transition to IFRSs is 1 January 2012 with its first IFRS financial statements presented for the year ended 31 December 2013.

In its first IFRS financial statements, Entity A would like to apply IFRS 9 *Financial Instruments*. IFRS 9 is being issued in phases. To date, two phases have been finalised and issued as follows.

- IFRS 9 *Financial Instruments* issued November 2009 (IFRS 9(2009)). This version of the Standard only includes requirements for the classification and measurement of financial assets.

- • IFRS 9 *Financial Instruments* issued October 2010 (IFRS 9(2010)). IFRS 9(2010) includes all of the requirements of IFRS 9(2009) with renumbering, with additional requirements for the recognition and measurement of financial liabilities. (It also includes requirements for recognition and derecognition, embedded derivatives, and fair value measurement, that were previously included in IAS 39 *Financial Instruments: Recognition and Measurement*. However, these items are unchanged (apart from renumbering). Consequently, whether an entity applies IFRS 9(2009) or IFRS 9(2010), the effect of these requirements is the same.)

Further phases of IFRS 9 will be issued on hedge accounting and amortised cost and impairment when the project to replace IAS 39 is complete.

Both IFRS 9(2009) and IFRS 9(2010) are effective for periods beginning on or after 1 January 2015 (i.e. after Entity A's first IFRS financial statements), with earlier application permitted.

Which version of IFRS 9 (2009 or 2010) should Entity A apply?

This question is not specifically addressed in IFRS 1. Note that neither version of IFRS 9 is effective for Entity A's first IFRS accounting period and, consequently, Entity A is not obliged to adopt either version in its first IFRS financial statements. In the absence of any specific requirement to the contrary (e.g. local regulatory requirements), Entity A has a choice as to which version of IFRS 9 to apply.

IFRS 1:BC11 explains that IFRS 1:7 to 9 require a first-time adopter to apply the current versions of IFRSs without considering superseded or amended versions with an objective, among others, of giving users comparative information that is prepared using later versions of IFRSs that the IASB regards as superior to superseded versions. However, IFRS 9(2009) and IFRS 9(2010) complement each other because the 2010 version builds on the 2009 version. Consequently, IFRS 9(2009) should not be considered as 'inferior' to IFRS 9(2010) — but as an earlier stage in the development of the IASB's comprehensive model for reporting financial instruments.

Allowing Entity A the choice as to which version of IFRS 9 to apply is consistent with the choice available to entities already applying IFRSs, which can choose to apply either IFRS 9(2009) or IFRS 9(2010) if they adopt IFRS 9 in a period beginning before 1 January 2015 (see IFRS 9(2010):7.3.2).

The transition provisions in other IFRSs apply to changes in accounting policies made by entities that already use IFRSs. They do not apply to a first-time adopter's transition to IFRSs except in certain specified circumstances that are explained in **sections 6** and **7** below. [IFRS 1:9]

For example, an entity with a 31 March year end prepares its first IFRS financial statements at 31 March 20X3. It presents a single year of comparative figures. The entity's date of transition to IFRSs is, therefore, 1 April 20X1.

The entity applies all of those IFRSs that are effective for years beginning on or before 1 April 20X2 (i.e. those that are effective at the end of its reporting period) and ignores any transition provisions in those IFRSs except when IFRS 1 specifies that they should be applied. Those IFRSs should be applied in preparing the opening statement of financial position at 1 April 20X1, the comparative statement of financial position at 31 March 20X2, and the statement of financial position at 31 March 20X3 in accordance with IFRSs. The entity is permitted, but not required, to apply any new IFRSs that have been issued but are not mandatory at the end of the reporting period, provided that the IFRSs in question permit early adoption.

5.2.1   New or amended IFRSs effective for the first IFRS reporting period issued after an interim financial report has been published

If an entity publishes an interim financial report during its first IFRS reporting period, it cannot be certain that there will be no subsequent changes to IFRSs that are effective for its first IFRS reporting period. In the event of such changes, the entity should revise its opening statement of financial position to comply with the new requirements and explain that it has done so in any subsequent interim financial report or its first annual financial statements under IFRSs. It is advisable for entities to include a statement in their interim financial reports to highlight the fact that the IFRS accounting policies may be subject to change.

5.2.2   Accounting policy changes after an entity has published an interim financial report in the year of adoption of IFRSs

IAS 8 *Accounting Policies, Changes in Accounting Estimates and Errors* does not apply to the changes in accounting policies that an entity makes when it adopts IFRSs or to changes in those policies until after it presents its first

IFRS financial statements. Therefore, IAS 8's requirements regarding changes in accounting policies do not apply in an entity's first IFRS financial statements. [IFRS 1:27]

Thus, when an entity has prepared an interim financial report under IFRSs during its first IFRS reporting period, it is acceptable for the entity to change the IFRS 1 elections and/or accounting policy choices reflected in that interim financial report in later reporting periods, leading up to and including its first annual financial statements. An entity's choices only need to be fixed by the time it prepares its first annual financial statements in accordance with IFRSs. The requirements of IAS 8 (both as regards justification for a change in accounting policy and disclosure) do not apply to any changes in accounting policies until after an entity presents its first IFRS financial statements (i.e. the first annual financial statements in which it adopts IFRSs).

If during the period covered by its first IFRS financial statements an entity changes its accounting policies or its use of the IFRS 1 exemptions, the effect of those changes should be explained and disclosed in the reconciliations required under IFRS 1, if appropriate (see **9.2.2** below).

5.2.3   Adjustments arising on the restatement of the opening statement of financial position

The adjustments arising on the restatement of the opening statement of financial position from previous GAAP to IFRSs should be recognised as an adjustment to retained earnings or, if appropriate, another category of equity, at the date of transition to IFRSs. [IFRS 1:11]

The adjustments are usually recognised in retained earnings except when another IFRS requires a separate component of equity to be recognised. For example, when an entity applies the revaluation model in IAS 16, the difference between fair value and depreciated cost at the date of transition is credited to a revaluation reserve. Similarly, a separate reserve is recognised in relation to derivatives classified as cash flow hedges. However, there is nothing to prevent a separate reserve being recognised within retained earnings in other circumstances. This may be appropriate, for example, if the reserve is not distributable or is subject to other legal restrictions.

6   Exceptions to retrospective application of other IFRSs

IFRS 1 prohibits retrospective application of some aspects of other IFRSs relating to:
[IFRS 1:13 and IFRS 1:B1]

- estimates (see **6.1** below);

- derecognition of financial assets and financial liabilities (see **6.2** below);

- hedge accounting (see **6.3** below);

- non-controlling interests (see **6.4** below);

- classification and measurement of financial assets (see **6.5** below);

- embedded derivatives (see **6.6** below); and

- government loans (see **6.7** below).

> The exceptions relating to classification and measurement of financial assets and embedded derivatives apply only to entities that adopt IFRS 9 *Financial Instruments* in their first IFRS financial statements.

6.1   Estimates

IFRS 1 requires estimates under IFRSs at the date of transition to IFRSs to be consistent with estimates made for the same date under previous GAAP, after adjustments to reflect any difference in accounting policies, unless there is objective evidence that those estimates were in error. [IFRS 1:14]

> Therefore, accounting estimates required under IFRSs that were made under previous GAAP may not be adjusted on transition except to reflect differences in accounting policies or unless there is objective evidence that the estimates were in error. The primary objective of this exception is to prevent entities using the benefit of hindsight to adjust estimates based on circumstances and information that were not known when the amounts were originally estimated under previous GAAP.

When restating the opening statement of financial position to IFRSs, an entity may have information about estimates it made under previous GAAP that was not available at the time when those estimates were made. This information is treated as non-adjusting (i.e. the amounts recognised are not adjusted). IFRS 1 gives the following example to illustrate this requirement.

Example 6.1

Consistency of estimates with previous GAAP

[IFRS 1:15]

Assume that an entity's date of transition to IFRSs is 1 January 20X4 and new information on 15 July 20X4 requires the revision of an estimate made in accordance with previous GAAP at 31 December 20X3. The entity shall not reflect that new information in its opening IFRS statement of financial position (unless the estimates need adjustment for any differences in accounting policies or there is objective evidence that the estimates were in error). Instead, the entity shall reflect the new information in profit or loss (or, if appropriate, other comprehensive income) for the year ended 31 December 20X4.

It may be necessary to make estimates under IFRSs at the date of transition to IFRSs that were not required at that date under previous GAAP. Those estimates should reflect conditions that existed at the date of transition to IFRSs. In particular, estimates of market prices, interest rates or foreign exchange rates should reflect market conditions at the date of transition to IFRSs. [IFRS 1:16]

The implementation guidance accompanying IFRS 1 explains that this exception does not override the requirements in other IFRSs to base classifications or measurements on circumstances existing at a particular date. Examples given are:
[IFRS 1:IG4]

- the distinction between finance leases and operating leases in IAS 17 *Leases*;

- the restrictions in IAS 38 *Intangible Assets* that prohibit capitalisation of expenditure on an internally generated intangible asset if the asset did not qualify for recognition when the expenditure was incurred; and

- the distinction between financial liabilities and equity instruments in IAS 32 *Financial Instruments: Presentation*.

The use of actuarial assumptions when applying IAS 19 *Employee Benefits* for the first time is considered at **7.6.3** below.

6.1.1   Correction of an error that occurred prior to the date of transition to IFRSs

If, when preparing its first IFRS financial statements, an entity discovers an error in an estimate made under previous GAAP, the effect of the correction of the error should be adjusted against retained earnings in the opening statement of financial position.

Such corrections should be disclosed separately in the reconciliations required under IFRS 1:24(a) and (b) (see **9.2.2** below). This disclosure should be on a gross basis; presentation of net errors is not acceptable.

6.1.2   Estimates made at the end of the comparative period

The principle also applies to comparative information presented in an entity's first IFRS financial statements. [IFRS 1:17] Therefore, estimates made at the end of the comparative period (in **example 6.1**, at 31 December 20X4) should follow the same rules as the opening IFRS statement of financial position as regards the use of hindsight.

6.2   Derecognition of financial assets and financial liabilities

A first-time adopter is required by IFRS 1:B2 to apply the derecognition rules in IFRS 9 (or, if the entity has not adopted IFRS 9, IAS 39) prospectively from the date of transition to IFRSs unless it elects to apply those derecognition rules retrospectively from a date of its choosing in accordance with IFRS 1:B3 (see **6.2.1** below). Therefore, if a first-time adopter derecognised financial assets or financial liabilities under its previous GAAP in a securitisation, transfer or other derecognition transaction that occurred before the date of transition to IFRSs (or an earlier date of the entity's choosing in accordance with IFRS 1:B3), it does not recognise those assets or liabilities at the date of transition (even if they would not have qualified for derecognition under IFRS 9 or IAS 39), unless they qualify for recognition as a result of a later transaction or event.

In applying this exception, it is important to note the following points.

- A first-time adopter must recognise any financial interest retained as a result of a derecognition transaction prior to the date of transition to IFRSs that still exists at the date of transition to IFRSs (e.g. any derivatives and other interests, such as servicing rights or servicing liabilities).

- The exemptions from retrospective application of the derecognition requirements do not extend to consolidation. A first-time adopter must consolidate all special purpose entities (SPEs) and structured entities that it controls at the date of transition to IFRSs, even if those entities existed before the date of transition to IFRSs or hold financial assets or financial liabilities that were derecognised under previous GAAP. [IFRS 1:IG26] Therefore, although a group may have derecognised financial assets under its previous GAAP as a result of a transfer of assets to a structured entity occurring before the date of transition to IFRSs, those assets may be consolidated back into the group's statement of financial position if the structured entity to which the financial assets were transferred is deemed to be controlled by the group in accordance with IFRS 10 *Consolidated Financial Statements* (or, for entities that have not adopted IFRS 10, SIC-12 *Consolidation – Special Purpose Entities*), and the structured entity did not derecognise the assets under its previous GAAP.

6.2.1   *Option to apply derecognition rules retrospectively from a chosen date*

Notwithstanding the requirement to apply the rules on derecognition prospectively from the date of transition to IFRSs, an entity may choose to apply them retrospectively from a date of the entity's choosing, provided that the information needed to apply IFRS 9 (or, if the entity has not adopted IFRS 9, IAS 39) to the financial assets and financial liabilities derecognised as a result of past transactions was obtained at the time of initially accounting for those transactions. [IFRS 1:B3]

For a more detailed discussion of the application of these derecognition rules on first-time adoption, see **section 3.1** of **chapter B13** or, for entities that have not adopted IFRS 9, **section 3.1** of **chapter C13**.

6.3   Hedge accounting

IFRS 1 prohibits retrospective application of IAS 39 in respect of hedge accounting. [IFRS 1:B4 – B6] This is consistent with the general hedging requirements in IAS 39 under which hedge accounting is only ever

available prospectively if the hedge relationship is appropriately designated, documented, is expected to be highly effective and satisfies all other
hedge accounting criteria.

> This exception applies equally to entities that adopt IFRS 9 in their
> first IFRS financial statements because, pending finalisation of the
> IASB's revised requirements regarding hedge accounting to be incor-
> porated into IFRS 9 in due course, such entities must apply IAS 39's
> requirements regarding hedge accounting.

At the date of transition to IFRSs, an entity is required to measure all
derivatives at fair value and eliminate all deferred gains and losses arising
on derivatives that were reported under previous GAAP as assets or
liabilities in the statement of financial position in respect of hedge relationships under previous GAAP because these do not qualify for recognition
as assets and liabilities under IFRSs. [IFRS 1:B4]

If, before the date of transition to IFRSs, a transaction had been designated
as a hedge of a type that qualifies for hedge accounting under IAS 39 but
the hedge does not meet all the specific conditions for hedge accounting in
IAS 39, the requirements of IAS 39:91 and IAS 39:101 should be applied to
discontinue hedge accounting. [IFRS 1:B6]

The designation and documentation of a hedge relationship must be
completed on or before the date of transition to IFRSs if the hedge
relationship is to qualify for hedge accounting from that date. Hedge
accounting can be applied prospectively only from the date that the hedge
relationship is fully designated and documented. [IFRS 1:IG60]

For a more detailed discussion of the application of IAS 39's hedge
accounting requirements on first-time adoption, see **section 3.3** of **chapter
B13** or, for entities that have not adopted IFRS 9, **section 3.3** of **chapter C13.**

6.4   Non-controlling interests

A first-time adopter should apply the following requirements of IFRS 10 (or, for entities that have not adopted IFRS 10, IAS 27(2008) *Consolidated and Separate Financial Statements*) prospectively from the date of transition to IFRSs:
[IFRS 1:B7]

- the requirement in IFRS 10:B94 (IAS 27(2008):28) that total comprehensive income be attributed to the owners of the parent and to the non-controlling interests even if this results in the non-controlling interests having a deficit balance;

- the requirements in IFRS 10:23 and B93 (IAS 27(2008):30 and 31) regarding the accounting for changes in the parent's ownership interest in a subsidiary that do not result in a loss of control; and

- the requirements in IFRS 10:B97 to B99 (IAS 27(2008):34 to 37) regarding the accounting for a loss of control over a subsidiary, and the related requirements in paragraph 8A of IFRS 5 *Non-current Assets Held for Sale and Discontinued Operations*.

However, if a first-time adopter elects to apply IFRS 3 *Business Combinations* retrospectively to past business combinations, it must also apply IFRS 10 (or, for entities that have not adopted IFRS 10, IAS 27(2008)) from the same date (see **section 7.1**). [IFRS 1:C1]

6.5   Classification and measurement of financial assets (entities applying IFRS 9)

A first-time adopter applying IFRS 9 is required to assess whether a financial asset meets the amortised cost criteria in IFRS 9(2010):4.1.2 on the basis of the facts and circumstances that exist at the date of transition to IFRSs. [IFRS 1:B8]

The criteria for qualification for amortised cost measurement under IFRS 9 are discussed in detail in **chapter B2**. In summary, IFRS 9(2010):4.1.2 requires an entity to assess whether the objective of its business model is to manage financial assets so as to collect the contractual cash flows. The requirement in IFRS 1:B8 for first-time adopters to make this assessment on the basis of facts and circumstances at the date of transition is consistent with the general transition requirement for continuing IFRS reporters in IFRS 9(2010):7.2.4 (which requires that the assessment be carried out at the date of initial application of the Standard). IFRS 9(2010):BC7.18 explains that the IASB believes that it would be "difficult, and perhaps impossible," to make the assessment on the basis of circumstances when the financial asset first qualified for recognition as a financial asset.

Once the classification of a financial asset has been determined on the basis described in IFRS 1:B8, that classification is applied retrospectively irrespective of the entity's business model in prior reporting periods.

6.6 Embedded derivatives (entities applying IFRS 9)

A first-time adopter applying IFRS 9 is required to assess whether an embedded derivative should be separated from the host contract and accounted for as a derivative on the basis of the conditions that existed at the later of the date it first became a party to the contract and the date a reassessment is required by IFRS 9(2010):B4.3.11. [IFRS 1:B9]

IFRS 9's requirements regarding the accounting for embedded derivatives are discussed in detail in **chapter B5**. In summary, IFRS 9 requires separate accounting for embedded derivatives not closely related to the host contract when the entire contract is not one measured at fair value through profit or loss and it is not a financial asset in the scope of IFRS 9. That assessment is generally made when the entity first becomes a party to a contract, and is revisited only when there has been a 'substantial modification' to the contract (see **section 3** of **chapter B5**). IFRS 1:B9 requires that a first-time adopter should make its assessment as to whether an embedded derivative is to be separated on the basis of conditions that existed at the later of the date it first became party to the contract and the date (if any) when the contract is substantially modified.

Once a first-time adopter has determined that an embedded derivative should be separated, the initial carrying amounts of the embedded derivative and the host contract should be determined based on the circumstances at the date the whole instrument satisfied the recognition criteria of IFRS 9. [IFRS 1:IG55]

If the entity cannot determine the initial carrying amounts of the embedded derivative and the host contract reliably, it treats the entire combined contract as a financial instrument as at fair value through profit or loss (see **section 12** of **chapter B5**). [IFRS 1:IG55]

6.7   Government loans

> Paragraph 10A of IAS 20 *Accounting for Government Grants and Disclosure of Government Assistance* requires the benefit of government loans advanced either interest-free or at a below-market rate of interest to be treated as a government grant, measured as the difference between the initial carrying amount of the loan determined in accordance with IFRS 9 (or IAS 39) and the proceeds received (see **section 4.3** of **chapter A36**). When this requirement was first introduced, the IASB decided on prospective application to avoid entities measuring the fair value of loans at an earlier date. However, no corresponding amendment was made to IFRS 1 at that time.
>
> A new exception added to IFRS 1 in March 2012 corrects this oversight by permitting first-time adopters of IFRSs to apply the requirements in paragraph 10A of IAS 20 only to new loans entered into after the date of transition to IFRSs. Specific requirements are established for government loans existing at the date of transition (see below).
>
> The March 2012 amendments are effective for annual periods beginning on or after 1 January 2013, with earlier application permitted.

A first-time adopter is required to classify all government loans received as either a financial liability or as an equity instrument in accordance with the requirements of IAS 32 *Financial Instruments: Presentation*. [IFRS 1:B10]

Except as permitted in IFRS 1:B11 (see **6.7.1**), first-time adopters should apply the requirements in IFRS 9 (or, for first-time adopters that have not adopted IFRS 9, IAS 39) and IAS 20 prospectively to government loans existing at the date of transition to IFRSs. When these requirements are applied prospectively:
[IFRS 1:B10]

- the first-time adopter should not recognise the corresponding benefit of the government loan at a below-market interest rate as a government grant;

- if the first-time adopter did not, under its previous GAAP, recognise and measure a government loan at a below-market rate of interest on a basis consistent with IFRSs, the previous GAAP carrying amount of the loan at the date of transition is used as the carrying amount of the loan in the opening IFRS statement of financial position; and

- IFRS 9 (or IAS 39) is applied in measuring the loan after the date of transition. For this purpose, the entity should calculate the effective interest rate on the loan by comparing the carrying amount of the loan at the date of transition to IFRSs with the amount and timing of expected repayments. [IFRS 1:IG66]

The following example, which is reproduced from the guidance accompanying IFRS 1, illustrates the application of these requirements for a first-time adopter.

Example 6.7

Government loan at a below-market rate of interest at the date of transition to IFRSs

[Guidance on implementing IFRS 1:Example 12]

To encourage entities to expand their operations in a specified development zone where it is difficult for entities to obtain financing for their projects, the government provides loans at a below-market rate of interest to fund the purchase of manufacturing equipment.

Entity S's date of transition is 1 January 20X2.

In accordance with the development scheme, in 20X0 Entity S receives a loan at a below-market rate of interest from the government for CU100,000. Under its previous GAAP, Entity S accounted for the loan as equity and the carrying amount under previous GAAP was CU100,000 at the date of transition to IFRSs. The amount repayable will be CU103,030 on 1 January 20X5.

No other payment is required under the terms of the loan and there are no further performance conditions attached to the loan. The information needed to measure the fair value of the loan was not obtained at the time of initially accounting for the loan.

The loan meets the definition of a financial liability in accordance with IAS 32. Entity S therefore reclassifies the government loan as a liability. It also uses the previous GAAP carrying amount of the loan at the date of transition to IFRSs as the carrying amount of the loan in the opening IFRS statement of financial position. Entity S therefore reclassifies the amount of CU100,000 from equity to liability in the opening IFRS statement of financial position. In order to measure the loan after the date of transition to IFRSs, the effective interest rate starting 1 January 20X2 is calculated as below:

$= (103,030 \, / \, 100,000)^{-3} - 1$

$= 0.01$

The carrying amounts of the loan are as follows:

Date	Carrying amount CU	Interest expense CU	Interest payable CU
1 January 20X2	100,000		
31 December 20X2	101,000	1,000	1,000
31 December 20X3	102,010	1,010	2,010
31 December 20X4	103,030	1,020	3,030

6.7.1   Option on a loan-by-loan basis to apply requirements re government loans retrospectively

Notwithstanding the requirement to apply the relevant requirements of IFRSs prospectively to government loans existing at the date of transition to IFRSs, an entity may choose to apply them retrospectively to any government loan originated before its date of transition to IFRSs, provided that the information needed to do so was obtained at the time of initially accounting for that loan. [IFRS 1:B11]

Consequently, if the information needed to apply IFRS 9 (or IAS 39) was obtained at the time of initially accounting for the loan, an entity can choose to apply the relevant requirements retrospectively – this option is available on a loan-by-loan basis.

7   Optional exemptions from retrospective application of other IFRSs

Retrospective application of IFRSs can require significant resources and could, in some circumstances, be impracticable. The IASB decided that the costs of applying IFRSs retrospectively may exceed the benefits in certain instances. IFRS 1 therefore provides a number of optional exemptions from the general principle of full retrospective application, as listed below.

A first-time adopter may elect to use one or more of the following exemptions:
[IFRS 1:18, IFRS 1:Appendices C & D]

- business combinations (see **7.1** below);

- share-based payment transactions (see **7.2** below);

- insurance contracts (see **7.3** below);

- deemed cost (see **7.4** below);

- leases (see **7.5** below);

- employee benefits (see **7.6** below);

- cumulative translation differences (see **7.7** below);

- investments in subsidiaries, associates and joint ventures* (see **7.8** below);

- assets and liabilities of subsidiaries, associates and joint ventures (see **7.9** below);

- compound financial instruments (see **7.10** below);

- designation of previously recognised financial instruments (see **7.11** below);

- fair value measurement of financial assets or financial liabilities at initial recognition (see **7.12** below);

- decommissioning liabilities included in the cost of property, plant and equipment (see **7.13** below);

- financial assets or intangible assets accounted for in accordance with IFRIC 12 *Service Concession Arrangements* (see **7.14** below);

- borrowing costs (see **7.15** below);

- transfers of assets from customers (see **7.16** below);

- extinguishing financial liabilities with equity instruments (see **7.17** below);

- severe hyperinflation (see **7.18** below);

- joint arrangements (see **7.19** below); and

- stripping costs in the production phase of a surface mine (see **7.20** below).

> *   For entities that do not adopt IFRS 11 *Joint Arrangements* in their first IFRS financial statements (required for annual periods beginning on or after 1 January 2013 with earlier adoption permitted), the reference to 'joint ventures' should be taken as a reference to 'jointly controlled entities'.

Appendix E to IFRS 1 sets out another category of 'short-term exemptions' which are applicable to users for a short time and which will be deleted once they become out of date (discussed in detail in **section 7.21** below).

> Unlike the mandatory exceptions discussed in **section 6** above, because the exemptions listed above are optional, entities may choose not to take advantage of them and instead to apply their IFRS accounting policies in these areas retrospectively, provided that the effects of retrospective application can be reliably estimated.
>
> If more than one optional exemption affects an account balance, more than one exemption may be applied. Each optional exemption is applied independently. There is no requirement to use a particular optional exemption as the result of choosing another exemption.
>
> For example, an entity might not restate a business combination prior to the date of transition so that the deemed cost of property, plant and equipment acquired in that business combination is the carrying amount under previous GAAP immediately after the business combination. The entity can override this deemed cost with a later deemed cost, such as fair value at the date of transition.

IFRS 1 states that the exemptions should not be applied by analogy to other items. [IFRS 1:D1]

> For example, a first-time adopter cannot use fair value or the previous GAAP carrying amount of an item as deemed cost except as specifically set out in the exemption (see **section 7.4**). The Standard specifies limited circumstances in which retrospective restatement in accordance with IFRSs does not apply. Unless the amount is immaterial, in all other circumstances IFRSs should be applied retrospectively.

Some of the optional exemptions refer to 'fair value'. For entities that adopt IFRS 13 *Fair Value Measurement* (see **3.3** above), fair value should be measured in accordance with the requirements of that Standard.

For entities that do not adopt IFRS 13, IFRS 1:19 (which is deleted as a consequential amendment arising from IFRS 13) requires that "[i]n determining fair values in accordance with this IFRS, an entity shall apply the definition of fair value in Appendix A [see **3.3** above] and any more specific guidance in other IFRSs on the determination of fair values for the asset or liability in question. Those fair values shall reflect conditions that existed at the date for which they were determined".

7.1   Business combinations

Note that the exemption discussed throughout this section only applies to business combinations to which IFRS 3 *Business Combinations* applies. The exemption does not apply, for example, to an investment entity's acquisition of a subsidiary to which, under IFRS 10:31, IFRS 3 should not be applied (see **15.2.1** in **chapter A24**).

7.1.1   Business combinations on or after the date of transition

For first-time adopters, irrespective of any exemptions applied, all business combinations on or after the date of transition to IFRSs should be accounted for in accordance with IFRS 3 *Business Combinations*.

Therefore, if an entity is preparing its first IFRS financial statements for the year ended 31 December 20X2, and its date of transition is 1 January 20X1, all business combinations on or after 1 January 20X1 are required to be accounted for in accordance with IFRS 3. If a business combination occurred in the comparative accounting period (20X1) and it was reported in the entity's previous GAAP financial statements for that period, the amounts previously reported will need to be restated if the application of IFRS 3 has a material effect.

7.1.2   Full retrospective application of IFRS 3 to business combinations before the date of transition

Entities that wish to apply IFRS 3 retrospectively to all business combinations prior to the date of transition to IFRSs may do so.

Any entity intending to opt for full retrospective application should ensure that it has the information needed to apply the acquisition method retrospectively in accordance with IFRS 3, which in particular includes:

- calculation of the cost of the business combination;

- identification of assets acquired (including any intangible assets), and liabilities assumed;

- measurement of fair value at the date of acquisition of assets acquired and liabilities assumed; and

- impairment test of goodwill each year subsequent to the date of acquisition.

Example 7.1.2

Full retrospective application of IFRS 3 – which version of IFRS 3?

Entity A is adopting IFRSs for the first time with a transition date of 1 January 2012 and its first IFRS financial statements will be prepared for the accounting period ended 31 December 2013. Entity A elects not to take the optional exemption in IFRS 1 and instead will apply IFRS 3 retrospectively to all past business combinations. Entity A has been involved in several business combinations dating back to 1990.

Which version of IFRS 3 should be applied to Entity A's business combinations before the effective date of IFRS 3 (as revised in 2008)?

If retrospective application of IFRS 3 is selected, IFRS 1 requires consistent application of the version of IFRS 3 that is adopted for the entity's first IFRS reporting period. Therefore, in the circumstances described, because IFRS 3 (as revised in 2008) is to be applied in the first IFRS reporting period, it must be applied retrospectively to all past business combinations (i.e. the previous version of IFRS 3 (issued in 2004) should *not* be applied to any of the entity's previous business combinations).

7.1.3   Optional exemption for business combinations – general

Rather than apply IFRS 3 retrospectively to business combinations prior to the date of transition to IFRSs, as an optional exemption first-time adopters are permitted to apply the requirements of Appendix C to IFRS 1, which are discussed for the remainder of this section. [IFRS 1:C1]

The most significant features of the accounting under Appendix C to IFRS 1 are that:

- the classification of former business combinations (acquisition or uniting of interests) under previous GAAP is maintained;

- there is no remeasurement of original 'fair values' determined at the time of the business combination (date of acquisition); and

- the carrying amount of goodwill recognised under previous GAAP is not adjusted, other than in specific instances.

It is important to understand that, although business combinations that occurred before the date of transition to IFRSs do not have to be 'restated' when the entity takes this optional exemption, this does not mean that all amounts recognised under previous GAAP relating to such business combinations can simply be carried forward under IFRSs. Adjustments may be required to the assets and liabilities recognised in such business combinations. These adjustments are discussed in the remainder of this section.

The decision to apply the business combinations exemption on first-time adoption, and the date from which the exemption is applied (see **7.1.4** below), can have a substantial impact on an entity's first IFRS financial statements. The following table summarises the key differences between using the exemption and restating business combinations to conform with the requirements of IFRS 3.

Subject	Optional exemption in IFRS 1 applied	IFRS 3 applied retrospectively
Classification (see **7.1.7**)	Keep the previous classification (acquisition/ pooling of interests/ reverse acquisition).	Identify the acquirer and the acquiree under IFRS 3.
Recognition (see **7.1.8** and **7.1.9**)	Identify assets and liabilities at the date of transition to IFRSs and: • recognise assets and liabilities in compliance with IFRSs (except for some financial assets and financial liabilities derecognised under previous GAAP and some assets and liabilities that were not recognised in the acquirer's statement of financial position under previous GAAP), which means that both recognition criteria – reliable measurement and probability – must be met for all assets and liabilities; and • exclude assets and liabilities not complying with IFRSs.	Identify assets and liabilities at the date of acquisition and: • recognise assets and liabilities in accordance with IFRS 3; and • exclude assets and liabilities not complying with IFRSs.
Measurement (see **7.1.10** to **7.1.12**)	**IFRS measurement basis other than cost:** these assets and liabilities are measured on that basis at the date of transition, e.g. fair value. **Cost-based measured assets and liabilities:** these assets and liabilities are measured at the carrying amount under previous GAAP immediately after the business combination less subsequent accumulated depreciation under IFRSs. **Assets and liabilities not recognised under previous GAAP:** these assets and liabilities are measured as if the acquiree had adopted IFRSs.	All identifiable assets and liabilities are measured in accordance with IFRS 3 (most at fair value at the date of acquisition).
Measurement of goodwill (see **7.1.13**)	Keep the carrying amount of goodwill at the date of transition, except adjust for: • recognition/ non-recognition of intangible assets at the date of transition; and • impairment of goodwill. Goodwill deducted from equity under previous GAAP remains deducted from equity at the date of transition.	Goodwill is determined at the date of acquisition in accordance with IFRS 3. This is likely to result in adjustments to the carrying amount of any goodwill recognised under previous GAAP, including reversals of goodwill previously deducted from equity. Reverse previous goodwill amortisation.

Subject	Optional exemption in IFRS 1 applied	IFRS 3 applied retrospectively
Subsidiaries not previously consolidated (see **7.1.14**)	Recognise and measure assets and liabilities at the date of transition as if the subsidiary always has applied IFRSs. Determine goodwill at the date of transition as the difference between: • the parent's interest in those adjusted carrying amounts; and • the cost of the investment in the subsidiary.	Apply the general rules as stated above.

7.1.4   Timing the use of the exemption

A first-time adopter may elect not to apply IFRS 3 retrospectively to business combinations that occurred before the date of transition to IFRSs. [IFRS 1:C1] In such circumstances, IFRS 3 is applied prospectively for business combinations on or after the date of transition.

However, the entity may elect to restate business combinations from any date prior to the date of transition. If any business combination is restated, then all later business combinations must also be restated. [IFRS 1:C1]

If business combinations prior to the date of transition are restated, they must be restated to conform with the requirements of the version of IFRS 3 that is being applied in the first-time adopter's first IFRS reporting period.

Therefore, if Entity B, with a first IFRS reporting period ending on 31 December 2013, elects to apply IFRS 3 for all business combinations occurring on or after 1 January 2005, IFRS 3 (as revised in 2008) is applied to all restated combinations. This is the case even though, for entities already applying IFRSs, the general transition provisions of IFRS 3 (as revised in 2008) do not permit that version of the Standard to be applied before 30 June 2007. Equally, Entity B must apply IFRS 10 *Consolidated Financial Statements* from 1 January 2005.

These requirements are illustrated in the following diagram.

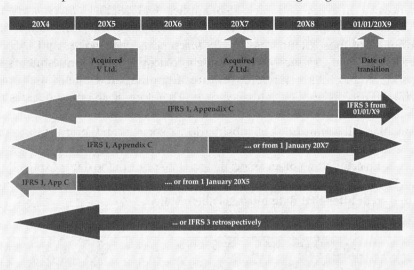

Example 7.1.4

Timing the use of the exemption for business combinations

Company A is adopting IFRSs for the year ended 31 December 20X5. Company A's date of transition is 1 January 20X4. Company A purchased Company B on 31 October 20X3, Company C on 15 March 20X4, Company D on 17 July 20X4 and Company E on 15 February 20X5.

The business combinations involving Company C and Company D must be restated in accordance with IFRS 3 because all business combinations on or after the date of transition (1 January 20X4) must be accounted for in accordance with the accounting requirements in force at the end of the entity's first IFRS reporting period (31 December 20X5). Similarly, the purchase of Company E will be accounted for in accordance with IFRS 3 when the purchase occurs because it is subsequent to the date of transition to IFRSs.

The purchase of Company B may also be restated if Company A elects to restate all business combinations from 31 October 20X3. If Company A does not restate the purchase of Company B, the requirements of Appendix C to IFRS 1 must be applied to the transaction in the first financial statements prepared in accordance with IFRSs.

7.1.5   Past acquisitions of investments in associates and interests in joint ventures

The exemption for past business combinations also applies to past acquisitions of investments in associates and of interests in joint ventures. The selected date (see **7.1.4**) applies equally for acquisitions of investments in associates and interests in joint ventures. [IFRS 1:C5] In such circumstances, a first-time adopter also applies IAS 28(2011) *Investments in Associates and Joint Ventures* and IFRS 11 *Joint Arrangements* (or, prior to the adoption of those Standards, IAS 28 *Investments in Associates* and IAS 31 *Interests in Joint Ventures*) retrospectively to acquisitions of investments in associates and interests in joint ventures from the same date as that from which IFRS 3 is applied retrospectively. Therefore, if an entity decides to restate an acquisition of a subsidiary at a date prior to the date of transition, all acquisitions of subsidiaries, associates and joint ventures on or after that date must also be restated. Equally, if an entity chooses to restate an acquisition of an associate at a date prior to the date of transition to IFRSs, all acquisitions of subsidiaries, other associates and joint ventures on or after that date must also be restated.

Example 7.1.5

The effect of a restatement of a business combination on the acquisition of an associate or a joint venture

Company D is adopting IFRSs with a date of transition of 1 January 20X5. It chooses to restate acquisitions of subsidiaries starting from 1 January 20X2. As a result, all acquisitions of associates and joint ventures from that date must also be restated.

7.1.6   Step acquisitions

For a step acquisition (i.e. the acquisition of another entity in stages), the timing of the exemption is determined by reference to the date of acquisition of the subsidiary, i.e. the date on which the acquirer obtains control.

Example 7.1.6

Step acquisition completed prior to the date of transition

Company C acquired Company T in stages, beginning with a 10 per cent share purchase on 30 June 20X5, 30 per cent on 31 December 20X5, and 20 per cent on 31 December 20X6. Company C obtained control of Company T on 31 December 20X6, which is its 'acquisition date' as defined in IFRS 3.

Company C is a first-time adopter with 1 January 20X7 as its date of transition to IFRSs and it has elected to restate all business combinations after 1 January 20X6 in accordance with IFRS 3.

In this example, the date of acquisition of Company T is 31 December 20X6 and, consequently, the business combination should be restated. Because the election to restate past business combinations is determined by reference to the date of acquisition of a subsidiary, the steps that occurred prior to

---

> 1 January 20X6 do not affect the date from which all business combinations are required to be restated. Therefore, in this example, restatement in accordance with IFRS 3 is not required for any other business combination prior to 1 January 20X6.

7.1.7   Classification of past business combinations

Under previous GAAP, a business combination may have been classified differently than IFRSs would require for the same business combination. For example, under previous GAAP an acquisition may have been classified as:

- a uniting of interests (also known as a 'pooling of interests'), which is not permitted for business combinations within the scope of IFRS 3; or

- an acquisition following the legal form, which would have been classified as a reverse acquisition under IFRS 3.

If an entity elects to apply the optional exemption for business combinations, the classification under previous GAAP is retained. [IFRS 1:C4(a)] If the entity instead elects to apply IFRS 3 retrospectively, the classification is changed retrospectively to comply with IFRS 3.

> The determination as to whether a transaction qualifies for the business combination exemption depends on whether that combination meets the definition of a business combination under IFRSs. If the transaction meets the definition, regardless of whether it met the definition under the entity's previous GAAP, use of the exemption for business combinations is permitted for that transaction.
>
> If a subsidiary was not previously consolidated (e.g. because the parent did not regard the entity as a subsidiary under previous GAAP), the requirements of IFRS 1:C4(j) regarding subsidiaries not previously consolidated should be applied (see **7.1.14** below).

7.1.8   Recognition of assets and liabilities

When IFRS 3 is not applied retrospectively to a past business combination, Appendix C to IFRS 1 requires that all of the assets acquired and liabilities assumed in that business combination that qualify for recognition under IFRSs should be recognised at the date of transition, other than:

- some financial assets and financial liabilities derecognised under previous GAAP (see **6.2** above); and

- assets, including goodwill, and liabilities that were not recognised in the acquirer's consolidated statement of financial position under previous GAAP and also would not qualify for recognition under IFRSs in the separate statement of financial position of the acquiree (see **7.1.12** and **7.1.13** below).

Therefore, even though IFRS 3 is not being applied retrospectively, application of Appendix C may result in the recognition of some assets and liabilities that were not recognised under previous GAAP (see **7.1.12**) and in the derecognition of some assets and liabilities that were recognised under previous GAAP (see **7.1.9**).

Note that the recognition criteria to be applied under Appendix C to IFRS 1 are those that generally apply to the specific asset or liability under consideration in accordance with relevant IFRSs rather than the recognition criteria set out in IFRS 3. In a limited number of cases, this can give rise to a different result than if IFRS 3 were applied to that business combination. For example, under Appendix C, the recognition requirements of IAS 37 *Provisions, Contingent Liabilities and Contingent Assets* are applied to contingent liabilities acquired in a business combination, with the result that some contingent liabilities that would have been recognised if IFRS 3 were applied for the same business combination may not be recognised (for further discussion, see **7.1.12**).

Any adjustments arising under Appendix C as a result of the recognition of assets acquired and liabilities assumed in a past business combination that were not recognised under previous GAAP should be made against retained earnings (or another appropriate category of equity), other than when the adjustment relates to an intangible asset that was previously subsumed within goodwill (see **7.1.13**). [IFRS 1:C4(b)]

Adjustments to deferred tax arising from the application of Appendix C to business combinations that occurred before the date of transition to IFRSs are considered at **7.1.17** below.

7.1.9   Assets and liabilities that should not be recognised

When Appendix C is applied to a past business combination, assets acquired and liabilities assumed in that business combination that do not

qualify for recognition under IFRSs, but that were recognised under previous GAAP, are required to be derecognised. The resulting adjustments should be accounted for as follows.
[IFRS 1:C4(c)]

- The first-time adopter may have classified a past business combination as an acquisition and recognised as an intangible asset an item that does not qualify for recognition as an asset under IAS 38 *Intangible Assets*. Such an item (and any related deferred tax and non-controlling interest) should be reclassified as part of goodwill unless the entity deducted goodwill directly from equity under previous GAAP (see **7.1.13** below).

- All other adjustments resulting from the derecognition of assets and liabilities arising from a past business combination that were recognised under previous GAAP should be made against retained earnings. Such changes include reclassifications from and to intangible assets if goodwill was not recognised under previous GAAP as an asset. This may arise if, under previous GAAP, goodwill was deducted directly from equity or the business combination was not treated as an acquisition.

Example 3 in the implementation guidance accompanying IFRS 1 illustrates the application of these requirements to a provision for restructuring costs which had been recognised under local GAAP but which would not be recognised under IFRSs.

7.1.10   Assets and liabilities subsequently measured on a basis other than historical cost

When IFRSs require subsequent measurement of an asset or a liability on a basis that is not based on original cost (e.g. fair value), that asset or liability should be measured on that basis in the opening IFRS statement of financial position even if it was acquired or assumed in a past business combination.

Therefore, when applying Appendix C for items that are required by IFRSs to be measured at fair value on an ongoing basis, the carrying amount established in the business combination under previous GAAP is effectively ignored and the IFRS carrying amount at the date of transition is established as its fair value at that date.

Any adjustment to the carrying amount of an asset or liability under this section is made against retained earnings (or, if appropriate, another category of equity) rather than goodwill. [IFRS 1:C4(d)]

7.1.11   Previous GAAP carrying amount to be treated as deemed cost

For assets and liabilities acquired in a past business combination and recognised under previous GAAP, other than those covered by **7.1.10** above and other than goodwill (see **7.1.14**), Appendix C requires that their IFRS carrying amounts should be determined by reference to their carrying amounts established in the business combination under previous GAAP.

Immediately after the business combination, the carrying amounts under previous GAAP of assets and liabilities assumed in that business combination are treated as their deemed cost under IFRSs at that date. If IFRSs require a cost-based measurement of those assets and liabilities at a later date, that deemed cost should be the basis for cost-based depreciation or amortisation from the date of the business combination. [IFRS 1:C4(e)]

It is therefore unnecessary to adjust such amounts even if they are calculated on a basis that would not have been acceptable under IFRS 3. For example, if previous GAAP required the assets and liabilities of an acquiree to be measured at the date of acquisition at the acquiree's book value instead of at fair value, those book values would be treated as the deemed cost of those assets and liabilities at the date of acquisition for subsequent accounting under IFRSs.

Note that the deemed cost is established at the date of acquisition of the acquiree; adjustments may be required to reflect depreciation or amortisation between that date and the date of transition to IFRSs.

The principle established in IFRS 1:C4(e) will generally apply to intangible assets acquired in a business combination and recognised under previous GAAP in the same way as other categories of assets and liabilities. However, an exception arises when the carrying amount recognised for the intangible asset under previous GAAP was zero. In such circumstances, the intangible asset should not be recognised in the opening IFRS statement of financial position unless it would qualify under IAS 38 (applying the criteria discussed at **8.7** below) for recognition in the separate statement of financial position of the acquiree at the date of transition to IFRSs. If those recognition criteria are met, the asset is measured on the basis that IAS 38 would require in the separate statement of financial position of the acquiree. The resulting adjustment affects goodwill. [IFRS 1:IG49]

> The effect of IFRS 1:IG49 is that intangible assets that were recognised in a past business combination under previous GAAP, but at a 'nil' carrying amount, will be dealt with under Appendix C in the same manner as if the intangible asset had not been recognised under previous GAAP (see **7.1.12**).

If there is any indication that the assets and liabilities arising from a past business combination that were recognised under previous GAAP are impaired, they should be tested for impairment based on conditions that existed at the date of transition to IFRSs in accordance with IAS 36 *Impairment of Assets*. [IFRS 1:IG Example 2]

7.1.12   Assets and liabilities not recognised under previous GAAP

If an asset acquired or a liability assumed in a past business combination was not recognised under previous GAAP, it does not have a deemed cost of zero in the opening IFRS statement of financial position. Instead, Appendix C to IFRS 1 requires that the asset or liability be recognised and measured in the consolidated statement of financial position on the basis that IFRSs would require in the separate statement of financial position of the acquiree.

For example, if a finance lease acquired in a business combination was not capitalised under previous GAAP, and the entity has elected not to restate past business combinations in accordance with IFRS 3, Appendix C requires that the lease should be capitalised in the IFRS consolidated statement of financial position because IAS 17 *Leases* would require the acquiree to do so in its own separate IFRS statement of financial position. [IFRS 1:C4(f)]

> **Example 7.1.12A**
>
> **Finance lease acquired in a business combination not capitalised under previous GAAP**
>
> Parent Company A's date of transition to IFRSs is 1 January 20X5. Parent Company A acquired Subsidiary B on 15 January 20X3 and, under previous

GAAP, did not capitalise Subsidiary B's finance leases entered into prior to 15 January 20X3. If Subsidiary B prepared separate financial statements under IFRSs, it would recognise finance lease obligations of CU750 and leased assets of CU625 at 1 January 20X5. On transition to IFRSs, Parent Company A has elected not to restate past business combinations in accordance with IFRS 3.

When applying Appendix C to IFRS 1 on transition to IFRSs, in its consolidated opening IFRS statement of financial position, Parent Company A is required to recognise Subsidiary B's finance lease obligations at CU750 and leased assets at CU625, and the net resulting adjustment of CU125 in retained earnings at that date.

Similarly, if the acquirer had not, under its previous GAAP, recognised a contingent liability assumed in a business combination that still exists at the date of transition to IFRSs, the acquirer should recognise that contingent liability at that date unless IAS 37 would prohibit its recognition in the financial statements of the acquiree. [IFRS 1:C4(f)]

This additional example of a contingent liability was added to IFRS 1:C4(f) when IFRS 3 was revised in 2008. Its application is unclear, because IAS 37:27 prohibits the 'recognition' of all contingent liabilities within its scope. Therefore, it appears that a contingent liability assumed in a past business combination not restated under IFRS 3 will be recognised under IFRS 1:C4(f) only when it is outside the scope of IAS 37 because it is covered by another Standard, in accordance with IAS 37:1(c).

If an asset acquired or a liability assumed in a past business combination was subsumed in goodwill under previous GAAP but would have been recognised separately under IFRS 3, that asset or liability remains in goodwill unless IFRSs would require its recognition in the separate financial statements of the acquiree. [IFRS 1:C4(f)]

Under this principle, when Appendix C to IFRS 1 is applied, intangible assets of the acquiree arising from a past business combination that were not separately recognised under previous GAAP are only recognised in the opening IFRS consolidated statement of financial position if they would have satisfied the criteria for recognition under IAS 38 in the statement of financial position of the acquiree. The criteria for recognition of such assets in the statement of financial position of the acquiree are the same as those explained in IFRS

1:IG46 and IFRS 1:IG48 (in the context of intangible assets arising other than in a business combination). Accordingly, unless they satisfied the criteria for recognition under IAS 38 at an earlier date (including an assessment and documentation at that date regarding the probability of future economic benefits as well as a reliable system of accumulating the costs – see **8.7** below), intangible assets generated internally by the acquiree will not be recognised at the date of transition. Conversely, intangible assets acquired by the acquiree externally will be recognised in most cases because the transaction and invoice are usually sufficient documentation and evidence of future economic benefits at that date.

In contrast, if the past business combination were restated in accordance with IFRS 3, all intangible assets acquired in the business combination would be recognised at the date of acquisition.

Example 7.1.12B

Deferred tax asset acquired in a past business combination

Company K acquired Company B on 1 January 20X4. Company K adopts IFRSs in 20X7 (date of transition is 1 January 20X6). Upon transition to IFRSs, Company K chooses not to restate this business combination in accordance with IFRS 3.

Company B has a tax loss that will expire if it is not used before 31 December 20X8. At the date of acquisition, Company K assessed that the tax loss carried forward in Company B could not be used before its expiry date. Consequently, Company K did not recognise the related deferred tax asset at the date of acquisition. The nominal value of the unused tax loss remains unchanged at the date of transition.

At the date of transition to IFRSs, Company K assesses that a portion of the unrecognised tax asset would probably be used before it expires at the end of 20X8.

A deferred tax asset should be recognised at the date of transition to IFRSs. IFRS 1 does not include any exceptions to the general principle for deferred tax assets. Therefore, a deferred tax asset is recognised in the opening IFRS statement of financial position for the amount the entity expects will be used at the date of transition to IFRSs. The resulting adjustment is recognised in retained earnings because this is not one of the permitted adjustments to goodwill under IFRS 1:C4(g) (see **7.1.13** below).

Example 7.1.12C

Asset acquired in a business combination but not recognised under previous GAAP for which recognition is required under IFRSs

Company D acquired Company Z and accounted for the transaction under previous GAAP three years prior to Company D's date of transition to IFRSs. Upon transition to IFRSs, Company D chooses not to restate this business combination in accordance with IFRS 3.

Two years prior to being acquired by Company D, Company Z purchased a licence for CU100 with a remaining useful life of 20 years. As part of its acquisition of Company Z, Company D obtained that licence with a remaining life of 18 years. Under previous GAAP, Company D did not (and was not required to) recognise the licence separately from goodwill.

Goodwill was amortised over 20 years under previous GAAP. The intangible asset does not meet the criteria for use of the revaluation model in IAS 38. The licence is not tax deductible.

How should the licence be accounted for in the opening statement of financial position at the date of transition to IFRSs?

For business combinations that occurred before the date of transition to IFRSs and that are not restated in accordance with IFRS 3, under IFRS 1:C4(b)(ii) assets and liabilities are *not* recognised if they (1) were not recognised separately in the acquirer's consolidated statement of financial position and (2) would not qualify for recognition under IFRSs in the separate statement of financial position of the acquiree.

In the circumstances described, although the licence was not recognised separately in Company D's consolidated statement of financial position, it would qualify for recognition in Company Z's statement of financial position under IFRSs; consequently, it fails the second condition in IFRS 1:C4(b)(ii). The licence should be recognised separately in Company D's consolidated financial statements under the requirements of IFRS 1:C4(f). At the date of transition to IFRSs, Company D should recognise the following adjustments:

- recognition of the intangible asset at its restated IFRS carrying amount of CU100 less accumulated amortisation of CU25 [(100÷20) × 5]; and

- adjustment of goodwill by the same amount (under IFRS 1:C4(g)(i), this is one of the limited circumstances in which the carrying amount of goodwill under previous GAAP is adjusted).

Although the amount recognised on restatement of the intangible asset's amortisation may differ from the amortisation that was recognised for the equivalent portion of goodwill recognised under previous GAAP, the previous amortisation of goodwill is not adjusted because that is not permitted under IFRS 1:C4(h)(ii); therefore, the restated goodwill is not necessarily what it would have been if the intangible asset had always been recognised separately.

If the amount to be recognised for the intangible asset exceeds the carrying amount of goodwill under previous GAAP, once goodwill has been reduced to zero the excess should be recognised as an adjustment to retained earnings.

Example 7.1.12D

Costs of development projects not recognised under previous GAAP

Parent Company C acquired Subsidiary D on 1 January 20X2. Parent Company C adopts IFRSs in 20X6 with a date of transition of 1 January 20X5. Upon transition to IFRSs, Parent Company C chooses not to restate this business combination in accordance with IFRS 3.

Under previous GAAP, all development costs were expensed as incurred. Had Subsidiary D applied IFRSs, development costs of CU20 related to a project completed at 31 December 20X1 would have been recognised as an internally generated intangible asset. The useful life of the intangible asset is 5 years. The fair value is assessed to be CU18 at 1 January 20X2 and CU10 at the date of transition (i.e. 1 January 20X5). No active market exists for this type of intangible asset.

The following journal entry is required at the date of transition in accordance with IFRS 1:C4(f).

		CU	CU
Dr	Development costs	20	
Cr	Accumulated amortisation		
	[CU20 x 3/5]		12
Cr	Goodwill [CU20 – CU12]		8

Recognition of the development cost asset.

Because the development costs were not recognised under previous GAAP, the acquirer (Parent Company C) recognises and measures the development costs in its consolidated IFRS statement of financial position on the basis that IFRSs would require in the statement of financial position of the acquiree (Subsidiary D). At the date of transition, this amount is CU8 (CU20 amortised over 3 out of 5 years). Goodwill is adjusted accordingly because the asset was previously subsumed within goodwill.

The option in IFRS 1 to measure intangible assets at fair value is not available in this case because no active market exists for these types of intangible assets.

Example 7.1.12E

Measurement of an asset acquired in a business combination but not recognised under previous GAAP for which recognition is required under IFRSs

Company A purchases a licence to operate a business in a particular jurisdiction for CU10 and recognises an intangible asset. Company A is subsequently acquired by Company B. Under its local GAAP, Company B does not recognise the licence as an intangible asset separately from goodwill.

Company B is subsequently acquired by Company C. Company C determines that the fair value of the licence at the date of acquisition of Company B is CU50 and recognises it as an intangible asset separately from goodwill.

Company C is subsequently acquired by Company D, but Company D does not recognise the licence as an intangible asset separately from goodwill.

The licence is therefore reported separately in the individual financial statements of Company A and in the consolidated financial statements of Company C.

Company D subsequently adopts IFRSs and chooses not to restate its acquisition of Company C in accordance with IFRS 3.

At what amount should the licence be recognised upon first-time adoption of IFRSs?

This example is similar to that discussed in **example 7.1.12C**. Although the intangible asset was not recognised in Company D's consolidated financial statements under previous GAAP, the second condition in IFRS 1:C4(b)(ii) is not met and, therefore, the licence should be recognised separately in Company D's consolidated financial statements under IFRSs.

However, this example raises an additional question because there are two alternatives available on which to base the measurement of the intangible asset in Company D's consolidated financial statements (the original cost of CU10 recognised by Company A and the fair value of CU50 recognised by Company C when it acquired Company B). IFRS 1 does not provide guidance as to which of these measures should be used. In many cases, the measurement would be based on the most reliable information. If both measurements were determined to be reliable, then the most recent fair value (CU50) would be the most relevant measurement and should be used. The amount recognised (and the equivalent adjustment to goodwill) will be adjusted for amortisation of the intangible asset in accordance with IFRSs from the date of the measurement to the date of transition to IFRSs.

7.1.13   Adjustments to goodwill

As a general principle, under the optional exemption for business combinations, the carrying amount of goodwill in the opening IFRS statement of financial position is its carrying amount under previous GAAP at the date of transition to IFRSs, adjusted only for the following items:
[IFRS 1:C4(g)]

- goodwill is increased when it is necessary to reclassify an item that was recognised as an intangible asset under previous GAAP (see **7.1.9** above);

- goodwill is decreased (and, if applicable, deferred tax and non-controlling interests adjusted) when it is necessary to recognise an intangible asset that was subsumed within recognised goodwill under previous GAAP (see **7.1.12** above); and

- regardless of whether there is any indication that goodwill may be impaired, IAS 36 should be applied in testing goodwill for impairment at the date of transition to IFRSs and in recognising any resulting impairment loss in retained earnings (or, if required by IAS 36, in revaluation surplus). The impairment test is based on conditions at the date of transition to IFRSs.

> Goodwill should not be subject to amortisation even if it includes a subsumed intangible asset with a finite life. All goodwill should be tested for impairment at the date of transition to IFRSs.

No other adjustments to goodwill are permitted at the date of transition to IFRSs. IFRS 1 highlights the following examples for which goodwill is not adjusted:
[IFRS 1:C4(h)]

- to exclude in-process research and development acquired in that business combination (unless the related intangible asset would qualify for recognition under IAS 38 in the separate statement of financial position of the acquiree);

- to adjust previous amortisation of goodwill; or

- to reverse adjustments to goodwill that IFRS 3 would not permit, but that were made under previous GAAP because of adjustments to assets and liabilities between the date of the business combination and the date of transition to IFRSs.

> Although there is no explicit prohibition in IFRS 1 on the reversal of a past impairment of goodwill, this is similar to a reversal of past amortisation which is explicitly prohibited by IFRS 1:C4(h)(ii). Also, the list of permitted adjustments to goodwill under IFRS 1:C4(g) refers only to "any resulting impairment loss" and does not envisage a profit arising from the impairment review of goodwill at the date of transition.

From the date of transition, goodwill is no longer amortised. As a result, IFRS 1 requires that goodwill be tested for impairment at the date of transition, in accordance with IAS 36, irrespective of whether there is any indication that goodwill may be impaired. The effect of any impairment loss identified is deducted from equity in the opening IFRS statement of financial position.

When goodwill has been amortised under previous GAAP, the carrying amount of accumulated amortisation at the date of transition is adjusted against the original cost of goodwill. The net amount is carried forward as the new carrying amount under IFRSs.

7.1.13.1 Amortisation recognised under previous GAAP after the date of application of IFRS 3

Example 7.1.13.1

Amortisation recognised under previous GAAP after the date of application of IFRS 3

Entity M is adopting IFRSs for the first time in its financial statements for the year ended 31 December 20X5; its date of transition is 1 January 20X4.

If Entity M uses the optional exemption under IFRS 1 not to apply IFRS 3 to business combinations before its date of transition, the carrying amount of goodwill under previous GAAP at 1 January 20X4 is the starting point for accounting for goodwill under IFRSs. No amortisation is recognised after that date.

Goodwill is required to be tested for impairment at 1 January 20X4 under IAS 36. Any impairment loss identified is recognised in retained earnings at 1 January 20X4.

However, if Entity M elects to apply IFRS 3 for all business combinations after an earlier date (say, 1 January 20X2), Entity M is also required to reverse the goodwill amortisation recognised under previous GAAP in 20X2 and 20X3 related to those business combinations for which the date of acquisition is on or after 1 January 20X2. Goodwill arising from business combinations with a date of acquisition before 1 January 20X2 will continue to be amortised until the date of transition.

If IFRS 3 is applied from 1 January 20X2, goodwill is tested annually for impairment as from 1 January 20X2 and any impairment loss in the period from 1 January 20X2 to 31 December 20X3 is recognised in retained earnings at 1 January 20X4.

7.1.13.2   *Goodwill previously deducted from equity*

If, under previous GAAP, goodwill was recognised as a deduction from equity and the entity has elected not to restate past business combinations in accordance with IFRS 3:
[IFRS 1:C4(i)]

- that goodwill is not recognised in the opening IFRS statement of financial position;

- that goodwill should not be reclassified to profit or loss if the subsidiary is disposed of or if the investment in the subsidiary becomes impaired; and

- adjustments resulting from the subsequent resolution of a contingency affecting the purchase consideration should be recognised in retained earnings.

7.1.13.3   *'Negative goodwill'*

If, under previous GAAP, an entity recognised any 'negative goodwill' in its statement of financial position, and the entity has elected not to restate past business combinations in accordance with IFRS 3, any 'negative goodwill' recognised under previous GAAP is derecognised with a corresponding adjustment to retained earnings at the date of transition.

7.1.13.4   *Reassessment of provisional fair values after the date of transition*

Example 7.1.13.4

Reassessment of provisional fair values after the date of transition

Under its previous GAAP, Entity A used provisional fair values at the time of a business combination occurring shortly prior to its date of transition to IFRSs.

How should Entity A measure goodwill in its first IFRS financial statements?

When IFRS 3 is not applied retrospectively to a business combination prior to the date of transition to IFRSs, the carrying amount of goodwill in the opening IFRS statement of financial position is its carrying amount under previous GAAP at the date of transition, adjusted only for three items specified in paragraph C4(g) of IFRS 1 (see above). If the business combination was in the period immediately prior to the date of transition, it is possible that adjustments would have been made in the next period, under previous GAAP, to the amount of goodwill because of a reassessment of provisional fair values. It may at first appear that IFRS 1 has the effect of prohibiting the adjustment of goodwill and that the amount would therefore have to remain as originally stated under previous GAAP at the date of transition. This is not so.

Under IFRS 3, adjustments to provisional fair values and goodwill may be made in the period subsequent to the business combination. The period during which such an adjustment is permitted is limited to twelve months from the date of acquisition, which may differ from the period during which such adjustments are permitted under previous GAAP. Under IFRS 3, the adjustment is reflected through a retrospective restatement of the previous period as if the initial accounting had been completed from the date of acquisition but previous GAAP may require the adjustment to be made as a current year adjustment to goodwill.

It is possible to adjust goodwill recognised in the opening IFRS statement of financial position if such an adjustment would be permitted by IFRS 3. The restriction on adjustments to goodwill in IFRS 1 applies only to the amount initially recognised and does not preclude subsequent adjustments as permitted or required by other IFRSs. The amount may be adjusted for the reassessment of fair values on the basis that IFRS 3 requires retrospective restatement for this. In other words, the provisional goodwill figure under previous GAAP is treated as the opening provisional goodwill figure under IFRSs.

7.1.14   Subsidiaries not consolidated under previous GAAP

Under previous GAAP, an entity may not have consolidated a subsidiary acquired in a past business combination because, for example, it did not regard the investment as a subsidiary, or because the subsidiary was exempted from consolidation under previous GAAP, or because the entity did not prepare consolidated financial statements under previous GAAP.

If a subsidiary has not previously been consolidated, and the acquirer has elected not to restate past business combinations in accordance with IFRS 3, at the date of transition the parent identifies the assets and liabilities of the subsidiary and adjusts the carrying amounts to the amounts that IFRSs would require in the subsidiary's separate financial statements.

The deemed cost of the goodwill relating to the previously unconsolidated subsidiary at the date of transition is calculated as the difference at the date of transition between:
[IFRS 1:C4(j)]

- the parent's interest in the adjusted carrying amounts of the net assets of the subsidiary; and

- the cost in the parent's separate financial statements of its investment in the subsidiary.

The practical effect of this requirement is to avoid the need to consider (and adjust for) the fair value of the assets and liabilities of the acquired entity either at its acquisition date or at the date of transition to IFRSs.

The procedures for determining goodwill for a subsidiary that was not previously consolidated could lead to the recognition of a significant amount of goodwill if the subsidiary has, subsequent to the date of acquisition, reduced the carrying amount of net assets either by distribution of pre-acquisition reserves or by incurring significant losses. In all cases, goodwill recognised is tested for impairment at the date of transition.

If, on the other hand, the subsidiary has generated a significant amount of profit subsequent to acquisition, goodwill could be very limited. 'Negative goodwill' at the date of transition is recognised directly in retained earnings.

Example 7.1.14A

Determining goodwill for a subsidiary not consolidated under previous GAAP

Parent Company T's date of transition to IFRSs is 1 January 20X9. Under its previous GAAP, Parent Company T did not consolidate its 75 per cent share of Subsidiary U, acquired in a business combination on 15 July 20X6. On 1 January 20X9:

- the cost of Parent Company T's investment in Subsidiary U is CU540 (based on the amount paid at the date of acquisition); and

- under IFRSs, Subsidiary U would measure its assets at CU1,500 and its liabilities at CU900. On this basis, the net assets of Subsidiary U under IFRSs at the date of transition are CU600.

On transition to IFRSs, Parent Company T has elected not to restate past business combinations in accordance with IFRS 3; nevertheless, it is required to consolidate Subsidiary U. The consolidated opening IFRS statement of financial position at 1 January 20X9 includes:

- the assets and liabilities of Subsidiary U at CU1,500 and CU900, respectively;

- non-controlling interests of CU150 (25 per cent of [CU1,500 – CU900]);

- goodwill of CU90 (cost of CU540 less 75 per cent of [CU1,500 – CU900]); and

- the elimination of the investment in Subsidiary U of CU540 (if the investment in Subsidiary U was recognised under previous GAAP at an amount other than its original cost, an additional entry would be recognised in retained earnings).

Parent Company T tests goodwill for impairment under IAS 36 based on conditions that existed at the date of transition and recognises any resulting impairment loss in retained earnings.

Example 7.1.14B

Measuring the assets of a subsidiary not consolidated under previous GAAP

Company A acquired a building in 20X1 at a cost of CU1 million. Under local GAAP, Company A did not depreciate the building. Company T subsequently acquired Company A on 1 January 20X5. Under local GAAP, Company T did not consolidate Company A. Company T will adopt IFRSs for its 31 December 20X9 annual financial statements with 1 January 20X8 as its date of transition. Company T has elected not to restate past business combinations in accordance with IFRS 3.

As a consequence of adopting IFRSs, Company T must consolidate Company A and consider whether it should depreciate the building.

In Company T's consolidated IFRS financial statements, how should the building be measured?

Because the asset belongs to a subsidiary that was not previously consolidated, it is subject to the requirements of IFRS 1:C4(j) and, in its consolidated financial statements, Company T is required to adjust the carrying amount of the building to the amount that IFRSs would require in Company A's statement of financial position.

The building should therefore be recognised either at:

- depreciated cost (measured at the date of the original purchase with subsequent depreciation); or

- the fair value of the asset at the date of transition.

Company T will consolidate Company A in its opening IFRS statement of financial position as required by IFRS 1:C4(j). The deemed cost of the goodwill is equal to the difference at the date of transition (i.e. 1 January 20X8) between Company T's interest in the adjusted carrying amounts of the assets and liabilities of Company A and the cost in Company T's separate financial statements of its investment in Company A.

Example 7.1.14C

Use of deemed cost to establish goodwill for subsidiaries not previously consolidated

Parent Company T's date of transition to IFRSs is 1 January 20X9. Under its previous GAAP, Parent Company T did not consolidate its 75 per cent share of Subsidiary U, acquired in a business combination on 15 July 20X6. Parent Company T has elected not to restate past business combinations in accordance with IFRS 3.

On transition, Parent Company T elects to recognise its investment in Subsidiary U at 'deemed cost', as permitted by IFRS 1:D15 (see **7.8** below).

When applying IFRS 1:C4(j), how should Parent Company T measure goodwill in respect of Subsidiary U?

IFRS 1:C4(j) requires a first-time adopter to calculate the deemed cost of goodwill on transition as the difference between its interest in the adjusted carrying amounts of a subsidiary's assets and liabilities and the cost of its investment in the subsidiary in its own separate financial statements.

IFRS 1:D15 provides first-time adopters who elect, under IAS 27(2011) *Separate Financial Statements* (or, for a first-time adopter that does not adopt IAS 27(2011), IAS 27(2008) *Consolidated and Separate Financial Statements*), to recognise investments in subsidiaries (or associates or joint ventures) at cost with options for establishing the 'cost' on first-time adoption in an entity's separate financial statements. In line with IAS 27(2011) (IAS 27(2008)), one of the allowed alternatives is the use of 'deemed cost' (either the fair value of the investment at the date of transition or the previous GAAP carrying amount at that date).

When the cost of an investment is measured using deemed cost, the same measurement is used to determine the amount of goodwill for the purposes of IFRS 1:C4(j), irrespective of whether the first-time adopter has actually prepared separate financial statements.

It is possible that the use of deemed cost will result in a larger amount being recognised as goodwill, for example, if the fair value of the investment in a subsidiary is higher than its cost under IAS 27(2011) (IAS 27(2008)).

As noted at **7.1.5** above, the requirements on restatement of business combinations in IFRS 1 apply to associates and joint ventures as well as to subsidiaries. A consequence of this is that if an associate (or a joint venture) was not accounted for using the equity method under previous GAAP but would have to be accounted for using the equity method under IFRSs, the approach adopted should be consistent with the approach prescribed by IFRS 1:C4(j) for subsidiaries not consolidated. This is illustrated in the following example.

> **Example 7.1.14D**
>
> **Restatement of investment in associate measured at cost under previous GAAP**
>
> Company F acquired 20 per cent of Company A (and obtained significant influence over it) prior to Company F's date of transition to IFRSs. Under local GAAP, Company F accounted for its investment in Company A at cost in its consolidated financial statements. Company F has elected not to restate past business combinations in accordance with IFRS 3.
>
> IAS 28 requires associates to be accounted for using the equity method in the consolidated financial statements (with certain limited exceptions). IFRS 1 provides guidance on investments in subsidiaries, including subsidiaries not previously consolidated, and consistently notes that this guidance should also be applied to investments in associates and joint ventures. Therefore, the guidance in IFRS 1:C4(j) should be applied.
>
> As a result, Company F should adjust the carrying amounts of the associate's assets and liabilities to the amounts that IFRSs would require in the associate's statement of financial position, as of the date of transition. Company F's share of the net assets of the associate so adjusted is included in Company F's consolidated opening IFRS statement of financial position, with the difference between this amount and the cost of the investment in the associate to be considered deemed cost of goodwill. Goodwill relating to an associate is included in the carrying amount of the investment, without subsequent amortisation.

7.1.14.1   Subsidiaries not previously consolidated – general guidance

IFRS 1 provides guidance relating to subsidiaries that were not consolidated prior to the adoption of IFRSs in more than one section of the Standard. IFRS 1:C4(j) (discussed above) only addresses subsidiaries that were not consolidated under previous GAAP in the context of business combinations before the date of transition to IFRSs. IFRS 1:IG27 (discussed below) addresses the issue of subsidiaries not previously consolidated more generally, referring to both those acquired in a business combination and those that were not acquired in business combinations. IFRS 1:IG27 refers to adjustment "for the effects of the business combination in which it acquired the subsidiary" but these words do not appear in IFRS 1:C4(j). This could be seen as conflicting guidance. However, because the purpose of the exemption in IFRS 1:C4(j) is to avoid the need to work out fair value adjustments that were not calculated under previous GAAP (see above), the words in IFRS 1:IG27 should not be read as requiring such acquisition-date fair value adjustments to be made, but only as requiring normal consolidation elimination entries.

A first-time adopter consolidates all subsidiaries that it controls, unless IFRS 10 *Consolidated Financial Statements* (or, if IFRS 10 is not adopted, IAS 27(2008)) requires otherwise. [IFRS 1:IG26]

This would apply to a subsidiary that was not consolidated under previous GAAP because it was acquired exclusively with a view to its subsequent disposal, for example as part of a business combination. As explained in **section 5** of **chapter A20**, in such circumstances, the disposal group (i.e. the subsidiary) will be classified as held for sale, in accordance with IFRS 5 *Non-current Assets Held for Sale and Discontinued Operations*, if certain conditions are met. However, a subsidiary that is classified as held for sale in accordance with IFRS 5 is still consolidated under IFRS 10 (IAS 27(2008)); it is just that IFRS 5 requires the amounts for such a subsidiary to be measured and presented in a particular way. If such a subsidiary was not consolidated under previous GAAP, it should be consolidated in accordance with the requirements set out below and IFRS 5.

If a first-time adopter did not consolidate a subsidiary under previous GAAP then, in its consolidated financial statements, it measures the subsidiary's assets and liabilities at the same carrying amounts as in the IFRS financial statements of the subsidiary, after adjusting for consolidation procedures and for the effects of the business combination in which it acquired the subsidiary. If the subsidiary has not adopted IFRSs in its financial statements, the carrying amounts required are those that IFRSs would require in those separate financial statements. [IFRS 1:IG27]

If the parent acquired the subsidiary in a business combination before the date of transition to IFRSs, the parent recognises goodwill as explained above. If the parent did not acquire the subsidiary in a business combination because it created the subsidiary, the parent does not recognise goodwill. [IFRS 1:IG27]

However, for a subsidiary that was not acquired in a business combination, a difference may still arise between the carrying amounts of the assets and liabilities and the cost of investment (e.g. because of accumulated profits of the subsidiary). IFRS 1:IG27(c) states that the parent does not recognise goodwill in this case but does not specify an alternative treatment for the difference. It should be taken to retained earnings or some other appropriate category of equity (e.g. if the entity maintains a specific reserve for IFRS 1 adjustments).

7.1.15   Effect of restatements on non-controlling interests and deferred tax

When a first-time adopter takes the exemption from full retrospective application of IFRS 3, the measurement of non-controlling interests (NCI) and deferred tax follows from the measurement of other assets and liabilities. Therefore, even if an entity decides to avail itself of the business combination exemption and not restate prior business combinations, some adjustments to non-controlling interests and deferred tax may still be required. [IFRS 1:C4(k)]

Example 7.1.15

Change in measurement of non-controlling interests on first-time adoption

Entity G adopts IFRSs in 20X9 with a date of transition of 1 January 20X8. Entity G acquired an 80 per cent interest in Entity H on 30 June 20X6 and has decided not to restate the business combination in accordance with IFRS 3.

Under previous GAAP, Entity G measured identifiable assets and liabilities acquired in a business combination at:

- the acquirer's interest obtained in the exchange transaction; plus

- the NCI's portion of the pre-acquisition carrying amounts.

Entity G's policy for measuring non-controlling interests under previous GAAP is not acceptable under IFRS 3, which requires that assets and liabilities acquired in a business combination be measured at their values at the date of acquisition. Under IFRS 3, there is a choice between measuring components of non-controlling interests that are present ownership interests at fair value or at the non-controlling interest's proportionate share of the fair value of the net identifiable assets acquired.

Although the manner in which the NCI in Entity H was calculated under previous GAAP is not supportable under IFRSs, Entity G is not required to adjust the amount attributed to NCI at the date of transition. Entity G has chosen not to restate business combinations that occurred before the date of transition to IFRSs in accordance with IFRS 3; therefore, it need not adjust NCI to conform to the measurement basis under IFRS 3.

> However, the requirements of IFRS 1:Appendix C may require some assets acquired, or liabilities assumed, in a business combination to be measured at amounts different from the carrying amounts immediately after the business combination under previous GAAP. In such circumstances, because the measurement of NCI follows the measurement of the other assets and liabilities, NCI will be adjusted for the effects of the differences.

7.1.16   Translation of goodwill and fair value adjustments arising in a business combination

Under paragraph 47 of IAS 21 *The Effects of Changes in Foreign Exchange Rates* (see **5.5.3** in **chapter A19**), any goodwill arising on the acquisition of a foreign operation and any fair value adjustments to the carrying amounts of assets and liabilities arising on the acquisition of that foreign operation should be treated as assets and liabilities of the foreign operation. They are therefore expressed in the functional currency of the foreign operation and retranslated at the closing rate at the end of the reporting period. An entity may, under previous GAAP, have treated such goodwill and fair value adjustments as assets and liabilities of the entity rather than as assets and liabilities of the foreign operation. If so, the requirements of IAS 21:47 may be applied prospectively to all acquisitions occurring after the date of transition to IFRSs. [IFRS 1:IG21A]

If this election is used, the fair value adjustments and goodwill arising in business combinations prior to the date of transition to IFRSs should be treated as assets and liabilities of the entity rather than assets and liabilities of the acquiree. Such goodwill and fair value adjustments are either already expressed in the entity's functional currency or are non-monetary foreign currency items, which are reported using the exchange rate applied under previous GAAP. [IFRS 1:C2]

Alternatively, IAS 21 may be applied retrospectively to goodwill and fair value adjustments arising in either:
[IFRS 1:C3]

- all business combinations that occurred before the date of transition to IFRSs; or

- all business combinations that the entity elects to restate to comply with IFRS 3 (see **7.1.4** above).

> **Example 7.1.16**
>
> **Treating goodwill relating to a foreign subsidiary as an asset of the acquirer**
>
> Entity A has previously recognised goodwill relating to a foreign subsidiary arising in a business combination that occurred before the date of transition

to IFRSs. Under previous GAAP, Entity A treated goodwill as its own asset and recognised goodwill in its functional currency based on the exchange rate at the date of acquisition.

On transition to IFRSs, Entity A is not required to restate the financial statements retrospectively to treat goodwill as an asset of the acquiree since the acquisition date and translate goodwill at the closing rate at the end of each reporting period.

Entity A can use the exemption in IFRS 1:C2 to avoid applying IAS 21 retrospectively to goodwill arising in business combinations that occurred before the date of transition.

When an entity does not apply IAS 21 retrospectively to goodwill, there are no further translation adjustments to the goodwill balance. Instead of treating goodwill as an asset of the acquiree and translating it at the end of each reporting period at the closing rate, Entity A treats the goodwill balance as its own asset and recognises goodwill in its functional currency at the exchange rate at the date of acquisition (in this case, the rate that was used under previous GAAP).

The exemption applies to goodwill that is deemed to be an asset of the acquirer at the date of transition. However, the exemption is not available for business combinations that occur after the date of transition. Therefore, for all acquisitions after the date of transition, IAS 21 must be fully complied with and goodwill must be treated as an asset of the acquiree (IFRS 1:IG21A).

Although the Standard is not completely clear, it is generally accepted that the exemption in respect of fair value adjustments and goodwill may be applied independently to fair value adjustments and to goodwill. In particular, if fair value adjustments were previously treated as foreign currency assets and liabilities, that treatment can be continued even if goodwill was denominated in the reporting entity's functional currency and the exemption from restatement is applied to this goodwill.

It is possible that under previous GAAP an entity was permitted to choose on an acquisition-by-acquisition basis whether to translate goodwill balances at each reporting date or leave them at the historical rate. It is possible to read IFRS 1:C2 as requiring all existing goodwill to be treated consistently as an asset of the entity when the exemption is used. This would mean that any amounts that had in fact been treated as foreign currency amounts would have to be restated to local currency denominated amounts based on the exchange rate at the date of the acquisition. However, given that the purpose of this exemption is to 'grandfather' the treatment under previous GAAP, it is regarded as acceptable to apply it only to those assets and liabilities that were not retranslated under previous

GAAP. Those that were retranslated under previous GAAP would continue to be retranslated in accordance with IAS 21.

In practice, the decision as to whether to apply IAS 21 retrospectively should not be taken in isolation, but in the light of all other factors affecting the transition to IFRSs. The choices made will have consequences in later reporting periods. For example, if goodwill is left denominated in the reporting entity's functional currency, there is a greater risk that it may become impaired in the future, merely as a result of adverse currency movements.

7.1.17   Deferred tax on pre-transition business combinations

On initial adoption of IFRSs, a number of amendments to deferred tax balances may need to be made. Such adjustments will be recognised directly in equity if the entity has elected not to restate its past business combinations in accordance with IFRS 3. If any past business combinations are restated in accordance with IFRS 3, the goodwill figure should be adjusted to take account of the deferred tax balances that would have been recognised at the date of the business combination if IFRS 3 had been applied.

Example 7.1.17A

Deferred tax on pre-transition business combinations (1)

Parent P is preparing its consolidated financial statements in accordance with IFRSs for the first time. Prior to its date of transition, it acquired Subsidiary S which, at the date of acquisition, owned items of property, plant and equipment that do not attract any tax relief. Parent P has chosen not to restate business combinations prior to the date of transition to IFRSs in accordance with IFRS 3.

When determining the temporary differences related to assets and liabilities of Subsidiary S at the date of transition, Parent P applies the general requirements of IAS 12. The initial recognition exception in IAS 12 *Income Taxes* (see **4.4.1** in **chapter A13**) does not apply because the assets were acquired and the liabilities assumed in a business combination. Accordingly, deferred tax assets and deferred tax liabilities are recognised in respect of the temporary differences identified. Because Parent P has elected not to restate the acquisition of Subsidiary S in accordance with IFRS 3, the effect of the recognition of the deferred tax assets and liabilities at the date of transition is recognised in retained earnings or another reserve used by Parent P for its IFRS 1 adjustments.

At the date of transition, a first-time adopter that has elected not to restate past business combinations in accordance with IFRS 3 will need to determine whether any tax loss carryforwards or other deferred tax assets not recognised at the date of acquisition of subsidiaries meet the recognition criteria under IAS 12. If so, they should be recognised at the date of transition.

When a deferred tax asset is recognised on transition that was not previously recognised in a past business combination, the resulting adjustment will be made in retained earnings or another reserve used by the entity for its IFRS 1 adjustments. The carrying amount of goodwill should not be adjusted because the recognition of previously unrecognised deferred tax assets is not one of the permitted adjustments to goodwill specifically identified in IFRS 1:C4 (see **7.1.13**). (But this does not preclude the adjustment of goodwill if the date of transition falls during the 'measurement period', as discussed in **example 7.1.13.4** above.)

The realisation of previously unrecognised deferred tax assets after the date of transition is accounted for in accordance with the general requirements of IFRS 3 and IAS 12:68 (IFRS 1 does not allow any ongoing exemptions from these requirements). Therefore, when an entity that has not restated a past business combination subsequently realises an unrecognised deferred tax asset that did not satisfy the recognition criteria at the date of transition, the impact will typically be recognised in profit or loss, and not as an adjustment to goodwill. The only exception to this will be when acquired deferred tax benefits are recognised within the 'measurement period' (generally 12 months after the date of the acquisition) that result from new information about facts and circumstances that existed at the acquisition date. These will be adjusted against goodwill.

Although the adjustment of goodwill for acquired deferred tax benefits recognised within the measurement period is not one of the adjustments to goodwill permitted under IFRS 1:C4(g) (see **7.1.13**), it is consistent with the treatment adopted for other adjustments to 'provisional' values (see **7.1.13.4**)

Example 7.1.17B

Deferred tax on pre-transition business combinations (2)

Entity B presents its first IFRS financial statements for the year ended 31 December 20X5 with a date of transition of 1 January 20X4. In preparing those financial statements, Entity B chooses not to restate business combinations prior to the date of transition in accordance with IFRS 3.

Entity B had previously acquired Entity C during 20X2 in a business combination in which CU300 of goodwill was recognised under previous GAAP, but CU500 of deferred tax assets arising from loss carryforwards were not recognised. The loss carryforwards expire on 31 December 20X6. Under Entity B's previous GAAP, goodwill amortisation was prohibited and the carrying amount of goodwill at the date of transition is CU300.

At the date of transition, Entity B assesses future profitability and determines that CU100 of the deferred tax benefit can be recovered by the end of 20X6. The following journal entry is recorded.

		CU	CU
Dr	Deferred tax asset	100	
Cr	Retained earnings		100

Recognition of the deferred tax asset.

During the year ended 31 December 20X6, Entity B's profitability is even higher than expected and, consequently, all of the tax loss carryforwards are utilised before they expire.

Entity B will account for the realisation of the deferred tax assets after the date of transition in accordance with IAS 12:68. Because the realisation occurs after the measurement period (i.e. more than 12 months after the date of the original acquisition of Entity C), it cannot be adjusted against goodwill.

A deferred tax asset may arise when goodwill has been written off directly to equity but attracts tax relief on an amortisation basis. Subject to the usual recoverability criteria, a deferred tax asset should be recognised, at the date of transition, based on the difference between the carrying amount (i.e. nil) and the tax base (i.e. the amount of future tax deductions). The adjustment is made against retained earnings (or another appropriate category of equity); the carrying amount of any other goodwill may not be adjusted because the recognition of previously unrecognised deferred tax assets is not one of the permitted adjustments to goodwill specifically identified in IFRS 1:C4.

Example 7.1.17C

Deferred tax assets relating to goodwill previously written off directly to equity

Company D operates in a jurisdiction in which, under previous GAAP, goodwill was written off directly to equity immediately following a business combination. The local tax law allows a deduction of 1/20 of the purchased goodwill in each of the 20 years following an acquisition. Company D acquired a business two years before the date of transition to IFRSs, and all related goodwill was written off directly to equity at that time. At the date of transition, Company D is still entitled to claim 18/20 of the amount of purchased goodwill as a deduction over the next 18 years. Company D has elected not to restate past business combinations prior to the date of transition in accordance with IFRS 3.

At the date of transition to IFRSs, should a deferred tax asset be recognised in respect of the goodwill previously written off directly to equity?

Yes, subject to IAS 12's general recognition criteria for deferred tax assets. Company D should recognise a deferred tax asset in respect of the deductible temporary difference between the carrying amount of the goodwill (nil) and its tax base. The adjustment is made against retained earnings (or another appropriate category of equity). As the deferred tax asset is subsequently reduced when tax deductions are received, the effect of the reduction in the deferred tax asset will be recognised in profit or loss for the period.

7.2   Share-based payment transactions

IFRS 2 *Share-based Payment* contains various transition provisions. The IASB decided that, in general, first-time adopters should be treated in the same way as entities already applying IFRSs in this regard. The exemptions set out in this section reflect that principle.

7.2.1   *Equity-settled transactions*

7.2.1.1   *Exemptions from retrospective application*

IFRS 1 includes two exemptions for equity-settled transactions. [IFRS 1:D2]

- First-time adopters are not required to apply IFRS 2 to equity-settled share-based payments granted on or before 7 November 2002.

- First-time adopters are not required to apply IFRS 2 to share-based payments granted after 7 November 2002 that vested before the date of transition to IFRSs.

Although entities are not required to apply IFRS 2 in the circumstances described, they are encouraged to do so. [IFRS 1:D2]

Under IFRS 1:D2, first-time adopters are also not required to apply IFRS 2 to share-based payments granted after 7 November 2002 that vested before 1 January 2005 (if the date of transition is earlier than 1 January 2005), but this is likely to be of limited relevance now.

The practical effect of the second exemption is that equity instruments that vested before the date of transition can be ignored. This is logical because, if IFRS 2 were applied to such instruments, no expense would be recognised in the statement of comprehensive income either in the first IFRS reporting period or in the comparative period. Equity instruments granted on or before 7 November 2002 can also be ignored, even if they have not vested at the date of transition, but this is likely to be of limited relevance now.

For share-based payment arrangements to which IFRS 2 must be applied, an entity may have recognised an expense for that share-based payment arrangement under previous GAAP. No adjustment will be necessary if previous GAAP is fully converged with IFRS 2. In other cases, the previous GAAP expense will often be calculated on a basis that is inconsistent with IFRS 2. Any such expense should generally be reversed and replaced with an expense in accordance with IFRS 2.

If a first-time adopter elects to apply IFRS 2 to the equity instruments referred to in IFRS 1:D2, it may do so only if the entity has disclosed publicly the fair value of those equity instruments, determined at the measurement date, as defined in IFRS 2. [IFRS 1:D2]

The effect of this requirement is to prohibit full retrospective application of IFRS 2 by many entities because they will not have disclosed publicly the fair value of the equity instruments granted in previous years. IFRS 1 does not elaborate on what is meant by 'disclosed publicly' but it appears that the IASB had in mind disclosure in the financial statements for the year in which the instruments were granted.

Example 7.2.1.1A

Transition to IFRS 2 for first-time adopter

Company L is a first-time adopter of IFRSs with a reporting date of 31 December 20X5 and a date of transition of 1 January 20X4 (which is after

7 November 2002). Company L has historically granted share-based payments to its employees. Some, but not all, of those grants have vested by 1 January 20X4.

Company L is required to apply IFRS 2 to all share-based payment transactions granted after 7 November 2002 that have not vested at 1 January 20X4. For share-based payment transactions granted before 7 November 2002, or granted after 7 November 2002 but vested before 1 January 20X4, Company L is not required to apply IFRS 2, but may choose to do so if the fair value of those share-based payments was previously disclosed publicly. The fair value must have been determined at the grant date, in accordance with IFRS 2.

Considerable judgement will be required to determine the appropriate valuation of share-based payment transactions retrospectively if valuations were not previously obtained. IFRS 1 provides some guidance in relation to estimates and restrictions on the use of hindsight, which is useful in the context of the measurement of fair value for equity-settled transactions.

Selective application of the IFRS 1 exemption for share-based payments is not acceptable. Electing to apply IFRS 2 to equity instruments covered by the exemption is an accounting policy choice that should be applied consistently to the extent possible. IFRS 1:D2 does not suggest that the exemption may be applied only to specific transactions or arrangements. If an entity has previously published fair values for all equity-settled share-based payments, and it elects to apply IFRS 2 to equity-settled share-based payment arrangements falling within the scope of the exemption, it must apply IFRS 2 to all such arrangements.

However, if the entity disclosed the fair value for some but not all of the equity-settled share-based payment arrangements falling within the scope of the exemption, it may apply IFRS 2 retrospectively only to those instruments for which the fair value had been disclosed.

Example 7.2.1.1B

Measurement of equity-settled share-based payments on first-time adoption

Company M is adopting IFRSs for the first time with a date of transition of 1 January 20X4 and a reporting date of 31 December 20X5. Company M issued share options on 30 June 20X3 (which was after 7 November 2002) that vest after four years (i.e. on 30 June 20X7). The transaction is classified as equity-settled. Under Company M's previous GAAP, Company M did not estimate (or disclose) the fair value of the share options determined as at 30 June 20X3 in accordance with IFRS 2.

> Company M is required to apply IFRS 2 to the June 20X3 grant of share options. Because estimates of fair value were not required under previous GAAP, in accordance with IFRS 1:16 the measurement should reflect conditions at the date of transition to IFRSs. Company M should use information available at 1 January 20X4 to determine expected volatility, expected dividends, and the expected life of the options under the equity-settled transaction. However, some inputs to the valuation model will be based purely on contractual or historical fact, in which case that contractual or historical information should be used. Therefore, the share price, exercise price and risk-free rate should be based on information available at grant date – in this case, 30 June 20X3.

For all grants of equity instruments to which IFRS 2 has not been applied (e.g. equity instruments granted on or before 7 November 2002), a first-time adopter should nevertheless disclose the information required by paragraphs 44 and 45 of IFRS 2 (see **chapter A16**). [IFRS 1:D2]

7.2.1.2   Modifications to terms and conditions

If a first-time adopter modifies the terms or conditions of a grant of equity instruments to which IFRS 2 has not been applied, paragraphs 26 to 29 of IFRS 2 (see **chapter A16**) need not be applied if the modifications occurred before the date of transition to IFRSs. [IFRS 1:D2]

> Paragraphs 26 to 29 of IFRS 2 deal with modifications to the terms and conditions on which equity instruments were granted, including cancellations and settlements. When a modification is beneficial to the employee, these paragraphs sometimes require additional share-based payment expense to be recognised; and in some other circumstances, they can require accelerated recognition of future share-based payment expense. However, a first-time adopter can ignore these paragraphs if IFRS 2 has not been applied to the share-based payment in question, provided that the modification occurred before the date of transition to IFRSs.

7.2.2   Cash-settled transactions

A first-time adopter is encouraged, but not required, to apply IFRS 2 to liabilities arising from share-based payment transactions that were: [IFRS 1:D3]

- settled before the date of transition to IFRSs; or

- settled before 1 January 2005.

For liabilities to which IFRS 2 is applied, a first-time adopter is not required to restate comparative information to the extent that the information relates to a period or date that is earlier than 7 November 2002. [IFRS 1:D3]

This exemption is now of limited relevance. The date of transition to IFRSs will invariably be later than 1 January 2005 so the practical effect is that liabilities can be ignored if they were settled before the date of transition to IFRSs. Such liabilities would have no effect on the financial statements even if an exemption did not exist.

Example 7.2.2

Measurement of cash-settled share-based payments on first-time adoption

Company N is adopting IFRSs for the first time with a date of transition of 1 January 20X4 and a reporting date of 31 December 20X5. Company N issued share options on 30 November 20X3 that do not vest until 30 November 20X6. The share options will be settled in cash. The vesting conditions are related to continued employment only. In accordance with IFRS 1, Company N is required to apply IFRS 2 to the November 20X3 grant of share options because the liability is not settled before the date of transition. Under previous GAAP, Company N had neither disclosed nor estimated fair value determined as at 30 November 20X3 in accordance with IFRS 2; however, it recognised and measured the liability in its previous GAAP financial statements at the difference between the exercise price and the current share price at 31 December 20X3.

At the date of transition (1 January 20X4) and at each reporting date until it is settled, Company N measures the liability at its fair value, by applying an option pricing model, taking into account the terms and conditions on which the share options were granted, and the extent to which the employees have rendered service to date. The fair value of the cash-settled share-based payments includes both intrinsic value and time value. Time value in this context is defined as "... the value of the right to participate in future increases in the share price, if any, that may occur between the valuation date and the settlement date". The exclusion of the time value would lead to an inadequate measure of the liability.

The amount recognised under previous GAAP at 31 December 20X3, which was based on the difference between the exercise price and the current share price at 31 December 20X3, cannot be used as an approximation to fair value of the options under IFRS 2 at 1 January 20X4.

> Similar to equity-settled transactions, judgement is required to determine the fair value in accordance with IFRS 2 of cash-settled-based payment transactions.

7.3   Insurance contracts

> The transition provisions in IFRS 4 *Insurance Contracts* allow entities already applying IFRSs when they adopt that Standard to continue to use their existing accounting policies for liabilities arising from insurance contracts as long as the existing policies meet certain minimum requirements as set out in IFRS 4. IFRS 4 also requires disclosures that identify and explain the amounts in an insurer's financial statements arising from insurance contracts. IFRS 4 is discussed in detail in **chapter A39**.

The IASB recognised that it could be quite onerous for first-time adopters to apply the requirements of IFRS 4 retrospectively. Therefore, IFRS 1 provides an optional exemption whereby an insurer may elect upon first-time adoption to apply the transition provisions of IFRS 4. [IFRS 1:D4]

The transition provisions in paragraphs 41 to 45 of IFRS 4 require an insurer to apply IFRS 4 prospectively for reporting periods beginning on or after 1 January 2005, with earlier application permitted. Therefore, the relief provided in IFRS 1:D4 allows a first-time adopter to apply the requirements of IFRS 4 prospectively from 1 January 2005 rather than applying the requirements of the Standard as if they had always been in place.

> While this may have represented significant relief for entities that adopted IFRSs in 2005, its benefit for later adopters is primarily in restricting the amount of retrospective application required (i.e. from 2005 to the date of transition).

One specific area of relief that continues to benefit first-time adopters is in the application of IFRS 4:39(c)(iii) (see **5.2** in **chapter A39**), under which first-time adopters are not required to disclose information about claims development that occurred earlier than five years before the end of the first financial year in which they apply IFRS 4. If it is impracticable when

an entity first applies IFRS 4 to prepare information about claims development that occurred before the beginning of the earliest period for which
the entity presents full comparative information that complies with IFRS 4,
that fact is required to be disclosed. [IFRS 4:44]

When an insurer changes its accounting policies for insurance liabilities, it
is permitted, but not required, to reclassify some or all of its financial
assets as measured at fair value under IFRS 9 *Financial Instruments*.
(Correspondingly, an insurer applying IAS 39 *Financial Instruments: Recognition and Measurement* is permitted, but not required, to reclassify some or
all of its financial assets as 'at fair value through profit or loss'.) This
reclassification is permitted:
[IFRS 4:45]

• if an insurer changes accounting policies when it first applies IFRS 4
  (e.g. on first-time adoption); and

• if it makes a subsequent policy change permitted by IFRS 4:22 (see
  4.3 in **chapter A39**), in which case the reclassification is a change in
  accounting policy and IAS 8 *Accounting Policies, Changes in Accounting Estimates and Errors* applies.

7.4 Deemed cost

In drafting IFRS 1, the IASB acknowledged that the costs of requiring
entities to reconstruct cost information or other transactional data for
property, plant and equipment and other long-term assets could be
particularly onerous when entities might not have retained the
necessary historical information. The IASB also noted that reconstructed data might be less relevant to users, and less reliable, than
current fair value data. As a result, IFRS 1 includes optional exemptions that relieve first-time adopters from the requirement to recreate
cost information for property, plant and equipment, investment
property and (to a much more limited extent) intangible assets.
When the exemptions are applied, deemed cost is the basis for
subsequent depreciation and impairment tests. Deemed cost is
defined by IFRS 1 as "the amount used as a surrogate for cost or
depreciated cost at a given date" (see **3.2** above).

There are four types of 'deemed cost' exemption under IFRS 1:

- IFRS 1:D5 to D7 allow fair value at the date of transition or previous GAAP revaluations to be taken as the deemed cost for specified categories of assets (detailed conditions discussed in **7.4.1** below);

- IFRS 1:D8 allows 'event-driven' fair values to be taken as the deemed cost at the date of that measurement (detailed conditions discussed in **7.4.2** below);

- IFRS 1:D8A deals specifically with oil and gas assets (see **7.4.3** below); and

- IFRS 1:D8B deals with assets used in operations subject to rate regulation (see **7.4.4** below).

When an asset is initially recognised under IFRSs on a deemed cost basis, subsequent depreciation is based on that deemed cost and starts from the date for which the fair value measurement or revaluation was established. [IFRS 1:IG9]

7.4.1   Fair value or revaluation as deemed cost

7.4.1.1   Scope

This exemption applies to:
[IFRS 1:D5 – D7]

- property, plant and equipment;

- investment property, if an entity elects to use the cost model in IAS 40 *Investment Property*; and

- intangible assets that meet:

    - the recognition criteria in IAS 38 *Intangible Assets* (including reliable measurement of original cost); and

    - the criteria in IAS 38 for revaluation (including the existence of an active market).

The exemption may be used selectively within the classes of assets described. IFRS 1:BC45 confirms that "the IFRS does not restrict the use of fair value as deemed cost to entire classes of assets". However, indications of impairment cannot be ignored for those assets that are not restated.

The ability to apply this exemption to intangible assets is likely to be of limited relevance given that IAS 38's restrictive criteria for use of the revaluation basis must be met.

The exemption cannot be applied to other classes of assets by analogy. [IFRS 1:D7] The exemption is available regardless of the IFRS accounting policy selected by the entity for ongoing reporting purposes.

IFRS 1:D5 provides the option to measure assets at deemed cost without specifying if the assets have been acquired, self-constructed or held under finance leases. Therefore, the exemption can also be applied to assets held under finance leases and capitalised in the financial statements. A first-time adopter may measure these items at fair value at the date of transition. However, the related finance lease liability is not measured at fair value; rather it is measured at the net present value of the lease payments in accordance with IAS 17 *Leases*.

The exemption in IFRS 1:D5 is not limited to property, plant and equipment within the scope of IAS 16. Consequently, an entity may elect to measure items of property, plant and equipment that are outside the scope of IAS 16 (e.g. certain mineral rights and reserves) at a deemed cost in accordance with IFRS 1:D5 (see also **7.4.3** below). Whether mineral rights and reserves are property, plant and equipment or intangible assets is considered in **section 2** of **chapter A7**. Property, plant and equipment used in exploration activities are within the scope of IAS 16.

7.4.1.2   Details of the exemption

IFRS 1:D5 permits any asset in the designated categories to be measured at the date of transition to IFRSs at its fair value and that fair value to be used as the asset's deemed cost at that date. When this election is made, the disclosures required by IFRS 1:30 should be made in the entity's first IFRS financial statements (see **9.2.4** below).

A first-time adopter may also elect to use a previous GAAP revaluation of any asset in the designated categories at, or before, the date of transition to IFRSs as deemed cost at the date of revaluation. This is, however, permitted only if the revaluation was, at the date of the revaluation, broadly comparable to:
[IFRS 1:D6]

• fair value; or

- cost or depreciated cost under IFRSs, adjusted to reflect, for example, changes in a general or specific price index.

The reference to the revaluation being 'broadly comparable' is explained in IFRS 1:BC47 as allowing a first-time adopter "to establish a deemed cost using a measurement that is already available and is a reasonable starting point for a cost-based measurement".

A previous GAAP valuation at a percentage of fair value (e.g. 80%) is not broadly comparable to fair value. IFRS 1:BC47 notes that it may not always be clear whether a previous revaluation was intended to be a measure of fair value. For the amount to be used as deemed cost, the measurement must represent a valid estimate of fair value. A percentage of fair value is not broadly comparable to fair value and, therefore, cannot be used as the asset's deemed cost.

However, a revaluation in accordance with previous GAAP that results in a carrying amount that is similar to fair value, such as the application of a price index to a previous carrying amount, may be considered broadly comparable.

In accordance with IFRS 1:D6, the previous GAAP revaluation must be "at, or before, the date of transition to IFRSs" and this would exclude a valuation carried out at the end of the last reporting period under previous GAAP. For example, if the end of the first IFRS reporting period is 31 December 20X8 and the date of transition to IFRSs is 1 January 20X7, a valuation carried out at 31 December 20X7 under previous GAAP would not comply with IFRS 1:D6. However, it might be possible instead to use the measurement at 31 December 20X7 under the exemption in IFRS 1:D8(b) (see **7.4.2** below).

Example 7.4.1.2

Accounting for previously recognised revaluation uplift

Under previous GAAP, Company G measured property, plant and equipment at a revalued amount that was broadly consistent with fair value and accumulated the difference between depreciated cost and the revalued amount within equity. Company G has elected to use the revalued amount as deemed cost under IFRS 1.

How should the revaluation uplift recognised under previous GAAP be accounted for at the date of transition to IFRSs?

IFRS 1:11 requires that the adjustments arising from first-time adoption be recognised in retained earnings or, if appropriate, another category of equity.

> The Standard does not specifically address the accounting for revaluation uplifts recognised under previous GAAP. The adjustment could be recognised as a separate component of equity but that is not required under IFRS 1.
>
> If a previous GAAP revaluation is used as deemed cost under IFRS 1:D6, any revaluation uplift accumulated in equity under previous GAAP does not form part of the revaluation surplus under IFRSs. Therefore, an impairment loss arising after the transition to IFRSs cannot be offset against the amount accumulated in equity under previous GAAP but instead should be recognised in profit or loss.

7.4.2 Event-driven fair value used as deemed cost

A first-time adopter may have established a deemed cost under previous GAAP for some or all of its assets and liabilities by measuring them at their fair value at one particular date because of an event such as a privatisation or initial public offering (IPO). IFRS 1 allows the following exemptions in respect of such event-driven fair values.

- If the measurement date is *at or before* the date of transition to IFRSs, the entity may use the event-driven fair value measurement as deemed cost for IFRSs at the date of that measurement. [IFRS 1:D8(a)]

- If the measurement date is *after* the date of transition to IFRSs, but during the period covered by the first IFRS financial statements, the event-driven fair value measurement may be used as deemed cost when the event occurs. In such circumstances, the entity should recognise the resulting adjustments directly in retained earnings (or, if appropriate, another category of equity) at the measurement date. At the date of transition to IFRSs, the entity should either establish the deemed cost by applying the criteria in paragraphs D5 to D7 or measure assets and liabilities in accordance with the other requirements in IFRS 1. [IFRS 1:D8(b)]

> The exemptions under IFRS 1:D8(a) and (b) can be applied broadly and are not limited to fair value measurements arising from privatisations and IPOs. The use of the expression 'an event such as' implies that these are examples of two such events, not a limitation on what events would qualify.

The scope of these exemptions differs from the exemption available under IFRS 1:D5 and D6, as illustrated in the following example.

Example 7.4.2A

Scope and applicability of the deemed cost exemption in IFRS 1:D8(a)

An entity plans to adopt IFRSs with a date of transition of 1 January 20X5. In November 20X4, the entity experiences financial difficulties and it is forced to file for protection from its creditors.

The entity undertakes a financial reorganisation under which there is a substantial realignment of the equity and non-equity interests in the entity. Under local GAAP, this leads to a comprehensive revaluation of the entity's assets and liabilities (including debt, intangible assets etc.) to fair value. These fair values are recognised in the entity's annual financial statements at 31 December 20X4 prepared under local GAAP.

For the purposes of the exemption in IFRS 1:D8(a), is the entity permitted to use the values established for the purposes of the financial reorganisation for all categories of assets and liabilities?

Yes. Unlike the exemptions available under IFRS 1:D5 and D6, application of the exemption under IFRS 1:D8(a) is not restricted to property, plant and equipment, investment property and certain intangible assets. The entity is permitted to use the IFRS 1:D8(a) exemption for any of its assets and liabilities provided that the conditions in that paragraph are met. Those conditions are:

- that the value established at the date of the reorganisation was the fair value; and

- that the value established at the date of the reorganisation was recognised in the entity's financial statements under previous GAAP (see below).

The application of the exemption under IFRS 1:D8(a) to intangible assets is not restricted to intangible assets meeting the revaluation criteria under IAS 38 (see IFRS 1:IG50).

If the entity elects to use the exemption under IFRS 1:D8(a), is it required to use all of the fair value measurements established for the purposes of the reorganisation or is it permitted to apply the exemption only to selected assets and liabilities?

The exemption may be applied to individual assets and liabilities (i.e. the entity is permitted to use the exemption selectively).

IFRS 1:D8(a) is not explicit in this regard. IFRS 1:BC45 clarifies that the exemption available under IFRS 1:D5 can be applied selectively – but it does not address the other deemed cost exemptions. However, in the absence of specific mention, it is reasonable to assume that the entity may choose to use only some of the fair value measurements established at the date of the reorganisation as deemed cost at the date of those measurements.

If a first-time adopter wishes to apply the IFRS 1:D8(a) exemption, it is necessary that the assets and liabilities have been recognised and measured at the event-driven fair value measurements in the first-time adopter's previous GAAP financial statements. It is not sufficient to have publicly disclosed the fair value (e.g. in the notes to the financial statements).

This is supported by IFRS 1:BC95 which states that, if this exemption is taken, it does not lead to a restatement on transition to IFRSs because the exemption applies "only if the measurement was already used in previous GAAP financial statements".

IFRS 1:D8(b) was added by *Improvements to IFRSs* issued in May 2010 to allow a first-time adopter to use an event-driven fair value as deemed cost at the measurement date for measurement events that occurred after the date of transition to IFRSs and to specify the accounting in such circumstances.

This extension of the scope of IFRS 1:D8 is aimed primarily at jurisdictions where local law requires an entity to revalue its assets and liabilities to fair value for a privatisation or IPO and to treat the revalued amounts as deemed cost for the entity's previous GAAP. Prior to the addition of IFRS 1:D8(b), if the revaluation occurred after the date of transition to IFRSs, the entity could not have used that revaluation as deemed cost under IFRSs. To avoid requiring the preparation of two sets of financial statements with different carrying amounts, the IASB amended paragraph D8 to allow an entity to recognise an event-driven fair value measurement as deemed cost when the event occurs, provided that this is during the period covered by its first IFRS financial statements. [IFRS 1:BC46A]

Notably, when IFRS 1:D8(b) was added, no changes were made to IFRS 1:BC95. Therefore, at first glance, it could be taken that IFRS 1:BC95 refers equally to the exemption in IFRS 1:D8(b) and, consequently, that IFRS 1:D8(b) can only be applied if the event-driven fair measurements have been recognised in the entity's financial statements under previous GAAP. However, because the IFRS 1:D8(b) exemption relates to event-driven fair value measurements after the date of transition, in the majority of cases these values will not have been recognised in previous GAAP financial statements and such a requirement would be counter-intuitive. If IFRS 1:BC95 were taken to apply to IFRS 1:D8(b), in practice the exemption could only be used in relation to event-driven fair values in the comparative period that were used in the previous GAAP financial statements for the comparative period. It seems clear that the IASB did not intend to restrict the application of the relief in this manner. Accordingly, unlike the

IFRS 1:D8(a) exemption, it is reasonable to assume that the event-driven fair value measurement is not required to have been recognised in the entity's previous GAAP financial statements.

Example 7.4.2B

Event-driven fair value established after the date of transition to IFRSs

Entity D is adopting IFRSs for the first time in its financial statements for the year ended 31 December 20X9. Its date of transition is 1 January 20X8. At 31 March 20X9, in producing financial information for an initial public offering (IPO), Entity D establishes fair values for property, plant and equipment.

The following information is relevant.

Fair value of assets established at 31 December 20X2 (recognised under previous GAAP)	CU750
Fair value of assets at 31 December 20X2 less accumulated depreciation and impairment to 1 January 20X8 (determined in accordance with IFRSs)	CU400
Fair value of assets at 31 December 20X2 less accumulated depreciation and impairment to 31 March 20X9 (determined in accordance with IFRSs)	CU300
Fair value of assets at 31 March 20X9	CU1,200

Under IFRS 1:D8(b), the fair value at 31 March 20X9 may be used as the deemed cost of the assets at that date for the purposes of the entity's first IFRS financial statements.

However, Entity D would still need to establish the carrying amount of the assets at the date of transition (1 January 20X8), and account for the assets under IFRSs from the date of transition to 31 March 20X9. For this purpose, Entity D has the usual options to establish the carrying amount of the assets by applying IAS 16 retrospectively or by reference to a deemed cost in accordance with IFRS 1:D5 to D7.

For example, using the exemption available under IFRS 1:D6, Entity D could use the fair value at 31 December 20X2 recognised under previous GAAP as the deemed cost at that date and establish the carrying amount at 1 January 20X8 by adjusting the 31 December 20X2 fair value for subsequent depreciation and impairment. When this option is taken, in the first IFRS financial statements, depreciation recognised from 1 January 20X8 to 31 March 20X9 will be based on the deemed cost at 31 December 20X2 (CU750).

> If the fair value at 31 March 20X9 is used as deemed cost for the assets at that date, the difference of CU900 between the carrying amount at 31 March 20X9 (CU300) and the fair value of the assets at 31 March 20X9 (CU1,200) is recognised in retained earnings or another category of equity (e.g. a reserve used for IFRS 1 adjustments). This is not considered to be a revaluation of the property, plant and equipment for the purposes of IAS 16 (and does not result in a requirement for subsequent regular revaluations). Subsequent depreciation (after 31 March 20X9) is based on the uplifted value. No adjustment is made to the depreciation recognised under IFRSs for the period from 1 January 20X8 to 31 March 20X9.

7.4.3   Oil and gas assets

Under some local GAAPs, exploration and development costs for oil and gas properties in the development or production phases are accounted for in cost centres that include all properties in a large geographical area (known as the 'full cost' method).

IFRS 1 permits a first-time adopter that has previously used this basis of accounting to elect to measure the related oil and gas assets at the date of transition to IFRSs on the following basis:
[IFRS 1:D8A]

- exploration and evaluation assets – at amounts determined under the entity's previous GAAP; and

- oil and gas assets in the development or production phases – at the amount determined for the cost centre under the entity's previous GAAP. This amount should be allocated to the cost centre's underlying assets pro rata using reserve volumes or reserve values as of that date.

For the purposes of this exemption, the term 'oil and gas assets' is limited to those assets used in the exploration, evaluation, development or production of oil and gas. [IFRS 1:D8A]

Entities electing to use the exemption are required to test both exploration and evaluation assets and assets in the development and production phases for impairment at the date of transition to IFRSs. The exploration and evaluation assets are tested in accordance with IFRS 6 *Exploration for and Evaluation of Mineral Resources*, and development and production assets are tested in accordance with IAS 36 *Impairment of Assets*. [IFRS 1:D8A]

Any identified impairment losses must be recognised at the date of transition. [IFRS 1:D8A]

7.4.4   Assets used in operations subject to rate regulation

The exemption applies for entities that:
[IFRS 1:D8B]

- hold items of property, plant and equipment that are used, or were previously used, in operations subject to rate regulation; and

- have included in the carrying amount of such items amounts that were determined under previous GAAP but do not qualify for capitalisation under IFRSs.

For this purpose, operations are subject to rate regulation if they provide goods or services to customers at prices (i.e. rates) established by an authorised body empowered to establish rates that bind the customers and that are designed to recover the specific costs the entity incurs in providing the regulated goods or services and to earn a specified return. The specified return could be a minimum or range and need not be a fixed or guaranteed return. [IFRS 1:D8B]

When a first-time adopter falls within the scope of this paragraph, it may elect to use the previous GAAP carrying amount of such an item at the date of transition to IFRSs as deemed cost. If an entity applies this exemption to an item, it need not apply it to all items. [IFRS 1:D8B]

When this option is taken, at the date of transition to IFRSs, the entity is required to test for impairment in accordance with IAS 36 each item to which the exemption is applied. [IFRS 1:D8B]

Subsequent depreciation or amortisation is based on the deemed cost and starts from the date of transition to IFRSs. [IFRS 1:IG51]

7.5   Leases

7.5.1   Determining whether an arrangement contains a lease

IFRS 1 allows two exemptions for first-time adopters applying IFRIC 4 *Determining whether an Arrangement contains a Lease*, which are discussed in the following sections.

7.5.1.1   Transition provisions of IFRIC 4

A first-time adopter may apply the transition provisions of IFRIC 4. Therefore, a first-time adopter may determine whether an arrangement existing at the date of transition to IFRSs contains a lease on the basis of the facts and circumstances existing at that date. [IFRS 1:D9]

IFRIC 4 specifies criteria for determining, at the inception of an arrangement, whether the arrangement contains a lease. It also specifies when an arrangement should be reassessed subsequently. IFRS 1 provides an exemption from these requirements. Instead of determining retrospectively whether an arrangement contained a lease at the inception of the arrangement and subsequently reassessing that arrangement as required in the periods prior to transition to IFRSs, entities may determine whether arrangements in existence on the date of transition contain leases by applying paragraphs 6 to 9 of IFRIC 4 to those arrangements on the basis of the facts and circumstances existing at that date (see **2.1.1** in **chapter A17**). [IFRS 1:IG204 – IG205]

7.5.1.2   *Assessment under previous GAAP made at a date other than that required under IFRIC 4*

An additional exemption is available for a first-time adopter that, under its previous GAAP, made an assessment as to whether an arrangement contained a lease at a date other than that required under IFRIC 4. In such circumstances, the first-time adopter is not required to reassess its previous determination if that previous determination made under its previous GAAP would have given the same outcome under IAS 17 *Leases* and IFRIC 4. [IFRS 1:D9A]

Example 7.5.1.2

Exemption from reassessment as to whether an arrangement contains a lease

Entity R is adopting IFRSs with a date of transition of 1 January 20X5. With effect from 1 January 20X3, Entity R's previous GAAP was amended to include guidance relating to whether an arrangement contains a lease. At the time the previous GAAP requirement became effective, Entity R assessed that it had only one arrangement which contained a lease. The arrangement was entered into on 30 June 20X2 and remains in existence at the date of transition to IFRSs. Other arrangements, which were determined not to contain a lease, are also ongoing at the date of transition to IFRSs.

Entity R has determined that the assessment as to whether the arrangement contained a lease under previous GAAP resulted in the same outcome as would have been arrived at under IAS 17 and IFRIC 4.

Therefore, under IFRS 1:D9A, upon adoption of IFRSs, Entity R is not required to reassess whether existing arrangements contain a lease. Instead, Entity R can rely on the assessment made under previous GAAP because that assessment resulted in the same outcome as would have been arrived at under IAS 17 and IFRIC 4.

Note that for the arrangement that was determined to contain a lease, IAS 17 must be applied retrospectively because IFRS 1 does not provide any exemptions in that regard.

7.5.2   *Other aspects of lease accounting*

Apart from the exemptions described in the previous sections regarding the application of IFRIC 4, no special exemptions for leases are available to a first-time adopter under IFRS 1. Accordingly, a first-time adopter is required to apply IAS 17 in full in its first IFRS financial statements, both in respect of the current period and any comparative periods.

A first-time adopter may, therefore, be required to recognise an asset (e.g. property, plant and equipment) on transition to IFRSs that it had not recognised under previous GAAP. This asset might be recognised by the first-time adopter in its role as the lessee under a finance lease (it may have treated the lease as an operating lease under previous GAAP) or as the lessor under an operating lease (it may have treated the lease as a finance lease under previous GAAP). In the former case, in the absence of other exemptions, the first-time adopter would be required to determine (1) the fair value of the asset at the inception of the lease (or the present value of the minimum lease payments, if lower) depreciated to the date of transition to IFRSs, and (2) the finance lease liability amortised at the rate implicit in the lease (or, if appropriate, the lessee's incremental borrowing rate). It may be difficult, and even impracticable, to determine the fair value of the leased asset at the inception of the lease; however, the entity might be able to elect to measure the asset capitalised under a finance lease at fair value at the date of transition to IFRSs in accordance with the optional exemption in IFRS 1 (see **7.4.1** above).

At the date of transition to IFRSs, leases should be classified as operating leases or finance leases (by both the lessee and the lessor) on the basis of circumstances existing at the inception of the leases (see IAS 17:13). The lessee and lessor may agree to amend the terms of the lease in a manner that would have resulted in a different classification had the amended terms been in effect at the inception of the lease. If so, the revised agreement is considered as a new agreement over its term, but changes in estimates (e.g. of the economic life or residual value of the leased property) or changes in circumstances (e.g. default by the lessee) do not give rise to a new lease classification. [IFRS 1:IG14]

When IAS 17 was revised in 1997, the net cash investment method for recognising finance income of lessors was eliminated. The transition provisions of IAS 17 permit finance lessors to eliminate this method prospectively. However, this transitional relief is not available to a first-time adopter when preparing its opening IFRS statement of financial position (see **5.2** above). Therefore, a finance lessor measures finance lease receivables in its opening IFRS statement of financial position as if the net cash investment method had never been permitted. [IFRS 1:IG15]

SIC-15 *Operating Leases – Incentives* (see **7.2.2** in **chapter A17**) applies to lease terms beginning on or after 1 January 1999. However, a first-time adopter must apply SIC-15 to all leases, irrespective of whether they started before or after that date. [IFRS 1:IG16]

7.6   Employee benefits

7.6.1   Entities that adopt IAS 19(2011)

Entities that adopt IAS 19(2011) *Employee Benefits* in their first IFRS financial statements are entitled to a short-term exemption as discussed at **7.21.1**.

7.6.2   Entities that do not adopt IAS 19(2011)

7.6.2.1   Option to recognise all past actuarial gains and losses for entities using the corridor approach

Under IAS 19(1998) *Employee Benefits*, an entity may elect to use a 'corridor' approach when measuring its obligations under defined benefit post-employment benefit plans (see **section 7.5.1** of **appendix A3**), which leaves some actuarial gains and losses unrecognised. Retrospective application of this approach would require the cumulative actuarial gains and losses from the inception of the plan until the date of transition to IFRSs to be split into a recognised portion and an unrecognised portion. A first-time adopter may elect to recognise all cumulative actuarial gains and losses at the date of transition to IFRSs (i.e. reset the corridor to zero), even if it uses the corridor approach for later actuarial gains and losses. If a first-time adopter uses this election, it must be applied to all of its plans. [IFRS 1:D10]

> As illustrated in **example 7.9.2** below, if a subsidiary is already reporting under IFRSs and has made an unreserved statement of compliance with IFRSs in previous years, it would not be acceptable to reset that subsidiary's defined benefit corridor to zero for the

purposes of the consolidated financial statements of the parent; in accordance with IFRS 1:D17, a parent adopting IFRSs later than its subsidiary is required to use the subsidiary's date of transition as its own for that subsidiary. It can be seen, therefore, that the reference in IFRS 1:D10 to 'all plans' excludes any plans that are subject to the more specific requirement in IFRS 1:D17.

Note, however, that when a subsidiary becomes a first-time adopter later than its parent, IFRS 1:D16 permits the subsidiary to measure its assets and liabilities at the carrying amount that would be included in the parent's consolidated financial statements, based on the parent's date of transition to IFRSs, if no adjustments were made for consolidation procedures and for the effects of the business combination in which the parent acquired the subsidiary (see **7.9.1** below).

Example 7.6.2.1

Date used to reset defined benefit corridor

Company Y is adopting IFRSs with a 1 January 20X4 date of transition. It selects as its accounting policy to recognise actuarial gains and losses arising on its defined benefit post-employment benefit plan using the corridor approach under IAS 19(1998) and it elects to reset the corridor to zero as permitted by IFRS 1:D10.

Is Company Y permitted to reset its defined benefit corridor from a date prior to its date of transition to IFRSs?

No. If Company Y elects to reset its defined benefit corridor in accordance with IFRS 1:D10, it must do so at its date of transition to IFRSs. It is not permitted to select any other date at which to reset the corridor. Although some of the other exemptions in IFRS 1 allow more flexibility (e.g. the flexibility provided by IFRS 1 for the restatement of past business combinations), it is not permissible to extend that flexibility to other scenarios by analogy.

The exemption refers only to cumulative actuarial gains and losses at the date of transition to IFRSs. It does not extend to any past service cost not recognised in accordance with IAS 19(1998):96 (see **7.6** in **appendix A3**). It will, therefore, be necessary to calculate, and adjust for, the amount of any unrecognised past service cost related to benefit changes that have not yet vested at the date of transition to IFRSs. This will mean that the asset or liability recognised for the defined benefit plan in the statement of financial position may differ from the surplus or deficit in the plan.

7.6.2.2   *Consequences of not using the exemption*

It is likely that most first-time adopters that apply the corridor approach will make use of the election to recognise all cumulative actuarial gains and losses at the date of transition. In practice, this typically means recognising the full amount of the surplus or deficit at the date of transition to IFRSs (subject to the detailed requirements of IAS 19(1998)).

If this option is not taken, it would be necessary to go back to the inception of the defined benefit plan (or, if later, the date on which the plan was acquired in a business combination) and obtain actuarial valuations at the end of each subsequent reporting period to apply the corridor approach with retrospective effect. For a defined benefit plan that has been established for more than a few years, this is likely to involve significant cost and may be impracticable.

If a plan was acquired in a business combination, the plan is only a plan of the consolidated entity from the date of acquisition. At the date of acquisition, the plan has a new measurement basis as required by IFRS 3 *Business Combinations* (or the equivalent value attributed to it under previous GAAP). Also, IFRS 1:IG Example 2 clarifies that the defined benefit obligation and corresponding entry to retained earnings are calculated from the date of acquisition.

7.6.2.3   *Exemption from IAS 19(1998) disclosure requirement*

IAS 19(1998) includes a requirement to disclose the following amounts for the current annual period and the previous four annual periods:

- the present value of the defined benefit obligation, the fair value of the plan assets and the surplus or deficit in the plan;

- the experience adjustments arising on the plan liabilities expressed either as an amount or as a percentage of plan liabilities at the end of the reporting period; and

- the experience adjustments arising on the plan assets expressed either as an amount or as a percentage of plan assets at the end of the reporting period.

To be consistent with the transition rules for this requirement in IAS 19(1998), IFRS 1 allows that a first-time adopter may disclose these amounts as they are determined for each accounting period prospectively from the transition date. [IFRS 1:D11]

7.6.3   Other aspects of accounting for employee benefits

The actuarial assumptions used at the date of transition to IFRSs should be consistent with the actuarial assumptions made for the same date under previous GAAP (after adjustments to reflect any differences in accounting policies) unless there is objective evidence that those assumptions were in error. The impact of any later revisions to those assumptions is an actuarial gain or loss of the period in which the entity makes the revisions. [IFRS 1:IG19]

It may be necessary to make actuarial assumptions at the date of transition to IFRSs that were not necessary under previous GAAP. Any such assumptions should not reflect conditions that arose after the date of transition to IFRSs. In particular, discount rates and the fair value of plan assets at the date of transition to IFRSs reflect market conditions at that date. Similarly, actuarial assumptions at the date of transition to IFRSs about future employee turnover rates should not reflect a significant increase in estimated employee turnover rates as a result of a curtailment of the pension plan that occurred after the date of transition to IFRSs. [IFRS 1:IG20]

An entity's first IFRS financial statements will usually reflect measurements of employee benefit obligations at three dates (the end of the reporting period, the date of the comparative statement of financial position and the date of transition to IFRSs). IAS 19 encourages the involvement of a qualified actuary in the measurement of all material post-employment benefit obligations. However, the implementation guidance accompanying IFRS 1 notes that, to minimise cost, an entity may request a qualified actuary to carry out a detailed actuarial valuation at one or two dates and roll the valuation(s) forward or back to other dates. Any such roll forward or roll back should reflect any material transactions and other material events (including changes in market prices and interest rates) between those dates. [IFRS 1:IG21]

7.7   Cumulative translation differences

Under IAS 21 *The Effects of Changes in Foreign Exchange Rates*, some translation differences are initially recognised in other comprehensive income and accumulated in a separate component of equity. On disposal of a foreign operation, IAS 21 requires an entity to reclassify the cumulative translation difference for that foreign operation (including, if applicable, gains and losses on related hedges) to profit or loss as part of the gain or loss on disposal. [IFRS 1:D12]

Retrospective application of IAS 21 could be very onerous for a
first-time adopter because it would require an entity retrospectively
to determine the translation differences arising on the translation of
the financial statements of a foreign operation in accordance with
IFRSs from the date on which the operation was formed or acquired.
Often, this information will not be readily available. IFRS 1 provides
an optional exemption relating to the treatment of cumulative translation differences upon first-time adoption.

A first-time adopter need not comply with these requirements for cumulative translation differences that existed at the date of transition to IFRSs. If
this exemption is applied, the cumulative translation differences for all
foreign operations are deemed to be zero at the date of transition to IFRSs.
The gain or loss on a subsequent disposal of any foreign operation will
include only foreign exchange differences that arose after the date of
transition. [IFRS 1:D13]

If the election is used to reset all cumulative translation differences
for all foreign operations to zero at the date of transition to IFRSs,
this treatment applies to translation differences that arise as a result
of first-time adoption of IFRSs. The election applies once all adjustments for first-time adoption have been recognised at the date of
transition. If the election is used, the balance of cumulative translation differences in the opening IFRS statement of financial position
will be zero.

7.7.1   Reassessment of functional currency on transition to IFRSs

The following example illustrates the application of the exemption when
an entity is required to change its functional currency on transition to
IFRSs to comply with IAS 21.

Example 7.7.1

Reassessment of functional currency on transition to IFRSs

Under previous GAAP, an entity had Sterling as its functional currency. At
the date of transition to IFRSs, when the requirements of IAS 21 are applied,
it is determined that the entity's functional currency is US dollars. The entity
chooses not to use the exemption available in IFRS 1:D13 but instead applies
IAS 21 retrospectively.

The Foreign Currency Translation Reserve (FCTR) should be recalculated from the date the functional currency (under IAS 21) is considered to be US dollars.

If the functional currency of the entity is determined always to have been US dollars, the FCTR at the date of transition will represent the effect of the movements in exchange rates since the acquisition of each asset and liability (including those disposed of before transition to IFRSs). The FCTR should be calculated based on the underlying measurement of assets and liabilities in the functional currency of the entity.

IFRS 1:D5 and D6 permit deemed cost to be used for certain assets. When this exemption is used, the FCTR will not be calculated from the date of acquisition, but from the date at which the deemed cost amount is determined for the assets to which deemed cost has been applied.

If it is determined that the functional currency changed from Sterling to US dollars at some point prior to the date of transition (ignoring the use of any deemed cost exemption), the FCTR is only calculated from the date of change because, under IAS 21:35, translation procedures are only applied prospectively.

Irrespective of whether the exemption in IFRS 1:D13 is used, balances in the financial statements must be recognised in the entity's functional currency following the IAS 21 requirements.

7.7.2   Application of exemption when parent becomes a first-time adopter later than its subsidiary

Example 7.7.2

Application of exemption when parent becomes a first-time adopter later than its subsidiary

Parent P is adopting IFRSs for the first time with a date of transition of 1 January 20X4. In its first IFRS consolidated financial statements, Parent P proposes to use the exemption in IFRS 1:D13 to reset the cumulative translation differences for its foreign operations to zero at 1 January 20X4.

Subsidiary S is a subsidiary of Parent P and a foreign operation of Parent P as defined in IAS 21:8. Subsidiary S adopted IFRSs with a date of transition of 1 January 20X1. Subsidiary S is itself a parent and it has interests in a number of subsidiaries (together forming the 'Subsidiary S sub-group') that are foreign operations of Subsidiary S as defined in IAS 21:8.

IFRS 1:D17 requires that when a parent becomes a first-time adopter later than its subsidiary, the parent should, in its consolidated financial statements, measure the assets and liabilities of the subsidiary at the same carrying amounts as in the financial statements of the subsidiary, after adjusting for consolidation and for the effects of the business combination in which the entity acquired the subsidiary (see **7.9.2** below).

Given the requirements of IFRS 1:D17, when considering whether to use the exemption in IFRS 1:D13 in the first IFRS consolidated financial statements for the larger group, is Parent P constrained by whether Subsidiary S elected to use that exemption in the first IFRS consolidated financial statements for the Subsidiary S sub-group?

No. The application of the exemption under IFRS 1:D13 is not affected by the requirements of IFRS 1:D17 because IFRS 1:D17 refers only to the measurement of assets and liabilities whereas IFRS 1:D13 is concerned with the classification of items within equity.

Irrespective of Subsidiary S's approach at its earlier date of transition, Parent P has a choice as to whether to use the exemption in IFRS 1:D13 in the first IFRS consolidated financial statements for the larger group. IFRS 1:D13 explicitly requires that when the exemption is applied, it should be applied to the cumulative translation differences for all of the foreign operations of the first-time adopter. Therefore, if it elects to use the exemption under IFRS 1:D13, Parent P should reset all of the cumulative translation differences for its group (including those relating to the Subsidiary S sub-group) to zero at 1 January 20X4.

7.8   Investments in subsidiaries, associates and joint ventures

Throughout this section, for entities that do not adopt IFRS 11 *Joint Arrangements* together with IAS 27(2011) *Separate Financial Statements* in their first IFRS financial statements (required for annual periods beginning on or after 1 January 2013 with earlier adoption permitted), references to 'joint ventures' should be taken as references to 'jointly controlled entities'.

When an entity prepares separate financial statements, IAS 27(2011) (or, if IAS 27(2011) is not adopted, IAS 27(2008) *Consolidated and Separate Financial Statements*) requires it to account for its investments in subsidiaries, associates and joint ventures either:
[IFRS 1:D14]

• at cost; or

• in accordance with IFRS 9 *Financial Instruments* (or, if IFRS 9 is not adopted, IAS 39 *Financial Instruments: Recognition and Measurement*).

This choice between measurement at cost or in accordance with IFRS 9 (or IAS 39) must be made consistently for all investments in the same category. [IAS 27(2011):10 (IAS 27(2008):38)]

If a first-time adopter chooses to measure its investments in subsidiaries, associates or joint ventures at cost, for the purposes of its opening IFRS statement of financial position, IFRS 1 requires that 'cost' to be either: [IFRS 1:D15]

- cost determined in accordance with IAS 27(2011) (or, if IAS 27(2011) is not adopted, IAS 27(2008)); or

- a deemed cost, determined as either:

  - fair value at the entity's date of transition to IFRSs for its separate financial statements; or

  - the previous GAAP carrying amount at the entity's date of transition to IFRSs for its separate financial statements.

> The exemption available under IFRS 1:D15 permits a first-time adopter to use a deemed cost based on either fair value or previous GAAP carrying amount for its investments in subsidiaries, associates or joint ventures. This exemption is intended to address concerns that it may be difficult, or even impossible, and costly to determine cost in accordance with IAS 27(2011) (or, if IAS 27(2011) is not adopted, IAS 27(2008)). The alternative available under IAS 27(2011):10 (IAS 27(2008):38) of accounting for such investments at fair value in accordance with IFRS 9 (or, if IFRS 9 is not adopted, IAS 39) on an ongoing basis will often be unattractive because of the cost of obtaining annual valuations.
>
> For entities that adopt IFRS 13 *Fair Value Measurement* in their first IFRS financial statements, when the option is taken to measure investments at a deemed cost based on fair value at the date of transition to IFRSs, that fair value is measured in accordance with the general principles of IFRS 13. For entities that do not adopt IFRS 13 in their first IFRS financial statements, fair value at the date of transition to IFRSs is determined in accordance with the measurement guidance in IFRS 9 (or, if IFRS 9 is not adopted, IAS 39).

A first-time adopter may choose either method for the determination of deemed cost (i.e. based on either fair value or previous GAAP carrying amount) to measure its investment in each subsidiary, joint venture or associate that it elects to measure using deemed cost. [IFRS 1:D15]

That is to say, first-time adopters are permitted to choose which cost measurement basis to use for each investment on an individual basis. Some could be measured at cost in accordance with IAS 27(2011) (or, if IAS 27(2011) is not adopted, IAS 27(2008)) and others at deemed cost. For those measured at deemed cost, the choice between fair value and previous GAAP carrying amount may also be made on an investment-by-investment basis.

If an entity uses this exemption, it must make the disclosures described at **9.2.9** below.

7.9   Assets and liabilities of subsidiaries, associates and joint ventures

This section deals with specific exemptions available to a first-time adopter when:

- the first-time adopter is a subsidiary and it is adopting IFRSs later than its parent (addressed in IFRS 1:D16); and

- the first-time adopter is a parent and it is adopting IFRSs later than its subsidiary (addressed in IFRS 1:D17).

The Standard does not specifically address circumstances in which a parent and a subsidiary are adopting IFRSs at the same date. However, considering the underlying objective of IFRS 1:D16 (i.e. to avoid the need to keep two parallel sets of records which the IASB accepted would be burdensome and not beneficial to users — see IFRS 1:BC60), it would appear reasonable to apply IFRS 1:D16 in such circumstances.

Application of this exemption when a parent and a subsidiary are adopting IFRSs at the same date might be helpful when the parent and the subsidiary have previously applied different GAAPs and, consequently, the accounting policies used in the subsidiary's financial statements differed from those in the consolidated financial statements. For example, if borrowing costs were capitalised under the subsidiary's, but not the parent's, previous GAAP this difference could be eliminated by excluding capitalised borrowing costs from the carrying amount of property, plant and equipment in its opening IFRS statement of financial position — an adjustment that would not otherwise be permitted by IFRS 1:D23(a) (see **7.15** below).

As explained in **example 7.9.4** below, in the consolidated financial statements of a first-time adopter, the exemptions in IFRS 1 must be applied consistently to all subsidiaries, associates and joint ventures except when the exemption permits otherwise (e.g. the election for deemed cost of property, plant and equipment may be applied on an individual asset basis). This is, however, subject to the requirements described at **7.9.2** below if the subsidiary, associate or joint venture becomes a first-time adopter before the investor.

7.9.1   Subsidiary becomes a first-time adopter later than its parent

If a subsidiary becomes a first-time adopter later than its parent, IFRS 1 permits a choice between two measurement bases in the subsidiary's financial statements. Note that this choice is not available to a subsidiary of an investment entity which is required to be measured at fair value through profit or loss under the *Investment Entities* amendments (see **15.2.1** in **chapter A24**). [IFRS 1:D16]

The *Investment Entities* amendments are effective for annual periods beginning on or after 1 January 2014, with earlier application permitted. It is expected that an entity adopting IFRSs for the first time in 2013 will adopt the *Investment Entities* amendments at the same time so as to avoid adopting IFRS 10 (with no exception from consolidation) in 2013 followed by the consolidation exception in the following year.

The subsidiary may measure its assets and liabilities at either:
[IFRS 1:D16]

(a)   the carrying amount that would be included in the parent's consolidated financial statements, based on the parent's date of transition to IFRSs, if no adjustments were made for consolidation procedures and for the effects of the business combination in which the parent acquired the subsidiary; or

(b)   the carrying amounts required by IFRS 1 based on the subsidiary's date of transition to IFRSs.

The carrying amounts under these alternatives could differ when the exemptions in IFRS 1 result in measurement that depends on the date of transition to IFRSs. They could also differ when the accounting policies used in the subsidiary's financial statements differ from those in the consolidated financial statements. [IFRS 1:D16]

> The purpose of this exemption is to avoid the need to keep two parallel sets of records which the IASB accepted would be burdensome and not beneficial to users. [IFRS 1:BC60]
>
> When the option to use the parent's date of transition to IFRSs is applied, the amounts recognised by the subsidiary are 'based on' the parent's date of transition. However, the amounts recognised by the subsidiary at its date of transition will not generally be the same amounts recognised as at the parent's date of transition because of the need to account for subsequent depreciation etc. up to the subsidiary's date of transition to IFRSs.

Example 8 in the implementation guidance accompanying IFRS 1 provides an illustration of this choice. The example notes that when the assets and liabilities are measured based on the subsidiary's (later) date of transition to IFRSs, this does not change the carrying amount of the assets and liabilities in the consolidated financial statements. [IFRS 1:IG29]

A similar election is available to an associate or a joint venture that becomes a first-time adopter later than an entity that has significant influence or joint control over it. [IFRS 1:D16]

Paragraphs D16 (discussed in this section) and D17 (discussed at **7.9.2** below) of IFRS 1 do not override the following requirements: [IFRS 1:IG30]

- to apply Appendix C to IFRS 1 (on business combinations – see **7.1** above) to assets acquired and liabilities assumed in a business combination that occurred before the acquirer's date of transition to IFRSs. But the acquirer should apply paragraph D17 to new assets acquired, and liabilities assumed, by the acquiree after that business combination and still held at the acquirer's date of transition to IFRSs;

- to apply the rest of IFRS 1 in measuring all assets and liabilities for which paragraphs D16 and D17 are not relevant; and

- to give all disclosures required by IFRS 1 as at the first-time adopter's own date of transition to IFRSs (see **section 9** below).

IFRS 1:D16 applies if a subsidiary becomes a first-time adopter later than its parent (e.g. if the subsidiary previously prepared a reporting package under IFRSs for consolidation purposes but did not present a full set of financial statements under IFRSs). The implementation guidance accompanying IFRS 1 notes that this may be relevant not only when a subsidiary's reporting package complies fully with the recognition and measurement requirements of IFRSs, but also when it is adjusted centrally for matters such as a review of events after the reporting period and central allocation of pension costs. The implementation guidance accompanying IFRS 1 explains that such adjustments to an unpublished reporting package are not the correction of errors for the purposes of the disclosure requirements of paragraph 26 of the Standard (see **9.2.2** below). However, paragraph D16 does not permit a subsidiary to ignore misstatements that are immaterial to the consolidated financial statements but are material to the subsidiary's own financial statements. [IFRS 1:IG31]

For example, if a subsidiary adopts IFRSs in its December 20X4 financial statements, its date of transition to IFRSs will be 1 January 20X3. Rather than applying IFRS 1 as at that date, the subsidiary can elect to use the assets and liabilities recorded in the group reporting package as at 31 December 20X2 as adjusted for any relevant central adjustments made to bring the reporting package into full compliance with the recognition and measurement requirements of IFRSs. However, if there was an error in the reporting package that was material to the subsidiary's financial statements (but ignored as immaterial to the consolidated financial statements) then the amounts would have to be adjusted to comply with IFRSs.

7.9.1.1   Subsidiary becomes a first-time adopter later than its parent – use of fair value as deemed cost exemption

Example 7.9.1.1

Subsidiary becomes a first-time adopter later than its parent – use of fair value as deemed cost exemption

Parent B's date of transition to IFRSs was 1 January 20X1. On 1 January 20X4, Parent B acquired Subsidiary M, which reports under local GAAP. For the purposes of its consolidated financial statements, Parent B measured the identifiable assets and liabilities of Subsidiary M at fair value at the acquisition date in accordance with the requirements of IFRS 3 *Business Combinations*.

Subsidiary M intends to adopt IFRSs in its financial statements for the year ended 31 December 20X8. Subsidiary M would like to reflect its property, plant and equipment on a fair value basis in its opening IFRS statement of financial position but without incurring the expense of commissioning additional valuations. Subsidiary M would like to use the January 20X4 valuations obtained by Parent B as the basis for an uplifted carrying amount in its first IFRS financial statements, rolling forward to reflect depreciation from 1 January 20X4 to the date of transition to IFRSs.

In the circumstances described, Subsidiary M is not permitted to apply the exemption available under IFRS 1:D16(a). The exemption set out in IFRS 1:D16 refers to circumstances in which a subsidiary becomes a first-time adopter later than its parent. The effect of the exemption is to allow the subsidiary to 'adopt' the parent's earlier date of transition as its own. This approach would not be appropriate in the circumstances described because Subsidiary M was not a subsidiary of Parent B at Parent B's date of transition to IFRSs. Consequently, Parent B's consolidated financial statements at Parent B's date of transition to IFRSs did not include the assets and liabilities of Subsidiary M.

Other IFRS 1 exemptions that allow previous valuations as the basis for an uplifted carrying amount in an entity's first IFRS financial statements are:

- IFRS 1:D6, which allows a previous GAAP revaluation of an item of property, plant and equipment before the date of transition to IFRSs to be taken as the deemed cost of the asset at the date of the revaluation (see **7.4.1** above); and

- IFRS 1:D8(a), which allows event-driven fair values on or before the date of transition to be taken as the deemed cost at the date of that measurement (see **7.4.2** above).

However, neither of these exemptions is available to Subsidiary M because both exemptions require that the amounts arising from the previous valuation to be taken as deemed cost have been recognised in the entity's previous GAAP financial statements. In the circumstances described, although the fair values at 1 January 20X4 have been incorporated into Parent B's consolidated financial statements since that date, they have not been recognised in Subsidiary M's local GAAP financial statements.

One option that is available to Subsidiary M is to elect as its date of transition to IFRSs the date at which Parent B obtained the valuations (i.e. 1 January 20X4). This would allow Subsidiary M to take advantage of the exemption under IFRS 1:D5 which permits an entity to use fair value at the date of transition as the deemed cost of an item of property, plant and equipment at that date (see **7.4.1**). However, if Subsidiary M were to elect 1 January 20X4 as its date of transition to IFRSs, it would be required to present:

- an opening statement of financial position under IFRSs at 1 January 20X4 prepared in accordance with the requirements of IFRS 1; and

- comparative information for the 20X4, 20X5, 20X6 and 20X7 reporting periods prepared in accordance with IFRSs effective at 31 December 20X8 (subject to the general exceptions and exemptions in IFRS 1).

7.9.2   Parent becomes a first-time adopter later than its subsidiary

If a parent becomes a first-time adopter later than its subsidiary, the parent should, in its consolidated financial statements, measure the assets and liabilities of the subsidiary at the same carrying amount as in the financial statements of the subsidiary, after adjusting for consolidation adjustments and for the effects of the business combination in which the parent acquired the subsidiary. The same approach applies in the case of associates and joint ventures. [IFRS 1:D17]

Note that this exemption does not permit a non-investment entity parent to apply the exception to consolidation used by any investment entity subsidiary following adoption of the *Investment Entities* amendments (see **15.2.1** in **chapter A24**). [IFRS 1:D17]

The *Investment Entities* amendments are effective for annual periods beginning on or after 1 January 2014, with earlier application permitted. It is expected that an entity adopting IFRSs for the first time in 2013 will adopt the *Investment Entities* amendments at the same time so as to avoid adopting IFRS 10 (with no exception from consolidation) in 2013 followed by the consolidation exception in the following year.

Although IFRS 1:D17 appears in an appendix to IFRS 1 dealing with optional exemptions, it is written as a requirement. The reason for this is unclear but the material was presumably included here to contrast with the situation when a subsidiary becomes a first-time adopter later than its parent. The Basis for Conclusions section of IFRS 1 devotes five paragraphs (BC59 to BC63) to explaining the reason for the exemption in the latter case. It then briefly adds "however, if a parent adopts IFRSs later than a subsidiary, the parent cannot, in its consolidated financial statements, elect to change IFRS measurements that the subsidiary has already used in its financial statements, except to adjust for consolidation procedures and for the effects of the business combination in which the parent acquired the subsidiary". This is a statement of fact rather than an explanation of the reason for the requirement.

The requirement for consistency with the financial statements of the subsidiary is subject to adjusting for "consolidation and equity accounting adjustments and for the effects of the business combination in which the entity acquired the subsidiary". These include, for example, accounting policy alignments and adjustments to eliminate profits on intragroup transactions. If the subsidiary was acquired in a business combination, the amounts may be determined after taking into account the IFRS 1 exemptions for business combinations (see **7.1** above). However, these exemptions apply only to assets and liabilities that existed at the date of the business combination. It may, therefore, be necessary to analyse the assets and liabilities of the acquired entity between those that existed at its date of acquisition and those that arose subsequently.

Example 9 in the implementation guidance accompanying IFRS 1 provides an illustration of this requirement. [IFRS 1:IG29]

The following example illustrates the effect of this requirement for the recognition of a defined benefit post-employment benefit plan surplus or deficit on transition to IFRSs.

Example 7.9.2

Effect on employee benefit exemption when a parent and subsidiary have different dates of transition to IFRSs

Company S is a subsidiary of Company P. Company S adopted IFRSs in 20X5, using 1 January 20X4 as its date of transition.

Company P is adopting IFRSs in 20X8, using 1 January 20X7 as its date of transition. Both Company P and Company S selected as their IFRS accounting policy for defined benefit post-employment benefit plans to recognise actuarial gains and losses using the 'corridor' approach permitted under IAS 19(1998) *Employee Benefits*. Company S elected to recognise all cumulative actuarial gains and losses at 1 January 20X4, as permitted by IFRS 1:D10 (thereby setting the corridor to zero at its date of transition). Company P has also elected to apply the IFRS 1:D10 exemption.

In its first IFRS consolidated financial statements, Company P is not permitted to reset Company S's corridor to zero at 1 January 20X7. IFRS 1:D10 states that if a first-time adopter chooses to reset the corridor to zero, that election should apply to all of its plans. However, 'all' plans in this context excludes any that are subject to the more specific requirements of IFRS 1:D17, which require the entity to measure the assets and liabilities of a subsidiary that is already applying IFRSs at the same carrying amounts as in the financial statements of the subsidiary. As a result, in the circumstances

---

described, Company P must measure the defined benefit liability or asset already accounted for in accordance with IAS 19(1998) by Company S at the current carrying amount in Company S' financial statements, regardless of whether it applies the IFRS 1:D10 exemption to its other plans.

However, this does not override the general principle that consolidated financial statements should be prepared using consistent accounting policies. For example, if Company P adopts a policy under IAS 19 of immediate recognition of all actuarial gains and losses without the use of the corridor, the amounts reported by Company S (using the corridor) would be adjusted to bring them in line with Company P's accounting policy for the purposes of Company P's consolidated financial statements.

As explained at **7.9.1** above, IFRS 1:D17 does not override certain other requirements of IFRS 1 as specified by IFRS 1:IG30.

7.9.3 Parent becomes a first-time adopter for its separate financial statements earlier or later than for its consolidated financial statements

If a parent becomes a first-time adopter for its separate financial statements earlier or later than for its consolidated financial statements, it should measure its assets and liabilities at the same amounts in both financial statements, except for consolidation adjustments. [IFRS 1:D17]

This might be relevant to a parent that is required to adopt IFRSs for its consolidated financial statements by local laws or regulations, but the requirement does not apply to separate financial statements. The parent may continue to prepare its separate financial statements under previous GAAP for a number of years and then decide to move to IFRSs.

It may not be immediately obvious how a parent could be a first-time adopter for its separate financial statements earlier than for its consolidated financial statements. Separate financial statements alone would not comply with IFRS 10 *Consolidated Financial Statements* (or, if IFRS 10 is not adopted, IAS 27(2008) *Consolidated and Separate Financial Statements*) when that Standard would require consolidated financial statements to be presented. However, the situation might arise if the parent was entitled to the exemption from preparation of consolidated financial statements in IFRS 10 (or, if IFRS 10 is not adopted, IAS 27(2008)) (i.e. because a higher parent prepares IFRS consolidated financial statements) but subsequently ceased to be entitled to the exemption or chose not to use it.

When a parent adopts IFRSs for its separate financial statements at a later date than for its consolidated financial statements, it is required by IFRS 1:D17 to measure its assets and liabilities at the amounts used in the consolidated financial statements, subject to any consolidation adjustments. This is different from the position for a subsidiary adopting IFRSs at a later date than its parent which has a choice (see **7.9.1** above) between using its own date of transition or that used for the consolidated financial statements of the group. In practice, it is likely that most entities will find it more convenient to use the amounts used in the IFRS-compliant consolidated financial statements and, therefore, will not be disadvantaged by this requirement.

7.9.4   Consistent application of IFRS 1 exemptions to subsidiaries, associates and joint ventures

Example 7.9.4

Consistent application of IFRS 1 exemptions to subsidiaries, associates and joint ventures

Investor I Limited is adopting IFRSs with a date of transition of 1 January 20X5. It has a number of subsidiaries, associates and joint ventures, both domestic and overseas, none of which applies IFRSs.

In I Limited's opening IFRS consolidated statement of financial position at 1 January 20X5, the IFRS 1 exemptions selected by the investor (which represent accounting policy choices) should be applied consistently to all of I Limited's subsidiaries, associates and joint ventures unless otherwise provided for in the specific exemption. This follows the general principle in IAS 8:13 that accounting policies should be applied consistently for similar transactions and events unless an IFRS specifically requires or permits otherwise, and the requirements of IFRS 10 (or, if IFRS 10 is not adopted, IAS 27(2008)) and IAS 28 for consistent application of accounting policies among group entities, associates and joint ventures.

Accordingly, I Limited should apply all of the exemptions in Appendix D consistently among its subsidiaries, associates and joint ventures in its consolidated financial statements except for the following, which make specific provision for selective application:

- fair value or revaluation as deemed cost (IFRS 1:D5 to D8) – the Standard provides that the deemed cost elections can be applied on an individual asset basis. Therefore, the application of the elections can vary among the various entities and within individual entities; and

- financial assets or intangible assets accounted for in accordance with IFRIC 12 *Service Concession Arrangements* (IFRS 1:D22) – the exemption permits the first-time adopter to apply the transition provisions of IFRIC 12. Because the transition provisions of IFRIC 12 provide relief from retrospective application of the Interpretation for any particular service arrangements for which retrospective application is impracticable, the election can vary for different arrangements in the various entities and within individual entities.

IFRS 1:D16 and D17 (see **7.9.1** and **7.9.2** above) set out specific rules for the measurement of assets and liabilities of subsidiaries, associates and joint ventures when the parent (investor) and the subsidiary, associate or joint venture adopt IFRSs at different dates. See **7.9** above for a discussion of the accounting required when a parent (investor) and its subsidiary, associate or joint venture adopt IFRSs at the same date.

With respect to the accounting for investments in subsidiaries, associates and joint ventures in I Limited's separate financial statements, IFRS 1:D14 and D15 set out the allowed alternative accounting treatments (see **7.8** above). If I Limited chooses to measure such investments in accordance with IFRS 9 (or, if IFRS 9 is not adopted, IAS 39) on an ongoing basis, it must apply that policy consistently for all investments in the same category. However, if I Limited chooses to measure its investments at cost, it is permitted to choose which 'cost' measure to use for each investment on an individual basis. Some may be measured at cost in accordance with IAS 27(2011) *Separate Financial Statements* (or, if IAS 27(2011) is not adopted, IAS 27(2008)) and others at deemed cost. For those measured at deemed cost, the choice between fair value and previous GAAP carrying amount may also be made on an investment-by-investment basis.

7.10   Compound financial instruments

IAS 32 *Financial Instruments: Presentation* requires an entity to split a compound financial instrument at inception into separate liability and equity components (see **chapter B3** or **chapter C3** for a detailed description of this requirement).

IFRS 1:D18 provides some relief for first-time adopters when applying IAS 32 for the first time. To the extent that the liability component of a compound instrument is no longer outstanding at the date of transition to IFRSs, retrospective application of IAS 32's requirement to split the instrument is not required. [IFRS 1:D18]

This exemption is justified on the basis of expediency. The only effect of retrospective application of IAS 32 in the circumstances described would be the separation of two components of equity: one portion representing the cumulative interest accrued on the liability component during its life using the effective interest method (which would normally reside in retained earnings) and the second portion representing the original equity component that would have been separated on initial recognition of the instrument.

See **section 2.7** of **chapter B13** or **section 2.7** of **chapter C13** for examples of the application of IAS 32 at the date of transition to IFRSs.

7.11   Designation of previously recognised financial instruments

7.11.1   Entities applying IFRS 9

IFRS 1 allows a number of optional exemptions in relation to the designation of previously recognised financial instruments for first-time adopters applying IFRS 9:

- a first-time adopter is permitted to designate any financial liability as at fair value through profit or loss (FVTPL) at the date of transition to IFRSs if it meets the criteria in IFRS 9(2010):4.2.2 (see **section 7.1.2** of **chapter B3**) at that date; [IFRS 1:D19]

- a first-time adopter is permitted to designate a financial asset that meets the conditions for amortised cost measurement as at FVTPL at the date of transition to IFRSs if the criteria in IFRS 9(2010):4.1.5 (see **section 5.2.1** of **chapter B2**) are met on the basis of the facts and circumstances that exist at the date of transition to IFRSs; [IFRS 1:D19A]

- a first-time adopter is permitted to designate an investment in an equity instrument as at fair value through other comprehensive income at the date of transition to IFRSs if the criteria in IFRS 9(2010):5.7.5 (see **section 5.3** of **chapter B2**) are met on the basis of the facts and circumstances that exist at the date of transition to IFRSs; [IFRS 1:D19B]

- if it is impracticable (as defined in IAS 8 *Accounting Policies, Changes in Accounting Estimates and Errors* – see **section 2.8** of **chapter A5**) for an entity to apply retrospectively the effective interest method (see **section 4.1** of **chapter B6**) or the impairment requirements of IAS 39 (see **section 5** of **chapter B6**), the fair value of the financial asset at the date of transition to IFRSs is taken to be the amortised cost of that financial asset at the date of transition to IFRSs; [IFRS 1:D19C] and

- when determining whether the presentation of changes in the fair value of a financial liability attributable to changes in credit risk in other comprehensive income would create or enlarge an accounting mismatch in profit or loss (see **section 7.1.2.5** of **chapter B3**), a first-time adopter is required to make that determination based on the facts and circumstances that exist at the date of transition to IFRSs. [IFRS 1:D19D]

Although IFRS 1:D19C and D19D appear in an appendix to IFRS 1 dealing with optional exemptions, they are written as requirements. IFRS 1:D19C specifies the required treatment when it is impracticable to apply the effective interest method or IAS 39's requirements regarding impairment retrospectively. Similarly, IFRS 1:D19D specifies that the determination to be made in the specific circumstances 'shall' be made on the basis of facts and circumstances at the date of transition to IFRSs rather than that it 'may' be made on that basis (as is the case for the exemptions in IFRS 1:D19A and 19B). These requirements are different because IFRS 1:D19, D19A, D19B and D19D relate to classification choices that an entity may, but is not obliged to, apply at the date of transition to IFRSs, whereas IFRS 1:D19C prescribes an alternative opening measurement basis only in circumstances when retrospective application is impracticable.

When the exemptions in IFRS 1:D19 and D19A are applied, specific disclosure requirements are triggered (see **9.2.3.1** below).

7.11.2   Entities applying IAS 39

IAS 39 permits any financial asset, other than an asset that meets the definition of held for trading, to be designated on initial recognition as available for sale (AFS). It also permits financial assets and financial liabilities to be designated as at fair value through profit or loss (FVTPL) provided that they meet specified criteria (see **chapters C2** and **C3** for a detailed description of these requirements). Entities are generally only permitted to make these designations when the financial instrument is first recognised.

IFRS 1 allows two optional exemptions in relation to the designation of previously recognised financial instruments for first-time adopters applying IAS 39:
[IFRS 1:D19]

- a first-time adopter is permitted to designate any financial asset, other than an asset that meets the definition of held for trading, as an AFS financial asset at the date of transition to IFRSs; and

- a first-time adopter is permitted to designate, at the date of transition to IFRSs, any financial asset or financial liability as at FVTPL if it meets the criteria for designation as at FVTPL in IAS 39:9 and 11A.

> When the exemptions in IFRS 1:D19 are applied, the designation is made at the date of transition as if the entity had never made a choice under previous GAAP, and this is so even if previous GAAP was identical to IAS 39. When the exemption in IFRS 1:D19 is applied, specific disclosure requirements are triggered (see **9.2.3.2** below).

7.12 Fair value measurement of financial assets or financial liabilities at initial recognition

IFRS 9 (or, if IFRS 9 is not adopted, IAS 39) requires that all financial assets and financial liabilities should be initially recognised at fair value. When determining the carrying amount of financial assets and financial liabilities at the date of transition to IFRSs, a first-time adopter must consider the guidance on measuring fair value in IFRS 13 *Fair Value Measurement* (or, for a first-time adopter that does not adopt IFRS 13 in its first IFRS financial statements, the guidance in IFRS 9 or IAS 39). This applies even if the financial asset or financial liability is not subsequently measured at fair value, because fair value at initial recognition will be the basis for the opening carrying amount at the date of transition to IFRSs.

IFRS 9 and IAS 39 limit up-front gain/loss recognition unless the fair value of the instrument is evidenced by comparison with other observable current market transactions in the same instrument (i.e. without modification or repackaging) or based on a valuation technique whose variables include only data from observable markets. This is often referred to as 'day 1 P&L' and is discussed in more depth at **7.1** in **chapter B7** or **7.1** in **chapter C7**.

For first-time adopters that have adopted IFRS 13, IFRS 1:D20 permits that the day 1 P&L guidance contained in IFRS 9(2010):B5.1.2A need not be applied to transactions entered into before the date of transition to IFRSs.

For first-time adopters that have not adopted IFRS 13, the equivalent references to the day 1 P&L guidance are to IFRS 9(2010):B5.4.8 and B5.4.9 (or, if IFRS 9(2010) is not adopted, IAS 39:AG76 and AG76A) .

7.13   Decommissioning liabilities included in the cost of property, plant and equipment

IFRIC 1 *Changes in Existing Decommissioning, Restoration and Similar Liabilities* (discussed at **4.4** in **chapter A7**) requires specified changes in a decommissioning, restoration or similar liability to be added to or deducted from the cost of the asset to which it relates; the adjusted depreciable amount of the asset is then depreciated prospectively over its remaining useful life. The exemption available under IFRS 1:D21 permits a first-time adopter to elect not to comply with the requirements of IFRIC 1 for changes in such liabilities that occurred before the date of transition to IFRSs. If this option is selected, the first-time adopter includes in the depreciated cost of the asset at the date of transition to IFRSs an amount calculated by the following steps:
[IFRS 1:D21]

- measuring its decommissioning liability as at the date of transition to IFRSs in accordance with IAS 37 *Provisions, Contingent Liabilities and Contingent Assets;*

- to the extent that the liability is within the scope of IFRIC 1, estimating the amount that would have been included in the cost of the related asset when the liability first arose by discounting the liability to that date using its best estimate of the historical risk-adjusted discount rate(s) that would have applied for that liability over the intervening period; and

- calculating the accumulated depreciation on that amount, as at the date of transition to IFRSs, on the basis of the current estimate of the useful life of the asset, using the depreciation policy adopted by the entity under IFRSs.

Example 7.13 below illustrates the application of this exemption. Note that, when discounting the liability to calculate the adjustment to the cost of the asset, it is necessary to take into account changes in the relevant discount rate between the date the asset was first recognised and the date of transition to IFRSs.

If a first-time adopter does not take the option available under IFRS 1:D21, IFRIC 1 should be applied retrospectively at the date of transition to IFRSs. If IFRIC 1 is applied retrospectively, in order to determine the portion of the decommissioning obligation to be included in the cost of the related asset, the first-time adopter will need to:

- determine the amount that would have been required to settle the obligation at the date the asset was acquired;

- construct a reliable historical record of any changes in the obligation between the date of the acquisition of the asset and the date of transition to IFRSs; and

- allocate those changes in accordance with IFRIC 1.

Whichever alternative is taken, if the deemed cost exemption (see **7.4** above) is used for the related asset, care is needed to ensure that the adjustment of the carrying amount related to the decommissioning liability is not counted twice. The valuation of the asset would be the gross amount without any adjustment for the costs of decommissioning. Any adjustment arising from recognition of the decommissioning liability is taken to retained earnings and is not added to the carrying amount of the asset.

Example 7.13

Decommissioning obligation not recognised under previous GAAP

Company A is adopting IFRSs with a 1 January 20X4 date of transition. Ten years before that date, Company A paid CU100,000 for an asset with a 40-year useful life. Company A has an obligation to decommission this asset at the end of its useful life, but it was not required to recognise that obligation under its previous GAAP.

Company A elects to take the exemption from retrospective application of IFRIC 1.

As a first step, Company A measures the decommissioning obligation at the date of transition in accordance with IAS 37 by estimating the present value of the expenditures expected to be required to settle the obligation in 30 years. Assume that Company A estimates this present value as CU25,000.

Next, Company A estimates the amount that would have been included in the cost of the asset when the liability first arose (in this example, when the asset was acquired) by discounting CU25,000 to the date on which the asset was acquired 10 years previously. The discount rate used will be Company A's best estimate of the historical risk-adjusted discount rate(s) that would have applied for that liability over the intervening period. Company A estimates this rate to be 5 per cent and that the rate has not changed since the date on which the asset was acquired. Consequently, Company A's estimate of the decommissioning obligation that would have been included in the cost of the asset when it was acquired is CU15,348 (CU25,000/1.05^{10}).

Finally, Company A calculates the accumulated depreciation on that amount, as at the date of transition to IFRSs, on the basis of the current estimate of the useful life of the asset, as CU3,837 (CU15,348 ÷ 40 × 10).

As a result of these calculations, Company A records the following journal entries in its opening statement of financial position as at 1 January 20X4.

		CU	CU
Dr	Cost of asset (the decommissioning portion of the asset)	15,348	
Dr	Retained earnings (the effect of the change)	13,489	
Cr	Provisions (the decommissioning obligation)		25,000
Cr	Accumulated depreciation (from the date of purchase to 31 Dec 20X3)		3,837

Recognition of the decommissioning obligation and the resultant adjustment to cost of asset.

When discounting the liability to calculate the adjustment to the cost of the asset, it is necessary to take into account changes in the relevant discount rate between the date the asset was first recognised and the date of transition to IFRSs. For example if, in the circumstances described in **example 7.13**, instead of a single rate of 5 per cent, Company A estimated that the historical risk-adjusted discount rate that would have applied for the first five years of owning the asset is 5 per cent and the rate that would have applied in the second five years of owning the asset is 7 per cent, the estimated decommissioning obligation that would have been included in the cost of the asset when it was acquired is CU13,966 [CU25,000/(1.05^5 x 1.07^5)].

The implementation guidance accompanying IFRS 1 includes another example illustrating the use of this exemption (IG Example 201).

7.13.1   Oil and gas assets

If an entity elects to use the deemed cost exemption (see **7.4.3** above) for oil and gas assets in the development or production phases, the entity is required to:
[IFRS 1:D21A]

•   measure decommissioning, restoration and similar liabilities as at the date of transition to IFRSs in accordance with IAS 37; and

- recognise directly in retained earnings any difference between that amount and the carrying amount of those liabilities at the date of transition to IFRSs determined under the entity's previous GAAP.

This treatment differs from the general exemption in IFRS 1:D21 which requires entities to measure the liability as at the date of transition to IFRSs in accordance with IAS 37 and then discount this to estimate the amount that would have been included in the cost of the related asset when the liability first arose, and to calculate accumulated depreciation on the latter amount to the date of transition.

7.14   Financial assets or intangible assets accounted for in accordance with IFRIC 12 *Service Concession Arrangements*

A first-time adopter may apply the transition provisions in IFRIC 12. [IFRS 1:D22]

The transition provisions in IFRIC 12 require that the Interpretation should be applied retrospectively, in accordance with IAS 8. However, if it is not practicable for an operator to apply the Interpretation retrospectively at the start of the earliest period presented, the entity should:
[IFRIC 12:30]

- recognise financial assets and intangible assets that existed at the start of the earliest period presented;

- use the previous carrying amounts of those financial and intangible assets (however previously classified) as their carrying amounts as at that date; and

- test financial and intangible assets recognised at that date for impairment, unless this is not practicable, in which case the amounts should be tested for impairment as at the start of the current period.

Therefore, if it is not practicable for a first-time adopter to apply IFRIC 12 retrospectively, the rules set out in IFRIC 12:30 should be applied. The 'start of the earliest period presented' in an entity's first IFRS financial statements is the date of transition to IFRSs.

7.15   Borrowing costs

IAS 23 *Borrowing Costs* prescribes the accounting treatment for borrowing costs and requires that borrowing costs directly attributable to the acquisition, construction or production of a qualifying asset form part of the cost of that asset. All other borrowing costs are expensed as incurred.

> The requirements in this section were amended by *Annual Improvements to IFRSs: 2009–2011 Cycle* issued in May 2012. Although paragraph IFRS 1:D23 has been rewritten in its entirety (see below), the requirements pre- and post-May 2012 amendments (set out under separate headings below) as they relate to borrowing costs incurred *prior* to the date of transition (or earlier date of application of IAS 23 – see detailed requirements in IFRS 1:D23 below) are unchanged. The effect of the May 2012 amendments is to specify new requirements for borrowing costs incurred *on or after* the date of transition (or earlier date of application of IAS 23, if relevant) that relate to qualifying assets under construction at that date. Prior to the May 2012 amendments, first-time adopters were not permitted to commence capitalisation (or change the capitalisation methodology) for such assets; following the May 2012 amendments, IAS 23 is applied to all borrowing costs incurred on or after the date of transition to IFRSs (or earlier date of application of IAS 23, if relevant), including those relating to qualifying assets under construction at that date. **Example 7.15.3** illustrates the impact of the May 2012 requirements.

The May 2012 amendments to IFRS 1:D23 are effective for annual periods beginning on or after 1 January 2013, with earlier application permitted. If a first-time adopter elects to apply the revised requirements for an accounting period beginning before 1 January 2013, that fact is required to be disclosed.

> Note that the decision to take the exemption under IFRS 1:D23 is an accounting policy choice which should be applied consistently for all borrowing costs. The entity is permitted to apply IAS 23 retrospectively at the date of transition to IFRSs but, if it chooses to do so, it must apply that Standard consistently to all qualifying assets.

7.15.1   *Entities that adopt the May 2012 amendments*

IFRS 1 permits a first-time adopter to choose either:
[IFRS 1:D23]

- to apply the requirements of IAS 23 retrospectively; or

- to apply the requirements of IAS 23 from the date of transition to IFRSs or from an earlier designated date, as permitted by IAS 23:28 (see **3.4.1.1** in **chapter A18**).

When a first-time adopter takes the option not to apply the requirements of IAS 23 retrospectively, from the date on which the first-time adopter begins to apply IAS 23 (date of transition to IFRSs or earlier designated date), the entity:

- should not restate any borrowing cost component that was capitalised under previous GAAP and that was included in the carrying amount of assets at that date; and

- should account for borrowing costs incurred on or after that date in accordance with IAS 23, including those borrowing costs incurred on or after that date on qualifying assets already under construction.

However, if the entity establishes a deemed cost for an asset, the entity should not capitalise borrowing costs incurred before the date of the measurement that established the deemed cost. [IFRS 1:IG23]

7.15.2   *Entities that do not adopt the May 2012 amendments*

IFRS 1 permits a first-time adopter to choose either:
[IFRS 1:D23]

- to apply the requirements of IAS 23 retrospectively; or

- to apply the transition provisions of IAS 23. When a first-time adopter chooses this option, references to the effective date are interpreted as references to 1 January 2009 or to the date of transition to IFRSs, whichever is later, or to an earlier date designated by the first-time adopter as the date from which it wishes to apply IAS 23.

When a first-time adopter takes the option under IFRS 1:D23 to apply the transition provisions of IAS 23, the entity:
[IFRS 1:IG23]

- should not restate any borrowing cost component that was capitalised under previous GAAP and that was included in the carrying amount of assets on the date on which the first-time adopter begins to apply IAS 23;

- should continue to apply its previous accounting method to all borrowing costs related to qualifying assets for which the commencement date for capitalisation is before the date on which the first-time adopter begins to apply IAS 23; and

- should account for borrowing costs related to qualifying assets for which the commencement date for capitalisation is on or after the date on which the first-time adopter begins to apply IAS 23 in accordance with IAS 23.

However, if the entity establishes a deemed cost for an asset, the entity should not capitalise borrowing costs incurred before the date of the measurement that established the deemed cost. [IFRS 1:IG23]

7.15.3   Application of borrowing costs exemption (pre- and post-May 2012 amendments)

Example 7.15.3

Application of borrowing costs exemption (pre- and post-May 2012 amendments)

Entity A's date of transition is 1 January 20X7 with its first IFRS financial statements to be prepared as at 31 December 20X8. It has the following assets in respect of which borrowing costs were either not capitalised under previous GAAP or were capitalised using a different methodology from that required by IAS 23.

- Asset 1 — construction commenced 1 January 20X4 and completed 30 June 20X6.

- Asset 2 — construction commenced 1 July 20X6 and not yet completed.

- Asset 3 — construction commenced 1 July 20X7 and completed 31 March 20X8.

In its first IFRS financial statements, Entity A wishes to use the optional exemption from retrospective application of IAS 23 and to apply IAS 23 from its date of transition.

All of these assets meet the definition of 'qualifying assets' under IAS 23 and the 'construction commenced' and 'construction completed' dates noted in each case are the appropriate dates for commencement and cessation of capitalisation of borrowing costs under IAS 23.

Application of the optional exemption in IFRS 1:D23		
	Pre-May 2012 amendments	**Post-May 2012 amendments**
Asset 1	The construction of Asset 1 began and ended before the date of transition. Entity A does not restate the borrowing costs capitalised in respect of Asset 1 (which may be zero if borrowing costs were not capitalised under previous GAAP).	
Asset 2	The construction of Asset 2 began before the date of transition and has extended beyond the end of the first IFRS reporting period.	The construction of Asset 2 began before the date of transition and has extended beyond the end of the first IFRS reporting period.
	Because the commencement date for capitalisation under IAS 23 is before the date of transition, Entity A does not restate any borrowing costs capitalised in respect of Asset 2 and continues to apply its previous GAAP capitalisation methodology (which may be not to capitalise any borrowing costs) until the asset is completed.	Any borrowing costs incurred in respect of Asset 2 before 1 January 20X7 are not restated. Any borrowing costs incurred in respect of Asset 2 on or after 1 January 20X7 are accounted for in accordance with IAS 23.
Asset 3	The construction of Asset 3 began after the date of transition; therefore, the requirements of IAS 23 must be applied. Any difference between the borrowing costs capitalised under previous GAAP (which may be zero) and the amount calculated under IAS 23 should be shown in the reconciliation of reported profit or loss for the comparative period in Entity A's first IFRS financial statements.	

7.16   Transfers of assets from customers

IFRIC 18 *Transfers of Assets from Customers* addresses the accounting by recipients for transfers of property, plant and equipment from 'customers'; the requirements of IFRIC 18 are discussed in detail at **2.3** in **chapter A14**.

In finalising IFRIC 18, the IFRIC (now the IFRS Interpretations Committee) noted that applying a change in accounting policy to comply with the requirements of IFRIC 18 retrospectively would require entities to establish a carrying amount for assets that had been transferred in the past. That carrying amount would be based on historical fair values which may or may not be based on an observable price or observable inputs. Therefore, the IFRIC concluded that retrospective application could be impracticable and that the Interpretation should require prospective application to transfers received after its effective date.

To provide first-time adopters with the same relief, an exemption was also added to IFRS 1 under which first-time adopters may also apply the transition provisions set out in IFRIC 18:22.

Therefore, IFRS 1 permits a first-time adopter to choose either: [IFRS 1:D24]

- to apply the requirements of IFRIC 18 retrospectively; or

- to apply the transition provisions of IFRIC 18. When a first-time adopter chooses this option, references to 1 July 2009 are interpreted as 1 July 2009 or the date of transition to IFRSs, whichever is later.

An entity is not, therefore, required to apply IFRIC 18 to transfers of assets that occurred before its date of transition to IFRSs.

A first-time adopter may also designate any date before the date of transition to IFRSs and apply IFRIC 18 to all transfers of assets from customers on or after that date. [IFRS 1:D24]

7.17   Extinguishing financial liabilities with equity instruments

IFRIC 19 *Extinguishing Financial Liabilities with Equity Instruments* addresses the accounting for entities that issue equity instruments in order to extinguish all or part of a financial liability (often referred to as 'debt for equity swaps'). The requirements of IFRIC 19 are discussed in **section 4.2** of **chapter B8** and **section 4.2** of **chapter C8**.

The transition provisions of IFRIC 19 require that an entity should apply any change in accounting policy arising from the application of the Interpretation from the beginning of the earliest comparative period presented.

In finalising IFRIC 19, the IFRIC (now the IFRS Interpretations Committee) concluded that it was preferable to require entities that could apply the Interpretation retrospectively to do so, rather than requiring all entities to apply it prospectively to future transactions; the Committee made specific reference to IAS 8's guidance on circumstances in which retrospective application might be impracticable. To simplify transition, the IFRIC also concluded that it should require retrospective application only from the beginning of the earliest comparative period presented because application to earlier periods would result only in a reclassification of amounts within equity. [IFRIC 19:BC33]

IFRS 1 permits first-time adopters to apply the transition provisions in IFRIC 19. [IFRS 1:D25]

First-time adopters therefore have a choice between full retrospective application of IFRIC 19 and application of the transition provisions of IFRIC 19. The option selected will have no impact on amounts reported for the first IFRS reporting period and for the comparative period, but full retrospective application could result in some additional reclassifications within equity.

7.18   Severe hyperinflation

This exemption (detailed below) provides relief for first-time adopters that experienced severe hyperinflation prior to the date of transition to IFRSs; such entities are not required to reconstruct historical values for the assets and liabilities held prior to the entity's emergence from severe hyperinflation. It is an optional exemption and therefore, in theory, the entity could instead opt to apply IFRS 1 in full when the entity resumes presenting IFRS financial statements after a period of severe hyperinflation. However, it is likely that such an approach would be impracticable.

If an entity has a functional currency that was, or is, the currency of a hyperinflationary economy, it is required to determine whether it was subject to severe hyperinflation before the date of transition to IFRSs. This applies to entities that are adopting IFRSs for the first time, as well as to entities that have previously applied IFRSs. [IFRS 1:D26]

The currency of a hyperinflationary economy is subject to 'severe hyperinflation' if it has both of the following characteristics:
[IFRS 1:D27]

- a reliable price index is not available to all entities with transactions and balances in the currency; and

- exchangeability between the currency and a relatively stable foreign currency does not exist.

The 'functional currency normalisation date' is the date when either or both of these characteristics no longer exist and, consequently, the currency is no longer subject to severe hyperinflation, or when the entity's functional currency changes to a currency that is not subject to severe hyperinflation. [IFRS 1:D28]

When an entity's date of transition to IFRSs is on or after the functional currency normalisation date, the entity may elect to measure all assets and liabilities held before the functional currency normalisation date at fair value on the date of transition to IFRSs and use that fair value as the deemed cost of those assets and liabilities in the opening IFRS statement of financial position. [IFRS 1:D29]

> The exemption allowing use of fair value as deemed cost should be applied only to those assets and liabilities that are held before the functional currency normalisation date, and not to other assets and liabilities held by the entity at the date of transition to IFRSs.
>
> Further, when a parent entity's functional currency has been subject to severe hyperinflation, but its subsidiary's functional currency has not, the subsidiary would not be able to apply this exemption.

Any adjustments arising from this election are recognised directly in equity at the date of transition to IFRSs and must be accompanied by an explanation of how, and why, the entity had, and then ceased to have, a functional currency that was subject to severe hyperinflation (see **9.2.7** below).

When the functional currency normalisation date falls within a 12-month comparative period, the comparative period may be less than 12 months, provided that a complete set of financial statements (as required by paragraph 10 of IAS 1) is provided for that shorter comparative period. [IFRS 1:D30]

7.19   Joint arrangements

IFRS 11 *Joint Arrangements* was issued in May 2011 and is effective for annual periods beginning on or after 1 January 2013, with earlier application permitted. The requirements of IFRS 11 are discussed in **chapter A27**.

IFRS 11 includes detailed transition provisions for entities that already use IFRSs, which are discussed in **section 9.2** of **chapter A27**. Full retrospective application is not required; specific rules are applied to establish the 'opening position' (i.e. at the beginning of the immediately preceding period) for the two circumstances when adoption of IFRS 11 results in a change in accounting model, i.e. when an entity is required to change:

- from proportionate consolidation to the equity method for 'joint ventures'; and

- from the equity method to accounting for asset and liabilities arising from interests in 'joint operations'.

IFRS 1 permits first-time adopters to apply the transition provisions in IFRS 11, subject to two exceptions (see below).
[IFRS 1:D31]

- A first-time adopter that does not apply IFRS 11 retrospectively in full is required to apply the transition provisions of IFRS 11 at the date of transition to IFRSs (i.e. at the beginning of the earliest IFRS period presented). [IFRS 1:D31(a)]

- A first-time adopter that does not apply IFRS 11 retrospectively in full, and that is required to change its accounting method for joint ventures from proportionate consolidation to the equity method, is required to test the investment for impairment in accordance with IAS 36 *Impairment of Assets* as at the date of transition to IFRSs, regardless of whether there is any indication that the investment may be impaired. Any resulting impairment should be recognised as an adjustment to retained earnings at the date of transition to IFRSs. [IFRS 1:D31(b)]

First-time adopters therefore have a choice between (1) full retrospective application of IFRS 11, and (2) application of the transition provisions of that Standard subject to the two exceptions set out above.

The requirements outlined above reflect consequential amendments to IFRS 1 in June 2012 arising from *Consolidated Financial Statements,*

Joint Arrangements and Disclosure of Interests in Other Entities: Transition Guidance (Amendments to IFRS 10, IFRS 11 and IFRS 12) (see **section 9** of **chapter A27** for details). Although detailed wording changes were made to IFRS 1:D31 as part of the June 2012 amendments, the effect is to clarify that there has been no change in the requirements for first-time adopters regarding first-time application of IFRS 11.

The exception in IFRS 1:D31(b) imposes a more stringent requirement for impairment testing on first-time adopters than applies for entities already applying IFRSs; the Board has opted for consistency with the requirement for first-time adopters to apply IAS 36 in testing goodwill for impairment at the date of transition to IFRSs regardless of whether there is any indication that the goodwill may be impaired. [IFRS 1:BC63L]

7.20   Stripping costs in the production phase of a surface mine

IFRIC 20 *Stripping Costs in the Production of a Surface Mine* addresses the accounting for waste removal costs that are incurred in surface mining activity during the production phase of a mine (production stripping costs). The requirements of IFRIC 20 are discussed in **section 10** of **chapter A7**.

IFRIC 20 is effective for annual periods beginning on or after 1 January 2013, with earlier application permitted. The transition provisions of IFRIC 20 require that an entity should apply the requirements of the Interpretation to production stripping costs incurred on or after the beginning of the earliest period presented. [IFRIC 20:A1 & A2]

When IFRIC 20 is first applied, as at the beginning of the earliest period presented, any predecessor stripping asset (i.e. any previously recognised asset balance that resulted from stripping activity undertaken during the production phase) is required to be reclassified as a part of an existing asset to which the stripping activity relates, and depreciated or amortised over the remaining expected useful life of the identified component of the ore body to which the predecessor stripping asset relates.

When there is no identifiable component of the ore body to which the predecessor stripping asset relates, it should be recognised in opening retained earnings at the beginning of the earliest period presented.

IFRS 1 permits first-time adopters to apply the transition provisions in IFRIC 20.

> First-time adopters therefore have a choice between full retrospective application of IFRIC 20 and application of the transition provisions of IFRIC 20.

For first-time adopters that take the option of applying the transition provisions of IFRIC 20, the requirements of IFRIC 20 should be applied from 1 January 2013 or the beginning of the first IFRS reporting period, whichever is later. [IFRS 1:D32]

> If a first-time adopter is preparing its first IFRS financial statements for a period beginning before 1 January 2013, it can elect to apply IFRIC 20 in advance of its effective date or to defer application of the Interpretation until its first accounting period for which IFRIC 20 is effective.

7.21   Other short-term exemptions

Appendix E to IFRS 1 includes short-term exemptions from IFRSs available to first-time adopters. The exemptions listed below are those that have continuing relevance for annual periods beginning on or after 1 January 2012.

7.21.1   Entities that adopt IAS 19(2011)

First-time adopters are permitted to apply the transition provisions in paragraph 173(b) of IAS 19(2011) *Employee Benefits*. [IFRS 1:E5] Consequently, in financial statements for periods beginning before 1 January 2014, a first-time adopter need not present comparative information for the disclosures required by IAS 19(2011):145 about the sensitivity of the defined benefit obligation (see **8.2.4** in **chapter A15**).

7.21.2   Investment entities

A first-time adopter that is a parent is required to assess whether it is an investment entity, as defined in IFRS 10 *Consolidated Financial Statements*, on the basis of the facts and circumstances that exist at the date of transition to IFRSs. [IFRS 1:E6]

A first-time adopter meeting the definition of an investment entity that prepares its first IFRS financial statements for an annual period ending on or before 31 December 2014 may apply the transition provisions in IFRS 10:C3C to C3D (see **16.3.2.3** and **16.3.2.4** in **chapter A24**) and paragraphs 18C to 18G of IAS 27(2011) *Separate Financial Statements* (see **section 7.3** in **chapter A29**). The references in those paragraphs to the annual period that immediately precedes the date of initial application should be read as the earliest annual period presented in the investment entity's first IFRS financial statements.

IFRS 10 was amended in October 2012 by the *Investment Entities* amendments which introduce an exception to IFRS 10's general consolidation requirements when the reporting entity is an 'investment entity' as defined (see **section 15** of **chapter A24** for detailed discussion).

The *Investment Entities* amendments are effective for annual periods beginning on or after 1 January 2014, with earlier application permitted. It is expected that an investment entity adopting IFRSs for the first time in 2013 will adopt the *Investment Entities* amendments at the same time so as to avoid adopting IFRS 10 (with no exception from consolidation) in 2013 followed by the consolidation exception in the following year.

First-time adopters with a first IFRS reporting period ending on or before 31 December 2014 are permitted to apply some of IFRS 10's transition provisions on the basis of practicability. However, this relief is temporary because the Board believes that it not necessary for first-time adopters who have sufficient time to adopt the requirements.

8   Other components of financial statements

The implementation guidance accompanying IFRS 1 does not form part of the Standard but it is nevertheless indicative of the way in which the IASB believes the IFRS should be implemented. It explains how the requirements of IFRS 1 interact with the requirements of some other IFRSs (those most likely to involve questions specific to first-time adopters). In addition, it provides an illustration of the reconciliations required under IFRS 1 (as described in **section 9**).

The following sections deal with specific components of financial statements not dealt with in other sections for which IFRS 1, or its implementation guidance, has specific requirements or guidance. Not all of the issues covered by the implementation guidance accompanying IFRS 1 are addressed.

8.1   IAS 12 *Income Taxes*

There are no exceptions or exemptions in IFRS 1 regarding the accounting for income taxes. An entity applies IAS 12 to temporary differences between the carrying amount of the assets and liabilities in its opening IFRS statement of financial position and their tax bases. Therefore, deferred tax is recognised in respect of adjustments to the carrying amounts of assets and liabilities recognised at the date of transition. However, if a first-time adopter recognised deferred tax under previous GAAP based on an accounting policy that is compliant with its IFRS accounting policy, it does not adjust its deferred tax estimate unless there is objective evidence that the estimate was in error.

The calculation of the deferred tax liability or asset at the date of transition, as well as the assessment of whether it is probable that a tax asset will be recovered, is based on facts, circumstances and probabilities that existed when the financial statements under previous GAAP were prepared for the same date, and should not take into account subsequent information available when the opening IFRS statement of financial position is actually prepared.

When calculating the deferred tax liability or asset to be included in its opening IFRS statement of financial position, a first-time adopter compares the carrying amounts of all assets and liabilities recognised in the opening IFRS statement of financial position (having made all the necessary adjustments and revaluations according to IFRS 1) with the tax bases of those assets and liabilities. [IFRS 1:IG5]

IAS 12 provides an exception (referred to as the 'initial recognition exception') from the requirement to recognise deferred tax arising on the initial recognition of an asset or a liability in a transaction that is not a business combination and that, at the time of the transaction, affects neither accounting profit nor taxable profit. The requirement in IFRS 1:IG5 to recognise deferred taxes on transition to IFRSs does not override the initial recognition exception in IAS 12. In restating deferred taxes under IAS 12, an entity considers whether each temporary difference arose in circumstances covered by the initial recognition exception (i.e. as though IAS 12 had been applied at the date of the transaction). When the temporary difference did arise in such circumstances, the requirements of paragraphs 15 and 24 of IAS 12 still apply and no deferred tax is recognised. In all other cases, the requirements of IFRS 1 to recognise deferred tax should be applied.

Under IAS 12, the measurement of current and deferred tax reflects tax rates and tax laws that have been enacted or substantively enacted by the end of the reporting period. The effects of changes in tax rates and tax laws are accounted for when those changes are enacted or substantively enacted. [IFRS 1:IG6]

The following examples illustrate the application of these requirements. Further examples dealing with deferred tax on pre-transition business combinations are provided at **7.1.17** above.

Example 8.1A

Deferred tax when valuation used as deemed cost

Entity G is adopting IFRSs for the first time. Entity G has previously purchased land for CU100. Under its previous GAAP, Entity G revalued the land to CU120, but did not recognise any deferred tax in respect of this revaluation. Entity G decides to obtain a valuation of the land at the date of transition to IFRSs and uses this value (CU150) as the deemed cost in accordance with IFRS 1:D5.

Part of the purchase price (CU10) is not allowable as a deduction by the local taxation authorities and, accordingly, the asset has a tax base at the date of purchase and the date of transition of CU90. The tax rate in the local jurisdiction is 30 per cent.

The initial recognition exception applies to the expenditure of CU10 that is not allowable. There is no temporary difference between the remainder of the initial cost and the tax base (both CU90). Therefore, on the date of transition, Entity G will recognise a deferred tax liability of CU15 [(CU150 − CU100) x 30%] being the deferred tax in respect of the difference between deemed cost and initial cost.

Example 8.1B

Deferred tax on intangible asset not recognised under previous GAAP

Under previous GAAP, Entity X incurred development expenditure, which it recognised immediately as an expense. The expenditure did not affect taxable profit at the time of the transaction – only 80 per cent is deductible over a period of five years.

On transition to IFRSs, Entity X recognises an intangible asset relating to the development expenditure.

Should Entity X recognise a deferred tax liability at the date of transition to IFRSs for the entire temporary difference between the carrying amount of the intangible asset in the opening IFRS statement of financial position and its tax base?

No. Under IFRSs, the intangible asset would have been recognised from the outset. Although a temporary difference (for 20 per cent of the expenditure) would have arisen initially, the transaction (restated to comply with IFRSs) would not have affected either accounting profit or taxable profit at that date; therefore, the initial recognition exception in IAS 12 would have applied. As discussed in **example 8.1A**, in circumstances covered by the initial recognition exception (i.e. as though IAS 12 had been applied at the date of the transaction), no deferred tax is recognised.

Entity X may, however, be required to account for any temporary differences that would have subsequently arisen (i.e. between the initial transaction date and the date of transition to IFRSs) as a result of differences between accounting amortisation under IFRSs and the tax write-off period.

Example 8.1C

Deferred tax asset not recognised under previous GAAP

Company X is a first-time adopter in 20X4. Under previous GAAP, deferred taxes were recognised based on timing differences. In 20X1, by means of an internal group reorganisation that had no effect for financial reporting purposes, Company X generated an asset for tax purposes that will be deductible in its tax return over three years. This asset is not recognised for financial reporting purposes under previous GAAP, and does not meet any asset recognition criteria under IFRSs. Therefore, the asset is not recognised on first-time adoption.

In its first IFRS consolidated financial statements, Company X should recognise a deferred tax asset at the date of transition to IFRSs for the net carrying amount of the tax asset that arose in 20X1. A temporary difference exists and a deferred tax asset should be recognised in the group's consolidated financial statements. The initial credit is an adjustment on first-time adoption of IFRSs and so will be recognised in retained earnings (or another appropriate reserve). Subsequent changes in the amount of the deferred tax asset will be recognised in profit or loss.

Paragraphs 9 and 17 of IAS 12 provide examples of one type of temporary difference (i.e. 'timing differences'). However, IAS 12 is, overall, driven by a 'balance sheet' approach, irrespective of whether an expense or income has previously been recognised, such that the comparison should follow an analysis of the tax consequences on settlement (i.e. deferred tax is recognised on the difference between the tax base and the carrying amount for accounting purposes). If a tax base exists for tax purposes and no asset or liability exists for accounting purposes, the carrying amount of the asset or liability should be deemed to be zero for the purposes of identifying temporary differences.

Example 8.1D

Deferred tax on share options not accounted for retrospectively on first-time adoption

Company A granted share options to employees prior to 7 November 2002 (i.e. before the mandatory application of IFRS 2 *Share-based Payment*). The options vest in 2006 subject to non-market vesting conditions. Company A did not recognise the transaction prior to 7 November 2002, and did not make a retrospective adjustment for the transaction on first-time adoption of IFRSs. On transition to IFRSs in 2005, there is consequently no expense recognised in profit or loss in respect of these options (the entity has not applied IFRS 2 to these options under the requirements of IFRS 2:54/IFRS 1:D2 – see **7.2.1.1**). However, on vesting, Company A will receive a tax deduction based on the intrinsic value at the date of exercise.

Does a temporary difference exist at the date of transition when there has been no accounting recognition of the share-option grant (i.e. no recognition of an asset or liability and no expense)?

Yes, there is a temporary difference. The principle of IAS 12:68A to 68C is to require deferred tax to be recognised on all temporary differences relating to share options. Therefore, when there is no remuneration expense recognised in the financial statements, but there is a future tax deduction, deferred tax on the entire temporary difference, equal to the expected tax deduction, is required to be recognised in equity at the date of transition.

8.2   IAS 16 *Property, Plant and Equipment*

8.2.1   *Depreciation methods and rates*

If an entity's depreciation methods and rates under previous GAAP are acceptable under IFRSs, it accounts for any change in estimated useful life or depreciation pattern prospectively from when it makes that change in estimate. This is consistent with the requirements of IFRS 1 on changes of estimates and with paragraph 61 of IAS 16. [IFRS 1:IG7]

Depreciation methods and rates under previous GAAP may differ from those that would be acceptable under IFRSs. For example, they may have been adopted solely for tax purposes and they may not reflect a reasonable estimate of the asset's useful life. In such cases, when the effect is material, the accumulated depreciation is adjusted retrospectively in the opening IFRS statement of financial position so that it complies with IFRSs. [IFRS 1:IG7]

IAS 16 requires each part of an item of property, plant and equipment with a cost that is significant in relation to the total cost of the item to be depreciated separately. But IAS 16 does not prescribe the unit of measure for recognition of an asset (i.e. what constitutes an item of property, plant and equipment). Thus, judgement is required in applying the recognition criteria to an entity's specific circumstances. [IFRS 1:IG12]

8.2.2 Assets measured under IAS 16's revaluation model

The use of fair value or previous revaluations as deemed cost on first-time adoption of IFRSs is considered at **7.4** above.

If the revaluation model in IAS 16 is used for some or all classes of property, plant and equipment, the cumulative revaluation surplus is presented as a separate component of equity. The revaluation surplus at the date of transition to IFRSs should be based on a comparison of the carrying amount of the asset at that date with its cost or deemed cost. If the deemed cost is the fair value at the date of transition to IFRSs, the disclosures required by IFRS 1:30 should be made (see **9.2.4** below). [IFRS 1:IG10]

If revaluations under previous GAAP did not satisfy the criteria in IFRS 1:D6 or D8, the revalued assets should be measured in the opening IFRS statement of financial position on one of the following bases: [IFRS 1:IG11]

- cost (or deemed cost) less any accumulated depreciation and any accumulated impairment losses under the cost model in IAS 16;

- deemed cost, being the fair value at the date of transition to IFRSs; or

- revalued amount, if the entity adopts the revaluation model in IAS 16 as its accounting policy under IFRSs for all assets in the same class.

8.2.3   Asset exchanges

Example 8.2.3

Asset exchanges

IAS 16 requires that an entity measure an item of property, plant and equipment acquired in exchange for a non-monetary asset or assets, or a combination of monetary and non-monetary assets, at fair value unless the exchange transaction lacks commercial substance.

Entity A, adopting IFRSs for the first-time in the current accounting period, acquired an asset via an asset exchange in a prior accounting period and recognised that asset at fair value in accordance with previous GAAP. If IAS 16 had been applied at the date of the asset exchange, the transaction would have been considered to lack commercial substance and the asset would have been recognised at the carrying amount of the asset given in exchange.

Should Entity A adjust accumulated depreciation in its opening IFRS statement of financial position retrospectively to comply with IAS 16?

Under previous GAAP, the acquired asset was recognised at fair value, but IAS 16 would have required it to be recognised at the carrying amount of the asset given up. IFRS 1 does not allow any exemption from retrospective application of the requirements of IAS 16 regarding asset exchanges. Therefore, in theory, restatement is required under IFRS 1. However, provided that the asset was measured at fair value at the date of the transaction, IFRS 1:D6 applies (see **7.4** above). Therefore, for the purposes of transition to IFRSs, Entity A may take the fair value at the date of the exchange transaction as the deemed cost of the asset at that date.

8.2.4   Separate recognition of land and building components of property

---

Example 8.2.4

Separate recognition of land and building components of property

Under local GAAP, an entity did not separately recognise the land and building components of a property asset, which was depreciated as a whole.

On first-time adoption of IFRSs, how should this asset be recognised in the opening IFRS statement of financial position?

At the date of transition, the first-time adopter should recognise the land and building components of the property asset separately. Each component should be measured using either:

- original cost less subsequent depreciation calculated using depreciation methods and rates acceptable under IFRSs; or

- one of the deemed cost measures available under IFRS 1:D5 to D8 (see
  7.4 above).

8.3   IAS 18 *Revenue*

Amounts may have been received that do not yet qualify for recognition as
revenue under IAS 18. An entity should recognise the amount received as
a liability in its opening IFRS statement of financial position and measure
the liability at the amount received. [IFRS 1:IG17]

8.4   IAS 29 *Financial Reporting in Hyperinflationary Economies*

The requirements of IAS 21 *The Effects of Changes in Foreign Exchange Rates*
should be applied to determine an entity's functional currency and presentation currency. IAS 29 should be applied to any periods during which
the economy of the functional or presentation currency was hyperinflationary. [IFRS 1:IG32]

An entity may elect to use the fair value of an item of property, plant and
equipment at the date of transition to IFRSs as its deemed cost at that date.
In such circumstances, it should make the disclosures required by IFRS
1:30 (see **9.2.4** below). [IFRS 1:IG33]

If the entity elects to use the exemptions in IFRS 1:D5 to D8 (i.e. fair value
or revaluation as deemed cost – see **7.4** above), it should apply IAS 29 to
periods after the date for which the revalued amount or fair value was
determined. [IFRS 1:IG34]

Example 8.4

Restatement of share capital for first-time adopters in hyperinflationary economies

Country A's economy was hyperinflationary until 31 December 20X1. An
entity operating in Country A with CU as its functional currency is a
first-time adopter of IFRSs with a transition date of 1 January 20X9. The
entity was established and its share capital was contributed by shareholders
before 31 December 20X1. The entity applies the IFRS 1:D5 fair value as
deemed cost exemption for property, plant and equipment, and does not
have any other non-monetary assets or liabilities acquired or originated prior
to 31 December 20X1.

The entity should inflate the historical cost amount of its share capital in its first IFRS financial statements. Unless there is a specific exemption, IFRS 1 requires full retrospective application of the Standards effective at the end of the reporting period of the entity's first IFRS financial statements. Therefore, IAS 29 should be applied for the period during which the CU was a hyperinflationary currency. Components of equity, such as share capital, should therefore be restated in accordance with IAS 29:24 from the transaction date to the end of the period of hyperinflation.

In the circumstances described, the entity should restate its share capital from the transaction date to 31 December 20X1. There is no exemption from restatement of the share capital, or any other component of equity except retained earnings (which are derived as a balancing figure based on the other amounts in the restated statement of financial position).

8.5   IAS 36 *Impairment of Assets*

A first-time adopter is required to apply IAS 36 at the date of transition. At that date, the first-time adopter:

- performs an impairment test on goodwill and intangible assets with indefinite useful lives regardless of whether an indication of impairment exists;

- determines whether there are any indications that other assets, groups of assets or cash-generating units are impaired at the date of transition;

- performs an impairment test on assets, groups of assets or cash-generating units for which indications of impairment have been identified;

- recognises any impairment losses in retained earnings; and

- reverses any impairment losses that no longer exist at that date except for previously recognised impairment losses on goodwill.

The estimates used at the date of transition to IFRSs to determine whether an impairment loss is recognised (and to measure any such impairment loss) should be consistent with estimates made for the same date under previous GAAP, after making adjustments to reflect differences in accounting policies. This applies unless there is objective evidence that those assumptions were in error. The impact of any later revisions to those estimates should be reported as an event of the period in which the revisions are made. [IFRS 1:IG40]

A first-time adopter recognises any impairment losses arising on transition to IFRSs as a result of changes in accounting policies in retained earnings at the date of transition. If a first-time adopter made a valid IFRS-compliant estimate of an impairment loss under previous GAAP at the date of transition, it does not recognise any additional impairment losses nor reverse any previously recognised impairment losses. Subsequent impairment losses or reversals of impairment losses, including reversals of losses recognised prior to transition, are recognised in profit or loss in accordance with IAS 36.

In assessing the need to recognise an impairment loss and in measuring any such impairment loss at the date of transition to IFRSs, it may be necessary to make estimates that were not necessary under previous GAAP. Such estimates and assumptions should not reflect conditions that arose after the date of transition to IFRSs. [IFRS 1:IG41]

The transition provisions of IAS 36 do not apply to the opening IFRS statement of financial position. [IFRS 1:IG42]

IAS 36 requires the reversal of impairment losses in some circumstances. If the opening IFRS statement of financial position reflects impairment losses, any later reversal of those losses should be reflected in profit or loss except when IAS 36 requires them to be treated as a revaluation. This applies to both impairment losses recognised under previous GAAP and to additional impairment losses recognised on transition to IFRSs. [IFRS 1:IG43]

8.6   IAS 37 *Provisions, Contingent Liabilities and Contingent Assets*

There are no exceptions or exemptions in IFRS 1 relating to provisions. Therefore, the general principle in IFRS 1 of retrospective application of the IFRSs effective at the reporting date applies to provisions, except that a first-time adopter may apply the transition provisions of IFRIC 1 *Changes in Existing Decommissioning, Restoration and Similar Liabilities* (see **7.13** above).

Therefore, at the date of transition, the first-time adopter analyses any provisions recognised under previous GAAP and assesses whether they meet the recognition criteria under IAS 37. If provisions recognised under previous GAAP do not meet these criteria (e.g. because the entity does not have a present obligation), they are removed from the opening IFRS statement of financial position with a corresponding adjustment to retained earnings at the date of transition.

Likewise, if the first-time adopter has incurred liabilities that meet the recognition criteria for provisions, but for which no provision had been recognised under previous GAAP, a provision is recognised in the opening IFRS statement of financial position measured in accordance with IAS 37 at the date of transition, with a corresponding adjustment to retained earnings.

The best estimate of a provision recognised under previous GAAP made on a basis similar to that required under IAS 37 is not adjusted at the date of transition. However, if a provision recognised under previous GAAP was estimated on a basis that is not similar to that required under IAS 37, the best estimate at the date of transition is determined in accordance with IAS 37 based on circumstances existing at the date of transition.

The estimates used to determine whether a provision is recognised, and to measure any such provision at the date of transition to IFRSs, should be consistent with estimates made for the same date under previous GAAP, after making adjustments to reflect differences in accounting policies. This applies unless there is objective evidence that those assumptions were in error. The impact of any later revisions to those estimates should be reported as an event of the period in which the revisions are made. [IFRS 1:IG40]

In assessing the need to recognise a provision, and in measuring any such provision at the date of transition to IFRSs, it may be necessary to make estimates that were not necessary under previous GAAP. Such estimates and assumptions should not reflect conditions that arose after the date of transition to IFRSs. [IFRS 1:IG41]

The transition provisions of IAS 37 do not apply to the opening IFRS statement of financial position. [IFRS 1:IG42]

8.7   IAS 38 *Intangible Assets*

The opening IFRS statement of financial position should:
[IFRS 1:IG44]

- exclude all intangible assets and other intangible items that do not meet the criteria for recognition in IAS 38 at the date of transition to IFRSs; and

- include all intangible assets that meet the recognition criteria in IAS 38 at the date of transition to IFRSs except as described below.

The exception in the second case is for intangible assets acquired in a business combination that were not recognised in the acquirer's consolidated statement of financial position under previous GAAP and also would not qualify for recognition under IAS 38 in the separate statement of financial position of the acquiree (see **section 7.1** above). [IFRS 1:IG44]

The criteria in IAS 38 require an entity to recognise an intangible asset if, and only if:

- it is probable that the future economic benefits that are attributable to the asset will flow to the entity; and

- the cost of the asset can be measured reliably.

8.7.1   *Internally generated intangible assets*

IAS 38 supplements its general recognition criteria with further, more specific criteria for internally generated intangibles. [IFRS 1:IG45] Under IAS 38, the costs of creating internally generated intangible assets are capitalised prospectively from the date when the recognition criteria are met. IAS 38 does not permit the use of hindsight to conclude retrospectively that the recognition criteria were met. Consequently, even if it is possible to conclude retrospectively that a future inflow of economic benefits is probable and the costs can be reconstructed reliably, IAS 38 does not permit the capitalisation of costs incurred before the date when the entity both:
[IFRS 1:IG46]

- concludes, based on an assessment made and documented at the date of that conclusion, that it is probable that future economic benefits from the asset will flow to the entity; and

- has a reliable system for accumulating the costs of internally generated intangible assets when, or shortly after, they are incurred.

If an internally generated intangible asset qualifies for recognition at the date of transition to IFRSs, the asset should be recognised in the opening IFRS statement of financial position even if the related expenditure had been recognised as an expense under previous GAAP. If the asset does not qualify for recognition under IAS 38 until a later date, its cost is the sum of the expenditure incurred from that date. [IFRS 1:IG47]

Example 8.7.1

Capitalisation of costs incurred prior to the date of transition on internally generated intangible assets

Company A adopts IFRSs with a date of transition of 1 January 20X4. At that date, certain internal development projects were determined to be in the development phase in accordance with IAS 38.

Is Company A required to recognise an asset for the development costs that would have been recognised under IAS 38 had Company A reported under IFRSs prior to the date of transition?

It depends. If Company A can reliably measure the development costs incurred, then recognition of the asset is required. However, IFRS 1 recognises that in many cases when prior cost data was not reliably segregated between research and development, the measurement of the development costs may not be reliable and should not be required. If measurement can be determined reliably from the date the recognition criteria were met, then restatement of the asset would be as if IAS 38 had always been applied; that is, only costs incurred during the development phase should be capitalised in the opening IFRS statement of financial position at 1 January 20X4.

The guidance in IFRS 1:IG46 prohibits recognition of an asset for development costs incurred before the date on which the entity concluded, based on an assessment made and documented at the date of that conclusion, that it was probable that future economic benefits from the asset would flow to the entity. In most cases when an entity had a policy of writing off development costs as incurred under previous GAAP, no such assessment would have been made at the time. No asset would therefore be recognised for development costs in the opening IFRS statement of financial position. But, in some cases, development costs may have been recorded and controlled through a system that involved such an assessment being made for commercial rather than financial reporting purposes. Such an assessment might, depending on the facts, constitute an appropriate basis for recognising an asset for development costs on transition to IFRSs.

8.7.2   Intangible assets acquired separately

The criteria described above for recognition of intangible assets under IAS 38 also apply to intangible assets acquired separately. Documentation prepared at the time to support the decision to acquire an asset will usually contain an assessment of the future economic benefits. Also, the cost of separately acquired intangible assets can usually be measured reliably. [IFRS 1:IG48]

8.7.3   Amortisation methods and rates

If the amortisation methods and rates used under previous GAAP would be acceptable under IFRSs, the accumulated amortisation should not be restated in the opening IFRS statement of financial position. Any change in estimated useful life or amortisation pattern should be accounted for prospectively from the period when the change of estimate is made. But in some cases the amortisation methods and rates under previous GAAP might not be acceptable under IFRSs (e.g. because they were adopted solely for tax purposes and do not reflect a reasonable estimate of the asset's useful life). In such cases, when the effect is material, the accumulated amortisation in the opening IFRS statement of financial position should be adjusted retrospectively so that it complies with IFRSs. [IFRS 1:IG51]

Example 8.7.3A

Indefinite-life intangible asset amortised under previous GAAP

A first-time adopter has an intangible asset. Under previous GAAP, the intangible asset was being amortised over 20 years. Previous GAAP required that all intangible assets be amortised and did not have the concept of indefinite-life intangible assets. On first-time adoption of IFRSs, the asset is determined to have an indefinite useful life.

The entity should treat the change of classification to indefinite life as a change in accounting policy. As discussed in IFRS 1:IG51, the entity's previous amortisation method under previous GAAP is not acceptable under IFRSs. Therefore, the change from finite to indefinite life is a change in accounting policy that should be accounted for retrospectively in accordance with IFRS 1.

The transition provisions in IAS 38:130 (which state that a change in useful life from a finite to an indefinite useful life should be accounted for as a change in accounting estimate) do not apply to first-time adopters of IFRSs. The entity must retrospectively restate the intangible as an indefinite-life asset, subject to mandatory annual impairment tests.

Example 8.7.3B

Restatement of an intangible asset as a result of prior impairments

Company N acquired Company U on 1 January 20X2. As part of the accounting for the business combination, CU100 was allocated to purchased in-process research and development (IPR&D) projects. In accordance with local accounting standards, this amount was expensed immediately in the entity's consolidated statement of comprehensive income.

Company N adopts IFRSs with a 1 January 20X4 date of transition, at which date the IPR&D projects are still in progress.

Should the amount allocated to IPR&D and expensed immediately subsequent to the acquisition of Company U under previous GAAP be recognised at the date of transition under IFRSs?

Yes. IFRS 1 requires the use of IFRS-compliant accounting policies in the opening IFRS statement of financial position and throughout the periods presented in the first IFRS financial statements. IFRS 1:IG51 requires that if an entity's amortisation methods and rates under previous GAAP differ from those that would be acceptable under IFRSs, and those differences have a material effect on the financial statements, the entity should retrospectively adjust the accumulated amortisation in its opening IFRS statement of financial position so that it complies with IFRSs.

The immediate impairment or write-off of IPR&D is not in accordance with IFRSs and, therefore, should be reversed in the opening IFRS statement of financial position. Amortisation should be appropriately recognised in accordance with IAS 38. The IPR&D should be tested at least annually for impairment until the asset to be developed is in the location and condition for it to be capable of operating in the manner intended by management, at which time amortisation should commence (assuming the developed asset has a finite useful life).

Because the write-off of IPR&D occurred outside of the business combination, the exemption from the general rules in Appendix C to IFRS 1 for a business combination does not apply.

This requirement also applies to other impairment losses and reversals recognised in prior periods for assets with continuing useful lives at the date of transition.

8.8   IAS 40 *Investment Property*

If the fair value model in IAS 40 is adopted, investment property should be measured at fair value at the date of transition to IFRSs. The transition requirements in IAS 40 do not apply. [IFRS 1:IG61]

If the cost model in IAS 40 is adopted, the requirements of IFRS 1 and related implementation guidance accompanying IFRS 1 for property, plant and equipment should be applied (see **8.2** above). [IFRS 1:IG62]

9   Presentation and disclosure

IFRS 1 does not provide exemptions from the presentation and disclosure requirements of other IFRSs. It imposes additional requirements on first-time adopters. There is an exception to this general rule which concerns non-IFRS comparative information and historical summaries as described at **9.1.1**. [IFRS 1:20]

Also, as explained at **7.6.2.3** above, IFRS 1 includes an exemption from the requirement to provide specified five-year trend information under IAS 19(1998) *Employee Benefits* for dates prior to the date of transition to IFRSs.

Example 9

Disclosure of key management personnel compensation for share-based payments when exemption regarding options granted prior to 7 November 2002 has been applied

Under an entity's executive share option plan, key management personnel received options that were granted prior to 7 November 2002 and that have not yet vested. The entity has elected to apply the exemption in IFRS 1:D2 to these options and, accordingly, has not recognised an expense in relation to them.

Is it appropriate for the entity to apply the exemption in IFRS 1 in determining the amount of key management personnel compensation to be disclosed?

Yes. IAS 24 *Related Party Disclosures* requires disclosure of key management personnel compensation, which is defined as including all employee benefits (as defined in IAS 19), including employee benefits to which IFRS 2 *Share-based Payment* applies (see **5.2** in **chapter A23**).

IAS 24 does not provide guidance on the measurement of amounts to be disclosed for compensation. Reference should therefore be made to the measurement guidance contained in other Standards (such as IAS 19 and IFRS 2) in order to determine the measurement of compensation to be disclosed. Accordingly, when the exemption in IFRS 1 has been applied so that amounts for options granted prior to 7 November 2002 have not been recognised as an expense, the amount disclosed as share-based payment compensation would similarly not include amounts relating to those options.

Entities should consider whether additional disclosures should be provided with respect to the unrecognised share-based payments.

9.1   Comparative information

An entity's first IFRS financial statements are required to include at least three statements of financial position, two statements of profit or loss and other comprehensive income, two separate statements of profit or loss (if presented), two statements of cash flows and two statements of changes in equity and related notes, including comparative information for all statements presented. [IFRS 1:21]

For an entity that does not adopt the amendments made to IAS 1 *Presentation of Financial Statements* in June 2011 (effective for annual periods beginning or on after 1 July 2012), the terminology is slightly different but the underlying requirements are the same. The first IFRS financial statements of such an entity are required to include three statements of financial position, two statements of comprehensive income, two income statements (if presented), two statements of cash flows and two statements of changes in equity and related notes, including comparative information.

The final four words ('for all statements presented') were added to IFRS 1:21 as part of *Annual Improvements to IFRSs: 2009–2011 Cycle* (the 2009–2011 Improvements), issued in May 2012, to clarify that a first-time adopter is required to present notes supporting its opening IFRS statement of financial position.

As part of the 2009–2011 Improvements, IAS 1 was amended to state that, when an entity already applying IFRSs is required to present a third statement of financial position in specified circumstances, it need not present related notes for that additional statement of financial position (see **2.10.4.3** in **chapter A4**). The Basis for Conclusions on IFRS 1 makes clear the IASB's view regarding notes supporting an opening IFRS statement of financial position by stating that "the requirements for comparative information for a first-time adopter should be different from the requirements for comparative information for an existing preparer. The Board noted that a first-time adopter should not be exempted from presenting three statements of financial position and related notes because it might not have presented this information previously on a basis consistent with IFRSs" (see IFRS 1:BC89B).

The amendment to IFRS 1:21 arising from the 2009–2011 Improvements is effective for annual periods beginning on or after 1 January 2013, with earlier application permitted. If the amendment is applied for a period beginning before 1 January 2013, that fact is required to be disclosed. [IFRS 1:39R]

9.1.1   *Historical summaries and previous GAAP comparatives*

Some entities present historical summaries of selected data for periods before the first period for which they present full comparative information under IFRSs. IFRS 1 does not require such summaries to comply with the recognition and measurement requirements of IFRSs. Also, some entities present comparative information under previous GAAP as well as the

comparative information required by IAS 1. In any financial statements containing historical summaries or comparative information under previous GAAP, an entity should:
[IFRS 1:22]

- label the previous GAAP information prominently as not being prepared under IFRSs; and

- disclose the nature of the main adjustments that would make it comply with IFRSs. The adjustments need not be quantified.

As part of *Annual Improvements to IFRSs: 2009–2011 Cycle*, the Basis for Conclusions on IFRS 1 was amended to confirm that a first-time adopter may provide additional comparative information that is presented in accordance with previous GAAP to help users of the financial statements understand the effects of the transition to IFRSs. It is noted that this is an exception to the general principle added to IAS 1 at the same time which, for entities already applying IFRSs, requires that all additional comparative information be prepared in accordance with IFRSs (see **2.10.3** in **chapter A4**).

9.2   Explanation of transition to IFRSs

Entities are required to explain how the transition from previous GAAP to IFRSs affected their reported financial position, financial performance and cash flows. [IFRS 1:23] The disclosures required to meet this objective are discussed in the following sections.

9.2.1   Repeated application of IFRS 1

An entity that has applied IFRSs in a previous reporting period, but whose most recent previous annual financial statements did not contain an explicit and unreserved statement of compliance with IFRSs (see **4.1** above), is required to disclose:
[IFRS 1:23A]

- the reason it stopped applying IFRSs; and

- the reason it is resuming the application of IFRSs.

If, as is permitted under IFRS 1:4A, an entity elects not to apply IFRS 1 when it resumes application of IFRSs, the entity is required to explain the reasons for electing to apply IFRSs as if it had never stopped applying IFRSs. [IFRS 1:23B]

The Standard states specifically that, if an entity elects not to apply IFRS 1 when it resumes application of IFRSs, it is required to provide the disclosures required under IFRS 1:23A and 23B (see above) as well as those required under IAS 8 *Accounting Policies, Changes in Accounting Estimates and Errors*. [IFRS 1:4B]

These disclosure requirements were added to IFRS 1 as part of *Annual Improvements to IFRSs: 2009-2011 Cycle*. They apply when an entity applies IFRS 1:4A (required for annual periods beginning on or after 1 January 2013, with earlier application permitted).

If an entity applies the requirements of IFRS 1:4A for a period beginning before 1 January 2013, it is required to disclose that fact. [IFRS 1:39P]

9.2.2   Reconciliations

An entity's first IFRS financial statements should include:
[IFRS 1:24]

- reconciliations of its equity reported under previous GAAP to its equity under IFRSs as at:

  - the date of transition to IFRSs; and

  - the end of the latest period presented in the entity's most recent annual financial statements under previous GAAP;

- a reconciliation to total comprehensive income under IFRSs for the latest period in the entity's most recent annual financial statements. The starting point for that reconciliation is total comprehensive income under previous GAAP for the same period or, if the entity did not report such a total, profit or loss under previous GAAP; and

- if the entity recognised or reversed any impairment losses for the first time in preparing its opening IFRS statement of financial position, the disclosures that IAS 36 *Impairment of Assets* would have required if the entity had recognised those impairment losses or reversals in the period beginning with the date of transition to IFRSs.

As explained in IFRS 1:BC94, the rationale for the last of these requirements is that there is inevitably subjectivity about impairment losses. The disclosure is intended to provide transparency about impairment losses recognised on transition to IFRSs. These losses might otherwise receive less attention than impairment losses recognised in earlier or later periods.

IFRS 1 requires the above reconciliations to be included in the financial statements. This contrasts with the requirements for an interim report in accordance with IAS 34 *Interim Financial Reporting* (see **9.2.8** below) when a cross reference to another published document is sufficient.

The reconciliations described above should give sufficient detail to enable users to understand the material adjustments to the statement of financial position and statement of comprehensive income. If a statement of cash flows was presented under previous GAAP, an explanation should be provided of the material adjustments to the statement of cash flows. [IFRS 1:25]

Example 11 in the implementation guidance accompanying IFRS 1 shows one way of satisfying these requirements.

An entity may become aware of errors made under previous GAAP. The reconciliations required by paragraphs 24(a) and (b) of IFRS 1 (i.e. the reconciliations of equity and profit or loss and/or total comprehensive income) should distinguish the correction of errors from changes in accounting policies. [IFRS 1:26]

If, during the period covered by its first IFRS financial statements, an entity changes its accounting policies or its use of the exemptions contained in IFRS 1, it is required to explain the changes between its first IFRS interim financial report and its first IFRS financial statements, in accordance with IFRS 1:23, and to update the reconciliations required by IFRS 1:24(a) and (b) (see **5.2.2** above). [IFRS 1:27A]

If an entity did not present financial statements for previous periods, its first IFRS financial statements should disclose that fact. [IFRS 1:28]

9.2.3 Designation of financial assets or financial liabilities

9.2.3.1 Entities applying IFRS 9

As discussed in **7.11.1** above, an entity that has adopted IFRS 9 *Financial Instruments* is permitted to designate a previously recognised financial asset as a financial asset measured at fair value through profit or loss in accordance with IFRS 1:D19A.

The entity is required to disclose the fair value of financial assets so designated at the date of designation and their classification and carrying amount in the previous financial statements. [IFRS 1:29]

An entity that has adopted IFRS 9 is also permitted to designate a previously recognised financial liability as a financial liability at fair value through profit or loss in accordance with IFRS 1:D19.

The entity is required to disclose the fair value of financial liabilities so designated at the date of designation and their classification and carrying amount in the previous financial statements. [IFRS 1:29A]

9.2.3.2 Entities applying IAS 39

As discussed in **7.11.2** above, an entity that applies IAS 39 *Financial Instruments: Recognition and Measurement* is permitted to designate a previously recognised financial asset or financial liability as a financial asset or financial liability at fair value through profit or loss or a financial asset as available for sale in accordance with IFRS 1:D19.

When such a designation is made, the entity is required to disclose the fair value of financial assets or financial liabilities designated into each category at the date of designation and their classification and carrying amount in the previous financial statements. [IFRS 1:29]

9.2.4 Use of fair value as deemed cost

If fair value is used in the opening IFRS statement of financial position as deemed cost for an item of property, plant and equipment, an investment property or an intangible asset (see **7.4** above), the first IFRS financial statements should disclose, for each item in the opening IFRS statement of financial position:
[IFRS 1:30]

- the aggregate of those fair values; and

- the aggregate adjustment to the carrying amounts reported under previous GAAP.

These disclosure requirements apply when fair value at the date of transition is used as deemed cost in accordance with IFRS 1:D5 or IFRS 1:D7. They do not apply when a first-time adopter uses a previous GAAP revaluation in accordance with IFRS 1:D6 or IFRS 1:D8.

9.2.5   Use of deemed cost for oil and gas assets

If an entity uses the exemption in IFRS 1:D8A(b) for oil and gas assets (see **7.4.3** above), that fact and the basis on which carrying amounts were determined under previous GAAP are required to be disclosed. [IFRS 1:31A]

9.2.6   Use of deemed cost for operations subject to rate regulation

If an entity uses the exemption in IFRS 1:D8B for operations subject to rate regulation (see **7.4.4** above), that fact and the basis on which carrying amounts were determined under previous GAAP are required to be disclosed. [IFRS 1:31B]

9.2.7   Use of deemed cost after severe hyperinflation

If an entity elects to measure assets and liabilities at fair value and to use that fair value as the deemed cost in its opening IFRS statement of financial position because of severe hyperinflation (see **7.18** above), the entity's first IFRS financial statements are required to include an explanation of how, and why, the entity had, and then ceased to have, a functional currency that is subject to 'severe hyperinflation' (as defined in IFRS 1:D27). [IFRS 1:31C]

9.2.8   Interim financial reports

When an interim financial report is presented under IAS 34 for part of the period covered by the first IFRS financial statements, the following additional requirements apply in addition to those in IAS 34.

Each such interim financial report should, if the entity presented an interim financial report for the comparable period of the immediately preceding financial year, include:
[IFRS 1:32]

- a reconciliation of its equity under previous GAAP at the end of that comparable interim period to its equity under IFRSs at that date;

- a reconciliation to its total comprehensive income under IFRSs for the comparable interim period (current and year to date). The starting point for that reconciliation is total comprehensive income under previous GAAP for that period or, if the entity did not report such a total, profit or loss under previous GAAP.

In addition, the first interim financial report under IAS 34 for part of the period covered by the first IFRS financial statements should include the reconciliations and other information described at **9.2.2** above. Alternatively, a cross-reference to another published document that includes these reconciliations may be provided. [IFRS 1:32]

If an entity changes its accounting policies or its use of the exemptions contained in IFRS 1, it is required to explain those changes in every interim financial report for part of the period covered by an entity's first IFRS financial statements and update the reconciliations required to be presented in interim financial reports. [IFRS 1:32(c)]

IAS 34 requires minimum disclosures that are based on the assumption that users of the interim financial report also have access to the most recent annual financial statements. But IAS 34 also requires disclosure of "any events or transactions that are material to an understanding of the current interim period". Therefore, if a first-time adopter did not, in its most recent annual financial statements under previous GAAP, disclose information material to an understanding of the current interim period, the interim report should disclose that information or include a cross-reference to another published document that includes it. [IFRS 1:33]

IAS 34:6 allows condensed financial statements and footnotes to avoid repetition of information previously reported. IAS 34:6 also states that "the interim financial report is intended to provide an update on the latest complete set of annual financial statements".

When no previous IFRS annual financial statements have been prepared, the first interim financial report under IFRSs will need to include additional information to assist users in understanding the financial statements.

For example, although condensed interim financial reports are generally only required to describe changes in accounting policies since the annual financial statements, an entity's first interim report under IFRSs should generally include a full description of the accounting policies adopted under IFRSs unless these had already been published in another document to which reference could be made. It would also be appropriate to include expanded notes disclosures on individual areas when information was not provided in the previous GAAP financial statements.

IAS 34 applies if an entity is required, or elects, to prepare an interim financial report in accordance with IFRSs. Therefore neither IAS 34 nor IFRS 1 requires an entity to present interim financial reports that comply with IAS 34. Neither do they require an entity to prepare a new version of interim financial reports presented under previous GAAP. [IFRS 1:IG37]

However, if an interim financial report is prepared under IAS 34 for part of the period covered by an entity's first IFRS financial statements, the comparative information presented should be restated so that it complies with IFRSs. [IFRS 1:IG37]

IFRS 1 should be applied in each interim financial report that is presented under IAS 34 for part of the period covered by the first IFRS financial statements. In particular, the requirements for reconciliations described above apply. [IFRS 1:IG38]

9.2.9   Use of deemed cost for investments in subsidiaries, associates and joint ventures

For entities that do not adopt IFRS 11 *Joint Arrangements* in their first IFRS financial statements (required for annual periods beginning on or after 1 January 2013 with earlier adoption permitted), the reference to a 'joint venture' below should be taken as a reference to a 'jointly controlled entity'.

If an entity uses a deemed cost in its opening IFRS statement of financial position for an investment in a subsidiary, associate or joint venture in its separate financial statements (see **7.8** above), it is required to disclose: [IFRS 1:31]

- the aggregate deemed cost of those investments for which deemed cost is their previous GAAP carrying amount;

- the aggregate deemed cost of those investments for which deemed cost is fair value; and

- the aggregate adjustment to the carrying amounts reported under previous GAAP.

10   Future developments

As part of *Annual Improvements to IFRSs: 2011–2013 Cycle* (expected to be issued in the fourth quarter of 2013), the IFRS Interpretations Committee proposes to clarify the meaning of 'effective IFRSs' in the context of first-time adoption. Specifically, the Committee has proposed an amendment to IFRS 1 which would confirm that a first-time adopter generally has the choice between applying an old Standard that is still effective or applying a new one that is permitted to be applied in advance of its effective date, provided that the same version of the Standard is applied throughout the periods covered by the entity's first IFRS financial statements (see also **5.2** above).

There are no other ongoing projects dealing specifically with IFRS 1. However, the IASB is working on a number of other new Standards which, when finalised, are likely to make consequential amendments to IFRS 1 regarding the application of the requirements of those Standards for first-time adopters.

A4 Presentation of financial statements

Contents

1   Introduction

IAS 1 *Presentation of Financial Statements* sets out overall requirements for the presentation of financial statements, guidelines for their structure and minimum requirements for their content.

IAS 1 was most recently amended in May 2012.

The implementation guidance accompanying IAS 1 sets out an illustrative structure for financial statements.

2   General requirements

2.1   Objective

The objective of IAS 1 is to prescribe the basis for presentation of general purpose financial statements so as to ensure comparability both with an entity's financial statements of previous periods and with the financial statements of other entities. [IAS 1:1]

2.2   Scope

IAS 1 is required to be applied in preparing and presenting general purpose financial statements in accordance with IFRSs. [IAS 1:2] The impact of the Standard is, therefore, pervasive and it affects every set of financial statements prepared under IFRSs.

Other IFRSs set out the recognition, measurement and disclosure requirements for specific transactions and other events. [IAS 1:3]

General purpose financial statements are defined in IAS 1 as "those intended to meet the needs of users who are not in a position to require an entity to prepare reports tailored to their particular information needs". References to 'financial statements' in IAS 1 should be taken as references to general purpose financial statements. [IAS 1:7]

The Standard applies equally to all entities, including those that present consolidated financial statements in accordance with IFRS 10 *Consolidated Financial Statements* and those that present separate financial statements in accordance with IAS 27(2011) *Separate Financial Statements* (or, prior to the adoption of IFRS 10 and IAS 27(2011), those entities that present consolidated financial statements and those that present separate financial statements in accordance with IAS 27(2008) *Consolidated and Separate Financial Statements*). [IAS 1:4]

The requirements of IFRSs apply equally to the financial statements of an individual entity and to consolidated financial statements for a group of entities. IFRSs contemplate three types of financial statements:

- 'individual' financial statements prepared by an entity that has no subsidiaries (which may incorporate the results of the entity's associates or joint ventures using the equity method or, prior to the adoption of IAS 28(2011) *Investments in Associates and Joint Ventures*, using proportionate consolidation for the entity's interests in jointly controlled entities under IAS 31 *Interests in Joint Ventures*);

- 'consolidated' financial statements for a parent with subsidiaries, prepared in accordance with IFRS 10 (or, prior to the adoption of IFRS 10, in accordance with IAS 27(2008)); and

- 'separate' financial statements presented by a parent or an investor with joint control of, or significant influence over, an investee, in which the investments are accounted for at cost or in accordance with IFRS 9 *Financial Instruments* (or, prior to the adoption of IFRS 9, IAS 39 *Financial Instruments: Recognition and Measurement*) (see **chapter A29** or, for entities that have not yet adopted IAS 27(2011), **appendix A1**).

IAS 1 does not preclude the presentation of consolidated financial statements complying with IFRSs and financial statements of the parent under national GAAP within the same document. In such circumstances, the basis of preparation for each should be clearly disclosed. In practice, the two sets of financial statements should generally be presented as separate sections of the document so as to avoid mixing information prepared under different GAAPs on the same page (e.g. columnar layouts mixing parent-only and consolidated information prepared under different GAAPs should be avoided). This would not preclude cross-references between the two sections of the document to avoid repetition of information that is the same on both bases.

The Standard does not apply to the structure and content of condensed interim financial statements prepared in accordance with IAS 34 *Interim Financial Reporting*. But paragraphs 15 to 35 of IAS 1 apply to such interim reports. [IAS 1:4]

Paragraphs 15 to 35 of IAS 1 are those dealing with fair presentation and compliance with IFRSs (see **section 3**), going concern (see **2.5**), accruals accounting (see **2.6**), materiality and aggregation (see **2.7**) and offsetting (see **2.8**).

IAS 1 uses terminology that is suitable for profit-oriented entities, including public sector business entities. The Standard notes that entities with not-for-profit activities in the private sector or public sector seeking to apply it may need to amend the descriptions used for particular line items in the financial statements and for the financial statements themselves. [IAS 1:5]

Similarly, entities that do not have equity as defined in IAS 32 *Financial Instruments: Presentation* (e.g. some mutual funds) and entities whose share capital is not equity (e.g. some co-operatives) may need to adapt the presentation in the financial statements of members' or unit holders' interests (see **2.1.2** in **chapter B3** or, for entities that have not yet adopted IFRS 9, **2.1.2** in **chapter C3**). [IAS 1:6]

2.3   Purpose of financial statements

Financial statements are a structured representation of the financial position and financial performance of an entity. The objective of financial statements is to provide information about the financial position, financial performance and cash flows of an entity that is useful to a wide range of users in making economic decisions. Financial statements also show the results of management's stewardship of the resources entrusted to it. IAS 1 explains that to meet this objective, financial statements provide information about an entity's:
[IAS 1:9]

- assets;
- liabilities;
- equity;
- income and expenses, including gains and losses;
- contributions by and distributions to owners in their capacity as owners; and
- cash flows.

This information, together with other information in the notes, assists users of financial statements in predicting the entity's future cash flows, including their timing and certainty. [IAS 1:9]

2.4   Complete set of financial statements

Amendments to paragraph 10 of IAS 1 in June 2011, which are effective for annual periods beginning on after 1 July 2012, introduced new titles for some of the financial statements to be presented. The requirements pre- and post-June 2011 amendments are set out separately below.

The only real effect of this portion of the June 2011 amendments is to introduce new titles for the 'statement of profit or loss and other comprehensive income' (previously called the 'statement of comprehensive income') and for the 'statement of profit or loss' (previously called the 'income statement').

Note that entities are not required to use the titles for financial statements as listed in IAS 1. IAS 1:10 (both pre- and post-June 2011 amendments) specifically permits the use of other titles for the statements. Therefore, for example, it is acceptable to use the term 'balance sheet' to describe the statement of financial position. Equally, for entities that have adopted the June 2011 amendments, it is acceptable to continue to use the title 'statement of comprehensive income' instead of 'statement of profit or loss and other comprehensive income'.

In fact, when the June 2011 amendments were issued, the IASB decided generally not to amend the titles used for these statements in other Standards, except when an IFRS made reference to the two-statement option (see IAS 1:BC20B). Therefore, IASB literature generally retains the previous titles for these statements. This chapter, and the remainder of this manual, follows the IASB lead and the titles of and references to these statements have only been amended when the IASB has done so.

The illustrative financial statements accompanying IAS 1 have been amended to reflect the new titles for the statements.

2.4.1   *Entities that have adopted the June 2011 amendments to IAS 1*

Following the amendments in June 2011, IAS 1 specifies that a complete set of financial statements comprises:
[IAS 1:10]

- a statement of financial position as at the end of the period (see **section 4**);

- a statement of profit or loss and other comprehensive income for the period (see **section 5**);

- a statement of changes in equity for the period (see **section 6**);

- a statement of cash flows for the period (see **chapter A21**);

- notes, comprising a summary of significant accounting policies and other explanatory information (see **section 7**);

- comparative information in respect of the preceding period as specified in IAS 1:38 and IAS 1:38A; and

- a statement of financial position as at the beginning of the preceding period when an entity applies an accounting policy retrospectively or makes a retrospective restatement of items in its financial statements, or when it reclassifies items in its financial statements (see **2.10.4**).

The requirements listed above reflect amendments arising from the *Annual Improvements to IFRSs: 2009-2011 Cycle*, issued in May 2012. Those amendments added the specific requirement for comparative information in the penultimate bullet above (but this has not changed the underlying requirements – see **section 2.10**), and amended the final bullet to refer to the presentation of a statement of financial position as at the beginning of the 'preceding' period in specified circumstances, rather than as at the beginning of the 'earliest comparative' period (see **2.10.4**).

An entity may either:
[IAS 1:10A]

- present a single statement of profit or loss and other comprehensive income, with profit or loss and other comprehensive income presented in two sections; or

- present the profit or loss section in a separate statement of profit or loss.

The exposure draft that preceded the June 2011 amendments to IAS 1 proposed to require the presentation of all of the components of comprehensive income (i.e. both profit or loss and other comprehensive income (OCI)) in a single statement, which would have eliminated the option to present a separate statement of profit or loss. However, the IASB decided to retain this option following negative responses to the proposal.

When a single statement is presented, the 'profit or loss' and 'other comprehensive income' sections are required to be presented together, with the profit or loss section presented first followed directly by the other comprehensive income section. [IAS 1:10A]

When a separate statement of profit or loss is presented, the separate statement of profit or loss should immediately precede the statement presenting comprehensive income, which should begin with profit or loss. [IAS 1:10A]

This requirement would not prevent the statements being presented on separate pages, although the statement of comprehensive income should be on the page following the statement of profit or loss and given equal prominence.

2.4.2   Entities that have not yet adopted the June 2011 amendments to IAS 1

Prior to the amendments in June 2011, IAS 1 specifies that a complete set of financial statements comprises:
[IAS 1:10]

- a statement of financial position as at the end of the period (see **section 4**);

- a statement of comprehensive income for the period (see **section 5**);

- a statement of changes in equity for the period (see **section 6**);

- a statement of cash flows for the period (see **chapter A21**);

- notes, comprising a summary of significant accounting policies and other explanatory information (see **section 7**); and

- a statement of financial position as at the beginning of the earliest comparative period when an entity applies an accounting policy retrospectively or makes a retrospective restatement of items in its financial statements, or when it reclassifies items in its financial statements (see **2.10.4**).

The requirements listed above do not reflect the amendments arising from *Annual Improvements to IFRSs: 2009-2011 Cycle* (the 2009–2011 Improvements). See **2.4.1** above for a discussion of the changes made to IAS 1:10 as a result of the 2009–2011 Improvements.

The components of profit or loss may be presented either as part of a single statement of comprehensive income or in a separate income statement. When an income statement is presented, it should immediately precede the statement of comprehensive income. [IAS 1:12]

> This requirement would not prevent the statements being presented on separate pages, although the statement of comprehensive income should be on the page following the income statement and given equal prominence.

2.4.3   Requirement to present all of the financial statements with equal prominence

In a complete set of financial statements, all of the financial statements should be presented with equal prominence. [IAS 1:11]

> IAS 1:BC22 explains that the reason for the requirement is that "the financial performance of an entity can be assessed only after all aspects of the financial statements are taken into account and understood in their entirety". In practice, the most significant effects of this requirement are that:
>
> - when an entity elects to present the components of profit or loss in a separate statement (the 'two-statement' approach), that statement and the statement of comprehensive income should be presented with equal prominence; and
>
> - the statement of changes in equity, which presents contributions from and distributions to owners, must be presented with equal prominence to the other statements.

2.4.4   Management commentary presented outside of the financial statements

IAS 1 notes that many entities present, outside of the financial statements, a review by management that describes and explains the main features of the entity's financial performance and financial position together with the principal uncertainties that it faces (generally referred to in international accounting literature as Management Commentary (MC)). Many entities also present, outside the financial statements, other statements, such as environmental reports and corporate governance statements. Reports and statements presented outside the financial statements are outside the scope of IFRSs. [IAS 1:13 – 14]

> Information presented in the MC, or other supplementary statement, may repeat information in the financial statements. All information required under IFRSs should be presented in the notes or elsewhere in the financial statements. Omission of a disclosure in the financial statements because it is included in the MC, or a similar statement, is not permitted. However, this may be included by way of cross-reference if allowed by specific Standards (e.g. IFRS 7:B6 – see **section 5** of **chapter B12** or, for entities that have not yet adopted IFRS 9, **section 5** of **chapter C12**).
>
> The IASB has issued a non-mandatory Practice Statement titled *Management Commentary* (see **chapter A33**).

2.5   Going concern

2.5.1   General

IAS 1 requires management to make an assessment of the entity's ability to continue as a going concern when preparing financial statements. Financial statements should be prepared on a going concern basis unless management intends either to liquidate the entity or to cease trading, or has no realistic alternative but to do so. [IAS 1:25]

The assessment as to whether the going concern basis is appropriate takes into account events after the end of the reporting period. Financial statements are not prepared on a going concern basis if management determines after the end of the reporting period either that it intends to liquidate the entity or to cease trading, or that it has no realistic alternative but to do so (see **section 5** of **chapter A22**). [IAS 10:14]

In assessing whether the going concern assumption is appropriate, management takes into account all available information about the future. IAS 1 states that the information should cover at least twelve months from the end of the reporting period but not be limited to that period. The degree of consideration depends on the facts in each case. When an entity has a history of profitable operations and ready access to financial resources, a conclusion that the going concern basis of accounting is appropriate may be reached without detailed analysis. In other cases, management may need to consider a wide range of factors relating to current and expected profitability, debt repayment schedules and potential sources of replacement financing before it can satisfy itself that the going concern basis is appropriate. [IAS 1:26]

When management is aware, in making its assessment, of material uncertainties related to events or conditions that may cast significant doubt upon the entity's ability to continue as a going concern, those uncertainties should be disclosed. [IAS 1:25]

IAS 1 does not explain what it means for an entity to 'continue as a going concern', so it is appropriate to look to the IASB's *Conceptual Framework for Financial Reporting*. Paragraph 4.1 of the Conceptual Framework explains that financial statements "are normally prepared on the assumption that an entity is a going concern and will continue in operation for the foreseeable future. Hence, it is assumed that the entity has neither the intention nor the need to liquidate or curtail materially the scale of its operations; …".

It is important to note that when an entity prepares financial statements on a going concern basis, this does not imply an absolute level of confidence that the entity will be able to continue as a going concern. Even when an entity is in severe financial difficulties, IAS 1:25 *requires* the going concern basis to be used unless management either intends to liquidate the entity or to cease trading, or has no realistic alternative but to do so.

Accordingly, an entity will depart from the going concern basis only when it is, in effect, clear that it is *not* a going concern. When there is significant uncertainty over whether an entity can continue in operational existence, IAS 1 requires the going concern basis to be used and appropriate disclosures to be made.

When there are doubts about an entity's ability to continue trading, the fact that the going concern basis must be used does not eliminate the need to consider whether any assets should be written down to their recoverable amounts and whether provision is required for any unavoidable costs under onerous contracts.

2.5.2   Departure from the going concern basis

If financial statements are not prepared on a going concern basis, the financial statements should disclose that fact, together with the basis on which the financial statements are prepared and the reason why the entity is not regarded as a going concern. [IAS 1:25]

Before considering further the appropriate basis of preparation for the financial statements of an entity that will cease or that has ceased trading, it is worth considering whether statutory financial statements will be required at all. This will depend on the legal and regulatory requirements in the jurisdiction concerned.

2.5.2.1   Recognition of impairment

It is always appropriate to consider the need to recognise impairment losses when an entity is planning to cease or has already ceased trading. This assessment will require a comparison of the carrying amount of an asset (or, when appropriate, cash-generating unit) with the higher of its value in use and fair value less costs of disposal (referred to as 'costs to sell' prior to the adoption of IFRS 13 *Fair Value Measurement*). The question arises as to whether, in such circumstances, it is possible to assess impairment by reference to a value in use calculation.

In theory, it is possible to assess impairment of assets by reference to a value in use calculation even when the financial statements are prepared on a basis other than that of a going concern. However, in practice, often the cash flows forecast to arise from the continuing use of such assets are not significant because the expectation is that the assets will be sold or abandoned in the near future. In such circumstances, the amounts arrived at using a value in use calculation will not be materially different from the fair value less costs of disposal.

Example 2.5.2.1

Recognition of impairment when directors are considering ceasing to trade

The directors of an entity are considering whether to cease trading. At the date of preparation of the financial statements, the directors have not yet reached a decision. There is a reasonable possibility that the entity will continue to trade and, therefore, the financial statements are being prepared on a going concern basis.

> *Should the fact that the directors are considering ceasing to trade be regarded as an indicator of impairment?*
>
> It is usually appropriate to regard the fact that the directors are considering ceasing to trade as an indicator of impairment. The directors of an entity do not usually consider ceasing to trade if the entity is expected to be profitable. The fact that the directors are considering ceasing to trade may call into question the ability of the entity to continue to trade profitably and, therefore, whether the carrying amounts of assets are recoverable.

2.5.2.2   Using a basis other than that of a going concern for preparing financial statements

Even if an entity has ceased trading, if the entity wishes to state compliance with IFRSs then its financial statements should be prepared on a basis that is consistent with IFRSs but amended to reflect the fact that the 'going concern' assumption is not appropriate. Among other things, such a basis requires writing assets down to their recoverable amounts. It also requires recognising a liability for contractual commitments that may have become onerous as a consequence of the decision to cease trading.

Although it is neither defined nor mentioned within IFRSs, some jurisdictions have a concept of financial statements prepared on a 'break-up' basis. Under this basis it is argued that the objective of the financial statements changes from reporting financial performance to (1) considering whether the assets of the entity are sufficient to meet its liabilities, and (2) quantifying the amount of any surplus that may, in due course, be available for distribution to the shareholders. Using this 'break-up' basis, a liability would be recognised for losses subsequent to the end of the reporting period and for the costs of winding up the business, irrespective of whether an irrevocable decision to terminate the business had been made at the end of the reporting period. Assets would also be restated to their actual or estimated sale proceeds, even if this was different from their market value at the end of the reporting period. In effect, on a 'break-up' basis, the accruals concept ceases to be of importance and the financial statements become a forecast of future realisation rather than a reflection of transactions and other events that have occurred in the reporting period.

The preparation of financial statements on this basis does not properly reflect the principles of IFRSs and is not considered appropriate under IFRSs except perhaps in very rare circumstances. This is because, under IFRSs, the financial statements should reflect the transactions and other events that have occurred in the reporting period and the circumstances existing at the end of the reporting period. For example, if the assets include quoted securities, it is difficult to see why these should be measured at above or below their market value even if they are sold for a higher or lower amount after the end of the reporting period. The gain or loss on disposal in the subsequent period reflects the decision to hold the securities rather than to sell them at the end of the reporting period. For similar reasons, it would not be appropriate to recognise provisions for future losses or liabilities for which there was no present legal or constructive obligation at the end of the reporting period.

When financial statements are being prepared under IFRSs but on a basis other than that of a going concern, another issue to consider is whether non-current assets and long-term liabilities should be reclassified as current assets and current liabilities. As discussed at **3.1.1** in **chapter A20**, assets classified as non-current in accordance with IAS 1 should not be reclassified as current assets unless and until they meet the 'held for sale' criteria in IFRS 5 *Non-current Assets Held for Sale and Discontinued Operations*. It is possible that the 'held for sale' criteria may be met for some non-current assets but not others, e.g. if the entity is actively marketing some of the assets but not others.

Long-term liabilities should be reclassified as current liabilities if they meet the criteria in IAS 1 to be presented as current liabilities (see **4.3** below). Reclassification may be required, for example, because of breaches of borrowing covenants or similar factors in existence at the end of the reporting period that accelerate the repayment requirements, with the result that the entity no longer has an unconditional right to defer settlement of the liability for at least twelve months after the end of the reporting period.

2.5.2.3   *Entities becoming dormant*

As explained above, IAS 1 and IAS 10 *Events after the Reporting Period* require a departure from the going concern basis in certain circumstances. In particular, an entity should not prepare its financial statements on a going concern basis if:

- at the end of the reporting period, management intends to liquidate the entity or to cease trading (or has no realistic alternative but to do so); or

- management determines after the reporting period that it intends to liquidate the entity or to cease trading (or has no realistic alternative but to do so).

Accordingly, when an entity ceases to trade during the year, or management has determined, either at the reporting date or after the reporting period, that it intends to liquidate the entity, any subsequent financial statements should also be prepared on a basis other than that of a going concern. However, there is no guidance in either IAS 1 or IAS 10 regarding the appropriate basis of preparation for the financial statements of an entity that has ceased to trade during the year but which management intends to keep in existence (e.g. as a dormant company).

Financial statements prepared on a going concern basis would be extremely unlikely to give a true and fair view when the entity had already ceased trading before the end of the reporting period. In fact, when an entity has ceased trading during the year, use of the going concern basis is likely to be very misleading to users of the financial statements who might reasonably assume that this basis implies that trading will continue in future periods. In the financial reporting period in which an entity ceases to trade it is, therefore, appropriate to prepare the financial statements on a basis other than that of a going concern in order to give sufficient emphasis to the effects of cessation of trading.

The question also arises as to what is an appropriate basis of preparation for such entities to use in later reporting periods when the entity is no longer trading but continues to exist (e.g. as a dormant company). Neither IAS 1 nor IAS 10 provides guidance for such circumstances. To provide clarity to users of the financial statements, and to avoid the risk of giving a misleading impression regarding the trading status of the entity, one possible approach would be for the financial statements to be prepared on a basis other than that of a going concern until such time as the only amounts reported in the current and prior year statements of comprehensive income and financial position relate to the entity's ongoing existence (i.e. any effects of ceasing to trade have been 'washed through'). Thereafter, the financial statements will no longer include any items relating to the trade that has ceased and, therefore, references to such cessation may be confusing. Instead, the financial statements should be prepared on a going concern basis, in accordance with IAS 1:25. This approach is illustrated in **example 2.5.2.3**.

Example 2.5.2.3

Departure from going concern basis

Company X has a December year end. It ceases trading during 20X1, and finishes disposing of its assets during 20X2. By the 20X2 year end, the only items in the statement of financial position are intragroup receivables and payables, which are not expected to be settled in the foreseeable future. The directors intend to keep Company X in existence for the foreseeable future.

If the directors choose to apply the possible approach suggested above, the financial statements for each of the 20X1, 20X2, 20X3 and 20X4 reporting periods would be prepared on the following bases.

20X1   A basis other than that of a going concern

20X2   A basis other than that of a going concern (because both the 20X2 and 20X1 statements of comprehensive income include effects of ceasing to trade, i.e. the disposal of the assets of Company X)

20X3   A basis other than that of a going concern (because the 20X2 statement of comprehensive income includes effects of ceasing to trade)

20X4   Going concern basis as explained above (all effects of ceasing to trade have been 'washed through' and there is no impact on either the 20X4 or 20X3 statements of comprehensive income)

Other approaches may also be acceptable.

2.5.2.4   Entities established as dormant

Example 2.5.2.4

Entity established as dormant

Company X is set up as a dormant company. It has never traded and the directors do not intend that it will trade in the future. The directors intend to keep Company X in existence as a dormant company for the foreseeable future.

On what basis should the financial statements of Company X be prepared?

The financial statements should be prepared on a going concern basis. The criteria to depart from the going concern basis in accordance with IAS 1:25 have not been met because the directors do not intend either to liquidate the entity or to cease trading.

2.6   Accruals basis of accounting

IAS 1 requires financial statements, except for cash flow information, to be prepared using the accruals basis of accounting. Under this basis, items are recognised as assets, liabilities, equity, income and expenses when they satisfy the definitions and recognition criteria for those elements in the IASB's *Conceptual Framework for Financial Reporting*. [IAS 1:27 – 28]

2.7   Materiality and aggregation

Each material class of similar items is presented separately in the financial statements. Items of a dissimilar nature or function are presented separately unless they are immaterial. [IAS 1:29]

Financial statements result from processing large numbers of transactions or other events that are aggregated into classes according to their nature or function. The final stage in this process is the presentation of condensed and classified data which form line items in the financial statements. If a line item is not individually material, it is aggregated with other items either in those statements or in the notes. An item that is not sufficiently material to warrant separate presentation in those statements may warrant separate presentation in the notes. [IAS 1:30]

IAS 1 confirms that a specific disclosure requirement in an IFRS need not be satisfied if the information is not material. [IAS 1:31]

IAS 1 defines 'material' as follows.
[IAS 1:7]

> "Omissions or misstatements of items are material if they could, individually or collectively, influence the economic decisions that users make on the basis of the financial statements. Materiality depends on the size and nature of the omission or misstatement judged in the surrounding circumstances. The size or nature of the item, or a combination of both, could be the determining factor."

Assessing whether an omission or misstatement could influence the economic decisions of users, and so be material, requires consideration of the characteristics of those users. The IASB's *Conceptual Framework for Financial Reporting* states that financial reports are prepared for "users who have a reasonable knowledge of business and economic activities and who review and analyse the information diligently". The assessment, therefore, needs to take into account how users with such attributes could reasonably be expected to be influenced in making economic decisions. [IAS 1:7]

2.8   Offsetting

Assets and liabilities, and income and expenses, are not offset unless required or permitted by an IFRS. [IAS 1:32] This basic principle is supplemented by some further guidance in IAS 1, as described below. IAS 32 *Financial Instruments: Presentation* sets out more detailed requirements regarding the offset of financial assets and financial liabilities (see **section 6** of **chapter B12** or, for entities that have not yet adopted IFRS 9, **section 6** of **chapter C12**).

It is important that assets and liabilities, and income and expenses, are reported separately. Offsetting in the statements of comprehensive income or financial position, except when this reflects the substance of the transactions or other events, detracts from the ability of users both to understand the transactions (or other events or conditions) that have occurred and to assess the entity's future cash flows. Measuring assets net of valuation allowances (e.g. inventories or receivables) is not regarded as offsetting for the purposes of applying IAS 1. [IAS 1:33]

Example 2.8A

Offsetting revenue and expenses when goods and services are sold at cost

An entity that sells goods and/or provides services as a principal to third parties at an amount equal to the cost of the goods or services is not permitted to present its revenues and expenses on a net basis. When an entity acts as a principal, the practice of selling goods or providing services at an amount equal to cost does not represent a contractual arrangement for reimbursement of the cost of goods and services. Revenues and expenses should, therefore, be presented gross.

Example 2.8B

Offsetting revenues and expenses for shared commissions

Company A has signed a contract with an insurance company whereby it receives a commission for every policy it sells on behalf of the insurance company. Company A contracts with individual agents to sell these insurance policies and agrees to split the commission evenly with the agents. Company A provides administrative facilities and office space to the agents. The insurance company is aware of the arrangements between Company A and the agents but pays the full commission to Company A which then pays half the commission to the agent who sold the policy.

Company A is not permitted to offset the amount it pays to the agents against the commission revenue it receives from the insurance company.. Company A is acting as a principal in its dealings with the individual agents, not as an agent for the insurer. Accordingly, a net presentation would not reflect the substance of the transactions and would detract from the ability of users to understand the transactions (see also **3.1** in **chapter A14**).

Example 2.8C

Presentation of withholding tax on revenue from investments

Company A pays dividends to Company B. Company B receives a net amount because Company A is required to deduct withholding tax on dividends and to pay the amount deducted to the tax authorities on Company B's behalf.

It is not acceptable for Company B to present its dividend revenue net of the tax withheld. Withholding tax is generally taken to mean tax on dividends (or other income) that has been deducted by the payer of the income (Company A) and is paid over to the tax authorities on behalf of the recipient of the dividends (Company B), so that the recipient receives the net amount. In accordance with paragraph 7 of IAS 18 *Revenue*, "[r]evenue is the gross inflow of economic benefits ...". When the withholding tax is tax actually suffered by Company B, it is appropriate to recognise the incoming dividends at an amount that is gross of the withholding tax and to present the tax withheld as part of the tax expense. Therefore, dividends from investments should be presented on a gross basis.

IAS 1:82(d) requires a specific line item for tax expense to be presented in the statement of comprehensive income (see **5.1** below). It follows that this line item should include all tax expenses, including withholding taxes suffered.

Example 2.8D

Presentation of shipping and handling costs billed to customers

Company S sells goods to a customer and bills the customer amounts for shipping and handling costs. The appropriate presentation of amounts billed to a customer for shipping and handling will depend on the circumstances and, in particular, whether the amounts billed represent a direct recharge of costs incurred on behalf of the customer by the seller (i.e. the seller is acting as the customer's agent).

When, in its capacity as principal, Company S bills the customer for shipping and handling costs arising on the transaction, and the goods are not derecognised by Company S until they are received by the customer, these amounts represent revenues earned for the goods provided and should be presented as revenue in the statement of comprehensive income.

Alternatively, when Company S has shipped the goods on behalf of the customer (e.g. when Company S is acting as an agent in relation to shipping the goods and the goods are derecognised by Company S at the point of despatch), and Company S has incurred shipping and handling charges that are to be recharged to the customer, then netting the amounts recharged

> against Company S's shipping and handling expense may be a more faithful representation.

IAS 18 (see **chapter A14**) defines revenue and requires it to be measured at the fair value of the consideration received or receivable, taking into account any trade discounts and volume rebates allowed to the customer. Other transactions may be undertaken that do not generate revenue but are incidental to the main revenue-generating activities. The results of such transactions are presented by netting any income and related expenses arising from the same transaction when this reflects the substance of the transactions or other events. For example:
[IAS 1:34]

- gains and losses on disposal of non-current assets, including investments and operating assets, are reported by deducting from the proceeds of disposal the carrying amount and related selling expenses; and

- expenditure related to a provision that is recognised in accordance with IAS 37 *Provisions, Contingent Liabilities and Contingent Assets* and reimbursed under a contractual arrangement with a third party (e.g. a supplier's warranty agreement) may be netted against the related reimbursement.

Also, gains and losses arising from a group of similar transactions are reported on a net basis. For example, foreign exchange gains and losses, and gains and losses arising on financial instruments held for trading, are presented net although they should be reported separately if material.
[IAS 1:35]

2.9   Frequency of reporting

IAS 1:36 states that a complete set of financial statements, including comparative information, should be presented at least 'annually'. However, as evidenced by the disclosure requirements of IAS 1:36 (see below), the Standard clearly envisages that the financial statements may cover a period longer or shorter than twelve months.

> IFRSs do not provide a definition for an 'annual' reporting period. However, they do provide a definition for an interim period – it is a "financial reporting period shorter than a full financial year" (see IAS 34:4). Therefore, the key feature that distinguishes 'annual' financial statements from interim financial statements is that the former cover a full *financial* year.

The circumstances in which a financial year can be longer or shorter than 12 months will generally be specified by local laws or regulations. Most commonly, a longer or shorter period will be permitted when there is a formal change in reporting date, or when an entity is presenting first-year or cessation financial statements.

Frequently, the transition provisions of new Standards and amendments to Standards refer to application for 'annual periods beginning on or after' a specified date. The reference to 'annual' periods in this context (which is intended to create a distinction from interim periods) is consistent with the reference to reporting 'annually' in IAS 1:36; an annual period for this purpose might therefore be a period of more or less than 12 months.

When the end of the reporting period is changed and the financial statements are presented for a period that is longer or shorter than one year, IAS 1 requires the following to be disclosed:
[IAS 1:36]

- the period covered by the financial statements;

- the reason for using a longer or shorter period; and

- the fact that the amounts presented in the financial statements are not entirely comparable.

For practical reasons, some entities prefer to report on a 52/53 week basis (e.g. always to the last Saturday in the month). IAS 1 does not preclude this practice. [IAS 1:37]

2.10   Comparative information

The section of IAS 1 dealing with comparative information has been rewritten as part of *Annual Improvements to IFRSs: 2009-2011 Cycle* (the 2009–2011 Improvements), issued in May 2012. The Standard has been substantively amended in three respects, each of which is discussed in more detail later in this section:

- clarification of the requirements when an entity provides comparative information beyond the minimum specified;

- clarification of the circumstances in which an entity is required to present a third statement of financial position; and

203

- amendment of the requirements regarding supporting notes for a third statement of financial position.

The May 2012 amendments are effective for annual periods beginning on or after 1 January 2013, with earlier application permitted. Note, however, that the first two items listed above are described in the Basis for Conclusions on IAS 1 as clarifications of existing requirements and, consequently, entities seeking guidance on these topics should refer to the more detailed requirements introduced as part of the 2009–2011 Improvements with immediate effect. If an entity previously followed a practice that is explicitly prohibited by the 2009–2011 Improvements (e.g. if it previously presented additional comparative information that was not prepared in accordance with IFRSs – see **2.10.3**), the entity is not required to change that presentation in annual financial statements beginning before 1 January 2013, although it is permitted to do so.

The third item listed represents an amendment to previous requirements such that, when an entity presents a third statement of financial position in its financial statements in one of the circumstances specified in IAS 1:40A (see **2.10.4**), the entity is not required to present supporting notes for that third statement of financial position. For many entities, this will result in a reduction in the amount of information disclosed. If an entity wishes to take advantage of this relief in annual financial statements beginning before 1 January 2013, it is permitted to do so (provided that the fact that the amendments have been adopted in advance of their effective date is disclosed).

Whenever the 2009–2011 Improvements are adopted, comparative information should be restated to achieve a consistent presentation.

Throughout this section, the descriptions of the requirements of IAS 1 reflect the May 2012 amendments. Significant amendments to previous wordings are explained.

2.10.1   *General requirements*

Except when IFRSs permit or require otherwise, comparative information in respect of the preceding period should be presented for all amounts reported in the financial statements. [IAS 1:38]

The 2009–2011 Improvements have made minor textual amendments to IAS 1:38 to clarify that the comparative information required is in respect of the immediately preceding period.

An entity is required to present the following statements, as a minimum, together with related notes:
[IAS 1:38A]

- two statements of financial position;

- two statements of profit or loss and other comprehensive income;

- two separate statements of profit or loss (if presented);

- two statements of cash flows; and

- two statements of changes in equity.

Paragraph 38A was added to IAS 1 as part of the 2009–2011 Improvements. It sets out the general requirements regarding the minimum statements to be presented on an ongoing basis (previously addressed in IAS 1:39, which has now been deleted). There has been no substantive change in this regard – the effect of the amendments is to state the requirements more clearly and to separate these general requirements from the more specific requirements in circumstances when a third statement of financial position is presented (see **2.10.4**).

2.10.2   Comparative information for narrative and descriptive information

Comparative information is included for narrative and descriptive information if it is relevant to understanding the current period's financial statements. [IAS 1:38]

Narrative information provided in the financial statements for the preceding period(s) may continue, in some cases, to be relevant in the current period. IAS 1 gives the example of a legal dispute, the outcome of which was uncertain at the end of the preceding period and is yet to be resolved. Users of the financial statements may benefit from the disclosure of information that the uncertainty existed at the end of the preceding period and from the disclosure of information about the steps that have been taken during the current period to resolve the uncertainty. [IAS 1:38B]

Note that paragraph 38B has been renumbered as part of the 2009–2011 Improvements (it was previously IAS 1:40). Although some minor wording amendments have been made, they have had no substantive effect.

The example given in IAS 1:38B is not particularly helpful because it suggests that the uncertainty has yet to be resolved and, therefore, it is clear that some disclosure would be required in the current year. A better example might be when the legal claim had been settled in the current year. In this case, it is likely that some disclosure would be judged relevant to an understanding of the current period's financial statements but the level of detail provided might be less than in the previous year given that the uncertainties have been resolved.

2.10.3   Additional comparative information

An entity may present comparative information in addition to the minimum required under IAS 1:38A (see **2.10.1**). [IAS 1:38C]

Such additional information might include, for example: [IAS 1:BC32E]

- additional information that is presented voluntarily; and

- additional comparative information that is required by law or other regulations.

If additional comparative information is presented: [IAS 1:38C]

- the information must be prepared in accordance with IFRSs;

- the information may consist of one or more statements referred to in IAS 1:10 (see **2.4.1** and **2.4.2**), but need not comprise a complete set of financial statements; and

- related note information should be presented for the additional statements.

The Standard cites as an example an entity that presents a third statement of profit of loss and other comprehensive income (i.e. it presents the statement for the current period, the preceding period and one additional comparative period). In such circumstances, the entity is not required to present a third statement of financial position, a third statement of cash flows or a third statement of changes in equity. However, the entity is required to present supporting notes for the additional statement of profit or loss and other comprehensive income. [IAS 1:38D]

2.10.4   Third statement of financial position required in the event of a change in accounting policy, retrospective restatement or reclassification

In specified circumstances, an entity is required to present a third statement of financial position as at the beginning of the preceding period in addition to the minimum comparative financial statements listed in IAS 1:38A (see **2.10.1**). This requirement applies when:
[IAS 1:40A]

- an entity applies an accounting policy retrospectively, makes a retrospective restatement of items in its financial statements or reclassifies items in its financial statements; and

- the retrospective application, retrospective restatement or the reclassification has a material effect on the information in the statement of financial position at the beginning of the preceding period.

Paragraph IAS 1:40A was added as part of the 2009–2011 Improvements in May 2012. The requirement to present a third statement of financial position in the event of a change in accounting policy, retrospective restatement or reclassification was first introduced in 2007. However, until the 2009–2011 Improvements, the Standard provided no further clarification as to when this requirement is triggered. Some observers considered that the third statement of financial position is always required when there has been a change in accounting policy, retrospective restatement or reclassification, even when there is no effect on the amounts in that third statement of financial position. The key clarification now added in IAS 1:40A (in the second bullet above) is that the third statement of financial position is only required when the change in accounting policy, retrospective restatement or reclassification has a material effect on the information reported in that statement of financial position.

Regardless of whether a third statement of financial position is required, an entity should provide the disclosures required under IAS 8 *Accounting Policies, Changes in Accounting Estimates and Errors* regarding the impact of changes in accounting policies and other restatements. IAS 1:41 sets out specific requirements when an entity has reclassified comparative amounts (see **2.10.5** below).

In the circumstances described in IAS 1:40A, an entity is therefore required to present statements of financial position as at:
[IAS 1:40B]

- the end of the current period;

- the end of the preceding period; and

- the beginning of the preceding period.

When presented, the date of the third statement of financial position is always at the beginning of the preceding period, regardless of whether the financial statements present comparative information for earlier periods. [IAS 1:40D]

Prior to the 2009–2011 Improvements, it was not clear whether the third statement of financial position should always be presented at the beginning of the preceding period (i.e. at the beginning of the period for which a statement of comprehensive income is required under IFRSs) or whether it should be at the beginning of the first period presented in the financial statements (which would be a different date if, for example, an entity presented a third statement of comprehensive income in accordance with the requirements of a regulator). Paragraph 40D provides clarification in this respect.

2.10.4.1   What is meant by a 'reclassification' in the context of the requirement for a third statement of financial position?

It appears that the phrase 'reclassifies items in its financial statements' in IAS 1:40A (or, prior to the 2009–2011 Improvements, in IAS 1:39) is intended to capture the types of 'reclassification' described in IAS 1:41 (see **2.10.5** below). In stating that the third statement of financial position is only required if it is materially affected by the reclassification, IAS 1:40A is clear that the following prospective event-driven reclassifications, for example, are not captured, because they do not affect the third statement of financial position:

- reclassification of an asset or liability from non-current to current under IAS 1 because of the passage of time;

- for entities applying IAS 39 *Financial Instruments: Recognition and Measurement*, reclassification of a financial asset from the held-to-maturity to the available-for-sale category and vice versa;

- for entities applying IAS 39, reclassification of cumulative gains or losses on an available-for-sale financial asset from equity to profit or loss as a reclassification adjustment on impairment or disposal of the asset;

- classification of an operation as discontinued with reclassification of the comparative period statement of comprehensive income; and

- reclassification of a property from inventories to investment property on commencement of an operating lease to another party.

2.10.4.2 Application of the requirement for a third statement of financial position to regulatory filings

Example 2.10.4.2

Application of the requirement for a third statement of financial position to regulatory filings

Entity A with a calendar year end prepares its financial statements in accordance with IFRSs. Entity A's securities are listed on a regulated exchange which requires two statements of financial position and three statements of comprehensive income and cash flows to be presented in the financial statements.

Scenario 1

In its 20X8 financial statements, Entity A has not applied an accounting policy retrospectively or made a retrospective restatement or reclassification requiring the presentation of a third statement of financial position at the beginning of the preceding period (i.e. as at 1 January 20X7) under IAS 1:40A.

As required by its regulator, Entity A presents statements of comprehensive income and cash flows for each of the years ending 31 December 20X8, 20X7 and 20X6.

Entity A is not required to present three statements of financial position. The third statements of comprehensive income and cash flows presented in respect of the earliest comparative period are supplementary information for regulatory purposes only. As clarified in IAS 1:38C (see **2.10.3** above), Entity A is only required under IAS 1:38 and 38A to present one year of comparative information for its 20X8 statement of financial position.

> *Scenario 2*
>
> In its 20X9 financial statements, Entity A makes a retrospective restatement that materially affects the statement of financial position at 1 January 20X8. As a result, IAS 1:40A requires the presentation of an additional statement of financial position at the beginning of the preceding period (i.e. at 1 January 20X8). For regulatory purposes, Entity A also presents the third statements of comprehensive income and cash flows for the year ending 31 December 20X7.
>
> Entity A is not required to present a fourth statement of financial position at 1 January 20X7. As clarified by IAS 1:40D (see **2.10.4** above), the additional statement of financial position is only required at the beginning of the preceding period (in this example, 20X8), not at the beginning of the earliest period presented (in this example, 20X7). It is acceptable for Entity A to present four statements of financial position if it chooses to do so, but this is not required.

2.10.4.3   Note disclosures required to support an additional statement of financial position

When an entity is required to present an additional statement of financial position as at the beginning of the preceding period in accordance with IAS 1:40A, it need not present notes supporting that opening statement of financial position. [IAS 1:40C]

However, in the circumstances when an additional statement of position is required to be presented, the entity is required to disclose the information required by IAS 1:41 to 44 (see **2.10.5** below) and also to comply with the relevant disclosure requirements of IAS 8 *Accounting Policies, Changes in Accounting Estimates and Errors* (see **chapter A5**). [IAS 1:40C]

Paragraph IAS 1:40C was added as part of the 2009–2011 Improvements in May 2012. The effect of IAS 1:40C is that, following the adoption of the 2009–2011 Improvements, an entity is no longer required to present notes supporting the additional statement of financial position. The revised requirements are effective for annual periods beginning on or after 1 January 2013, with earlier application permitted. If an entity adopts the 2009–2011 Improvements in an annual period beginning before 1 January 2013, that fact is required to be disclosed.

For entities that have not adopted the 2009–2011 Improvements, IAS 1:39 states that, when the requirements of IAS 1:10(f) are triggered, the entity should present "as a minimum, three statements of financial position, two of each of the other statements, *and related notes*" (emphasis added). Therefore, supporting notes are required. Although the Standard is not explicit, it appears that only those notes that may be described as supporting the statement of financial position are required to be presented, i.e. those disclosures required by IAS 1:77 to 80A.

2.10.5 *Reclassification of comparative amounts*

If the presentation or classification of items in the financial statements is amended, comparative amounts are reclassified unless this is impracticable. When comparative amounts are reclassified, the following information is required to be disclosed (including as at the beginning of the preceding period):
[IAS 1:41]

- the nature of the reclassification;

- the amount of each item or class of items that is reclassified; and

- the reason for the reclassification.

The phrase 'including as at the beginning of the preceding period' was added to IAS 1:41 as part of the 2009–2011 Improvements. The intention is to clarify that an entity is required to explain the effect (if any) of the reclassification on the third statement of financial position presented under IAS 1:40A (see **2.10.4**).

Applying a requirement is impracticable for this purpose "when the entity cannot apply it after making every reasonable effort to do so". [IAS 1:7]

Enhancing the inter-period comparability of information assists users in making economic decisions, especially by allowing the assessment of trends in financial information for predictive purposes. But in some circumstances it is impracticable to reclassify comparative information to achieve comparability. For example, data may not have been collected in the prior period in a way that allows reclassification and it may be impracticable to recreate the information. [IAS 1:43]

It is not appropriate to conclude that restatement is impracticable merely because of the cost or effort involved. When revising IAS 1 in

2003, the IASB considered replacing the exemption from restating comparative amounts on the basis of 'impracticability' with one based on 'undue cost or effort'. However, based on comments received on the exposure draft, the IASB decided that an exemption based on management's assessment of undue cost or effort was too subjective to be applied consistently by different entities. The IASB decided that balancing costs and benefits was a task for the Board when it sets accounting requirements rather than for entities when they apply those requirements. Therefore, although the Standard does not explicitly say that undue cost or effort does not alone make restatement impracticable, this is the clear intention of the Board and is consistent with the definition of 'impracticable' in IAS 1:7. [IAS 1:BC34 – BC36]

When comparative amounts have been restated in accordance with IAS 1:41, there is no explicit requirement for columns of comparative information to be headed up (e.g. as 'represented', 'restated' or 'adjusted'), although the inclusion of such headings is common practice. Whether the comparative information should be headed up in this way depends on the significance of the change (e.g. its impact on either the entity's results or equity). In each case, it is a matter of judgement and consideration of any local regulatory requirements.

Irrespective of whether comparative information is headed up as discussed above, entities are required to provide the disclosures regarding reclassified comparative amounts set out in IAS 1:41 (see above).

When it is impracticable to reclassify comparative amounts, disclosure is required of:
[IAS 1:42]

• the reason for not reclassifying the amounts; and

• the nature of the adjustments that would have been made if the amounts had been reclassified.

IAS 8 sets out adjustments to comparative information required when an entity changes an accounting policy or corrects an error (see **chapter A5**). [IAS 1:44]

The reference to the more specific requirements of IAS 8 within IAS 1 appears to envisage that it is possible to have a 'reclassification' that is not a change in accounting policy. No examples are given in IAS 1.

2.11   Consistency of presentation

The presentation and classification of items in the financial statements should be retained from one period to the next unless:
[IAS 1:45]

- it is apparent, following a significant change in the nature of the entity's operations (e.g. a major acquisition or disposal) or a review of its financial statements, that another presentation or classification would be more appropriate having regard to the criteria for selection and application of accounting policies in IAS 8 *Accounting Policies, Changes in Accounting Estimates and Errors* (see **section 3** of **chapter A5**); or

- an IFRS requires a change in presentation.

The presentation of the financial statements is changed only if the changed presentation provides information that is reliable and is more relevant to users of the financial statements and the revised structure is likely to continue, so that comparability is not impaired. When making such a change of presentation, the comparative information is reclassified in accordance with IAS 1:41 and 42 (see **2.10.5**). [IAS 1:46]

2.12   General requirements regarding disclosure and presentation

IAS 1 requires particular disclosures in the statement of financial position, the statement(s) presenting profit or loss and other comprehensive income, and the statement of changes in equity. It also requires disclosure of other line items either in those statements or in the notes. Presentation and disclosure requirements for the statement of cash flows are contained in IAS 7 (see **chapter A21**). [IAS 1:47]

IAS 1 sometimes uses the term 'disclosure' in a broad sense, encompassing items presented in the financial statements. Disclosures are also required by other IFRSs. Unless specified to the contrary in IAS 1 or another IFRS, such disclosures may be made in the financial statements. [IAS 1:48]

> The intention of this paragraph in IAS 1 (as revised in 2007) is not very clear from its wording. However, the equivalent paragraph in the previous version of the Standard made the point much more clearly that, unless specified otherwise, disclosures may be made either on the face of statements such as the statement of profit or loss and the statement of financial position, or in the notes.

IAS 1 does not prescribe a fixed format for the presentation of the statement of comprehensive income, the statement of financial position and the statement of changes in equity. It does, however, set out minimum disclosures in those statements (see **5.2**, **4.4** and **section 6** below). In addition, it establishes further items that may be presented either in those financial statements or in the notes (see **5.4** and **4.5**).

The illustrative financial statements accompanying IAS 1 include examples of ways in which the requirements for the statement of profit or loss and other comprehensive income, the statement of financial position and the statement of changes in equity might be presented in the primary financial statements. These are illustrative only and the order of presentation and the descriptions used for line items should be changed when necessary to achieve a fair presentation in an entity's particular circumstances.

2.13   Identification of the financial statements

The financial statements should be identified clearly and distinguished from other information in the same published document. [IAS 1:49] IFRSs apply only to financial statements. They do not necessarily apply to other information provided in an annual report, a regulatory filing or other document. Therefore, it is important that users can distinguish information that is prepared using IFRSs from other information that may be useful to users but is not subject to those requirements. [IAS 1:50]

Information given outside of the financial statements may be subject to separate regulatory requirements. For example, there may be a requirement for such information to be consistent with the financial statements.

IAS 1 requires that each financial statement and the notes should be identified clearly. In addition, the following information is required to be 'displayed prominently' and repeated when it is necessary for the information presented to be understandable:
[IAS 1:51]

- the name of the reporting entity or other means of identification;

- any change in that information from the end of the preceding reporting period;

- whether the financial statements are of an individual entity or a group of entities;

- the date of the end of the reporting period or the period covered by the set of financial statements or notes;

- the presentation currency, as defined in IAS 21; and

- the level of rounding used in presenting amounts in the financial statements.

IAS 1 explains that these requirements are normally met by presenting appropriate headings for pages, statements, notes, columns and the like. Judgement is required in determining the best way of presenting such information. For example, when the financial statements are presented electronically, separate pages are not always used. The items listed above are then presented to ensure a proper understanding of the information. [IAS 1:52]

Financial statements may be made more understandable by presenting information in thousands or millions of units of the presentation currency. This is acceptable as long as the level of rounding is disclosed and material information is not omitted. [IAS 1:53]

Different levels of rounding may be appropriate for different disclosures. For example, while it may be appropriate to disclose line items in the statements of financial position and comprehensive income in millions of units of the presentation currency for a very large group, a greater level of detail is likely to be necessary for disclosure of management remuneration and some other related party transactions. In all cases, the level of rounding should be disclosed and care should be exercised to ensure that no material disclosures are omitted.

3 Fair presentation and compliance with IFRSs

Financial statements should not be described as complying with IFRSs unless they comply with all of the requirements of IFRSs. IAS 1 requires an entity whose financial statements comply with IFRSs to make an explicit and unreserved statement of such compliance in the notes. [IAS 1:16]

An entity cannot claim compliance with IFRSs if it states that it complies with IFRSs 'except for' one or more Standards. Compliance with IFRSs is clearly defined in IAS 1:16 which, taken together with the requirements of paragraphs 11 and 12 of IAS 8 *Accounting Policies, Changes in Accounting Estimates and Errors*, means that financial statements must:

- comply with relevant IASs and IFRSs;

- comply with all relevant IFRICs and SICs; and

- in the absence of specific guidance in IFRSs:

  - apply by analogy other IFRSs;

  - apply the IASB's *Conceptual Framework for Financial Reporting*; or

  - apply pronouncements of national standard-setters to the extent that these are consistent with other IFRSs, other SICs, other IFRICs and the IASB's *Conceptual Framework for Financial Reporting*.

Financial statements should not be described as complying with IFRSs unless they comply with all the applicable requirements.

This principle applies equally to departures from IFRSs that are necessary to comply with national law. For example, consider an entity that is incorporated in a country where legislation does not permit unrealised gains to be reported in profit or loss. The entity prepares its financial statements in compliance with IFRSs including measuring derivatives at fair value; however, to comply with the national laws, fair value gains on those derivatives are taken directly to equity and are not recognised in profit or loss until the derivatives are derecognised. The entity cannot claim compliance with IFRSs. The fact that an entity is prevented by legislation from complying with IFRSs does not change the requirement in IFRSs.

Financial statements should present fairly the financial position, financial performance and cash flows of an entity. Fair presentation requires the faithful representation of the effects of transactions, other events and conditions in accordance with the definitions and recognition criteria set out in the Conceptual Framework. The application of IFRSs, with additional disclosure when necessary, is presumed to result in financial statements that achieve a fair presentation. [IAS 1:15]

3.1   Substance over form

Prior to the September 2010 release of sections of the IASB's *Conceptual Framework for Financial Reporting* (see **chapter A2**), the Board's predecessor framework (the *Framework for the Preparation and Presentation of Financial Statements*) stated that "[i]n order to ensure a faithful representation, transactions and other events should be accounted for and presented in accordance with their substance and economic reality, and not merely their legal form". This reference to 'substance over form' has been omitted from the *Conceptual Framework for Financial Reporting* because the Board determined that 'substance over form' should not be presented as a separate component of faithful representation because it would be redundant (see **section 5** of **chapter A2**).

However, it is still a very useful concept to consider in the context of the faithful representation of information, and the following paragraphs provide some guidance in this regard.

For the vast majority of routine transactions, substance and form will be the same, and the application of the principle of substance over form will not alter the established method of accounting. However, there will be transactions for which the substance and the legal form differ, or for which the substance is not readily apparent. In practice, common features of such transactions often include:

- the deliberate separation of legal title and the underlying benefits (e.g. leases, consignment inventories, factored debts and the use of structured or special purpose entities);

- options granted for which the exercise of the option can be considered a virtual certainty (e.g. sale with put and call options to repurchase); and

- a series of transactions designed so that the commercial effect can only be appreciated when the series is taken as a whole (e.g. securitisations, project financing and circular finance structures).

The key to accounting in accordance with the principle of substance over form is to obtain a full understanding of the rationale behind the transaction as a whole, including the role of each of the parties, and the commercial logic for their involvement. This requires:

- a realistic appreciation of why the transaction exists and why each party is involved. In determining the substance of a transaction, all of its aspects and implications should be identified and greater weight given to those more likely to have a commercial effect in practice;

- placing the transaction in context. A group or series of transactions that achieves or is designed to achieve an overall commercial effect should be viewed as a whole;

- an assessment of what has been achieved by the transaction. To determine the substance of a transaction, it is necessary to establish whether it has given rise to new assets or liabilities for the reporting entity or whether it has changed the entity's existing assets or liabilities;

- identification of the risk-takers. Evidence that an entity has rights or other access to benefits (and hence has an asset) is provided if the entity is exposed to the risks inherent in the benefits, taking into account the likelihood of those risks having a commercial effect in practice. Similarly, evidence that an entity has an obligation to transfer benefits (and hence has a liability) is given if there is some circumstance in which the entity is unable to avoid, legally or commercially, an outflow of benefits; and

- a realistic appraisal of conditional events. When a transaction incorporates one or more options, guarantees or conditional provisions, their commercial effect should be assessed in the context of all of the aspects and implications of the transaction, in order to determine what assets and liabilities exist.

In practice, the following analysis will assist in understanding the commercial effects of the transaction:

- obtain all relevant documentation and agreements, including side letters, which affect the likely course of events. Documents should always be in final form and include monetary details when relevant;

- identify the role played by each party to the transaction (in particular, the equity participants to a transaction) and the reason for their involvement. It is reasonable to suppose that a financial institution will limit its interest to that of financier – any assertion to the contrary should be supported by clear evidence. If a transaction appears to lack logic from the point of view of one or more participants, then it is likely that either all of the relevant parts of the transaction have not been identified, or that the commercial effect of some aspect of the transaction has been incorrectly assessed;

- assess the likely course of action (including options) – place greater emphasis on the probable course of events and, accordingly, little or no emphasis on unlikely events. The consequences of liquidation of one of the parties should only be considered when this is a likely event; and

- test the transaction's responsiveness, and the return for each participant, in the event of marginal changes in variables, such as interest rates, asset values and the timing of events. This provides useful insight into the role of the parties involved (e.g. whether a participant obtains a risk-taker's return or a financier's return).

3.2   Fair presentation generally achieved by compliance with IFRSs

In virtually all circumstances, a fair presentation is achieved by compliance with applicable IFRSs. A fair presentation also requires an entity: [IAS 1:17]

- to select and apply accounting policies in accordance with IAS 8, which sets out a hierarchy of authoritative guidance that management considers in the absence of an IFRS that specifically applies to the item (see **chapter A5**);

- to present information, including accounting policies, in a manner that provides relevant, reliable, comparable and understandable information; and

- to provide additional disclosures when compliance with the specific requirements in IFRSs is insufficient to enable users to understand the impact of particular transactions, other events or conditions on the entity's financial position or financial performance.

Inappropriate accounting policies are not rectified either by disclosure of the accounting policies used or by notes or explanatory material. [IAS 1:18]

3.3   Departure from IFRSs when compliance would be misleading

In extremely rare circumstances, management may conclude that compliance with a requirement in an IFRS would be so misleading that it would conflict with the objective of financial statements set out in the IASB's *Conceptual Framework for Financial Reporting*. In such circumstances, IAS 1 requires the entity to depart from that requirement "if the relevant regulatory framework requires, or otherwise does not prohibit, such a departure". [IAS 1:19]

IAS 1 explains that an item of information would conflict with the objective of financial statements when it does not represent faithfully the transactions, other events and conditions that it either purports to represent or could reasonably be expected to represent and, consequently, it would be likely to influence economic decisions made by users of financial statements. When assessing whether complying with a specific requirement of an IFRS would be so misleading that it would conflict with the objective of financial statements set out in the Conceptual Framework, management should consider:
[IAS 1:24]

- why the objective of financial statements is not achieved in the particular circumstances; and

- how the entity's circumstances differ from those of other entities that comply with the requirement. If other entities in similar circumstances comply with the requirement, there is a rebuttable presumption that the entity's compliance with the requirement would not be so misleading that it would conflict with the objective of financial statements set out in the Conceptual Framework.

When a departure is made from a requirement of an IFRS in the circumstances described above, the following disclosures are required:
[IAS 1:20]

- a statement that management has concluded that the financial statements present fairly the entity's financial position, financial performance and cash flows;

- a statement that the entity has complied with applicable IFRSs, except that it has departed from a particular requirement to achieve a fair presentation;

- the title of the IFRS from which there has been a departure;

- the nature of the departure, including the treatment that the IFRS would require;

- the reason why that treatment would be so misleading in the circumstances that it would conflict with the objective of financial statements set out in the Conceptual Framework;

- the treatment adopted; and

- for each period presented, the financial effect of the departure on each item in the financial statements that would have been reported in complying with the requirement.

IAS 1 also requires disclosures to be made when there was a departure from a requirement of a Standard or an Interpretation in a prior period that affects the amounts recognised in the financial statements for the current period. In such cases, the disclosures listed above should be made excluding the first two items. [IAS 1:21 – 22]

3.4   Compliance with IFRSs misleading but regulatory framework prohibits departure from IFRSs

IAS 1 specifies additional disclosures that apply in those extremely rare circumstances in which management concludes that compliance with a requirement in a Standard or an Interpretation would be so misleading that it would conflict with the objective of financial statements set out in the Conceptual Framework but the relevant regulatory framework prohibits departure from the requirement. In this case the entity should, to the extent possible, reduce the perceived misleading aspects of compliance by disclosing:
[IAS 1:23]

- the title of the IFRS in question;

- the nature of the requirement;

- the reason why management has concluded that complying with that requirement is so misleading in the circumstances that it conflicts with the objectives of financial statements set out in the Conceptual Framework; and

- for each period presented, the adjustments to each item in the financial statements that management has concluded would be necessary to achieve a fair presentation.

IAS 1:BC28 explains that departing from a requirement in a Standard or an Interpretation when considered necessary to achieve a fair presentation would conflict with the regulatory framework in some jurisdictions. But the departure would be required (and not just permitted) by IAS 1 when the relevant conditions are met. Arguably, this is no more of a departure from a Standard than when an exemption is given in specified circumstances. However, the IASB acknowledged these concerns and drafted the Standard to enable entities to comply with the requirements of the Standard when the relevant regulatory framework prohibits departures from accounting standards, while retaining the principle that entities should, to the extent possible, ensure that financial statements provide a fair presentation.

4   Statement of financial position

IAS 1 uses the title 'statement of financial position' rather than 'balance sheet', although they have the same meaning. As discussed at 2.4 above, the use of IAS 1's terminology is not mandatory and it is acceptable to use the title 'balance sheet' or other similar expressions. However, in this manual, IAS 1's terminology is used except when the context requires otherwise.

4.1   Current/non-current distinction

Current and non-current assets, and current and non-current liabilities, are presented as separate classifications in the statement of financial position. Further detailed requirements are set out below. This is subject to an exception when a presentation based on liquidity provides information that is reliable and is more relevant. When this exception applies, all assets and liabilities are presented in order of liquidity. [IAS 1:60]

For some entities (e.g. financial institutions), a presentation of assets and liabilities in increasing or decreasing order of liquidity provides information that is reliable and is more relevant than a current/non-current presentation. This is because the entity does not supply goods or services within a clearly identifiable operating cycle (see below). [IAS 1:63]

Whichever method of presentation is adopted (i.e. current/non-current or liquidity), for each asset and liability line item that combines amounts expected to be recovered or settled:
[IAS 1:61]

- no more than twelve months after the reporting period; and

- more than twelve months after the reporting period,

the amount expected to be recovered or settled after more than twelve months should be disclosed.

> This disclosure may be given in the notes and does not have to be in the statement of financial position itself. As explained later in this section, current assets and current liabilities may include amounts due after twelve months.

When an entity supplies goods or services within a clearly identifiable operating cycle, separate classification of current and non-current assets and liabilities provides useful information by distinguishing the net assets that are continually circulating as working capital from those used in the entity's long term operations. It also highlights assets that are expected to be realised within the current operating cycle and liabilities that are due for settlement within that same period. [IAS 1:62]

The operating cycle of an entity is the time between the acquisition of assets for processing and their realisation in cash or cash equivalents. When an entity's normal operating cycle is not clearly identifiable, its duration is assumed to be twelve months. [IAS 1:68]

IAS 1 permits an entity to present some assets and liabilities using a current/non-current classification and others in order of liquidity when this provides information that is reliable and more relevant. [IAS 1:64]

> IAS 1 states that such a mixed basis may be appropriate "when an entity has diverse operations". In practice it is likely to be a combination of financial and non-financial operations, rather than just 'diversity', that would make such an approach necessary.

Information about the expected realisation dates of assets and liabilities is useful in assessing liquidity and solvency. IFRS 7 *Financial Instruments:*

Disclosures (see **chapter B12** or, for entities that have not yet adopted IFRS 9, **chapter C12**) requires disclosure of the maturity dates of financial assets and financial liabilities. Financial assets include trade and other receivables. Financial liabilities include trade and other payables. Information about the expected date of recovery of non-monetary assets such as inventories and the expected date of settlement for liabilities such as provisions is also useful, whether assets and liabilities are classified as current or as non-current. For example, the amount of inventories that is expected to be recovered more than twelve months after the reporting period should be disclosed. [IAS 1:65]

4.1.1   *Employee benefits*

4.1.1.1   *Post-employment benefits*

When an entity uses a current/non-current distinction to present the statement of financial position (i.e. rather than a liquidity presentation), it is not required to analyse assets and liabilities arising from post-employment benefits accounted for under IAS 19 between current and non-current, either in the statement of financial position or in the notes.

IAS 19(2011):133 (previously IAS 19(1998):118) states that the Standard does not specify whether an entity should distinguish current and non-current portions of assets and liabilities arising from post-employment benefits. IAS 19(2011):BC200 (previously IAS 19(1998):BC81) states that the IASC (the IASB's predecessor) decided not to specify whether an entity should distinguish between the current and non-current portions of such assets and liabilities because such a distinction may sometimes be arbitrary.

Although IAS 1 has not been modified to reflect this exemption, the more specific references of IAS 19 apply. Similarly, IAS 1:61 is not considered to require separate disclosure of the portions of the employment benefit assets and liabilities that are expected to be recovered or settled before and after twelve months from the end of the reporting period because the concepts of 'recovery' and 'settlement' for such assets and liabilities are unclear.

IAS 19 requires the disclosure of the employer's best estimate of contributions expected to be paid to defined benefit plans during the annual period beginning after the reporting period, as soon as that information can reasonably be determined (see IAS 19(2011):147(b), previously IAS 19(1998):120A(q)).

4.1.1.2   Other employee benefits

The exemption in IAS 19(2011):133 (previously IAS 19(1998):118) discussed in the previous section applies only to post-employment benefits. There is no exemption from the requirements in IAS 1 for short-term and other long-term employee benefit liabilities such as annual leave, long-term disability leave and long-service leave. In respect of such benefits:

- to the extent that employees are entitled to take their annual/long-service leave in the next twelve months, whether they are expected to take it or not, the liability should be presented as a 'current' liability. The entity does not have an unconditional right to defer settlement of the liability for at least twelve months after the end of the reporting period;

- to the extent that employees are not entitled to take a portion of their annual/long-service leave during the next twelve months because, for example, additional years of service must first be rendered (i.e. the leave has not yet vested), and the employer is not expected to allow such leave to be taken early, that portion should be presented as a 'non-current' liability; and

- employees do not have an unconditional right to long-term disability benefits. Those rights arise when employees fall ill. IAS 19(2011):157 (previously IAS 19(1998):130) requires the measurement for long-term disability benefits to reflect the probability of payment/right arising. Consistent with this is a split between 'current' and 'non-current' based on the expected payment profile at the end of the reporting period.

As discussed further below, prior to the June 2011 revisions to IAS 19, the basis for classifying benefits as short- and long-term benefits when an arrangement is first entered into is consistent with the basis for presenting liabilities as current and non-current under IAS 1 (i.e. based on when the employee is entitled to the benefit). However, the bases are no longer consistent for entities that have adopted IAS 19(2011), under which short- and long-term benefits are distinguished based on when the benefit is *expected* to be settled.

Entities that have adopted the June 2011 revision of IAS 19

The definitions of short-term and 'other long-term' employee benefits set out in IAS 19(2011):8 are as follows (emphasis added).

Short-term employee benefits are "employee benefits (other than termination benefits) that are expected to be settled wholly before twelve months after the end of the annual reporting period in which the employees render the related service".

Other long-term employee benefits are "all employee benefits other than short-term employee benefits, post-employment benefits and termination benefits".

Therefore, the focus in IAS 19(2011) is on the timing of the *expected* settlement, rather than on when the benefits are *due to be settled*. Classification on this basis is different from the basis for presentation as current vs non-current under IAS 1. This will not have any effect when a benefit cannot be carried forward beyond twelve months from the end of the annual period in which it is earned (both the 'expected' and the 'due' settlement dates are within twelve months). It will have an effect when employees are entitled to carry forward a benefit beyond twelve months from the end of the annual period in which it is earned (e.g. in some cases, unused holiday entitlement) and some employees are expected to do so, but the employees are also entitled to immediate settlement (e.g. if they were to leave the entity's employment). Under IAS 19(2011), such a benefit is classified as an other long-term employee benefit even though, under IAS 1, it is presented entirely as a current liability.

Entities that have not yet adopted the June 2011 revision of IAS 19

The definitions of short-term and 'other long-term' employee benefits set out in IAS 19(1998):7 are as follows (emphasis added).

Short-term employee benefits are "employee benefits (other than termination benefits) that are due to be settled within twelve months after the end of the period in which the employees render the related service".

Other long-term employee benefits are "employee benefits (other than post-employment benefits and termination benefits) that are not due to be settled within twelve months after the end of the period in which the employees render the related service".

The phrase 'due to be settled' is also used in IAS 1:69(c) to define current liabilities. This indicates the IASB's intention that, prior to the June 2011 revisions, the classification of employee benefits (other than post-employment and termination benefits) when an arrangement is first entered into should be consistent with that under IAS 1 (i.e. current vs. non-current). This is also supported by IAS 19(1998):BC4C, which states that "this distinction between short-term and long-term benefits is consistent with the current/non-current liability distinction in IAS 1 *Presentation of Financial Statements*". However, unlike under IAS 1, once an employee benefit has been determined to be long-term for IAS 19 classification purposes, that classification is not changed as time passes and the date of settlement draws near; although part or all of it may be presented as a current liability, it continues to be measured as an other long-term employee benefit.

4.1.2   Derivatives

The presentation of derivatives in the statement of financial position is considered generally in **section 5** of **chapter B4** (or, for entities that have not yet adopted IFRS 9, **section 5** of **chapter C4**). Guidance on the presentation of embedded derivatives is set out in **section 13** of **chapter B5** (or, for entities that have not yet adopted IFRS 9, **section 13** of **chapter C5**).

4.1.3   Deferred tax assets and liabilities

When current and non-current assets and current and non-current liabilities are presented as separate classifications in the statement of financial position, deferred tax should not be classified as a current asset or a current liability. [IAS 1:56]

Given that the Standard does not require deferred tax assets or liabilities to be analysed as current, it follows that an entity is not required to disclose under IAS 1:61 (see above) the amount of deferred tax assets (liabilities) that are expected to be recovered (settled) within twelve months after the reporting period. Such a disclosure requirement would negate the relief provided in IAS 1:56 (although such information may be presented if the entity wishes to do so).

4.2   Current assets

An asset is classified as a current asset when it satisfies any of the following criteria:
[IAS 1:66]

- it is expected to be realised in the entity's normal operating cycle;

- it is intended for sale or consumption in the entity's normal operating cycle;

- it is held primarily for the purpose of trading;

- it is expected to be realised within twelve months of the reporting period; or

- it is cash or a cash equivalent (as defined in IAS 7 *Statement of Cash Flows* – see **chapter A21**) unless it is restricted from being exchanged or used to settle a liability for at least twelve months after the reporting period.

All other assets are classified as non-current. [IAS 1:66]

> The IFRIC (now the IFRS Interpretations Committee) was asked to consider whether the 'normal operating cycle' criterion in IAS 1:66 applies only if an entity has a predominant operating cycle. This is particularly relevant to the inventories of conglomerates which, on a narrow reading of the wording, might always have to refer to the twelve-month criteria, rather than the operating-cycle criterion. The Committee decided not to consider the question further because, in its view, it was clear that the wording should be read in both the singular and the plural and that it is the nature of the asset in relation to the operating cycle that is relevant for classification. Furthermore, if an entity holds assets (e.g. inventories) related to different operating cycles, and it is material to readers' understanding of an entity's financial position, further information should be disclosed under the general requirements of IAS 1:57. This rejection was published in the June 2005 edition of *IFRIC Update*.
>
> When an entity uses a current/non-current distinction to present the statement of financial position, immature agricultural produce should not be presented as a current asset separate from the agricultural asset to which it is attached. Until harvest, agricultural produce forms part of the total biological asset. This asset should be presented as a single asset in the statement of financial position and classified as either current or non-current in accordance with IAS 1. Long-term biological assets (e.g. fruit trees and vines) should be classified as

non-current assets, because the requirements of IAS 1:66 are not met for the asset as a whole. In all cases, if material, biological assets should be presented as a separate line item in the statement of financial position in accordance with IAS 1:54(f) (see **4.4** below).

The Standard uses the term 'non-current' to include tangible, intangible and financial assets of a long-term nature. It does not prohibit the use of alternative descriptions provided that the meaning is clear. [IAS 1:67]

Current assets include assets (e.g. inventories and trade receivables) that are sold, consumed or realised as part of the normal operating cycle even when they are not expected to be realised within twelve months after the reporting period. Current assets also include assets primarily held for the purpose of trading (examples include some financial assets that meet the definition of held for trading in IFRS 9 or, prior to the adoption of IFRS 9, IAS 39) and the current portion of non-current financial assets. [IAS 1:68]

Current assets include some, but not necessarily all, financial assets classified as held for trading in accordance with IFRS 9 (or, prior to the adoption of IFRS 9, IAS 39). Further detail in the context of derivatives is given in **section 5** of **chapter B4** (or, for entities that have not yet adopted IFRS 9, **section 5** of **chapter C4**).

4.3   Current liabilities

A liability is classified as a current liability when it satisfies any of the following criteria:
[IAS 1:69]

- it is expected to be settled in the entity's normal operating cycle;

- it is held primarily for the purposes of trading;

- it is due to be settled within twelve months after the reporting period; or

- the entity does not have an unconditional right to defer settlement of the liability for at least twelve months after the reporting period. Terms of a liability that could, at the option of the counterparty, result in its settlement by the issue of equity instruments do not affect its classification.

All other liabilities are classified as non-current. [IAS 1:69]

Example 4.3A

Classification of refundable deposits

A primary school requires a deposit to be paid upon enrolment into the school. Should the student leave the school, this deposit is refundable with one school-term's notice (four months). The majority of students enrol into just one primary school and, having completed the seven-year study period, receive the deposit back at the end of that seven-year period.

Despite the historical evidence that indicates that the majority of the deposits are only repaid after the seven-year period, the deposits are repayable on four months' notice. IAS 1:69 states that a liability should be classified as current when the entity does not have an unconditional right to defer settlement of the liability for at least twelve months after the reporting period. Therefore, the deposits should be classified as current liabilities.

It may be appropriate to disclose why the amounts are presented as current liabilities.

Example 4.3B

Current/non-current classification of a callable term loan

Entity A borrows funds from Bank B for which repayment is scheduled over five years. However, Bank B retains a right (either by means of a specific clause in the loan agreement or by inclusion of a cross-reference to the bank's general terms of business) to call for repayment at any time without cause.

Should the loan be classified as current or non-current by Entity A?

The loan should be classified as current if the right to call for repayment at any time without cause is enforceable. IAS 1:69 (see above) requires that a liability should be classified as current if the borrowing entity "does not have an unconditional right [at the reporting date] to defer settlement of the liability for at least twelve months after the reporting period".

The conclusion above was published as a rejection in the November 2010 *IFRIC Update*.

Some current liabilities, such as trade payables and some accruals for employee and other operating costs, are part of the working capital used in the entity's normal operating cycle. Such items are classified as current liabilities even if they are due to be settled more than twelve months after the reporting period. The same normal operating cycle applies to the classification of an entity's assets and liabilities. When the normal operating cycle is not clearly identifiable, its duration is assumed to be twelve months. [IAS 1:70]

Other current liabilities are not settled as part of the normal operating cycle but are due for settlement within twelve months after the reporting period or held primarily for the purpose of trading (examples include some financial liabilities classified as held for trading in accordance with IFRS 9 or, prior to the adoption of IFRS 9, IAS 39), bank overdrafts, the current portion of non-current financial liabilities, dividends payable, income taxes and other non-trade payables). Financial liabilities that provide financing on a long-term basis (i.e. not working capital used in the normal operating cycle) and are not due for settlement within twelve months after the reporting period are non-current liabilities. This is subject to an exception when the entity breaches an undertaking under a long-term loan arrangement (see **4.3.1** below). [IAS 1:71]

> Current liabilities include some, but not necessarily all, financial liabilities classified as held for trading in accordance with IFRS 9 (or, prior to the adoption of IFRS 9, IAS 39). Further detail in the context of derivatives is given in **section 5** of **chapter B4** (or, for entities that have not yet adopted IFRS 9, **section 5** of **chapter C4**).

The following example considers the situation in which the amortised cost of a liability at the end of the reporting period exceeds its principal amount (e.g. due to accrued unpaid interest).

Example 4.3C

Current/non-current presentation of non-derivative financial liabilities

An entity issues a 6 per cent CU100 million bond at par on 30 June 20X0. The bond is repayable at par 10 years after issuance on 30 June 20Y0. Interest of CU6 million is paid annually. There are no issue costs. The liability is measured at amortised cost using an effective interest rate of 6 per cent. For illustrative purposes only, it is assumed the amortised cost of the bond is CU103 million at 31 December 20X0.

How should the entity disclose the carrying amount of the bond in its statement of financial position at 31 December 20X0? Specifically, how is the presentation of the bond in the financial statements affected by IAS 1:71 which refers to the inclusion of the "current portion of non-current financial liabilities" in current liabilities?

Two methods of classification are acceptable under IFRSs. An entity should adopt one of the following methods as an accounting policy choice and should apply it consistently in accordance with IAS 8:13.

One approach is to present the entire amortised cost carrying amount of CU103 million in non-current liabilities. IAS 1:71 supports this classification because:

> - the liability is not expected to be settled in the entity's normal operating cycle;
>
> - the liability is not held primarily for the purpose of trading;
>
> - the liability is not due until 20Y0 (i.e. the principal is not expected to be settled within twelve months of the end of the reporting period); and
>
> - the entity has the unconditional right to defer settlement of the liability for at least twelve months after the reporting period.
>
> Under this approach, interest on the bond is viewed as servicing of the liability instead of its settlement. Therefore, the amount of interest to be paid within twelve months of the end of the reporting period does not constitute the 'current portion of non-current financial liabilities' described in IAS 1:71. The current portion of the bond would be the portion of its principal amount repayable within twelve months of the reporting period.
>
> The alternative method is to present CU3 million (i.e. the difference between the amortised cost carrying amount and the par value repayable on maturity) separately as a current liability. This current liability represents interest accrued at the year end. The remaining carrying amount of CU100 million would be classified as a non-current liability.

Financial liabilities are classified as current when they are due to be settled within twelve months after the reporting period even if:
[IAS 1:72]

- the original term was for a period longer than twelve months; and

- an agreement to refinance, or to reschedule payments, on a long-term basis is completed after the reporting period and before the financial statements are authorised for issue.

> Therefore, a refinancing after the reporting period should not to be taken into account in assessing whether a liability should be classified as current or non-current. As explained in IAS 1:BC44, the IASB concluded that the reporting of an entity's liquidity and solvency at the end of a reporting period should reflect contractual arrangements in force on that date. A refinancing after the reporting period is a non-adjusting event in accordance with IAS 10 *Events after the Reporting Period* and should not affect the presentation of the entity's statement of financial position.

If an entity expects, and has the discretion, to refinance or roll over an obligation for at least twelve months after the reporting period under an existing loan facility, it classifies the obligation as non-current. This is so even if it would otherwise be due within a shorter period. But when refinancing or rolling over the obligation is not at the discretion of the entity (e.g. there is no arrangement for refinancing), the potential to refinance is not considered (and the obligation is therefore classified as current). [IAS 1:73]

Example 4.3D

Current/non-current classification of a short-term loan with a rollover option subject to meeting defined conditions

Entity A has a variable rate loan from Bank B that is due for repayment six months after the end of the reporting period. Entity A may roll over the loan on the same terms for another 12 months from the due date, provided that it passes a specified financial test at that date. Entity A has concluded that the extension option is not a separable embedded derivative.

Should the loan be classified as current or non-current?

It depends on the nature of the conditions attached to the extension option. In circumstances in which the conditions are substantive (which would normally be the case for any financial condition), or management does not expect to extend, the loan should be classified as current.

However, if (1) the conditions are entirely within Entity A's control or totally perfunctory, and (2) management expects to exercise its option, the substance of the option is that the rollover is at Entity A's discretion. The loan would therefore be classified as non-current in accordance with the requirements of IAS 1:73.

With respect to (1) above, when assessing whether the conditions are within the control of Entity A, the following factors should be considered:

- the defined conditions are customary for these types of financing arrangements;

- the assessment as to whether Entity A has met the conditions (i.e. the result of the 'test') is objectively determinable (e.g. it is not a subjective acceleration clause);

- the conditions are related to Entity A and its operations (e.g. there are no broad economic conditions or lender conditions); and

- it is reasonable to assume, based on facts and circumstances that exist at the end of the reporting period, that meeting the conditions at the rollover date is reasonably possible.

For loans classified as current liabilities, IAS 1 states that if the following events occur between the end of the reporting period and the date the

financial statements are authorised for issue, those events are disclosed as non-adjusting events in accordance with IAS 10:
[IAS 1:76]

- refinancing on a long-term basis;

- rectification of a breach of a long-term loan arrangement; and

- the granting by the lender of a period of grace to rectify a breach of a long-term loan arrangement ending at least twelve months after the reporting period.

4.3.1   Breaches of covenants

When a provision of a long-term loan arrangement is breached on or before the end of the reporting period with the effect that the liability becomes payable on demand, the liability is classified as current. This is so, even if the lender has agreed, after the reporting period and before authorisation of the financial statements for issue, not to demand payment as a consequence of the breach. The liability is classified as current because, at the end of the reporting period, the entity does not have an unconditional right to defer settlement for at least twelve months after that date. [IAS 1:74]

The liability is classified as non-current if the lender agreed before the end of the reporting period to provide a period of grace (i.e. a period within which the entity can rectify the breach and during which the lender cannot demand immediate repayment) ending at least twelve months after the reporting period. [IAS 1:75]

Example 4.3.1

Overdraft facility with 'lock-box' arrangement

Company A has a 5-year, CU50 million overdraft facility with Bank B that includes a 'lock-box' account arrangement. Under the terms of the lock-box arrangement, Company A's customers are required to remit payments directly to a designated lock-box account, and the amounts received are applied to reduce the debt outstanding under the overdraft facility. At the end of each day, because Company A may request additional borrowings under the facility (Company A is permitted to withdraw an amount equal to the daily cash receipts), the outstanding balance due under the facility could remain unchanged.

Company A uses the overdraft facility as a source of long-term financing and has maintained a minimum balance of CU20 million. Neither Company A nor Bank B expects the balance to be below CU20 million in the next 12 months. Total cash receipts exceed the overdraft facility in any given year.

Should Company A's overdraft be presented as a current or a non-current liability?

The overdraft facility should be presented as a current liability. IAS 1:69 requires an entity to classify a liability as current if it expects to settle the liability in its normal operating cycle. Because the customer remittances represent current working capital of Company A that is being used to settle its obligation, the obligation is considered a short-term obligation of the borrower.

In many situations, entities maintain a minimum balance payable to a trading partner. Similar to the accounting for trade payables, the balance is classified based on the terms of the underlying arrangements or invoices payable – consequently, they are generally classified as current liabilities.

4.3.2   Expected voluntary repayment of a loan not due to be settled within twelve months after the reporting period

Example 4.3.2

Expected voluntary repayment of a loan not due to be settled within twelve months after the reporting period

On 1 January 20X1, Entity X borrows funds from a third-party bank for long-term financing purposes. The loan is due for repayment in 20X5. The loan is classified as a non-current liability in Entity X's financial statements for the year ended 31 December 20X1.

At 31 December 20X2, Entity X has not breached any provisions of the loan agreement and does not expect to do so in the foreseeable future. However, at that date, Entity X intends to enter into a refinancing arrangement that will involve voluntary repayment of the loan and taking out a new loan with a different lender. Entity X has notified the bank of its intentions, but has not entered into an irrevocable commitment to repay within 12 months.

In January 20X3 (before the 31 December 20X2 financial statements are authorised for issue), the refinancing is completed as planned and the loan repaid.

How should Entity X classify the loan in its financial statements at 31 December 20X2?

Entity X should classify the loan as a non-current liability. As at 31 December 20X2, the loan is still due to be settled in 20X5 (i.e. more than twelve months after the reporting period) and Entity X has not given up its unconditional right to defer settlement.

The voluntary repayment after the reporting period is a non-adjusting event which, if material, should be disclosed (including, potentially, the impact on

> liquidity) in accordance with paragraph 21 of IAS 10 *Events after the Reporting Period* (see **chapter A22**).

4.4   Information to be presented in the statement of financial position

IAS 1 uses the expression 'in the statement of financial position' rather than 'on the face of the statement of financial position'. However, it is clearly the intention that these items are shown 'on the face of' the statement itself. Disclosure in the notes would not be adequate to comply with the Standard in this regard.

The statement of financial position should include, at a minimum, line items that present the following amounts:
[IAS 1:54]

(a)   property, plant and equipment;

(b)   investment property;

(c)   intangible assets;

(d)   financial assets (other than investments accounted for using the equity method, trade and other receivables and cash and cash equivalents, which are presented separately);

(e)   investments accounted for using the equity method;

(f)   biological assets;

(g)   inventories;

(h)   trade and other receivables;

(i)   cash and cash equivalents;

(j)   the total of assets classified as held for sale and assets included in disposal groups classified as held for sale in accordance with IFRS 5 *Non-current Assets Held for Sale and Discontinued Operations* (see **chapter A20**);

(k)   trade and other payables;

(l)   provisions;

(m)   financial liabilities (other than trade and other payables, and provisions, which are presented separately);

(n)   liabilities and assets for current tax, as defined in IAS 12;

(o)   deferred tax liabilities and deferred tax assets, as defined in IAS 12;

(p)   liabilities included in disposal groups classified as held for sale in accordance with IFRS 5 (see **chapter A20**);

(q)   non-controlling interests, presented within equity; and

(r)   issued capital and reserves attributable to owners of the parent.

4.4.1   General requirements

Additional line items, headings and subtotals are presented in the statement of financial position when such presentation is relevant to an understanding of the entity's financial position. [IAS 1:55]

> For example, retirement benefit obligations under a defined benefit pension scheme might be very material and so would be presented separately in the statement of financial position.

The Standard does not prescribe the order or the format in which items are to be presented. The Standard merely provides a list of items (see above) that are sufficiently different in nature or function to warrant separate presentation in the statement of financial position. In addition:
[IAS 1:57]

- line items are included when the size, nature or function of an item or aggregation of similar items is such that separate presentation is relevant to an understanding of the entity's financial position; and

- the descriptions used and the ordering of items or aggregation of similar items may be amended according to the nature of the entity and its transactions, to provide information that is relevant to an understanding of the entity's financial position. For example, a financial institution may amend the above descriptions to provide information that is relevant to the operations of a financial institution.

The judgement as to whether additional items are presented separately is based on an assessment of:
[IAS 1:58]

- the nature and liquidity of the assets;

- the function of the assets within the entity; and

- the amounts, nature and timing of liabilities.

The use of different measurement bases for different classes of assets suggests that their nature or function differs and, therefore, that they should be presented as separate line items. For example, different classes of property, plant and equipment can be carried at cost or revalued amounts in accordance with IAS 16 *Property, Plant and Equipment*. [IAS 1:59]

4.4.2 Cash and cash equivalents

The separate line item in the statement of financial position for 'cash and cash equivalents' does not necessarily correspond to 'cash and cash equivalents' as defined in IAS 7 *Statement of Cash Flows*. IAS 7:45 acknowledges this fact by requiring a reconciliation of the amount of cash and cash equivalents in the statement of cash flows with the equivalent line item reported in the statement of financial position.

IAS 7:8 states that bank overdrafts repayable on demand may be classified as a component of cash and cash equivalents for the purposes of the statement of cash flows when they form an integral part of an entity's cash management. IAS 7:8 notes that a characteristic of such banking arrangements is that the balance often fluctuates from being positive to overdrawn.

Even when such overdrafts are classified as a component of cash and cash equivalents under IAS 7, it will not generally be appropriate for them to be netted against cash and cash equivalent assets for the purposes of presenting the 'cash and cash equivalents' line item in the statement of financial position. Such overdrafts should be netted against positive cash balances only when the more restrictive offset criteria in paragraph 42 of IAS 32 *Financial Instruments: Presentation* are met (see **section 6** of **chapter B12** or, for entities that have not yet adopted IFRS 9, **section 6** of **chapter C12**).

When the amounts presented for cash and cash equivalents in the statements of financial position and cash flows are different, entities may wish to consider using different descriptions so as to avoid confusion; for example, the amount presented in the statement of financial position could be described as 'cash and bank balances'. IAS 1:57 permits the use of alternative descriptions in this manner. However, even when different descriptions are used in the two statements, the requirement to present a reconciliation under IAS 7:45 applies.

4.5 Information to be presented in the statement of financial position or in the notes

4.5.1 General requirements

Further sub-classifications of the line items presented should be disclosed either in the statement of financial position or in the notes, classified in a manner that is appropriate to the entity's operations. [IAS 1:77]

The details provided depend on the requirements of IFRSs and on the size, nature and function of the amounts involved. The factors set out in IAS 1:58 (see **4.4.1** above) are also used to decide on the basis of sub-classifications. IAS 1 gives the following examples:
[IAS 1:78]

- items of property, plant and equipment are disaggregated into classes in accordance with IAS 16 *Property, Plant and Equipment*;

- receivables are disaggregated into amounts receivable from trade customers, receivables from related parties, prepayments and other amounts;

- inventories are sub-classified, in accordance with IAS 2 *Inventories*, into classifications such as merchandise, production supplies, materials, work in progress and finished goods;

- provisions are disaggregated into provisions for employee benefits and other items; and

- equity capital and reserves are disaggregated into various classes, such as paid-in capital, share premium and reserves.

4.5.2 Share capital and reserves

4.5.2.1 Presentation when 'legal' share capital is classified as liabilities

IAS 1 requires several disclosures about share capital and reserves. These are described at **4.5.2.4** and **4.5.2.5** below.

In straightforward cases, these disclosures will be made in respect of the amounts included in the statement of financial position caption 'issued capital and reserves attributable to owners of the parent'. However, this will not always be the case, because amounts that are legally share capital will sometimes be presented, in whole or in part, as liabilities in the statement of financial position in accordance with IAS 32 *Financial Instruments: Presentation.*

There are a number of ways in which the requirements of IAS 1 can be met. For example, it is generally acceptable to present a single line item on the face of the statement of financial position for 'issued share capital and reserves attributable to owners of the parent'. When this approach is taken, the amount presented on the face of the statement of financial position is the 'net' amount (i.e. excluding amounts that are legally share capital but presented as financial liabilities). Further details (e.g. analysing legal share capital between amounts classified as equity and liabilities) can be shown in the notes. This approach may not be appropriate in some jurisdictions; regulatory requirements or general practice may be such that entities present greater detail in the statement of financial position (e.g. share capital, share premium and specified reserves).

When an expanded analysis of equity items is shown on the face of the statement of financial position (either because this is a regulatory requirement or because the entity wishes to present more detail on the face of the statement of financial position), the question arises as to which line items should be reduced by the amounts presented as liabilities.

When the amounts presented as liabilities represent the proceeds of issue of a class (or classes) of shares, the most common approach is that the amounts presented as 'share capital' and 'share premium' on the face of the statement of financial position exclude those amounts (i.e. they relate to equity shares only). Alternatively, the gross amounts for 'share capital' and 'share premium' may be presented on the face of the statement of financial position, with amounts classified as liabilities shown as a separate deduction. In such circumstances, the supplementary disclosures required by IAS 1 regarding share capital (see **4.5.2.4** below) can be presented separately in the relevant notes for the 'equity' and 'liability' classes of shares. Alternatively, details about all classes of share capital may be presented in a single note, but distinguishing separately those classes and amounts that have been presented as liabilities.

The position is more complicated when a class of shares (e.g. redeemable convertible preference shares) is accounted for as a compound financial instrument with both equity and liability components. There are several possibilities for presentation in such circumstances, including:

- the share capital and share premium could be shown on the face of the statement of financial position at their 'legal' amounts, with a separate negative reserve equal to the liability recognised; or

- the share capital and share premium could be shown on the face of the statement of financial position as those amounts that relate to equity shares, with a separate line item such as 'equity component of preference shares'; or

- the deduction for the liability might be made first from the share premium and then from share capital; or

- the deduction for the liability might be made from share capital and share premium in proportion to the allocation of the original proceeds of issue between those captions.

All of these are acceptable provided that adequate explanation is provided and that all of IAS 1's disclosure requirements are met. The key point is that the total amount presented as equity is unaffected by these choices.

4.5.2.2   Analysis of reserves

There are some specific instances when IFRSs require a separate component of equity to be maintained. For example, IAS 21 *The Effects of Changes in Foreign Exchange Rates* requires certain exchange differences to be accumulated in a separate component of equity and IAS 16 requires a surplus on revaluation of an asset to be recognised in other comprehensive income and accumulated in equity under the heading of revaluation surplus. Subject to these (and other) specific requirements, there is some flexibility about which items are accounted for as separate components within equity.

See **4.5.2.5** below for a discussion of the disclosure requirements regarding reserves within equity.

4.5.2.3   Meaning of 'retained earnings'

When IFRSs require amounts to be accumulated in equity, in the absence of specific requirements in IFRSs (see previous section), and subject to local regulatory requirements, it is generally acceptable for these amounts to be included within retained earnings.

For example, the credit to equity required by IFRS 2 *Share-based Payment* for equity-settled share-based payments may either be credited to a separate reserve or to retained earnings. This issue is considered further at **4.1.2** in **chapter A16**.

4.5.2.4   Disclosures about share capital

For each class of share capital, the following should be disclosed, either in the statement of financial position or in the notes:
[IAS 1:79(a)]

- the number of shares authorised;

- the number of shares issued and fully paid;

- the number of shares issued but not fully paid;

- the par value per share, or the fact that the shares have no par value;

- a reconciliation of the number of shares outstanding at the beginning and at the end of the period;

- the rights, preferences and restrictions attaching to that class including restrictions on distributions of dividends and the repayment of capital;

- shares in the entity held by the entity or by its subsidiaries or associates; and

- shares reserved for issue under options and contracts for the sale of shares, including the terms and amounts.

In accordance with IAS 32, all or part of the amounts recognised for shares in the statement of financial position may be classified as liabilities. The above disclosure requirements apply irrespective of whether the shares are classified as equity or debt or a combination of the two (see also **4.5.2.1** above).

It is unclear whether the requirement to disclose 'shares in the entity held by the entity or by its subsidiaries or associates' refers to the number of shares held or the amount of the deduction from equity in respect of such holdings. In the context of the other disclosures required by this paragraph of IAS 1, the text appears to refer to the number of shares. This would be appropriate for all of the types of holding referred to in IAS 1:79(a), including shares held by associates of the entity which are not deducted from equity as is required for shares held by the entity and its subsidiaries under IAS 32:33.

However, IAS 32:34 states that "[t]he amount of treasury shares held is disclosed separately either in the statement of financial position or in the notes, in accordance with IAS 1". This text refers to the 'amount' of treasury shares rather than their number, but it appears to be a reminder of the disclosure requirement in IAS 1 rather than an additional requirement.

Because of the uncertainty regarding this disclosure requirement, it is recommended that both of the following be disclosed: (1) the number of shares held by the entity and by its subsidiaries and associates, and (2) when relevant, the amount of any deduction from equity in respect of treasury shares.

Some entities such as partnerships or trusts do not have share capital. In such cases, information equivalent to that described above for share capital should be disclosed, showing changes during the period in each category of equity interest and the rights, preferences and restrictions attaching to each category of equity interest. [IAS 1:80]

If an entity has reclassified:

- a puttable instrument classified as an equity instrument, or

- an instrument that imposes on the entity an obligation to deliver to another party a pro rata share of the net assets of the entity only on liquidation and is classified as an equity instrument,

between financial liabilities and equity, the amount reclassified into and out of each category (financial liabilities or equity), and the timing and reason for that reclassification, should be disclosed. [IAS 1:80A]

The terms used in the two bullet points above have the meaning specified in IAS 32 (see **2.1.2** and **2.1.3** in **chapter B3** or, for entities that have not yet adopted IFRS 9, **2.1.2** and **2.1.3** in **chapter C3**).

4.5.2.5   Disclosures about reserves

Entities are required to provide a description of the nature and purpose of each reserve within equity, either in the statement of financial position or in the notes. [IAS 1:79(b)]

While IAS 1 requires financial statements to include additional information as to the nature and purpose of each reserve, it does not provide any further clarification regarding what information is needed.

By allowing this information to be disclosed in the statement of financial position, the IASB has indicated that the required information might be sufficiently disclosed by a precise wording of the name of the reserve. Thus, for reserves that are commonly encountered (revaluation reserves on property, plant and equipment, share premium account, translation reserves in respect of foreign operations etc.), no further explanation is necessary for investors to understand the nature and purpose of the reserves.

However, if, for example, the entity wishes to designate special reserves within equity that are not familiar to users of financial statements, supplementary information should be provided regarding the purpose of the reserve, and how it will be utilised.

5   Statement of profit or loss and other comprehensive income

As discussed at **2.4** above, the June 2011 amendments to IAS 1 introduced a new title for the 'statement of profit or loss and other comprehensive income' (previously the 'statement of comprehensive income'). However, use of the new title is not mandatory.

The option to present components of profit or loss in a separate statement has been retained (see **2.4.1**) following the June 2011 amendments. The title for that separate statement introduced by the June 2011 amendments is the 'statement of profit or loss'; again, entities are not required to use this title.

Amendments have also been made to the paragraphs of the Standard dealing with the presentation of items in the statement of profit or loss and other comprehensive income. Most of these arise from changes in terminology; the only substantive change relates to the presentation of items in other comprehensive income (see **5.3**).

The sections below are structured as follows:

- the minimum contents for the statement of profit or loss and other comprehensive income are set out in **5.1** – these are listed separately for entities that have adopted the June 2011 amendments to IAS 1 and those that have not;

- detailed requirements regarding the presentation of items in the profit or loss section or the separate statement of profit or loss (income statement) are discussed in **5.2** – these have not been affected by the June 2011 amendments;

- detailed requirements regarding the presentation of items of other comprehensive income are discussed in **5.3** – identifying the impact of the June 2011 amendments to IAS 1; and

- information required to be presented either in the statement of profit or loss and other comprehensive income or in the notes is discussed in **5.4** – this has not been affected by the June 2011 amendments.

The June 2011 amendments are effective for annual periods beginning on or after 1 July 2012, with earlier application permitted. If an entity applies the amendments for an earlier period, it is required to disclose that fact. [IAS 1:139J]

In the absence of specific transition provisions, the June 2011 amendments should be applied retrospectively, which means that amounts presented for comparative periods are required to be restated in the period in which the amendments are first applied.

Whichever approach is adopted to the presentation of the statement of profit or loss and other comprehensive income, and irrespective of whether the entity has adopted the June 2011 amendments, the objective is to arrive at an amount for 'total comprehensive income', which is defined as "the change in equity during a period resulting from transactions and other events, other than those changes resulting from transactions with owners in their capacity as owners. Total comprehensive income comprises all components of 'profit or loss' and 'other comprehensive income'". [IAS 1:7]

Although IAS 1 uses the terms 'profit or loss', 'other comprehensive income' and 'total comprehensive income', other terms may be used to describe the totals as long as the meaning is clear. For example, the term 'net income' may be used to describe profit or loss. [IAS 1:8]

The following sections cover the minimum requirements regarding the presentation of profit or loss and other comprehensive income. Additional line items, headings and sub-totals should be presented in the statement(s) presenting profit or loss and other comprehensive income when such a presentation is relevant to an understanding of the entity's financial performance. [IAS 1:85]

Disclosing the components of financial performance assists users in understanding the financial performance achieved and in making projections of future financial performance. To explain the elements of financial performance, it may be necessary to:
[IAS 1:86]

- include additional line items in the statement(s) presenting profit or loss and other comprehensive income;

- amend the descriptions used; and/or

- amend the ordering of items.

Factors to be considered include materiality and the nature and function of the items of income and expense. For example, a financial institution may amend the descriptions of line items to provide information that is relevant to the operations of such an institution. However, income and expense items should not be offset unless the criteria in IAS 1 are met (see **2.8** above). [IAS 1:86]

5.1 Minimum contents for the statement of profit or loss and other comprehensive income

5.1.1 *Entities that have adopted the June 2011 amendments to IAS 1*

The statement of profit or loss and other comprehensive income (statement of comprehensive income) is required to present, in addition to the profit or loss and other comprehensive income sections:
[IAS 1:81A]

- profit or loss;

- total other comprehensive income; and

- comprehensive income for the period, being the total of profit or loss and other comprehensive income.

If an entity presents a separate statement of profit or loss, it should not present the profit or loss section in the statement presenting comprehensive income. [IAS 1:81A]

The requirements of IAS 1:81A are essentially the same as the equivalent requirements prior to the June 2011 amendments (see **5.1.2**). If a one-statement approach is adopted, the single statement presents separate sections for (1) profit or loss, and (2) other comprehensive income, with totals shown for each and the aggregate of the two presented as a final total. If a two-statement approach is adopted, the separate statement of profit or loss is presented to arrive at a total for profit or loss; this total is then the starting point for the second statement which presents items of other comprehensive income, a total for other comprehensive income, and a total for comprehensive income (the aggregate of profit or loss and other comprehensive income). Both of these approaches are illustrated in the illustrative financial statements accompanying the amended Standard.

The following items are required to be presented as allocation of profit or loss and other comprehensive income for the period:
[IAS 1:81B]

- profit or loss for the period attributable to:

  - non-controlling interests; and

  - owners of the parent; and

- comprehensive income for the period attributable to:

  - non-controlling interests; and

  - owners of the parent.

If an entity presents profit or loss in a separate statement, the allocation of the profit or loss for the period should be presented in that separate statement. [IAS 1:81B]

The reference to presentation 'as allocation of profit or loss' means that these items are not items of income or expense. This presentation is consistent with IFRS 10 *Consolidated Financial Statements* (or, for entities that have not yet adopted IFRS 10, IAS 27(2008) *Consolidated and Separate Financial Statements*), which requires non-controlling interests to be presented within equity because they do not meet the definition of a liability in the IASB's *Conceptual Framework for Financial Reporting* (see IAS 1:BC59).

The illustrative financial statements accompanying IAS 1 show how these requirements can be met. A presentation that shows the profit for the period as a sub-total and then deducts non-controlling interests to arrive at the profit attributable to the equity holders of the parent would not be regarded as meeting the requirements of IAS 1.

In addition to items required by other IFRSs, the profit or loss section or the statement of profit or loss is required to present the following line items:
[IAS 1:82]

- revenue;

- finance costs;

- share of the profit or loss of associates and joint ventures accounted for using the equity method;

- tax expense; and

- a single amount for the total of discontinued operations (see **6.2.1** in **chapter A20**).

Entities applying IFRS 9 *Financial Instruments* are also required to disclose:

- gains and losses arising from the derecognition of financial assets measured at amortised cost; [IAS 1:82(aa)] and

- if a financial asset is reclassified so that it is measured at fair value, any gain or loss arising from a difference between the previous carrying amount and its fair value at the reclassification date (as defined in IFRS 9). [IAS 1:82(ca)]

5.1.2   *Entities that have not yet adopted the June 2011 amendments to IAS 1*

An entity should present all items of income and expense recognised in a period:
[IAS 1:81]

- in a single statement of comprehensive income; or

- in two statements: a statement displaying components of profit or loss (separate income statement) and a second statement beginning with profit or loss and displaying components of other comprehensive income (statement of comprehensive income).

As a minimum, the statement of comprehensive income is required to include line items that present the following amounts for the period:
[IAS 1:82]

- revenue;

- finance costs;

- share of the profit or loss of associates and joint ventures accounted for using the equity method;

- tax expense;

- a single amount comprising the total of:

  - the post-tax profit or loss of discontinued operations; and

  - the post-tax gain or loss recognised on the measurement to fair value less costs to sell, or on the disposal of the assets or disposal groups constituting the discontinued operation;

- profit or loss;

- each component of other comprehensive income, classified by nature (excluding amounts included in the next item below);

- share of other comprehensive income of associates and joint ventures accounted for using the equity method; and

- total comprehensive income.

Entities applying IFRS 9 *Financial Instruments* are also required to disclose:

- gains and losses arising from the derecognition of financial assets measured at amortised cost; [IAS 1:82(aa)] and

- if a financial asset is reclassified so that it is measured at fair value, any gain or loss arising from a difference between the previous carrying amount and its fair value at the reclassification date (as defined in IFRS 9). [IAS 1:82(ca)]

IAS 1 requires the following items to be disclosed in the statement of comprehensive income as allocations for the period:
[IAS 1:83]

- profit or loss for the period attributable to:

    - non-controlling interests; and

    - owners of the parent; and

- total comprehensive income for the period attributable to:

    - non-controlling interests; and

    - owners of the parent.

The reference to presentation 'as allocations' means that these items are not items of income or expense. This presentation is consistent with IFRS 10 *Consolidated Financial Statements* (or, for entities that have not yet adopted IFRS 10, IAS 27(2008) *Consolidated and Separate Financial Statements*), which requires non-controlling interests to be presented within equity because they do not meet the definition of a liability in the IASB's *Conceptual Framework for Financial Reporting* (see IAS 1:BC59).

The illustrative financial statements accompanying IAS 1 show how these requirements can be met. A presentation that shows the profit for the period as a sub-total and then deducts non-controlling interests to arrive at the profit attributable to the equity holders of the parent would not be regarded as meeting the requirements of IAS 1.

A separate income statement may be presented including the first six main bullets from IAS 1:82 listed above. When this presentation is adopted, the disclosures required by IAS 1:83(a) concerning non-controlling interests should be presented as part of the income statement. [IAS 1:84]

5.2   Items to be presented in profit or loss

5.2.1   Income and expenses to be recognised in profit or loss unless an IFRS requires or permits otherwise

All items of income or expense recognised in a period are recognised in profit or loss unless an IFRS requires or permits otherwise. [IAS 1:88]

Some IFRSs specify circumstances in which particular items are recognised outside profit or loss in the current period. IAS 8 *Accounting Policies, Changes in Accounting Estimates and Errors* deals with two such circumstances – the correction of errors and changes in accounting policies (see **chapter A5**). Other IFRSs require or permit components of other comprehensive income that meet the definition of income or expense in the *Conceptual Framework for Financial Reporting* to be excluded from profit or loss. [IAS 1:89]

Examples of such items include:

- revaluation surpluses under IAS 16 (see **chapter A7**);

- certain gains and losses arising from the translation of the financial statements of a foreign operation under IAS 21 (see **chapter A19**);

- for entities that have adopted IFRS 9, gains and losses from investments in equity instruments measured at fair value through other comprehensive income (see **chapter B2**); and

- for entities that have not yet adopted IFRS 9, gains and losses on remeasuring available-for-sale financial assets under IAS 39 (see **chapter C2**).

5.2.2   Presentation of net finance costs

At its October 2004 meeting, the IFRIC (now the IFRS Interpretations Committee) discussed a potential agenda topic regarding whether it is acceptable to present a line item for 'net finance costs' in profit or loss without presenting separately the finance revenue and finance costs comprising the net amount. The Committee noted that, at that time, IAS 1(2003):81 required line items for revenue and finance costs to be presented on the face of the income statement (correspondingly, IAS 1:82 now requires line items for revenue and finance costs to be presented on the face of the statement of comprehensive income). The Committee therefore agreed that:

- taken together with the requirements of IAS 1:32 (prohibition on netting of income and expenses unless required or permitted by a Standard or an Interpretation –see **2.8** above), this precludes the presentation of 'net finance costs' (or a similar term) in the income statement (similar logic now applies for the statement of comprehensive income) without showing the finance revenue and finance costs comprising the net amount; but

- this does not preclude the presentation of finance revenue followed immediately by finance costs and a sub-total (e.g. 'net finance costs') in the income statement (and similarly now the statement of comprehensive income), as illustrated below.

	20X1 CU'000	20X0 CU'000
Operating profit	126,342	49,774
Investment revenues	3,501	717
Finance costs	(36,187)	(32,165)
Net finance costs	(32,686)	(31,448)
Share of profit of associates	12,763	983
Other gains and losses	(563)	(44)
Profit before tax	105,856	19,265

The IFRIC decided not to develop an Interpretation on this issue but the above conclusion was set out in the October 2004 edition of *IFRIC Update*.

5.2.3 Presentation of revenue

IAS 1:82 requires revenue to be presented as a separate line item in profit or loss. When the entity has more than one category of revenue (e.g. both trading and finance revenue), the question arises as to whether it is necessary to present a single line item that includes the combined revenue from all sources, or whether it is acceptable to present different categories of revenue as individual line items, without presenting a total for revenue.

It is not necessary for there to be a single total for each of the items listed in IAS 1:82 in the statement of comprehensive income. For example, revenue from sales of goods to customers may be presented separately from interest received (which falls within the definition of revenue in IAS 18 *Revenue*). However, it is necessary to be able to arrive at the total by adding together items that appear in the statement of comprehensive income.

Before the IFRIC's conclusion on net finance costs (see **5.2.2**), there had been some uncertainty regarding whether IAS 1:82 should be interpreted as requiring a single total for each item listed or whether several 'line items' could be presented to represent a single requirement in IAS 1:82 (e.g. revenue). The Committee's conclusion on net finance costs effectively confirms that it is acceptable to present different categories of revenue as individual line items without presenting a total in the statement of comprehensive income.

5.2.4   Results of operating activities

IAS 1 does not require the results of operating activities to be disclosed as a line item on the face of the income statement. The IASB has omitted this requirement on the basis that the term is not defined and that it is inappropriate to require disclosure of an undefined item.

However, the IASB recognises that an entity may elect to disclose the results of operating activities, or a similar line item, even though the term is not defined. IAS 1:BC56 notes that, in such cases, it is necessary to ensure the amount presented is representative of activities that would normally be considered as 'operating'. In the IASB's view, it would be misleading and would impair the comparability of financial statements if items of an operating nature were excluded from the results of operating activities, even if that had been industry practice. For example, it would be inappropriate to exclude items clearly related to operations (e.g. inventory write-downs and restructuring or relocation expenses) because they occur irregularly or infrequently or are unusual in amount. Similarly, it would be inappropriate to exclude items on the grounds that they do not involve cash flows, such as depreciation and amortisation expenses.

A line item 'profit from operations' is often presented after all income and expenses other than finance costs and income from associates and joint ventures. Investment income would usually be shown below profit from operations (unless the entity is a financial institution or similar entity). Based on the IASB's views expressed in IAS 1:BC56, it would not be appropriate to exclude items such as restructuring costs. There does, however, appear to be flexibility to disclose the results of associates and joint ventures either within or below profit from operations (see **5.2.6** below).

5.2.5   Extraordinary items

IAS 1 states that items of income and expense should not be presented as 'extraordinary items' in the statement(s) presenting profit or loss and other comprehensive income, or in the notes. [IAS 1:87]

This may appear to be a slightly odd requirement in that IAS 1 does not define what is meant by 'extraordinary items' or say how such items might be presented if they were not prohibited. To understand the requirements of IAS 1:87, it is necessary to be aware that a previous version of IAS 8 included a definition of extraordinary items as "income and expenses that arise from events or transactions that are clearly distinct from the ordinary activities of the enterprise and, therefore, are not expected to recur frequently or regularly". It required such items to be disclosed on the face of the income statement separately from the profit or loss on ordinary activities (normally as a single net-of-tax number after profit from ordinary activities and before net profit). As part of the revisions of IAS 1 and IAS 8 in 2003, the IASB decided to prohibit the presentation of extraordinary items because they result from the normal business risks faced by an entity and do not warrant presentation in a separate component of the income statement. The reasons are more fully set out in IAS 1:BC60 to BC64.

5.2.6   Results of associates and joint ventures accounted for using the equity method

The share of the profit or loss of associates and joint ventures accounted for using the equity method is one of the line items required to be presented in profit or loss.

This item should be presented on an after-tax basis. The separate statement of profit or loss shown in the illustrative financial statements accompanying IAS 1 notes that "[t]his means the share of associates' profit attributable to owners of the associates, ie it is after tax and non-controlling interests in the associates". The same principle applies for the share of profits or losses of joint ventures accounted for using the equity method (not shown in the illustrative financial statements accompanying IAS 1).

The investor's share of the profit or loss of an individual associate or a joint venture accounted for using the equity method should be presented within a single line item in the profit or loss section of the statement of comprehensive income (or, when relevant, the separate statement of profit or loss) and should not be separated over different line items (revenue, expenses etc.).

However, there is nothing to prevent the disaggregation of the investor's share of the profits or losses of different associates or joint ventures so that they are presented in different line items. For example, an entity might choose to show separately the profits or losses for associates and for joint ventures accounted for using the equity method. Segregation on this basis would ensure compliance with the requirement under paragraph B16 of IFRS 12 *Disclosure of Interests in Other Entities* to disclose the investor's share of the profits or losses of associates separately from its share of the profits or losses of joint ventures (or, prior to the adoption of IFRS 12, under paragraph 38 of IAS 28(2003) *Investments in Associates* to disclose separately the investor's share of the profits or losses of associates accounted for using the equity method).

Equally, an entity might present its share of the profits or losses of different associates and joint ventures in different line items if such presentation would be considered relevant to an understanding of the financial statements. For example, an entity might present its share of the profits or losses of some of its associates or joint ventures as part of profit from operations, when such a sub-total is presented (see **5.2.4**). Such a presentation might be useful for any of an entity's associates or joint ventures that are considered to be part of its operations.

When an entity chooses to segregate the profits or losses of different associates and joint ventures over different line items, it is not necessary to present a total for all such items. Before the IFRIC conclusion on net finance costs (see **5.2.2**), there had been some uncertainty regarding whether IAS 1:82 should be interpreted as requiring a single total for each item listed or whether several line items could be presented to represent a single requirement in IAS 1:82 (e.g. share of the profit or loss of associates and joint ventures accounted for using the equity method). The IFRIC conclusion on net finance costs effectively confirms that it is acceptable to present different categories of such items as individual line items without presenting a total.

Given that the results of equity method investments are presented on an after-tax basis (see above), the question arises as to whether these amounts are required to be presented above the tax expense line in profit or loss. In the list of items in IAS 1:82 (see **5.1.1** and **5.1.2** above), the share of profits or losses of investments accounted for using the equity method appears above tax expense. In the statement of comprehensive income shown in the illustrative financial statements accompanying IAS 1, the item is presented before the tax expense but after all other expenses (including finance costs). However, there is no requirement in the Standard that the items listed in IAS 1:82 must appear in any particular order. Therefore, it would be acceptable to present the share of profits or losses of investments accounted for using the equity method below the tax expense line (although, under IAS 1:88, it must always be presented before the 'profit for the period').

5.2.7   Presentation of tax-based structuring income

Example 5.2.7

Presentation of tax-based structuring income

Bank A undertakes to lend money to Company B. Under its general lending rates, Bank A would charge 12 per cent interest to a customer with Company B's credit profile. However, Bank A structures the loan so that it receives a favourable tax deduction and recovers half of the interest that it would have charged Company B from this deduction. Consequently, it charges Company B interest at 6 per cent and requires Company B to agree that if the tax deduction does not arise, or it is less than anticipated, Company B will pay the difference to Bank A as an increased interest charge.

Is it acceptable for Bank A to recognise interest income of 12 per cent in respect of its loan to Bank B and increase its tax expense accordingly?

No. The substance of the transaction is that Bank A has originated a loan that bears interest at 6 per cent. Tax and interest are separate items; they should be accounted for separately and presented in the tax line and the interest line, respectively, of the statement of comprehensive income.

5.2.8   Investment income as revenue

IAS 18:7 defines revenue as the gross inflow of economic resources during the period arising from ordinary activities, excluding inflows from equity participants. IAS 1:82 requires the disclosure of revenue in the statement of comprehensive income but IAS 1:85 requires the presentation of additional line items when necessary to explain the financial performance of the entity.

Paragraphs 4:29 and 4:30 of the *Conceptual Framework for Financial Reporting* distinguish 'revenue' from 'gains'. Investment income may include elements of both investment revenue (e.g. interest and dividends received) and other 'gains' (such as profits on sale of investments and gains on remeasurement to fair value).

Unless investment is one of the principal activities of the entity, in most circumstances it will be necessary to present investment revenue as a separate line item to explain the entity's financial performance. IAS 1:82 does not preclude the segregation of different types of revenue in this manner (see also **5.2.3** above).

Other gains and losses that do not meet the definition of revenue might be separately presented in the statement of comprehensive income, or they might be presented in a more general 'other gains and losses' line item, according to their materiality.

Note that IAS 18:35(b) (see **section 11** of **chapter A14**) requires entities to disclose the amount of each significant category of revenue recognised during the period, including revenue arising from interest and revenue arising from dividends.

5.2.9   Exchange gains and losses

Paragraph 52(a) of IAS 21 *The Effects of Changes in Foreign Exchange Rates* requires an entity to disclose the amount of exchange differences recognised in profit or loss, except for those arising on financial instruments measured at fair value through profit or loss in accordance with IFRS 9 (or, prior to the adoption of IFRS 9, IAS 39).

IAS 21 is silent regarding the appropriate classification in profit or loss of foreign exchange gains and losses. Foreign exchange gains and losses should be classified based on the nature of the transactions or events which give rise to those foreign exchange gains or losses. For example, it may be appropriate to recognise foreign exchange gains and losses on operational items (trade receivables, payables etc.) within income from operations, and foreign exchange gains and losses on issued debt as part of finance costs (but not within interest payable).

Classification of foreign exchange gains or losses in profit or loss is a matter of accounting policy which must be disclosed and applied consistently year-on-year. In addition, when the impact of foreign exchange gains or losses is material, in accordance with IAS 1:97 (see **5.4.1** below), their nature and amount should be disclosed separately, either in the statement of comprehensive income or in the notes. Therefore, for example, when an entity classifies foreign exchange gains or losses on operating items within income from operations, and the impact of these is material, the entity may elect to present foreign exchange gains and losses on operating items as a separate line item within income from operations.

5.2.10 Fair value gains and losses on derivatives that are economic hedges

The presentation of gains and losses on derivatives that are economic hedges when hedge accounting is not applied is discussed at **5.2.2** in **chapter B4** (or, for entities that have not yet adopted IFRS 9, **5.2.2** in **chapter C4**).

5.2.11 Release of provisions

A provision should be used only for expenditures for which the provision was originally recognised. [IAS 37:61] This means that when an entity finally settles the liability, the payment should be recorded against the provision.

However, the amount of cash paid does not always equal the amounts of provisions at the date of the payment, as illustrated in the following example.

Example 5.2.11

Amount of cash payment differs from provision amount

Company A recognised a restructuring provision under IAS 37 in 20X1 and the amount was included in 'other expenses'. In 20X2, the expenditure was

---

> paid in cash and the amount paid was different from the amount recognised as a provision in the previous year. The difference between the two amounts will be recognised in 20X2, either as an additional expense or as a gain due to the release of the provision, in the same line item in which the related restructuring expense was recorded in 20X1 (i.e. it should be included in 'other expenses').

Section 6 of chapter A12 addresses changes in provisions.

5.3   Other comprehensive income

5.3.1   Items to be presented in other comprehensive income

Other comprehensive income (OCI) comprises items of income and expense (including reclassification adjustments) that are not recognised in profit or loss as required or permitted by IFRSs and includes:
[IAS 1:7]

- changes in revaluation surplus (see IAS 16 *Property, Plant and Equipment* and IAS 38 *Intangible Assets*);

- for entities that have adopted IAS 19(2011) *Employee Benefits*, remeasurements of defined benefit plans (see IAS 19(2011));

- for entities that have not yet adopted IAS 19(2011), actuarial gains and losses on defined benefit plans (see IAS 19(1998));

- gains and losses arising from translating the financial statements of a foreign operation (see IAS 21 *The Effects of Changes in Foreign Exchange Rates*);

- for entities that have adopted IFRS 9 *Financial Instruments*, gains and losses from investments in equity instruments measured at fair value through other comprehensive income;

- for entities that have not yet adopted IFRS 9, gains and losses on remeasuring available-for-sale financial assets (see IAS 39 *Financial Instruments: Recognition and Measurement*);

- the effective portion of gains and losses on hedging instruments in a cash flow hedge (see IAS 39); and

- for entities that have adopted IFRS 9, for particular liabilities designated as at fair value through profit or loss, the amount of the change in fair value that is attributable to changes in the liability's credit risk (see IFRS 9(2010):5.7.7).

The credit recognised in equity for equity-settled share-based payments in accordance with IFRS 2 *Share-based Payment* should not be included in OCI. This is because it arises from a transaction with owners in their capacity as such. The net credit represents either the proceeds of the grant of an equity instrument or, when a subsidiary recognises an expense for a grant of its parent's equity instruments, a capital contribution from the parent.

5.3.2   Information to be presented in the other comprehensive income section

The other comprehensive income section of the statement of comprehensive income is required to present line items for amounts of OCI in the period (see **5.3.1**), classified by nature and including the entity's share of the OCI of associates and joint ventures accounted for using the equity method). [IAS 1:82A]

Paragraph IAS 1:82A was added to the Standard as part of the June 2011 amendments to IAS 1. The general requirements regarding the amounts to be presented in the other comprehensive income section as set out above are unchanged (see **5.1.2** for the details required to be presented under the Standard prior to the June 2011 amendments). However, the grouping of items also required under IAS 1:82A (see below) is new. Further, the requirements regarding the presentation of an investor's share of the OCI of associates and joint ventures accounted for using the equity method have been amended, although the intentions of the Board in this regard are not very clear (see **5.3.2.1**).

The June 2011 amendments are effective for annual periods beginning on or after 1 July 2012, with earlier application permitted. If an entity applies the amendments for an earlier period, it is required to disclose that fact. [IAS 1:139J]

In the absence of specific transition provisions, the June 2011 amendments should be applied retrospectively, which means that amounts presented for comparative periods are required to be restated in the period in which the amendments are first applied.

For entities that have adopted the June 2011 amendments to IAS 1, the line items presented for amounts of OCI are required to be grouped into those that, in accordance with other IFRSs:
[IAS 1:82A]

- will not be reclassified subsequently to profit or loss; and

- will be reclassified subsequently to profit or loss when specific conditions are met.

5.3.2.1 Presentation of investor's share of OCI of associates and joint ventures

Prior to the June 2011 amendments, the requirements of IAS 1 regarding the presentation of an investor's share of the OCI of associates and joint ventures accounted for using the equity method are clear. IAS 1:82 (see **5.1.2**) includes within the minimum line items to be presented in the statement of comprehensive income "share of the other comprehensive income of associates and joint ventures accounted for using the equity method". Consistent with the equivalent requirement for the investor's share of the profit or loss of associates and joint ventures (see **5.2.6**), this should be interpreted as requiring a single line item rather than individual line items (for example, the investor's share of gains or losses on revaluation of property, plant and equipment, or relevant gains or losses on cash flow hedges). However, there is nothing to prevent disaggregation of this line item to show the OCI of associates separately from the OCI of joint ventures, or to present the OCI of different associates and joint ventures in different line items if such presentation would be considered relevant to an understanding of the financial statements (see **5.2.6**).

The 2011 amendments to IAS 1 made the following changes regarding the presentation of an investor's share of the OCI of associates and joint ventures accounted for using the equity method:

- paragraph 82A of the Standard now states that the OCI section should "present line items for amounts of other comprehensive income in the period, classified by nature (including share of the other comprehensive income of associates and joint ventures accounted for using the equity method", with no reference to a separate line item for associates and joint ventures;

- paragraph 82A of the Standard now requires items of OCI to be grouped into those that may and those that will not be reclassified subsequently to profit or loss. OCI of an associate or joint venture could include items in both of those categories; and

- the illustrative statement of comprehensive income in the implementation guidance accompanying the Standard now includes a line for "share of the gain (loss) on property revaluation of associates".

This may suggest a change in the requirements for presentation of an entity's share of OCI of associates and joint ventures. However:

- it appears counter intuitive to continue to prohibit presentation of the individual line items (i.e. revenue, finance costs etc.) of profit or loss of associates and joint ventures (the Standard has not changed in this respect) but to require such a presentation in OCI;

- the wording of the requirement to present items of OCI "classified by nature (including share of the other comprehensive income of associates and joint ventures ...)" could be read as stating that the investor's share of the OCI of associates and joint ventures is itself different in nature to the investor's own items of OCI;

- the illustrative presentation in the implementation guidance accompanying IAS 1 is inconclusive because, in the example provided, the associate has only one item of OCI (property revaluation movements); and

- the Basis for Conclusions on the June 2011 amendments to IAS 1 makes no reference to a change in the requirements regarding the presentation of items of OCI of associates and joint ventures.

Alternative approaches that seem to be acceptable under IAS 1:82A include the following.

- The investor presents separate line items for its share of each item of OCI of associates and joint ventures. This approach would require separate lines for each item because the investor's share of, for example, property revaluation movements of an associate is of a different 'nature' to the investor's share of relevant gains or losses on cash flow hedges of an associate.

This approach would be consistent with the presentation illustrated in the implementation guidance accompanying IAS 1.

- The investor presents a single line item for its share of OCI of associates and joint ventures (consistent with the approach prior to the June 2011 amendments); this line item would, when appropriate, be split between items that may be subsequently reclassified to profit or loss and those that will not.

5.3.3   Income tax

The amount of income tax relating to each item of OCI, including reclassification adjustments, should be disclosed either in the statement of profit or loss and other comprehensive income or in the notes. [IAS 1:90]

As explained in IAS 1:IN14, the purpose of this requirement is to provide users with tax information relating to the items of OCI because they often have tax rates different from those applied to profit or loss.

Paragraph IAS 1:90 has been updated by the June 2011 amendments to IAS 1 to reflect the revised title of the statement of profit or loss and other comprehensive income, but the underlying requirement is unchanged. However, the requirement in some circumstances to provide a further analysis of the tax (see below), which follows from the requirements of IAS 1:82A set out in the previous section, only applies to entities that have adopted the June 2011 amendments.

The items of OCI may be presented either:
[IAS 1:91]

- net of related tax effects; or

- before related tax effects with one amount shown for the aggregate amount of income tax relating to those items.

This permits a choice of presentation in the statement of comprehensive income. As explained in IAS 1:BC65, there are advantages to each method of presentation and the IASB decided to permit either to be used. However, when the income tax effects are aggregated into a single item on the face of the statement of comprehensive income, it is still necessary to disclose in the notes the amount of tax attributable to each item of OCI as required by IAS 1:90.

For entities that have adopted the June 2011 amendments to IAS 1, if the latter approach is taken (i.e. items of OCI are presented gross with a single amount shown for the aggregate amount of income tax), the amount of tax is required to be allocated between the items that might be reclassified subsequently to the profit or loss section and those that will not be reclassified subsequently to the profit or loss section. [IAS 1:91]

5.3.4   Reclassification adjustments

Reclassification adjustments are amounts reclassified to profit or loss in the current period that were recognised in OCI in the current or previous periods. [IAS 1:7]

Other IFRSs specify whether and when amounts previously recognised in other comprehensive income are reclassified to profit or loss. Such reclassifications are referred to in IAS 1 as 'reclassification adjustments'. A reclassification adjustment is included with the related component of OCI in the period that the adjustment is reclassified to profit or loss. [IAS 1:93]

The amounts that are reclassified may have been recognised in OCI as unrealised gains in the current or previous periods. Those unrealised gains must be deducted from OCI in the period in which the realised gains are reclassified to profit or loss to avoid including them twice in total comprehensive income. [IAS 1:93]

Reclassification adjustments arise, for example, on disposal of a foreign operation and when a hedged forecast transaction affects profit or loss. [IAS 1:95] Reclassification adjustments do not arise on changes in revaluation surplus recognised in accordance with IAS 16 or IAS 38. They also do not arise on remeasurements of defined benefit plans recognised in accordance with IAS 19(2011) (or, for entities that have not yet adopted IAS 19(2011), actuarial gains and losses on defined benefit plans recognised in accordance with IAS 19(1998):93A). These components are recognised in OCI and are not reclassified to profit or loss in subsequent periods. Changes in revaluation surplus may be transferred to retained earnings in subsequent periods as the asset is used or when it is derecognised. [IAS 1:96]

IAS 1 requires reclassification adjustments relating to components of OCI to be disclosed. [IAS 1:92] Such reclassification adjustments may be presented in the statement(s) of profit or loss and other comprehensive income or in the notes. When reclassification adjustments are presented in the notes, the items of OCI are stated after any related reclassification adjustments. [IAS 1:94]

5.3.5   *Entity has no items of other comprehensive income in the current or prior periods*

When an entity has no items of OCI to recognise in either the current or the comparative reporting period, the question arises as to how the statement of comprehensive income should be presented. In the absence of explicit guidance in IAS 1, the following treatments, among others, are acceptable (subject to regulatory/jurisdictional requirements):

- presentation of a statement of profit or loss ending with 'profit for the year', followed by a narrative statement to the effect that there were no items of comprehensive income in the current or prior year other than the profit for the year and, accordingly, no statement of comprehensive income is presented; or

- presentation of a single statement of comprehensive income ending with a total line for 'profit for the year and total comprehensive income'.

5.4   Information to be presented in the statement of profit or loss and other comprehensive income or in the notes

5.4.1   *General requirements*

IAS 1 requires that, when items of income and expense are material, their nature and amount should be disclosed separately. [IAS 1:97] The Standard lists the following items as examples of circumstances that would give rise to separate disclosure:
[IAS 1:98]

- write-downs of inventories to net realisable value, and reversals of such write-downs;

- write-downs of property, plant and equipment to recoverable amount, and reversals of such write-downs;

- restructuring of activities and reversals of any provisions for such costs;

- disposals of items of property, plant and equipment;

- disposals of investments;

- discontinued operations;

- litigation settlements; and

- other reversals of provisions.

5.4.2   Analysis by nature and function

An analysis of expenses recognised in profit or loss should be provided using a classification based on either the nature of the expenses (e.g. depreciation, employee costs etc.) or their function within the entity (e.g. cost of sales, administrative expenses etc.). The choice of classification method should be based on whichever provides information that is reliable and more relevant. [IAS 1:99] IAS 1 encourages, but does not require, this analysis to be in the statement(s) presenting profit or loss and other comprehensive income. [IAS 1:100]

IAS 1 explains that there are two forms of analysis whereby expenses are sub-classified to highlight components of financial performance that may differ in terms of their frequency, potential for gain or loss and predictability; these are analysis by nature and analysis by function. [IAS 1:101]

The first method of analysis is by the nature of expenses (e.g. depreciation, purchases of materials, transport costs, employee benefits and advertising costs). This method is simple to apply because no allocation of expenses to functional classifications is necessary. IAS 1 gives the following example of a classification using the nature of expense method. [IAS 1:102]

Example 5.4.2A
Analysis by nature of expense
[IAS 1:102]

Revenue		X
Other income		X
Changes in inventories of finished goods and work in progress	X	
Raw materials and consumables used	X	
Employee benefits expense	X	
Depreciation and amortisation expense	X	
Other expenses	X̲	
Total expenses		(X̲)
Profit before tax		X̲

The second method of analysis is by function (e.g. cost of sales, distribution costs and administrative expenses). At a minimum, cost of sales must be disclosed separately from other expenses when expenses are analysed by their function. This method can provide more relevant information to users than classification by nature. But allocating costs to functions may require arbitrary allocations and involve considerable judgement. IAS 1 gives the following example of a classification using the function of expense method. [IAS 1:103]

Example 5.4.2B

Analysis by function of expense
[IAS 1:103]

Revenue	X
Cost of sales	(X)
Gross profit	X
Other income	X
Distribution costs	(X)
Administrative expenses	(X)
Other expenses	(X)
Profit before tax	X

When an entity chooses to classify expenses by function, it is also required to disclose additional information on the nature of the expenses, including:
[IAS 1:104]

• depreciation and amortisation expense; and

• employee benefits expense (as defined in IAS 19 *Employee Benefits*).

Example 5.4.2C

Shipping and handling costs

Company A, acting in the capacity of principal, sells goods to a customer. Company A classifies expenses by function in its statement of comprehensive income. Company A may adopt a policy of including shipping and handling costs in cost of sales. This treatment is permitted by paragraph 38 of IAS 2 *Inventories*, which states that the circumstances of the entity may warrant the inclusion of distribution costs in cost of sales.

Alternatively, shipping and handling costs may be included in a separate 'distribution costs' classification or, if insignificant, in 'other operating expenses'. The key points are to ensure that:

- the classification is appropriate to the entity's circumstances;

- the classification is consistent from year to year; and

- material items are separately identified, as required by IAS 1:97 (see **5.4.1** above).

The presentation of shipping and handling costs as a deduction from revenue is not usually permitted (see **2.8** above). However, when Company A is acting as agent in relation to shipping the goods, it may be appropriate to net the shipping costs incurred and the shipping costs recharged (see **example 2.8D** above).

The choice between the two methods of analysis depends on historical and industry factors and the nature of the entity. Both methods provide an indication of those costs that might vary, directly or indirectly, with the level of sales or production. IAS 1 requires management to select the more relevant and reliable presentation because each method has merit for different types of entities. However, additional disclosure about the nature of the expenses is required when the primary analysis is by function because information on the nature of expenses is useful in predicting future cash flows. [IAS 1:105]

Ad hoc mixing of classifications of expenses by nature and function should be avoided. For example, it is not appropriate for an entity to classify expenses on a functional basis but exclude certain 'unusual' expenses from the functional classification to which they relate and present those items separately by nature. Examples are inventory write-downs, employee termination benefits and impairments.

This also applies in the consolidated financial statements of groups when some of the subsidiaries report their expenses by function and other subsidiaries report expenses by nature in their own IFRS financial statements. Management should select one method of presentation for expenses in the consolidated statement of comprehensive income (i.e. either by function or by nature). The financial statements of those subsidiaries using the other basis should be adjusted for the purposes of consolidation.

5.4.3   Columnar presentation in the statement of comprehensive income

There is nothing in IAS 1 to prevent the presentation of additional information in the statement of comprehensive income provided that it is not misleading. Such additional information is sometimes presented using a columnar layout, where the total column gives the amounts required by IAS 1 and the additional columns provide an analysis of some or all of those amounts. For example, separate columns might be used to present the results of two operating segments in the statement of comprehensive income. They may also be used to segregate certain types of income or expense such as those required to be disclosed separately under IAS 1:97 (see **5.4.1** above).

However, to avoid the risk that the additional information may be misleading, when this approach is used, the description of the columns should be unambiguous and as factual as possible. The descriptions should be clear enough to be understood by a general reader of the financial statements without further explanation. The use of terms such as 'core performance', 'underlying performance' and 'special items' should be avoided because they may be ambiguous or, in the extreme, misleading. When necessary, a clear definition should be provided for those items included in a separate column.

Entities should also consider the requirements of local regulators, particularly as regards the inclusion and labelling of non-GAAP measures in financial statements.

6   Statement of changes in equity

Changes in an entity's equity between the beginning and end of the reporting period reflect the increase or decrease in its net assets during the period. Except for changes resulting from transactions with owners in their capacity as owners (e.g. equity contributions and distributions), the overall change in equity during a period represents the total amount of income and expense, including gains and losses, generated by the entity's activities during that period. [IAS 1:109]

IAS 1 requires the presentation of a statement of changes in equity, to include the following information:
[IAS 1:106]

- total comprehensive income for the period, showing separately the total amounts attributable to owners of the parent and to non-controlling interests;

- for each component of equity, the effects of retrospective application or retrospective restatement recognised in accordance with IAS 8 *Accounting Policies, Changes in Accounting Estimates and Errors*; and

- for each component of equity, a reconciliation between the carrying amount at the beginning and the end of the period, separately disclosing changes resulting from:

  - profit or loss;

  - other comprehensive income; and

  - transactions with owners in their capacity as owners, showing separately contributions by and distributions to owners and changes in ownership interests in subsidiaries that do not result in a loss of control.

> The statement must present a reconciliation for each component of equity. It is not, therefore, acceptable to present a simple statement showing only the movements in total equity, with details of movements on individual components of equity provided in the notes. In fact, there is no explicit requirement in the Standard to provide totals, across all components of equity, for each type of movement. However, this is likely to be helpful in practice. For example, it will eliminate the effects of amounts transferred between different components of equity which have no effect on total equity.
>
> The statement of changes in equity set out in the illustrative financial statements accompanying IAS 1 adopts a columnar layout with a column for each component of equity and a total column. This format is not prescribed by the Standard but is commonly adopted in practice.

For the purpose of IAS 1:106, components of equity include, for example, each class of contributed equity, the accumulated balance of each class of OCI and retained earnings. [IAS 1:108]

The amount of dividends recognised as distributions to owners during the period, and the related amount of dividends per share, must be shown either in the statement of changes in equity or in the notes (see **6.1**). [IAS 1:107]

> It is necessary to show dividends, at least in aggregate, in the statement because they are one of the owner changes in equity.

However, details of individual dividends and the amounts per share will typically be shown in the notes, combined with the disclosures about dividends proposed or declared after the reporting period required by IAS 1:137(a) (see **7.4.2** below).

IAS 8 requires that changes in accounting policies be applied retrospectively, to the extent practicable, except when the transition provisions in another IFRS require otherwise. IAS 8 also requires that restatements to correct errors be made retrospectively, to the extent practicable. The effects of such retrospective adjustments and retrospective restatements are not changes in equity in the period, but they are included in the statement of changes in equity because they provide a reconciliation between the previous period's closing balance and the opening balance in the statement of changes in equity. [IAS 1:BC74]

IAS 1:106(b) requires disclosure in the statement of changes in equity of the total adjustment to each component of equity resulting, separately, from changes in accounting policies and from correction of errors. These adjustments are disclosed for each prior period and the beginning of the period. [IAS 1:110]

6.1   Dividends

6.1.1   General requirements

IAS 1 requires the amount of dividends recognised as distributions to owners during the period, and the related amount of dividends per share, to be presented either in the statement of changes in equity or in the notes. [IAS 1:107]

The presentation of such disclosures in the statement of comprehensive income is not permitted. IAS 1:BC75 explains that this is because dividends are distributions to owners in their capacity as owners and the statement of changes in equity presents all owner changes in equity. The Board concluded that an entity should not present dividends in the statement of comprehensive income because that statement presents non-owner changes in equity.

Further disclosures relating to dividends are considered at **7.4.2** below.

6.1.2   Distributions of non-cash assets to owners

6.1.2.1   Introduction

IFRIC 17 *Distributions of Non-cash Assets to Owners* addresses the following issues:

- when should the entity recognise the dividend payable?

- how should the entity measure the dividend payable?

- when it settles the dividend payable, how should the entity account for any difference between the carrying amount of the assets distributed and the carrying amount of the dividend payable?

IFRS 5 *Non-current Assets Held for Sale and Discontinued Operations* applies to a non-current asset (or disposal group) that is classified as held for distribution to owners acting in their capacity as owners (see **3.5** and **4.8** in **chapter A20**).

> Subject to certain scope exclusions, IFRIC 17 requires distributions of non-cash assets to be accounted for at the fair value of the assets concerned. This will often result in a profit being recognised when the distribution is settled.

6.1.2.2   Scope

IFRIC 17 applies to the following types of non-reciprocal distributions of assets by an entity to its owners acting in their capacity as owners: [IFRIC 17:3]

- distributions of non-cash assets (e.g. items of property, plant and equipment, businesses, ownership interests in another entity, or disposal groups as defined in IFRS 5); and

- distributions that give owners a choice of receiving either non-cash assets or a cash alternative.

The Interpretation applies only to distributions in which all owners of the same class of equity instruments are treated equally. [IFRIC 17:4]

> IFRIC 17:BC6 explains that distributions when owners of the same class of equity are treated differently may imply that at least some of the owners receiving the distribution gave up something to the entity

and/or to the other owners. In other words, such distributions might be more in the nature of exchange transactions.

In practice, such transactions are likely to be rare and will usually be with a controlling shareholder.

The Interpretation does not apply to a distribution of a non-cash asset that is ultimately controlled by the same party or parties before and after the distribution. This exclusion applies to the separate, individual and consolidated financial statements of an entity that makes a distribution. [IFRIC 17:5]

For the purpose of this scope exclusion, a group of individuals is regarded as controlling an entity when, as a result of contractual arrangements, they collectively have the power to govern its financial and operating policies so as to obtain benefits from its activities. This is consistent with the requirement in IFRS 3:B2 for the identification of common control transactions. Therefore, for a distribution to be outside the scope of IFRIC 17 on this basis, a group of individual shareholders receiving the distribution must have, as a result of contractual arrangements, such ultimate collective power over the entity making the distribution. [IFRIC 17:6]

Therefore, IFRIC 17 applies in the common situation of a demerger of a subsidiary by a listed entity that has no single controlling party. However, it will not apply to intragroup transactions when a subsidiary makes a distribution to its parent. Nor will it apply to distributions by private entities when there is a single controlling shareholder.

Similarly, IFRIC 17 does not apply when an entity distributes some of its ownership interests in a subsidiary but retains control of the subsidiary. The entity making a distribution that results in the entity recognising a non-controlling interest in its subsidiary should account for the distribution in accordance with IFRS 10 *Consolidated Financial Statements* (or, for entities that have not yet adopted IFRS 10, IAS 27(2008) *Consolidated and Separate Financial Statements*). [IFRIC 17:7]

For example, if a parent distributes 25 per cent of the shares in its wholly-owned subsidiary to its shareholders but retains control of that subsidiary, the transaction will be outside the scope of IFRIC 17.

In accordance with IFRS 10 (or, for entities that have not yet adopted IFRS 10, IAS 27(2008)), no profit or loss should be recognised on the transaction. In such circumstances, although there is a reallocation between parent and non-controlling interests, the assets and liabilities of the group do not change.

IFRIC 17 addresses only the accounting by the entity that makes the non-cash distribution. It does not address the accounting by shareholders who receive such a distribution. [IFRIC 17:8]

However, IFRIC 17:BC33 notes that dividend income, regardless of whether it is in the form of cash or non-cash assets, is within the scope of IAS 18 *Revenue* and is required to be measured at the fair value of the consideration received.

IFRIC 17 includes some simple examples regarding the application of these scope exclusions which are not reproduced here because they provide no significant interpretational guidance. The first example considers a distribution of available-for-sale securities and contrasts the position when there is not a controlling shareholder (i.e. the distribution is within the scope of IFRIC 17) and when there is a controlling shareholder (i.e. the distribution is not within the scope of IFRIC 17). The second example contrasts the distribution of the whole of a subsidiary by a parent that has no controlling party (i.e. the distribution is within the scope of IFRIC 17) with the distribution of shares in a subsidiary without loss of control by the parent (i.e. the distribution causes a non-controlling interest in the subsidiary to be recognised, and is not within the scope of IFRIC 17). [IFRIC 17:IE1 – IE4]

IFRIC 17 does not include an exemption on the grounds of cost or effort or practicality. The reasons for this are explained in IFRIC 17:BC28 to BC34. IFRIC 17:BC30 states that management would be expected to know the fair value of the asset because management has to ensure that all owners of the entity are informed of the value of the distribution. The IFRIC (now the IFRS Interpretations Committee), therefore, concluded that it would be difficult to argue that the fair value of the asset cannot be determined reliably. It is arguable that when all shareholders are treated in the same way they do not need to know the fair value of the distribution because the value of their total investment will be unaffected. Nevertheless, no scope exclusion is provided for these circumstances.

6.1.2.3 When to recognise a dividend

The liability to pay a dividend is recognised when the dividend is appropriately authorised and no longer at the discretion of the entity, which is the date:
[IFRIC 17:10]

- when declaration of the dividend (e.g. by management or the board of directors) is approved by the relevant authority (e.g. the shareholders) if the jurisdiction requires such approval; or

- when the dividend is declared (e.g. by management or the board of directors) if the jurisdiction does not require further approval.

As explained at **4.1** in **chapter A22**, the principle that a dividend is recognised when it is appropriately authorised and no longer at the discretion of the entity was previously in IAS 10 *Events after the Reporting Period* but has been removed as a consequential amendment of IFRIC 17. The reasons for this are given in IFRIC 17:BC18 to BC20 which explain that the Interpretation did not change the principle as to when to recognise a dividend payable. The principle was moved from IAS 10 into the Interpretation and clarified but without changing the principle. The 'declaration' of a dividend by management does not, therefore, result in a liability when that decision is subject to further approval or when management retains discretion to reverse its decision.

6.1.2.4 Measurement of a dividend payable

A liability to distribute a non-cash asset to owners should be measured at the fair value of the asset to be distributed. [IFRIC 17:11]

If the owners of the entity are given a choice of receiving either a non-cash asset or a cash alternative, the liability for the dividend payable is estimated by considering both the fair value of each alternative and the associated probability of owners selecting each alternative. [IFRIC 17:12]

The carrying amount of the dividend payable is reviewed and adjusted at the end of each reporting period and at the date of settlement. Any changes in the carrying amount are recognised in equity as adjustments to the amount of the distribution. [IFRIC 17:13]

6.1.2.5   Accounting for any difference on settlement

The difference, if any, between the carrying amount of the assets distributed and the carrying amount of the dividend payable is recognised in profit or loss when the dividend is settled. [IFRIC 17:14]

> When the fair value of the asset is higher than its carrying amount, the application of IFRIC 17:14 results in the recognition of a profit when the dividend is settled. It will be less usual for a loss to arise. If the fair value of the asset is less than its carrying amount, it will often have been written down for impairment prior to the distribution unless, depending on the nature of the asset, a higher value in use could be justified.

6.1.2.6   Presentation and disclosure

The difference arising on settlement of the dividend described at **6.1.2.5** above should be presented as a separate line item in profit or loss. [IFRIC 17:15]

The following information should be disclosed, if applicable: [IFRIC 17:16]

- the carrying amount of the dividend payable at the beginning and end of the period; and

- the increase or decrease in the carrying amount recognised in the period in accordance with IFRIC 17:13 as a result of a change in the fair value of the assets to be distributed.

If, after the end of the reporting period but before the financial statements are authorised for issue, an entity declares a dividend to distribute a non-cash asset, the financial statements should disclose: [IFRIC 17:17]

- the nature of the asset to be distributed;

- the carrying amount of the asset to be distributed as at the end of the reporting period;

- the estimated fair value of the asset to be distributed as at the end of the reporting period, if different from its carrying amount;

- for entities that have adopted IFRS 13 *Fair Value Measurement*, the information about the method(s) used to measure that fair value required by IFRS 13:9(b), (d), (g) and (i) and IFRS 13:99; and

- for entities that have not yet adopted IFRS 13, the information about the method used to determine that fair value required by IFRS 7:27(a) and (b).

6.1.3 Stock or scrip dividends

Companies sometimes issue shares as an alternative to a cash dividend. This is often termed a 'stock dividend', a 'share dividend' or a 'scrip dividend'. Shareholders are usually offered a choice between a cash dividend and a stock dividend alternative. When the dividend is structured such that it is probable that most of the shareholders will decide to take the shares, because the market value of the share alternative is above the cash alternative, the dividend is referred to as an 'enhanced stock dividend'.

Stock dividends may take different legal forms in different jurisdictions. How they affect, for example, distributable reserves and the balance on the share premium reserve will be governed by local legal requirements.

Pure stock dividends (i.e. those without a cash alternative) do not result in a reduction in equity and are not, therefore, strictly 'distributions to owners'. The statement of changes in equity will, therefore, show no net movement for a pure stock dividend.

However, when shareholders have a choice between receiving cash and receiving shares, this will typically involve a distribution to owners. IFRSs do not include any specific guidance on the appropriate accounting in such cases, but the choice of accounting policy may be restricted by local legal or regulatory requirements. One common approach is for the dividend to be shown in the statement of changes in equity, or the note required by IAS 1:137 (see **7.4.2** below), at its full 'cash equivalent' amount, irrespective of the extent to which shareholders choose to receive shares rather than cash. When the dividend is presented at its 'gross' or' full' amount in this manner, there will be also be a credit item in the statement of changes in equity to reflect the stock element of the dividend. The notes to the financial statements should provide an explanation of the stock dividend and the policy adopted to account for it. In the absence of clear guidance, other approaches may also be acceptable.

See **10.2** in **chapter A14** for a discussion of the appropriate accounting for stock dividends in the financial statements of the recipient.

6.2   Capital contributions

The term 'capital contribution' is not defined in IFRSs but is generally accepted as meaning a contribution by owners (i.e. a gift made to an entity by an owner which increases the entity's equity without any obligation for the entity to make repayment or to do anything in consideration for receiving it). Capital contributions are most often made by parent entities to their wholly-owned subsidiaries but they may be made in other circumstances. For example, a majority owner might make a capital contribution to an entity in some situations, even though this would result in the benefits being shared with the other owners.

The term 'capital contribution' may be used in some jurisdictions to include arrangements allowing for the contribution to be returned in certain circumstances. The assessment of whether such a contribution is classified as a liability or as equity is made in accordance with IAS 32 *Financial Instruments: Presentation* (see **chapter B3** or, for entities that have not yet adopted IFRS 9 *Financial Instruments*, **chapter C3**). For the purposes of the analysis below, it is assumed that the contribution is classified as equity in accordance with IAS 32.

Capital contributions are sometimes made for the purpose of improving the financial position of a subsidiary by increasing its net assets without formally increasing its issued share capital (e.g. so as to improve its credit rating). However, in some jurisdictions, capital contributions often serve another purpose which is to eliminate a deficit on distributable profits so that the payment of dividends can be resumed. This may not be achievable by an issue of shares.

Not all non-arm's length transactions between an entity and its owners are in the nature of capital contributions (or distributions). IFRSs do not impose a general requirement to reflect the fair value of such transactions although they require disclosure of related party transactions. Whether a particular transaction should be recognised as a capital contribution is a matter of judgement in the context of the particular facts and circumstances. As explained at **6.2.1** below, a waiver of inter-company debt is a common form of capital contribution.

6.2.1   Accounting for a waiver of intragroup debt

A capital contribution can arise from the waiver of a debt due by a subsidiary to its parent or through the assumption of the subsidiary's liabilities by the parent. A capital contribution can also arise if a subsidiary waives debt due from a fellow subsidiary in the same group. In this case, the waiver of the intragroup debt in one subsidiary is in effect a dividend up to the parent and a subsequent capital contribution from the parent to the fellow subsidiary. While each case should be considered based on the specific facts and circumstances, such transactions should generally be viewed as capital contributions unless there is clearly some other commercial purpose.

The actual amount of debt waived is determined by considering the specific circumstances. For example, in the case of an interest-bearing loan, the amount waived may consist of any principal not yet repaid together with any unpaid interest that has accrued up to the date of waiver. It would not be appropriate to recognise further interest income or expense on such a loan after it has been waived. Accordingly, it is important to establish the date on which the waiver was actually granted, based on a careful assessment of the facts, in order to establish the date on which the capital contribution should be recognised. Separately, the lender should consider whether the loan was already impaired and, if so, recognise any associated impairment loss before accounting for the waiver. (For further discussion of the appropriate accounting entries, see **4.2** and **example 4.2E** in **chapter B8** or, for entities that have not yet adopted IFRS 9, **4.2** and **example 4.2E** in **chapter C8**).

More generally, when a waiver or gift relates to a recent transaction, care should be taken to consider whether the waiver should be accounted for as the reversal of that recent transaction or as a capital contribution. Transactions that are conducted on a non-arms' length basis should be considered on a case-by-case basis to determine whether they result in a capital contribution. It will not usually be appropriate for the borrower to record credits in profit or loss as a result of a waiver of intragroup debt.

6.2.2   Accounting treatment of a capital contribution

A capital contribution should not be included in profit or loss for the period, nor within other comprehensive income. Instead, it should be shown as part of the statement of changes in equity (i.e. like the proceeds of a share issue). This is because the increase in shareholders' funds is not 'income' as defined in the *Conceptual Framework for Financial Reporting*. The Conceptual Framework defines income as follows.

[CF:4.25(a)]

> "Income is increases in economic benefits during the accounting period in the form of inflows or enhancements of assets or decreases of liabilities that result in increases in equity, other than those relating to contributions from equity participants."

Therefore, income cannot result from 'contributions from equity participants'.

There is no formal financial reporting guidance on the treatment of a capital contribution by the donor (parent) entity, although it is usually capitalised as part of the cost of investment. This is reasonable because, all other things being equal, the net assets of the subsidiary, and therefore its value as an investment, will have increased by the amount of the contribution. However, when the investment is accounted for at cost, it is important to consider whether the investment has suffered an impairment, particularly if the reason for making the contribution is to eliminate the effect of losses made by the subsidiary. An impairment loss should be recognised in respect of the investment, if necessary.

6.2.3   Capital contribution made by a parent to a subsidiary as part of a group share-based payment arrangement

When a parent enters into a share-based payment arrangement with employees of its subsidiary and the parent has the obligation to those employees, the subsidiary in its own financial statements measures the services received from its employees in accordance with the requirements of IFRS 2 *Share-based Payment* for equity-settled share-based payment arrangements. There is a corresponding increase recognised in equity as a capital contribution from the parent. The accounting by entities within groups for share-based payment arrangements is addressed in **section 8** of **chapter A16**.

There is no requirement within IFRSs to credit the capital contribution to a separate component of equity but this may be affected by local legal and regulatory requirements.

7   The notes

7.1   Structure

Notes contain information in addition to that presented in:
[IAS 1:7]

- the statement of financial position;

- the statement(s) of profit or loss and other comprehensive income (or, for entities that have not yet adopted the June 2011 amendments to IAS 1, the statement of comprehensive income and, if presented, the separate income statement);

- the statement of changes in equity; and

- the statement of cash flows.

Notes provide narrative descriptions or disaggregations of items presented in those statements and information about items that do not qualify for recognition in those statements. [IAS 1:7]

The notes are required to:
[IAS 1:112]

- present information about the basis of preparation of the financial statements and the specific accounting policies used in accordance with the relevant paragraphs of IAS 1 (see **7.2** below);

- disclose the information required by IFRSs that is not presented elsewhere in the financial statements; and

- provide additional information that is not presented elsewhere in the statements but is relevant to an understanding of any of them.

The notes should, so far as practicable, be presented in a systematic manner. Each item in the statement of financial position, the statement(s) of profit or loss and other comprehensive income (or, for entities that have not yet adopted the June 2011 amendments to IAS 1, the statement of comprehensive income and, if presented, the separate income statement), the statement of changes in equity and the statement of cash flows should be cross referenced to any related information in the notes. [IAS 1:113] The

281

notes are normally presented in the following order, which assists users to understand the financial statements and compare them with financial statements of other entities:
[IAS 1:114]

- a statement of compliance with IFRSs (see **section 3** above);

- a summary of significant accounting policies applied (see **7.2** below);

- supporting information for items presented in the financial statements in the order in which each statement and each line item is presented; and

- other disclosures including:

  - contingent liabilities (see **chapter A12**) and unrecognised contractual commitments; and

  - non-financial disclosures, for example an entity's financial risk management objectives and policies (see **chapter B12** or, for entities that have not yet adopted IFRS 9 *Financial Instruments*, **chapter C12**).

In some circumstances, it may be necessary or desirable to vary the order of specific items within the notes. For example, information on changes in fair value recognised in profit or loss may be combined with information on maturities of financial instruments, although the former disclosures relate to the statement(s) presenting profit or loss and other comprehensive income, whereas the latter relate to the statement of financial position. Nevertheless, a systematic structure for the notes should be retained as far as practicable. [IAS 1:115]

> There is a case for putting all of the disclosures about financial instruments required by IFRS 7 in a single note (or a series of notes). This will combine the disclosures about the impact of financial instruments on the statement of financial position and the statement of comprehensive income in one place.

Notes providing information about the basis of preparation of the financial statements and specific accounting policies may be presented as a separate section of the financial statements. [IAS 1:116]

> That is to say, it is acceptable to present a statement of accounting policies that does not form one of the numbered notes to the financial statements.

7.1.1   *Non-current assets held for sale and discontinued operations*

IFRS 5 *Non-current Assets Held for Sale and Discontinued Operations* clarifies the extent to which the disclosures required by other Standards apply to non-current assets (or disposal groups) held for sale and discontinued operations. It confirms that disclosures required by other IFRSs do not apply to such assets (or disposal groups) or operations unless those IFRSs require:
[IFRS 5:5B]

* specific disclosures in respect of non-current assets (or disposal groups) classified as held for sale or discontinued operations; or

* disclosures about measurement of assets and liabilities within a disposal group that are not within the scope of the measurement requirements of IFRS 5 and such disclosures are not already provided in the other notes to the financial statements.

IFRS 5 also notes that additional disclosures about non-current assets (or disposal groups) classified as held for sale or discontinued operations may be necessary to comply with the general requirements of IAS 1, particularly paragraphs 15 (see **section 3** above) and 125 (see **7.3** below).

> The notes supporting the statement of comprehensive income as required by IAS 1 and other Standards will therefore exclude amounts for any discontinued operations. For example, the analysis of expenses by nature and function (see **5.4.2** above) will include only amounts for continuing operations. However, it may be helpful, in some cases, to use a columnar layout to present amounts for continuing operations, discontinued operations and the combined total. This will enable the total amount to be reconciled with other disclosures such as depreciation disclosed in the note for property, plant and equipment.

(For further discussion related to this topic, see **6.2.1** and **section 7** in **chapter A20**.)

7.2   Disclosure of accounting policies

The financial statements should include a summary of significant accounting policies that includes:
[IAS 1:117]

* the measurement basis (or bases) used in preparing the financial statements; and

- the other accounting policies used that are relevant to an understanding of the financial statements.

7.2.1 Measurement bases

It is important that users of the financial statements are informed about the measurement basis or bases used because the basis will significantly affect their analysis. Examples of measurement bases are historical cost, current cost, net realisable value, fair value and recoverable amount. When more than one measurement basis is used in the financial statements (e.g. when particular classes of assets are revalued), it is sufficient to provide an indication of the categories of assets and liabilities to which each measurement basis is applied. [IAS 1:118]

7.2.2 Accounting policies

In deciding whether a particular accounting policy should be disclosed, management considers whether disclosure would assist users in understanding how transactions, other events and conditions are reflected in the reported financial performance and position. Disclosure of particular accounting policies is especially useful to users when those policies are selected from alternatives allowed in IFRSs. For example, an entity would disclose whether it applies the fair value or cost model to its investment property. Some IFRSs that permit a choice of policies contain specific disclosure requirements about those choices. For example, IAS 16 *Property, Plant and Equipment* requires disclosure of the measurement bases used for classes of property, plant and equipment. [IAS 1:119]

Each entity considers the nature of its operations and the policies that the users of its financial statements would expect to be disclosed for that type of entity. For example, an entity that is subject to income taxes would be expected to disclose its policies for accounting for taxes, including those for deferred tax. Similarly, an entity with significant foreign operations or transactions in foreign currencies should disclose its policies for the recognition of foreign exchange gains and losses. [IAS 1:120]

An accounting policy may be significant because of the nature of an entity's operations even if amounts for current or prior periods are not material. It is also appropriate to disclose each significant policy that is not specifically required by IFRSs but is selected and applied in accordance with IAS 8 *Accounting Policies, Changes in Accounting Estimates and Errors*. [IAS 1:121]

Although IAS 1 highlights the particular importance of the disclosure of policies if there is a choice under the relevant IFRS, it is clear that significant policies should be disclosed even if there is no choice. This is required by the Standard and is useful for users of the financial statements who may not be familiar with all of the requirements of the applicable Standards.

7.2.3 *Judgements that management has made*

The summary of significant accounting policies or other notes should disclose the judgements management has made, in the process of applying the entity's accounting policies, that have the most significant effect on the amounts recognised in the financial statements. This requirement excludes judgements involving estimations, which are subject to a separate disclosure requirement (see **7.3** below). [IAS 1:122]

In the process of applying the entity's accounting policies, management makes various judgements, apart from those involving estimations, that can significantly affect the amounts recognised in the financial statements. Examples given in IAS 1 include:
[IAS 1:123]

* for entities that have not yet adopted IFRS 9, whether financial assets are held-to-maturity investments;

* when substantially all the significant risks and rewards of ownership of financial assets and lease assets are transferred to other entities; and

* whether, in substance, particular sales of goods are financing arrangements and, therefore, do not give rise to revenue.

In some instances, similar disclosures are specifically required by other IFRSs. For example, IAS 40 *Investment Property* requires, when classification is difficult, disclosure of the criteria developed to distinguish investment property from owner-occupied property and property held for sale in the ordinary course of business. [IAS 1:124]

Disclosure of the most important judgements helps users of financial statements to understand how accounting policies have been applied and to make comparisons between entities. Accordingly, such disclosures are most useful when they avoid 'boilerplate' and explain clearly the most important judgements made.

7.3   Key sources of estimation uncertainty

When there are uncertainties that have a significant risk of causing material adjustment to the carrying amount of assets and liabilities within the next financial year, the notes should disclose:
[IAS 1:125]

- information about the assumptions concerning the future; and

- other major sources of estimation uncertainty at the end of the reporting period.

In respect of those assets and liabilities, the notes should include details of:
[IAS 1:125]

- their nature; and

- their carrying amount at the end of the reporting period.

The disclosures of particular judgements that management made in the process of applying the entity's accounting policies (see **7.2.3** above) do not relate to the disclosures of sources of estimation uncertainty described in this section. [IAS 1:132]

Determining the carrying amount of some assets and liabilities requires estimation of the effects of uncertain future events. For example, in the absence of recently observed market prices, future-oriented estimates are necessary to measure:

- the recoverable amount of classes of property, plant and equipment;

- the effect of technological obsolescence on inventories;

- provisions subject to the future outcome of litigation in progress; and

- long-term employee benefit liabilities such as pension obligations.

These estimates involve assumptions about such items as the risk adjustment to cash flows or discount rates, future changes in salaries and future changes in prices affecting other costs. [IAS 1:126]

The assumptions and other sources of estimation uncertainty to be disclosed relate to the estimates that require management's most difficult, subjective or complex judgements. Those judgements become more subjective and complex as the number of variables and assumptions affecting the possible future resolution increases. The potential for a consequential material adjustment to the carrying amount of assets and liabilities normally increases accordingly. [IAS 1:127]

These disclosures are not required for assets or liabilities that are measured at fair value based on a quoted price in an active market for an identical asset or liability. This is so even if there is a significant risk that their carrying amounts might change materially within the next financial year. This is because these changes would not arise from assumptions or other sources of estimation uncertainty at the end of the reporting period. [IAS 1:128]

These disclosures should be presented in a manner that helps users of the financial statements to understand the judgements management makes about the future and about other key sources of estimation uncertainty. The nature and extent of the information to be disclosed will vary according to the nature of the assumptions and the other circumstances. Examples in IAS 1 of the types of disclosures to be made are: [IAS 1:129]

- the nature of the assumption or other estimation uncertainty;

- the sensitivity of the carrying amounts to the methods, assumptions and estimates underlying their calculation, including the reasons for the sensitivity;

- the expected resolution of an uncertainty and the range of reasonably possible outcomes within the next financial year in respect of the carrying amounts of the assets and liabilities affected; and

- an explanation of changes made to past assumptions concerning those assets and liabilities, if the uncertainty remains unresolved.

However, the Standard confirms that it is not necessary to disclose budget information or forecasts in making these disclosures. [IAS 1:130]

It may be impracticable to disclose the extent of the possible effects of an assumption or another key source of estimation uncertainty at the end of the reporting period. In this case, the entity discloses that it is reasonably possible, based on existing knowledge, that outcomes within the next financial year that are different from assumptions could require a material adjustment to the carrying amount of the affected asset or liability. In all cases, the nature and the carrying amount of the specific asset or liability (or class of assets or liabilities) is disclosed. [IAS 1:131]

Some other IFRSs include specific requirements for disclosures that would otherwise be required by IAS 1. The following examples are given in IAS 1: [IAS 1:133]

- IAS 37 *Provisions, Contingent Liabilities and Contingent Assets* requires disclosures, in specified circumstances, of major assumptions concerning future events affecting classes of provisions;

- for entities that have adopted IFRS 13 *Fair Value Measurement*, that Standard requires disclosure of significant assumptions (including the valuation technique(s) and inputs) the entity uses when measuring the fair values of assets and liabilities that are carried at fair value;

- for entities that have not yet adopted IFRS 13, IFRS 7 *Financial Instruments: Disclosures* requires disclosure of significant assumptions used in estimating fair values of financial assets and financial liabilities that are carried at fair value; and

- for entities that have not yet adopted IFRS 13, IAS 16 requires disclosure of significant assumptions used in estimating fair values of revalued items of property, plant and equipment.

It is noteworthy that IAS 1:BC81 states that the disclosures described in this section would be made "in respect of relatively few assets and liabilities (or classes of them)" because they relate only to the most difficult, subjective or complex judgements.

It is also important to understand that the scope of the disclosure is limited to items that have a significant risk of causing material adjustment to the carrying amount of assets or liabilities "within the next financial year". IAS 1:BC84 explains that the longer the future period to which the disclosures relate, the greater the range of items that would qualify for disclosure and the less specific those disclosures could be made. Therefore, the IASB decided to limit the scope of the requirement in this way, noting that a period longer than the next financial year might obscure the most relevant information with other disclosures.

7.4   Other disclosures

7.4.1   *Details about the entity*

The following should be disclosed in the financial statements, unless disclosed elsewhere in information published with the financial statements:
[IAS 1:138]

- the domicile and legal form of the entity;

- its country of incorporation;

- the address of its registered office (or principal place of business, if different);

- a description of the nature of the entity's operations and its principal activities;

- the name of the parent and the ultimate parent of the group; and

- if the entity is a limited life entity, information about the length of its life.

7.4.2 Dividends

IAS 1 requires disclosure in the notes of:
[IAS 1:137]

- the amount of dividends proposed or declared before the financial statements were authorised for issue but not recognised as a distribution to owners;

- the related amount per share; and

- the amount of any cumulative preference dividends not recognised.

These disclosures are in addition to the disclosure required for the amount of dividends recognised as distributions to owners during the period and the related amount per share (see **6.1** above).

7.4.3 Disclosures about service concession arrangements

SIC-29 *Service Concession Arrangements: Disclosures* specifies the disclosures that are required for such arrangements to meet the requirements of IAS 1:112(c) (see **7.1** above). These paragraphs require disclosures to provide additional information that is not presented in the primary financial statements but is relevant to an understanding of them.

Examples of service concession arrangements given in SIC-29 are water treatment and supply facilities, motorways, car parks, tunnels, bridges, airports and telecommunications networks. SIC-29 also explains that outsourcing the operation of an entity's internal services (e.g. employee restaurant, building maintenance, accounting or IT functions) are not service concession arrangements. [SIC-29:1]

Certain aspects and disclosures relating to some service concession arrangements are addressed in other Standards. For example, IAS 16 would apply to property, plant and equipment used in a service concession arrangement. However, SIC-29 points out that service concession arrangements may involve executory contracts that are not addressed in IFRSs, unless the contracts are onerous, in which case IAS 37 applies.

SIC-29, therefore, addresses additional disclosures that are relevant to service concession arrangements. [SIC-29:5]

All aspects of service concession arrangements should be considered in determining the appropriate disclosure in the notes. An operator and a grantor should disclose the following in each period:
[SIC-29:6]

- a description of the arrangement;

- significant terms of the arrangement that may affect the amount, timing and certainty of future cash flows (e.g. the period of the concession, repricing dates and the basis upon which repricing or renegotiation is determined);

- the nature and extent (e.g. quantity, time period or amount as appropriate) of:

  - rights to use specified assets;

  - obligations to provide or rights to expect provision of services;

  - obligations to acquire or build items of property, plant and equipment;

  - obligations to deliver or rights to receive specified assets at the end of the concession period;

  - renewal and termination options; and

  - other rights and obligations (e.g. major overhauls);

- changes in the arrangement occurring during the period; and

- how the service arrangement has been classified.

In addition, an operator discloses the amount of revenue and profits or losses recognised in the period on exchanging construction services for a financial asset or an intangible asset. [SIC-29:6A]

These disclosures are required to be provided individually for each service concession arrangement or in aggregate for each class of service concession arrangements. For this purpose, a class is a grouping of service concession arrangements involving services of a similar nature. For example, arrangements for water treatment services could be treated as a class. [SIC-29:7]

The accounting for certain infrastructure relating to service concession arrangements is dealt with by IFRIC 12 *Service Concession Arrangements* (see **chapter A35**).

IFRIC 12 explains how an operator should account for infrastructure that it constructs or acquires from a third party for the purpose of the service arrangement, but which is controlled by the grantor. The scope of SIC-29 is wider than this and includes, for example, arrangements in which the operator controls the infrastructure and also applies to the grantor in service concession arrangements.

7.4.4   Capital disclosures

An entity is required to disclose information that enables users of its financial statements to evaluate the entity's objectives, policies and processes for managing capital. [IAS 1:134]

To comply with this principle, IAS 1 requires an entity to disclose the following:
[IAS 1:135]

- qualitative information about its objectives, policies and processes for managing capital, including but not limited to:

    - a description of what it manages as capital;

    - when an entity is subject to externally imposed capital requirements, the nature of those requirements and how those requirements are incorporated into the management of capital; and

    - how it is meeting its objectives for managing capital;

- summary quantitative data about what it manages as capital. Some entities regard some financial liabilities (e.g. some forms of subordinated debt) as part of capital. Other entities regard capital as excluding some components of equity (e.g. components arising from cash flow hedges);

- any changes in the foregoing from the previous period;

- whether, during the period, it has complied with any externally imposed capital requirements to which it is subject; and

- when the entity has not complied with the externally imposed capital requirements to which it is subject, the consequences of such non-compliance.

The Standard requires these disclosures to be based on the information provided internally to the entity's key management personnel.

Loan covenants that affect how an entity manages its capital are conditions of a contract between the entity and the lender and are not 'capital requirements'. Consequently, the requirement of IAS 1:135 to disclose the nature of capital requirements and how those requirements are incorporated into the management of capital does not apply. Only capital requirements imposed by external regulators are required to be disclosed under IAS 1:135.

Although IAS 1:134 and 135 do not provide any further guidance regarding what is meant by 'externally imposed capital requirements', paragraphs BC92 to BC97 of the Basis for Conclusions on IAS 1 effectively narrow the scope of the requirements to "entity-specific requirement[s] imposed on a particular entity by its prudential supervisor or other regulator".

Although disclosure of details regarding loan covenants is not required under IAS 1:135, entities should consider whether such details should nevertheless be disclosed in line with the requirements in IAS 1:17 (see **3.2**) to provide additional information to enable users of the financial statements to understand the impact of particular transactions, other events and conditions on the entity's financial position and financial performance.

An entity may manage capital in a number of ways and be subject to a number of different capital requirements. A conglomerate may include entities that undertake banking activities and insurance activities. Those entities may operate in several jurisdictions. When an aggregate disclosure of capital requirements and how capital is managed would not provide useful information or distorts a financial statement user's understanding of an entity's capital resources, the entity should disclose separate information for each capital requirement to which it is subject. [IAS 1:136]

These disclosures are required for all entities, not just regulated entities.

7.4.5   Puttable financial instruments classified as equity

The following disclosures are required for puttable financial instruments classified as equity instruments:
[IAS 1:136A]

- summary quantitative data about the amount classified as equity;

- the entity's objectives, policies and processes for managing its obligation to repurchase or redeem the instruments when required to do so by the instrument holders, including any change from the previous period;

- the expected cash outflow on redemption or repurchase of that class of financial instruments; and

- information about how the expected cash outflow on redemption or repurchase was determined.

Puttable financial instruments have the same meaning as in IAS 32 *Financial Instruments: Presentation* (see **2.1.2** in **chapter B3** or, for entities that have not yet adopted IFRS 9, **2.1.2** in **chapter C3**). [IAS 1:8A]

7.4.6   Employee benefit expense

Whether management elects to report expenses by their nature or by function, the entity will need to disclose an employee benefit expense. Employee benefits in IAS 1 have the same meaning as employee benefits in IAS 19 (see **chapter A15** and **appendix A3**). [IAS 1:104 & 105]

7.4.7   Disclosures for joint operations or proportionately consolidated jointly controlled entities

IFRS 11 *Joint Arrangements* requires a joint operator to recognise its share of the assets, liabilities, revenues and expenses of a joint operation in accordance with the IFRSs applicable to those revenues and expenses. For an entity that has not yet adopted IFRS 11, IAS 31 *Interests in Joint Ventures* requires a similar approach for any jointly controlled entities that are proportionately consolidated, any jointly controlled assets and any jointly controlled operations. In such circumstances, line items in the entity's financial statements may include amounts relating to operations that are jointly controlled. IAS 1, IFRS 11 and IAS 31 do not provide any guidance on whether amounts disclosed in the notes required by IAS 1 should include amounts for such operations.

The supporting notes are generally expected to reconcile with the totals presented in the primary financial statements, so they should include amounts in relation to such operations. In some cases, this may lead to a higher level of disclosure in relation to such amounts than would have been required under the equity method.

This approach should also be used for other note disclosures that are not directly linked to totals that appear in the primary financial statements. For example, this would apply to the disclosure of employee benefits expense required by IAS 1:104. However, because IAS 1 is not explicit in this regard, it is important that the basis used (i.e. included or excluded) is explained in the financial statements if this could have a material effect on the amounts disclosed.

A5 Accounting policies, changes in accounting estimates and errors

Contents

1   Introduction

IAS 8 *Accounting Policies, Changes in Accounting Estimates and Errors* was published in 2003. It was most recently amended in May 2011.

The objective of IAS 8 is to prescribe the criteria for selecting and changing accounting policies. IAS 1 *Presentation of Financial Statements* (see **chapter A4**) sets out the disclosure requirements for accounting policies (excluding changes in accounting policies); IAS 8 deals with the accounting and disclosure requirements regarding changes in accounting policies, changes in accounting estimates and the correction of errors.

2   Definitions

IAS 8:5 contains definitions of certain terms used in the Standard. This section sets out these definitions with further explanations when necessary.

2.1   Accounting policies

Accounting policies are defined as follows.
[IAS 8:5]

> "[T]he specific principles, bases, conventions, rules and practices applied by an entity in preparing and presenting financial statements."

This definition is fundamental to the sections of IAS 8 dealing with the selection of accounting policies (see **3.1** below) and changes in accounting policies (see **3.2** below). In particular, it is necessary to distinguish between changes in accounting policies and changes in accounting estimates (see **2.2** below).

2.2   Changes in accounting estimates

A change in an accounting estimate is defined as follows.
[IAS 8:5]

> "[A]n adjustment of the carrying amount of an asset or a liability, or the amount of the periodic consumption of an asset, that results from the assessment of the present status of, and expected future benefits and obligations associated with, assets and liabilities. Changes in accounting estimates result from new information or new developments and, accordingly, are not corrections of errors."

The identification, recognition and disclosure of changes in accounting estimates are considered in **section 4** below.

2.3   International Financial Reporting Standards (IFRSs)

International Financial Reporting Standards are defined as follows.
[IAS 8:5]

> "[T]he Standards and Interpretations adopted by the International Accounting Standards Board (IASB). They comprise:
>
> a)   International Financial Reporting Standards;
>
> b)   International Accounting Standards;
>
> c)   IFRIC Interpretations; and
>
> d)   SIC Interpretations."

IFRSs are accompanied by guidance to assist entities applying their requirements. All such guidance states whether it is an integral part of IFRSs. Guidance that is an integral part of IFRSs is mandatory. Guidance that is not an integral part of IFRSs does not contain requirements for financial statements. [IAS 8:9]

IAS 8:9 is clear that implementation guidance published with an IFRS does not form part of that IFRS and, therefore, is not mandatory.

However, although such guidance does not contain mandatory requirements, it is nevertheless indicative of the way in which the IASB believes the Standard should be implemented. Departures from such guidance should, therefore, be made only after careful consideration and when they can be demonstrated to be fully justified.

Agenda decisions issued by the IFRS Interpretations Committee do not form part of IFRSs. However, these agenda decisions can be considered when selecting a suitable accounting policy for a transaction not specifically addressed by a Standard or Interpretation (see **3.1** below).

2.4   Material

The term 'material' is defined as follows.
[IAS 8:5]

> "Omissions or misstatements are material if they could, individually or collectively, influence the economic decisions that users make on the basis of

the financial statements. Materiality depends on the size and nature of the omission or misstatement judged in the surrounding circumstances. The size or nature of the item, or both, could be the determining factor."

The concept of materiality is also considered in the IASB's Conceptual Framework (see **5.1.1** in **chapter A2**). The definition of material omissions or misstatements is relevant to the determination of whether prior period errors (see **2.5** below) are material. This, in turn, determines whether retrospective restatement is required when such errors have arisen in a prior period (see **section 5** below).

2.5   Prior period errors

Prior period errors are defined as follows.
[IAS 8:5]

"[O]missions from, and misstatements in, the entity's financial statements for one or more prior periods resulting from a failure to use, or misuse of, reliable information that:

a)   was available when financial statements for those periods were authorised for issue; and

b)   could reasonably be expected to have been obtained and taken into account in the preparation and presentation of those financial statements.

Such errors include the effects of mathematical mistakes, mistakes in applying accounting policies, oversights or misinterpretations of facts, and fraud."

As explained at **5.2** below, IAS 8 requires all material prior period errors to be corrected by retrospective restatement unless this is impracticable.

2.6   Retrospective application and restatement

Retrospective application is defined as follows.
[IAS 8:5]

"Retrospective application is applying a new accounting policy to transactions, other events and conditions as if that policy had always been applied."

Retrospective restatement is defined as follows.
[IAS 8:5]

> "Retrospective restatement is correcting the recognition, measurement and disclosure of amounts of elements of financial statements as if a prior period error had never occurred."

2.7 Prospective application

Prospective application is defined as follows.
[IAS 8:5]

> "Prospective application of a change in accounting policy and of recognising the effect of a change in an accounting estimate, respectively, are:
>
> a) applying the new accounting policy to transactions, other events and conditions occurring after the date as at which the policy is changed; and
>
> b) recognising the effect of the change in the accounting estimate in the current and future periods affected by the change."

2.8 Impracticable

The term 'impracticable' is defined as follows.
[IAS 8:5]

> "Applying a requirement is impracticable when the entity cannot apply it after making every reasonable effort to do so. For a particular prior period, it is impracticable to apply a change in accounting policy retrospectively or make a retrospective restatement to correct an error if:
>
> a) the effects of the retrospective application or retrospective restatement are not determinable;
>
> b) the retrospective application or retrospective restatement requires assumptions about what management's intent would have been in that period; or
>
> c) the retrospective application or retrospective restatement requires significant estimates of amounts and it is impossible to distinguish objectively information about those estimates that:
>
>> i. provides evidence of circumstances that existed on the date(s) as at which those amounts are to be recognised, measured or disclosed; and
>>
>> ii. would have been available when the financial statements for that prior period were authorised for issue
>
> from other information."

For some types of estimates (e.g. a fair value measurement that uses significant unobservable inputs), it is impracticable to distinguish these types of information. When retrospective application or retrospective restatement would require making a significant estimate for which it is impossible to distinguish these two types of information, it is impracticable to apply the new accounting policy or correct the prior period error retrospectively. [IAS 8:52]

> This definition is relevant to exemptions from the general rule of retrospective application for changes in accounting policies (see **3.2** below) and the correction of material prior period errors (see **5.2** below). Impracticability in respect of retrospective application and retrospective restatement are considered further in **section 6** below.

3   Accounting policies

3.1   Selection of accounting policies

When an IFRS specifically applies to a transaction, other event or condition, the accounting policy or policies applied to that item are determined by applying the IFRS. [IAS 8:7]

It is not necessary to apply these policies if the effect of applying them is immaterial. But this does not mean that immaterial departures from IFRSs can be made, or left uncorrected, in order to achieve a particular presentation of an entity's financial position, performance or cash flows. [IAS 8:8]

> In practice, an entity will sometimes wish to consider applying the requirements of IFRSs even when the effect is immaterial. This is in part because materiality is subject to judgement based on both quantitative and qualitative factors, but also because items that are not material in the current period may become material in a subsequent period.

If there is no IFRS that specifically applies to the transaction, event or condition under consideration, judgement is required by management in developing and applying an accounting policy that results in information that is:
[IAS 8:10]

- relevant to the economic decision-making needs of users; and

- reliable, in that the financial statements:

  - represent faithfully the financial position, financial performance and cash flows of the entity;

  - reflect the economic substance of transactions, other events and conditions, and not merely the legal form;

  - are neutral (i.e. free from bias);

  - are prudent; and

  - are complete in all material respects.

IAS 8:10 continues to refer to the selection of an accounting policy with a view to reporting information that is 'prudent' and has not been amended to reflect the changes made in the IASB's *Conceptual Framework for Financial Reporting* (see **chapter A2**). Specifically, no reference is made in the Conceptual Framework to prudence (or conservatism) as an aspect of faithful representation because the Board considered that including either would be inconsistent with neutrality. The Board concluded that, even with the prohibitions against deliberate misstatement that appear elsewhere, an admonition to be prudent would be likely to lead to a bias. [CF:BC3.27 – 29]

It seems likely that the Board will process required amendments to IFRSs for consistency with the Conceptual Framework when resources are available to make further progress on the Conceptual Framework project. In the meantime, it is useful to refer to the wording in paragraph 37 of the *Framework for the Preparation and Presentation of Financial Statements* (the IASB's predecessor framework): "[p]rudence is the inclusion of a degree of caution in the exercise of the judgements needed in making the estimates required under conditions of uncertainty, such that assets or income are not overstated and liabilities or expenses are not understated. However, the exercise of prudence does not allow . . . the creation of hidden reserves or excessive provisions, the deliberate understatement of assets or income, or the deliberate overstatement of liabilities or expenses, because the financial statements would not be neutral and, therefore, not have the quality of reliability".

In practical terms, in forming a judgement about a suitable accounting policy, management should refer to, and consider the applicability of, the following sources in descending order:
[IAS 8:11]

• requirements in IFRSs dealing with similar and related issues; and

• the definitions, recognition criteria and measurement concepts for assets, liabilities, income and expenses in the Conceptual Framework.

Agenda decisions issued by the IFRS Interpretations Committee form an important source of guidance although they do not form part of IFRSs. Relevant agenda decisions should be carefully considered as indicative (but not definitive) guidance when selecting a suitable accounting policy for a transaction not specifically addressed by a Standard or an Interpretation.

In the absence of specifically applicable requirements, when an entity is making reference to and considering the applicability of IFRS requirements for similar and/or related issues, the question arises as to whether it is necessary to apply all aspects of the IFRS to the issues being analogised, or could it be appropriate to consider only certain aspects of that IFRS. This issue was considered by the IFRS Interpretations Committee in March 2011. The Committee observed that "when management develops an accounting policy through analogy to an IFRS dealing with similar and related matters, it needs to use its judgement in applying all aspects of the IFRS that are applicable to the particular issue".

Therefore, when analogising to the requirements of an IFRS, an entity is not necessarily bound to apply all of the requirements of that IFRS. Rather, the entity should use its judgement in determining which aspects of that IFRS are applicable to the particular issue and then apply all those aspects of the IFRS that it judges to be applicable.

The most recent pronouncements of other standard-setting bodies that use a similar conceptual framework to develop accounting standards, accounting literature and accepted industry practices may also be considered, provided that they do not conflict with the above sources. [IAS 8:12]

Example 3.1

Selection of accounting policy for combinations of entities under common control – requirement to restate comparative information

Entities S1 and S2 are two subsidiaries of holding company H. Following a decision by H to reorganise the legal structure of the group, S1 acquires S2 (i.e. H now holds an indirect interest in S2 in place of the direct interest it held before the reorganisation). The acquisition of S2 by S1 is considered a combination of entities under common control and, under paragraph 2(c) of IFRS 3 *Business Combinations*, is excluded from the scope of that Standard.

This is the first time that S1 has entered into a transaction of this nature and, therefore, it is required to develop a new accounting policy. In the absence of specific IFRS literature on the topic, S1 has applied the requirements of IAS 8:10 to 12 and has chosen to account for the transaction at S2's carrying amounts at the date of the transaction (i.e. as a pooling of interests).

Is S1 obliged to restate the comparative periods in its consolidated financial statements as if S1 had acquired S2 at the beginning of the earliest period presented?

No. Even if S1 has developed its accounting policy by reference to a pronouncement of another standard-setting body that requires restatement of comparatives when the pooling-of-interests method is applied, S1 is not bound to apply all of the requirements of that pronouncement.

However, the decision-usefulness of the restated comparative information should be considered by management when developing its accounting policy and, if the failure to restate comparative information would be detrimental to the users of the financial statements, restatement should be considered. In addition, S1 should consider local regulatory requirements that may require (or prohibit) restatement of comparative periods for such transactions.

Accounting policies should be applied consistently for similar transactions, other events and conditions, unless an IFRS specifically requires or permits categorisation of items for which different policies may be appropriate. If this is the case, an appropriate accounting policy should be selected and applied consistently to each category. [IAS 8:13]

IFRS 10 *Consolidated Financial Statements* requires that consolidated financial statements should be prepared using uniform accounting policies for like transactions and other events in similar circumstances. [IFRS 10:19] Similarly, for entities that have not yet adopted IFRS 10, IAS 27(2008) *Consolidated and Separate Financial Statements* requires that consistent accounting policies should be applied within a group for the purposes of consolidated financial statements. [IAS 27(2008):24 & 25] There is no such requirement for the individual or separate financial statements of a parent and its subsidiaries.

In practice, most subsidiaries will choose to apply accounting policies that are applied by their parent because this will simplify the consolidation process. Also, the factors that determine the most appropriate policy for the group will often also determine that the same policy is the most appropriate for the subsidiary.

3.2   Changes in accounting policies

An accounting policy can be changed only if the change:
[IAS 8:14]

- is required by an IFRS; or

- results in the financial statements providing reliable and more relevant information about the effects of transactions, other events or conditions on the entity's financial position, financial performance or cash flows.

It is important that changes in accounting policies are only made if one of the above criteria is met; otherwise comparability over time within the financial statements will be lost. [IAS 8:15]

One consequence of the requirements of IAS 8:14 is that if a policy is changed in one year, it is unlikely to be justifiable to change it back to the original policy in a subsequent year. Similarly, it would be difficult to justify the adoption of a policy that would have to be changed again in a subsequent year because of a new Standard or an Interpretation that had been issued but was not yet effective at the date of the first change.

Example 3.2A

Application of a new IFRS in advance of its effective date

Company M's reporting period ended on 31 December 20X1 and it has applied IFRSs for several years. On 15 January 20X2, a new Standard is issued by the IASB which is effective for annual periods beginning on or after 1 January 20X3, with earlier application permitted. Company M will not issue its 20X1 financial statements until 1 March 20X2.

Is Company M permitted to apply this new Standard issued after the reporting period, but prior to the issue of financial statements, in its 20X1 financial statements?

Yes. Because the new Standard allows for application in advance of its effective date, Company M has the option to apply the new Standard for

---

periods in respect of which financial statements have not yet been issued. If the new Standard did not allow for application in advance of its effective date, early application would not be permitted.

Company M may not adopt exposure drafts or other guidance that has not been issued in its final form by the date of issue of its financial statements if this would conflict with the requirements of IFRSs in effect at the reporting date.

IAS 8:20 specifically states that early application of an IFRS is not a voluntary change in accounting policy. Therefore, any specific transition provisions in the new Standard should be applied for Company M's 20X1 financial year. If the new Standard does not include any specific transition provisions relating to the change in accounting policy, the change should be applied retrospectively.

If the entity decides not to apply the Standard in advance of its effective date, the requirements of IAS 8:30 apply (see **3.4.3** below).

Example 3.2B

Voluntary change in accounting policy for investment property

Entity R has applied IFRSs for a number of years. Prior to its 20X3 reporting period, Entity R's policy was to account for all of its investment property using the cost model, as permitted by IAS 40 *Investment Property*. Most of the other participants in Entity R's business sector apply the alternative model permitted under IAS 40 (i.e. the fair value model). In 20X3, because of this prevalence, Entity R decides to change its accounting policy for all investment property to the fair value model on the basis that this model will provide reliable and more relevant information for the users of its financial statements.

Because this is a voluntary change in accounting policy rather than first-time application of the Standard, the transition provisions in IAS 40:80 to 84 do not apply. Consequently, the new accounting policy should be applied retrospectively for all Entity R's investment property, except to the extent that retrospective application is impracticable. (In this scenario, retrospective application will typically be possible because the necessary fair value information in respect of prior periods will have been obtained and disclosed in accordance with IAS 40:79(e), other than in the exceptional cases described in IAS 40:53 (see **5.2.4** in **chapter A8**). Note that the exception from retrospective application in IAS 8:17 (see below) applies only to assets within the scope of IAS 16 *Property, Plant and Equipment* and IAS 38 *Intangible Assets* and, accordingly, is not available for investment property.)

It should be noted that the application of an accounting policy to a transaction, other event or condition that differs in substance from those previously occurring in an entity does not qualify as a change in accounting policy. Equally, the application of a new accounting policy to a transaction, event or condition that had not previously occurred in an entity (or was previously immaterial) does not qualify as a change in accounting policy. [IAS 8:16]

Example 3.2C

Change in use of property

Entity N owns an office building that in previous reporting periods has been classified as property, plant and equipment and accounted for under IAS 16 using the cost model. During the current reporting period, Entity N has vacated the property and it has been leased to a third party. Entity N's accounting policy for investment property under IAS 40 is to use the fair value model.

Is the change in the accounting treatment for the office building from the cost model under IAS 16 to the fair value model under IAS 40 a change in accounting policy?

No. The change in accounting treatment has arisen because of a change in circumstances rather than a change in accounting policy. Entity N's policy for each type of property remains unchanged but the office building in question is accounted for as an investment property from the date of change of use. No retrospective restatement should be made in these circumstances.

IAS 8 states that the initial application of a policy to revalue assets in accordance with IAS 16 or IAS 38 is a change in accounting policy to be dealt with as a revaluation in accordance with those Standards rather than in accordance with IAS 8. IAS 8 also states that its requirements in paragraphs 19 to 31 do not apply to such changes in accounting policy. [IAS 8:17 – 18]

Application of the exception in IAS 8:17 is restricted to assets within the scope of IAS 16 and IAS 38; it does not apply, for example, when an entity revalues investment property under IAS 40's fair value model for the first time (see **example 3.2B**).

There is no further guidance in IAS 16 or IAS 38 as to how the initial application of a policy to revalue assets under those Standards should be recognised or disclosed; however, Example 3 in the implementation guidance accompanying IAS 8 (see **3.3.1** below) notes that such a change from the cost model to the revaluation model is required to be accounted for prospectively.

3.2.1   *Applying changes in accounting policies*

When an entity initially applies an IFRS, the change is accounted for in accordance with the specific transition provisions of that IFRS. If the IFRS does not contain transition provisions, the change is applied retrospectively. [IAS 8:19] Early application of a Standard does not constitute a voluntary change in accounting policy. [IAS 8:20]

If an entity changes an accounting policy voluntarily, the change is applied retrospectively. [IAS 8:19]

As noted in **section 3.1**, in the absence of an IFRS that applies to a specific transaction, other event or condition, the pronouncements of standard-setters using a similar conceptual framework may be considered in selecting an appropriate accounting policy. If, following an amendment of such a pronouncement, an entity chooses to change an accounting policy, this change is accounted for, and disclosed, as a voluntary change in accounting policy in accordance with IAS 8. [IAS 8:21]

> In other words, the entity may not apply any transition provisions in the pronouncement of the other standard-setter.

3.3   Retrospective application

Except when the impracticability exception discussed at **3.3.1** below applies, if retrospective application of an accounting policy is required by the criteria in **3.2.1** above, it is accounted for as follows:
[IAS 8:22]

- the opening balance of each affected component of equity for the earliest prior period presented is adjusted as if the new accounting policy had always been applied; and

- the other comparative amounts disclosed for each prior period presented are adjusted as if the new accounting policy had always been applied.

As explained further at **3.3.1** below, an entity applies a new accounting policy retrospectively to comparative information for prior periods as far back as is practicable. The amount of the resulting adjustment relating to periods before those presented in the financial statements is made to the opening balance of each affected component of equity of the earliest period presented. Usually the adjustment is made to retained earnings. However, the adjustment may be made to another component of equity (e.g. to comply with an IFRS). Any other information about prior periods, such as historical summaries of financial data, is also adjusted as far back as practicable. [IAS 8:26]

> When it is impracticable to restate the earlier periods of any historical summaries in the financial statements, this should be made clear and the affected periods identified.

Entities are required to present an additional statement of financial position, as at the beginning of the preceding period, when a new accounting policy is applied retrospectively and the retrospective application has a material effect on the statement of financial position at the beginning of the preceding period (see **2.10.4** in **chapter A4**).

3.3.1   Limitations on retrospective application

When retrospective application of a change in accounting policy is required by IAS 8:19, the change is applied retrospectively except to the extent that it is impracticable to determine either the period-specific effects or the cumulative effect of the change. [IAS 8:23] The definition of 'impracticable' is considered at **2.8** above and further guidance is provided in **section 6** below.

The impracticability exemption applies both to voluntary changes in accounting policies and to those made in accordance with the transition provisions in a new or revised IFRS.

When it is impracticable to determine the period-specific effects of changing an accounting policy on comparative information for one or more prior periods presented, the new accounting policy is applied to the carrying amounts of assets and liabilities as at the beginning of the earliest period for which retrospective application is practicable. This may be the current period. Corresponding adjustments are made to the opening balance of each affected component of equity for that period. [IAS 8:24]

When a new policy is applied retrospectively, it is applied to comparative periods as far back as is practicable. Retrospective application to a prior period is not practicable unless it is practicable to determine the cumulative effect on the amounts in both the opening and closing statements of financial position for that period. [IAS 8:26]

When it is impracticable to determine the cumulative effect, at the beginning of the current period, of applying a new accounting policy to all prior periods, the comparative information is adjusted to apply the new accounting policy prospectively from the earliest date practicable. [IAS 8:25] That is to say, the new policy is applied prospectively from the start of the earliest period practicable. The portion of the cumulative adjustment to assets, liabilities and equity arising before that date is therefore disregarded. Changing an accounting policy is permitted even if it is impracticable to apply the policy prospectively for any prior period. [IAS 8:27]

Example 3.3.1

Prospective application of a change in accounting policy when retrospective application is not practicable

[Example 3 from the implementation guidance accompanying IAS 8]

During 20X2, Delta Co changed its accounting policy for depreciating property, plant and equipment, so as to apply much more fully a components approach, whilst at the same time adopting the revaluation model.

In years before 20X2, Delta's asset records were not sufficiently detailed to apply a components approach fully. At the end of 20X1, management commissioned an engineering survey, which provided information on the components held and their fair values, useful lives, estimated residual values and depreciable amounts at the beginning of 20X2. However, the survey did not provide a sufficient basis for reliably estimating the cost of those components that had not previously been accounted for separately, and the existing records before the survey did not permit this information to be reconstructed.

Delta's management considered how to account for each of the two aspects of the accounting change. They determined that it was not practicable to account for the change to a fuller components approach retrospectively, or to account for that change prospectively from any earlier date than the start of 20X2. Also, the change from a cost model to a revaluation model is required to be accounted for prospectively. Therefore, management concluded that it should apply Delta's new policy prospectively from the start of 20X2.

Additional information:

Delta's tax rate is 30 per cent.

	CU
Property, plant and equipment at the end of 20X1:	
Cost	25,000
Depreciation	(14,000)
Net book value	11,000
Prospective depreciation expense for 20X2 (old basis)	1,500
Some results of the engineering survey:	
Valuation	17,000
Estimated residual value	3,000
Average remaining asset life (years)	7
Depreciation expense on existing property, plant and equipment for 20X2 (new basis)	2,000

Extract from the notes

From the start of 20X2, Delta changed its accounting policy for depreciating property, plant and equipment, so as to apply much more fully a components approach, whilst at the same time adopting the revaluation model. Management takes the view that this policy provides reliable and more relevant information because it deals more accurately with the components of property, plant and equipment and is based on up-to-date values. The policy has been applied prospectively from the start of 20X2 because it was not practicable to estimate the effects of applying the policy either retrospectively, or prospectively from any earlier date. Accordingly, the adoption of the new policy has no effect on prior years. The effect on the current year is to increase the carrying amount of property, plant and equipment at the start of the year by CU6,000; increase the opening deferred tax provision by CU1,800; create a revaluation surplus at the start of the year of CU4,200; increase depreciation expense by CU500; and reduce tax expense by CU150.

3.3.2 Tax effects of retrospective adjustments

IAS 8 states that the tax effects of corrections of prior period errors and of retrospective adjustments made to apply changes in accounting policies are accounted for and disclosed in accordance with IAS 12 *Income Taxes*. [IAS 8:4] Accounting for the current and deferred tax effects of a transaction or other event should be consistent with the accounting for the transaction or event itself. [IAS 12:57] The implementation guidance accompanying IAS 8 provides an example of a retrospective restatement, which clearly demonstrates that the income tax effect is part of the retrospective adjustment.

Therefore, if an adjustment is recognised against opening retained earnings, the tax effect should also be recognised against opening retained earnings.

As explained at **4.7** in **chapter A13**, subsequent movements in the deferred tax balance follow the item to which the deferred tax balance relates. For the purpose of subsequent movements (reversals or remeasurements), a deferred tax balance that was recognised through a retrospective adjustment against retained earnings is, nonetheless, considered to have been established in profit or loss if the retrospective adjustment was made in respect of a transaction that affected profit or loss. For example, an item of property, plant and equipment that is recognised at fair value as its deemed cost at the date of transition to IFRSs in accordance with IFRS 1 *First-time Adoption of International Financial Reporting Standards* may give rise to a deferred tax liability. Although the additional deferred tax liability arising on transition is recognised in opening retained earnings, the reversal of that deferred tax balance relates to depreciation of the item of property, plant and equipment. Consequently, it should be recognised in profit or loss, consistent with the recognition of the depreciation expense.

3.4   Disclosure

3.4.1   Initial application of an IFRS

The requirements in this section apply on the initial application of an IFRS. They do not apply on first-time adoption of IFRSs, when the disclosure requirements in IFRS 1 apply instead (see **chapter A3**). However, the disclosures detailed below are required when an entity applies a new Standard in advance of its effective date (which, as noted at **3.2.1** above, is not regarded as a voluntary change of policy for the purposes of IAS 8).

If the initial application of an IFRS:

- has an effect on the current period or any prior period; or

- would have such an effect except that it is impracticable to determine the amount of any adjustment; or

- may have an effect on future periods,

the following should be disclosed:
[IAS 8:28]

- the title of the IFRS;

- when applicable, that the change in accounting policy is made in accordance with its transition provisions;

- the nature of the change in accounting policy;

- when applicable, a description of the transition provisions;

- when applicable, the transition provisions that might have an effect on future periods; and

- for the current period and each prior period presented, to the extent practicable, the amount of the adjustment:

  - for each financial statement line item affected; and

  - if IAS 33 *Earning per Share* applies to the entity, for basic and diluted earnings per share:

    - the amount of the adjustment relating to periods before those presented, to the extent practicable; and

    - if retrospective application is impracticable for a particular prior period, or for periods before those presented, the circumstances that led to the existence of that condition and a description of how and from when the change in accounting policy has been applied.

Financial statements of subsequent periods need not repeat these disclosures. [IAS 8:28]

When adopting a new Standard or Interpretation with specific transition provisions, the entity should still follow the disclosure requirements of IAS 8:28 to the extent that the transition provisions do not override those requirements or make them inapplicable. For example, if a new Standard requires prospective application only, the disclosures regarding the amount of the adjustments and line items affected in prior periods will not be relevant.

3.4.2   *Voluntary change in accounting policy*

Early application of a new IFRS is not a voluntary change in accounting policy for the purposes of IAS 8. [IAS 8:20] Therefore, the requirements at **3.4.1** apply to such changes instead of the requirements in this section.

When a voluntary change in accounting policy:

- has an effect on the current period or any prior period; or

- would have such an effect except that it is impracticable to determine the amount of any adjustment; or

- may have an effect on future periods,

the following should be disclosed:
[IAS 8:29]

- the nature of the change in accounting policy;

- the reasons why applying the new accounting policy provides reliable and more relevant information; and

- for the current period and each prior period presented, to the extent practicable, the amount of the adjustment:

  - for each financial statement line item affected; and

  - if IAS 33 applies to the entity, for basic and diluted earnings per share:

    - the amount of the adjustment relating to periods before those presented, to the extent practicable; and

    - if retrospective application is impracticable for a particular prior period, or for periods before those presented, the circumstances that led to the existence of that condition and a description of how and from when the change in accounting policy has been applied.

Financial statements of subsequent periods need not repeat these disclosures. [IAS 8:29]

3.4.3   IFRSs in issue but not yet effective

When an entity has not applied a new Standard or an Interpretation that has been issued but is not yet effective, the following should be disclosed by the entity:
[IAS 8:30]

- this fact; and

- known or reasonably estimable information relevant to assessing the possible impact that application of the new IFRS will have on the entity's financial statements in the period of initial application.

The disclosures required by IAS 8:30 should be made in respect of all IFRSs issued before the date of issue of the financial statements that are not yet effective.

It will be helpful if the relevant note to the financial statements either specifies the date at which the details are given or refers explicitly to them being as at the date of authorisation of the financial statements.

In complying with the general requirement of IAS 8:30, an entity should consider disclosing:
[IAS 8:31]

- the title of the new IFRS;

- the nature of the impending change or changes in accounting policy;

- the date by which application of the IFRS is required;

- the date as at which it plans to apply the IFRS initially; and

- either:

  - a discussion of the impact that initial application of the IFRS is expected to have on the entity's financial statements; or

  - if that impact is not known or reasonably estimable, a statement to that effect.

It is clear from BC31 in the Basis for Conclusions on IAS 8 that the matters listed in IAS 8:31 (see above) are not intended to be mandatory disclosure requirements; they are instead matters that an entity 'considers' in applying IAS 8:30.

The question arises as to whether it is necessary for the financial statements to list every new or amended IFRS that has been issued but is not yet effective, even if it is expected to have no material effect on the entity's financial statements. The safest approach is to provide a complete list because this clearly meets the requirements of the Standard and reduces the risk that some new pronouncements might be overlooked.

However, a briefer disclosure may be acceptable in some circumstances; for example, it may be acceptable not to mention a pronouncement that plainly does not affect the entity because of its scope. Another factor to consider is that when a new pronouncement has no material effect, it may be acceptable to adopt it in advance of its effective date (which would have no material effect) and so exclude it from the disclosures required by IAS 8:30.

When a complete list is not provided, it may be wise to include a statement to the effect that the impact of all other IFRSs not yet adopted is not expected to be material.

4   Changes in accounting estimates

4.1   Identification of accounting estimates

The definition of a change in an accounting estimate is set out at 2.2 above.

Accounting estimates arise from inherent uncertainties in business activities which mean that many items in financial statements cannot be measured with precision but can only be estimated. Estimates are formed using judgements based on the latest available, reliable information. Common examples of estimates in the financial statements include: [IAS 8:32]

- allowances for bad debts;

- allowances for inventory obsolescence;

- the fair value of financial assets or financial liabilities;

- the useful lives of, or the expected pattern of consumption of the future economic benefits embodied in, depreciable assets; and

- warranty obligations.

The use of reasonable estimates is essential in the preparation of financial statements. A revision of an estimate may be required if the circumstances on which the estimate was based change, or if new information or experience is gained. The revision of an estimate does not relate to prior periods and is not equivalent to the correction of an error. [IAS 8:34]

It should be noted that a change in the measurement basis applied to an item in the financial statements constitutes a change in accounting policy, not a change in accounting estimate. In circumstances when it is difficult to distinguish between a change in an accounting policy and a change in an accounting estimate, the change is treated as a change in an accounting estimate. [IAS 8:35]

4.2   Recognition of changes in accounting estimates

The effect of a change in an accounting estimate is recognised prospectively by including it in profit or loss in: [IAS 8:36 – 38]

- the period of the change, if the change affects that period only (e.g. revision of a bad debts estimate); or

- the period of the change and future periods, if the change affects both (e.g. revision of the estimated useful economic life of a depreciable asset).

Example 4.2

Change in estimate of a provision for a lawsuit

Should a change in the estimate of the outcome of a pending lawsuit be recognised in profit or loss in the year of the change?

Yes. Even though the original estimate of the outcome may have been made several years previously, and the case may continue for a number of years, a change in the estimate of the outcome should be recognised in profit or loss in the period (year) of the change.

However, to the extent that a change in an accounting estimate gives rise to changes in assets and liabilities, or relates to an item of equity, it should be recognised by adjusting the carrying amount of the related asset, liability or equity item in the period of the change. [IAS 8:37]

In other words, a change in accounting estimate need not be reported in profit or loss when it is appropriately reflected in the carrying amount of other assets or liabilities, or taken directly to equity, in accordance with the requirements of other IFRSs.

When a change in an accounting estimate is recognised in profit or loss, the change should be recognised in the same line item as the underlying item, except when an IFRS requires a different treatment. For example, if the best estimate of a provision for a legal claim is reduced, the credit in profit or loss should be included within the same expense heading as the original expense was recognised. This ensures that the cumulative expense recognised under that heading is correct.

The disclosure requirements of IAS 8:39 and 40 (see **4.3** below) should be complied with. In addition, if the change in accounting estimate causes a material distortion in a particular expense heading, additional disclosure may be required in accordance with paragraph 97 of IAS 1 *Presentation of Financial Statements* (see **5.4.1** in **chapter A4**).

4.3   Disclosure

An entity discloses the nature and amount of a change in an accounting estimate that has an effect in the current period or is expected to have an effect in future periods. The disclosure of the effect on future periods is not required when it is impracticable to estimate that effect. [IAS 8:39]

If the amount of the effect in future periods is not disclosed because estimating it is impracticable, the entity should disclose this fact. [IAS 8:40]

5   Errors

5.1   Material errors

Financial statements do not comply with IFRSs if they contain either:

- material errors; or

- immaterial errors made intentionally in order to achieve a particular presentation of an entity's financial position, financial performance or cash flows.

The definition of 'material' for this purpose is considered at **2.4** above.

Errors can occur in respect of the recognition, measurement, presentation or disclosure of elements of the financial statements. [IAS 8:41]

Errors are distinguished from changes in accounting estimates because accounting estimates, by their very nature, are items that may need to be revised as additional information becomes known. For example, the gain or loss recognised on the outcome of a contingency is not the correction of an error. [IAS 8:48]

Although, in principle, the distinction between errors and corrections of estimates is clear, it may sometimes be difficult in practice to establish what information was available, or should have been available, at the time when an estimate was made.

5.2   Correction of errors

If a current period error is discovered before the financial statements are authorised for issue, it is corrected in that period. However, if a material error remains undetected until a subsequent period, the prior period error

is corrected retrospectively in the first set of financial statements authorised for issue after its discovery. [IAS 8:41]

Except when it is impracticable to do so (see below), material prior period
errors are corrected by:
[IAS 8:42]

- restating the comparative amounts for the prior period(s) presented
  in which the error occurred; or

- if the error occurred before the earliest prior period presented,
  restating the opening balances of assets, liabilities and equity for the
  earliest prior period presented.

The correction of the prior period error is excluded from profit or loss in
the period of discovery. [IAS 8:46]

The tax effects of retrospective adjustments are discussed at **3.3.2**
above.

IAS 8 does not differentiate between fundamental errors and other
material prior period errors; the IASB concluded that the definition
of 'fundamental errors' in the previous version of the Standard was
difficult to interpret consistently because the main feature of the
definition (that the error causes the financial statements of one of
more prior periods no longer to be considered to have been reliable)
was also a feature of all material prior period errors. [IAS 8:BC12]

IAS 8 refers to the correction of material prior period errors by
retrospective restatement but does not say that *only* material errors
may be corrected in this way. It is silent on the correction of
immaterial errors which is consistent with the fact that IFRSs do not
apply to immaterial items. Nevertheless, the explicit reference to
'material' in IAS 8:42 suggests that only material errors should be
corrected in this way. This is the way in which the requirement is
normally interpreted.

A prior period error is corrected by retrospective restatement, except to the
extent that it is impracticable to determine either:
[IAS 8:43]

- the period-specific effects; or

- the cumulative effect of the error.

The definition of 'impracticable' is considered at **2.8** above and further guidance is provided in **section 6** below.

If it is impracticable to determine the period-specific effects of an error on comparative information for one or more prior periods presented, the opening balances of assets, liabilities and equity are restated for the earliest period for which retrospective restatement is practicable. This may be the current period. [IAS 8:44]

If it is impracticable to determine the cumulative effect on all prior periods of a prior period error at the beginning of the current period, the comparative information is restated to correct the error prospectively from the earliest date practicable. [IAS 8:45] The entity therefore disregards the portion of the cumulative restatement of assets, liabilities and equity arising before that date. [IAS 8:47]

Any information presented about prior periods, including any historical summaries of financial data, is restated as far back as practicable. [IAS 8:46]

> When it is impracticable to restate the earlier periods of any historical summaries in the financial statements, this should be made clear and the affected periods identified.

5.3 Disclosure of prior period errors

When a material prior period error is corrected in accordance with IAS 8, the following should be disclosed:
[IAS 8:49]

- the nature of the prior period error; and

- for each prior period presented, to the extent practicable, the amount of the correction:

  - for each financial statement line item affected; and

  - if IAS 33 *Earning per Share* applies to the entity, for basic and diluted earnings per share:

    - the amount of the correction at the beginning of the earliest prior period presented; and

- if retrospective restatement is impracticable for a particular prior period, the circumstances that led to the existence of that condition and a description of how and from when the error has been corrected.

Financial statements of subsequent periods need not repeat these disclosures. [IAS 8:49]

Entities are required to present an additional statement of financial position, as at the beginning of the preceding period, when an error is corrected by retrospective restatement and the retrospective restatement has a material effect on the statement of financial position at the beginning of the preceding period (see **2.10.4** in **chapter A4**).

6   Impracticability in respect of retrospective application and retrospective restatement

6.1   Obstacles faced in retrospective application and restatement

The term 'impracticable' is defined in **2.8** above. It may be impracticable to adjust comparative information for one or more prior periods to achieve comparability with the current period. This may be the case because data was not collected in the prior period(s) in a way that allows either retrospective application of a new accounting policy, or retrospective restatement to correct a prior period error, and it may be impracticable to recreate the information. [IAS 8:50]

Restatement is not impracticable just because of the cost or effort involved. When revising IAS 8 in 2003, the IASB considered replacing the exemption from retrospective application or restatements on the basis of 'impracticability' with one based on 'undue cost or effort'. However, based on comments received on the exposure draft, the IASB decided that an exemption based on management's assessment of undue cost or effort was too subjective to be applied consistently by different entities. The IASB decided that balancing costs and benefits was a task for the Board when it sets accounting requirements rather than for entities when they apply those requirements. Therefore, although the Standard does not explicitly state that undue cost or effort alone does not render restatement impracticable,

> this is the clear intention of the Board and is consistent with the definition in the Standard. [IAS 8:BC24]

6.1.1   Estimates

It is often necessary to make estimates in applying an accounting policy to elements of financial statements recognised or disclosed in respect of transactions, other events or conditions. Estimation is inherently subjective, and estimates may be developed after the reporting period.

Further, developing estimates is potentially more difficult when retrospectively applying an accounting policy or making a retrospective restatement to correct a prior period error, because of the longer period of time that may have passed since the affected transaction, other event or condition occurred. However, the objective of estimates relating to prior periods remains the same as for estimates made in the current period, i.e. for the estimate to reflect the circumstances that existed *when the transaction, other event or condition occurred.* [IAS 8:51]

As explained at **2.8** above, it may sometimes be impracticable to distinguish information that:

- provides evidence of circumstances that existed on the date(s) as at which the transaction, other event or condition occurred; and

- would have been available when the financial statements for that period were authorised for issue,

from other information. [IAS 8:52]

Nevertheless, IAS 8 notes that the fact that significant estimates are frequently required when amending comparative information presented for prior periods does not prevent reliable adjustment or correction of the comparative information. [IAS 8:53]

6.2   Use of hindsight

Hindsight should not be used when applying a new accounting policy to, or correcting amounts for, a prior period, either in making assumptions about what management's intentions would have been in a prior period or estimating the amounts recognised, measured or disclosed in a prior period.

IAS 8 cites the example of an entity's calculation of its liability for employees' accumulated sick leave in accordance with IAS 19 *Employee*

Benefits. When correcting a prior period error in relation to this calculation, the entity disregards information about an unusually severe influenza season during the next period that became available after the financial statements for the prior period were authorised for issue. [IAS 8:53]

A6 Fair value measurement

Contents

1   Introduction

This chapter deals with the requirements of IFRS 13 *Fair Value Measurement* which was issued in May 2011. IFRS 13 establishes a single framework for measuring fair value when that is required or permitted by other Standards. It replaces the guidance on measuring fair value previously included in other Standards.

IFRS 13 defines fair value, provides guidance on *how* fair value should be measured, and establishes consistent requirements for disclosures regarding fair value measurements. The requirements of IFRS 13 apply whenever an entity is required or permitted to use fair value for measurement or disclosure purposes, whether in respect of a financial or a non-financial item, other than in the limited circumstances listed in IFRS 13:6 and IFRS 13:7 (see **section 2**). However, IFRS 13 does not mandate *when* fair value measurements should be used; requirements regarding when it is appropriate to measure particular categories of assets, liabilities or an entity's own equity instruments at fair value continue to be dealt with in other IFRSs.

Prior to the issue of IFRS 13, guidance on how to measure fair value was included in the various IFRSs that require or permit its use. Because those IFRSs were developed over many years, the requirements for measuring fair value were dispersed and did not necessarily articulate a clear measurement objective. Further, the guidance in the various IFRSs was not always consistent. IFRS 13 was developed to address these issues and to provide a single source of guidance and a coherent framework for measuring fair value.

Historically, much of the guidance on the measurement of fair value was developed in the context of financial instruments. One of the most significant features of IFRS 13 is that it establishes principles that are equally applicable to financial and non-financial items. More detailed guidance is then provided separately for financial and non-financial items. This chapter covers the general principles of IFRS 13, the general requirements applicable to both financial and non-financial items, and the specific requirements regarding the measurement of fair value for non-financial items. IFRS 13's specific requirements regarding the measurement of financial instruments at fair value, and more detailed application guidance, are set out in **chapter B7** (for entities that have adopted IFRS 9 *Financial Instruments*) and **chapter C7** (for entities that have not yet adopted IFRS 9).

IFRS 13 is required to be applied for annual periods beginning on or after 1 January 2013, with earlier application permitted (see **section 12**).

1.1   Summary of IFRS 13 framework

The table and flow chart below set out a step-by-step approach to applying the basic measurement principles of IFRS 13. The table also provides a high level summary of some of the key concepts underlying IFRS 13 and illustrates the framework for measuring fair value. The summary does not address all of the requirements of the Standard – users should refer to the more detailed discussions later in this chapter and to the text of the Standard for a fuller understanding.

Note that Steps 2 to 4 do not necessarily occur in the order set out in the table and flow chart (i.e. they are inter-related).

#	Step	Explanation
1.	Identify the 'asset' or 'liability' being measured (i.e. the **unit of account**) (see **3.1** below).	IFRS 13 notes that the asset or liability measured at fair value may be (1) a stand-alone asset or liability (e.g. an investment property), (2) a group of assets or a group of liabilities, or (3) a group of assets and liabilities (e.g. a cash-generating unit). The level at which fair value is measured will depend on the 'unit of account' specified in other IFRSs (typically, the level at which the asset or liability is aggregated or disaggregated for recognition or disclosure purposes). For example: <ul><li>in accordance with IAS 36 *Impairment of Assets*, an entity may be required to measure fair value less costs of disposal for a cash-generating unit (CGU) when assessing its recoverable amount; and</li><li>under IFRS 9 *Financial Instruments* (or, prior to the adoption of IFRS 9, IAS 39 *Financial Instruments: Recognition and Measurement*), the unit of account is generally an individual financial instrument.</li></ul>

#	Step	Explanation
2a.	For non-financial assets, determine the asset's **highest and best use** (see **section 4** below).	A fair value measurement of a non-financial asset is based on its 'highest and best use'. This concept is not relevant for financial assets, liabilities or an entity's own equity instruments because those items do not have alternative uses as contemplated in IFRS 13. The highest and best use must be determined from the perspective of market participants, even if an entity intends a different use. However, there is a presumption that an entity's current use of a non-financial asset is its highest and best use, unless there is evidence to suggest otherwise. Consequently, IFRS 13 does not require an entity to perform an exhaustive search for other potential uses of a non-financial asset. The highest and best use of an asset might provide maximum value through either (1) its use in combination with other assets or other assets and liabilities, or (2) on a stand-alone basis.
2b.	For **financial assets and financial liabilities with offsetting market risks or counterparty credit risk**, evaluate the criteria for the fair value exception and establish a policy (see **section 6** of **chapter B7** (for entities that have adopted IFRS 9) or **section 6** of **chapter C7** (for entities that have not yet adopted IFRS 9)).	IFRS 13 permits an exception to the general fair value measurement requirements for financial assets and financial liabilities if an entity: • manages the group of assets and liabilities on the basis of its net exposure to market risks or counterparty credit risk; • provides information on that basis to key management personnel; and • measures those assets and liabilities at fair value in the statement of financial position. In summary, the exception permits an entity to measure the fair value of the group of assets and liabilities (i.e. the portfolio) rather than the individual assets and liabilities within the portfolio. Details of the exception, including the detailed criteria for qualification, are set out in IFRS 13:48 to 56 (see **section 6** of **chapter B7** (for entities that have adopted IFRS 9) or **section 6** of **chapter C7** (for entities that have not yet adopted IFRS 9)).

#	Step	Explanation
		The application of this exception is an accounting policy choice in accordance with IAS 8 *Accounting Policies, Changes in Accounting Estimates and Errors* and must be applied consistently from period to period for a particular portfolio.
		This exception does not change the *unit of account* (which continues to be the individual instrument determined under IFRS 9 or IAS 39), but changes the *unit of measurement* from the individual financial instrument to the group (portfolio) of financial instruments.
2c.	For liabilities and an entity's own equity instruments, assume the liabilities or equity instruments are **transferred to market participants at the measurement date** (see **section 5** below).	IFRS 13 requires that the fair value of a liability or an entity's own equity instrument be based on an assumed transfer to a market participant even if the entity does not intend to transfer the liability or equity instrument to a third party or it is unable to do so.
		Under this assumption, the fair value of a liability should be measured on the basis that the liability would remain outstanding and the transferee would be required to fulfil the obligation; it should not be assumed that the liability would be settled or otherwise extinguished. Similarly, the fair value of an entity's own equity instrument should be measured on the basis that the equity instrument would remain outstanding and the transferee would take on the rights and responsibilities associated with the instrument; it should not be assumed that the instrument would be cancelled or otherwise extinguished.
		In addition, the measurement of liabilities and own equity instruments depends on whether identical liabilities or equity instruments are held by other parties as assets.

#	Step	Explanation
3.	Identify the market in which to price the asset or liability – i.e. either (1) the **principal market**, or (2) if no principal market exists, the **most advantageous market** (see **3.2** below).	The principal market is "[t]he market with the greatest volume and level of activity for the asset or liability". The most advantageous market is "[t]he market that maximises the amount that would be received to sell the asset or minimises the amount that would be paid to transfer the liability . . .".
		If there is a principal market for the asset or liability, the fair value measurement should reflect the price in that market, even if the price in a different market is potentially more advantageous at the measurement date. In the absence of evidence to the contrary, the market in which an entity would normally enter into a transaction to sell the asset or to transfer the liability is presumed to be the principal (or most advantageous) market. Therefore, an entity is permitted to use the price in the market in which it normally enters into transactions unless there is evidence that the principal (or most advantageous) market and that market are not the same.
		A market cannot be identified as the principal (or most advantageous) market unless the entity has access to that market at the measurement date.
4.	Develop assumptions that **market participants** in the principal (or most advantageous) market would use when pricing the asset or liability (see **3.3** below).	'Market participants' are buyers and sellers in the principal (or most advantageous) market for the asset or liability that are (1) independent of each other, (2) knowledgeable, (3) able to enter into a transaction for the asset or liability, and (4) willing to enter into such a transaction.
		An entity need not identify specific market participants, but should identify characteristics that distinguish market participants generally.

#	Step	Explanation
5.	Estimate fair value using appropriate **valuation techniques** and related **inputs** (see **sections 8** and **9** below).	When the price for an asset or a liability cannot be observed directly, it must be estimated using a valuation technique. Entities should use valuation techniques that are appropriate in the circumstances and for which sufficient data are available to measure fair value, maximising the use of relevant observable inputs and minimising the use of unobservable inputs. Highest priority should be given to unadjusted quoted prices in active markets for identical assets or liabilities.
		IFRS 13 refers to three widely used valuation techniques: • the market approach (see **8.1**); • the cost approach (see **8.2**); and • the income approach (see **8.3**). Any valuation technique used to measure fair value should be consistent with one or more of these approaches. IFRS 13 does not set out a hierarchy of valuation techniques because particular valuation techniques may be more appropriate in some circumstances than in others.
		The use of multiple valuation techniques may be appropriate in certain circumstances. In those cases, the results should be evaluated considering the reasonableness of the range of values indicated by those results. A fair value measurement is the point within that range that is most representative of the fair value in the circumstances.
		Once a valuation technique has been selected, it should be applied consistently. A change in a valuation technique or its application (e.g. a change in its weighting when multiple valuation techniques are used or a change in an adjustment applied to a valuation technique) is only appropriate if the change results in a measurement that is equally or more representative of fair value in the circumstances.
		An entity should evaluate the factors listed in IFRS 13:B37 (see **9.4** below) to determine whether there has been a significant decrease in the volume or level of activity for the asset or liability relative to normal market activity. When such a decrease has occurred, this will affect the entity's selection of techniques and/or inputs and the weight placed on quoted prices.

6.	If the exception in Step 2b applies, **allocate the fair value** calculated in Step 5 (which might include several units of account) **to the individual units of account** that are the subject of the fair value measurement (as determined in Step 1 above) (see **section 6** of **chapter B7** (for entities that have adopted IFRS 9) or **section 6** of **chapter C7** (for entities that have not yet adopted IFRS 9)).

	If the fair value calculated in Step 5 is for multiple units of account, the fair value should be allocated to the individual units of account that are the subject of the fair value measurement on a reasonable and consistent basis.

7.	Classify the fair value measurement within the **fair value hierarchy** (see **section 10** below) and prepare the disclosures required by IFRS 13 (see **section 11** below).

	IFRS 13 establishes a fair value hierarchy that categorises into three levels the inputs to valuation techniques used to measure fair value (see **10.1**). When several inputs are used to measure the fair value of an asset or a liability, those inputs may be categorised within different levels of the fair value hierarchy (e.g. the valuation may be based on some Level 2 and some Level 3 inputs). In such circumstances, the categorisation of the fair value measurement in its entirety is based on the lowest level input that is significant to the entire measurement.

	IFRS 13 sets out disclosure requirements in respect of fair value measurements. The disclosures vary depending on whether the assets or liabilities are measured at fair value on a recurring or non-recurring basis.

Fair value measurement framework

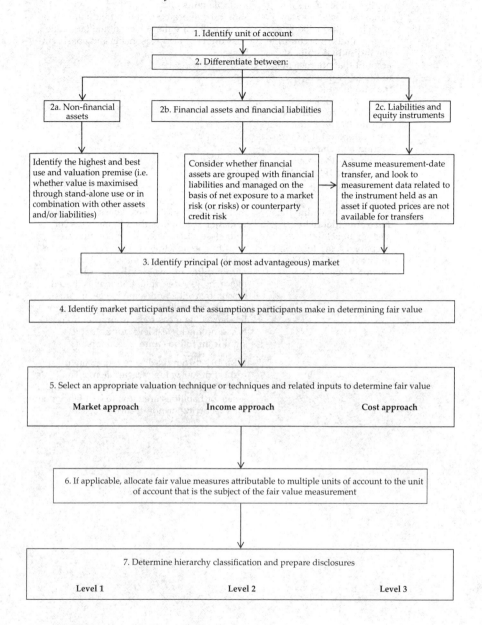

2   Objective and scope

The objective of IFRS 13 is to:
[IFRS 13:1]

- define fair value;

- set out in a single IFRS a framework for measuring fair value; and

- require disclosures about fair value measurements.

IFRS 13 applies when another IFRS requires or permits fair value measurements or disclosures about fair value measurements except in the limited circumstances specified in IFRS 13:6 and 7 (see below). [IFRS 13:5]

> The measurement requirements in IFRS 13 apply when measuring the fair value of:
>
> - items that are measured at fair value in the statement of financial position; and
>
> - items for which the fair value is disclosed, even if the item is not measured at fair value in the statement of financial position (e.g. investment property measured subsequent to initial recognition using the cost model in IAS 40 *Investment Property*). [IFRS 13:BC25]

IFRS 13 also applies to measurements and disclosures about measurements that are *based on* fair value (e.g. 'fair value less costs to sell' in IFRS 5 *Non-current Assets Held for Sale and Discontinued Operations* and IAS 41 *Agriculture*). [IFRS 13:5]

> When determining the scope of IFRS 13, the IASB concluded that the Standard should apply to all measurements for which fair value is the "underlying measurement basis". However, IFRS 13:6 (see below) clarifies that the requirements of IFRS 13 do not apply to measurements that have similarities to fair value but are not fair value. [IFRS 13:BC24]

The measurement and disclosure requirements of IFRS 13 do not apply to the following:
[IFRS 13:6]

- share-based payment transactions within the scope of IFRS 2 *Share-based Payment*;

- leasing transactions within the scope of IAS 17 *Leases*; and

- measurements that have some similarities to fair value but are not fair value (e.g. net realisable value in IAS 2 *Inventories* or value in use in IAS 36 *Impairment of Assets*).

The disclosures specified by IFRS 13 are not required for: [IFRS 13:7]

- plan assets measured at fair value in accordance with IAS 19 *Employee Benefits*;

- retirement benefit plan investments measured at fair value in accordance with IAS 26 *Accounting and Reporting by Retirement Benefit Plans*; and

- assets for which recoverable amount is fair value less costs of disposal in accordance with IAS 36.

The measurement requirements of IFRS 13 apply equally when an item is measured at fair value at initial recognition and for measurement at fair value subsequent to recognition. [IFRS 13:8]

Some Standards (e.g. IAS 40) require items to be measured at fair value on an ongoing basis (IFRS 13 refers to this as 'fair value on a recurring basis'); some (e.g. IFRS 5) require fair value only in specified circumstances (IFRS 13 refers to this as 'fair value on a non-recurring basis'); and some (e.g. IFRS 3 *Business Combinations*) require fair value only on initial recognition of an item. IFRS 13 applies in all of these circumstances (subject to the exceptions in IFRS 13:6 and 7 listed above).

The discussion in IFRS 13 (and, consequently, throughout this chapter) focuses on assets and liabilities. Note, however, that the Standard also applies when an entity's own equity instruments are measured at fair value. [IFRS 13:4]

Examples of fair value measurements that are within the scope of IFRS 13 include, but are not limited to:

- identifiable assets and liabilities of an acquiree measured at fair value at the acquisition date under IFRS 3 (but see **2.5** below regarding the application of IFRS 13's disclosure requirements);

- non-current assets and disposal groups classified as held for sale measured at fair value less costs to sell under IFRS 5;

- property, plant and equipment and intangible assets measured using the revaluation models in IAS 16 *Property, Plant and Equipment* and IAS 38 *Intangible Assets,* respectively;

- revenue measured at the fair value of the consideration received or receivable in accordance with IAS 18 *Revenue;*

- the measurement by the issuer of the fair value of a compound financial instrument and the fair value of the liability component of that compound financial instrument, for the purpose of measuring the debt and equity components of the instrument at initial recognition under IAS 32 *Financial Instruments: Presentation;*

- the recoverable amount of an asset or a cash-generating unit determined under IAS 36 when it is based on its fair value less costs of disposal (see **2.1** below);

- financial assets and financial liabilities within the scope of IFRS 9 *Financial Instruments* (or, for entities that have not yet adopted IFRS 9, IAS 39 *Financial Instruments: Recognition and Measurement*) required to be measured at fair value at initial recognition or at subsequent reporting dates;

- investment property measured subsequent to initial recognition using the fair value model under IAS 40 or investment property measured using the cost model under IAS 40 (for which the fair value is disclosed even though the investment property is not measured at fair value in the statement of financial position); and

- biological assets and agricultural produce measured at fair value less costs to sell at initial recognition or at subsequent reporting dates under IAS 41.

2.1   Impact of IFRS 13 on impairment testing under IAS 36

In specified circumstances, IAS 36 requires an entity to estimate the recoverable amount of an asset or a cash-generating unit (CGU). The recoverable amount of an asset or a CGU is the higher of its fair value less costs of disposal and its value in use (see **chapter A10** for detailed requirements).

IFRS 13's measurement requirements will affect the impairment testing of assets or CGUs under IAS 36 when an entity is required to estimate the asset's (or the CGU's) fair value less costs of disposal. This will be the case when an entity is required by IAS 36 to estimate the recoverable amount of the asset or CGU, unless it has already been determined that the value in use of the asset or CGU is higher than its carrying amount (see **section 6** of **chapter A10**).

One aspect of the IFRS 13 model that has particular significance in the context of impairment testing is that, when measuring fair value, an entity is required to use the assumptions that market participants would use, even if the entity has no intention of selling the asset (see **3.3** below). If unobservable inputs (i.e. inputs for which market data are not available) are used, IFRS 13:89 states that "an entity may begin with its own data, but it shall adjust those data if reasonably available information indicates that other market participants would use different data or there is something particular to the entity that is not available to other market participants". Therefore, an entity may need to adjust its internally developed assumptions to reflect the assumptions that market participants would use.

In addition, when measuring the fair value of a non-financial asset, the entity must consider the highest and best use of the non-financial asset from the perspective of market participants, even if the entity intends a different use (see **section 4** below). However, an entity's current use of a non-financial asset can be presumed to be its highest and best use unless market or other factors suggest that a different use by market participants would maximise the value of the asset (see IFRS 13:29).

Note that, in accordance with IFRS 13:7 (see above), IFRS 13's disclosure requirements do not apply to assets or CGUs for which an entity is required to estimate the fair value less costs of disposal. Instead, an entity should comply with the disclosure requirements in IAS 36.

2.2   Application of IFRS 13 to provisions within the scope of IAS 37

Provisions falling within the scope of IAS 37 *Provisions, Contingent Liabilities and Contingent Assets* are not measured at fair value. Such provisions are measured at the entity's best estimate of the expenditure required to settle the present obligation at the end of the reporting period (see **section 4** of **chapter A12**). Consequently, the measurement and disclosure requirements of IFRS 13 do not apply to provisions within the scope of IAS 37.

IAS 37:37 states that the best estimate of the expenditure required to settle the present obligation is "the amount that an entity would rationally pay to settle the obligation at the end of the reporting period or to transfer it to a third party at that time". Although this measure may have some similarities to fair value, it is not fair value or based on fair value and, consequently, in accordance with IFRS 13:6 (see above), IFRS 13 does not apply.

2.3   Application of IFRS 13 to the net defined benefit liability (asset) for a defined benefit retirement benefit plan

IFRS 13 does not apply to the net defined benefit liability (asset) reported in the statement of financial position for a defined benefit retirement benefit plan under IAS 19. However, the measurement requirements of IFRS 13 do apply to plan assets, which is the only component of the net defined benefit liability (asset) that is measured at fair value.

For the other components of the net defined benefit liability (asset) (i.e. those that are not measured at fair value), employers should follow the measurement requirements set out in IAS 19.

Although plan assets are subject to the measurement requirements in IFRS 13, in accordance with IFRS 13:7 (see above), IFRS 13's disclosure requirements do not apply.

2.4   Application of IFRS 13 to fair value information disclosed in the financial statements that is not required by IFRSs

An entity may disclose in its financial statements fair value information that is not required to be disclosed by IFRSs. Such 'supplementary' fair value information is generally presented in the notes to the financial statements and it is most commonly presented in one of the following circumstances:

- the disclosure is encouraged (but not required) by an IFRS. For example, IAS 16:79(c) suggests that, when the cost model is being used, a disclosure that might be relevant for users of the financial statements is "the fair value of property, plant and equipment when this is materially different from the carrying amount"; or

- the disclosure is required by local legislation or by a regulator; or

- the entity wishes to draw attention to particular circumstances (e.g. a significant shift in the fair value of assets measured on a cost basis in the financial statements).

The requirements of IFRS 13 generally apply to such supplementary fair value information. IFRS 13 applies "when another IFRS requires or permits fair value measurements or disclosures about fair value measurements" other than in the limited circumstances listed in IFRS 13:6 and 7 (see above). Therefore, when an entity presents supplementary fair value information that is encouraged by another IFRS (e.g. under IAS 16:79(c) as described above), the fair value measure that is disclosed should comply with the measurement requirements of IFRS 13 and certain of the disclosures required under IFRS 13 as specified in IFRS 13:97 (see **11.5** below) should be presented.

Equally, when an entity voluntarily presents information about fair value, a user of the financial statements will generally be entitled to assume, unless otherwise stated, that the term has the same meaning as elsewhere in the financial statements, and the entity should comply with the requirements of IFRS 13 as described in the previous paragraph.

In some circumstances, local legislation or other regulations may require that the financial statements should disclose an amount described by the relevant authority as 'fair value' but for which the relevant authority specifies a measurement basis that differs from the basis of measurement for fair value under IFRS 13. In such circumstances, while the entity is obliged to comply with the requirements imposed by the relevant authority, the measurement basis used for the specified disclosure, and the fact that the basis differs from that which would be used under IFRSs, should be clearly disclosed.

2.5   Application of the disclosure requirements of IFRS 13 to assets and liabilities acquired in a business combination

IFRS 3 generally requires the identifiable assets and liabilities of an acquiree to be measured at fair value at the date of acquisition. As a result, the acquirer is required to apply the measurement requirements of IFRS 13 to these acquisition date fair values in its consolidated financial statements. However, in the acquirer's consolidated financial statements, the disclosure requirements of IFRS 13 do not apply to the fair value measurements of the acquiree's identifiable assets and liabilities at the acquisition date.

IFRS 13:91 establishes that the disclosure requirements of IFRS 13 apply to assets and liabilities that are measured at fair value on a recurring or non-recurring basis in the statement of financial position *after* initial recognition (see **11.1** below). Further, IFRS 13:BC184 clarifies that the disclosure requirements in IFRS 13 apply only to fair value measurements made after initial recognition in the financial statements because other IFRSs address the disclosures at initial recognition.

When an acquiree's identifiable assets and liabilities are measured at fair value at the date of acquisition, this is for the purpose of their initial recognition in the consolidated financial statements of the acquirer. Consequently, the disclosure requirements of IFRS 13 need not be applied to those acquisition-date measurements.

2.6   Application of the disclosure requirements of IFRS 13 to assets and liabilities measured at fair value and included within a disposal group classified as held for sale

Under IFRS 5, assets and liabilities that are excluded from the scope of the measurement requirements of that Standard may nevertheless be included within a disposal group classified as held for sale and the disposal group as a whole is subject to the measurement requirements and the classification and presentation requirements of IFRS 5 (see **section 2** of **chapter A20** for details).

Items included within a disposal group that are not subject to the measurement requirements of IFRS 5 are measured in accordance with applicable IFRSs (see **2.2.1** in **chapter A20** for details); some items (e.g. financial instruments) may be measured at fair value. If assets and liabilities that are measured at fair value on a recurring or non-recurring basis are part of a disposal group classified as held for sale, the question arises as to whether the disclosure requirements of IFRS 13 apply to those assets and liabilities.

The extent to which the disclosure requirements of other IFRSs apply to assets or liabilities included within disposal groups classified as held for sale is addressed in IFRS 5:5B which states that "[d]isclosures in other IFRSs do not apply to [non-current assets held for sale] (or disposal groups) unless those IFRSs require . . . disclosures about measurement of assets and liabilities within a disposal group that are not within the scope of the measurement requirement of IFRS 5".

For assets and liabilities excluded from the scope of the measurement requirement of IFRS 5 that are included within a disposal group classified as held for sale and that are measured at fair value, the effect of IFRS 5:5B is that the disclosure requirements of IFRS 13 apply *to the extent that those disclosure requirements relate to measurement*.

Given that IFRS 13 as a whole is concerned with the measurement of fair value, and with disclosures regarding the measurement of fair value, all of the disclosure requirements of IFRS 13 relate to 'measurement' and, consequently, should be applied.

When determining the classes of assets and liabilities as required by IFRS 13:94 (see **11.3** below), and preparing the fair value measurement disclosures, an entity should distinguish assets and liabilities that are part of a disposal group classified as held for sale from its other assets and liabilities. The classes determined in accordance with IFRS 13:94 should be consistent with the major classes of assets and liabilities disclosed separately in accordance with IFRS 5:38 (see **7.2.1** in **chapter A20**).

3   Definition of fair value

Fair value is defined as "[t]he price that would be received to sell an asset or paid to transfer a liability in an orderly transaction between market participants at the measurement date". [IFRS 13:Appendix A]

This basis for measuring fair value is commonly referred to as an *exit price* approach because it reflects the price at which a market participant that holds the asset or owes the liability could *exit* that asset or liability by selling the asset or transferring the liability to a third party.

Note that the definition assumes a hypothetical and orderly exchange transaction (i.e. it is not an actual sale or a forced transaction or distress sale). [IFRS 13:BC30]

Fair value as defined above is a market-based measurement (not an entity-specific value). [IFRS 13:2] It is therefore measured using the assumptions that market participants would use when pricing the asset or liability, including assumptions about risk. Consequently, an entity's intention to hold an asset or to settle or otherwise fulfil a liability is not relevant when measuring fair value. [IFRS 13:3]

IFRS 13's definition clarifies that fair value should reflect current market conditions (which reflect the current expectations of market participants about future market conditions, rather than those of the reporting entity). [IFRS 13:BC31]

The extent to which market information is available can vary between different types of assets and liabilities. For some assets and liabilities, observable market transactions or market information may be available. For other assets and liabilities, observable market transactions and market information may not be available. However, the objective under IFRS 13 in both cases is the same – to estimate the price at which an orderly transaction to sell the asset or to transfer the liability would take place between market participants at the measurement date under current market conditions (i.e. an exit price at the measurement date from the perspective of a market participant that holds the asset or owes the liability). [IFRS 13:2] When a price for an identical asset or liability is not observable, an entity measures fair value using another valuation technique that maximises the use of relevant observable inputs and minimises the use of unobservable inputs. [IFRS 13:3]

A fair value measurement requires an entity to determine all the following: [IFRS 13:B2]

- the particular asset or liability that is the subject of the measurement (consistently with its unit of account);

- for a non-financial asset, the valuation premise that is appropriate for the measurement (consistently with its highest and best use);

- the principal (or most advantageous) market for the asset or liability; and

- the valuation technique(s) appropriate for the measurement, considering the availability of data with which to develop inputs that represent the assumptions that market participants would use when pricing the asset or liability and the level of the fair value hierarchy within which the inputs are categorised.

Key elements of the definition of fair value are discussed in the following sections, namely:

- the asset or liability that is being measured (see **3.1**);

- the market in which the transaction is assumed to occur (see **3.2**);

- the market participants that are assumed to enter into the transaction (see **3.3**); and

- the 'price' at which the transaction is assumed to occur (see **3.4**).

3.1   Identifying the asset or liability

3.1.1   Determining the appropriate unit of account

The asset or liability being measured at fair value may be (1) a stand-alone asset or liability (e.g. an investment property), (2) a group of assets or a group of liabilities, or (3) a group of assets and liabilities (e.g. a cash-generating unit). The level at which fair value is measured will depend on the 'unit of account' (typically, the level at which the asset or liability is aggregated or disaggregated for recognition or disclosure purposes). [IFRS 13:13 and Appendix A]

The unit of account is determined in accordance with the IFRS that requires or permits the fair value measurement, except as provided in IFRS 13. [IFRS 13:14]

> IFRS 13 does not generally prescribe the unit of account. The IASB concluded that IFRS 13 should describe how to measure fair value, not what is being measured at fair value. Other IFRSs specify whether a fair value measurement considers an individual asset or liability or a group of assets or liabilities (i.e. the unit of account). For example:
> [IFRS 13:BC47]
>
> - IAS 36 *Impairment of Assets* states that an entity should measure the fair value less costs of disposal for a cash-generating unit when assessing its recoverable amount; and
>
> - under IFRS 9 *Financial Instruments* (or, for entities that have not yet adopted IFRS 9, IAS 39 *Financial Instruments: Recognition and Measurement*), the unit of account is generally an individual financial instrument.
>
> The following examples set out considerations for determining the appropriate unit of account for equity interests held by an entity in various scenarios and how the fair value of those interests should be measured.

Scenario	Unit of account prescribed in the applicable IFRS
Scenario 1	
Entity A owns a 16 per cent equity interest in Entity B (160 million ordinary shares). Entity B's ordinary shares are traded in an active market. The share price at the measurement date is CU0.5. Entity A accounts for the 16 per cent equity interest at fair value at initial recognition and at the end of each reporting period in accordance with IFRS 9 (or, prior to the adoption of IFRS 9, IAS 39).	IFRS 9 (or IAS 39) is the applicable Standard that requires the fair value measurement. IFRS 13:80 specifically discusses the measurement of fair value for a holding of financial instruments that are traded in an active market when the unit of account is the individual financial instrument (see **10.1** below). Such holdings are required to be measured within Level 1 as the product of the quoted price (P) for the individual financial instrument and the quantity (Q) held by the entity (i.e. P × Q). Therefore, in this scenario, the fair value of the 16 per cent equity interest in Entity B is measured as 160 million × CU0.5 = CU80 million.

Scenario	Unit of account prescribed in the applicable IFRS
Scenario 2	
Entity C owns a 54 per cent equity interest in Entity D (300 million ordinary shares). Entity D is a subsidiary of Entity C. Entity D's ordinary shares are traded in an active market. The share price at the measurement date is CU0.5.	Based on Entity C's accounting policy, IFRS 9 (or IAS 39) is the applicable Standard that requires the fair value measurement in Entity C's separate financial statements.
In its separate financial statements, Entity C has chosen to account for its investments in subsidiaries in accordance with IFRS 9 (or, prior to the adoption of IFRS 9, IAS 39) at fair value at initial recognition and at the end of each reporting period.	Consistent with the conclusion under Scenario 1 above, the unit of account for Entity C's investment in Entity D is the individual share in Entity D, and the fair value of the 54 per cent equity interest in Entity D is determined as the product of the quoted price (P) for the individual shares and the quantity (Q) held by Entity C (i.e. P × Q = 300 million × CU0.5 = CU150 million).
	This conclusion is equally applicable for fair value measurements in accordance with IFRS 9 (or IAS 39) of investments in associates or joint ventures in an entity's separate financial statements when the shares of the associate or the joint venture are traded in an active market.
	The measurement of such interests is the subject of ongoing discussion by the IASB (see below).
	Note that this question concerns measurement in the separate financial statements of Entity C only. The accounting in the consolidated financial statements is specified in IFRS 10 *Consolidated Financial Statements* (or, prior to the adoption of IFRS 10, IAS 27(2008) *Consolidated and Separate Financial Statements*).

Scenario	Unit of account prescribed in the applicable IFRS
Scenario 3 Entity E owns a 60 per cent equity interest in Entity F (120 million ordinary shares). Entity F is a subsidiary of Entity E. Entity F's ordinary shares are traded in an active market. The share price at the measurement date is CU0.5. For the purposes of Entity E's consolidated financial statements, the operations of Entity F represent a separate cash-generating unit (CGU) in accordance with IAS 36. There is an indication that this CGU may be impaired and, consequently, Entity E is required to estimate the recoverable amount of Entity F. IAS 36 defines the recoverable amount of a CGU as the higher of its value in use and fair value less costs to sell. For the purpose of measuring fair value less costs to sell, Entity E is required to apply the requirements of IFRS 13.	IAS 36 is the applicable Standard that requires Entity E to measure the fair value less costs to sell of Entity F in the circumstances described. What is being measured in this scenario is a CGU that represents the operations of Entity F; accordingly, the unit of account is the CGU and not the individual shares of Entity F. In this scenario, for impairment purposes, the CGU consists of Entity F's assets and liabilities that are recognised in Entity E's consolidated financial statements, together with any goodwill allocated to the CGU. Consequently, the fair value of the CGU for impairment assessment purposes should be the price that a market participant would pay to acquire a 100 per cent interest in Entity F in a single transaction. Because the unit of account is the CGU as a whole, appropriate adjustments should be made to reflect factors such as a control premium and liquidity risk if market participants would make such adjustments when pricing the 100 per cent interest in Entity F.

In March 2013, the IASB discussed the unit of account for investments in subsidiaries, joint ventures and associates. The IASB was asked whether the unit of account for such investments is the investment as a whole or the individual financial instruments that make up the investment. The IASB also discussed the interaction between the unit of account of those investments and their fair value measurement.

The IASB tentatively decided that the unit of account for investments in subsidiaries, joint ventures and associates is the investment as a whole. Secondly, the IASB tentatively decided that the fair value measurement of an investment composed of financial instruments quoted in an active market should be the product of the quoted price of the financial instrument (P) multiplied by the quantity (Q) of instruments held (i.e. P × Q) because Level 1 inputs should be given priority over the unit of account.

This issue is the subject of ongoing discussions by the IASB.

3.1.2   Determining the characteristics of an asset or a liability to be taken into account

When measuring fair value, the characteristics of an asset or a liability that should be taken into account are those that market participants would consider when pricing that asset or liability at the measurement date. Such characteristics could include, for example:
[IFRS 13:11]

- the condition and location of an asset; and

- restrictions, if any, on the sale or use of an asset.

The effect on the measurement arising from a particular characteristic will differ depending on how that characteristic would be taken into account by market participants. [IFRS 13:12]

3.1.2.1   Restrictions on the sale or use of an asset

Following the principle set out in IFRS 13:11 (see above), a legal or contractual restriction on the sale or use of an asset should be incorporated in the asset's fair value measurement if the restriction is a characteristic of the asset and market participants would take the effect of the restriction into account when pricing the asset.

The following examples, reproduced from the illustrative examples accompanying IFRS 13, illustrate the effect of restrictions on the fair value measurement of an asset. **Example 3.1.2.1A** considers a restriction that is a characteristic of the asset being measured and that would transfer to market participants with the asset; such restrictions should be taken into account when measuring the fair value of the asset. **Example 3.1.2.1B** considers a restriction that is specific to the entity holding the asset and that would not transfer to market participants; such entity-specific restrictions should not be taken into account when measuring the fair value of the asset.

Example 3.1.2.1A

Restriction on the sale of an equity instrument

[IFRS 13:IE28, Example 8]

An entity holds an equity instrument (a financial asset) for which sale is legally or contractually restricted for a specified period. (For example, such a restriction could limit sale to qualifying investors.) The restriction is a characteristic of the instrument and, therefore, would be transferred to market participants. In that case, the fair value of the instrument would be measured on the basis of the quoted price for an otherwise identical unrestricted equity instrument of the same issuer that trades in a public market, adjusted to reflect the effect of the restriction. The adjustment would reflect the amount market participants would demand because of the risk relating to the inability to access a public market for the instrument for the specified period. The adjustment will vary depending on all the following:

(a)   the nature and duration of the restriction;

(b)   the extent to which buyers are limited by the restriction (eg there might be a large number of qualifying investors); and

(c)   qualitative and quantitative factors specific to both the instrument and the issuer.

Example 3.1.2.1B

Restrictions on the use of an asset

[IFRS 13:IE29, Example 9]

A donor contributes land in an otherwise developed residential area to a not-for-profit neighbourhood association. The land is currently used as a playground. The donor specifies that the land must continue to be used by the association as a playground in perpetuity. Upon review of relevant documentation (e.g. legal and other), the association determines that the fiduciary responsibility to meet the donor's restriction would not be transferred to market participants if the association sold the asset, i.e. the donor restriction on the use of the land is specific to the association. Furthermore, the association is not restricted from selling the land. Without the restriction on the use of the land by the association, the land could be used as a site for residential development. In addition, the land is subject to an easement (i.e. a legal right that enables a utility to run power lines across the land). Following is an analysis of the effect on the fair value measurement of the land arising from the restriction and the easement:

(a)   *Donor restriction on use of land.* Because in this situation the donor restriction on the use of the land is specific to the association, the restriction would not be transferred to market participants. Therefore, the fair value of the land would be the higher of its fair value used as a playground (i.e. the fair value of the asset would be maximised through its use by market participants in combination with other assets or with other assets and liabilities) and its fair value as a site for residential development (i.e. the fair value of the asset would be maximised through its use by market participants on a stand-alone basis), regardless of the restriction on the use of the land by the association.

(b)   *Easement for utility lines.* Because the easement for utility lines is specific to (i.e. a characteristic of) the land, it would be transferred to market participants with the land. Therefore, the fair value measurement of the land would take into account the effect of the easement, regardless of whether the highest and best use is as a playground or as a site for residential development.

Sometimes it is immediately clear whether a restriction is a characteristic of an asset and would transfer to market participants. In other circumstances, significant judgement may be required to make the assessment and it may be necessary to obtain expert advice.

Consistent with **example 3.1.2.1A**, when a restriction is a characteristic of an asset and would transfer to a market participant and, consequently, needs to be taken into account when measuring the fair value of the asset, this is achieved by adjusting the fair value of an identical unrestricted asset to reflect the 'compensation' that a market participant would require because of the restriction. The adjustment will vary depending on (1) the nature and duration of the restriction, (2) the extent to which buyers are limited by the restriction, and (3) qualitative and quantitative factors specific to the asset (including factors specific to the issuer of the asset, as appropriate).

When categorising the fair value measurement for the purposes of the fair value hierarchy under IFRS 13:72, an entity will need to evaluate the significance of any adjustment made to reflect a restriction on the sale or use of the asset (see **10.2.2.1** below for additional guidance regarding such evaluations).

Below are some additional common examples of restrictions on the sale of assets.

Restriction on the sale of securities specified in contractual terms   When a restriction on the sale of securities (e.g. prohibiting sale of the securities to specified groups of investors or only permitting the securities to be sold to specified groups of investors) is embedded in the contractual terms of the securities, the restriction is a characteristic of the securities and would transfer to market participants. Consequently, the fair value measurement of the securities should reflect the asset-specific restriction.

Founders' shares   Founder shareholders may be contractually prevented from selling their shares immediately following an initial public offering (IPO). Such a restriction may be outlined in the IPO prospectus. Assuming that the restriction is not embedded in the contractual terms of the shares (and, accordingly, would not transfer to a market participant in a hypothetical sale of the shares), the restriction is specific to the founder shareholders and is not a characteristic of the shares. In such circumstances, the restriction on the sale of the shares would not be taken into account when measuring the fair value of the shares.

Directors' shareholdings   Assume that Company A owns ordinary shares issued by Company B and Company A is entitled to appoint a member of its management team to Company B's board of directors. Because Company A appoints a director of Company B, Company A is restricted from selling any of its shares in Company B during the period surrounding Company B's periodic release of earnings. Other market participants that are not directors of Company B or do not have a right to appoint directors of Company B would not be subject to this restriction. Because the restriction is entity-specific (i.e. it is not a characteristic of the shares) and would not transfer with the shares, Company A should not reflect the effect of the restriction in the fair value measurement of its investment in Company B.

Assets pledged as collateral   An entity may enter into a borrowing arrangement that requires assets to be pledged as collateral. The borrowing arrangement may restrict the entity from selling or transferring the assets during the term of the arrangement. Other market participants, however, would not be subject to this restriction. Because the restriction is entity-specific (i.e. it is not a characteristic of the assets) and would not transfer with the assets, it should not be reflected in the fair value measurement of the pledged assets.

3.2   Identifying the market in which to price the asset or liability

IFRS 13 requires an entity to consider the market in which the sale of an asset or the transfer of a liability will take place. The Standard

introduces the concepts of a 'principal market' and a 'most advantageous market'. Both terms are important in establishing the market
in which the particular asset will be sold or liability transferred and,
therefore, in determining what price will be achieved if the sale or
transfer occurs in that market at the measurement date.

3.2.1   Principal market versus most advantageous market

For the purposes of measuring fair value, the transaction to sell the asset
or transfer the liability is assumed to take place either:
[IFRS 13:16]

- in the 'principal market' for the asset or liability; or

- in the absence of a principal market, in the 'most advantageous
  market' for the asset or liability.

The principal market is defined as "[t]he market with the greatest volume
and level of activity for the asset or liability". [IFRS 13:Appendix A].

The most advantageous market is defined as "[t]he market that maximises
the amount that would be received to sell the asset or minimises the
amount that would be paid to transfer the liability, after taking into
account transaction costs and transport costs". [IFRS 13:Appendix A].

The exposure draft preceding IFRS 13 proposed that the transaction
should be assumed to take place in the most advantageous market to
which the entity has access. This presented some difficulties for
respondents to the exposure draft, particularly regarding the identification of the most advantageous market when the asset or liability
is exchanged in multiple markets throughout the world, and the
potential disconnect between the most advantageous market and the
market in which the entity normally enters into such transactions.
Consequently, in the final Standard, the focus has been shifted to the
principal market. [IFRS 13:BC48 – BC51]

Note that, although transaction costs are not deducted (for an asset)
or added (for a liability) when measuring fair value, they are considered when identifying the most advantageous market for an asset or
a liability (see 3.4.2).

The principal market should be identified on the basis of the volume
or level of activity for the asset or liability rather than the volume or
level of activity of the reporting entity's transactions in a particular

market. [IFRS 13:BC52] Therefore, the assessment as to which of two or more accessible markets is the principal market is made from the perspective of market participants rather than the entity.

Equally, in the absence of a principal market, the most advantageous market is identified using the assumptions that market participants would use.

A principal market may not exist, for example, when the volume or level of activity for the asset or liability is the same in two different markets to which the entity has access, or when there is no observable market for the asset or liability. In such circumstances, an entity needs to identify the most advantageous market or develop assumptions from the perspective of a market participant in a hypothetical most advantageous market. IFRS 13 does not require an entity to conduct an exhaustive search of all possible markets to identify the principal market or, in the absence of a principal market, the most advantageous market, but an entity is required to take into account all information that is reasonably available. In the absence of evidence to the contrary, the market in which an entity would normally enter into a transaction to sell the asset or to transfer the liability is presumed to be the principal (or most advantageous) market. [IFRS 13:17]

Therefore, an entity is permitted to use the price in the market in which it normally enters into transactions unless there is evidence that the principal market and that market are not the same. [IFRS 13:BC53]

If there is evidence that the market in which an entity would normally transact is not the principal (or most advantageous) market, the principal (or most advantageous) market should be identified by:

- firstly, identifying other markets to which the entity has access; and

- secondly, when relevant, assessing which of two or more accessible markets is the principal (or most advantageous) market.

If there is a principal market for the asset or liability, the fair value measurement should reflect the price in that market, even if the price in a different market is potentially more advantageous at the measurement date. [IFRS 13:18]

3.2.2   Access to the market

To use the price in the principal (or most advantageous) market as the basis for measuring fair value, an entity must have access to that market at the measurement date. Because different entities (and businesses within those entities) with different activities may have access to different markets, the principal (or most advantageous) market for the same asset or liability might be different for different entities (and businesses within those entities). Therefore, the principal (or most advantageous) market (and thus, market participants) should be considered from the perspective of the entity, thereby allowing for differences between and among entities with different activities. [IFRS 13:19]

> Example 7 of the illustrative examples accompanying IFRS 13 (summarised at **section 7** below) illustrates a scenario in which two entities measure the same instrument differently because each identifies its principal market on the basis of the market to which it has access.

Although an entity must be able to access the market, the entity does not need to be able to sell the particular asset or transfer the particular liability on the measurement date to be able to measure fair value on the basis of the price in that market. [IFRS 13:20]

> For example, as discussed in **example 3.1.2.1A**, an entity may be restricted from selling a particular asset at the measurement date. Nevertheless, if the entity has access to the principal market at that date, the entity could measure the asset's fair value using observed prices for sales of similar (but unrestricted) assets in that market. If the restriction is a characteristic of the asset (i.e. it would transfer with the asset in a hypothetical sale), an entity should make an adjustment to observed market prices for similar (but unrestricted) assets to reflect the restriction (see **3.1.2.1** above for further details).

3.2.3   Measuring fair value when no apparent exit market exists

Even when there is no observable market to provide pricing information about the sale of an asset or the transfer of a liability at the measurement date, a fair value measurement should assume that a transaction takes place at that date, considered from the perspective of a market participant that holds the asset or owes the liability. That assumed transaction establishes a basis for estimating the price to sell the asset or to transfer the liability. [IFRS 13:21]

> When an observable market for an asset or a liability does not exist, an entity must assume a hypothetical transaction at the measurement date. This is consistent with the fair value objective in IFRS 13 to measure fair value as "the price that would be received to sell an asset or paid to transfer a liability in an orderly transaction between market participants at the measurement date" (see IFRS 13:Appendix A). See **3.3.1** below for guidance on how an entity might identify market participants when no apparent exit market exists.

3.2.4   Factors indicating a change in the principal (or most advantageous) market

> While it is presumed that the market in which an entity normally transacts is the principal (or most advantageous) market (see **3.2.1** above), an entity should reassess the principal (or most advantageous) market for an asset or a liability at each measurement date based on reasonably available information. Factors indicating that there may have been a change in the principal (or most advantageous) market include the following (the list is not exhaustive):
>
> - a significant change in market conditions;
>
> - a decrease in the volume or level of activity relative to other markets;
>
> - the development of a new market (see below);
>
> - a change in the entity's ability to access particular markets (e.g. an entity loses access to a market or gains access to a market to which it did not previously have access); and

- when there is no principal market, a change in value such that the price for the asset or liability in a market previously considered most advantageous is no longer the most advantageous.

Events such as those listed above may indicate that there has been a change in the principal (or most advantageous) market for the asset or liability, or that circumstances have changed such that there is no longer a principal market for the asset or liability (in which case the entity should refer instead to the most advantageous market).

When a market first develops (e.g. for a new form of securities), it may operate primarily as a principal-to-principal or over-the-counter market. However, the volume and level of activity in the exchange market may increase over time. As the volume and level of activity change, and the balance of market activity shifts, an entity should take this into account when reassessing the principal (or most advantageous) market for an asset or a liability.

3.3   Market participants

IFRS 13 requires an entity to use the assumptions that 'market participants' would use when pricing the asset or liability, assuming that market participants act in their economic best interest. [IFRS 13:22]

Market participants are defined as "[b]uyers and sellers in the principal (or most advantageous) market for the asset or liability that have all of the following characteristics:

(a) They are independent of each other, i.e. they are not related parties as defined in IAS 24, although the price in a related party transaction may be used as an input to a fair value measurement if the entity has evidence that the transaction was entered into at market terms.

(b) They are knowledgeable, having a reasonable understanding about the asset or liability and the transaction using all available information, including information that might be obtained through due diligence efforts that are usual and customary.

(c) They are able to enter into a transaction for the asset or liability.

(d) They are willing to enter into a transaction for the asset or liability, i.e. they are motivated but not forced or otherwise compelled to do so". [IFRS 13:Appendix A]

In developing those assumptions, an entity is not required to identify specific market participants, but is expected to identify characteristics that distinguish market participants generally, considering factors specific to: [IFRS 13:23]

- the asset or liability;

- the principal (or most advantageous) market for the asset or liability; and

- market participants with whom the entity would enter into a transaction in that market.

Example 3.3

Use of assumptions that market participants would use

Entity F uses a discounted cash flow model to measure the fair value of a financial asset. Entity F has obtained information about the assumptions that market participants would use to measure the fair value of the asset. However, Entity F believes that some of those assumptions are not appropriate.

Entity F is not permitted to rely on its own internal data rather than use the assumptions that market participants would use. A fair value measurement is a market-based measurement and not entity-specific. IFRS 13:22 requires that the fair value of an asset or a liability should be measured using the assumptions that market participants would use when pricing the asset or liability, assuming that market participants act in their economic best interest.

When using a discounted cash flow model to measure the fair value of a financial asset, Entity F should incorporate relevant observable inputs whenever available. Any unobservable inputs used in the fair value measure (e.g. estimated future cash flows or risk adjustments incorporated into the discount rate) should be based on management's estimate of assumptions that market participants would use in pricing the asset in a current transaction at the measurement date. If market data from transactions involving comparable assets indicate, for example, that a significant liquidity discount applies at the measurement date to compensate for the difficulty in selling assets under current market conditions, Entity F should incorporate that information in its cash flow model (e.g. through an adjustment to the discount rate) even if management's internal data would not result in such a liquidity adjustment.

3.3.1 Identifying market participants when no apparent exit market exists

IFRS 13:21 requires that, even when there is no observable market to provide pricing information about the sale of an asset or the transfer of a liability at the measurement date, a fair value measurement should assume that a transaction takes place at that date, considered from the perspective of a market participant that holds the asset or owes the liability. That assumed transaction establishes a basis for estimating the price to sell the asset or to transfer the liability (see **3.2.3** above).

In such circumstances, the entity is not required to identify specific market participants. Instead, the entity should consider the characteristics of potential market participants who would purchase the asset or accept a transfer of the liability being measured. In addition, the entity should identify the assumptions that such market participants would make in a transaction that maximises the amount received to sell an asset or minimises the amount paid to transfer a liability.

Potential market participants include the following (the list is not exhaustive).

- For non-financial assets, groups of non-financial assets, or groups of non-financial assets and liabilities in a business or cash-generating unit:

  - **strategic buyers:** these buyers have related assets and the asset being measured would enhance the value of the business unit within which the buyer would use the asset. Examples of strategic buyers are direct competitors or others with characteristics similar to those of the entity; and

  - **financial buyers:** these buyers do not have related or substitute assets. Examples of financial buyers are financial institutional investors and private equity and venture capital investors.

- For financial instruments: counterparties to a derivative instrument, investors maximising return, investors trying to establish a strategic relationship with an investee, or a range of other participants with a specific objective.

When identifying a potential market participant, care should be taken to ensure that the unit of account from the perspective of the market participant is consistent with the unit of account of the item being measured.

When developing assumptions that market participants would use in such a hypothetical transaction, an entity may start with its own assumptions and make adjustments for factors specific to the asset or liability being measured, including (the list is not exhaustive):

- transportation costs necessary to transfer an asset from its current location to the hypothetical market (if location is a characteristic of the asset);

- conversion costs to transform a non-financial asset from its current condition to its highest and best use from the perspective of potential market participants;

- synergies that are specific to the entity and not available to market participants and thus would not be taken into account in the hypothetical transaction (e.g. cost savings from synergies related to other groups of assets held by the entity);

- growth rates and risk adjustments to reflect market participant assumptions; and

- performance and risk indicators (e.g. delinquencies, defaults, prepayment speeds and interest rates).

Market participant assumptions that are developed when no apparent market exists may be based on unobservable inputs or adjustments. An entity needs to evaluate the significance of these inputs or adjustments when determining the appropriate level in the fair value hierarchy within which the measurement should be categorised (see **10.2.2.1** below for additional guidance regarding such evaluations).

3.4   The price at which a transaction is assumed to occur

The price at which a transaction is assumed to occur in the principal or most advantageous market is the price:
[IFRS 13:24]

- in an 'orderly' transaction (see **3.4.1**); and

- under current market conditions at the measurement date.

The price may be directly observable or estimated using another valuation technique (see **section 8**). [IFRS 13:24]

The price should not be adjusted for 'transaction costs', but it should be adjusted for 'transport costs' in specified circumstances (see **3.4.2**). [IFRS 13:25 & 26]

3.4.1   An 'orderly' transaction

A fair value measurement assumes that the asset or liability is exchanged in an 'orderly' transaction in the principal (or most advantageous) market. An orderly transaction is defined as "[a] transaction that assumes exposure to the market for a period before the measurement date to allow for marketing activities that are usual and customary for transactions involving such assets or liabilities; it is not a forced transaction (e.g. a forced liquidation or distress sale)". [IFRS 13:Appendix A]

Appendix B to the Standard provides additional guidance regarding the identification of orderly transactions (see **9.5**).

3.4.2   Transaction costs and transport costs

Transaction costs are defined as "[t]he costs to sell an asset or transfer a liability in the principal (or most advantageous) market for the asset or liability that are directly attributable to the disposal of the asset or the transfer of the liability and meet both of the following criteria:

(a)   They result directly from and are essential to that transaction.

(b)   They would not have been incurred by the entity had the decision to sell the asset or transfer the liability not been made (similar to costs to sell, as defined in IFRS 5)". [IFRS 13:Appendix A]

Transaction costs do not include transport costs. [IFRS 13:26] Transport costs are defined as "[t]he costs that would be incurred to transport an asset from its current location to its principal (or most advantageous) market". [IFRS 13:Appendix A]

IFRS 13 specifies that, when measuring fair value, the relevant market price should *not* be reduced (for an asset) or increased (for a liability) for transaction costs. Because such costs are specific to a transaction and will differ depending on how an entity enters into a transaction for an asset or a liability, they are not considered to be a characteristic of the asset or liability. [IFRS 13:25]

The appropriate treatment for transaction costs should be determined in accordance with other relevant IFRSs. [IFRS 13:25]

> Note, however, that transaction costs are considered when identifying the most advantageous market for an asset or a liability (see **3.2.1** above and **example 3.4.2A** below).

In contrast, the price in the principal (or most advantageous) market used to measure the fair value of an asset or liability *is* adjusted for any transport costs (as defined above) *if* location is a characteristic of the asset (which might be the case, for example, for a commodity). [IFRS 13:26]

> The appropriate treatments for transaction and transport costs are illustrated in the following example, which is reproduced from the illustrative examples accompanying the Standard.

Example 3.4.2A

Level 1 principal (or most advantageous) market

[IFRS 13:IE19 – IE22, Example 6]

An asset is sold in two different active markets at different prices. An entity enters into transactions in both markets and can access the price in those markets for the asset at the measurement date. In Market A, the price that would be received is CU26, transaction costs in that market are CU3 and the costs to transport the asset to that market are CU2 (ie the net amount that would be received is CU21). In Market B, the price that would be received is CU25, transaction costs in that market are CU1 and the costs to transport the asset to that market are CU2 (ie the net amount that would be received in Market B is CU22).

If Market A is the principal market for the asset (ie the market with the greatest volume and level of activity for the asset), the fair value of the asset would be measured using the price that would be received in that market, after taking into account transport costs (CU24).

If neither market is the principal market for the asset, the fair value of the asset would be measured using the price in the most advantageous market. The most advantageous market is the market that maximises the amount

---

that would be received to sell the asset, after taking into account transaction costs and transport costs (ie the net amount that would be received in the respective markets).

Because the entity would maximise the net amount that would be received for the asset in Market B (CU22), the fair value of the asset would be measured using the price in that market (CU25), less transport costs (CU2), resulting in a fair value measurement of CU23. Although transaction costs are taken into account when determining which market is the most advantageous market, the price used to measure the fair value of the asset is not adjusted for those costs (although it is adjusted for transport costs).

IFRS 13 requires entities to reflect characteristics specific to the asset or liability being measured when measuring fair value. Consequently, *if* location is a characteristic of an asset, an entity should adjust the price in the principal (or most advantageous) market for transport costs when measuring the fair value of the asset.

The following two examples illustrate how transport costs may be a subtractive input or an additive input as an adjustment to an observable market price for an asset.

Example 3.4.2B

Transport costs are a subtractive input

Company A has agricultural produce ready for harvesting at Location 1. As required under IAS 41 *Agriculture*, the agricultural produce is measured at fair value less costs to sell at the point of harvest. The fair value less costs to sell at that date will subsequently be used as the cost when applying IAS 2 *Inventories* to the harvested produce.

Company A has identified Location 2 as the principal market for sale of its produce. The quoted price for the produce in Location 2 is CU100 per unit. Company A determines that transport costs of CU5 per unit would be incurred to move the produce from Location 1 to Location 2. Therefore, the fair value of the produce at its current location would be CU95 per unit (i.e. CU100 per unit quoted price at Location 2 less CU5 per unit to transport the produce to the principal market at Location 2). Note that this represents the fair value before deduction of costs to sell in accordance with IAS 41.

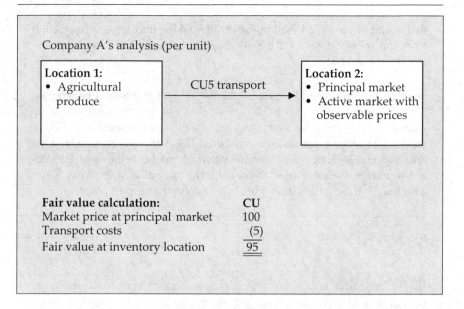

Company A's analysis (per unit)

Location 1:
- Agricultural produce

CU5 transport →

Location 2:
- Principal market
- Active market with observable prices

Fair value calculation:	CU
Market price at principal market	100
Transport costs	(5)
Fair value at inventory location	95

Example 3.4.2C

Transport costs are an additive input

Company B has agricultural produce ready for harvesting at Location 1. As required under IAS 41, the agricultural produce at the point of harvest is measured at fair value less costs to sell.

Location 1 is a developing retail market for Company B's produce with a relatively low level of activity. Location 1 is the only market to which Company B has access and therefore it is identified as Company B's principal market.

There is also a wholesale market for the agricultural produce at Location 2 which is an active market. Although Company B does not have access to the wholesale market at Location 2, that market provides an observable current price for comparable produce of CU100 per unit. Company B determines that this price represents a more reliable input for the fair value measurement of its produce because of the higher level of activity in the market at Location 2 compared to Location 1.

However, when measuring the fair value of its produce, Company B must apply an adjustment to the prices quoted at Location 2, because they reflect a location other than its principal market. Company B determines that the cost to transport the produce from Location 2 to Location 1 is CU5 per unit. Based on observations in Company B's principal market at Location 1, it can be corroborated that market participants in the principal market would be willing to pay a retail price that is based on the wholesale price in Location 2 plus the cost to transport the produce from Location 2 to Location 1. Accordingly, the fair value of the produce at Location 1 is measured at CU105 per unit (i.e. CU100 per unit at Location 2 plus CU5 per unit to transport the produce to Company B's principal market at Location 1).

Company B's analysis (per unit)

Location 1:
- Agricultural produce
- Principal market

CU5 transport ←

Location 2:
- Active market with observable prices

Fair value calculation:	CU
Market price at principal market	100
Transport costs	5
Fair value at inventory location	105

4   Measuring the fair value of non-financial assets – highest and best use

A fair value measurement of a non-financial asset is based on its 'highest and best use' (see below). This concept is not relevant for financial assets, liabilities or an entity's own equity instruments because those items do not have alternative uses as contemplated in IFRS 13. [IFRS 13:BC63]

When measuring the fair value of a non-financial asset, an entity is required to take into account a market participant's ability to generate economic benefits by using the asset in its 'highest and best use' or by selling it to another market participant that would use the asset in its highest and best use. [IFRS 13:27]

The highest and best use of a non-financial asset is defined as "[t]he use of a non-financial asset by market participants that would maximise the value of the asset or the group of assets and liabilities (eg a business) within which the asset would be used". [IFRS 13:Appendix A]

365

The highest and best use takes into account the use of the non-financial asset that is:
[IFRS 13:28]

- physically possible (taking into account the physical characteristics of the asset that market participants would consider when pricing the asset – e.g. the location or size of a property);

- legally permissible (taking into account any legal restrictions on the use of the asset that market participants would consider when pricing the asset – e.g. the zoning regulations applicable to a property); and

- financially feasible (taking into account whether a use of the asset that is physically possible and legally permissible generates an adequate investment return that market participants would require from an investment in that asset put to that use).

For the purposes of the final bullet above, the income or cash flows producing the investment return should take into account the costs of converting the asset to that use. [IFRS 13:28]

In the context of IFRS 13:28, the question arises as to whether the term 'legally permissible' should be taken to refer to a use of the asset that is currently legally permitted, or should be more broadly interpreted to mean a use that may be permitted in the future.

This question is not specifically addressed in the body of IFRS 13, but it is referred to in the Basis for Conclusions, as follows.

> "Some respondents asked for further guidance about whether a use that is legally permissible must be legal at the measurement date, or if, for example, future changes in legislation can be taken into account. The IASB concluded that a use of an asset does not need to be legal at the measurement date, but must not be legally prohibited in the jurisdiction (eg if the government of a particular country has prohibited building or development in a protected area, the highest and best use of the land in that area could not be to develop it for industrial use). The illustrative examples that accompany IFRS 13 show how an asset can be zoned for a particular use at the measurement date, but how a fair value measurement can assume a different zoning if market participants would do so (incorporating the cost to

convert the asset and obtain that different zoning permission, including the risk that such permission would not be granted)." [IFRS 13:BC69]

This discussion clarifies that the term 'legally permissible' is not restricted to uses that are legal at the measurement date. For example, in the context of zoning regulations and depending on the rules in the particular jurisdiction, if a property is zoned only for commercial use at the measurement date, but market participants would take a potential change in use into account in pricing the property, the illustrative example set out in IFRS 13:IE7 and 8 (see **example 4A** below) indicates that such a potential change in use should be incorporated in the fair value measurement.

The key to determining whether a particular use should be considered to be legally permissible is set out in IFRS 13:28: "[a] use that is legally permissible takes into account any legal restrictions on the use of the asset that market participants would take into account when pricing the asset (eg the zoning regulations applicable to a property)". In line with the general requirement under IFRS 13:22 to measure fair value using the assumptions that market participants would use, if market participants in pricing an asset would factor in the possibility that current legal restrictions might change in the future, then that potential for future changes in restrictions should be incorporated into the fair value measurement.

Example 4A

Land

[IFRS 13:IE7 & IE8, Example 2]

An entity acquires land in a business combination. The land is currently developed for industrial use as a site for a factory. The current use of land is presumed to be its highest and best use unless market or other factors suggest a different use. Nearby sites have recently been developed for residential use as sites for high-rise apartment buildings. On the basis of that development and recent zoning and other changes to facilitate that development, the entity determines that the land currently used as a site for a factory could be developed as a site for residential use (ie for high-rise apartment buildings) because market participants would take into account the potential to develop the site for residential use when pricing the land.

The highest and best use of the land would be determined by comparing both of the following:

(a)   the value of the land as currently developed for industrial use (ie the land would be used in combination with other assets, such as the factory, or with other assets and liabilities).

(b)   the value of the land as a vacant site for residential use, taking into account the costs of demolishing the factory and other costs (including the uncertainty about whether the entity would be able to convert the asset to the alternative use) necessary to convert the land to a vacant site (ie the land is to be used by market participants on a stand-alone basis).

The highest and best use of the land would be determined on the basis of the higher of those values. In situations involving real estate appraisal, the determination of highest and best use might take into account factors relating to the factory operations, including its assets and liabilities.

Highest and best use is determined from the perspective of market participants, even if the entity intends a different use. However, an entity's current use of a non-financial asset is presumed to be its highest and best use unless market or other factors suggest that a different use by market participants would maximise the value of the asset. [IFRS 13:29]

IFRS 13 does not require an entity to perform an exhaustive search for other potential uses of a non-financial asset if there is no evidence to suggest that the current use of an asset is not its highest and best use. The IASB concluded that an entity that seeks to maximise the value of its assets would use those assets at their highest and best use and that it would be necessary for an entity to consider alternative uses of those assets only if there was evidence that the current use of the assets is not their highest and best use (i.e. an alternative use would maximise their fair value). [IFRS 13:BC71]

There may be reasons why an entity intends not to use an acquired non-financial asset actively or according to its highest and best use (e.g. if an entity acquires an intangible asset solely in order to protect its competitive position by preventing others from using the intangible asset). Nevertheless, in such circumstances, the entity is required to measure the fair value of the asset assuming its highest and best use by market participants. [IFRS 13:30]

The requirements of IFRS 13:30, which are illustrated in **example 4B**, are consistent with guidance already included in IFRS 3 *Business*

Combinations regarding assets acquired in a business combination that the acquirer intends not to use or to use in a way that is different from the way other market participants would use them (see also **7.2.2** in **chapter A25**).

Example 4B

Research and development project

[IFRS 13:IE9, Example 3]

An entity acquires a research and development (R&D) project in a business combination. The entity does not intend to complete the project. If completed, the project would compete with one of its own projects (to provide the next generation of the entity's commercialised technology). Instead, the entity intends to hold (ie lock up) the project to prevent its competitors from obtaining access to the technology. In doing this, the project is expected to provide defensive value, principally by improving the prospects for the entity's own competing technology. To measure the fair value of the project at initial recognition, the highest and best use of the project would be determined on the basis of its use by market participants. For example:

(a)   The highest and best use of the R&D project would be to continue development if market participants would continue to develop the project and that use would maximise the value of the group of assets or of assets and liabilities in which the project would be used (ie the asset would be used in combination with other assets or with other assets and liabilities). That might be the case if market participants do not have similar technology, either in development or commercialised. The fair value of the project would be measured on the basis of the price that would be received in a current transaction to sell the project, assuming that the R&D would be used with its complementary assets and the associated liabilities and that those assets and liabilities would be available to market participants.

(b)   The highest and best use of the R&D project would be to cease development if, for competitive reasons, market participants would lock up the project and that use would maximise the value of the group of assets or of assets and liabilities in which the project would be used. That might be the case if market participants have technology in a more advanced stage of development that would compete with the project if completed and the project would be expected to improve the prospects for their own competing technology if locked up. The fair value of the project would be measured on the basis of the price that would be received in a current transaction to sell the project, assuming that the R&D would be used (ie locked up) with its complementary assets and the associated liabilities and that those assets and liabilities would be available to market participants.

(c)   The highest and best use of the R&D project would be to cease development if market participants would discontinue its development. That might be the case if the project is not expected to provide a market rate of return if completed and would not otherwise provide defensive value if locked up. The fair value of the project would be measured on the basis of the price that would be received in a current transaction to sell the project on its own (which might be zero).

4.1   Highest and best use as a stand-alone asset

If the highest and best use of the asset is on a stand-alone basis, the fair value of the asset is the price that would be received in a current transaction to sell the asset to market participants that would use the asset on a stand-alone basis. [IFRS 13:31(b)]

4.2   Highest and best use as part of a group of assets or in combination with other assets and liabilities

If the highest and best use of the asset is in combination with other assets or with other assets and liabilities, the fair value of the asset is the price that would be received in a current transaction to sell the asset assuming that the asset would be used with other assets or with other assets and liabilities and that those assets and liabilities would be available to market participants. [IFRS 13:31(a)(i)]

Therefore, in such circumstances, the price used would be the price for a sale to a market participant that has, or can obtain, the other assets and liabilities needed to generate cash inflows by using the asset (i.e. its complementary assets and the associated liabilities). [IFRS 13:BC74(a)]

When the highest and best use of a non-financial asset is in combination with other assets and liabilities, the liabilities associated with the asset and with the complementary assets include liabilities that fund working capital, but do not include liabilities used to fund assets other than those within the group of assets. [IFRS 13:31(a)(ii)]

Assumptions about the highest and best use of a non-financial asset should be consistent for all the assets (for which highest and best use is relevant) of the group of assets or the group of assets and liabilities within which the asset would be used. [IFRS 13:31(a)(iii)]

Even when it is considered that the highest and best use of a non-financial asset is in combination with other assets, or with other assets and liabilities, the unit of account for the purposes of the fair value measurement (see **3.1** above) is the unit of account specified in other IFRSs (which may be an individual asset). Specifically, the fair value measurement assumes that the market participant already holds the complementary assets and the associated liabilities and, therefore, that the non-financial asset is sold by itself. [IFRS 13:32]

It is assumed that the non-financial asset being measured at fair value is sold on its own (at the unit of account level) even if transactions in the asset are typically the result of sales of the asset as part of a group of assets or a business. Even when an asset is used in combination with other assets, the exit price for the asset is a price for that asset individually because a fair value measurement assumes that a market participant (buyer) of the asset already holds the complementary assets and the associated liabilities. Because the buyer is assumed to hold the other assets (and liabilities) necessary for the asset to function, that buyer would not be willing to pay more for the asset solely because it was sold as part of a group. [IFRS 13:BC77]

When measuring the fair value of a non-financial asset used in combination with other assets or with other assets and liabilities, the effect of the requirements in IFRS 13:31 and 32 (as described above) depends on the circumstances. The fair value of the asset may be the same whether the asset is used on a stand-alone basis or in combination with other assets or with other assets and liabilities. That might be the case if the asset is a business that market participants would continue to operate. In such circumstances, the business should be valued in its entirety, thus reflecting the synergies that would be available to market participants. [IFRS 13:B3]

The Standard provides the following examples of how an asset's use in combination with other assets or with other assets and liabilities might be incorporated into the fair value measurement.
[IFRS 13:B3]

- It might be incorporated through adjustments to the value of the asset used on a stand-alone basis. That might be the case if the asset is a machine and the fair value measurement is determined using an observed price for a similar machine (not installed or otherwise configured for use), adjusted for transport and installation costs so that the fair value measurement reflects the current condition and location of the machine (installed and configured for use).

- It might be incorporated through the market participant assumptions used to measure the fair value of the asset. For example, if the asset is work in progress inventory that is unique and market participants would convert the inventory into finished goods, the fair value of the inventory would assume that market participants have acquired or would acquire any specialised machinery necessary to convert the inventory into finished goods.

- It might be incorporated into the valuation technique used to measure the fair value of the asset. That might be the case when using the multi-period excess earnings method to measure the fair value of an intangible asset because that valuation technique specifically takes into account the contribution of any complementary assets and the associated liabilities in the group in which such an intangible asset would be used.

- In more limited situations, when an entity uses an asset within a group of assets, the entity might measure the asset at an amount that approximates its fair value when allocating the fair value of the asset group to the individual assets of the group. That might be the case if the valuation involves real property and the fair value of improved property (i.e. an asset group) is allocated to its component assets (such as land and improvements).

The following example, reproduced from the illustrative examples accompanying IFRS 13, describes the measurement of the fair value of an asset that is used as part of a group of assets.

Example 4.2

Asset group

[IFRS 13:IE3 – IE6, Example 1]

An entity acquires assets and assumes liabilities in a business combination. One of the groups of assets acquired comprises Assets A, B and C. Asset C is billing software integral to the business developed by the acquired entity for its own use in conjunction with Assets A and B (ie the related assets). The entity measures the fair value of each of the assets individually, consistently with the specified unit of account for the assets. The entity determines that the highest and best use of the assets is their current use and that each asset would provide maximum value to market participants principally through its use in combination with other assets or with other assets and liabilities

---

(ie its complementary assets and the associated liabilities). There is no evidence to suggest that the current use of the assets is not their highest and best use.

In this situation, the entity would sell the assets in the market in which it initially acquired the assets (ie the entry and exit markets from the perspective of the entity are the same). Market participant buyers with whom the entity would enter into a transaction in that market have characteristics that are generally representative of both strategic buyers (such as competitors) and financial buyers (such as private equity or venture capital firms that do not have complementary investments) and include those buyers that initially bid for the assets. Although market participant buyers might be broadly classified as strategic or financial buyers, in many cases there will be differences among the market participant buyers within each of those groups, reflecting, for example, different uses for an asset and different operating strategies.

As discussed below, differences between the indicated fair values of the individual assets relate principally to the use of the assets by those market participants within different asset groups:

(a)   Strategic buyer asset group. The entity determines that strategic buyers have related assets that would enhance the value of the group within which the assets would be used (ie market participant synergies). Those assets include a substitute asset for Asset C (the billing software), which would be used for only a limited transition period and could not be sold on its own at the end of that period. Because strategic buyers have substitute assets, Asset C would not be used for its full remaining economic life. The indicated fair values of Assets A, B and C within the strategic buyer asset group (reflecting the synergies resulting from the use of the assets within that group) are CU360, CU260 and CU30, respectively. The indicated fair value of the assets as a group within the strategic buyer asset group is CU650.

(b)   Financial buyer asset group. The entity determines that financial buyers do not have related or substitute assets that would enhance the value of the group within which the assets would be used. Because financial buyers do not have substitute assets, Asset C (ie the billing software) would be used for its full remaining economic life. The indicated fair values of Assets A, B and C within the financial buyer asset group are CU300, CU200 and CU100, respectively. The indicated fair value of the assets as a group within the financial buyer asset group is CU600.

The fair values of Assets A, B and C would be determined on the basis of the use of the assets as a group within the strategic buyer group (CU360, CU260 and CU30). Although the use of the assets within the strategic buyer group does not maximise the fair value of each of the assets individually, it maximises the fair value of the assets as a group (CU650).

5   Measuring the fair value of liabilities and an entity's own equity instruments

Except when indicated otherwise, the guidance in this section regarding liabilities applies equally to financial and non-financial liabilities.

5.1   General principles

The fair value of a liability or an entity's own equity instrument (e.g. equity interests issued as consideration in a business combination) is measured based on the assumption that the liability or equity instrument is transferred to a market participant at the measurement date. [IFRS 13:34]

For a liability, it is assumed that the liability would remain outstanding and the market participant transferee would be required to fulfil the obligation. It would not be settled with the counterparty or otherwise extinguished on the measurement date. [IFRS 13:34(a)]

IFRS 13 is clear that the fair value of a liability is based on a transfer amount, i.e. the amount the reporting entity would need to pay a third party to take on the obligation, and that obligation remains outstanding and contractually unaltered before and after transfer. Fair value is therefore not based on the premise of settling the liability with the counterparty at the measurement date.

For an entity's own equity instrument, it is assumed that the equity instrument would remain outstanding and the market participant transferee would take on the rights and responsibilities associated with the instrument. The instrument would not be cancelled or otherwise extinguished on the measurement date. [IFRS 13:34(b)]

When an entity is required to measure a liability or its own equity instrument at fair value under another IFRS, IFRS 13 requires that the fair value measure be based on an assumed transfer to a market participant even if an entity does not intend to transfer its liability or own equity instrument to a third party (e.g. because the entity has advantages relative to the market that make it more beneficial for the entity to fulfil the liability using its own internal resources) or it is unable to do so (e.g. because the counterparty would not permit the liability to be transferred to another party). [IFRS 13:BC81 & 82]

Even when there is no observable market to provide pricing information about the transfer of a liability or an entity's own equity instrument (e.g. because contractual or other legal restrictions prevent the transfer of such items), there might be an observable market for such items if they are held by other parties as assets (see **5.1.1**). [IFRS 13:35]

Consistent with the objective of fair value measurement and the prioritisation in the fair value hierarchy (see **section 10**), when measuring the fair value of a liability or an entity's own equity instrument, the entity should maximise the use of relevant observable inputs and minimise the use of unobservable inputs. [IFRS 13:36]

5.1.1   Liabilities and equity instruments held by other parties as assets

When a quoted price for the transfer of an identical or a similar liability or an entity's own equity instrument is not available, and the identical item is held by another party as an asset, an entity is required to measure the fair value of the liability or equity instrument from the perspective of a market participant that holds the identical item as an asset at the measurement date. [IFRS 13:37] This requirement could be relevant, for example, when measuring the fair value of corporate bonds or a call option on an entity's shares. [IFRS 13:35]

Determining the fair value of a liability or an entity's own equity instrument from the perspective of the counterparty holding the same instrument as an asset reinforces the notion that the fair value ascribed to the contract is the same irrespective of whether the entity is the issuer or the holder. This is based on the theory that fair value is based on a transaction in which the contract is transferred, as opposed to being settled or extinguished with the holder. In all cases, the fair value is based on the premise that the instrument remains outstanding and therefore is a theoretical transfer value.

In the circumstances described above, the appropriate bases for measuring the fair value of the liability or the entity's own equity instrument are listed below, in descending order of preference:
[IFRS 13:38]

(a) using the quoted price in an active market (see below) for the identical item held by another party as an asset, if that price is available;

(b) if that price is not available, using other observable inputs, such as the quoted price in a market that is not active for the identical item held by another party as an asset; and

(c) if the observable prices in (a) and (b) above are not available, using another valuation technique, such as:

(i) an income approach (e.g. a present value technique that takes into account the future cash flows that a market participant would expect to receive from holding the liability or equity instrument as an asset – see **8.3** below); or

(ii) a market approach (e.g. using quoted prices for similar liabilities or equity instruments held by other parties as assets – see **8.1** below).

An active market is defined as "[a] market in which transactions for the asset or liability take place with sufficient frequency and volume to provide pricing information on an ongoing basis". [IFRS 13:Appendix A]

A quoted price of a liability or an entity's own equity instrument held by another party as an asset should be adjusted only if there are factors specific to the asset that are not applicable to the fair value measurement of the liability or equity instrument. An entity should ensure that the price of the asset does not reflect the effect of a restriction preventing the sale of an asset. [IFRS 13:39]

The Standard provides the following examples of factors that might indicate that the quoted price of the asset should be adjusted.
[IFRS 13:39]

• The quoted price for the asset relates to a similar (but not identical) liability or equity instrument held by another party as an asset. For example, the liability or equity instrument may have a particular characteristic (e.g. the credit quality of the issuer) that is different from that reflected in the fair value of the similar liability or equity instrument held as an asset.

- The unit of account for the asset is not the same as for the liability or equity instrument. For example, for liabilities, in some cases the price for an asset reflects a combined price for a package comprising both the amounts due from the issuer and a third-party credit enhancement. If the unit of account for the liability is not for the combined package, the objective is to measure the fair value of the issuer's liability, not the fair value of the combined package. In such circumstances, the entity would adjust the observed price for the asset to exclude the effect of the third-party credit enhancement.

5.1.2   Liabilities and equity instruments not held by other parties as assets

When a quoted price for the transfer of an identical or a similar liability or entity's own equity instrument is not available, and the identical item is not held by another party as an asset, the fair value of the liability or equity instrument is required to be measured using a valuation technique from the perspective of a market participant that owes the liability or has issued the claim on equity. [IFRS 13:40]

This requirement could be relevant, for example, for measuring the fair value of a decommissioning liability. [IFRS 13:B31]

For example, when applying a present value technique, an entity might take into account either of the following:
[IFRS 13:41]

- the future cash outflows that a market participant would expect to incur in fulfilling the obligation, including the compensation that a market participant would require for taking on the obligation (see **5.1.2.1**); or

- the amount that a market participant would receive to enter into or issue an identical liability or equity instrument, using the assumptions that market participants would use when pricing the identical item (e.g. having the same credit characteristics) in the principal (or most advantageous) market for issuing a liability or an equity instrument with the same contractual terms.

5.1.2.1   Estimating future cash outflows

IFRS 13's general guidance regarding the use of present value techniques is discussed in detail in **8.3.1** to **8.3.3** below. This section covers the Standard's specific guidance for applying present value techniques to liabilities and an entity's own equity instruments not held by other parties as assets.

When using a present value technique to measure the fair value of a liability that is not held by another party as an asset, an entity should, among other things, estimate the future cash outflows that market participants would expect to incur in fulfilling the obligation. [IFRS 13:B31]

Those future cash outflows should include:
[IFRS 13:B31]

• market participants' expectations about the costs of fulfilling the obligation; and

• the compensation that a market participant would require for taking on the obligation.

The compensation that a market participant would require for taking on the obligation should include the return that a market participant would require for the following:
[IFRS 13:B31]

• undertaking the activity (i.e. the value of fulfilling the obligation – for example by using resources that could be used for other activities); and

• assuming the risk associated with the obligation (i.e. a risk premium that reflects the risk that the actual cash outflows might differ from the expected cash outflows).

The Standard cites as an example a non-financial liability that does not contain a contractual rate of return and for which there is no observable market yield. In some cases, the components of the return that market participants would require will be indistinguishable from one another (e.g. when using the price a third-party contractor would charge on a fixed fee basis). In other cases, an entity needs to estimate those components separately (e.g. when using the price a third-party contractor would charge on a cost plus basis, because the contractor in that case would not bear the risk of future changes in costs). [IFRS 13:B32]

IFRS 13 defines a risk premium (also referred to as a 'risk adjustment') as "[c]ompensation sought by risk-averse market participants for bearing the uncertainty inherent in the cash flows of an asset or a liability". [IFRS

13:Appendix A] A risk premium can be included in the fair value measurement of a liability or an entity's own equity instrument that is not held by another party as an asset in one of the following ways:
[IFRS 13:B33]

- by adjusting the cash flows (i.e. as an increase in the amount of cash outflows); or

- by adjusting the rate used to discount the future cash flows to their present values (i.e. as a reduction in the discount rate).

An entity should ensure that it does not double-count or omit adjustments for risk. For example, if the estimated cash flows are increased to take into account the compensation for assuming the risk associated with the obligation, the discount rate should not be adjusted to reflect that risk. [IFRS 13:B33]

The following example, reproduced from the illustrative examples accompanying IFRS 13, describes the use of the present value technique to measure the fair value of a decommissioning liability.

Example 5.1.2.1

Decommissioning liability

[IFRS 13:IE35 – IE39, Example 11]

On 1 January 20X1 Entity A assumes a decommissioning liability in a business combination. The entity is legally required to dismantle and remove an offshore oil platform at the end of its useful life, which is estimated to be 10 years.

On the basis of IFRS 13:B23 – B30, Entity A uses the expected present value technique to measure the fair value of the decommissioning liability.

If Entity A was contractually allowed to transfer its decommissioning liability to a market participant, Entity A concludes that a market participant would use all the following inputs, probability-weighted as appropriate, when estimating the price it would expect to receive:

(a)   labour costs;

(b)   allocation of overhead costs;

(c)   the compensation that a market participant would require for undertaking the activity and for assuming the risk associated with the obligation to dismantle and remove the asset. Such compensation includes both of the following:

　　(i)   profit on labour and overhead costs; and

    (ii)   the risk that the actual cash outflows might differ from those expected, excluding inflation;

(d)   effect of inflation on estimated costs and profits;

(e)   time value of money, represented by the risk-free rate; and

(f)   non-performance risk relating to the risk that Entity A will not fulfil the obligation, including Entity A's own credit risk.

The significant assumptions used by Entity A to measure fair value are as follows:

(a)   Labour costs are developed on the basis of current marketplace wages, adjusted for expectations of future wage increases, required to hire contractors to dismantle and remove offshore oil platforms. Entity A assigns probability assessments to a range of cash flow estimates as follows:

Cash flow estimate (CU)	Probability assessment	Expected cash flows (CU)
100,000	25%	25,000
125,000	50%	62,500
175,000	25%	43,750
		131,250

    The probability assessments are developed on the basis of Entity A's experience with fulfilling obligations of this type and its knowledge of the market.

(b)   Entity A estimates allocated overhead and equipment operating costs using the rate it applies to labour costs (80 per cent of expected labour costs). This is consistent with the cost structure of market participants.

(c)   Entity A estimates the compensation that a market participant would require for undertaking the activity and for assuming the risk associated with the obligation to dismantle and remove the asset as follows:

    (i)   A third-party contractor typically adds a mark-up on labour and allocated internal costs to provide a profit margin on the job. The profit margin used (20 per cent) represents Entity A's understanding of the operating profit that contractors in the industry generally earn to dismantle and remove offshore oil platforms. Entity A concludes that this rate is consistent with the rate that a market participant would require as compensation for undertaking the activity.

    (ii)   A contractor would typically require compensation for the risk that the actual cash outflows might differ from those expected because of the uncertainty inherent in locking in today's price for a project that will not occur for 10 years. Entity A estimates the amount of that premium to be 5 per cent of the expected cash flows, including the effect of inflation.

(d)   Entity A assumes a rate of inflation of 4 per cent over the 10-year period on the basis of available market data.

(e)   The risk-free rate of interest for a 10-year maturity on 1 January 20X1 is 5 per cent. Entity A adjusts that rate by 3.5 per cent to reflect its risk of non-performance (ie the risk that it will not fulfil the obligation), including its credit risk. Therefore, the discount rate used to compute the present value of the cash flows is 8.5 per cent.

Entity A concludes that its assumptions would be used by market participants. In addition, Entity A does not adjust its fair value measurement for the existence of a restriction preventing it from transferring the liability. As illustrated in the following table, Entity A measures the fair value of its decommissioning liability as CU194,879.

	Expected cash flows (CU) 1 January 20X1
Expected labour costs	131,250
Allocated overhead and equipment costs (0.80 × CU131,250)	105,000
Contractor's profit mark-up [0.20 × (CU131,250 + CU105,000)]	47,250
Expected cash flows before inflation adjustment	283,500
Inflation factor (4% for 10 years)	1.4802
Expected cash flows adjusted for inflation	419,637
Market risk premium (0.05 × CU419,637)	20,982
Expected cash flows adjusted for market risk	440,619
Expected present value using discount rate of 8.5% for 10 years	194,879

5.2   Non-performance risk

The fair value of a liability should reflect the effect of non-performance risk. [IFRS 13:42]

Non-performance risk is defined as "[t]he risk that an entity will not fulfil an obligation. Non-performance risk includes, but may not be limited to, the entity's own credit risk". [IFRS 13:Appendix A]

Credit risk is defined in IFRS 7 *Financial Instruments: Disclosures* as "[t]he risk that one party to a financial instrument will cause a financial loss for the other party by failing to discharge an obligation". [IFRS 7:Appendix A]

The explicit statement in IFRS 13:42 clarifies that the fair value of a liability should include an entity's own credit risk. This principle is consistent with fair value measurement guidance already included in IFRSs but was previously subject to inconsistent application. [IFRS 13:BC92 & BC93]

Non-performance risk is assumed to be the same before and after the transfer of the liability. [IFRS 13:42]

The IASB acknowledges in the Basis for Conclusions on IFRS 13 that it is unlikely that non-performance risk is the same before and after the transfer of the financial liability. However, the IASB concluded that such an assumption was necessary when measuring the fair value of a financial liability in order for the transfer concept to apply. If the transferee, acting as a market participant, had a different credit standing to the transferor it would not take on the obligation of the transferor because either (1) the counterparty to the obligation would not permit the transfer to take place, in the case of the transferee's credit standing being worse than the transferor's, or (2) in the case of the transferee's credit standing being better than the transferor's, the transferee would not choose to take on the obligation without renegotiating the terms to reflect the difference in credit standing. Furthermore, if it is assumed that market participants have different credit standings, this would result in fundamentally different valuations depending on the identity of the transferee. It was also noted that those that hold the entity's obligations as assets do consider the effect of an entity's credit risk and other risk factors when pricing those assets and, therefore, this effect should be equally reflected in the fair value of the entity's obligations to those holders of assets. [IFRS 13:BC94]

Example 5.2

Impact of guarantee by acquirer on the fair value of an acquiree's loan

Entity A acquires 100 per cent of Entity B from Entity C in a business combination. One of the identifiable liabilities of Entity B is a loan owed to a third party. The loan was originally guaranteed by Entity C as part of the loan terms. However, as a result of the business combination, the terms of the loan are revised so that Entity A becomes the guarantor of the loan (i.e. the guarantee by Entity A becomes part of the revised loan terms).

IFRS 3 *Business Combinations* requires that the third party loan is measured at fair value at the date of acquisition. The measurement requirements of IFRS 13 apply.

There are no quoted prices available for the transfer of an identical or a similar liability.

When measuring the fair value of the loan at the date of acquisition for the purpose of preparing consolidated financial statements, Entity A should take into account the effect of its own guarantee of the loan because the guarantee is part of the loan terms.

As discussed at **5.1.1** above, IFRS 13:37 requires that when a quoted price for the transfer of an identical or a similar liability is not available, and the identical item is held by another party as an asset, an entity should measure the fair value of the liability from the perspective of a market participant that holds the identical item as an asset at the measurement date.

In the circumstances described, the loan is guaranteed by Entity A from the date of acquisition. From the perspective of a market participant holding the loan as an asset, the fact that the loan is guaranteed by Entity A would be taken into account when measuring the fair value of the loan receivable because the market participant would expect to recover the loan from Entity A if Entity B defaulted on the loan. Consequently, when measuring the fair value of the loan, a market participant would take into account (1) the credit standing of Entity B, and (2) the guarantee provided by Entity A.

This is also consistent with the requirement in IFRS 13:43 (see below) that an entity should take into account the effect of its own credit risk (credit standing) and any other factors that might influence the likelihood that the obligation will or will not be fulfilled.

The effect of an entity's credit standing and other factors that might influence the likelihood that the obligation will or will not be fulfilled may differ depending on the nature of the liability (e.g. whether it is a financial or a non-financial liability, or whether any credit enhancements are attached). [IFRS 13:43]

To understand non-performance risk, it is necessary to consider the specific terms of the instrument rather than simply looking at the overall credit standing of the issuing entity. Focusing on the standing of the entity will generally obscure the particular credit characteristics of the instrument itself, like credit enhancements, or fail to reflect the priority of the liability relative to the other liabilities of the entity.

The fair value measurement for a liability should reflect the effect of non-performance risk based on the unit of account for financial reporting purposes specified in relevant IFRSs (see also **3.1**). The issuer of a liability issued with an inseparable third-party credit enhancement (e.g. a third-party guarantee of debt) that is accounted for separately from the liability should not include the effect of the credit enhancement in the fair value measurement of the liability; in such circumstances, the fair value measurement should reflect the credit standing of the issuer and not that of the third-party guarantor. [IFRS 13:44]

> As required under IFRS 13:44, when an entity has in issue a liability with a third-party guarantee, and the liability and the guarantee are accounted for separately under relevant IFRSs, the fair value of the liability should not reflect the effect of the guarantee. In such circumstances, the fair value of the liability from the issuer's perspective will not equal its fair value as a guaranteed liability held by another party as an asset. [IFRS 13:BC98]

5.2.1   Effect of collateral on fair value measurement of liabilities

> When an entity has provided collateral in respect of a liability, this will affect the fair value measurement of the liability under IFRS 13. As discussed above, IFRS 13:42 requires that the fair value of a liability should reflect the effect of non-performance risk, and that non-performance risk is assumed to be the same before and after the transfer of the liability. The definition of non-performance risk in IFRS 13:Appendix A (see 5.2 above) clarifies that it encompasses an entity's own credit risk (credit standing) and any other factors that might influence the likelihood that the obligation will be fulfilled. One factor specifically mentioned in IFRS 13:43(b) is "the terms of credit enhancements related to the liability, if any".
>
> Collateral is a form of credit enhancement that is contractually linked to a liability (i.e. the terms of the obligation require a lien on the collateral until settlement of the obligation). The fact that an entity has provided collateral typically means that the stated terms of the liability (e.g. the interest rate charged) differ from the terms of an identical liability that is not supported by collateral. The collateral is a characteristic of the liability and, consequently, it should be reflected in the fair value measurement of the collateralised liability.
>
> Example 5.2.1 illustrates how collateral might affect the fair value of a liability on initial recognition.

Example 5.2.1

Effect of collateral on fair value measurement of liabilities

On 1 January 20X1, Company A borrows CU10 million repayable in five years. The fixed interest rate is one-year LIBOR plus 125 basis points. Company A is required to pledge specified property interests as collateral. Management estimates that Company A could have arranged a similar loan with no collateral at a 200 basis point spread to LIBOR. On 1 January 20X1, the one-year LIBOR rate is 1.5 per cent. For simplicity, transaction costs are ignored.

At 1 January 20X1, the fair value of the loan (including any impact from the collateral) is CU10 million. The present value of the loan's contractual cash flows, discounted at Company A's unsecured borrowing rate of 3.5 per cent (i.e. 1.5 per cent LIBOR plus 200 basis points), is CU9.7 million.

This example illustrates that the effect of an issuer's credit standing as well as the effect of credit enhancements should be taken into account in measuring the fair value of the liability. If Company A ignored the reduction in the interest rate attributable to the collateral, it would mistakenly conclude that the fair value of its debt was CU9.7 million rather than CU10 million.

5.2.2 Risks associated with entity's ability to deliver goods or perform services

The definition of non-performance risk in IFRS 13:Appendix A (see **5.2** above) clarifies that it encompasses an entity's own credit risk (credit standing) and any other factors that might influence the likelihood that the obligation will be fulfilled. Therefore, in addition to an entity's own credit risk, non-performance risk may include the risk associated with the entity's ability to deliver goods or perform services.

For example, consider a contract for the delivery of a commodity (e.g. oil, natural gas, electricity) that is measured as a derivative liability at fair value in accordance with IFRS 9 *Financial Instruments* (or, prior to the adoption of IFRS 9, IAS 39 *Financial Instruments: Recognition and Measurement*). When measuring the fair value of the liability, the entity is required to reflect its own credit risk (i.e. the risk that there will be financial loss for the counterparty because the entity fails to meet its financial obligation). In addition, there is the risk that the entity will not be able to obtain and deliver the commodity to the counterparty (e.g. because of supply issues for the commodity) which is also part of non-performance risk.

Such contracts may contain 'make-whole' or other default clauses to mitigate the risk of non-delivery because the entity would be required to compensate the counterparty for damages incurred if the entity is unable to deliver the commodity. The effect of such clauses will need to be considered in assessing the non-performance risk.

5.2.3   Effect of changes in non-performance risk

Changes in the fair value of collateral or an entity's credit standing should be taken into account in measuring the fair value of a liability on an ongoing basis. This is to ensure that the fair value measurement reflects market participant assumptions at the measurement date.

Examples 5.2.3A and **5.2.3B** below illustrate the effect of some of these factors on the fair value of collateralised obligations.

Example 5.2.3A

Effect of a decline in the fair value of collateral

On 1 January 20X1, Company B issues CU100 million of bonds collateralised by a portion of its aircraft fleet. On 30 September 20X3, there has been a substantial decline in the fair value of the aircraft that serve as collateral for the bonds. Assume that Company B's credit standing remains unchanged and all other stated terms of the bonds represent current market conditions for the remaining term of the obligation.

When measuring the fair value of the bonds at 30 September 20X3, Company B must do so from the perspective of a market participant that holds the bonds as an asset (i.e. a bondholder) – see **5.1.1** above. A market participant would reflect the reduced level of collateral in the price at which a transfer of the bond would take place.

Company B determines that the hypothetical market participant would be willing to transfer the liability for only CU80 million. In other words, the fair value of the bonds has decreased by CU20 million due to the decline in value of the collateral even though Company B's credit standing remains unchanged.

> **Example 5.2.3B**
>
> **Effect of a decline in the borrower's credit standing**
>
> The facts are the same as in **example 5.2.3A**, except that, at 30 September 20X3, the fair value of the aircraft pledged as collateral remains unchanged. Instead, the credit standing of Company B has declined from AAA to AA-.
>
> When measuring the fair value of the bonds at 30 September 20X3, Company B is required to consider the effect of the decline in its credit standing but also the fact that the fair value of the collateral has not changed.
>
> Company B observes that the wider credit spread for uncollateralised AA- corporate bonds suggests that the fair value of the bonds has declined by 10 per cent (i.e. to CU90 million). However, because the fair value of the collateral has not changed, the note remains well collateralised. Consequently, the fair value of the note may not have declined by as much as 10 per cent. Company B determines that the increase in non-performance risk arising from the decline in its own credit standing is partially offset by the collateral. Based on credit spreads observed for similar, collateralised bonds, Company B concludes that the fair value of the notes has decreased by CU7 million to CU93 million.

5.2.4   Additional examples

IFRS 13 provides many examples of measuring the fair value of financial liabilities. These examples are included at **5.2** in **chapter B7** (for entities that have adopted IFRS 9) and at **5.2** in **chapter C7** (for entities that have not yet adopted IFRS 9).

5.3   Restriction preventing the transfer of a liability or an entity's own equity instrument

When measuring the fair value of a liability or an entity's own equity instrument, no separate input or adjustment to other inputs should be included to reflect the existence of a restriction that prevents the transfer of the item. The effect of a restriction that prevents the transfer of a liability or an entity's own equity instrument is either implicitly or explicitly included in the other inputs to the fair value measurement. [IFRS 13:45]

For example, at the transaction date for a liability, both the creditor and the obligor accepted the transaction price for the liability with full knowledge that the obligation includes a restriction that prevents its transfer. As a result of the restriction being included in the transaction price, a separate input or an adjustment to an existing input is not required at the transaction date to reflect the effect of the restriction on transfer. Similarly, a separate input or an adjustment to an existing input is not required at subsequent measurement dates to reflect the effect of the restriction on transfer. [IFRS 13:46]

5.4 Financial liability with a demand feature

The fair value of a financial liability with a demand feature (e.g. a demand deposit) is not less than the amount payable on demand, discounted from the first date that the amount could be required to be paid. [IFRS 13:47]

6 Measuring the fair value of financial assets and financial liabilities with offsetting positions in market risks or counterparty credit risk

The application of IFRS 13's requirements under this heading is limited to financial assets and financial liabilities. Consequently, they are not dealt with in this chapter but are discussed separately in **section 6** of **chapter B7** (for entities that have adopted IFRS 9 *Financial Instruments*) and in **section 6** of **chapter C7** (for entities that have not yet adopted IFRS 9).

7 Fair value measurement at initial recognition

Some IFRSs require or permit assets or liabilities to be recognised initially on the basis of 'fair value'. If the asset has been acquired, or the liability assumed, in a market transaction, it might be assumed that the transaction price (i.e. the price paid to acquire an asset or received to assume a liability) can be taken to be the fair value of the asset or the liability. However, the price paid to acquire an asset, or received to assume a liability, is an *entry* price and, consequently, it is not necessarily the same as the fair value of the asset or liability for IFRS 13 purposes (which is an *exit* price – see **section 3**). The Standard notes that entities do not necessarily sell assets at the prices paid to acquire them; nor do they necessarily transfer liabilities at the prices received to assume them. [IFRS 13:57]

In many cases, the transaction price and the fair value will be equal (e.g. when the transaction date is the same as the measurement date and an asset is acquired in the market in which it would be sold). [IFRS 13:58] However, when the amounts are not equal, the asset or liability should be measured at fair value and the difference between the transaction price and fair value (generally referred to as a 'day 1 gain or loss', 'day 1 profit or loss, or 'day 1 p&l') is required to be recognised as a gain or loss in profit or loss unless the relevant IFRS specifies otherwise. [IFRS 13:60]

For example, IFRS 9 *Financial Instruments* and IAS 39 *Financial Instruments: Recognition and Measurement* state that an entity cannot recognise a day 1 gain or loss for a financial instrument unless the instrument's fair value is evidenced by a quoted price in an active market for an identical asset or liability or based on a valuation technique that uses only data from observable markets. In contrast, IFRS 3 *Business Combinations* and IAS 41 *Agriculture* require the recognition of day 1 gains or losses even when fair value is measured using unobservable inputs (see IFRS 13:BC135).

When, in accordance with the relevant IFRS, a day 1 gain or loss is not recognised, the asset or liability should be measured at fair value and the day 1 gain or loss deferred and accounted for separately under the relevant Standard (see **7.1** in **chapter B7** for entities that have adopted IFRS 9, and **7.1** in **chapter C7** for entities that have not yet adopted IFRS 9).

When determining whether the fair value at initial recognition equals the transaction price, an entity should take into account factors specific to the transaction and to the asset and liability. [IFRS 13:59]

IFRS 13:B4 lists a number of factors which may suggest that the transaction price is not the fair value of the asset or liability at initial recognition.

The following table repeats the factors listed in IFRS 13:B4 and provides examples for each. Note that this list of indicators is not exhaustive, and other factors may exist that should be considered in evaluating whether a transaction price represents fair value (see IFRS 13:BC133).

Factor (IFRS 13:B4)	Example
The transaction is between related parties, although the price in a related party transaction may be used as an input into a fair value measurement if the reporting entity has evidence that the transaction was entered into at market terms.	An entity purchases a portfolio of troubled loans from an unconsolidated investee. The parties meet the definition of related parties under IAS 24 *Related Party Disclosures*. The fact that the parties are related may indicate that the transaction price does not reflect fair value. However, this alone would not be determinative. Evidence that the transaction was entered into at market terms may include: • the appointment of third parties to negotiate or measure fair value; or • the terms of the transaction are consistent with available market data for similar transactions between unrelated parties; or • there is no evidence that one of the parties to the transaction is under duress (see the next factor).
The transaction takes place under duress or the seller is forced to accept the price in the transaction (e.g. if the seller is experiencing financial difficulty).	A hedge fund must sell all of its non-marketable assets in response to a spike in redemptions that may lead to a liquidity crisis. A liquidity crisis may be an indicator of financial difficulty. The factors in IFRS 13:B43 indicating that a transaction is not orderly (see **9.5** below) may also indicate that the transaction price does not represent fair value.

Factor (IFRS 13:B4)

The unit of account represented by the transaction price is different from the unit of account for the asset or liability measured at fair value. For example, this might be the case if the asset or liability measured at fair value is only one of the elements in the transaction (e.g. in a business combination), if the transaction includes unstated rights and privileges that are measured separately in accordance with another IFRS, or if the transaction price includes transaction costs.

Example

IFRS 13:14 requires that the unit of account for an asset or a liability should be determined in accordance with the IFRS that requires or permits the fair value measurement, except as provided in IFRS 13 (see **3.1.1** above).

The following example illustrates a scenario in which the unit of account for the asset is different from the unit of account represented by the transaction price.

On 30 June 20X1, Company A acquires a 3 per cent equity interest (3 million shares) in Company B from an independent third party. Quoted prices in an active market are available for Company B's shares. Company A pays CU100 million for the entire 3 per cent equity interest (the transaction price is determined based on a negotiated arm's length price for the entire 3 per cent equity interest). The quoted price for Company B's shares on 30 June 20X1 is CU36 per share. Company A needs to identify the unit of account in order to measure the fair value of the 3 per cent equity interest on initial recognition.

In identifying the unit of account for fair value measurement purposes, IFRS 9 (or, if IFRS 9 has not yet been adopted, IAS 39) is the applicable Standard.

Factor (IFRS 13:B4)	Example
	IFRS 13:BC47 states, in part, that "[i]n IAS 39 and IFRS 9... the unit of account is generally an individual financial instrument". This guidance is also consistent with the guidance set out in IFRS 13:80 which states that "[i]f an entity holds a position in a single asset . . . and the asset . . . is traded in an active market, the fair value of the asset . . . shall be measured within Level 1 as the product of the quoted price for the individual asset . . . and the quantity held by the entity".
	Therefore, notwithstanding the fact that Company A paid a transaction price of CU100 million for the entire 3 million shares, the unit of account in this example is each individual share, not the entire 3 per cent equity interest acquired. Specifically, the fair value of the 3 per cent equity interest in Company B is measured as the product of the quoted price for each individual share and the quantity held ('P × Q') (i.e. CU108 million = 3 million shares × CU36 per share).
The market in which the transaction takes place is different from the principal market (or most advantageous market). For example, those markets might be different if the entity is a dealer that enters into transactions with customers in the retail market, but the principal (or most advantageous) market for the exit transaction is with other dealers in the dealer market.	Entity A (a retail counterparty) enters into an interest rate swap in a retail market with Entity B (a dealer) for no initial consideration (i.e. the transaction price is zero). Entity A can access only the retail market. Entity B can access both the retail market (i.e. with retail counterparties) and the dealer market (i.e. with dealer counterparties).

Factor (IFRS 13:B4)	Example
	From the perspective of Entity A, the fair value at initial recognition is zero because Entity A does not have access to the dealer market.
	From Entity B's perspective, the transaction price of the interest rate swap (i.e. zero) does not represent fair value at initial recognition if prices observed or market participant assumptions in the dealer market (i.e. Entity B's principal market) indicate that fair value is something other than zero.
	Note: This final scenario is a summary of Example 7 from the illustrative examples accompanying IFRS 13 (see IFRS 13:IE24 to IE26).

8   Valuation techniques

When the price for an asset or a liability cannot be observed directly, it must be estimated using a valuation technique. When used in the context of fair value measurement, 'valuation technique' is a generic term and its application is not limited to complex fair valuation models. For example, valuing an asset or a liability using quoted prices in an active market for identical assets and liabilities is a valuation technique. In other cases, when prices cannot be observed directly and more judgement is required, it will be appropriate to use more complex valuation techniques.

An entity is required to use valuation techniques that are appropriate in the circumstances and for which sufficient data are available to measure fair value, maximising the use of relevant observable inputs and minimising the use of unobservable inputs. [IFRS 13:61]

Observable inputs are defined as "[i]nputs that are developed using market data, such as publicly available information about actual events or transactions, and that reflect the assumptions that market participants would use when pricing the asset or liability". [IFRS 13:Appendix A]

Unobservable inputs are defined as "[i]nputs for which market data are not available and that are developed using the best information available about the assumptions that market participants would use when pricing the asset or liability". [IFRS 13:Appendix A]

IFRS 13 refers to three widely used valuation techniques: [IFRS 13:62]

- the market approach (see **8.1** below);

- the cost approach (sometimes referred to as 'replacement cost') (see **8.2** below); and

- the income approach (see **8.3** below)

Any valuation technique used to measure fair value should be consistent with one or more of the above approaches. [IFRS 13:62]

Note that IFRS 13 does not set out a hierarchy of valuation techniques; this is because particular valuation techniques may be more appropriate in some circumstances than in others (see IFRS 13:BC142).

Each valuation technique has its own merits and may or may not be suitable for measuring the fair value of a specified item or items in particular circumstances. In practice, different valuation techniques can give rise to different estimates of fair value and, therefore, it is important to select the most appropriate methodology for the particular circumstances.

Choosing a valuation technique requires judgement and involves the selection of a method, formulae and assumptions. The reliability of a fair value measurement derived from a valuation technique is dependent on both the reliability of the valuation technique and the reliability of the inputs used. Consequently, when selecting a valuation technique, it will be important to consider the availability of reliable inputs for that valuation (see **section 9**). In addition to selecting a technique that maximises the use of relevant observable inputs and minimises the use of unobservable inputs, an entity must also ensure that the best possible evidence is used to support unobservable inputs.

In assessing the appropriateness of each valuation technique, an entity should also evaluate all available inputs significant to the valuation technique and compare the technique with other valuation techniques. For example, in a given situation, an entity may conclude that it is appropriate to use a market approach rather than an income approach because the market approach uses superior market information as inputs.

An entity should consider using a valuation specialist, when appropriate.

See **8.4** below for a discussion of when it is appropriate to use multiple valuation techniques.

Example 8 illustrates how an entity might approach the selection of a valuation technique (or techniques) for unquoted equity securities in specified circumstances.

Example 8

Selecting an appropriate valuation technique or techniques for unquoted equity securities

Company A holds equity investments in two entities – Company B and Company C. Company A measures these investments at fair value on a recurring basis.

- Company B is a clothing retailer that operates in the niche market of the baby clothing industry. Quoted prices are not available for Company B's shares. Most of Company B's competitors are either privately held or are subsidiaries of larger publicly traded clothing retailers. Company B is similar to two other organisations, whose shares are thinly traded in an observable market.

- Company C is a retailer that operates in the competitive consumer electronics industry. Although quoted prices are not available for Company C's shares, Company C is comparable to many entities whose shares are actively traded.

Because the prices of Company B's and Company C's shares cannot be observed directly, Company A must measure the fair value of these investments using a valuation technique (or techniques).

Company A is considering a market approach, an income approach or a combination of these two approaches. The market approach and the income approach are common valuation techniques for equity investments that are not publicly traded. Under the market approach, entities use prices and other relevant information generated by market transactions involving identical or comparable securities. Under the income approach, future amounts are converted into a single present amount (e.g. discounted cash flows model). Company A is not considering the cost approach to value its equity securities because it is not considered relevant. (See **8.1** to **8.3** below for

---

detailed descriptions of these valuation techniques. See also **8.4** below for a discussion of when it is appropriate to use multiple valuation techniques.)

Company A should select the valuation technique (or techniques) that is (are) appropriate in the circumstances and for which sufficient data are available to measure fair value, maximising the use of relevant observable inputs and minimising the use of unobservable inputs.

Investment in Company B

Using a market approach, the fair value measurement of Company A's investment in Company B would involve an analysis of market prices and other relevant information for the two similar organisations that are traded (albeit thinly) in an observable market. It is likely that the observable market data would need to be adjusted to reflect differences between Company B and the two similar organisations that are traded. For example, Company A might consider that market participants would incorporate significant entity-specific adjustments into the valuation of Company B's shares (e.g. adjustments to reflect the relative illiquidity of Company B's shares, profitability, net assets, unrecognised assets such as internally generated intangible assets, and differences in business model between Company B and the two traded organisations). These adjustments would be made using Company A's own assumptions. Consequently, in such circumstances, a market approach would rely on unobservable inputs that are significant to the fair value measurement.

Using an income approach based on discounted cash flows, the fair value measurement of Company A's investment in Company B would also be based on significant entity-specific assumptions in forecasting Company B's future cash flows. As a result, the income approach would also rely on unobservable inputs that are significant to the fair value measurement.

Based on the above information, it is likely that Company A would conclude that both the market approach and the income approach are appropriate techniques for measuring the fair value of its investment in Company B. In making its selection, Company A would consider the reliability of the evidence supporting the inputs used in each of the valuation techniques. Provided that relevant and reliable inputs are available, and there are no other factors indicating that one of the approaches is superior, it would seem appropriate to use a combination of both approaches, even if one approach is used only to corroborate the results of the other.

Investment in Company C

When selecting an appropriate approach to measure the fair value of its investment in Company C, Company A should perform an analysis similar to that outlined above.

Using a market approach, it is more likely that market participants would incorporate fewer unobservable adjustments into the valuation of Company C's shares because of the large number of comparable traded entities and the high trading volume of the shares of those comparable entities. However, Company A should consider whether to make an adjustment for illiquidity to reflect the fact that Company C's shares are unquoted whereas those of comparable entities in the same sector are listed and actively traded.

Using an income approach based on discounted cash flows, the fair value measurement of Company A's investment in Company C would be based on forecasted future cash flows. This forecast would include projections of future profitability and, therefore, would be likely to include entity-specific assumptions that are not observable.

As a result, it is likely that Company A would conclude that it is appropriate to measure the fair value of its investment in Company C using the market approach because it uses more observable inputs (i.e. in terms of the hierarchy described in **section 10** below, 'Level 2' inputs vs. 'Level 3' inputs) with a significant effect.

8.1   Market approach

The 'market approach' is defined as "[a] valuation technique that uses prices and other relevant information generated by market transactions involving identical or comparable (ie similar) assets, liabilities or a group of assets and liabilities, such as a business". [IFRS 13:Appendix A]

A quoted price for an identical asset or liability in an active market that the entity can access at the measurement date provides the most reliable evidence of fair value. [IFRS 13:77] Quoted prices for an identical asset or liability are regarded as Level 1 inputs within the fair value hierarchy (see **10.1.1** below). When a quoted price exists for an identical asset or liability, it should be used without adjustment, except in the circumstances described at **10.1.1** below. [IFRS 13:77] When a quoted price for an asset or a liability exists in multiple active markets, it will be necessary to identify the market and price which represents fair value for the specific facts and circumstances. [IFRS 13:78]

Valuation techniques consistent with the market approach often use market multiples derived from a set of comparable assets or liabilities. A range of multiples may be derived, with a different multiple for each comparable asset or liability. The selection of the appropriate multiple within the range requires the exercise of judgement – with appropriate consideration of the qualitative and quantitative factors specific to the measurement. [IFRS 13:B6]

One valuation technique that is consistent with the market approach is 'matrix pricing'; matrix pricing is a mathematical technique used principally to value some types of financial instruments, such as debt securities, without relying exclusively on quoted prices for the specific securities, but rather relying on the securities' relationship to other benchmark quoted securities. [IFRS 13:B7]

8.2   Cost approach

The 'cost approach' is defined as "[a] valuation technique that reflects the amount that would be required currently to replace the service capacity of an asset (often referred to as current replacement cost)". [IFRS 13:Appendix A] This method is often used to measure the fair value of tangible assets that are used in combination with other assets or with other assets and liabilities. [IFRS 13:B9]

When the cost approach is applied, the fair value of the asset is based on what it would cost a market participant buyer to acquire or construct a substitute asset of comparable utility, adjusted for obsolescence (i.e. its current replacement cost). The approach is based on the rationale that a market participant buyer would not pay more for an asset than the amount for which it could replace the service capacity of that asset. [IFRS 13:B9]

For the purpose of measuring an asset's current replacement cost, obsolescence encompasses (1) physical deterioration, (2) functional (technological) obsolescence and (3) economic (external) obsolescence; obsolescence is a broader concept than depreciation for financial reporting purposes or tax purposes. [IFRS 13:B9]

> The inclusion of the cost approach as an appropriate valuation technique may seem counter-intuitive in the light of IFRS 13's exit price definition of fair value. However, the IASB points out that an entity's cost to replace an asset would equal the amount that a market participant buyer of that asset would pay to acquire it (i.e. the entry price and the exit price would be equal in the same market). Therefore, the cost approach is considered to be consistent with an exit price definition of fair value. [IFRS 13:BC141]

8.3   Income approach

The 'income approach' is defined as "[v]aluation techniques that convert future amounts (eg cash flows or income and expenses) to a single current (ie discounted) amount. The fair value measurement is determined on the basis of the value indicated by current market expectations about those future amounts". [IFRS 13:Appendix A]

Income approaches that are used for measuring fair value include, for example:
[IFRS 13:B11]

- present value techniques (see below);

- option pricing models, such as the Black-Scholes-Merton formula or a binomial model (i.e. a lattice model), that incorporate present value techniques and reflect both the time value and the intrinsic value of an option; and

- the multi-period excess earnings method, which is used to measure the fair value of some intangible assets.

IFRS 13 describes two types of present value technique:

- the discount rate adjustment technique (see **8.3.3.1** below); and

- the expected cash flow (expected present value) technique (see **8.3.3.2** below).

IFRS 13 does not specifically require that one of these present value techniques be used. The most appropriate present value technique for the measurement of fair value in a particular scenario will depend on the facts and circumstances specific to the asset or liability being measured (e.g. whether prices for comparable assets or liabilities can be observed in the market) and the availability of sufficient data. [IFRS 13:B12]

8.3.1   *Components of a present value measurement*

Present value is a tool used to link future amounts (e.g. cash flows or values) to a present amount using a discount rate. A fair value measurement of an asset or a liability using a present value technique captures all of the following elements from the perspective of market participants at the measurement date:
[IFRS 13:B13]

- an estimate of future cash flows for the asset or liability being measured;

- expectations about possible variations in the amount and timing of the cash flows representing the uncertainty inherent in the cash flows;

- the time value of money, represented by the rate on risk-free monetary assets that have maturity dates or durations that coincide with the period covered by the cash flows and pose neither uncertainty in timing nor risk of default to the holder (i.e. a risk-free interest rate);

- the price for bearing the uncertainty inherent in the cash flows (i.e. a risk premium);

- other factors that market participants would take into account in the circumstances; and

- for a liability, the non-performance risk relating to that liability, including the obligor's own credit risk.

When using post-tax cash flows (and a post-tax discount rate) to measure the fair value of a depreciable asset, an entity should include all relevant cash flows. These would include cash inflows resulting from future tax deductions for the asset's depreciation or amortisation expense that a market participant would expect to receive. A market participant would expect to receive the future tax deductions if the depreciation or amortisation is deductible for tax purposes in the jurisdiction in which the transaction is entered into. Judgement will be required to determine which jurisdiction should be considered from a market participant perspective.

This conclusion is consistent with the following guidance in paragraph C35 of IVS 210 *Intangible Assets* issued by the International Valuation Standards Council.

> "In many tax regimes, the amortisation of an *intangible* asset can be treated as an expense in calculating taxable income. This "tax amortisation benefit" can have a positive impact on the value of the asset. When an *income approach* is used, it will be necessary to consider the impact of any available tax benefit to buyers and make an appropriate adjustment to the cash flows."

8.3.2   *General principles underlying present value measurement*

Present value techniques differ in how they capture the elements listed in **8.3.1**. However, all of the following general principles govern the application of any present value technique used to measure fair value.
[IFRS 13:B14]

- Cash flows and discount rates should reflect assumptions that market participants would use when pricing the asset or liability.

- Cash flows and discount rates should take into account only the factors attributable to the asset or liability being measured.

- To avoid double-counting or omitting the effects of risk factors, discount rates should reflect assumptions that are consistent with those inherent in the cash flows. For example, a discount rate that reflects the uncertainty in expectations about future defaults is appropriate if using contractual cash flows of a loan (i.e. a discount rate adjustment technique). That same rate should not be used if using expected (i.e. probability-weighted) cash flows (i.e. an expected present value technique) because the expected cash flows already reflect assumptions about the uncertainty in future defaults; instead, a discount rate that is commensurate with the risk inherent in the expected cash flows should be used.

- Assumptions about cash flows and discount rates should be internally consistent. For example, nominal cash flows, which include the effect of inflation, should be discounted at a rate that includes the effect of inflation. The nominal risk-free interest rate includes the effect of inflation. Real cash flows, which exclude the effect of inflation, should be discounted at a rate that excludes the effect of inflation. Similarly, after-tax cash flows should be discounted using an after-tax discount rate. Pre-tax cash flows should be discounted at a rate consistent with those cash flows.

> Care should be taken in determining a pre-tax discount rate by adjusting a post-tax rate. Because the tax consequences of cash flows may occur in different periods, the pre-tax rate of return is not always the post-tax rate of return grossed up by the standard rate of tax. See **8.3.1** in **chapter A10** for further guidance on how to adjust a post-tax discount rate to arrive at a pre-tax discount rate.

- Discount rates should be consistent with the underlying economic factors of the currency in which the cash flows are denominated.

8.3.3 Risk and uncertainty

A fair value measurement using present value techniques is made under conditions of uncertainty because the cash flows used are estimates rather than known amounts. In many cases, both the amount and timing of the cash flows are uncertain. Even contractually fixed amounts, such as the payments on a loan, are uncertain if there is risk of default. [IFRS 13:B15]

Market participants generally seek compensation (i.e. a risk premium) for bearing the uncertainty inherent in the cash flows of an asset or a liability. A fair value measurement should include a risk premium reflecting the amount that market participants would demand as compensation for the uncertainty inherent in the cash flows. Otherwise, the measurement would not faithfully represent fair value. In some cases, determining the appropriate risk premium may be difficult. However, the degree of difficulty alone is not a sufficient reason to exclude a risk premium. [IFRS 13:B16]

Present value techniques differ in how they adjust for risk and in the type of cash flows they use. For example, the discount rate adjustment technique described in **8.3.3.1** below uses contractual, promised or most likely cash flows and a risk-adjusted discount rate. [IFRS 13:B17(a)]

Expected present value techniques incorporate the effects of risk and uncertainty in one of two ways. The calculation either uses risk-adjusted expected cash flows and a risk-free rate to discount them or uses expected cash flows that are not risk-adjusted and a discount rate adjusted to include the risk premium that market participants require (see **8.3.3.2** below). That rate is different from the rate used in the discount rate adjustment technique described immediately below. [IFRS 13:B17(b)&(c)]

8.3.3.1   *Discount rate adjustment technique*

The discount rate adjustment technique uses a single set of cash flows from the range of possible estimated amounts, whether contractual or promised (as is the case for a bond) or most likely cash flows. In all cases, those cash flows are conditional upon the occurrence of specified events (e.g. contractual or promised cash flows for a bond are conditional on the event of no default by the debtor). The discount rate used in the discount rate adjustment technique is derived from observed rates of return for comparable assets or liabilities that are traded in the market. Accordingly, the contractual, promised or most likely cash flows are discounted at an observed or estimated market rate for such conditional cash flows (i.e. a market rate of return). [IFRS 13:B18]

The discount rate adjustment technique requires an analysis of market data for comparable assets or liabilities. Comparability is established by considering the nature of the cash flows (e.g. whether the cash flows are contractual or non-contractual and are likely to respond similarly to changes in economic conditions), as well as other factors (e.g. credit standing, collateral, duration, restrictive covenants and liquidity). Alternatively, if a single comparable asset or liability does not fairly reflect the risk inherent in the cash flows of the asset or liability being measured, it may be possible to derive a discount rate using data for several comparable assets or liabilities in conjunction with the risk-free yield curve (i.e. using a 'build-up' approach). [IFRS 13:B19]

Example 8.3.3.1

Deriving a discount rate using a build-up approach

[Based on IFRS 13:B20 – B21]

Assume that Asset A is a contractual right to receive CU800 in one year (i.e. there is no timing uncertainty). There is an established market for comparable assets, and information about those assets, including price information, is available.

(a)   Asset B is a contractual right to receive CU1,200 in one year and has a market price of CU1,083. Thus, the implied annual rate of return (i.e. a one-year market rate of return) is 10.8 per cent [(CU1,200/CU1,083) – 1].

(b)   Asset C is a contractual right to receive CU700 in two years and has a market price of CU566. Thus, the implied annual rate of return (i.e. a two-year market rate of return) is 11.2 per cent [(CU700/CU566)^0.5 – 1].

(c)   All three assets are comparable with respect to risk (i.e. dispersion of possible pay-offs and credit).

On the basis of the timing of the contractual payments to be received for Asset A relative to the timing for Asset B and Asset C (i.e. one year for Asset B versus two years for Asset C), Asset B is deemed more comparable to Asset A. Using the contractual payment to be received for Asset A (CU800) and the one-year market rate derived from Asset B (10.8 per cent), the fair value of Asset A is CU722 (CU800/1.108).

Alternatively, in the absence of available market information for Asset B, the one-year market rate could be derived from Asset C using the build-up approach. In that case, the two-year market rate indicated by Asset C (11.2 per cent) would be adjusted to a one-year market rate using the term structure of the risk-free yield curve. Additional information and analysis might be required to determine whether the risk premiums for one-year and two-year assets are the same. If it is determined that the risk premiums for one-year and two-year assets are not the same, the two-year market rate of return would be further adjusted for that effect.

When the discount rate adjustment technique is applied to fixed receipts or payments, the adjustment for risk inherent in the cash flows of the asset or liability being measured is included in the discount rate. In some applications of the discount rate adjustment technique to cash flows that are not fixed receipts or payments, an adjustment to the cash flows may be necessary to achieve comparability with the observed asset or liability from which the discount rate is derived. [IFRS 13:B22]

8.3.3.2   *Expected present value technique*

The expected present value technique uses as a starting point a set of cash flows that represents the probability-weighted average of all possible future cash flows (i.e. the expected cash flows). The resulting estimate is identical to expected value, which, in statistical terms, is the weighted average of a discrete random variable's possible values with the respective probabilities as the weights. All possible cash flows are probability-weighted; consequently, the resulting expected cash flow is not conditional upon the occurrence of any specified event (unlike the cash flows used in the discount rate adjustment technique described in **8.3.3.1** above). [IFRS 13:B23]

In making an investment decision, risk-averse market participants would take into account the risk that the actual cash flows may differ from the expected cash flows. Portfolio theory distinguishes between unsystematic (diversifiable) risk, which is the risk specific to a particular asset or liability, and systematic (non-diversifiable) risk, which is the common risk shared by an asset or a liability with the other items in a diversified portfolio. Portfolio theory holds that in a market in equilibrium, market participants will be compensated only for bearing the systematic risk inherent in the cash flows. In markets that are inefficient or out of equilibrium, other forms of return or compensation might be available. [IFRS 13:B24]

IFRS 13 describes two methods for applying the expected present value technique. Both methods are illustrated in **example 8.3.3.2** below. [IFRS 13:B25 & B26]

- Method 1 adjusts the expected cash flows of an asset for systematic (i.e. market) risk by subtracting a cash risk premium (i.e. risk-adjusted expected cash flows). Those risk-adjusted expected cash flows represent a certainty-equivalent cash flow, which is discounted at a risk-free interest rate. A certainty-equivalent cash flow refers to an expected cash flow (as defined), adjusted for risk so that a market participant is indifferent to trading a certain cash flow for an expected cash flow. For example, if a market participant were willing to trade an expected cash flow of CU1,200 for a certain cash flow of CU1,000, the CU1,000 is the certainty equivalent of the CU1,200 (i.e. the CU200 would represent the cash risk premium). In that case, the market participant would be indifferent as to the asset held.

- Method 2 adjusts for systematic (i.e. market) risk by adding a risk premium to the risk-free interest rate. Accordingly, the expected cash flows are discounted at a rate that corresponds to an expected rate associated with probability-weighted cash flows (i.e. an expected rate of return). Models used for pricing risky assets, such as the capital asset pricing model, can be used to estimate the expected rate of return. Because the discount rate used in the discount rate adjustment technique (see **8.3.3.1** above) is a rate of return relating to conditional cash flows, it is likely to be higher than the expected rate of return relating to expected or probability-weighted cash flows.

Example 8.3.3.2

Present value techniques: discounting risk-adjusted expected cash flows by the risk-free rate vs. discounting unadjusted expected cash flows by a risk-adjusted discount rate

[Based on IFRS 13:B27 – B30]

Assume that an asset has expected cash flows of CU780 in one year determined on the basis of the possible cash flows and probabilities shown below. The applicable risk-free interest rate for cash flows with a one-year horizon is 5 per cent, and the systematic risk premium for an asset with the same risk profile is 3 per cent.

Possible cash flows	Probability	Probability-weighted cash flows
CU500	15%	CU75
CU800	60%	CU480
CU900	25%	CU225
Expected cash flows:		CU780

In this simple illustration, the expected cash flows (CU780) represent the probability-weighted average of the three possible outcomes. In more realistic situations, there could be many possible outcomes. However, to apply the expected present value technique, it is not always necessary to take into account distributions of all possible cash flows using complex models and techniques. Rather, it might be possible to develop a limited number of discrete scenarios and probabilities that capture the array of possible cash flows. For example, an entity might use realised cash flows for some relevant past period, adjusted for changes in circumstances occurring subsequently (e.g. changes in external factors, including economic or market conditions, industry trends and competition as well as changes in internal factors affecting the entity more specifically), taking into account the assumptions of market participants.

In theory, the present value (i.e. the fair value) of the asset's cash flows is the same whether determined using Method 1 or Method 2, as follows.

(a) Using Method 1, the expected cash flows are adjusted for systematic (i.e. market) risk. In the absence of market data directly indicating the amount of the risk adjustment, such adjustment could be derived from an asset pricing model using the concept of certainty equivalents. For example, the risk adjustment (i.e the cash risk premium of CU22)

---

could be determined using the systematic risk premium of 3 per cent (CU780 – [CU780 × (1.05/1.08)]), which results in risk-adjusted expected cash flows of CU758 (CU780 – CU22). The CU758 is the certainty equivalent of CU780 and is discounted at the risk-free interest rate (5 per cent). The present value (i.e the fair value) of the asset is CU722 (CU758/1.05).

(b)   Using Method 2, the expected cash flows are not adjusted for systematic (i.e. market) risk. Rather, the adjustment for that risk is included in the discount rate. Thus, the expected cash flows are discounted at an expected rate of return of 8 per cent (i.e. the 5 per cent risk-free interest rate plus the 3 per cent systematic risk premium). The present value (i.e. the fair value) of the asset is CU722 (CU780/1.08).

When using an expected present value technique to measure fair value, either Method 1 or Method 2 could be used. The selection of Method 1 or Method 2 will depend on facts and circumstances specific to the asset or liability being measured, the extent to which sufficient data are available, and the judgements applied.

8.4   Use of multiple valuation techniques

In some cases, it is appropriate to use a single valuation technique (e.g. when valuing an asset or a liability using quoted market prices in an active market for identical assets or liabilities). However, in other circumstances, it is appropriate to use multiple valuation techniques to arrive at an appropriate measure of fair value. [IFRS 13:63]

When multiple valuation techniques are used to measure fair value, the results (i.e. the fair value measurements) should be evaluated taking into account the reasonableness of the range of values indicated by those results. A fair value measurement is the point within that range that is most representative of the fair value in the circumstances. [IFRS 13:63]

In determining whether it is more appropriate to use a single approach or multiple approaches, an entity should consider the appropriateness (i.e. relevance and applicability) of each valuation technique and the observability of the available inputs that are significant to the valuation technique. If one valuation technique is clearly superior to the other techniques (e.g. because it uses more observable inputs), it may be appropriate to use a single valuation technique. Conversely, if no valuation technique is superior (e.g. because all techniques use unobservable inputs that are significant to the measurement), it may be appropriate to use a combination of valuation techniques provided that reliable and relevant inputs are available.

Examples **8.4A** and **8.4B**, which are reproduced from the illustrative examples accompanying the Standard, illustrate the use of multiple valuation techniques.

Example 8.4A

Machine held and used

[IFRS 13:IE11 – IE14, Example 4]

An entity acquires a machine in a business combination. The machine will be held and used in its operations. The machine was originally purchased by the acquired entity from an outside vendor and, before the business combination, was customised by the acquired entity for use in its operations. However, the customisation of the machine was not extensive. The acquiring entity determines that the asset would provide maximum value to market participants through its use in combination with other assets or with other assets and liabilities (as installed or otherwise configured for use). There is no evidence to suggest that the current use of the machine is not its highest and best use. Therefore, the highest and best use of the machine is its current use in combination with other assets or with other assets and liabilities.

The entity determines that sufficient data are available to apply the cost approach and, because the customisation of the machine was not extensive, the market approach. The income approach is not used because the machine does not have a separately identifiable income stream from which to develop reliable estimates of future cash flows. Furthermore, information about short-term and intermediate-term lease rates for similar used machinery that otherwise could be used to project an income stream (ie lease payments over remaining service lives) is not available. The market and cost approaches are applied as follows:

(a)   The market approach is applied using quoted prices for similar machines adjusted for differences between the machine (as customised) and the similar machines. The measurement reflects the price that would be received for the machine in its current condition (used) and location (installed and configured for use). The fair value indicated by that approach ranges from CU40,000 to CU48,000.

(b)   The cost approach is applied by estimating the amount that would be required currently to construct a substitute (customised) machine of comparable utility. The estimate takes into account the condition of the machine and the environment in which it operates, including physical wear and tear (ie physical deterioration), improvements in technology (ie functional obsolescence), conditions external to the condition of the machine such as a decline in the market demand for similar machines (ie economic obsolescence) and installation costs. The fair value indicated by that approach ranges from CU40,000 to CU52,000.

The entity determines that the higher end of the range indicated by the market approach is most representative of fair value and, therefore, ascribes

---

more weight to the results of the market approach. That determination is made on the basis of the relative subjectivity of the inputs, taking into account the degree of comparability between the machine and the similar machines. In particular:

(a)   the inputs used in the market approach (quoted prices for similar machines) require fewer and less subjective adjustments than the inputs used in the cost approach.

(b)   the range indicated by the market approach overlaps with, but is narrower than, the range indicated by the cost approach.

(c)   there are no known unexplained differences (between the machine and the similar machines) within that range.

Accordingly, the entity determines that the fair value of the machine is CU48,000.

If customisation of the machine was extensive or if there were not sufficient data available to apply the market approach (eg because market data reflect transactions for machines used on a stand-alone basis, such as a scrap value for specialised assets, rather than machines used in combination with other assets or with other assets and liabilities), the entity would apply the cost approach. When an asset is used in combination with other assets or with other assets and liabilities, the cost approach assumes the sale of the machine to a market participant buyer with the complementary assets and the associated liabilities. The price received for the sale of the machine (ie an exit price) would not be more than either of the following:

(a)   the cost that a market participant buyer would incur to acquire or construct a substitute machine of comparable utility; or

(b)   the economic benefit that a market participant buyer would derive from the use of the machine.

Example 8.4B

Software asset

[IFRS 13:IE15 – IE17, Example 5]

An entity acquires a group of assets. The asset group includes an income-producing software asset internally developed for licensing to customers and its complementary assets (including a related database with which the software asset is used) and the associated liabilities. To allocate the cost of the group to the individual assets acquired, the entity measures the fair value of the software asset. The entity determines that the software asset would provide maximum value to market participants through its use in combination with other assets or with other assets and liabilities (ie its complementary assets and the associated liabilities). There is no evidence to suggest that the current use of the software asset is not its highest and best use. Therefore, the highest and best use of the software asset is its current use. (In this case, the licensing of the software asset, in and of itself, does not indicate that the fair value of the asset would be maximised through its use by market participants on a stand-alone basis.)

The entity determines that, in addition to the income approach, sufficient data might be available to apply the cost approach but not the market approach. Information about market transactions for comparable software assets is not available. The income and cost approaches are applied as follows:

(a)   The income approach is applied using a present value technique. The cash flows used in that technique reflect the income stream expected to result from the software asset (licence fees from customers) over its economic life. The fair value indicated by that approach is CU15 million.

(b)   The cost approach is applied by estimating the amount that currently would be required to construct a substitute software asset of comparable utility (ie taking into account functional and economic obsolescence). The fair value indicated by that approach is CU10 million.

Through its application of the cost approach, the entity determines that market participants would not be able to construct a substitute software asset of comparable utility. Some characteristics of the software asset are unique, having been developed using proprietary information, and cannot be readily replicated. The entity determines that the fair value of the software asset is CU15 million, as indicated by the income approach.

8.5   Calibration of valuation techniques

If the transaction price is fair value at initial recognition and a valuation technique that uses unobservable inputs will be used to measure fair value in subsequent periods, the valuation technique should be calibrated so that at initial recognition the result of the valuation technique equals the transaction price. Calibration ensures that the valuation technique reflects current market conditions, and it helps an entity to determine whether an adjustment to the valuation technique is necessary (e.g. there might be a characteristic of the asset or liability that is not captured by the valuation technique). After initial recognition, when measuring fair value using a valuation technique or techniques that use unobservable inputs, an entity should ensure that those valuation techniques reflect observable market data (e.g. the price for a similar asset or liability) at the measurement date. [IFRS 13:64]

Some IFRSs require or permit assets or liabilities to be recognised initially at fair value. When an asset is acquired or a liability assumed in a market transaction, it cannot be assumed that the price paid to acquire the asset or received to assume the liability (i.e. transaction or entry price) is the same as the fair value of the asset or liability in accordance with IFRS 13 (an exit price) (see **section 7** above for further discussion).

IFRS 13:64 deals specifically with circumstances in which:

- a valuation technique that uses unobservable inputs is used to measure the fair value of an asset or a liability in subsequent periods; and

- the transaction price for the asset or liability *is* an appropriate measure of fair value at initial recognition in accordance with IFRS 13.

In such circumstances, IFRS 13:64 requires that the valuation technique should be calibrated (i.e. adjusted) so that, at initial recognition, the result of the valuation technique equals the transaction price.

If the transaction price is fair value at initial recognition, calibration of an entity's pricing model eliminates differences between the transaction price and the model's output (the 'inception difference'). IFRS 13 does not prescribe any specific method for the calibration of pricing models. Therefore, an entity should select the most appropriate method for the particular circumstances.

Factors to consider when selecting the calibration method include:

- the valuation technique used;

- the availability of information about market participant assumptions (e.g. relevant observable inputs, estimated timing of when unobservable inputs may become observable);

- the complexity involved (i.e. complexity in different calibration methods, or in the identification of the causes underlying differences between transaction price and fair value estimates based on the entity's pricing model);

- the terms of the instrument; and

- the nature of the entity's portfolio.

In outline, calibration might be approached in the following manner.

- **Step 1** Identify the source of the inception difference.

- **Step 2** Adjust the unobservable inputs or establish valuation adjustments such that the adjusted model result equals the transaction price at inception (i.e. the inception difference is eliminated).

- **Step 3** Changes in fair value measured using the entity's pricing model will be recognised subsequent to initial recognition. The adjustments identified at Step 2 may be reversed or modified when (1) unobservable inputs become observable, or (2) unobservable inputs or valuation adjustments are adjusted to reflect new information (e.g. through subsequent calibration of the model or model inputs to reflect new transaction data).

Step 2 may result in either direct adjustment to model inputs or an adjustment to the model's output (a valuation adjustment).

When calibration is achieved through direct adjustment to model inputs, an entity should consider the impact of such adjustments on the valuation of other instruments in its portfolio (e.g. instruments valued using the same or similar pricing inputs). The calibration may affect the valuation of other instruments because the calibrated inputs may replace or supersede the assumptions previously used for unobservable inputs.

When calibration is achieved through a valuation adjustment, the entity should review the valuation adjustment periodically to ensure that the adjustment reflects any new information and that it is consistent with the exit price notion in IFRS 13.

See **example 8.5** for an illustration of a model calibration approach that may be acceptable when the inception difference can be isolated to a particular unobservable model input.

Example 8.5

Calibration of models or model inputs

Entity X enters into an electricity forward contract to purchase 100 megawatts of electricity (daily) for a 10-year term. The electricity forward contract is within the scope of IFRS 9 *Financial Instruments* (or, if IFRS 9 has not yet been adopted, IAS 39 *Financial Instruments: Recognition and Measurement*) and is measured at fair value.

No cash is exchanged between the parties at the inception of the forward contract. Using the guidance in IFRS 13:B4 (see **section 7** above), Entity X determines that the transaction price equals the exit price (i.e. the fair value of the forward contract equals zero at inception).

Entity X develops its own valuation technique to measure the fair value of the forward contract at subsequent reporting dates. At inception, there are three years of observable forward prices available in the relevant market. Entity X's model uses estimated forward electricity prices beyond three years. At inception, and prior to calibration, the pricing model values the forward contract as an asset of CU1 million. Consequently, Entity X needs to calibrate its model so that the model result at inception equals the transaction price of zero.

In this simple scenario, Entity X might calibrate its model as follows.

- **Step 1** Entity X establishes that the only unobservable input that significantly affects the model value is forward electricity prices. Consequently, Entity X attributes the inception difference of CU1 million (i.e. the difference between the model's result and the fair value of zero) to its estimate of unobservable forward electricity prices for Years 4 to 10 of the contract.

- **Step 2** Entity X adjusts the unobservable forward price points at Years 4 to 10 on the forward price curve such that the model produces a fair value of zero.

  Because Entity X attributed the inception difference solely to the unobservable electricity prices in the relevant market, any calibration adjustment represents a calibration of these unobservable electricity prices to the most recent available information (the forward contract's transaction price). As a result, if Entity X owns a portfolio of contracts whose fair values are estimated using long-dated electricity prices in the same market, the calibration adjustment to the electricity forward prices would most likely also affect the fair value of those other long-dated contracts.

  Similar considerations are also relevant when a calibration results in valuation adjustments to the pricing model's output. In general, calibration adjustments provide updated information about assumptions used by market participants in assessing unobservable inputs or valuation adjustments. Therefore, calibration adjustments may have an effect beyond the recently executed transaction.

- **Step 3** Assuming no other calibration adjustments are made and that observable forward prices remain available for the next three years, the calibration adjustments would be removed as the inputs for Years 4 to 10 become observable. (For example, at the end of Year 1 of the contract, observable forward prices would be available for Years 2 to 4, and unobservable inputs for Years 5 to 10 would be used. As a result, the calibration adjustments for Year 4 should be removed from the valuation as this input has become observable.) All calibration adjustments should be removed once all the unobservable inputs become observable (e.g. in the last 3 years of the contract). In addition, no calibration adjustments should remain in the model in a period in which settlement has occurred.

8.6   Changes in valuation techniques

Once a valuation technique has been selected, it should be applied consistently. A change in a valuation technique or its application (e.g. a change in its weighting when multiple valuation techniques are used or a change in an adjustment applied to a valuation technique) is only appropriate if the change results in a measurement that is equally or more representative of fair value in the circumstances. [IFRS 13:65]

The Standard provides the following examples of events that might appropriately lead to a change in valuation technique:
[IFRS 13:65]

● new markets develop;

● new information becomes available;

● information previously used is no longer available;

● valuation techniques improve; or

● market conditions change.

If a valuation technique does not use unadjusted quoted prices, and in a subsequent period a quoted price in an active market becomes available, the quoted price should be used because IFRS 13:77 states that "a quoted price in an active market provides the most reliable evidence of fair value and shall be used without adjustment to measure fair value whenever available", with limited exceptions.

Depending on the particular circumstances, a change from a valuation technique that uses unadjusted quoted prices to a different valuation technique (such as a discounted cash flow technique) may be appropriate when:

● quoted prices for an identical asset or liability are no longer available; or

- quoted prices are available, but the market is no longer active. Note, however, that prices from relevant observable transactions must be considered in determining fair value even if the market is not active (see **9.4** below); or

- the entity no longer has access to the market in which the prices are quoted. The entity must be able to access the market in order to use a quote from that market without adjustment to reflect the lack of access, but the entity does not need to be able to sell the particular asset or transfer the particular liability on the measurement date (see **3.2** above for further details); or

- quoted prices are no longer based on relevant observable market data and do not reflect assumptions that market participants would make in pricing the asset at the measurement date. As discussed at **9.6** below, an entity cannot necessarily assume that a price provided by an external source is representative of fair value at the measurement date.

A decrease in the volume or level of activity in a market does not necessarily mean that the market is no longer active (see **10.1.1** for a discussion of active vs. inactive markets) and, consequently, that a change in the valuation technique is warranted.

In selecting another valuation technique, when appropriate, an entity should maximise the use of relevant observable inputs (e.g. quoted prices for a similar asset or liability with adjustments as appropriate) and minimise the use of unobservable inputs.

If there is a change in the valuation technique used or its application, any resulting difference should be accounted for as a change in accounting estimate in accordance with IAS 8 *Accounting Policies, Changes in Accounting Estimates and Errors*; however, the disclosures generally required under IAS 8 regarding a change in accounting estimate are not required for revisions resulting from a change in a valuation technique or its application. [IFRS 13:66]

9   Inputs to valuation techniques

Inputs are defined as "[t]he assumptions that market participants would use when pricing the asset or liability, including assumptions about risk, such as the following:

(a)   the risk inherent in a particular valuation technique used to measure fair value (such as a pricing model); and

(b)   the risk inherent in the inputs to the valuation technique". [IFRS 13:Appendix A]

Inputs may be observable or unobservable. [IFRS 13:Appendix A] Valuation techniques used to measure fair value are required to maximise the use of relevant observable inputs and minimise the use of unobservable inputs (see **section 8**). [IFRS 13:67]

> Valuation inputs that are observable are more reliable than those that are unobservable (sometimes referred to as 'entity-specific' because these inputs are derived by an entity rather than by the 'market').

The inputs used should be consistent with the characteristics of the asset or liability that market participants would take into account in a transaction for the asset or liability (see **3.1** above). [IFRS 13:69]

9.1   Observable inputs

Examples of markets in which inputs might be observable for some assets and liabilities include the following.
[IFRS 13:68 & B34]

- **Exchange markets** In an exchange market, closing prices are both readily available and generally representative of fair value (e.g. the London Stock Exchange).

- **Dealer markets** In a dealer market, dealers stand ready to trade (either buy or sell for their own account), thereby providing liquidity by using their capital to hold an inventory of the items for which they make a market. Typically, bid and ask prices (representing the price at which the dealer is willing to buy and the price at which the dealer is willing to sell, respectively) are more readily available than closing prices. Over-the-counter markets (for which prices are publicly reported) are dealer markets. Dealer markets also exist for some other assets and liabilities, including some financial instruments, commodities and physical assets (e.g. used equipment).

- **Brokered markets** In a brokered market, brokers attempt to match buyers with sellers but do not stand ready to trade for their own account. Brokers do not use their own capital to hold an inventory of the items for which they make a market. The broker knows the prices bid and asked by the respective parties, but each party is typically unaware of another party's price requirements. Prices of completed transactions are sometimes available. Brokered markets include electronic communication networks, in which buy and sell orders are matched, and commercial and residential real estate markets.

- **Principal-to-principal markets** In a principal-to-principal market, transactions (both originations and re-sales) are negotiated independently with no intermediary. Little information about those transactions may be made available publicly.

9.2   Applying a premium or discount

In some cases, the characteristics of an asset or a liability that market participants would take into account in a transaction for the asset or liability result in the application of an adjustment, such as a premium or discount (e.g. a control premium or non-controlling interest discount). However, a fair value measurement should not incorporate a premium or discount that is inconsistent with the unit of account in the IFRS that requires or permits the fair value measurement (see **3.1**). [IFRS 13:69]

Premiums or discounts that reflect size as a characteristic of the entity's holding (specifically, a blockage factor that adjusts the quoted price of an asset or a liability because the market's normal daily trading volume is not sufficient to absorb the quantity held by the entity) are not permitted in a fair value measurement. [IFRS 13:69]

For example, an investor holding one share that is quoted in an active market may receive a different amount of consideration per share compared to an investor that sells 20 per cent of the total equity shares. The difference between the two holdings is simply the size of the investor's holding, which IFRS 13 states is not a characteristic of the financial asset and thus cannot be considered in the fair value measurement. For both investors, the fair value measurement of the shares is the price for disposing of a single share multiplied by the quantity held.

In contrast, when measuring the fair value of a controlling interest, it is appropriate to incorporate a control premium because IFRS 13 regards the control premium as a characteristic of the asset or liability. [IFRS 13:69]

In all cases, if there is a quoted market price in an active market for an asset or a liability, the entity should use that price without adjustment when measuring fair value, except as specified in IFRS 13:79 (see **10.1.1** below). [IFRS 13:69]

9.3   Bid price and ask price inputs

If an asset or a liability measured at fair value has a bid price and an ask price (e.g. an input from a dealer market), the price within the bid-ask spread that is most representative of fair value in the circumstances should be used to measure fair value regardless of where the input is categorised within the fair value hierarchy (i.e. Level 1, 2 or 3 – see **section 10** below). [IFRS 13:70]

IFRS 13 permits, but does not require, that asset positions may be measured at bid prices and that liability positions may be measured at ask prices. [IFRS 13:70]

IFRS 13 allows an entity to use mid-market pricing or other pricing conventions that are used by market participants as a practical expedient for fair value measurements within a bid-ask spread. [IFRS 13:71]

An entity does not need to meet any specific qualifying criteria to use mid-market pricing or other pricing conventions as a practical expedient for measuring fair value, provided that the selected pricing convention:

- is used by market participants (e.g. an industry-accepted pricing convention); and

- is consistent with the fair value measurement objective of IFRS 13. For example, it would not be appropriate to use ask prices for recognised assets or bid prices for recognised liabilities because such a pricing approach would be inconsistent with the IFRS 13 objective that fair value is an exit price.

The decision to use a particular pricing convention is an accounting policy choice that should be consistently applied from period to period and for assets or liabilities with similar characteristics and risk. The policy should also be disclosed, if appropriate.

> **Example 9.3**
>
> **Mid-market prices**
>
> Entity X and Entity Y hold the same debt security as an asset. Entity Y, a broker-dealer, is a market-maker in the debt security. Entity X is not. The debt security is traded in an active market by Entity Y (and other broker-dealers) using bid and ask prices.
>
> Even though Entity X would most likely sell the debt security at or close to the bid price, Entity X may select a policy to use the mid-market price as the fair value of the debt security as a practical expedient. However, it would not be appropriate to use the ask price for the debt security because this would be inconsistent with the objective of fair value being an exit price.
>
> Even though Entity Y may be able to exit at a price greater than the bid price, Entity Y may choose as its policy to measure the debt security by using the bid price as a practical expedient.

IFRS 13 also contains detailed guidance for circumstances when an entity may fair value a portfolio of similar items together that have offsetting market risks and in doing so use mid-market prices for the offsetting market risks. This detailed guidance applies to financial assets and financial liabilities and is dealt with in **section 6** of **chapter B7** (or, for entities that have not yet adopted IFRS 9 *Financial Instruments*, in **section 6** of **chapter C7**).

9.3.1   Changes in the use of bid, ask or mid-market pricing or other pricing conventions

When an entity has in the past complied with the requirements of IFRS 13:70 (see above) and measured fair value at the price within the bid-ask spread that is most representative of fair value in the circumstances, it is not generally appropriate for the entity to change its accounting policy to using the practical expedient of mid-market pricing or another pricing convention as permitted by IFRS 13:71.

Once a valuation technique has been selected, it should generally be applied consistently. A change in a valuation technique is only appropriate if the change results in a measurement that is equally or more representative of fair value in the circumstances (see IFRS 13:65).

Having established a policy of measuring fair value at the price within the bid-ask spread that is most representative of fair value in the circumstances, a change to using a practical expedient such as mid-market pricing or another pricing convention would generally be inappropriate because it would not typically result in a measurement that is equally or more representative of fair value.

9.4   Measuring fair value when the volume or level of activity for an asset or a liability has significantly decreased

IFRS 13 notes that the fair value of an asset or a liability might be affected when there has been a significant decrease in the volume or level of activity for that asset or liability in relation to normal market activity for the asset or liability (or similar assets or liabilities). [IFRS 13:B37]

The consequence of a significant decrease in the volume or level of activity could be that a transaction price or a quoted price for that item is not representative of fair value. However, a decrease in the volume or level of activity on its own may not indicate that a transaction price or quoted price does not represent fair value or that a transaction in that market is not orderly. [IFRS 13:B38]

The following are examples of factors that can help determine whether, on the basis of the evidence available, there has been a significant decrease in the volume or level of activity for the asset or liability:
[IFRS 13:B37]

- there are few recent transactions;

- price quotations are not developed using current information;

- price quotations vary substantially either over time or among market-makers (e.g. some brokered markets);

- indices that previously were highly correlated with the fair values of the asset or liability are demonstrably uncorrelated with recent indications of fair value for that asset or liability;

- there is a significant increase in implied liquidity risk premiums, yields or performance indicators (such as delinquency rates or loss severities) for observed transactions or quoted prices when compared with the entity's estimate of expected cash flows, taking into account all available market data about credit and other non-performance risk for the asset or liability;

- there is a wide bid-ask spread or a significant increase in the bid-ask spread;

- there is a significant decline in the activity of, or there is an absence of, a market for new issues (i.e. a primary market) for the asset or liability or similar assets or liabilities; and

- little information is publicly available (e.g. for transactions that take place in a principal-to-principal market).

In assessing whether there has been a significant decrease in the volume or level of activity, an entity should evaluate the significance and relevance of factors such as those listed above. [IFRS 13:B37]

> Note that the presence of one or more of the factors listed in IFRS 13:B37 alone is not sufficient to conclude that a market is not 'active' (see **10.1.1** below for further discussion).

If it is concluded that there has been a significant decrease in the volume or level of activity for the asset or liability in relation to normal market activity for the asset or liability (or similar assets or liabilities), further analysis of the transactions or quoted prices is needed. If it is determined that a transaction or quoted price does not represent fair value (e.g. there may be transactions that are not orderly), an adjustment to the transactions or quoted prices will be necessary if those prices are to be used as a basis for measuring fair value. The adjustment can be significant to the fair value measurement in its entirety. [IFRS 13:B38]

Adjustments also may be necessary in other circumstances (e.g. when a price for a similar asset requires significant adjustment to make it comparable to the asset being measured, or when the price is 'stale'). [IFRS 13:B38]

IFRS 13 does not prescribe a methodology for making significant adjustments to transactions or quoted prices. Consistent with valuation techniques, as discussed in **section 8** above, appropriate risk adjustments should be applied, including a risk premium reflecting the amount that market participants would demand as compensation for the uncertainty inherent in the cash flows of an asset or a liability. Otherwise, the measurement does not faithfully represent fair value. In some cases, determining the appropriate risk adjustment may be difficult. However, the degree of difficulty alone is not a sufficient basis on which to exclude a risk adjustment. The risk adjustment should be reflective of an orderly transaction between market participants at the measurement date under current market conditions. [IFRS 13:B39]

If there has been a significant decrease in the volume or level of activity for the asset or liability, a change in valuation technique or the use of multiple valuation techniques may be appropriate (e.g. the use of a market approach and an income approach – see **8.1** and **8.3,** respectively). When weighting indications of fair value resulting from the use of multiple valuation techniques (see **8.4**), an entity should consider the reasonableness of the range of fair value measurements. The objective is to determine the point within the range that is most representative of fair value under current market conditions. A wide range of fair value measurements may be an indication that further analysis is needed. [IFRS 13:B40]

Even when there has been a significant decrease in the volume or level of activity for the asset or liability, the objective of a fair value measurement remains the same. Fair value is the price that would be received to sell an asset or paid to transfer a liability in an orderly transaction (i.e. not a forced liquidation or distress sale) between market participants at the measurement date under current market conditions. [IFRS 13:B41]

Estimating the price at which market participants would be willing to enter into a transaction at the measurement date under current market conditions if there has been a significant decrease in the volume or level of activity for the asset or liability depends on the facts and circumstances at the measurement date and requires judgement. An entity's intention to hold the asset or to settle or otherwise fulfil the liability is not relevant when measuring fair value because fair value is a market-based measurement, not an entity-specific measurement. [IFRS 13:B42]

If an entity is unwilling to transact at a price from an external source (such as a quoted market price or a price provided by a broker, pricing service or potential buyer), the entity's unwillingness to transact at that price is not sufficient evidence for the entity to disregard that price in measuring fair value. If the best information available in the circumstances indicates that market participants would transact at a price from an external source, an entity is not permitted to disregard that price simply because it is not willing to transact at that price.

Examples 9.4A and **9.4B** explore this issue further.

Example 9.4A

Assumptions can be readily derived from current observable market data

Entity A is using a valuation model to measure the fair value of its investment in privately placed corporate debt securities issued by Entity X.

No quoted price for identical securities is available. Entity A's valuation model uses assumptions about default rates and discount rates. Default rate assumptions can be readily derived from current observable market data for actively traded credit default swaps on publicly traded bonds of Entity X. When measuring the fair value of its investment, Entity A cannot disregard this market data even if Entity A would not be willing to transact at a price consistent with this market data.

Example 9.4B

Active markets for similar securities

Entity A holds distressed debt securities. Transactions in the securities occur infrequently and there is no active market for the securities, but there are active markets for similar securities. Entity A's own valuation model, which is based on observable Level 2 inputs current at the measurement date, indicates that market participants would be willing to buy and sell the debt for CU30 at the measurement date. Entity A has calibrated the model to the best information available at the measurement date (including transaction prices in similar securities and risk premiums).

At the measurement date, a potential buyer provides an unsolicited bid to buy the securities for CU20. When measuring the fair value of the debt securities, Entity A can neither disregard this bid price simply because it is not willing to transact at that price, nor can it assume that the bid price provides better evidence of fair value than its own model. Although the bid price is the price one potential buyer would be willing to pay for Entity A's asset, it may not necessarily be the price at which market participants (buyers and sellers) would be willing to transact on the measurement date.

Valuation techniques to measure fair value should maximise the use of relevant observable inputs (i.e. Level 1 and Level 2 inputs that do not require significant adjustment) and minimise the use of unobservable inputs (Level 3 inputs). If the bid price is classified as a Level 3 input, it may be appropriate for Entity A to place less weight on the bid price in measuring the fair value of its debt securities given that Entity A's own model is based on Level 2 inputs. However, if Entity A obtains several bid prices and the fair value indicated by the valuation model is not in the range of the bid prices obtained, Entity A may need to consider whether its model is valid and identify the reasons for the discrepancy between the model amount and the bid prices.

IFRS 13 provides an illustrative example of estimating a market rate of return when the volume or level of activity for a financial asset has significantly decreased (see **example 9.4C** in **chapter B7** for entities that have adopted IFRS 9 *Financial Instruments*, or **example 9.4C** in **chapter C7** for entities that have not yet adopted IFRS 9).

9.5   Identifying transactions that are not orderly

The determination as to whether a transaction is orderly is more difficult if there has been a significant decrease in the volume or level of activity for the asset or liability in relation to normal market activity. In such circumstances, it is not appropriate to conclude that all transactions in that market are not orderly (i.e. forced liquidations or distress sales). [IFRS 13:B43]

IFRS 13 does not require an entity to undertake exhaustive efforts to determine whether a transaction is orderly, although the entity should not ignore information that is reasonably available. However, the Standard does establish a presumption that, when an entity is a party to a transaction, it has sufficient information to conclude whether the transaction is orderly. [IFRS 13:B44]

An entity is expected to evaluate the circumstances to determine whether, on the weight of the evidence available, the transaction is orderly. [IFRS 13:B43]

The Standard identifies the following circumstances that may indicate that a transaction is not orderly:
[IFRS 13:B43]

- there was not adequate exposure to the market for a period before the measurement date to allow for marketing activities that are usual and customary for transactions involving such assets or liabilities under current market conditions;

- there was a usual and customary marketing period, but the seller marketed the asset or liability to a single market participant;

- the seller is in or near bankruptcy or receivership (i.e. the seller is distressed);

- the seller was required to sell to meet regulatory or legal requirements (i.e. the seller was forced); or

- the transaction price is an outlier when compared with other recent transactions for the same or a similar asset or liability.

If a transaction is determined not to be orderly, little if any weight (compared to other indications of fair value) is placed on that transaction price. [IFRS 13:B44(a)]

If a transaction is determined to be orderly, that transaction price is taken into account in estimating fair value. However, the amount of weight placed on that transaction price when compared with other indications of fair value will depend on the facts and circumstances, such as: [IFRS 13:B44(b)]

- the volume of the transaction;

- the comparability of the transaction to the asset or liability being measured; and

- the proximity of the transaction to the measurement date.

If there is not sufficient information available to conclude whether a transaction is orderly, the transaction price should be taken into account in estimating fair value. However, the transaction price may not represent fair value and, consequently, would not necessarily be the sole or primary basis for measuring fair value or estimating market risk premiums and less weight should be placed on it when compared with other transactions that are known to be orderly. [IFRS 13:B44(c)]

Example 9.5

Determining whether a transaction is orderly

Entity A is acting as an administrator on behalf of the creditors of Entity B, which is subject to bankruptcy proceedings. The administrator's role is to seek to maximise the return to Entity B's creditors. As part of Entity A's responsibilities, it auctions a portfolio of Entity B's financial assets. Entity A promotes the auction to interested parties with the expectation of receiving bids for the financial assets over a specified period.

Even though the financial assets are being sold as part of bankruptcy proceedings, the auction process may be considered to be an orderly trans-action provided that all of the necessary conditions are met.

IFRS 13:Appendix A defines an orderly transaction as "[a] transaction that assumes exposure to the market for a period before the measurement date to allow for marketing activities that are usual and customary for transactions involving such assets or liabilities; it is not a forced transaction (eg a forced liquidation or distress sale)".

In the circumstances described, it seems possible that the auction process may be considered to be an orderly transaction because the sale is not immediate and there is sufficient (i.e. usual and customary) time to market the assets to other market participants.

If transactions in assets or liabilities occur between willing buyers and sellers in a manner that is usual and customary for transactions involving such assets or liabilities, these should be considered to be orderly transactions. Persuasive evidence is required to establish that an observable transaction is not an orderly transaction.

See **10.2.3** below for the effect of observable transactions in inactive markets on the categorisation of the fair value measurement within the fair value hierarchy.

9.6   Quoted prices provided by third parties

IFRS 13 does not preclude the use of quoted prices provided by third parties, such as pricing services or brokers, if it is determined that the quoted prices provided by those parties are developed in accordance with IFRS 13. [IFRS 13:B45]

However, if there has been a significant decrease in the volume or level of activity for the asset or liability, an entity is required to evaluate whether the quoted prices provided by third parties are developed using current information that reflects orderly transactions or a valuation technique that reflects market participant assumptions (including assumptions about risk). In weighting a quoted price as an input to a fair value measurement, an entity should place less weight (when compared with other indications of fair value that reflect the results of transactions) on quotes that do not reflect the result of transactions. [IFRS 13:B46]

Further, the nature of a quote (e.g. whether the quote is an indicative price or a binding offer) should be taken into account when weighting the available evidence, with more weight given to quotes provided by third parties that represent binding offers. [IFRS 13:B47]

Broker or pricing service quotes are not necessarily determinative of fair value if an active market (as defined in IFRS 13:Appendix A – see **10.1.1** below) does not exist for the item being measured. In assessing whether a broker or pricing service quote appropriately represents fair value, an entity needs to understand how the broker or pricing service has arrived at the quoted price, and the inputs and other information used.

Quote based on information from an active market

Consistent with IFRS 13:77 (see **10.1.1** below), when a broker or pricing service quote represents the unadjusted price quoted for an identical asset, liability or equity instrument in an active market to which the entity has access at the measurement date, the entity is required to use the quoted price without adjustment when measuring fair value, subject to limited exceptions as discussed in IFRS 13:79. Such a quote represents a Level 1 input.

If any adjustment is made to the broker or pricing service quote in the circumstances specified in IFRS 13:79, or in the absence of an active market, a broker or pricing service quote does not represent a Level 1 input. However, it may nevertheless be determinative of fair value.

Quote based on valuation technique(s)

If a quote is based on a valuation technique that is used by market participants and uses market-observable or market-corroborated inputs that reflect the assumptions of market participants, it is determinative of fair value if no significant adjustment to the quote is needed. If a significant adjustment is needed, the quote is not determinative of fair value but it could represent a relevant observable input into the entity's fair value measurement.

General considerations

In assessing whether a quote is determinative of fair value, the entity should consider all relevant circumstances, including the following questions (the list is not exhaustive).

- Are there differences between the asset or liability being measured and the item for which a quote is available (e.g. differences in the terms or risk attributes)? Such differences may necessitate adjustments to the price quoted by the broker or pricing service.

- Does the quote reflect currently occurring orderly transactions for the asset or liability being measured? That is, are market participants currently transacting in the asset or liability at the price quoted by the broker or pricing service or does the quote reflect 'stale' information or transactions that are not orderly? IFRS 13:B46 (see above) provides specific guidance for circumstances in which there has been a significant decrease in the volume or level of activity for the asset or liability.

- Is the broker or pricing service using a valuation technique that complies with the fair value measurement principles in IFRS 13? For example, does the valuation technique used by the broker or pricing service (1) reflect market participant assumptions, including assumptions about risk, (2) maximise the use of relevant observable inputs, and (3) minimise the use of unob-servable inputs? If the valuation technique does not reflect the assumptions market participants would use in pricing the asset or liability, the price quoted by the broker or pricing service may need adjustment or may not be relevant to the entity's fair value measurement.

- Is the quote provided by the broker or pricing service an indicative price or a binding offer? That is, does the broker or another market participant stand ready to transact at the price quoted by the broker or pricing service? As noted above, IFRS 13:B47 indicates that more weight should be given to quotes based on binding offers. Typically, a quote obtained from a broker or pricing service is an indicative price and not a binding offer (unless the broker is a market-maker).

- Does the quote come from a reputable broker or pricing service that has a substantial presence in the market and the experience and expertise to provide a representationally faithful quote for the asset or liability being measured? An entity may place more weight on a quote from a broker or pricing service that has more experience and expertise related to the asset or liability being measured.

As the number of market transactions decreases, brokers or pricing services may rely more on proprietary models based on their own assumptions to arrive at a quote. The entity should evaluate how the quote has been arrived at and whether it reflects market participant assumptions, including assumptions about risk. This information may be difficult to obtain if quotes are based on proprietary models that brokers or pricing services may not be willing to share. How-ever, even when brokers or pricing services do not wish to share detailed information about their models, it may still be possible to obtain information about the nature of the assumptions and the inputs used in the model. If the quote does not reflect assumptions that market participants would use in pricing the asset or liability, the quote will most likely not be determinative of fair value because adjustments may be required. In such cases, the quote may be an input to the entity's fair value measurement, but other indications of fair value may be equally or more useful when estimating fair value (e.g. a valuation based on the entity's own estimates of the inputs that market participants would use in pricing the asset or liability).

Multiple quotes

An entity may need to perform additional analysis when quotes for an individual asset or liability are obtained from different brokers or pricing services. Multiple quotes within a narrow range constitute stronger evidence of fair value than multiple quotes that are widely dispersed. IFRS 13:B40 states that a wide range of measurements may be an indication that further analysis is needed. The entity should consider the reasonableness of the range of fair value measurements, with the objective of determining the point within the range that is most representative of fair value under current market conditions.

In addition, if an entity's own estimate of fair value is outside the range of broker or pricing service quotes, the entity should understand the reason(s) for such a difference. If the range of quotes provides strong evidence of fair value, the entity may need to make adjustments to its valuation technique to reflect current market information.

10 Fair value hierarchy

To increase consistency and comparability in fair value measurements and related disclosures, IFRS 13 establishes a fair value hierarchy that categorises into three levels the inputs to valuation techniques used to measure fair value, as follows:
[IFRS 13:72]

- Level 1 inputs comprise unadjusted quoted prices in active markets for identical assets and liabilities that the entity can access at the measurement date (see **10.1.1**);

- Level 2 inputs comprise other observable inputs not included within Level 1 of the fair value hierarchy (see **10.1.2**); and

- Level 3 inputs comprise unobservable inputs (including the entity's own data, which are adjusted, if necessary, to reflect the assumptions market participants would use in the circumstances) (see **10.1.3**).

Observable inputs are defined as "[i]nputs that are developed using market data, such as publicly available information about actual events or transactions, and that reflect the assumptions that market participants would use when pricing the asset or liability". [IFRS 13:Appendix A]

Unobservable inputs are defined as "[i]nputs for which market data are not available and that are developed using the best information available about the assumptions that market participants would use when pricing the asset or liability". [IFRS 13:Appendix A]

The fair value hierarchy gives the highest priority to Level 1 inputs and the lowest priority to Level 3 inputs. [IFRS 13:72]

When an entity approaches the measurement of an asset, or a liability, or an entity's own equity instrument, at fair value, it looks at the available valuation techniques and at the inputs available for those techniques. When selecting the techniques and inputs to be used, the entity is required to maximise the use of observable inputs and minimise the use of unobservable inputs (see **section 8** above). Once the selection has been made, each of the inputs is categorised within the fair value hierarchy outlined above; **section 10.1** below summarises IFRS 13's requirements regarding the categorisation of inputs.

When an entity has determined the appropriate categorisation of the inputs into a fair value measurement, and has arrived at a measure of fair value using those inputs, it is then necessary to determine the appropriate categorisation of the fair value measurement in its entirety; this topic is discussed in **section 10.2**.

10.1   Categorisation of inputs to valuation techniques within the fair value hierarchy

10.1.1   Level 1 inputs

Level 1 inputs are quoted prices (unadjusted) in active markets for identical assets or liabilities that the entity can access at the measurement date. [IFRS 13:76 & Appendix A]

A quoted price for an identical asset or liability in an active market provides the most reliable evidence of fair value. Such prices should be used without adjustment to measure fair value whenever available, except in any of the circumstances described in IFRS 13:79 (see below). [IFRS 13:77]

Therefore, when a Level 1 input is available, it must be used without adjustment, except in any of the circumstances described in IFRS 13:79.

An active market is defined as "[a] market in which transactions for the asset or liability take place with sufficient frequency and volume to provide pricing information on an ongoing basis". [IFRS 13:Appendix A]

Determining whether a market is active focuses on the trading activity for the individual asset or liability being measured and not on the general levels of activity in the market in which the asset or liability is traded. For example, a security listed on the FTSE in London or HKEx in Hong Kong could be considered to be traded in an inactive market if the security itself is traded infrequently.

IFRS 13:B37 sets out a list of factors that may indicate that there has been a significant decrease in the volume or level of activity for an asset or liability relative to normal market activity for that asset or liability (or similar assets or liabilities) (see **9.4** above).The presence of one or more of the factors listed in IFRS 13:B37 alone is not sufficient to conclude that a market is not active. An entity should evaluate the relevance and significance of these factors to the individual asset or liability measured at fair value in order to determine whether the market for that asset or liability is inactive. A market is not deemed inactive simply because of insufficient trading volume relative to the size of an entity's position.

The characterisation of a market as 'active' or 'inactive' may change as market conditions change. However, a decline in the volume of transactions for a particular asset or liability does not automatically mean that the market has become inactive. A market would still be considered active as long as the frequency and volume of relevant transactions are sufficient to provide ongoing pricing information.

Further, quoted prices from a market affected by a decline in the volume or level of activity should not be ignored unless the price is associated with a transaction that is not orderly. It is not appropriate to conclude automatically that all transactions occurring in a market exhibiting a significant decline in volume or level of activity are not orderly. IFRS 13:B43 sets out a list of factors that may indicate that a transaction is not orderly (see **9.5** above). Very little weight should be given to prices observed for a transaction that is not orderly; more weight may be given to a price observed for an orderly transaction. However, the entity should evaluate carefully whether an adjustment may be needed to that price to ensure the fair value measurement is consistent with the objectives in IFRS 13.

When an asset or a liability could be exchanged in a number of markets (e.g. a financial asset or a financial liability that could be exchanged on a number of exchanges), the entity will need to consider which market is the most relevant for measuring fair value. IFRS 13 states explicitly that the emphasis within Level 1 is on determining both of the following:
[IFRS 13:78]

- the principal market for the asset or liability or, in the absence of a principal market, the most advantageous market for the asset or liability (see **3.2** above); and

- whether the entity can enter into a transaction for the asset or liability at the price in that market at the measurement date.

When a quoted price in an active market is available, it should not be adjusted except in the circumstances listed below.
[IFRS 13:79]

- When an entity holds a large number of similar (but not identical) assets or liabilities (e.g. debt securities) that are measured at fair value and a quoted price in an active market is available but not readily accessible for each of those assets or liabilities individually (i.e. given the large number of similar assets or liabilities held by the entity, it would be difficult to obtain pricing information for each individual asset or liability at the measurement date). In such cir-cumstances, as a practical expedient, an entity may measure fair value using an alternative pricing method that does not rely exclu-sively on quoted prices (e.g. matrix pricing – see **8.1** above). How-ever, the use of an alternative pricing method results in a fair value measurement categorised within a lower level of the fair value hierarchy.

- When a quoted price in an active market does not represent fair value at the measurement date. That might be the case if, for example, significant events (such as transactions in a principal-to-principal market, trades in a brokered market or announcements) take place after the close of a market but before the measurement date. An entity should establish and consistently apply a policy for identifying those events that might affect fair value measurements. However, if the quoted price is adjusted for new information, the adjustment results in a fair value measurement categorised within a lower level of the fair value hierarchy.

- When measuring the fair value of a liability or an entity's own equity instrument using the quoted price for the identical item traded as an asset in an active market and that price needs to be adjusted for factors specific to the item or the asset (see **5.1.1** above). If no adjustment to the quoted price of the asset is required, the result is a fair value measurement categorised within Level 1 of the fair value hierarchy. However, any adjustment to the quoted price of the asset results in a fair value measurement categorised within a lower level of the fair value hierarchy.

If an entity holds a position in a single asset or liability (including a position comprising a large number of identical assets or liabilities, such as a holding of financial instruments) and the asset or liability is traded in an active market, the fair value of the asset or liability should be measured within Level 1 as the product of the quoted price for the individual asset or liability and the quantity held by the entity. That is the case even if a market's normal daily trading volume is not sufficient to absorb the quantity held and placing orders to sell the position in a single transaction might affect the quoted price. [IFRS 13:80]

10.1.1.1 Published net asset values for open-ended investment funds as Level 1 inputs

Some open-ended investments funds not listed on a stock exchange may publish daily quotations of their net asset values (NAVs) at which redemptions or purchases of units occur without any adjustments to the published NAV. The redemptions and unit purchases may take place regularly at the quoted NAVs and there is no secondary market for the units because they are not transferrable (i.e. the sole transactions are issuances and redemptions of the units by the fund). These quoted NAVs may meet the definition of a Level 1 input provided that all of the elements of the definition in IFRS 13:76 (see above) are met.

Consequently, the following criteria must be satisfied:

- the price must be quoted in an active market (see above);

- the price must be unadjusted;

- the price must be for an asset or liability that is identical to the asset or liability being measured; and

- the entity must have access to the price at the measurement date.

1 April 20X3 to 31 December 20X6) using a model that relies on pricing data and weather patterns from the previous four years. The model also incorporates all relevant physical constraints (capacity of existing power plants and power plants expected to be completed near location ABC, projected supply and demand etc.).

In the circumstances described, the five-year and nine-month forward price curve represents a Level 3, rather than a Level 2, input.

An input for an item with a specified contractual term falls within Level 2 of the hierarchy only if it meets both of the following criteria:

- as required by IFRS 13:82 (see above), the input must be observable for substantially the full term of the asset or liability; and

- the impact of the unobservable period must not be significant to the fair value of the asset or liability. The guidance set out in **10.2.2.1** below should be applied when evaluating whether the effect of the unobservable period is significant.

IFRS 13:B35(b) cites as an example an interest rate swap with a term of 10 years and for which the fair value is determined using a swap rate based on a yield curve that is observable at commonly quoted intervals for 9 years. The swap rate input is a Level 2 input provided that any reasonable extrapolation of the yield curve for Year 10 would not be significant to the fair value measurement of the swap in its entirety.

In contrast, in the circumstances described, Company X can observe forward prices for only 24 months of the remaining 69-month term of the agreement (i.e. 35 per cent of the term). Because this does not represent substantially the full term, the first criterion above is not met. An analysis of the second criterion is unnecessary; the forward price curve is considered a Level 3 input. However, if the forward price curve had been observable for substantially the full term, Company X would need to consider the second criterion (i.e. whether the effect of the unobservable term is significant to the fair value of the agreement) to determine whether the forward price curve is a Level 2 or Level 3 input.

Adjustments to Level 2 inputs will vary depending on factors specific to the asset or liability. Those factors include the following: [IFRS 13:83]

- the condition or location of the asset;

- the extent to which inputs relate to items that are comparable to the asset or liability (including those factors described in IFRS 13:39 – see **5.1.1** above); and

- the volume or level of activity in the markets within which the inputs are observed.

An entity should consider whether adjustments to the quoted price for a similar asset or liability are necessary to reflect differences between the terms of the items being compared and other factors that may affect the fair values of those items. For example, the entity may need to make adjustments to reflect differences in the condition, location or risks (including non-performance risk and liquidity risk) of the items being compared.

Under IFRS 13:37, an entity should measure the fair value of a liability by reference to the quoted price of a similar item that is held by another party as an asset. In such circumstances, the quoted price of the similar item held by another party as an asset should be adjusted for factors specific to the asset that are not applicable to the fair value measurement of the liability. IFRS 13:39 provides a number of examples of such factors (see **5.1.1** above).

In addition, if an entity uses a quoted price for a similar item in its valuation technique, the entity may need to make adjustments to reflect differences in risk, including liquidity differences. For example, the item being measured may be in shorter supply (relative to demand) than the similar item for which a quoted price exists. In this situation, a liquidity risk premium exists for the item being measured that should be factored into the fair value measurement as an adjustment to the quoted price of the similar item.

Example 10.1.2B provides an illustration of circumstances in which the quoted price for a similar asset needs to be adjusted to reflect the different characteristics of the asset being measured.

Example 10.1.2B

Using quoted prices for a similar asset or liability

Sales of genetically modified wheat are increasing globally. However, there are no separate markets for genetically modified wheat and wheat that is not genetically modified. Thus, when measuring their agricultural produce at the time of harvest at fair value less costs to sell under IAS 41 *Agriculture*, sellers of genetically modified wheat use quoted prices for wheat that is not genetically modified. Because the quoted price is for a similar asset, that price would generally represent a Level 2 input. However, because genetically modified wheat has different characteristics to the wheat for which a quoted price exists, an adjustment should be made to reflect market participant assumptions about the price that would be received for selling genetically modified wheat. If the adjustment is significant to the entire measurement and based on unobservable data, the entire measurement would be classified as a Level 3 measurement.

An adjustment to a Level 2 input that is significant to the entire measurement might result in a fair value measurement categorised within Level 3 of the fair value hierarchy if the adjustment uses significant unobservable inputs. [IFRS 13:84] See **10.2.2.1** for further discussion.

IFRS 13 provides the following examples of Level 2 inputs for particular assets and liabilities.
[IFRS 13:B35]

- **Receive-fixed, pay-variable interest rate swap based on the London Interbank Offered Rate (LIBOR) swap rate** A Level 2 input would be the LIBOR swap rate if that rate is observable at commonly quoted intervals for substantially the full term of the swap.

- **Receive-fixed, pay-variable interest rate swap based on a yield curve denominated in a foreign currency** A Level 2 input would be the swap rate based on a yield curve denominated in a foreign currency that is observable at commonly quoted intervals for substantially the full term of the swap. That would be the case if the term of the swap is 10 years and that rate is observable at commonly quoted intervals for 9 years, provided that any reasonable extrapolation of the yield curve for year 10 would not be significant to the fair value measurement of the swap in its entirety (but see **example 10.1.2A** above for circumstances when observable data is not available for substantially the full term of the agreement).

- **Receive-fixed, pay-variable interest rate swap based on a specific bank's prime rate** A Level 2 input would be the bank's prime rate derived through extrapolation if the extrapolated values are corroborated by observable market data, e.g. by correlation with an interest rate that is observable over substantially the full term of the swap.

- **Three-year option on exchange-traded shares** A Level 2 input would be the implied volatility for the shares derived through extrapolation to year 3 if both of the following conditions exist:

  - prices for one-year and two-year options on the shares are observable; and

  - the extrapolated implied volatility of a three-year option is corroborated by observable market data for substantially the full term of the option.

In that case, the implied volatility could be derived by extrapolating from the implied volatility of the one-year and two-year options on the shares and corroborated by the implied volatility for three-year options on comparable entities' shares, provided that correlation with the one-year and two-year implied volatilities is established.

- **Licensing arrangement** For a licensing arrangement that is acquired in a business combination and was recently negotiated with an unrelated party by the acquired entity (the party to the licensing arrangement), a Level 2 input would be the royalty rate of the contract with the unrelated party at inception of the arrangement.

- **Finished goods inventory at a retail outlet** For finished goods inventory that is acquired in a business combination, a Level 2 input would be either a price to customers in a retail market or a price to retailers in a wholesale market, adjusted for differences between the condition and location of the inventory item and the comparable (i.e. similar) inventory items so that the fair value measurement reflects the price that would be received in a transaction to sell the inventory to another retailer that would complete the requisite selling efforts. Conceptually, the fair value measurement will be the same, whether adjustments are made to a retail price (downward) or to a wholesale price (upward). Generally, the price that requires the least amount of subjective adjustments should be used for the fair value measurement.

- **Building held and used** A Level 2 input would be the price per square metre for the building (a valuation multiple) derived from observable market data, e.g. multiples derived from prices in observed transactions involving comparable (i.e. similar) buildings in similar locations.

- **Cash-generating unit** A Level 2 input would be a valuation multiple (e.g. a multiple of earnings or revenue or a similar performance measure) derived from observable market data, e.g. multiples derived from prices in observed transactions involving comparable (i.e. similar) businesses, taking into account operational, market, financial and non-financial factors.

10.1.3 Level 3 inputs

Level 3 inputs are unobservable inputs for the asset or liability. [IFRS 13:86 & Appendix A]

Unobservable inputs should be used to measure fair value to the extent that relevant observable inputs are not available (e.g. when there is little, if any, market activity for the asset or liability at the measurement date). However, unobservable inputs should reflect the assumptions that market participants would use when pricing the asset or liability, so as to achieve the general fair value measurement objective (i.e. an exit price at the measurement date from the perspective of a market participant that holds the asset or owes the liability). [IFRS 13:87]

Unobservable inputs should reflect, among others, assumptions that market participants would make about risk. Assumptions about risk include the risk inherent in a particular valuation technique used to measure fair value (such as a pricing model) and the risk inherent in the inputs to the valuation technique. A measurement that does not include an adjustment for risk would not represent a fair value measurement if market participants would include one when pricing the asset or liability. For example, it might be necessary to include a risk adjustment when there is significant measurement uncertainty (e.g. when there has been a significant decrease in the volume or level of activity when compared with normal market activity for the asset or liability (or similar assets or liabilities) and the entity has determined that the transaction price or quoted price does not represent fair value – see **9.4** to **9.6** above). [IFRS 13:88]

Unobservable inputs should be developed using the best information available in the circumstances, which might include an entity's own data. In developing unobservable inputs, an entity's own data should be adjusted if reasonably available information indicates that other market participants would use different data or there is something particular to the entity that is not available to other market participants (e.g. an entity-specific synergy). IFRS 13 does not require an entity to undertake exhaustive efforts to obtain information about market participant assumptions. However, the entity is required to take into account all information about market participant assumptions that is reasonably available. Unobservable inputs developed in the manner described above are considered market participant assumptions and meet the objective of a fair value measurement. [IFRS 13:89]

IFRS 13 provides the following examples of Level 3 inputs for particular assets and liabilities.
[IFRS 13:B36]

- **Long-dated currency swap** A Level 3 input would be an interest rate in a specified currency that is not observable and cannot be corroborated by observable market data at commonly quoted intervals or otherwise for substantially the full term of the currency swap. The interest rates in a currency swap are the swap rates calculated from the respective countries' yield curves.

- **Three-year option on exchange-traded shares** A Level 3 input would be historical volatility, i.e. the volatility for the shares derived from the shares' historical prices. Historical volatility typically does not represent current market participant expectations about future volatility, even if it is the only information available to price an option.

- **Interest rate swap** A Level 3 input would be an adjustment to a mid-market consensus (non-binding) price for the swap developed using data that are not directly observable and cannot otherwise be corroborated by observable market data.

- **Decommissioning liability assumed in a business combination** A Level 3 input would be a current estimate using the entity's own data of the future cash outflows to be paid to fulfil the obligation (including market participants' expectations about the costs of fulfilling the obligation and the compensation that a market participant would require for taking on the obligation to dismantle the asset) if there is no reasonably available information that indicates that market participants would use different assumptions. That Level 3 input would be used in a present value technique together with other inputs, e.g. a current risk-free interest rate or a credit-adjusted risk-free rate if the effect of the entity's credit standing on the fair value of the liability is reflected in the discount rate rather than in the estimate of future cash outflows.

- **Cash-generating unit** A Level 3 input would be a financial forecast (e.g. of cash flows or profit or loss) developed using the entity's own data if there is no reasonably available information that indicates that market participants would use different assumptions.

10.1.4 Determining the level within the fair value hierarchy when broker or pricing service quotes are used

IFRS 13 allows the use of quoted prices provided by brokers or pricing services if the entity has determined that the quoted prices provided by a broker or pricing service are developed in accordance with IFRS 13. See **9.6** above for more detailed guidance regarding when a quoted price provided by a broker or pricing service can be considered to be determinative of fair value.

When quoted prices are provided by a broker or pricing service, and are used by an entity in measuring the fair value of an asset or a liability, the following considerations are relevant for the entity's assessment of the level within the fair value hierarchy in which the quoted prices fall.

Level 1 inputs

Level 1 inputs are unadjusted quoted prices in active markets for identical assets or liabilities. If the quote provided by a broker or pricing service is a Level 1 input, the quoted price should be used to measure the fair value of the asset or liability without adjustment, subject to limited exceptions as discussed in IFRS 13:79 (see **10.1.1** above).

If an adjustment is necessary in accordance with IFRS 13:79, or if the quoted price originates from a market that is not active, the broker or pricing service quote does not represent a Level 1 input.

Level 2 inputs

Level 2 inputs are inputs other than quoted prices included within Level 1 that are observable for the asset or liability, either directly or indirectly. Observable inputs are defined in IFRS 13:Appendix A as "[i]nputs that are developed using market data, such as publicly available information about actual events or transactions, and that reflect the assumptions that market participants would use when pricing the asset or liability [or own equity instrument]".

If a quote from a broker or pricing service meets any of the following criteria, it represents a Level 2 input.

- The entity can determine that the broker or pricing service quote itself represents a quoted price for similar assets or liabilities in active markets.

- The entity can determine that the quote is based on quoted prices for identical or similar assets or liabilities in markets that are not active, from transactions that are orderly and for which adjustments are based only on information that is (1) observable, or (2) market-corroborated, or (3) unobservable, but insignificant to the measurement.

- The entity can determine that the quote was established using a valuation technique and that the inputs the broker or pricing service used to arrive at the quoted price are observable or market-corroborated and any unobservable inputs do not have a significant effect on the measurement.

- The entity can corroborate the broker or pricing service quote or inputs using prices (1) from orderly transactions in an active market, or (2) from orderly transactions in an inactive market for which any adjustment needed to ensure the price is representative of fair value is insignificant to the measurement.

In some circumstances, adjustments to the Level 2 inputs may be necessary, for example if the quoted price is based on a similar (but not identical) asset or liability. If an adjustment is required, an entity should determine whether the adjustment is significant to the entire measurement and whether it is based on unobservable inputs (see **10.2.2.1**). If this is the case, the entire measurement will be categorised within Level 3.

Level 3 inputs

Level 3 inputs are unobservable inputs for the asset or liability. Broker or pricing service quotes meeting any of the following criteria are categorised in Level 3 of the fair value hierarchy.

- The entity can determine that the quote is based on a Level 1 or Level 2 input but an adjustment is required that is significant to the measurement and based on unobservable inputs.

- The entity can determine that the quote is based on unobservable inputs with a significant effect.

Regardless of whether the entity determines that the broker or pricing service quote is based on observable or unobservable inputs, it is not appropriate for an entity to accept, without further analysis, that the inputs used are appropriate in the circumstances. The entity must gain sufficient understanding of the inputs to be able to conclude that they reflect assumptions market participants would use, including assumptions about risks inherent in a particular valuation technique and the inputs used. Further, an entity must be able to conclude that the inputs used are based on the best information available. Adjustments should be made if reasonably available information, including the entity's own data, indicates that other market participants would use different inputs.

Other considerations

Depending on the asset or liability being measured at fair value, a quote from a broker or pricing service may be the only input, or one of many inputs, into an entity's fair value measurement of that asset or liability. All inputs must be considered before determining the level within the fair value hierarchy for measurement of the asset or liability (see **10.2** below).

Other factors indicating that a broker or pricing service quote may be given more weight in the fair value measurement include that:

- the quote is binding on the entity making the quote; or

- the quote is available from more than one broker or pricing service.

Disclosure

IFRS 13:IE64(b) in the illustrative examples accompanying IFRS 13 suggests that, in order to comply with the disclosure requirements in IFRS 13:92(d), an entity may disclose "how third-party information such as broker quotes, pricing services, net asset values and relevant market data was taken into account when measuring fair value" as part of the entity's additional information about significant unobservable inputs. Further, IFRS 13:IE65(d) suggests that, in order to comply with the disclosure requirements in IFRS 13:93(g), an entity may disclose how the entity determined that third-party information, such as broker quotes or pricing services, used in the fair value measurement was developed in accordance with IFRS 13 as part of the entity's description of its valuation process for Level 3 fair value measurements. See **section 11** for IFRS 13's disclosure requirements.

10.2   Categorisation of fair value measurements within the fair value hierarchy

The categorisation of a fair value measurement within the fair value hierarchy is a two-step process. Initially, the entity determines the appropriate categorisation of the inputs to the valuation techniques used in the fair value measurement (see **10.1** above). Once the valuation techniques have been applied, and the fair value measured, it is then necessary to determine the appropriate categorisation of the fair value measurement in its entirety. This is required in order to arrive at the appropriate analysis of the fair value measurements for disclosure purposes (see **section 11**).

As can be seen from the discussion in the remainder of this section, the appropriate categorisation of a fair value measurement is determined by the 'mix' of inputs used. For example, if only Level 1 inputs are used, the fair value measurement will be categorised as a Level 1 measurement (see **10.2.1**). The same principle applies if only Level 2 or only Level 3 inputs are used. Alternatively, the fair value measurement may be derived from several inputs from different categories, in which case it will be necessary to consider the significance of each of those inputs (see **10.2.2**).

10.2.1   *Categorisation of measurements made using Level 1 inputs*

A fair value measurement can only be categorised as a Level 1 measurement when only Level 1 inputs are used, and no adjustments are made.

In any of the circumstances described in IFRS 13:79 (see **10.1.1** above), a Level 1 input cannot be used without adjustment. IFRS 13:79 outlines the appropriate adjustments for each circumstance. Note that any adjustment to a Level 1 input, regardless of its significance, means that the resulting fair value measurement cannot be categorised as a Level 1 measurement.

Based on the definition in IFRS 13:76 and Appendix 1 (see **10.1.1** above), for a fair value measurement to be categorised in Level 1 of the fair value hierarchy, the following criteria must be satisfied:

- the only input used must be a price (or prices) quoted in an active market;

- the price must be unadjusted. IFRS 13:79 (see above) requires that any adjustment to a fair value measurement (regardless of its significance) that would otherwise meet the Level 1 criteria results in the fair value measurement being categorised as a lower-level measurement;

- the price must be for an asset or liability that is identical to the asset or liability being measured (see **examples 10.2.1A** to **10.2.1D** below); and

- the entity must have access to the price at the measurement date. For example, an entity has access to the price if it has the ability to transact at that price in an exchange market. In addition, an entity has access to the price if there are dealers who stand ready to transact with the entity at that price. However, broker quotes by themselves are not sufficient evidence that the entity has access to the price if the brokers do not stand ready to transact at that price. Any adjustment made to a quoted price in an active market because the entity has limited or no access to that market results in a Level 2 or a Level 3 measurement, depending on the nature of the adjustment. Further, although a quoted price in an active market may be available, such pricing may not be readily accessible for all of the assets and liabilities being measured, if an entity holds a large volume of similar (but not identical) instruments. As a result, the entity may measure fair value using alternative pricing (e.g. matrix pricing) as a practical expedient, which would result in a lower level measurement in the fair value hierarchy.

Example 10.2.1A

Application of Level 1 classification criteria — debt security

Entity P holds a debt security that is traded in a dealer market in which bid and ask prices are available. The market is an active market and it is the principal market for the security. The market is accessible by Entity P. No adjustments have been made to the quoted price.

If the quoted price used to measure the fair value of the debt security is for a debt security identical to that held by Entity P, the measurement of the debt security should be classified within Level 1 of the fair value hierarchy. The fact that a price is derived from a dealer market (rather than an 'exchange' market) does not in itself preclude classification as a Level 1 measurement because such dealer markets may be active and accessible to the entity (see also **10.1.1** above).

Example 10.2.1B

Application of Level 1 classification criteria — issued debt security with identical instrument traded as an asset

Entity Q has issued an exchange-traded debt security. Entity Q has elected to account for this instrument using the fair value option under IFRS 9 *Financial Instruments* (or, prior to adoption of IFRS 9, IAS 39 *Financial Instruments: Recognition and Measurement*). A quoted price for the transfer of an identical or similar liability is not available; however, an identical instrument is currently trading as an asset in an active market. Entity Q uses the quoted price for the asset as its initial input for the fair value measurement of the issued debt security. Entity Q also evaluates whether the quoted price for the asset requires adjustment for factors, such as third-party credit enhancements, that would not be applicable to the issued debt security. Entity Q determines that no adjustments are required to the quoted price of the asset.

Because the quoted price used to measure the fair value of the issued debt security is for an identical debt security (e.g. the identical ISIN*) traded as an asset, and no adjustments to the quoted price of the instrument are required, the resulting measurement of the issued debt security should be classified as a Level 1 measurement in the fair value hierarchy.

*   ISIN refers to the International Securities Identification Number, a 12-character alpha-numerical code that does not contain information

---

characterising financial instruments but serves for uniform identification of a security at trading and settlement.

Example 10.2.1C

Application of Level 1 classification criteria — 'look-alike' forward contract

Entity R holds an over-the-counter (OTC) 'look-alike' forward contract (i.e. it mirrors another contract). The counterparty to this contract is contractually obligated to settle it on the basis of the quoted price for a similar futures contract traded on an active futures exchange. The forward contract meets the definition of a derivative and is therefore measured at fair value.

While the look-alike forward contract mirrors the exchange-traded futures contract, and the value of the look-alike forward contract is intended to approximate the quoted price for the exchange-traded futures contract, the forward and futures contracts are not identical. Even if the parties to the forward contract both have the highest credit quality (resulting in the same level of credit risk as the exchange-traded futures contract), the forward contract is not considered identical because (1) the counterparties are different, and (2) Entity R cannot sell the forward contract on the futures exchange (i.e. the forward contract has different levels of counterparty and liquidity risk when compared to the futures contract). While the quoted price for the futures contract may be a Level 1 input (when the market for it is active), the fair value measurement of the look-alike forward contract can only be classified as Level 2 or 3.

Example 10.2.1D

Application of Level 1 classification criteria — interest rate swap

Entity S is a party to an interest rate swap that is transacted on an over-the-counter (OTC) market. The OTC market does not quote prices for interest rate swaps. Entity S would determine the fair value of the swap by using either (1) a discounted cash flow approach based on market-based yield curves, or (2) the price at which a similar swap was exchanged on the OTC market. While similar swaps may have been exchanged on the OTC market, the similar swaps would have different counterparties and would, therefore, not be identical to the swap held by Entity S.

The price at which Entity S would be able to sell the swap would result from a negotiated transaction contemplating the credit standings of the two parties to the swap as well as the terms of the specific swap. Because the swap held by Entity S is not identical to any similar swap for which there may be transactions on the OTC market, the measurement of the swap by Entity S would be classified as a Level 2 or 3 measurement, depending on the inputs that are significant to the measurement.

10.2.2   Determining the level within the fair value hierarchy when several inputs are used

When several inputs are used to measure the fair value of an asset or a liability, those inputs may be categorised within different levels of the fair value hierarchy (e.g. the valuation may be based on some Level 2 and some Level 3 inputs). In such circumstances, the categorisation of the fair value measurement in its entirety is based on the lowest level input that is significant to the entire measurement. [IFRS 13:73] See **10.2.2.1** below for a discussion of the meaning of the term 'significant'.

Example 10.2.2

Classification of fair value measurements within the fair value hierarchy

Entity I holds an investment in equity instruments that are not traded in an active market (e.g. equity instruments issued by a private entity). In accordance with IFRS 9 (or, prior to the adoption of IFRS 9, IAS 39), the investment is measured at fair value subsequent to initial recognition.

How should Entity I classify the fair value measurement of its investment within the fair value hierarchy (i.e. as Level 1, Level 2 or Level 3)?

The examples below illustrate the application of the guidance in IFRS 13 on the classification of measurements within the fair value hierarchy.

Note that, because the equity instruments are not traded in an active market, Level 1 inputs are not available.

Scenario 1 — Fair value is estimated based on recent transactions

If Entity I estimates the fair value of its investment based on recent transactions between independent third parties (e.g. quoted prices in an inactive market, privately negotiated acquisitions or disposals of the equity instruments etc.), these transaction prices would be considered Level 2 inputs if they meet the definition of fair value. This would be the case if the price represents an exit price for the equity instruments at the date of the transaction, the transaction is executed at terms that are consistent with how other market participants would transact, and the transaction is not executed under duress.

Similarly, prices based on recent transactions between Entity I and third parties may be considered Level 2 inputs if they meet the criteria above. For example, Entity I owns a 5 per cent equity investment in Entity X and measures that investment at fair value. Entity I acquires an additional 10 per cent of Entity X. If the transaction price for the additional 10 per cent meets the definition of fair value, Entity I may use that price as a basis for valuing its entire 15 per cent investment at the next reporting date.

In either case, it may be necessary to adjust the recent transaction price to measure the investment appropriately at fair value at the reporting date. For

---

example, the recent transaction price should be adjusted for events or changes in the entity's financial position that have occurred since the date of the transaction that would affect the value of the equity investment in the entity. Unobservable adjustments to a Level 2 input that are significant to the entire measurement would change the categorisation to Level 3.

Scenario 2 — Fair value is determined based on a discounted cash flow technique

IFRS 13:B36 (see **10.1.3** above) cites as an example of a Level 3 input "a financial forecast (eg of cash flows or earnings) developed using the entity's own data if there is no reasonably available information that indicates that market participants would use different assumptions". While certain information used in the model may be observable (e.g. interest rate curves), the entity's projected cash flows (which are not observable) would probably be significant to the entire fair value measurement. Therefore, the measurement of the investment would probably be classified as Level 3.

Scenario 3 — Fair value is determined based on a market-based multiple applied to a financial measure

IFRS 13:B35 (see **10.1.2** above) cites as an example of a Level 2 input "a valuation multiple (eg a multiple of earnings or revenue or a similar performance measure) derived from observable market data, eg multiples derived from prices in observed transactions involving comparable (that is, similar) businesses, taking into account operational, market, financial, and non-financial factors". The market-derived multiple may thus be considered a Level 2 input. However, the historical financial measure (i.e. earnings or EBITDA) and any adjustments needed to reflect differences between the entity and comparable entities would probably be Level 3 inputs because they are entity-specific and are not considered market-observable data. Therefore, the measurement of the investment would probably be classified within Level 3 of the fair value hierarchy.

For measurements such as 'fair value less costs to sell' that are based on fair value, the adjustments to fair value (e.g. for costs to sell) to arrive at the required measurement are not taken into account when determining the level of the fair value hierarchy within which the measurement is categorised. [IFRS 13:73]

Therefore, for example, if an asset is required to be measured at fair value less costs to sell, and the fair value of the asset can be measured by reference solely to Level 1 inputs, the valuation at fair value less costs to sell is categorised within Level 1, notwithstanding that the adjustment for costs to sell may be based on unobservable inputs.

The availability of relevant inputs and their relative subjectivity might affect the selection of appropriate valuation techniques. However, the fair value hierarchy prioritises the inputs to valuation techniques, not the valuation techniques used to measure fair value. For example, a fair value measurement developed using a present value technique might be categorised within Level 2 or Level 3, depending on the inputs that are significant to the entire measurement and the level of the fair value hierarchy within which those inputs are categorised. [IFRS 13:74]

> In other words, the categorisation of the fair value measurement in the fair value hierarchy is based on inputs, not on the valuation technique in which they are used.

If an observable input requires an adjustment using an unobservable input and that adjustment results in a significantly higher or lower fair value measurement, the resulting measurement is a Level 3 measurement. For example, if a market participant would take into account the effect of a restriction on the sale of an asset when estimating the price for the asset, an entity would adjust the quoted price to reflect the effect of that restriction. If that quoted price is a Level 2 input and the adjustment is an unobservable input that is significant to the entire measurement, the measurement would be categorised within Level 3 of the fair value hierarchy. [IFRS 13:75]

10.2.2.1   Determining the 'significance' of an input or an adjustment

The Standard does not expand on what is meant by 'significant' in the context of IFRS 13:73, other than to state that the assessment of the significance of a particular input to the entire measurement requires judgement, taking into account factors specific to the asset or liability. [IFRS 13:73]

> To determine the level in which the fair value measurement should be categorised, an entity should aggregate the inputs to the measurement by level and determine the lowest level of inputs that are significant to the fair value measurement in its entirety. For example, a measurement that includes inputs with significant effect from Levels 2 and 3 would be classified in its entirety in Level 3, because Level 3 is the lowest level input with a significant effect.

Entities should establish a methodology for determining whether an input or aggregated inputs are significant to the measurement in its entirety. The methodology should be applied consistently.

In some cases, a qualitative assessment of the inputs used may be sufficient. For example, changes in discount rates generally have a significant effect on fair value measurements determined using a discounted cash flow model.

In other cases, a quantitative analysis of the inputs may be required. One quantitative approach might involve the following steps.

- **Step 1** Select a threshold or percentage of the overall fair value measurement as a benchmark for significance.

- **Step 2** Perform a sensitivity analysis, calculating the percentage change in the fair value measurement arising from reasonably possible changes to each input.

- **Step 3** Compare the percentage change in the fair value measurement for each input calculated under Step 2 to the benchmark selected under Step 1. If the percentage change in the fair value measurement for a particular input exceeds the selected benchmark, that input would be considered significant. If none of the individual Level 3 inputs are considered significant, the combined effect of all the Level 3 inputs should be considered to determine whether they have a significant effect in aggregate on the fair value measurement.

When this approach is used, the benchmark should represent a percentage of the overall measurement and not a percentage of a particular component of the fair value measurement. In addition, the threshold should not represent a percentage of total assets, total liabilities, gains or losses, or other line items in the statement of financial position or the statement of comprehensive income because this would not be specific to the fair value measurement.

Example 10.2.2.1 illustrates this approach.

Example 10.2.2.1

Determining the significance of an input

Entity A holds a hybrid instrument which includes an embedded option. Entity A is measuring the instrument at fair value in its entirety. One of the inputs to its valuation model is the volatility of the embedded option for which market data are not available (i.e. it is unobservable and, consequently, a Level 3 input).

Entity A is evaluating whether the unobservable volatility input is significant to the overall fair value measurement for the hybrid instrument. In making its assessment, Entity A considers the significance of the volatility in relation to the hybrid instrument in its entirety and not solely in relation to the embedded option.

Entity A uses a quantitative methodology and selects a threshold or percentage of the overall fair value measurement of the hybrid instrument as a benchmark for significance. Entity A then performs a sensitivity analysis to determine how the volatility input affects the overall fair value of the hybrid instrument within a reasonably possible range of values for the volatility input.

If reasonable changes in the volatility input cause the percentage change in the fair value measurement of the hybrid instrument to exceed the selected threshold, Entity A would conclude that the unobservable volatility input is significant to the measurement in its entirety. In that case, the fair value measurement of the hybrid instrument would represent a Level 3 measurement within the fair value hierarchy.

10.2.3   Observable transactions in inactive markets

The level of market activity does not affect the IFRS 13 measurement objective, i.e. fair value is the price in an orderly transaction between market participants at the measurement date under current market conditions.

Observable transactions are relevant inputs to a fair value measurement when they reflect market participants' assumptions in orderly transactions and, thus, are representative of fair value. Relevant observable inputs should be given priority when measuring fair value in accordance with IFRS 13. IFRS 13:67 (see **section 9**) states that "[v]aluation techniques used to measure fair value shall maximise the use of relevant observable inputs and minimise the use of unobservable inputs". Further, IFRS 13:87 (see **10.1.3**) states, in part, that "[u]nobservable inputs [Level 3] shall be used to measure fair value to the extent that relevant observable inputs [Level 1 and 2] are not available . . .".

However, when the volume and level of activity in a market have significantly decreased and the market is not active, observable transactions may not be representative of fair value because of increased instances of transactions that are not orderly (e.g. forced liquidations or distress sales). Consequently, an entity should perform further analysis of the transactions or quoted prices available to determine whether they represent fair value. In some circumstances, a change in valuation technique or the use of multiple valuation techniques may be appropriate, as discussed below.

Transaction is not orderly

If the observable transactions are not orderly, IFRS 13:B44(a) states that "the entity shall place little, if any, weight (compared with other indications of fair value) on that transaction price" (see **9.5**). If an entity previously used quoted prices to measure fair value, and quoted prices from orderly transactions are no longer available, the entity may need to change its valuation technique or use multiple valuation techniques. If the entity measures fair value by using the price from a transaction that is not orderly, the price should be adjusted to reflect the assumptions that market participants would use in pricing the asset or liability in an orderly transaction. The resulting measurement would generally be classified as a Level 3 measurement.

Transactions are orderly

If the observable transactions are orderly, the entity should consider the transaction price when estimating fair value. However, the entity may also need to adjust the transaction price when measuring fair value to meet the measurement objective. IFRS 13:B44(b) states that the "amount of weight placed on that [orderly] transaction price when compared with other indications of fair value will depend on the facts and circumstances" (see **9.5**).

If an entity determines that it does not need to make any significant adjustment to the transaction price using unobservable inputs to arrive at the fair value of the asset or liability, the transaction price represents a relevant observable input and the measurement would be classified as a Level 2 measurement. However, if the entity determines that it needs to make a significant adjustment to the transaction price using unobservable inputs, the measurement would be classified as a Level 3 measurement.

Insufficient information to determine whether transactions are orderly

If an entity is unable to obtain, without undue cost and effort, sufficient information to determine whether the transaction is orderly, the entity must consider the transaction price in determining fair value; however, the transaction price may not be the 'sole or primary' basis for estimating fair value. In such circumstances, because the transaction price may not reflect the assumptions that market participants would use, a fair value measurement that has this price as its principal input would most likely represent a Level 3 measurement. As above, the use of multiple valuation techniques may be appropriate in this case.

11   Disclosure

IFRS 13's disclosure requirements replace many of the fair value measurement disclosures previously required by other IFRSs.

The disclosures required in respect of a fair value measurement vary depending on whether the fair value measurement is recognised in the statement of financial position on a recurring or a non-recurring basis or is only disclosed in the notes to the financial statements. See **11.6** below for a table summarising the application of IFRS 13's disclosure requirements.

11.1   General

IFRS 13 requires that the entity should disclose information that helps users of its financial statements to assess both of the following: [IFRS 13:91]

- for assets and liabilities that are measured at fair value on a recurring or non-recurring basis in the statement of financial position after initial recognition, the valuation techniques and inputs used to develop those measurements; and

- for recurring fair value measurements using significant unobservable inputs (Level 3) (see **10.1.3** above), the effect of the measurements on profit or loss or other comprehensive income for the period.

See **11.2** for an explanation of what is meant by measurement of fair value on a 'recurring' and a 'non-recurring' basis.

To meet the objectives of IFRS 13:91, the entity is required to consider all the following:
[IFRS 13:92]

- the level of detail necessary to satisfy the disclosure requirements;

- how much emphasis to place on each of the various requirements;

- how much aggregation or disaggregation to undertake; and

- whether users of financial statements need additional information to evaluate the quantitative information disclosed.

To meet the objectives of IFRS 13:91, the Standard sets out minimum disclosure requirements that are aggregated by class of assets and liabilities. If the specific disclosures provided in accordance with IFRS 13 and other IFRSs are insufficient to meet the objectives described in IFRS 13:91, the entity should disclose whatever additional information is necessary to meet those objectives. [IFRS 13:92]

The quantitative disclosures required under IFRS 13 should be presented in a tabular format unless another format is more appropriate. [IFRS 13:99]

11.2   Scope of disclosure requirements

In line with the general scope of IFRS 13 (see **section 2**), the disclosure requirements of IFRS 13 generally apply whenever assets or liabilities are measured at fair value (or using a measurement based on fair value). The general disclosure requirements of IFRS 13 do not apply to the following:
[IFRS 13:7]

- plan assets measured at fair value in accordance with IAS 19 *Employee Benefits*;

- retirement benefit plan investments measured at fair value in accordance with IAS 26 *Accounting and Reporting by Retirement Benefit Plans*; and

- assets for which recoverable amount is fair value less costs of disposal in accordance with IAS 36 *Impairment of Assets*.

The majority of IFRS 13's disclosure requirements apply only to assets and liabilities measured in the statement of financial position at fair value. Certain of these requirements are specified for assets and liabilities not measured at fair value in the statement of financial position but for which the fair value is disclosed (see **11.5**).

IFRS 13's disclosure requirements do not apply to fair value measurements at initial recognition; the disclosures required when a fair value measurement is used at initial recognition are dealt with in other IFRSs (e.g. IFRS 3 *Business Combinations* regarding the measurement of assets acquired and liabilities assumed in a business combination). [IFRS 13:BC184]

For each disclosure requirement, the Standard is explicit as to whether it applies in respect of 'recurring' fair value measurements, 'non-recurring' fair value measurements, or both.

Recurring fair value measurements are those that other IFRSs require or permit in the statement of financial position at the end of each reporting period (e.g. investment property measured at fair value at the end of each reporting period under IAS 40 *Investment Property*). Non-recurring fair value measurements are those that other IFRSs require or permit in the statement of financial position in particular circumstances (e.g. an asset held for sale measured at fair value less costs to sell under IFRS 5 *Non-current Assets Held for Sale and Discontinued Operations* because it meets the criteria for classification as held for sale and fair value less costs to sell is lower than its carrying amount). [IFRS 13:93(a)]

11.3   Classes of assets and liabilities

For the purposes of IFRS 13's disclosure requirements, assets and liabilities are segregated into 'classes'. Entities are required to determine appropriate classes of assets and liabilities on the basis of:
[IFRS 13:94]

- the nature, characteristics and risks of the asset or liability; and

- the level of the fair value hierarchy within which the fair value measurement is categorised.

The following additional guidance is provided:
[IFRS 13:94]

- a class of assets and liabilities will often require greater disaggregation than the line items presented in the statement of financial position. However, the entity is required to provide information sufficient to permit reconciliation to the line items presented in the statement of financial position;

- if another IFRS specifies the class for an asset or a liability, the entity may use that class for the purpose of providing the disclosures under IFRS 13 if that class meets the requirements set out in IFRS 13:94; and

- the number of classes may need to be greater for fair value measurements classified within Level 3 of the fair value hierarchy because those measurements have a greater degree of uncertainty and subjectivity.

The identification of appropriate classes of assets and liabilities for which disclosures about fair value measurements should be provided requires the exercise of judgement. [IFRS 13:94]

11.4   Financial and non-financial items measured at fair value

At a minimum, the information set out in sections **11.4.1** to **11.4.11** is required to be disclosed for each class of assets and liabilities measured at fair value in the statement of financial position after initial recognition (including measurements based on fair value within the scope of IFRS 13, e.g. fair value less costs to sell). [IFRS 13:93]

11.4.1   Fair value measurements by class of assets or liabilities

For recurring and non-recurring fair value measurements, an entity is required to disclose the fair value measurement at the end of the reporting period. [IFRS 13:93(a)]

11.4.2   Reasons underlying non-recurring measurements

For non-recurring fair value measurements (see **11.2** above), an entity is required to disclose the reasons for the measurement. [IFRS 13:93(a)]

11.4.3   Level within the fair value hierarchy

For recurring and non-recurring fair value measurements, an entity is required to disclose the level within the fair value hierarchy within which the fair value measurements are categorised in their entirety (i.e. Level 1, 2 or 3). [IFRS 13:93(b)]

> IFRS 13:IE60 provides an illustrative example of the disclosures required by IFRS 13:93(a) and (b) in the case of assets measured at fair value (see **example 4.3.3.3A** in **chapter B12** or **example 4.3.3.3A** in **chapter C12**).

11.4.4   *Transfers within the fair value hierarchy*

For assets and liabilities held at the end of the reporting period that are measured at fair value on a recurring basis, an entity is required to disclose:
[IFRS 13:93(c)]

- the amounts of any transfers between Level 1 and Level 2 of the fair value hierarchy;

- the reasons for those transfers; and

- the entity's policy for determining when transfers between levels are deemed to have occurred (see below).

Transfers into each level are required to be disclosed and discussed separately from transfers out of each level. [IFRS 13:93(c)]

An entity is required to disclose and consistently follow its policy for determining when transfers between levels of the fair value hierarchy are deemed to have occurred. The policy must be the same for transfers in and transfers out of the levels. Examples of policies for determining the timing of transfers include the following:
[IFRS 13:95]

- the date of the event or change in circumstances that caused the transfer;

- the beginning of the reporting period; and

- the end of the reporting period.

See **11.4.7** below for a discussion as to how an entity should determine the amounts to be reported for transfers between levels of the fair value hierarchy.

11.4.5   *Valuation techniques and inputs (Levels 2 and 3)*

For recurring and non-recurring fair value measurements categorised within Level 2 and Level 3 of the fair value hierarchy, an entity is required to disclose:
[IFRS 13:93(d)]

- a description of the valuation technique(s) and the inputs used in the fair value measurement; and

- if there has been a change in valuation technique (e.g. changing from a market approach to an income approach or the use of an additional valuation technique), details of the change and the reason(s) for making the change.

The objective of these disclosures is to help users of the financial statements understand not only the valuation techniques and inputs used, but also the judgements made by the entity when measuring fair value.

When developing the disclosures required under IFRS 13 about valuation techniques and the overall valuation process, entities may wish to consider the description of valuation techniques and processes in the IASB Expert Advisory Panel's October 2008 report *Measuring and disclosing the fair value of financial instruments in markets that are no longer active*. This report notes that a description of valuation techniques is important to enable users to understand the subjectivity and the judgements that are a part of measuring fair values. Specifically, for fair value measurements in Level 2 or Level 3 of the fair value hierarchy, the report indicates that information that an entity might consider disclosing about the valuation techniques and inputs used includes:

- whether the entity can choose between various valuation techniques and how it makes that choice;

- a description of the valuation techniques selected and the risks or shortcomings (if any) of those techniques. When a model is used, a description of the model and related inputs, and how the inputs are sourced by the entity;

- if the valuation technique has changed since previous reporting periods, the reason why the entity made the change and a quantification of the change's impact on the financial statements;

- the methods the entity uses to calibrate models to market prices, and the frequency of calibration;

- a description of the use of broker quotes or pricing services, which may include how many quotes were obtained, how these quotes were verified, what brokers or pricing services the entity used and why, whether quotes are adjusted, whether a quote is binding or non-binding and how the ultimate fair value used was determined;

• when an entity measures fair value by using prices for similar instruments, how the entity adjusts these prices to reflect the characteristics of the instruments subject to the measurement;

• the key drivers of value for each significant Level 2 and Level 3 asset/liability class and the extent to which the inputs used are observable or unobservable;

• an entity's consideration of illiquidity when performing the valuation; and

• a description of how the entity's and counterparty's non-performance risk was taken into consideration in the valuation (e.g. for derivatives or debt instruments).

11.4.6   *Quantitative information about significant unobservable inputs (Level 3)*

For recurring and non-recurring fair value measurements categorised within Level 3 of the fair value hierarchy, an entity is required to provide quantitative information about the significant unobservable inputs used in the fair value measurement. [IFRS 13:93(d)]

An entity is not required to create quantitative information to comply with this disclosure requirement if quantitative unobservable inputs are not developed by the entity when measuring fair value (e.g. when an entity uses prices from prior transactions or third-party pricing information without adjustment). However, when providing this disclosure, an entity cannot ignore quantitative unobservable inputs that are significant to the fair value measurement and are reasonably available to the entity. [IFRS 13:93(d)]

IFRS 13:IE63 provides an illustrative example of the disclosures required by IFRS 13:93(d) in respect of unobservable inputs for Level 3 valuations.

Having regard to the general requirements of IFRS 13:92 (see **11.1** above), an entity might disclose some or all of the following information in order

to help users of its financial statements to evaluate the quantitative information disclosed under IFRS 13:93(d):
[IFRS 13:IE64]

- the nature of the item being measured at fair value, including the characteristics of the item being measured that are taken into account in the determination of relevant inputs. For example, for residential mortgage-backed securities, an entity might disclose the following:

  - the types of underlying loans (e.g. prime loans or sub-prime loans);

  - collateral;

  - guarantees or other credit enhancements;

  - seniority level of the tranches of securities;

  - the year of issue;

  - the weighted-average coupon rate of the underlying loans and the securities;

  - the weighted-average maturity of the underlying loans and the securities;

  - the geographical concentration of the underlying loans; and

  - information about the credit ratings of the securities; and

- how third-party information such as broker quotes, pricing services, net asset values and relevant market data was taken into account when measuring fair value.

11.4.7   Reconciliation of fair value measurements (Level 3 recurring)

For recurring fair value measurements categorised within Level 3 of the fair value hierarchy, IFRS 13 requires a reconciliation from the opening to the closing balances. [IFRS 13:93(e)]

The reconciliation should include separate disclosure of changes during the period attributable to the following:
[IFRS 13:93(e)]

- total gains or losses for the period recognised in profit or loss, and the line item(s) in profit or loss in which those gains or losses are recognised;

- total gains or losses for the period recognised in other comprehensive income, and the line item(s) in other comprehensive income in which those gains or losses are recognised;

- purchases, sales, issues and settlements (each of those types of changes disclosed separately); and

- the amounts of any transfers into or out of Level 3 of the fair value hierarchy, the reasons for those transfers and the entity's policy for determining when transfers between levels are deemed to have occurred (see **11.4.4** above).

Transfers into Level 3 are required to be disclosed and discussed separately from transfers out of Level 3. [IFRS 13:93(e)]

The Standard cites the following examples of policies for determining the timing of transfers:
[IFRS 13:95]

- the actual date of the event or change in circumstances that caused the transfer;

- the beginning of the reporting period; and

- the end of the reporting period.

> The 'amounts' to be disclosed for transfers between the levels of the fair value hierarchy should be the fair values of the items transferred. However, IFRS 13 is not prescriptive as to the timing of the recognition of the transfers (i.e. the date at which the fair values of the transferred items should be measured).

In addition, IFRS 13:95 requires that:

- an entity should disclose and consistently follow its policy for determining when transfers between levels of the fair value hierarchy are deemed to have occurred; and

- the entity's policy regarding the timing of recognising transfers should be the same for transfers into the levels as that for transfers out of the levels.

> Accordingly, it would not be appropriate for an entity to determine the amount of 'transfers in' by using the beginning-of-period fair

value and the amount of 'transfers out' by using the end-of-period fair value.

Example 11.4.7

Disclosure of transfers into and out of Level 3

Entity R holds two securities and is preparing its quarterly financial statements for the period ended 30 September.

- Security A was a Level 2 measurement at the beginning of the period (1 July) and transferred into Level 3 on 15 July.

- Security B was a Level 3 measurement at the beginning of the period (1 July) and transferred out of Level 3 into Level 2 on 15 August.

The fair values of Securities A and B at the beginning and end of the period, and at the actual dates of transfer, are set out below.

	Fair value		
	At date of transfer	**At 1 July**	**At 30 September**
	CU	**CU**	**CU**
Security A	125 (15 July)	150	50
Security B	250 (15 August)	150	300

The following table sets out the amounts that would be disclosed by Entity R for transfers into and out of the Level 3 hierarchy using each of the example methods identified in IFRS 13:95. The table also sets out the amount of gain/(loss) included in profit or loss that would be reflected in the reconciliation of fair value changes in Level 3 as required by IFRS 13:93(e).

	Method 1 Fair value at actual date of transfer	**Method 2** Fair value at beginning of reporting period	**Method 3** Fair value at end of reporting period
Impact on levels	**CU**	**CU**	**CU**
Security A			
Level 2			
transfer-out			
value	(125)	(150)	(50)
Level 3			
transfer-in value	125	150	50
Loss reflected in			
Level 3			
reconciliation	(75)	(100)	–

Impact on levels	Method 1 Fair value at actual date of transfer CU	Method 2 Fair value at beginning of reporting period CU	Method 3 Fair value at end of reporting period CU
Security B			
Level 2			
transfer-in value	250	150	300
Level 3			
transfer-out			
value	(250)	(150)	(300)
Gain reflected in			
Level 3			
reconciliation	100	–	150

> IFRS 13:IE61 provides an illustrative example of the reconciliation required to be presented under IFRS 13:93(e) for Level 3 measurements.

In addition, an entity is required to disclose the amount of the total gains or losses recognised in profit or loss in the period (and included in the Level 3 reconciliation) that is attributable to the change in unrealised gains or losses relating to those assets and liabilities held at the end of the reporting period, and the line item(s) in profit or loss in which those unrealised gains or losses are recognised. [IFRS 13:93(f)]

> IFRS 13:IE62 provides an illustrative example of information required to be disclosed under IFRS 13:93(f).

11.4.8   Valuation processes (Level 3)

For recurring and non-recurring fair value measurements categorised within Level 3 of the fair value hierarchy, an entity is required to disclose a description of the valuation processes used (including, for example, how an entity decides its valuation policies and procedures and analyses changes in fair value measurements from period to period). [IFRS 13:93(g)]

An entity might disclose the following information in order to comply with IFRS 13:93(g):
[IFRS 13:IE65]

- for the group within the entity that decides the entity's valuation policies and procedures:

- its description;

- to whom that group reports; and

- the internal reporting procedures in place (e.g. whether and, if so, how pricing, risk management or audit committees discuss and assess the fair value measurements);

- the frequency and methods for calibration, back testing and other testing procedures of pricing models;

- the process for analysing changes in fair value measurements from period to period;

- how the entity determined that third-party information, such as broker quotes or pricing services, used in the fair value measurement was developed in accordance with IFRS 13; and

- the methods used to develop and substantiate the unobservable inputs used in a fair value measurement.

For further guidance based on the IASB Expert Advisory Panel's October 2008 report *Measuring and disclosing the fair value of financial instruments in markets that are no longer active*, see **11.4.5** above.

11.4.9   Sensitivity to changes in significant unobservable inputs (*Level 3 recurring*)

For recurring fair value measurements categorised within Level 3 of the fair value hierarchy, an entity is required to provide a narrative description of the sensitivity of the fair value measurement to changes in unobservable inputs if a change in those inputs to a different amount might result in a significantly higher or lower fair value measurement. If there are interrelationships between those inputs and other unobservable inputs used in the fair value measurement, the entity is also required to provide a description of those interrelationships and of how they might magnify or mitigate the effect of changes in the unobservable inputs on the fair value measurement. To comply with that disclosure requirement, the narrative description of the sensitivity to changes in unobservable inputs should include, at a minimum, the unobservable inputs disclosed when complying with IFRS 13:93(d) (see **11.4.6** above). [IFRS 13:93(h)(i)]

IFRS 13:IE66 provides an illustrative example of the information required to be disclosed about sensitivity to changes in significant unobservable inputs under IFRS 13:93(h)(i).

11.4.10   *Sensitivity to changes in significant unobservable inputs* (*Level 3 recurring – financial assets and financial liabilities*)

For recurring fair value measurements of financial assets and financial liabilities categorised within Level 3 of the fair value hierarchy, if changing one or more of the unobservable inputs to reflect reasonably possible alternative assumptions would change fair value significantly, an entity is required to state that fact and disclose the effect of those changes. [IFRS 13:93(h)(ii)]

The entity is required to disclose how the effect of a change to reflect a reasonably possible alternative assumption was calculated. For that purpose, significance is required to be judged with respect to profit or loss, and total assets or total liabilities, or, when changes in fair value are recognised in other comprehensive income, total equity. [IFRS 13:93(h)(ii)]

11.4.11   *Highest and best use of non-financial asset differs from its current use*

For recurring and non-recurring fair value measurements, if the highest and best use of a non-financial asset differs from its current use, an entity should disclose that fact and why the non-financial asset is being used in a manner that differs from its highest and best use. [IFRS 13:93(i)]

11.4.12   *Liability measured at fair value and issued with an inseparable third-party credit enhancement*

For a liability measured at fair value and issued with an inseparable third-party credit enhancement, an issuer is required to disclose the existence of that credit enhancement and whether it is reflected in the fair value measurement of the liability. [IFRS 13:98]

11.5   Financial and non-financial items for which fair value is disclosed

For each class of assets and liabilities not measured at fair value in the statement of financial position but for which the fair value is disclosed, an entity is required to disclose the information required by IFRS 13:93(b), (d) and (i) (see **11.4.3**, **11.4.5** and **11.4.11** above). [IFRS 13:97]

However, an entity is not required to provide the quantitative disclosures about significant unobservable inputs used in fair value measurements categorised within Level 3 of the fair value hierarchy required by IFRS 13:93(d). [IFRS 13:97]

For such assets and liabilities, an entity does not need to provide the other disclosures required by IFRS 13. [IFRS 13:97]

11.6   Summary of the application of IFRS 13's disclosure requirements

The disclosures required in respect of a fair value measurement vary depending on whether the fair value measurement is recognised in the statement of financial position on a recurring or a non-recurring basis or is only disclosed in the notes to the financial statements.

The following table summarises the application of the disclosure requirements in IFRS 13. The quantitative disclosures should be presented in a tabular format unless another format is more appropriate.

Required disclosure	Assets and liabilities measured at fair value (FV) in the statement of financial position after the date of initial recognition		FV disclosed in notes only
	Recurring	Non-recurring	
Fair value at the reporting date [IFRS 13:93(a)]	X	X	X
Reason for the fair value measurement [IFRS 13:93(a)]		X	
The level of the fair value measurement in the fair value hierarchy [IFRS 13:93(b)]	X	X	X
For assets and liabilities held at the reporting date, amounts of transfers between Levels 1 and 2 (separately for transfers into and out of each level), the reasons for those transfers, and the entity's policy for determining that a transfer has occurred [IFRS 13:93(c)]	X		

| Required disclosure | Assets and liabilities measured at fair value (FV) in the statement of financial position after the date of initial recognition | | FV disclosed in notes only |
	Recurring	Non-recurring	
For Level 2 and 3 measurements, a description of the valuation techniques and inputs used [IFRS 13:93(d)]	X	X	X
For Level 2 and 3 measurements for which there has been a change in valuation technique, the nature of that change and reason for it [IFRS 13:93(d)]	X	X	X
For non-financial assets with a highest and best use that differs from its current use, that fact and why the asset is being used in a manner different from its highest and best use [IFRS 13:93(i)]	X	X	X
Information sufficient to permit a reconciliation between the amounts disclosed for classes of assets and liabilities by level of the fair value hierarchy and the line items presented in the statement of financial position [IFRS 13:94]	X	X	Not required by IFRS 13 but may be required by other IFRSs
If an entity chooses as its accounting policy to use the portfolio valuation exception permitted by IFRS 13:48, that fact [IFRS 13:96]	X		
For liabilities measured at fair value, the existence of inseparable third-party credit enhancements and whether they are reflected in the fair value measurement of the liabilities [IFRS 13:98]	X	X	
The disclosures below only apply to Level 3 fair value measurements			
Quantitative information about the significant unobservable inputs used in the fair value measurement [IFRS 13:93(d)]	X	X	

Required disclosure	Assets and liabilities measured at fair value (FV) in the statement of financial position after the date of initial recognition		FV disclosed in notes only
	Recurring	Non-recurring	
Reconciliation of movements in fair value from opening to closing balances, showing separately: [IFRS 13:93(e)] • total gains and losses recognised in profit or loss (including the line items in profit or loss); • total gains and losses recognised in other comprehensive income (including the line items in other comprehensive income); • purchases, sales, issues, settlements (each disclosed separately); and • the amounts of transfers into and out of Level 3 separately (including the reasons for those transfers and the entity's policy for determining that a transfer has occurred)	X		
Amount of total gains and losses for the period recognised in profit or loss that is attributable to the change in unrealised gains or losses for those assets or liabilities held at the reporting date, and the line items in profit or loss in which those unrealised gains or losses are recognised [IFRS 13:93(f)]	X		
Description of the valuation processes used, including a discussion of how the entity decides on valuation policies and procedures and how it analyses changes in fair value from period to period [IFRS 13:93(g)]	X	X	

| Required disclosure | Assets and liabilities measured at fair value (FV) in the statement of financial position after the date of initial recognition | | FV disclosed in notes only |
	Recurring	Non-recurring	
Narrative description of the sensitivity of the fair value measurement to changes in unobservable inputs if a change in those inputs might result in a significantly different fair value measurement and a description of the interrelationships between those inputs and other unobservable inputs, if any, including how those interrelationships might magnify or mitigate the impact on fair value arising from changes in such inputs. The narrative description of the sensitivity should include, as a minimum, all significant unobservable inputs used in the fair value measurement [IFRS 13:93(h)(i)]	X		
For financial assets and liabilities, when a change in one or more of the unobservable inputs to reflect reasonably possible alternative assumptions would change fair value significantly, that fact, the effect of those changes, and how the effect of such a change is calculated [IFRS 13:93(h)(ii)]	X		

12   Effective date and transition

IFRS 13 is effective for annual periods beginning on or after 1 January 2013, with earlier application permitted. If an entity applies IFRS 13 for an earlier period, it is required to disclose that fact. [IFRS 13:C1]

The Standard should be applied prospectively as of the beginning of the annual period in which it is initially applied; however, the disclosure requirements need not be applied in comparative information provided for periods before initial application of the Standard. [IFRS 13:C2 & C3]

The IASB considered that a change in the methods used to measure fair value would be inseparable from a change in the fair value measurements (i.e. as new events occur or as new information is obtained, e.g. through better insight or improved judgement) and therefore IFRS 13 should be applied prospectively (in the same way as a change in accounting estimate). [IFRS 13:BC229] IAS 8 *Accounting Policies, Changes in Accounting Estimates and Errors* requires that the effects of a change in accounting estimate are recognised in the current period and in future periods affected by the change.

A7 Property, plant and equipment

Contents

1   Introduction

IAS 16 *Property Plant and Equipment* specifies the required accounting treatment for property, plant and equipment, and addresses issues such as the recognition of assets, the determination of their carrying amounts, and the depreciation charges and impairment losses to be recognised in relation to them.

The Standard was most recently amended in May 2012.

2   Scope

IAS 16 is applicable in accounting for property, plant and equipment, which it defines as tangible items that:
[IAS 16:6]

- are held for use in the production or supply of goods or services, for rental to others, or for administrative purposes; and

- are expected to be used during more than one period.

IAS 16 is applied except when another Standard requires or permits a different accounting treatment. [IAS 16:2] An example of another Standard requiring a different accounting treatment for property, plant and equipment is IAS 17 *Leases* which prescribes a different approach as regards recognition for assets held under leases.

The Standard excludes the following from its scope:
[IAS 16:3]

- property, plant and equipment classified as held for sale in accordance with IFRS 5 *Non-current Assets Held for Sale and Discontinued Operations* (see **chapter A20**);

- biological assets related to agricultural activity (addressed by IAS 41 *Agriculture*– see **chapter A38**); and

- mineral rights and mineral reserves such as oil, natural gas and similar non-regenerative resources.

Although biological assets and mineral rights and reserves are excluded from the scope of IAS 16, the Standard does apply to property, plant and equipment used to develop or maintain those assets. [IAS 16:3] Thus, for example, it applies to agricultural land.

The term 'mineral rights' is not defined in IFRSs. In practice, it is often used to refer to both an 'intangible' right to explore or mine and the 'tangible' underlying mineral reserve. The illustrative examples accompanying IFRS 3 *Business Combinations* list 'use rights' such as drilling rights as an example of a contract-based intangible asset that should be recognised separately from goodwill in a business combination. However, it is not always possible to distinguish the intangible right from the tangible element. In accordance with paragraph 4 of IAS 38 *Intangible Assets*, an entity should assess which element is more significant when an asset incorporates both intangible and tangible elements. For that reason, the entity should assess whether the underlying reserve or the right to mine is more significant. If the tangible resource/reserve is the more significant element, the combined mineral rights should be classified as tangible.

Factors to consider in this assessment include:

- whether the rights are granted for extraction of the mineral resource;

- whether the rights include ownership of the land on which the mineral resources are located; and

- whether the rights are granted for exploration only.

Investment property, including property being constructed or developed for future use as investment property, is within the scope of IAS 40 *Investment Property*. When an entity chooses to apply the cost model to investment properties under IAS 40, it should use the cost model as specified in IAS 16.

2.1 Classification of hotel properties

The question is often asked as to whether hotel properties should be classified as property, plant and equipment within the scope of IAS 16 or as investment properties within the scope of IAS 40. The key determinant is whether the owner acts primarily as the hotel operator or as a landlord. If the property owner's primary source of income from the property depends on day-to-day or week-by-week occupancy of hotel rooms and usage of restaurants and other facilities, and the property owner is providing services directly to hotel guests and diners, the hotel is likely to be property held by the entity for use in the production of services, in which case IAS 16 applies. On the other hand, if the owner's primary source of income from the property comes from longer-term leases (months and years rather than days or weeks), the hotel is likely to be an investment property, in which case IAS 40 applies. That is the case even if the property owner provides a relatively insignificant amount of ancillary services such as cleaning. Management should make the determination based on facts and circumstances. It is not a matter of accounting policy choice.

IAS 40 acknowledges that it may be difficult to determine when ancillary services are so significant that a property does not qualify as an investment property. For example, the owner of the hotel may transfer certain responsibilities to a third party under a management contract. The terms of such management contracts vary widely. At one end of the spectrum, the owner's position may, in substance, be that of a passive investor. At the other end of the spectrum, the owner may simply have outsourced certain day-to-day functions, while retaining significant exposure to variations in the cash flows generated by the operations of the hotel. In the latter case, classification as an investment property is not appropriate.

Classification as an investment property may also be acceptable if the direct involvement of the reporting entity in the operation of the property is short-term. For example, following the acquisition of a hotel, if the reporting entity continues to operate it while seeking a suitable third party manager, the operation of the hotel can be seen to be incidental to the underlying objective of investment return.

2.2   Base stock of assets

It is common for restaurants and similar operations to maintain a base stock inventory of items such as silverware and dishes in an unchanging amount. Additions to the stock are recognised in profit or loss. On average, the turnover of the items is likely to exceed one year. These items are tangible assets held for use in the supply of goods and services and are expected to be used for more than one period. They are therefore appropriately classified as property, plant and equipment and should not be included in current assets.

2.3 Property, plant and equipment used in research activities

Property, plant and equipment used in research activities should be accounted for in the same way as other property, plant and equipment under IAS 16. IAS 38:54, which requires all expenditure on research to be recognised as an expense when it is incurred, does not require that expenditure on property, plant and equipment used in research activities should be recognised in profit or loss when acquired. However, the depreciation of property, plant and equipment used in research activities constitutes a research expense to which IAS 38 applies.

2.4 Gold bullion held by a central bank

Central banks commonly hold significant gold reserves to support the national currency. Such reserves are not traded and the levels frequently do not change from one year to the next.

The gold bullion should be classified as property, plant and equipment, and accounted for under IAS 16, using either the cost model or the revaluation model. Gold bullion meets the definition of property, plant and equipment in that it is a tangible item, held for use in the supply of services (stabilisation of the exchange rates for the benefit of entities operating in the jurisdiction) and can be expected to be used during more than one period.

IFRS 9(2010):IG B.1 *Definition of a financial instrument: gold bullion* (which is also included in the implementation guidance accompanying IAS 39 *Financial Instruments: Recognition and Measurement*) states that gold bullion "... is a commodity. Although bullion is highly liquid, there is no contractual right to receive cash or another financial asset inherent in bullion". Accordingly, gold bullion is not a financial instrument and is outside the scope of IFRS 9 *Financial Instruments* (or, for entities that have not yet adopted IFRS 9, IAS 39).

In the circumstances described, the gold bullion is not held for sale; it is not in the process of production for sale, nor is it to be consumed in a production process or the rendering of services. Therefore, it does not meet the definition of inventories in paragraph 6 of IAS 2 *Inventories*.

3   Recognition

3.1   General recognition criteria

The recognition criteria for property, plant and equipment are derived from the general principles for asset recognition reflected in the *Conceptual Framework for Financial Reporting* (see **chapter A2**). An item of property, plant and equipment is to be recognised as an asset if, and only if: [IAS 16:7]

- it is probable that future economic benefits associated with the asset will flow to the entity; and

- the cost of the asset to the entity can be measured reliably.

3.2   Spare parts, stand-by equipment and servicing equipment

Items such as spare parts, stand-by equipment and servicing equipment should be recognised as property, plant and equipment when they meet the definition of property, plant and equipment. Otherwise, they should be classified as inventories in accordance with IAS 2 *Inventories*. [IAS 16:8]

The requirements of IAS 16:8 described above reflect amendments made by *Annual Improvements to IFRSs: 2009–2011 Cycle* (the 2009–2011 Improvements) issued in May 2012. The amendments are effective for annual periods beginning on or after 1 January 2013, with earlier application permitted. An entity should apply the amendments retrospectively as a change in accounting policy in accordance with IAS 8 *Accounting Policies, Changes in Accounting Estimates and Errors* (see **chapter A5**).

Previously, IAS 16:8 stated that spare parts would usually be carried as inventories and recognised as an expense as they are consumed. Major spare parts and stand-by equipment would qualify for recognition as property, plant and equipment when the entity expects to use them during more than one period. Similarly, if the spare parts and servicing equipment could be used only in connection with a particular item of property, plant and equipment, they would be accounted for as property, plant and equipment. The IASB was made aware of a perceived inconsistency in the classification requirements for servicing equipment which led some to classify servicing equipment used during more than one period as inventories. The IASB amended IAS 16:8 to clarify that servicing equipment should be classified as property, plant and equipment when it is used during more than one period; otherwise, it should be classified as inventories.

Example 3.2

Classification of stand-by equipment

An entity has installed two turbines. One will produce energy for the plant, and the other will be used as a back-up in case the first turbine fails, or is otherwise rendered out of service. The probability that the spare turbine will ever be used is very low. The spare turbine is necessary, however, to ensure the continuity of the production process if the first turbine fails. The useful life of the stand-by turbine will equal the life of the plant, which is the same as the useful life of the primary turbine.

IAS 16:8 states that stand-by equipment qualifies as property, plant and equipment when it meets the definition of property, plant and equipment. Although the definition in IAS 16:6 (see **section 2** above) requires that the entity should expect to use the turbine during more than one period, it does not state that such use should be regular. Therefore, the spare turbine is classified as property, plant and equipment and should be depreciated from the date it becomes available for use (i.e. when it is in the location and condition necessary for it to be capable of operating in the manner intended by management). (See also **7.5.5** for a discussion of depreciation of stand-by equipment.)

3.3 Items acquired for safety or environmental reasons

The acquisition of property, plant and equipment for safety or environmental reasons, while not directly increasing the future economic benefits of any particular existing item of property, plant and equipment, may be necessary in order for the entity to obtain the future economic benefits from its other assets. Such acquisitions qualify for recognition as assets, in that they enable future economic benefits to be derived from related assets in excess of what could otherwise have been derived. The resulting carrying amount of such an asset and the related assets is reviewed for impairment in accordance with IAS 36 *Impairment of Assets*. [IAS 16:11] The Standard cites the following example.

Example 3.3

Items acquired for safety or environmental reasons
[IAS 16:11]

A chemical manufacturer is required to install certain new chemical-handling processes in order to comply with environmental requirements in relation to the production and storage of dangerous chemicals. Related plant enhancements are recognised as an asset because, without them, the entity is unable to manufacture and sell chemicals.

3.4   Aggregation of individually insignificant items

The Standard does not prescribe what constitutes a separate item of property, plant and equipment, and allows a degree of judgement according to the entity's circumstances. It does, however, suggest that, for individually insignificant items (such as moulds, tools and dies), it may be appropriate to aggregate the items and to apply the recognition criteria to the aggregate value. [IAS 16:9]

However, IAS 16:43 requires that each part of an item of property, plant and equipment with a cost that is significant in relation to the cost of the item should be depreciated separately. Componentisation is therefore implicitly required under IAS 16:43 for all significant components of property, plant and equipment.

The determination as to whether an item is significant requires a careful assessment of the facts and circumstances. This assessment would include, at a minimum:

- comparison of the cost allocated to the item to the total cost of the aggregated property, plant and equipment; and

- consideration of the potential impact of componentisation on the depreciation expense.

3.5   Subsequent costs

IAS 16 also deals with the recognition of costs incurred subsequently to add to, replace part of, or service a previously recognised item of property, plant and equipment. The general recognition criteria set out in **3.1** above are applied to such expenditure. If the recognition criteria are met, the expenditure should be added to the carrying amount of the property, plant and equipment. If the recognition criteria are not met, the expenditure should be expensed when incurred.

3.5.1   Repairs and maintenance

The costs of the day-to-day servicing, repair or maintenance of an item of property, plant and equipment should not be recognised in the carrying amount of the item. These costs are primarily the cost of labour and other items consumed in the service/repair. They may also include the cost of small parts. [IAS 16:12]

3.5.2 Replacement parts

Costs incurred on a replacement part for property, plant and equipment are recognised in the carrying amount of the affected item of property, plant and equipment when the costs are incurred if the recognition criteria set out in **3.1** above are met. [IAS 16:13]

If the cost of the replacement part is recognised in the carrying amount of an asset, the carrying amount of what was replaced should be derecognised (regardless of whether it had been identified as a component and depreciated separately), so that the replacement and the replaced item are not both carried as assets. [IAS 16:13] When it is not practicable to determine the carrying amount of the replaced part, the cost of the replacement may be used as an indication of what the cost of the replaced part was at the time it was acquired or constructed. [IAS 16:70]

Example 3.5.2

Replacement costs

A hotel operator refurbishes its hotels every ten years, on average. The cost of refurbishment is considered a replacement of assets capitalised (i.e. the recognition criteria in IAS 16:7 are met). The replacement indicates, however, that previously recognised assets may now be required to be derecognised, typically giving rise to a loss to the extent that they have not already been depreciated.

3.5.3 Major inspections or overhauls

Major inspections or overhauls may be required at regular intervals over the useful life of an item of property, plant and equipment to allow the continued use of the asset. For example, an entity might acquire a ship that requires a major overhaul, say, once every five years. When each major inspection or overhaul is performed, its cost is recognised in the carrying amount of the item of property, plant and equipment as a replacement if the recognition criteria set out at **3.1** above are met. [IAS 16:14]

Any remaining carrying amount of the cost of the previous inspection is derecognised, regardless of whether the previous inspection was separately identified at the time that the asset was acquired or constructed. If the previous inspection was not separately identified, the estimated cost of a similar future inspection may, if necessary, be used as an indication of what the cost of the existing inspection component was when the asset was acquired or constructed. [IAS 16:14]

3.5.4   Substantial modifications

IAS 16 does not distinguish between subsequent expenditure that maintains the existing service potential of an asset ('repairs and maintenance') and subsequent expenditure that enhances that service potential ('improvements'). Instead, all major subsequent expenditure should be capitalised, provided that it is probable that future economic benefits will flow to the entity, and any part of the existing asset that has been replaced should be derecognised, irrespective of whether it has been depreciated separately. However, the costs of the day-to-day servicing of property, plant and equipment are not capitalised, even though they are arguably incurred in the pursuit of future economic benefits, because they are not sufficiently certain to be recognised in the carrying amount of an asset under the general recognition principle. [IAS 16:BC5 – BC12]

Accordingly, when an entity incurs both maintenance costs and substantial modification costs in relation to a specific item of property, plant and equipment, the expenditure should be analysed according to its nature. Any costs of day-to-day servicing should be accounted for in profit or loss, but substantial modification costs should be capitalised as part of the cost of the asset if it is probable that future economic benefits associated with the modification will flow to the entity.

Example 3.5.4

Substantial modification costs

A retail outlet needs to be redecorated each year. Because the expenditure is incurred on a regular basis and is not particularly large, the retailer treats the redecoration as part of the day-to-day servicing of the store and recognises an expense as it is incurred. In the current year, the entity has asked the supplier carrying out the redecoration work to install new partitioning, which is intended to make the outlet more profitable and result in additional future economic benefits.

The redecoration costs should be recognised in profit or loss as an expense under IAS 16:12, while the incremental partitioning costs should be capitalised if they satisfy the recognition criteria set out in IAS 16:7 (i.e. the cost incurred to install new partitioning can be measured reliably and it is probable that future economic benefits associated with the partitioning will flow to the entity). To the extent that the new partitioning replaces existing partitioning, the partitioning being replaced should be derecognised.

3.5.5   Subsequent expenditure on an impaired asset

When an entity incurs capital expenditure on an item of property, plant and equipment in respect of which an impairment loss has previously been recognised, the expenditure should be recognised in accordance with IAS 16 and included in the cost of the asset if the criteria in IAS 16:7 are met (see **3.1**).

In order for those criteria to be met, it must be probable that the future economic benefits associated with the expenditure will flow to the entity. An entity will generally only choose to incur additional expenditure on an impaired asset when it expects that expenditure to generate net future economic benefits. If this is the case, the criteria in IAS 16:7 are likely to be met.

Note that this analysis applies equally to subsequent expenditure on a completed asset and continuing expenditure on an asset in the course of construction.

4   Measurement at recognition

4.1   Measurement at cost

When an item of property, plant and equipment qualifies for recognition as an asset, it should initially be measured at its cost. [IAS 16:15]

Cost is defined as the amount of cash or cash equivalents paid or the fair value of the other consideration given to acquire an asset at the time of its acquisition or construction or, when applicable, the amount attributed to that asset when initially recognised in accordance with the specific requirements of other IFRSs (e.g. IFRS 2 *Share-based Payment*). [IAS 16:6]

4.2   Elements of cost

4.2.1   *Cost of an acquired asset*

In the case of an acquired asset, cost comprises:
[IAS 16:16]

- the purchase price, including import duties and non-refundable purchase taxes, after deducting trade discounts and rebates;

- any directly attributable costs of bringing the asset to the location and condition necessary for it to be capable of operating in the manner intended by management; and

- the initial estimate of the costs of dismantling and removing the item and restoring the site on which it is located, the obligation for which the entity incurred either when the item was acquired, or as a consequence of having used the item during a particular period for purposes other than to produce inventories during that period. (See **4.4** for guidance on how to deal with subsequent changes in the estimate of these costs and **4.2.10** for guidance regarding the cost of obligations that did not exist when the item was acquired.)

> It is perhaps worth emphasising that the final element noted above should be included only when, and to the extent that, the entity has an obligation to dismantle and remove the asset, and has therefore recognised a provision in accordance with IAS 37 *Provisions, Contingent Liabilities and Contingent Assets*. For many assets, no such obligation will exist.

Costs cited by IAS 16 as suitable for inclusion in the cost of an item of property, plant and equipment are:
[IAS 16:17]

- costs of employee benefits arising directly from the construction or acquisition of the item of property, plant and equipment;

- costs of site preparation;

- initial delivery and handling costs;

- installation and assembly costs;

- costs of testing whether the asset is functioning properly, after deducting the net proceeds from selling any items produced while bringing the asset to that location and condition (e.g. samples produced when testing equipment) (see **4.2.1.1** below); and

- professional fees.

Example 4.2.1A

Land clearing costs

A ski slope operator has developed a piece of land into a ski resort. To do that, the operator has cut the trees, cleared and graded the land and hills, and constructed ski lifts.

Should the tree cutting, land clearing, and grading costs be capitalised as part of the cost of land or as part of the cost of the ski lifts?

The tree cutting, land clearing, and grading costs should be capitalised as part of the cost of the land. These costs are expenditures directly attributable to bringing the land to working condition for its intended use and, therefore, are part of the cost of the land, not the ski lifts.

As required under IAS 16:59, when the cost of site dismantlement, removal and restoration is included in the cost of land, that portion of the land asset is depreciated over the period of benefits obtained by incurring those costs.

Example 4.2.1B

Compensation for late delivery of an asset

When, under the terms of a contract for the purchase of an asset, a supplier is required to compensate the purchaser because the asset is not delivered on time (e.g. in the form of penalty payments or additional discounts), how should the purchaser account for such compensation?

In the vast majority of cases, such compensation will represent a reduction in the cost of the asset for the purchaser and it should be accounted for accordingly. For example, when compensation is calculated as a percentage of the contract price or based on notional damages suffered by the purchaser (e.g. a fixed rate per day), the compensation represents a penalty imposed on the supplier for the delayed delivery of the asset and it should be accounted for as a reduction in the cost of the asset.

However, in very limited circumstances when the contract specifies that the supplier will reimburse actual costs incurred by the purchaser as a result of the delayed delivery, it may be appropriate to account for those elements as reimbursements of costs under IAS 37:53 and 54 (see **section 5** of **chapter A12**). Such a treatment may be appropriate if:

- the costs being reimbursed are clearly identifiable and are actual incremental costs incurred by the purchaser as a result of the delay; and

- the compensation is payable whether or not the asset is eventually delivered to the purchaser.

If it is determined that the amounts are appropriately accounted for as reimbursements, they should be recognised in profit or loss when it is virtually certain that they will be received (see IAS 37:53). Under IAS 37:54, they may be offset against the related costs in profit or loss or presented as 'other income'.

Costs listed in IAS 16 as unsuitable for capitalisation and, therefore, to be expensed are:
[IAS 16:19]

- costs of opening a new facility;

- costs of introducing a new product or service (including costs of advertising and promotional activities);

- costs of conducting business in a new location, or with a new class of customer (including costs of staff training); and

- administration and other general overhead costs.

Example 4.2.1C

Training cost as a component of the cost of an asset

An entity acquires equipment of a type that its employees have never operated before. During the installation period, the employees receive extensive training on the equipment. The cost to the entity includes the incremental cost of hiring experts to conduct the training, and the directly attributable cost of wages of the employees during the training period. The equipment could not be used by the entity unless its employees received the training.

These training costs do not qualify as a component of the cost of the equipment; they do not fall within the scope of costs directly attributable to bringing the asset to the location and condition necessary for it to be capable of operating in the manner intended by the management. The equipment would be capable of operating in the manner intended by the management without the entity incurring the training cost – even though the employees would not know how to operate the equipment.

In accordance with paragraphs 15 and 69 of IAS 38 *Intangible Assets*, the training costs will typically be recognised as an expense when incurred.

4.2.1.1   Offsetting proceeds from selling output against costs of testing property, plant and equipment

Example 4.2.1.1

Offsetting proceeds from selling output against costs of testing property, plant and equipment

Entity R is constructing a petrochemical complex with several autonomous manufacturing facilities. Construction of some of the facilities has been completed; these have been certified as ready for commercial production by the relevant authority and they have commenced producing chemicals that are sold on the market. Other facilities are still in the commissioning phase and they are not yet ready for production.

IAS 16:16 states that the cost of an item of property, plant and equipment comprises "any costs directly attributable to bringing the asset to the location and condition necessary for it to be capable of operating in the manner intended by management". IAS 16:17 states that costs directly attributable to bringing an asset to the location and condition necessary for it to be capable of operating in the manner intended by management include "costs of testing whether the asset is functioning properly, <u>after deducting the net proceeds from selling any items produced while bringing the asset to that location and condition (such as samples produced when testing equipment)</u>" (emphasis added).

In the circumstances described, is it appropriate to offset the proceeds received from selling chemicals produced by the completed manufacturing facilities against the costs of testing the other facilities still in the commissioning phase (i.e. could such proceeds be accounted for as a reduction in the cost of facilities under construction, rather than recognised as revenue in profit or loss)?

IAS 16 does not provide any specific guidance in respect of assets or projects that are completed in parts and the extent to which one part can be considered to be "in the location and condition necessary for it to be capable of operating in the manner intended by management" while construction of other parts continues. Paragraphs 24 and 25 of IAS 23 *Borrowing Costs* do, however, address this topic in the context of capitalising borrowing costs on qualifying assets, as follows (see **3.4.3** in **chapter A18**).

> "When an entity completes the construction of a qualifying asset in parts and each part is capable of being used while construction continues on other parts, the entity shall cease capitalising borrowing costs when it completes substantially all the activities necessary to prepare that part for its intended use or sale.
>
> A business park comprising several buildings, each of which can be used individually, is an example of a qualifying asset for which each part is capable of being usable while construction continues on other parts. An example of a qualifying asset that needs to be complete before any part can be used is an industrial plant involving several

processes which are carried out in sequence at different parts of the plant within the same site, such as a steel mill."

Applying this principle to the circumstances under consideration, it is likely that the petrochemical complex should be thought of as consisting of a number of parts (the autonomous manufacturing facilities), each of which is capable of operating in the manner intended by management while construction of the other parts continues. Consequently, when an individual facility has been completed and is ready for commercial use, it should be considered to be in the location and condition necessary for it to be capable of operating in the manner intended by management. Once that position has been reached, proceeds received from the sale of chemicals produced by that facility should be recognised as revenue in profit or loss (subject to the general conditions of IAS 18 *Revenue* – see **chapter A14**) because those chemicals were produced after the facility is operational and, consequently, proceeds from their sale do not qualify for deduction from the cost of the asset in accordance with IAS 16:17(e).

4.2.2   Cost of a self-constructed asset

The cost of a self-constructed asset is determined using the same principles as for an acquired asset, as set out at **4.2.1** above. The Standard states that if an entity makes similar assets for sale in the normal course of business, the cost of the asset is usually the same as the cost of constructing the asset for sale, in accordance with the principles of IAS 2 *Inventories*. [IAS 16:22]

For example, if the entity were a car manufacturer, the costs used to determine the cost of a car for sale under IAS 2 could also be used in determining the cost of a car that will be held as property, plant and equipment.

However, if the entity does not construct similar assets for sale, only those elements of costs described in IAS 16:16 (see **4.2.1**) can be incorporated in the cost of a self-constructed asset. Accordingly, costs which can be included are:

- direct materials;

- direct labour costs; and

- unavoidable costs that are directly attributable to the construction activity (i.e. costs that would have been avoided if the asset had not been constructed).

This concept of 'directly attributable' costs is different from the concepts applied in the measurement of costs of conversion in IAS 2. The latter includes a systematic allocation of fixed and variable production overheads that are incurred in converting materials into finished goods. Such systematic allocation of fixed overheads is not appropriate under IAS 16, because IAS 16 looks to capitalise only directly attributable costs.

The Standard gives no further guidance on how to determine which costs should be viewed as 'directly attributable'. Costs that are directly incremental as a result of the construction of a specific asset would generally be eligible, if they relate to bringing the asset to working condition. When an entity regularly constructs assets, however, it is possible that some element of apparently 'fixed' costs may also be directly attributable. In such circumstances, an entity should consider which costs would have been avoided if none of those assets had been constructed. For example, a construction company may employ builders who are normally engaged on the construction of properties for sale. If those builders are engaged for part of the year on the construction of a new head office for the entity, their direct employment costs should be capitalised as part of the cost of the new head office.

It is, therefore, likely that some variable production overheads may be incorporated into the cost of a self-constructed asset (depending on whether they could have been avoided absent the self-construction of the asset) but that no fixed production overheads can be incorporated.

Administration and other general overhead costs are not a component of the cost of property, plant and equipment because they cannot be directly attributed to the acquisition of the asset or bringing the asset to its working condition.

The costs that may be included in the carrying amount of an asset are limited to those that arise directly from the construction or acquisition of the asset. When, for example, costs are incurred to demolish existing structures in order to build on a site, the cost of demolition may be incremental to the construction cost or it may be associated with derecognition of a previously held asset. It depends on whether the existing structures were previously used in the entity's business, or were acquired as part of the site with the specific intention of demolishing them. In the latter case, the demolition costs are clearly incremental and should be included in the cost of the new asset. In the former case, the cost of the old asset should be written off to profit or loss through accelerated depreciation once the decision to demolish is made; the demolition costs incurred relate to the derecognition of the old asset and should be expensed when incurred.

Example 4.2.2A

Existing building demolished in order to construct new building

In 20X1, Company E purchased land and buildings for CU100 million (land: CU40 million and building: CU60 million). The building is used by Company E in its business; it is classified as property, plant and equipment and is depreciated over its estimated useful life. In 20X3, Company E demolishes the building and constructs a new building for its own use on the same piece of land. The carrying amount of the old building prior to demolition was CU55 million.

Should the CU55 million be written off to profit or loss or be capitalised as part of the cost of the new building?

The carrying amount of CU55 million should be written off to profit or loss. Under IAS 16, Company E is required to depreciate the building to its residual value over its useful life. The remaining useful life of Company E's building is equivalent to the period from when Company E decided to demolish the building to the demolition date in 20X3. The residual value of the building is zero because the building will be demolished. Therefore, after management's decision to demolish the building, Company E should revise both the remaining useful life and the residual value of the building and should adjust the depreciation expense accordingly, resulting in a write-down of the building to zero before demolition.

The following principles also apply in relation to self-constructed assets: [IAS 16:22]

- any internal profits are eliminated in arriving at the cost of an asset;

- the costs of abnormal amounts of wasted material, labour or other resources incurred in the production of the self-constructed asset are excluded from its cost; and

- borrowing costs incurred during the period of production should be included in accordance with IAS 23 if the self-constructed asset meets the definition of a qualifying asset (see **chapter A18**).

> **Example 4.2.2B**
>
> **Cost of abnormal amounts of waste in producing a self-constructed asset**
>
> A power company, Company P, signed a contract with a contractor to construct a power plant. Company P believed that the quality of the construction work was poor and terminated the construction contract. The contractor sued Company P for breach of contract and Company P lost. Company P then paid a lump sum to the contractor as compensation for the breach of contract, and the construction work was resumed thereafter.
>
> *Should the lump sum compensation paid to the contractor be recognised immediately as an expense or added to the construction cost of the power plant?*
>
> The amount does not fall within the scope of costs that are directly attributable to bringing the asset to the location and condition necessary for it to be capable of operating in the manner intended by management. This cost is similar in nature to the cost of abnormal amounts of wasted material, labour or other resources described in IAS 16:22 and, therefore, should be expensed.

See **3.5.5** for a discussion of the appropriate accounting when an entity continues to incur capital expenditure on an item of property, plant and equipment in respect of which an impairment loss has previously been recognised.

4.2.3 Cost of dismantling, removal and site restoration

Costs incurred by an entity in respect of obligations for dismantling, removing and restoring the site on which an item of property, plant and equipment is located are recognised and measured in accordance with IAS 37 *Provisions, Contingent Liabilities and Contingent Assets*. If the obligations are incurred when the asset is acquired, or during a period when the item is used other than to produce inventories, they are included in the cost of the item of property, plant and equipment, as specified in **4.2.1** above. If the obligations are incurred during a period when the entity uses the item of property, plant and equipment to produce inventories, the costs are accounted for under IAS 2 *Inventories*. [IAS 16:18]

The accounting for changes in such obligations is discussed at **4.4** below and accounting for the cost of obligations that did not exist when the item was acquired is discussed at **4.2.10**.

4.2.4   *Start-up or commissioning period*

It is appropriate to recognise directly attributable costs in the carrying amount of an item of property, plant and equipment during a commissioning period in which it is not possible to operate at normal levels because of the need to run machinery, test equipment, or ensure the proper operation of the equipment. This circumstance generally relates to the physical preparation for use. An example would be a printing press if it is necessary to run it for a period in order to achieve the necessary level of performance.

The following are examples of costs that are *not* included in the carrying amount of an item of property, plant and equipment:
[IAS 16:20]

- costs incurred while an item capable of operating in the manner intended by management has yet to be brought into use or is operated at less than full capacity;

- initial operating losses, such as those incurred while demand for the item's output builds up; and

- costs of relocating or reorganising part or all of an entity's operations.

> See **4.2.1.1** above for an example addressing whether proceeds from selling output can be offset against the costs of testing an item of property, plant and equipment.

4.2.5   *Incidental operations*

Some operations occur in connection with the construction or development of an item of property, plant and equipment, but are not necessary to bring the item to the location and condition necessary for it to be capable of operating in the manner intended by management. These incidental operations may occur before or during the construction or development activities. For example, income may be earned through using a building site as a car park until construction starts. Because these incidental operations are not necessary to bring an item of property, plant and equipment to the location and condition necessary for it to be capable of operating in the manner intended by management, the income and related expenses of incidental operations are recognised in profit or loss, and included in their respective classifications of income or expense. [IAS 16:21]

4.2.6   *Reimbursement of part of the cost of an asset*

Example 4.2.6

Reimbursement of part of the cost of an asset

Company A enters into a contract with Company B to produce and sell a specific product. Company A needs to transform a major part of its plant to be able to produce that product, and commissions that transformation work from a third party, Company C, unconnected with Company A and Company B. The transformation costs are significant and exclusively for the purpose of this sales contract. As a result, Company A and Company B enter into an agreement under which Company B will reimburse Company A for a portion of the transformation costs. The cash received from Company B can only be used to offset the costs of the transformation for Company A.

Should the reimbursement be deducted from the cost of the transformation.

From the perspective of Company A, two transactions are occurring: the purchase of services (transformation costs) from Company C, and the supply of products to Company B. Accordingly, Company A must determine whether the amount receivable from Company B relates to the former or to the latter.

The arrangement between Company A and Company B is within the scope of IFRIC 18 *Transfers of Assets from Customers*. IFRIC 18:6 states that the Interpretation "also applies to agreements in which an entity receives cash from a customer when that amount of cash must be used only to construct or acquire an item of property, plant and equipment and the entity must then use the item of property, plant and equipment either to connect the customer to a network or to provide the customer with ongoing access to a supply of goods or services, or to do both". In this case, the cash from Company B must be used to acquire transformation services from Company C that will create assets to be used exclusively to provide Company B with the supply of a specific product.

Accordingly, Company A applies IFRIC 18 as described below.

- Company A has received an asset (cash) from Company B and it must recognise that asset.

- The cost of the transformation will be recognised as property, plant and equipment, without any offset of the amount received from Company B.

- Instead, the amount received from Company B is deferred, to be recognised as revenue when the conditions in IAS 18 *Revenue* are met.

- No separate service is being provided to Company B other than the supply of the specified product, so the amount received from Company B should be regarded as revenue relating to the supply of that specified product.

Therefore, the amount received as a reimbursement from Company B should be treated as revenue in accordance with IAS 18, and not as a reduction in the cost of the transformation. Because the payment is an integral part of the contract to produce and sell the product, the two agreements should be accounted for together in accordance with IAS 18:13 (see **section 5** of **chapter A14**). The total revenue (i.e. the price per the sales contract plus the reimbursement) should be recognised when the conditions for revenue recognition set out in IAS 18 are met.

IFRIC 18 is discussed at **2.3** in **chapter A14**.

4.2.7   Broker's commission rebate to purchaser of property

Example 4.2.7

Broker's commission rebate to purchaser of property

During negotiations to purchase a property, the purchaser was unwilling to accept the seller's best offer. To induce the purchaser to proceed with the transaction, the broker agreed to rebate a portion of the seller-paid commission to the purchaser.

As far as the purchaser is concerned, only one transaction has occurred – the purchase of property. The commission rebate is not immediate income to the purchaser. The seller's best offer is not the price that the purchaser actually paid. If the purchaser had been required to pay a brokerage commission, that commission would have been part of the cost of the property as a cost necessarily incurred to obtain the asset. In the circumstances described, the commission rebate is similarly a component of the cost of the property.

4.2.8   Utility fees paid to a government

In some jurisdictions, developers of factories, offices, apartment buildings and shopping malls must pay a 'capacity fee' to the government for the privilege of being able to purchase, on an ongoing basis, defined quantities of electricity and other utilities beyond certain minimum quantities that can be purchased without paying the fee. The fee is paid on a one-off basis and covers supply, either on an indefinite basis or at least for a substantial number of years. However, the building owner still pays the market rate to purchase the electricity and other utilities. The capacity fee attaches

493

to the entity that owns the building, and it can be transferred to another building if the capacity allowed by the fee is not fully utilised.

Because a capacity fee is transferable between buildings, it is not part of the cost of the building but should be recognised as a purchased intangible asset in its own right. As such, it is subject to the requirements of IAS 38 *Intangible Assets* relating to amortisation and impairment (see **chapter A9**).

If, instead, a capacity fee were attached to the building and not transferable, it would be recognised as part of the cost of the building and depreciated.

4.2.9 *Cessation of capitalisation*

Recognition of costs in the carrying amount of an item of property, plant and equipment ceases when the item is in the location and condition necessary for it to be capable of operating in the manner intended by management. Therefore, costs incurred in using or redeploying an item are not included in the carrying amount of that item. [IAS 16:20]

In the case of a self-constructed asset, or the installation of a major asset, a policy decision should be made and applied consistently as to what event or activity characterises the point at which an asset's physical construction/installation is complete (i.e. when the item is in the location and condition necessary for it to be capable of operating in the manner intended by management), so that all costs incurred after that point are identified and expensed. When a commissioning period is involved, it will similarly be essential to determine in principle the point that characterises reaching the capability of operating at normal levels, and then to ensure that costs incurred after reaching that point are captured and expensed.

When there is delay in achieving final physical completion, costs arising during the period of delay are likely to fall into the category of abnormal costs and so be expensed as incurred. Borrowing costs incurred during such a period of delay will not qualify for capitalisation under IAS 23 *Borrowing Costs*, which requires that capitalisation should cease when active development is suspended (see **chapter A18**).

Regulatory consents (e.g. health and safety clearance) are sometimes required before an asset may be used legally. Cost capitalisation will not necessarily continue until such consents are in place. Management will normally seek to ensure that such consents are in place very close to the time-frame for physical completion and testing, and that they do not delay the commencement of operations. Avoidable delays in obtaining consents which prevent the start of operations should be seen as abnormal and similar in effect to an industrial dispute, with the result that capitalisation should cease (see **example 4.2.9**).

The words 'capable of operating in the manner intended by management' in IAS 16 cannot be used to justify ongoing capitalisation of costs (and postponement of depreciation) once the asset has actually been brought into use just because the asset does not live up to management's original intentions. This may, however, constitute an impairment trigger under IAS 36 *Impairment of Assets*.

Example 4.2.9

Capitalisation of costs incurred between the completion of a building and the date of approval for occupation

On 20 September 20X0, Company A completed the construction of a building intended for use as its administrative headquarters.

By law, the local health and safety authority must approve the offices for occupation before any activity can commence. This approval can be requested only when the building is physically complete, and it takes on average three months to obtain the approval.

The health and safety authority issued the approval for occupation on 20 December 20X0. In the three months from 20 September 20X0, Company A incurred CU10 of building management costs (e.g. utility and security expenses) and interest expenses. (The building is identified as a qualifying asset under IAS 23.)

Should the costs incurred by Company A between 20 September 20X0 (when the building was physically completed) and 20 December 20X0 (when the approval for occupation was issued) be included in the initial cost of the building?

Yes. The management costs incurred are considered "directly attributable to bringing the asset to the location and condition necessary for it to be capable of operating in the manner intended by management" (IAS 16:16(b)). In addition, obtaining the approval for occupation is considered to be an activity "necessary to prepare the qualifying asset for its intended use or sale" (IAS 23:25); therefore, Company A should continue to capitalise borrowing costs until the approval is obtained.

However, any abnormal amounts of wasted resources incurred in obtaining that approval should not be capitalised (IAS 16:22). For example, if the approval for occupation had taken longer than the customary three-month period from the completion of construction, due to avoidable delays caused by Company A failing to provide the required information to the health and safety authority, Company A could include in the original cost of the building only costs incurred during the time usually required to obtain the approval for occupation (in the circumstances under consideration, three months).

If the delays were due to a slow response from the health and safety authority (without cause by Company A), the capitalisation period would be extended.

4.2.10   Rehabilitation liability – change in legislation

Example 4.2.10

Rehabilitation liability – change in legislation

Company X acquired a building in 20X1. Asbestos was used in the construction of the building. During 20X5, legislation is enacted which requires Company X either to remove the asbestos or to vacate the building.

Company X obtains a reliable estimate of the costs of removing the asbestos. In accordance with IAS 37, Company X recognises a provision for the cost of removing the asbestos.

Should Company X capitalise the estimated cost of removing the asbestos from the building?

IAS 16:16 states that the cost of an item of property, plant and equipment should include the initial estimate of the costs of dismantling and removing the item and restoring the site on which it is located, the obligation for which the entity incurred either when the item was acquired, or as a consequence of having used the item during a particular period for purposes other than to produce inventories during that period (see **4.2.1**). IAS 16:BC14 confirms that IAS 16:16 does not specifically address how an entity should account for the "cost of obligations an entity did not face when it acquired the item, such as an obligation triggered by a law change enacted after the asset was acquired".

Company X should therefore assess whether the costs of removing the asbestos meet the general recognition criteria in IAS 16:7. In this scenario:

- the cost of removing the asbestos can be reliably measured; and

- it is probable that economic benefits associated with the asbestos removal will flow to Company X (because the building would otherwise be vacated).

Therefore, Company X should capitalise the estimated cost of removing the asbestos.

The change in legislation is also an indicator of impairment; consequently, when the legislation is enacted, Company X should estimate the recoverable amount of the building.

4.3   Measurement of cost

The cost of an item of property, plant and equipment (or of an element of an item) is the cash price equivalent (i.e. the amount that the entity would need to pay if it were to purchase the asset by paying cash immediately upon purchase) at the date on which the asset is recognised. [IAS 16:23]

4.3.1   Payments deferred beyond normal credit terms

When payment for an item of property, plant and equipment is deferred beyond normal credit terms, the difference between the cash price equivalent and the total payments is recognised as an interest expense over the period of credit, unless it is capitalised in accordance with the requirements of IAS 23 *Borrowing Costs* (see **chapter A18**). [IAS 16:23]

Example 4.3.1A

Deferred payment terms

On 1 January 20X1, an item of property is offered for sale at CU10 million, with payment terms being three equal instalments of CU3,333,333 over a two year period (payments are made on 1 January 20X1, 31 December 20X1 and 31 December 20X2). The property developer is offering a discount of 5 per cent (i.e. CU500,000) if payment is made in full at the time of completion of the sale and purchase agreement (which corresponds to an implicit interest rate of 5.36 per cent per annum).

The purchaser will recognise the acquisition of the asset as follows.

	CU	CU
Dr Property, plant and equipment	9,500,000	
Cr Cash		3,333,333
Cr Accounts payable		6,166,667
Initial recognition of property.		

The following entry will be required at the end of 20X1.

	CU	CU
Dr Interest expense	330,459	
(5.36% × CU6,166,667)		
Dr Accounts payable	3,002,874	
Cr Cash		3,333,333

Recognition of interest expense and payment of second instalment.

The following entry will be required at the end of 20X2.

	CU	CU
Dr Interest expense	169,541	
Dr Accounts payable	3,163,793	
Cr Cash		3,333,334

Recognition of interest expense and payment of final instalment.

Example 4.3.1B

Payment for an asset deferred beyond 'normal credit terms'

The commercial property market in a particular city is very slow. As an inducement to potential purchasers, a seller of commercial property in that city advertises a property for sale at 'no interest for the first three years after purchase, market rate of interest thereafter'. Other property sellers in the city are making similar offers. A buyer purchases a property on those terms. IAS 16:23 requires imputation of interest if payment for an item of property is 'deferred beyond normal credit terms'.

In this circumstance, is the three-year interest-free period 'normal credit terms'?

No. The intent of IAS 16:23 is to ensure that the asset is recognised at its current cash sale price. The 'normal credit terms' requirement is intended to recognise that settlement of cash purchases often takes a few days, weeks, or even months (depending on the industry and national laws), and imputation of interest is not required in those circumstances. Particularly for a large item such as a property, however, the cash sale price would be significantly lower if cash payment is made up-front rather than deferred for three years. If the deferral period is greater than what can be considered normal credit terms, the imputed interest element should be recognised.

Example 4.3.1C

Time value of money on deposit paid for the acquisition of an asset

Company A has two choices regarding payment for an item of property, plant and equipment:

- it can pay the list price of CU10,000 when the asset is delivered in 2 years' time; or

- it can pay CU5,000 as an up-front, non-refundable deposit, and make a final payment of CU3,500 when the asset is delivered.

If Company A chooses to pay the up-front deposit, how should the time value of money associated with the deposit be accounted for?

Because such a substantial deposit is paid up-front, the total amount that Company A is required to pay is reduced; that is, the time value of money associated with the up-front payment is reflected in the total amount payable.

The deposit is non-refundable and, therefore, it is not a financial asset. Nevertheless, the deposit represents not only a payment on account for the asset but also, in effect, provides financing to the supplier. Therefore, it will be appropriate to recognise the implicit financing as part of the cost of the asset by unwinding the time value of money over time, using the discount rate implicit in the original transaction (14 per cent in the above example), as follows.

Year	Carrying amount of deposit b/fwd	Interest income at 14%	Final payment	Carrying amount of deposit/asset c/fwd
1	CU5,000	CU700		CU5,700
2	CU5,700	CU800	CU3,500	CU10,000

Including the time value of money as part of the cost of the asset is consistent with IAS 16:23, as discussed earlier in this section.

4.3.2 Exchanges of assets

When an item of property, plant and equipment is acquired in exchange for a non-monetary asset or assets, or a combination of monetary and non-monetary assets, the cost of that item is measured at fair value (even if the entity cannot immediately derecognise the asset given up) unless: [IAS 16:24]

- the exchange transaction lacks commercial substance; or

- the fair value of neither the asset received nor the asset given up is reliably measurable.

If the acquired item is not measured at fair value, its cost is measured at the carrying amount of the asset given up.

The entity should determine whether an exchange transaction has commercial substance by considering the extent to which its future cash flows are expected to change as a result of the transaction. An exchange transaction has commercial substance if: [IAS 16:25]

- either:

- the configuration (risk, timing and amount) of the cash flows of the asset received differs from the configuration of the cash flows of the asset transferred; *or*

- the entity-specific value of the portion of the entity's operations affected by the transaction changes as a result of the exchange; *and*

- the difference arising in either of the two circumstances outlined above is significant relative to the fair value of the assets exchanged.

Entity-specific value is the present value of the cash flows an entity expects to arise from the continuing use of an asset and from its disposal at the end of its useful life or expects to incur when settling a liability. [IAS 16:6] For the purpose of assessing commercial substance, post-tax cash flows are used. [IAS 16:25]

Example 4.3.2

Exchange of assets

A ship charterer owns land and buildings which are carried in its statement of financial position at an aggregate carrying amount of CU10 million, but which have a fair value of CU15 million. It exchanges the land and buildings for a ship, which has a fair value of CU18 million, and pays an additional CU3 million cash.

Provided that the transaction has commercial substance, the entity should recognise the ship at a cost of CU18 million (its fair value) and should recognise a profit on disposal of the land and buildings of CU5 million, calculated as follows:

	CU'000
Consideration received	18,000
less:	
– carrying amount of land and building disposed of	(10,000)
– cash paid	(3,000)
	5,000

The required journal entry is therefore as follows.

	CU'000	CU'000
Dr Property, plant and equipment (ship)	18,000	
Cr Property, plant and equipment (land and buildings)		10,000
Cr Cash		3,000
Cr Profit on exchange of assets (profit or loss)		5,000

The fair value of an asset is reliably measurable if:
[IAS 16:26]

- the variability in the range of reasonable fair value measurements is not significant for that asset; or

- the probabilities of the various estimates within the range can be reasonably assessed and used when measuring fair value.

If an entity is able to measure reliably the fair value of either the asset received or the asset given up, then the fair value of the asset given up is used to measure the cost of the asset received, unless the fair value of the asset received is more clearly evident. [IAS 16:26]

> Some terminology changes have been made in IAS 16:26 as consequential amendments arising from IFRS 13 *Fair Value Measurement*, and those changes are reflected above. However, the approach required by IAS 16:26 is not affected by the introduction of IFRS 13.

4.3.3   Assets held under finance lease

The cost of assets held under finance leases is determined using the principles set out in IAS 17 *Leases* (see **chapter A17** for details). [IAS 16:27]

4.3.4   Government grants

The carrying amount of an item of property, plant and equipment may be reduced by government grants, in accordance with IAS 20 *Accounting for Government Grants and Disclosure of Government Assistance* (see **chapter A36**). [IAS 16:28]

4.3.5   Assets acquired as part of a business combination

IFRS 3 *Business Combinations* requires that property, plant and equipment of a subsidiary acquired as part of a business combination be measured initially at fair value for the purpose of inclusion in the consolidated financial statements (see **chapter A25** for detailed discussion). This fair value is the cost of the asset for the purpose of subsequent accounting under IAS 16. All other aspects of the accounting treatment for these assets, including depreciation, are determined by reference to the requirements of IAS 16.

The fair value exercise does not amount to a revaluation of the assets concerned. Accordingly, it is not necessary thereafter to comply with the revaluation model prescribed in IAS 16 merely because the assets have been recognised initially at fair value. As discussed in **section 5**, an entity makes an accounting policy choice whether to apply the cost model or the revaluation model to a particular class of assets.

4.4 IFRIC 1 *Changes in Existing Decommissioning, Restoration and Similar Liabilities*

IFRIC 1 *Changes in Existing Decommissioning, Restoration and Similar Liabilities* provides guidance on how to account for the effect of changes in the measurement of existing decommissioning, restoration and similar liabilities. For example, such liabilities may exist for decommissioning a plant, rehabilitating environmental damage in extractive industries, or removing equipment. IFRIC 1 applies to changes in the measurement of any existing decommissioning, restoration or similar liability that is both:
[IFRIC 1:2]

- recognised as part of the cost of an item of property, plant and equipment in accordance with IAS 16; and

- recognised as a liability in accordance with IAS 37.

The guidance below deals with how to account for changes in the measurement of an existing decommissioning, restoration or similar liability that result from changes in the estimated timing or amount of the outflow of resources required to settle the obligation, or a change in the discount rate.

4.4.1 Cost model

If the related asset is measured using the cost model:
[IFRIC 1:5]

- changes in the liability are added to, or deducted from, the cost of the related asset in the current period, except that the amount deducted from the cost of the asset must not exceed its carrying amount. If a decrease in the liability exceeds the carrying amount of the asset, the excess is recognised immediately in profit or loss; and

- if the adjustment results in an addition to the cost of an asset, the entity should consider whether this may indicate that the new carrying amount of the asset may not be fully recoverable. If so, the asset should be tested for impairment in accordance with IAS 36 (see **chapter A10**).

4.4.2 Revaluation model

If the related asset is measured using the revaluation model:
[IFRIC 1:6]

- changes in the liability alter the revaluation surplus or deficit previously recognised on that asset, so that:

  - a decrease in the liability is generally recognised in other comprehensive income and increases the revaluation surplus within equity, but is recognised immediately in profit or loss:

    - to the extent that it reverses a revaluation deficit on the asset that was previously recognised in profit or loss; or

    - to the extent that it exceeds the carrying amount that would have been recognised had the asset been carried under the cost model; and

  - an increase in the liability is recognised in other comprehensive income and reduces the revaluation surplus within equity to the extent of any credit balance relating to that asset, with the balance being recognised in profit or loss;

- a change in the liability is an indication that the asset may have to be revalued in order to ensure that the carrying amount does not differ materially from fair value at the end of the reporting period. Any such revaluation is taken into account in determining the amounts to be recognised in profit or loss or in other comprehensive income. If a revaluation is necessary, all assets of that class are revalued; and

- to comply with IAS 1 (see **5.3.1** in **chapter A4**), the change in the revaluation surplus arising from a change in the liability is separately identified and disclosed as a component of other comprehensive income.

4.4.3 Other requirements

The adjusted depreciable amount of the asset is depreciated over its useful life. Accordingly, once the related asset has reached the end of its useful life, all subsequent changes in the liability are recognised in profit or loss as they occur. This applies under both the cost model and the revaluation model. [IFRIC 1:7]

The periodic unwinding of the discount is recognised in profit or loss as a finance cost as it occurs. Capitalisation under IAS 23 *Borrowing Costs* is not permitted. [IFRIC 1:8]

5   Alternatives for measurement after recognition

IAS 16 permits two different bases for the determination of the carrying amount of property, plant and equipment at the end of subsequent reporting periods – a cost model and a revaluation model. Whichever accounting policy is selected, it is required to be applied to entire classes of property, plant and equipment. [IAS 16:29]

5.1   Cost model

When the cost model is selected, after recognition as an asset an item of property, plant and equipment is carried at cost less any accumulated depreciation and any accumulated impairment losses. [IAS 16:30]

When the cost model is used, the cost of the asset normally remains unchanged until it is derecognised. The treatment of subsequent costs is considered at **3.5** above.

5.2   Revaluation model

When the revaluation model is selected, after recognition as an asset an item of property, plant and equipment whose fair value can be measured reliably is carried at a revalued amount, being its fair value at the date of the revaluation less any subsequent accumulated depreciation and any subsequent accumulated impairment losses. Revaluations are required to be carried out with sufficient regularity to ensure that the carrying amount does not differ materially from that which would be determined using fair value at the end of the reporting period. [IAS 16:31]

6   Revaluation model

6.1   Initial adoption of revaluation basis

When an entity initially adopts a policy to measure property, plant and equipment using the revaluation model, this initial adoption of the valuation basis represents a change in accounting policy. IAS 8:17 specifies, however, that it should be dealt with as a revaluation rather than as a prior period adjustment. Consequently, the valuation uplift or write-down occurring on the initial adoption of the revaluation basis is dealt with in other comprehensive income (and accumulated in the revaluation surplus) or in profit or loss, as appropriate, in accordance with the requirements of IAS 16 (see **6.8** below). Prior period amounts are not restated.

This is a practical and helpful exemption from the general rules for changes in accounting policies, which means that it will not be necessary to obtain valuations at the end of earlier reporting periods. One side effect of the approach, however, is that the amounts of depreciation included in current and prior year profit or loss may not be comparable, because they are likely to be based on revaluation and on cost, respectively. When the impact is significant, the entity may wish to provide a brief explanation.

6.2   Measuring fair value

IAS 16's requirements for measuring fair value have been amended as a result of the issue of IFRS 13 *Fair Value Measurement*. In **6.2.1** and **6.2.2** below, the requirements for entities that have adopted IFRS 13 and those that have not yet adopted that Standard are set out separately. Essentially, the effect of IFRS 13 has been to remove the detailed guidance on the measurement of fair value from IAS 16 so that, following the adoption of IFRS 13, entities measuring property, plant and equipment at fair value should refer to the guidance in that Standard.

IFRS 13 is effective for annual periods beginning on or after 1 January 2013, with earlier application permitted.

As discussed in **section 12** of **chapter A6**, when IFRS 13 is first adopted, it is required to be applied prospectively and it need not be applied to comparative information provided for periods before the initial application of IFRS 13; therefore, amounts reported in prior annual periods are not required to be restated.

6.2.1   *Entities that have adopted IFRS 13*

Fair value is defined as "the price that would be received to sell an asset or paid to transfer a liability in an orderly transaction between market participants at the measurement date. (See IFRS 13 *Fair Value Measurement*.)" [IAS 16:6]

6.2.2 Entities that have not yet adopted IFRS 13

Fair value is defined as "the amount for which an asset could be exchanged between knowledgeable, willing parties in an arm's length transaction". [IAS 16:6]

The fair value of land and buildings is usually determined from market-based evidence by appraisal that is normally undertaken by professionally qualified valuers. The fair value of items of plant and equipment is usually their market value determined by appraisal. [IAS 16:32]

If there is no market-based evidence of fair value, because of the special-ised nature of the item of property, plant and equipment, and the item is rarely sold, except as part of a continuing business, the entity may need to estimate fair value using an income or a depreciated replacement cost approach. [IAS 16:33]

> The depreciated replacement cost valuation method is defined in the International Valuation Glossary, as produced by the International Valuation Standards Council, as "the current replacement cost of an asset less deductions for physical deterioration and all relevant forms of obsolescence". In accordance with International Valuation Stand-ard IVS 220 *Plant and Equipment*, paragraphs C11 and C12, it involves determining the cost of obtaining a modern equivalent asset provid-ing the same functionality or reproducing an exact replica of the property, plant and equipment item and deducting an allowance for depreciation, based on age, physical, functional and economic obso-lescence.
>
> The depreciated replacement cost valuation method is generally relevant when an item of property, plant and equipment is identified as a specialised asset. In particular, specialised properties are defined in the International Valuation Standard IVS 230 *Real Property Interests* as "property that is rarely if ever sold in the market, except by way of sale of the business or entity of which it is part". Examples of specialised assets may include a nuclear power station, a chemical plant or a film studio.

6.3 Frequency of revaluations

IAS 16:31 requires that revaluations should be made with sufficient regularity such that the carrying amount does not differ materially from that which would be determined using fair value at the end of the reporting period.

In order to meet this requirement, an entity must estimate the fair value of its revalued items of property, plant and equipment at the end of each reporting period. This does not mean, however, that revaluation adjustments must be made every year, unless the estimate of fair value differs significantly from the carrying amount of the intangible asset.

The Standard therefore does not require annual revaluations. The frequency of revaluations will depend upon fluctuations in the fair values of the items of property, plant and equipment under consideration. Some items of property, plant and equipment (e.g. properties situated in countries with high capital asset inflation rates) may experience significant and volatile movements in fair value, thus necessitating annual revaluations. Such frequent revaluations would be unnecessary for items of property, plant and equipment with only insignificant movements in fair value (e.g. machinery situated in countries with relatively low capital asset inflation rates).

When items of property, plant and equipment have only insignificant changes in fair value, the Standard indicates that it may be necessary to revalue them only every three or five years. [IAS 16:34]

6.4   Accumulated depreciation at the date of revaluation

IAS 16:35 allows that any depreciation accumulated on an asset at the date of revaluation can be dealt with in one of two ways, i.e. either:

- restated proportionately with the change in the gross carrying amount of the asset so that the carrying amount of the asset after revaluation equals its revalued amount (Method A). The carrying amount is increased to the revalued amount by restating the cost and depreciation proportionately. This method is often used when an asset is revalued by means of applying an index to determine its replacement cost; or

- eliminated against the gross carrying amount of the asset and the resulting net amount restated to the revalued amount of the asset (Method B). The accumulated depreciation is eliminated, and any remaining surplus is used to increase cost. This method is often used for buildings. It is the most commonly used method in practice.

Example 6.4 illustrates the alternative methods permitted under the Standard.

Example 6.4

Accumulated depreciation at the date of revaluation

A property has a carrying amount of CU10 million, represented by cost of CU12 million and accumulated depreciation of CU2 million. It is revalued to its fair value of CU13 million.

	Method A CU'000	Method B CU'000
Cost or valuation		
Before revaluation	12,000	12,000
Revaluation adjustment	3,600*	1,000
After revaluation	15,600	13,000
Accumulated depreciation		
Before revaluation	2,000	2,000
Revaluation adjustment	600*	(2,000)
After revaluation	2,600	0
Revalued amount	13,000	13,000

*   30 per cent increase in carrying amount results in a 30 per cent increase in both cost and accumulated depreciation.

See **12.1** for details of proposed amendments to IAS 16:35 which are expected to be finalised in the fourth quarter of 2013.

6.5   Revaluation to be made for entire class of assets

When an item of property, plant and equipment is revalued, the entire class of property, plant and equipment to which that asset belongs is required to be revalued. [IAS 16:36] Items within a class of property, plant and equipment are revalued simultaneously to avoid selective revaluation of assets and the reporting of amounts in the financial statements that are a mixture of costs and valuations at different dates. [IAS 16:38] This is intended to prevent the distortions caused by the selective use of revaluation, also referred to as 'cherry-picking', so as to take credit for gains without acknowledging falls in the value of similar assets.

6.5.1   Definition of a 'class' of assets

A class of property, plant and equipment is defined as a grouping of assets of a similar nature and use in an entity's operations. [IAS 16:37] The following examples of separate classes are cited:

• land;

- land and buildings;

- machinery;

- ships;

- aircraft;

- motor vehicles;

- furniture and fixtures; and

- office equipment.

The examples cited as separate classes are not intended to be pre-scriptive or comprehensive. In practice, it is not uncommon for some of these classes to be combined. For example, when motor vehicles are not significant to an entity, motor vehicles and machinery may be combined in a plant and machinery class. For similar reasons, office equipment may be included in the furniture and fixtures class.

6.5.2   Disclosure of classes

As discussed in **11.2** below, detailed disclosures are specified for each class of property, plant and equipment. This should be borne in mind when distinguishing classes, because multiple classes could lead to voluminous disclosures.

6.5.3   Revaluation on a rolling basis

The requirement to revalue entire classes of assets is a potentially onerous requirement because, for some reporting entities, a class of assets could comprise a large number of items. For this reason, IAS 16:38 allows a class of assets to be revalued on a rolling basis, provided that revaluation of the class of assets is completed within a short period of time and that the revaluations are kept up to date.

No further guidance is provided as to how a 'short period' should be interpreted for the purposes of IAS 16:38 although, given the drafting of the Standard, it is presumably less than a financial year. The general approach of IAS 16:38 is, however, to require simultaneous valuations so as to avoid the reporting of amounts that are a mixture of costs and values as at different dates. Accordingly, it would seem appropriate:

- for all such valuations to take place in the same accounting period (and in the same interim period when an entity presents interim financial statements); and

- for the acceptable length of the period to take into account how stable fair values are, so that greater volatility requires a shorter period over which to perform valuations.

6.6   Assets for which fair value cannot be reliably measured

Even when an entity has selected the revaluation model for its property, plant and equipment, only those assets whose fair value can be measured reliably are carried at revalued amounts. [IAS 16:31]

The Standard provides no guidance as to the circumstances in which it is appropriate to conclude that the fair value of an item of property, plant and equipment cannot be measured reliably, nor does it address the appropriate accounting for those assets whose fair value cannot be measured reliably.

However, IAS 40 *Investment Property* contains useful guidance on the circumstances in which it is appropriate to conclude that the fair value of an item of property, plant and equipment cannot be measured reliably. Under that Standard, the exception is allowed when, and only when, comparable market transactions are infrequent and alternative reliable estimates of fair value (e.g. based on discounted cash flow projections) are not available. IAS 40 is very restrictive, and allows this exception to be invoked only when an entity first acquires an investment property. IAS 16 is not so explicit, and seems to permit a greater degree of flexibility. It seems, however, that the intention of the IASB is that, when the entity has selected the revaluation model as its accounting policy for a particular class of assets, there should be a rebuttable presumption that all of the assets within that class will be carried at revalued amounts. The 'not reliably measurable' exception should be invoked only in exceptional circumstances. When the entity holds particular types of assets for which it will frequently be difficult to establish fair values (e.g. specialised plant and machinery), then it is preferable to adopt the cost basis for that entire class of assets, so as to avoid the reporting of amounts in the financial statements that are a mixture of costs and valuations at different dates.

When fair value cannot be reliably measured, the only reasonable approach is to account for those assets using IAS 16's cost model. This is consistent with the treatment required by IAS 40 for those investment properties whose fair value is not reliably measurable. To assist users of the financial statements, additional disclosures should be provided in respect of those assets carried at cost less accumulated depreciation and accumulated impairment losses. Again, useful guidance can be found in IAS 40 which requires that such assets be disclosed separately. In addition, entities are required by IAS 40 to disclose:

- a description of the property;

- an explanation of why fair value cannot be determined reliably;

- if possible, the range of estimates within which fair value is highly likely to lie; and

- on disposal of the property:

  - the fact that the entity has disposed of property not carried at fair value;

  - the carrying amount of the property at the time of sale; and

  - the amount of gain or loss recognised.

Although IAS 16 does not require equivalent disclosures, they should be seen as best practice. In addition, some of these disclosures may on occasions be necessary in order to comply with IAS 1:97, which requires that when items of income and expense are material, their nature and amount should be separately disclosed.

6.7   Voluntary disclosure of revalued amounts

Entities that adopt the cost model of accounting for their property, plant and equipment may wish to disclose the fair value of their property, plant and equipment in a note to the financial statements, when this is materially different from the carrying amount. Such disclosures are encouraged by IAS 16:79(d). In disclosing such fair values, such entities are not strictly bound by IAS 16's revaluation rules. However, when the amounts disclosed do not represent current fair values, they could mislead users of the financial statements. Therefore, the entity should either disclose the current fair values of the assets concerned, or not disclose revalued amounts at all. Similar considerations apply when an entity engages in 'cherry-picking', by disclosing current values only for those assets whose fair values are significantly above carrying amounts and ignoring those assets whose fair values are significantly below their carrying amounts. Accordingly, when fair values are disclosed voluntarily under IAS 16:79(d), they should normally be disclosed for an entire class of assets.

6.8   Treatment of surplus or deficit arising on revaluation

6.8.1   Revaluation surplus

IAS 16 requires that when an asset's carrying amount is increased as a result of a revaluation, the increase (being the difference between the fair value at the date of revaluation and the carrying amount at that date) should generally be recognised in other comprehensive income and accumulated in equity, under the heading of revaluation surplus. [IAS 16:39]

A revaluation increase should be recognised in profit or loss, however, to the extent that it reverses a revaluation decrease of the same asset previously recognised as an expense. [IAS 16:39]

When a revaluation surplus is recognised, no amendment is made to profit or loss to reverse depreciation previously recognised.

6.8.2   Revaluation deficit

The Standard requires that when an asset's carrying amount is decreased as a result of a revaluation, the decrease should generally be recognised in profit or loss. [IAS 16:40]

A revaluation decrease should be recognised in other comprehensive income, however, to the extent of any credit balance existing in the revaluation surplus in respect of that same asset. The decrease reduces the amount of the revaluation surplus accumulated in equity. [IAS 16:40]

6.8.3   Illustrative examples

The following examples illustrate the appropriate treatment of valuation movements in a number of circumstances. In each case, the deferred tax implications are ignored.

Example 6.8.3A

Revaluation surplus

An entity purchased a parcel of land on 1 July 20X1 for CU125 million. At 31 December 20X1, the land was valued at CU150 million.

The revaluation surplus of CU25 million is recognised in other comprehensive income and credited to a property revaluation reserve within equity.

Example 6.8.3B

Revaluation surplus reversing previous deficit

An entity purchased a parcel of land on 1 July 20X1 for CU140 million. At 31 December 20X1, the land was valued at CU125 million. At 31 December 20X2, the fair value of the land had increased to CU150 million.

20X1: Revaluation deficit of CU15 million is recognised in profit or loss.

20X2: Revaluation surplus is treated as follows:

- CU15 million is credited to profit or loss (i.e. reversal of the previous deficit).

- CU10 million is recognised in other comprehensive income and credited to the property revaluation reserve within equity.

Example 6.8.3C

Revaluation deficit reversing previous surplus

An entity purchased a parcel of land on 1 July 20X1 for CU60 million. At 31 December 20X1, the land was valued at CU70 million. At 31 December 20X2, the fair value of the land had decreased to CU55 million.

20X1:   Revaluation surplus of CU10 million is recognised in other comprehensive income and credited to the property revaluation reserve within equity.

513

20X2: Revaluation deficit is treated as follows:

- CU10 million is recognised in other comprehensive income and debited to the property revaluation reserve within equity (i.e. reversal of the previous surplus).
- CU5 million is recognised in profit or loss (i.e. excess of deficit over available surplus attributable to the same parcel of land).

Example 6.8.3D

Revaluation surplus reversing previous deficit: effect of depreciation

The cost of a property with a useful life of 20 years is CU10 million. Depreciation each year is CU0.5 million.

At the end of Year 5, the property has a carrying amount of CU7.5 million and a fair value of CU6 million. At that date, the directors move to the revaluation basis of accounting. The deficit on revaluation of CU1.5 million is recognised in profit or loss.

At the end of Years 6 through 9, the directors determine that there is no material difference between the carrying amount of the property and its fair value and, therefore, no valuation adjustments are required. Depreciation of CU2 million (i.e. 5 × CU0.4 million) is recognised in the periods up to the end of Year 10, at which time the property has a carrying amount of CU4 million. During Year 10, however, the value of the property increases sharply to a closing fair value of CU7 million.

Applying the basic principle as stated in IAS 16:39, the portion of the revaluation surplus that is to be credited to profit or loss at the end of Year 10 might appear to be CU1.5 million (i.e. the amount of the deficit previously recognised in profit or loss). In effect, however, part of this revaluation decrease has already been reversed through the recognition of a lower depreciation charge for Years 6 to 10.

Accordingly, the amount of the revaluation surplus that is credited to profit or loss should be reduced by the cumulative reduction in depreciation in Years 6 to 10 as a result of recognising the revaluation deficit (i.e. (CU0.5 million less CU0.4 million) × 5 years). Therefore the amount of the revaluation surplus credited to profit or loss is CU1 million. The remaining CU2 million of the revaluation surplus is recognised in other comprehensive income and credited to the revaluation reserve within equity. The end result is that the balance on the revaluation reserve (CU2 million) is the excess of the carrying amount (CU7 million) over what it would have been had the property never been revalued (CU5 million).

This treatment is consistent with the treatment prescribed for the reversal of an impairment loss under IAS 36 *Impairment of Assets* (see **chapter A10**).

6.8.4   Utilisation of revaluation reserve

Under IAS 16:41, the revaluation reserve may be transferred directly to retained earnings when the asset is derecognised. The reserve may be transferred on the retirement or disposal of the asset. Part of the reserve may, however, be transferred over the period for which the asset is used by the entity. In such circumstances, the amount of the reserve transferred is the difference between the depreciation charge based on the revalued carrying amount of the asset and the depreciation charge based on the asset's original cost. The transfer from revaluation reserve to retained earnings, whether on disposal or on a systematic basis over the life of the asset, is not made through profit or loss.

The reserve transfers referred to in IAS 16:41 are implied to be at the option of the reporting entity, rather than being mandated by the Standard. There would, therefore, appear to be another alternative – to make no reserve transfer. That option would, however, result in the permanent retention of the portion of the revaluation reserve relating to assets that have been fully depreciated or disposed of.

Any transfer between the revaluation reserve and retained earnings, which should be made on a net of tax basis, will reduce the amount that is available for offset against future revaluation deficits in respect of individual assets.

Example 6.8.4

Transfer from revaluation reserve to retained earnings

The cost of a property with a useful life of 20 years is CU10 million. Depreciation each year is CU0.5 million.

At the end of Year 5, the property has a carrying amount of CU7.5 million and a fair value of CU12 million. The surplus on revaluation of CU4.5 million is credited to the revaluation reserve and the property will be depreciated over its remaining 15-year useful life at the rate of CU0.8 million per annum. Assume that, for the remainder of its useful life, the depreciated carrying amount of the property is not materially different from its fair value. Therefore, no further revaluation adjustments are required.

In Years 6 through 20, depreciation has been increased by CU0.3 million per annum as a result of the revaluation. Therefore, at the end of each of those years, it is acceptable to make a transfer from the revaluation reserve to retained earnings of an amount of CU0.3 million, to reflect the realisation of the revaluation surplus. If such periodic transfers are made, then the revaluation reserve will have been reduced to zero at the point that the property is fully depreciated.

> Alternatively, if no annual transfers are made, the reserve may be transferred in its entirety on the retirement or disposal of the asset.

6.9   Deferred tax impact

> The revaluation of assets is also likely to have deferred tax implications. For the purposes of the examples in this chapter the deferred tax impact is ignored. Readers should refer to **chapter A13** for a detailed discussion of the deferred tax impact of revaluations.

7   Depreciation

If an item of property, plant and equipment has a limited useful economic life, then its cost or, if applicable, its fair value, is reduced to its estimated residual value by the systematic allocation of depreciation over the asset's useful economic life. [IAS 16:50]

The depreciation charge for each period should be recognised in profit or loss, unless it qualifies to be capitalised in the carrying amount of another asset. [IAS 16:48] For example, the depreciation of plant and machinery used for construction purposes may be included in the cost of a self-constructed property.

Depreciation, as defined in IAS 16:6, is the systematic allocation of the depreciable amount of an asset (i.e. the cost of the asset, or other amount substituted for cost, less its residual value) over its useful life. In order to comply with the requirements of IAS 16 relating to depreciation, it is necessary to identify:

- the parts (components) of each item of property, plant and equipment that are to be depreciated separately;

- the cost or valuation of each separately depreciable component;

- the estimated residual value of each separately depreciable component;

- the length of time during which each separately depreciable component will be commercially useful to the entity; and

- the most appropriate depreciation method for each separately depreciable component.

7.1   Each significant component to be depreciated separately

IAS 16 requires that each part of an item of property, plant and equipment with a cost that is significant in relation to the total cost of the item should be depreciated separately. [IAS 16:43]

When an item of property, plant and equipment is first recognised, the Standard requires that the entity should allocate the amount initially recognised between the item's significant parts (i.e. those separately identifiable components of the item with a cost that is significant to the total cost of the item). Each significant part is required to be depreciated separately. [IAS 16:44]

There may be some significant parts which, although separately identifiable, have the same useful life and which are appropriately depreciated using the same depreciation method. Such items will generally be grouped together for the purposes of calculating the depreciation charge. [IAS 16:45]

Once the individually significant parts have been identified, the remaining parts that are not individually significant are grouped together. Although the entity may have varying expectations as to the useful lives and pattern of consumption of the benefits of these remaining components, because they are not individually significant, the Standard allows that they can be depreciated as a group, provided that the depreciation rate and method selected result in a faithful representation of the pattern of consumption of benefits. [IAS 16:46]

A common example of the allocation of the cost of an item of property, plant and equipment is that of an aircraft, as mentioned in IAS 16:44. The airframe, engines and cabin interior of a single plane are likely to have significantly different useful lives. Under IAS 16, these parts are separately identified at the time that the aircraft is acquired, and each is depreciated separately over an appropriate useful life.

This approach of depreciating separate parts of a single item of property, plant and equipment is easily understood in relation to the physical components of a single item, as in the aircraft example discussed above. There will, however, also be 'parts' that are less tangible. An entity may purchase an item of property, plant and equipment that is required to undergo major inspections or over-hauls at regular intervals over its useful life. For example, an entity might acquire a ship that requires a major overhaul, say, once every five years. Part of the cost of the ship may be allocable to a separate component representing the service potential required to be restored by the periodic overhauls. That separate component is isolated when the asset is acquired, and depreciated over the period to the next overhaul.

The identification of this inherent component at the time of acquisition may not be simple, because it will generally not have been separately invoiced. Therefore, an estimate of the cost will be required. This will generally be based on the current cost of the expected overhaul or inspection (i.e. the estimated cost of those activities if they were performed at the time of the purchase).

As discussed at **3.5** above, expenditure incurred subsequently on the major inspection or overhaul is capitalised provided that the recognition criteria set out in IAS 16:7 are met. To the extent that the separate component representing the estimated cost of the inspection or overhaul has not been fully depreciated by the time that the inspection/overhaul expenditure is incurred, it is derecognised and will therefore give rise to a loss.

Example 7.1 illustrates the accounting treatment for major inspection or overhaul costs that qualify for separate recognition.

Example 7.1

Separate depreciation of cost of major overhaul

An entity purchases a ship for CU40 million. This ship will be required to undergo a dry dock overhaul every five years to restore its service potential. At the time of purchase, the service potential that will be required to be restored by the overhaul can be measured based on the cost of the dry docking if it had been performed at the time of the purchase of the ship, say CU4 million.

The following shows the calculation of the depreciation of the ship for Years 1 to 5, using the straight-line method.

	Amount	Useful life
	CU'000	(years)
Purchase price of ship	40,000	
Comprising:		
– the ship, excluding projected overhaul cost	36,000	30
– projected overhaul cost	4,000	5
For Years 1 to 5, depreciation charges per annum are:		
– ship (excluding the service potential component)	1,200	
– service potential	800	

By the end of Year 5, the service potential would be fully depreciated. When a dry docking is carried out in Year 6, the expenditure is capitalised to reflect the restoration of service potential, which is then depreciated over the period to the next overhaul in Years 6 to 10.

The process in Years 6 to 10 repeats every five years from Year 11 onwards until Year 30, when both the ship and the cost of dry docking are fully depreciated and a new ship is acquired.

Note that the entity is required to use its best efforts to identify separately components such as the service potential component, as described in **example 7.1**, when the asset is first acquired or constructed. That separate identification, and the subsequent separate depreciation of the service potential component, is not, however, a necessary condition for the capitalisation of the subsequent expenditure on the overhaul as part of the cost of the asset. For example, if the entity described in **example 7.1** had failed to identify the service potential component at the date of acquisition, because it was not considered significant, and had not depreciated it separately during Years 1 to 5, the expenditure on the overhaul in Year 6 would still be capitalised as part of the cost of the asset, provided that the general recognition criteria were met. In this circumstance, the entity would be required to estimate the remaining carrying amount of the service potential component at the date of the first overhaul (which would be approximately CU3.33 million, i.e. CU4 million depreciated for 5 years out of 30), and to derecognise that carrying amount at the same time as the expenditure on the overhaul is capitalised.

IAS 16 gives a further example of circumstances in which cost may need to be allocated to significant parts of an asset. If an entity acquires property, plant and equipment subject to an operating lease in which it is the lessor, it may be appropriate to depreciate separately amounts reflected in the cost of the item that are attributable to favourable or unfavourable lease terms relative to market terms. [IAS 16:44]

Land and buildings acquired in such circumstances might qualify as investment property, in which case this guidance would apply when the cost model within IAS 40 *Investment Property* is adopted (see **example 5.3** in **chapter A8**).

When lease terms are unfavourable for the lessor (e.g. fixed rentals are below market terms), this will tend to depress the fair value of the asset, so that the component relating to the unfavourable terms will be a credit. Separate depreciation of such a credit component will reduce the total depreciation charge during the period for which unfavourable terms apply.

7.2 Residual value

IAS 16 defines residual value as the estimated amount that an entity would currently obtain from disposal of the asset, after deducting the estimated costs of disposal, if the asset were already of the age and in the condition expected at the end of its useful life. [IAS 16:6]

In practice, the residual value of an asset is often insignificant and, therefore, is immaterial in the calculation of the depreciable amount. However, when the residual value is significant, then it will directly affect the depreciation recognised over the life of the asset.

The residual value of an asset is required to be reviewed at least at each financial year end. [IAS 16:51] The revised estimate should be based on market conditions current at the end of the reporting period. If the revised estimate differs significantly from previous estimates of residual value, the effect is accounted for prospectively as a change in estimate, in accordance with the requirements of IAS 8 *Accounting Policies, Changes in Accounting Estimates and Errors*. [IAS 16:51] Effectively, the depreciation recognised over the remaining useful life of the asset is adjusted to take account of the revised estimate of residual value.

If the revised estimate of residual value is equal to or greater than the asset's carrying amount, whether due to inflation or otherwise, then the asset's depreciation charge is zero unless and until its residual value subsequently decreases to an amount below the asset's carrying amount. [IAS 16:54]

The definition of residual value refers to the potential disposal value of the asset if it were already of the age and in the condition expected at the end of its useful life. The amount is therefore quite separate from the current fair value of the asset. If the fair value of the asset exceeds its carrying amount (generally because the entity has adopted the cost model for accounting for its property, plant and equipment), this does not remove the obligation to recognise depreciation. [IAS 16:52]

Further, the definition focuses on the amount that could currently be obtained on disposal of the asset, rather than the amount that is expected to be obtained at the end of the asset's useful life. Therefore, expectations as to future increases or decreases in that disposal value are not taken into account. Thus, an increase in the expected residual value of an asset because of past events will affect the depreciable amount; expectations of future changes in residual value other than the effects of wear and tear will not. [IAS 16:BC29]

7.3   Estimates of useful lives

The useful life of an asset is defined as:
[IAS 16:6]

- the period over which an asset is expected to be available for use by an entity; or

- the number of production or similar units expected to be obtained from the asset by an entity.

7.3.1   Commencement of depreciation

Depreciation of an asset commences when it is available for use, i.e. when it is in the location and condition necessary for it to be capable of operating in the manner intended by management. [IAS 16:55] This is the same point in time at which the entity is required to cease capitalising costs within the carrying amount of the asset. (See **4.2.9** above for guidance as to when this point in time occurs.)

7.3.2   Cessation of depreciation

Depreciation of an asset ceases at the earlier of:
[IAS 16:55]

- the date that the asset is classified as held for sale (or included in a disposal group that is classified as held for sale) in accordance with IFRS 5 *Non-current Assets Held for Sale and Discontinued Operations* (see **9.1**); and

- the date that the asset is derecognised.

IFRS 5 requires that a non-current asset (or disposal group) be classified as held for sale if its carrying amount will be recovered principally through a sale transaction rather than through continuing use. [IFRS 5:6] For this to be the case, the asset (or disposal group) must be available for immediate sale in its present condition, and its sale must be 'highly probable' (see **chapter A20** for further guidance).

IAS 16 sets out requirements in respect of the derecognition of items of property, plant and equipment – see **section 9** below.

Therefore, depreciation of an asset does not cease when an asset becomes idle or is retired from active use unless the asset is fully depreciated. If the depreciation is calculated by reference to the usage of the asset, however, the depreciation recognised may be zero while there is no production. [IAS 16:55] In any case, when an asset becomes idle, or is retired from active use, this may trigger an impairment loss which will result in the reduction of the carrying amount of the asset to its estimated recoverable amount.

Example 7.3.2

Depreciation of an asset retired from active use

Company Q uses specialised machinery to manufacture its products and is the only entity in its market that operates this type of machinery.

Company Q plans to increase its production capacity by introducing new specialised machinery with improved technology. As a result, Company Q will discontinue using the specialised machinery currently in use. However, in order to protect its competitive advantage and deny other market participants access to the technology, Company Q will not sell the machinery currently in use, even though it is still in good working condition; instead, the machinery will be retired from active use and 'mothballed' by Company Q for potential further use or sale at a later date.

At the date of retirement, the fair value less costs to sell of the specialised machinery exceeds its carrying amount.

Should Company Q continue to depreciate the machinery when it is retired from active use and, if so, over what period?

Company Q should continue to depreciate the depreciable amount of the machinery on a systematic basis over its estimated useful life. The useful life of the machinery is defined in terms of its expected utility to Company Q (see IAS 16:57). This utility may be either the use of the asset by Company Q or alternatively the retention of a competitive advantage by denying others access to such machinery. However, the useful life of the machinery will be limited to its economic life.

IAS 16:55 (see above) specifies that deprecation of an asset should cease only at the earlier of (1) the date the asset is classified as held for sale (or is included in a disposal group classified as held for sale) under IFRS 5, and (2) the date that the asset is derecognised. Neither of these conditions is met in the circumstances under consideration.

IAS 16:55 also states explicitly that "depreciation does not cease when the asset becomes idle or is retired from active use unless the asset is fully depreciated".

Note that the retirement of the asset from active use is likely to be an indicator of impairment under paragraph 12 of IAS 36 *Impairment of Assets*. However, in the circumstances under consideration, because the fair value less costs to sell of the machinery is greater than its carrying amount, no impairment loss will be recognised.

7.3.3   Factors affecting the useful life of an asset

The consumption of the future economic benefits embodied in an asset occurs principally through usage. Other factors should also be taken into account, however, such as technical obsolescence and wear and tear while an asset remains idle, because they may result in a reduction in the economic benefits expected to be derived from the asset. Consequently, all of the following factors need to be considered in determining the useful life of an asset:
[IAS 16:56]

- the expected usage of the asset by the entity. Usage is assessed by reference to the asset's expected capacity or physical output;

- the expected physical wear and tear, which depends on operational factors such as the number of shifts for which the asset is to be used and the repair and maintenance programme of the entity, and the care and maintenance of the asset while idle;

- technical or commercial obsolescence arising from changes or improvements in production, or from a change in the market demand for the product or service output of the asset; and

- legal or similar limits on the use of the asset, such as the expiry dates of related leases.

Because the useful life of an asset is defined in terms of its expected utility to the entity, the asset management policy of the reporting entity should be taken into account when estimating the useful life of an asset. For example, an entity may have a policy of disposing of assets after a specified time or after consumption of a specified proportion of the economic benefits embodied in the assets. In such circumstances, the useful life of an asset may be shorter than its economic life. [IAS 16:57] For example, it is often the case that company cars are disposed of well before the end of their economic life.

7.3.4   Change in estimate of useful life

IAS 16 requires that the estimate of the useful life of an item of property, plant and equipment should be reviewed at least at the end of each financial year. If expectations differ from previous estimates, the change is accounted for as a change in accounting estimate in accordance with IAS 8. [IAS 16:51]

> Estimates of useful lives require adjustment from time to time in the light of changes in experience and knowledge. These changes may reflect the extension of estimated useful lives due to exceptional maintenance expenditure, curtailment of estimated useful lives due to excessive use, or obsolescence not included in the original esti-mates. When the original estimate of the useful life of an asset is revised, the undepreciated cost (or valuation) should be recognised in profit or loss over the revised remaining useful life, except to the extent that the depreciation expense qualifies for capitalisation into the cost of other assets, such as inventories.

Example 7.3.4

Change in estimate of useful life

An entity purchased an item of plant at a cost of CU1.2 million with an estimated useful life of 10 years.

At the end of Year 3, the asset has a carrying amount of CU840,000. During Year 4, on the basis of experience of similar assets, the item of plant is now estimated to have a remaining useful life of 4 years. The asset is determined not to be impaired. Consequently, the carrying amount of CU840,000 is depreciated over the remaining 4 years at CU210,000 per annum.

Depreciation charges for Years 1 to 7 will be as follows:

	CU'000		CU'000
Year 1	120	Year 5	210
Year 2	120	Year 6	210
Year 3	120	Year 7	210
Year 4	210		

A significant reduction in the estimated useful life of an asset may indicate that the asset has been impaired because the amount that the entity expects to generate from the use of the asset may have been reduced below its carrying amount (see IAS 36:12(f)). In such circumstances, a detailed impairment test should be performed and, if necessary, an impairment loss recognised to reduce the carrying amount of the asset to its recoverable amount (see **chapter A10**). The recoverable amount is then depreciated over the revised estimate of the useful life of the asset.

7.3.5   Fully-depreciated assets

If estimates of the useful lives of items of property, plant and equipment are made realistically, and kept under regular review as required by IAS 16:51, there should be few fully depreciated assets still in use. If fully-depreciated assets are no longer in use, they should either be classified as held for sale in accordance with IFRS 5, or they should be derecognised (see **section 9** below).

7.4   Methods of depreciation

It is necessary to select a method of applying depreciation that results in the carrying amount of the asset being allocated as fairly as possible to the periods expected to benefit from the use of the asset. The method used should be that which reflects most closely the pattern in which the asset's economic benefits are expected to be consumed by the entity. [IAS 16:60]

> See **12.2** below for a discussion of proposed amendments to IAS 16 regarding the selection of depreciation methods.

7.4.1   Alternative methods of apportioning depreciation

There are several methods of apportioning depreciation over the antici-pated useful life of the asset. Those most commonly employed are the straight-line method and the reducing balance (diminishing balance) method. Straight-line depreciation results in a constant charge over the useful life of the asset, because the annual depreciation charge is a fixed percentage of the original cost (or revalued amount). The reducing balance method results in a decreasing charge over the life of the asset, because the annual depreciation charge is a fixed percentage of the opening carrying amount. The straight-line method is the most popular, principally because of its simplicity.

Another useful basis is the unit of production method, which apportions the cost of the asset over its productive life measured in terms of the units produced or machine hours utilised in relation to the total of such units or hours estimated to comprise the productive life of the asset. This method is theoretically superior to the straight-line and reducing balance methods in that it more accurately matches costs with revenue, if the life of the asset can be measured with some precision in terms of its ultimate total output. This method is commonly used in the oil, gas and other extractive industries, where the life of an asset may be expressed in terms of a quantity of output and production assets have no further value once mineral reserves have been extracted.

More generally, alternative methods of depreciation (e.g. decreasing charge depreciation and the sum-of-digits method, or 'rule of 78') are acceptable under IFRSs only if they reflect the pattern in which the asset's economic benefits are expected to be consumed. As a consequence, a method based on tax allowances granted (e.g. the double declining balance method) is not permitted unless it also reflects the expected consumption pattern of the asset.

7.4.2   Increasing charge depreciation

Entities will often construct items of property, plant and equipment that are expected to generate benefits over many years. Customer demand to use the assets may, however, be expected to start slowly and take a number of years to reach an expected 'normal' level. An example of this might be a cable-television distribution network. In such cases, an entity may wish the depreciation charge for the asset to increase gradually to reflect customers' expected phased-in demand.

The appropriateness of such a policy will depend on how the asset's benefits are being consumed. IAS 16:60 requires that depreciation reflect the pattern in which the asset's economic benefits are consumed by the entity. Those benefits should be viewed in terms of physical capacity or physical output (using up physical capability, wear and tear, technical obsolescence) and legal limits on the physical use of the asset (such as by a lease).

While an 'increasing charge' or 'sinking fund' method of calculating depreciation is not appropriate under IAS 16, a unit of production method of calculating depreciation is appropriate if it reflects the pattern of benefit consumption. This method is more likely to be justified for a physical asset, reflecting wear and tear, than for an intangible asset (see chapter A9).

The depreciation method adopted should be based on the economic depreciation of the asset, rather than the return from the asset (e.g. the annuity method). Therefore, consideration of the time value of money in determining the depreciation method is not appropriate.

7.4.3   *Change in depreciation method*

IAS 16 requires that the depreciation method applied to an item of property, plant and equipment should be reviewed at least at the end of each financial year. Except when there is a change in the expected pattern of consumption of economic benefits embodied in the asset, the depreciation method adopted should be applied consistently from period to period. If there has been a significant change in the expected pattern of consumption of benefits, the depreciation method is changed to reflect the changed pattern. The change is accounted for as a change in accounting estimate in accordance with IAS 8 *Accounting Policies, Changes in Accounting Estimates and Errors*. [IAS 16:61]

Therefore, a change from one method of recognising depreciation to another does not constitute a change in accounting policy but is accounted for as a change in accounting estimate in accordance with IAS 8. The carrying amount of the asset is written off using the new method over the remaining useful life, commencing with the period in which the change takes place. Separate disclosure of the impact of the change is required if the change has a material effect in the current period or is expected to have a material effect in subsequent periods.

Example 7.4.3

Change in depreciation method

An entity acquired an asset 3 years ago at a cost of CU5 million. The depreciation method adopted for the asset was 10 per cent reducing balance.

At the end of Year 3, the carrying amount of the asset is CU3,645,000. The entity estimates that the remaining useful life of the asset is 8 years and determines to adopt straight-line depreciation from that date so as to reflect better the revised estimated pattern of recovery of economic benefits.

Depreciation charges for years 1 to 11 will be as follows:

	CU'000		CU'000
Year 1	500	Year 7	456
Year 2	450	Year 8	456
Year 3	405	Year 9	455
Year 4	456	Year 10	455
Year 5	456	Year 11	455
Year 6	456		

7.5   Depreciation of particular classes of asset

7.5.1   Freehold land

Freehold land that is not subject to depletion (e.g. by the extraction of minerals) does not have a limited useful life and, therefore, should not be depreciated. In consequence, it is necessary, when freehold property is purchased, to allocate the purchase consideration between the value of the land and that of the buildings. Similarly, any revaluations of freehold property should distinguish between land and buildings.

When the cost of site dismantlement, removal and restoration is included in the cost of land, that portion of the land asset is depreciated over the period of benefits obtained by incurring those costs. In some cases, the land itself may have a limited useful life, in which case it is depreciated in a manner that reflects the benefits to be derived from it. [IAS 16:59]

When the value of freehold land is adversely affected by long-term environmental factors, an impairment loss should be recognised to reflect any decline in its estimated recoverable amount below its carrying amount.

7.5.2   Freehold buildings

Buildings have limited useful economic lives and are no different from other depreciable assets. Although their estimated useful lives are usually significantly longer than other items of property, plant and equipment, they should nevertheless be depreciated in a similar manner, generally using the straight-line method. IAS 16 emphasises that an increase in the value of the land on which a building stands does not affect the determination of the useful life of the building. [IAS 16:58] An exception to the general requirement to depreciate buildings is allowed for those properties that qualify as investment properties and that are accounted for using the fair value model (see **chapter A8** for details).

> IAS 16 does not grant an exemption in respect of historic buildings: the fact that they may have been built centuries earlier, and may be expected to last for centuries more, does not exempt them from depreciation. It is possible that the useful life of such a building may be very long. Also, when an entity intends to sell such a building in due course, rather than use it for the remainder of its physical life, it is possible that the residual value may be relatively high. Both of these factors may lead to the depreciation recognised being relatively small. Care should be taken to identify any components (e.g. roofs)

that may require replacement at periodic intervals, which need to be depreciated over a shorter period (see **7.1**).

7.5.3   *Plant and machinery, tools and equipment, ships, vehicles etc.*

Depreciation recognised is, in general, computed using the straight-line method, but the reducing balance and unit of production methods are also suitable in appropriate circumstances. Some small assets with very short useful lives, such as loose tools, jigs and patterns may, however, be dealt with more satisfactorily in aggregate, as discussed at **3.4**.

7.5.4   *Leased assets*

Tangible assets that are held under finance leases are required by IAS 17 *Leases* to be depreciated. That Standard requires that the depreciation policy adopted for depreciable leased assets should be consistent with that for similar assets that are owned, and that the depreciation recognised should be calculated in accordance with the principles of IAS 16, as discussed throughout this section. [IAS 17:27]

IAS 17 also stipulates that, if there is reasonable certainty that the lessee will obtain ownership by the end of the lease term, the period of expected use is the useful life of the asset; otherwise, the asset is to be depreciated over the shorter of the lease term and its useful life. [IAS 17:28]

IAS 16:56(d) states that the expiry dates of related leases should be taken into account in determining the useful life of a depreciable asset. The question arises as to whether a renewal option in a lease contract be considered in estimating the useful life of leasehold improvements.

The renewal period(s) should be taken into account if, at the inception of the lease, it is 'reasonably certain' that the lessee will exercise the renewal option. For property acquired by a lessee under a finance lease, IAS 17:27 states that "if there is no reasonable certainty that the lessee will obtain ownership by the end of the lease term, the asset shall be fully depreciated over the shorter of the lease term and its useful life". IAS 17:4 defines lease term to include "any further terms for which the lessee has the option to continue to lease the asset, with or without further payment, when at the inception of the lease it is reasonably certain that the lessee will exercise the option". This 'reasonable certainty of renewal' test should be applied at the commencement of the lease both in accounting for the lease itself and in assessing the depreciable life of leasehold improvements relating to both finance and operating leases. In particular, therefore, the assumption regarding the lease term should be applied consistently for the lease and for any leasehold improvements.

7.5.5   Stand-by equipment

The useful life of stand-by equipment should be determined by the useful life of the equipment for which it serves as a back-up. In the example cited at **3.2** above (entity has installed two turbines), one turbine produces energy for the plant, and the other is used as a back-up in case the first turbine fails or is otherwise rendered out of service. The stand-by equipment should be depreciated from the date it is made available for use (i.e. when it is in the location and condition necessary for it to be capable of operating in the manner intended by management) over the shorter of the life of the turbine and the life of the plant of which the turbine is part (assuming the turbine cannot be removed and used in another plant). Note that, if the residual value of the stand-by turbine is estimated to be significantly higher than the residual value of the primary turbine (because it is expected to be in better condition at the end of the asset's useful life due to lower usage), this will affect the depreciation charged over that useful life.

7.5.6   Spare parts

In contrast to the depreciation of stand-by equipment, the useful life of spare parts classified as property, plant and equipment commences when they are put into use, rather than when they are acquired.

Example 7.5.6

Depreciation of spare parts classified as property, plant and equipment

An entity buys five new machines for use in its production facility. Simultaneously, it purchases a spare motor to be used as a replacement if a motor on one of the five machines breaks. The motor will be used in the production of goods and, once brought into service, will be operated during more than one period. It is therefore classified as property, plant and equipment.

The motor does not qualify as stand-by equipment because it will not be ready for use until it is installed. Therefore, the useful life of the motor commences when it is available for use within the machine rather than when it is acquired. It should be depreciated over the period starting when it is brought into service and continuing over the shorter of its useful life and the remaining expected useful life of the asset to which it relates. If the asset to which it relates will be replaced at the end of its useful life and the motor is expected to be used or usable for the replacement asset, a longer depreciation period may be appropriate. During the period before the motor is available for service, any reduction in value should be reflected as an impairment loss under IAS 36 at the time impairment is indicated.

---

8   Impairment

An entity should refer to the requirements of IAS 36 *Impairment of Assets* to determine whether an item of property, plant and equipment is impaired. IAS 36 explains how an entity reviews the carrying amount of its assets, how it determines the recoverable amount of an asset, and when it recognises or reverses an impairment loss (see **chapter A10**). [IAS 16:63]

8.1   Compensation for impairment or loss

When an asset is impaired, lost or given up, any compensation from third parties is included in profit or loss when the compensation becomes receivable. [IAS 16:65]

Examples of such circumstances include:

- reimbursements by insurance companies after the impairment or loss of items of property, plant and equipment (e.g. due to natural disasters, theft etc.);

- indemnities by governments for items of property, plant and equipment that are expropriated (e.g. compulsory purchase of land to be used for public purposes);

- compensation related to the involuntary conversion of items of property, plant and equipment (e.g. relocation of facilities from a designated urban area to a non-urban area in accordance with government land policy); and

- physical replacement in whole or in part of an impaired or lost asset.

The Standard emphasises that impairments or losses of items of property, plant and equipment, related claims for or payments of compensation from third parties, and any subsequent purchase or construction of replacement assets are separate economic events and should be accounted for as such. The three economic events should be accounted for separately as follows:
[IAS 16:66]

- in respect of impairment or loss:

  - impairments of items of property, plant and equipment should be recognised in accordance with IAS 36; and

  - derecognition of items of property, plant and equipment retired or disposed of should be determined in accordance with IAS 16;

- compensation from third parties for items of property, plant and equipment that were impaired, lost or given up should be included in determining profit or loss when it becomes receivable; and

- the cost of items of property, plant and equipment restored, purchased or constructed as replacements should be determined in accordance with IAS 16.

9 Derecognition

IAS 16 requires that the carrying amount of an item of property, plant and equipment should be derecognised:
[IAS 16:67]

- on disposal; or

- when no future economic benefits are expected from its use or disposal.

Example 9

Disposal of property, plant and equipment

An entity enters into a transaction whereby it sells an item of property, plant and equipment to a third party. It concurrently enters into a contract with the third party to buy all of the actual output of the asset over its remaining

---

useful life at a fixed per-unit price, but in total not less than a minimum payment equal to the value of 90 per cent of the expected output. The minimum payment must be made even if the actual output is below expectation.

Should the entity recognise the sale of the asset by removing it from its statement of financial position?

In this situation, the entity should consider the requirements of IFRIC 4 *Determining Whether an Arrangement Contains a Lease* (see **2.1** in **chapter A17**). If it is concluded that the supply arrangement involves a finance lease, the requirements of IAS 17 *Leases* regarding sale and leaseback transactions apply, and the entity will still recognise the asset in its statement of financial position after title has been transferred to the third party.

Except when IAS 17 *Leases* requires otherwise in the circumstances of a sale and leaseback, the gain or loss arising on the derecognition of an item of property, plant and equipment should be included in profit or loss when the amount is derecognised. [IAS 16:68]

On the derecognition of an item of property, plant and equipment, the gain or loss arising is determined as the difference between the net disposal proceeds, if any, and the carrying amount of the item. [IAS 16:71] As discussed at **6.8.4** above, when a revalued asset is disposed of, any credit balance on the revaluation reserve attributable to that asset may be transferred directly to retained earnings, though such a transfer is not mandatory, but must not be reflected in profit or loss.

The disposal consideration received is measured at its fair value. If payment is deferred beyond normal credit terms, the consideration received is recognised initially at the cash price equivalent. The difference between the nominal amount of the consideration and the cash price equivalent is recognised as interest income on an effective yield basis, in accordance with IAS 18 *Revenue*. [IAS 16:72]

IAS 16 specifically prohibits the classification as revenue of gains arising on the derecognition of property, plant and equipment (but see **9.2** below). [IAS 16:68] The Standard does, however, require that the date of disposal of an item of property, plant and equipment be determined using the criteria for recognising revenue from the sale of goods, as set out in IAS 18 (see **chapter A14**). [IAS 16:69]

9.1   Application of IFRS 5 to 'in-period' disposals of assets

It is necessary to consider the requirements of IFRS 5 *Non-current Assets Held for Sale and Discontinued Operations* not only for items meeting the criteria for classification as held for sale at the end of the reporting period, but also for all 'in-period' disposals, including assets sold during the reporting period that were not classified as held for sale at the previous reporting date.

The following example illustrates how the requirements of IFRS 5 are applied to an asset that was not classified as held for sale at the previous reporting date.

Example 9.1

Application of IFRS 5 to in-period disposals of assets

Entity R prepares its financial statements to 31 December and it does not prepare interim financial reports. At 31 December 20X1, Entity R carried a property asset in its statement of financial position at its revalued amount of CU2 million in accordance with IAS 16. Depreciation is CU60,000 per year. In April 20X2, management decides to sell the property and it is advertised for sale. By 30 April 20X2, the sale is considered to be highly probable. At that date, the asset's fair value is CU2.6 million and its value in use is CU2.8 million. Costs of disposal of the asset are estimated at CU100,000. On 15 June 20X2, the property is sold for CU2.75 million.

Is Entity R required to apply IFRS 5 to the disposal of the property?

Yes. When the effect is material, the requirements of IFRS 5 should be applied to in-period disposals of assets.

In the circumstances described, the following steps are required.

- Entity R should determine the date at which the IFRS 5 criteria for classification as held for sale are met (assume the date is determined to be 30 April 20X2 in this case).

- Entity R should depreciate the property until the date of reclassification as held for sale. Accordingly, the depreciation charge is CU60,000 × 4/12 = CU20,000.

- The property should be revalued to its fair value at that date of CU2.6 million if the difference between the property's carrying amount at that date and its fair value is material (see **4.2** in **chapter A20**). The revaluation increase should be recognised in other comprehensive income in accordance with IAS 16.

- Entity R should consider whether the property is impaired by comparing its carrying amount (fair value) with its recoverable amount (higher of value in use and fair value less costs of disposal). In the above example, no impairment loss is recognised because value in use of CU2.8 million is higher than fair value less costs of disposal of CU2.5 million. If any impairment loss were identified at this point, it would be accounted for as a revaluation decrease under IAS 16.

- The property should be reclassified as held for sale and remeasured to fair value less costs to sell (CU2.5 million). Because, in this example, the property is already carried at fair value, the requirement to deduct costs to sell results in the immediate recognition of a loss of CU100,000. In accordance with IFRS 5, this write down to fair value less costs to sell should be recognised in profit or loss.

- When the property is disposed of on 15 June 20X2, a profit on disposal of CU150,000 is recognised (net proceeds of CU2.65 million less carrying amount of CU2.5 million). Any remaining revaluation reserve relating to the property is not recognised in profit or loss, but it may be transferred to retained earnings in accordance with IAS 16.

The application of IFRS 5 in the above example affects the amounts reported in profit or loss, because the valuation movement prior to the date of reclassification (CU620,000) is recognised in other comprehensive income and is not subsequently reclassified to profit or loss. In addition to the depreciation expense of CU20,000, a net gain is recognised of CU50,000 in profit or loss which is comprised of the fair value movement after reclassification (CU150,000) less costs of disposal (CU100,000). If IFRS 5 had not been applied, in addition to the depreciation expense of CU27,500 (CU60,000 × 5.5/12), the net gain recognised in profit or loss would have been CU677,500 (net proceeds of CU2.65 million less the carrying amount at 15 June 20X2 of CU1,972,500).

For assets measured under IAS 16's cost model, the application will not affect the net amount reported in profit or loss for the period. However, it will affect the amounts disclosed under IFRS 5:41(c) (see **7.3** in **chapter A20**) and, when disclosed separately, amounts reported for gains or losses arising on the disposal of property, plant and equipment (see **5.4.1** in **chapter A4**).

9.2   Sales of property, plant and equipment held for rental

When an entity, in the course of its ordinary activities, routinely sells items that it has held for rental to others, it transfers those assets to inventories at their carrying amount when they cease to be rented and become held for sale. Sale proceeds from such assets are recognised as revenue in accordance with IAS 18. When such assets are transferred to inventories, IFRS 5 does not apply to them. [IAS 16:68A]

10   IFRIC 20 *Stripping Costs in the Production Phase of a Surface Mine*

IFRIC 20 *Stripping Costs in the Production Phase of a Surface Mine* aims to address diversity in practice in the accounting for costs of removing waste material to gain access to mineral ore deposits ('stripping activity') incurred during the production phase of a surface mine ('production stripping costs'). The Interpretation concludes that costs related to stripping activity should be recognised as an asset if specified criteria are met.

IFRIC 20 applies to waste removal costs that are incurred in surface mining activity during the production phase of a mine. [IFRIC 20:6] It does not apply to waste removal costs during the development phase of the mine, i.e. before production begins; but it acknowledges that such costs are usually capitalised as part of the depreciable cost of building, developing and constructing the mine. [IFRIC 20:2]

Material removed during stripping activity in the production phase of the mine will often be a combination of mineral ore and waste. The ratio of mineral ore to waste can range from uneconomic low grade to profitable high grade. The material removed may result in some useable mineral ore that can be used to produce inventory. In addition, the removal of material may also provide improved access to deeper levels of mineral ore deposits that have a higher ratio of mineral ore to waste. Therefore, stripping activity may result in two benefits: useable mineral ore for the production of inventory and improved access to the mineral ore body that will be mined in future periods. [IFRIC 20:4] IFRIC 20 addresses the accounting for these two benefits.

10.1   Recognition of production stripping costs as an asset

To the extent that the benefit from the stripping activity relates to useable mineral ore for the production of inventory, the costs of the stripping activity should be accounted for in accordance with the principles of IAS 2 *Inventories* (see **chapter A11**). [IFRIC 20:8]

To the extent that the benefit from the stripping activity relates to improved access to the mineral ore body, the costs of the stripping activity should be recognised as a non-current asset (referred to as the 'stripping activity asset'), if, and only if, all of the following criteria are met: [IFRIC 20:9]

- it is probable that the future economic benefit (improved access to the ore body) associated with the stripping activity will flow to the entity;

- the entity can identify the component of the ore body for which access has been improved; and

- the costs relating to the stripping activity associated with that component can be measured reliably.

> Therefore, a stripping activity asset should only be recognised if the definition of an asset in the *Conceptual Framework for Financial Reporting* is met and the component of the ore body for which access is improved can be specifically identified. Otherwise, the costs of the stripping activity should be expensed as incurred. [IFRIC 20:BC7]

The stripping activity asset should be accounted for as an addition to, or an enhancement of, an existing asset, i.e. it should be accounted for as part of an existing asset. [IFRIC 20:10] IFRIC 20:BC10 states that the stripping activity asset may add to or improve a range of existing assets (e.g. the mine property (land), the mineral deposit itself, an intangible right to extract the ore, or an asset that originated in the mine development phase). Classification of the stripping activity asset as a tangible or an intangible asset will be determined consistent with the nature of the existing asset to which it relates. [IFRIC 20:11]

10.2   Initial measurement of the stripping activity asset

The stripping activity asset should be measured initially at cost, being the accumulated costs directly incurred in performing the stripping activity that improves access to the identified component of the ore body, plus an allocation of directly attributable overhead costs. However, costs associated with incidental operations that take place at the same time as the stripping activity but that are not necessary for the stripping activity to continue as planned should not be included in the cost of the stripping activity asset. [IFRIC 20:12]

In practice, it may be difficult to identify separately the costs associated with any inventory produced (i.e. useable mineral ore for the production of inventory) and the stripping activity asset (i.e. improved access to the specified component of the ore body). When the costs of the stripping activity asset and the inventory produced are not separately identifiable, a relevant production measure should be used as the basis to allocate the production stripping costs between the inventory produced and the stripping activity asset. The production measure should be calculated for the identified component of the ore body and used as a benchmark to identify the extent to which activity has taken place beyond what would otherwise be expected for the inventory production in the period, and that therefore may have created future access benefit (i.e. the stripping activity asset). [IFRIC 20:13 & BC16] Examples of production measures include: [IFRIC 20:13]

- cost of inventory produced compared with expected cost;

- volume of waste extracted compared with expected volume, for a given volume of ore production; and

- mineral content of the ore extracted compared with expected mineral content to be extracted, for a given quantity of ore produced.

10.3 Subsequent measurement of the stripping activity asset

After initial recognition, the stripping activity asset should be measured at cost or revalued amount, less depreciation or amortisation and less impairment losses in the same way as the existing asset of which it is a part. [IFRIC 20:14]

The stripping activity asset should be depreciated or amortised on a systematic basis over the expected useful life of the identified component of the ore body to which access is improved as a result of the stripping activity. [IFRIC 20:15] The expected useful life of the identified component of the ore body to which the stripping activity asset relates will usually differ from the expected useful life of the mine itself and the related life-of-mine assets, unless the stripping activity improves access to the entire remaining ore body. This might be the case, for example, towards the end of the mine's useful life when the identified component represents the final part of the ore body to be extracted. [IFRIC 20:16]

An entity should use the units of production method of depreciation, unless another method is more appropriate. [IFRIC 20:15]

10.4 Effective date and transition

IFRIC 20 is effective for periods beginning on or after 1 January 2013, with earlier application permitted. If an entity applies the Interpretation for an annual period beginning before 1 January 2013, it should disclose that fact. [IFRIC 20:A1]

An entity should apply the accounting required by IFRIC 20 to production stripping costs incurred on or after the beginning of the earliest period presented. [IFRIC 20:A2]

For any previously recognised asset balances as at the beginning of the earliest period presented which resulted from production stripping activity in previous periods (the 'predecessor stripping assets'), an entity should determine whether there is an identifiable component of the ore body with which that asset can be associated.

If there is an identifiable component of the ore body, the predecessor stripping asset as at the beginning of the earliest period presented should be reclassified as a part of the existing asset to which the stripping activity related. Each such predecessor stripping asset should be depreciated or amortised over the remaining useful life of the identified component of the ore body to which it relates. [IFRIC 20:A3]

If there is no identifiable component of the ore body to which a predecessor stripping asset relates, the asset should be derecognised with a corresponding entry to opening retained earnings at the beginning of the earliest period presented. [IFRIC 20:A4]

11   Presentation and disclosure

11.1   Presentation

IAS 1 *Presentation of Financial Statements* requires that, if material, the aggregate carrying amount of the entity's property, plant and equipment should be presented in the statement of financial position. [IAS 1:54(a)]

11.2   Disclosure

11.2.1   General

In respect of each class of property, plant and equipment, an entity is required to disclose:
[IAS 16:73]

- the measurement bases (i.e. cost or valuation) used for determining the gross carrying amount;

- the depreciation methods used;

- the useful lives or the depreciation rates used; and

- the gross carrying amount and the accumulated depreciation (aggregated with accumulated impairment losses) at the beginning and end of the period.

An entity is also required to provide a reconciliation of the carrying amount at the beginning and end of the period, in respect of each class of property, plant and equipment, showing:
[IAS 16:73(e)]

- additions;

- assets classified as held for sale, or included as a disposal group classified as held for sale in accordance with IFRS 5 *Non-current Assets held for Sale and Discontinued Operations*, and other disposals;

- acquisitions through business combinations;

- increases or decreases resulting from revaluations and from impairment losses recognised or reversed in other comprehensive income;

- impairment losses recognised in profit or loss during the period;

- impairment losses reversed in profit or loss during the period;

- depreciation;

- the net exchange differences arising on the translation of the financial statements from the functional currency into a different presentation currency, including the translation of a foreign operation into the presentation currency of the reporting entity; and

- other changes.

The financial statements are also required to disclose:
[IAS 16:74]

- the existence and amounts of restrictions on title, and property, plant and equipment pledged as security for liabilities;

- the amount of expenditures recognised in the carrying amount of an item of property, plant and equipment in the course of its construction;

- the amount of contractual commitments for the acquisition of property, plant and equipment; and

- if not disclosed separately in the statement of comprehensive income, the amount of compensation from third parties for items of property, plant and equipment that were impaired, lost or given up that is included in profit or loss.

Although the drafting is a little unclear in the Standard, it appears that the second bullet above requires disclosure of the cost of assets that are still in the course of construction at the end of the reporting period (i.e. rather than those that were in the course of construction when the costs were incurred). The drafting is also unclear whether it is the costs incurred in the year or the total cumulative costs incurred on such assets which should be disclosed, although the latter inter-pretation appears more logical.

Disclosures may also be required by IAS 8 *Accounting Policies, Changes in Accounting Estimates and Errors* in respect of changes in accounting esti-mates for residual values, useful lives, depreciation methods or provisions for dismantling, removing or restoring assets (see **chapter A5**), or by IAS 36 *Impairment of Assets* (see **chapter A10**). [IAS 16:76 & 78]

11.2.2   *Items stated at revalued amounts*

In respect of items of property, plant and equipment stated at revalued amounts, the entity is required to disclose:
[IAS 16:77]

(a)   the effective date of the revaluation;

(b)   whether an independent valuer was involved;

(c)   the methods and significant assumptions applied in estimating the items' fair values (*);

(d)   the extent to which the items' fair values were determined directly by reference to observable prices in an active market or recent market transactions on arm's length terms or were estimated using other valuation techniques (*);

(e)   for each revalued class of property, plant and equipment, the carry-ing amount that would have been recognised had the assets been carried under the cost model; and

(f)   the revaluation surplus, indicating the movement for the period and any restrictions on the distribution of the balance to shareholders.

* Entities that have adopted IFRS 13 are not required to provide disclosures under IAS 16:77(c) and (d), but will instead provide additional disclosures as required by IFRS 13 (see **chapter A6**).

The disclosures required under IAS 16:77(f) could be made in the reserves note rather than the property, plant and equipment note.

11.2.3   Additional recommended disclosures

IAS 16:79 also encourages, but does not require, the disclosure of the following information:

- the carrying amount of temporarily idle property, plant and equipment;

- the gross carrying amount of any fully depreciated property, plant and equipment that is still in use;

- the carrying amount of property, plant and equipment retired from active use and not classified as held for sale in accordance with IFRS 5; and

- when the cost model is used, the fair value of property, plant and equipment when this is materially different from the carrying amount.

The IFRIC (now called the IFRS Interpretations Committee) was asked to consider to what extent disclosures are required for property, plant and equipment that is temporarily idle and for assets under construction when additional construction has been postponed.

Although the item was not taken onto the IFRIC agenda, the Committee did note that IAS 16:74(b) requires an entity to disclose the amount of expenditures recognised in the carrying amount of an item of property, plant and equipment in the course of its construction. IAS 16:79(a) encourages an entity to disclose the amount of property, plant and equipment that is temporarily idle. IAS 1:112(c) requires an entity to provide in the notes to the financial statements information that is not presented elsewhere in the financial statements but is relevant to an understanding of any of the financial statements.

The IFRIC concluded that, in combination, the requirements of IAS 16 and IAS 1 lead to an expectation that, when the amount of idle assets or postponed construction projects becomes significant, such amounts will be separately disclosed.

The conclusions above were set out in the May 2009 edition of *IFRIC Update*.

12   Future developments

12.1   Annual Improvements 2010–2012 Cycle

In May 2012, the IASB issued an exposure draft (ED/2012/1 *Annual Improvements to IFRSs: 2010–2012 Cycle*) proposing changes to a number of Standards as part of its Annual Improvements project. Amendments are proposed for IAS 16 to clarify that, when an item of property, plant and equipment is revalued, accumulated depreciation should be computed as the difference between the gross and the net carrying amounts of the revalued asset, after restating the gross carrying amount in a manner consistent with the revaluation of the net carrying amount (see **6.4** above). The amendments are proposed to address divergent views in practice on how to calculate accumulated depreciation for a revalued asset when the residual value, the useful life or the depreciation method has been re-estimated prior to revaluation.

Finalised amendments are expected in the fourth quarter of 2013.

12.2   Acceptable methods of depreciation

In December 2012, the IASB issued an exposure draft (ED/2012/5 *Clarification of Acceptable Methods of Depreciation and Amortisation* (*Proposed Amendments to IAS 16 and IAS 38*)). The exposure draft proposes to amend IAS 16 (and IAS 38 *Intangible Assets*) to the effect that when selecting a depreciation (or an amortisation) rate, a revenue-based method should not be used, because such methods reflect a pattern of economic benefits being generated from the asset, rather than the expected pattern of consumption of the future economic benefits embodied in the asset. The proposed amendments also provide some further guidance on the application of the diminishing balance method.

The deadline for comments on these proposals was 2 April 2013.

A8   Investment property

Contents

1 Introduction

IAS 40 *Investment Property* prescribes the accounting treatment and disclosure requirements for investment property, which is property held to earn rentals, or for capital appreciation, or both.

The Standard was most recently amended in May 2011.

2 Scope

IAS 40 is to be applied in the recognition, measurement and disclosure of 'investment property' (see **2.1** below). [IAS 40:2]

The Standard also deals with the measurement in the lessee's financial statements of investment property interests held under a lease accounted for as a finance lease, and with the measurement in a lessor's financial statements of investment property leased out under an operating lease. The more general requirements regarding the classification and measurement of leased investment property are not dealt with in IAS 40 but fall within the general requirements of IAS 17 *Leases*. In particular, the following matters are dealt with in IAS 17 rather than in IAS 40:
[IAS 40:3]

- classification of leases as finance leases or operating leases;

- recognition of lease income from investment property;

- measurement in a lessee's financial statements of property interests held under a lease accounted for as an operating lease (but see **2.2**);

- measurement in a lessor's financial statements of its net investment in a finance lease;

- accounting for sale and leaseback transactions; and

- disclosures regarding finance leases and operating leases.

Also specifically excluded from the scope of IAS 40 are:
[IAS 40:4]

- biological assets related to agricultural activity (see the discussion of IAS 41 *Agriculture* in **chapter A38**); and

- mineral rights and mineral reserves such as oil, natural gas, and similar non-regenerative resources.

2.1   Investment property – definition

Investment property is defined in IAS 40 as follows.
[IAS 40:5]

> "Investment property is property (land or a building – or part of a building – or both) held (by the owner or by the lessee under a finance lease) to earn rentals or for capital appreciation or both, rather than for:
>
> (a)   use in the production or supply of goods or services or for administrative purposes; or
>
> (b)   sale in the ordinary course of business."

Included within this definition are:
[IAS 40:8]

- land held for long-term capital appreciation, and not for short-term sale in the ordinary course of business;

- land held for a currently undetermined future use. If an entity has not decided whether land will be used for owner-occupation or for short-term sale in the ordinary course of business, it should be regarded as held for capital appreciation;

- a building owned or held under a finance lease by an entity and leased out under operating lease(s);

- a vacant building that is being held to be leased out under an operating lease (or leases); and

- property that is being constructed or developed for future use as investment property.

Examples of items that are *not* investment property include:
[IAS 40:9]

- property that is being held for sale in the ordinary course of business, or that is under construction or development for such sale (within the scope of IAS 2 *Inventories*, see **chapter A11**). This means that properties acquired specifically for the purpose of subsequent disposal in the near future, or for development and resale, are excluded from the scope of IAS 40;

- property being constructed or developed on behalf of third parties (within the scope of IAS 11 *Construction Contracts*, see **chapter A34**);

- owner-occupied property, which includes property held for future development and subsequent use as owner-occupied property, property held for future use as owner-occupied property, employee-occupied property (whether or not the employees pay rent at market rates) and owner-occupied property awaiting disposal; and

- property leased to another entity under a finance lease.

The Standard acknowledges that judgement is often required to determine whether a property qualifies as an investment property and requires entities to develop criteria to enable them to make that determination in a consistent manner. Disclosure of such criteria is required when classification is difficult (see **8.2**). [IAS 40:14]

2.2   Property held under an operating lease

A property interest that is held by a lessee under an operating lease may be classified and accounted for as an investment property if, and only if, the property would otherwise meet the definition of an investment property and the lessee uses IAS 40's fair value model (see **5.2**) for the asset recognised. It is important to note that:
[IAS 40:6]

- this is an option (a 'classification alternative'). Entities may elect whether they wish to classify such interests as investment property;

- the classification alternative is available on a property-by-property basis;

- the classification alternative is not available for assets not accounted for using the fair value model;

- once this classification alternative is selected for one property interest held under an operating lease, all property classified as investment property must be accounted for using the fair value model; and

- property interests accounted for under the classification alternative are considered to be part of the entity's investment property for the purposes of IAS 40's disclosure requirements (see **8.2**).

The option discussed above to classify certain property interests under operating leases as investment property is intended to facilitate the classification of assets such as land held under long-term operating leases as investment property, provided that the general criteria for such classification are met. This is particularly relevant in jurisdictions such as Hong Kong and the United Kingdom where interests in property are commonly – or, in the former case, exclusively – held under long-term lease arrangements.

In contrast to the option available in relation to property held under an operating lease under IAS 40:6 (see above), IAS 40:8 *requires* that property held under a finance lease be treated as investment property, provided that the property otherwise meets the definition of an investment property. IAS 40:8 also applies to property held under a lease that is classified as a finance lease because the lease payments cannot be allocated reliably between the land and buildings elements (see **5.2.1** in **chapter A17**).

The detailed requirements when property or property interests held under leases are classified as investment property are considered further at **4.3** below.

Example 2.2

Classification – lease of an investment property

Company A (as lessee) leases a property which meets the definition of an investment property.

Company A is unable to obtain a reliable allocation between the land element and the buildings elements of the leased property. Therefore, in accordance with IAS 17:16, the entire lease is classified as a finance lease (it is *not* clear that both elements are operating leases, otherwise the entire lease would be classified as an operating lease).

The requirement in IAS 40:6 (also referred to in IAS 17:19) to adopt the fair value model applies when an entity chooses to account for a property interest held under an operating lease as an investment property. Because, in the circumstances described, Company A classifies the entire lease as a finance lease, IAS 40 permits a choice between the cost model and the fair value model. This option is available for finance leases (as determined by IAS 17) irrespective of whether there may be an 'operating lease' component for land which cannot be reliably determined.

2.3   Property held for more than one purpose

In circumstances when property is held partly for capital appreciation and/or rentals, and partly for the production of goods or services or administrative purposes, the two parts are accounted for separately if they could be sold, or leased out under a finance lease, separately. If they could not be sold (or leased out under a finance lease) separately, the property is accounted for as an investment property only if an insignificant portion is held for use in the production or supply of goods or services or for administrative purposes. [IAS 40:10]

The Standard does not include any guidance as to what constitutes an 'insignificant' portion for this purpose. This is a deliberate omission – the Basis for Conclusions on IAS 40 explains that quantitative guidance has not been provided because the Board concluded that such guidance could lead to arbitrary distinctions.

2.4 Ancillary services

If an entity provides ancillary services to the occupants of its property, the property is accounted for as investment property provided that the services are an 'insignificant' portion of the arrangement. [IAS 40:11]

Example 2.4A

Services provided by the owner of an office building

The owner of an office building provides cleaning services for the lessees of the building and these services are 'insignificant' in the context of the total arrangement. Therefore, the building is classified and accounted for as an investment property.

As indicated in the above example, it would be unusual for cleaning services to be so material that they would prevent a property from being classified as an investment property. A similar conclusion is likely for security and maintenance services. At the other extreme, some entities rent out fully furnished offices including a whole range of services such as IT systems and secretarial services. Such arrangements are in the nature of the rendering of a service rather than property investment and the property would be classified as owner-occupied and accounted for under IAS 16 *Property, Plant and Equipment*. However, there are many instances in between these extremes for which the appropriate classification can only be determined based on a detailed assessment of the arrangements and whether or not the services provided are judged to be 'insignificant'.

Example 2.4B

Hotel property as investment property

A hotel operator owns a significant number of buildings. The hotel operator seeks to maximise revenue by selling room occupancy.

Is it acceptable for the hotel operator to classify these buildings as investment properties?

> The property is for use by the hotel operator in the normal course of business and, therefore, is not investment property. IAS 40:12 cites the direct provision of services to hotel guests as services that will generally be considered to be 'significant'. Although the hotel operator may hold the buildings for long-term appreciation, that is not the principal reason for holding them.

The determination as to whether ancillary services are significant (thus excluding the property from the scope of IAS 40) requires the exercise of judgement. The Standard considers the case of hotels and acknowledges the variety of arrangements that may exist. For example, the owner of a hotel property may transfer some responsibilities to third parties under a management contract. The terms of such contracts may vary widely. The owner's role may be restricted to that of a passive investor, in which case the property would be more likely to qualify as investment property. At the other extreme, the contract may simply result in the outsourcing of some day-to-day responsibilities, while the owner retains significant exposure to variations in the cash flows generated by the operation of the hotel. In the latter case, the contract has little effect on the substance of the owner's interest and the property is likely to be classified as owner-managed. [IAS 40:13]

2.5   Property leased to other group members

If an entity owns a property that is leased to, and occupied by, another group member (e.g. a parent or another subsidiary), the property is not recognised as an investment property in the consolidated financial statements because it will be treated as owner-occupied from the perspective of the group. However, from an individual-entity perspective, the property is treated as an investment property if it meets the requirements of IAS 40:5. [IAS 40:15]

2.6   Property accepted as loan settlement

> **Example 2.6**
>
> **Property accepted as loan settlement**
>
> Entity A, a financial institution, provides mortgage loans to individuals and corporate entities to finance the acquisition of properties. The terms of these mortgage loans require the property to be pledged as collateral for the loan. If a counterparty defaults under the terms of a mortgage loan and is no longer entitled to redeem the collateral, Entity A accepts the property as settlement of the loan receivable. The former owner ceases to have any rights over the property or over the income that it generates. The derecognition

criteria in paragraph 17 of IAS 39 *Financial Instruments: Recognition and Measurement* are met and Entity A derecognises the loan receivable. In accordance with IAS 39:37, Entity A recognises the property as its asset, initially measured at fair value. Under local regulations, Entity A is required to sell the asset within two years.

Should Entity A classify the property as an investment property in accordance with IAS 40 or as inventories in accordance with IAS 2? How should Entity A account for any rental income received during the period for which it holds the asset?

The appropriate classification of the property as investment property or inventories depends on management's intent. If management intends to hold the property to earn rentals or for capital appreciation (or both), the property would meet the definition of an investment property and should be accounted for under IAS 40. In contrast, if the property is being actively marketed for sale, but it is not sold within a short timeframe (e.g. because of seasonal fluctuations in the property market), such activity would indicate that Entity A views the property as a form of settlement of amounts due under the defaulted mortgage loan and that it is an asset acquired and held for sale in the ordinary course of business. In such circumstances, the property should be accounted for as inventories under IAS 2.

Regardless of the classification of the property as investment property or inventories, any rentals received should be recognised as rental income in profit or loss.

2.7 Group of assets leased under a single operating lease

Example 2.7

Group of assets leased under a single operating lease

IAS 40:5 defines investment property as "property (land or a building – or part of a building – or both) held (by the owner or by the lessee under a finance lease) to earn rentals or for capital appreciation or both".

IAS 40:50 states (see **5.2.1** and **5.2.2.2**) that "[i]n determining the carrying amount of investment property under the fair value model, an entity does not double-count assets or liabilities that are recognised as separate assets or liabilities. For example:

a.   equipment such as lifts or air conditioning is often an integral part of a building and is generally included in the fair value of the investment property, rather than recognised separately as property, plant and equipment.

b.   if an office is leased on a furnished basis, the fair value of the office generally includes the fair value of the furniture, because the rental income relates to the furnished office. When furniture is included in the fair value of investment property, an entity does not recognise that furniture as a separate asset."

Consider the following example:

- a lessor leases out a farm for the purpose of earning rentals;

- the farm is made up of the following assets: (1) land and agricultural buildings; and (2) agricultural fittings, fixtures and machinery that are an integral part of the agricultural buildings;

- the lease agreement meets the definition of an operating lease for the lessor; and

- the lessor measures investment property after initial recognition at fair value.

The lessor should account for all the assets included in the operating lease agreement as a unique investment property and, as a consequence, measure it using the fair value model.

Although agricultural fittings, fixtures and machinery do not meet the definition of an investment property in their own right, the lessor should follow the requirements in IAS 40:50 to determine the fair value of its investment property, including the other assets that form part of the lease agreement.

In the above example, the lease agreement includes all the assets (i.e. land and agricultural buildings and fittings, fixtures and machinery) that are an integral part of the farm and are necessary for operating the farm. Therefore, the rental income reflects the right to use of the complete set of assets. Consequently, the lessor should recognise investment property comprising all the assets (i.e. the land and agricultural buildings and the agricultural fittings, fixtures and machinery), measured in accordance with IAS 40.

Specific facts and circumstances should be considered by the lessor in each operating lease agreement covering a piece of land or a building, or part of a building, or both together with property, plant and equipment items held to earn rentals, in order to establish which assets covered by the agreement should be regarded as investment property.

3   Recognition

3.1   General requirements

Investment property is recognised as an asset when: [IAS 40:16]

- it is probable that the future economic benefits that are associated with the investment property will flow to the entity; and

- the cost of the investment property can be measured reliably.

This general principle is used to consider whether capitalisation is appropriate both in respect of the costs incurred initially to acquire or construct an investment property, and costs incurred subsequently to add to, replace part of, or service a property. [IAS 40:17]

3.2   Subsequent costs

Appropriate application of the principle set out at **3.1** results in:
[IAS 40:19]

- the immediate expensing of the costs of the day-to-day servicing of a property (e.g. the costs of labour, consumables and minor parts used for repairs and maintenance); and

- costs incurred to replace parts of the original property being recognised in the investment property if they meet the recognition criteria.

When the costs of replacement parts are capitalised, the carrying amounts of the replaced parts are derecognised. [IAS 40:19]

If the entity has been using the cost model to measure its investment property, but the replaced part was not being depreciated separately, and the carrying amount of the replaced part cannot be determined, the cost of the replacement may be used as an indication of what the cost of the replaced part would have been at acquisition. [IAS 40:68]

When the fair value model is being used, the carrying amount of the investment property may already reflect the deterioration in value of the replaced part. In other cases it may be difficult to discern how much fair value should be reduced for the part being replaced. An alternative to reducing fair value for the replaced part, when it is not practical to do so, is to include the cost of the replacement in the carrying amount of the investment property, and then to reassess the fair value of the property (i.e. in the same way as would be required for additions not involving replacement). [IAS 40:68]

3.3   Investment property in the course of construction

The Standard does not deal specifically with the recognition of the cost of a self-constructed investment property. The appropriate accounting for such property is therefore determined in accordance with general principles.

Over the period of construction, the costs of construction will be capitalised as part of the cost of the investment property in accordance with the general principle outlined at **3.1**. Paragraphs 16 to 22 of IAS 16 *Property, Plant and Equipment* (see **section 4.2** of **chapter A7**) provide guidance as to what is appropriately included within such costs.

The capitalisation of borrowing costs is considered in accordance with the general requirements of IAS 23 *Borrowing Costs* (see **chapter A18**). IAS 23:4 provides an optional exemption from the requirement to capitalise borrowing costs for qualifying assets that are measured at fair value (which would include investment property under construction if an entity follows the fair value model for investment property). Therefore, entities can choose, as a matter of accounting policy, whether to capitalise borrowing costs in respect of such assets. When relevant to an understanding of the financial statements, that accounting policy should be disclosed.

If an entity follows the fair value model in accounting for its investment property (see **5.2**), provided that the fair value of the property under construction can be measured reliably, the costs capitalised during the course of construction do not affect the carrying amount of the investment property under construction, which is remeasured to fair value at the end of each reporting period. Therefore, any costs capitalised during the reporting period simply reduce the amount recognised in profit or loss for any gain (or increase the amount recognised for any loss) arising on remeasurement to fair value at the end of the reporting period. Although the amount reported in the statement of financial position is not affected, it is important to capitalise construction costs when appropriate, because this may affect the classification of amounts in the statement of comprehensive income (e.g. any gain on remeasurement may be overstated and property expenses overstated by the same amount).

4   Measurement at recognition

4.1   General requirements

An investment property is measured initially at its cost. Transaction costs are included in the initial measurement. [IAS 40:20]

When investment property is acquired, it is necessary to consider whether the transaction is the acquisition of an asset or a group of assets, or a business combination in the scope of IFRS 3 *Business Combinations*. IAS 40 does not currently contain any guidance regarding how an entity should make this determination. However, proposals issued in November 2012 would amend IAS 40 to clarify that such a determination should be made based on the guidance in IFRS 3 (see **section 9** below). If a transaction is identified as a business combination, the investment property acquired as part of that transaction should initially be recognised and measured in accordance with IFRS 3 rather than in accordance with the requirements of IAS 40 discussed in this section.

The cost of an investment property includes its purchase price (if purchased) and other directly attributable expenditure, e.g. professional fees for legal services, property transfer taxes and other transaction costs. [IAS 40:21]

Start-up costs are not included unless they are necessary to bring the asset to the condition required for its intended operation. Abnormal costs, and operating losses incurred before the property reaches its required level of occupancy, are excluded from the cost of the investment property. [IAS 40:23]

Example 4.1A

Expenditure to be capitalised as part of the cost of an investment property

Entity R acquires a building for CU95 million in March 20X1 as an investment property. In June 20X1, Entity R refurbishes entirely the building at a cost of CU5 million to bring it to the condition required by the rental market. Entity R will pay an estate agent two months' rent if the agent locates a lessee. In December 20X1, Entity R (the lessor) finally rents the property under an operating lease to Entity S (the lessee).

Is it appropriate for Entity R to include the refurbishment costs and the estate agent's fees as part of the initial cost of the investment property?

Yes. When it buys the building, Entity R should recognise the purchase price as the initial cost of the building under IAS 40. The refurbishment costs are necessary to bring the property to a condition suitable for renting out and, therefore, these costs should also be included in the initial cost of the building.

The estate agent's fees are not part of the initial cost of the building but they are considered to be "initial direct costs incurred in negotiating and arranging an operating lease" under IAS 17 *Leases*. They are, therefore, capitalised as part of the leased building in accordance with IAS 17:52. When the cost model is used, the expenditure should be depreciated over the lease term.

When the fair value model is used, the costs should be capitalised and will, therefore, result in a smaller revaluation gain (or larger revaluation loss) when the building is next remeasured to fair value.

Example 4.1B

Termination payments by a lessor to a lessee

Company A owns an office building that it leases to Company B. The lease is classified as an operating lease in accordance with IAS 17. Company A would like to convert the office building into a block of flats, believing that this will attract significantly higher rental income. First, however, Company A must terminate the lease contract with Company B.

Company A applies the cost model as its accounting policy for the measurement of its investment property subsequent to initial recognition.

Should Company A capitalise the lease termination costs as part of the cost of converting the office building into a block of flats?

Yes. Paragraph 16(b) of IAS 16 *Property, Plant and Equipment* states that the cost of an item of property, plant and equipment includes "any costs directly attributable to bringing the asset to the location and condition necessary for it to be capable of operating in the manner intended by management". IAS 16:7 requires that the cost of an item of property, plant and equipment be recognised as an asset if "it is probable that future economic benefits associated with the item will flow to the entity" and if "the cost of the item can be measured reliably".

Therefore, if Company A's cost of terminating Company B's operating lease meets the recognition criteria for property, plant and equipment in IAS 16:7, Company A should capitalise this cost because it is a directly attributable cost of enabling operation of the asset in the manner intended by management.

Company A should also consider whether there is an indicator of impairment and whether any further impairment testing should be performed to ensure that the building is not recognised at a carrying amount higher than its recoverable amount as a result of capitalising the lease termination costs.

4.2   Deferred payments

The cost of an investment property for which payment is deferred is the cash price equivalent of the deferred payments. The difference between the cash price equivalent recognised at initial measurement, and the total payments made, is recognised as an interest expense over the period of credit, i.e. the period from the point of receipt of the property until the point of settlement of the related liability. [IAS 40:24]

There is no definition of 'cash price equivalent' in IAS 40. It is presumably intended to equate to the present value of the deferred payment but might also encompass a cash price offered by the vendor as an alternative to the deferred payment terms.

4.3   Property held under lease and classified as investment property

The initial cost of a property interest held under a lease and classified as an investment property is prescribed by IAS 17:20. The property is recognised at the lower of its fair value and the present value of the minimum lease payments. An equivalent amount is recognised as a liability in accordance with the same paragraph. [IAS 40:25]

IAS 40:25 applies to all property interests held under leases (whether operating or finance) and classified as investment property. Therefore, in effect, such interests are recognised as if the underlying lease were a finance lease, even if it would be classified as an operating lease under the general requirements of IAS 17.

When a premium is paid on the lease, it is treated as part of the minimum lease payments for this purpose. It is included within the cost of the asset, but excluded from the liability (because it has already been paid). If a property interest held under a lease is classified as an investment property, the item accounted for at fair value is that interest and not the underlying property. [IAS 40:26]

This means that it is the fair value of the leasehold interest, rather than the fair value of the property, that is recognised in the financial statements. Normally, in a very long lease with only nominal 'ground rent', the difference between these two values is very small. However, IAS 40 allows any property held under an operating lease to be classified as an investment property provided that certain criteria are met (see **2.2**). In some cases, therefore, the difference between the fair value of the leasehold interest and the fair value of the property can be significant. For example, in the case of a short lease at market rent, the market value of the leasehold interest will be small compared to the value of the freehold interest in the property.

4.3.1   Gross value of leasehold interest

As noted above, a liability should be recognised in the statement of financial position for the present value of the minimum lease payments. If the property is subsequently accounted for under the fair value model, it is important to ensure that the valuation reflected in the statement of financial position is consistent with this. Valuers may value very long leasehold interests on the basis of the freehold interest and then deduct from that value the present value of the ground rent on the head lease and the present value of the estimated residual value at the end of the lease term. But if the liability for the ground rent is recognised separately in the financial statements, it is the gross valuation before any such deduction (but excluding any amount attributable to the residual value) that should be recognised as an asset to avoid double-counting the liability.

4.4   Investment property acquired through exchange of another asset

When an investment property is exchanged for an asset (assets), whether monetary or non-monetary, IAS 40 prescribes the treatment for such an exchange. The cost of the investment property is measured at fair value unless either:
[IAS 40:27]

- the exchange transaction lacks commercial substance; or

- the fair value of neither the asset received nor the asset given up is reliably measurable.

The acquired asset is measured in this way even if an entity cannot derecognise immediately the asset given up. If the acquired asset is not measured at fair value, its cost is measured at the carrying amount of the asset given up. [IAS 40:27]

Whether an exchange transaction has commercial substance is determined by considering the extent to which the future cash flows are expected to change as a result of the transaction. IAS 40 states that a transaction has commercial substance if:
[IAS 40:28]

- the configuration (risk, timing and amount) of the cash flows of the asset received differs from the configuration of the cash flows of the transferred asset; or

- the entity-specific value of the portion of the entity's operations affected by the transaction changes because of the exchange; and

- the difference in either of these is significant relative to the fair value of the assets exchanged.

In determining whether an exchange transaction has commercial substance, the entity-specific value of the portion of the entity's operations affected by the transaction should reflect post-tax cash flows. The Standard notes that the results of these analyses may be clear without having to perform detailed calculations. [IAS 40:28]

In most instances, it will be readily apparent whether a transaction lacks commercial substance. The reference in the Standard to the entity-specific value of the portion of the entity's operations affected by the transaction is not explained in detail but clearly is intended to indicate that a transaction will have substance when it has a significant effect on the present value of the entity's future cash flows.

The fair value of the asset is reliably measurable if:
[IAS 40:29]

- the variability in the range of reasonable fair value measurements is not significant for the asset; or

- the probabilities of the various estimates within the range can be reasonably assessed and used when measuring fair value.

If the fair value of either the asset received or the asset given up can be measured reliably, then the fair value of the asset given up is used to measure cost unless the fair value of the asset received is more clearly evident. [IAS 40:29]

Some detailed wording changes have been made in IAS 40:29 as consequential amendments arising from IFRS 13 *Fair Value Measurement*, and those changes are reflected above; however, the general principle set out in IAS 40:29 is not affected by the introduction of IFRS 13.

5   Measurement after recognition

5.1   Accounting policy

In general, IAS 40 (1) allows an entity to choose whether it adopts a fair value model or a cost model for investment property, and (2) requires that, having decided on its policy, an entity should apply that model to all of its investment property. [IAS 40:30]

There are two exceptions to this general principle. These are:
[IAS 40:30]

- when a lessee chooses to classify a property interest held under an operating lease as investment property, the lessee automatically forfeits the choice of model offered by IAS 40 – the fair value model must be used for all investment property (see **2.2**); [IAS 40:6 & 34] and

- when an entity has investment property backing liabilities that pay a return linked directly to the fair value of, or returns from, specified assets including that investment property, the entity is not required to apply the same policy for that property as it does for its other investment property (see **5.1.1**). [IAS 40:32A]

Note also that one of the criteria for qualification as an investment entity under IFRS 10 *Consolidated Financial Statements* (see **section 15** of **chapter A24** for details) is that an entity should measure and evaluate substantially all of its investments on a fair value basis. Accordingly, in order to meet the investment entity exception in IFRS 10, and measure its investments in subsidiaries (other than subsidiaries that provide investment-related services or activities) at fair value through profit or loss rather than consolidating them, an entity will need to select IAS 40's fair value model for its investment property.

Once a policy has been adopted, any change will be considered a voluntary change in accounting policy which, under IAS 8 *Accounting Policies, Changes in Accounting Estimates and Errors*, is permitted only if it will result in financial statements providing reliable and more relevant information. IAS 40 notes that it is highly unlikely that a change from the fair value model to the cost model will result in a more relevant presentation. [IAS 40:31]

If an entity adopts the cost model, it must still measure the fair value of all of its investment property for disclosure purposes, other than in exceptional circumstances when the fair value cannot be reliably measured (see **5.2.4** below).

5.1.1 Investment property linked to liabilities

When an entity has investment property backing liabilities that pay a return linked directly to the fair value of, or returns from, specified assets including that investment property, the entity may choose a model for all such investment property and independently choose a different model for all other investment property. The choice of policy made by an entity for such property does not affect the entity's choice for the rest of its property, e.g. the entity could choose the fair value model for its investment property linked to liabilities, but choose the cost model for the rest of its investment property. [IAS 40:32A]

> This choice is typically applicable to vehicles that have been set up to own investment property and that are funded by debt instruments instead of equity instruments (see **2.1.2** in **chapter B3** (or, for entities that have not yet adopted IFRS 9 *Financial Instruments*, **2.1.2** in **chapter C3**) for the classification of puttable instruments).

For an entity that operates an internal property fund that issues notional units whereby some units are held by investors and others are held by the entity, the property held by the fund cannot be held partly at cost and partly at fair value. [IAS 40:32B]

If different models are chosen, sales of investment property between pools of assets are recognised at fair value and the cumulative change in fair value is recognised in profit or loss. [IAS 40:32C]

5.1.2 Investment property classified as held for sale

Investment property accounted for under IAS 40's cost model falls within the scope of IFRS 5 *Non-current Assets Held for Sale and Discontinued Operations*, both as regards measurement and as regards presentation in the statement of financial position. Therefore, from the point at which an investment property accounted for under the cost model meets the criteria for classification as held for sale (or is included within a disposal group meeting the criteria for classification as held for sale), the asset is accounted for under that Standard (see **chapter A20**).

Investment property accounted for under IAS 40's fair value model is excluded from the measurement requirements of IFRS 5, but is otherwise subject to the requirements of that Standard. [IFRS 5:5] Therefore, from the point at which investment property accounted for under the fair value model meets the criteria for classification as held for sale (or is included in a disposal group meeting the criteria for classification as held for sale), the asset is presented as held for sale in the statement of financial position, as required by IFRS 5:38 (see **7.2.1** in **chapter A20**), but it continues to be measured at fair value in accordance with the entity's accounting policy for investment property.

5.2   Fair value model

After initial recognition, an entity that chooses the fair value model measures all of its investment property at fair value, except when the requirements of IAS 40:53 apply (inability to determine fair value reliably – see **5.2.4**). [IAS 40:33]

The requirements for measuring fair value have been amended by IFRS 13 *Fair Value Measurement* which establishes a single framework for measuring fair value when that is required by other Standards. It replaces the guidance regarding the measurement of fair value previously included in other Standards (including IAS 40). Essentially, the effect of IFRS 13 has been to remove the detailed guidance on the measurement of fair value from IAS 40 so that, following the adoption of IFRS 13, entities measuring investment property at fair value should refer to the guidance in IFRS 13.

In **5.2.1** and **5.2.2** below, the requirements for entities that have adopted IFRS 13 and those that have not yet adopted that Standard are set out separately.

IFRS 13 is effective for annual periods beginning on or after 1 January 2013, with earlier application permitted.

When IFRS 13 is first adopted, it is required to be applied prospectively and it need not be applied to comparative information provided for periods before the initial application of IFRS 13; therefore, amounts reported in prior annual periods are not required to be restated.

5.2.1   *Measurement of fair value – entities that have adopted IFRS 13*

Fair value is defined as "the price that would be received to sell an asset or paid to transfer a liability in an orderly transaction between market participants at the measurement date. (See IFRS 13 *Fair Value Measurement*.)" [IAS 40:5]

When measuring the fair value of investment property, an entity should ensure that the fair value reflects, among other things, rental income from current leases and other assumptions that market participants would use when pricing the investment property under current market conditions. [IAS 40:40]

Assets or liabilities recognised elsewhere in the financial statements (e.g. prepaid or accrued operating lease income) should not be double-counted in determining the carrying amount of investment property under the fair value model. For example, if the lifts and air-conditioning system in a property are considered an integral part of the building, they are generally included in the fair value of the investment property and are not recognised as separate assets. Similarly, if an office is leased on a furnished basis, and the rental income relates to the furnished office, the fair value of the office generally includes the fair value of the furniture, and the furniture is, therefore, not recognised as a separate asset. [IAS 40:50]

> These requirements would extend to lease incentives. That is to say that assets/liabilities recognised for lease incentives received/given should not be double-counted in the statement of financial position.

Example 5.2.1

Acquisition of investment property with existing operating lease in place

Company C acquires an investment property with an operating lease that is not at current market rates.

IAS 40:40 states as follows.

> "When measuring the fair value of investment property in accordance with IFRS 13, an entity shall ensure that the fair value reflects, among other things, rental income from current leases and other assumptions that market participants would use when pricing the investment property under current market conditions."

In addition, IAS 40:26 states that a premium paid for a lease should be included in the cost of an investment property. This acknowledges the fact that an investment property includes not only land and buildings but other

---

assets (customer relationships, furniture and favourable leases) and liabilities (unfavourable leases) that are interrelated in determining the fair value of the investment property. Therefore, the fair value of operating leases at above or below market rates should be incorporated into the fair value of the investment property.

The requirements of IAS 40:50 regarding double-counting of assets or liabilities recognised elsewhere in the financial statements (see above) also apply.

Example 2.7 above addresses whether a group of assets leased under a single operating lease (e.g. agricultural machinery leased together with agricultural land and buildings) meets the definition of investment property.

The fair value of an investment property held under a lease reflects expected cash flows (including contingent rent that is expected to become payable). Thus, if a valuation obtained for a property is net of all payments expected to be made, any recognised lease liability must be added back to arrive at the carrying amount of the investment property using the fair value model. [IAS 40:50(d)]

If, at the time of initial recognition, an entity incurred other expenditure directly attributable to the acquisition of an investment property (e.g. professional fees for legal services, property transfer taxes and other transaction costs – see **example 4.1A**), these additional costs are included in the original carrying amount of the investment property, in accordance with IAS 40:21.

These additional costs should not be considered separately from the fair value of the related investment property because they are included in the net carrying amount of the asset. Accordingly, when an investment property is acquired immediately before the end of an accounting period, such that its fair value is unlikely to change between the date of acquisition and the end of the accounting period, it is likely that a downward revaluation will be recognised that is equal and opposite to the capitalised acquisition costs.

5.2.2   Measurement of fair value – entities that have not yet adopted IFRS 13

5.2.2.1   Definition of fair value

Fair value is defined as "the amount for which an asset could be exchanged between knowledgeable, willing parties in an arm's length transaction". [IAS 40:5]

For this definition, 'knowledgeable' means that both the willing buyer and the willing seller are reasonably informed about the investment property's nature, characteristics, and actual and potential uses, as well as the market conditions at the end of the reporting period. [IAS 40:42]

A 'willing' buyer is motivated, but not compelled, nor over-eager to buy, nor determined to buy at any price. A 'willing' seller is not compelled, nor over-eager to sell, and is not prepared to sell at any price, nor prepared to hold out for a price not considered reasonable in current market conditions. [IAS 40:42 & 43]

An 'arm's length transaction' is one between parties that do not have a particular or special relationship that would make the prices of the transaction uncharacteristic of market conditions. The transaction is presumed to be between unrelated parties, each acting independently. [IAS 40:44]

If, at the time of initial recognition, an entity incurred other expenditure directly attributable to the acquisition of an investment property (e.g. professional fees for legal services, property transfer taxes and other transaction costs – see **example 4.1A**), these additional costs are included in the original carrying amount of the investment property, in accordance with IAS 40:21.

These additional costs should not be considered separately from the fair value of the related investment property because they are included in the net carrying amount of the asset. Accordingly, when an investment property is acquired immediately before the end of an accounting period, such that its fair value is unlikely to change between the date of acquisition and the end of the accounting period, it is likely that a downward revaluation will be recognised that is equal and opposite to the capitalised acquisition costs.

'Fair value' is different from 'value in use' as defined in IAS 36 *Impairment of Assets*. Fair value is based on the knowledge and estimates of willing

and knowledgeable buyers and sellers. Value in use reflects the entity's estimates, including the effects of factors that may be specific to the entity. This means that the following items would be taken into account in determining value in use, but not in assessing fair value to the extent that they would not be generally available to knowledgeable, willing buyers and sellers:
[IAS 40:49]

- additional value derived from the creation of a portfolio of properties in different locations;

- synergies between investment property and other assets;

- legal rights or legal restrictions that are specific only to the current owner; and

- tax benefits or tax burdens that are specific to the current owner.

5.2.2.2   Determining fair value

The Basis for Conclusions on IAS 40 explains, at paragraphs B52 to B54, that when developing the guidance in the Standard on the fair value of investment property, reference was made to the International Valuation Standards (IVS) issued by the International Valuations Standards Committee (IVSC). The guidance in paragraphs 36, 37 and 39 to 44 of IAS 40 was, in substance and largely in wording, developed to be identical to the guidance in IVS 1. In practice, professional valuers will usually be engaged to perform the required valuations in accordance with IVS (see **5.2.3**). Further details about IVS can be found at *www.ivsc.org*.

When determining the fair value of an investment property, special terms or circumstances such as atypical financing, sales and leaseback arrangements, special considerations or concessions granted by anyone associated with the sale are ignored. [IAS 40:36]

Fair value is determined without any deduction for transaction costs that may be incurred on sale or other disposal. [IAS 40:37]

The fair value of investment property should reflect market conditions at the end of the reporting period. [IAS 40:38] Fair value is time-specific at a given date because the amount reported as fair value may be incorrect or inappropriate if estimated at another time, due to a change in market conditions. The definition of fair value assumes simultaneous exchange and completion of the contract, without any variation in price that might be made in an arm's length transaction between knowledgeable, willing parties if exchange and completion are not simultaneous. [IAS 40:39]

The fair value of investment property reflects, among other things, rental income from current leases and reasonable and supportable assumptions that represent what reasonable and knowledgeable, willing parties would assume about rental income from future leases in the light of current conditions. It also reflects, on a similar basis, any cash outflows (including rental payments and other outflows) that could be expected for the property. Some of these outflows are reflected in the liability whereas others relate to outflows that are not recognised in the financial statements until a later date (e.g. contingent rents). [IAS 40:40]

The best evidence of fair value is given by current prices in an active market for similar property in the same location and condition and subject to similar lease and other contracts. When reference is made to transactions in 'similar' properties that are subject to 'similar' contractual arrangements, care is required to ensure that there are no significant variations, whether as regards the characteristics of the property or the contractual obligations applying to the property. [IAS 40:45]

In the absence of current prices in an active market as described above, an entity may consider information from a variety of other sources, including: [IAS 40:46]

- current prices in an active market for properties of different nature, condition or location (or subject to different lease or other contracts), adjusted to reflect those differences;

- recent prices of similar properties on less active markets, with adjustments to reflect any changes in economic conditions since the date of the transactions that occurred at those prices; and

- discounted cash flow projections based on reliable estimates of future cash flows, supported by the terms of any existing lease and other contracts and (when possible) by external evidence such as current market rents for similar properties in the same location and condition, and using discount rates that reflect current market assessments of the uncertainty in the amount and timing of the cash flows.

In some cases, the various sources listed in IAS 40:46 may suggest different estimates for the fair value of an investment property. An entity will need to consider the reasons for those differences, in order to arrive at the most reliable estimate of fair value within a range of reasonable fair value estimates. [IAS 40:47]

In such circumstances, an entity will also need to ensure that the variability in the range of reasonable fair value estimates is not so great, and the assessment of the probabilities of the various outcomes so difficult, that the fair value of the property is not reliably measurable (see **5.2.4**).

Assets or liabilities recognised elsewhere in the financial statements (e.g. prepaid or accrued operating lease income) should not be double-counted in determining the carrying amount of investment property under the fair value model. For example, if the lifts and air-conditioning system in a property are considered an integral part of the building, they are generally included in the fair value of the investment property and are not recognised as separate assets. Similarly, if an office is leased on a furnished basis, and the rental income relates to the furnished office, the fair value of the office generally includes the fair value of the furniture, and the furniture is, therefore, not recognised as a separate asset. [IAS 40:50]

These requirements would extend to lease incentives. That is to say that assets/liabilities recognised for lease incentives received/given should not be double-counted in the statement of financial position.

Example 5.2.2.2A

Acquisition of investment property with existing operating lease in place

Company C acquires an investment property with an operating lease that is not at current market rates.

IAS 40:40 states as follows.

> "The fair value of investment property reflects, among other things, rental income from current leases and reasonable and supportable assumptions that represent what knowledgeable, willing parties would assume about rental income from future leases in the light of current conditions. It also reflects, on a similar basis, any cash outflows (including rental payments and other outflows) that could be expected in respect of the property. Some of those outflows are reflected in the liability whereas others relate to outflows that are not recognised in the financial statements until a later date (e.g. periodic payments such as contingent rents)."

Additionally, IAS 40:26 states that a premium paid for a lease should be included in the cost of an investment property. This acknowledges the fact that an investment property includes not only land and buildings but other assets (customer relationships, furniture and favourable leases) and liabilities (unfavourable leases) that are interrelated in determining the fair value of the investment property. Therefore, the fair value of operating leases at above or below market rates should be incorporated into the fair value of the investment property.

The requirements of IAS 40:50 regarding double-counting of assets or liabilities recognised elsewhere in the financial statements (see above) also apply.

Example 2.7 above addresses whether a group of assets leased under a single operating lease (e.g. agricultural machinery leased together with agricultural land and buildings) meets the definition of investment property.

The fair value of an investment property held under a lease reflects expected cash flows (including contingent rent that is expected to become payable). Thus, if a valuation obtained for a property is net of all payments expected to be made, any recognised lease liability must be added back to arrive at the carrying amount of the investment property using the fair value model. [IAS 40:50(d)]

Neither future capital expenditure intended to improve or enhance a property, nor related future benefits, should be reflected in the fair value of an investment property. [IAS 40:51]

In many jurisdictions, the tax consequences that would flow from acquiring, holding and selling an investment property will have a significant impact on the value a market participant would be willing to pay to acquire the property. It is common that the difference in the market price will not be directly equal to the tax consequences under existing tax law because market participants will also factor into the price they are willing to pay the risk that tax law may change. In determining the fair value of an investment property, the valuation should take account of all tax consequences that are available to all market participants, but should not reflect those tax consequences that are unique to the buyer. For example, when the acquisition of the property will enable the entity to recover some unused tax losses, this should not be taken into account in the valuation of the investment property (although such deferred tax assets may have to be recognised under IAS 12 *Income Taxes*). But when there is a tax benefit from holding the property that is available to all market participants, that should be taken into account in determining the fair value in accordance with IAS 40:49(d).

Example 5.2.2.2B

Use of 'highest and best value'

In recent years, a local authority has been prepared to grant planning permission to redevelop petrol station sites for residential purposes. To obtain planning permission, an entity must make a formal application and meet whatever specific requirements are imposed by the local authority (i.e. the application is not a mere formality). Company A owns a petrol station site, which it currently leases to a third party and classifies as an investment property for reporting purposes. Company A intends to sell the site to a construction and development entity after the end of the reporting period.

Company A determines that:

- the value of the petrol station site in its current use and condition is CU10,000 (i.e. this is the value if the property is intended to be used as a petrol station for the foreseeable future);

- the value of the petrol station site for residential use, if planning permission had already been granted to Company A, would be CU15,000; and

- the costs to be incurred in applying for planning permission are expected to be CU1,000.

Accordingly, the fair value of the petrol station site to be reported in Company A's financial statements will lie in the range from CU10,000 (value based on existing use) to CU14,000 (value based on alternative use, after taking account of necessary costs). Whether the value is at the lower or upper end of this range will depend on how likely it is that the application for planning permission will be successful.

It is appropriate to include in the fair value calculation an element of 'hope value', if the property has a reasonable prospect of securing an uplift in value on the completion of specific events, but only to the extent that this is generally recognised by market participants. Such events could include the granting of a planning consent that would allow a more valuable, alternative use or the relaxation of restrictive covenants. In most instances, however, hope value will be more appropriately defined within a market valuation on the basis of a special assumption that an alternative, more valuable use is possible.

Hope value might also relate to the realisation of 'synergy value' arising from a merger with another property or property interests. In practice, however, it is difficult to envisage a situation where the synergy value will not be related to entity-specific synergies, which does not meet the arm's length transaction requirement of fair value. Consequently, synergy values would not normally be included in the fair value calculation.

Finally, when a valuation on the basis of fair value is required, planning consent should not be assumed unless the market would make such an assumption, and even then an allowance for risk is appropriate to the extent that the market would make such an allowance. For example, prospective purchasers in the market might make an assumption that planning permission would be granted, but nevertheless would make an allowance or deduction from the amount of their offers to reflect the risks involved and the likelihood of delay in obtaining an acceptable permission. In such circumstances, a valuation on the basis of market value, subject to the assumption that planning permission would be granted, should only be made with a corresponding discount for risk and delay, thus reflecting the view that would be taken in the market.

5.2.2.3   Additional guidance

IAS 40:33 to 52 set out the key considerations in respect of determining the fair value of an investment property. In the absence of current prices in an active market, IAS 40:46 gives guidance as to what information should be considered to determine the fair value of an investment property. This guidance sets out a number of sources of evidence that an entity should consider in determining fair value (see **5.2.2.2** above).

Further, the Basis for Conclusions on IAS 40 confirms that, although obtaining a third party valuation is encouraged, it is not required. Accordingly, entities may use their own analysis to underpin their assessment of fair value, assuming that the valuation in question appropriately reflects the underlying information, for example through a discounted cash flow assessment based on underlying rental agreements. Appropriate disclosures in accordance with IAS 40:75(e) should be included in the financial statements, including the entity's policy on the use of independent valuers.

Some of the guidance contained in the IASB Expert Advisory Panel's October 2008 report titled *Measuring and disclosing the fair value of financial instruments in markets that are no longer active* may also be useful in the determination of fair value of investment property when property market activity is very low. Several sections, in particular, are concerned with issues that may also be relevant to the valuation of investment property such as:

- considerations with regard to forced transactions (paragraph 21 onwards); and

- valuation adjustments as market conditions change (paragraph 29 onwards).

Similar to the approach in the IASB Expert Advisory Panel's report, enhanced disclosures become key.

Entities may wish to consider splitting their investment property valuations balance into those that are supported by observable market data and those that are not, thereby giving the reader of the financial statements a detailed understanding of the source of the valuation figures. This split would need to be determined through consultation with the valuers themselves.

Enhanced disclosures may be appropriate to draw readers' attention to the increased uncertainty around fair values of investment property. The objective of the disclosure is to give readers enough information as to the uncertainties, assumptions and market conditions at the reporting date that affect the fair values of investment properties. Depending on the particular circumstances, it may be useful to include:

- the professional rules applicable to valuers facing increased uncertainty with respect to their valuations;

- a sensitivity analysis on property yields or an indication of the range of potential valuation outcomes to the extent valuers are willing to provide this information within their valuation reports; and

- a reproduction of any additional wording included in the valuation report by the valuers regarding valuation uncertainties, if the report is not reproduced within the annual financial statements, or a suitable cross reference if it is.

In addition, the valuation of investment properties may be a critical accounting judgement and/or key source of estimation uncertainty required to be disclosed in accordance with IAS 1 *Presentation of Financial Statements* (see **7.2.3** and **7.3** in **chapter A4**). For some entities in the real estate sector, investment property is likely to be the most significant item in the statement of financial position and it is reasonable to conclude that the increased uncertainty when market activity is very low represents "estimation uncertainty at the end of the reporting period" that has "a significant risk of resulting in a material adjustment to the carrying amounts of assets and liabilities within the next financial year" for which additional disclosure is required by IAS 1:125. For entities not in the real estate sector, but with significant investment property portfolios, this could also be the case.

5.2.2.4 *Investment property valuation – material considerations*

The valuation of investment property should have due regard to the material considerations affecting the property interest. While each property interest will have some unique characteristics, material considerations usually fall into the following categories:

- site characteristics and location;

- building characteristics such as form of construction, size, specification, services, state of repair;

- nature of interest – freehold, leasehold, restrictive covenants etc.;

- planning permission and legal constraints;

- environmental issues and potential contamination;

- market condition and trends; and

- comparable evidence.

5.2.2.5 *Investment property valuation – evidence of open market transactions*

Generally, valuations on the basis of fair value are based on comparable evidence of open market transactions in similar property. However, given the heterogeneous nature of the commercial real estate market, no two properties will be identical in terms of location, condition, specification and other factors. Therefore, a valuation is an exercise of subjective judgement and should represent the price that would have been obtained if the property had been sold on the valuation date in an arm's length transaction between knowledge-able and willing market participants.

Evidence of market transactions should not be followed unquestion-ingly. Trends in value and the market evidence available (whether for directly comparable transactions or not) should be taken into account. The valuation should be done adjusting such evidence to reflect the fair value definition and attach more or less weight to some pieces of evidence, according to judgement.

Market trends will also dictate whether historical transactions are relevant to the valuation of the property concerned. In both a falling and a rising market, historical transactions will not necessarily reflect the upward or downward trend of the market. Growth assumptions should be adjusted to reflect the trends of the market when consider-ing historical comparable transactions.

However, in a depressed market, transaction prices may still be relevant in determining fair values of investment property. Although a significant proportion of sales may be made by vendors who are obliged to sell, such as liquidators or receivers, such transactions may be considered transactions at fair value. Liquidators and receiv-ers are normally under a duty to obtain the best price and their sales should be regarded generally as open market transactions when there has been a reasonable period for marketing the property and the transactions are on an arm's length between knowledgeable and willing market participants.

In addition, the valuation should reflect a full analysis of all rental market transactions to understand the 'net effective rent' rather than the headline (gross) rent because headline (gross) rent may be agreed but significant incentives may be offered to the tenants to accept the headline rent. Incentives can take the form of, for example, cash payments, enhanced fit-out specification from the market norm, surrender of existing leases with the same landlords and transfer of liabilities to the landlord. How these incentives are deemed to reflect an adjustment to the market rent is a matter of judgement but, in practice, most incentives are spread over the term of the lease (or until the first break option) and deducted from the headline rent to calculate the 'net effective rent'.

5.2.2.6 Investment property valuation – valuation methodology

Most valuations are prepared by capitalising the rental income stream at an 'all risk yield' or capitalisation factor to produce a net present value. The current rental income will reflect the rent payable under a lease and, when a property is unoccupied, the valuation will take into account the timing and amount of rent expected to become payable, based on comparable evidence. Future income from rent review or lease expiry dates will be similarly estimated.

The 'all risk yield' takes account of all risk factors that an investor will consider if purchasing a real estate asset, and includes the age, condition, location, manner in which it is let (including the quality of the tenant's covenant and the security of the rental profile), frequency of rent reviews and timing of future reversions. Usually, property investment is subject to borrowing of one kind or another and, therefore, in determining an investment yield a key factor will be the perceived ability of a purchaser to fund the property in the event of a sale.

The yield is, therefore, a measure, in the valuer's opinion, of the risks and rewards of the investment in the property. The greater the rewards (e.g. potential for rental growth) and the smaller the perceived risk (e.g. quality of the covenant strength and likelihood of the income being received), the lower the yield and the higher the capital value.

The 'all risk yield' is inextricably linked with the general marketplace, including the financial markets, economic prospects for growth and the likelihood of future rental growth of the income stream. It is the annual percentage return expected to be produced by a specific property interest (in simple terms, the annual net rental income divided by the capital value) and is generally derived from comparison with market transactions having the same characteristics as the property interest being valued.

To give an example of this valuation methodology, consider a property with a net rental income stream of CU100,000 per annum in perpetuity. A comparable property with an income stream of CU120,000 per annum has been sold for CU1.5 million, implying a yield of 8 per cent. Applying this yield to the original property would indicate a capital value of CU1.25 million.

Invariably, a valuation based on vacant possession will result in a higher yield and lower value than a valuation of the same property subject to an existing lease (assuming the same level of rent and all other factors remain constant).

Commonly three types of yields are used:

- initial yield: the initial net income at the date of purchase/ valuation expressed as a percentage of the purchase price/ valuation;

- equivalent yield: the average expected rent over the current lease term divided by the purchase price/valuation. The average and current rent will often differ due to, for example:

    - a currently vacant property, which is expected to be let at a given point in the future;

    - an initial rent-free period that will lapse at some point in time; or

    - a rent review, where market rent is above the rent passing; and

- revisionary yield: yield that takes account of the rent likely to be obtained at the next rent review or lapse of lease (e.g. yield based upon the anticipated rental value at the rent review or lease expiry).

When a property is multi-let or a portfolio is of a significant size, valuers may consider using a discounted cash flow approach to valuation, rather than using a single yield. This approach allows the valuer to show explicitly:

- the potential growth in the income stream;

- the extent of any void periods;

- costs of marketing or securing a tenant;

- dilapidation or refurbishment costs; and

- increases in rental at review.

Once this data has been input against a timeline and projected rental income, usually over a period of up to 25 years, a traditional 'all risk yield' calculation is typically undertaken to establish the sale price at the end of the term by multiplying the annual income (anticipated at the end of the term) by an initial yield. The net present value of the rental income and sale price is then calculated using a discount rate reflecting cost of capital and market evidence to arrive at an estimate of the value of the projected income stream (rental income and sale price). This value is then considered to be the market value of the property.

5.2.2.7   *Investment property valuation – land and buildings in the course of development*

In practice, there are likely to be only few transactions in partially completed investment properties. Even if there is evidence of such transactions near the reporting date, the stage of completion of such properties will almost certainly be different, resulting in the trans-action prices not being directly comparable in determining the fair value of investment property under construction. As a result, a higher degree of estimation and the use of one or more market-based valuation approaches may be necessary in arriving at a fair value for partially completed investment property.

In light of the need for guidance in this area, in 2011 the International Valuation Standards Council (IVSC) published International Valua-tion Standard (IVS) 233 *Investment Property under Construction*. IVS 233 contains the valuation principles that should be applied to estimate the market value of investment property that is under construction at the valuation date. The principles of IVS 233 are summarised below.

- The objective of the valuation is to estimate the price that would be paid and received in a hypothetical exchange of the partially completed property in the market as of the date of valuation. Consequently, fair value cannot be determined by reference to the original project plan or feasibility study pro-duced at the commencement of the project, as any resulting value would be based on historical inputs. An approach based on estimating the percentage of the project that has been completed prior to the valuation date is therefore unlikely to be relevant in determining the current market value.

- Instead, the market value of a partially completed investment property will reflect the expectations of market participants of the value of the property when complete, less deductions for the costs required to complete the project and appropriate adjustments for profit and risk and time value of money, if significant.

- IVS 233 permits using a growth-implicit model, which uses current cost and value inputs, or a growth-explicit model which uses estimated future costs and value inputs depending on the prevailing method used in the market for the class of property at the valuation date. The valuation and all key assumptions used in the valuation should reflect market conditions at the valuation date. The following valuation inputs would normally be required to estimate the fair value of an investment property under construction.

  - Completed property: this reflects the value on the assumption that the property is complete with its current specification.

  - Leasing: if not all lessees have been identified, adjustments should be made to reflect time and costs (including incentives and fees) that would be realistic to reach realistic long-term occupancy levels. Lease agreements that are conditional on completion of the project, or part thereof, should be reflected in the fair value of the partially completed property.

  - Construction costs: all construction and other project costs still to be incurred to complete the project. These costs should be based on contracted terms or current best estimates, reflecting expectations of market prices on the dates when they are likely to be incurred.

  - Finance costs: the valuation should reflect the cost of finance for the project from acquisition through to the anticipated repayment of the loan. As the lender may perceive the risks during construction to differ substantially from the risks following completion of construction, the finance cost during each period should be considered separately. If the entity is funding the project from existing funds, finance costs should be based on an appropriate market rate of interest that would be obtainable by a typical buyer of the partially completed property in the market at the valuation date.

- Other costs: the valuation should also reflect other costs that are directly attributable to the project, such as legal and professional costs that would be reasonably incurred in completing the construction and letting the investment property. This may also include reasonable marketing costs where lease agreements are not yet in place. However, in accordance with IAS 40:37, transaction costs incurred on sale or disposal of the property should not be taken into consideration.

- Risk: all significant risks should be identified and evaluated. Typical risks associated with any partially completed construction project will include variations in construction cost, finance costs and the construction programme as well as fluctuations in the value of the completed project between inception and completion, and the time that will be required to secure lessees and a stabilised income. The risks associated with generating income from the property after completion should be identified and evaluated separately from the risks associated with completing construction.

- Investor's return: allowance should be made for the return that a reasonable buyer would expect to achieve on the partially completed property. This allowance should reflect the current market conditions at the valuation date and, consequently, the profit anticipated by the entity at the start of the development project is no longer relevant once construction has commenced. The valuation should reflect all those significant risks associated with completing the project and achieving the expected income or capital appreciation that remain at the valuation date. Risks that have been minimised or eliminated should not be taken into account. The investor's return can be expressed as a target profit (either a lump sum or a percentage return on cost or value) or, alternatively, if a discounted cash flow approach is used to produce the valuation, it may be the minimum rate of return that would be required by a typical buyer in the market.

- Other considerations: a change in market since the beginning of the project may mean that the partially completed property no longer represents the highest and best use of the land. In such cases, the costs to complete the property as originally planned may be irrelevant because any buyer would either adapt any partially completed structures for an alternative project or demolish those structures. If this is the case, the valuation of the partially completed property should reflect the current value of the alternative project and any costs and risks associated with completing the alternative project.

5.2.2.8   Investment property valuation – portfolio valuations

A sale of a portfolio may attract a premium or a discount on the aggregate value of the separate properties. In a bull market, a purchaser may be willing to pay a premium for a portfolio which it would otherwise take significant time and resources to amass. Nevertheless, for the purposes of IAS 40, fair value should be determined for each property and not for the portfolio as a whole.

5.2.2.9   Investment property valuation – break-up value

This term is used when the optimum value of the property lies in selling its constituent parts separately rather than as a whole. Such a value should be included in a valuation if the market would take this into account in its purchase decision. According to the anticipated timescale and difficulties of break-up, a valuation on this basis, either in aggregate or if separated into its constituent parts, would normally be subject to discount for delay, uncertainty and risk.

5.2.3   Use of independent valuers

Apart from minor wording changes, the guidance below is not amended as a result of the issue of IFRS 13.

Entities are encouraged (but not required) to use, as the basis for measuring fair value, a valuation by an independent valuer "who holds a recognised and relevant professional qualification and has recent experience in the location and category of the investment property being valued". [IAS 40:32]

The IASB decided that an independent valuation would not be required by the Standard because of the following considerations:

- the cost-benefit ratio of an independent valuation may be inappropriate for some entities; and

- independent valuers with appropriate expertise are not available in some markets.

Thus, paragraphs B55 and B56 of the Basis for Conclusions on IAS 40 explain that it is for the preparers of financial statements to decide, in consultation with auditors, whether an entity has sufficient internal resources to determine reliable fair values. This approach is consistent with the approach to actuarial valuations in IAS 19 *Employee Benefits*.

5.2.4   Inability to measure fair value reliably

There is a rebuttable presumption that the fair value of an investment property can be measured reliably on a continuing basis. But in exceptional cases, when an investment property is first acquired (or when an existing property first becomes an investment property after a change of use), there may be clear evidence that the fair value of the property is not reliably measurable on a continuing basis. [IAS 40:53]

The requirement above is not affected by the adoption of IFRS 13. However, the description of the circumstances in which there is clear evidence that the fair value of the property is not reliably measurable on a continuing basis has been amended:
[IAS 40:53]

- for entities that have adopted IFRS 13, such circumstances are said to arise when, and only when, the market for comparable properties is inactive (e.g. there are few recent transactions, price quotations are not current or observed transaction prices indicate that the seller was forced to sell) and alternative reliable measurements of fair value (e.g. based on discounted cash flows) are not available; and

- for entities that have not yet adopted IFRS 13, such circumstances are said to arise when, and only when, comparable market transactions are infrequent, and alternative reliable estimates of fair value (e.g. based on discounted cash flows) are not available.

Note that the exception under IAS 40:53 is available only when the investment property is first recognised as such. If an investment property has previously been measured at fair value, it should continue to be measured at fair value until disposal (or until it otherwise ceases to be an investment property, for example because it becomes owner-occupied) even if comparable market transactions become less frequent or market prices become less readily available. [IAS 40:55]

When, in the circumstances described above, it is not possible for an entity that uses the fair value model to measure the fair value of a particular property (other than an investment property under construction) reliably on initial recognition, that particular investment property is measured using the cost model in IAS 16 *Property, Plant and Equipment*. In accounting for the property under IAS 16, the entity is required to assume that the residual value of the property is zero. IAS 16 is then applied until the disposal of the property. [IAS 40:53] Special rules apply for investment properties under construction – see **5.2.5**.

When an entity is compelled, for the reasons set out above, to measure an investment property using the cost model under IAS 16, it continues to measure all of its other investment property at fair value. [IAS 40:54]

The circumstances described above are also relevant to determining the circumstances in which an entity using the cost model would be exempt from disclosing the fair value of investment property (see **8.2.3** below).

An economic downturn may increase the volatility of prices in real estate markets and restrict the level of comparator transactions against which to assess value. This may increase uncertainty around reported investment property fair value compared to 'normal' market conditions. For this reason, third party valuers may include valuation uncertainty paragraphs in their reports in order to draw the reader's attention to the financial backdrop against which the valuations have been assessed. Generally, this type of uncertainty paragraph may not caveat the valuation opinion provided, but it may make reference to major upheaval in the financial sector, reduced liquidity in the market place, restricted availability of debt and similar factors, and may state that these factors have caused increased uncertainty in respect of current real estate prices.

There is a rebuttable presumption in IAS 40:53 that the fair value of an investment property can be determined reliably on a continuing basis; there is no exemption in a period of significant valuation uncertainty, even if comparable market transactions become less frequent or market prices become less readily available. The reclassifications available for certain financial instruments out of fair value measurement under the amendments made to IAS 39 *Financial Instruments: Recognition and Measurement* in October 2008 (see **section 4** of **chapter C2**) are not available for investment property. IAS 40 only permits the transfer of investment property to another asset category in the event of an evidenced change in use. It is only in exceptional cases, when there is clear evidence when the entity first acquires an investment property (or when an existing property first becomes an investment property after an evidenced change in use) that fair value is not reliably determinable, that the entity is permitted to measure that investment property at cost, while measuring its other investment properties at fair value. These exceptional cases are expected to be very rare.

5.2.5   Investment property in the course of construction

If an entity determines that the fair value of an investment property under construction is not reliably measurable but expects the fair value to be reliably measurable when construction is complete, the entity measures the investment property under construction at cost until the earlier of the fair value becoming reliably measurable or the completion of construction. [IAS 40:53]

Once the entity is able to measure reliably the fair value of the investment property under construction, that property should be measured at fair value. Once construction is complete, it is presumed that fair value can be measured reliably. If this is not the case, following completion, the property is accounted for using the cost model in accordance with IAS 16, under the general requirements of IAS 40:53 (see **5.2.4**). [IAS 40:53A]

The presumption that the fair value of investment property under construction can be measured reliably can be rebutted only on initial recognition. An entity that has measured such property at fair value may not conclude that the fair value of the completed investment property cannot be determined reliably. [IAS 40:53B]

5.2.6   Changes in fair value

Changes in the fair value of investment property are recognised in profit or loss in the period in which they arise. [IAS 40:35]

5.2.7   *Property held under a lease and classified as investment property*

When a property held under a lease that is negotiated at market rates is classified as an investment property (i.e. accounted for as a finance lease), the fair value of the interest in the leased property at acquisition, net of all expected lease payments including those relating to recognised liabilities, should be zero. This fair value does not change, regardless of whether the leased asset and liability are recognised at fair value or at the present value of minimum lease payments as per paragraph 20 of IAS 17 *Leases*. This means that there should be no initial gain or loss arising from the remeasurement of a leased asset from cost to fair value unless fair value is measured at different times. This could occur when an election to apply the fair value model is made after initial recognition. [IAS 40:41]

5.2.8   *Anticipated liabilities*

When an entity expects that the present value of its payments relating to an investment property (excluding payments relating to recognised liabilities) will exceed the present value of the related cash receipts, IAS 37 *Provisions, Contingent Liabilities and Contingent Assets* should be applied to determine whether a liability should be recognised and, if so, how that liability should be measured. [IAS 40:52]

5.3   Cost model

IAS 40:5 defines cost as "the amount of cash or cash equivalents paid or the fair value of other consideration given to acquire an asset at the time of its acquisition or construction or, where applicable, the amount attributed to that asset when initially recognised in accordance with the specific requirements of other IFRSs ...".

> For example, if the consideration for the purchase of a property was an issue of equity shares in the entity, IFRS 2 *Share-based Payment* should be applied to establish the cost of the property.

After initial recognition, an entity that chooses the cost model measures all of its investment property in accordance with IAS 16's requirements for that model, other than investment property classified as held for sale or included in a disposal group classified as held for sale, which is measured in accordance with IFRS 5 (see **5.1.2**). [IAS 40:56]

> **Example 5.3**
>
> **Component accounting for in-place leases**
>
> Entity A acquires a building with a number of operating leases for tenants already in place. Entity A applies the cost model for investment property under IAS 40 (i.e. Entity A measures the property in accordance with IAS 16's cost model).
>
> *Should Entity A depreciate separately the different amounts reflected in the cost of the building attributable to the in-place leases (above and below market rentals, direct costs associated with obtaining new tenants etc.)?*
>
> IAS 16:44 states that, in the circumstances described, "it may be appropriate to depreciate separately amounts reflected in the cost [of the property] that are attributable to favourable or unfavourable lease terms relative to market terms". If Entity A determines, through the exercise of judgement, that the components of cost attributable to favourable or unfavourable lease terms are significant, those components should be depreciated separately.
>
> However, IAS 16 is silent with respect to other amounts related to the value of in-place leases that may be reflected in the cost of the property. Therefore, whether Entity A recognises such amounts as separate components for depreciation purposes is an accounting policy choice to be applied consistently for all similar transactions.

6   Transfers

Transfers to, or from, investment property are made when, and only when, there is a change in use evidenced by one of the following:
[IAS 40:57]

- commencement of owner-occupation, for a transfer from investment property to owner-occupied property;

- commencement of development with a view to sale, for a transfer from investment property to inventories;

- end of owner-occupation, for a transfer from owner-occupied property to investment property; or

- commencement of an operating lease to another party, for a transfer from inventories to investment property.

These circumstances are discussed more fully below.

Paragraphs 60 to 65 of IAS 40 apply to recognition and measurement issues that arise when the fair value model is used for investment property and transfers are made to or from investment property (see **6.1** to **6.4** below). When the cost model is used, transfers between investment property, owner-occupied property and inventories do not change the carrying amount of the property transferred. They do not, therefore, change the cost of the property for measurement or disclosure purposes. [IAS 40:59]

6.1   Transfer from investment property to owner-occupied property

The Standard requires an investment property to be transferred to owner-occupied property only when there is a change of use evidenced by commencement of owner-occupation. [IAS 40:57(a)]

When an investment property carried at fair value is transferred to owner-occupied property, the property's deemed cost for subsequent accounting in accordance with IAS 16 *Property, Plant and Equipment* is its fair value at the date of change in use. [IAS 40:60]

6.2   Transfer from investment property to inventories

The Standard requires an investment property to be transferred to inventories only when there is a change of use evidenced by commencement of development with a view to sale. [IAS 40:57(b)]

When an investment property carried at fair value is transferred to inventories, the property's deemed cost for subsequent accounting in accordance with IAS 2 *Inventories* is its fair value at the date of change in use. [IAS 40:60]

6.3   Transfer from owner-occupied property to investment property

End of owner-occupation signals a potential transfer to investment property. If an owner-occupied property becomes an investment property that will be carried at fair value, IAS 16 is applied up to the date of change of use. Any difference at that date between the carrying amount of the property in accordance with IAS 16 and its fair value is treated in the same way as a revaluation in accordance with IAS 16. [IAS 40:61]

This means that any decrease in the carrying amount of the property is recognised in profit or loss, unless the decrease is the reversal of a previous revaluation surplus, in which case the decrease is recognised in other comprehensive income and reduces that revaluation surplus within equity. [IAS 40:62]

Any increase in the carrying amount is recognised in other comprehensive income and increases the revaluation surplus within equity, unless the increase reverses a previous impairment loss on that property in which case the increase is recognised in profit or loss. The amount recognised in profit or loss should not exceed the amount needed to restore the carrying amount to the amount that would have been determined (net of depreciation) had no impairment loss been recognised. [IAS 40:62]

On subsequent disposal of such a property, the revaluation surplus may be transferred to retained earnings, but not through profit or loss. [IAS 40:62]

6.4   Transfer from inventories to investment property

A transfer from inventories to investment property should be made when, and only when, there is a change in use, evidenced by the commencement of an operating lease to another party. For a transfer to investment property, if the property will be carried at fair value, any difference between the fair value and the carrying amount of the property at the date of transfer is recognised in profit or loss. [IAS 40:63] This is consistent with the treatment of sales of inventories. [IAS 40:64]

6.5   Continued classification as investment property

If an entity decides to dispose of an investment property without development, the property continues to be treated as an investment property until its disposal. It is not treated as inventories. [IAS 40:58]

> When an entity has decided to dispose of an investment property through sale, the requirements of IFRS 5 *Non-current Assets Held for Sale and Discontinued Operations* need to be considered (see **5.1.2** above and **chapter A20**).

Similarly, if redevelopment of an existing investment property commences but the property is intended for future use as an investment property, the property continues to be recognised as an investment property. [IAS 40:58]

> When the fair value model is used, expenditure incurred in the redevelopment of an investment property which remains classified as an investment property (e.g. rebuilding costs) should initially be capitalised (see **3.2**). The effect of remeasuring the asset to fair value is that any resulting gain or loss will be taken to profit or loss.

Disclosures required by IAS 40:76 distinguish between the cost of additions and fair value movements (see **8.2.2.1**).

Undeveloped land may fall within the definition of investment property in IAS 40 (see **2.2** above) although this will depend on the particular circumstances. When such land is subsequently developed for future use as an investment property, the property continues to be recognised as an investment property while the development takes place.

7   Disposals

An investment property is derecognised (i.e. removed from the statement of financial position) on disposal or when it is permanently withdrawn from use and no future economic benefits are expected from its disposal. [IAS 40:66]

The disposal of an investment property may occur through sale of the property or through entering into a finance lease. In determining the date of disposal for an investment property, the criteria in IAS 18 *Revenue* for recognising revenue from the sale of goods should be applied and the related guidance in the appendix to IAS 18 should be considered (see **chapter A14**). IAS 17 *Leases* applies to a disposal effected by entering into a finance lease and to a sale and leaseback (see **chapter A17**). [IAS 40:67]

7.1   Consideration, gains and losses on disposal

The gain or loss on the retirement or disposal of an investment property is calculated as the difference between the net disposal proceeds and the carrying amount of the property and is recognised in profit or loss in the period of the retirement or disposal. This is subject to the requirements of IAS 17 in the case of a sale and leaseback transaction. [IAS 40:69]

The consideration receivable on the disposal of an investment property is recognised initially at fair value. In particular, if payment is deferred, the consideration is recognised initially at its cash price equivalent. The difference between this amount and the nominal amount is recognised as interest revenue under the effective interest method in accordance with IAS 18. [IAS 40:70]

There is no definition of 'cash price equivalent' in IAS 40. It is presumably intended to equate to the present value of the deferred payment but might also encompass a cash price offered by the vendor as an alternative to the deferred payment terms.

When any liabilities are retained relating to the property after its disposal, IAS 37 *Provisions, Contingent Liabilities and Contingent Assets* or other relevant Standards are applied to those liabilities. [IAS 40:71]

7.2   Compensation for impairment of investment property

Impairments or losses of investment property, related claims for or payment of compensation from third parties and any subsequent purchase or construction of replacement assets are separate economic events and are accounted for separately. Therefore:
[IAS 40:73]

- impairments of investment property are recognised in accordance with IAS 36 *Impairment of Assets*;

- retirements or disposals of investment property are recognised as set out at **7.1** above in accordance with IAS 40:66 to 71;

- compensation from third parties for investment property that was impaired, lost or given up is recognised in profit or loss when it becomes receivable; and

- the cost of assets restored, purchased or constructed as replacements is determined as set out in **section 4** above in accordance with IAS 40:20 to 29.

Example 7.2

Insurance claim

A building carried as an investment property burns down during the reporting period. A valuation of the building in its damaged state is performed at the end of the reporting period.

Should the value of the property at the end of the reporting period include any amount receivable from insurance?

The amount receivable from insurance should be recognised separately in the statement of financial position if it meets the relevant recognition criteria. Any valuation of the property recognised as an investment property should not include the insurance receivable.

---

8   Presentation and disclosure

8.1   Presentation

IAS 1 *Presentation of Financial Statements* requires that, when material, the aggregate carrying amount of the entity's investment property should be presented in the statement of financial position. [IAS 1:54(b)]

8.2   Disclosure

The disclosures required by IAS 40 are made in addition to the disclosures required by IAS 17 *Leases* for leases entered into by lessees and lessors.

8.2.1   General disclosures

An entity is required to disclose:
[IAS 40:75]

- whether it applies the fair value or the cost model;

- whether, and in what circumstances, properties held under operating leases are classified as investment property when the fair value model is used;

- the criteria used to distinguish investment property from owner-occupied property or property held for sale in the normal course of business, when that classification is difficult;

- the methods and significant assumptions applied in determining the fair value of investment property, including a statement of whether the determination of fair value was supported by market evidence or was more heavily based on other factors, which are disclosed, because of the nature of the property and lack of comparable market data;

> This disclosure regarding the methods and significant assumptions underlying the determination of fair value is not required for entities that have adopted IFRS 13 *Fair Value Measurement*. Such entities should instead provide the disclosures required under IFRS 13 (see **section 11** of **chapter A6**).

- the extent to which the fair value of investment property (as measured or disclosed in the financial statements) is based on a valuation by an independent valuer who holds a recognised and relevant professional qualification and has recent experience in the location and category of the investment property being valued. If there has been no such valuation, that fact should be disclosed;

- the amounts recognised in profit or loss for:

  - rental income from investment property;

  - direct operating expenses (including repairs and maintenance) arising from investment property that generated rental income during the period;

  - direct operating expenses (including repairs and maintenance) arising from investment property that did not generate rental income during the period; and

  - the cumulative change in fair value recognised in profit or loss on a sale of investment property from a pool of assets, in which the cost model is used, into a pool in which the fair value model is used (i.e. on investment property linked to liabilities – see **5.1.1** above);

- the existence and amounts of restrictions on the realisability of investment property or the remittance of income and proceeds of disposal; and

- contractual obligations to purchase, construct or develop investment property or for repairs, maintenance or enhancements.

In addition, if there has been a material reduction in asset values after the reporting date, whether arising from a specific event or not, disclosure of the non-adjusting event is required in accordance with IAS 10 *Events after the Reporting Period* (see **sections 4** and **6.1** of **chapter A22**).

8.2.1.1   Service charge income and expense

Property investment entities often make service charges to their tenants (e.g. to cover the cost of repairs and maintenance) which are the responsibility of the tenants under the terms of the lease but which are arranged and managed by the lessor. These costs are typically passed on at cost or with a fixed percentage mark-up under the terms of the lease. When the lessor is in substance merely acting as agent for the payment of these costs, the reimbursement will generally not be recognised as revenue under IAS 18 *Revenue*. Nevertheless, it would be helpful to disclose the amount of such receipts and related costs in the notes to the financial statements.

8.2.2   Fair value model

8.2.2.1   Reconciliation of movements in carrying amount

In addition to the general disclosure requirements set out at **8.2.1** above, an entity that applies the fair value model is required to present a reconciliation between the carrying amounts of investment property at the beginning and end of the period, showing the following:
[IAS 40:76]

- additions, disclosing separately those additions resulting from acquisitions, those resulting from subsequent expenditure recognised in the carrying amount of an asset and those resulting from acquisitions through business combinations;

- assets classified as held for sale, or included in a disposal group classified as held for sale, in accordance with IFRS 5 *Non-current Assets Held for Sale and Discontinued Operations* and other disposals;

- net gains or losses from fair value adjustments;

- the net exchange differences arising on the translation of the financial statements into a different presentation currency and on translation of a foreign operation into the presentation currency of the entity;

- transfers to and from inventories and owner-occupied property; and

- other changes.

8.2.2.2   Reconciliation of adjustments to valuation of property

When a valuation obtained for investment property is adjusted significantly for the purpose of the financial statements (e.g. to avoid double-counting of assets or liabilities that are recognised as separate assets and liabilities), the entity is required to present a reconciliation between the valuation obtained and the adjusted valuation included in the financial statements, showing separately the aggregate amount of any recognised lease obligations that have been added back, and any other significant adjustments. [IAS 40:77]

8.2.2.3   Details about property exceptionally stated at cost

In the exceptional circumstances referred to at **5.2.4** above, when an entity applying the fair value model measures investment property using the cost model in IAS 16 *Property, Plant and Equipment*, the reconciliation described at **8.2.2.1** should disclose amounts relating to that investment property separately from amounts relating to other investment property. In addition, the following should be disclosed:

- a description of the investment property;

- an explanation of why fair value cannot be measured reliably; and

- if possible, the range of estimates within which fair value is highly likely to lie.

On disposal of such investment property not carried at fair value, the following should be disclosed:
[IAS 40:78]

- the fact that the entity has disposed of investment property not carried at fair value;

- the carrying amount of that investment property at the time of sale; and

- the amount of gain or loss recognised.

8.2.3   Cost model

In addition to the general disclosure requirements set out at **8.2.1** above, an entity that applies the cost model is required to disclose:
[IAS 40:79]

- the depreciation methods used;

- the useful lives or the depreciation rates used; and

- the gross carrying amount and the accumulated depreciation (aggregated with accumulated impairment losses) at the beginning and end of the period.

An entity that applies the cost model is also required to provide a reconciliation of the carrying amount of investment property at the beginning and end of the period, showing:
[IAS 40:79(d)]

- additions, disclosing separately those additions resulting from acquisitions and those resulting from subsequent expenditure recognised as an asset;

- additions resulting from acquisitions through business combinations;

- assets classified as held for sale, or included in a disposal group classified as held for sale, in accordance with IFRS 5 and other disposals;

- depreciation;

- the amount of impairment losses recognised, and the amount of impairment losses reversed, during the period in accordance with IAS 36 *Impairment of Assets*;

- the net exchange differences arising on the translation of the financial statements into a different presentation currency, and on translation of a foreign operation into the presentation currency of the entity;

- transfers to and from inventories and owner-occupied property; and

- other changes.

An entity that applies the cost model is also required to disclose the fair value of its investment property. In the exceptional cases described at **5.2.4** above, when an entity cannot measure the fair value of the investment property reliably, it should disclose:

- a description of the investment property;

- an explanation of why fair value cannot be measured reliably; and

- if possible, the range of estimates within which fair value is highly likely to lie.

9   Future developments

In November 2012, the IASB issued an exposure draft (ED/2012/2 *Annual Improvements to IFRSs: 2011-2013 Cycle*) proposing changes to a number of Standards as part of its Annual Improvements project. Amendments are proposed to IAS 40 to clarify that:

- judgement is required to determine whether the acquisition of investment property is the acquisition of an asset or a group of assets, or a business combination in the scope of IFRS 3 *Business Combinations*; and

- this judgement should be based on the guidance in IFRS 3 rather than on the requirements in paragraphs 7 to 15 of IAS 40 (see **2.1** above).

Finalised amendments are expected in the fourth quarter of 2013.

A9   Intangible assets

Contents

1   Introduction

IAS 38 *Intangible Assets* establishes general principles for the recognition and measurement of intangible assets. The Standard requires an entity to recognise an intangible asset if, and only if, specified criteria are met. The Standard also specifies how to measure the carrying amount of intangible assets, and requires certain disclosures about intangible assets.

The Standard was most recently amended in May 2011.

2   Scope

IAS 38 applies to all intangible assets, except:
[IAS 38:2& 3]

- intangible assets that are within the scope of another Standard, for example:

    - intangible assets held by an entity for sale in the ordinary course of business (addressed by IAS 2 *Inventories* and IAS 11 *Construction Contracts*);

    - deferred tax assets (addressed by IAS 12 *Income Taxes*);

    - leases that fall within the scope of IAS 17 *Leases*;

    - assets arising from employee benefits (addressed by IAS 19 *Employee Benefits*);

    - goodwill acquired in a business combination (addressed by IFRS 3 *Business Combinations*);

    - deferred acquisition costs, and intangible assets arising from an insurer's contractual rights under insurance contracts within the scope of IFRS 4 *Insurance Contracts*; and

    - non-current intangible assets classified as held for sale (or included in a disposal group that is classified as held for sale) in accordance with IFRS 5 *Non-current Assets Held for Sale and Discontinued Operations*;

- financial assets, as defined in IAS 32 *Financial Instruments: Presentation*;

- the recognition and measurement of exploration and evaluation assets (addressed by IFRS 6 *Exploration for and Evaluation of Mineral Resources*); and

- expenditure on the development and extraction of minerals, oil, natural gas and similar non-regenerative resources.

When an intangible asset is contained in or on a physical substance (such as computer software on a compact disc or a motion picture on film), management must assess which element is more significant. For example, software that controls machinery would normally be considered an integral part of the machinery and, therefore, would be treated as property, plant and equipment rather than as an intangible asset. The same would normally be true for the operating system for a computer. When the software does not form an integral part of the machinery or computer hardware to which it relates, it is separately accounted for under IAS 38. [IAS 38:4]

Research and development activities may give rise to an asset with physical substance (e.g. a prototype). Because the activities are primarily directed to the development of knowledge, the physical element of the asset is secondary to its intangible component, i.e. the knowledge embodied in it. In such circumstances, the activities are accounted for under IAS 38. [IAS 38:5]

A reporting entity may enter into a lease in respect of an intangible asset. The appropriate classification of the lease is determined in accordance with the requirements of IAS 17. When the lease is a finance lease, IAS 17 directs the lessee to IAS 38 for the appropriate accounting treatment after initial recognition. However, certain rights are specifically excluded from the scope of IAS 17 (rights under licensing agreements for items such as motion picture films, video recordings, plays, manuscripts, patents and copyrights) and are accounted for under IAS 38. [IAS 38:6]

> Programme rights meet the definition of an intangible asset (see **section 3** below). However, if they are held or developed for sale, or 'consumption' through broadcasting, in the ordinary course of business, they may also meet the definition of inventories (e.g. a right to broadcast a particular programme only once is an asset that will be consumed in the rendering of broadcasting services). Judgement is required in determining whether classification as an intangible asset or as inventories is appropriate. When classified as inventories, programme rights should not be amortised. An entity may be able to demonstrate that a programme right comprises identifiable components (e.g. different transmission rights) which should be accounted for separately.

Although certain specialised activities and transactions associated with the extractive and insurance industries are excluded from the scope of IAS 38, the Standard does apply to other intangible assets used in such industries (such as computer software) and other expenditure incurred (such as start-up costs).

> IFRIC 20 *Stripping Costs in the Production Phase of a Surface Mine* (effective for annual periods beginning on or after 1 January 2013, with earlier application permitted) addresses the appropriate treatment for waste removal costs that are incurred in surface mining activity during the production phase of a surface mine (referred to as 'production stripping costs'). If specified criteria are met, the requirements of that Interpretation may result in production stripping costs being accounted for as an addition to, or an enhancement of, existing intangible assets or existing property, plant and equipment – see **section 10** of **chapter A7** for details.

3   Definition of an intangible asset

An intangible asset is defined as an identifiable non-monetary asset without physical substance. [IAS 38:8]

The key components of this definition are:

• identifiability; and

• asset (the definition of which encompasses control).

3.1   Identifiability

Identifiability is the characteristic that conceptually distinguishes other intangible assets from goodwill. [IAS 38:11] In a business combination, it is often difficult to determine whether an intangible item qualifies for recognition as an intangible asset or whether it is merely part of goodwill. The word 'identifiable' in the definition is intended to help in such situations.

An asset is identifiable if either:
[IAS 38:12]

• it is separable, i.e. it is capable of being separated or divided from the entity and sold, transferred, licensed, rented or exchanged, either individually or together with a related contract, identifiable asset or liability, regardless of whether the entity intends to do so; or

- it arises from contractual or other legal rights, regardless of whether those rights are transferable or separable from the entity or from other rights and obligations.

3.1.1   Identifying intangible assets in a business combination

The IASB has concluded that all assets that are separable, as defined above, are identifiable. Therefore, any intangible asset that has that characteristic and that is acquired in a business combination should be recognised as an asset separate from goodwill.

However, separability is not the only indication of identifiability. The Standard is clear that, while an asset that is separable meets the identifiability criterion, there are other ways to meet that criterion. For example, a legal right, such as a broadcasting licence, may give rise to future benefits that are 'identifiable' under IAS 38, even if they are not separable from the underlying broadcasting business, because it is unlikely that the broadcasting licence could be sold without disposing of the underlying broadcasting business. Therefore, in a business combination, all intangible assets that arise from contractual or other legal rights, whether or not they are separable, should be identified as assets separate from goodwill.

The illustrative examples accompanying IFRS 3 *Business Combinations* provide a number of examples of items acquired in a business combination that meet the definition of an intangible asset. These examples are not exhaustive, but they do illustrate many of the more common items that arise in the circumstances of a business combination, and they provide a very useful framework for the determination as to whether particular items qualify for recognition as intangible assets (see **7.4.2.3 in chapter A25**).

3.2   Asset (control)

IAS 38 takes its definition of an asset from the *Conceptual Framework for Financial Reporting*, i.e. an asset is defined as a resource controlled by an entity as a result of past events and from which future economic benefits are expected to flow to the entity. [IAS 38:8] In the context of intangible assets, it is sometimes difficult to determine whether an entity can exert control over the expected future economic benefits. Control in this context means that the entity has the power to obtain the economic benefits that the asset will generate and to restrict the access of others to those benefits. [IAS 38:13]

> Normally, control of an intangible asset is achieved through legal rights (e.g. a brand name is protected by a trademark, a publishing title by copyright, a licence by contract). Less frequently, an intangible asset may be controlled merely through custody (e.g. a product formula or intellectual property may be controlled simply by keeping it a secret from outsiders).

3.2.1   Assembled workforce

Certain intangible items of value to an entity may not be controlled by it. For example, it is unusual for an entity to have control over its employees – usually employee contracts can be terminated with a short period of notice and without penalty. Therefore, when a business combination is accounted for as an acquisition, the benefit of an assembled workforce is more likely to fall to be treated as goodwill than as an intangible asset, because the workforce cannot normally be controlled (at least in the IAS 38 sense). This is consistent with IFRS 3:11 which only permits those identifiable assets acquired that meet the asset definition in the *Conceptual Framework for Financial Reporting* to be recognised at the acquisition date. For similar reasons, specific management or technical talent is unlikely to meet the definition of an intangible asset, unless it is protected by legal rights to use it and to obtain the future economic benefits expected from it, and it also meets the other parts of the definition. [IAS 38:15]

> However, occasionally, an entity may be able to demonstrate that it has sufficient control to be able to capitalise an employee contract as an asset. For example, when a football club acquires a new player, the contract negotiated may give the club exclusive rights to use the player for a specified period of time, and the club may also be entitled to sell that contract to a third party.

3.2.2   Customer relationships and similar items

IAS 38 allows that customer relationships and similar items may meet the definition of intangible assets when either:
[IAS 38:16]

- they are protected or otherwise controlled by legal rights; or

- the ability to control the expected benefits flowing from the relationships, and the separability of the relationships, have been evidenced by exchange transactions for the same or similar non-contractual customer relationships (other than as part of a business combination).

An established customer base or market share is not usually controlled by the entity. There may be an expectation that customers will continue to buy from the entity but, usually, they are under no obligation to do so. Clearly, when the relationship is protected by a legal right, the entity has control over the future economic benefits. However, such control may also be evidenced when the entity has acquired a non-contractual customer relationship in a separate exchange transaction, or when there have been exchange transactions for similar relationships. Because these exchange transactions also provide evidence that the customer relationships are separable, such customer relationships meet the definition of an intangible asset. [IAS 38:16]

> For example, in some industries, such as those providing mobile telephone services, one service provider may purchase subscriber bases of existing customers from another. The price paid for the subscriber bases usually exceeds the value of the existing contracts, the difference representing the expectation that existing subscribers will renew their contracts. The exchange transaction may provide sufficient evidence to enable the entity to recognise this difference as a separable intangible asset in its own right, even if the existing customers are under no obligation to renew their contracts. (However, this should not be confused with the situation when payments are made directly to potential customers as an incentive to enter into a contract.)
>
> Another example of a common scenario when a non-contractual relationship may qualify for recognition as a separate intangible in a business combination is when the acquiree has an established customer loyalty programme to which IFRIC 13 *Customer Loyalty Programmes* applies.

The illustrative examples accompanying IFRS 3 address various types of customer-related intangible assets acquired in a business combination and whether they meet the definition of an intangible asset (see **7.4.2.3** in **chapter A25**).

3.2.2.1   Commissions paid to acquire contracts

Example 3.2.2.1

Commissions paid to acquire contracts

Company A pays commission to an external party, Company B, which markets its security contracts. When a customer commits to a security contract, the customer agrees to use Company A's security services for a minimum of two years and Company B earns a commission of CU100. If, for any reason, the customer cancels within those two years, it is required to pay in full for the unexpired term of the contract. Company A has a history of enforcing these payments in the event of cancellation.

The commission is paid to acquire an asset (the ability to obtain revenues over a minimum two-year period.) The asset is controlled by Company A as evidenced by the enforcement of cancellation penalties, and it has arisen as a result of past events (the signing of the contract) from which future economic benefits (security contract revenues) are expected to flow.

More specifically, the asset meets the definition of an intangible asset because it is "an identifiable non-monetary asset without physical substance". The amount, which represents a right to receive future revenue from customers, is clearly identifiable; it is non-monetary, because it cannot be readily converted into cash; and it does not have physical substance. [IAS 38:8]

3.2.3   Non-competition agreements

Non-competition agreements (NCAs) are often entered into in conjunction with a business combination and can be structured in a variety of ways. For example, a subsidiary and its parent (the vendor) may enter into an NCA prior to the subsidiary being sold to an unrelated third party. Alternatively, the acquirer may enter into an NCA with the vendor.

It is presumed for the purposes of the following discussion that a reliable valuation of an NCA can be obtained.

Consolidated financial statements

The illustrative examples accompanying IFRS 3 cite non-competition agreements as items that, when acquired in a business combination, meet the definition of an intangible asset because they arise from contractual or other legal rights. While they may not be separable assets, separability is not a necessary condition to satisfy the recognition criteria for intangible assets in IAS 38 (see **3.1** above). Because they are contractual rights, NCAs should be recognised separately as intangible assets in the consolidated financial statements.

The value of an NCA will depend on a number of different factors, such as barriers to entry in the market in which the entities operate. For example, the existence of a customer list in the acquired entity alone does not indicate that the NCA is valuable.

When an NCA is recognised as a separate intangible asset, it forms part of the same cash-generating unit (or units) as the underlying assets of the acquired business to which it relates for the purposes of impairment testing in the consolidated financial statements (see **chapter A10**).

Separate financial statements of acquirer

When the NCA is between the subsidiary and the vendor, the acquirer does not have the legal rights arising from the contract. In such circumstances, the acquirer should simply recognise an investment in a subsidiary in its separate financial statements (i.e. it should not recognise a separate intangible asset for the NCA).

When the NCA is between the acquirer and the vendor, the acquirer does have a separately identifiable legal right with respect to the NCA in addition to its investment in the subsidiary. The right has a value in the separate financial statements of the acquirer. Therefore, in these circumstances, the acquirer should recognise a separate intangible asset for the NCA in accordance with IAS 38 in addition to the investment in its subsidiary. If the NCA and the investment are acquired at the same time, which will usually be the case, it will be necessary to consider whether the amounts specified in the acquisition agreement/NCA are the appropriate amounts for inclusion in the financial statements. In some cases, a different allocation of the total amount payable between the two items may be necessary in order to reflect the substance of the transaction.

When an NCA is recognised as a separate intangible asset, the NCA and the investment in the subsidiary will be tested for impairment jointly.

3.2.4 *Regulatory assets*

The appropriate accounting for rate-regulated activities is the subject of a major IASB project; the Board has issued proposals for an interim Standard for first-time adopters of IFRSs, and a more comprehensive project is at the research stage (see **section 14** below for details).

An example of a rate-regulated scenario is set out in **example 3.2.4**.

Example 3.2.4

Regulatory assets

Company X, an electricity producer, operates in Country B. Electricity producers in Country B are subject to government regulation of electricity charges. Company X has incurred operating losses in the two years ending 20X0 as a consequence of the regulatory pricing mechanism.

The government of Country B subsequently approves a regulatory agreement allowing the electricity producers to increase their prices in future years to offset losses incurred for the previous two years ending 20X0.

Company X should not recognise an asset and associated revenues at the end of 20X0 for the recovery of past operating losses through invoicing future consumption at higher prices. In order to recover operating losses incurred, electricity producers are required to produce electricity for their clients in the future. Even though it is arguable that electricity producers will recover the operating losses, Company X has not, at the end of 20X0, provided the service for which the customers will be paying and, therefore, the regulatory asset cannot be recognised because it does not qualify for recognition as an asset in accordance with the *Conceptual Framework for Financial Reporting*. Moreover, customers can choose not to purchase electricity from this producer even if electricity is produced. In other words, it is not just a matter of producing electricity for clients in the future but clients purchasing electricity.

Consequently, the authorisation given by the government to increase prices in the future is merely a pricing mechanism that regulates prices for the following periods, and does not give rise to an asset and additional revenue in the current period (i.e. 20X0). The recovery of the operating loss is included in the calculation of the price the regulated entity may charge to its customers and should be recognised only when such revenues are received or receivable.

---

4   Recognition and initial measurement

IAS 38 establishes general principles for the recognition and measurement of intangible assets, as set out in **4.1** below, and discusses the treatment of subsequent expenditure as set out in **4.2**. The Standard then considers in detail the following situations:

- separate acquisition (see **4.3**);

- acquisition as part of a business combination (see **4.4**);

- acquisition by way of a government grant (see **4.5**);

- exchanges of assets (see **4.6**); and

- internally generated intangible assets (see **4.7**).

These detailed requirements are dealt with in the following sections.

4.1   General principles

Provided that an item meets the definition of an intangible asset, as discussed in **section 3** above, it should be recognised in the financial statements if, and only if:
[IAS 38:18 & 21]

- it is probable that the expected future economic benefits that are attributable to the asset will flow to the entity (the probability criterion); and

- the cost of the asset can be measured reliably.

> While the term 'probable' is not defined in IAS 38, it should be interpreted as 'more likely than not', consistent with the definition in the IASB Glossary of Terms.

These recognition criteria apply both to costs incurred to acquire an intangible asset and those incurred to generate an asset internally. The Standard imposes additional criteria, however, for the recognition of internally generated intangible assets (see **4.7** below).

When assessing the probability of expected future economic benefits, reasonable and supportable assumptions should be used, representing management's best estimate of the set of economic conditions that will exist over the useful life of the asset. [IAS 38:22]

Intangible assets are initially recognised at cost. [IAS 38:24]

4.2   Subsequent expenditure

The recognition criteria set out above apply equally to those costs incurred to add to, replace part of, or service an intangible asset. [IAS 38:18] Unlike a physical asset, it is not common to add to or replace parts of an intangible asset. Most expenditure incurred on an acquired intangible asset subsequent to its initial recognition, or on an internally generated intangible asset after completion, is incurred to maintain the benefits expected from the asset, and therefore will not meet the recognition criteria set out above. Additionally, expenditure incurred on intangible assets can be difficult to differentiate from expenditure related to the business as a whole. Therefore, IAS 38 concludes that only rarely should subsequent expenditure on an intangible asset be recognised in the carrying amount of the asset. [IAS 38:20]

> One of the rare circumstances in which subsequent costs may be added to the carrying amount of an intangible asset is in the case of waste removal costs falling within the scope of IFRIC 20 *Stripping Costs in the Production Phase of a Surface Mine*, provided that specified criteria are met (see **section 10** of **chapter A7** for details).

Specifically, the Standard prohibits the capitalisation of any subsequent expenditure incurred on brands, mastheads, publishing titles, customer lists and items similar in substance (whether externally acquired or internally generated). Because such expenditure cannot be distinguished from expenditure to develop the business as a whole, it is always recognised in profit or loss as incurred. [IAS 38:20]

The Standard also addresses specifically subsequent expenditure on an in-process research and development project acquired separately or in a business combination that has been recognised as an intangible asset. Such expenditure is subject to the additional recognition criteria established for internally generated intangible assets (see **4.7** below). [IAS 38:42] Therefore, the expenditure is:

* recognised as an expense when it is incurred if it is research expenditure;

* recognised as an expense when it is incurred if it is development expenditure that does not satisfy the recognition criteria set out in IAS 38:57 (see **4.7.4** below); and

- added to the carrying amount of the acquired in-process research or development project if it is development expenditure that satisfies the recognition criteria set out in IAS 38:57 (see **4.7.4** below).

If the cost of a replacement for part of an intangible asset is capitalised, in accordance with IAS 38:21, the carrying amount of the replaced part is derecognised. If it is not practicable to determine the carrying amount of the replaced part, the cost of the replacement may be used as an indication. [IAS 38:115]

4.3   Separate acquisition

4.3.1   Recognition criteria

Assuming that the asset acquired meets IAS 38's definition of an intangible asset, it should be recognised in the financial statements provided that (1) it is probable that expected future economic benefits will flow to the entity, and (2) the cost of the asset can be measured reliably (see **4.1** above).

These conditions are generally met when an asset is acquired separately. The anticipation of future economic benefits, even if there is uncertainty about the timing or the amount, is built into the price paid for the asset. Therefore, the probability criterion is always considered to be satisfied for separately acquired intangible assets. [IAS 38:25]

Cash or other monetary assets expended will establish a reliable measure of the cost of the asset. [IAS 38:26] The only circumstance when it may not be possible to measure the cost of the asset reliably is when the purchase consideration comprises non-monetary assets (see **4.6** below).

4.3.2   Measurement of cost

4.3.2.1   Elements of cost

When an intangible asset is purchased separately, and the consideration given is in the form of cash or other monetary assets, the determination of cost is relatively straight-forward. The cost of the intangible asset comprises:
[IAS 38:27]

- its purchase price, including import duties and non-refundable purchase taxes, after deducting trade discounts and rebates; and

- any directly attributable expenditure on preparing the asset for its intended use.

Examples of directly attributable expenditure are:
[IAS 38:28]

- the salaries, wages and other employment-related costs of personnel directly engaged in bringing the asset to its working condition;

- professional fees arising directly from bringing the asset to its working condition; and

- costs of testing whether the asset is functioning properly.

Examples of expenditure that *does not* form part of the cost of an intangible asset are:
[IAS 38:29]

- costs of introducing a new product or service (including costs of advertising and promotional activities);

- costs of conducting business in a new location or with a new class of customer (including the cost of staff training); and

- administration and general overhead costs.

4.3.2.2   Deferred consideration

If the payment of consideration is deferred beyond normal credit terms, the asset is recognised at the equivalent cash price and the difference between this amount and the amount actually paid is recognised as interest expense (unless capitalised in accordance with IAS 23 *Borrowing Costs*). [IAS 38:32]

> See **4.3.1** in **chapter A7** for further discussion of the application of this principle (in the context of measuring the cost of an item of property, plant and equipment, which is subject to equivalent requirements).

4.3.2.3   Cessation of capitalisation

Recognition of cost in the carrying amount of an intangible asset ceases when the asset is in the condition necessary for it to be capable of operating in the manner intended by management. The following costs are excluded from the carrying amount of an intangible asset:
[IAS 38:30]

- costs incurred in using or redeploying an asset;

- costs incurred while an asset capable of operating in the manner intended by management has yet to be brought into use; and

- initial operating losses, such as those incurred while demand for the asset's output builds up.

4.4   Acquisition as part of a business combination

4.4.1   Recognition criteria

IFRS 3 *Business Combinations* stipulates that, if an intangible asset is acquired in a business combination, the cost of that intangible asset is its fair value at the acquisition date. The fair value of the asset reflects market participants' expectations at the acquisition date as to the economic benefits that will flow from it, even if there is uncertainty about the timing or the amount of those benefits. Therefore, the probability criterion, as set out in **4.1** above, is always considered to be satisfied for intangible assets acquired in a business combination. [IAS 38:33]

The acquirer should recognise an intangible asset acquired in a business combination, separately from goodwill, irrespective of whether the asset was previously recognised by the acquiree. This should include any in-process research and development project of the acquiree if the project meets the definition of an intangible asset, and its fair value can be measured reliably. [IAS 38:34]

4.4.2   Measuring fair value

When an asset acquired in a business combination is separable or arises from contractual or other legal rights, sufficient information always exists to measure reliably the asset's fair value. [IAS 38:33]

IAS 38:33 was amended as a consequential amendment arising from IFRS 3 (as revised in 2008) so as to be clear that it should always be possible to reach a reliable measure of the fair value of an intangible asset acquired in a business combination. The effect of the amendment was to remove the possibility of arguing for the non-recognition of such intangible assets on the basis that their value cannot be measured reliably.

When the estimates used to measure the fair value of an intangible asset indicate that there is a range of possible outcomes with different probabilities, that uncertainty should be incorporated into the measurement of fair value. [IAS 38:35]

When an intangible asset acquired in a business combination is separable, but only together with a related contract, identifiable asset or liability, the acquirer should recognise the intangible asset separately from goodwill, but together with the related item. [IAS 38:36] Similarly, a group of complementary intangible assets (e.g. a trademark and its related trade name, formulas, recipes and technological expertise) may be combined into a single asset (often described as a 'brand') if the individual assets have similar useful lives. [IAS 38:37]

4.4.3 Measuring fair value: additional guidance for entities that have not yet adopted IFRS 13

IFRS 13 *Fair Value Measurement* establishes a single framework for measuring fair value when that is required by other Standards. It replaces the guidance regarding the measurement of fair value previously included in IAS 38.

For entities that have not yet adopted IFRS 13 (required for annual periods beginning on or after 1 January 2013, with earlier adoption permitted), IAS 38:39 to 41 provide additional guidance on the measurement of fair value, as set out below. With effect from the adoption of IFRS 13, paragraphs 39 to 41 are deleted from the Standard and entities should instead refer to IFRS 13 for guidance on the measurement of fair value. (See **7.2** below for the transition provisions of IFRS 13.)

An intangible asset acquired in a business combination is recognised at its fair value determined:

- by reference to an active market (see **7.1.2** below). While quoted market price (usually, current bid price) in an active market provides the most reliable measurement, when current bid prices are unavailable, the price of a similar recent transaction may provide a basis from which to estimate fair value, provided that there has not been a significant change in economic circumstances since the date of the original transaction; [IAS 38:39] or

- if no active market exists for the asset, the fair value reflects the amount that the entity would have paid for the asset, at the date of acquisition, in an arm's length transaction between knowledgeable and willing parties, based on the best information available. In determining this amount, the entity should consider the outcome of recent transactions for similar assets. For example, an entity may apply multiples reflecting current market transactions to factors that drive the profitability of the asset (such as revenue, operating profit or earnings before interest, tax, depreciation and amortisation). [IAS 38:40]

In certain industries, techniques have been developed for estimating the fair values of intangible assets indirectly. Such techniques may be used for the initial measurement of an intangible asset acquired in a business combination if their objective is to estimate fair value and if they reflect current transactions and practices in the industry. Such techniques include, for example, discounting estimated future net cash flows from the asset or estimating the costs the entity avoids by owning the intangible asset and, therefore, not needing either to license it from another party in an arm's length transaction (as in the 'relief from royalty' approach, using dis-counted net cash flows) or to recreate or replace it (as in the cost approach). [IAS 38:41]

4.4.3.1   Approaches for determining fair value

Three approaches that might be considered for determining fair value are set out below:

- if observable prices for market transactions for identical assets or liabilities at or near the measurement date are available, fair value would be estimated by reference to these prices;

- if observable prices for market transactions for similar assets or liabilities at or near the measurement date are available, fair value could be estimated by reference to these prices, making the necessary adjustments; and

- if the first two approaches do not apply, other valuation meth-odologies will need to be adopted.

In the majority of cases, there are unlikely to be identical assets with observable prices that can be relied upon to estimate the fair values of the intangible assets of the business being acquired. Some exam-ples of assets for which there may be directly comparable prices that could be relied on include taxi licences, allowances for emission rights and fishing rights in some markets.

Other assets can be considered similar by reference to their legal nature (e.g. patents, licences), intended uses, useful economic life, pattern of cash flows, risks and opportunities etc. Identifying similar assets for which observable prices exist can also be difficult, however, because there are few markets for intangible assets and a majority of asset acquisitions are 'private' transactions for which information is not publicly available. In addition, making adjustments to the observable prices so that they may be used to assess the value of the asset in question can be highly subjective and requires detailed analysis.

Accordingly, in a majority of cases, it should be expected that intangible asset valuations will need to be performed using other valuation methodologies for the purposes of IFRS 3. There are various valuation techniques that might be appropriate for the purposes of assessing the fair value of intangible assets, which are discussed below. When possible, more than one of the valuation techniques may be applied to arrive at fair value. This approach is designed to provide additional support, by way of a cross-check, for the fair value assessment made.

4.4.3.2   *Valuation techniques for the purposes of assessing the fair value of intangible assets*

When applying valuation techniques for the purposes of assessing the fair value of intangible assets, the objective of fair value measurement must be considered. Accordingly, the assumptions used should reflect market assumptions.

The most common generally accepted valuation methodologies for the purposes of assessing the fair value of intangible assets include:

- **market methods** – value intangible assets by reference to transactions, or benchmarks, involving similar assets that have occurred recently in similar markets; and

- **income methods** – value intangible assets on the basis of the future economic benefits derived from ownership of the asset. The main income methods include Relief from Royalty and Premium Profits (Excess Earnings).

Note that cost-based methods (which value intangible assets by aggregating the cost of developing the asset to its current condition, or replacing that asset) are sometimes, though not often, used in intangible asset valuations. Paragraph BCZ29 of IAS 36 *Impairment of Assets* states, however, that the "IASC believed that replacement cost techniques are not appropriate to measure the recoverable amount of an asset".

There is a further category of 'hybrid' methods which use elements from more than one method above. These are included below in the category to which they are most closely related (e.g. relief from royalty and avoided cost under income methods, replacement cost plus lost profits under cost-based methods).

Neither IFRS 3 nor IAS 38 sets out detailed criteria for performing a valuation. Listed below, however, are some key criteria, based on common valuation practice, that need to be considered in undertaking a valuation of an intangible asset:

- *credibility* – the valuation methodology should be credible and respectable from both a theoretical and commercial perspective;

- *objectivity* – the choice of methodology may necessitate a trade-off between the intellectual rigour of the methodology and the inherent degree of subjectivity. The valuer must be guided by the quality and quantity of objective information available;

- *versatility* – credibility will be enhanced if standard approaches can be applied across entities, industries and classifications of intangible assets;

- *consistency* – the methodologies should be applicable on a consistent basis year-on-year, and thus facilitate the updating of the valuation;

- *reliability* – the valuation should be verifiable, such that other valuers may replicate the process using similar measurement principles;

- *relevance* – the valuation basis and methodology selected should be relevant to the requirements of the user; and

- *practicability* – the methods and underlying parameters should be clear and relatively easy to apply in practice.

One of the key elements of any valuation exercise is a thorough understanding of the business that is the subject of the transaction. Having obtained this, a valuer will have a better appreciation of the approach that may be adopted for the purposes of the valuation exercise and be able to identify the intangible assets that are important to the business. This will assist in applying the appropriate valuation methodology and assessing the information that will be required, subject to availability. In addition it will help in assessing the lives of the intangible assets that are in existence by understanding their nature and importance to the business.

4.4.3.3 *The process of assessing the fair value of intangible assets*

The approaches set out above include a number of steps that identify and collate the information to enable the valuer to make an assessment of the fair value of the intangible assets. These steps may be summarised as follows.

Below are set out brief comments on the application of different valuation methodologies.

4.4.3.4   *Market value method*

Under the comparable market value methodology, the value of an intangible asset is determined by reference to the prices obtained for comparable assets in recent transactions. The methodology is, therefore, theoretically attractive: it is credible, objective and, because the valuation basis is fair value, relevant.

Appropriate adjustments for entities using this method should be made by reference to known, quantifiable differences between the transaction being accounted for and the comparable transaction. (If the differences between the transactions are not capable of quantification, an entity will need to adopt other valuation methodologies.)

The main issues with this methodology are that:

- its use in practice is often limited by the scarcity of comparable transactions and publicly disclosed information on any such transactions; and

- it can be difficult to ensure that the asset under consideration and the market transaction are sufficiently comparable.

Transactions in the shares of entities owning similar assets are more frequent. In the majority of these circumstances, separation of the value attributable to the intangible asset from the underlying assets of the business will not be straightforward, particularly for those not party to the transaction. However, the valuer will often find the component parts of the transaction data useful. For example, the multiple of earnings at which the business is sold may be an important reference point when determining an appropriate rate at which to capitalise the intangible asset's earnings.

4.4.3.5   *Income-based methods*

The economic / income-based valuation of any intangible asset has two distinct components:

- identification, separation and quantification of the cash flows (or earnings) attributable to the intangible asset; and

- capitalisation of those cash flows (or earnings).

The main income methods are:

- relief from royalty; and

- premium profits (excess earnings).

Relief from royalty

Principle: the value of an intangible asset to an entity is what it would pay to use it under a licence if it did not own it, or the cost savings of not having to pay a royalty.

Generally applicable to: technologies, patents, brands, know-how.

Steps

- research licensing transactions with comparable assets to establish a range of market levels for royalty rates;

- analyse the strength and importance of the asset and its contribution to the overall economics of the owning entity to determine an applicable royalty rate;

- select a royalty rate or range of royalty rates;

- apply the selected royalty rate to the future revenue stream attributable to the asset;

- use the appropriate marginal tax rate to arrive at an after-tax royalty rate;

- discount the resulting cash flow stream to the present value at an appropriate risk-adjusted discount rate; and

- if appropriate, apply a factor to adjust the value of the asset for the effect of tax amortisation.

Issues

- the value of an owned asset may exceed the value of a licensed asset, because ownership may provide additional options, which can be difficult to value separately;

- the process of selecting an appropriate royalty rate range based on market evidence needs to be rigorous because the value implications of a small change in the royalty rate can be significant;

- factors to consider in establishing the appropriate royalty rate range include the asset's strengths and weaknesses, competing assets etc.;

- what discount rate to use:

  - entity-specific?

  - cash-generating unit-specific? (This may include an additional premium linked to the size of the cash-generating unit.)

  - asset-specific? (This may include an additional premium due to the higher risks of an intangible asset compared to a business as a whole.)

Premium profits (excess earnings)

Principle: the value of an asset is the capitalised amount of incremental profits achievable through use of the intangible asset as compared with the profits of the same business not using it, or the value of an asset is the capitalised amount of earnings relating to that asset less the returns on all other assets that contribute to that earnings stream.

Generally applicable to: customer relationships, technology, know-how, brands.

Two approaches:

- profit or loss based (forecasting profits in excess of 'normal' profits that would be obtained by a business producing a similar good or rendering a similar service, without the use of this intangible asset); and

- balance sheet (i.e. net asset) based (comparing the return on capital of the cash-generating unit using the intangible asset with the return on capital of businesses not using the respective intangible assets).

Steps

- forecast a normalised level of income for the cash-generating unit;

- apply an appropriate or 'fair' rate of return to the net asset base to compute the economic income attributable to the tangible and the other intangible assets of the cash-generating unit;

- subtract the fair return on assets from the normalised level of economic income for the cash-generating unit to arrive at the excess earnings;

- capitalise the resulting excess earnings using an appropriate risk-adjusted discount rate to calculate fair value; and

- if appropriate, apply a factor to adjust the value of the asset for the effect of tax amortisation.

Issues

- difficult to find relevant entities which do not own/use a similar intangible asset;

- estimation of discount rate;

- if a business has several intangible assets, how should 'premium profits' value be allocated amongst them?

- what is an appropriate rate of return on other intangible assets?

4.4.3.6 Some useful information sources used for intangible asset valuations

For the purposes of valuing intangible assets, various sources can be used for certain elements of the exercise, including:

- third-party licensing agreements;

- *www.royaltysource.com* (a fee is charged for this service);

- *www.royaltystat.com* (a fee is charged for this service);

- Licensing Economics Review;

- in respect of franchise fees:

  - *www.minorityfranchising.com;*

  - *www.franchisingamerica.com;*

- SEC EDGAR database for any information filed by comparable entities.

4.5   Acquisition by way of a government grant

An intangible asset may be granted to an entity free of charge or for nominal consideration by a government. This may be the case for assets such as airport landing rights, broadcasting licences, import licences or quotas, or rights to access other restricted resources.

In these circumstances, an entity may either:
[IAS 38:44]

- recognise both the grant and the intangible asset at fair value; or

- recognise both the grant and the intangible asset at a nominal amount plus any expenditure that is directly attributable to preparing the asset for its intended use.

The alternatives allowed for under IAS 38:44 are consistent with those allowed for non-monetary government grants under IAS 20 *Accounting for Government Grants and Disclosure of Government Assistance* (see **section 5** of **chapter A36**).

4.6   Exchanges of assets

When an intangible asset is acquired in exchange for a non-monetary asset or assets, or a combination of monetary and non-monetary assets, the cost of the asset received is measured at fair value (even if the entity cannot immediately derecognise the asset given up), unless either:
[IAS 38:45]

- the exchange transaction lacks commercial substance; or

- the fair value of neither the asset received nor the asset given up is reliably measurable.

In either of these circumstances, which result in the acquired asset not being measured at fair value, its cost is measured at the carrying amount of the asset given up. [IAS 38:45]

Whether or not a transaction has commercial substance is determined by considering the extent to which the entity's future cash flows are expected to change as a result of the transaction. An exchange transaction is considered to have commercial substance if:
[IAS 38:46]

- the configuration (i.e. risk, timing and amount) of the cash flows of the asset received differs from the configuration of the cash flows of the asset transferred; or

- the entity-specific value (reflecting post-tax cash flows) of the portion of the entity's operations affected by the transaction changes as a result of the exchange; and

- the difference arising in either of the two circumstances outlined is significant relative to the fair value of the assets exchanged.

As set out in **4.1** above, no intangible asset can be recognised unless its cost can be measured reliably. In an exchange transaction, if an entity is able to measure reliably the fair value of either the asset received or the asset given up, the fair value of the asset given up should be used to measure cost, unless the fair value of the asset received is more clearly evident. Fair value can be measured reliably if either (1) the variability in the range of reasonable fair value measurements is not significant for that asset, or (2) the probabilities of the various estimates within the range can be reasonably assessed and used when measuring fair value. [IAS 38:47]

4.7   Internally generated intangible assets

Inherently, it is more difficult to assess whether an internally generated intangible asset qualifies for recognition because of problems in identifying whether and when there is an identifiable asset that will generate future economic benefits, and in determining the cost of the asset reliably. Therefore, IAS 38 includes additional recognition criteria for internally generated intangible assets which expand on the general recognition criteria. It is assumed that these additional criteria are met implicitly whenever an entity acquires an intangible asset.

Example 4.7

Development costs paid to an external party

Company A pays Company B, an external party, to develop an asset that would meet the requirements of IAS 38 for recognition as an internally generated intangible asset in Company A's financial statements (see **4.7.4** below). Company B is performing only development work; all the associated research has already been performed, and the costs expensed, by Company A.

Company A should recognise an internally generated intangible asset for these development costs under IAS 38. Whether Company A incurs the costs directly via an internal development function or outsources the development process to an external party does not influence how Company A should account for the asset in its financial statements.

Therefore, because the expenditure meets the requirements for the recognition of an internally generated intangible asset under IAS 38, Company A should recognise the asset as an internally generated intangible asset in its financial statements. If the asset being developed did not meet the requirements for recognition of an internally generated intangible asset under IAS 38, the costs would be considered research expenditures and would be expensed as incurred. Similarly, if Company B was paid by Company A to perform both research and development activities, the research element would be expensed as incurred, but the development element would be capitalised provided that it met the requirements of IAS 38.

4.7.1 Items that should not be recognised as internally generated intangible assets

The Standard prohibits the recognition of internally generated goodwill as an asset. [IAS 38:48]

Some other internally generated items are specifically identified in IAS 38 as not capable of being distinguished from the cost of developing the business as a whole and therefore are prohibited from being capitalised as internally generated intangible assets. These are internally generated: [IAS 38:63]

- brands;

- mastheads;

- publishing titles;

- customer lists; and

- items similar in substance to any of the above.

Although IAS 38 bans these items from recognition as internally generated assets, when such assets are purchased either individually or as part of a business combination, they may meet the general recognition criteria for intangible assets and, therefore, potentially may be recognised. This difference means that intangible assets such as brands can be recognised as intangible assets if acquired but should be expensed if they are generated internally.

4.7.2   Distinction between research and development

The Standard distinguishes between two phases in the generation of an intangible asset internally – the research phase and the development phase. Capitalisation is only permitted during the development phase. The additional recognition criteria are discussed at **4.7.4** below.

Research is defined as original and planned investigation undertaken with the prospect of gaining new scientific or technical knowledge and understanding. [IAS 38:8]

Development is the application of research findings or other knowledge to a plan or design for the production of new or substantially improved materials, devices, products, processes, systems or services prior to the commencement of commercial production or use. [IAS 38:8]

If it is not possible to distinguish the research phase from the development phase of an internal project to create an intangible asset, the expenditure on that project is treated as relating only to the research phase. [IAS 38:53]

The following examples of research activities given in the Standard illustrate that the main objective of research activities is the discovery of something new:
[IAS 38:56]

- activities aimed at obtaining new knowledge;

- the search for, evaluation and final selection of, applications of research findings or other knowledge;

- the search for alternatives for materials, devices, products, processes, systems or services; and

- the formulation, design, evaluation and final selection of possible alternatives for new or improved materials, devices, products, processes, systems or services.

The following examples of development activities illustrate that the main objective of development activities is to apply research findings for a business purpose:
[IAS 38:59]

- the design, construction and testing of pre-production or pre-use prototypes and models;

- the design of tools, jigs, moulds and dies involving new technology;

- the design, construction and operation of a pilot plant that is not of a scale economically feasible for commercial production; and

- the design, construction and testing of a chosen alternative for new or improved materials, devices, products, processes, systems or services.

4.7.3   Research phase

Research costs are, by their nature, incurred with the intent of gaining new knowledge rather than creating a practical application from which future economic benefits will flow. Therefore, research costs do not meet the criteria for recognition of an internally generated asset. Costs incurred during the research phase are required to be expensed. [IAS 38:54]

4.7.4   Development phase (additional recognition criteria)

In limited circumstances, during the development phase of a project, an entity is able to identify an intangible asset and demonstrate that the asset will generate probable future economic benefits. [IAS 38:58] However, criteria in addition to those for externally acquired intangible assets must be met in order to recognise an internally generated intangible asset.

Specifically, an intangible asset arising from development (or from the development phase of an internal project) should be recognised if, and only if, an entity can demonstrate all of the following:
[IAS 38:57]

- the technical feasibility of completing the intangible asset so that it will be available for use or sale;

- its intention to complete the intangible asset and use or sell it;

- its ability to use or sell the intangible asset;

- how the intangible asset will generate probable future economic benefits. Among other things, the entity can demonstrate the existence of a market for the output of the intangible asset or the intangible asset itself or, if it is to be used internally, the usefulness of the intangible asset;

- the availability of adequate technical, financial and other resources to complete the development and to use or sell the intangible asset; and

- its ability to measure the expenditure attributable to the intangible asset during the development phase.

IAS 38 does not provide any guidance in respect of the first criterion as to when technical feasibility is established. Although it is difficult to set one guideline, due to the differing types of internally generated intangible assets, when the asset is the product of 'traditional' research and development activities or software development activities, an appropriate point may be when the entity has completed all the planning, design and testing activities that are necessary to establish that an asset can be produced to meet its design specifications, including functions, features and technical performance requirements.

If regulatory approval is required before the technical feasibility can be established, the entity should consider carefully the process involved and the likelihood of achieving approval. If there is significant uncertainty regarding the approval process or outcome at any time during the development process, it is unlikely that the entity has met the criteria to recognise an internally generated asset. However, if the entity is confident it will obtain approval, and has evidence to support this, it may be more likely that the technical feasibility criterion has been met.

In respect of the fourth criterion, IAS 38 suggests that an entity can demonstrate that the asset will generate future economic benefits by using the principles in IAS 36 *Impairment of Assets* relating to the estimation of future cash flows. [IAS 38:60] As discussed in more detail in **chapter A10**, cash flow projections should be based on reasonable and supportable assumptions that represent management's best estimate of the set of economic conditions that will exist over the useful life of the asset, with greater weight given to external evidence. Such projections should not normally cover a period of more than five years. The cash flows should be discounted using a pre-tax rate that reflects current market assessments of the time value of money and the risks specific to the asset. If the internally generated intangible asset will only produce economic benefits together with other assets (e.g. new computer software that will significantly reduce overhead costs), its cash flows cannot be independently assessed. Therefore, it is included in its cash-generating unit and the unit as a whole is evaluated. (See **chapter A10** for further discussion of cash-generating units.)

The fifth criterion (availability of resources) would normally be met by a business plan that details the planned expenditure on the project and the resources that will be available to fund it. If the project is being financed externally, a lender's indication of its willingness to finance the business plan may be sufficient to demonstrate availability of external finance. [IAS 38:61]

In order to meet the final criterion (ability to measure attributable expenditure), an entity should have a costing system to track costs incurred related to the specific development project. In many cases, this can be a simple system based on the time sheets of the employees involved in the development of the intangible asset but, on more complex projects, the system should also track direct expenses incurred.

In practice, in different industries, the relative lengths of the research and development phases of a project are likely to be significantly different. In some industries (e.g. the pharmaceutical industry), some of the criteria will only be met very late in the process so that, of the total research and development costs incurred, only a small proportion will form part of the cost of an internally generated intangible asset. In other industries, the criteria may be met at a much earlier stage in the process and an intangible asset may be recognised for a higher proportion of the costs incurred. Often, this is influenced by how early, or late, in the overall process it is possible to be confident that the project outcome will be successful.

4.7.4.1 *Impairment indicators identified during development phase*

If an impairment indicator has been identified in respect of an internally generated intangible asset that is currently being developed for internal use as part of a cash-generating unit (and for which

IAS 38's criteria for recognition of an internally generated intangible asset have been met), but no impairment loss has been recognised because the recoverable amount of the cash-generating unit as a whole is greater than its carrying amount, the entity should generally include subsequent expenditure in the cost of the intangible asset.

Usually, an entity will only continue with such a development project if it expects the future benefits from completing the project to exceed the additional costs that will need to be incurred (even though those benefits may not be sufficient also to cover costs already incurred, i.e. 'sunk' costs). When the future benefits are expected to exceed the additional costs, it is appropriate to capitalise the subsequent costs in accordance with the requirements of IAS 38:57. **Example 4.7.4.1** illustrates the approach taken in such circumstances.

If, exceptionally, an entity decides to continue with a development project even though it does not expect the future benefits from completing the project to exceed the additional costs that will need to be incurred, then the entity will need to consider carefully whether the fourth criterion in IAS 38:57 (probability of future economic benefits) is met. If it is not, subsequent expenditure should be recognised as an expense.

Example 4.7.4.1

Subsequent expenditure on an internally generated intangible asset under development for use in a cash-generating unit after impairment indicators are identified

Entity R is developing computer software for use in its business. On 1 January 20X1, the criteria for recognition as an internally generated intangible asset are met and expenditure on the development incurred after that date is included in the cost of the asset. Budgeted total expenditure to completion of the project at the end of 20X3 is CU3 million and the incremental benefits to be derived from the software are expected to be approximately CU5 million.

At 31 December 20X1, the intangible asset is tested for impairment as required by IAS 36:10(a), but no impairment loss is identified.

At 31 May 20X2, the carrying amount of the intangible asset is CU1.5 million. In June 20X2, estimates of the additional costs to complete the project are increased to CU4.5 million (i.e. total project costs of CU6 million). (Note that this is not as a result of operating inefficiencies or error.) A decision is taken to proceed with the project because the expected incremental benefits (CU5 million) are still in excess of the costs not yet incurred (CU4.5 million).

However, the directors consider that this is an indication of impairment and that the recoverable amount of the software should be estimated.

The software does not generate independent cash flows, and its fair value less costs of disposal is estimated to be lower than its carrying amount; accordingly, the software asset is tested for impairment as part of its cash-generating unit.

The recoverable amount of the cash-generating unit as a whole is determined to be CU100 million and its carrying amount is CU75 million; therefore, no impairment loss is recognised.

As additional expenditure is incurred on completion of the software development, Entity R should continue to include that expenditure in the cost of the software asset in accordance with IAS 38:57. In addition, although the total costs are significantly in excess of the original budget, and are expected to exceed the incremental benefits that will be generated by the software, no impairment loss is required to be recognised unless the carrying amount of the cash-generating unit as a whole exceeds its recoverable amount.

4.7.5   Cost of an internally generated intangible asset

The requirement that an intangible asset should be initially recognised at its cost applies equally to internally generated intangible assets. Cost includes all costs incurred from the date on which all of the recognition criteria (i.e. those for purchased as well as for internally generated intangible assets) are met. If costs have been expensed prior to the recognition criteria being met, they may not be reinstated upon satisfaction of the criteria. [IAS 38:65 & 71]

Similar to self-constructed items of property, plant and equipment, the cost of an internally generated intangible asset includes all directly attributable costs necessary to create, produce and prepare an asset to be capable of operating in the manner intended by management. These costs may include:
[IAS 38:66]

- expenditure on materials and services used or consumed in generating the intangible asset;

- the salaries, wages and other employment-related costs of personnel directly engaged in generating the asset;

- borrowing costs, in accordance with the requirements of IAS 23 *Borrowing Costs* – see **chapter A18**; and

- any other expenditure that is directly attributable to generating the asset, such as fees to register a legal right and the amortisation of patents and licences that are used to generate the asset.

IAS 38 specifically prohibits the inclusion of the following items in the cost of an internally generated intangible asset:
[IAS 38:67]

- selling, administrative and other general overhead expenditure unless this expenditure can be directly attributed to preparing the asset for use;

- clearly identified inefficiencies and initial operating losses incurred before an asset achieves planned performance; and

- expenditure on training staff to operate the asset.

Example 4.7.5

Evaluating whether overheads are 'directly attributable costs'

Company A is developing a product in premises used solely for the product's development. The criteria in IAS 38 for the recognition of an intangible asset arising from the development activities have been met. Company A expects to continue to use the premises after the product's development is completed.

Is it acceptable for the costs of these premises to be included in the cost of the internally generated development asset?

IAS 38:66 states that "the cost of an internally generated intangible asset comprises all directly attributable costs necessary to create, produce and prepare the asset to be capable of operating in the manner intended by management". Premises costs are more likely to fall under IAS 38:67, which states that selling, administrative and other general overhead costs are not part of the cost of an internally generated intangible asset "unless this expenditure can be directly attributed to preparing the asset for use". Whether such costs can be considered 'directly attributable' is a matter of judgement in the particular circumstances. However, to qualify as directly attributable, it would be expected that the costs would have been avoided had the entity not engaged in the development activities.

Therefore, if the premises are rented, it may be possible to demonstrate that the rental costs are directly attributable costs if they would not have been incurred had the entity not engaged in the development activities. For example, Company A might be able to demonstrate that:

- it did not rent the premises until commencement of the development activities; and

- had it not engaged in the development activities, it would not have rented the premises until a later date for use in other activities.

Alternatively, if the development activities take place in a property owned by Company A, prior to commencing those activities, Company A would need to demonstrate that the costs of the building (or portion of the building)

---

in which the development activities are carried out would have been avoided, such as in one of the following scenarios:

- the building (or portion of the building) is separately identifiable and could have been separately subleased if not used for the development activities; or

- the building (or portion of the building) would have been used to house other activities for which Company A has rented additional premises.

4.7.6   *Research and development activities performed under contract for others*

When an entity carries out research and development activities for others, the substance of the arrangement dictates the accounting treatment of the research and development expenditure for both entities. If the entity carrying out the research and development activities is retaining the risks and rewards of the activities and will control any asset that is developed, it should account for the expenditure on the research and development activities in accordance with IAS 38. If the entity carrying out the research and development activities is not retaining the risks and rewards of the activities and control of any asset that is developed will lie with the other party, the entity carrying out the activities is providing a service to that other party and should account for its activities in accordance with IAS 18 *Revenue* or IAS 11 *Construction Contracts*, as appropriate (see **chapters A14** and **A34**, respectively). The following factors may indicate that the risks and rewards of the research and development activities are retained by the entity carrying out the activities:

- the entity conducting the research and development activities will retain full rights to any intellectual property that is developed;

- the entity conducting the research and development activities will only receive payment from the other entity if the outcome of the research and development activities is successful (i.e. the outcome meets criteria specified by that other entity);

- the entity conducting the research and development activities is contractually obliged to repay any of the funds provided by the other entity, regardless of the outcome of the research and development activities; or

- even though the contract does not require the entity conducting the research and development activities to repay any of the funds provided by the other entity, repayment could be required at the option of the other entity or the surrounding conditions indicate that repayment is probable.

4.7.7   Web site costs

SIC-32 *Intangible Assets – Web Site Costs* addresses the appropriate accounting treatment for internal expenditure to develop, enhance and maintain a web site incurred by an entity (whether for internal or external access). Specifically, the Interpretation addresses the application of IAS 38 to web site development costs.

The Interpretation does not apply to purchasing, developing and operating the hardware associated with a web site (accounted for under IAS 16 *Property, Plant and Equipment*), nor to expenditure on the development or operation of a web site for sale to another entity (accounted for under IAS 2 *Inventories* and IAS 11 *Construction Contracts*).

SIC-32 identifies the following stages of web site development: [SIC-32:2]

- Planning (including undertaking feasibility studies, defining objectives and specifications, evaluating alternatives and selecting preferences);

- Application and Infrastructure Development (including obtaining a domain name, purchasing and developing hardware and operating software, installing developed applications and stress testing);

- Graphical Design (including designing the appearance of web pages);

- Content Development (including creating, purchasing, preparing and uploading information, either textual or graphical in nature, on the web site before the completion of the web site's development. This information may either be stored in separate databases that are integrated into, or accessed from, the web site or coded directly into the web pages); and

- Operating (including maintaining and enhancing the applications, infrastructure, graphical design and content of the web site).

The Interpretation states that:
[SIC-32:7 & 8]

- a web site developed by an entity for its own use (whether for internal or external access) is an internally generated intangible asset that is subject to the requirements of IAS 38;

- future economic benefits, as envisaged by IAS 38's criteria for recognition of internally generated intangible assets, will be generated from a web site only when the web site is capable of generating revenue. For example, the requirement may be satisfied when the web site is capable of generating direct revenues from enabling orders to be placed; and

- if the web site has been developed solely or primarily for promoting or advertising the entity's products and services, the entity will be unable to demonstrate that such a web site will generate future economic benefits, and costs incurred on the development of the web site should be expensed as incurred.

SIC-32 concludes as follows:
[SIC-32:9]

- the nature of each activity for which expenditure is incurred (e.g. training employees and maintaining the web site) and the web site's stage of development or post-development are evaluated to determine the appropriate accounting treatment (additional guidance is provided in the appendix to SIC-32);

- the Planning stage of a web site development is similar to the research phase described at **4.7.3** above and, therefore, any expenditure incurred in this stage is recognised as an expense when it is incurred;

- the Application and Infrastructure Development stage, the Graphical Design stage and the and Content Development stage are similar in nature to the development phase described at **4.7.4** above. Therefore, expenditure incurred in these stages is recognised as an intangible asset if the expenditure can be directly attributed and is necessary to creating, producing or preparing the web site for it to be capable of operating in the manner intended by management. For example, expenditure on purchasing or creating content (other than content that advertises and promotes an entity's own products and services) specifically for a web site, or to enable use of the content (e.g. a fee for acquiring a licence to reproduce) on the web site, is included in the cost of development when this condition is met; and

- expenditure incurred in the Content Development stage, to the extent that content is developed to advertise and promote an entity's own products and services (e.g. digital photographs of products), is recognised as an expense when incurred. For example, when accounting for expenditure on professional services for taking digital photographs of an entity's own products and for enhancing their display, expenditure is recognised as an expense as the professional services are received during the process, not when the digital photographs are displayed on the web site.

In accordance with IAS 38:71 (see **4.7.5**), expenditure on web site development that has previously been recognised as an expense should not be recognised as part of the cost of the web site intangible asset at a later date.

> The Operating stage commences once the web site is available for use and, therefore, expenditure to maintain or enhance the web site after development has been completed should be recognised as an expense when it is incurred, unless it meets the criteria discussed at **4.2** above (criteria for recognising subsequent expenditure as an asset). Similarly, when an entity incurs expenditure on an Internet service provider hosting the entity's web site, the expenditure is recognised as an expense when the services are received.

SIC-32 indicates that the best estimate of a web site's useful life, for the purpose of amortisation, is short. [SIC-32:10]

4.7.8   *Accounting for costs related to compliance with REACH*

> The Registration, Evaluation, Authorisation and Restriction of Chemicals (REACH) regulation requires commercial users of chemical substances in the European Union (EU) to perform studies demonstrating the properties of each of the substances they use or sell and to pay a one-time fee to register each of the chemical substances. The registration process (the performance of the studies and the one-time registration fee) is required for all chemical substances already in use and those that will be developed. If the registration process is not followed for a substance, a commercial user cannot market that chemical substance or the products containing the substance.

In addition, the REACH regulation allows studies performed by one commercial user to be sold to other users as a means of sharing costs among users.

In the July 2009 edition of *IFRIC Update*, the IFRIC (now the IFRS Interpretations Committee) announced its rejection of a request to provide guidance on the appropriate accounting for the costs of complying with the REACH regulation. The IFRIC noted that IAS 38 includes definitions and recognition criteria for intangible assets that provide guidance to enable entities to account for the costs of complying with the REACH regulation.

The appropriate accounting for the costs of the registration process depends on whether the costs incurred relate to chemical substances (and products made with such substances) already in commercial use when the REACH regulation came into effect or to new substances (and new products made with such substances) developed after the effective date of the REACH regulation.

4.7.8.1   *Existing chemical substances and existing products made with chemical substances*

The preferred treatment is to recognise the REACH costs relating to existing chemical substances and products in profit or loss as incurred because those costs do not add value to the entity's business but rather enable the entity to continue its operations.

However, because there is no clear guidance on the issue, it would also be acceptable to recognise an intangible asset arising from the costs incurred to comply with the REACH regulation, provided that the recognition criteria of IAS 38 are met. This is because the costs incurred under REACH result in an entity obtaining identifiable rights for the commercial use of a specific substance that are necessary to earn benefits from that substance or the product that embodies the substance.

The accounting policy adopted should be disclosed and applied consistently.

4.7.8.2   New chemical substances and new products made with chemical substances

The REACH costs are necessary for the development of new chemical substances (or new products) and their commercial use. Therefore, if the recognition criteria in IAS 38 are met, an intangible asset should be recognised arising from the costs incurred to comply with the REACH regulation.

4.7.8.3   Income from sale of the studies

In either case, any income received from the sale of the studies should be recognised in profit or loss as 'other income' because it is incidental to the development of the studies.

5   Items to be recognised as an expense

As a general rule, expenditure on an intangible item should be recognised as an expense as incurred unless:
[IAS 38:68]

- it forms part of the cost of an intangible asset that meets the appropriate definition and recognition criteria; or

- the item is acquired in a business combination and does not meet the criteria for separate recognition. In such cases, it forms part of the amount recognised as goodwill at the acquisition date.

IAS 38 states that the following types of expenditure should always be recognised as an expense:
[IAS 38:69]

- research (except to the extent that it relates to an intangible acquired in a business combination);

- start-up activities, unless the expenditure qualifies to be included in the cost of an item of property, plant and equipment. Start-up costs include:

  - establishment costs such as legal and secretarial costs incurred in establishing a legal entity;

- expenditure to open a new facility or business (i.e. pre-opening costs); and

- expenditure prior to starting new operations or launching new products or processes (i.e. pre-operating costs);

- training activities;

- advertising and promotional activities (including mail order catalogues); and

- relocating or reorganising part or all of an entity.

More generally, if expenditure does not give rise to an intangible asset: [IAS 38:69 & 69A]

- for a supply of goods, an expense is recognised when the entity has a right to access those goods. This is when the entity owns the goods or, if they have been constructed by a supplier in accordance with the terms of a supply contract, when the entity could demand delivery of them in return for payment; and

- for a supply of services, an expense is recognised when the entity receives the services. Services are received when they are performed by a supplier in accordance with a contract to deliver them to the entity and not when the entity uses them to deliver another service, for example to deliver an advertisement to customers.

This does not, however, preclude the recognition of a prepayment asset when payment for goods or services has been made in advance of the entity obtaining a right to access those goods, or in advance of receiving those services. [IAS 38:70]

The specific reference to mail order catalogues being part of advertising and promotional activities (and, consequently, always required to be recognised as an expense) is designed specifically to prohibit entities from recognising a prepayment asset for the costs of production of mail order catalogues or advertising, and only recognising those costs as an expense when the catalogues are distributed to the end-customer or when the advertisements are broadcast or published. Once an entity has a right to access, or has taken delivery of, mail order catalogues or advertisements, any associated expenditure is required to be recognised as an expense immediately.

Example 5

Selling and marketing costs

Entity A, a real estate developer, has incurred selling and marketing costs during the construction of a block of units that relate to the specific real estate construction project. These costs include:

- advertising costs for the project;

- sales commissions paid for selling the units; and

- fees paid to the bank to list the property to enable buyers to get mortgages.

The construction of the units does not fall within the scope of IAS 11 *Construction Contracts*. Following the guidance in IFRIC 15 *Agreements for the Construction of Real Estate*, revenue from the construction of the units is recognised as a 'sale of goods' in accordance with IAS 18 *Revenue* rather than in accordance with IAS 11.

There may be very limited circumstances in which the capitalisation of selling and marketing costs is appropriate. Although IFRIC 15 and IAS 18 are both silent regarding the accounting for the costs of real estate projects that are not in the scope of IAS 11, other Standards do provide guidance on the capitalisation of costs.

The following Standards specifically prohibit the capitalisation of selling and marketing costs:

- if the real estate units are accounted for as inventories, paragraph 16 of IAS 2 *Inventories* prohibits selling costs from being included in the cost of inventories;

- IAS 16 *Property, Plant and Equipment* does not permit selling costs to be recognised as part of the cost of property, plant and equipment unless they are directly attributable to preparing the asset for use; and

- IAS 11:20 excludes selling costs from the cost of a construction contract.

No Standard permits the capitalisation of advertising or other costs incurred in attempting to obtain customer contracts.

However, other Standards permit some direct and incremental costs recoverable as a result of securing a specifically identifiable contract with a customer to be capitalised in narrow circumstances. For example, IAS 11:21 permits costs incurred in securing a contract to be included as part of contract costs provided that specified conditions are met; and paragraph 14(b)(iii) of the illustrative examples accompanying IAS 18 indicates that the incremental costs of securing an investment management contract may be capitalised provided that specific conditions are met. In these circumstances, when the specified conditions are met, capitalised costs may represent an identifiable intangible asset arising from contractual or other legal rights in accordance with IAS 38.

> The appropriate accounting for selling and marketing costs is dependent on the specific facts and circumstances. Each situation should be carefully assessed to determine if capitalisation of such costs is appropriate.
>
> The conclusions above were set out in the May 2009 edition of *IFRIC Update*.

6 Alternatives for measurement after initial recognition

> IAS 38 sets out two alternatives for subsequent measurement – the cost model and the revaluation model. However, the conditions imposed for use of the revaluation model are strict and this alternative is unlikely to be available in practice other than in very rare cases (see **7.1** below).

6.1 Cost model

If an intangible asset is accounted for using the cost model, after initial recognition, it is carried in the statement of financial position at its cost (measured as described in **section 4** above) less any accumulated amortisation and any accumulated impairment losses. [IAS 38:74]

6.2 Revaluation model

If the revaluation model is adopted, the intangible asset is carried at a revalued amount, which is its fair value at the date of the revaluation less any subsequent accumulated amortisation and any subsequent accumulated impairment losses. [IAS 38:75] The revaluation model is described in **section 7**.

7 Revaluation model

7.1 Which intangible assets can be revalued?

In order to use the revaluation model, the fair value of an intangible asset is required to be measured by reference to an active market. Therefore, only intangible assets that are traded on an active market can be revalued under the Standard.

This requirement has not been changed as a result of the issue of IFRS 13 *Fair Value Measurement*. However, the definition of an 'active market' has been amended by that Standard. For entities that have adopted IFRS 13, the definition in IFRS 13 (see **7.1.1**) should be applied. For entities that have not yet adopted IFRS 13, the definition in IAS 38 (see **7.1.2**) should be applied.

See **7.2** below for a discussion of the transition provisions of IFRS 13.

7.1.1   Definition of an active market – entities that have adopted IFRS 13

An active market is defined as "[a] market in which transactions for the asset or liability take place with sufficient frequency and volume to provide pricing information on an ongoing basis". [IFRS 13:Appendix A]

7.1.2   Definition of an active market – entities that have not yet adopted IFRS 13

An active market is defined as a market where all of the following conditions are present:
[IAS 38:8]

- the items traded within the market are homogeneous;

- willing buyers and sellers can normally be found at any time; and

- prices are available to the public.

7.1.3   Active markets for intangible assets expected to be rare

IAS 38 permits no basis for the measurement of fair value other than by reference to an active market. It is quite rare for an active market to exist for intangible assets. Therefore, the revaluation of intangible assets is not expected to be common. Examples of intangible assets for which the revaluation option might be available are freely transferable taxi licenses, fishing licenses or production quotas. [IAS 38.78]

Other intangible assets may be traded in private transactions, with such intangible assets being unique and the price for each transaction being specifically negotiated. In such circumstances, the price paid for one asset may not provide sufficient evidence of the fair value of another. [IAS 38.78]

> **Example 7.1.3**
>
> **Revaluation of internally generated intangible assets**
>
> Over the past two years, a group has developed various items of computer software to be used internally and/or to be sold to prospective buyers. In accordance with IAS 38, the group capitalised the development costs incurred during the development phase and recognised an intangible asset of CU1 million. After the reporting date, the group began discussions with a third party for the sale of the subsidiary that owns the software, or the sale of that subsidiary's assets. The selling price under negotiation is much higher than the carrying amount of the subsidiary's assets (which mainly relate to the internally generated intangible asset and other computer equipment).
>
> The group is not permitted to revalue its internally generated intangible asset because no active market exists. [IAS 38:75] Although the entity has entered into sale negotiations, this is not sufficient to indicate an active market. If an active market, as defined, genuinely existed, the price for which the asset could be sold would be publicly available and would not be a matter for negotiation. Indeed, IAS 38:78 states that the fact that there is a sale agreement between an entity and a buyer does not provide evidence of an active market.

IAS 38 specifically states that, due to their unique nature, an active market cannot exist for any of the following items:
[IAS 38:78]

- brands;

- newspaper mastheads;

- music and film publishing rights; and

- patents or trademarks.

7.1.4   *Revaluation not permitted for items that have not previously been recognised as assets*

The revaluation model does not permit:
[IAS 38:76]

- the revaluation of intangible assets that have not previously been recognised as assets; or

- the initial recognition of intangible assets at amounts other than their cost.

Therefore if, in developing an asset internally, the criteria for recognition as set out at **4.7.4** above are not met, and all of the costs are written off as incurred, the asset should not be subsequently measured at fair value. If, however, part of the asset was initially recognised as an asset (e.g. because the recognition criteria were met part way through the project), the whole of that asset can be revalued, if the conditions for revaluation are met. [IAS 38:77]

7.1.5   Intangible assets received by government grant

If the conditions for revaluation are met, the Standard states specifically that the revaluation model may be adopted for intangible assets received by way of government grant and recognised at a nominal amount (see **4.5** above). [IAS 38:77]

7.2   Basis for revaluation

When an intangible asset is revalued, it is revalued to its fair value. As discussed at **7.1** above, for the purpose of revaluing intangible assets, such fair values can only be measured by reference to an active market.

The definition of fair value is amended by IFRS 13. For entities that have adopted IFRS 13, fair value is defined as "the price that would be received to sell an asset or paid to transfer a liability in an orderly transaction between market participants at the measurement date. (See IFRS 13 *Fair Value Measurement*.)" [IAS 38:8]

For entities that have not yet adopted IFRS 13, fair value of an asset is defined as "the amount for which that asset could be exchanged between knowledgeable, willing parties in an arm's length transaction". [IAS 38:8]

IFRS 13 is effective for annual periods beginning on or after 1 January 2013, with earlier application permitted.

> As discussed in **section 12** of **chapter A6**, when IFRS 13 is first adopted, it is required to be applied prospectively and it need not be applied to comparative information provided for periods before the initial application of IFRS 13; therefore, amounts reported in prior annual periods are not required to be restated.

7.3   Frequency of revaluations

IAS 38 does not set a specific requirement for the frequency of revaluations, but states that they should be carried out with sufficient regularity so that, at the end of each reporting period, the carrying amount of a revalued intangible asset does not differ materially from its fair value. [IAS 38:75]

In order to meet this requirement, an entity must estimate the fair value of its revalued intangible assets at the end of each reporting period. This does not mean, however, that revaluation adjustments must be made every year, unless the estimate of fair value differs significantly from the carrying amount of the intangible asset.

When permitted, the revaluation of intangible assets should, in practice, be a straightforward matter, because it is a pre-requisite that an active market exists.

The frequency of revaluations depends on the volatility in the active market on which the intangible asset is traded. Some intangible assets may experience significant and volatile movements in fair value, thus necessitating annual revaluation. Such frequent revaluations are unnecessary for intangible assets with only insignificant movements in fair value. [IAS 38:79]

7.4   Scope of revaluations

When an intangible asset is accounted for using the revaluation model, all of the other assets in its class should also be accounted for using the revaluation model, unless there is no active market for those assets. [IAS 38:72] If there is no active market for a particular intangible asset which is included in a revalued class of intangible assets, that asset is carried at its cost less any accumulated amortisation and any accumulated impairment losses. [IAS 38:81]

A class of intangible assets is defined as a grouping of assets of a similar nature and use in the operations of an entity. Examples of separate classes may include:
[IAS 38:119]

- brand names;

- mastheads and publishing titles;

- computer software;

- licences and franchises;

- copyrights, patents and other industrial property rights, service and operating rights;

- recipes, formulae, model designs and prototypes; and

- intangible assets under development.

If the fair value of a revalued intangible asset can no longer be measured by reference to an active market, the intangible asset is carried at its fair value at the date of the last revaluation by reference to the active market less any subsequent accumulated amortisation and any subsequent impairment losses. [IAS 38:82] The disappearance of the active market may be an indicator of impairment which triggers an impairment review under IAS 36 *Impairment of Assets* (see **chapter A10**). If the active market re-emerges, the intangible asset should once again be revalued by reference to the active market. [IAS 38:84]

7.5   Accumulated amortisation at the date of revaluation

IAS 38:80 allows the accumulated amortisation relating to an intangible asset that has been revalued to be dealt with in two ways – either:

- restated proportionately with the change in the gross carrying amount of the asset so that the carrying amount of the asset after revaluation equals its revalued amount. The carrying amount is increased to the revalued amount by restating the cost and amortisation proportionately; or

- eliminated against the gross carrying amount of the asset and the resulting net amount restated to the revalued amount of the asset. The accumulated amortisation is eliminated, and any remaining surplus is used to increase cost.

These treatments are similar to those permitted for accumulated depreciation when an item of property, plant and equipment is revalued. (See **example 6.4** in **chapter A7** for a comparison of the two methods described above.)

See **14.1** for details of proposed amendments to IAS 38:80 which are expected to be finalised in the fourth quarter of 2013.

7.6 Treatment of surplus or deficit arising on revaluation

7.6.1 Revaluation surplus

When a valuation indicates that the fair value of an intangible asset is greater than its carrying amount, the amount of the surplus is generally recognised in other comprehensive income and accumulated in equity as a revaluation surplus. [IAS 38:85]

If the increase in the fair value of the asset reverses a previously recognised decrease in the fair value of the same asset, however, the increase is recognised in profit or loss to the extent that the previous decrease was recognised in profit or loss. [IAS 38:85]

7.6.2 Revaluation deficit

When a revaluation indicates that the fair value of an intangible asset is less than its carrying amount, the amount of the deficit is generally recognised in profit or loss. [IAS 38:86]

If the decrease in the fair value of the intangible asset reverses a previously recognised increase in the fair value of the same asset, however, the decrease is recognised in other comprehensive income to the extent of any credit balance in the revaluation surplus in respect of that asset. The decrease reduces the amount of revaluation surplus. [IAS 38:86]

The treatment of revaluation surpluses and deficits arising on intangible assets is the same as that for items of property, plant and equipment (see the illustrative examples at **6.8.3** in **chapter A7**).

7.6.3 Realisation of the revaluation surplus

The revaluation surplus may be transferred to retained earnings as the surplus is realised, though such a transfer is not mandatory. Realisation of the entire surplus may occur on the retirement or disposal of the asset. Some realisation of the revaluation surplus may occur, however, through the use of the intangible asset. The amount of the surplus that is realised through use of the asset is calculated as the difference between the amortisation calculated on the historical cost of the asset and the amortisation calculated on the revalued amount. This difference may be transferred from the revaluation surplus to retained earnings in each period. [IAS 38:87]

If an entity chooses to make such periodic transfers, when a revalued intangible asset is fully amortised in the statement of financial position, the related revaluation surplus will have been reduced to zero.

Whether the revaluation surplus is realised on disposal or on a systematic basis over the life of the asset, any transfer from revaluation reserve to retained earnings is not made through profit or loss. [IAS 38:87]

8   Determining the useful life of an intangible asset

The subsequent accounting for an intangible asset is determined on the basis of its useful life. If the useful life of the asset is determined to be finite, the asset is amortised over that useful life. If the useful life of the asset is determined to be indefinite, the asset is not amortised. [IAS 38:89] IAS 38 provides a significant amount of guidance to assist in this determination, which is summarised in the following sections.

8.1   Finite or indefinite useful life?

Entities are required to assess whether the useful life of an intangible asset is finite or indefinite and, if finite, the length of, or number of production or similar units constituting, that useful life. [IAS 38:88]

An intangible asset should be regarded as having an indefinite useful life when, based on all of the relevant factors, there is no foreseeable limit to the period over which the asset is expected to generate net cash inflows for the entity. [IAS 38:88] Therefore, if management has the intention and the ability to maintain an intangible asset so that there is no foreseeable limit on the period over which the asset is expected to generate net cash inflows for the entity, the asset is regarded as having an indefinite useful life.

Note that the term 'indefinite' does not mean 'infinite'. [IAS 38:91] There does not need to be an expectation that the cash inflows generated by the asset will go on forever – simply that, at the date of assessment, there is no foreseeable point at which the cash inflows will cease.

If there is a foreseeable limit to the period over which net cash inflows are expected to flow to the entity, the asset is regarded as having a finite life.

The assessment as to whether an intangible asset has an indefinite useful life is clearly crucial for the purposes of the subsequent accounting treatment for the intangible asset. IAS 38 provides a number of illustrative examples for this determination, which are summarised at **8.4** below.

8.2   Factors for consideration in determining useful life

The useful life of an intangible asset is either:
[IAS 38:8]

- the period over which the asset is expected to be available for use by the entity; or

- the number of production or similar units expected to be obtained from the asset by an entity.

Factors to consider in estimating the useful life of an intangible asset include:
[IAS 38:90]

- the expected usage of the asset by the entity and whether the asset could be efficiently managed by another management team;

- typical product life cycles for the asset and public information on estimates of useful lives of similar types of assets that are used in a similar way;

- technical, technological, commercial or other types of obsolescence;

- the stability of the industry in which the asset operates and changes in the market demand for the products or services output from the asset;

- expected actions by competitors or potential competitors;

- the level of maintenance expenditure required to obtain the expected future economic benefits from the asset and the entity's ability and intent to reach such a level;

- the period of control over the asset, and legal or similar limits on the use of the asset, such as the expiry dates of related leases; and

- whether the useful life of the asset is dependent on the useful life of other assets of the entity.

The useful life of an intangible asset reflects only that level of future maintenance expenditure required to maintain the asset at its standard of performance assessed at the time of estimating the asset's useful life, and the entity's ability and intention to reach such a level. A conclusion that the useful life of an intangible asset is indefinite should not depend on planned future expenditure in excess of that required to maintain the asset at that standard of performance. [IAS 38:91]

The Standard notes that, given the history of rapid changes in technology, computer software and many other intangible assets are susceptible to technological obsolescence. Therefore, it is likely that their useful lives will be short. [IAS 38:92] Uncertainty may lead to estimating the useful life of an intangible asset on a prudent basis; however, it is not appropriate to choose a useful life that is unrealistically short. [IAS 38:93]

8.3   Assets arising from contractual or other legal rights

Control over the future economic benefits from an intangible asset is often achieved through legal rights that have been granted for a finite period. Under most circumstances, the estimated useful life of the intangible asset is the shorter of the period of the legal rights and the period over which economic benefits are expected to be generated. [IAS 38:94]

In some cases, however, the legal rights may be renewable. The question then arises as to whether it is appropriate to assume that the legal rights will be extended. IAS 38:94 stipulates that the useful life of an intangible asset should include the renewal period(s) only if there is evidence to support renewal by the entity without significant cost. The following factors are listed which indicate that an entity would be able to renew the contractual or other legal rights without significant cost:
[IAS 38:96]

- there is evidence (possibly based on past experience) that the legal rights will be renewed. If renewal is contingent upon the consent of a third party, this includes evidence that the third party will give its consent;

- there is evidence that the conditions necessary to obtain the renewal of the legal right (if any) will be satisfied; and

- the cost to the entity of renewal is not significant when compared with the future economic benefits expected to flow to the entity from renewal.

If the cost of renewal is significant when compared with the future economic benefits expected to flow to the entity from renewal, the 'renewal' represents, in substance, the acquisition of a new intangible asset at the renewal date. [IAS 38:96]

The useful life of a reacquired right recognised as an intangible asset in a business combination is the remaining contractual period of the contract in which the right was granted, and does not include renewal periods. [IAS 38:94]

8.4   Illustrative examples

The illustrative examples accompanying IAS 38 provide guidance for the determination of the useful life of an asset in accordance with the Standard. Each example details the specific facts and circumstances surrounding the determination of the asset's useful life. The following table summarises the key determinants for each example. Readers should refer to the text of the Standard, however, to obtain a full understanding of each of the circumstances and of the factors assessed in each scenario.

Asset description	Finite or indefinite life?	Amortisation period
Acquired customer list – anticipated to generate benefits for between 1 and 3 years. [IAS 38 Illustrative examples: Example 1]	Finite. Although the entity will expect to generate further benefits when new customers are added to the list, the useful life is determined by reference only to customers on the list at the acquisition date.	Management's best estimate of the useful life – say 18 months.

Asset description	Finite or indefinite life?	Amortisation period
Acquired patent that expires in 15 years. The entity intends to sell the patent to a committed third party in five years for 60 per cent of its fair value at the date of acquisition. [IAS 38 Illustrative examples: Example 2]	Finite	The period over which the patent is expected to generate cash inflows for the entity, i.e. five years. The residual value should equal the present value of 60 per cent of the fair value at the date of acquisition.
Copyright with remaining legal life of 50 years, but management estimates that net cash inflows will only be generated for 30 years. [IAS 38 Illustrative examples:Example 3]	Finite	30 years

Asset description	Finite or indefinite life?	Amortisation period
Broadcasting licence that expires in five years. Can be renewed indefinitely, at little cost every 10 years, provided that certain conditions are met. Management intends to renew the licence indefinitely, and evidence supports its ability to do so. No third party or obsolescence issues that would indicate a problem with indefinite renewal. [IAS 38 Illustrative examples: Example 4]	Indefinite. Potential to renew indefinitely is taken into account.	N/a
Same licence as previous example but, when licence has three years remaining, licensing authority decides to auction licences at future renewal dates. [IAS 38 Illustrative examples: Example 5]	Finite. No potential to renew the existing arrangement.	Three years

Asset description	Finite or indefinite life?	Amortisation period
Acquired airline route authority that expires in three years. Renewable indefinitely, at minimal cost, every five years provided that conditions are complied with. Management expects to renew indefinitely, and no indication that they will not be able to do so. [IAS 38 Illustrative examples: Example 6]	Indefinite. Potential to renew indefinitely is taken into account.	N/a
Acquired trademark for a market-leading consumer product with a remaining legal life of five years, but renewable every 10 years at little cost. Management intends to renew indefinitely and market indicators support cash inflows for an indefinite period. [IAS 38 Illustrative examples: Example 7]	Indefinite. Potential to renew indefinitely is taken into account.	N/a

Asset description	Finite or indefinite life?	Amortisation period
Acquired trademark for leading consumer product previously regarded as having an indefinite life. Increased competitor activity indicates reduced future cash inflows for an indefinite period. [IAS 38 Illustrative examples: Example 8]	Indefinite. Impairment loss recognised for impact of reduced cash inflows.	N/a
Trademark acquired in a business combination some years ago, previously considered to have an indefinite life. Management decides to discontinue related product line over the next four years. [IAS 38 Illustrative examples: Example 9]	Finite	Four years

8.5   Subsequent reassessment of useful life

Whether an intangible asset is determined to have a finite useful life, or an indefinite useful life, IAS 38 requires that the initial determination be reviewed at least annually (see **section 9** and **10.2.3** below).

The determination of useful life for each intangible asset requires a comprehensive consideration of all pertinent factors surrounding the assets. Subsequent to the initial determination of useful life, entities must establish sufficient procedures to identify and evaluate appropriately those events or circumstances that, if occurring after, or changed from, the initial determination, may affect the remaining useful life. Some events or circumstances will represent both discrete and readily identifiable events to which the entity should respond (e.g. a change in regulation). Other events or circumstances may develop more gradually over time but, nevertheless, must be monitored and given appropriate consideration by the entity (e.g. obsolescence, competition and demand). Given the varying nature of the intangible assets, and each entity's unique background and circumstances, procedures employed by entities to evaluate useful lives of intangible assets are expected to vary.

9   Subsequent accounting for assets with indefinite useful lives

Entities are not permitted to amortise intangible assets that have been assessed as having an indefinite useful life. [IAS 38:107] Rather, in accordance with the requirements of IAS 36 *Impairment of Assets*, such assets are tested for impairment by comparing their recoverable amounts with their carrying amounts once a year, at a minimum. An additional impairment test is required whenever there is an indication that an intangible asset may be impaired. [IAS 38:108] The requirements of IAS 36 are dealt with in detail in **chapter A10**.

If an asset has been assessed as having an indefinite useful life, resulting in the asset not being amortised in accordance with IAS 38:107, that assessment is revisited each period to determine whether events and circumstances continue to support an indefinite useful life for that asset. If not, the change in the indefinite life assessment is accounted for as a change in accounting estimate in accordance with IAS 8 *Accounting Policies, Changes in Accounting Estimates and Errors*. [IAS 38:109]

When the useful life of an intangible asset is reassessed as finite rather than indefinite, this is an indicator that the asset may be impaired. Accordingly, the asset is tested for impairment by comparing its recoverable amount, determined in accordance with IAS 36, with its carrying amount, and recognising any excess of the carrying amount over the recoverable amount as an impairment loss. [IAS 38:110]

Following the annual reassessment of the useful life of an intangible asset previously considered to have an indefinite useful life:

- if the intangible asset still has an indefinite useful life, it should be tested for impairment in accordance with the requirements of IAS 36; and

- if the intangible asset is determined to have a finite useful life, it should be tested for impairment, and should be amortised over its estimated remaining useful life and accounted for in the same manner as other intangible assets that are subject to amortisation, including further impairment testing when indicators of impairment exist.

10   Subsequent accounting for assets with finite useful lives

The depreciable amount of an intangible asset with a finite useful life is required to be amortised on a systematic basis over its useful life. [IAS 38:97] The depreciable amount of an asset is defined as the cost of the asset, or other amount substituted for cost, less its residual value. [IAS 38:8]

In the majority of cases, amortisation is recognised in profit or loss. If the economic benefits of the intangible asset are used by the entity in the production of other assets, however, the amortisation is added to the cost of the other assets and included in their carrying amount. For example, if a patented production process has been capitalised as an intangible asset, as the relevant inventory items are produced using the patented process, the amortisation of the intangible asset is added to the cost of the inventories. [IAS 38:99]

10.1   Residual value

IAS 38 defines residual value as the estimated amount that an entity would currently obtain from disposal of the asset, after deducting the estimated costs of disposal, if the asset were already of the age and in the condition expected at the end of its useful life. [IAS 38:8]

Under most circumstances, the residual value of an intangible asset with a finite life is zero. A residual value of greater than zero, which implies that the entity expects to dispose of the intangible asset before the end of its useful life, may arise if:
[IAS 38:100]

- there is a commitment by a third party to purchase the asset at the end of its useful life; or

- there is an active market for the asset, and:

- residual value can be determined by reference to that market; *and*

- it is probable that such a market will exist at the end of the asset's useful life.

For entities that have adopted IFRS 13 *Fair Value Measurement,* an active market is defined in that Standard (see **7.1.1**). For entities that have not yet adopted IFRS 13, the definition and guidance in IAS 38 should be followed (see **7.1.2**).

If residual value is significant, it has a direct impact on the amortisation recognised over the life of the asset.

The residual value of an asset is required to be reviewed at least at each financial year end. The revised estimate should be based on conditions and prices current at the end of the reporting period. When the revised estimate differs significantly from previous estimates of residual value, the effect is accounted for prospectively as a change in estimate, in accordance with the requirements of IAS 8 *Accounting Policies, Changes in Accounting Estimates and Errors.* [IAS 38:102] Effectively, the amortisation recognised over the remaining useful life of the asset is adjusted to take account of the revised estimate of residual value.

When the revised estimate of residual value is equal to or greater than the asset's carrying amount, whether due to inflation or otherwise, then no amortisation is recognised unless and until the asset's residual value subsequently decreases to an amount below the asset's carrying amount. [IAS 38:103]

IAS 38 does not allow a reversal of earlier amortisation in these circumstances.

10.2   Amortisation period

The factors to be considered in determining the useful life of an intangible asset are discussed in **section 8** above.

10.2.1   Commencement of amortisation

Amortisation commences from the date the asset is available for use, i.e. when it is in the location and condition necessary for it to be capable of operating in the manner intended by management. [IAS 38:97]

It is important to distinguish the date an asset is available for use from the date on which it is actually brought into use. Amortisation will commence from the former.

Example 10.2.1

Date of commencement of amortisation of an intangible asset

Operators usually are required to purchase a telecom licence prior to the provision of services in a particular location or prior to the provision of certain types of services (e.g. 4G services). Because telecom licences normally are granted for a specified period of time, the cost of the licence has to be amortised over the best estimate of its useful life. The operator is generally required to build and commission its network before it can earn revenues from the use of its licence.

The ability to receive economic benefits from the licence is linked directly to the ability to use the network; therefore, the licence is only available for use when the network is in place. Consequently, amortisation of the licence should commence at the date the network is available for use (i.e. it is in the location and condition necessary for it to be capable of operating in the manner intended by management).

In some countries, the full network may not be operational in the entire targeted areas until a certain date. However, as soon as one area (one connection) is in place and working, the amortisation of the licence should commence. In most instances, the amortisation of the licence should begin before the full commercial launch.

10.2.2   Cessation of amortisation

Amortisation ceases at the earlier of:
[IAS 38:97]

- the date that the asset is classified as held for sale (or included in a disposal group that is classified as held for sale) in accordance with IFRS 5 *Non-current Assets Held for Sale and Discontinued Operations*; and

- the date that the asset is derecognised (see **section 12** below).

Amortisation does not cease when an intangible asset is taken out of use, unless one of these conditions is met. [IAS 38:117]

> The circumstances that cause an intangible asset to be taken out of use could also indicate that it may be impaired, in which case an impairment review may be required in accordance with IAS 36 *Impairment of Assets*.

10.2.3   *Review of amortisation period*

At least at each financial year end, the amortisation periods for intangible assets with finite lives should be reviewed. If the expected useful life of the asset is different from previous estimates, the amortisation period should be adjusted accordingly. Any such change is accounted for as a change in estimate in accordance with IAS 8, by adjusting current and future periods. [IAS 38:104]

> When the annual review of the amortisation period of a previously-amortised intangible asset results in a determination that the asset has an indefinite useful life:
>
> * it should be tested for impairment;
>
> * it should no longer be amortised, but should be accounted for in the same manner as other intangible assets that are not subject to amortisation; and
>
> * previous amortisation of that asset is not reversed.

10.3   Amortisation method

There are several methods of apportioning amortisation over the anticipated useful life of the asset. Those most commonly employed are the straight-line method and the reducing balance (diminishing balance) method. These, and other, methods of depreciation and amortisation are discussed in **section 7.4** of **chapter A7**. IAS 38 requires that the entity should select an amortisation method that reflects the pattern in which the asset's future economic benefits are expected to be consumed by the entity. [IAS 38:97]

At least at the end of each financial year, the amortisation methods for intangible assets with finite useful lives should be reviewed. If there has been a change in the expected pattern of consumption of the future economic benefits embodied in an asset, the amortisation method should be changed to reflect the changed pattern. Any such change is accounted for as a change in estimate in accordance with IAS 8, by adjusting current and future periods. [IAS 38:104]

Example 10.3

Amortisation method for intangible assets in the entertainment industry

Entity A holds an exclusive three-year licence for the distribution of a film. Typically, the volume of sales declines over the life of the licence, such that Entity A recognises the majority of its revenue in the first two years of distribution of a new film. Entity A typically lowers its per-unit selling price over time, in response to the declining volume of sales.

If Entity A were to use the straight-line method of amortisation, it is likely that Entity A would need to recognise significant impairment losses towards the end of the distribution agreement.

It is acceptable for Entity A to use an amortisation method other than straight-line. The amortisation method for an intangible asset should be selected, as described in IAS 38:97, so as to "reflect the pattern in which the asset's future economic benefits are expected to be consumed by the entity". It is not acceptable to base amortisation directly on revenue. Amortisation should reflect the consumption of the future economic benefits inherent in the intangible asset, not the revenue generated from the use of that asset. However, methods such as the unit-of-production method, whose application may consider how revenue will be generated, may be used if they result in a pattern of amortisation that complies with the principle established in IAS 38:97. When such methods are adopted, this sometimes results in revenue and amortisation being recognised on a similar basis – but that is because both are being driven by the underlying consumption of benefits (e.g. production), not because amortisation is being driven by revenue.

In the specific fact pattern described above, the film distribution licence may be amortised using a unit-of-production method of amortisation, adjusted to take into account the typical life cycle of the product as contemplated in IAS 38:90(b).

For example, assume that a film is expected to be in high demand in the first two years following its launch. In the third year, the distributor estimates that it will be able to match the volume of sales in the second year but only if it drops the price by 50 per cent. Using this data (assumed to be supported by historical data for similar products), the distributor may appropriately conclude that the intangible asset should be amortised 40 per cent (10/25) in Year 1, 40 per cent (10/25) in Year 2, and 20 per cent (5/25) in Year 3.

> In this example, the projected revenue as assessed at each reporting date (rather than actual revenue) is used to establish the expected remaining consumption of the asset such that the resulting pattern of amortisation reflects the consumption of the benefits embodied in the exclusive distribution right.
>
> If, at the end of Year 1, actual revenue achieved is less than originally projected and the distributor now expects to generate equal revenue in Years 2 and 3, the amortisation recognised in Year 1 would remain at 40 per cent and would not be revised. However, the amortisation pattern would be adjusted prospectively to reflect the change in projected revenues. Therefore, the amortisation recognised in each of Years 2 and 3 would represent 30 per cent of the original cost of the film distribution licence.

In some circumstances, it may be difficult to determine reliably the expected pattern of consumption. In such circumstances, use of the straight-line method is mandatory. [IAS 38:97]

Prior to May 2008, the Standard noted that there would rarely, if ever, be persuasive evidence to support an amortisation method for intangible assets (e.g. the annuity method) that results in a lower amount of accumulated amortisation than under the straight-line method. This statement was deleted by *Improvements to IFRSs* issued in May 2008.

See **14.2** below for a discussion of proposed amendments to IAS 38 regarding the selection of amortisation methods.

11   Impairment

The requirements of IAS 36 *Impairment of Assets* are applied to determine whether an intangible asset is impaired and to measure any such impairment loss (see **chapter A10**). Any impairment loss is then recognised in accordance with the requirements of IAS 36.

For intangible assets with indefinite lives, an impairment review is required at least annually (see **section 9** above).

12   Derecognition

IAS 38 requires that the carrying amount of an intangible asset should be derecognised:
[IAS 38:112]

- on disposal; or

- when no future economic benefits are expected from its use or disposal.

The gain or loss arising from the derecognition of an intangible asset is to be recognised in profit or loss when the asset is derecognised (unless IAS 17 *Leases* requires otherwise in the circumstances of a sale and leaseback). [IAS 38:113]

IAS 38 specifically prohibits the classification as revenue of gains arising on the derecognition of intangible assets. [IAS 38:103] The Standard does require, however, that the date of disposal of an intangible asset be determined using the criteria for recognising revenue from the sale of goods, as set out in IAS 18 *Revenue* (see **chapter A14**). [IAS 38:114]

The gain or loss arising from the derecognition of an intangible asset is determined as the difference between the net disposal proceeds, if any, and the carrying amount of the item. [IAS 38:113] Therefore, as discussed at **7.6.3** above, when a revalued asset is disposed of, any credit balance on the revaluation reserve attributable to that asset may be transferred directly to retained earnings, but should not be reflected in profit or loss. [IAS 38:87]

In the case of a reacquired right in a business combination, if the right is subsequently reissued (i.e. sold) to a third party, the related carrying amount, if any, is used in determining the gain or loss on reissue. [IAS 38:115A]

The disposal consideration received is measured at its fair value. If payment is deferred beyond normal credit terms, the consideration received is recognised initially at the cash price equivalent. The difference between the nominal amount of the consideration and the cash price equivalent is recognised as interest income in accordance with IAS 18. [IAS 38:116]

13   Presentation and disclosure

13.1   Presentation

IAS 1 *Presentation of Financial Statements* requires that, if material, the aggregate carrying amount of the entity's intangible assets should be presented in the statement of financial position (see **chapter A4**). [IAS 1:54(c)]

13.2   Disclosure

13.2.1   *General*

The following disclosures should be made for each class of intangible assets, distinguishing between internally generated intangible assets and other intangible assets:
[IAS 38:118]

- whether the useful lives are indefinite or finite and, if finite, the useful lives or amortisation rates used;

- the amortisation methods used for intangible assets with finite useful lives;

- the gross carrying amount and any accumulated amortisation (aggregated with accumulated impairment losses) at the beginning and end of the period; and

- the line item(s) of the statement of comprehensive income in which any amortisation of intangible assets is included.

An entity is also required to provide a reconciliation of the carrying amount at the beginning and end of the period, in respect of each class of intangible assets, showing:
[IAS 38:118(e)]

- additions, indicating separately those from internal development, those acquired separately, and those acquired through business combinations;

- assets classified as held for sale or included in a disposal group classified as held for sale in accordance with IFRS 5 *Non-current Assets Held for Disposal and Discontinued Operations*, and other disposals;

- increases or decreases during the period resulting from revaluations and from impairment losses recognised or reversed in other comprehensive income;

- impairment losses recognised in profit or loss during the period;

- impairment losses reversed in profit or loss during the period;

- any amortisation recognised during the period;

- net exchange differences arising on the translation of the financial statements into the presentation currency, and on the translation of a foreign operation into the presentation currency of the entity; and

- other changes in the carrying amount during the period.

Examples of classes of intangible assets are listed at **7.4**. Those classes are disaggregated (aggregated) into smaller (larger) classes if this results in more relevant information for the users of the financial statements. [IAS 38:119]

13.2.2 *Intangible assets having an indefinite useful life*

For an intangible asset assessed as having an indefinite useful life, the financial statements should disclose the carrying amount of the asset and the reasons supporting the assessment of an indefinite useful life. In giving these reasons, the entity should describe the factor(s) that played a significant role in determining that the asset has an indefinite useful life. [IAS 38:122(a)] The factors listed in **8.2** above should be considered. [IAS 38:123]

13.2.3 *Intangible assets that are individually material*

For any individual intangible asset that is material to the entity's financial statements, the financial statements should disclose a description of the asset, its carrying amount and its remaining amortisation period. [IAS 38:122(b)]

13.2.4 *Intangible assets acquired by way of government grant and initially recognised at fair value*

For intangible assets acquired by way of government grant and initially recognised at fair value (see **4.5** above), the financial statements should disclose:
[IAS 38:122(c)]

- the fair value initially recognised for those assets;

- their carrying amount; and

- whether they are measured after recognition under the cost model or the revaluation model.

13.2.5   Title restrictions and capital commitments

The financial statements should also disclose:

- the existence and carrying amount of intangible assets whose title is restricted and the carrying amounts of intangible assets pledged as security for liabilities; [IAS 38:122(d)] and

- the amount of contractual commitments for the acquisition of intangible assets. [IAS 38:122(e)]

13.2.6   Changes in estimates

In addition to the disclosure requirements included in IAS 38, if there has been a change in estimate during the period, the disclosure requirements set out in IAS 8 *Accounting Policies, Changes in Accounting Estimates and Errors* apply (see **section 4.3** of **chapter A5**). Changes in estimate related to intangible assets include changes regarding:

- the assessment of an intangible asset's useful life;

- the amortisation method; and

- residual values.

13.2.7   Impairment losses

If an intangible asset has suffered an impairment loss, the disclosure requirements set out in IAS 36 *Impairment of Assets* apply (see **section 11** of **chapter A10**).

13.2.8   Intangible assets carried at revalued amounts

In addition to the disclosures listed in the previous sections, if an entity accounts for any intangible assets at revalued amounts, the following disclosures are required:
[IAS 38:124]

- by class of intangible assets:

  - the effective date of the revaluation;

  - the carrying amount of revalued intangible assets; and

- the carrying amount that would have been included in the financial statements had the revalued intangible assets been accounted for under the cost model;

- the amount of the revaluation surplus that relates to intangible assets at the beginning and end of the period, indicating the changes during the period and any restrictions on the distribution of the balance to shareholders; and

- the methods and significant assumptions applied in estimating the assets' fair values.

For entities that have adopted IFRS 13 *Fair Value Measurement*, the final requirement in IAS 38:124 (i.e. to disclose the methods and significant assumptions underlying fair value measurements) no longer applies. Such entities should instead provide the disclosures required under IFRS 13 (see **section 11** of **chapter A6**).

If necessary, it is acceptable to aggregate the classes of revalued assets into larger classes for disclosure purposes. Classes are not aggregated, however, if this would result in the combination of a class of intangible assets that includes amounts measured under both the cost and revaluation models. [IAS 38:125]

13.2.9   *Research and development expenditure*

The aggregate amount of research and development expenditure recognised as an expense during the period should be disclosed. [IAS 38:126]

Note that the requirement is to disclose the amount expensed rather than the amount incurred. Therefore, when development expenditure is capitalised, the disclosure will occur in subsequent periods as the resulting intangible asset is amortised.

13.2.10   *Additional recommended disclosures*

The following disclosures are encouraged but not required: [IAS 38:128]

- a description of any fully amortised intangible asset that is still in use; and

667

- a brief description of significant intangible assets controlled by the entity but not recognised as assets because they did not meet the recognition criteria in IAS 38 or because they were acquired or generated before the 1998 version of IAS 38 (which prohibited retrospective recognition) became effective.

14   Future developments

14.1   Annual Improvements 2010–2012 Cycle

In May 2012, the IASB issued an exposure draft (ED/2012/1 *Annual Improvements to IFRSs: 2010–2012 Cycle*) proposing changes to a number of Standards as part of its Annual Improvements project. Amendments are proposed for IAS 38 to clarify that, when an intangible asset is revalued, accumulated amortisation should be computed as the difference between the gross and the net carrying amounts of the revalued asset, after restating the gross carrying amount in a manner consistent with the revaluation of the net carrying amount (see **7.5** above). The amendments are proposed to address divergent views in practice on how to calculate accumulated amortisation for a revalued asset when the residual value, the useful life or the amortisation method has been re-estimated prior to revaluation.

Finalised amendments are expected in the fourth quarter of 2013.

14.2   Acceptable methods of depreciation

In December 2012, the IASB issued an exposure draft (ED/2012/5 *Clarification of Acceptable Methods of Depreciation and Amortisation* (*Proposed Amendments to IAS 16 and IAS 38*)). The exposure draft proposes to amend IAS 38 (and IAS 16 *Property, Plant and Equipment*) to the effect that when selecting an amortisation (or a depreciation) rate, a revenue-based method should not be used, because such methods reflect a pattern of economic benefits being generated from the asset, rather than the expected pattern of consumption of the future economic benefits embodied in the asset. The proposed amendments also provide some further guidance on the application of the diminishing balance method.

The deadline for comments on these proposals was 2 April 2013.

14.3   Rate-regulated activities

The issue to be addressed by this project is whether IFRSs should require entities with rate-regulated activities (i.e. activities subject to restrictions on prices that can be charged to customers) to recognise assets and liabilities arising from the effects of rate regulation. Some national GAAPs provide specific guidance on this matter, but there is no equivalent guidance in IFRSs.

The IASB reactivated this project following its Agenda Consultation in 2011. A new comprehensive project was initiated in September 2012; this comprehensive project is currently at the research stage, with the objective of releasing a discussion paper before the end of 2013.

In addition, the Board has released proposals for an interim Standard that would allow entities adopting IFRSs to continue to use their local GAAP requirements for rate-regulated activities until the comprehensive project is completed. Key aspects of the exposure draft (ED/2013/5 *Regulatory Deferral Accounts*) issued in April 2013 are as follows.

- The proposed interim Standard is only applicable upon the initial adoption of IFRSs and cannot be applied by entities that have previously adopted IFRSs.

- Entities applying the interim Standard, if approved, must meet specified eligibility criteria. Specifically, there must be an authorised body (i.e. the rate regulator) that restricts the price that the entity can charge its customers for the goods or services that the entity provides and the price established by regulation is designed to recover the entity's allowable costs of providing the regulated goods or services.

- The proposed interim Standard:

    - permits (but does not require) an entity that adopts IFRSs to continue to use its previous GAAP accounting policies as accepted in its local jurisdiction for the recognition, measurement and impairment of regulatory deferral account balances;

    - requires entities to present regulatory deferral account balances as separate line items in the statement of financial position and to present movements in those account balances as a separate line item in the statement of profit of loss and other comprehensive income; and

    - requires specific disclosures to identify clearly the nature of, and risks associated with, the rate regulation that has resulted in the recognition of regulatory deferral account balances.

- The draft interim Standard replaces the commonly used phrases 'regulatory assets' and 'regulatory liabilities' with the terms 'regulatory deferral account debit balances' and 'regulatory deferral account credit balances', respectively. The issue of whether such regulatory balances meet the conceptual definitions of assets and liabilities is part of the comprehensive project.

The comment period for the exposure draft ends on 4 September 2013.

A10 Impairment of assets

Contents

1   Introduction

The objective of IAS 36 *Impairments of Assets* is to prescribe the procedures that an entity applies to ensure that its assets are carried at no more than their recoverable amount. The Standard was most recently amended in May 2013 when the IASB provided clarification on a number of the disclosure requirements in the Standard (see **section 11** below).

IAS 36 was also amended in May 2011 when a number of new Standards were issued, including IFRS 13 *Fair Value Measurement*. Substantive consequential amendments to IAS 36 at that time are highlighted throughout this chapter. One non-substantive, but pervasive, change to the language in IAS 36 as a consequence of the issue of IFRS 13 is that the term 'fair value less costs to sell' has been replaced by 'fair value less costs of disposal'. This change has no real effect in practice because, prior to the adoption of IFRS 13, 'fair value less costs to sell' is defined as "[fair value] less the costs of disposal" and there has been no change in the guidance regarding what constitutes 'costs of disposal' (see **section 4** below).

For ease of reading, throughout this chapter the term 'fair value less costs to sell' has generally been replaced by 'fair value less costs of disposal' (unless the context requires otherwise); the only consequence of this change is that, following the adoption of IFRS 13, 'fair value' is measured in accordance with the requirements in that Standard rather than the guidance previously included in IAS 36.

2   Summary of IAS 36 approach

The principles of IAS 36 apply to a wide range of assets (those assets outside its scope are described in **section 3**). The idea is that, for those assets within its scope, the requirements for the recognition of impairment losses should be specified in a single Standard. Thus, other Standards dealing with such asset categories (e.g. IAS 16 *Property, Plant and Equipment*) simply refer to IAS 36 for the requirements regarding impairment testing.

IAS 36 requires that a review for impairment be carried out if events or changes in circumstances indicate that the carrying amount of an asset may not be recoverable. The review will compare the carrying amount of the asset with its recoverable amount, which is the higher of its value if sold (if known) and its value in use.

Any shortfall is deemed an impairment loss which, for assets carried at cost, is recognised in profit or loss and, for assets carried at a revalued amount, is treated as a revaluation decrease (which may or may not lead to an expense being recognised in profit or loss).

3   Scope

IAS 36 applies to all assets except:
[IAS 36:2]

- inventories (dealt with in IAS 2 *Inventories* – see **chapter A11**);

- assets arising from construction contracts (dealt with in IAS 11 *Construction Contracts* – see **chapter A34**);

- deferred tax assets (dealt with in IAS 12 *Income Taxes* – see **chapter A13**);

- assets arising from employee benefits (dealt with in IAS 19 *Employee Benefits* – see **chapter A15** and **appendix A3**);

- financial assets that are within the scope of IFRS 9 *Financial Instruments* (see **chapter B2** and **chapter B6**) or, for entities that have not yet adopted IFRS 9, IAS 39 *Financial Instruments: Recognition and Measurement* (see **chapter C2** and **chapter C6**);

- investment property that is measured at fair value (dealt with in IAS 40 *Investment Property* – see **chapter A8**);

- biological assets related to agricultural activity that are measured at fair value less costs of disposal (dealt with in IAS 41 *Agriculture* – see **chapter A38**);

- deferred acquisition costs, and intangible assets, arising from an insurer's contractual rights under insurance contracts within the scope of IFRS 4 *Insurance Contracts* (see **chapter A39**); and

- non-current assets (or disposal groups) classified as held for sale in accordance with IFRS 5 *Non-current Assets Held for Sale and Discontinued Operations* (see **chapter A20**).

Therefore, IAS 36 applies to (among other assets):

- land carried at cost or revalued amounts;

- buildings carried at cost or revalued amounts;

- machinery and equipment carried at cost or revalued amounts;

- investment property carried at cost;

- biological assets carried at cost;

- intangible assets carried at cost or revalued amounts;

- goodwill; and

- investments in subsidiaries, associates and joint ventures (other than those accounted for in accordance with IFRS 9 or, for entities that have not yet adopted IFRS 9, IAS 39).

Note that, although investments in subsidiaries, associates and joint ventures are financial assets, they are included within the scope of IAS 36 unless they are accounted for in accordance with IFRS 9 (or, for entities that have not yet adopted IFRS 9, IAS 39).

4   Definitions

The terms used in IAS 36 have specific meanings within the context of the Standard. Therefore, the more important definitions, as set out in IAS 36:6, are set out below for reference.

- **Recoverable amount** for an asset or a cash-generating unit is the higher of its fair value less costs of disposal and its value in use.

- **Fair value*** is the price that would be received to sell an asset or paid to transfer a liability in an orderly transaction between market participants at the measurement date (see IFRS 13 *Fair Value Measurement* – **chapter A6**).

- **Costs of disposal** are incremental costs directly attributable to the disposal of an asset or cash-generating unit, excluding finance costs and income tax expense.

- **Value in use** is the present value of the future cash flows expected to be derived from an asset or cash-generating unit.

- An **impairment loss** is the amount by which the carrying amount of an asset or cash-generating unit exceeds its recoverable amount.

- **Carrying amount** is the amount at which an asset is recognised in the statement of financial position after deducting any accumulated depreciation (amortisation) and accumulated impairment losses thereon.

- A **cash-generating unit** (**CGU**) is the smallest identifiable group of assets that generates cash inflows that are largely independent of the cash inflows from other assets or groups of assets.

- **Corporate assets** are assets other than goodwill that contribute to the future cash flows of both the cash-generating unit under review and other cash-generating units.

> *   The definition of fair value has been amended by IFRS 13. Previously, IAS 36 included a definition of 'fair value less costs to sell' as "the amount obtainable from the sale of an asset or cash-generating unit in an arm's length transaction between knowledgeable, willing parties, less the costs of disposal". This IAS 36 definition (and the supplementary guidance in IAS 36 regarding the measurement of fair value – see later sections) should be applied prior to the adoption of IFRS 13.

The consequential amendments arising from IFRS 13 have also resulted in the removal of the definition of an 'active market' from IAS 36 (an amended definition is included in IFRS 13 – see **5.1.1** in **chapter A6**). Prior to the adoption of IFRS 13, entities should apply the definition previously included in IAS 36, which is as follows.

> "An active market is a market where all of the following conditions exist:
>
> - the items traded within the market are homogeneous;

- willing buyers and sellers can normally be found at any time; and

- prices are available to the public."

5 Identifying an asset that may be impaired

5.1 Requirements for impairment reviews

An asset is impaired when its carrying amount exceeds its recoverable amount. [IAS 36:8] At the end of each reporting period, entities are required to assess whether there is any indication that an asset may be impaired. If any such indication exists, the entity is required to estimate the recoverable amount of the asset. [IAS 36:9]

Example 5.1

Decline in demand for output

An entity has a machine that was purchased in January 20X1 for CU1 million. It is being depreciated over its estimated useful life of 10 years on a straight-line basis. The carrying amount at 31 December 20X3 is therefore CU700,000.

At 31 December 20X3, the directors become aware that a new technological development means that demand for the output produced by the machine is likely to decline significantly. Consequently, under IAS 36:9, they are required to estimate the asset's recoverable amount.

The following items are required to be tested for impairment at least annually, irrespective of whether there is any indication of impairment: [IAS 36:10]

- intangible assets with an indefinite useful life;

- intangible assets that are not yet available for use; and

- goodwill acquired in a business combination.

Other than in these three specific circumstances (which are discussed at **5.3** below), there is no requirement to make a formal estimate of an asset's recoverable amount if no indication of an impairment loss is present. [IAS 36:8]

5.2   Indications of impairment

The following sections describe a number of indications that an impairment loss may have occurred. In making its assessments as to the possibility of impairment losses having arisen, the entity is required, at a minimum, to consider the indications listed. The lists are not exhaustive, however, and all of the items listed will not apply to every entity. If an impairment indicator that is not on these lists exists at the end of the reporting period, a detailed impairment review is required nonetheless. [IAS 36:13]

5.2.1   *Internal sources of information*

The following internal sources of information may indicate that an asset is impaired:
[IAS 36:12]

- evidence is available of obsolescence or physical damage of the asset;

- significant changes with an adverse effect on the entity have taken place during the period, or are expected to take place in the near future, in the extent to which, or the manner in which, an asset is used or is expected to be used. These changes include the asset becoming idle, plans to discontinue or restructure the operation to which an asset belongs, plans to dispose of an asset before the previously expected date, and reassessing the useful life of an asset as finite rather than indefinite; or

- evidence is available from internal reporting that indicates that the economic performance of an asset is, or will be, worse than expected.

Such evidence may include:
[IAS 36:14]

- cash flows for acquiring the asset, or subsequent cash needs for operating or maintaining it, that are significantly higher than those originally budgeted; or

- actual net cash flows or operating profit or loss flowing from the asset that are significantly worse than those budgeted; or

- a significant decline in budgeted net cash flows or operating profit, or a significant increase in budgeted loss, flowing from the asset; or

- operating losses or net cash outflows for the asset, when current period figures are aggregated with budgeted figures for the future.

Impairment indicators related to obsolescence or physical damage may be the easiest to identify because they can be observed physically. Items such as unused factory equipment or equipment that has been damaged by fire are two examples that may indicate impairment.

An impairment indicator may also arise because an asset is to be taken out of use to be sold. If the asset qualifies as held for sale, in accordance with IFRS 5 *Non-current Assets Held for Sale and Discontinued Operations*, it will be measured under the rules of that Standard (see **chapter A20**) and will fall outside the scope of IAS 36. However, immediately before this reclassification, IFRS 5:18 requires the asset to be measured in accordance with other applicable Standards. If the requirements of IAS 36 result in the recognition of an impairment loss before reclassification, that loss should be reported separately as an impairment loss and should not be included as part of the gain or loss disclosed in accordance with IFRS 5:41(c) (see **7.3** in **chapter A20**) or as part of any subsequent gain or loss on disposal disclosed in accordance with paragraph 98(c) of IAS 1 *Presentation of Financial Statements* (see **5.4.1** in **chapter A4**).

5.2.2   *External sources of information*

The following external sources of information may indicate that an asset is impaired:
[IAS 36:12]

• there are observable indications that the asset's value has declined during the period significantly more than would be expected as a result of the passage of time or normal use;

The wording of this requirement has been amended as a consequence of the issue of IFRS 13 *Fair Value Measurement* and those amendments are reflected above. Previously the paragraph read "during the period, an asset's market value has declined significantly more than would be expected as a result of the passage of time or normal use". The changes have been made to reflect the revised model for fair value measurement established in IFRS 13.

Such a decline could be caused by a decrease in the external market value for an asset (e.g. a head office building), or by a decrease in the sales price of items produced by a group of assets, such as the property, plant and equipment making up a factory.

- significant changes with an adverse effect on the entity have taken place during the period, or will take place in the near future, in the technological, market, economic or legal environment in which the entity operates or in the market to which the asset is dedicated;

> For example, if a factory produces a product that is judged harmful to the environment, and the government introduces a ban on the use of such equipment after a phase-out period, the carrying amount of the factory and the associated plant and equipment would need to be assessed for impairment. As another example, the value of a luxury hotel would need to be assessed if occupancy rates are declining as a result of a downturn in the economy.

- the carrying amount of the net assets of the entity is more than its market capitalisation;

> In some cases, the business prospects of the entity may not have changed, but the sector in which the entity operates may be 'out of favour' with market analysts, resulting in a decline in share price. In such circumstances, a write-down may not be required, but a formal review should be carried out. In particular, great care should be taken in determining the appropriate discount rate with which to calculate value in use, to ensure that it is consistent with current market assessments.

- for an investment in a subsidiary, joint venture or associate, the investor recognises a dividend from the investment and evidence is available that:

  - the carrying amount of the investment in the separate financial statements exceeds the carrying amounts in the consolidated financial statements of the investee's net assets, including associated goodwill; or

  - the dividend exceeds the total comprehensive income of the subsidiary, joint venture or associate in the period the dividend is declared; and

Dividends are recognised in profit or loss, rather than as a reduction of the cost of the associated investment. Accordingly, when a
dividend reduces the recoverable amount of an investment to
below its carrying amount, the investment is impaired.

- market interest rates or other market rates of return on investments
  have increased during the period, and those increases are likely to
  affect the discount rate used in calculating the asset's value in use
  and decrease the asset's recoverable amount materially.

If in prior years an asset has been the subject of an impairment
test, and there is a change in market interest rates in the current
period that will affect the discount rate used in the previous
calculation, it is appropriate to revisit the calculation. However,
this does not necessarily mean that, once an impairment review
has been carried out, it must be revisited each year or whenever
market rates move. The review in subsequent periods is required
only when the change in rates is likely to affect materially the
recoverable amount of the asset.

IAS 36:16 specifically states that no formal review is required when the
discount rate used in calculating the asset's value in use is:

- unlikely to be affected by the increase in market interest rates or
  other market rates of return on investments. For example, increases
  in short-term interest rates may not have a material effect on the
  discount rate used for an asset that has a long remaining useful life;
  or

- likely to be affected by the increase in these market rates, but
  previous sensitivity analysis of recoverable amount shows that:

  - it is unlikely that there will be a material decrease in the
    recoverable amount because future cash flows are also likely to
    increase. For example, in some cases, an entity may be able to
    demonstrate that it adjusts its revenues to compensate for any
    increase in market rates; or

  - the decrease in recoverable amount is unlikely to result in a
    material impairment loss.

If there is an indication that the asset may be impaired, the underlying
facts should be kept in mind when performing the annual reviews of the

useful life of the asset, the depreciation or amortisation method used and the estimated residual value. These items may need to be adjusted even if no impairment loss is recognised. [IAS 36:17]

5.2.3 Other examples of impairment indicators

5.2.3.1 Investment property carried at depreciated cost

It is necessary to exercise careful judgement when identifying impairment indicators for investment property carried at depreciated cost. In addition to the events and circumstances detailed in IAS 36:12, the following conditions may indicate that an investor may be unable to realise the carrying amount of an investment property carried at depreciated cost (list is not exhaustive):

- the investor recently sold a portion of its similar income-generating investment properties and realised losses on the sale transactions;

- income-generating properties have significant vacancy rates or are expected to be vacant in the near future (e.g. because of non-competitive lease terms);

- depressed market conditions are adversely affecting the rental or sale activities of significant properties;

- the investor does not appear to have the ability to recover the current net carrying amount of investment properties from future cash flows due to a decline in rental rates or occupancy rates; or

- the investor is encountering cash flow difficulties, which may require forced sale of some or all of its investment properties.

5.2.3.2 Appraisal or valuation below carrying amount

The existence of an appraisal or other independent valuation information indicating that the fair value less costs of disposal of a held-and-used asset is below its carrying amount does not, in itself, require that an impairment loss be recognised. When the asset's recoverable amount was previously based on value in use, the entity should consider whether the appraisal is an indication of impairment; it is possible that the factors resulting in the lower valuation do not affect the value in use calculations. When the entity does consider the lower valuation to be an indication of impairment, the entity should calculate the value in use of the asset (or, when appropriate, of the cash-generating unit to which it belongs – see **8.1** below). If the recoverable amount of the asset (i.e. the higher of the asset's fair value less costs of disposal and its value in use) is less than its carrying amount, an impairment loss should be recognised.

5.2.3.3   *Computer software asset developed (or under development) or purchased for internal use*

It is necessary to exercise careful judgement when identifying impairment indicators for recognised computer software assets developed or purchased for internal use. In addition to the events and circumstances detailed in IAS 36:12, the following conditions may indicate that the entity may not be able to recover the amounts recognised as an asset (list is not exhaustive):

- the internal-use computer software is not expected to provide service potential as originally planned;

- a significant change occurs in the extent to which, or the manner in which, the software is used or is expected to be used such that the future benefits expected to be generated are reduced;

- a significant change is made or will be made to the software program such that the future benefits expected to be generated are reduced; or

- the cost of developing or modifying the software significantly exceeded the amount originally budgeted.

Specifically in connection with software currently in development for internal use, indications that the software may no longer be expected to be completed and placed into service include the following:

- no expenditures budgeted or being incurred for the project;

- programming difficulties that cannot be resolved on a timely basis;

- significant cost overruns;

- the costs of internally developed software will significantly exceed the costs of comparable third-party software, and management intends to acquire the third-party software instead of completing the internally developed software;

- technologies are introduced in the marketplace so that management now intends to obtain third-party software instead of completing the internally developed software; or

- the business segment or unit to which the software relates, or relates in part, is unprofitable and has been or will be discontinued.

If events and circumstances indicate that the carrying amount of software recognised as an asset may not be recoverable, the entity will need to determine whether an impairment loss should be recognised (see **8.1**)

5.2.3.4   *Impairment indicators after the reporting period*

If information is received after the reporting period, but before the financial statements are authorised for issue, indicating that an asset is impaired, management should consider whether that information is indicative of impairment that existed at the end of the reporting period. If so, an impairment review should be carried out.

Even if management has already undertaken an impairment review in respect of that asset as at the end of the reporting period, additional information received after the reporting period that is indicative of impairment that existed at the end of the reporting period should lead management to re-perform that impairment review.

If the information received after the reporting period is not indicative of conditions existing at the end of the reporting period, it should not trigger an impairment test (or the re-performance of any impairment test already carried out). Rather, the information should be disclosed as a non-adjusting event after the reporting period when it is of such importance that non-disclosure would affect decisions of users of the financial statements (see **section 6** of **chapter A22** for further discussion of the disclosure requirements for events occurring after the reporting period).

Example 5.2.3.4

Closure announcement after the reporting date

An entity is a manufacturer of aircraft engines. After the reporting date, management decides and announces its intention to close its operations in Country A. Closure of the operation will not be completed within three years. The equipment and fixtures will only have a remaining life of three years, and there is no alternative use for the property.

The decision after the reporting date to close the operations in Country A is an indication of impairment. Any assessment of recoverable amounts should be based on the conditions and commitments existing at the reporting date. In accordance with IAS 10 *Events after the Reporting Period*, if the decision was made after the reporting date then any impairment resulting only from that decision (i.e. that was not already present in the business) is a non-adjusting event after the reporting period, although disclosure may be required. For further guidance on whether an entity was committed to a restructuring at the end of the reporting period, see **3.9.3** in **chapter A12**.

Although, in the circumstances described, the decision to close the operations in Country A may have been made after the reporting date, the decision may have resulted from conditions that existed at the reporting date (e.g. poor trading performance). Recognition of an impairment loss may therefore still be required to reflect those conditions that existed at the reporting date.

It will also be necessary to establish revised depreciation rates for the fixtures and equipment based on revised estimates of the useful lives and residual values of the affected assets, and those revised depreciation rates should be applied prospectively.

5.2.3.5   *Events and circumstances indicating that goodwill is impaired*

In addition to testing goodwill for impairment annually, goodwill should be tested for impairment whenever there is an indication that it might be impaired (as for other assets). It is necessary to exercise careful judgement when identifying impairment indicators for goodwill. The following are examples of events and circumstances that might indicate that goodwill is impaired (list is not exhaustive):

- the merger of business information systems does not occur as planned, and the acquirer does not achieve the savings that were expected from operating a merged system;

- industrial agreements do not permit the level of workplace reform that the acquirer had planned, and the employee head-count is higher than that planned at acquisition;

- the acquirer identified at acquisition the feasibility of developing several research projects, and these projects subsequently have been abandoned;

- a regulatory ruling prevents the acquirer from operating in certain markets, and the acquirer will not achieve the level of sales planned at acquisition; or

- a competitor introduces a new product earlier than expected, and the acquirer will not achieve the level of sales planned at acquisition.

5.2.3.6   Asset life shortened by physical damage

Example 5.2.3.6

Asset life shortened by physical damage

An entity has an asset that has been damaged such that the life of the asset has been shortened, but the carrying amount of the asset will still be recovered by the cash flows over the shortened life. The damage to the asset is an indication of impairment in accordance with IAS 36:12 (see **5.2.1**) and, therefore, the asset must be tested for impairment.

Because the carrying amount of the asset will be recovered by the cash flows over the asset's revised useful life, no impairment loss should be recognised. Nevertheless, the useful life of the asset is changed and the depreciation amount should be recalculated prospectively and accounted for as a change in estimate in accordance with the requirements of IAS 8 *Accounting Policies, Changes in Accounting Estimates and Errors*.

5.2.3.7   *Competitor enters an existing market*

Example 5.2.3.7

Competitor enters an existing market

An entity has several retail outlets in an area where no other significant competition has previously existed. During the current period, a large well-established competitor opens two stores in the region, selling similar products at similar prices.

The entrance into the market of a competitor is an impairment indicator. In determining value in use, revised cash flow forecasts should be prepared and new estimations of assets' recoverable amounts should be calculated, based on the best information available.

5.2.3.8   *Increase in sales tax*

Example 5.2.3.8

Increase in sales tax

An entity operates a chain of bookshops. Under the local tax regulations, a sales tax payable by purchasers of books is increased in the current period from 5 per cent to 10 per cent.

The change in tax rates may affect levels of demand for books and is an impairment indicator. Revised cashflow forecasts should be prepared by management, based on the best information available, so as to determine the value in use of the assets.

5.3   Requirements for annual reviews

As noted at **5.1** above, irrespective of whether there is any indication of impairment, the following items are required to be tested for impairment at least annually:
[IAS 36:10]

- intangible assets with an indefinite useful life;

- intangible assets that are not yet available for use; and

- goodwill acquired in a business combination.

5.3.1   Intangible assets

Intangible assets with an indefinite useful life and intangible assets not yet available for use are tested for impairment by comparing their carrying amounts with their recoverable amounts both:
[IAS 36:10(a)]

- annually; and

- whenever there is an indication, at the end of a reporting period, that the asset may be impaired.

The Standard allows that the annual impairment test may be performed at any time during the annual period, provided that it is performed at the same time every year. Different intangible assets may be tested for impairment at different times. [IAS 36:10(a)]

In the case of a newly recognised intangible asset (e.g. an intangible asset with an indefinite useful life purchased in the current period), an impairment test must be carried out before the end of the current annual period. [IAS 36:10(a)]

Although the Standard requires an annual review for the specified intangible assets, it does allow that the most recent detailed calculation of an asset's recoverable amount made in a preceding period may be used in the impairment test for that asset in the current period, provided that the following criteria are met:
[IAS 36:24]

- the most recent recoverable amount calculation resulted in an amount that exceeded the asset's carrying amount by a substantial margin;

- based on an analysis of events that have occurred and circumstances that have changed since the most recent recoverable amount calculation, the likelihood that a current recoverable amount determination would be less than the asset's carrying amount is remote; and

- for intangible assets tested for impairment as part of a cash-generating unit (see **8.1** below), the assets and liabilities making up that unit have not changed significantly since the most recent recoverable amount calculation.

5.3.2   Goodwill

Impairment testing for goodwill is always carried out in the context of a cash-generating unit (CGU) or a group of CGUs because goodwill does not generate cash flows independently of other assets. The detailed rules for the allocation of goodwill to cash-generating units are set out in **8.1.2** below.

5.3.2.1   CGUs to which goodwill has been allocated

When goodwill has been allocated to a CGU, or to a group of CGUs (in the circumstances discussed at **8.1.2**), that unit or group of units is tested for impairment both:
[IAS 36:90]

- annually; and

- whenever there is an indication that the unit, or group of units, may be impaired.

The impairment test is carried out by comparing the carrying amount of the unit (or group of units), including the goodwill, with the recoverable amount of the unit(s). If the recoverable amount of the unit(s) exceeds the carrying amount of the unit(s), the unit(s) and the goodwill allocated to the unit(s) are not regarded as impaired. If the carrying amount of the unit, or group of units, exceeds its (their) recoverable amount, the entity recognises an impairment loss in accordance with the requirements set out in **9.2** below. [IAS 36:90]

5.3.2.2   Timing of impairment tests

The annual impairment test for a CGU to which goodwill has been allocated may be performed at any time during the annual period, provided that it is performed at the same time every year. Different CGUs may be tested for impairment at different times. [IAS 36:96]

When some or all of the goodwill allocated to a CGU was acquired in a business combination during the current annual period, that CGU must be tested for impairment before the end of the current annual period. [IAS 36:96]

Example 5.3.2.2

Impairment testing for goodwill acquired in the period

An entity routinely tests goodwill for impairment in the second quarter of its annual reporting period. During the third quarter of 20X0, the entity makes an acquisition in which goodwill arises. The acquired goodwill (determined

---

on a provisional basis) is allocated to CGUs in accordance with the requirements of IAS 36. There is no indication that the acquired or existing goodwill
is impaired.

In 20X0, although there is no indication that the acquired goodwill is
impaired, and the annual impairment test for goodwill has already been
performed, a further impairment test must be conducted before the end of
the 20X0 reporting period on each CGU to which the newly acquired
goodwill has been allocated.

5.3.2.3   Individual assets to be tested before CGU

When assets within a CGU to which goodwill has been allocated (such as
intangible assets with indefinite lives) are tested for impairment at the
same time as the CGU containing the goodwill, the assets should be tested
for impairment before the CGU containing the goodwill. Similarly, when
CGUs are tested for impairment at the same time as the group of CGUs to
which they belong and to which goodwill has been allocated in aggregate,
the individual CGUs should be tested for impairment first (see **9.3**). [IAS
36:97]

In addition, at the time of testing a CGU to which goodwill has been
allocated, there may be an indication that a specific asset within the CGU
is impaired. In such circumstances, the individual asset is tested for
impairment first (and any identified impairment loss relating to that asset
is recognised) before the CGU is tested for impairment. This requirement
is imposed so as to ensure that any losses that can be identified with a
specific asset are not 'lost' in the testing of the CGU. Similarly, when
goodwill has been allocated to a group of CGUs, and there is an indication
that an individual CGU within the group is impaired, the individual CGU
is tested for impairment first (and any identified impairment loss relating
to the individual CGU recognised) before testing for impairment the
group of units to which goodwill has been allocated. [IAS 36:98]

Example 5.3.2.3A

Asset within cash-generating unit that provides no future benefit

An entity provides worldwide wireless communications to its customers
through a network of 10 satellites. The entity has determined appropriately
that its satellite business as a whole represents a 'lowest level' for which
identifiable cash flows are largely independent of the cash flows of other
assets and liabilities. A meteor destroys one satellite. However, the entity can
continue to provide worldwide service with the remaining 9 satellites.

Should the entity continue to recognise the satellite that has been destroyed as part of the cash-generating unit if the recoverable amount of the cash-generating unit exceeds its carrying amount?

No. IAS 36 is not intended to allow an entity to continue to recognise as an asset an item that does not meet the definition of an asset. If no future benefits are expected to be gained from holding or disposing of the satellite, it is likely that the asset should be written off in full in accordance with the derecognition requirements of paragraph 67 of IAS 16 *Property, Plant and Equipment* (see **section 9** of **chapter A7**). In such circumstances, even though the entity continues to have positive cash flows from its satellite communications business, the entity must recognise the loss of a satellite.

Example 5.3.2.3B

Asset within cash-generating unit that no longer contributes to cash flows

A machine within a cash-generating unit has become redundant and is no longer contributing to cash flows. Its carrying amount exceeds its recoverable amount. However, the recoverable amount of the CGU is above its carrying amount.

The entity should recognise an impairment loss for the machine because its carrying amount is above its recoverable amount. The general principle is that impairment should be identified at the individual asset level, if possible. The recoverable amount should be calculated for the smallest CGU to which the asset belongs only when the recoverable amount for the individual asset cannot be identified. The machine is no longer in use and, therefore, no longer belongs to the CGU. The smallest CGU is now the machine itself. The entity is able to determine the future cash inflows arising from using this machine; they are nil. Therefore, the entity should determine the fair value less costs of disposal of the machine (because it is possible the machine has some scrap or resale value), and it should recognise the impairment loss identified.

5.3.2.4   Rolling forward detailed calculations from a preceding period

Although the Standard requires an annual review for CGUs to which goodwill has been allocated, it does allow that the most recent detailed calculation of a unit's recoverable amount made in a preceding period may be used when testing that unit for impairment in the current period, provided that the following criteria are met:
[IAS 36:99]

- the assets and liabilities making up the unit have not changed significantly since the most recent recoverable amount calculation;

- the most recent recoverable amount calculation resulted in an amount that exceeded the unit's carrying amount by a substantial margin; and

- based on an analysis of events that have occurred and circumstances that have changed since the most recent recoverable amount calculation, the likelihood that a current recoverable amount determination would be less than the unit's carrying amount is remote.

5.3.2.5 *CGUs to which it has not been possible to allocate goodwill*

As discussed in **8.1.2**, it may not be possible to allocate goodwill to an individual CGU to which it relates. In such circumstances, the unit concerned is tested for impairment whenever there is an indication that the unit may be impaired by comparing the unit's carrying amount, excluding any goodwill, with its recoverable amount. Any impairment loss is recognised in accordance with the rules set out in **9.2** below. [IAS 36:88]

If no goodwill has been allocated to a CGU but the CGU includes an intangible asset that has an indefinite life or that is not yet available for use, it will be necessary to carry out an annual impairment test for that CGU if that asset can be tested for impairment only as part of the CGU. [IAS 36:89] In such circumstances, the rules described at **5.3.1** above apply.

6 Measurement of recoverable amount

An asset or CGU is considered to be impaired when its recoverable amount declines below its carrying amount. Following the identification of any indication of impairment, the entity is required to make a formal estimate of the recoverable amount of the asset or CGU. [IAS 36:8] It is only by making such an estimate that the entity can determine whether an impairment loss has occurred.

> The recoverable amount of an asset is the higher of its fair value less costs of disposal and its value in use. The Standard measures impairment loss based on an assumption that the entity will choose to recover the carrying amount of the asset in the most beneficial way. Therefore, if the entity could earn more by selling the asset than by continuing to use it, it would choose to sell the asset, and vice versa.

Example 6A

Measurement of recoverable amount

An entity buys a machine for CU7 million on 1 January 20X1. The asset has a seven-year life, with nil residual value. The carrying amount at 31 December 20X3 is CU4 million. The machine generates largely independent cash inflows and, therefore, is tested for impairment as a stand-alone asset.

Due to changes in market conditions, the entity considers that the machine may be impaired. It is determined that the asset could be sold for CU2 million (with costs of disposal of CU200,000). The directors have estimated that the value in use of the asset is CU3.5 million.

First, the fair value less costs of disposal of the asset (CU1.8 million) is compared with the estimated value in use (CU3.5 million). The recoverable amount is the higher of these, i.e. CU3.5 million.

The recoverable amount is then compared with the carrying amount and an impairment loss of CU500,000 is recognised.

Example 6B

Recoverable amount based on fair value less costs of disposal

Entity A is reviewing all of its assets for impairment as a result of a fall in the demand for its products. One item of machinery is 10 years old and has a carrying amount of CU80 million and a value in use of CU75 million (calculated on the basis of revised sales estimates). The fair value of the machine is CU82 million.

It is estimated that if the machine were to be disposed of, costs attributable to the disposal would be approximately CU1 million. Management has no intention of selling the machine.

The fair value less costs of disposal of the machine (CU81 million) is higher than its value in use; therefore, the fair value less costs of disposal represents the machine's recoverable amount. The carrying amount is less than the recoverable amount; consequently, no impairment loss should be recognised.

For the purposes of an impairment review, it is not always necessary to calculate both fair value less costs of disposal and value in use.

- If either the fair value less costs of disposal or the value in use is found to be higher than the carrying amount, the asset is not impaired, and there is no need to calculate the other amount. [IAS 36:19]

693

- If there is no basis for making a reliable estimate of fair value less costs of disposal, recoverable amount is measured by reference to value in use alone. [IAS 36:20]

- The detailed calculations involved in measuring value in use may be avoided if a simple estimate is sufficient to show either that value in use is higher than the carrying amount (in which case there is no impairment) or that it is lower than fair value less costs of disposal (in which case recoverable amount is the fair value less costs of disposal). [IAS 36:23]

Recoverable amount is determined for an individual asset, unless the asset does not generate cash inflows that are largely independent of those from other assets or groups of assets. If this is the case, recoverable amount is determined for the cash-generating unit to which the asset belongs (see **8.1** below), unless either:
[IAS 36:22]

- the asset's fair value less costs of disposal is higher than its carrying amount; or

- the asset's value in use can be estimated to be close to its fair value less costs of disposal and fair value less costs of disposal can be measured.

For example, a CGU may include an office building whose fair value can be readily determined. If either (1) the fair value less costs of disposal of the office building is higher than its carrying amount, or (2) its value in use can be estimated to be close to its fair value less costs of disposal, the building is first considered by itself for impairment testing. In addition, if an impairment test is required for the CGU of which the building forms part, the building should be included within the carrying amount of the CGU for the purpose of that impairment test. However, any loss identified for the CGU (in excess of any loss already recognised for the building) should be allocated to other assets.

As explained at **9.2** below, when allocating an impairment loss to an individual asset within a CGU, the carrying amount of such an asset should not be reduced below its fair value less costs of disposal.

6.1   Impairment of goodwill in associates and joint ventures

As described at **4.4.3.6** in **chapter A26**, the entire carrying amount of an investment in an associate or a joint venture accounted for using the equity method, including any goodwill, is tested for impairment as a whole. Impairment losses recognised in respect of such investments may be reversed, as described in **section 10** below.

Prior to the adoption of IFRS 11 *Joint Arrangements* (required for annual periods beginning on or after 1 January 2013, with earlier adoption permitted), if an interest in a joint venture is accounted for using proportionate consolidation, any goodwill is held separately and, therefore, tested for impairment annually.

7   Fair value less costs of disposal

This section discusses the measurement of fair value less costs of disposal for an asset or CGU. For guidance on the identification of CGUs, see **8.1**.

Prior to the adoption of IFRS 13 *Fair Value Measurement*, the term 'fair value less costs to sell' was used instead of 'fair value less costs of disposal'. As can be seen from the definitions below, the only effect of this change is that, following the adoption of IFRS 13, 'fair value' is measured in accordance with the requirements in that Standard rather than the guidance previously included in IAS 36.

7.1   Entities that have adopted IFRS 13 (fair value less costs of disposal)

7.1.1   *Definition*

Fair value is defined as the price that would be received to sell an asset or paid to transfer a liability in an orderly transaction between market participants at the measurement date. [IAS 36:6] No further guidance is provided on the measurement of fair value – the reader is directed to IFRS 13 (see **chapter A6**).

Although IFRS 13 amended the definition of fair value in IAS 36, it did not change the definition and guidance in respect of costs of disposal, as set out below.

Costs of disposal are defined as incremental costs directly attributable to the disposal of an asset or CGU, excluding finance and income tax expense. [IAS 36:6]

Costs of disposal to be deducted in arriving at fair value less costs of disposal include:
[IAS 36:28]

- legal costs;

- stamp duty or similar transaction taxes;

- costs of removing the asset; and

- other direct incremental costs to bring the asset into condition for its sale.

Costs such as termination benefits to employees and reorganisation expenses following a disposal are not considered direct, incremental costs of sale and, as such, are not deducted in arriving at fair value less costs of disposal. [IAS 36:28]

Costs of disposal that have been recognised as liabilities should not be deducted in measuring fair value less costs of disposal. [IAS 36:28]

For example, when an entity already had an obligation to remove an asset at the end of its life, a provision will have been recognised and those costs will already be included in the carrying amount of the asset. Accordingly, in such circumstances, either:

- the costs should not be included as costs of disposal in arriving at fair value less costs of disposal; or

- in some cases (e.g. when the buyer will have to assume the liability), it may be necessary to deduct the carrying amount of the liability from that of the asset in order to determine a carrying amount that can be compared with fair value less costs of disposal, in accordance with IAS 36:29 and IAS 36:78 (see 8.1.1).

7.1.2   Revalued assets

As discussed in **section 3**, the scope of IAS 36 includes some assets carried at a revalued amount (e.g. property, plant and equipment accounted for under the revaluation model in IAS 16 *Property, Plant and Equipment* – see **chapter A7**).

The only difference between a revalued asset's fair value and its fair value less costs of disposal is the direct incremental costs attributable to the disposal of the asset.
[IAS 36:5]

- If the disposal costs are negligible, the recoverable amount of a revalued asset is, by definition, close to, or greater than, its revalued amount. In this case, after the revaluation requirements have been applied, it is unlikely that the revalued asset is impaired and recoverable amount need not be estimated.

- If the disposal costs are not negligible, the fair value less costs of disposal of the revalued asset is necessarily less than its fair value. Therefore, the revalued asset will be impaired if its value in use is less than its revalued amount. In this case, after the revaluation requirements have been applied, the entity should apply IAS 36 to determine whether the asset may be impaired.

> The guidance in IAS 36:5 set out above reflects consequential amendments to IAS 36 arising from IFRS 13. Prior to amendment, the text distinguished between circumstances when the asset's fair value is its market value and when the asset's fair value is determined on a basis other than its market value. This distinction does not arise under the revised IAS 36, which takes its single definition of fair value from IFRS 13 (see **7.1.1** above).

7.1.3   Contrasting fair value and value in use

Fair value differs from value in use. Fair value reflects the assumptions market participants would use when pricing the asset. In contrast, value in use reflects the effects of factors that may be specific to the entity and not applicable to entities in general. For example, fair value does not reflect any of the following factors to the extent that they would not be generally available to market participants:
[IAS 36:53A]

- additional value derived from the grouping of assets (such as the creation of a portfolio of investment properties in different locations);

- synergies between the asset being measured and other assets;

- legal rights or legal restrictions that are specific only to the current owner of the asset; and

- tax benefits or tax burdens that are specific to the current owner of the asset.

7.2 Entities that have not yet adopted IFRS 13 (fair value less costs to sell)

7.2.1 Definition

The fair value less costs to sell of an asset or CGU is the amount obtainable from the sale of the asset or CGU in an arm's length transaction between knowledgeable, willing parties, less costs of disposal. [IAS 36:6]

Costs of disposal are defined as incremental costs directly attributable to the disposal of an asset or CGU, excluding finance and income tax expense. [IAS 36:6]

Costs of disposal to be deducted in arriving at fair value less costs to sell include:
[IAS 36:28]

- legal costs;

- stamp duty or similar transaction taxes;

- costs of removing the asset; and

- other direct incremental costs to bring the asset into condition for its sale.

Costs such as termination benefits to employees and reorganisation expenses following a disposal are not considered direct, incremental costs of sale and, as such, are not deducted in arriving at fair value less costs to sell. [IAS 36:28]

Costs of disposal that have been recognised as liabilities should not be deducted in determining fair value less costs to sell. [IAS 36:28]

> For example, when an entity already had an obligation to remove an asset at the end of its life, a provision will have been recognised and those costs will already be included in the carrying amount of the asset. Accordingly, these costs should not be included as costs of disposal in arriving at fair value less costs to sell.

However, in some cases (e.g. when buyers assume the liability to remove the asset), it may be that the fair value would necessarily reflect the fact that the liability is attached to the asset. In such circumstances, it would be necessary to deduct the carrying amount of the liability from that of the asset in order to determine a carrying amount that can be compared with fair value less costs to sell, in accordance with IAS 36:29 and IAS 36:78 (see **8.1.1**).

7.2.2   Revalued assets

As discussed in **section 3**, the scope of IAS 36 includes some assets carried at a revalued amount (e.g. property, plant and equipment accounted for under the revaluation model in IAS 16 *Property, Plant and Equipment* – see **chapter A7**).

Identifying whether a revalued asset may be impaired depends on the basis used to determine fair value:
[IAS 36:5]

- if the asset's fair value is its market value, the only difference between the asset's fair value and its fair value less costs to sell is the direct incremental costs to dispose of the asset:

  - if the disposal costs are negligible, the recoverable amount of a revalued asset is, by definition, close to, or greater than, its revalued amount (i.e. fair value). In this case, after the revaluation requirements have been applied, it is unlikely that the revalued asset is impaired and recoverable amount need not be estimated; but

  - if the disposal costs are not negligible, the fair value less costs to sell of the revalued asset is necessarily less than its fair value. Therefore, the revalued asset will be impaired if its value in use is less than its revalued amount (i.e. fair value). In this case, after the revaluation requirements have been applied, the entity will apply IAS 36 to determine whether the asset may be impaired; and

- if the asset's fair value is determined on a basis other than its market value, its revalued amount (i.e. fair value) may be greater than or lower than its recoverable amount. Hence, after the revaluation requirements have been applied, the entity should apply IAS 36 to determine whether the asset may be impaired.

7.2.3   Guidance on measurement of fair value

If an estimate of fair value less costs to sell is required, the following sources represent the best evidence (in descending order of preference):

- a price in a binding sale agreement in an arm's length transaction, adjusted for incremental, directly attributable disposal costs; [IAS 36:25]

- the bid price in an active market less costs of disposal. If current bid prices are unavailable, the price of the most recent transaction may provide a basis from which to estimate fair value less costs to sell, if there has not been a significant change in economic circumstances between the transaction date and the estimation date; [IAS 36:26] and

- the best information available to reflect the amount that the entity could obtain, at the end of the reporting period, for the disposal of the asset in an arm's length transaction after deducting the costs of disposal. The outcome of recent transactions for similar assets within the same industry may provide a basis for the estimate. Unless management is compelled to sell immediately, the estimate should not reflect a forced sale. [IAS 36:27]

8   Value in use

The calculation of value in use can be broken down into four stages:

- identification of cash-generating units (see **8.1**);

- estimation of expected future cash flows (see **8.2**);

- determination of an appropriate discount rate (see **8.3**); and

- discounting and aggregating expected cash flows to arrive at value in use (see **8.4**).

8.1   Stage 1: Identification of cash-generating units (CGUs)

If the recoverable amount of an asset can be individually determined, this stage is omitted.

It is often not possible to estimate the recoverable amount of an individual asset because assets frequently generate cash when working together rather than singly. When this is the case, an entity should determine the recoverable amount of the CGU to which the asset belongs. [IAS 36:66]

A cash-generating unit is defined as the smallest identifiable group of assets that generates cash inflows that are largely independent of the cash inflows from other assets or groups of assets. [IAS 36:6]

IAS 36:67 specifically states that the recoverable amount of an individual asset cannot be determined when both of the following conditions exist:

- the value in use of the asset cannot be estimated to be close to its fair value less costs of disposal (e.g. when the future cash flows from the continuing use of the asset are not negligible); and

- the asset does not generate cash inflows that are largely independent of those from other assets.

Examples **8.1A** and **8.1B** below are reproduced from the Standard.

Example 8.1A

Recoverable amount cannot be determined
[IAS 36:67]

A mining entity owns a private railway to support its mining activities. The private railway could be sold only for scrap value and it does not generate cash inflows that are largely independent of the cash inflows from the other assets of the mine.

It is not possible to estimate the recoverable amount of the private railway because its value in use cannot be determined and is probably different from scrap value. Therefore, the entity estimates the recoverable amount of the cash-generating unit to which the private railway belongs, i.e. the mine as a whole.

Example 8.1B

Lowest aggregation of assets that generate largely independent cash flows
[IAS 36:68]

A bus company provides services under contract with a municipality that requires minimum service on each of five separate routes. Assets devoted to each route and the cash flows from each route can be identified separately. One of the routes operates at a significant loss.

Because the entity does not have the option to curtail any one bus route, the lowest level of identifiable cash inflows that are largely independent of the cash inflows from

> *other assets or groups of assets is the cash inflows generated by the five routes together. The cash-generating unit for each route is the bus company as a whole.*

When the recoverable amount of an individual asset cannot be determined, its CGU should be identified as the lowest aggregation of assets that generates largely independent cash inflows. [IAS 36:68]

If events and circumstances indicate that the carrying amount of an asset may not be recoverable, the appropriate accounting will depend on whether the entity expects to continue to use the asset and, if so, whether it will be used as part of a cash-generating unit.

For example, consider the situation in which events and circumstances indicate that the carrying amount of a computer software asset developed (or under development) or purchased for internal use may not be recoverable. The appropriate accounting will depend on whether the entity expects to continue to use the software and, if so, whether it will be used as part of a cash-generating unit.

The outcome of events and circumstances of the nature described in **5.2.3.3** above may result in a determination, either during development or after development is completed, that the software is no longer expected to be placed into service or that it will be removed from service. In such circumstances, the entity should determine whether the software asset should be derecognised in accordance with paragraph 112 of IAS 38 *Intangible Assets* (see **example 5.3.2.3A**).

Alternatively, it may be determined that the software will continue to be used.

- If the software generates cash flows independently, the entity should estimate the software's recoverable amount, which will be the higher of its fair value less costs of disposal (based on selling the software) and its value in use (based on the cash flows that it is expected to generate from use, less any associated costs). An impairment loss should be recognised if the software's carrying amount is in excess of recoverable amount.

- If the software does not generate cash flows independently, it should generally be tested for impairment as part of the cash-generating unit to which it relates (see IAS 36:66 and 67). In such circumstances, whether it is necessary to recognise an impairment loss will depend on the recoverable amount of the cash-generating unit as a whole. If the recoverable amount of the cash-generating unit as a whole exceeds its carrying amount, no impairment loss is recognised. This may be the case even though the software will be used less frequently than was originally intended and even though, had they foreseen this, the directors might not have been prepared to incur the costs of the software.

Example 8.1C

Group of interchangeable assets

A national wireless communication provider owns a number of sets of antennae, radio transmitters and receivers (collectively referred to as 'antennae sets') installed on cell towers which together provide the infrastructure for its telecommunications network. If a specific antennae set is damaged or otherwise is not capable of operating, its output can be delivered from a similar antennae set on another cell tower so that services are virtually uninterrupted, and all cash flow streams will remain intact. This interchangeability is a feature deliberately built into the integrated logistical design of the network.

In the circumstances described, the cash flows generated by each individual antennae set are not 'largely independent' as contemplated in the definition for a cash-generating unit; it is not appropriate to attribute specific cash flows to individual antennae sets because the sets are almost instantaneously interchangeable and, as a result, whether an individual antennae set is capable of operating does not affect cash inflows. However, each antennae set is part of a group of assets that make up the entity's national network of towers and antennae. Because the wireless communication provider operates using a national network, the national network infrastructure asset group would be the smallest identifiable asset group that generates cash flows that are largely independent; therefore, the national network infrastructure asset group is a cash-generating unit and it is at that level that the network should be assessed for impairment.

Example 8.1D

Identification of cash-generating units in the retail industry

Entity A, a retail company, operates three stores that generate largely independent cash inflows. The three stores share expenditures (cash outflows) such as on infrastructure, marketing and human resources.

When Entity A is tested for impairment under IAS 36, should Entity A's cash-generating unit be composed of the three stores, on the basis that the net cash flows associated with the stores are interdependent?

No. IAS 36:6 defines a cash-generating unit as "the smallest identifiable group of assets that generates cash inflows that are largely independent of the cash inflows from other assets or groups of assets".

The definition of a cash-generating unit requires the identification of an asset's cash-generating unit on the basis of independent cash inflows generated by the asset, not independent net cash flows (i.e. cash inflows and outflows). Therefore, outflows such as shared infrastructure and marketing expenditures are not considered when identifying a cash-generating unit. When a store is tested for impairment under IAS 36, the store's cash-generating unit is the store itself.

Cash inflows are inflows of cash and cash equivalents received from parties outside the reporting entity. In general terms, cash inflows are likely to follow the way in which management monitors and makes decisions about continuing or closing the different lines of business of the entity. [IAS 36:69]

Unique intangible assets, such as brands and mastheads, are generally seen to generate cash independently of each other and are usually monitored separately. Hence, they can often be used to identify CGUs. Other CGUs may be identified by reference to major products or services.

If an active market exists for the output produced by an asset or a group of assets, it should be identified as a CGU, even if some or all of the output is used internally. The asset or group of assets forms a separate CGU if the entity could sell this output in an active market. This is because this asset or group of assets *could* generate cash inflows that would be largely independent of the cash flows from other assets or groups of assets. [IAS 36:70 & 71]

In the circumstances described in the previous paragraph, management estimates the expected market price for the output of the unit and uses that estimate not only when determining the value in use of the supplying unit, but also when determining the value in use of the other CGU that is using the output. In other words, market prices rather than internal transfer prices are used when estimating the recoverable amount of a CGU. [IAS 36:70]

For entities that have not yet adopted IFRS 13 *Fair Value Measurement*, the definition of an 'active market' is as set out in **section 4** above.

For entities that have adopted IFRS 13, an amended definition is included in that Standard – see **5.1.1** in **chapter A6**).

Example 8.1E

Active market for product used internally

An entity manufactures two products – Product 1 and Product 2. Product 1 is manufactured in the entity's factory in Country A, and all of the items produced are transferred to the entity's factory in Country B where they are used in the assembly of Product 2. The entity does not sell Product 1.

If there is an active market for Product 1, the factory in Country A is treated as a separate CGU. The value in use of the factory in Country A is calculated using the market price of the units of Product 1 produced. The estimated value in use of the factory in Country B will be calculated using the market price of the units of Product 1 purchased as the basis for estimating cash outflows for the purchase of subcomponents.

CGUs should be identified consistently from period to period for the same asset or types of assets, unless a change is justified. [IAS 36:72] When a change is made during a period in which an impairment loss is recognised or reversed, disclosure is required of the current and former ways of aggregating assets and the reasons for changing the way the CGU is identified (see **11.3** below).

The first of the illustrative examples accompanying IAS 36 includes several examples of the identification of CGUs.

8.1.1   Allocation of assets and liabilities to CGUs

The allocation of assets and liabilities to a CGU, so as to establish the carrying amount of the CGU, should be determined on a basis consistent with the way the recoverable amount of the CGU is determined. [IAS 36:75]

As a general rule, the carrying amount of a CGU:
[IAS 36:76]

- includes the carrying amount of only those assets that can be attributed directly, or allocated on a reasonable and consistent basis, to the CGU and that will generate the future cash inflows used in determining the CGU's value in use; and

- does not include the carrying amount of any recognised liability, unless the recoverable amount of the CGU cannot be determined without consideration of this liability.

This allocation is consistent with the calculation of fair value less costs of disposal and value in use of a CGU, which both exclude cash flows that relate to assets outside the CGU and liabilities that have already been recognised in the financial statements (see Stage 2 at **8.2** below). [IAS 36:76]

> There will be some assets that contribute to cash flows, such as goodwill and corporate assets, which cannot be allocated to the CGU on a reasonable and consistent basis. These are discussed in **8.1.2** (goodwill) and **8.1.3** (corporate assets) below.

In some situations, due to the nature of a particular recognised liability, it may be appropriate to include it in the carrying amount and the recoverable amount of a CGU. This will be the case when a CGU could not be sold without the assumption of the related liability by the buyer. In such circumstances, the fair value less costs of disposal (or the estimated cash flow from ultimate disposal) of the CGU is the price to sell the assets and the liability together, less disposal costs. In order to be consistent and compare like items, the carrying amount of the liability should be deducted in determining both the value in use and carrying amount of the CGU. [IAS 36:78]

Example 8.1.1 below is reproduced from the Standard.

Example 8.1.1

Liability included in CGU
[IAS 36:78]

A company operates a mine in a country where legislation requires that the owner must restore the site on completion of its mining operations. The cost of restoration includes the replacement of the overburden, which must be removed before mining operations commence. A provision for the costs to replace the overburden was recognised as soon as the overburden was removed. The amount provided was recognised as part of the cost of the mine and is being depreciated over the mine's useful life. The carrying amount of the provision for restoration costs is CU500, which is equal to the present value of the restoration costs.

The entity is testing the mine for impairment. The cash-generating unit for the mine is the mine as a whole. The entity has received various offers to buy the mine at a price of around CU800. This price reflects the fact that the buyer will assume the obligation to restore the overburden. Disposal costs for the mine are negligible. The value in use of the mine is approximately CU1,200, excluding restoration costs. The carrying amount of the mine is CU1,000.

The cash-generating unit's fair value less costs of disposal is CU800. This amount considers restoration costs that have already been provided for. As a consequence, the value in use for the cash-generating unit is determined after consideration of the restoration costs and is estimated to be CU700 (CU1,200 less CU500). The carrying amount of the cash-generating unit is CU500, which is the carrying amount of the mine (CU1,000) less the carrying amount of the provision for restoration costs (CU500). Therefore, the recoverable amount of the cash-generating unit exceeds its carrying amount.

IAS 36:79 states that, for practical purposes, it is sometimes necessary to include assets that are not part of the CGU (e.g. receivables or other financial assets) or liabilities that have already been recognised in the financial statements (e.g. payables, pensions and other provisions) when determining recoverable amount. When this is the case, these items are also included in the carrying amount of the CGU.

Therefore, although best practice is to exclude these items, if they are included they should be included consistently, i.e. both in the carrying amount of the CGU and in the estimation of recoverable amount. To do otherwise would be to compare unlike items.

8.1.2   Allocation of goodwill to CGUs

For the purpose of impairment testing, goodwill acquired in a business combination is, from the acquisition date, required to be allocated to each of the acquirer's CGUs, or groups of CGUs, that are expected to benefit from the synergies of the combination, irrespective of whether other assets or liabilities of the acquiree are assigned to those units or groups of units. [IAS 36:80]

Goodwill recognised in a business combination is an asset representing the future economic benefits arising from other assets acquired in a business combination that are not individually identified and separately recognised. Goodwill does not generate cash flows independently of other assets or groups of assets and, therefore, it will always be tested for impairment as part of a CGU or a group of CGUs. [IAS 36:81]

In fact, it may not be possible to allocate goodwill to individual CGUs on a reasonable basis and it will often be the case that goodwill can only be allocated to a group of CGUs. IAS 36 permits such aggregation provided that the CGU or group of CGUs to which goodwill is allocated:
[IAS 36:80]

- represents the lowest level within the entity at which goodwill is monitored for internal management purposes; and

- is not larger than an operating segment, as defined by paragraph 5 of IFRS 8 *Operating Segments*, before aggregation (see **chapter A30**).

> The objective of the IASB in setting these conditions is to require entities to allocate goodwill to the lowest possible level without resorting to arbitrary allocations and without, generally, having to develop new or additional reporting systems to perform impairment testing. The Board's approach is that goodwill should be tested for impairment at a level at which information about the operations of the entity and the assets that support them is provided for internal reporting purposes.
>
> In many cases, the goodwill purchased in a business combination enhances the value of all of the acquirer's pre-existing cash-generating units. Some might argue that, in such circumstances, goodwill should be tested for impairment at the entity level. The Board has rejected this argument and determined that the highest level at which goodwill should be tested for impairment is the operating segment level, before aggregation. If the entity monitors goodwill at a level higher than the operating segment level, it may be necessary to develop additional reporting systems to perform the impairment testing of goodwill mandated by IAS 36.

Example 8.1.2A

Level at which goodwill is tested for impairment

Company A has three retail divisions, each of which is classified for reporting purposes as an operating segment under IFRS 8. All three divisions consist of a number of individual stores that operate independently of one another. Goodwill was recognised on the acquisition of each division. Management does not monitor goodwill for internal purposes.

However, under the requirements of IAS 36, goodwill is monitored and assessed for impairment annually for financial reporting purposes. Management currently only monitors goodwill for impairment at an operating segment level. However, management also has the ability to allocate goodwill to each store within each operating segment and to monitor goodwill for impairment at that lower level.

Given that management is capable of monitoring the impairment of goodwill at a lower level than is currently the case, should management perform its goodwill impairment assessment at that lower level?

Management's current practice is appropriate. IAS 36:80 requires goodwill to be assessed for impairment at a level no larger than an operating segment determined under IFRS 8, and which represents the lowest level at which goodwill is monitored for internal management purposes. Company A complies with both requirements and does not need to alter the level at which goodwill is currently assessed for impairment.

Example 8.1.2B

Allocation of goodwill by unlisted entities

Group A is an unlisted entity. It is therefore not within the scope of IFRS 8; nor does it choose to apply that Standard voluntarily. Group A acquired a subsidiary some years ago, which resulted in the recognition of goodwill.

Management generally monitors Group A's activities on a country-by-country basis. However, goodwill has not been allocated to individual countries for internal management purposes. If Group A were to apply IFRS 8, each country would represent an operating segment under that Standard.

Should Group A test goodwill for impairment at the reporting entity (group) level, or should it test for impairment at a lower operating segment (individual country) level, i.e. at the level at which management generally monitors activities?

IAS 36:82 clarifies that the objective of the guidance in IAS 36 on allocating goodwill is to ensure that goodwill is tested for impairment "at a level that reflects the way an entity manages its operations and with which the goodwill would naturally be associated".

In specifying the level at which goodwill should be allocated, IAS 36:80(b) requires that the unit or group of units to which goodwill is allocated "not be larger than an operating segment as defined by paragraph 5 of IFRS 8 *Operating Segments*, before aggregation". Note that this requirement does not refer to the level of *reported* operating segments. Therefore, irrespective of whether an entity reports segment information in respect of its operating segments in accordance with IFRS 8, it should assess its goodwill at the operating segment level in accordance with IAS 36:80(b).

In the circumstances described, the internal management reporting system on an individual country basis appears to represent an appropriate operating segment level for Group A. Therefore, goodwill should be tested for impairment at the country level.

Example 8.1.2C

Goodwill allocation methodologies

Entity M is a mining conglomerate. Entity M acquires Entity N, which operates a number of mines remotely located from each other, for consideration of CU10 million. For the purpose of accounting for the acquisition under IFRS 3 *Business Combinations*, Entity M measures the fair value of the net identifiable assets of Entity N at CU8 million. Goodwill of CU2 million is therefore recognised at the acquisition date.

IAS 36:80 requires that "[f]or the purpose of impairment testing, goodwill acquired in a business combination shall, from the acquisition date, be allocated to each of the acquirer's cash-generating units, or groups of cash-generating units, that is expected to benefit from the synergies of the combination, irrespective of whether other assets or liabilities of the acquiree are assigned to those units or groups of units".

Entity M determines that each independently operating mine is a CGU.

How should Entity M allocate the goodwill arising on the acquisition of Entity N among its CGUs?

Entity M should first identify the CGUs or groups of CGUs throughout the group that are expected to benefit from the synergies of the combination, irrespective of whether other assets and liabilities of Entity N are allocated to those CGUs or groups of CGUs.

The level at which goodwill is required to be allocated to a CGU or group of CGUs is determined by the level at which management monitors goodwill and the operating segments of the entity. When it is necessary to allocate goodwill among individual CGUs or groups of CGUs, because that is the level at which the goodwill is monitored for internal management purposes, the Standard does not specify any particular method of allocation.

In the circumstances described, assume that Entity M has concluded that only the newly acquired CGUs will benefit from the synergies of the combination. Consequently, Entity M needs to identify an appropriate method to allocate the goodwill among the Entity N mines that are expected to benefit from those synergies.

For Entity M, appropriate methods of allocating the goodwill may include:

- in proportion to the relative fair value of the identifiable net assets in each CGU; or

- in proportion to the relative fair values of the CGUs; or

- in proportion to the possible reserves beyond proven and probable (whether or not used in determining the value of the purchased assets) in each CGU; or

- in proportion to proven reserves in each CGU.

None of these allocation methods is prohibited by the Standard. However, other considerations to take into account include that:

- the method used to determine the purchase price may indicate an appropriate allocation methodology, which could include any of those proposed; and

- the allocation methodology used should not be inconsistent with any disclosed factors that support the goodwill figure.

Note that paragraph 21 of IFRS 6 *Exploration for and Evaluation of Mineral Resources* addresses the determination of an accounting policy for allocating exploration and evaluation assets to CGUs or groups of CGUs for the purpose of assessing such assets for impairment (see **5.2** in **chapter A40** for further guidance). However, the allocation of any goodwill arising on the acquisition of a mining entity remains within the scope of IAS 36 rather than IFRS 6.

8.1.2.1 *Completing the initial allocation of goodwill*

Ideally, the initial allocation of goodwill recognised in a business combination to CGUs should be completed before the end of the annual period in which the business combination is effected. If this is not possible, the initial allocation should be completed before the end of the first annual period beginning after the acquisition date. [IAS 36:84]

This rule differs from that specified by IFRS 3 when the initial accounting for a business combination can be determined only provisionally by the end of the period in which the combination is effected. In such circumstances, IFRS 3 requires the acquirer to:

- account for the combination using the provisional values; and

- recognise any adjustments to those provisional values as a result of completing the initial accounting within the measurement period, which is not to exceed twelve months from the acquisition date.

Therefore, the period allowed to complete the initial allocation of goodwill to CGUs is longer than the period to complete the initial accounting for a business combination. The Board decided to allow this longer period because the allocation of goodwill will often not be possible until after the initial accounting for the combination is complete.

8.1.2.2   Disposal of a portion of a CGU including goodwill

If goodwill has been allocated to a CGU, or a group of CGUs, and the entity disposes of an operation within that unit or group, the goodwill associated with the operation disposed of should be:
[IAS 36:86]

- included in the carrying amount of the operation when determining the gain or loss on disposal; and

- measured on the basis of the relative values of the operation disposed of and the portion of the CGU retained, unless the entity can demonstrate that some other method better reflects the goodwill associated with the operation disposed of.

> In accordance with the requirements set out in the previous sections, the entity will already have allocated goodwill to the CGU, or group of CGUs, at the lowest level at which goodwill is monitored for internal management purposes. It may be that goodwill cannot easily be identified with smaller operations within that unit or group, except in an arbitrary fashion. However, even if this is the case, when such smaller operations are being disposed of, it is appropriate to assume that some amount of goodwill is associated with the operation being disposed of, and to make an allocation of goodwill for that purpose.

The following example is included in the Standard.

Example 8.1.2.2

Goodwill measured on basis of relative values
[IAS 36:86]

An entity sells for CU100 an operation that was part of a CGU to which goodwill has been allocated. The goodwill allocated to that unit cannot be identified or associated with an asset group at a level lower than that unit, except arbitrarily. The recoverable amount of the portion of the CGU retained is CU300.

Because the goodwill allocated to the CGU cannot be non-arbitrarily identified or associated with an asset group at a level lower than that unit, the goodwill associated with the operation disposed of is measured on the basis of the relative values of the operation disposed of and the portion of the unit retained. Therefore, 25 per cent of the goodwill allocated to the CGU is included in the carrying amount of the operation that is sold.

When goodwill cannot be allocated, except arbitrarily, at a lower level than that at which it is monitored for internal management purposes, the most appropriate method of allocation will generally be based on the relative values of the operation disposed of and the portion of the CGU retained. There may be circumstances when some other method better reflects the amount of goodwill associated with the operation disposed of, and the Standard allows the use of another method of allocation, provided that the superiority of the chosen method can be demonstrated. For example, assume that a CGU is acquired and integrated with a pre-existing CGU that did not include any goodwill. Assume that, almost immediately after the business combination, the entity disposes of a pre-existing loss-making operation from within the integrated CGU. In such circum-stances, it might reasonably be argued that no part of the goodwill has been disposed of and, therefore, no part of its carrying amount should be derecognised by being included in the determination of the gain or loss on disposal.

8.1.2.3   Reorganisation of reporting structure

An entity may reorganise its reporting structure in a way that changes the composition of one or more CGUs to which goodwill has been allocated. In these circumstances, the goodwill should be reallocated to the units affected. Unless the entity can demonstrate that some other method better reflects the goodwill associated with the reorganised units, the reallocation should be performed using a relative value approach similar to that discussed in **8.1.2.2** above. [IAS 36:87]

The following example is set out in the Standard.

Example 8.1.2.3

Reorganisation of reporting structure
[IAS 36:87]

Goodwill had previously been allocated to CGU A. The goodwill allocated to A cannot be identified or associated with an asset group at a level lower than A, except arbitrarily. A is to be divided and integrated into three other CGUs, B, C and D.

Because the goodwill allocated to A cannot be non-arbitrarily identified or associated with an asset group at a level lower than A, it is reallocated to units B, C and D on the basis of the relative values of the three portions of A before those portions are integrated with B, C and D.

713

8.1.2.4   Goodwill relating to non-wholly-owned subsidiaries

IFRS 3 requires goodwill to be measured as of the acquisition date as the excess of (a) over (b) below:
[IAS 36:C1]

(a)   the aggregate of:

    (i)   the consideration transferred measured in accordance with IFRS 3, which generally requires acquisition-date fair value;

    (ii)   the amount of any non-controlling interest in the acquiree measured in accordance with IFRS 3; and

    (iii)   in a business combination achieved in stages, the acquisition-date fair value of the acquirer's previously held equity interest in the acquiree.

(b)   the net of the acquisition-date amounts of the identifiable assets acquired and liabilities assumed measured in accordance with IFRS 3.

Goodwill acquired in a business combination is allocated to each of the acquirer's cash-generating units, or groups of cash-generating units, expected to benefit from the synergies of the combination, irrespective of whether other assets or liabilities of the acquiree are assigned to those units, or groups of units. It is possible that some of the synergies resulting from a business combination will be allocated to a cash-generating unit in which the non-controlling interest does not have an interest. [IAS 36:C2]

Example 8.1.2.4A

Allocation of goodwill relating to non-wholly owned subsidiary

Entity A has an existing wholly-owned subsidiary, Entity B. Subsequently, Entity A acquires 80 per cent of Entity C in a business combination. Synergies arising from that business combination are expected to benefit Entity B.

Accordingly, some of the goodwill acquired in the business combination may be allocated to CGUs within Entity B.

When an entity chooses to measure components of non-controlling interests that are present ownership interests at their proportionate interest in the net identifiable assets of a subsidiary at the acquisition date, rather than at fair value, goodwill attributable to non-controlling interests is included in the recoverable amount of the related cash-generating unit but is not recognised in the parent's consolidated financial statements. To deal with this mismatch, for the purpose of impairment testing, the carrying amount of goodwill allocated to the unit is grossed up to include the goodwill attributable to the non-controlling interest. This adjusted carrying amount is then compared with the recoverable amount of the unit to determine whether the cash-generating unit is impaired. [IAS 36:C4]

Example 8.1.2.4B

Gross-up of goodwill for impairment testing when components of non-controlling interests that are present ownership interests arising in a business combination are measured at their proportionate interest in the net identifiable assets of the subsidiary

Entity A acquires 80 per cent of Entity B in a business combination. On acquisition, Entity A chooses to measure the components of non-controlling interests (NCI) that are present ownership interests in Entity B at their proportionate interest in the net identifiable assets of Entity B. This results in goodwill of CU20,000, which is allocated in its entirety to Entity B for the purposes of impairment testing under IAS 36.

IAS 36:C4 requires the carrying amount of goodwill to be grossed up to include the goodwill attributable to the NCI. The adjusted carrying amount should then be compared with the recoverable amount of Entity B to determine whether there is impairment.

IAS 36 does not prescribe a method for grossing up goodwill to include the amount attributable to NCI when the components of NCI that are present ownership interests arising in a business combination are measured at the proportionate interest in the net identifiable assets of the subsidiary.

Example 7A in the illustrative examples accompanying IAS 36 demonstrates a mathematical gross-up based on ownership interests. Therefore, in the above example, it would be appropriate to gross up goodwill to CU25,000 (being CU20,000 x 100/80).

However, in the absence of guidance to the contrary, Entity A could gross up goodwill based on the fair value of NCI at the acquisition date (i.e. the amount of goodwill that would have been recognised if NCI had been measured at fair value at the acquisition date), if that information can be determined reliably.

IAS 36:C4 does not apply to situations in which the non-controlling interests arise from transactions or events other than a business combination (e.g. a decrease in ownership in a subsidiary without loss of control) even if the components of non-controlling interests that are present ownership interests are measured at the proportionate share of a subsidiary's net assets.

This is because the purpose of IAS 36:C4 is to ensure consistency (for the purpose of impairment testing) between the goodwill included in the recoverable amount of a CGU and the goodwill included in the carrying amount of that CGU. The cash flows used to determine the recoverable amount of a CGU reflect 100 per cent of its activities; as a result, the recoverable amount includes 100 per cent of the goodwill attributable to the CGU.

When components of non-controlling interests that are present ownership interests arise as a result of a business combination and are measured at the proportionate share of the acquiree's identifiable net assets, the goodwill recognised in the consolidated financial statements reflects only the parent's share of the goodwill. Therefore, there is a potential mismatch for the purpose of impairment testing, which is avoided by IAS 36:C4's requirement to gross up the goodwill included in the carrying amount of the CGU.

However, when a parent initially purchases 100 per cent of the subsidiary, the goodwill recognised in the consolidated financial statements represents 100 per cent of the goodwill of the subsidiary. This remains the case after a disposal of a non-controlling interest in the subsidiary, even when components of non-controlling interests that are present ownership interests recognised subsequent to the acquisition are measured at the proportionate share of the net assets. Therefore, grossing up goodwill for the purpose of impairment testing would not be appropriate.

This is illustrated in **example 8.1.2.4C**.

Example 8.1.2.4C

Application of IAS 36:C4 when components of non-controlling interests that are present ownership interests arise subsequent to a business combination

On 1 January 20X3, Parent P acquires 100 per cent of Subsidiary S for CU1,900. At that date, the fair value of Subsidiary S's net identifiable assets is CU1,500. Parent P recognises goodwill of CU400 in its consolidated financial statements as a result of the business combination.

On 1 July 20X3, Parent P disposes of 20 per cent of its interest in Subsidiary S for CU380. For simplicity, it is assumed that the fair value of Subsidiary S's net identifiable assets on that date is still CU1,500. Parent P recognises non-controlling interests of CU300 (20% × CU1,500) and the difference of CU80 between this amount and the proceeds received is recognised in equity. Because control is retained, there is no adjustment to the carrying amount of goodwill (i.e. goodwill remains at CU400).

At the end of 20X5, Parent P determines that the recoverable amount of Subsidiary S is CU1,000. The carrying amount of the net assets of Subsidiary S, excluding goodwill, is CU1,350.

Because all of the goodwill attributable to Subsidiary S is included in the recoverable amount of Subsidiary S and is also recognised in Parent P's consolidated financial statements, no adjustment is required to gross up goodwill for the purpose of impairment testing. In the circumstances described, an impairment loss of CU750 should be recognised, calculated as follows.

End of 20X5	Goodwill of Subsidiary S	Net identifiable assets	Total
	CU	CU	CU
Carrying amount	400	1,350	1,750
Recoverable amount			1,000
			750

In accordance with IAS 36:104, the impairment loss of CU750 is allocated to the assets in Subsidiary S by first reducing the carrying amount of goodwill (see **9.2** below). Therefore, CU400 of the CU750 impairment loss is allocated to the goodwill and the remaining impairment loss of CU350 is recognised by reducing the carrying amounts of Subsidiary S's identifiable assets.

If a subsidiary, or part of a subsidiary, with a non-controlling interest is itself a cash-generating unit, the impairment loss is allocated between the parent and the non-controlling interest on the same basis as that on which profit or loss is allocated. [IAS 36:C6]

When non-controlling interests (NCI) are measured at fair value, paragraph B45 of IFRS 3 indicates that the fair values of the parent's interest in an entity and the NCI on a per-share basis may differ (e.g. due to the inclusion of a control premium in fair value of the parent's interest or, conversely, the inclusion of a discount to reflect its lack of control in the fair value of the NCI). In such circumstances, the goodwill attributable to the parent's interest is not necessarily pro-portional to the goodwill attributable to the NCI.

Despite this fact, in line with the explicit requirement in IAS 36:C6, any impairment loss arising on the goodwill should be allocated to the parent and to the NCI on the same basis as that on which profit or loss is allocated (i.e. in proportion to their respective present ownership interests).

Example 8.1.2.4D provides an illustration of such circumstances.

Example 8.1.2.4D

Allocation of goodwill impairment loss when non-controlling interests are measured at fair value

Entity A acquires 80 per cent of Entity B for CU1,250. Entity B has identifiable net assets with a fair value of CU1,000 and the fair value of the non-controlling interests (NCI) is determined to be CU250.

	Ownership	Share of identifiable net assets	Fair value	Goodwill	Goodwill
	%	CU	CU	CU	%
Parent interest	80	800	1,250	450	90
NCI	20	200	250	50	10
		1,000	1,500	500	

If an impairment loss of CU100 subsequently arises on Entity B's goodwill, it is allocated 80 per cent to Entity A (CU80) and 20 per cent to the NCI (CU20).

Equally, if the impairment loss arising on Entity B's goodwill is CU300, CU60 (i.e. 20 per cent) is allocated to the NCI and CU240 (i.e. 80 per cent) is allocated to Entity A. This is so even though, in this example, the goodwill impairment allocated to the NCI exceeds the goodwill originally included in the NCI.

If a subsidiary, or part of a subsidiary, with a non-controlling interest is part of a larger cash-generating unit, goodwill impairment losses are allocated to the parts of the cash-generating unit that have a non-controlling interest and the parts that do not. The impairment losses should be allocated to the parts of the cash-generating unit on the basis of: [IAS 36:C7]

- to the extent that the impairment relates to goodwill in the cash-generating unit, the relative carrying values of the goodwill of the parts before the impairment; and

- to the extent that the impairment relates to identifiable assets in the cash-generating unit, the relative carrying values of the net identifiable assets of the parts before the impairment. Any such impairment is allocated to the assets of the parts of each unit pro rata on the basis of the carrying amount of each asset in the part.

In those parts that have a non-controlling interest, the impairment loss is allocated between the parent and the non-controlling interest on the same basis as that on which profit or loss is allocated.

If an impairment loss attributable to a non-controlling interest relates to goodwill that is not recognised in the parent's consolidated financial statements, that impairment is not recognised as a goodwill impairment loss. In such cases, only the impairment loss relating to the goodwill that is allocated to the parent is recognised as a goodwill impairment loss. [IAS 36:C8]

Example 8.1.2.4E

Allocation of impairment loss

Entity A has an existing wholly-owned subsidiary, Entity B. Subsequently, Entity A acquires 80 per cent of Entity C in a business combination. Synergies arising from that business combination are expected to benefit Entity B. Accordingly, under IAS 36:C2, some of the goodwill acquired in the business combination is allocated to cash-generating units within Entity B.

Following the allocation of goodwill, Entity A compares the adjusted carrying amounts of the cash-generating units with their recoverable amounts. Entity A has chosen to measure the components of non-controlling interests that are present ownership interests at their proportionate interest in the net identifiable assets of Entity C at the acquisition date. Therefore, in accordance with IAS 36:C4, the carrying amount of goodwill allocated to Entity C is grossed up to include the goodwill attributable to the non-controlling interests (see **example 8.1.2.4B**). On the basis of this comparison, Entity C is determined to be impaired.

	Adjusted carrying amount	Recoverable amount	Impairment
	CU	CU	CU
Entity C	29,500	25,000	(4,500)
Entity B	32,500	40,000	–

The impairment of CU4,500 for Entity C relates to goodwill, and is allocated between the parent and the non-controlling interests on the same basis as that on which profit or loss is allocated, i.e. 80 per cent to the parent (CU3,600) and 20 per cent to the non-controlling interests (CU900). But, because the impairment loss attributable to the non-controlling interests relates to goodwill that is not recognised in the parent's consolidated financial statements, that impairment is not recognised as a goodwill impairment loss.

Accordingly, CU3,600 is recognised as a goodwill impairment loss in the consolidated financial statements, being the impairment loss relating to the goodwill that is allocated to the parent (Entity A).

Examples 8.1.2.4F to **H** reproduce illustrative examples 7A to 7C accompanying IAS 36, which illustrate the impairment testing of a non-wholly-owned CGU.

Example 8.1.2.4F

Non-controlling interests measured initially as a proportionate share of the net identifiable assets
[IAS 36 Illustrative examples: Example 7A]

In this example, tax effects are ignored.

Background

Parent acquires an 80 per cent ownership interest in Subsidiary for CU2,100 on 1 January 20X3. At that date, Subsidiary's net identifiable assets have a fair value of CU1,500. Parent chooses to measure the non-controlling interests as the proportionate interest of Subsidiary's net identifiable assets of CU300 (20% of CU1,500). Goodwill of CU900 is the difference between the aggregate of the consideration transferred and the amount of the non-controlling interests (CU2,100 + CU300) and the net identifiable assets (CU1,500).

The assets of Subsidiary together are the smallest group of assets that generate cash inflows that are largely independent of the cash inflows from other assets or groups of assets. Therefore Subsidiary is a cash-generating unit. Because other cash-generating units of Parent are expected to benefit from the synergies of the combination, the goodwill of CU500 related to those synergies has been allocated to other cash-generating units within Parent. Because the cash-generating unit comprising Subsidiary includes goodwill within its carrying amount, it must be tested for impairment annually, or more frequently if there is an indication that it may be impaired (see paragraph 90 of IAS 36).

At the end of 20X3, Parent determines that the recoverable amount of cash-generating unit Subsidiary is CU1,000. The carrying amount of the net assets of Subsidiary, excluding goodwill, is CU1,350.

Testing Subsidiary (cash-generating unit) for impairment

Goodwill attributable to non-controlling interests is included in Subsidiary's recoverable amount of CU1,000 but has not been recognised in Parent's consolidated financial statements. Therefore, in accordance with paragraph C4 of Appendix C of IAS 36, the carrying amount of Subsidiary is grossed up to include goodwill attributable to the non-controlling interest, before being compared with the recoverable amount of CU1,000. Goodwill attributable to Parent's 80 per cent interest in Subsidiary at the acquisition date is CU400 after allocating CU500 to other cash-generating units within Parent. Therefore, goodwill attributable to the 20 per cent non-controlling interest in Subsidiary at the acquisition date is CU100.

Schedule 1. Testing Subsidiary for impairment at the end of 20X3

End of 20X3	Goodwill of Subsidiary CU	Net identifiable assets CU	Total CU
Carrying amount	400	1,350	1,750
Unrecognised non-controlling interests	100	–	100
Adjusted carrying amount	500	1,350	1,850
Recoverable amount			1,000
Impairment loss			850

Allocating the impairment loss

In accordance with paragraph 104 of IAS 36, the impairment loss of CU850 is allocated to the assets in the unit by first reducing the carrying amount of goodwill.

Therefore, CU500 of the CU850 impairment loss for the unit is allocated to the goodwill. In accordance with paragraph C6 of Appendix C of IAS 36, if the partially-owned subsidiary is itself a cash-generating unit, the goodwill impairment loss is allocated to the controlling and non-controlling interests on the same basis as that on which profit or loss is allocated. In this example, profit or loss is allocated on the basis of relative ownership interests. Because the goodwill is recognised only to the extent of Parent's 80 per cent ownership interest in Subsidiary, Parent recognises only 80 per cent of that goodwill impairment loss (i.e. CU400).

The remaining impairment loss of CU350 is recognised by reducing the carrying amounts of Subsidiary's identifiable assets (see Schedule 2).

Schedule 2. Allocation of the impairment loss for Subsidiary at the end of 20X3

End of 20X3	Goodwill CU	Net identifiable assets CU	Total CU
Carrying amount	400	1,350	1,750
Impairment loss	(400)	(350)	(750)
Carrying amount after impairment loss	–	1,000	1,000

Example 8.1.2.4G

Non-controlling interests measured initially at fair value and the related subsidiary is a stand-alone cash-generating unit
[IAS 36 Illustrative examples: Example 7B]

In this example, tax effects are ignored.

Background

Parent acquires an 80 per cent ownership interest in Subsidiary for CU2,100 on 1 January 20X3. At that date, Subsidiary's net identifiable assets have a fair value of CU1,500. Parent chooses to measure the non-controlling interests at fair value, which is CU350. Goodwill of CU950 is the difference between the aggregate of the consideration transferred and the amount of the non-controlling interests (CU2,100 + CU350) and the net identifiable assets (CU1,500).

The assets of Subsidiary together are the smallest group of assets that generate cash inflows that are largely independent of the cash inflows from other assets or groups of assets. Therefore, Subsidiary is a cash-generating unit. Because other cash-generating units of Parent are expected to benefit from the synergies of the combination, the goodwill of CU500 related to those synergies has been allocated to other cash-generating units within Parent. Because Subsidiary includes goodwill within its carrying amount, it must be tested for impairment annually, or more frequently if there is an indication that it might be impaired (see paragraph 90 of IAS 36).

Testing Subsidiary for impairment

At the end of 20X3, Parent determines that the recoverable amount of cash-generating unit Subsidiary is CU1,650. The carrying amount of the net assets of Subsidiary, excluding goodwill, is CU1,350.

Schedule 1. Testing Subsidiary for impairment at the end of 20X3

End of 20X3	Goodwill	Net identifiable assets	Total
	CU	CU	CU
Carrying amount	450	1,350	1,800
Recoverable amount			1,650
Impairment loss			150

Allocating the impairment loss

In accordance with paragraph 104 of IAS 36, the impairment loss of CU150 is allocated to the assets in the unit by first reducing the carrying amount of goodwill. Therefore, the full amount of impairment loss of CU150 for the unit is allocated to the goodwill. In accordance with paragraph C6 of Appendix C of IAS 36, if the partially-owned subsidiary is itself a cash-generating unit, the goodwill impairment loss is allocated to the controlling and non-controlling interests on the same basis as that on which profit or loss is allocated.

Example 8.1.2.4H

Non-controlling interests measured initially at fair value and the related subsidiary is part of a larger cash-generating unit
[IAS 36 Illustrative examples:Example 7C]

In this example, tax effects are ignored.

Background

Suppose that, for the business combination described in paragraph IE68A of Example 7B [**example 8.1.2.4G**], the assets of Subsidiary will generate cash inflows together with other assets or groups of assets of Parent. Therefore, rather than Subsidiary being the cash-generating unit for the purposes of impairment testing, Subsidiary becomes part of a larger cash-generating unit, Z. Other cash-generating units of Parent are also expected to benefit from the synergies of the combination. Therefore, goodwill related to those synergies, in the amount of CU500, has been allocated to those other cash-generating units. Z's goodwill related to previous business combinations is CU800.

Because Z includes goodwill within its carrying amount, both from Subsidiary and from previous business combinations, it must be tested for impairment annually, or more frequently if there is an indication that it might be impaired (see paragraph 90 of IAS 36).

Testing Subsidiary for impairment

At the end of 20X3, Parent determines that the recoverable amount of cash-generating unit Z is CU3,300. The carrying amount of the net assets of Z, excluding goodwill, is CU2,250.

Schedule 3. Testing Z for impairment at the end of 20X3

End of 20X3	Goodwill	Net identifiable assets	Total
	CU	CU	CU
Carrying amount	1,250	2,250	3,500
Recoverable amount			3,300
Impairment loss			200

Allocating the impairment loss

In accordance with paragraph 104 of IAS 36, the impairment loss of CU200 is allocated to the assets in the unit by first reducing the carrying amount of goodwill. Therefore, the full amount of impairment loss of CU200 for cash-generating unit Z is allocated to the goodwill. In accordance with

> paragraph C7 of Appendix C of IAS 36, if the partially-owned subsidiary forms part of a larger cash-generating unit, the goodwill impairment loss would be allocated first to the parts of the cash-generating unit, Z, and then to the controlling and non-controlling interests of the partially owned Subsidiary.
>
> Parent allocates the impairment loss to the parts of the cash-generating unit on the basis of the relative carrying values of the goodwill of the parts before the impairment. In this example Subsidiary is allocated 36 per cent of the impairment (450/1,250). The impairment loss is then allocated to the controlling and non-controlling interests on the same basis as that on which profit or loss is allocated.

8.1.3   Allocation of corporate assets to CGUs

Corporate assets are assets other than goodwill that contribute to the future cash flows of both the CGU under review and other CGUs. [IAS 36:6] Such assets may include group or divisional assets such as a headquarters building or a research centre. Key characteristics of corporate assets are that:
[IAS 36:100]

- they do not generate cash inflows independently from other assets or groups of assets; and

- their carrying amount cannot be fully attributed to the cash-generating unit under review.

> Other examples of corporate assets may include brands and operating licences.

Because corporate assets do not generate separate cash flows, they are tested for impairment in the context of the CGU or group of CGUs to which the asset belongs. If a portion of the carrying amount of a corporate asset:
[IAS 36:102]

- can be allocated on a reasonable and consistent basis to a CGU, the entity compares the carrying amount of the unit (including the allocated portion of the carrying amount of the corporate asset) with its recoverable amount. Any impairment loss is recognised in accordance with **9.2** below;

- cannot be allocated on a reasonable and consistent basis to that unit, the entity:

- compares the carrying amount of the unit, excluding the corporate asset, with its recoverable amount, and recognises any impairment loss in accordance with **9.2** below;

- identifies the smallest group of CGUs that includes the CGU under review and to which a portion of the carrying amount of the corporate asset can be allocated on a reasonable and consistent basis; and

- compares the carrying amount of that group of CGUs, including the allocated portion of the carrying amount of the corporate asset, with the recoverable amount of the group of units. Any impairment loss is recognised in accordance with **9.2** below.

Illustrative example 8 accompanying IAS 36 illustrates the application of the requirements for corporate assets.

8.2   Stage 2: Estimation of expected future cash flows

8.2.1   *General approach to present value*

Appendix A to IAS 36 (which is an integral part of the Standard) provides some guidance on the use of present value techniques in measuring value in use. In particular, it considers some of the practical difficulties in estimating future cash flows and arriving at an appropriate discount rate for those cash flows. This section provides a brief summary of the guidance in Appendix A to IAS 36 as regards the general approach to present value. The selection of an appropriate discount rate is dealt with in **8.3**.

IAS 36 identifies the following elements which, taken together, capture the economic differences between assets:
[IAS 36:A1]

- an estimate of the future cash flows the entity expects to derive from the asset;

- the time value of money, represented by the current market risk-free rate of interest;

- expectations about possible variations in the amount or timing of the future cash flows;

- the price for bearing uncertainty inherent in the asset; and

- other factors, such as illiquidity, that market participants would reflect in pricing the future cash flows that the entity expects to derive from the asset.

When estimating the value in use of an asset, the last three elements described in the previous paragraph can be reflected either:

- as adjustments to the discount rate (called the 'traditional' approach); or

- as adjustments to the future cash flows (called the 'expected cash flow' approach).

The traditional approach involves the use of a single set of estimated cash flows, and a single discount rate. It emphasises the selection of an appropriate discount rate, assuming that a single discount rate can incorporate all the expectations about the future cash flows and appropriate risk premium. However, the traditional approach may not be easy to apply, for example, in the case of non-financial assets when no market for the item or a comparable item exists.

IAS 36 supports the expected cash flow approach as being, in some situations, a more effective measurement tool. This approach uses all expectations about possible cash flows instead of the single most likely cash flow. For example, a cash flow might be CU100, CU200 or CU300, with probabilities of 10 per cent, 60 per cent and 30 per cent, respectively. The expected cash flow is CU220, i.e. (CU100 x 10%) + (CU200 x 60%) + (CU300 x 30%). The expected cash flow approach therefore differs from the traditional approach by focusing on a direct analysis of the cash flows in question and on more explicit statements of the assumptions used in the measurement. It is highly dependent on assigning probabilities to estimates of future cash flows.

Appendix A to IAS 36 provides a more detailed discussion and comparison of the two approaches. Whichever approach the entity adopts to reflect expectations about possible variations in the amount or timing of future cash flows, the objective is to arrive at an estimate that best reflects the expected present value of future cash flows, i.e. the weighted average of all possible outcomes. [IAS 36:A2]

Whichever approach is selected, key principles to be borne in mind are: [IAS 36:A3]

- consistent assumptions should be used for the estimation of cash flows and the selection of an appropriate discount rate in order to avoid any double-counting or omissions. For example, a discount rate of 12 per cent might be applied to the contractual cash flows of a loan receivable. That rate reflects expectations about future defaults from loans with particular characteristics. That same 12 per cent should not be used to discount expected cash flows because those cash flows already reflect assumptions about future defaults;

- estimated cash flows and discount rates should be free from both bias and factors unrelated to the asset in question. For example, deliberately understating estimated net cash flows to enhance the apparent future profitability of an asset introduces a bias into the measurement; and

- estimated cash flows or discount rates should reflect a range of possible outcomes, rather than a single, most likely, minimum or maximum possible amount.

8.2.2   Use of forecasts/budgets/cash flow projections

When estimating expected future cash flows, the following rules apply.

- Projections of cash flows should be based on reasonable and support-able assumptions that represent management's best estimate of the range of economic conditions that will exist over the remaining useful life of the asset. Greater weight should be given to external evidence. [IAS 36:33(a)] The reasonableness of the assumptions on which current cash flow projections are based should be assessed by examining the causes of differences between past cash flow projec-tions and actual cash flows. The assumptions used should be consist-ent with past actual outcomes, provided the effects of subsequent events or circumstances that did not exist when those actual cash flows were generated make this appropriate. [IAS 36:34]

- Cash flow projections should be based on the most recent financial budgets/forecasts that have been approved by management. Projec-tions based on these budgets/forecasts should cover a maximum period of five years, unless a longer period can be justified. [IAS 36:33(b)] Detailed budgets/forecasts for a period of greater than five years are generally not available and, if they are available, are less likely to be accurate. If management has produced budgets/forecasts for a period greater than five years, however, and can demonstrate, based on past experience, that its forecasting methods are reliable for such extended periods, it can use forecasts for periods exceeding five years if it is confident that these projections are reliable. [IAS 36:35] This is expected to be very much the exception, not the rule.

- Projections of cash flows beyond the period covered by the most recent budgets/forecasts should be estimated by extrapolating the projections based on the budgets/forecasts using a steady or declining growth rate for subsequent years, unless an increasing rate can be justified based on objective information about patterns over a product or industry lifecycle. This growth rate should not be overly optimistic and should not exceed the long-term average growth rate for the products, industries, or country or countries in which the entity operates, or for the market in which the asset is used, unless a higher rate can be justified. [IAS 36:33(c)] In some cases, it may be appropriate for the growth rate to be zero or negative. [IAS 36:36]

- Projections of cash flows should be consistent with the discount rate assumptions as regards price increases due to general inflation. Thus, if the discount rate includes the effect of price increases due to general inflation, future cash flows are estimated in nominal terms. If the discount rate excludes the effect of price increases due to general inflation, cash flows are estimated in real terms (but including future specific price increases or decreases). [IAS 36:40]

In principle, the guidance in the final bullet above also applies when a currency is hyperinflationary. However, in the case of hyperinflation, frequently there will be difficulties in determining the likely future rate of inflation and the relevant nominal interest rate. Calculating the value in use generally will be easier in real terms.

8.2.2.1   Impact of inflation

As noted above, IAS 36:40 sets out two ways to deal with inflation when estimating future cash flows.

The first method is to forecast cash flows in real terms – i.e. forecast cash flows that are increased or decreased in real terms, to reflect the likely relation between future changes in specific prices and general inflation. These cash flows are then discounted at a real discount rate (i.e. a rate that excludes general inflation).

Alternatively, the forecast cash flows can reflect the estimated increase or decrease in specific prices in nominal terms, but those 'nominal cash flows' then need to be discounted at a nominal rate of interest (i.e. a rate that includes general inflation).

Care will be needed when revenues and costs are expected to change at different rates in the future. This would happen when there are specific factors applicable to the different cash flow streams that will make them vary, other than general price level changes (the general price level change will be the same for all cash flow streams). For example, the regulator may restrict the revenues of a regulated entity, but its costs will be unrestricted. The entity's costs and revenues, therefore, will be subject to different assumptions as to the rates at which they will change. In such circumstances:

- if the first method described above is used, it will be necessary to reflect the different estimated rates of variation of revenues and costs in real terms; and

- if the second method is used, it will be necessary to reflect the different estimated changes to revenues and costs in nominal terms.

Example 8.2.2.1 illustrates the application of these two methods.

Example 8.2.2.1

Taking inflation into account when forecasting cash flows – illustration of alternative methods

Entity A is estimating the value in use of a machine with four years of remaining expected useful life.

The following general information is relevant:

- forecast inflation for the next four years – 3 per cent per year;

- forecast interest (nominal rate) for the next four years – 9 per cent per year; and

- forecast interest (real rate) for the next four years – 5.8252* per cent per year.

The specific revenues and costs of Entity A are expected to increase at the following rates for the next four years.

Year	1	2	3	4
Revenues	3%	2%	2%	1%
Raw material	4%	4%	5%	6%
Labour	3%	3%	3%	3%

*   Forecast real rate is calculated as follows.

$$\frac{1 + \text{nominal interest rate}}{1 + \text{inflation rate}} - 1 = \frac{1 + 0.09}{1 + 0.03} - 1 = 0.058252 \ or \ 5.8252\%$$

Method 1 – real cash flows discounted using real rate of interest

The following are the cash flows expected to be generated by the machine in real terms.

Cash flows forecast in real terms

	Base (Year 0)	Year 1	Year 2	Year 3	Year 4	Total (Years 1 to 4)
Revenues	100,000	100,000	99,029	98,068	96,163	
Raw material	-35,000	-35,340	-35,683	-36,376	-37,435	
Labour	-25,000	-25,000	-25,000	-25,000	-25,000	
Net cash flows	40,000	39,660	38,346	36,692	33,728	148,426

When these 'real' cash flows are discounted at the real interest rate, the outcome is as follows.

Cash flows forecast in real terms discounted at the real interest rate (5.8252% per year)

	Year 1	Year 2	Year 3	Year 4	Total (Years 1 to 4)
Revenues	94,495	88,427	82,748	76,675	
Raw material	-33,394	-31,863	-30,693	-29,849	
Labour	-23,624	-22,323	-21,095	-19,933	Value in use
Net cash flows	37,477	34,241	30,960	26,893	129,571

Method 2 – nominal cash flows discounted using nominal rate of interest

The following are the cash flows expected to be generated by the machine in nominal terms.

Cash flows forecast in nominal terms

	Base (Year 0)	Year 1	Year 2	Year 3	Year 4	Total (Years 1 to 4)
Revenues	100,000	103,000	105,060	107,161	108,233	
Raw material	-35,000	-36,400	-37,856	-39,749	-42,134	
Labour	-25,000	-25,750	-26,522	-27,318	-28,138	
Net cash flows	40,000	40,850	40,682	40,094	37,961	159,587

When these nominal cash flows are discounted at the nominal interest rate, the outcome is as follows.

Cash flows forecast in nominal terms discounted at the nominal interest rate (9% per year)

	Year 1	Year 2	Year 3	Year 4	Total (Years 1 to 4)
Revenues	94,495	88,427	82,748	76,675	
Raw material	-33,394	-31,863	-30,693	-29,849	
Labour	-23,624	-22,323	-21,095	-19,933	Value in use
Net cash flows	37,477	34,241	30,960	26,893	129,571

8.2.3 Cash flows to be included

Estimates of future cash flows should include:

- projections of cash inflows from the continuing use of the asset; [IAS 36:39(a)]

- projections of cash outflows that are necessarily incurred to generate the cash inflows from continuing use of the asset. This includes cash outflows to prepare the asset for use (if such preparation has not yet been completed), and future overheads that can be directly attributed, or allocated on a reasonable and consistent basis, to the asset (see **example 8.2.3** below); [IAS 36:39(b)]

- net cash flows, if any, to be received (or paid) for the disposal of the asset at the end of its useful life. [IAS 36:39(c)] This is the amount that an entity expects to obtain from the disposal of the asset in an arm's length transaction between knowledgeable, willing parties, after deduction of the estimated costs of disposal. [IAS 36:52] In estimating these net cash flows, the same approach is taken as for estimates of fair value less costs of disposal, except that:

  - prices used are those prevailing at the date of the estimate for similar assets that have reached the end of their useful life and that have operated under similar conditions; [IAS 36:53(a)] and

  - the prices are adjusted for the effect of both future price increases due to general inflation and specific future price increases/decreases. However, if estimates of future cash flows from the asset's continuing use and the discount rate exclude the effect of general inflation, this effect is also excluded from the estimate of net cash flows on disposal; [IAS 36:53(b)]

- projections of cash outflows for the day-to-day servicing of the asset as well as future overheads that can be attributed directly, or allocated on a reasonable and consistent basis, to the use of the asset; [IAS 36:41] and

- in the same way that corporate assets can be allocated to a CGU's carrying value, the CGU's cash flows should also include an appropriate apportionment of corporate overheads when calculating value in use. However, care should be taken around internal charges for using the asset as explained in **8.2.4** below.

Example 8.2.3

Testing an asset under construction for impairment – costs of construction not yet incurred

Company D designs, develops and manufactures components for high speed optical networks. The majority of Company D's customers are building communication infrastructures. In December 20X1, Company D purchased a

---

plot of land in an industrial complex with the intent to build a state-of-the-art production facility for its integrated circuit and module products.

Construction of the new facility began in March 20X2 and is expected to be completed by the end of August 20X2. In June 20X2, a number of Company D's customers announced plans to cut the level of capital expenditures related to their infrastructure development, and Company D received several order cancellations. At 30 June 20X2, due to the significant change in business climate, Company D identified indications of impairment of the new production facility under IAS 36.

Company D should include the remaining costs associated with completing the production facility in its estimates of future cash flows when assessing the asset group for impairment. IAS 36:42 clearly states that when the carrying amount of an asset does not yet include all the cash outflows to be incurred before it is ready for use, the estimate of future cash outflows includes an estimate of any further cash outflow that is expected to be incurred before the asset is ready for use.

8.2.4   Cash flows to be excluded

Estimates of future cash flows should exclude:

- cash inflows from assets that generate cash inflows that are largely independent of the cash inflows from the asset under review (e.g. financial assets such as receivables); [IAS 36:43(a)]

- cash outflows that relate to obligations that have already been recognised as liabilities (e.g. payables, pensions or provisions), except in the limited circumstances described at **8.1.1** above; [IAS 36:43(b)]

- cash outflows or related cost savings (e.g. reductions in staff costs) or benefits that are expected to arise from a future restructuring to which an entity is not yet committed. [IAS 36:45(a)] The guidance in IAS 37 *Provisions, Contingent Liabilities and Contingent Assets* should be used to determine when an entity is committed to a restructuring (see **chapter A12**). Once an entity is committed to the restructuring, estimates of future cash inflows and cash outflows reflect the cost savings and other benefits from the restructuring based on the most recent financial budgets/forecasts that have been approved by management. [IAS 36:47(a)] An entity's internal forecasts may include the impact of a restructuring before the financial statements. Such forecasts may, therefore, need to be adjusted to comply with the principles of IAS 37;

- estimated future cash flows that are expected to arise from improving or enhancing an asset's performance. [IAS 36:44(b)]

Estimates of future cash flows do, however, include future cash flows necessary to maintain the level of economic benefits expected to arise from the asset in its current condition, for example overhauls or fault inspections. In practice it may not be easy to distinguish between maintenance and improvements, which are addressed in **example 8.2.4A** below.

When a CGU consists of assets with different estimated useful lives, the replacement of assets with shorter lives is considered to be part of the day-to-day servicing of the unit when estimating the future cash flows associated with the unit. Similarly, when a single asset consists of components with different estimated useful lives, the replacement of components with shorter lives is considered to be part of the day-to-day servicing of the asset when estimating the future cash flows generated by the asset; [IAS 36:49]

Example 8.2.4A

Expenditure on maintaining and improving assets

The assets of a CGU comprise a factory and plant and machinery. The factory is expected to last 50 years, but will need a new roof in 30 years, and the machinery needs to be replaced every 10 years. The entity expects to be able to reduce costs per unit of production by extending the factory to double production in a few years, but is not yet committed to such a restructuring.

The replacement expenditure for the 50 years, including the new roof and new machinery, should be included in the cash flows.

Neither the expenditure to increase the size of the factory nor the additional income and revenue expenditure consequent on that expansion should be included.

- cash inflows or outflows from financing activities. [IAS 36:50(a)] The assumptions underlying the discount rate must be consistent with the estimated future cash flows. Therefore, because the time value of money is considered by discounting the estimated future cash flows, these cash flows exclude cash inflows/outflows from financing activities; [IAS 36:51]

IAS 36:50(a) prohibits the inclusion of financing cash outflows or inflows in a value in use calculation and does not provide for any exceptions to this rule. Therefore, borrowing costs that will be capitalised as part of the cost of an asset under IAS 23 *Borrowing*

> *Costs* are excluded from estimates of future cash flows when testing an asset under development for impairment.

- income tax receipts or payments. [IAS 36:50(b)] As discussed in Stage 3 (see **8.3** below), a pre-tax discount rate is used and, therefore, future cash flows are also estimated on a pre-tax basis; [IAS 36:51] and

- when corporate assets have been allocated to a CGU's carrying amount, any internal charges incurred by the CGU for using such assets should not be included in the CGU's expected future cash flows. To do so would be to double-count the impact of the corporate assets and could result in an impairment loss being recognised incorrectly.

Example 8.2.4B

Payments for corporate assets

The present value of the net cash inflows of a CGU is CU220 before charges for the use of corporate assets, and the carrying amount of the assets of the CGU (excluding corporate assets) is CU140. The present value of the cash outflows for the use of the corporate assets is CU50, and the carrying amount of the portion of the corporate assets allocated to the CGU is CU45. The corporate assets can be allocated to the CGU on a reasonable and consistent basis.

In these circumstances, IAS 36:102 requires that the portion of the corporate assets allocated to the CGU should be included in its carrying amount. Therefore, the value in use of CU220 is compared to the CGU's carrying amount of CU185 (CU140 + CU45). The headroom is CU35 and there is no impairment loss.

The entity should *not* factor into the determination of recoverable amount both the portion of the corporate assets and the related outflows; if it does so, it will incorrectly recognise an impairment loss of CU15 (value in use of CU170 (CU220 – CU50) compared to carrying amount of CU185 (CU140 + CU45)).

Illustrative examples 5 and 6 accompanying IAS 36 illustrate, respectively, how future restructurings and improvements or enhancements to asset performance affect a value in use calculation.

8.2.5 *Foreign currency cash flows*

Future cash flows are estimated in the currency in which they will be generated and then discounted using a discount rate appropriate for that currency. The present value obtained is then translated using the spot exchange rate at the date of the value in use calculation. [IAS 36:54]

If goodwill or intangible assets are being assessed for impairment during the year rather than at the reporting date, the rate used will be the spot rate at the time that the testing is performed.

It is not appropriate to use a forward exchange rate to translate the value in use expressed in a foreign currency. A forward rate reflects the market's adjustment for the differential in interest rates, so using such a rate would double-count the time value of money (in the discount rate and also in the forward rate). [IAS 36:BCZ49]

8.2.6   Impact of leases on the calculation of value in use

Although IAS 36 does not explicitly discuss the treatment of leased assets, applying the principles that do exist would suggest the following approach:

- for a lessee, assets under an operating lease should not be included in a CGU's carrying amount, but the lease payments should be included in the CGU's cash outflows;

- for a lessor, an asset leased out under an operating lease should be included in its CGU's carrying amount, and the cash flows arising from the lease should also be included in the CGU's future cash inflows;

- for a lessee, assets under a finance lease should be included in a CGU's carrying amount, but the lease payments (and the associated finance lease creditor) should be excluded from the cash flows on the grounds that they represent financing activities (see **8.2.4** above) and do not affect the economic benefits that can be derived from the assets; and

- for a lessor, receivables under a finance lease are scoped into IAS 39 *Financial Instruments: Recognition and Measurement* for the purpose of impairment testing (see IAS 39:2(b)(i) and **section 3** above).

When a lessee has operating lease accruals in its statement of financial position, it is important to compare like items. It is usually appropriate to include these balances in the carrying amount of the CGU. But, if they are excluded, it is necessary to adjust the cash outflows accordingly. For example, if a lessee excludes an accrual of CU100 for an operating lease, the future cash outflows of CU100 that will settle this liability should also be excluded.

8.2.7   Impact of cash flow hedges on the calculation of value in use

When an entity has entered into derivative contracts to hedge cash flows related to the purchase and sale of goods within a specific CGU, and the contracts are designated and qualify as cash flow hedges, the entity may either include or exclude the cash flows on the hedging contracts in determining the value in use of the CGU, as long as the carrying amount of the CGU is established in a consistent manner.

IAS 36:68 defines a cash-generating unit as "the smallest group of assets that includes the asset and generates cash inflows that are largely independent of the cash inflows from other assets or groups of assets". IAS 36:69 explains that "[i]n identifying whether cash inflows from an asset (or group of assets) are largely independent of the cash inflows from other assets (or groups of assets), an entity considers various factors including how management monitors the entity's operations (such as by product lines, businesses, individual locations, districts or regional areas) or how management makes decisions about continuing or disposing of the entity's assets and operations" (see **8.1** above).

Accordingly, the decision to include or exclude the effect of hedging instruments and associated cash flows for the purpose of testing the carrying amount of a CGU for impairment should reflect how management defines its CGUs.

Example 8.2.7

Impact of cash flow hedges on the calculation of value in use

Entity A has entered into derivative contracts to hedge the cash flows related to the purchase and sale of commodities in a specific CGU. These contracts are designated and qualify as cash flow hedges.

Entity A may either include or exclude the cash flows on the hedging contracts in determining the value in use of the CGU, as long as the carrying amount of the CGU is established in a consistent manner.

If Entity A includes the cash flows on the hedging contracts in determining the value in use of the CGU, it must also include the fair value of the hedging contracts in the carrying amount of the CGU. Conversely, if the cash flows on the hedging contracts are excluded, it would be appropriate also to exclude the hedging contracts from the carrying amount of the CGU.

Entity A may define its CGU strictly based on the independence of cash flows (i.e. by including only those assets that may not be operated without other assets). When this approach is taken, Entity A may consider that the CGU could operate without the hedging instruments and that the hedging instruments generate their own independent cash flows. Therefore, it would exclude the hedging instruments and their cash flows in testing the CGU for impairment.

Alternatively, Entity A may define its CGU based on the manner in which it operates the assets. When this approach is taken, Entity A may consider that the CGU should include the hedging contracts if they are acquired specifically for the operations of a specific CGU and have no other business purposes.

Both approaches are acceptable.

8.2.8   Dividend discount models

When calculating the value in use of a CGU in accordance with IAS 36:33, estimated future cash flows expected to arise from dividends calculated using dividend discount models (DDMs) represent an appropriate cash flow projection in some circumstances.

IAS 36:30 to 57 and IAS 36:74 to 79 provide guidance on the principles to be applied in calculating the value in use of a CGU. Calculations using a DDM that values shares at the discounted value of future dividend payments may be appropriate when calculating the value in use of a single asset (e.g. when an entity applies IAS 36 in determining whether an investment is impaired in the separate financial statements of an entity).

Some DDMs focus on future cash flows that are expected to be available for distribution to shareholders rather than future cash flows from dividends. Such a DDM could be used to calculate the value in use of a CGU in consolidated financial statements, if it is consistent with the principles and requirements in IAS 36.

This was confirmed in an agenda decision of the IFRS Interpretations Committee published in the November 2010 *IFRIC Update*.

8.3   Stage 3: Determination of an appropriate discount rate

IAS 36:55 specifies that the discount rate (or rates) used should be:

- a pre-tax rate (or rates);

- that reflect(s) current market assessments of:

  - the time value of money; and

  - the risks specific to the asset for which the future cash flow estimates have not been adjusted (but not those for which the cash flows have been adjusted).

Effectively, the discount rate used is an estimate of the rate that the market would expect on an equally risky investment. This rate is ideally estimated from either:
[IAS 36:56]

- the rate implicit in current market transactions for similar assets; or

- the weighted average cost of capital (WACC) of a listed entity that has a single asset (or portfolio of assets) similar in terms of service potential and risks to the asset under review.

In practice, asset-specific rates, such as those suggested in the previous paragraph, will seldom be available due to the unique nature of different transactions and the fact that there are likely to be few listed entities that offer a readily usable comparison because listed entities generally have a wider product/service base, wider markets and potentially lower risk profile. When an asset-specific rate is unavailable, a discount rate must be estimated. Appendix A to IAS 36, which is an integral part of the Standard, provides additional guidance on estimating the discount rate in such circumstances. This guidance is summarised in the following sections.

8.3.1   Estimation of a market rate

The entity may consider one of the following rates as a 'starting point' for its estimation. The rates would then be adjusted as discussed below. The starting-point rates include:
[IAS 36:A17]

- the WACC of the entity determined using techniques such as the Capital Asset Pricing Model;

- the entity's incremental borrowing rate; and

- other market borrowing rates.

This starting-point rate is then adjusted:
[IAS 36:A18]

- to reflect the way that the market would assess the specific risks associated with the asset's estimated cash flows (such as country risk, currency risk and price risk); and

- to exclude risks that are not relevant to the asset's estimated cash flows or for which the estimated cash flows have been adjusted.

If the starting-point rate is post-tax, it must be adjusted to arrive at a pre-tax rate. [IAS 36:A20]

In practice, estimating a suitable pre-tax rate is far from straightforward. The pre-tax discount rate is the rate of return that will, after tax has been deducted, give the post-tax rate of return. However, the pre-tax discount rate is generally not the post-tax rate grossed up by a standard rate of tax – IAS 36:BCZ85 includes an example illustrating this point.

Conceptually, discounting post-tax cash flows at a post-tax discount rate should give the same result as discounting pre-tax cash flows at a pre-tax discount rate, provided that the pre-tax discount rate is the post-tax discount rate adjusted to reflect the specific amount and timing of the future tax cash flows (see IAS 36:BC94).

In the example set out in IAS 36:BCZ85, one of the reasons for the difference between the grossed-up post-tax discount rate and the 'real' pre-tax discount rate is that the tax deductions for the asset do not arise evenly over its life. In practice, in a cash-generating unit comprised of a group of assets acquired at different times, it is possible that the overall pattern of tax deduction for assets will be more even and that a simple grossed-up post-tax rate may give a reasonable approximation of the actual pre-tax rate of return.

Example 8.3.1 illustrates the calculation of a pre-tax discount rate.

Example 8.3.1

Calculating a pre-tax discount rate from a post-tax rate – asset is not deductible for tax purposes

At the end of 20X0, an asset has a remaining useful life of 5 years. The asset is not deductible for tax purposes. The tax rate is 20 per cent. The discount rate for the asset can be determined only on a post-tax basis and is estimated to be 10 per cent. Therefore, the pre-tax discount rate grossed-up at the standard rate of tax is 12.5 per cent [10 per cent/(100 per cent – 20 per cent)].

At the end of 20X0, cash flow projections determined on a pre-tax basis are as follows.

	20X1	20X2	20X3	20X4	20X5
(1) Pre-tax cash flows (CF)	500	500	500	500	500

Value in use calculated using post-tax cash flows and post-tax discount rate

	20X1	20X2	20X3	20X4	20X5
(2) Tax CF [(1) x 20 per cent]	100	100	100	100	100
(3) Post-tax CF [(1) – (2)]	400	400	400	400	400
(4) Post-tax CF discounted at 10% to the end of 20X0	364	331	300	273	248

Value in use [Σ(4)] = 1,516

Value in use calculated using pre-tax cash flows and the grossed-up pre-tax discount rate

	20X1	20X2	20X3	20X4	20X5
(5) Pre-tax CF discounted at 12.5% to the end of 20X0	444	395	351	312	278

Value in use [Σ(5)] = 1,780

Calculating the 'real' pre-tax discount rate by iteration

Using iterative computation (i.e. so that the value in use determined using pre-tax cash flows and a pre-tax discount rate equals the value in use determined using post-tax cash flows and a post-tax discount rate), the pre-tax discount rate would be 19.4 per cent.

	20X1	20X2	20X3	20X4	20X5
(6) Pre-tax CF discounted at 19.4% to the end of 20X0	419	351	294	246	206

Value in use [Σ(6)] = 1,516

The 'real' pre-tax discount rate differs from the post-tax discount rate grossed up by the standard rate of tax depending on the tax rate, the post-tax discount rate and the useful life of the asset.

Similar calculations to those outlined above were carried out, but with the asset assumed to have a 10, 15 and 20 years life (and be worth nil at the end of that life).

A post-tax discount rate of 10 per cent in these similar scenarios equated to the following 'real' pre-tax discount rates:

Assumed life	Pre-tax discount rate
10 years	15.5 per cent
15 years	14.2 per cent
20 years	13.5 per cent

The discount rate is independent of the capital structure of the entity and of the way in which the entity financed the purchase of the asset because the future cash flows expected to arise from an asset do not depend on the way in which the entity financed the purchase of the asset. [IAS 36:A19]

Generally, a single discount rate is used to estimate the value in use of an asset. Separate discount rates for different future periods should be used, however, when value in use is sensitive to a difference in risks for different periods or to the term structure of interest rates. [IAS 36:A21]

8.4   Stage 4: Discounting and aggregating expected cash flows to arrive at value in use

The formulae for calculating value in use are derived from the following formulae:

Single cash flow

Present value of a single cash flow occurring in n years =

$$\frac{\text{Cashflow}}{(1 + d)^n}$$

Series of equal cash flows

Present value of n annual cash flows =

$$\text{Cashflow} \times \frac{1 - (1 + d)^{-n}}{d}$$

Perpetuity

Present value of fixed annual cash flow, in perpetuity =

$$\frac{Cashflow}{d}$$

Where d = annual discount rate

In the first (single cash flow) formula, the cash flow is an actual cash flow. The discount rate will therefore be a nominal rate, matching the cash flow by including a compatible estimate of the effect of inflation.

In the second (series) and third (perpetuity) formulae, it is assumed that all cash flows are the same, with the first cash flow occurring at the end of Year 1. When these cash flows will increase due to growth and inflation, this effect can be achieved by using a cash flow for Year 1 and reducing the nominal discount rate by both growth and inflation rates. When the actual cash flow for the previous period is used, it will first be necessary to increase it by the first year's growth and inflation in order to find the cash flow at the end of Year 1. (This adjustment of the discount rate for growth is a substitute for building growth into the cash flows. It should not be confused with a real rate of return that would adjust for inflation only.)

At a discount rate of 10 per cent, perpetuity can be assumed to approximate to 35 years or more, since any amounts beyond that horizon will be immaterial.

Example 8.4A

Assumed steady growth in cash flows to perpetuity

The calculation is based on the perpetuity formula. Cash flow is for Year 1. Thus, when the previous year's actual cash flow is used, it is first necessary to increase it to reflect growth and inflation in Year 1.

Value in use =

$$\frac{CF_o}{d_a}(1 + g)(1 + i)$$

Where:

CF_0 = actual cash flow for previous period

i   = annual inflation rate

g   = annual growth rate in cash flows

d_a = nominal pre-tax discount rate adjusted to reflect inflation and growth in cash flows.

Example 8.4B

Cash flows forecast for five years and assumed steady growth thereafter

The calculation is the sum of individual present values for the first 5 years, plus a perpetuity from Year 6 onwards re-expressed from Year 5 back to present value at time 0.

Value in use = Present value of each cash flow for Years 1–5

+ Present value of cash flows from Year 6 onwards

$$= \frac{CF_1}{1 + d_n} + \frac{CF_2}{(1 + d_n)^2} + \frac{CF_3}{(1 + d_n)^3} + \frac{CF_4}{(1 + d_n)^4} + \frac{CF_5}{(1 + d_n)^5} + \frac{CF_5(1 + g)(1 + i)}{d_a \times (1 + d_n)^5}$$

Where:

CF_n = Cash flow in nth year

i   = annual inflation rate after Year 5

g   = annual growth rate in cash flows after Year 5

d_n = nominal pre-tax discount rate

d_a = nominal pre-tax discount rate adjusted to reflect growth and inflation in cash flows

Note:

The sixth term in the formula above,

$$\frac{CF_5(1 + g)(1 + i)}{d_a \times (1 + d_n)^5}$$

is a compound of two functions.

$$\frac{CF_5(1 + g)(1 + i)}{d_a}$$

is the present value of cash flows from Year 6 onwards expressed as a present value at the beginning of Year 6. Further adjustment to multiply by

$$\frac{1}{(1 + d_n)^5}$$

re-expresses this as a present value at the beginning of Year 1.

743

Example 8.4C

Cash flows are forecast for 2 years and assumed steady growth thereafter

Assume:

Cash flow for Year 1	CU20 million
Cash flow for Year 2	CU24 million
Assumed steady growth thereafter	2.5 per cent
Inflation	2.5 per cent
Nominal pre-tax discount rate	15 per cent
Adjusted pre-tax discount rate	10 per cent

Value in use =

$$\frac{CU20m}{1.15} + \frac{CU24m}{1.15^2} + \frac{CU24m \times 1.025 \times 1.025}{0.1 \times 1.15^2} = CU226m$$

---

9   Recognition and measurement of an impairment loss

The following sections discuss the recognition and measurement of an impairment loss for an individual asset (other than goodwill) and for a CGU, respectively.

9.1   Individual asset

If, and only if, the recoverable amount of an asset is less than its carrying amount, the carrying amount of the asset should be reduced to its recoverable amount. That reduction is an impairment loss. [IAS 36:59]

An impairment loss should be recognised in profit or loss immediately unless it relates to an asset carried at a revalued amount. If an asset has been revalued (e.g. an item of property, plant and equipment), the impairment loss is dealt with as a revaluation decrease in accordance with the relevant Standard (in this case IAS 16 *Property, Plant and Equipment* – see **chapter A7**). [IAS 36:60] Generally, an impairment loss will first result in a decrease in any revaluation surplus related to the asset. This decrease is recognised in other comprehensive income rather than in profit or loss. When no related revaluation surplus exists, or to the extent that the impairment loss is greater than the related revaluation surplus, the excess impairment loss is recognised in profit or loss. [IAS 36:61]

If the impairment loss is greater than the carrying amount of the asset, a liability should be recognised only if it is required by another Standard. [IAS 36:62] A liability will only be recognised in respect of present obligations arising as a result of past events. IAS 37 *Provisions, Contingent Liabilities and Contingent Assets* describes the appropriate recognition criteria (see **chapter A12**). When a provision is required to be recognised, it is measured in accordance with the general requirements of IAS 37.

IAS 16 requires that the estimated useful life, the depreciation method and residual value of an item of property, plant and equipment should be reviewed at the end of each reporting period. After an impairment loss is recognised, these three items are reviewed, and the new carrying amount is depreciated over the asset's remaining useful life. [IAS 36:63] Similar rules for intangible assets are set out in IAS 38 *Intangible Assets*.

Because an impairment loss affects the carrying amount of an asset, it affects the relationship between the asset's carrying amount and its tax base. Therefore, any deferred tax asset or liability is determined by comparing the revised carrying amount of the asset with its tax base (see **chapter A13**). [IAS 36:64]

Example 9.1

Recognition of an impairment loss creates a deferred tax asset
[IAS 36 Illustrative examples: Example 3B]

An entity has an identifiable asset with a carrying amount of CU1,000. Its recoverable amount is CU650. The tax rate is 30 per cent and the tax base of the asset is CU800. Impairment losses are not deductible for tax purposes. The effect of the impairment loss is as follows:

	Before impairment CU	Effect of impairment CU	After impairment CU
Carrying amount	1,000	(350)	650
Tax base	800	–	800
Taxable (deductible) temporary difference	200	(350)	(150)
Deferred tax liability (asset) at 30%	60	(105)	(45)

In accordance with IAS 12, the entity recognises the deferred tax asset to the extent that it is probable that taxable profit will be available against which the deductible temporary difference can be utilised.

When an entity incurs capital expenditure on an item of property, plant and equipment in respect of which an impairment loss has previously been recognised, the expenditure should be recognised in accordance with IAS 16 and included in the cost of the asset if the criteria in IAS 16:7 are met (see **3.1** and **3.5.5** in **chapter A7**). For intangible assets, similar considerations apply and the expenditure should be recognised in accordance with IAS 38 and included in the cost of the asset if the criteria in IAS 38:57 are met (see **example 4.7.4.1** in **chapter A9**).

9.2   Cash-generating unit

An impairment loss should be recognised for a CGU (or the smallest group of CGUs to which goodwill or a corporate asset has been allocated) if, and only if, its recoverable amount is less than its carrying amount. The impairment loss should be allocated to reduce the carrying amount of the assets of the unit or group of units in the following order:
[IAS 36:104]

- first, to goodwill allocated to the CGU (group of CGUs); and

- then, to the other assets of the unit or group on a pro rata basis based on the carrying amount of each asset in the unit or group of units.

Example 9.2A

Allocation of impairment loss within a cash-generating unit

Entity C has a soft drinks cash-generating unit which contains both goodwill and intangible assets in the form of brands with indefinite lives. Entity C tests the CGU for impairment and determines that an impairment loss has occurred. The directors attribute the impairment loss to the poor performance of a particular brand, B.

In the light of the directors' belief that the impairment is attributable to brand B, is it acceptable for Entity C to allocate the impairment loss to the carrying amount of that brand, rather than following the allocation specified in IAS 36:104?

No. Because it is not practicable to estimate the recoverable amount of each individual asset, the rules set out in IAS 36:104 (see above) result in an arbitrary allocation of any impairment loss between the assets of the unit (including brand B) other than goodwill. These reductions in carrying amounts should be dealt with in the same manner as impairment losses on individual assets as discussed at **9.1**.

Therefore, in the circumstances described, the impairment loss identified must first be allocated to goodwill. Following this, any excess is then available for allocation against the carrying amount of Entity C's other assets (including brand B).

When allocating an impairment loss to individual assets within a CGU, the carrying amount of an individual asset should not be reduced below the highest of:
[IAS 36:105]

- its fair value less costs of disposal (if measurable);

- its value in use (if determinable); and

- zero.

If this results in an amount being allocated to an asset which is less than its pro rata share of the impairment loss, the excess is allocated to the remaining assets within the CGU on a pro rata basis. [IAS 36:105]

If the recoverable amount of an individual asset cannot be determined:
[IAS 36:107]

- an impairment loss is recognised for the asset if its carrying amount is greater than the higher of its fair value less costs of disposal and the results of the allocation procedures described above; and

- no impairment loss is recognised for the asset if the related CGU is not impaired. This applies even if the asset's fair value less costs of disposal is less than its carrying amount.

After the allocation procedures have been applied, a liability is recognised for any remaining impairment loss for a CGU if, and only if, that is required by another Standard. [IAS 36:108] A liability will only be recognised in respect of present obligations arising as a result of past events. IAS 37 describes the appropriate recognition criteria (see **chapter A12**). When a provision is required to be recognised, it is measured in accordance with the general requirements of IAS 37.

Example 9.2B

Corporate assets

An entity produces different types of packaging based on paper. The three main types of packaging materials produced for its customers are the following:

- tubes;

- corrugated board; and

- solid board.

Each of the three main types of packaging associated with the business is identified as an operating segment under IFRS 8 *Operating Segments*, and as a

---

cash-generating unit under IAS 36. Asset M is partly used for the production of tubes (CGU T) and corrugated board (CGU C).

The following information relates to CGU T.

- Goodwill = zero

- Carrying amount of machinery used exclusively in manufacturing tubes (excluding Asset M) = CU4,500

- Carrying amount of Asset M = CU1,000

- Capacity of Asset M used for the tubes production = 60 per cent

- Recoverable amount of CGU T (including Asset M) = CU4,000

For CGU C, the excess of value in use over the carrying amount is CU2,000.

In accordance with IAS 36, Asset M should be allocated on a reasonable and consistent basis to CGUs T and C. The entity should compare the carrying amount of each CGU, including the portion of the carrying amount of the corporate asset allocated to the CGU, with its recoverable amount. In this case, 60 per cent of Asset M's capacity is used for the production of the tubes; accordingly, it seems reasonable to allocate 60 per cent of the carrying amount of Asset M to CGU T. Therefore, the carrying amount of CGU T is CU5,100 (CU1,000 × 60% + CU4,500) which exceeds its recoverable amount (CU4,000) by CU1,100.

An impairment loss should be recognised and should be allocated to all assets of CGU T (including Asset M) pro rata based on the carrying amount of each asset in the unit:

- to Asset M: CU1,100 x CU600 / CU5,100 = CU129
- to other assets: CU1,100 x CU4,500 / CU5,100 = CU971

However, if the entity were able to determine the fair value less costs of disposal of Asset M, and that number was CU1,000 or more, the impairment loss in respect of CGU T would be allocated on a pro rata basis to the other assets of CGU T in accordance with the requirements of IAS 36:104 and 105.

No impairment loss is recognised in respect of CGU C because the amount of Asset M to be allocated (CU400) is less than the excess of CGU C's value in use over CGU C's carrying amount (CU2,000).

Even though the difference between the carrying amount and the recoverable amount (CU2,000) of CGU C is higher than the impairment loss of CGU T, an impairment loss should be recognised in CGU T. The entity cannot test for impairment at a higher level to avoid the impairment loss.

9.3 Two-step approach for goodwill allocated to a group of CGUs

When goodwill is allocated to a group of CGUs for the purpose of impairment testing but cannot be allocated on a non-arbitrary basis to individual CGUs, the individual CGUs must be tested for impairment before the group of CGUs containing the associated goodwill. [IAS 36:81, 88 and 97 – 98] The allocation of goodwill to CGUs is discussed at **8.1.2** above. This two-step approach is illustrated in the following example.

Example 9.3

Two-step approach for goodwill allocated to a group of CGUs

In 20X0, Entity X acquires a business comprising three cash-generating units, A, B and C. The entire goodwill arising in the business combination is allocated to the three CGUs as a group (this allocation complies with the requirements of IAS 36:80). At the end of 20X5, the carrying amount of the net assets in each CGU and the associated goodwill and the value in use of each CGU is as set out below. Entity X has determined that the fair value less costs of disposal of each of the CGUs and of the business as a whole is less than the value in use of each CGU and of the business, respectively.

Cash-generating unit	A	B	C	Goodwill	Total
	CU	CU	CU	CU	CU
Carrying amount	80	120	140	50	390
Value in use	100	140	120		360

Step 1

Firstly, Entity X assesses each individual CGU for impairment. This first assessment results in an impairment loss of CU20 being recognised in respect of cash-generating unit C, thereby reducing its carrying amount from CU140 to CU120, and the total carrying amount of the group of CGUs (including goodwill) from CU390 to CU370.

Cash-generating unit	A	B	C	Goodwill	Total
	CU	CU	CU	CU	CU
Original carrying amount	80	120	140	50	390
Impairment recognised in Step 1	–	–	(20)	–	(20)
Carrying amount following Step 1	80	120	120	50	370
Value in use	100	140	120		360

Step 2

Secondly, the group of CGUs including the associated goodwill is tested for impairment. This second assessment gives rise to an impairment loss of CU10 in respect of the goodwill, reducing its carrying amount from CU50 to CU40. The total carrying amount of the group of CGUs including goodwill is reduced to CU360.

Cash-generating unit	A	B	C	Goodwill	Total
	CU	CU	CU	CU	CU
Carrying amount	80	120	140	50	390
Impairment recognised in Step 1	–	–	(20)	–	(20)
Impairment recognised in Step 2	–	–	–	(10)	(10)
Carrying amount following Step 2	80	120	120	40	360
Value in use	100	140	120		360

10   Reversals of impairment losses

10.1   General rules

An impairment loss on goodwill should not be reversed. This is discussed in **10.5** below. [IAS 36:124] Note that, for entities that have not yet adopted IFRS 9 *Financial Instruments*, paragraph 66 of IAS 39 *Financial Instruments: Recognition and Measurement* applies a similar requirement to an unquoted equity instrument that is not carried at fair value because its fair value cannot be reliably measured, and to a derivative asset that is linked to, and must be settled by delivery of, such an unquoted equity instrument (see **5.3** in **chapter C6**).

When an impairment loss was recognised for an asset other than goodwill (or for a CGU) in prior years, an entity is required to assess at the end of each reporting period whether there is any indication that the impairment loss may no longer exist or may have decreased. If such an indication exists, the entity should estimate the recoverable amount of that asset (or CGU). [IAS 36:110]

An impairment loss recognised in a prior period for an asset other than goodwill (or for a CGU) may be reversed if, and only if, there has been a change in the estimates used to determine the recoverable amount of the asset (or CGU) since the last impairment loss was recognised. When this is the case, the carrying amount of the asset (or CGU) is increased to its recoverable amount in accordance with the rules set out in **10.3** below (or in **10.4** below for a CGU). [IAS 36:114]

Example 10.1A

Determining whether the reversal of an impairment loss is appropriate

An acquired business produces bottled mineral water. Just before the year end, a consumer group tests the water and publicises the fact that it contains high levels of a harmful chemical. Sales of the mineral water plummet.

Situation 1

Assume that there is great uncertainty about the validity of the consumer group's claim, but it is assumed to be valid and that sales of the product will recover only after the problem has been sorted out, and the product has been re-tested and re-marketed. The future cash flows indicate that the recoverable amount of the CGU (which consists mainly of an intangible asset, being the brand of mineral water) is less than its carrying amount, so the CGU/intangible asset is written down by the entity.

However, in the next period, further tests demonstrate that the consumer group had been wrong in its claims and it retracts them publicly. Sales of the mineral water recover very quickly and soon are back to the previous level.

In this specific case, it is clear that an unforeseen change in the estimates of future cash flows used in determining the recoverable amount has resulted in the recognition of the impairment loss, and later in the reversal of that impairment loss. The CGU/intangible asset can be written back up to the value that would have been recognised had the impairment never occurred (refer to **example 10.3A** below). This write-up is recognised immediately in profit or loss.

Situation 2

Assume that, by year end, the mineral water company has conducted its own tests and satisfied both itself and independent experts that the consumer group was wrong in its claims. So the entity forecasts that, although there has been a temporary reduction in sales, sales will soon recover when the consumer group retracts the claims.

The temporary reduction in sales has caused a small temporary impairment in the value of the CGU/intangible asset as measured at the end of the reporting period. The CGU/intangible asset is written down by this small amount to its recoverable amount.

In the next period, sales increase back to their previous levels in line with expectations and the value of the CGU/intangible asset recovers to its original level. But, the (small) impairment loss cannot be reversed in the financial statements. Its reversal was foreseen in the original impairment calculations and has occurred simply because of the passing of time; therefore, the reversal does not arise from a change in the estimates used in the original recoverable amount calculation.

A reversal of an impairment loss must reflect an increase in the estimated service potential of an asset (or CGU), either from use or sale. Examples of such changes in estimate include:
[IAS 36:115]

- a change in the basis for recoverable amount (i.e. whether recoverable amount is based on fair value less costs of disposal or value in use);

- if recoverable amount was based on value in use, a change in the amount or timing of estimated future cash flows or in the discount rate; or

- if recoverable amount was based on fair value less costs of disposal, a change in estimate of the components of fair value less costs of disposal.

An increase in the recoverable amount of the asset due to the passage of time does not, however, represent an increase in the estimated service potential of an asset and, therefore, it is not acceptable to recognise a reversal of an impairment loss on this basis. In other words, the value in use of an asset may increase and even become greater than the carrying amount of the asset simply because the present value of future cash inflows increases as they become closer (i.e. 'the discount unwinds'). This does not, however, represent an economic change in the value of the asset. Therefore, a reversal of an impairment loss should not be recognised on this basis. [IAS 36:116]

Example 10.1B

Unwinding of discounted cash flows does not reverse an impairment loss

At the beginning of 20X0, Entity X acquires a machine with an expected useful life of four years for CU1,000. Depreciation is charged on a straight-line basis. At the end of 20X0, there is an indication that the machine may be impaired and consequently its recoverable amount is assessed by Entity X. Entity X determines that the fair value less costs of disposal is lower than the value in use of the machine. The value in use of the machine is determined using estimated future cash flows and a discount rate of 10 per cent as follows.

	20X1	20X2	20X3	Total
	CU	CU	CU	CU
Estimated future cash flows	250	250	300	800
Present value at 20X0	227	207	225	659

The carrying amount of the machine of CU750 is higher than its value in use of CU659. Therefore, Entity X should recognise an impairment loss of CU91 to reduce the machine's carrying amount to its value in use. The revised

---

carrying amount is then depreciated over the remaining useful life of three years. The cash flows and discount rate used in estimating the value in use of the machine do not change in subsequent years. The value in use based on the original estimated future cash flows and discount rate in each of the subsequent years is as follows.

	20X1	20X2	20X3
	CU	CU	CU
Carrying amount at year end	439	220	–
Estimated future cash flows	550	300	–
Value in use at year end	475	273	–

Although the machine's value in use exceeds its carrying amount in 20X1 and 20X2, this increase simply arises from the unwinding of the discount relating to the future cash flows. Consequently, the impairment loss of CU91 should not be reversed.

10.2   Indications of reversals of impairment losses

The indications of the reversal of impairment losses listed in IAS 36:111 are broadly the mirror image of the impairment indicators discussed at **5.2** above, and are reproduced in the following paragraphs.

The following external sources of information may indicate that an impairment loss previously recognised for an asset other than goodwill (or for a CGU) no longer exists or has decreased:
[IAS 36:111]

- there are observable indications that the asset's (or CGU's) value has increased significantly during the period;

The wording of this requirement has been amended as a consequence of the issue of IFRS 13 *Fair Value Measurement* and those amendments are reflected above. Previously the paragraph read "the asset's market value has increased significantly during the period". The changes have been made to reflect the revised model for fair value measurement established in IFRS 13.

- significant changes with a favourable effect on the entity have taken place during the period, or will take place in the near future, in the technological, market, economic or legal environment in which the entity operates or in the market to which the asset (or CGU) is dedicated; and

- market interest rates or other market rates of return on investments have decreased during the period, and those decreases are likely to affect the discount rate used in calculating the asset's (or CGU's) value in use and increase the asset's (or CGU's) recoverable amount materially.

The following internal sources of information may indicate that an impairment loss previously recognised for an asset other than goodwill (or for a CGU) no longer exists or has decreased:
[IAS 36:111]

- significant changes with a favourable effect on the entity have taken place during the period, or are expected to take place in the near future, in the extent to which, or the manner in which, the asset (or CGU) is used or is expected to be used. These changes include costs incurred during the period to improve or enhance the asset's (or CGU's) performance or restructure the operation to which the asset (or CGU) belongs; and

- evidence is available from internal reporting that indicates that the economic performance of the asset (or CGU) is, or will be, better than expected.

If there is an indication that an impairment loss previously recognised for an asset other than goodwill may no longer exist or may have decreased, this may indicate that the remaining useful life, the depreciation/amortisation method or the residual value may need to be reviewed and adjusted in accordance with the Standard applicable to the asset, even if no impairment loss is reversed for the asset. [IAS 36:113]

10.3   Reversal for an individual asset

The increased carrying amount of an asset other than goodwill due to a reversal of an impairment loss should not exceed the carrying amount that would have been determined (net of amortisation or depreciation) had no impairment loss been recognised for the asset in prior years. [IAS 36:117] Any increase in excess of this amount would be a revaluation and would be accounted for under the appropriate Standard (e.g. IAS 16 *Property, Plant and Equipment* for an item of property, plant and equipment). [IAS 36:118]

Example 10.3A

Reversal of an impairment loss

Entity A holds an intangible asset and accounts for it under the cost model of IAS 38 *Intangible Assets*. The intangible asset cost CU10 million and it is amortised over 10 years. Two years after it is purchased, the intangible asset becomes impaired and it is written down from its carrying amount of CU8 million to its estimated recoverable amount of CU4 million. Its estimated useful life is unchanged (8 years remaining). Two years after the recognition of the impairment loss, with the carrying amount at CU3 million, the recoverable amount of the intangible asset is estimated to be CU7 million, following a change in estimates of the future cash flows arising from this asset.

Because the reversal of the impairment loss arises from a change in the estimates used to determine the recoverable amount, the impairment loss should be reversed. However, the impairment loss can only be reversed to the extent that it does not increase the carrying amount above what it would have been had the impairment loss never been recognised. Had the impairment loss never been recognised, the carrying amount would be CU6 million (CU8 million less two further years depreciation at CU1 million per annum); therefore, only CU3 million of the original CU4 million impairment loss can be reversed.

Example 10.3B

Limited reversal of impairment loss

Entity A holds a property and accounts for it under IAS 16's cost model. The cost of the property is CU10 million and its useful life is 20 years. Depreciation each year is, therefore, CU0.5 million.

At the end of Year 5, the property has a carrying amount of CU7.5 million. Due to changes in the economic environment, the directors perform a detailed impairment review and determine that the property's recoverable amount is its value in use, which is CU5 million. Their estimate of the remaining useful life of the asset is 10 years.

Therefore an impairment loss of CU2.5 million is recognised in Year 5. In Years 6 and 7 the property is depreciated by CU0.5 million per year so that its carrying amount at the end of Year 7 is CU4 million.

Due to shortages in the supply of properties, the directors determine that the fair value less costs of disposal of the property at the end of Year 7 is CU8 million. The recoverable amount of the asset has therefore increased to CU8 million.

The reversal of the impairment loss is limited, however, to the amount that would restore the carrying amount to what it would have been had no

> impairment loss been recognised (i.e. CU7.5 million – (CU7.5 million x 2/10) = CU6 million). Therefore, only CU2 million of the impairment loss is reversed.
>
> If the entity wishes to recognise the market value of the property in its statement of financial position, the remainder of the uplift would be treated as a revaluation movement. (This will only be possible, however, if the entity decides to adopt the revaluation model for all assets in that class.)

A reversal of an impairment loss for an asset other than goodwill is recognised immediately in profit or loss unless the asset is carried at a revalued amount in accordance with another Standard. When an asset is carried at a revalued amount, the reversal is considered a revaluation increase and treated accordingly. [IAS 36:119] Normally, a revaluation increase is recognised in other comprehensive income and increases the revaluation surplus within equity. But to the extent that an impairment loss on the same revalued asset was previously recognised in profit or loss, a reversal of that impairment loss is recognised in profit or loss. [IAS 36:120]

After the reversal of an impairment loss, the depreciation (amortisation) charge for the asset is adjusted in future periods to allocate the asset's revised carrying amount, less its residual value (if any), on a systematic basis over its remaining useful life. [IAS 36:121]

10.4   Reversal for a CGU

A reversal of an impairment loss for a CGU should be allocated to increase the carrying amount of the assets of the unit, except for goodwill, pro rata based on the carrying amount of each asset in the unit. These increases in carrying amounts should be dealt with as reversals of impairment losses for individual assets in the same manner as discussed at **10.3**. [IAS 36:122]

In allocating a reversal of an impairment loss for a CGU, the carrying amount of an asset should not be increased above the lower of: [IAS 36:123]

- its recoverable amount (if determinable); and

- the carrying amount that would have been determined (net of amortisation/ depreciation) had no impairment loss been recognised for the asset in prior years. (Any further increase would constitute a revaluation.)

It follows, therefore, that the reversal of the impairment loss will be allocated only between those assets (excluding goodwill) against which the original loss was allocated, though not necessarily in the same proportions.

If this results in a reversal being allocated to an asset which is less than its pro rata share of the reversal, the amount of the reversal of the impairment loss that would otherwise have been allocated to the asset should be allocated to the other assets of the unit, other than goodwill, on a pro rata basis. [IAS 36:123]

10.5   Reversal for goodwill

When an impairment loss has previously been recognised for goodwill, that impairment loss should not be reversed in a subsequent period. [IAS 36:124]

The IASB has concluded that, because any increase in the recoverable amount of goodwill in the periods following the recognition of an impairment loss is likely to be an increase in internally generated goodwill, rather than a reversal of an impairment loss, it is inappropriate to recognise any such increase in recoverable amount (because it would result in the recognition of internally generated goodwill, which is prohibited by IAS 38).

IFRIC Interpretation 10 *Interim Financial Reporting and Impairment* states that an entity should not reverse an impairment loss recognised in a previous interim period in respect of goodwill. For entities that have not yet adopted IFRS 9, a similar requirement applies in respect of investments in equity instruments and financial assets carried at cost. For further discussion of IFRIC 10, see **5.6.16.1** in **chapter A32**.

11   Disclosure

IAS 36 was amended in May 2013 when the IASB provided clarification on a number of the disclosure requirements in the Standard. These amendments are effective for annual periods beginning on or after 1 January 2014, with earlier application permitted. Entities are not permitted to apply the May 2013 amendments to IAS 36 unless they have also adopted IFRS 13 *Fair Value Measurement*.

The amendments made in May 2013 have the following effects:

- to restrict the requirement to disclose the recoverable amount of an asset or a CGU to periods in which an impairment loss has been recognised or reversed. Consequential amendments to IAS 36 in May 2011 arising from IFRS 13 had a broader impact than the IASB had intended; in particular, they introduced a requirement to disclose in every reporting period the recoverable amount of each CGU or group of CGU's to which a significant portion of the overall carrying amount of goodwill (or other intangible assets with indefinite useful lives) had been allocated. The IASB had intended to limit such disclosures to reporting periods in which an impairment loss was recognised or reversed. Amendments to IAS 36:130(e) and IAS 36:134(c) (see **11.3.1** and **11.6.1**, respectively, below) are designed to achieve this objective; and

- to expand and clarify the disclosure requirements applicable when the recoverable amount of an asset or a CGU has been determined on the basis of fair value less costs of disposal (see amendments to IAS 36:130(f) in **11.3.1** below).

Entities are not permitted to apply the May 2013 amendments unless they have also adopted IFRS 13 *Fair Value Measurement*. In the period in which an entity applies the May 2013 amendments for the first time, it should not restate disclosures for comparative period(s) unless it also applies IFRS 13 in those comparative period(s).

11.1   General

For each class of assets (defined as a grouping of assets of similar nature and use in the operations of the entity), the financial statements should disclose the amount of:
[IAS 36:126]

(a) impairment losses recognised in profit or loss during the period and the line item(s) of the statement of comprehensive income in which those impairment losses are included;

(b) reversals of impairment losses recognised in profit or loss during the period and the line item(s) of the statement of comprehensive income in which those impairment losses are reversed;

(c) impairment losses on revalued assets recognised in other comprehensive income during the period; and

(d)   reversals of impairment losses on revalued assets recognised in other comprehensive income during the period.

This information may be presented in the reconciliation of the carrying amounts of property, plant and equipment, intangible assets, or elsewhere as appropriate. [IAS 36:128]

Example 11.1

Impairment loss not included within depreciation expense

An entity recognises an impairment loss in respect of certain intangible assets with indefinite useful lives in the fourth quarter of 20X1 in accordance with IAS 36. The entity has certain debt covenants that state that it must maintain a specified multiple of EBITDA (earnings before interest, taxes, depreciation and amortisation).

Impairment losses recognised in accordance with IAS 36 should not be included within depreciation expense. IAS 16 *Property, Plant and Equipment* defines depreciation as the systematic allocation of the depreciable amount of an asset over its useful life. The recognition of an impairment loss is as a result of a valuation exercise, rather than an allocation exercise, and should not be presented in a manner that might encourage the belief that it is part of the regular allocation (i.e. the depreciation expense).

11.2   Entities reporting segment information

Entities that report segment information in accordance with IFRS 8 *Operating Segments* (see **chapter A30**) are required to disclose the following for each reportable segment:
[IAS 36:129]

(a)   the amount of impairment losses recognised in profit or loss and in other comprehensive income during the period; and

(b)   the amount of reversals of impairment losses recognised in profit or loss and in other comprehensive income during the period.

11.3   Impairment losses recognised or reversed in the period

11.3.1   Entities that have adopted the May 2013 amendments to IAS 36

The following disclosures are required in respect of an individual asset (including goodwill) or a CGU for which an impairment loss has been recognised or reversed during the period:
[IAS 36:130]

(a)   the events and circumstances that led to the recognition (reversal) of the loss;

(b)   the amount of the loss recognised (reversed);

(c)   for an individual asset:

   (i)   the nature of the asset; and

   (ii)   for entities that apply IFRS 8, the reportable segment to which the asset belongs (see **chapter A30**);

(d)   for a CGU:

   (i)   a description of the CGU (such as whether it is a product line, a plant, a business operation, a geographical area, a reportable segment or other);

   (ii)   the amount of the loss recognised or reversed by class of assets and, for entities that apply IFRS 8, by reportable segment; and

   (iii)   if the aggregation of assets for identifying the CGU has changed since the previous estimate of the CGU's recoverable amount (if any), the entity should describe the current and former ways of aggregating assets and the reasons for changing the way the CGU is identified;

(e)   the recoverable amount of the asset or CGU, and whether the recoverable amount of the asset or CGU is its fair value less costs of disposal or its value in use;

(f)   if the recoverable amount is fair value less costs of disposal:

   (i)   the level of the fair value hierarchy (see IFRS 13) within which the fair value measurement of the asset or CGU is categorised in its entirety (without taking into account whether the 'costs of disposal' are observable);

   (ii)   for fair value measurements categorised within Level 2 and Level 3 of the fair value hierarchy, a description of the valuation technique(s) used to measure fair value less costs of disposal. If

11.4   Other impairment losses/reversals material in aggregate to the financial statements

If impairment losses recognised (reversed) during the period, other than those disclosed under **11.3**, are material in aggregate to the financial statements taken as a whole, the entity should disclose a brief description of the following:
[IAS 36:131]

(a)   the main classes of assets affected by those impairment losses (reversals); and

(b)   the main events and circumstances that led to the recognition (or reversal) of those impairment losses.

> Prior to the May 2013 amendments to IAS 36, there was a clear dividing line between the requirements of IAS 36:130 (which applied to impairment losses or reversals recognised in the period that were individually material) and those of IAS 36:131 (which applied to impairments or reversals, other than those disclosed under IAS 36:130, that were material in aggregate). The May 2013 amendments removed the explicit reference to materiality in IAS 36:130, on the basis that all IFRSs are governed by the concept of materiality. In the Basis for Conclusions on the May 2013 amendments, the IASB confirmed that the amendments are not intended to change the scope of the disclosure requirements in IAS 36:130, and that the amendments to IAS 36:130 should not affect the disclosure requirements in IAS 36:131. [IAS 36:BC209M & N] Consequently, it appears that the previous segregation continues to apply between losses or reversals that are individually material (covered by IAS 36:130), and other losses or reversals that are material in aggregate (covered by IAS 36:131).

11.5   Unallocated goodwill

If any portion of the goodwill acquired in a business combination during the period has not been allocated to a CGU (group of CGUs) at the end of the reporting period (see **8.1.2.1** above), the amount of the unallocated goodwill should be disclosed, together with the reasons why that amount remains unallocated. [IAS 36:134]

11.6   CGUs containing goodwill or intangible assets with indefinite useful lives

Some of the disclosure requirements under this heading have been amended as a consequence of the issue of IFRS 13. For ease of reading, the requirements of IAS 36:134 are set out twice below; the listing in **11.6.1** reflects the revisions made as a result of IFRS 13. The changes have been made to reflect the revised model for fair value measurement established in IFRS 13.

11.6.1   *Information to be disclosed for CGUs to which significant goodwill or indefinite-life intangible assets have been allocated (entities applying IFRS 13)*

The wording below reflects the amendments to IAS 36:134(c) in May 2013 (see also the discussion at the beginning of this section). Previously, the Standard required disclosure, in every reporting period, of the recoverable amount of each CGU or group of CGU's to which a significant portion of the overall carrying amount of goodwill (or other intangible assets with indefinite useful lives) had been allocated. The IASB had intended to limit such disclosures to reporting periods in which an impairment loss was recognised or reversed. To achieve this effect, the requirement to disclose the recoverable amount of each CGU or group of CGUs has been moved from IAS 36:134(c) to IAS 36:130(f) (see **11.3.1** above)

The following information should be disclosed for each CGU (or group of CGUs) for which the carrying amount of goodwill or intangible assets with indefinite useful lives allocated to that unit (or group of units) is significant in comparison with the entity's total carrying amount of goodwill or intangible assets with indefinite useful lives:
[IAS 36:134]

(a)   the carrying amount of goodwill allocated to the unit (or group of units);

(b)   the carrying amount of intangible assets with indefinite useful lives allocated to the unit (or group of units);

(c)   the basis on which the unit's (or group of units') recoverable amount has been determined (i.e. value in use or fair value less costs of disposal);

(d)   if the unit's (or group of units') recoverable amount is based on value in use:

   (i)   each key assumption on which management has based its cash flow projections for the period covered by the most recent budgets/forecasts. Key assumptions are those to which the unit's (or group of units') recoverable amount is most sensitive;

   (ii)   a description of management's approach to determining the value(s) assigned to each key assumption, whether those value(s) reflect past experience or, if appropriate, are consistent with external sources of information, and, if not, how and why they differ from past experience or external sources of information;

   (iii)   the period over which management has projected cash flows based on financial budgets/forecasts approved by management and, when a period greater than five years is used for a CGU (or group of CGUs), an explanation as to why that longer period is justified;

   (iv)   the growth rate used to extrapolate cash flow projections beyond the period covered by the most recent budgets/ forecasts, and the justification for using any growth rate that exceeds the long-term average growth rate for the products, industries, or country or countries in which the entity operates, or for the market to which the unit (or group of units) is dedicated; and

   (v)   the discount rate(s) applied to the cash flow projections;

(e)   if the unit's (or group of units') recoverable amount is based on fair value less costs of disposal, the valuation technique(s) used to measure fair value less costs of disposal. An entity is not required to provide the disclosures required by IFRS 13. If fair value less costs of disposal is not measured using a quoted price for an identical unit (or group of units), the following information should also be disclosed:

   (i)   each key assumption on which management has based its determination of fair value less costs of disposal. Key assumptions are those to which the unit's (or group of units') recoverable amount is most sensitive;

   (ii)   a description of management's approach to determining the value (or values) assigned to each key assumption, whether those values reflect past experience or, if appropriate, are consistent with external sources of information, and, if not, how and why they differ from past experience or external sources of information;

(iii) the level of the IFRS 13 fair value hierarchy (see **section 10** of **chapter A6**) within which the fair value measurement is categorised in its entirety (without giving regard to the observability of 'costs of disposal'); and

(iv) if there has been a change in valuation technique, the change and the reason(s) for making it.

In addition, if fair value less costs of disposal is measured using discounted cash flow projections, the following information should also be disclosed:

(v)   the period over which management has projected cash flows;

(vi) the growth rate used to extrapolate cash flow projections; and

(vii) the discount rate(s) applied to the cash flow projections; and

(f)   if a reasonably possible change in a key assumption on which management has based its determination of the unit's (or group of units') recoverable amount would cause the unit's (or group of units') carrying amount to exceed its recoverable amount:

(i)   the amount by which the unit's (or group of units') recoverable amount exceeds its carrying amount;

(ii)   the value assigned to the key assumption; and

(iii) the amount by which the value assigned to the key assumption must change, after incorporating any consequential effects of that change on the other variables used to measure recoverable amount, in order for the unit's (or group of units') recoverable amount to be equal to its carrying amount.

11.6.2   Information to be disclosed for CGUs to which significant goodwill or indefinite-life intangible assets have been allocated (entities that have not adopted IFRS 13)

The following information should be disclosed for each CGU (or group of CGUs) for which the carrying amount of goodwill or intangible assets with indefinite useful lives allocated to that unit (or group of units) is significant in comparison with the entity's total carrying amount of goodwill or intangible assets with indefinite useful lives: [IAS 36:134]

(a) the carrying amount of goodwill allocated to the unit (or group of units);

(b) the carrying amount of intangible assets with indefinite useful lives allocated to the unit (or group of units);

(c) the basis on which the unit's (or group of units') recoverable amount has been determined (i.e. value in use or fair value less costs to sell);

(d) if the unit's (or group of units') recoverable amount is based on value in use:

   (i) a description of each key assumption on which management has based its cash flow projections for the period covered by the most recent budgets/forecasts. Key assumptions are those to which the unit's (or group of units') recoverable amount is most sensitive;

   (ii) a description of management's approach to determining the value(s) assigned to each key assumption, whether those value(s) reflect past experience or, if appropriate, are consistent with external sources of information, and, if not, how and why they differ from past experience or external sources of information;

   (iii) the period over which management has projected cash flows based on financial budgets/forecasts approved by management and, when a period greater than five years is used for a CGU (or group of CGUs), an explanation as to why that longer period is justified;

   (iv) the growth rate used to extrapolate cash flow projections beyond the period covered by the most recent budgets/forecasts, and the justification for using any growth rate that exceeds the long-term average growth rate for the products, industries, or country or countries in which the entity operates, or for the market to which the unit (or group of units) is dedicated; and

   (v) the discount rate(s) applied to the cash flow projections;

(e) if the unit's (or group of units') recoverable amount is based on fair value less costs to sell, the methodology used to determine fair value less costs to sell. If fair value less costs to sell is not determined using an observable market price for the unit (or group of units), the following information should also be disclosed:

(i)   a description of each key assumption on which management has based its determination of fair value less costs to sell. Key assumptions are those to which the unit's (or group of units') recoverable amount is most sensitive; and

(ii) a description of management's approach to determining the value (or values) assigned to each key assumption, whether those values reflect past experience or, if appropriate, are consistent with external sources of information, and, if not, how and why they differ from past experience or external sources of information.

In addition, if fair value less costs to sell is determined using discounted cash flow projections, the following information should also be disclosed:

(iii) the period over which management has projected cash flows;

(iv) the growth rate used to extrapolate cash flow projections; and

(v)   the discount rate(s) applied to the cash flow projections; and

(f) if a reasonably possible change in a key assumption on which management has based its determination of the unit's (or group of units') recoverable amount would cause the unit's (or group of units') carrying amount to exceed its recoverable amount:

(i)   the amount by which the unit's (or group of units') recoverable amount exceeds its carrying amount;

(ii) the value assigned to the key assumption; and

(iii) the amount by which the value assigned to the key assumption must change, after incorporating any consequential effects of that change on the other variables used to measure recoverable amount, in order for the unit's (or group of units') recoverable amount to be equal to its carrying amount.

11.6.3 Information to be disclosed for CGUs to which insignificant goodwill or indefinite-life intangible assets have been allocated

The disclosure requirements below are not amended by IFRS 13.

If some or all of the carrying amount of goodwill or intangible assets with indefinite useful lives is allocated across multiple CGUs (or groups of

CGUs), and the amount so allocated to each unit (or group of units) is not significant in comparison with the entity's total carrying amount of goodwill or intangible assets with indefinite useful lives, that fact should be disclosed, together with the aggregate carrying amount of goodwill or intangible assets with indefinite useful lives allocated to those units (or groups of units). [IAS 36:135]

In addition to the requirements set out in the previous paragraph, if the recoverable amounts of any such units (or groups of units) are based on the same key assumption(s) and the aggregate carrying amount of goodwill or intangible assets with indefinite useful lives allocated to them is significant in comparison with the entity's total carrying amount of goodwill or intangible assets with indefinite useful lives, the entity should disclose that fact, together with:
[IAS 36:135]

(a)   the aggregate carrying amount of goodwill allocated to those units (or groups of units);

(b)   the aggregate carrying amount of intangible assets with indefinite useful lives allocated to those units (or groups of units);

(c)   a description of each key assumption;

(d)   a description of management's approach to determining the value assigned to each key assumption, whether those value(s) reflect past experience or, if appropriate, are consistent with external sources of information, and, if not, how and why they differ from past experience or external sources of information; and

(e)   if a reasonably possible change in the key assumptions would cause the aggregate of the units' (or groups of units') carrying amounts to exceed the aggregate of their recoverable amounts:

   (i)   the amount by which the aggregate of the units' (or groups of units') recoverable amounts exceeds the aggregate of their carrying amounts;

   (ii)   the value(s) assigned to the key assumption(s); and

   (iii)   the amount by which the value(s) assigned to the key assumption(s) must change, after incorporating any consequential effects of that change on the other variables used to measure recoverable amount, in order for the aggregate of the units' (or groups of units') recoverable amounts to be equal to the aggregate of their carrying amounts.

As discussed at **5.3.1** and **5.3.2.4** above, provided that specified criteria are met, the most recent detailed calculation made in a preceding period of the recoverable amount of a CGU (or group of CGUs) may be carried forward and used in the impairment test for that unit (or group of units) in the current period. When this is the case, the information for that unit (or group of units) that is incorporated into the disclosures required by IAS 36:134 and IAS 36:135 (set out above) relates to the carried forward calculation of recoverable amount. [IAS 36:136]

The comprehensive disclosures required by this section are illustrated in illustrative example 9 accompanying IAS 36.

A11   Inventories

Contents

1   Introduction

The accounting treatment for inventories is prescribed in IAS 2 *Inventories*, which provides guidance for determining the cost of inventories and for subsequently recognising an expense, including any write-down to net realisable value. It also provides guidance on the cost formulas that are used to assign costs to inventories.

IAS 2 was most recently amended in May 2011.

2   Scope

IAS 2 defines inventories as assets:
[IAS 2:6]

- held for sale in the ordinary course of business;

- in the process of production for such sale; or

- in the form of materials or supplies to be consumed in the production process or in the rendering of services.

Inventories held for sale include inventories held by retailers and finished goods of a manufacturer. Inventories in the process of production for such sale may include both work in progress of a manufacturing entity and the labour costs of a service provider related to revenue not yet recognised for a particular project. Inventories in the form of materials or supplies to be consumed in the production process or in the rendering of services are generally referred to as raw materials.

See **example 6.1E** in **chapter A14** for discussion of retention of title clauses.

The classification of spare parts, stand-by equipment and servicing equipment as inventories or property, plant and equipment is addressed at **3.2** in **chapter A7**.

IFRIC 20 *Stripping Costs in the Production Phase of a Surface Mine* addresses the classification of costs relating to production stripping activity in a surface mine as inventories or as a non-current asset – see **section 10** of **chapter A7**.

IAS 2 applies to all inventories, except:
[IAS 2:2]

- work in progress arising under construction contracts, including directly related service contracts (addressed by IAS 11 *Construction Contracts* – see **chapter C34**);

- financial instruments (addressed by IAS 32 *Financial Instruments: Presentation* and either IFRS 9 *Financial Instruments* or, for entities that have not yet adopted IFRS 9, IAS 39 *Financial Instruments: Recognition and Measurement* – see **Volume B** or **Volume C**); and

- biological assets related to agricultural activity and agricultural produce at the point of harvest (addressed by IAS 41 *Agriculture* – see **chapter A38**).

The Standard does not apply to the measurement of inventories held by:
[IAS 2:3]

- producers of agricultural and forest products, agricultural produce after harvest, and minerals and mineral products, to the extent that they are measured at net realisable value in accordance with well-established practices in those industries; or

- commodity broker-traders who measure their inventories at fair value less costs to sell.

Although inventories held by these entities are excluded from the measurement requirements of IAS 2, the Standard requires that when such inventories are measured at net realisable value/fair value less costs to sell, changes in those values are to be recognised in profit or loss in the period of change. [IAS 2:3] The other requirements of IAS 2 (e.g. regarding presentation and disclosure) apply in the normal way to such inventories.

For the avoidance of doubt, note that the requirements of IAS 2 apply in their entirety to:

- property intended for sale in the ordinary course of business or in the process of construction or development for such sale (e.g. property acquired exclusively with a view to subsequent disposal in the near future or for development and resale); and

- inventories held by producers of agricultural and forest products, agricultural produce after harvest, and minerals and mineral products, when they are not measured at net realisable value in accordance with well-established practices in those industries.

Example 2A

Classification and measurement of pipeline fill

Company A operates a pipeline to transport crude oil. Company A does not produce or distribute crude oil; it merely provides the use of its pipeline to the buyer and seller in a contract for a usage fee. The seller and buyer independently negotiate the sales price, and either the buyer or the seller pays a fee to Company A for transporting the oil purchased/sold through its pipeline.

The pipeline needs to be full of oil at all times to be operational. Therefore, during initial construction of the pipeline, Company A purchases oil to fill the pipeline. Once the pipeline is operational, Company A charges a fixed fee for its transportation services and, in effect, swaps crude oil pushed into the pipeline by a seller for crude oil of the same grade and quality delivered to the customer at the exit point of the pipeline. Company A bears the risk of loss due to theft or line loss in excess of the maximums allowed under the contract. Such losses are rare and normally arise as the result of a pipeline spill that is covered by insurance.

The pipeline fill meets the definition of an asset and should be recognised at cost when acquired. In accordance with IAS 16 *Property, Plant and Equipment*, the pipeline fill does not meet the definition of property, plant and equipment (see IAS 16:6). Rather, it should be classified as inventories because it is held "in the form of materials or supplies to be consumed in the production process or in the rendering of services" (see IAS 2:6).

Because an accounting transaction does not take place at the time of each swap of crude oil, no step-up in the value of inventories is recognised. The pipeline fill is measured at the lower of cost and net realisable value throughout the term of the pipeline's operations in accordance with IAS 2:9.

Example 4.3A in **chapter A14** addresses the question of revenue recognition in these circumstances.

Example 2B

Classification of assets acquired for sale in the ordinary course of business

Entity X, a lessor, leases assets ordinarily under three-year agreements. At the end of the lease term, the lessee has the option either to return or to acquire the asset. Some of the leases contain an extension option, which allows the lessee an additional three months to return or to acquire the asset. The extension option must be exercised prior to the end of the main lease term.

Entity X enters into 'residual value guarantee' contracts with Entity A, a third party. Under these contracts, Entity A will purchase the assets from Entity X at the end of each lease term at a predetermined price. Entity A receives a fee in return for providing the residual value guarantee.

When an extension option is exercised by the lessee, ownership of the asset is transferred to Entity A at the end of the main lease term for the predetermined price. During the extension period, Entity X passes the rental income to Entity A. At the end of the extension period, Entity A sells the asset either in the market or to the lessee. Rental income received by Entity A during the extension period is considered incidental to Entity A's principal activities, which are the provision of residual value guarantee contracts and selling the assets acquired.

In order to determine how to recognise the assets in the period from acquisition at the end of the main lease term to the point of sale, Entity A must establish how the assets are used in the business, i.e. whether they represent inventories or property, plant and equipment.

In the circumstances described, Entity A acquires the assets at the end of the main lease term to profit from selling them in the market. In accordance with IAS 2, the assets are classified as inventories because they are assets "held for sale in the ordinary course of business".

The assets acquired do not represent property, plant and equipment, in accordance with IAS 16, because they are not held primarily for rental by Entity A to others and are not expected to be used during more than one period.

2.1   Inventories on consignment

In some industries, it is common for a manufacturer to supply goods to a distributor 'on consignment'; the manufacturer retains the substantial risks and rewards of ownership and legal title to the goods until some future predetermined event occurs (e.g. sale to a third-party customer) which triggers transfer of the legal title to the distributor.

The distributor should recognise the goods as an asset only when the substantial risks and rewards of ownership have been transferred. IAS 18 *Revenue* provides specific guidance on consignment sales under which the recipient of the goods (the buyer) undertakes to sell goods on behalf of the shipper (the seller), and requires that revenue be recognised by the shipper when the goods are sold by the recipient to a third party (see IAS 18:Appendix Example 2(c)). Equally, the risks and rewards of consignment inventories may not pass to the distributor until it has sold the inventories to a third-party customer and the manufacturer (the seller) would therefore not derecognise the inventories until that stage in the arrangement.

IFRSs do not provide any other guidance on accounting for consignment arrangements and, therefore, in accordance with IAS 8 *Accounting Policies, Changes in Accounting Estimates and Errors*, the distributor (the buyer) should determine an accounting treatment for inventories on consignment that results in information that is relevant and reliable (see **3.1** in **chapter A5**). Until it is established that the transfer to the distributor is substantive and that the risks and rewards of the inventories have passed to the distributor, the goods should be treated as the manufacturer's inventories and excluded from the distributor's statement of financial position.

3   Measurement of inventories

Inventories are measured at the lower of cost and net realisable value. [IAS 2:9] The comparison of cost with net realisable value should, in principle, be carried out on an item-by-item basis but, if this is impracticable, groups of similar items may be considered together. It is unacceptable to compare the total net realisable value of all inventories with their total purchase price or production cost.

The introduction to IAS 2 makes clear that, with the limited exception of the classes of inventory listed in **section 2** above (i.e. those outside the scope of the Standard and those exempt from its measurement rules), it is not acceptable to adopt an accounting policy of carrying inventories at a current value.

3.1   Components of cost

IAS 2:10 specifies that the cost of inventories comprises:

- all costs of purchase (see **3.1.1**);

- costs of conversion (see **3.1.2**); and

- other costs incurred in bringing the inventories to their present location and condition (see **3.1.3**).

3.1.1   Costs of purchase

The costs of purchase of inventories include:
[IAS 2:11]

- purchase price;

- import duties and other taxes that are not recoverable by the entity (e.g. associated VAT paid to the extent that an entity cannot reclaim it);

- transport and handling costs; and

- other costs directly attributable to the acquisition of finished goods, materials and services.

Any trade discounts or rebates received are deducted in determining the costs of purchase of inventory.

Example 3.1.1A

Discounts and rebates

Entity A is a retailer that acquires products from manufacturers, which are sold to end users. The manufacturers grant incentives to Entity A on one of two bases:

- a 10 per cent prompt settlement discount on all purchases of inventories settled within 30 days of purchase; or

- rebates based on the volume of merchandise purchased or sold.

How should these discounts and rebates be accounted for by Entity A in each of the following circumstances:

- *Entity A acts as principal in the purchase of products from manufacturers and the sale of products to end users?*

- *Entity A acts as an agent of the manufacturers in making sales to end users?*

Entity A acts as principal

If Entity A acts as principal in the sale and purchase of products then, in accordance with IAS 2:11, rebates and discounts that have been received as a reduction in the purchase price of inventories should be taken into consideration in the measurement of the cost of those inventories.

Prompt settlement (cash) discount

Entity A should deduct prompt settlement discounts from the cost of the inventories. When measuring the cost of the inventories, Entity A should estimate the expected settlement discount to be received from the supplier.

This is consistent with the accounting by the supplier required by paragraph 10 of IAS 18 *Revenue*, which states that a transaction should be measured "at the fair value of the consideration received or receivable taking into account the amount of any trade discounts and volume rebates allowed by the entity" (see also **example 4.1** in **chapter A14**).

This issue was addressed by the IFRIC (now the IFRS Interpretations Committee), and an IFRIC agenda rejection was published in the August 2002 *IFRIC Update*.

Volume rebates

Similarly, volume rebates should be deducted from the cost of inventories. See **example 3.1.1B** for more detailed considerations regarding when the rebate should be recognised.

Entity A acts as agent

If Entity A is not purchasing the products as principal, and its sales to end users are as agent for the manufacturers, then it will not account for the products sold on a gross basis. Instead, the rebates will form part of the net commission revenue earned by Company A.

The distinction between an entity acting as a principal or as an agent is addressed at **3.1** in **chapter A14**.

Example 3.1.1B

Cash refund based on volume of purchases

On 1 July 20X1, in a binding arrangement, a vendor offers a cash refund of CU1,000 to a customer if during the 12 months to 30 June 20X2 the customer purchases 1,000 units of a particular product. Historically, on average, the customer has purchased 1,700 units each year and there have been no significant changes in the trading relationship in the current period.

How should the customer account for the refund to be received from the vendor in its financial statements for the year ending 31 December 20X1 if the 1,000 unit threshold has not yet been reached?

The cash refund constitutes a volume rebate, to be accounted for as a reduction in the cost of inventories (see IAS 2:11, as discussed above). IAS 2:11 does not, however, specify the treatment of refunds or rebates that are anticipated but have not yet been 'earned' or the allocation of refunds or rebates to items of inventory.

Anticipation of refunds not yet 'earned'

The question regarding refunds or rebates that are anticipated but that have not yet been 'earned' in full is addressed in IAS 34 *Interim Financial Reporting* in the context of the preparation of interim financial statements, and it is appropriate to apply the principle established in IAS 34 to the preparation of annual financial statements in the circumstances described.

IAS 34:B23 states as follows.

> "Volume rebates or discounts and other contractual changes in the prices of raw materials, labour, or other purchased goods and services are anticipated in interim periods, by both the payer and the recipient, if it is probable that they have been earned or will take effect. Thus, contractual rebates and discounts are anticipated but discretionary rebates and discounts are not anticipated because the resulting asset or liability would not satisfy the conditions in the *Conceptual Framework* that an asset must be a resource controlled by the entity as a result of a past event and that a liability must be a present obligation whose settlement is expected to result in an outflow of resources."

Therefore, in the circumstances described, if it is probable that the customer will purchase at least 1,000 units in the specified period (e.g. forecast purchase levels are in line with historical volumes), the refund (which is contractual) should be accrued as the units are purchased.

Units to which the refund should be allocated

The refund should be allocated to the units of inventory purchased on a systematic and rational basis. If the vendor's offer of a cash refund is a one-off incentive, and not expected to be repeated, it may be appropriate to account for the refund as a reduction in the cost of the first 1,000 units purchased, because the customer's entitlement to the refund is based only on the purchase of 1,000 units of inventory. Conversely, if the vendor routinely offers such a refund on an annual basis but on the condition that the customer purchases all inventories of this type from the vendor (i.e. an exclusive supply arrangement), it may be more appropriate to regard the refund as relating to all purchases in the year and account for it as a reduction in the cost of all units purchased. This assessment should be made on the basis of the specific facts and circumstances, including all relevant contractual terms.

3.1.1.1   *Direct materials and wastage*

When raw material is unavoidably subject to wastage and spoilage during production, it is generally appropriate to include the cost of such normal scrapping and wastage as part of the direct material cost of the product. Alternatively, if more practicable, the cost of direct materials unavoidably wasted or spoiled may be included in overheads as part of the costs of conversion. It is not appropriate, however, to include abnormal wastage in the carrying amount of inventories (see IAS 2:16(a)).

3.1.2   Costs of conversion

The costs of conversion of inventories include costs directly related to the units of production such as:
[IAS 2:12]

- direct labour, including all related employment taxes, and benefits and any share-based payment costs; and

- a systematic allocation of the fixed and variable production overheads incurred in converting materials into finished goods.

> It is sometimes argued that overheads should be excluded from the cost of inventories on the grounds of prudence. Such an approach (sometimes called 'direct costing') is not acceptable under IAS 2, which requires a systematic allocation of production overheads.
>
> Similarly, 'marginal costing' approaches, under which only costs that vary directly with volume of output are included in the measurement of inventories and costs that accrue on a time basis (such as some overheads) are excluded, are not acceptable under IAS 2 because they do not result in the allocation of fixed production overheads.

3.1.2.1   Direct labour

The cost of wages of employees directly engaged in production should be allocated to production activities on the basis of normal operating conditions. Labour costs that are the result of operating inefficiencies, such as abnormal idle capacity or abnormal rectification work, should not be included in inventory valuation. [IAS 2:13]

3.1.2.2   Overhead costs

Fixed production overheads are those indirect costs of production that remain relatively constant regardless of the volume of production. They may include:

- depreciation;

> When an entity adopts the revaluation model for certain items of property, plant and equipment (see **section 6** of **chapter A7**), it should consider, for the purpose of inventory valuation, depreciation based on the revalued amounts of those items.

- rent and rates of the factory building;

- maintenance of the factory building and equipment; and

- factory management and administration.

The allocation of fixed production overheads to inventories should be based on the normal capacity of the production facilities, which is the production expected to be achieved on average over a number of periods under normal circumstances, taking into account the loss of capacity resulting from planned maintenance. The actual level of production may be used if it approximates to normal capacity. [IAS 2:13]

When production levels are abnormally low, unallocated fixed overheads are recognised in profit or loss in the period in which they are incurred. In periods of abnormally high production, the amount of fixed overhead allocated to each unit of production is decreased so that inventories are not measured at above cost.

Variable production overheads are those indirect costs of production that vary directly, or nearly directly, with the volume of production. [IAS 2:12] Variable overheads may include indirect materials and indirect labour. They are allocated to each unit of production on the basis of the actual use of the production facilities.

Overheads that are properly classified as selling costs should not be included in the cost of inventories

Other non-production overheads should only be included when this is justified by exceptional circumstances. When firm sales contracts have been entered into for the provision of goods or services to customer specification, overheads (other than selling costs) relating to design, incurred before manufacture, may be included in arriving at cost.

The process for determining the amount of overheads to be carried forward in inventories can be considered under two headings: (1) identifying the overheads to be included, and (2) allocating those overheads to production in a logical manner. It is necessary first to analyse overheads by function between production, marketing and distribution, and administration. There are practical problems in performing this analysis. For example, management salaries may include an element of supervision of production as well as of administration, and pension costs are likely to cover employees in the production function as well as those in sales and general administration departments. Central services departments, such as accounts, may provide identifiable services for production. Costs should be allocated over the functions on a reasonable basis, which should be applied consistently and reviewed regularly.

The method for allocating overheads to production should be one that is appropriate to the nature of the product and the method of production. The most popular methods for allocating overheads are:

- by way of a labour-hour or machine-hour rate;

- in proportion to direct labour costs;

- in proportion to material costs;

- in proportion to prime costs; and

- equally to each unit of production. (This is only appropriate when a single product is being produced in a given cost centre.)

Whichever method for allocating overheads is adopted, the overheads should be allocated on the basis of the entity's normal level of activity. Overhead costs that are the result of operating inefficiencies, such as abnormal idle capacity or abnormal rectification work, should not be included in the inventory carrying amount.

Example 3.1.2.2

Lease costs included in the cost of inventories

An entity enters into a 99-year lease of land with the intention of constructing a building. The building will be sold together with any remaining lease interest over the land and is, therefore, classified as inventories when construction commences. Because of various required legal permits, construction begins in Year 6 of the lease and is completed in Year 10.

The operating lease expense incurred for the land (as determined in accordance with paragraph 33 of IAS 17 *Leases*) should be included in the cost of inventories. IAS 2:10 states that the cost of inventories should include all costs of "bringing the inventories to their present location and condition". The operating lease expense incurred for the land is required to construct the building and is, therefore, a cost of bringing the building to a condition in which it can be sold. However, only the operating lease expense incurred during the period of construction (i.e. Years 6 to 10 – the period during which the entity undertakes activities that are necessary to prepare the asset

> for intended sale) should be capitalised. All operating lease expense incurred
> outside of this period must be recognised in profit or loss.

3.1.2.3   Allocation of cost to joint products and by-products

Sometimes two products may result from the production process when
joint products are produced or when a product and a by-product are
produced. In such cases, when it is difficult to allocate costs between the
two, a rational and consistent allocation method is chosen. For example,
the cost of joint products may be allocated on the basis of relative sales
values either at the stage in production when each product becomes
identifiable or when production is complete. If an immaterial by-product
results from production of the main product, the net realisable value of the
by-product is often deducted from the cost of the main product. Because
the value of the by-product is immaterial, this deduction does not result in
the cost of the main product being understated. [IAS 2:14]

3.1.3   Other costs

Other costs are included in the cost of inventories only to the extent that
they are incurred in bringing the inventories to their present location and
condition.

IAS 2:16 gives the following as examples of costs that should be excluded
from the cost of inventories and recognised as expenses in the period in
which they are incurred:

- abnormal amounts of wasted materials, labour, or other production
  costs;

- storage costs, unless those costs are necessary in the production
  process before a further production stage;

- administrative overheads that do not contribute to bringing inventories to their present location and condition; and

- selling costs.

Example 3.1.3

**Other costs incurred in bringing inventories to their present location and
condition**

Company A, which redevelops and then sells real estate, purchases a disused
petrol station and obtains planning permission from the local authority to
redevelop the site for residential purposes. Planning permission is granted

---

subject to the condition that Company A will also develop a recreation amenity on an adjacent site owned by the local authority.

Company A should include the costs incurred in developing the adjacent recreation amenity in the cost of its development property inventories. These costs meet the definition of "costs incurred in bringing inventories to their present location and condition" because they were a necessary cost of redeveloping the disused petrol station into a residential site.

Specific attention should be paid to costs of distribution and transportation associated with moving inventories to their present location and condition for sale, which may include the following:

- transportation of goods from the supplier;

- transportation or distribution at an intermediate stage in the production process;

- transportation or distribution of inventories to a temporary storage location (e.g. warehouse), including costs incurred for receiving, marking, processing, picking and repackaging; and

- transportation or distribution of inventories from a warehouse or distribution centre to the initial point of sale.

Costs incurred in transporting an item from a warehouse to its initial point of sale should be capitalised to inventories. However, costs associated with moving inventories from one point of sale to another (e.g. transport of goods between stores) should not be included in the cost of inventories because the goods were already in a condition and location for sale before the move.

3.1.4   Borrowing costs

The extent to which borrowing costs should be included in the cost of inventories is determined on the basis of the requirements of IAS 23 *Borrowing Costs*.

IAS 23 expressly states that "inventories that are manufactured, or otherwise produced, over a short period of time, are not qualifying assets". Only inventories that take a 'substantial' period of time to get ready for their intended sale or use can meet the definition of a qualifying asset (see **section 3.1** of **chapter A18** for a discussion of what should be considered a 'substantial' period of time).

An example of circumstances when it would be appropriate to include borrowing costs in the cost of inventories is when the reporting entity holds maturing inventories (such as whisky). The maturing period is a necessary part of the period of production and borrowing costs incurred during that period are attributable to bringing the product to its existing condition. Such borrowing costs may therefore appropriately be included in the cost of inventories under IAS 2. See **3.4.3** in **chapter A18** for a discussion of the appropriate timing for cessation of capitalisation of borrowing costs incurred in respect of such inventories.

IAS 23 includes an optional scope exemption which allows an entity not to apply that Standard to inventories that are manufactured, or otherwise produced, in large quantities on a repetitive basis. The exemption is optional; therefore, an entity can choose, as a matter of accounting policy, whether to apply the requirements of IAS 23 to borrowing costs that relate to inventories produced in large quantities on a repetitive basis.

3.1.5   Inventories acquired on deferred settlement terms

When an entity acquires inventories on deferred settlement terms, the transaction may involve a financing element (e.g. when there is a difference between the amount paid and the amount that would have been paid if the inventories had been acquired on normal credit terms). In such circumstances, the financing element is not included in the cost of the inventories, but is recognised as an interest expense over the period of the financing. [IAS 2:18]

3.1.6   Inventories invoiced in a foreign currency

When inventories are invoiced in a foreign currency, the cost of those inventories should not include exchange differences.

Although this matter is not addressed directly in the body of IAS 2, the introduction to the Standard states that the capitalisation of such exchange differences is not permitted (see IAS 2:IN10). Prior to the revision of IAS 21 *The Effects of Changes in Foreign Exchange Rates* in 2003, that Standard had permitted the capitalisation of exchange differences in very limited circumstances. That exception to the general rule has been removed from IAS 21.

However, when the purchase of inventories in a foreign currency has been cash flow hedged and the entity has a policy of basis adjusting (see **2.2.3** in **chapter B9** or **2.2.3** in **chapter C9**), then the effective portion of hedging gains and losses previously accumulated in equity can be included in the amount initially recognised for the inventories.

3.1.7   Transfer pricing

When the manufacturing process involves the transfer of work from one department to another, the transfer may be made at a price different from the cost incurred by the transferring department, either for reasons of convenience in accounting or as part of the system of management control. When this occurs, it is necessary for the purpose of determining the cost of closing inventories to adjust the carrying amount to actual cost, by eliminating any profits or losses arising at the separate department levels.

3.1.8   Costs of service providers

To the extent that service providers have inventories, they measure them at the costs of their production. These costs consist mainly of labour and overhead costs related to any parts of service projects for which revenue has not yet been recognised. The bulk of such costs would relate to the labour costs attributable to the personnel performing the work, with other overheads such as costs associated with photocopying and telephoning allocated to each assignment as appropriate. [IAS 2:19]

Prices charged by service providers will generally reflect a profit margin and an allocation for non-attributable overheads. These items will often be allocated to specific service projects in the internal costing system of the service provider. However, IAS 2 specifically prohibits their inclusion in the cost of inventories of service providers for reporting purposes. [IAS 2:19]

3.1.9   Cost of agricultural produce harvested from biological assets

Consistent with IAS 41 *Agriculture*, agricultural produce that an entity has harvested from its biological assets is measured on initial recognition at its fair value less costs to sell at the point of harvest. This is considered the cost of those inventories at that date for application of IAS 2. [IAS 2:20]

3.1.10   Techniques for the measurement of cost

Techniques for the measurement of cost, such as the standard cost method or the retail method, may be used provided that the results approximate to actual cost. [IAS 2:21]

The standard cost method is a method often used by manufacturing entities to allocate fixed and variable production overheads to each item of inventory produced. The standard cost of a unit of production is based on the budgeted amount of fixed production overheads and the normal capacity of the production facilities. Standard costs are revised to take account of variances that arise when actual performance varies from the budgeted figures on which the standard cost was based.

> Standard costs should only be used for year-end inventory valuation purposes if they relate to actual costs incurred during the period. This can be achieved by frequent updating of standards or adjusting for the recorded variances.

The retail method may often be used by retailers who sell a large number of relatively homogeneous items with similar gross profit margins. The cost of inventories is determined by deducting the average margin from the selling price of the inventories. Such average margins take into account any reductions from the original selling price of items due to sales or other promotions. When the retail method is used, average margins are often determined on a departmental basis.

Example 3.1.10

Retail method

	Cost CU'000	Retail price CU'000
Opening inventories	300	400
Purchases	1,000	1,600
Total	1,300	2,000
Sales		(1,500)
Closing inventories at retail value		500

To convert closing inventories at retail value to closing inventories at cost, multiply by the ratio of cost:retail price for the year as follows.

CU1,300,000 / CU2,000,000 = 65%

65% × CU500,000 = CU325,000 = closing value of inventories

This method results in a valuation of inventories that approximates to average price and is, therefore, acceptable subject to certain constraints. The method only works satisfactorily for an entire department or shop if all of the lines held are expected to generate similar profit margins. For example, the inventories of a newsagent and confectioner normally include lines of widely differing profit margins; therefore, to arrive at an acceptable inventory valuation using the retail method, it is necessary to divide the inventories into categories according to the profit margin achieved. A further problem with the retail method arises if the selling price on slow-moving items has been marked down. If the normal gross profit percentage is then deducted from such items, this will result in them being valued below cost, giving a result that may well be excessively prudent and, accordingly, unacceptable. It is, therefore, necessary to ensure that the volume of marked-down items is insignificant or, alternatively, they should be segregated and valued separately.

3.2   Cost formulas

Cost may be assigned to individual items of inventory, depending on their nature, either by the specific identification method or by the use of a cost formula. When the use of the specific identification method is inappropriate, IAS 2 allows a choice between two cost formulas: the weighted average formula and the first-in, first out (FIFO) formula. The use of the last-in, first out (LIFO) formula is prohibited under IAS 2. [IAS 2:IN13]

Although the Standard permits a choice between the weighted average formula and FIFO for those inventories not measured by specific identification, it requires that the same cost formula is used for all inventories having a similar nature and use to the entity. For inventories with a different nature or use, a different cost formula may be justified. [IAS 2:25] Differences of geographical location or of tax rules will not, by themselves, justify the use of different cost formulas. [IAS 2:26]

3.2.1   Specific identification

IAS 2:23 requires that the cost of inventories of items that are not ordinarily interchangeable, and of goods or services produced and segregated for specific projects, should be assigned by using specific identification of their individual costs. The specific identification method entails assigning specific costs to identified items of inventory. Thus, this method is appropriate when items of inventory are produced for specific projects or when other items of inventory held could not be substituted for those items (e.g. antique cars or works of art).

> The specific identification method is not appropriate for the routine production of inventories that are ordinarily interchangeable, because it would allow an entity to influence its reported profits by choosing which specific units to sell – and, hence, which otherwise identical products remain in inventory at the end of the reporting period – based on those products having higher or lower specific costs. Some entities may nevertheless have set up computer systems that allocate specific costs to inventories that are ordinarily interchangeable. Whether the valuations produced by such systems will be acceptable will depend on whether they reasonably approximate those that would have resulted from the use of cost formulas.

3.2.2   Weighted average cost

The weighted average cost formula assigns a value to each item of inventory based on the weighted average of items in inventories at the beginning of the period and the weighted average of items of inventories purchased or produced during the period. Depending on the inventory system of the reporting entity, the weighted average cost is calculated either on a periodic basis or on a perpetual basis as the inventories are received.

Example 3.2.2

Weighted average cost

An entity had opening inventories of 15,000 units at a weighted average cost of CU4 per unit, and made the following purchases during the year:

Date of purchases	Number of units	Cost per unit CU	Total cost CU
1 January	15,000	4.20	63,000
1 April	20,000	4.50	90,000
1 May	25,000	4.10	102,500
1 July	10,000	4.40	44,000
1 October	5,000	4.50	22,500
Total	75,000		322,000

Closing inventories are 20,000 units.

Under the weighted average formula, the number of units in closing inventories is multiplied by the weighted average cost per unit for the year.

	Number of units	Cost per unit CU	Total cost CU
Opening inventories	15,000	4.00	60,000
Date of purchase:			
1 January	15,000	4.20	63,000
1 April	20,000	4.50	90,000
1 May	25,000	4.10	102,500
1 July	10,000	4.40	44,000
1 October	5,000	4.50	22,500
Total	90,000		382,000

The weighted average cost per unit for the year is calculated as follows.

CU382,000 / 90,000 = CU4.24

The value of closing inventories is CU4.24 x 20,000 = CU84,800.

3.2.3   FIFO

The FIFO cost formula assumes that the items of inventory that were purchased or produced first are sold first. Therefore, at the end of the period, the items in inventory are valued using the prices for the most recent purchases.

Example 3.2.3

FIFO

The facts are the same as in **example 3.2.2**.

Under the FIFO formula, the first units held are the first units sold. Therefore, closing inventories are valued at the cost per unit of the latest purchases.

If 20,000 units are on hand at year end, the value of closing inventories is calculated as follows.

Date of purchases	Number of units	Cost per unit CU	Total cost CU
October	5,000	4.50	22,500
July	10,000	4.40	44,000
May	5,000	4.10	20,500
Total	20,000		87,000

Thus, closing inventories are valued at CU87,000.

3.2.4   Changing from one cost formula to another

A reporting entity may decide to change from one cost formula to another (e.g. from the weighted average formula to FIFO) on the basis that the latter is more widely used in its particular industry and will, therefore, enhance comparability. A common question is whether such a change constitutes a change in accounting policy or a change in estimate. It is sometimes argued that it merely represents a change in estimate, in that it is a revision of the method of estimating cost. On balance, however, it seems appropriate to treat this as a change of accounting policy, for the following reasons.

- For inventories that are ordinarily interchangeable, IAS 2:24 states that a specific identification approach is inappropriate. Accordingly, the use of cost formulas is not merely a method of estimating the aggregate actual cost of individual items, because otherwise a specific identification approach would not be inappropriate, but would instead give the best possible estimate. Rather, cost formulas are used to arrive at a different figure that avoids the unacceptable distortions that would occur if a specific identification approach were adopted.

- IAS 2:36(a) requires disclosure of the accounting policies used for measuring inventories "including the cost formula used", which reinforces the view that the cost formula selected is a matter of accounting policy.

Requirements and disclosures relating to changes in accounting policies are discussed in **chapter A5**.

Other changes to the way in which inventories are measured (e.g. any changes to the basis for allocation of overheads or other costs of conversion to inventories) are likely to be changes of estimate rather than matters of accounting policy. Under IAS 8:39, the effect of a change in estimate should be separately disclosed, when material.

3.3   Determination of net realisable value

3.3.1   *Measurement of net realisable value*

IAS 2:6 defines net realisable value as "the estimated selling price in the ordinary course of business less the estimated costs of completion and the estimated costs necessary to make the sale". The net realisable value of an item of inventory may fall below its cost for many reasons, including damage, obsolescence, a decline in selling prices, or an increase in the estimate of costs to complete and market the inventories.

The Standard highlights the distinction between net realisable value (as defined in the previous paragraph) and the fair value of inventory. It explains that fair value reflects:
[IAS 2:7]

- for entities applying IFRS 13 *Fair Value Measurement* (effective for annual periods beginning on or after 1 January 2013, with earlier application permitted), "the price at which an orderly transaction to sell the same inventory in the principal (or most advantageous) market for that inventory would take place between market partici-pants at the measurement date"; and

- for entities that have not yet adopted IFRS 13, "the amount for which the same inventory could be exchanged between knowledgeable and willing buyers and sellers in the marketplace".

Net realisable value is the net amount that an entity expects to realise from the sale of inventories in the ordinary course of business and is, therefore, an entity-specific value. Fair value is not an entity-specific value. The net realisable value of inventories may not equal their fair value less costs to sell. [IAS 2:7] This will occur, for example, when the reporting entity has secured favourable binding sales contracts that have not been affected by more recent adverse market conditions.

Generally, estimates of net realisable value are made on an item-by-item basis. In some circumstances, however, it may be appropriate to group items of similar or related inventories. This may be the case when items of inventory:
[IAS 2:29]

- relate to the same product line and have similar purposes or end uses;

- are produced and marketed in the same geographical area; and

- cannot be practicably evaluated separately from other items in that product line.

Service providers generally accumulate costs for each service for which a separate selling price is charged. Thus, when determining net realisable value, it is appropriate to consider separately each service.

Example 3.3.1A

Determination of the net realisable value of an item of inventory with a long operating cycle

An entity is engaged in the production of an item of inventory with a long operating cycle. Production of the item normally takes six years to complete. Costs are accumulated over time and recognised as inventory. At the end of the second year of production, a further four years of work is required for the inventory item to be completed. No relevant market exists for the inventory in its current state.

IAS 2:30 states that estimates of net realisable value should be based on the most reliable evidence available at the time the estimates are made of the amounts the inventories are expected to realise.

At the end of the second year of production, how should the net realisable value of the inventory item be determined under IAS 2?

When estimating the net realisable value of inventories, management should consider all of the facts relating to the type of inventory and the operating environment at the time the estimates are made.

In the circumstances described, because no relevant market exists for the two-year work in progress, it may be the case that, in order to determine the net realisable value of the inventory at the end of the reporting period, the entity uses as its starting point the current selling price for the inventory in

---

its completed state, deducting expected holding costs (including finance costs), outstanding costs of conversion and costs to sell.

An entity might alternatively use the forward price for sales of the completed inventory in four years' time. When this approach is adopted, the cash flows associated with the net realisable value should be discounted at an appropriate rate to determine an estimate of the net realisable value of the inventory in its present location and condition, consistent with IAS 2:30 and paragraph BCZ4 of IAS 36 *Impairment of Assets*. Consequently, it will be necessary to adjust the forward price for the effect of the time value of money and also for outstanding costs of conversion and costs to sell.

When estimating the net realisable value of inventories, management should consider all of the facts relating to the inventories and the operating environment at the time the estimates are made. Estimates are based on the most reliable evidence available at that time as to the amount that the inventories are likely to realise. These estimates take into consideration fluctuations in price or cost directly relating to events occurring after the reporting period to the extent that such events confirm conditions existing at the end of the reporting period. [IAS 2:30]

Example 3.3.1B

Sales after the reporting period

An item of inventory which cost CU100 is sold after the reporting period for CU80. A sale after the reporting period at a lower price generally provides evidence of the net realisable value of the inventories at the end of the reporting period and the closing inventories should therefore be carried at CU80 less any costs to sell.

However, this will not always be the case. If, for example, further investigation shows that the decrease in sales price arose because of damage to the inventories that occurred after the reporting period, this would indicate that the CU80 sales price did not reflect conditions existing at the end of the reporting period and that the loss in value should not be accounted for until the next period. In these circumstances, it would be necessary to assess whether the item could have been sold undamaged for an amount at or in excess of its cost (CU100) plus any costs to sell. If so, no write-down to net realisable value would be required at the end of the reporting period.

Example 3.3.1C

Decrease in net realisable value after the end of the reporting period for inventories under development

Entity P is a property developer. It is preparing its financial statements for the year ended 31 December 20X0, which will be authorised for issue on 31 March 20X1.

At 31 December 20X0, Entity P holds a property as development work in progress. Costs incurred to date are CU20 million. Estimated costs to complete are CU10 million (therefore, total costs will be CU30 million). Completion and sale of the development are expected within 18 to 24 months.

Entity P estimates net realisable value for development work in progress based on the projected sales price for the property when it is complete, discounted back to current value. Based on market information on sales prices for similar, finished properties at 31 December 20X0, net realisable value is estimated at CU32 million (implying a net development profit of CU2 million).

However, property prices in the relevant market are falling. At 31 March 20X1 (date of authorisation of financial statements), the observed sales prices for similar, finished properties have declined to CU27 million (implying a net development loss of CU3 million). Estimated costs to complete (and other applicable factors) are unchanged since year end.

Should Entity P recognise an inventory write-down in its 31 December 20X0 financial statements?

Yes. The development property is not available for sale at the year end. IAS 2:30 acknowledges that "fluctuations of price or cost directly relating to events occurring after the end of the period" are relevant to estimates of net realisable value "to the extent that such events confirm conditions existing at the end of the period". Because Entity P estimates net realisable value based on projected sales prices of completed property, discounted back to current value, information received after the end of the reporting period (including revised sales price estimates) provides further evidence as to conditions that existed at the end of the reporting period, unless the changes in sales prices clearly relate to a separate event subsequent to the period end.

When estimating the net realisable value of inventories, the purpose for which the inventories are held is taken into consideration. For example, if the inventories are held to satisfy firm sales contracts, the sales prices agreed in those contracts form the basis of the estimation. If the sales contracts are for less than the inventory quantities held, the net realisable value of the excess is based on general selling prices. [IAS 2:31]

3.3.2   Writing inventories down to net realisable value

When the net realisable value of an item of inventory is less than its cost, the excess is written off immediately in profit or loss.

Items of inventory are generally written down on an item-by-item basis. IAS 2 indicates that it is generally inappropriate to write down entire classifications of inventories, such as finished goods, or all of the inventories in a particular operating segment. [IAS 2:29]

Materials and other supplies held for use in the production of inventories are not written down below cost if the finished products in which they will be incorporated are expected to be sold at or above cost. However, when a decline in the price of materials indicates that the cost of the finished products will exceed net realisable value, the materials are written down to net realisable value. In such circumstances, the replacement cost of the materials may be the best available measure of their net realisable value. [IAS 2:32]

The costs necessary to make the sale should be determined in a manner consistent with the definition of 'costs of disposal' in IAS 36, which states that these are "incremental costs directly attributable to the disposal of an asset, excluding finance costs and income tax expense". An incremental cost is one that would not be incurred if the activity was not undertaken. General overheads, therefore, may not be allocated for the purposes of determining costs to sell. Direct transaction costs must be allocated for the purposes of determining costs to sell.

3.3.3   Reversals of write-downs

Net realisable value estimates are made at the end of each reporting period. When subsequent evaluations show that the circumstances that previously caused inventories to be written down below cost no longer exist, or when there is clear evidence of an increase in net realisable value because of changed economic circumstances, write-downs of inventories previously recognised are required to be reversed. [IAS 2:33] This occurs, for example, when an item of inventory that is carried at net realisable value because its selling price had declined is still on hand in a subsequent period and its selling price has increased (though it would still be necessary, if the item had been on hand for a long time, to consider whether there might be obsolescence issues).

The amount of the write-down should be reversed through profit or loss so that the new carrying amount is the lower of the cost and the revised net realisable value. Therefore, the amount of the reversal is limited to the amount of the original write-down.

Example 3.3.3

Increase in net realisable value for inventories acquired in an exchange transaction

Company A exchanges inventories with Company B. IAS 18:12 states that "[w]hen goods or services are exchanged or swapped for goods or services which are of a similar nature and value, the exchange is not regarded as a transaction which generates revenue". IAS 18 includes no further guidance on when goods or services should be considered 'similar' and that determination will be a matter of judgement. The directors of Company A have judged the inventories exchanged to be similar (but not identical) and, consequently, no revenue is recognised on the transaction.

Company A originally purchased the inventories it exchanges for CU50. Prior to the exchange with Company B, the inventories were written down to their net realisable value of CU40. Both Company A's inventories and the inventories acquired from Company B in the exchange have a fair value at the date of exchange of CU40.

If the net realisable value of the inventories were to subsequently increase to CU50, would it be acceptable for Company A to recognise in profit or loss a reversal of the CU10 write-down previously recognised?

No, because the inventories acquired from Company B are similar, but not identical, to the inventories originally held by Company A and, consequently, CU40 represents the cost of the inventories to Company A of the inventories acquired from Company B.

While IAS 18:12 states that an exchange of similar goods such as in the circumstances described "is not a transaction which gives rise to revenue", an exchange transaction with commercial substance has nevertheless occurred. Accordingly, the inventories originally held by Company A should be derecognised and the inventories acquired from Company B should be recognised. The acquired inventories should be initially recognised at their cost to Company A, which is CU40. If the net realisable value of the inventories subsequently increases, there can be no reversal of the write-down to net realisable value previously recognised.

In contrast, if the inventories acquired from Company B were determined to be identical to those originally held by Company A, then the exchange would lack commercial substance. In such circumstances, no accounting transaction would be recognised and the acquired inventories would 'inherit' the previous carrying amounts of the inventories originally held by Company A – including any valuation allowance. As a result, if the net realisable value of the inventories were to increase following the exchange with Company B, the write-down to net realisable value previously recognised by Company A would be reversed.

Example 2A provides an example of an exchange of identical goods.

3.4   Recognition as an expense

The amount of inventories recognised as an expense in the period will generally be:
[IAS 2:34]

- the carrying amount of inventories sold in the period; and

- the amount of any write-down of inventories to net realisable value and all losses of inventories in the period; less

- the amount of any reversal in the period of any write-down of inventories, arising from an increase in net realisable value.

If inventories are used by the entity rather than being sold, their cost may be capitalised as part of the cost of another asset (e.g. property, plant and equipment). Their cost is then recognised as an expense through depreciation of that asset.

4   Presentation and disclosure

4.1   Presentation

IAS 1:54 requires that, when material, the total carrying amount of inventories (other than those included in disposal groups that are classified as held for sale – see **chapter A20**) should be presented as a separate item in the statement of financial position. The analysis of items between current and non-current is discussed at **4.1** in **chapter A4**.

4.2   Disclosure

4.2.1   Accounting policies

IAS 2:36(a) requires that financial statements should disclose the accounting policies adopted in measuring inventories, including the cost formula used.

The description of the accounting policies should be succinct, while making clear to the reader which of the different policies permissible under IAS 2 have been adopted.

4.2.2   *Analysis of carrying amount*

IAS 2:36(b) requires the total carrying amount of inventories to be disclosed, together with an analysis of the carrying amount in a manner appropriate to the entity.

Common classifications of inventories are as follows:

- merchandise;

- production supplies;

- materials;

- work in progress; and

- finished goods.

Entities in specialist industries should use a classification that is meaningful in the context of their operations; for example, property development entities could analyse their development portfolio as:

- land held for development;

- properties under construction; and

- completed properties held for sale.

The inventories of a service provider may simply be described as work in progress.

4.2.3   *Expected realisation*

IAS 1:61 requires that an entity should disclose for each asset that combines amounts expected to be recovered both within twelve months of and after twelve months from the end of the reporting period, the amount expected to be recovered after more than twelve months. It is appropriate for an entity to disclose the amount of inventories expected to be recovered after more than one year from the end of the reporting period. [IAS 1:65]

4.2.4   *Inventories carried at fair value less costs to sell*

IAS 2:36(c) requires separate disclosure of the carrying amount of inventories carried at fair value less costs to sell.

As discussed in **section 2**, this requirement should in practice apply only to certain inventories held by commodity broker-traders. (As explained in **chapter A20**, when inventories are classified as held for sale as part of a disposal group, they continue to be measured in accordance with IAS 2. The disposal group itself may then be written down to fair value less costs to sell, but not the inventories per se.)

4.2.5   Amounts recognised in profit or loss

The Standard requires separate disclosure of:

- the amount of inventories recognised as an expense during the period; [IAS 2:36(d)]

- the amount of any write-down of inventories to net realisable value recognised as an expense in the period; [IAS 2:36(e)] and

- the amount of any reversal of any write-down recognised as a reduction in the inventories expense for the period. [IAS 2:36(f)]

In addition, disclosure is required of the circumstances or events that led to any recognised reversal of a write-down of inventories. [IAS 2:36(g)]

IAS 2:38 specifies that the amount of inventories recognised as an expense during the period, which is commonly described as cost of sales, consists of:

- the costs that have previously been included in the measurement of inventories that have now been sold;

- unallocated production overheads; and

- abnormal amounts of production costs of inventories.

4.2.6   Inventories pledged as security

IAS 2:36(h) requires entities to disclose the carrying amount of inventories pledged as security for liabilities.

A12 Provisions, contingent liabilities and contingent assets

Contents

1   Introduction

IAS 37 *Provisions, Contingent Liabilities and Contingent Assets* deals with the appropriate recognition criteria, measurement bases and the disclosure requirements applied to provisions, contingent liabilities and contingent assets. It was most recently amended in October 2010.

IFRIC 21 *Levies* was issued in May 2013 and provides guidance on when to recognise a liability for a levy imposed by a government, both for levies that are accounted for in accordance with IAS 37 and those for which the timing and amount of the levy is certain (see **section 9.4** for details). IFRIC 21 is effective for annual periods beginning on or after 1 January 2014, with earlier application permitted.

2   Scope

The requirements of IAS 37 apply to all provisions, contingent liabilities and contingent assets other than those:
[IAS 37:1]

- resulting from executory contracts, except when the contract is onerous; and

- covered by another Standard.

Unlike IAS 16 *Property, Plant and Equipment* (see **section 2** of **chapter A7**), IAS 37 does not include a scope exclusion for the extractive industries. Therefore, the requirements of IAS 37 should be applied and liabilities recognised for restoration costs, for example, when the recognition and measurement criteria are met. Refer to Examples 2A, 2B and 3 in Section C of the implementation guidance accompanying IAS 37 for illustrations of the application of IAS 37 to the extractive industries (see **section 8** below).

When a provision meets the definition of a financial instrument in IAS 32 *Financial Instruments: Presentation*, but is accounted for under IAS 37 because it is not within the scope of IFRS 9 *Financial Instruments* (or, prior to the adoption of IFRS 9, IAS 39 *Financial Instruments: Recognition and Measurement*), the disclosure requirements of IFRS 7 *Financial Instruments: Disclosures* apply in addition to those of IAS 37.

2.1 Executory contracts

Executory contracts are contracts under which neither party has performed any of its obligations, or both parties have partially performed their obligations to an equal extent. [IAS 37:3] Executory contracts do not fall within the scope of IAS 37 unless they are onerous (see **3.9.2** below).

Examples of executory contracts include:

- employee contracts in respect of continuing employment;

- contracts for future delivery of services such as gas and electricity;

- obligations to pay local authority charges and similar levies; and

- most purchase orders.

Example 2.1

Executory contract

On 1 January 20X0, Company A enters into a contract with Company B for the manufacture and delivery of 100 units of component Q at five different dates in the future, i.e. 500 units are to be delivered in total. Payment is due on delivery of the units.

On 1 January 20X0, the contract between Company A and Company B is executory because neither party has performed any of its obligations; Company B has not manufactured or delivered any of the units, nor has Company A paid for any of them.

By 1 March 20X0, Company B has produced and delivered 200 of the units and Company A has paid in full for those 200 units. At this date, the contract between Company A and Company B continues to be executory because both parties have partially performed their obligations to an equal extent.

By 1 June 20X0, Company B has produced and delivered the full 500 units, but Company A has only paid for 400 units in total. The contract between Company A and Company B no longer meets the definition of an executory contract because the two parties have not performed under the terms of the contract to an equal extent. Company A is required to recognise a liability for the final 100 units of component Q for which it has not yet paid.

2.2   Provisions, contingent liabilities and contingent assets covered by other Standards

When another Standard deals with a specific type of provision, contingent liability or contingent asset, the more specific Standard should be applied, as follows:
[IAS 37:5]

- provisions relating to construction contracts are dealt with under IAS 11 *Construction Contracts* (see **chapter A34**);

- provisions relating to income taxes are dealt with under IAS 12 *Income Taxes* (see **chapter A13**);

- provisions relating to leases generally fall within the scope of IAS 17 *Leases* (see **chapter A17**). However, because IAS 17 contains no specific requirements to deal with operating leases that have become onerous, IAS 37 applies to such onerous contracts;

- provisions relating to employee benefits are dealt with under IAS 19 *Employee Benefits* (see **chapter A15** and **appendix A3**); and

- provisions relating to insurance contracts are dealt with under IFRS 4 *Insurance Contracts* (see **chapter A39**). However, IAS 37 applies to provisions, contingent liabilities and contingent assets of an insurer other than those arising from its contractual obligations and rights under insurance contracts within the scope of IFRS 4.

> In addition, the acquirer's treatment of contingent liabilities assumed in a business combination is addressed by IFRS 3 *Business Combinations* (see **chapter A25**).

IAS 37 *does* apply to provisions for restructurings (including discontinued operations). When a restructuring meets the definition of a discontinued operation, additional disclosures may be required by IFRS 5 *Non-current Assets Held for Sale and Discontinued Operations* (see **chapter A20**). [IAS 37:9]

2.3   Financial instruments

IAS 37 does not apply to financial instruments (including guarantees) that fall within the scope of IFRS 9 or, prior to the adoption of IFRS 9, IAS 39 (see **chapter B1** and **chapter C1**, respectively). [IAS 37:2]

Financial guarantee contracts are not within the scope of IAS 37. They are within the scope of IFRS 9 (or, prior to the adoption of IFRS 9, IAS 39), except in certain limited circumstances when the issuer may instead elect to apply IFRS 4 (see the discussion at **2.3.2** in **chapter B1** or 2.3.2 in **chapter C1**).

Example 2.3

Liability with payment linked to future sales

Entity A faces a claim for an alleged infringement of intellectual property (IP) rights. On 31 December 20X1, in settlement of the claim, Entity A agrees to pay the claimant a fixed sum plus a variable amount calculated as 1 per cent of any revenue generated by Entity A over the next five years from sales of a specified product.

At 31 December 20X1, Entity A must consider whether to recognise a liability for the obligation to pay a variable amount on the basis of future sales. This will depend on whether the variable amount to be paid based on future sales represents a settlement for use of the IP in the past or compensation for the future use by Entity A of the underlying IP:

- if the sales-linked feature is a mechanism for determining the amount due for past use by Entity A of the IP (plus any compensatory or punitive element), Entity A should recognise a liability under IFRS 9 or IAS 39 at 31 December 20X1; whereas

- if the sales-linked payments relate to future use by Entity A of the underlying IP, the obligation arises as new sales are realised and represents an executory contract under IAS 37. In such circumstances, Entity A should not recognise a liability for the variable amount to be paid based on future sales at 31 December 20X1, unless the executory contract is determined to be onerous.

In practice, situations in which entities would recognise immediately a liability for the variable amount to be paid on the basis of future sales are expected to be rare.

2.4   Use of the term 'provision'

The use of the term 'provision' is restricted to liabilities of uncertain timing or amount. It does not cover adjustments to the carrying amounts of assets (such as depreciation, impairment and allowances for doubtful debts) for which the term 'provision' is used in some jurisdictions. [IAS 37:7]

2.5   Related income and expenditure

Although some amounts treated as provisions may relate to the recognition of revenue (e.g. when an entity gives guarantees in exchange for a fee), IAS 37 does not deal with revenue recognition. IAS 18 *Revenue* identifies the circumstances in which revenue is recognised and provides practical guidance on the application of the recognition criteria (see **chapter A14**). [IAS 37:6]

IAS 37 does not specify whether expenditure should be capitalised as an asset or treated as an expense. These issues are addressed in other Standards. Therefore, IAS 37 itself neither prohibits nor requires capitalisation of the costs recognised when a provision is made. [IAS 37:8]

3   Definition and recognition of provisions, contingent liabilities and contingent assets

3.1   Provisions

IAS 37 defines a provision as a liability of uncertain timing or amount, i.e. a subset of liabilities. [IAS 37:10] The Standard repeats the definition of a liability found in the *Conceptual Framework for Financial Reporting*, i.e. a present obligation of the entity arising from past events, the settlement of which is expected to result in an outflow from the entity of resources embodying economic benefits. [IAS 37:10]

A provision should be recognised when and only when:
[IAS 37:14]

* an entity has a present obligation (legal or constructive) as a result of a past event;

* it is probable that an outflow of resources embodying economic benefits will be required to settle the obligation; and

* a reliable estimate can be made of the amount of the obligation.

These recognition criteria cover two elements: the existence of a liability and the measurement of that liability.

Provision = | Liability | + | Ability to measure |

The existence element is further subdivided into two conditions.

	Liability				
Provision =	Present obligation from past event	+	Outflow is probable	+	Ability to measure

3.2   Contingent liabilities

A contingent liability is defined as:
[IAS 37:10]

- a possible obligation that arises from past events and whose existence will be confirmed only by the occurrence or non-occurrence of one or more uncertain future events not wholly within the control of the entity; or

- a present obligation that arises from past events that is not recognised because:

  - it is not probable that an outflow of resources embodying economic benefits will be required to settle the obligation; or

  - the amount of the obligation cannot be measured with sufficient reliability.

Under IAS 37, a reporting entity should not recognise a contingent liability in its statement of financial position. [IAS 37:27]

Therefore, a contingent liability, which is not recognised but is disclosed by way of note, results when one or more of the three recognition criteria for a provision, as outlined at **3.1** above, is not met.

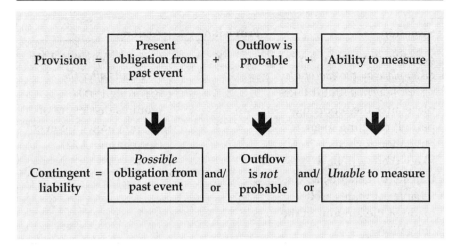

The table below illustrates the application of the recognition criteria.

Situation	Provision?	Action
Past event has occurred, resulting in a *possible* obligation for which a transfer of benefits is possible but not probable (see **3.6** below).	✗	Unless the possibility of a transfer of benefits is remote, disclose a contingent liability.
Past event has occurred, resulting in a present obligation for which there may *possibly* be a transfer of benefits, but for which there probably will not.	✗	Unless the possibility of a transfer of benefits is remote, disclose a contingent liability.
Past event has occurred, resulting in a present obligation for which it is likely there will be a transfer of benefits, but a *reliable estimate cannot be made* of the amount of the obligation.	✗	Disclose a contingent liability. (N.B. This situation is likely to be very rare – see **3.8** below).
Past event has occurred, resulting in a present obligation for which it is likely there will be a transfer of benefits; a reliable estimate can be made of the amount of the obligation.	✔	Recognise provision and make necessary disclosures.

Situation	Provision?	Action
An obligating event *has not taken place by the end of the reporting period,* but it takes place after the reporting period, resulting in an obligation for which it is likely there will be a transfer of benefits; a reliable estimate can be made of the amount of the obligation.	✗	Consider whether IAS 10 *Events after the Reporting Period* requires disclosure of the non-adjusting event (see **chapter A22**).

3.3   Contingent assets

A contingent asset is defined as a possible asset that arises from past events and whose existence will be confirmed only by the occurrence or non-occurrence of one or more uncertain future events not wholly within the control of the entity. [IAS 37:10]

Contingent assets are not recognised, but are disclosed by way of note when an inflow of economic benefits is probable. When the realisation of income is virtually certain, however, the related asset is not a contingent asset and its recognition is appropriate. [IAS 37:33]

3.4   Distinguishing provisions from other liabilities

Provisions can be distinguished from other types of liability, including those that involve uncertain amounts, by considering the events that give rise to the obligation and also the degree of uncertainty as to the amount of the liability. In each case, the definition of a liability will be met through the existence of a present obligation arising from a past event.

For example, trade payables are liabilities to pay for goods/services already received/supplied and which have been invoiced or otherwise agreed with the supplier. Accruals, on the other hand, are liabilities to pay for goods/services already received/supplied but which have not been invoiced or otherwise agreed with the supplier. Although it is sometimes necessary to estimate the amount or timing of accruals, the uncertainty is generally much less than for provisions. Accruals are often reported as part of trade and other payables, whereas provisions are reported separately. [IAS 37:11]

Example	Classification	Degree of uncertainty
Goods or services received and invoiced	Trade payable	None
Goods or services received, but not invoiced	Accrual	Some
Legal claim from supplier for breach of exclusive supply agreement	Provision (if conditions met)	Significant

Amounts recognised as provisions will often relate to items such as legal claims, warranties given in respect of goods sold or services provided, restructurings and decommissioning obligations.

3.5   Present obligations and past events

As will be clear from the table set out at **3.2** above, the existence of a present obligation arising from a past obligating event is a key consideration when determining whether classification as a provision or as a contingent liability is appropriate.

As defined in IAS 37:10, an obligating event is an event that creates a legal or constructive obligation that results in an entity having no realistic alternative to settling that obligation. A legal obligation derives either from the terms of a contract (either explicit or implicit), or legislation or other operation of the law. A constructive obligation is an obligation deriving from an entity's actions when:

- by an established pattern of past practice, published policies or a sufficiently specific current statement, the entity has indicated to other parties that it will accept certain responsibilities; and

- as a result, the entity has created a valid expectation on the part of those other parties that it will discharge those responsibilities.

3.5.1   *Events before the end of the reporting period*

Financial statements deal with the financial position of an entity at the end of its reporting period and not its possible position in the future. The only liabilities recognised in an entity's statement of financial position are those that exist at the end of the reporting period. Therefore, no provision is recognised for costs that need to be incurred to operate in the future, notwithstanding that such costs may be necessary to continue as a going concern. [IAS 37:18]

Accordingly, if an obligation exists at the end of the reporting period, that obligation will exist irrespective of whether the reporting entity continues to trade after the end of the reporting period. Conversely, any outflow that can be avoided by ceasing to trade will not be an obligation at the end of the reporting period.

A reporting entity may be aware of some future commitment to spend money, and may even feel less well off at the prospect of the expense. But future expenditure, however necessary, does not justify the recognition of a provision unless a liability exists at the end of the reporting period.

3.5.2 Future actions

It is only those obligations arising from past events that exist independently of the reporting entity's future actions that are recognised as provisions. [IAS 37:19] One example in which a provision is recognised might be for clean-up costs relating to environmental damage. Even if the entity changes its future business activities (at an extreme, by ceasing to trade), it will still incur the expenses relating to cleaning up, because of its past activities.

This can be contrasted with the circumstances in which ships and aircraft are required to undergo major work at regular intervals due to maritime and aviation law. No present obligation is created by the legal requirement to do the major work until the requisite number of hours or days have been completed. The cost of the major work is not recognised because, at the end of the reporting period, no obligation to undertake such major work exists independently of the entity's future actions — the entity could avoid the future expenditure by its future actions, for example by selling the ship or aircraft (see also **example 8.1**).

3.5.3   Role of third parties

An obligation always involves a commitment to another party. It is not necessary, however, to know the identity of the party to whom the obligation is owed – the obligation may be to the public at large. [IAS 37:20]

3.5.4   Management decisions

It is because of the requirement for a clear commitment to another party, referred to in **3.5.3**, that a decision made by management before the end of the reporting period does not of itself give rise to a present obligation, unless it is communicated to those affected by it in a sufficiently specific manner to raise a valid expectation in them that the entity will discharge its responsibilities. [IAS 37:20]

3.5.5   New legislation

It is possible that an event may not give rise to an obligation immediately, but may do so at a later date. This could be as a result of changes in the law or because an act (e.g. a sufficiently specific public statement) by the entity gives rise to a constructive obligation. For example, when an entity causes environmental damage, this may not give rise to an obligation for remedial costs if there is no applicable legislation. The causing of the damage will become an obligating event at a later date, however, if a new law requires the existing damage to be rectified or if the entity publicly accepts responsibility for rectification in a way that creates a constructive obligation. [IAS 37:21]

When details of new legislation have yet to be finalised, an obligation arises only when the legislation is virtually certain to be enacted as drafted. Under IAS 37, such an obligation is treated as a legal obligation. In many cases, however, it will be impossible to be virtually certain of the enactment of a law until it is actually enacted. [IAS 37:22]

3.5.6   Smoothing of results

IAS 37 seeks to prevent artificial 'smoothing' of results. By basing the recognition of a provision on the existence of a present obligation, it rules out the recognition of any provision made simply to allocate expenses over more than one period or otherwise to smooth the results reported. For example, entities are not permitted to provide on an annual basis for items such as future repairs to assets, so as to produce a reasonably level charge each year. Unless dealt with through a component approach to depreciation (see **chapter A7**), such costs will instead generally be recognised in profit or loss when they are actually incurred, i.e. when the work is done. (Repairs and maintenance obligations under leases are discussed at **8.1**.)

3.6   Situations of uncertainty regarding present obligations

IAS 37:15 states that there will, on rare occasions, be circumstances when it is unclear whether a present obligation exists. In order to determine whether a present obligation exists under such circumstances (e.g. when the facts in a lawsuit are disputed), the Standard advises that account should be taken of all available evidence. Such evidence may include, for example, the opinion of experts. It will also include additional evidence contributed by events occurring after the reporting period. Preparers of financial statements should look at all of the available evidence and come to a reasoned judgement as to whether it is more likely than not that a present obligation exists. If it is more likely than not that a present obligation exists, a provision should be recognised. Otherwise, a contingent liability is disclosed, unless the possibility of any transfer of economic benefits in settlement is remote. [IAS 37:16]

3.7   Transfer of economic benefits

An essential element of the definition of a liability is the existence of an obligation to transfer economic benefits. Recognition of a provision is conditional on the transfer of economic benefits being 'probable'. For the purpose of IAS 37, probable is taken to mean more likely than not to occur. [IAS 37:23]

Thus, 'more likely than not' means that the probability that a transfer of economic benefits will occur is more than 50 per cent.

When a number of similar obligations exist (e.g. product warranties), the overall probability that a transfer of economic benefits will be made is determined by looking at the class of obligations as a whole. A typical situation will be that, despite the likelihood of an outflow of resources for any one item being small, it may well be probable that a transfer of some economic benefits will be needed to settle the class of obligations as a whole. When this is the case, assuming that the other recognition criteria are met, a provision is recognised (see **4.2** below). [IAS 37:24]

3.8   Reliable estimate

The use of estimates is an inherent part of preparing financial statements. Provisions are clearly uncertain by nature, but IAS 37 emphasises that it should not be impossible to determine a range of possible outcomes and, from this range, to reach an appropriate conclusion that is sufficiently reliable for the provision to be recognised. IAS 37:26 concludes that the circumstances in which it will not be possible to reach a reliable estimate will be extremely rare. In those extremely rare circumstances, a liability exists that cannot be recognised. That liability will instead be disclosed as a contingent liability.

3.9   Specific applications of recognition criteria

3.9.1   Future operating losses

IAS 37 sets out two prohibitions on the recognition of provisions for future operating losses:

- a general prohibition, on the grounds that there is no present obligation and thus no liability (albeit that the expectation of future operating losses may indicate a need to test whether assets have been impaired); [IAS 37:63 – 65] and

- a specific prohibition in respect of future operating losses up to the date of a restructuring – again on grounds that there is no present obligation, unless the losses relate to an onerous contract (see **3.9.2** below). [IAS 37:82]

In both circumstances, future operating losses relate to an activity that will continue, albeit in a restructured form, and are presumed to be avoidable (e.g. by an immediate closure of the loss-making activities). They are, therefore, appropriately recognised as the activity occurs.

3.9.2   Onerous contracts

A provision should be recognised for the present obligation arising under an onerous contract. [IAS 37:66] When assets dedicated to a contract are involved, however, a separate provision is recognised only after any impairment loss has been recognised in respect of those assets. [IAS 37:69]

An onerous contract is defined in IAS 37:10 as a contract in which the unavoidable costs of meeting the obligations under the contract exceed the economic benefits expected to be received under it. In other words, a provision should be recognised for any unavoidable net loss arising from the contract. The unavoidable costs under a contract reflect the least net cost of exiting from the contract, i.e. the lower of:
[IAS 37:68]

- the cost of fulfilling the contract; and

- any compensation or penalties arising from failure to fulfil the contract.

It is not appropriate to test for an onerous contract only by comparing the value of the goods or services to be received or provided with the amount to be paid or received. A mere fall in price does not necessarily mean that a contract is onerous. Instead, the test of whether a contract is onerous focuses on how the goods or services that are the subject of the contract will be used within the business.

Depending on the facts and circumstances, a contract may or may not relate to a cash-generating unit (CGU) and this will affect the determination as to whether the contract is onerous. For example, a vacant leasehold property is not part of any CGU of a lessee because it is not being used in the business. Accordingly, the assessment as to whether the lease contract is onerous will be carried out by comparing the cash flows to be generated through sub-letting with those to be paid out as rent. When the forecast cash outflows exceed the forecast cash inflows, a provision should be recognised at the lower of the net rent payable (i.e. rent payable net of forecast rental income) and any penalty payable for early termination of the lease.

In contrast, a contract to buy goods or services that will be used by a CGU is directly related to that CGU. Such a contract will be assessed as onerous if the cost of the items purchased causes the CGU to report a loss or increases the loss to be reported by the CGU.

It does not necessarily follow that a CGU reporting a loss has an onerous contract or contracts. Rather, it will always be necessary to consider individual contracts to assess whether the unavoidable costs of meeting the obligations under any contract exceed the economic benefits expected to be received under it. Onerous contracts may arise when an entity prepares financial statements on a basis other than that of a going concern. In those circumstances, contracts that would not normally be onerous (e.g. employee contracts) may become onerous (see **2.5** in **chapter A4** for further guidance).

Long-term contracts for the supply of goods or services when costs have risen or current market prices have fallen may be onerous and, if so, a provision is recognised to the extent that future supplies must be made at a loss. No provision is recognised under a contract for the supply of goods which is profitable but at a reduced margin compared to other contracts, because there is no probable net transfer of economic benefits by the reporting entity.

Example 3.9.2A

Recognition and measurement of onerous contracts

Entity A has entered into a contract with Entity B to supply goods for a fixed price of CU100. Because of price inflation, Entity A's expenditure to meet its obligations under the contract is expected to be CU120. No other benefits are expected under the contract. Therefore, the contract is considered to be onerous, and a provision should be recognised. Entity A estimates that any compensation or penalties arising from failure to fulfil the contract are equal to the cost of fulfilling the contract (i.e. CU120).

At the end of the reporting period, Entity A has commenced negotiations with Entity B with a view to increasing the price at which the goods are supplied under the contract. Entity A expects that Entity B will be willing to agree to such a price increase so as to avoid Entity A ceasing to trade as a result of the losses incurred under the contract (and, consequently, cutting off the source of supply of goods necessary for Entity B's own business).

Should the potential renegotiation of the supply contract between Entity A and Entity B be reflected in the amount of provision recognised for the onerous contract?

No. The onerous contract should be measured based on the contractual terms in existence at the end of the reporting period because that is Entity A's 'present obligation' required to be recognised and measured in accordance with IAS 37:66. Any future amendment to the terms of the contract would be a change in the obligation resulting in remeasurement of the provision when the amendment occurs.

As discussed in **4.5** below, IAS 37:48 states that "future events that may affect the amount required to settle an obligation shall be reflected in the amount of a provision where there is sufficient objective evidence that they will occur". However, this reference to future events is not to changes in the underlying obligation, but to those future events that are factors in estimating the costs of meeting a present obligation (e.g. developments in the technology used to clean up a site – see **4.5.1** below) or in assessing the extent to which a present contractual obligation is onerous (e.g. an expectation of subleasing a vacant property – see **example 3.9.2B**).

Should the provision recognised by Entity A be the entire cost of fulfilling the contract (CU120) or only the expected loss (CU20)?

Entity A should recognise a provision for the onerous contract equal to the expected loss of CU20.

IAS 37:10 defines an onerous contract as "a contract in which the unavoidable costs of meeting the obligations under the contract exceed the economic benefits expected to be received under it". IAS 37:68 further states that "[t]he unavoidable costs under a contract reflect the least net cost of exiting from the contract, which is the lower of the cost of fulfilling it and any compensation or penalties arising from failure to fulfil it" (emphasis added).

Because IAS 37 refers to the net cost rather than the gross cost associated with the contract, the provision for the onerous contract should reflect the costs required to fulfil the contract net of any income that the entity will receive as a consequence of fulfilling the contract.

Example 3.9.2B

Vacant property

Company X has an operating lease over a property which it entered into several years ago. The property is now surplus to requirements and Company X has vacated it. The lease has three years to run with an associated expense of CU10,000 per year.

Company X believes it may be able to find a tenant to take a sublease of the property but that it might only receive CU8,000 per year from the sublease. Alternatively, the landlord is prepared to terminate the lease, and forgive the future rentals of CU30,000, if Company X makes a termination payment of CU5,500.

Because the property has been vacated, and the continuing rentals are not expected to be recoverable from subleasing the property, a provision should be recognised. The provision should represent the best estimate of the expenditure required to settle the obligation at the end of the reporting period. If Company X subleases the property, it expects to pay CU30,000 in lease rentals and receive CU24,000 in sublease rentals, which would leave a deficit of CU6,000 to be provided. However, in this case, the amount the landlord would accept to terminate the lease is CU5,500, which is lower. Accordingly, Company X should recognise an onerous lease provision of CU5,500, irrespective of whether it intends to terminate the lease or enter into a sublease.

(For simplicity, this example ignores the time value of money. If the effect of discounting is material, the future rental payments and receipts are discounted to their present value. If the net present value of future rental payments less receipts is less than CU5,500, provision is made for that lower amount. Present value calculations are discussed at **4.7**.)

Examples of contracts that do not meet the criteria for recognition of a provision are:

- those routine purchase orders, and similar contracts, which realistically could be cancelled by agreement with the vendor without paying compensation; and

- purchase orders when the future benefits from use of the asset exceed its cost, notwithstanding that compensation must be paid if the order is cancelled.

Executory contracts (i.e. contracts under which neither party has performed any of its obligations or both parties have performed their obligations to an equal extent) that are not onerous are excluded from the scope of IAS 37 (see **2.1**).

> With the exception of onerous contracts, therefore, an entity will recognise no liability in respect of the purchase of goods or services until those goods or services are supplied, notwithstanding that the entity may become committed to paying for them at an earlier date.

3.9.3   Restructuring provisions

IAS 37 provides specific guidance on how the general recognition criteria for provisions should be applied to restructurings.

3.9.3.1   Definition of a restructuring

A restructuring is defined as a programme that is planned and controlled by management, and materially changes either:
[IAS 37:10]

- the scope of a business undertaken by an entity; or

- the manner in which that business is conducted.

The term 'restructuring' therefore includes events such as:
[IAS 37:70]

- the sale or termination of a line of business;

- the closure of business locations in a country or region or the relocation of business activities from one country or region to another;

- changes in management structure (e.g. the elimination of a layer of management); and

- fundamental reorganisations that have a material effect on the nature and focus of the entity's operations.

3.9.3.2   Specific recognition criteria for restructuring provisions

The two principal requirements for the recognition of a provision for a restructuring are that the entity:
[IAS 37:72]

- has a detailed formal plan; and

- has raised a valid expectation in those affected that the plan will be carried out by starting to implement that plan or by announcing its main features to those affected by it.

The detailed formal plan must identify:
[IAS 37:72]

- the business or part of a business concerned;

- the principal locations affected;

- the location, function and approximate number of employees who will be compensated for terminating their services;

> Generally, it is not necessary for the plan to be so detailed that it identifies which individual employees will be leaving. However, it must be sufficiently detailed that those employees in the employee groups affected by the restructuring plan have a valid expectation that either they or their colleagues in the group will be affected.

- the expenditures that will be undertaken; and

- when the plan will be implemented.

Suitable evidence that an entity has started to implement a restructuring plan will, for example, be provided by:
[IAS 37:73]

- dismantling plant; or

- selling assets; or

- the public announcement of the main features of the plan.

Note, however, that a public announcement of a detailed plan to restructure constitutes a constructive obligation to restructure only if it is made in such a way and in sufficient detail (i.e. setting out the main features of the plan) that it gives rise to valid expectations in other parties such as customers, suppliers and employees (or their representatives) that the entity will carry out the restructuring. [IAS 37:73] Accordingly, for a plan to be sufficient to give rise to a constructive obligation when it is communicated to those affected by it, implementation of the plan should be planned to begin as soon as possible and to be completed within a timeframe that makes significant change to the plan unlikely. When either there is a long delay before commencement, or execution of the plan will take an unreasonably long time, the timeframe allows opportunities for the plan to be changed. Thus, it is unlikely that the reporting entity has raised a valid expectation that it is sufficiently committed to the restructuring. [IAS 37:74]

When a restructuring plan will take quite a long time to be completed, it is possible that the entity may be demonstrably committed to earlier actions in the plan but not to later actions in the plan. In such circumstances, a provision should be recognised only for those actions to which the entity is committed (i.e. the earlier actions in the restructuring plan).

The requirement for the existence of a valid expectation in those affected relates to the situation at the end of the reporting period. The fact that implementation has commenced by the date that the financial statements are authorised for issue does not, by itself, provide evidence that a present obligation existed at the end of the reporting period.

A management or board decision to go ahead with its plan does not, by itself, give rise to a constructive obligation, unless it is accompanied by commencement of the plan, or by a suitable announcement. [IAS 37:75] An obligation may, however, result from earlier events taken together with such a decision. For example, negotiations with employee representatives for termination payments, or with purchasers for the sale of an operation, may have been concluded subject only to board approval. Once that approval has been obtained and communicated to the other parties, the entity has a constructive obligation to restructure if the general conditions set out above have been met. [IAS 37:76] In addition, a constructive obligation could arise if, as happens in some countries, a board includes non-management representatives such as employees, because a decision by such a board involves communication to those representatives. [IAS 37:77]

A valid expectation is unlikely to exist in either of the following circumstances:

- management has developed a detailed plan, but has not notified those affected by it, even though it can point to previous instances when it has proceeded with a plan; or

- management has developed a plan that involves the closure of one of two possible sites. It has made general indications to employees that one site will close, but has not communicated which of the two sites will close, in order to avoid alienation of employees at that site before implementation commences.

Example 3.9.3.2

Lease termination

An entity has developed a detailed formal plan for restructuring a business, and has announced the key features of the restructuring to all affected by it in a manner that meets the criteria of IAS 37. As part of the restructuring, the entity has entered into an oral agreement (i.e. a commitment has been established) with the landlord to terminate a lease and pay a settlement fee of CU1 million to the landlord. The settlement fee represents a direct cost resulting from the restructuring. The entity does not expect to be able to sublet the property; therefore, CU1 million represents the minimum expected obligation.

A provision should be recognised for the CU1 million settlement fee for the lease because a valid expectation has been created between the lessor and lessee that the lease will be terminated. The entity has a constructive restructuring obligation because it has publicly announced the plan to restructure. Such an announcement gives rise to valid expectations in other parties (e.g. the lessor) that the entity will carry out the restructuring, which includes the termination of the lease.

3.9.3.3   Sale of an operation as part of a restructuring

IAS 37:78 specifies that an obligation does not exist for the sale of an operation until the reporting entity is committed to the sale, i.e. there is a binding sale agreement. Until there is such an agreement, the reporting entity will be able to change its mind and, indeed, will be required to take another course of action if a purchaser cannot be found on acceptable terms. [IAS 37:79]

When a sale is only one element of a restructuring plan, a constructive obligation can arise for the other parts of the restructuring before a binding sale agreement exists. In such circumstances, the assets of the operation should be reviewed for impairment. [IAS 37:79]

3.9.3.4   Amounts to be included in a restructuring provision

The amounts to be included in a restructuring provision are restricted to the direct expenditures arising from the restructuring, i.e. those that are both:
[IAS 37:80]

- necessarily entailed by the restructuring; and

- not associated with the ongoing activities of the reporting entity.

3.9.3.5   Amounts to be excluded from a restructuring provision

Specific items that are excluded from restructuring provisions under IAS 37, on the basis that they relate to the ongoing activities of the business, are:
[IAS 37:81]

- retraining or relocating continuing staff;

- marketing; and

- investment in new systems and distribution networks.

Example 3.9.3.5

Relocation costs

An entity has decided to relocate one of its employees. The employee is aware of the impending move.

No provision should be recognised until the relocation occurs, because the relocation relates to the ongoing activities of the business.

3.9.3.6   Restructuring provision flowchart

The flowchart set out below details the steps necessary to determine whether a restructuring provision should be recognised.

Recognition of restructuring provisions

START

Is there a detailed formal plan for the restructuring identifying at least:
(i)   the business or part of a business concerned;
(ii) the principal locations affected;
(iii) the location, function, and approximate number of employees who will be compensated for terminating their services;
(iv) the expenditures that will be undertaken; and
(v) when the plan will be implemented? [IAS 37:72]

No

Yes

Will implementation of the plan begin as soon as possible and be completed in a timeframe that makes significant changes to the plan unlikely? [IAS 37:74]

No

Yes

Has the entity started to implement the plan by, for example, dismantling plant or selling assets? [IAS 37:73]

Yes

No

Has the entity made a public announcement of the main features of the plan in such a way and in sufficient detail that it gives rise to valid expectations in other parties such as customers, suppliers and employees (or their representatives) that the entity will carry out the restructuring? [IAS 37:73]

No

Yes

Do not recognise provision.

No

Overall, has the entity raised a valid expectation in those affected that it will carry out the restructuring? [IAS 37:72]

Yes

Recognise provision for restructuring.

4   Measurement of provisions

4.1   Best estimate

The amount to be recognised as a provision under IAS 37 is the 'best estimate' of the expenditure required to settle the present obligation at the end of the reporting period. [IAS 37:36] The reference to the end of the reporting period does not preclude use of later additional evidence or better information, but indicates that the best estimate will be the amount that a reporting entity would rationally pay at the end of the reporting period to have the obligation taken away – by settlement or by transfer to a third party. [IAS 37:37]

The addition of 'rationally' in IAS 37:37 suggests that, although it may be difficult to arrange settlement or transfer, there is nevertheless a point of balance, and thus a price, at which management, taking all possible outcomes into account, could be willing to settle.

Ultimately, the best estimate will be determined based on the judgement of management and will reflect experience of similar transactions. In reaching that judgement, reports of independent experts may be required. Examples of relevant independent experts are:

- solicitors and barristers;

- surveyors and valuers;

- loss adjusters;

- actuaries; and

- technical experts (e.g. regarding a decommissioning process).

4.2   Use of expected value

4.2.1   *Large populations*

When the provision relates to a large population of items, the use of an 'expected value' is appropriate to arrive at a best estimate of the obligation. This is the amount that takes account of all possible outcomes, using probabilities to weight the outcomes. [IAS 37:39] When there is a continuous range of possible outcomes, and each point in that range is as likely as any other, the mid-point of the range is used.

Expected value, as a method of estimation, has a number of desirable features. The method provides an estimate that reflects the entire probability distribution, i.e. all the possible outcomes weighted by their probabilities. For a given assessed distribution, the method has the advantage of objectivity in that different measurers would calculate the same estimate. Furthermore, expected value is additive (i.e. the expected value of a number of items is the sum of the expected values of the individual items).

Example 4.2.1

Best estimate: large populations

An entity faces 100 unrelated legal claims, each with an independent 40 per cent likelihood of success with no cost and a 60 per cent likelihood of failure with the cost of each claim to be CU1 million.

Using expected value, the statistical likelihood is that 60 per cent of the claims will result in a cost of CU1 million. Thus, the best estimate of the provision should be calculated as 60 per cent × 100 × CU1 million = CU60 million.

4.2.2   Single obligations

When a single obligation is being measured, IAS 37:40 indicates that the individual most likely outcome may be the best estimate of the liability. Even in such a case, however, it will be necessary to consider other possible outcomes. When the other possible outcomes are either mostly higher or mostly lower than the most likely outcome, the best estimate will be a higher or lower amount.

Thus, when the provision relates to a single event, or a small number of events, expected value as described in **4.2.1** above is not a valid technique.

Example 4.2.2A

Best estimate: single obligation

An entity faces a single legal claim, with a 40 per cent likelihood of success with no cost and a 60 per cent likelihood of failure with a cost of CU1 million.

Expected value is not valid in this case because the outcome will never be a cost of CU600,000 (60 per cent × CU1 million); the outcome will either be nil or CU1 million. IAS 37:40 indicates that the provision may be estimated at the individual most likely outcome. In this example, it is more likely that a

---

cost of CU1 million will result and, therefore, a provision for CU1 million should be recognised.

Generally, when the most likely outcome is close to the expected value, it will be appropriate to provide for the most likely outcome because expected value provides evidence of the probable outflow of benefits.

Example 4.2.2B

Best estimate: expected value (1)

An entity is required to replace a major component in an asset under warranty. Each replacement costs CU1 million. From experience, there is a 30 per cent chance of a single failure, a 50 per cent chance of two failures, and a 20 per cent chance of three failures.

The most likely outcome is two failures, costing CU2 million. The expected value is CU1.9 million ((30 per cent × CU1 million) + (50 per cent × CU2 million) + (20 per cent × CU3 million)). The expected value supports the provision for the most likely outcome of CU2 million.

When the most likely outcome and the expected value are not close together, it will often be appropriate to provide for whichever possible outcome is nearest to the expected value.

Example 4.2.2C

Best estimate: expected value (2)

An entity is required to replace a major component in an asset under a warranty. Each replacement costs CU1 million. From experience, there is a 40 per cent chance of a single failure, a 30 per cent chance of two failures, and a 30 per cent chance of three failures.

The most likely outcome is a single failure, costing CU1 million. The expected value is CU1.9 million ((40 per cent × CU1 million) + (30 per cent × CU2 million) + (30 per cent × CU3 million)). In this case, the most likely outcome of CU1 million has only a 40 per cent probability. There is a 60 per cent probability that the cost will be higher. The outcome closest to expected value is CU2 million (i.e. two failures) and, therefore, a provision for CU2 million should be recognised.

Irrespective of the method applied, in relation to very material items, entities may wish to consider whether it would be appropriate to provide any further information, e.g. the range of possible outcomes.

4.3   Tax

Under IAS 37, provisions are measured before tax. The tax consequences of the provision, and of changes in the provision, are considered separately under IAS 12 *Income Taxes* (see **chapter A13**). [IAS 37:41]

4.4   Risks and uncertainties

IAS 37 indicates that the "risks and uncertainties that inevitably surround many events and circumstances shall be taken into account in reaching the best estimate of a provision". [IAS 37:42] Caution is needed in making judgements under conditions of uncertainty, so that income or assets are not overstated and expenses or liabilities are not understated. However, uncertainty does not justify the creation of excessive provisions or a deliberate overstatement of liabilities. [IAS 37:43]

Also, adjustments for risk and uncertainty should not be double-counted. The most obvious situation in which this may happen is when risk is reflected both in estimated future cash flows and in the discount rate (see **4.7** below). Disclosures regarding uncertainty required by the Standard should act as a safeguard against obvious error (see **10.2** below).

4.5   Future events

In many cases, future events do not represent present obligations and, therefore, they are not provided for. Future events may, however, affect the measurement of a present obligation. IAS 37 requires that future events that may affect the amount required to settle an obligation should be reflected in the amount of a provision when there is sufficient objective evidence that they will occur. [IAS 37:48]

> The reference to future events in IAS 37:48 is to those future events that are factors in estimating the costs of meeting a present obligation (e.g. developments in technology used to clear up a site – see **4.5.1** below) or in assessing the extent to which a present contractual obligation is onerous (e.g. an expectation of subleasing a property – see **example 3.9.2B**). However, it does not refer to possible future changes in the underlying obligation (e.g. to the potential for renegotiating the terms of an onerous contract – see **example 3.9.2A**).

4.5.1   Changes in technology

A common example is the impact of future technology changes on site clean-up costs at the end of a site's life. The amount recognised as a provision for site clean-up costs should reflect the reasonable expectations of technically qualified, objective observers, taking account of all available evidence, as to the technology that will be available at the time of the clean-up. In this situation, IAS 37:49 requires the provision recognised to reflect the reduced costs arising from technology expected to be available at the time of the future clean-up. This allows cost reductions to be recognised for:

- increased experience in applying existing technology; and

- applying existing technology to a larger or more complex clean-up operation than has been carried out to date.

The development of a completely new technology should only be taken into account, however, when there is sufficient objective evidence that it will be available and that it will be effective for the required task. [IAS 37:49]

4.5.2   Changes in legislation

New legislation should be reflected in the measurement of a provision for an existing obligation when there is sufficient objective evidence that the legislation is virtually certain to be enacted. IAS 37 specifies that this will require evidence:
[IAS 37:50]

- of what the legislation will demand; and

- that the legislation will be enacted and implemented.

In practice, because of varying circumstances, there is no single event in the passage of new legislation prior to enactment that provides a general trigger point. In many cases, sufficient objective evidence will not exist until the new legislation is enacted.

4.6   Expected disposals of assets

Gains from expected disposals of assets should not be taken into account in measuring a provision, even if the expected disposal is closely linked to the event giving rise to the provision. [IAS 37:51 & 52]

Example 4.6

Expected disposals of assets

At the end of 20X1, an entity is demonstrably committed to the closure of some facilities, having drawn up a detailed plan and made appropriate announcements. The expected impact of the plan is as follows.

	20X2 CUm	20X3 CUm
Committed closure costs	-100	
Gain from sale of property		+20

The provision required at the end of 20X1 is CU100 million (ignoring discounting). The expected gain on the sale of the property is dealt with separately under the derecognition criteria in IAS 16 *Property, Plant and Equipment*.

4.7   Present value

IAS 37 requires provisions to be discounted to present value when the effect of the time value of money is material. [IAS 37:45]

It will usually be appropriate to make an initial assessment as to whether the impact of discounting might be material before embarking on a potentially complex calculation. Quantifying materiality will depend on a range of factors, e.g. the size of the provision relative to other items in the statement of financial position and the impact of any adjustment on profit for the year. The following table summarises the impact of discounting a single future cash flow for a range of future dates and for a range of possible discount rates. Over a 40-year period, discounting typically reduces an amount to less than 15 per cent of its nominal amount (with the effect that most of the charge would be recognised through the unwinding of the discount).

Cash flow of 100 after:	Discount rate		
	5 per cent	7.5 per cent	10 per cent
1 year	95	93	91
2 years	91	87	83
3 years	86	80	75
4 years	82	75	68
5 years	78	70	62
10 years	61	49	39
15 years	48	34	24
20 years	38	24	15
40 years	14	6	2

4.7.1   Choice of discount rate

The discount rate (or rates) selected should:
[IAS 37:47]

- be pre-tax;

- reflect current market assessments of the time value of money; and

- reflect risks specific to the liability.

4.7.2   Adjusting for risk

Under IAS 37, it is acceptable to reflect risk either in the estimation of cash flows or by adjusting the discount rate. The estimation of an adjusted discount rate is not a precise science. It may, therefore, be preferable, on grounds of simplicity, to deal with risk through a detailed estimation of cash flows to include the impact of risk, coupled with the use of a risk-free discount rate. Whichever method is used, care should be taken to avoid double-counting (or omitting) the effect of any risks.

It follows that, when risk is reflected in estimates of cash flows, the appropriate discount rate will be a pre-tax risk-free rate such as a current government bond rate.

Example 4.7.2A

Risk-free rate

An entity sells goods subject to a warranty. A provision is calculated for warranty claims based on detailed records of past faults in products. Because the estimation of cash flows takes account of risks specific to the warranty, the appropriate discount rate will be a risk-free rate (e.g. a government bond rate).

Example 4.7.2B

Risk-adjusting the discount rate

An entity's best estimate of the amount that it will have to pay to settle a liability in two years' time is CU1,000. The actual liability could be anything between CU500 and CU1,500. At the end of the reporting period, the entity knows that it could transfer the liability to a third party immediately if it agrees to pay that third party CU1,075 in two years' time. Accordingly, before taking the time value of money into account, the entity's best estimate of the outflow is CU1,000, excluding any risk adjustment, and the equivalent certain amount payable in two years' time is CU1,075, i.e. including an adjustment for risk of CU75. The amount of the provision recognised at the end of the reporting period should be the same whether the unadjusted best estimate or the risk-adjusted best estimate is used as the basis for the net present value calculation. The appropriate risk-free rate is 4 per cent per annum.

	Undiscounted amount CU	Net present value CU
Risk-adjusted cash flow	1,075	994*
Expected cash flow (unadjusted for risk)	1,000	994#

*   Using a risk-free rate of 4% on the risk-adjusted cash flow of CU1,075 gives a net present value of CU994.

\#   To arrive at the same net present value (CU994), a risk-adjusted rate of 0.3% must be used to discount the expected cash flow of CU1,000.

As illustrated by this example, the risk-adjusted discount rate will generally be lower than the risk-free rate when discounting liabilities.

4.7.2.1   Effect of own credit risk

At its March 2011 meeting, the IFRS Interpretations Committee considered the question as to whether, if the discount rate is to be adjusted for risk, an entity's own credit risk (performance risk) should be considered a risk 'specific to the liability' as contemplated in IAS 37:47 (and, therefore, be taken into account in measuring the present value of the expenditures expected to be required to settle the obligation).

The Interpretations Committee noted that IAS 37 does not explicitly state whether an entity's own credit risk should be included as an adjustment to the discount rate used to measure non-financial liabilities.

Despite there being no explicit statement in IAS 37, the Committee did note its understanding that predominant practice is to exclude the effect of an entity's own credit risk, which is generally viewed in practice as a risk of the entity rather than a risk specific to the liability.

4.7.3   Pre-tax rates calculated from post-tax rates

Care should be taken in determining a pre-tax discount rate by adjusting a post-tax rate. Because the tax consequences of cash flows may occur in different periods, the pre-tax rate of return is not always the post-tax rate of return grossed up by the standard rate of tax. See **8.3.1** in **chapter A10** for further guidance on how to adjust a post-tax discount rate to arrive at a pre-tax discount rate.

4.7.4   Impact of inflation

When estimated cash flows are expressed in current prices, a real discount rate (i.e. reduced for the impact of future inflation) will be used. Alternatively, when cash flows are expressed in expected future prices (normally higher than current prices), a nominal discount rate will be used. The effects of inflation specific to the cash flows on the present value of those cash flows will be the same provided that one of the following methods is used:

- current (lower) prices discounted at a real (lower) rate; or

- future (higher) prices discounted at a nominal (higher) rate.

The real rate can be estimated by deducting the inflation rate from the nominal rate. Mathematically, the relationship between the nominal rate and the real rate is expressed by the following formula:

$$(1+ \text{ real rate}) = (1+ \text{ nominal rate})/(1+ \text{ inflation rate}).$$

Example 4.7.4

Impact of inflation

Company A estimates that it will pay CU1,000 (in current prices) at the end of each of the next three years to settle a present obligation. If it takes into account inflation, assumed at 1.5 per cent per annum, these cash flows will increase to the amounts illustrated in the table below. Company A has established that the nominal discount rate (which includes inflation) is 4 per cent. By discounting the cash flows the net present value is CU2,858. By iteration, it is possible to calculate the real discount rate, i.e. the rate that would have to be applied to the cash flows excluding inflation to arrive at the same present value.

	Net present value	Year 1	Year 2	Year 3
	CU	CU	CU	CU
Cash flows adjusted for inflation of 1.5% per annum		1,015	1,030	1,046
NPV @ nominal discount rate of 4%	2,858			
Cash flows excluding inflation		1,000	1,000	1,000
NPV@ real discount rate of 2.46%	2,858			

The equivalent real rate is 2.46 per cent. It would be incorrect to discount the cash flows that exclude inflation (i.e. CU1,000 per year) using the nominal discount rate of 4 per cent because this would give an understated net present value of CU2,776.

Assuming no change in discount rate and no change in expected cash flows (i.e. inflation proves to be as assessed on initial recognition of the provision), the amount recognised each year to unwind the discount will be as follows:

	NPV @ 4% at start of the year	Cash flow	Year end carrying amount	Unwind of discount
	CU	CU	CU	CU
Year 1	2,858	(1,015)	1,957	114
Year 2	1,957	(1,030)	1,006	79
Year 3	1,006	(1,046)	–	40

The interest cost is made up of a discount factor being the real interest rate of 2.46 per cent and an inflation factor of 1.5 per cent. The interest cost should not be split between these elements for reporting purposes. Rather, the full nominal amount of the discount should be included as a borrowing cost consistent with other external borrowing costs.

5   Reimbursements

An entity with a present obligation may be able to seek reimbursement of part or all of the expenditure from another party, for example via:

- an insurance contract arranged to cover a risk; or

- an indemnity clause in a contract; or

- a warranty provided by a supplier.

The basis underlying the recognition of a reimbursement is that any asset arising is separate from the related obligation. Consequently, such a reimbursement should be recognised only when it is virtually certain that it will be received if the entity settles the obligation. [IAS 37:53] This treatment is also consistent with the guidance on contingent assets.

When a provision has been recognised, the occurrence of the expenditure is taken to be certain for the purposes of assessing the probability of receiving reimbursement and judging whether it is virtually certain.

Note that it is the existence of the reimbursement asset that must be virtually certain, rather than its amount. An entity may be virtually certain that it has insurance to cover a particular provision, but it may not be certain of the precise amount that would be received from the insurer. Provided that the range of possible recoveries is such that the entity can arrive at a reliable estimate, it will be able to recognise this as an asset, even though the amount ultimately received may be different.

The appropriate presentation of a reimbursement is as follows:

- in the statement of financial position, a separate asset is recognised (which must not exceed the amount of the provision); [IAS 37:53] and

- in profit or loss, a net amount may be presented, being the anticipated cost of the obligation less the reimbursement. [IAS 37:54]

Example 5

Recognition of reimbursement due from insurance company

An entity has a high probability of losing a lawsuit in which it is the defendant. The entity's insurance company is expected to cover any loss incurred.

What amounts, if any, should the entity recognise in its statement of financial position in respect of the anticipated loss and reimbursement?

The outflow of resources expected on the loss of the lawsuit and the amounts expected to be recovered from the insurance company arise from the same past event. When the conditions of IAS 37:14 (see **3.1** above) are met, the entity should recognise a liability for the expected outflow of resources, measured at the best estimate of the expenditure required to settle the obligation at the end of the reporting period as stated in IAS 37:36.

In respect of the expected recovery from the insurance company, the entity should assess the effectiveness of its insurance policy. Under IAS 37:53, it should recognise the amount expected to be reimbursed (as a separate asset) when, and only when, it is virtually certain that the claim will be received (i.e. unless there is doubt regarding the insurance claim).

The amount recognised for the reimbursement should not exceed the amount of the provision.

Offset of a provision and the related reimbursement is never appropriate. If a reporting entity can avoid making payment in respect of an obligation in all circumstances (i.e. there can never be any recourse to the entity), then it has no liability and hence neither a provision nor a reimbursement asset should be recognised. In most cases, however, the entity will remain liable for the whole amount in question and will have to settle the full amount if the third party fails to pay for any reason. In these circumstances, no offset is permitted, irrespective of how unlikely it is that the entity will have to settle the obligation directly. [IAS 37:56 & 57]

If a reporting entity is jointly and severally liable for an obligation, it should provide for that part of the obligation which it is probable will be settled by the entity. The remainder, expected to be paid by other parties, is a contingent liability. [IAS 37:29 & 58]

If an entity has a provision and a matching reimbursement, and the time value of money is material to both, the question arises as to whether both should be discounted. In principle, both the asset and the liability should be discounted. If there will be a significant interval between the cash outflows and receiving the reimbursement, the reimbursement will be more heavily discounted; in such circumstances, if the gross inflows and outflows are the same, on initial recognition there will be a net cost. If (presumably rarely) the reimbursement will be received first, IAS 37:53 will restrict the discounted amount of the reimbursement so that it does not exceed the discounted amount of the provision. In profit or loss, the unwinding of the discount on the reimbursement may be offset against that on the provision.

When a reimbursement will not be received until some significant time after the outflows to which it relates, it is possible (though perhaps rare) that it may carry interest, or in some other way be increased, so as to reimburse the entity for the lost time value of money. The only restriction in IAS 37 is that the asset recognised (i.e. the discounted amount) must not exceed the provision recognised. It is, in principle, possible for the gross amount of reimbursement used in the discounting calculation to exceed the gross outflows expected (i.e. for the undiscounted asset to be greater than the undiscounted liability).

5.1   Collateralised or guaranteed loan commitments

Example 5.1

Collateralised or guaranteed loan commitments

Entity A has issued a non-cancellable loan commitment at market terms to Entity B. The loan commitment cannot be settled net, and Entity A has no past practice of selling the assets resulting from its loan commitments shortly after origination. Entity A did not designate this loan commitment at fair value through profit or loss; therefore in accordance with paragraphs 2(h) and 4 of IAS 39 *Financial Instruments: Recognition and Measurement*, this loan commitment is scoped out of IAS 39 (and, when adopted, IFRS 9 *Financial Instruments*) and should be accounted for under IAS 37.

Scenario 1

The loan subject to the loan commitment is guaranteed by another party (e.g. the parent of the borrowing entity or an insurer). That party will reimburse Entity A for any loss incurred if Entity B fails to make payments when due (i.e. if there is a breach of contract). The loan commitment has not been settled at the end of the reporting period; however, Entity A assesses that Entity B will not be able to repay the loan that it has committed to grant to Entity B.

Scenario 2

The loan subject to the loan commitment is a collateralised loan; that is, if Entity B fails to make payments when due, the legal ownership of the collateral (e.g. property) will be transferred to Entity A. The loan commitment has not been settled at the end of the reporting period; however, Entity A assesses that Entity B will not be able to repay the loan that it has committed to grant to Entity B.

How should Entity A account for the loan commitments under Scenarios 1 and 2 at the end of the reporting period?

General

In general, a provision should be recognised when the conditions set out in IAS 37:14 (see **3.1** above) are met. That is, if Entity A has assessed at the end of the reporting period that Entity B will not be able to repay the loan that it has committed to grant to Entity B, a provision should be recognised.

Scenario 1:

- The provision should be measured according to IAS 37:36 at "the best estimate of the expenditure required to settle the present obligation at the end of the reporting period". In accordance with IAS 37:53, Entity A should not take into account the guarantee provided by the parent or insurer when assessing the amount of the provision necessary at the end of the reporting period.

- The guarantee provided by the parent or insurer is a reimbursement right because Entity A "is able to look to another party to pay part or all of the expenditure required to settle a provision". [IAS 37:55] The guarantee, therefore, should be recognised as a separate asset. However, this should only be done when the criteria in IAS 37:53 are met, which requires that a reimbursement from another party is recognised only when it is virtually certain that reimbursement will be received if Entity B fails to make payment when due. The 'virtually certain' criteria may be met once Entity B's breach of contract has occurred (e.g. at the first interest payment date).

- If the guarantee was part of the same contractual arrangement (e.g. when the loan commitment issued to Entity B is guaranteed by the parent of Entity B, and the guarantee is part of the same contractual arrangement), then it would be bundled and an alternative treatment would be appropriate (see the answer for scenario 2 below).

Scenario 2:

- Collateral held on the loan is not a reimbursement right because Entity A is not "able to look to another party to pay part or all of the expenditure required to settle a provision". [IAS 37:55] Accordingly, this collateral is not separate from the loan commitment and, when accounting for the provision, it should be treated as a net arrangement with a single counterparty (i.e. the collateral should be taken into account when measuring the provision amount).

- The provision is measured in accordance with IAS 37:36. Although the loan commitment is within the scope of IAS 37, in practice, a provision will be recognised at the amount equivalent to the impairment that would have been required under IAS 39:63, which states that "the amount of the loss is measured as the difference between the asset's carrying amount and the present value of estimated future cash flows". Additionally, IAS 39:AG84 indicates that "the calculation of the present value of the estimated future cash flows of a collateralised financial asset reflects the cash flows that may result from foreclosure, less costs for obtaining and selling the collateral, whether or not foreclosure is probable". Accordingly, the provision is recognised for the present value of the net non-recoverable amount (taking into account the value of the collateral, less the cost for obtaining and selling it).

6   Changes in provisions

Provisions should be reviewed at the end of each reporting period and adjusted to reflect current best estimates. [IAS 37:59]

Adjustments to provisions arise from three sources:

- revisions to estimated cash flows (both amount and likelihood);

- changes to present value due to the passage of time; and

- revisions of discount rates to reflect prevailing current market conditions.

In the years following the initial measurement of a provision at a present value, the present value will be restated to reflect estimated cash flows being closer to the measurement date. This unwinding of the discount relating to the passage of time should be recognised as a finance cost. [IAS 37:60] The effect of revising estimates of cash flows is not part of this unwinding and should be dealt with as part of any adjustment to the previous provision.

When a provision is no longer required (e.g. if it is no longer probable that a transfer of economic benefits will be required to settle the obligation), the provision should be reversed. [IAS 37:59]

The disclosure requirements in respect of changes in provisions are dealt with in **10.2** below.

The degree of uncertainty associated with an obligation can change over time. In some cases, an obligation will be recognised initially as a provision due to the uncertainty surrounding the amount payable. Subsequently, after negotiation with the counterparty, an exact amount may be agreed. To the extent that the agreed amount is not settled immediately, it no longer meets the definition of a provision and, therefore, should be reclassified to another appropriate category within liabilities.

7   Use of provisions

One of the objectives of IAS 37 is to increase the transparency of accounting for provisions and, in particular, to prevent the use of an existing provision to meet a different undisclosed obligation. Accordingly, the Standard requires a provision to be used only for expenditures for which the provision was originally recognised. [IAS 37:61]

The disclosure requirements for provisions (see **10.2** below), particularly the requirement to identify movements on each class of provision, are intended to reinforce this requirement.

8   Illustrative examples

The examples set out in Section C of the implementation guidance accompanying IAS 37 are summarised below, but in a tabular format, in order to identify reasons for particular items meeting, or not meeting, the definition of a provision. In all cases, it is assumed that a reliable estimate can be made.

Type of risk or cost	Present obligation as a result of a past event?	Probable transfer of benefits?	Conclusion
Warranty Example 1: Warranty given by a manufacturer under the terms of a contract for sale. Past experience shows that it is probable that claims will be received.	✔	✔	Provide at date of sale for legal obligation.
Contaminated land (1) Example 2A: Contaminated land – entity cleans up only to meet legal requirements, which are virtually certain to be enacted soon after the end of the reporting period.	✔	✔	Provide for expected legal obligation.
Contaminated land (2) Example 2B: Contaminated land – entity has no legal obligation, but meets widely publicised clean-up policy.	✔	✔	Provide for constructive obligation.
Decommissioning Example 3: Decommissioning – terms of a licence impose a legal obligation to remove an oil rig at the end of its life.	✔	✔	Provide on commissioning of asset and include in cost of oil rig.
Refunds policy Example 4: Refunds – retail store follows a published policy of providing refunds, even though there is no legal obligation.	✔	✔	Provide for constructive obligation.
Closure of a division (1) Example 5A: Closure of a division – board decision taken before the end of the reporting period, but not communicated to those affected and plan not commenced.	✘		No obligating event before the end of the reporting period.
Closure of a division (2) Example 5B: Closure of a division – board decision, detailed plan completed, staff and customers notified before the end of the reporting period.	✔	✔	Provide for expected costs of closure.

Type of risk or cost	Present obligation as a result of a past event?	Probable transfer of benefits?	Conclusion
Legal requirement to fit smoke filter Example 6: Introduction of legal requirement to fit smoke filters by 30 June 20X1.			
(a) At 31 December 20X0, the end of the reporting period.	✗		No obligating event at the end of the reporting period.
(b) At 31 December 20X1, the end of the reporting period (assuming filters not yet fitted).	✗		– no obligating event in respect of filters, but
	✔	✔	– provision may be required for any fines and penalties likely to be suffered.
Staff retraining Example 7: Staff retraining – need to retrain staff to meet new system requirements imposed by change in the law.	✗		No obligating event until training occurs.
Onerous contract Example 8: Onerous contract – operating lease rental payments on vacated property.	✔	✔	Provide for unavoidable lease payments.
Guarantee Example 9: Guarantee – provided for another entity's borrowings. Although such guarantees were within the scope of IAS 37 when the Standard was originally issued, they are now within the scope of IFRS 9 *Financial Instruments* (or, prior to the adoption of IFRS 9, IAS 39 *Financial Instruments: Recognition and Measurement*), except in limited circumstances in which IFRS 4 *Insurance Contracts* applies (see the discussion at **2.3.2** in **chapter B1** or at **2.3.2** in **chapter C1**). Example 9 provides an example of an accounting policy that IFRS 4 permits and that also complies with the requirements in IFRS 9 (or IAS 39) for financial guarantee contracts within the scope of IFRS 9 (or IAS 39).			

Type of risk or cost	Present obligation as a result of a past event?	Probable transfer of benefits?	Conclusion
Court case Example 10: Unsettled court case (a) At 31 December 20X0, the end of the reporting period – lawyers advise that no liability will be proved.	✗		No obligation exists based on evidence.
(b) At 31 December 20X1, the end of the reporting period – lawyers advise that liability will be proved.	✔	✔	Provide for estimated settlement.
Repairs and maintenance Example 11A: Repairs and maintenance – a furnace has a lining that needs to be replaced every five years for technical reasons. At the end of the reporting period, the lining has been in use for three years.	✗		No obligation exists independently of future actions. Expenditure capitalised when incurred and depreciated.
Refurbishment costs Example 11B: Refurbishment costs – legislative requirement – an airline is required by law to overhaul its aircraft once every three years.	✗		No obligation exists independently of future actions (the entity could sell the aircraft). Expenditure capitalised when incurred and depreciated.

8.1   Repairs and maintenance obligations under leases

Under some operating leases, the lessee is required to incur periodic charges for maintenance of the leased asset or to make good dilapidations or other damage occurring during the rental period. Because the lease is a legal contract, it may give rise to legal obligations. Accordingly, the principles of IAS 37, which generally preclude the recognition of provisions for repairs and maintenance, do not preclude the recognition of such liabilities in a lease once the event giving rise to the obligation under the lease has occurred.

Example 8.1

Lease of aircraft

An entity leases an aircraft under an operating lease. The aircraft has to undergo an expensive 'C check' after every 2,400 flying hours.

The requirement to perform a 'C check' does not give rise to a present obligation at the time the lease is signed because, until 2,400 hours have been flown, there is no obligation which exists independently of the entity's future actions. Even the intention to incur the cost of a 'C check' depends on the entity deciding to continue flying the aircraft. Therefore, no provision should be recognised for a future 'C check'. The cost of each successive 'C check' will instead be capitalised when it is incurred and amortised over the period to the next 'C check'.

This leaves the question of the condition in which the aircraft must be returned to the lessor at the end of the lease and of whether this creates a present obligation, and thus the requirement for a provision, at the time the lease is signed. The answer depends on what the lease terms state will happen when the aircraft is returned at the end of the lease. If no final 'C check' is required (i.e. in the final period, the client can use the aircraft for up to 2,399 flying hours and then return it without bearing any cost), no provision should be recognised because there is no legal obligation.

If a 'C check' is required at the end of the lease, irrespective of how many hours have been flown, full provision for the cost should be recognised at the start of the lease. The costs should be carried forward and written off over the shorter of the next 2,400 flying hours and the number of flying hours to the end of the lease – and similarly each time a 'C check' is carried out.

If, on returning the aircraft, the entity must make a payment towards the 'C check' which is in proportion to the number of hours flown (e.g. 75 per cent of the cost of a 'C check' for 1,800 hours flown), then an obligation is created as the aircraft is used. It will be appropriate to build up a provision based on the number of hours flown.

8.1.1   Obligations to restore leased property

Example 8.1.1

Obligations to restore leased property

Entity A is a lessee in a lease contract. As a condition of the lease and prior to return of the property to the lessor, Entity A is required to:

- remove any leasehold improvements, such as additional internal walls or partitioning fitted by the lessee; and

- repair the fabric of the building so that it is restored to its original condition at the date of inception of the lease, i.e. to make good any dilapidations.

When should Entity A recognise any provision in relation to restoration of the leased property?

If a lease agreement requires an item to be replaced if its standard falls below a specified level, no provision should be recognised until the point at which it is no longer possible for the entity to avoid replacing the item.

Generally, it will not be appropriate to recognise a provision for restoring leased property on a straight-line basis over the lease term, because typically the obligation will not arise on a straight-line basis. For example, if a lease agreement requires carpets to be replaced or walls to be repainted at the end of the lease period, full provision for the associated cost will be required from the outset, because the outflow cannot be avoided.

Typically, a provision will be recognised on a straight-line basis only when the associated costs are directly proportional to the length of time for which the associated asset has been used. This may be true for some elements of restoration relating to, for example, oil wells and landfill sites, but it is less common for property leases.

Accordingly, Entity A should provide for the cost of removing leasehold improvements when those leasehold improvements are first made (e.g. when additional internal walls and partitioning are fitted). Entity A should only provide for repairs to the fabric of the building once it is no longer possible for Entity A to avoid making those repairs.

8.2   Self-insurance – cost of accidents

When an entity self-insures (e.g. a retailer might decide not to insure itself in respect of the risk of minor accidents to its customers), it should recognise a provision each year for the costs of accidents that have occurred prior to the end of the reporting period. This provision should cover not only those claims that have been made prior to the end of the reporting period, but also claims potentially incurred but not reported (IBNR) at that date. It will be common that an accident has happened but the entity does not know of its occurrence. This in itself does not preclude the entity from recognising a provision – as long as a reliable estimate can be made of IBNR claims, probably based on past experience. Because the IBNR provision is, by definition, in respect of claims incurred before the end of the reporting period, the obligating event will have occurred by that date. IAS 37 does not, however, permit the recognition of a provision for the excess of the 'normal annual cost' over the cost of actual accidents in the year. In other words, a self-insuring entity is prevented from 'smoothing' the cost of accidents by making a buffer provision in a year when actual costs are low.

When a group self-insures by setting up a separate captive insurance subsidiary, any intragroup premiums charged or received will be eliminated on consolidation, reflecting the fact that, for the group, this is not external insurance cover.

Example 8.2

Adjustment of insurance premiums

Entity A has an insurance policy with premiums that are adjusted on the basis of actual losses incurred in that year. For example, if losses for a specific period exceed 100, Entity A will have to pay the insurer 80 per cent of the excessive losses in the form of additional premiums in that year.

Entity A should recognise a provision at the end of each reporting period for the additional premiums due as a result of losses in that year. In measuring that provision, Entity A should consider not only known losses but also losses incurred but not yet reported.

8.3   Vouchers issued for no consideration

A reporting entity may, for no consideration, distribute vouchers that can be used, sometimes within a set period, to obtain discounts on the entity's products and/or a third party's products. (Note that when such vouchers are issued as part of a sales transaction, it will be necessary to consider the unbundling implications of IFRIC 13 *Customer Loyalty Programmes* – see **5.5** in **chapter A14**.)

Applying IAS 37's recognition criteria, the questions to be considered are as follows.

- *Is there a present obligation?* Generally, the answer will be yes. But if the reporting entity reserves the right to terminate the scheme at any time, thus invalidating existing vouchers, there may or may not be a constructive obligation. In the absence of evidence that schemes have been terminated (and existing vouchers invalidated) in the past, however, it should be presumed that an obligation exists.

- *Is it probable that economic benefits will be transferred?* If, after vouchers are deducted, the entity's products are still being sold at a profit, the answer will be no – in which case no provision will be recognised. To the extent that products will be sold at a loss, however, or that a third party will be reimbursed for discounts, there will be a transfer of economic benefits.

- *Can a reliable estimate be made?* The answer here should be presumed to be yes, but in making the estimate the entity should consider how many vouchers are expected to be used.

In summary, if the criteria are met, provision should be recognised for the best estimate of the cost to the entity (which may not be the face value of the discounts). The entity will need to form a view as to how many vouchers are expected to be used and should also consider whether discounting is appropriate.

8.4   Costs of decommissioning an oil rig

Commissioning of a new oil rig creates an obligation to incur costs of decommissioning in the future, but also gives access to future economic benefits. A provision for the present value of costs of decommissioning should be recognised at the time of commissioning the oil rig and the amount recognised should be added to the cost of the rig. The provision should only include the costs that are an obligation resulting from commissioning the rig. The provision should not include any additional costs that will only be triggered by further drilling until that further drilling occurs.

IFRIC 1 *Changes in Existing Decommissioning, Restoration and Similar Liabilities* (see **4.4** in **chapter A7**) and IFRIC 5 *Rights to Interests arising from Decommissioning, Restoration and Environmental Rehabilitation Funds* (see **9.2** below) address related issues.

8.5   Late delivery penalties

In some circumstances, a late delivery penalty may be incurred when goods are not supplied by a specified delivery date. At the end of its reporting period, an entity may know that it will not be able to meet the delivery date for goods to be supplied in the next year.

At its year end, before the original delivery date, should the entity recognise a provision for the penalty that will be payable when, as is expected, the goods are delivered late?

No. There is no past event because the late delivery of goods has not yet occurred. Consequently, there is neither a legal nor a constructive obligation to pay the penalty at the end of the current reporting period and no basis for recognising a provision for the penalty.

However, if the remaining part of the contract has, as a whole, become onerous as a result of the penalty clause, a provision should be recognised for any overall loss expected to result.

Example 8.5

Late delivery penalties

Entity A (which has a December year end) signed a firm sales contract with one of its major clients on 1 February 20X1. This contract specifies that 100 units of a product must be delivered before 1 February 20X2 at a fixed price of CU10 per unit. The costs of production are CU9 per unit. If the products are delivered more than 10 days late, the client will be given a discount of 50 per cent on each delayed product.

At the time Entity A signed the contract, it had the ability and the intention to produce the 100 units on time. However, at the end of 20X1, it has only been able to deliver 80 units, and expects to deliver only 10 more before 1 February 20X2 due to manufacturing constraints. Therefore, at the end of the reporting period, Entity A expects to deliver 10 of the remaining 20 units at the discounted price of CU5 per unit.

Total revenue from this contract will be CU950 $[(90 \times 10) + (10 \times 5)]$ and total costs will be CU900 (100×9). Therefore, the overall contract is profitable. However, the situation at the end of the 20X1 reporting period is as follows:

- Entity A has recognised CU800 revenue and CU720 costs (i.e. profit of CU80) in 20X1;

- Entity A expects to deliver 10 units on time at a profit of CU10 $[(10 \times 10) - (10 \times 9)]$; and

- Entity A expects to deliver 10 units after the deadline at a loss of CU40 $[(10 \times 5) - (10 \times 9)]$.

The remaining part of the contract is therefore onerous and a provision of CU30 (discounted if material) should be recognised to cover the potential loss arising from the outstanding obligations under the contract. If Entity A is able and expects to mitigate damages by purchasing suitable replacement products and delivering them prior to 1 February, the provision should be adjusted to reflect the expected economic loss anticipated to be incurred by Entity A.

If Entity A had entered into this contract knowing that it would not be able to deliver on time, this would have been dealt with under the revenue recognition criteria of IAS 18 *Revenue*. If, from the outset, Entity A expected to sell 100 units at an average price of CU9.50 (CU950 ÷ 100) per unit, then revenue of only CU9.50 would have been recognised for each unit sold (both in 20X1 and 20X2) and there would have been no need to consider a separate provision.

8.6   Repurchase agreements – trade-in right

Example 8.6

Repurchase agreements – trade-in right

In order to facilitate vehicle sales, a motor dealer offers specified-price trade-in arrangements on vehicles for sale that give a customer the right to trade in his or her vehicle toward the purchase of a new vehicle at some point in the future. The trade-in may be exercisable by the customer at a specified point in time or during a specified period of time.

Should the dealer recognise a provision for the cost of the guaranteed vehicle repurchases?

If the amount of credit that will be received upon exercise of a specified-price trade-in right is equal to or less than the estimated fair value of the vehicle at the trade-in date (determined on the date of the original sale of the vehicle subject to the specified-price trade-in right) and if the customer is required to pay a significant incremental amount in addition to the trade-in credit for the new vehicle at the trade-in date, then no revenue from the original sale of the vehicle should be allocated to the trade-in right and no provision should be recognised for the trade-in right at the time of the original sale. If the motor dealer subsequently determines, however, that the trade-in arrangement has become onerous, the motor dealer should recognise a provision for the onerous contract. In assessing whether, and to what extent, the trade-in arrangement has become onerous, the motor dealer should consider the net of:

- any loss that may be incurred upon the customer's exercise of the specified-price trade-in right (i.e. the difference between the trade-in price and the resale value at that date of the vehicle traded-in); and

- any profit that may be expected on the sale of the new vehicle to the customer at the trade-in date.

8.7   Employment disputes

> **Example 8.7**
>
> **Employment disputes**
>
> An entity employs three professional seamen. Maritime law prescribes that registered professionals are paid a premium over unregistered professionals. The entity subsequently discovers that the professionals are not registered and, therefore, have been overpaid. The entity consequently reduces the salaries of these professionals who then take the matter to court. One employee wins the case and is awarded a CU70,000 retrenchment package. The other two lose on a technicality, but will appeal the decision. Lawyers are certain that the appeal will be successful.
>
> A provision should be recognised for the best estimate of the costs to settle the appeal. The past event is the underpayment of the employees (after it was thought they were overpaid), and therefore occurred during the year. As a result of the court proceedings, a legal obligation to compensate one employee exists in the current year (for CU70,000). With regard to the other two seamen, the past event is the constructive dismissal (i.e. the reduction in salaries) that occurred during the year. Because it is probable (more likely than not) that the entity will be found liable, a present obligation exists. It is probable that economic benefits will flow from the entity.

8.8   Recognition of construction obligations associated with a construction contract

> **Example 8.8**
>
> **Recognition of constructive obligations associated with a construction contract**
>
> Entity X is in the construction industry. It stores plant and machinery at its site, Site A, and transports certain plant and machinery (e.g. cranes) to a construction site (Site B), where it is in the process of constructing a hotel. At the end of construction, Entity X will be required to remove the crane from Site B and transport it back to Site A, or to the site of another contract.
>
> A liability should be recognised for transporting the crane back to Site A. IAS 11 *Construction Contracts* does not deal specifically with this type of provision, and so it falls within the scope of IAS 37.
>
> IAS 37:19 states that "[i]t is only those obligations arising from past events existing independently of an entity's future actions (i.e. the future conduct of its business) that are recognised as provisions". Because the crane cannot be left at Site B, Entity X has a constructive obligation to remove the crane. Therefore, Entity X should recognise a liability for the removal of the crane

as soon as it is installed at Site B and measure that liability at the best estimate of the cost of transporting the crane back to Site A (or to the next site at which it is required).

The liability cannot be capitalised to the cost of the crane under the cost model of IAS 16 *Property, Plant and Equipment*. In accordance with IAS 16:16(c), the cost of an item of property, plant and equipment comprises, inter alia:

> "the initial estimate of the costs of dismantling and removing the item and restoring the site on which it is located, the obligation for which an entity incurs either when the item is acquired or as a consequence of having used the item during a particular period for purposes other than to produce inventories during that period".

The cost of removal of the crane in this instance relates to its redeployment post inventory production, not to restoring the site on which it was located for construction purposes. However, the cost may represent a contract cost under IAS 11 and, if so, would be included in the associated construction asset.

8.9   Warranties

Although IAS 37 gives warranties as an example of an item for which provisions should be recognised, it is important to distinguish between the types of warranty to which IAS 37 should be applied and those that should properly be regarded as a separately identifiable component of a revenue transaction.

For example, a warranty that merely reflects the rights that a customer would have in any case under local sale of goods legislation would not be a separately identifiable component (because no customer would ever choose to pay extra for it), so IAS 37 will apply for the purposes of estimating the costs to satisfy this obligation. However, some 'extended warranties' should be regarded as separately identifiable components of a revenue transaction because the customer can choose whether to pay for such an 'extended warranty'. IAS 18 should be applied in these circumstances (see **5.1 in chapter A14**). The appropriate accounting will depend on the specific facts and circumstances but often it will be appropriate to recognise the amount paid by the customer for the extended warranty over the period of extended warranty cover. Typically, this will not commence with the sale of goods but will instead commence once the 'statutory warranty period' in the local jurisdiction has expired.

9   IFRIC Interpretations

9.1   Emission Rights (IFRIC 3, since withdrawn)

In December 2004, IFRIC 3 *Emission Rights* was issued to deal with the accounting by participants in a 'cap and trade' scheme. The Interpretation specified that a cap and trade scheme gives rise to an asset for allowances held, a government grant in respect of any allowances granted free of charge, and a liability for the obligation to deliver allowances, equal to the emissions made. However, the accounting required by IFRIC 3 led to a perceived mismatch: assets would either be recognised at historical amounts or revalued with changes recognised in other comprehensive income, whereas liabilities would be remeasured to fair value through profit or loss. Thus, an entity holding precisely the level of assets required to settle its liabilities would nevertheless report gains or losses if there were changes in fair value.

In 2005, as a result of these perceived problems with IFRIC 3, the Interpretation was withdrawn. The IASB has stated its intention to conduct a broader assessment of the nature of the various volatilities resulting from the application of IFRIC 3 and to consider whether and how it might be appropriate to amend existing Standards to reduce or eliminate some of those volatilities.

In the meantime, entities participating in cap and trade schemes will need to give careful thought to how they account for the assets and liabilities arising. One possible approach would be to follow the guidance set out in IFRIC 3 (see **9.1.1** below). Two other possible approaches are outlined at **9.1.2** and **9.1.3** below. The accounting policy adopted should be applied to all emission allowances and related liabilities on a consistent basis.

Although emission rights are typically regarded as intangible assets for most entities, if an entity is acting as a broker or trader, such that it acquires rights from one market participant and sells them on to another, the emission rights are likely to be inventories for that entity. In the event that an entity acquires emission rights far in excess of the emissions it is likely to make, with a view to selling those rights, those excess rights may qualify as inventories.

9.1.1   Approach 1: apply IFRIC 3

Emission rights are intangible assets that are accounted for in accordance with IAS 38 *Intangible Assets* and would be recognised initially at fair value. When allowances are issued for less than fair value, the difference between the amount paid (if any) and fair value would be accounted for as a government grant within the scope of IAS 20 *Accounting for Government Grants and Disclosure of Government Assistance*.

As emissions are made, a liability would be recognised for the obligation to deliver allowances equal to emissions that have been made. This liability would be a provision within the scope of IAS 37, and would be measured at the best estimate of the expenditure required to settle the present obligation at the end of the reporting period. This would usually be the present market price of the number of allowances required to cover emissions made up to the end of the reporting period.

Offset of the asset (emission credits held) and the liability (to deliver credits to the value of emissions made) would not be permitted.

9.1.2   Approach 2: government grant and an intangible asset initially at fair value, emission liability reflects carrying amounts

9.1.2.1   Intangible asset

Allowances allocated free of charge or for nominal consideration would be measured under the alternatives permitted in IAS 20 and IAS 38. It would seem preferable for allowances to be recognised as an asset only when issued. But an acceptable alternative would be for the entire period allocation to be recognised as an asset at the point at which the relevant authority finalises the allocation plan for the allowances.

Allowances allocated represent an intangible asset acquired by an entity free of charge or for nominal consideration. IAS 38:44 sets out two possible treatments. The entity could choose to recognise both the intangible asset and the government grant initially at fair value; alternatively, nominal value could be used (see **9.1.3** below). The fair value approach might be considered as providing better accounting information, in that it results in a better representation of the economic resources and obligations of the entity.

Subsequent to initial recognition, the general requirements for intangible assets in IAS 38 would apply.

- IAS 38 permits an intangible asset to be remeasured at fair value when this can be measured by reference to an active market. Remeasurements are recognised in other comprehensive income. [IAS 38:75] The revalued amount is subject to amortisation and impairment testing between remeasurements. This accounting treatment precludes any reclassification to profit or loss of fair value increments accumulated in equity.

- IAS 38 also permits an intangible asset to be measured at cost less amortisation / impairment. [IAS 38:74] If an entity were to use this method, any difference between the carrying amount of the asset and the liability would be recognised in profit or loss upon settlement of the obligation (or sale of the allowances).

For most allowances traded in an active market, no amortisation will be required because the residual value will be the same as cost and, therefore, the depreciable amount will be zero. If the market value of the allowances falls below cost, or other indicators of impairment exist, then the guidance in IAS 36 *Impairment of Assets* should be followed to determine whether the assets are impaired.

9.1.2.2   Government grant

Allowances represent a non-monetary government grant and could be recognised at the fair value of the related asset or at a nominal amount. [IAS 20:23] For the reasons noted above, it might be preferable for the government grant to be measured initially at fair value. The grant would be recognised as deferred income and recognised in profit or loss on a systematic basis over the compliance period, regardless of whether the allowances received continue to be held by the entity.

9.1.2.3   Emission liability

A liability for emissions would be recognised as incurred and measured at the best estimate of the expenditure required to settle the present obligation at the end of the reporting period, in accordance with IAS 37:36. Under cap and trade schemes, entities generally can settle the obligation created by the emission of pollutants only by surrendering allowances to the appropriate authority and cannot settle their obligations by making a cash payment or by transferring other assets.

When an entity measures allowances at fair value, the liability would be measured at the same amount, because this is the best estimate of the expenditure (economic resources) required to settle the obligation.

When an entity measures allowances at cost then, provided that it has sufficient allowances to satisfy the emission liability, the liability would be measured at the same amount (i.e. as the sum of the cost of the initial allowances received and the cost of any additional allowances purchased). If at the end of the reporting period the liability to deliver allowances exceeds the amount of allowances on hand, then the shortfall would be measured at the current fair (market) value of the short position. Consequently, if an entity chose to sell allowances during the year, and in doing so created a shortfall in the number of allowances held as compared to the total pollutants emitted at that date, it would remeasure the portion of the obligation related to the shortfall at the current market value of the allowances.

9.1.3   Approach 3: government grant and an intangible asset measured at nominal amounts (net liability approach)

Under this approach, when allowances are allocated free of charge or for nominal consideration, an intangible asset would be recognised and measured at a nominal amount when allowances are issued or allocated (i.e. the cost / nominal amount alternatives are adopted in IAS 20 and IAS 38). A credit entry for the government grant would be recognised in the statement of financial position at a nominal amount equal to the carrying amount of the allowances. [IAS 20:23]

No liability for emissions would be recognised provided that the entity has sufficient allowances to satisfy the emission liability, because the allowances granted (which are recognised only at a nominal amount) will be used to settle the liability. Therefore, no entries are required as long as the entity holds sufficient allowances to meet its emission obligations.

If at the end of the reporting period the liability to deliver allowances exceeds the amount of allowances on hand, then the shortfall should be measured at the current fair (market) value of the short position (as in **9.1.2** above).

9.2   IFRIC 5 *Rights to Interests arising from Decommissioning, Restoration and Environmental Rehabilitation Funds*

IFRIC 5 deals with the accounting, in the financial statements of the contributor, for interests in decommissioning, restoration and environmental rehabilitation funds established to fund some or all of the costs of decommissioning assets or to undertake environmental rehabilitation. Contributions to such funds may be voluntary or required by law. Funds may be established by a single contributor, or they may be established by multiple contributors. Such funds are generally separately administered by trustees. Entities make contributions that are invested on behalf of the fund by the trustees. The contributors retain the obligation to pay decommissioning costs, but they are able to obtain reimbursement from the fund up to the lower of the decommissioning costs incurred and the contributor's share of the assets of the fund. The contributors may have restricted access or no access to any surplus of assets of the fund over those used to meet eligible decommissioning costs.

The issues under consideration in IFRIC 5 are:
[IFRIC 5:6]

- how should a contributor account for its interest in a fund; and

- when a contributor has an obligation to make additional contributions (e.g. in the event of the bankruptcy of another contributor), how should that obligation be accounted for?

Note that the scope of IFRIC 5 is restricted to funds with separately-administered assets, when the contributor's right to access the assets is restricted. [IFRIC 5:4] A residual interest in a fund that extends beyond a right to reimbursement, such as a contractual right to distributions once all the decommissioning has been completed or on winding up the fund, may be an equity instrument within the scope of IFRS 9 *Financial Instruments* (or, prior to the adoption of IFRS 9, IAS 39 *Financial Instruments: Recognition and Measurement*), and is not within the scope of IFRIC 5. [IFRIC 5:5]

9.2.1   Assessing the relationship between the contributor and the fund

The contributor is required to assess whether it has control or joint control of, or significant influence, over the fund, in accordance with relevant IFRSs, and to account for its interest by consolidation, proportionate consolidation, or the equity method, as appropriate under those Standards. [IFRIC 5:8]

> The option of proportionate consolidation is not available for entities that have adopted IFRS 11 *Joint Arrangements* (see **chapter A27**).

9.2.2   Accounting for the obligation to pay decommissioning costs

The contributor's obligation to pay decommissioning costs should be recognised as a liability, separately from its interest in the fund, unless its contributions to the fund have extinguished its obligation to pay decommissioning costs (even in the event that the fund fails to pay). [IFRIC 5:7] Therefore, when an entity remains liable for expenditure, a provision should be recognised, even when reimbursement is available.

When a contributor has an obligation to make potential additional contributions (e.g. in the event of the bankruptcy of another contributor, or if the value of the investments held by the fund decreases to an extent that they are insufficient to fulfil the fund's reimbursement obligations) this obligation is a contingent liability that is accounted for under IAS 37. The contributor will recognise a liability only if it is probable that additional contributions will be made. [IFRIC 5:10]

9.2.3   Accounting for the contributor's interest in the fund

In the absence of control, joint control or significant influence, the contributor's right to reimbursement from the fund is accounted for in accordance with the rules set out in IAS 37 in respect of reimbursements. [IFRIC 5:9] Therefore, if the reimbursement is virtually certain to be received when the obligation is settled, it should be treated as a separate asset.

The reimbursement should be measured at the lower of the amount of the decommissioning obligation recognised, and the contributor's share of the fair value of the net assets of the fund attributable to contributors. [IFRIC 5:9] Therefore, recognition of an asset in excess of the recognised liability is prohibited. For example, rights to receive reimbursement to meet decommissioning liabilities that have yet to be recognised as a provision are not recognised.

Changes in the carrying amount of the right to receive reimbursement other than contributions to and payments from the fund should be recognised in profit or loss in the period in which those changes occur. [IFRIC 5:9]

9.2.4   Disclosure

Contributors are required to disclose the nature of interests in funds, and any restrictions on access to the assets in the funds. [IFRIC 5:11] In addition, when the arrangements give rise to contingent liabilities or reimbursement rights that are accounted for under IAS 37, the relevant disclosure requirements of IAS 37 apply.

9.3   IFRIC 6 *Liabilities arising from Participating in a Specific Market – Waste Electrical and Electronic Equipment*

IFRIC 6 addresses the recognition of liabilities for waste management under the European Union's Directive on Waste Electrical and Electronic Equipment (the WE&EE Directive). Specifically, the Interpretation deals with waste from private households arising from products sold on or before 13 August 2005. It does not apply to waste from sources other than private households, nor to household waste arising from products sold after 13 August 2005.

The Interpretation is therefore quite narrow in scope. The general principles in IAS 37 should be applied to determine the appropriate recognition point for other remediation and recycling obligations. However IFRIC 6:7 states that "if, in national legislation, new waste from private households is treated in a similar manner to historical waste from private households, the principles of the Interpretation apply by reference to the hierarchy in paragraphs 10 – 12 of IAS 8". Therefore, before determining an accounting policy for 'new' household waste, entities will need to determine how the WE&EE Directive has been transposed into local law. The Interpretation will also be a source of authoritative guidance on the appropriate accounting for obligations that are imposed by similar cost attribution models.

Under the WE&EE Directive, the obligation to contribute to waste management costs is allocated proportionately to producers of the relevant type of equipment who participate in the market during a specified period (the measurement period). The IFRIC (now the IFRS Interpretations Committee) was asked to determine what constitutes the obligating event for the recognition of a provision for the waste management costs.

The IFRIC decided that the event that triggers liability recognition is participation in the market during a measurement period (and not the production of the equipment, nor the actual incurrence of waste management costs).

9.4   IFRIC 21 *Levies*

IFRIC 21 *Levies* was issued in May 2013 and is effective for annual periods beginning on or after 1 January 2014, with earlier application permitted. IFRIC 21 provides guidance on when to recognise a liability for a levy imposed by a government; it applies both for levies that are accounted for in accordance with IAS 37 and those for which the timing and amount of the levy is certain.

The consensus in IFRIC 21 is consistent with the consensus in IFRIC 6 (see **9.3** above). However, the Interpretations Committee decided not to withdraw IFRIC 6 because it provides useful information on the accounting for liabilities within its scope. [IFRIC 21:BC10]

9.4.1   Scope

IFRIC 21 addresses the accounting for a liability to pay a levy if either: [IFRIC 21: 2]

- the liability is within the scope of IAS 37 (i.e. the timing or amount of the levy is uncertain); or

- both the timing and the amount of the levy are certain.

IFRIC 21 does not address the appropriate accounting for the costs that arise from recognising a liability to pay a levy; the determination as to whether the recognition of a such a liability gives rise to an asset or an expense is made in accordance with other IFRSs. [IFRIC 21:3]

For the purposes of IFRIC 21, a levy is defined as "an outflow of resources embodying economic benefits that is imposed by governments on entities in accordance with legislation (ie laws and/or regulations), other than:

(a) those outflows of resources that are within the scope of other Standards(such as income taxes that are within the scope of IAS 12 Income Taxes); and

(b) fines or other penalties that are imposed for breaches of the legislation.

'Government' refers to government, government agencies and similar bodies whether local, national or international." [IFRIC 21:4]

The Interpretation was issued in response to a request to the IFRS Interpretations Committee to determine whether, under specified circumstances, IFRIC 6 (see **9.3** above) should be applied by analogy to other levies charged for participation in a market on a specified date in order to identify the event that gives rise to a liability. The specific examples provided to the Committee in this regard included the United Kingdom bank levy, fees paid to the Federal Government by pharmaceutical manufacturers in the United States, a bank levy in Hungary, and the railway tax in France. The final Interpretation covers a broad range of levies, rather than focussing on levies charged to participate in a market.

Any 'levy' imposed by a government that meets the definition of an income tax (see **section 2** of **chapter A13**) is accounted for in accordance with IAS 12 rather than in accordance with IFRIC 21.

Amounts that are collected by entities on behalf of governments and remitted to governments (e.g. value added taxes) are not an 'outflow of resources' for the entity collecting and remitting those amounts. [IFRIC 21:BC6]. Consequently, they do not fall within the scope of IFRIC 21.

Note that:
[IFRIC 21:5, 6 & BC7]

• a payment made by an entity for the acquisition of an asset, or for the rendering of services, under a contractual agreement with a government, does not meet the definition of a levy because it is not 'imposed' by the government; and

• an entity is not required to apply IFRIC 21 to liabilities that arise from emissions trading schemes.

9.4.2 Obligating event that gives rise to the recognition of a liability to pay a levy

The obligating event that gives rise to a liability to pay a levy is the activity that triggers the payment of the levy, as identified by the legislation. [IFRIC 21:8]

If the activity that triggers the payment of the levy is the generation of revenue in the current period and the calculation of that levy is based on the revenue that was generated in a previous period, the obligating event for that levy is the generation of revenue in the current period. The generation of revenue in the previous period is necessary, but not sufficient, to create a present obligation. [IFRIC 21:8]

Example 9.4.2

A levy is triggered in full as soon as the entity generates revenue

[Illustrative examples accompanying IFRIC 21, Example 2]

Entity B has an annual reporting period that ends on 31 December. In accordance with legislation, a levy is triggered in full as soon as an entity generates revenue in 20X1. The amount of the levy is calculated by reference to revenue generated by the entity in 20X0. Entity B generated revenue in 20X0 and in 20X1 starts to generate revenue on 3 January 20X1.

In this example, the liability is recognised in full on 3 January 20X1 because the obligating event, as identified by the legislation, is the first generation of revenue in 20X1. The generation of revenue in 20X0 is necessary, but not sufficient, to create a present obligation to pay a levy. Before 3 January 20X1, Entity B has no present obligation to pay a levy. In other words, the activity that triggers the payment of the levy, as identified by the legislation, is the point at which Entity B first generates revenue in 20X1. The generation of revenue in 20X0 is not the activity that triggers the payment of the levy and the recognition of the liability. The amount of revenue generated in 20X0 only affects the measurement of the liability.

In the interim financial report (if any), the liability is recognised in full in the first interim period of 20X1 because the liability is recognised in full on 3 January 20X1.

The date on which the levy is paid does not affect the timing of recognition of the liability to pay a levy, because the obligating event is the activity that triggers the payment of the levy, and not the payment of the levy itself. [IFRIC 21:BC13]

9.4.3   *Economic compulsion to continue to operate does not result in a constructive obligation*

An entity does not have a constructive obligation to pay a levy that will be triggered by operating in a future period as a result of the entity being economically compelled to continue to operate in that future period. [IFRIC 21:8]

When drafting IFRIC 21, the Interpretations Committee considered an argument that, if it would be necessary for an entity to take unrealistic action in order to avoid an obligation to pay a levy that would otherwise be triggered by operating in the future, then a constructive obligation to pay the levy exists and a liability should be recognised (see IFRIC 21:15 for further discussion). However, the Committee rejected this argument, noting that if this rationale were applied, many types of future expenditure within the scope of IAS 37 would be recognised as liabilities. The Interpretations Committee noted that, in accordance with IAS 37:18 and 19:
[IFRIC 21:BC16]

• no provision is recognised for costs that need to be incurred to operate in the future; and

• it is only those obligations arising from past events existing independently of an entity's future conduct of its business that are recognised as provisions.

The Basis for Conclusions on IFRIC 21 further emphasises that there is no constructive obligation to pay a levy that relates to the future conduct of the business, even if:
[IFRIC 21:BC18]

• it is economically unrealistic for the entity to avoid the levy if it has the intention of continuing in business;

• there is a legal requirement to incur the levy if the entity does continue in business;

• it would be necessary for an entity to take unrealistic action to avoid paying the levy, such as to sell, or stop operating, property, plant and equipment;

• the entity made a statement of intent (and has the ability) to operate in the future period(s); or

- the entity has a legal, regulatory or contractual requirement to operate in the future period(s).

Example 9.4.3

A levy is triggered in full if the entity operates as a bank at a specified date

[Illustrative examples accompanying IFRIC 21, Example 3]

Entity C is a bank and has an annual reporting period that ends on 31 December. In accordance with legislation, a levy is triggered in full only if an entity operates as a bank at the end of the annual reporting period. The amount of the levy is calculated by reference to the amounts in the statement of financial position of the entity at the end of the annual reporting period. The end of the annual reporting period of Entity C is 31 December 20X1.

In this example, the liability is recognised on 31 December 20X1 because the obligating event, as identified by the legislation, is Entity C operating as a bank at the end of the annual reporting period. Before that point, Entity C has no present obligation to pay a levy, even if it is economically compelled to continue to operate as a bank in the future. In other words, the activity that triggers the payment of the levy, as identified by the legislation, is the entity operating as a bank at the end of the annual reporting period, which does not occur until 31 December 20X1. The conclusion would not change even if the amount of the liability is based on the length of the reporting period, because the obligating event is the entity operating as a bank at the end of the annual reporting period.

In the interim financial report (if any), the liability is recognised in full in the interim period in which 31 December 20X1 falls because the liability is recognised in full on that date.

The preparation of financial statements under the going concern assumption does not imply that an entity has a present obligation to pay a levy that will be triggered by operating in a future period. [IFRIC 21:10]

9.4.4   Obligating event that occurs over a period of time

The liability to pay a levy is recognised progressively if the obligating event occurs over a period of time (i.e. if the activity that triggers the payment of the levy, as identified by the legislation, occurs over a period of time). For example, if the obligating event is the generation of revenue over a period of time, the corresponding liability is recognised as the entity generates that revenue. [IFRIC 21:11]

Example 9.4.4

A levy is triggered progressively as the entity generates revenue

[Illustrative examples accompanying IFRIC 21, Example 1]

Entity A has an annual reporting period that ends on 31 December. In accordance with legislation, a levy is triggered progressively as an entity generates revenue in 20X1. The amount of the levy is calculated by reference to revenue generated by the entity in 20X1.

In this example, the liability is recognised progressively during 20X1 as Entity A generates revenue, because the obligating event, as identified by the legislation, is the generation of revenue during 20X1. At any point in 20X1, Entity A has a present obligation to pay a levy on revenue generated to date. Entity A has no present obligation to pay a levy that will arise from generating revenue in the future.

In the interim financial report (if any), the liability is recognised progressively as Entity A generates revenue. Entity A has a present obligation to pay the levy on revenue generated from 1 January 20X1 to the end of the interim period.

9.4.5   Levy triggered when a minimum threshold is reached

If an obligation to pay a levy is triggered when a minimum threshold is reached, the principles discussed in the previous sections should be applied. For example, if the obligating event is the reaching of a minimum activity threshold (such as a minimum amount of revenue or sales generated or outputs produced), the corresponding liability is recognised when that minimum activity threshold is reached. [IFRIC 21:12]

Example 9.4.5

A levy is triggered in full if the entity generates revenue above a minimum amount of revenue

[Illustrative examples accompanying IFRIC 21, Example 4]

Entity D has an annual reporting period that ends on 31 December. In accordance with legislation, a levy is triggered if an entity generates revenue above CU50 million in 20X1.[(a)] The amount of the levy is calculated by reference to revenue generated above CU50 million, with the levy rate at 0 per cent for the first CU50 million revenue generated (below the threshold) and 2 per cent above CU50 million revenue. Entity D's revenue reaches the revenue threshold of CU50 million on 17 July 20X1.

In this example, the liability is recognised between 17 July 20X1 and 31 December 20X1 as Entity D generates revenue above the threshold because the obligating event, as identified by the legislation, is the activity undertaken after the threshold is reached (ie the generation of revenue after the threshold is reached). The amount of the liability is based on the revenue generated to date that exceeds the threshold of CU50 million revenue.

In the interim financial report (if any), the liability is recognised between 17 July 20X1 and 31 December 20X1 as Entity D generates revenue above the threshold.

Variation:

Same fact pattern as above (ie a levy is triggered if Entity D generates revenue above CU50 million in 20X1), except that the amount of the levy is calculated by reference to all revenue generated by Entity D in 20X1 (ie including the first CU50 million revenue generated in 20X1).

In this example, the liability for the payment of the levy related to the first CU50 million revenue is recognised on 17 July 20X1 when the threshold is met, because the obligating event, as identified by the legislation, for the payment of that amount is the reaching of the threshold. The liability for the payment of the levy related to revenue generated above the threshold is recognised between 17 July 20X1 and 31 December 20X1 as the entity generates revenue above the threshold, because the obligating event, as identified by the legislation, is the activity undertaken after the threshold is reached (ie the generation of revenue after the threshold is reached). The amount of the liability is based on the revenue generated to date, including the first CU50 million revenue. The same recognition principles apply in the interim financial report (if any) as in the annual financial statements.

(a) In this Interpretation, currency amounts are denominated in 'currency units' (CU).

9.4.6   *Levy prepaid in advance of present obligation*

An entity should recognise an asset if it has prepaid a levy but does not yet have a present obligation to pay that levy. [IFRIC 21:14]

9.4.7   *Recognising a liability to pay a levy in an interim financial report*

An entity is required apply the same recognition principles in the interim financial report that it applies in the annual financial statements. As a result, in the interim financial report, a liability to pay a levy: [IFRIC 21:13]

- should not be recognised if there is no present obligation to pay the levy at the end of the interim reporting period; and

- should be recognised if a present obligation to pay the levy exists at the end of the interim reporting period.

9.4.8   *Effective date and transition*

IFRIC 21 is effective for annual periods beginning on or after 1 January 2014, with earlier application permitted. If an entity applies IFRIC 21 for an earlier period, it is required to disclose that fact. [IFRIC 21:A1]

Changes in accounting policies resulting from the initial application of IFRIC 21 are required to be accounted for retrospectively in accordance with IAS 8 *Accounting Policies, Changes in Accounting Estimates and Errors.* [IFRIC 21:A2]

10   Presentation and disclosure

10.1   Presentation

IAS 1 *Presentation of Financial Statements* requires that, when material, the aggregate carrying amount of the entity's provisions should be presented in the statement of financial position. [IAS 1:54(l)]

10.2   Disclosure

The objective of IAS 37 with respect to disclosure is to ensure that sufficient information is disclosed in the notes to the financial statements to enable users to understand the nature, timing and amount of provisions, contingent liabilities and contingent assets.

10.2.1   *Provisions*

For each class of provision, the following should be disclosed (comparative information is not required):
[IAS 37:84]

- the carrying amount at the beginning and end of the period;

- additional provisions recognised in the period, including increases to existing provisions;

- amounts used (i.e. incurred and charged against the provision) during the period;

- unused amounts reversed during the period; and

- the increase during the period in the discounted amount arising from the passage of time and the effect of any change in the discount rate.

The following should also be disclosed for each class of provision:
[IAS 37:85]

- a brief description of the nature of the obligation and the expected timing of any resulting outflows of economic benefits;

- an indication of the uncertainties about the amount or timing of those outflows. When necessary to provide adequate information, the entity should disclose the major assumptions made concerning future events (see **4.5**); and

- the amount of any expected reimbursement, stating the amount of any asset that has been recognised for that expected reimbursement.

In determining which provisions may be aggregated to form a class, it is necessary to consider whether the nature of the items is sufficiently similar for a single statement about them to fulfil the requirements outlined above with respect to disclosure of the nature of and uncertainties surrounding such liabilities. [IAS 37:87]

When a provision meets the definition of a financial instrument in IAS 32 *Financial Instruments: Presentation*, but is accounted for under IAS 37 because it is not within the scope of IFRS 9 *Financial Instruments* (or, prior to the adoption of IFRS 9, IAS 39 *Financial Instruments: Recognition and Measurement*), the disclosure requirements of IFRS 7 *Financial Instruments: Disclosures* will apply in addition to those of IAS 37.

10.2.2   Contingent liabilities

For each class of contingent liability (unless the possibility of an outflow in settlement is remote), a brief description of the nature of the contingent liability should be provided. The following information should also be disclosed, if practicable:
[IAS 37:86]

- an estimate of its financial effect (based on the measurement requirements of IAS 37);

- an indication of the uncertainties relating to the amount or timing of any outflow; and

- the possibility of any reimbursement.

In determining which contingent liabilities may be aggregated to form a class, it is necessary to consider whether the nature of the items is sufficiently similar for a single statement about them to fulfil the requirements outlined above with respect to disclosure of the nature of and uncertainties surrounding such items. [IAS 37:87]

When a provision and a contingent liability arise from the same set of circumstances, the reporting entity should make the required disclosures in a way that clearly shows the link between the provision and the contingent liability. [IAS 37:88]

10.2.3 Contingent assets

When an inflow of economic benefits is probable, the entity should disclose a brief description of the nature of the contingent assets at the end of the reporting period and, if practicable, an estimate of their financial effect (based on the measurement requirements of IAS 37), taking care to avoid giving misleading indications of the likelihood of income arising. [IAS 37:89 & 90]

10.2.4 Exemptions from disclosure requirements

10.2.4.1 Exemption applying to disclosure of contingent liabilities and contingent assets

When any of the information required in respect of contingent liabilities and contingent assets, as set out in **10.2.2** and **10.2.3** above, is not disclosed because it is not practicable to do so, that fact should be stated. [IAS 37:91]

10.2.4.2 Exemption applying to all disclosures

In extremely rare cases, it is conceivable that some or all of the disclosures required by IAS 37 can be expected to prejudice seriously the position of the entity in a dispute with other parties on the subject matter of the provision, contingent liability or contingent asset. In such cases, the reporting entity need not disclose the information, but it should disclose the general nature of the dispute, together with the fact that the information has not been disclosed and the reason why. [IAS 37:92]

11 Future developments

In 2005, the IASB published an exposure draft (the '2005 ED') that proposed to replace IAS 37. Following consideration of the responses received to the 2005 ED, in January 2010 the IASB published ED/2010/1 (the '2010 ED') *Measurement of Liabilities in IAS 37* (*Limited re-exposure of proposed amendment to IAS 37*). The 2010 ED addressed only one section of the proposed replacement Standard – the measurement requirements for liabilities that are within the scope of IAS 37.

The comment letters received demonstrated strong opposition to the proposed Standard (not limited to the 2010 ED but also to aspects of the 2005 ED that were not re-exposed). Some constituents also argued that, given the time that had elapsed since the 2005 ED, the Board should re-expose the entire proposed IFRS.

During their joint meeting in November 2010, the IASB and FASB decided to defer further work on this project. In December 2012, as part of the response to its Agenda Consultation in 2011, the IASB formally reactivated this project as an IASB-only research project; at that time, the IASB confirmed it will not amend IAS 37 without a full re-exposure.

The reactivated project will focus on identifying examples that are continuing to cause difficulty in applying IAS 37 in practice. These examples will initially be used as 'test cases' in developing the elements and measurement chapters of the *Conceptual Framework for Financial Reporting* (see **chapter A2**).

A13   Income taxes

Contents

1   Introduction

This chapter sets out the accounting treatment for both current and deferred tax under IAS 12 *Income Taxes* and SIC-25 *Income Taxes – Changes in the Tax Status of an Entity or its Shareholders*.

IAS 12 was most recently amended in October 2012 for consequential amendments arising from the *Investment Entities* amendments to IFRS 10 *Consolidated Financial Statements*. Those *Investment Entities* amendments require that an investment entity parent should measure its investments in subsidiaries (other than subsidiaries that provide investment-related services or activities) at fair value through profit or loss (see **section 15** of **chapter A24** for details). The consequential amendments to IAS 12 specify that the general exceptions allowed in IAS 12 in respect of current and deferred tax arising from a business combination do not apply to the acquisition by an investment entity of a subsidiary that is required to be measured at fair value through profit or loss (see **3.2.2** and **4.7**).

The consequential amendments arising from the *Investment Entities* amendments are effective for annual periods beginning on or after 1 January 2014, with earlier application permitted. If an entity applies the *Investment Entities* amendments for a period beginning before 1 January 2014, it should apply all amendments included in the *Investment Entities* amendments at the same time. [IAS 12:98C]

2   Scope

IAS 12 deals with accounting for income taxes. The Standard defines income taxes as including "all domestic and foreign taxes which are based on taxable profits. Income taxes also include taxes, such as withholding taxes, that are payable by a subsidiary, associate or joint arrangement on distributions to the reporting entity". [IAS 12:2]

> For entities that have not yet adopted IFRS 11 *Joint Arrangements* (effective for annual periods beginning on or after 1 January 2013, with earlier adoption permitted), the reference to 'joint arrangement' in IAS 12:2 should be read as a reference to a 'joint venture'.

> The determination as to whether a tax is an 'income tax' is a matter requiring careful judgement based on the specific facts and circumstances. Factors to consider in making this determination include, but are not limited to, whether:

- the 'starting point' for determining the taxable amount is based on taxable profits rather than another metric (e.g. units of production);

- the tax is based on a 'taxable profit' notion, implying a net rather than a gross amount;

- the tax is based on actual income and expenses rather than a notional amount (e.g. on a tonnage capacity);

- the legal description or characteristics of the tax imply that the tax is calculated based on taxable profits; and

- there is any withholding related to the tax.

The IFRIC (now the IFRS Interpretations Committee) referred to this topic in a rejection notice published in the March 2006 *IFRIC Update*. The IFRIC noted that the definition of taxable profit implies that not all taxes are in the scope of IAS 12, and that the requirement to disclose an explanation of the relationship between the tax expense and the accounting profit implies that taxable profit need not be the same as accounting profit.

Taxes that are unlikely to meet the definition of an income tax include:

- sales taxes (because they are transactional taxes based on sales value rather than on taxable profits);

- production-based taxes (see **example 2.4A** below); and

- 'tonnage' taxes (see **2.2** below).

Care should be exercised in respect of taxes imposed in different jurisdictions that are referred to by common titles but for which the detailed application varies significantly between jurisdictions (such as 'petroleum revenue taxes' – see **example 2.4B** below). The determination as to whether such taxes are income taxes should be made on a case-by-case basis.

2.1   Levies

IFRIC 21 *Levies*, which was issued in May 2013, provides guidance on when to recognise a liability for a 'levy' imposed by a government; a levy is defined as "an outflow of resources embodying economic benefits that is imposed by governments on entities in accordance with legislation (ie laws and/or regulations), other than:

(a)   those outflows of resources that are within the scope of other Standards (such as income taxes that are within the scope of IAS 12); and

(b)   fines or other penalties that are imposed for breaches of the legislation".

Therefore, any 'levy' imposed by a government needs to be assessed to determine if it meets the definition of an income tax (see above). If it does, it should be accounted for in accordance with IAS 12 rather than in accordance with IFRIC 21.

Section 9.4 in **chapter A12** provides a detailed description of the requirements of IFRIC 21.

2.2   Tonnage tax

In some jurisdictions, shipping entities can choose to be taxed by means of a 'tonnage tax' instead of under general corporate income tax regulations. Tonnage tax may be paid on the basis of tonnage transported, tonnage capacity or a notional profit.

The IFRIC (now the IFRS Interpretations Committee) considered tonnage taxes in a rejection notice published in the May 2009 *IFRIC Update*. The IFRIC noted that taxes based on tonnage transported or tonnage capacity are based on a gross rather than a net amount, and taxes on notional income are not based on the entity's actual income and expenses. Such taxes should not be considered income taxes in accordance with IAS 12 and should not be presented as part of tax expense in the statement of comprehensive income. However, the IFRIC also noted that an entity subject to tonnage tax might present additional subtotals in the statement of comprehensive income if that presentation is relevant to an understanding of its financial performance.

2.3   Interest and penalties

In many jurisdictions, interest and penalties are assessed on under-payments or late payments of income tax. In some circumstances, interest and penalties arise because the tax amount payable could not be agreed with the tax authority until significantly after the due date and, therefore, the interest and penalties could not have been avoided by the entity. Alternatively, interest and penalties may arise because the entity has made a deliberate choice not to make the appropriate tax payments before the due date.

Interest and penalties assessed on underpayments or late payments of income tax do not meet the definition of current or deferred tax under IAS 12:5 (see **3.1** and **4.1** below), regardless of the circum-stances in which they arise, and they should be presented in the financial statements based on their nature, i.e. either as a finance cost (interest) or an operating cost (penalties).

2.4   Hybrid taxes

Entities are sometimes subject to a tax that has different components. It is necessary to exercise careful judgement when determining whether each of the components meets the definition of an income tax under IAS 12.

Example 2.4A

Tax comprising both production and profit-based components

Company A is subject to a tax made up of two discrete components – a production-based component and a profit-based component. The production-based component is a fixed minimum amount per tonne of product sold. The total tax, however, may exceed the fixed minimum per tonne depending on the entity's profitability.

The production-based component of the tax should not be considered an income tax because it is based on the weight of product sold rather than taxable profits; it is, therefore, outside the scope of IAS 12. On the other hand, any amounts due as a result of the profit-based component should be considered an income tax and within the scope of IAS 12.

The production-based component of the tax may be reported within either 'cost of goods sold' or 'operating expenses', though the former is preferable.

In either case, the presentation should reflect the substance of the entity's operations and should be consistently applied.

Example 2.4B

Petroleum revenue tax

In many jurisdictions, taxes are imposed on 'petroleum revenue'; these taxes are generally designed to ensure that the tax authority benefits from 'super profits' generated by entities in certain resource sectors.

Petroleum revenue taxes vary from jurisdiction to jurisdiction, but they are generally determined based on revenue from extraction activities reduced by specified items of deductible expenditure. The deductions are often limited to items relating to the extraction activities, but may also include other amounts such as administration expenses and deductions based on assets held in the industry.

In addition, the amount of petroleum revenue tax paid will often itself be deductible when computing the entity's 'general' income tax liability.

The key characteristic that defines an income tax is that it is based on a measure of taxable profit. Whether a petroleum revenue tax in a particular jurisdiction is considered to be an income tax will depend on the rules in that specific jurisdiction and whether the basis for the tax is judged to be closer to a measure of revenue or a measure of net profit.

The fact that the 'taxable profit' for the purposes of the petroleum revenue tax differs from 'taxable profit' for the purpose of a jurisdiction's general income tax regime (e.g. because it relates to only part of the operations or because different deductions or allowances are available) is not in itself relevant because the basis for the petroleum revenue tax may still be considered to be a measure of net profit (albeit a different measure than that used as the basis for general income tax).

If the petroleum revenue tax is allowed as a deduction when computing the entity's general income tax liability, this does not preclude the petroleum revenue tax from being considered an income tax for the purposes of IAS 12. The reference in IAS 12:2 to 'all' domestic taxes indicates that there may be more than one form of income tax in a particular jurisdiction.

2.5 Investment tax credits

IAS 12:4 states that the Standard does not deal with methods of accounting for government grants or 'investment tax credits'. IAS 12 does not provide a definition for 'investment tax credits', which is a term used in many tax jurisdictions to describe a wide range of tax arrangements. Accordingly, in practice, the first step in accounting for an 'investment tax credit' is to determine whether it is within the scope of IAS 12. Even if a tax benefit is referred to by a tax authority as an investment tax credit, it is important to consider the substance to determine whether the tax benefit is outside the scope of IAS 12. A tax credit (outside the scope of IAS 12) provides a reduction to taxes payable and can be distinguished from a tax deduction (within the scope of IAS 12) which is factored into the determination of taxable income.

IAS 20 *Accounting for Government Grants and Disclosure of Government Assistance* (see **chapter A36**) has a broad scope exemption, not just for investment tax credits, but also for "government assistance that is provided for an entity in the form of benefits that are available in determining taxable income or are determined or limited on the basis of income tax liability".

When a tax credit is determined to be an investment tax credit (and, consequently, outside the scope of IAS 12 and IAS 20), it is a matter of judgement under IAS 8 *Accounting Policies, Changes in Accounting Estimates and Errors* to determine the most appropriate accounting treatment. It may be appropriate to analogise to IAS 12 or IAS 20. Generally, if an approach similar to IAS 12 is adopted, a credit will be recognised in profit or loss, and the related asset in the statement of financial position, when the entity satisfies the criteria to receive the credit. If the substance of the arrangement is considered to be closer to a government grant, and an IAS 20 approach is adopted, the credit will be recognised within profit or loss over the periods necessary to match the benefit of the credit with the costs for which it is intended to compensate.

2.6   Refundable tax credits

In some jurisdictions, tax credits may arise that have either or both of the following characteristics.

- The credit may be utilised to obtain a cash payment, rather than solely to reduce income tax payable in the year in which the credit is generated or to reduce income tax payable over a number of years. Therefore, the benefit is not dependent entirely on the entity having a future or past income tax liability against which the credit can be utilised (e.g. an entity may receive a full or partial cash payment despite being in a tax loss position).

- The credit may be utilised to receive a refund of a combination of income taxes and other non-income taxes paid during the year. For example, the tax credit may be offset first against income tax payable for the year, then against some other taxes (e.g. payroll taxes) incurred in the year, with any unused credit carried forward to subsequent years.

Such credits are often referred to as 'refundable' tax credits.

Whether refundable tax credits come within the scope of IAS 12 depends on the specific terms of the particular tax credits under consideration. The most appropriate accounting treatment for such refundable tax credits will be a matter of judgement to be determined under IAS 8. It will be necessary to look carefully at the substance of the particular credit, including the requirements that must be met in order to generate the credit and how the credit will be realised in practice. IAS 12 and IAS 20 are likely to provide the most appropriate references for the purpose of determining an appropriate accounting policy. For example, if the credit can be used to generate a cash payment and realisation is not dependent on any past or future income tax liability, then it may be reasonable to conclude that the credit is in the nature of a government grant and is not within the scope of IAS 12.

2.7 Additional tax deductions

Example 2.7

Accounting for additional tax deductions

Entity A will receive an additional tax deduction if it invests in more than 25 per cent of an investee abroad and it meets a number of specified conditions. The deduction is granted to encourage investment in foreign entities.

If the specified conditions are met, the additional tax deduction is 50 per cent of the cost of the investment. Entity A is permitted to use the deduction in the calculation of its current year's tax liability; alternatively, it can defer claiming the deduction, but only for a maximum of five years.

IAS 12:7 defines the tax base of an asset as "the amount that will be deductible for tax purposes against any taxable economic benefits that will flow to an entity when it recovers the carrying amount of the asset" (see also **4.2.1** below).

In the circumstances described, the deduction is available independently of the recovery of the investment either through use or sale, and it is therefore not part of the tax base of the asset.

The incentive is not directly linked to any underlying asset. If deferred, it represents an unused tax deduction and, in accordance with IAS 12:34 (see **4.6**), a deferred tax asset should be recognised to the extent that it is probable that future taxable profit will be available against which the unused tax deduction can be used.

Note that arrangements of the type described in **example 2.7** are sometimes referred to as 'investment tax credits'; however, use of the term 'investment tax credit' in local tax legislation is not necessarily consistent with the term's use in IAS 12 and it is necessary to review the detailed application of tax incentives referred to as investment tax credits in order to determine whether they are within the scope of IAS 12 (see **2.5** above).

2.8   Classification of payments in a tax structuring transaction

When implementing tax planning strategies, entities will often incur costs payable to the designer of the strategy. In determining whether such costs meet the definition of income tax or should be treated as an operating expense, the entity will need to have regard to whether the payment is to the designer, or whether it is paid to the designer to be paid to the tax authorities on the entity's behalf.

Example 2.8

Classification of payments in a tax structuring transaction

Entity A has an effective domestic tax rate of 40 per cent. Entity A enters into a transaction with an investment bank which enables a portion of its activities (generating profit of CU1,000) to be taxed in a tax-haven jurisdiction rather than under Entity A's domestic tax regime.

The investment bank receives a 30 per cent fee based on total taxable profits before the transaction, of which it pays 10 per cent (CU30) over to the tax authorities in the tax-haven jurisdiction. The net result of the transaction on domestic tax is that tax is paid on 10 per cent of the original profit. The following table illustrates the effect of the transaction on taxable profits and tax payments.

	Before structuring CU	After structuring CU
Taxable profit before structuring	1,000	1,000
Fee payable to investment bank	–	(300)
Domestic tax (40%)	(400)	(40)
Profit after fee payable to investment bank and domestic tax	600	660

Should the fee payable by Entity A to the investment bank be classified as income tax expense?

No, but consideration should be given to whether the tax paid by the investment bank was paid on Entity A's behalf.

Only amounts that are ultimately paid to tax authorities on Entity A's behalf should be considered as tax expenses. In the circumstances described, an evaluation needs to be performed as to whether, in substance, Entity A continues to bear the tax risk associated with the tax payment by the investment bank, or whether the bank makes the tax payment of CU30 on its own behalf. If Entity A retains substantially all of the tax risk associated with the tax payment by the investment bank, all direct and indirect payments to the tax authorities should be considered as a tax expense, resulting in the recognition of a tax expense of CU70 (CU40 domestic tax paid by Entity A and CU30 tax in the tax-haven jurisdiction paid on Entity A's behalf by the investment bank). If the investment bank takes over substantially all the tax risk, the entire fee paid to the investment bank will be an operating expense and the tax expense will be only the domestic tax of CU40.

In determining whether Entity A has retained the tax risk, the following factors should be considered:

- whether the tax authority has any power to demand payment from Entity A if the investment bank does not pay; and

- whether Entity A could be required to make further payments for the tax (or be entitled to refunds) if the onward payment proves to have been miscalculated.

2.9 Classification of payments to acquire tax losses

Example 2.9

Classification of payments to acquire tax losses

In some jurisdictions, the tax authority requires each entity to file its tax return as if it is a stand-alone tax payer which is taxed and pays income tax separately. However, within a tax group (e.g. a group of entities under common control), tax losses may be transferred between entities and used to offset the taxable income in the purchasing entity. The price to be paid for the tax losses is determined by agreement between the seller and the purchaser.

For example, Entity A and Entity B are both direct subsidiaries of Entity P. The tax rate in their jurisdiction is 30 per cent. Entity A acquires tax losses of CU100 from Entity B at an agreed price of CU50 and utilises the tax losses immediately.

In its separate financial statements, how should Entity A classify the payment made to Entity B to acquire the tax losses?

In this example, the payment of CU50 exceeds the tax benefit that Entity A has acquired (which is 30% × CU100 = CU30). The payment can only be considered a settlement of Entity A's income tax liability to the extent of that tax benefit. Therefore, only CU30 of the payment should be offset against Entity A's tax liability.

The accounting treatment for the excess payment of CU20 should reflect the substance of the transaction. In particular, it is necessary to consider whether Entity A has acquired anything else from Entity B that would correspond to the excess payment of CU20. If not, the substance of the transaction would seem to be that the excess payment of CU20 represents a distribution by Entity A which has been directed to Entity B in accordance with the wishes of their common parent, Entity P. Entity A should therefore recognise the CU20 as a distribution in equity.

In practice, the losses will be included in the tax return and Entity A will have recognised a lower tax expense and tax liability on the basis of the amounts in the tax return. The entries to reflect the cash payment of CU50 will therefore be as follows.

		CU	CU
Dr	Tax expense	30	
Dr	Distribution	20	
Cr	Cash		50

3   Current tax

3.1   Definitions

Current tax is defined as the amount of income taxes payable (recoverable) in respect of the taxable profit (tax loss) for a period. [IAS 12:5] It is the tax that the entity expects to pay (recover) in respect of a financial period.

Taxable profit (tax loss) is defined as the profit (loss) for a period, determined in accordance with the rules established by the tax authorities, upon which income taxes are payable (recoverable). [IAS 12:5]

3.2 Recognition of current tax assets and liabilities

IAS 12's basic requirement is that, to the extent that current tax for the current and prior reporting periods is unpaid, it should be recognised as a liability. Conversely, if the amount already paid in respect of current and prior periods exceeds the amount due for those periods, the excess should be recognised as an asset. [IAS 12:12]

Similarly, an asset is recognised if a tax loss can be carried back to recover the current tax paid in an earlier period. [IAS 12:13] Thus, if an entity has a tax loss in one year (e.g. 20X3), and this is carried back and used to recover tax paid in an earlier period (e.g. 20X2), the current tax benefit of the recovery is recognised in the year in which the loss arises (i.e. 20X3).

Generally, current tax is recognised in profit or loss. There are two exceptions:
[IAS 12:58]

- when the current tax arises as a result of a transaction or event that is recognised, in the same or a different period, outside profit or loss, either in other comprehensive income or directly in equity (see **3.2.1**); and

- when the current tax arises from a business combination (see **3.2.2**).

For entities that have adopted the *Investment Entities* amendments (effective for annual periods beginning on or after 1 January 2014, with earlier adoption permitted – see **section 15** of **chapter A24** for details), IAS 12:58 is amended to clarify that the exception for business combinations does not apply to the acquisition by an investment entity (as defined in IFRS 10 *Consolidated Financial Statements*) of a subsidiary that is required to be measured at fair value through profit or loss.

3.2.1 *Items recognised outside profit or loss*

Current tax is recognised outside profit or loss if the tax relates to items that are recognised, in the same or a different period, outside profit or loss. When the current tax relates to items that are recognised in other comprehensive income, the tax is also recognised in other comprehensive income; when the tax relates to items that are recognised directly in equity, the tax is also recognised directly in equity. [IAS 12:61A]

3.2.1.1   Items recognised in other comprehensive income

Items required or permitted under IFRSs to be recognised in other comprehensive income include:
[IAS 12:62]

- revaluations of property, plant and equipment under IAS 16 *Property, Plant and Equipment*; and

- exchange differences on the translation of the financial statements of a foreign operation under IAS 21 *The Effects of Changes in Foreign Exchange Rates*.

> Other items recognised in other comprehensive income that may affect current tax are movements in fair value on investments in equity instruments designated at fair value through other comprehensive income under IFRS 9 *Financial Instruments* (or, for entities that have not yet adopted IFRS 9, movements in fair value on available-for-sale securities) when gains and losses are assessed for tax in the same period in which they are recognised in other comprehensive income.

3.2.1.2   Items recognised directly in equity

Items required or permitted under IFRSs to be credited or charged directly to equity include:
[IAS 12:62A]

- an adjustment to the opening balance of retained earnings resulting from a change in accounting policy that is accounted for retrospectively or the correction of an error under IAS 8 *Accounting Policies, Changes in Accounting Estimates and Errors*; and

- the initial recognition of the equity component of a compound financial instrument under IAS 32 *Financial Instruments: Presentation* (see **5.3.4**).

Another common situation when tax is charged directly to equity is when an entity is required to pay a portion of its dividends over to the tax authorities on behalf of the shareholders (often referred to as a 'withholding tax'). The amount paid or payable to the tax authorities is charged to equity as part of dividends (see also **4.7.2.1**). [IAS 12:65A]

> The circumstances in which current tax is recognised directly in equity are quite limited. This treatment will be required when, under

the tax rules in a particular jurisdiction, an item recognised directly in equity for accounting purposes affects the current tax expense or income for the period, for example:

- the transaction costs associated with the issue of an equity instrument are deductible for tax purposes in the period in which they are incurred;

- capital gains tax is charged relating to transactions in the entity's own equity instruments (see **example 3.2.1.2**); or

- the current tax deduction for an equity-settled share-based payment exceeds the cumulative profit or loss expense recognised in respect of that share-based payment (see **5.6**).

Example 3.2.1.2

Tax arising on sale of treasury shares held by a subsidiary

Company S (a subsidiary) holds 10 per cent of the ordinary shares of its parent (Company P). These shares are classified as treasury shares by the group. Company P buys back the shares from Company S. After the buy-back, the shares are cancelled, and the treasury shares in the consolidated financial statements are derecognised.

In accordance with the law in the tax jurisdiction in which the group operates, an entity is liable for capital gains tax (CGT) if it sells an asset for more than its base cost. In the circumstances under consideration, Company S sells the shares for more than their base cost and, therefore, incurs CGT on the sale. The group therefore incurs CGT on the sale.

In the consolidated financial statements, a transfer from one equity classification (the treasury share reserve) to another equity classification (share capital or another reserve as required by local law) is made to reflect the cancellation of shares. The CGT represents a transaction cost relating to the cancellation and should therefore be recognised directly in equity.

3.2.1.3   Uncertainty regarding amount to be recognised outside profit or loss

If an entity cannot determine the amount of current tax that relates to items recognised outside of profit or loss (either in other comprehensive income or directly in equity), the amount may be based on a reasonable pro rata allocation, or some other method achieving a more appropriate allocation. These circumstances are assumed to arise only rarely; such an uncertainty could arise, for example, when there are graduated rates of income tax and it is impossible to determine the rate at which a specific component of taxable profit (tax loss) has been taxed. [IAS 12:63]

Example 3.2.1.3

Pro rata allocation of tax between profit or loss and other comprehensive income

Entity A operates in a jurisdiction in which revaluations of property, plant and equipment are taxed when they are recognised for accounting purposes. In 20X1, Entity A recognises an accounting profit of CU1,000 and a revaluation gain in other comprehensive income of CU200. Total taxable profit is therefore CU1,200. Tax is charged at 20 per cent on the first CU600 of taxable profit and 30 per cent on any taxable profit above CU600.

Total tax for the year   CU600 × 20% + CU600 × 30% = CU300

In this graduated tax regime, it is not possible to make a determination as to which component of total taxable profit was taxed at each particular rate. Entity A therefore needs to allocate the current tax liability of CU300 between profit or loss and other comprehensive income on a reasonable pro rata basis. Entity A's overall average tax rate is 25 per cent (CU300 tax payable on CU1,200 taxable profit), and the entity could use this average rate to make a reasonable allocation. The journal entry to recognise the current tax liability for the year would be as follows.

		CU	CU
Dr	Current income tax – profit or loss (CU1,000 × 25%)	250	
Dr	Current income tax – other comprehensive income (CU200 × 25%)		50
Cr	Taxes payable – statement of financial position		300

To recognise the current tax liability for the year.

3.2.1.4 Reclassification from equity to profit or loss of current tax effects of gains and losses previously recognised in other comprehensive income

As discussed at **3.2.1** above, IAS 12:61A requires that current tax relating to items that are recognised in the same or a different period in other comprehensive income should be recognised in other comprehensive income.

In some cases, IFRSs require that gains or losses initially recognised in other comprehensive income be subsequently reclassified to profit or loss. For example:

- gains or losses arising on cash flow hedges previously recognised in other comprehensive income are reclassified from equity to profit or loss when the hedged forecast cash flows affect profit or loss (subject to the conditions in IAS 39 *Financial Instruments: Recognition and Measurement*);

- gains or losses arising on net investment hedges previously recognised in other comprehensive income are reclassified from equity to profit or loss when the net investment affects profit or loss;

- for entities that have not yet adopted IFRS 9, gains or losses arising on available-for-sale financial assets previously recognised in other comprehensive income are reclassified from equity to profit or loss when the asset is disposed of or is determined to be impaired; and

- on disposal or partial disposal of a foreign operation (other than a partial disposal of a subsidiary when control is retained), all or a portion of the foreign currency translation reserve is reclassified from equity to profit or loss as part of the gain or loss on disposal.

Whether such gains and losses are included in the determination of taxable profit in the period in which they are initially recognised in other comprehensive income depends on the rules in the particular tax jurisdiction.

If such gains and losses are subject to current tax when they are recognised in other comprehensive income, the question arises as to whether that current tax (initially recognised in other comprehensive income in accordance with IAS 12:61A) should be subsequently reclassified to profit or loss when the related gains and losses are reclassified.

The most appropriate treatment is that any current tax expense or benefit relating to the gains or losses reclassified should also be reclassified to profit or loss. Even though IAS 12 makes no reference to reclassification of the current tax effects previously recognised in other comprehensive income, the principle in IAS 12 is clear that the tax effects of a transaction (if any) should be reported in a consistent manner with the gains or losses to which they relate. This principle is applied when the gains and losses are initially recognised in other comprehensive income, and equally can be applied when the gains and losses are subsequently reclassified to profit or loss.

See **example 3.2.1.4** for an illustration of this approach. Note that, in the example, there is no impact on the effective tax rate of the entity, because both the realised loss and the related tax are recognised in profit or loss.

Example 3.2.1.4

Reclassification from equity to profit or loss of current tax effects of gains and losses previously recognised in other comprehensive income

Company Y has a portfolio of financial assets classified as available for sale in accordance with IAS 39. For financial reporting purposes, unrealised gains and losses on the assets are recognised in other comprehensive income. In accordance with IAS 12, any tax consequences are also recognised in other comprehensive income.

Under local tax laws, unrealised gains and losses on investment portfolios are included in the determination of taxable income or loss; consequently, the movement in the value of financial assets each year affects the current taxes payable.

In 20X1, the unrealised loss on the assets is CU5 million. There is no movement in the market value of the assets during 20X2. On the last day of 20X2, Company Y sells the assets, thereby crystallising the previously recognised pre-tax loss of CU5 million.

The tax rate for 20X1 and 20X2 is 30 per cent. Company Y has net taxable income in 20X1.

The journal entries for 20X1 are as follows.

		CU'000	CU'000
Dr	Unrealised loss on investments (other comprehensive income)	5,000	
Cr	Investment portfolio		5,000

To recognise the unrealised loss on the available-for-sale assets in other comprehensive income.

		CU'000	CU'000
Dr	Current tax liability	1,500	
Cr	Current tax benefit (other comprehensive income)		1,500

To recognise the tax consequences of the unrealised losses – computed based on mark-to-market accounting under local tax law (CU5 million × 30%).

The journal entries for 20X2 are as follows.

		CU'000	CU'000
Dr	Loss on sale (profit or loss)	5,000	
Cr	Unrealised loss on investments (other comprehensive income)		5,000

To recognise the reclassification from equity to profit or loss of the pre-tax loss on sale of the asset portfolio in 20X2.

		CU'000	CU'000
Dr	Current tax expense (other comprehensive income)	1,500	
Cr	Current tax benefit (profit or loss)		1,500

To recognise the reclassification from equity to profit or loss of the tax consequences of the realised loss on sale of the assets in 20X2.

3.2.1.5 Dividends

In some jurisdictions, income taxes are payable at a higher or lower rate if part or all of the net profit or retained earnings is paid out as a dividend to shareholders of the entity. In some other jurisdictions, income taxes may be refundable or payable if part or all of the net profit or retained earnings is paid out as a dividend to shareholders of the entity. In these circumstances, current and deferred tax assets and liabilities are measured at the tax rate applicable to undistributed profits. [IAS 12:52A]

In the circumstances described above, the income tax consequences of dividends are recognised when a liability to pay the dividend is recognised. The income tax consequences of dividends are more directly linked to past transactions or events than to distributions to owners. Therefore, the income tax consequences of dividends are recognised in profit or loss for the period as required by IAS 12:58 except to the extent that the income tax consequences of dividends arise from the circumstances described in IAS 12:58(a) and (b) (see **3.2**). [IAS 12:52B]

3.2.2 Current tax arising from business combinations

Current tax arising from a business combination should not be recognised in profit or loss. [IAS 12:58(b)]

For entities that have adopted the *Investment Entities* amendments (effective for annual periods beginning on or after 1 January 2014, with earlier adoption permitted – see **section 15** of **chapter A24** for details), IAS 12:58 is amended to clarify that the exception for business combinations does not apply to the acquisition by an investment entity, as defined in IFRS 10 *Consolidated Financial Statements*, of a subsidiary that is required to be measured at fair value through profit or loss.

IAS 12 does not specifically address the appropriate treatment in the consolidated financial statements of the acquirer for adjustments arising when a business combination has direct current tax consequences for the acquiree (paragraphs IAS 12:66 to 68, to which reference is made from IAS 12:58(b), only address the accounting for deferred tax). However, it can be assumed that adjustments to current tax should be treated consistently with adjustments to deferred tax; therefore, adjustments to current tax should also be accounted for as part of the initial accounting for the business combination.

For example, a change of ownership may result in a change in tax rate or loss of tax incentives. When those consequences result in an adjustment to current tax assets or liabilities, the remeasured current tax assets or liabilities should be included in the identifiable net assets recognised for the acquiree, and the adjustment will therefore affect the amount of the goodwill or the bargain purchase gain recognised in the consolidated financial statements.

The appropriate accounting in the financial statements of the acquiree will be determined in accordance with SIC-25 *Income Taxes – Changes in the Tax Status of an Entity or its Shareholders* (see **4.7.8** below).

3.3   Measurement of current tax assets and liabilities

Current tax assets and liabilities for both the current and prior periods are measured at the amounts that are expected to be paid to (recovered from) the tax authorities, using the tax rates (and tax laws) that have been enacted or substantively enacted by the end of the reporting period. [IAS 12:46] See **4.5.2** below for a discussion of the general issues that arise in respect of the appropriate tax rate to be used. **Section 4.5.2.2** discusses the meaning of 'substantively enacted'.

When current tax amounts fall due to be paid in future periods, the current tax should be recognised at a discounted amount if the effect of discounting is material. This may be contrasted with the accounting for deferred tax which, as required under IAS 12:53, is never discounted (see **4.5.5**).

Example 3.3

Discounting current tax payable

Entity A is a start-up entity. The local tax authority has granted a five-year partial deferral of tax payments to new businesses in the jurisdiction, for which Entity A is eligible. Under this arrangement, Entity A must pay

60 per cent of its current year tax bill at the end of the tax year, and 40 per cent is deferred until the end of the tax year five years later.

When measuring its liability for current tax, if the effect is material, Entity A should discount the amount deferred for five years. Entity A should recognise a current tax liability of 60 per cent of the total current tax bill, plus 40 per cent of the total current tax bill discounted for five years as a non-current tax liability.

The unwinding of the discount in subsequent periods should be presented as a finance cost, because it does not meet the definition of income tax expense in IAS 12.

3.3.1   Uncertain tax positions

Entities are required to calculate and pay income taxes in accordance with applicable tax law in each relevant tax jurisdiction. However, no tax legislation can clearly articulate the tax consequences of every possible transaction. Accordingly, the application of tax rules to complex transactions is sometimes open to interpretation, both by the preparers of financial statements (and the tax return) and by the tax authorities.

The tax authorities may challenge positions taken by an entity in determining its current income tax expense and either require further payments or disallow tax losses or other tax attributes. Tax positions taken by an entity when measuring its tax assets and liabilities for financial statement purposes (and when submitting its tax return) for which the interpretation of tax law is unclear are generally referred to as 'uncertain tax positions'.

Uncertain tax positions affect the amount recognised for current tax liabilities or assets, and are within the scope of IAS 12. IAS 12:46 provides that "[c]urrent tax liabilities (assets) for the current and prior periods shall be measured at the amount expected to be paid to (recovered from) the taxation authorities".

IAS 12 does not include explicit guidance regarding the recognition and measurement of uncertain tax positions. While income taxes are outside the scope of IAS 37 *Provisions, Contingent Liabilities and Contingent Assets*, the guidance in IAS 37:10 is considered relevant to uncertain tax positions because they may give rise to "a liability of uncertain timing or amount". Consequently, preparers may use the recognition and measurement criteria of IAS 37 by analogy when determining the appropriate recognition and measurement of uncertain tax positions. It would be inappropriate, however, to present the resulting liabilities with other provisions recognised under IAS 37, because IAS 37:5(b) specifically excludes from the scope of that Standard provisions that are addressed in IAS 12.

It should be presumed that any uncertain tax positions taken by an entity in determining its current tax liabilities (assets) will be examined by the appropriate tax authority having full knowledge of all relevant information.

Accordingly, an entity should follow a two-step process in accounting for its uncertain tax positions.

- Having already presumed 100 per cent detection risk by the relevant tax authority, the entity should determine whether, under IAS 37:14(b), it is *probable* that an outflow of economic resources will occur (i.e. the entity should consider whether it is probable that upon examination of the uncertain tax position by the tax authority, the entity would, for example, not be entitled to a particular tax credit or deduction or it would be assessed for tax on a particular income stream). Note that, under IAS 37, an outflow of economic resources is considered to be 'probable' if it is more likely than not to occur.

- If the probability threshold is met, the entity will need to measure the potential impact of the relevant tax authority's examination of the uncertain tax position; that is to say, the entity will need to make its best estimate of the amount of the tax benefit that will be lost. That amount may be determined in accordance with the guidance set out in IAS 37:39 and 40.

As stated in IAS 37:38, the best estimate of the amount to be provided is "determined by the judgement of the management of the entity, supplemented by experience of similar transactions and, in some cases, reports from independent experts".

Disclosure requirements for uncertain tax positions are governed not only by IAS 12, but also by the requirement under IAS 1:125 to disclose key sources of estimation uncertainty when there is a significant risk of a material adjustment in carrying amounts of assets and liabilities within the next financial year.

When the uncertain tax position gives rise to a contingent tax liability for which no provision is recognised (e.g. because it is not probable that a payment will be made to the tax authority), an entity must still consider the requirements of IAS 12:88, which states that "[a]n entity discloses any tax-related contingent liabilities and contingent assets in accordance with IAS 37 . . . contingent liabilities and contingent assets may arise, for example, from unresolved disputes with the taxation authorities".

The recognition and measurement in a business combination of the potential liability arising from an uncertain tax position is addressed at **5.1.8** below.

3.3.1.1   *Recognition of an asset in relation to an uncertain tax position*

Example 3.3.1.1

Recognition of an asset in relation to an uncertain tax position

Entity X is involved in a dispute with its local tax authority over a sum of CU100 and has, as required by local law, made a payment of that amount. This money will be held in escrow by the tax authority pending resolution of the dispute, at which point it will either be returned to Entity X or used to settle any tax liability arising from the dispute.

Entity X does not believe it to be probable that any tax liability will arise in relation to the disputed amount and, consequently, it has not recognised any obligation in this regard (see **3.3.1** above for a discussion of the appropriate recognition criteria for such 'uncertain tax positions').

Should Entity X recognise the payment of CU100 as an asset?

Yes. This asset is not a contingent asset as defined in IAS 37 because, although the outcome of the uncertain future event (i.e. the resolution of the tax dispute) will confirm the means of recovery, there is no uncertainty regarding the 'existence' of the asset. The asset will either be recovered in the form of a cash refund from the tax authority or it will be used to settle the tax liability that may arise on resolution of the dispute.

Entity X should continue to monitor the underlying uncertain tax position, and should recognise an income tax expense if and when it is considered probable that the dispute will result in some or all of the CU100 being retained by the tax authority to settle any tax liability arising from the dispute.

3.4   Changes in the tax status of an entity or its shareholders

SIC-25 *Income Taxes – Changes in the Tax Status of an Entity or its Shareholders* deals with the appropriate accounting for the consequences of such changes. SIC-25, which applies equally to current and deferred taxes, is discussed in detail in **4.7.8** below.

4   Deferred tax

4.1   General approach

IAS 12 focuses on the statement of financial position by recognising the tax effects of temporary differences, i.e. differences between the carrying amount of an asset or a liability and its tax base.

Deferred tax liabilities are defined as the amounts of income taxes payable in future periods in respect of taxable temporary differences. [IAS 12:5]

Deferred tax assets are defined as the amounts of income taxes recoverable in future periods in respect of:
[IAS 12:5]

- deductible temporary differences;

- the carryforward of unused tax losses; and

- the carryforward of unused tax credits.

Deferred tax assets and liabilities are calculated using the following formulas.

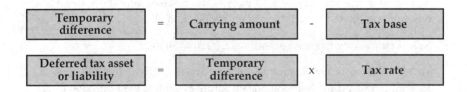

The recognition of deferred tax, therefore, relies on two central concepts:

- tax bases (as defined in **4.2.1** below); and

- temporary differences (as defined in **4.3** below).

The principal steps in arriving at deferred tax assets and liabilities under IAS 12 are as follows.

Step 1

Calculate the tax base of each asset and liability in the statement of financial position (see **4.2** below). Note that temporary differences can also arise when there is no associated asset or liability recognised for accounting purposes (see **4.2.4** below).

Step 2

Calculate the temporary difference (if any) for each of the above items (see **4.3** below).

Step 3

Identify those temporary differences that will give rise to deferred tax assets or liabilities taking into account the recognition criteria and initial exceptions laid down in the Standard (see **4.4** below).

Step 4

Calculate the deferred tax attributable to those temporary differences by multiplying each temporary difference by the tax rate that is expected to apply when the temporary difference reverses based on enacted or substantively enacted tax rates (see **4.5** below).

Step 5

Assess the recoverability of deferred tax assets arising from deductible temporary differences, carried forward unused tax losses and unused tax credits (see **4.6** below).

Step 6

Recognise the movement between the deferred tax balances in the opening and closing statements of financial position in profit or loss, in other comprehensive income, in equity, or as part of the initial accounting for a business combination (thus affecting the goodwill or bargain purchase gain recognised) (see **4.7** below).

4.2   Calculation of tax bases

4.2.1   Definition of tax base

The tax base of an asset or a liability is the amount attributed to that asset or liability for tax purposes. [IAS 12:5] IAS 12 describes separately the tax base of assets (see **4.2.2** below), and of liabilities and revenue received in advance (see **4.2.3** below).

4.2.2   Assets

The tax base of an asset is the amount that will be deductible for tax purposes against any taxable economic benefits that will flow to an entity when it recovers the carrying amount of the asset. [IAS 12:7] Taxable economic benefits could take the form of proceeds on disposal of an asset, or income earned through the use of an asset (e.g. manufacturing profits).

Future tax consequences are always calculated based on the realisation of the asset at its carrying amount. In reality, an entity will often generate economic benefits in excess of the carrying amount through use or sale. For example, a property may have a market value that is substantially greater than its carrying amount. IAS 12 does not require an estimate of the benefits that will be generated by the asset. Rather, deferred tax is calculated on the assumption that those benefits will be equal to the carrying amount of the asset.

When the economic benefits that flow from an asset are not taxable, the tax base of the asset is equal to its carrying amount. [IAS 12:7] Deferred taxes only arise when the tax base of an asset or a liability differs from its carrying amount. If the economic benefits that flow from an asset are not taxable (and the tax base of the asset is, therefore, equal to its carrying amount), the recovery of the asset will not have any deferred tax consequences.

Paragraph 7 of IAS 12 contains the following examples of the calculation of the tax base of an asset.

Example 4.2.2A

Tax base of an asset

[Examples following IAS 12:7]

1   A machine cost 100. For tax purposes, depreciation of 30 has already been deducted in the current and prior periods and the remaining cost will be deductible in future periods, either as depreciation or through a deduction on disposal. Revenue generated by using the machine is taxable, any gain on disposal of the machine will be taxable and any loss on disposal will be deductible for tax purposes. *The tax base of the machine is 70.*

2   Interest receivable has a carrying amount of 100. The related interest revenue will be taxed on a cash basis. *The tax base of the interest receivable is nil.*

3   Trade receivables have a carrying amount of 100. The related revenue has already been included in taxable profit (tax loss). *The tax base of the trade receivables is 100.*

---

4   Dividends receivable from a subsidiary have a carrying amount of 100. The dividends are not taxable. *In substance, the entire carrying amount of the asset is deductible against the economic benefits. Consequently, the tax base of the dividends receivable is 100.*[a]

5   A loan receivable has a carrying amount of 100. The repayment of the loan will have no tax consequences. *The tax base of the loan is 100.*

a   Under this analysis, there is no taxable temporary difference. An alternative analysis is that the accrued dividends receivable have a tax base of nil and that a tax rate of nil is applied to the resulting taxable temporary difference of 100. Under both analyses, there is no deferred tax liability.

Sometimes, the manner in which the carrying amount of an asset is recovered can affect the tax base of the asset. When this is the case, the tax base used should be consistent with the expected manner of recovery (see also **4.2.6** below). [IAS 12:51A]

Example 4.2.2B

Expected manner of recovery of asset

[Based on IAS 12:51A, Example C]

An item of property, plant and equipment with a cost of 100 and a carrying amount of 80 is revalued to 150. No equivalent adjustment is made for tax purposes. Cumulative depreciation for tax purposes is 30. If the item is sold for more than cost, the cumulative tax depreciation of 30 will be included in taxable income and the sale proceeds in excess of an inflation-adjusted cost of 110 will also be taxed.

If the entity expects to recover the carrying amount by selling the item, the tax base is 80 (indexed cost of 110 less tax depreciation of 30).

If the entity expects to recover the carrying amount of the item by using the asset, its tax base is 70 (100 less tax depreciation of 30).

4.2.3   Liabilities

The tax base of a liability is its carrying amount, less any amount that will be deductible for tax purposes in respect of that liability in future periods. In the case of revenue received in advance, the tax base of the resulting liability is its carrying amount, less any amount of the revenue that will not be taxable in future periods. [IAS 12:8]

Future tax consequences are always calculated based on the settlement of the liability at its carrying amount. There may be occasions when the settlement of a liability is expected to exceed its current carrying amount (e.g. when a settlement premium is being accrued over the life of a debt instrument). IAS 12 does not require anticipation of the expected settlement amount. Instead, deferred tax is calculated on the assumption that the liability will be settled at its carrying amount.

When settlement of the liability at its carrying amount would have no tax consequences, the tax base of the liability is equal to its carrying amount. This will be the case when either the transaction has no tax implications (e.g. accrual of fines and penalties that are not tax deductible), or when the accounting and tax implications occur in the same period (e.g. accrued wages in respect of which a tax deduction is allowed at the same time as the expense is recognised).

Paragraph 8 of IAS 12 contains the following examples of the calculation of the tax base of a liability.

Example 4.2.3A

Tax base of a liability

[Examples following IAS 12:8]

1   Current liabilities include accrued expenses with a carrying amount of 100. The related expense will be deducted for tax purposes on a cash basis. *The tax base of the accrued expenses is nil.*

2   Current liabilities include interest revenue received in advance, with a carrying amount of 100. The related interest revenue was taxed on a cash basis. *The tax base of the interest received in advance is nil.*

3   Current liabilities include accrued expenses with a carrying amount of 100. The related expense has already been deducted for tax purposes. *The tax base of the accrued expenses is 100.*

4   Current liabilities include accrued fines and penalties with a carrying amount of 100. Fines and penalties are not deductible for tax purposes. *The tax base of the accrued fines and penalties is 100.*[a]

5   A loan payable has a carrying amount of 100. The repayment of the loan will have no tax consequences. *The tax base of the loan is 100.*

    a   Under this analysis, there is no deductible temporary difference. An alternative analysis is that the accrued fines and penalties payable have a tax base of nil and that a tax rate of nil is applied

---

> to the resulting deductible temporary difference of 100. Under both analyses, there is no deferred tax asset.

In the case of revenue received in advance, the tax base of the liability is the carrying amount of the liability less the portion of the revenue received that has already been taxed (or is never taxable) and, consequently, will not be taxed in the future.

| Tax base | = | Carrying amount | - | The amount of the revenue that will not be taxable in future periods |

Example 4.2.3B

Revenue received in advance

On 31 December 20X1, Company A receives CU100 revenue in advance of performing services. The amount is recognised as deferred revenue in Company A's statement of financial position and it will be recognised in profit or loss as services are performed during the 20X2 reporting period. The revenue is taxed on receipt.

At 31 December 20X1, the carrying amount of the deferred revenue is CU100; the amount that will not be taxable in future periods is CU100 (because this has already been taxed). Therefore, the tax base of the deferred revenue is nil and a deductible temporary difference arises. A deferred tax asset is recognised in respect of this temporary difference subject to IAS 12's general recognition criteria; the 'initial recognition exception' (see **4.4.5** below) does not apply because the recognition of the revenue affected taxable profit.

Example 4.2.3C

Government grant recognised as deferred income

Company B receives a government grant of CU150 to purchase a specified property. Company B recognises the government grant as deferred income in its statement of financial position, as permitted under paragraph 24 of IAS 20 *Accounting for Government Grants and Disclosure of Government Assistance.*

If the government grant is taxed on receipt, the same analysis as set out in **example 4.2.3B** applies, and a temporary difference equal to the carrying amount of the deferred income arises. A deferred tax asset is recognised in respect of this temporary difference subject to IAS 12's general recognition criteria; the 'initial recognition exception' (see **4.4.5** below) does not apply because the receipt of the grant affected taxable profit.

If the government grant is taxed at the same time as it is recognised in profit or loss over the life of the related asset, all of the grant is taxable in future periods. Therefore, on initial recognition, the tax base will equal the carrying amount of the deferred income and no temporary difference arises.

If the government grant is not taxable, either on receipt or when it is recognised in profit or loss over the useful life of the related property, applying the formula above will give a tax base of nil. Consequently, a deductible temporary difference arises. However, because this difference arises on the initial recognition of the deferred income and the conditions in IAS 12:24 are met (see **4.4.2** below), no deferred tax is recognised.

4.2.4 Tax bases without an associated carrying amount

Some items have a tax base but have no carrying amount (i.e. they are not recognised in the statement of financial position for accounting purposes). When a transaction does not give rise to, or affect the carrying amount of, an asset or a liability, but does affect the taxable income of future reporting periods, the tax base is calculated as the amount of the effect on taxable income in future reporting periods. In this case, the carrying amount of the asset or liability associated with the tax base is zero for the purposes of calculating temporary differences. [IAS 12:9]

Examples of such items include the following:

- research costs recognised as an expense in determining accounting profit in the period in which they are incurred but for which a tax deduction is allowed in a later period (see IAS 12:9);

- goodwill or other intangible assets recognised for local tax purposes, but not meeting the recognition criteria under IFRSs; and

- reserves in the local statutory books of the entity that will be taxable upon the occurrence of certain events (e.g. reclassification of the reserve, or upon liquidation of the entity). Such reserves are generally established upon receipt of a tax benefit.

A temporary difference may also arise when a transaction has given rise to an asset or a liability in previous reporting periods that is no longer included in the statement of financial position, but will affect taxable income in future reporting periods (e.g. an asset that is fully depreciated for accounting purposes but for which tax depreciation may still be claimed).

> **Example 4.2.4**
>
> **Pre-operating costs expensed but not deductible in current period**
>
> An entity may incur pre-operating costs. Under IAS 38 *Intangible Assets*, these costs are required to be recognised as an expense when incurred. If local tax laws do not allow an immediate deduction, but do allow a future deduction, the difference between the tax base of the pre-operating costs (i.e. the amount that the tax authorities will permit as a deduction in future periods) and the carrying amount (nil) is a temporary difference.

The basic principle of IAS 12 is that, unless specifically exempted under IAS 12, entities should recognise deferred tax liabilities (assets) whenever settlement or recovery of the carrying amount of an asset or a liability would make future tax payments larger (smaller) than they would be if such recovery or settlement were to have no tax consequences. This may be helpful to remember when the tax base of an asset or a liability is not immediately apparent. [IAS 12:10]

4.2.5   Tax bases for the purpose of consolidated financial statements

For an entity preparing consolidated financial statements, temporary differences are calculated using:
[IAS 12:11]

- carrying amounts taken from the consolidated statement of financial position; and

- tax bases as determined by reference to the method of tax computation. If the tax authorities calculate tax by reference to each individual entity in the group, the tax bases will be taken from the individual entities' tax computations. If the tax authorities calculate tax using consolidated amounts, the tax bases will be taken from the consolidated tax amounts.

> **Example 4.2.5**
>
> **Tax base generated as a result of intragroup transfer**
>
> A group undertakes an internal restructuring whereby Subsidiary A sells an item of intellectual property with no carrying amount to Subsidiary B for

CU100. Subsidiary B is able to claim a tax deduction for the amortisation of the purchased intangible asset over 5 years.

IFRS 10 *Consolidated Financial Statements* (or, for entities that have not yet adopted IFRS 10, IAS 27(2008) *Consolidated and Separate Financial Statements*) requires that intragroup profits be eliminated in full. Therefore, from the group perspective, the intellectual property has a carrying amount of nil and a tax base of CU100. Accordingly, a deductible temporary difference has arisen in respect of which a deferred tax asset should be recognised provided that it is probable that taxable profit will be available against which the deductible temporary difference can be utilised. The corresponding gain should be recognised in profit or loss.

The deferred tax impact of eliminations of unrealised profits arising on intragroup transfers is discussed in detail at **5.2** below.

4.2.6   *Alternative tax rates and tax bases according to management intent*

When the amount of tax payable or receivable is dependent upon how the entity recovers the asset or settles the liability, the rate and tax base used to calculate the deferred tax balances should reflect the manner in which the entity expects, at the end of the reporting period, to recover the asset or settle the liability. [IAS 12:51] IAS 12:51A indicates that the manner of recovery or settlement may affect either, or both, the applicable tax rate and the tax base of an asset or a liability.

Specific rules apply in relation to the recovery of non-depreciable assets (see **4.2.6.1**) and investment property (see **4.2.6.2**).

Example 4.2.6A

Alternative tax rates for use and disposal of an item of property, plant and equipment (1)

The carrying amount of an item of property, plant and equipment is CU400,000 (cost of CU500,000 less accumulated depreciation of CU100,000). The asset's tax base is CU300,000 (tax depreciation of CU200,000 having been claimed to date).

Income generated from the use of the asset is taxed at 25 per cent and, therefore, the tax depreciation will be recovered at 25 per cent. If the asset were sold, any excess of the disposal proceeds over the asset's tax base would be taxed at 30 per cent.

The taxable temporary difference is CU100,000. If the entity intends to continue to use the asset in its business, generating taxable income, the deferred tax liability is CU25,000 (CU100,000 at 25 per cent). If, instead, the entity intends to dispose of the asset, the deferred tax liability is CU30,000 (CU100,000 at 30 per cent).

Further examples are given in IAS 12:51A.

Example 4.2.6B

Alternative tax rates for use and disposal of an item of property, plant and equipment (2)

The facts are as in **example 4.2.6A**, except that the entity intends to use the asset until its carrying amount is CU300,000 and its tax base is CU100,000. At that point, the entity will sell the asset, and will be taxed on the difference between the amount recovered through sale and the tax base.

In accordance with the general principles of IAS 12, deferred tax is calculated on the assumption that the value of the asset will be recovered at its carrying amount. The entity will therefore recover another CU100,000 from the asset through its use, and receive CU200,000 of allowable deductions during that period. The entity will then recover CU300,000 from the sale of the asset, and receive CU100,000 of allowable deductions. In total, the entity expects to recover CU400,000 from the asset and receive CU300,000 of deductions.

The tax rate applicable at the time the temporary difference reverses is 25 per cent in respect of use and 30 per cent in respect of sale. The entity must therefore use both tax rates in determining the deferred tax balance to take account of the fact that the temporary difference will reverse at different rates. Accordingly, the entity's deferred tax liability in respect of the asset is calculated as follows.

$$[(CU100,000 - CU200,000)] \times 25\% + [(CU300,000 - CU100,000)] \times 30\% = CU35,000$$

A more complicated situation arises when, in a particular tax jurisdiction, the recovery of an asset through use is subject to one type of income tax and recovery through sale is subject to another type of income tax (potentially at a different rate). In such circumstances, it is often necessary to consider separately the tax bases and temporary differences arising from recovery through use and recovery through sale, particularly when the tax regime is such that there are effectively two distinct tax systems applicable to the recovery of the asset. Any deductible temporary differences need to be assessed for recognition in accordance with the usual requirements, separately from any taxable temporary difference arising. This is illustrated in **example 4.2.6C**.

Example 4.2.6C

Recovery through sale and use under different income taxes

Company D acquires machinery in a business combination. The machinery is initially recognised in the consolidated financial statements at its fair value at the date of acquisition of CU150. Company D is not entitled to claim any tax deductions if the machinery is used in its operations and, therefore, the machinery's tax base for recovery through use is nil.

Company D expects to use the asset for a number of years and then sell it for its currently estimated residual value of CU50. The income on sale of the machinery is subject to a different type of income tax and, when the machinery is sold, a tax deduction of CU100 (the original cost of the asset when purchased by the acquiree) will be available. Therefore, the asset's tax base for recovery through sale is CU100.

The tax rates expected to apply when the temporary differences reverse are 10 per cent in respect of use and 30 per cent in respect of sale. In the tax jurisdiction in which Company D operates, losses on sale of this type of property, plant and equipment can only be recovered against gains on disposal of similar assets and not against general operating profits.

Company D should recognise deferred tax as follows.

	Carrying amount	Tax base	Taxable (deductible) temporary difference	Deferred tax liability (asset)
	CU	CU	CU	CU
Recovery through use	100	Nil	100	10
Recovery through sale	50	**100**	(50)	(15)*

*   The possible deferred tax asset that is expected to arise from the sale of the machinery must be assessed for recoverability. If it is not probable that suitable future taxable profit will be available against which the deductible temporary difference can be utilised, the deferred tax asset should not be recognised.

4.2.6.1   *Non-depreciable assets measured under the revaluation model in IAS 16*

A specific issue arises in respect of non-depreciable assets. As discussed in the previous section, the measurement of deferred tax should generally reflect the manner in which the entity intends to recover the carrying amount of the asset. However, when an asset has an unlimited life (i.e. it is non-depreciable), the question arises as to how the term 'recovery' should be interpreted.

The topic of revalued non-depreciable assets was previously addressed in SIC-21 *Income Taxes – Recovery of Revalued Non-Depreciable Assets*. In December 2010, SIC-21 was withdrawn and replaced by a new paragraph IAS 12:51B. Although there have been some changes to the detailed wording, the requirements of SIC-21 and IAS 12:51B (set out below) are essentially consistent. What has changed is the scope of the requirements: in addition to non-depreciable assets carried at a revalued amount under IAS 16 *Property, Plant and Equipment*, SIC-21 included within its scope investment property carried at a revalued amount under paragraph 33 of IAS 40 *Investment Property* that would be considered non-depreciable if IAS 16 were to be applied (e.g. land held for rental to others). Under the revised requirements, such 'non-depreciable investment property' falls within the scope of a general exception for investment property carried at fair value (see **4.2.6.2**).

The measurement of deferred tax liabilities or assets arising from non-depreciable assets measured at a revalued amount under IAS 16 should reflect the tax consequences of recovering the carrying amount of the non-depreciable asset through sale, regardless of the basis of measuring the carrying amount of that asset. [IAS 12:51B]

Accordingly, if the tax consequences that would arise from the sale of a revalued non-depreciable asset differ from the tax consequences of using the asset, the deferred tax asset or liability arising should be measured based on the assumption that the asset will be sold. [IAS 12:51B]

Generally, the future economic benefits will be derived from an asset (and, therefore, the carrying amount of the asset will be recovered) through sale, through use, or through use and subsequent sale. Recognition of depreciation implies that the carrying amount of a depreciable asset is expected to be recovered through use to the extent of its depreciable amount, and through sale at its residual value. Consistently with this, the carrying amount of a non-depreciable asset, such as land having an unlimited life, will be recovered only through sale. In other words, because the asset is not depreciated, no part of its carrying amount is expected to be recovered (i.e. consumed) through use. [IAS 12:BC6]

Example 4.2.6.1A

Non-depreciable asset – freehold land

Company E holds freehold land and accounts for it on a revaluation basis under IAS 16. The carrying amount of the land is CU900,000, which is its current market value. The tax base on sale of the land will be its original cost of CU500,000. The land is used for the storage of Company E's raw materials. The tax rate applicable to manufacturing income is 25 per cent but, on disposal of a capital asset, any proceeds in excess of cost are taxed at 30 per cent. There is currently no intention to sell the land.

The taxable temporary difference between the carrying amount and the tax base of the freehold land is CU400,000. Although the asset is being used by Company E to generate manufacturing income, the carrying amount of the land is not being recovered in that way; the value of the land does not diminish over time through use. All of the value of the land will be recovered through its eventual sale and, therefore, the applicable tax rate is 30 per cent, and the deferred tax liability arising is CU120,000.

If, for tax purposes, there was an indexation allowance on the land for the purposes of calculating the gain on disposal of the land, this indexed amount would be the tax base of the land.

IAS 12:BC6 points to land having an unlimited life and being non-depreciable. Land is the only asset that should be assumed to be non-depreciable (with some exceptions such as quarries and landfill sites – see IAS 16:58). Assets such as some intangible assets that are simply not being depreciated because they have an indefinite life, or because their current residual value is at or above carrying amount, are not non-depreciable for the purposes of these requirements. IAS 12's general principles apply to such assets, namely that temporary differences should be recognised based on the expected manner of recovery.

Example 4.2.6.1B

Brand with an indefinite useful life

Company F has a brand that is considered to have an indefinite useful life and, in accordance with the requirements of IAS 38:107, is therefore not being amortised. The carrying amount of the brand is its original cost of CU900,000. Under local tax law, the brand is being amortised over 10 years. At 31 December 20X3, the tax base of the brand after three years' tax amortisation is CU630,000. This tax base is either deductible over the life of the asset or upon sale. The tax rate applicable to trading profits is 25 per cent but, if the intangible asset were to be disposed of, the capital gain arising would be taxed at 30 per cent. There is currently no intention to dispose of the brand.

In accordance with the general requirements of IAS 12:51, the measurement of deferred tax should reflect the tax consequences that would follow from the manner in which the entity expects to recover the asset. In the circumstances described, the brand is expected to be recovered through use in Company F's trading operations. The brand is not considered to be a non-depreciable asset for the purposes of IAS 12:51B (see discussion above).

On this basis, the taxable temporary difference between the carrying amount and the tax base of the brand is CU270,000. The applicable tax rate is 25 per cent and the deferred tax liability arising is CU67,500.

4.2.6.2 Investment property measured at fair value

In December 2010, IAS 12 was amended to provide an additional exception to the Standard's general principle that the measurement of deferred tax should reflect the manner in which an entity expects to recover the carrying amount of an asset. The amendments established a rebuttable presumption that the carrying amount of an investment property measured using the fair value model in IAS 40 *Investment Property* will be recovered entirely through sale.

As discussed at **4.2.6.1** above, non-depreciable investment property (e.g. land held for rental to others) previously fell within the scope of SIC-21; following the December 2010 amendments, non-depreciable investment property is accounted for under the new exception for investment property in IAS 12:51C. [IAS 12:BC5] The principal difference between the requirements previously included in SIC-21 and the exception for investment property introduced in December 2010 is that SIC-21 set an absolute rule for the determination of the deferred tax effects of the recovery of non-depreciable assets (always on the basis that recovery would be through sale) whereas IAS 12:51C establishes this as a rebuttable presumption.

The December 2010 amendments to IAS 12 are effective for annual periods beginning on or after 1 January 2012.

If a deferred tax liability or asset arises from investment property that is measured using the fair value model in IAS 40, there is a rebuttable presumption that the carrying amount of the investment property will be recovered through sale. Accordingly, unless the presumption is rebutted, the measurement of the deferred tax liability or deferred tax asset is required to reflect the tax consequences of recovering the carrying amount of the investment property entirely through sale. [IAS 12:51C]

The rebuttable presumption established in IAS 12:51C is rebutted if the investment property is depreciable and the investment property is held within a business model whose objective is to consume substantially all of the economic benefits embodied in the investment property over time, rather than through sale. [IAS 12:51C]

The question arises as to whether the presumption can be rebutted in circumstances other than those explicitly described in the previous paragraph. Provided that sufficient evidence is available to support the rebuttal, the presumption could be rebutted in other circumstances.

This conclusion was confirmed by the IFRS Interpretations Committee in November 2011. The Committee noted that a presumption is a matter of consistently applying a principle (or an exception) in IFRSs in the absence of acceptable reasons to the contrary and that it is rebutted when there is sufficient evidence to overcome the presumption. Because IAS 12:51C is expressed as a rebuttable presumption, and because the sentence explaining the rebuttal of the presumption does not express the rebuttal as 'if and only if', the Committee considered that the presumption could be rebutted in other circumstances, provided that sufficient evidence is available to support that rebuttal.

If the presumption is rebutted, the general requirements of IAS 12:51 and IAS 12:51A apply (i.e. expected manner of recovery is based on management intent – see **4.2.6** above).

The rebuttable presumption in IAS 12:51C also applies when a deferred tax liability or a deferred tax asset arises from measuring investment property in a business combination if the entity will use the fair value model when subsequently measuring that investment property. [IAS 12:51D]

For entities applying the specific requirements for investment properties measured at fair value in accordance with IAS 12:51B to 51D, the general principles regarding the recognition and measurement of deferred tax assets in IAS 12:24 to 36 still apply. [IAS 12:51E]

The following example from IAS 12 illustrates the application of IAS 12:51C.

The example illustrates the distinction, when the presumption in IAS 12:51C is rebutted, between the treatment of buildings, which are depreciable, and land, which is not depreciable.

Example 4.2.6.2

Investment property measured at fair value

[Example illustrating IAS 12:51C]

An investment property has a cost of 100 and fair value of 150. It is measured using the fair value model in IAS 40. It comprises land with a cost of 40 and fair value of 60 and a building with a cost of 60 and fair value of 90. The land has an unlimited useful life.

Cumulative depreciation of the building for tax purposes is 30. Unrealised changes in the fair value of the investment property do not affect taxable profit. If the investment property is sold for more than cost, the reversal of the cumulative tax depreciation of 30 will be included in taxable profit and taxed at an ordinary tax rate of 30%. For sales proceeds in excess of cost, tax law specifies tax rates of 25% for assets held for less than two years and 20% for assets held for two years or more.

Because the investment property is measured using the fair value model in IAS 40, there is a rebuttable presumption that the entity will recover the carrying amount of the investment property entirely through sale. If that presumption is not rebutted, the deferred tax reflects the tax consequences of recovering the carrying amount entirely through sale, even if the entity expects to earn rental income from the property before sale.

The tax base of the land if it is sold is 40 and there is a taxable temporary difference of 20 (60 – 40). The tax base of the building if it is sold is 30 (60 – 30) and there is a taxable temporary difference of 60 (90 – 30). As a result, the total taxable temporary difference relating to the investment property is 80 (20 + 60).

In accordance with paragraph 47, the tax rate is the rate expected to apply to the period when the investment property is realised. Thus, the resulting deferred tax liability is computed as follows, if the entity expects to sell the property after holding it for more than two years:

	Taxable Temporary Difference	Tax Rate	Deferred Tax Liability
Cumulative tax depreciation	30	30%	9
Proceeds in excess of cost	50	20%	10
Total	80		19

If the entity expects to sell the property after holding it for less than two years, the above computation would be amended to apply a tax rate of 25%, rather than 20%, to the proceeds in excess of cost.

If, instead, the entity holds the building within a business model whose objective is to consume substantially all of the economic benefits embodied in the building over time, rather than through sale, this presumption would be rebutted for the building. However, the land is not depreciable. Therefore the presumption of recovery through sale would not be rebutted for the land. It follows that the deferred tax liability would reflect the tax consequences of recovering the carrying amount of the building through use and the carrying amount of the land through sale.

The tax base of the building if it is used is 30 (60 − 30) and there is a taxable temporary difference of 60 (90 − 30), resulting in a deferred tax liability of 18 (60 at 30%).

The tax base of the land if it is sold is 40 and there is a taxable temporary difference of 20 (60 − 40), resulting in a deferred tax liability of 4 (20 at 20%).

As a result, if the presumption of recovery through sale is rebutted for the building, the deferred tax liability relating to the investment property is 22 (18 + 4).

In many jurisdictions, it is common for an investment property to be sold within its corporate structure – that is, the corporate structure will hold only one material asset, the investment property itself. When the parent disposes of the property, it will dispose of it within that corporate shell because, in many cases, this will shield the parent entity from adverse tax consequences.

Generally, any deferred tax liabilities or assets relating to the investment property are recognised in the individual financial statements of the property-holding subsidiary, calculated based on the tax rate applicable to that entity, and such deferred tax will be reflected in the parent's financial statements on consolidation. In addition, the consolidated financial statements may reflect deferred tax liabilities or assets in respect of the parent's investment in the property-holding subsidiary, calculated based on the tax rate applicable to the parent entity.

However, if it is the case that, in a particular jurisdiction, all market participants will purchase and sell investment property within a corporate shell, such that the purchase of a corporate entity holding only an investment property will always be viewed as the purchase of an asset (and not a business combination), in the consolidated financial statements of the parent, it may be appropriate to recognise deferred tax in respect of the property on the basis of the rate applicable to the sale of the shares.

4.2.6.3   *Convertible instrument with different tax treatments on redemption and conversion*

Under IAS 32 *Financial Instruments: Presentation*, the requirement to separate the equity and financial liability components of a compound instrument is consistent with the principle that a financial instrument should be classified in accordance with its substance, rather than its legal form. The expected manner of recovery is not taken into account in establishing this classification.

> In some jurisdictions, the tax treatment for a convertible instrument may differ depending on whether the instrument is settled in cash or by the delivery of shares. Unlike IAS 32, IAS 12:51 and 51A require that the tax base and the rate used to determine the deferred tax assets and liabilities reflect the manner in which the entity expects to settle the instrument.
>
> However, when settlement is outside the control of the issuer, the presumed settlement should be aligned with the IAS 32 classification (i.e. cash settlement should be presumed) unless there is strong evidence that the instrument will be settled by the delivery of shares.

4.2.6.4   *Changes of intention*

> When there is a change in management's expectation as to the manner in which an asset will be recovered, or a liability settled, the change may affect the measurement of the related deferred tax balances.
>
> The deferred tax impact should be remeasured based on management's revised intentions and the adjustment recognised in profit or loss or, to the extent that it relates to items previously recognised outside profit or loss, in other comprehensive income or directly in equity. Amounts reported in prior periods are not restated.

4.2.7   *Rollover relief*

> In some jurisdictions, an entity may be entitled to 'rollover relief' when it disposes of a capital asset for a profit and replaces it with an

equivalent asset. In such circumstances, the gain on disposal may not have any impact for tax purposes until the replacement asset is disposed of, when it is taken into account via the 'capital' (or sale) tax base of the replacement asset. When the entity disposes of the replacement asset, it is required to pay the tax on the gain on disposal of the replacement asset together with the tax on the gain on disposal of the original asset.

In many cases, the 'rollover' of the gain on the disposal of the original asset into the tax base of the replacement asset merely postpones, rather than eliminates, the payment of tax, and IAS 12:20(b) requires that a deferred tax liability be recognised.

In some jurisdictions, the manner of recovery of the replacement asset will determine whether the rollover relief gives rise to a postponement of tax or to permanent relief. However, until the replacement asset is acquired, deferred tax should be recognised on the basis that rollover relief will give rise only to postponement of tax, i.e. the potential permanent relief should not be anticipated. If the original asset is sold and there is a time delay before the replacement asset is acquired, the entity should continue to recognise the deferred tax.

If the replacement asset is recovered entirely through use, an entity should give careful consideration to the effect of rollover relief on the tax payments flowing from its recovery when determining the tax base of a replacement asset based on the expected manner of recovery.

4.2.8   Revaluation of the tax base

The tax base of an asset may change as a result of a revaluation of the asset for tax purposes. For example, local tax law may specify that the tax base of a particular type of asset is adjusted for inflation each year (see 4.4.6.6). The effects of other revaluations for tax purposes are discussed at 4.7.6.

See also 4.4.6.5 for the impact of foreign currency adjustments when the tax base of an asset or a liability is determined in a currency other than the entity's functional currency.

4.3   Calculation of temporary differences

Under IAS 12, deferred tax balances are recognised in respect of temporary differences. A temporary difference arises when the carrying amount of an asset or a liability differs from its tax base. For many transactions, there is no difference between the accounting and the tax treatment; no temporary difference and, consequently, no deferred tax balance arises.

4.3.1   Definition of temporary difference

IAS 12 defines a temporary difference as the difference between the carrying amount of an asset or a liability in the statement of financial position and its tax base. [IAS 12:5]

Temporary differences can arise in a number of circumstances, for example:

- when income or expenses are included in accounting profit in one period but included in taxable profit in a different period (i.e. timing differences);

- in a business combination, when the carrying amounts of assets and liabilities are adjusted to their fair values at the date of acquisition, but the tax bases of those assets and liabilities are not affected by the business combination or are affected differently;

- when an asset or a liability is revalued, but the tax base of the asset or liability is not adjusted;

- when the tax authority permits indexation of, or other adjustments to, the cost of an asset for tax purposes, but the asset is not revalued for accounting purposes;

- in respect of non-tax deductible goodwill which arises in a business combination; and

- on the initial recognition of an asset or a liability, for example, if part or all of the cost of an asset will not be deductible for tax purposes.

Temporary differences are determined by reference to the carrying amount of an asset or a liability. [IAS 12:55]

The carrying amounts used in the calculation of temporary differences are determined from the accounting records. If applicable, carrying amounts are calculated net of any allowances or deductions, such as allowances for doubtful debts or impairment losses.

There are two types of temporary differences – taxable temporary differences and deductible temporary differences. These are discussed in detail in the following sections.

4.3.2   Taxable temporary differences

Taxable temporary differences are temporary differences that will result in taxable amounts in determining the taxable profit (tax loss) of future periods when the carrying amount of the asset or liability is recovered or settled. [IAS 12:5]

Taxable temporary differences are, therefore, differences that will give rise to taxable income in the future; they increase future taxable profit, and so give rise to deferred tax liabilities.

In the context of an asset, a taxable temporary difference arises when the carrying amount of the asset exceeds its tax base (e.g. an asset is depreciated more quickly for tax purposes than for accounting purposes). As the carrying amount of the asset is recovered, the economic benefits subject to tax (i.e. the profits generated by the use of the asset equal to the carrying amount of the asset) will exceed the remaining future tax deductions available (the tax base). The tax effect of this taxable temporary difference gives rise to a deferred tax liability.

In the context of a liability, a taxable temporary difference arises when the tax base of the liability exceeds its carrying amount (e.g. a foreign currency loan payable which has been reduced for accounting purposes by an exchange gain that will be taxable when the loan is settled). If the loan is settled at its carrying amount, a taxable gain will arise; this is a taxable temporary difference.

4.3.3   Deductible temporary differences

Deductible temporary differences are temporary differences that will result in amounts that are deductible in determining the taxable profit (tax loss) of future periods when the carrying amount of the asset or liability is recovered or settled. [IAS 12:5]

Deductible temporary differences are, therefore, differences that decrease taxable income in the future, and so they give rise to deferred tax assets. IAS 12:26 gives some examples of deductible temporary differences that result in deferred tax assets, as follows.

- Retirement benefit costs may be deducted in determining accounting profit as service is provided by the employee, but deducted in determining taxable profit either when contributions are paid to a fund by the entity or when retirement benefits are paid by the entity. A temporary difference exists between the carrying amount of the liability and its tax base – the tax base of the liability is usually nil. Such a deductible temporary difference results in a deferred tax asset because economic benefits will flow to the entity in the form of a deduction from taxable profits when contributions are made to the plan or retirement benefits are paid.

- Research costs are recognised as an expense in determining accounting profit in the period in which they are incurred but may not be permitted as a deduction in determining taxable profit (tax loss) until a later period. The difference between the tax base of the research costs (i.e. the amount the tax authorities will permit as a deduction in future periods) and the carrying amount of nil is a deductible temporary difference that results in a deferred tax asset.

- With limited exceptions, an entity recognises the identifiable assets acquired and liabilities assumed in a business combination at their fair values at the acquisition date. When a liability assumed is recognised at the acquisition date but the related costs are not deducted in determining taxable profits until a later period, a deductible temporary difference arises which results in a deferred tax asset. A deferred tax asset also arises when the fair value of an identifiable asset acquired is less than its tax base. In both cases, the resulting deferred tax asset affects the goodwill or bargain purchase gain recognised.

- Assets may be carried at fair value, or may be revalued, without an equivalent adjustment being made for tax purposes. A deductible temporary difference arises if the tax base of the asset exceeds its carrying amount.

In the context of an asset, a deductible temporary difference arises when the tax base of the asset exceeds its carrying amount (e.g. when the carrying amount of a financial asset has been reduced by an allowance for irrecoverable amounts, but the allowance is not deductible for tax purposes until settlement). If the asset is settled at its carrying amount, a net deduction will arise; this is a deductible temporary difference.

In the context of a liability, a deductible temporary difference arises when the carrying amount of the liability exceeds its tax base (e.g. when interest payable has been accrued, but no tax deduction is available until the interest is paid). If the liability is settled at its carrying amount, a net deduction will arise; this is a deductible temporary difference.

A useful guide for determining whether temporary differences are taxable or deductible is set out below.

	Carrying amount – tax base	Type of temporary difference	Gives rise to ...
Asset	Positive	Taxable	Deferred tax liability
Asset	Negative	Deductible	Deferred tax asset
Liability	Positive	Deductible	Deferred tax asset
Liability	Negative	Taxable	Deferred tax liability

4.4   Recognition of deferred taxes on temporary differences identified

Having identified all of the temporary differences that exist at the end of the reporting period (see **section 4.3** above), the next step is to pinpoint those temporary differences that will give rise to deferred tax assets or liabilities in the statement of financial position, using the recognition criteria laid down in the Standard.

4.4.1   Recognition of taxable temporary differences

A deferred tax liability should be recognised for all taxable temporary differences, unless the deferred tax liability arises from:
[IAS 12:15]

• the initial recognition of goodwill; or

• the initial recognition of an asset or a liability in a transaction which:

  • is not a business combination; and

  • at the time of the transaction affects neither accounting profit nor taxable profit (tax loss).

An entity should recognise a deferred tax liability for all taxable temporary differences associated with investments in subsidiaries, branches and

associates, and interests in joint arrangements, except to the extent that both of the following conditions are satisfied:
[IAS 12:39]

- the parent, investor, joint venturer or joint operator is able to control the timing of the reversal of the temporary difference; and

- it is probable that the temporary difference will not reverse in the foreseeable future.

For entities that have not yet adopted IFRS 11 *Joint Arrangements* (effective for annual periods beginning on or after 1 January 2013, with earlier adoption permitted), the reference to 'interests in joint arrangements' in IAS 12:39 should be read as a reference to 'interests in joint ventures' and the reference to a 'joint venturer or joint operator' should be read as a reference to a 'venturer'.

4.4.2   *Recognition of deductible temporary differences*

A deferred tax asset should be recognised for all deductible temporary differences to the extent that it is probable that taxable profit will be available against which the deductible temporary difference can be utilised, unless the deferred tax asset arises from the initial recognition of an asset or a liability in a transaction that:
[IAS 12:24]

- is not a business combination; and

- at the time of the transaction, affects neither accounting profit nor taxable profit (tax loss).

IAS 12 is silent with regard to the meaning of 'probable' in the context of IAS 12:24. IAS 37 *Provisions, Contingent Liabilities and Contingent Assets* defines the term 'probable' as 'more likely than not'. [IAS 37:23] The footnote to IAS 37:23 acknowledges that this definition is not necessarily applicable to other IFRSs. However, in the absence of any other guidance, the term 'probable' should be applied as 'more likely than not'.

In March 2009, the IASB issued an exposure draft (ED) containing proposals for an IFRS that would replace IAS 12. Although a replacement Standard was not finalised, the ED provides useful guidance on the meaning of 'probable' because it uses the term 'more likely than not' and notes in the Basis for Conclusions that this is consistent with the term 'probable' as used in IAS 37 and IFRS 3 *Business Combinations*.

See **section 4.6.1** for a discussion of factors to be considered when assessing the availability of future taxable profit.

An entity should recognise a deferred tax asset for all deductible temporary differences arising from investments in subsidiaries, branches and associates, and interests in joint arrangements, to the extent that, and only to the extent that, it is probable that:
[IAS 12:44]

- the temporary difference will reverse in the foreseeable future; and

- taxable profit will be available against which the temporary difference can be utilised.

For entities that have not yet adopted IFRS 11, the reference to 'interests in joint arrangements' in IAS 12:44 should be read as a reference to 'interests in joint ventures'.

The availability of future taxable profits is discussed in **section 4.6.1** below.

4.4.3   Recognition exceptions – general

As detailed in **4.4.1** and **4.4.2** above, deferred tax assets and liabilities should be recognised on all temporary differences except for those arising from:

- in relation to deferred tax liabilities only, the initial recognition of goodwill (see **section 4.4.4**); or

- the initial recognition of an asset or a liability in a transaction which (i) is not a business combination and (ii) at the time of the transaction affects neither accounting profit nor taxable profit (tax loss) (see **4.4.5**); or

- certain differences associated with investments in subsidiaries, branches and associates, and interests in joint arrangements (see **4.4.6**).

For entities that have not yet adopted IFRS 11, the reference to 'interests in joint arrangements' should be read as a reference to 'interests in joint ventures'.

In addition to the exceptions noted, a further condition must be met before a deferred tax asset can be recognised in respect of deductible temporary differences – it must be probable that taxable profit will be available against which the deferred tax asset can be utilised. This probability criterion is discussed in detail in **4.6** below.

Deferred tax liabilities are recognised for all taxable temporary differences except for those meeting the exceptions described above. Tax planning opportunities, as referred to in IAS 12:30 and discussed at **4.6.4**, relate only to the determination of taxable profits available to support the recognition of deferred tax assets. Tax planning opportunities should not be used to justify non-recognition of a deferred tax liability on a taxable temporary difference that exists at the end of the reporting period.

4.4.4   Recognition exceptions – the initial recognition of goodwill

4.4.4.1   Taxable temporary differences arising on the initial recognition of goodwill

The tax deductibility of reductions or impairments in the carrying amount of goodwill varies among jurisdictions according to the tax laws. When a reduction of goodwill is not deductible against taxable income, the tax base of the goodwill is nil, and a taxable temporary difference arises equal to the carrying amount of the goodwill.

Although a taxable temporary difference exists at initial recognition, IAS 12 prohibits the recognition of the resulting deferred tax liability. The underlying rationale for this exception is that, if a deferred tax liability were set up in respect of the goodwill at the time of the business combination, this would decrease the total for the net assets recognised. Because goodwill is a residual, this would further increase goodwill and the increase would also need to be tax-effected. [IAS 12:21 & 21A]

Subsequent reductions in a deferred tax liability that is unrecognised because it arises from the initial recognition of goodwill are also regarded as arising from the initial recognition of goodwill and, therefore, they are not recognised. [IAS 12:21A]

In contrast, deferred tax liabilities associated with goodwill are recognised to the extent that they do not arise from the initial recognition of that goodwill. [IAS 12:21B] This is illustrated in **examples 4.4.4.1A** to **C** below.

Example 4.4.4.1A

Taxable temporary difference arising on the initial recognition of non-tax deductible goodwill

Company A acquires Company B for consideration of CU500. The fair value of the identifiable net assets of Company B at the acquisition date is CU400, resulting in goodwill of CU100. The goodwill is not tax deductible and, therefore, has a tax base of nil, but IAS 12:15 prohibits the recognition of the resulting deferred tax liability on the temporary difference of CU100.

Subsequently, the goodwill is impaired by CU20 and, therefore, the amount of the taxable temporary difference relating to the goodwill is reduced from CU100 to CU80, with a resulting decrease in the value of the unrecognised deferred tax liability. The decrease in the value of the unrecognised deferred tax liability is also regarded as relating to the initial recognition of the goodwill and is not recognised.

Example 4.4.4.1B

Taxable temporary difference arising on goodwill that is wholly tax deductible

The facts are as for **example 4.4.4.1A**, except that the goodwill is deductible for tax purposes at 20 per cent per year starting in the year of acquisition. Thus, the tax base of the goodwill is CU100 on initial recognition and CU80 at the end of the year of acquisition. If the carrying amount of goodwill at the end of the year of acquisition remains unchanged at CU100 (i.e. it has not been impaired), a taxable temporary difference of CU20 arises in that year. That taxable temporary difference does not relate to the initial recognition of the goodwill and, therefore, the resulting deferred tax liability is recognised. The temporary difference will reverse when the acquired business (including the goodwill) is sold or the goodwill is impaired.

Example 4.4.4.1C

Taxable temporary difference arising on goodwill that is partially tax deductible

The facts are as for **example 4.4.4.1A**, except that CU80 of the goodwill is deductible for tax purposes at 25 per cent per year starting in the year of acquisition. The carrying amount of the goodwill that is non-tax deductible is CU20, but no deferred tax liability is initially recognised on this temporary difference of CU20. The tax rate is 30 per cent.

At the end of the year of acquisition, the carrying amount of the total goodwill remains CU100 (i.e. it has not been impaired). No deferred tax liability is recognised for the initial temporary difference of CU20 in relation to the non-tax deductible goodwill. A deferred tax liability of CU6 (30% × CU20) is recognised for the temporary difference between the carrying amount (CU80) and the tax base (CU60) of the tax deductible goodwill because that taxable temporary difference does not relate to the initial recognition of the goodwill. The temporary difference will reverse when the acquired business (including the goodwill) is sold or the goodwill is impaired.

4.4.4.2   Deductible temporary differences arising on the initial recognition of goodwill

As discussed above and illustrated in **examples 4.4.4.1A** and **4.4.4.1C**, IAS 12:15 prohibits the recognition of a deferred tax liability in relation to a taxable temporary difference arising on the initial recognition of goodwill. There is no equivalent prohibition on the recognition of deferred tax assets arising from deductible temporary differences in such circumstances.

IAS 12:32A specifically addresses the circumstances in which the carrying amount of goodwill arising in a business combination is less than its tax base and states that the difference gives rise to a deferred tax asset that should be recognised as part of the accounting for the business combination to the extent that it is probable that it will be recovered.

Example 4.4.4.2

Tax deductible goodwill exceeds the carrying amount of goodwill

Company A acquires Company B for consideration of CU500. The fair value of the identifiable net assets of Company B at the acquisition date is CU400, resulting in goodwill of CU100 (before any adjustment for a deferred tax asset arising on that goodwill). For tax purposes, a deduction of CU120 is available in respect of the goodwill. The tax rate is 30 per cent.

Following the requirements of IAS 12:32A, a deferred tax asset is recognised for the deductible temporary difference between the carrying amount and tax base of the goodwill, subject to the general recognition requirements of IAS 12. Because the carrying amount of goodwill is generally the residual purchase price over fair value of identifiable assets acquired and liabilities assumed (including deferred tax balances), a simultaneous equation (as illustrated below) is used to determine the final carrying amount of goodwill to be recognised in the business combination.

Equation 1 – Calculation of goodwill

	CU
Consideration	500
Less: Fair value of identifiable net assets	(400)
Less: Deferred tax asset on goodwill	(DTA)
Goodwill (GW)	100 – DTA

Equation 2 – Calculation of deferred tax asset

	CU
Tax base of goodwill	120
Less: Carrying amount of goodwill	(GW)
Deductible temporary difference	120 – GW
Tax rate	30%
Deferred tax asset on goodwill (DTA)	**0.3 × (120 – GW)**

Substituting Equation 2 into Equation 1

$$GW = 100 - DTA = 100 - 0.3(120 - GW) = 100 - 36 + 0.3(GW) = 64 + 0.3(GW)$$

Rearranged to

$$0.7(GW) = 64 \rightarrow GW = CU91.43$$

The calculated goodwill figure is then used to determine the deferred tax asset.

$$DTA = 0.3(120 - GW) = 0.3(120 - 91.43) = CU8.57$$

Therefore, the final goodwill calculation is as follows.

	CU
Consideration	500.00
Less: Fair value of identifiable net assets	(400.00)
Deferred tax asset	(8.57)
Goodwill (GW)	91.43

See **7.1.17** in **chapter A3** for a discussion of the accounting, on transition to IFRSs, for deferred tax relating to goodwill that has previously been written off directly to equity.

4.4.5   Recognition exceptions – initial recognition of an asset or a liability

IAS 12 requires the recognition of deferred tax in respect of temporary differences arising when an asset or a liability results from any one of the following:

- a transaction that affects accounting profit (e.g. anticipation of income receivable (asset), or accrual of costs payable (liability)); or

- a transaction that affects taxable profit (e.g. expenditure on assets such as computer equipment allowed for tax purposes when paid (asset), or deferral of income recognition in respect of funds that are taxable when received (liability)); or

- a business combination.

IAS 12 prohibits the recognition of deferred tax on the initial recognition of an asset or a liability in any other circumstances. [IAS 12:22] The flowchart below illustrates these rules.

Temporary difference arising on the initial recognition of an asset or liability

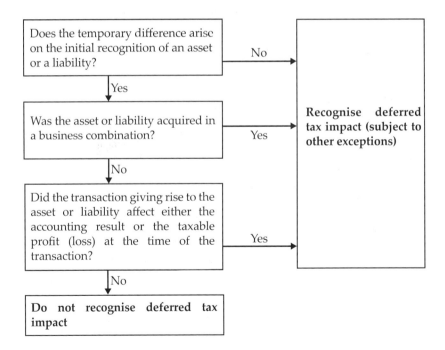

One example given in IAS 12 is that of an asset for which there is no deduction against taxable profits for depreciation. Assuming that the entity intends to recover the value of the asset through use, the tax base of the asset is nil. Therefore, a taxable temporary difference equal to the cost of the asset arises on initial recognition. However, the Standard does not permit a deferred tax liability to be recognised because the initial recognition of the asset is not part of a business combination and does not affect either accounting profit or taxable profit. Further, no deferred tax is recognised as a result of depreciating the asset.

The prohibition on recognition is based on the argument that, if a deferred tax liability were recognised, the equivalent amount would have to be added to the asset's carrying amount in the statement of financial position, or be recognised in profit or loss at the date of initial recognition, and this would make the financial statements 'less transparent'. [IAS 12:22(c)] This exception is based on pragmatism and the desire to avoid the particular financial statement effects discussed above, rather than any particular conceptual basis. The exception has a particular effect in jurisdictions where some or all of the initial expenditure on assets is disallowed for tax purposes.

Example 4.4.5A

Deferred tax liability arising on the recognition of an asset – asset depreciated at the same rate for tax and accounting purposes

Company A purchases an asset for CU100,000 at the end of 20X0. Only CU60,000 is qualifying expenditure for tax purposes. The carrying amount of the asset will be recovered through use in taxable manufacturing operations. The asset is depreciated on a straight-line basis at 25 per cent for both tax and accounting purposes.

Year	Carrying amount CU	Tax base CU	Temporary difference CU	Unrecognised temporary difference CU	Recognised temporary difference CU	Deferred tax liability CU
	A	B	A – B = C	D*		
20X0	100,000	60,000	40,000	40,000	–	–
20X1	75,000	45,000	30,000	30,000	–	–
20X2	50,000	30,000	20,000	20,000	–	–
20X3	25,000	15,000	10,000	10,000	–	–
20X4	–	–	–	–	–	–

*   The unrecognised temporary difference reflects the proportion of the asset's carrying amount that represents the original unrecognised temporary difference, as reduced by subsequent depreciation. No deferred tax is ever recognised in respect of the original temporary difference.

Subsequent to initial recognition, additional temporary differences may arise in respect of the same asset or liability (e.g. due to different depreciation rates for accounting and tax purposes). In such circumstances, the deferred tax effect of those additional temporary differences is recognised in accordance with the usual requirements.

Effectively what is required, as illustrated in **example 4.4.5B**, is to deduct from the temporary difference at each period end the proportion of the asset's (or the liability's) carrying amount that represents the unrecognised temporary difference at the date of acquisition, as reduced by subsequent depreciation or amortisation. Deferred tax is provided in respect of the remainder of the temporary difference (the recognised temporary difference) in accordance with the usual requirements.

Example 4.4.5B

Deferred tax liability arising on the recognition of an asset – different deprecation rates for tax and accounting purposes

The facts are as per **example 4.4.5A**, but the asset is depreciated on a straight-line basis at 25 per cent for accounting purposes and 33⅓ per cent for tax purposes. The tax rate is 30 per cent.

Year	Carrying amount CU	Tax base CU	Temporary difference CU	Unrecognised temporary difference CU	Recognised temporary difference CU	Deferred tax liability CU
	A	B	A – B = C	D*	C – D = E**	E × 30%
20X0	100,000	60,000	40,000	40,000	–	–
20X1	75,000	40,000	35,000	30,000	5,000	1,500
20X2	50,000	20,000	30,000	20,000	10,000	3,000
20X3	25,000	–	25,000	10,000	15,000	4,500
20X4	–	–	–	–	–	–

*   As per **example 4.4.5A**

**   The recognised temporary difference reflects the difference between cumulative tax and cumulative accounting depreciation on the original tax base of the asset.

Additional temporary differences will also arise when the asset is subsequently revalued, as illustrated below.

Example 4.4.5C

Deferred tax liability arising on the recognition of an asset – asset subsequently revalued

The facts are as per **example 4.4.5A** (i.e. depreciation on a straight-line basis at 25 per cent for both tax and accounting purposes), but the asset is revalued for accounting purposes to CU120,000 at the end of 20X1. The tax rate is 30 per cent.

925

Year	Carrying amount CU	Tax base CU	Temporary difference CU	Unrecognised temporary difference CU	Recognised temporary difference CU	Deferred tax liability CU
	A	B	A − B = C	D*	C − D = E**	E × 30%
20X0	100,000	60,000	40,000	40,000	−	−
20X1	120,000	45,000	75,000	30,000	45,000	13,500
20X2	80,000	30,000	50,000	20,000	30,000	9,000
20X3	40,000	15,000	25,000	10,000	15,000	4,500
20X4	−	−	−	−	−	−

*   As per **example 4.4.5A**

**   The recognised temporary difference is the amount by which the asset has been revalued upwards in comparison with the depreciated original cost (i.e. the difference between CU120,000 and CU75,000, being the carrying amount of the asset at the time of the revaluation), less depreciation of the revaluation uplift.

4.4.5.1   Available tax deductions exceed the cost of the asset ('super deductions')

Example 4.4.5.1A

Additional tax deduction available when assets are brought into use

On 31 December 20X0, Manufacturing Entity A enters into a capital expansion project that qualifies for tax deductions based on 150 per cent of the cost of new manufacturing assets (CU80,000). The deduction in excess of the cost of the assets (the additional tax deduction) is deductible in the determination of taxable income in the period when the assets are brought into use (20X1).

The carrying amount of the assets will be recovered through use in taxable manufacturing operations. The cost of the assets is depreciated on a straight-line basis at 25 per cent for accounting purposes and 33⅓ per cent for tax purposes.

The tax rate is 30 per cent.

Note that the tax deduction in excess of the cost of the assets (available when the assets are brought into use in 20X1) satisfies the conditions for the initial recognition exception under IAS 12:24 because the transaction (i.e. the incurrence of capital expenditure) (1) is not a business combination, and (2) affects neither accounting nor taxable profit on initial recognition.

Year	Carrying amount CU	Tax base CU	Temporary difference CU	Unrecognised temporary difference CU	Recognised temporary difference CU	Deferred tax liability CU
	A	B	A − B = C	D*	C − D = E	E × 30%
20X0	80,000	120,000	−40,000	−40,000	−	−
20X1	60,000	53,333	6,667	−	6,667	2,000
20X2	40,000	26,667	13,334	−	13,334	4,000
20X3	20,000	−	20,000	−	20,000	6,000
20X4	−	−	−	−	−	−

* The unrecognised temporary difference represents the proportion of the additional tax deduction not yet claimed.

The accounting treatment described results in a lower effective tax rate in 20X1 when the assets are brought into use (and the additional tax deduction of CU40,000 is claimed) and a constant effective tax rate from 20X2 to 20X4.

Example 4.4.5.1B

Additional tax deduction available over several periods

The facts are as per **example 4.4.5.1A**, except the additional tax deduction is claimed evenly over three years, commencing when the assets are brought into use in 20X1.

Year	Carrying amount CU	Tax base CU	Temporary difference CU	Unrecognised temporary difference CU	Recognised temporary difference CU	Deferred tax liability CU
	A	B	A – B = C	D*	C – D = E	E × 30%
20X0	80,000	120,000	-40,000	-40,000	–	–
20X1	60,000	80,000	-20,000	-26,667	6,667	2,000
20X2	40,000	40,000	–	-13,333	13,334	4,000
20X3	20,000	–	-20,000	–	20,000	6,000
20X4	–	–	–	–	–	–

* The unrecognised temporary difference reflects the proportion of the additional tax deduction not yet claimed.

The additional tax deduction is allowed over several periods, resulting in the reversal of the temporary difference that is subject to the initial recognition exception over time. This reduces the effective tax rate evenly throughout the period over which the tax deductions are realised.

4.4.5.2   Acquisition of investment property

At the time of acquisition of an investment property, an entity should determine whether the acquisition is considered to be the acquisition of a single asset, or whether it is considered to be a business combination as defined in accordance with IFRS 3. The acquisition of a single asset is a transaction to which the initial recognition exception would generally apply and, if so, no deferred tax would be recognised for any taxable temporary difference at the date of acquisition. Conversely, the acquisition of assets in a business combination does not attract the initial recognition exception and, therefore, deferred tax would be recognised on any taxable temporary differences arising at the date of acquisition.

In determining whether the acquisition of an investment property is a business combination, an entity might examine the ancillary activities related to the property. For example, if an entity simply purchases a property with tenancy agreements in place and all other services are carried out by a third party contracting with the tenant, it is likely that the acquisition would be considered to be the acquisition of a single asset. If a property is acquired that necessarily involves the entity in a number of service arrangements, it is more likely that the transaction would be considered to be a business combination. (See **section 4** of **chapter A25** for a discussion of the guidance in IFRS 3 on whether a transaction is a business combination.)

The deferred tax accounting for the acquisition will automatically follow the accounting determination as to whether the acquisition meets the definition of a business combination under IFRS 3; it is not an independent decision for the purposes of applying IAS 12.

4.4.5.3   Government grants

The above examples all deal with deferred tax liabilities arising on the initial recognition of an asset. More rarely, deferred tax assets can arise in such circumstances. The example cited in IAS 12 for a deferred tax asset arising on initial recognition is when a non-taxable government grant related to an asset is deducted in arriving at the carrying amount of the asset but, for tax purposes, is not deducted from the asset's depreciable amount (i.e. its tax base). The carrying amount of the asset is less than its tax base, giving rise to a deductible temporary difference. Under IAS 20 *Accounting for Government Grants and Disclosure of Government Assistance*, the government grant may also be set up as deferred income, in which case the difference between the deferred income and its tax base of nil is a deductible temporary difference. Whichever method of presentation is adopted, the entity does not recognise the resulting deferred tax asset. [IAS 12:33]

4.4.5.4   Recognition exceptions applied by an acquiree prior to a business combination

An entity acquired in a business combination may not have recognised deferred taxes on temporary differences related to some assets or liabilities in its individual financial statements because, when the asset or liability was first recognised, the initial recognition exception applied.

Although the acquired entity does not recognise deferred tax on these items in its individual financial statements, the recognition exception does not apply when the assets and liabilities of the acquired entity are initially recognised in the new consolidated group. Deferred tax will be recognised on any temporary differences at the date of acquisition because, from the group's perspective, the assets and liabilities are initially recognised as part of a business combination and, therefore, the conditions for the initial recognition exception are not met.

4.4.5.5   Transfers of assets between group entities

In some circumstances, an entity within a group will acquire assets and liabilities in a business combination and subsequently transfer one or more of the acquired assets to another entity within the group. In the consolidated financial statements of the group, because the assets were acquired in a business combination, the initial recognition exception does not apply and deferred tax should be recognised on any taxable temporary difference arising at the date of acquisition and subsequently (including any difference arising on the subsequent transfer of the assets between entities within the group).

However, from the perspective of the individual entity within the group to which assets have been subsequently transferred, often the transfer will not constitute a business combination, but rather the acquisition of individual assets. In such circumstances, in the individual financial statements of the entity to which the assets have been transferred, any taxable temporary difference arising on the initial recognition of the assets is subject to the initial recognition exception and no deferred tax liability should be recognised at the point of transfer. In the consolidated financial statements of the group, the unrecognised deferred tax liability would then be reinstated as a consolidation adjustment.

A similar analysis applies when an intragroup transfer results in a deductible temporary difference, with the recognition of any deferred tax asset in the consolidated financial statements being subject to IAS 12's general recognition criteria (see **4.6** below).

4.4.6   *Recognition exceptions – investments in subsidiaries, branches and associates, and interests in joint arrangements*

Temporary differences arise when the carrying amount of an investment differs from its tax base (which is often cost). Examples of circumstances in which temporary differences may arise include:
[IAS 12:38]

- the existence of undistributed profits in the subsidiary, branch, associate or joint arrangement (when profits have been consolidated or accounted for using the equity method);

- movements in the carrying amount of a foreign operation due to changes in foreign exchange rates when a parent and its subsidiary have different functional currencies; or

- a reduction in the carrying amount of an investment in an associate to its recoverable amount without a corresponding change in its tax base.

For entities that have not yet adopted IFRS 11, the reference to a 'joint arrangement' in IAS 12:38 should be read as a reference to a ' joint venture'.

Additionally, temporary differences can arise due to adjustments made to the tax base of the investment as a result of local tax law. These may include adjustments as a result of controlled foreign company laws, deemed taxable distributions of dividends, or tax elections.

A temporary difference arising in consolidated financial statements may be different from that in the parent's separate financial statements if the parent carries the investment at cost or revalued amount. [IAS 12:38]

Differences associated with investments in subsidiaries, associates and joint arrangements (or, for entities that have not yet adopted IFRS 11, joint ventures) generally arise in consolidated financial statements because the profits of the investee have been recognised (whether by consolidation or the equity method) but the tax base of the investment remains unchanged. The tax effects that would arise if those profits were distributed (e.g. withholding tax) should be considered. Unlike the 'general' recognition exceptions (see **4.4.3** above), IAS 12 does not prohibit the recognition of deferred tax assets and liabilities in respect of these differences. Instead, it imposes particular conditions for such recognition.

An entity should recognise a deferred tax liability for all *taxable* temporary differences associated with investments in subsidiaries, branches and associates, and interests in joint arrangements, except to the extent that both of the following conditions are satisfied:
[IAS 12:39]

- the parent, investor, joint venturer or joint operator is able to control the timing of the reversal of the temporary difference; and

- it is probable that the temporary difference will not reverse in the foreseeable future.

> For entities that have not yet adopted IFRS 11, the reference to 'interests in joint arrangements' in IAS 12:39 should be read as a reference to 'interests in joint ventures' and the reference to a 'joint venturer or joint operator' should be read as a reference to a 'venturer'.

An entity should recognise a deferred tax asset for all *deductible* temporary differences arising from investments in subsidiaries, branches and associates, and interests in joint arrangements, to the extent that, and only to the extent that, it is probable both:
[IAS 12:44]

- that the temporary difference will reverse in the foreseeable future; and

- that taxable profit will be available against which the temporary difference can be utilised.

> For entities that have not yet adopted IFRS 11, the reference to 'interests in joint arrangements' in IAS 12:44 should be read as a reference to 'interests in joint ventures'.

> IAS 12 does not define 'foreseeable future'. However, it is reasonable to analogise to the guidance in IAS 1 *Presentation of Financial Statements* regarding the going concern assumption underlying the preparation of financial statements. IAS 1:26 refers to a period that "is at least, but not limited to, twelve months from the end of the reporting

period". Therefore, for the purposes of applying IAS 12, it is reasonable to expect that the 'foreseeable future' would be at least twelve months from the end of the reporting period. However, depending on the facts and circumstances (including management intent), it may be a longer period.

4.4.6.1   Investments in subsidiaries

For investments in subsidiaries, the temporary difference generally represents the difference between the net investment accounted for in the consolidated financial statements (effectively the parent's share of the subsidiary's net assets including any associated goodwill) and the tax base of the investment.

A parent/subsidiary relationship involves the parent controlling its subsidiary, including the subsidiary's dividend policy. Accordingly, the Standard provides that when a parent has determined that it is probable that undistributed profits in a subsidiary will not be distributed in the foreseeable future, the parent does not recognise deferred tax on those undistributed profits. The same considerations apply to investments in branches. [IAS 12:40]

The Standard provides no specific guidance regarding the factors to be considered by the parent in order to determine whether distribution of the subsidiary's profits (and, therefore, reversal of a taxable temporary difference) is probable. Factors that might be considered in making the assessment include, but are not limited to:

- any plans for reinvestment to grow the business of the subsidiary;

- the past pattern of dividend payments;

- whether the parent needs the funds that would be generated by a dividend from its subsidiary to enable it to make a dividend payment or satisfy any other cash requirement;

- whether cash and distributable profits are available to pay dividends;

- whether a binding agreement exists regarding the amount of dividends to be paid out;

- whether there is a policy of paying out a certain percentage of profits each year;

- whether there is intent to dispose of the subsidiary before any distribution is made; and

- whether any legal or taxation requirements effectively create an economic compulsion to pay distributions.

When a parent requires its subsidiary to remit only a portion of undistributed earnings, the parent should recognise a deferred tax liability only for the portion of the undistributed earnings expected to be remitted in the foreseeable future.

If circumstances change, and it becomes probable that some or all of the undistributed earnings of the subsidiary in respect of which deferred tax has not been recognised will be remitted in the foreseeable future, the parent should recognise the additional deferred tax liability as an expense of the current period; prior year amounts are not restated.

If a subsidiary is classified as a discontinued operation under IFRS 5 *Non-current Assets Held for Sale and Discontinued Operations* (see **chapter A20**), this does not affect the requirements regarding the recognition of deferred tax assets. Therefore, a deferred tax asset should be recognised to the extent that it is probable that a temporary difference will reverse in the foreseeable future, and that taxable profit will be available against which the temporary difference can be utilised.

If a parent has recognised deferred tax in relation to its investment in a subsidiary classified as a discontinued operation, that deferred tax should be included in the accounting for the disposal of the subsidiary through sale or otherwise. Particular considerations apply when the parent retains an interest such that the investee is accounted for subsequently as an associate (see **4.4.6.4** below).

Example 4.4.6.1A

Profits in a subsidiary not expected to be distributed in the foreseeable future

Company A has a subsidiary with a carrying amount of CU200 and a tax base of CU100. Company A controls the distribution of dividends by the subsidiary. Company A does not have any need for the subsidiary to make a distribution, and in fact has active plans for the undistributed profits to be

---

reinvested to grow the business of the subsidiary. In these circumstances, Company A should not recognise a deferred tax liability in respect of the temporary difference of CU100, because Company A can control the timing of the reversal and the temporary difference is not expected to reverse in the foreseeable future.

Example 4.4.6.1B

Profits in a subsidiary expected to be distributed in the foreseeable future

The facts are as per **example 4.4.6.1A**, except that Company A has encountered a cash flow problem. In order to resolve this problem, Company A needs to extract the increased value in the subsidiary in the form of cash dividends. In these circumstances, Company A should recognise the deferred tax liability for the portion of the earnings to be remitted because, although it can control the timing of the reversal, it is probable that the temporary difference will reverse in the foreseeable future.

Example 4.4.6.1C

Parent does not control timing of payment of dividends

The facts are as per **example 4.4.6.1A**, except that the subsidiary operates in a foreign jurisdiction. In that jurisdiction, the determination as to whether profits are returned to foreign investors or are reinvested in the business is made through regulatory channels. While Company A can express a preference, it is the local regulator who determines when profits are paid out as dividends. In these circumstances, Company A should recognise the deferred tax liability for all unremitted earnings of the subsidiary because it does not control the timing of the reversal of the temporary difference.

Example 4.4.6.1D

Temporary difference arising in relation to a loan forming part of net investment

Company B has a functional currency of US dollars. It makes a loan in Euros to its wholly-owned subsidiary, Company D, which has a functional currency of Euros. The loan is assessed under IAS 21 *The Effects of Changes in Foreign Exchange Rates* to be part of Company B's net investment in Company D.

In Company B's separate financial statements, in accordance with IAS 21:32, the loan is retranslated at the end of the reporting period, with exchange differences recognised in profit or loss. The exchange differences arising from the loan will only be assessed for tax purposes when the loan is repaid.

Because the loan forms part of Company B's net investment in Company D, the requirements of IAS 12:39 (see **4.4.1** above) should be applied in relation to the loan.

Company B can control the repayment of the loan which forms part of its net investment in the subsidiary. Therefore, Company B is able to control when tax will be incurred on the exchange differences, and is able to control the timing of the reversal of the temporary difference. Because settlement is neither planned nor likely to occur in the foreseeable future (a condition for the loan to qualify as part of Company B's net investment under IAS 21:15), it is probable that the temporary difference arising from the exchange differences will not reverse in the foreseeable future.

Consequently, Company B should not recognise deferred tax on the exchange differences arising on the foreign currency loan to Company D. In addition, Company B should comply with the disclosure requirements of IAS 12:81(f).

Example 4.4.6.1E

Deferred tax on overseas income derived from a subsidiary that is only taxed on repatriation

Company A has a subsidiary, Company C, which operates in a foreign tax jurisdiction. During the year, Company A made an interest earning loan of CU100,000 to Company C that is not considered to be part of its net investment in Company C for the purposes of IAS 21:15. The interest income from the loan is not taxable while held in the foreign tax jurisdiction and is only taxed on repatriation. Company A has no current intention to repatriate the interest income.

At the end of the current financial year, the total interest earned is CU10,000 and the carrying amount of the loan is CU110,000. The tax base of the interest earned is nil.

Company A should recognise a deferred tax liability in respect of the interest earned on the loan; Company A is required to recognise a tax liability on the difference between the carrying amount of CU10,000 and the tax base of nil.

The exception in IAS 12:38 to 45 relates to differences between the carrying amount and the tax base of investments in subsidiaries, branches, associates, and interests in joint arrangements (or, for entities that have not yet adopted IFRS 11, joint ventures); the exception does not apply to temporary differences that exist between the carrying amount of amounts receivable from or payable to the investee and their tax bases.

Measurement considerations are discussed further in **4.5.3** below.

4.4.6.2   Investments in associates

In consolidated financial statements, investments in associates are generally accounted for using the equity method of accounting. Under the equity method, the investment is initially recognised at cost and the carrying amount is then increased or decreased by the investor's share of the profit or loss and other comprehensive income of the investee, less any distributions received from the associate. The tax arising in respect of the investee's profit or loss and other comprehensive income is recognised in the financial statements of the investee, and is therefore reflected in the amounts accounted for by the investor using the equity method of accounting, which are reported net of tax. Any additional tax arising on any dividends received by the investor from the associate will also be reflected in the investor's own financial statements.

It may be that additional tax implications would arise if the investor were to realise its investment in the associate – whether through distribution of the retained profits of the associate or through disposal. For example, dividend income might be taxable or partially taxable in the hands of the investor; withholding taxes might be applied in the associate's country of operation; capital gains tax might be payable on disposal of the investment. In any of these circumstances, a temporary difference may exist.

Under IAS 12's recognition rules (see **4.4.1** above), taxable temporary differences associated with investments in associates should be accounted for except when:

- the investor controls the timing of the reversal of the temporary difference; and

- it is probable that the temporary difference will not reverse in the foreseeable future.

Because an investor/associate relationship does not involve control, an investor in an associate should normally recognise deferred tax arising in relation to the undistributed profits of an associate, unless there is strong evidence of an agreement that profits will not be distributed in the foreseeable future.

Example 4.4.6.2

Investment in associate

Company B has an associate, Company A, which operates in Country Z. In its consolidated financial statements for the year ended 31 December 20X3, Company B recognised its CU20,000 share of the profits of Company A for that period using the equity method of accounting.

During the period, Company A paid interim dividends of CU5,000 to Company B out of its current year profits. No tax arises in Company B's country of operation on receipt of the dividends. However, under the laws of Country Z, additional tax is payable on distributed profits at 25 per cent and is not recoverable.

Because Company B is not able to control the timing of the reversal of the taxable temporary difference, in its consolidated financial statements it must also recognise the tax consequences that would arise if the remainder of its share of Company A's current year profits (i.e. CU15,000) were distributed. A deferred tax liability of CU3,750 (CU15,000 × 25%) should therefore be recognised in the consolidated financial statements to 31 December 20X3, in addition to the recognition of the tax consequences arising from the remittance of CU5,000.

For deductible temporary differences arising in relation to investments, it is not necessary to consider the investor's ability to control distributions from the investee. Recognition of the deferred tax asset is only required if it is probable that the temporary difference will reverse in the foreseeable future and that taxable profit will be available against which the temporary difference can be utilised.

The determination of the expected manner of recovery of an investment in an associate will often require careful judgement. Factors to consider in making this judgement include, but are not limited to:

- whether the investor intends to sell its interest;

- the dividend yield on the investment; and

- the reason for acquiring and holding the investment.

When, for example, there has been a regular flow of dividends from the investment in the past, and there is no evidence of an intention to dispose of the associate (even though a disposal may be a possibility at some future point), this may lead to a determination that the investment will be recovered via remittance of earnings by dividend.

4.4.6.3 Interests in joint arrangements (or, for entities that have not yet adopted IFRS 11, joint ventures)

Under IFRS 11 *Joint Arrangements* (effective for annual periods beginning on or after 1 January 2013, with earlier adoption permitted), the accounting for a joint arrangement is determined by whether the arrangement is classified as a joint venture or a joint operation (as defined in that Standard). Entities that have not yet adopted IFRS 11 apply IAS 31 *Interests in Joint Ventures*, under which the accounting for a joint venture is determined by whether the joint venture is classified as a jointly controlled entity, a jointly controlled operation or a jointly controlled asset.

Irrespective of the method of accounting for joint arrangements (under IFRS 11) or joint ventures (under IAS 31), the same general considerations apply in respect of deferred tax.

The arrangement between the parties to a joint arrangement usually deals with the distribution of the profits and identifies whether decisions on such matters require the consent of all of the parties or a group of the parties. When the joint venturer or joint operator can control the timing of the distribution of its share of profits of the joint arrangement, and it is probable that its share of the profits will not be distributed in the foreseeable future, a deferred tax liability is not recognised. [IAS 12:43]

For entities that have not yet adopted IFRS 11, the reference to a 'joint arrangement' in IAS 12:43 should be read as a reference to a 'joint venture' and the reference to a 'joint venturer or joint operator' should be read as a reference to a 'venturer'.

Interests in joint ventures (or, for entities that have not yet adopted IFRS 11, jointly controlled entities)

The determination as to who controls the timing of the reversal of the temporary difference in the case of joint ventures (jointly controlled entities) is not as clear-cut as it is for associates. Investments in joint ventures (jointly controlled entities) involve joint control, i.e. there is a contractual agreement to share control and no joint venturer (venturer) exercises unilateral control.

The arrangements for distributions or disposals of shareholdings are generally dealt with in the joint venture agreement. In most cases, although each joint venturer (venturer) cannot unilaterally declare a dividend, neither can such dividend be declared without each joint venturer's (venturer's) agreement. Therefore, each joint venturer (venturer) has the ability to prevent distributions and, accordingly, prevent the reversal of the temporary difference. If this is the case, no deferred tax liability should be recognised if the joint venturer (venturer) does not anticipate that such distributions will be authorised in the foreseeable future.

Interests in joint operations (or, for entities that have not yet adopted IFRS 11, jointly controlled operations and jointly controlled assets)

Under IFRS 11, the determination of the tax implications for joint operations will depend on whether the joint operation is structured through a legal entity.

For joint arrangements that are structured through a legal entity but are determined to be joint operations because of other facts and circumstances (see **chapter A27**), the same considerations apply as above for joint ventures.

For joint operations that are not structured through a legal entity, the absence of a legal entity would mean that the joint operator does not generally have the ability to control the reversal of the temporary difference. Accordingly, deferred tax should normally be recognised. This also applies to jointly controlled operations and jointly controlled assets under IAS 31.

4.4.6.4   *Change in investment from subsidiary to associate*

A parent may cease to have control over a subsidiary (e.g. because the parent sells a portion of the investment or because the subsidiary issues additional shares to a third party) but may retain some of its ownership interest such that the investment is subsequently classified as an associate and is, therefore, accounted for using the equity method. This change from subsidiary to associate may have deferred tax consequences.

When the parent did not previously recognise deferred tax in respect of temporary differences associated with the investment in the subsidiary (on the basis that it could control the timing of the reversal of such differences and it was not considered probable that the temporary differences would reverse in the foreseeable future), the change in status will generally require this determination to be revisited. Because an investor/associate relationship does not involve control, it will be determined in the majority of cases that the investor no longer has control over the timing of the reversal of the temporary differences associated with the investment, and deferred tax will need to be recognised in respect of the difference between the carrying amount of the investment in the associate and its tax base.

Under IFRS 10 *Consolidated Financial Statements* (or, for entities that have not yet adopted IFRS 10, IAS 27(2008) *Consolidated and Separate Financial Statements*), when a transaction results in a parent losing control of a subsidiary, any investment retained in the former subsidiary is recognised at its fair value at the date when control is lost. In such circumstances, there is a change in the temporary differences associated with the investment; after the transaction, the temporary differences will include not only the investor's share of the undistributed profits of the associate and foreign exchange differences etc., but also the fair value uplift of the investment.

4.4.6.5   Foreign currency adjustments

The non-monetary assets and liabilities of an entity are measured in its functional currency (see **chapter A19**). If an entity's taxable profit or tax loss (and, consequently, the tax base of its non-monetary assets and liabilities) is determined in a different currency, changes in the exchange rate give rise to temporary differences that result in a recognised deferred tax liability or asset (subject to the general recognition criteria). The resulting deferred tax is recognised in profit or loss. [IAS 12:41]

IAS 12 is clear that when the tax base of a non-monetary asset is determined in a different currency from the functional currency of the entity, temporary differences will arise and deferred tax should be calculated. However, there is no guidance on how the deferred tax should be calculated.

In general, the most appropriate methodology will be to convert the tax base into the functional currency using the closing rate. This should be compared with the asset's carrying amount in the financial statements, which will have been converted at the rate ruling on the date of recognition. The deferred tax is then calculated at the tax rate expected to apply when the temporary difference reverses.

Example 4.4.6.5A

Tax base of asset denominated in a foreign currency

Company B, a Sterling functional currency entity, owns an asset in the United States. At 1 January 20X1, the tax base of the asset is US$120 and the carrying amount is £50. The exchange rate is £0.5 = US$1, resulting in a temporary difference of £10 (US$120 × 0.5 = £60 less £50).

At 31 December 20X1, the carrying amount and the US$ tax base of the asset have not changed, but the exchange rate is now £0.52 = US$1, resulting in a temporary difference of £12 (US$120 × 0.52 = £62 less £50). The movement of £2 represents an increase in the temporary difference as a result of the movement in the exchange rate.

Company B's tax rate will be applied to the movement of £2 and the resulting value recognised as part of deferred tax expense for the year, even though the movement is attributable to an exchange rate movement.

The asset may be subject to depreciation; if so, part of the movement in the temporary difference would arise from the depreciation of the carrying amount.

When an entity owns a subsidiary that is taxed in a currency other than that subsidiary's functional currency, a translation difference will arise on the calculated deferred tax balance in that subsidiary's financial statements. On consolidation, that exchange difference is recognised in profit or loss; it is not transferred to the foreign currency translation reserve because the translation difference does not result from the accounting for the reporting entity's net investment in a foreign operation.

Example 4.4.6.5B

Tax base of subsidiary's assets and liabilities denominated in a foreign currency

Group A prepares consolidated financial statements which are presented in Sterling, and include a subsidiary with a functional currency of US dollars. However, that subsidiary pays taxes that are calculated and denominated in Sterling (the local currency of the subsidiary). Accordingly, the tax bases of the assets and liabilities in the subsidiary's financial statements are denominated in Sterling. Therefore, changes in exchange rates give rise to temporary differences. The resulting deferred tax is recognised in profit or loss in the financial statements of the subsidiary.

The amount is also recognised as part of the tax expense (income) in profit or loss in Group A's consolidated financial statements (rather than being recognised in other comprehensive income) because it reflects the genuine foreign currency exposure between the functional currency of the subsidiary and the tax cash flows of that subsidiary.

In some jurisdictions, tax returns and tax bases are permitted to be calculated in an entity's functional currency, even if that currency is not the local currency. The current tax liability is then translated into local currency for payment to the tax authorities. In such circum-stances, foreign exchange gains and losses will not generally arise on the entity's temporary differences (which are computed in the func-tional currency), but a foreign exchange gain or loss can arise on differences between the accrual of the income tax provision in the functional currency and the payment of the liability in local currency. This is a genuine foreign currency exposure between the functional currency and the tax cash flows and is recognised in profit or loss.

4.4.6.6   *Inflation adjustments*

The tax law for a particular foreign jurisdiction may permit or require the taxpayer to adjust the tax base of an asset or a liability to take into account the effects of inflation. The inflation-adjusted tax base of an asset or a liability would be used to determine the future taxable or deductible amounts. If a foreign subsidiary has such inflation-indexed assets or liabilities, it cannot use the exceptions from recognition of deferred tax associated with investments in subsidiaries under IAS 12:39 and IAS 12:44 (see **4.4.1** and **4.4.2** above) to avoid recognising the related deferred tax liabilities or assets.

The temporary differences relate to the foreign operation's own assets and liabilities, rather than to the reporting entity's investment in that foreign operation. Consequently, the foreign subsidiary recog-nises the resulting deferred tax liability or asset as appropriate in its domestic financial statements. The resulting deferred tax is recog-nised in profit or loss.

Example 4.4.6.6

Tax base of assets adjusted for inflation

Company X (with Sterling as its functional currency) has an overseas subsidiary (in a country where the inflation rate is not considered hyperin-flationary) whose functional currency is the Euro.

At the beginning of 20X2, the foreign jurisdiction enacted tax legislation that increased the tax base of depreciable assets by 10 per cent. That increase will permit the overseas subsidiary to deduct additional depreciation in the current and future years. Immediately prior to the change in tax legislation, the base of the overseas subsidiary's depreciable assets is €1,000 for both tax and financial reporting purposes; the foreign tax rate is 50 per cent, and the current exchange rate between Sterling and the Euro is £1 = €2.

Therefore, at the beginning of 20X2, the overseas subsidiary should recognise a deferred tax asset resulting from the temporary difference between the carrying amount of the depreciable asset and the indexed tax base of €50 ([€1,000 × 10 per cent] × 50%) (subject to IAS 12's general recognition criteria for deferred tax assets).

In the consolidated financial statements, the deferred tax asset of the subsidiary should be translated to £25 (€50 × 0.5) based on the current exchange rate.

In certain jurisdictions, the indexation allowance is only available upon sale, and does not affect the tax base available for tax depreciation. Therefore, if the expected manner of recovery of the asset (and, consequently, the deferred tax associated with the asset) is based on use, the indexation allowance should not be considered.

4.5   Measurement of deferred tax assets and liabilities

4.5.1   Computation of deferred tax assets and liabilities

To calculate the amount of a deferred tax asset or liability, the following formula may be useful.

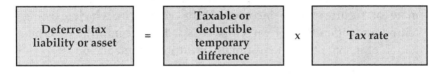

A deferred tax asset can also arise from unused tax losses and tax credits that have been carried forward. These deferred tax assets are calculated as follows.

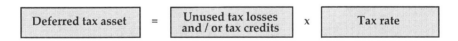

Thus, an important consideration is what tax rate should be used. This is considered in **section 4.5.2** below.

4.5.2   Tax rates and laws

Deferred tax balances are calculated using the tax rates that are expected to apply to the reporting period or periods when the temporary differences reverse, based on tax rates and tax laws enacted or substantively enacted at the end of the reporting period. [IAS 12:47]

When the tax rates that will apply to the entity are expected to vary in coming years (e.g. in start-up situations when tax concessions are granted in the early years), it is necessary to anticipate the year in which the temporary difference will reverse so that the deferred tax asset or liability can be calculated at the appropriate rate.

4.5.2.1   *Progressive or graduated tax rates*

In some jurisdictions, the tax rate varies according to the amount of taxable profit earned in a period. This creates a potential issue when it is necessary to predict the tax rate that will apply when a temporary difference reverses. IAS 12 addresses this situation and requires that, in such circumstances, deferred tax assets and liabilities should be measured using the average rates that are expected to apply in the periods in which the temporary differences are expected to reverse. [IAS 12:49]

For entities that expect graduated tax rates to be a significant factor, careful judgement should be exercised in determining the appropriate average tax rate to be used when measuring deferred tax assets and liabilities.

The determination of the appropriate tax rate may require an estimate of future taxable income for the year(s) in which existing temporary differences or carryforwards will enter into the determination of income tax. That estimate of future income includes:

- income or loss excluding reversals of temporary differences; and

- reversals of existing taxable and deductible temporary differences.

The following example illustrates the measurement of deferred tax assets and liabilities when graduated tax rates are a significant factor.

Example 4.5.2.1

Graduated tax rates

At the end of 20X1, Company X has CU30,000 of deductible temporary differences that are expected to result in tax deductions of CU10,000 for each of the next three years – 20X2, 20X3 and 20X4.

Company X operates in a jurisdiction that has a graduated tax rate structure. The graduated tax rates are as follows.

Income >	Income ≤	Tax rate
CU	CU	
–	50,000	15%
50,000	75,000	25%
75,000	100,000	34%
100,000	335,000	39%
335,000	10,000,000	34%
10,000,000	15,000,000	35%
15,000,000	18,333,333	38%
18,333,333	–	34%

Company X's estimates for pre-tax income for the three years 20X2, 20X3 and 20X4 are CU410,000, CU110,000 and CU60,000, respectively, exclusive of reversing temporary differences. The estimated taxable income and income taxes payable for those years is computed as follows.

	Future years		
	20X2	20X3	20X4
	CU	CU	CU
Estimated pre-tax income	410,000	110,000	60,000
Reversing deductible temporary differences	(10,000)	(10,000)	(10,000)
Estimated taxable income (A)	400,000	100,000	50,000
Tax based on graduated tax rates:			
(CU50,000 × 15%)	7,500	7,500	7,500
(CU25,000 × 25%)	6,250	6,250	–
(CU25,000 × 34%)	8,500	8,500	–
(CU235,000 × 39%)	91,650	–	–
(over CU335,000 × 34%)	22,100	–	–
Estimated tax (B)	136,000	22,250	7,500
Applicable tax rate (C = B/A)	34%	22.25%	15%
Deferred tax credit (CU10,000 × C), CU	3,400	2,225	1,500

Provided that the probable realisation criterion established under IAS 12 is met, Company A should recognise a deferred tax asset at the end of 20X1 of CU7,125 (CU3,400 + CU2,225 + CU1,500).

4.5.2.2   Substantively enacted tax rates

The Standard requires that deferred tax assets and liabilities be measured based on rates and laws that have been 'enacted or substantively enacted' by the end of the reporting period. It is not appropriate to anticipate changes to tax rates or laws that have not been substantively enacted.

Whether or not a law has actually been enacted by the end of the reporting period is a fact that will be immediately clear. However, when a new rate or law is announced at or before the end of the reporting period, but the formalities of the enactment process have not been finalised, it will be necessary to determine whether such announcement and any procedures or processes that have occurred prior to the end of the reporting period constitute substantive enactment.

> The determination as to whether new tax rates are considered to be 'substantively enacted' is a matter requiring careful judgement, based on the specific facts and circumstances. Factors to consider in assessing that determination include, but are not limited to, the following:
>
> • the legal system and related procedures or processes necessary for enactment of the tax law change;
>
> • the nature and extent of the remaining procedures or processes;
>
> • the extent to which the remaining procedures or processes are perfunctory; and
>
> • the timing of the remaining procedures or processes.

IAS 12 acknowledges that, in some jurisdictions, the announcement of new tax rates and tax laws by the government may have the substantive effect of enactment, even if formal enactment takes place some months later. In these circumstances, tax assets and liabilities are measured using the announced rates. [IAS 12:48] In other countries, it may be necessary for virtually all of the legal stages towards enactment to have been completed before the rates can be considered to be substantively enacted.

> The IASB decided as part of the US/IFRS convergence project to clarify that 'substantively enacted' means that any expected change in the tax rate is virtually certain. This proposed clarification was included in the exposure draft for the replacement Standard for IAS 12 (which, although a replacement Standard was not finalised, provides useful guidance on the meaning of 'substantive enactment'). The IASB noted that in some jurisdictions (e.g. the US) enactment may not be virtually certain until the change is signed into law. The Board discussed whether 'substantively enacted' should be based on the probability of enactment or on the process of enactment. The

Board decided that reaching a specified stage in the process should be required. It further decided that the specified stage should be that the process of enactment is complete, which is when the remaining steps will not change the outcome.

4.5.2.3   Changes in tax rates after the reporting period

When there is a change in tax rates or laws after the reporting period, no adjustment is made to the carrying amounts of deferred tax assets and liabilities. However, when the effect of the change is such that "non-disclosure could influence the economic decisions of users taken on the basis of the financial statements", disclosure will be required in accordance with IAS 10 *Events after the Reporting Period*. [IAS 10:21]

Example 4.5.2.3

Change in tax rate after the reporting period

Company D has recognised interest receivable of CU1,000 in its statement of financial position as at 31 March 20X3. The interest will be taxed when it is received, which will be during the year ending 31 March 20X4. At 31 March 20X3, the tax rate is 16 per cent. On 5 April 20X3, it is announced that the tax rate for the year ending 31 March 20X4 will be increased to 17.5 per cent; the change is enacted on 25 April 20X3. The financial statements for the year ended 31 March 20X3 are authorised for issue on 30 June 20X3.

The taxable temporary difference in respect of the interest receivable is CU1,000. A deferred tax liability of CU160 will be included in Company D's financial statements for the year ended 31 March 20X3. Although it is known at the time that the financial statements are authorised for issue that the interest income will be taxed at 17.5 per cent when it is received, IAS 12 precludes using the 17.5 per cent rate to calculate the deferred tax liability because this rate was neither enacted nor substantively enacted by 31 March 20X3. If the effect of the change is sufficiently significant, disclosure will be required in accordance with IAS 10.

4.5.2.4   Phased-in tax rates

A phased-in change in tax rates occurs when the tax law specifies that in future periods the tax rate applied to taxable income will change (e.g. the tax law provides that the corporate tax rate will be 43 per cent in 20X1, 38 per cent in 20X2 and 35 per cent for 20X3 and later years).

IAS 12:47 requires deferred tax assets and liabilities to be measured using the enacted (or substantively enacted) tax rates expected to apply to taxable income in the years in which the temporary differences are expected to reverse. Consequently, enacted or substantively enacted changes in tax laws or rates that become effective for particular future years must be considered when determining the tax rate to apply when measuring the tax consequences of temporary differences that are expected to reverse in those years. This exercise may require assumptions to be made regarding tax elections that will be made in future years (based on management expectations), and estimates to be made for the amounts of profit or loss anticipated in the future years when those temporary differences are expected to reverse.

4.5.3   Tax rate varies according to whether profits are distributed

In some jurisdictions, income taxes are payable at a higher or lower rate if part or all of the net profit or retained earnings are paid out as a dividend to shareholders. Equally, income taxes may be refundable or payable if part or all of the net profit or retained earnings is paid out as a dividend to shareholders of the entity. In such circumstances, IAS 12 stipulates that the rate to be used for the purposes of measurement of both current and deferred tax assets and liabilities is the tax rate applicable to undistributed profits. [IAS 12:52A]

The income tax consequences of a dividend should only be accounted for when the dividend is recognised as a liability in the financial statements. [IAS 12:52B]

Example 4.5.3A

Higher income tax rate on undistributed profits

Company G has undistributed profits of CU1,000 in its statement of financial position at 31 December 20X3. Under local tax regulations, income taxes are payable at a higher rate on undistributed profits (50 per cent) than on distributed profits (35 per cent). Company G has traditionally paid dividends to shareholders equivalent to 25 per cent of the taxable profit for the year. It continues that dividend policy by paying an interim dividend in March 20X4, before the 31 December 20X3 financial statements are authorised for issue.

A current tax liability of CU500 (CU1,000 × 50 per cent) will be included in the financial statements for the year ended 31 December 20X3, even though

---

Company G knows that a portion of the taxable profit will be taxed at a lower rate due to the interim dividend payment.

In accordance with IAS 10, the liability for the 20X4 interim dividend is not recognised in the financial statements for the year ended 31 December 20X3 and, therefore, the tax consequences of that dividend are not taken into account at 31 December 20X3. The impact of the reduction in tax rates will be recognised at the time the dividend is recognised, which will be when the criteria for recognition of a liability are met.

Although the current and deferred tax assets and liabilities of an entity are always measured at the undistributed rate in its individual financial statements, future distributions are anticipated to some extent when those financial statements are subsequently incorporated into consolidated financial statements of a group or are incorporated into the financial statements of an investor using the equity method. If, for example, Entity A is an associate of Investor I and Entity A's financial statements are incorporated into the financial statements of Investor I using the equity method, the application of IAS 12:39 and IAS 12:44 (see **4.4.1** and **4.4.2** above) may require deferred tax to be recognised presuming the distribution of earnings from Entity A. To the extent that such distribution is assumed, Investor I should use the 'distributed tax rate' to measure the resulting deferred tax assets or liabilities.

IAS 12:52B clarifies that the income tax consequences of dividends are more directly related to the past events and transactions that gave rise to the tax liability or asset than to the distributions to owners. If additional income taxes are payable or refundable when profits are distributed, although the timing of the recognition of the rate change is related to the recognition of the dividend in the financial statements, the incremental tax effect should not be dealt with in equity. Rather, it should generally be dealt with in profit or loss for the period, unless it arose as a result of an underlying transaction or event recognised outside profit or loss, or a business combination, in line with the general rules set out in IAS 12:58 (see **4.7** below).

Example 4.5.3B

Recognition of incremental tax effect of dividend payment

Company A has undistributed profits of CU1,500 in its statement of financial position at 31 December 20X3, all distributable under local law. CU500 of those profits were recognised in other comprehensive income because they arose from the revaluation of an item of property, plant and equipment that was subsequently sold (the revaluation uplift of CU500 was transferred from revaluation surplus to retained earnings when the asset was disposed of and was not recognised in profit or loss). Under local tax regulations, income taxes are payable at a higher rate on undistributed profits (50 per cent) than on distributed profits (35 per cent).

Prior to any dividend being declared, at 31 December 20X3, a current tax liability of CU750 was recognised on these earnings. Of this amount, CU250 (CU500 × 50%) was recognised in other comprehensive income and CU500 (CU1,000 × 50%) was recognised in profit or loss.

The distribution of all available profits in March 20X4 results in a reduction of the tax liability of CU225 [CU1,500 × 15%]. The reduction should be allocated between profit or loss and other comprehensive income based on the original recognition of the tax liability, resulting in the following journal entry.

		CU	CU
Dr	Current tax liability	225	
Cr	Income tax (profit or loss)		150
Cr	Income tax (other comprehensive income)		75

To recognise the reduction in the tax liability.

4.5.4   Tax holidays

When a tax jurisdiction grants an exemption from an income tax for a specified period, the event is sometimes referred to as a 'tax holiday'. For example, the jurisdiction may, for economic reasons, provide the exemption from income taxes for a specified period if an entity constructs a manufacturing facility located within the jurisdiction.

IAS 12 does not specifically address the subject of tax holidays; consequently, the general principles of IAS 12 should be applied.

An entity that is entitled to a tax holiday should calculate temporary differences in the usual manner if temporary differences originating during the tax holiday period will affect future taxable income. However, assuming that the conditions for exemption from taxation continue to be met, deferred tax should not be recognised in respect of temporary differences that are scheduled to reverse during the tax holiday period, because no net expense or benefit will result (e.g. because a zero per cent tax rate will apply to taxable income or deduction upon reversal).

See **example 4.5.4A** for two illustrative examples of tax holiday regimes.

Example 4.5.4A

Tax holidays – examples

Example 1

In Jurisdiction X, under the terms of the its tax holiday programme, an entity meeting the required criteria will be exempt from income taxes for the first 5 years of operation in Jurisdiction X.

During the tax holiday period, an entity is required to compute its tax liability in the usual manner, but a zero per cent tax rate is applied to the taxable profit. If an entity incurs tax losses during the tax holiday period, the losses will be available for carryforward and use after the tax holiday without restriction.

Under this system, temporary differences may arise during the tax holiday and reverse after the tax holiday, with tax consequences. To the extent that temporary differences are expected to reverse after the tax holiday, deferred tax assets and liabilities should be recognised for any temporary differences. Similarly, tax losses generated during the tax holiday period that are expected to be utilised after the tax holiday should be recognised as deferred tax assets (subject to the general recognition criteria for deferred tax assets).

Example 2

In Jurisdiction Y, under the terms of the its tax holiday programme, an entity meeting the required criteria will be exempt from income taxes for the first 5 years of operation in Jurisdiction Y.

During the tax holiday period, an entity is not required to compute an income tax liability (e.g. it may file no income tax return or simply file an income tax return reporting its statutory profit and with a copy of the tax holiday agreement). If an entity incurs losses during the tax holiday period, the losses are not available for carryforward after the tax holiday. Tax depreciation (capital allowances) on the entity's assets commences following the tax holiday. Once the tax holiday expires, the entity computes its tax liabilities in the usual manner.

Under this system, no deferred tax assets will be recognised for losses arising during the tax holiday. The tax base of assets and liabilities may not change during the tax holiday, but the carrying amounts of the entity's assets and liabilities will still change, and temporary differences may arise. Deferred taxes should be recognised for any temporary differences arising during the tax holiday period that will reverse after the tax holiday.

Example 4.5.4B

Tax holiday period not yet commenced

Entity A is a start-up entity. The tax laws in the relevant jurisdiction state that start-up entities are exempt from taxation for five years, commencing from the year in which the entity begins to generate taxable income.

Entity A is currently generating losses and it expects to continue to do so for three years. Therefore, it expects that it will not be required to pay tax for the next eight years.

When determining to what extent deferred tax should be recognised, when should Entity A assume that the tax holiday period begins?

As discussed above, deferred tax should not be recognised in respect of temporary differences that are scheduled to reverse during a tax holiday period, assuming that the conditions for exemption from taxation continue to be met.

In the circumstances described, when considering which temporary differences will reverse during the tax holiday period, Entity A should assume that the holiday period begins immediately and lasts for five years. To extend the assumed holiday period to take account of future periods in which losses are anticipated (i.e. in this example, to extend the holiday period to eight years) would be equivalent to anticipating future tax losses, which is not permitted.

In the circumstances described, at each reporting date until the entity produces taxable profit, the applicable tax holiday period should be assumed to be five years from that date.

4.5.5   *Discounting*

IAS 12 prohibits the use of discounting for the measurement of deferred tax assets and liabilities. [IAS 12:53]

This prohibition is not based on any conceptual argument. Rather, it reflects the practical issues involved in arriving at a reliable determination of deferred tax assets and liabilities on a discounted basis, which would require detailed scheduling of the expected timing of the reversal of every temporary difference. Having concluded that such detailed scheduling would be impracticable or highly complex in many circumstances (and, therefore, that it would be inappropriate to require discounting), the Standard removes the option to discount deferred tax balances because that would reduce comparability of deferred tax balances between entities.

4.6   Recognition of deferred tax assets

Deferred tax assets can arise from deductible temporary differences (e.g. when the carrying amount of an asset is less than its tax base), or from the ability to carry forward unused tax losses and unused tax credits.

Under IAS 12, subject to the exceptions listed at **4.4.2** above, deferred tax assets are recognised for all deductible temporary differences and all unused tax losses and tax credits, to the extent that it is probable that future taxable profit will be available against which they can be utilised. [IAS 12:24 & 34]

When an entity has a deferred tax asset that has not been recognised because it failed this recoverability test, the entity is required to reassess the position at the end of each subsequent reporting period. When the test is subsequently met, the asset is recognised at that later date; this may occur, for example, if there is an improvement in trading conditions such that it becomes more likely that sufficient taxable profits will be generated in the future. [IAS 12:37]

Conversely, when a deferred tax asset has been recognised in the statement of financial position, its carrying amount should be reviewed at the end of each subsequent reporting period and reduced to the extent that it is no longer probable that sufficient taxable profit will be available to enable its recovery. [IAS 12:56]

4.6.1   Availability of future taxable profits

A deferred tax asset represents a future tax deduction. It is, therefore, only valuable if the entity will have sufficient future taxable profits against which the deduction can be offset. Therefore, an important question to answer is when it can be considered probable that an entity will have sufficient taxable profits available in the future to enable the deferred tax asset to be recovered.

> The term 'probable' is not defined in IAS 12. As noted at **4.4.2** above, the term is subject to varying interpretations, but is generally agreed to mean at least more likely than not (i.e. a probability of greater than 50 per cent).

IAS 12 states that it is probable that an entity will have sufficient taxable profit available in the future to enable a deferred tax asset to be recovered when:

- there are sufficient taxable temporary differences relating to the same tax authority and the same taxable entity that are expected to reverse either in the same period as the expected reversal of the deductible temporary difference or in periods into which a tax loss arising from the deferred tax asset can be carried back or forward; [IAS 12:28] or

- it is probable that the entity will have sufficient taxable profit, relating to the same tax authority and the same taxable entity, in the same period as the reversal of the deductible temporary difference (or in the periods into which a tax loss arising from the deferred tax asset can be carried back or forward). In making this evaluation, taxable amounts arising from deductible temporary differences that are expected to originate in future periods should be ignored (because these will need further future taxable profits in order to be utilised); [IAS 12:29(a)] or

- tax planning opportunities are available to the entity that will create taxable profit in appropriate periods. [IAS 12:29(b)]

Thus, when looking for future taxable income to justify the recognition of a deferred tax asset, entities can look to:

- future reversals of existing taxable temporary differences (see **4.6.2**);

- future taxable profit (see **4.6.3**); and

- tax planning opportunities, i.e. actions that the entity could take to create or increase taxable profits in future periods so as to utilise the available tax deductions before they expire (see **4.6.4** below).

4.6.2   Future reversals of existing taxable temporary differences

As noted above, in order to justify the anticipated recovery of a deductible temporary difference against existing taxable differences, the following conditions must be met:
[IAS 12:28]

- the taxable differences must relate to the same tax authority and the same taxable entity; and

- the taxable differences must be expected to reverse either in the same period as the deferred tax asset reverses, or in a period into which any tax loss arising from the reversal of the deferred tax asset can be carried forward or back.

IAS 12 does not specifically address how an entity should schedule the reversal pattern for existing temporary differences. It is generally only necessary to schedule the reversal of taxable temporary differences when deferred tax assets have limited lives (i.e. they are subject to expiry). Because of cost benefit considerations, there may be more than one approach to scheduling reversal patterns. However, it is apparent from the discussion in IAS 12:35 and 36 that two concepts underlie the determination of the reversal patterns for existing temporary differences:

- the year(s) in which temporary differences result in taxable or deductible amounts generally are determined by the timing of the recovery of the related asset or the settlement of the related liability; and

- the tax law determines whether future reversals of temporary differences will result in taxable and deductible amounts that offset each other in future years.

Note that an entity may not take account of future originating temporary differences (e.g. planned future capital expenditure) when assessing future reversals of temporary differences, because those differences will only arise as a result of future events or transactions.

Example 4.6.2

Forecasting future reversals of existing taxable temporary differences

Company C has made a tax loss for the year and has identified the following temporary differences at 31 December 20X3:

- taxable temporary differences related to accelerated tax depreciation, expected to reverse in 20X4 and 20X5 – CU4,000; and

- deductible temporary differences in respect of pre-operating costs expensed for accounting purposes in 20X3 but allowed for tax purposes over five years – CU2,800.

Company C is expected to make losses for the foreseeable future. Tax is payable at 20 per cent. Tax losses may be carried forward, but not back.

Anticipated reversals of Company C's existing temporary differences are as follows.

	20X4	20X5	20X6	20X7
	CU	CU	CU	CU
Accelerated tax depreciation	(2,000)	(2,000)	–	–
Pre-operating costs	700	700	700	700

At 31 December 20X3, a deferred tax liability is recognised in respect of the accelerated tax depreciation, amounting to CU800 (CU4,000 × 20%). The

---

deferred tax asset recognised in respect of the pre-operating costs is limited to CU280 (CU1,400 × 20%). Future tax deductions are available for the remainder of the pre-operating costs. However, because the reversals occur in periods when they cannot be used against existing taxable temporary differences, their recognition cannot be justified on the basis of those temporary differences. Other expected sources of taxable income or tax planning opportunities would need to be identified in order to support the recognition of the remainder of the deferred tax asset. In the above example this seems unlikely because Company C is, and is forecast to continue to be, a loss-making entity (see **4.6.3.3** below).

4.6.3   Future taxable profits

In general, entities should consider all currently available information about the availability of future taxable profits. However, certain future events should not be anticipated or considered in determining the realisability of deferred tax assets. These items include, but are not limited to, the following:

- changes in tax laws or rates (except those that are substantively enacted);

- expected business combinations;

- anticipated future income from events beyond the entity's control and that are non-recurring or unusual in nature (e.g. forgiveness of indebtedness for purposes of avoiding derecognition of a deferred tax asset); and

- events dependent on future market conditions or otherwise not within the entity's control.

4.6.3.1   Indicators of future taxable profits

In evaluating whether it is probable that taxable profit will be available, the nature and timing of such profit should be considered.

The following are some examples of factors that may support the assertion that it is probable that taxable profit will be available.

Contracts or firm sales backlog that will produce sufficient taxable income to realise the deferred tax asset based on existing sales prices and cost structures:

- an entity enters into a long-term contract that will generate sufficient future taxable income to enable it to utilise all existing operating loss carryforwards; or

- during the current year, an entity acquired another entity that operates in a different industry that is characterised by stable profit margins. Assuming that the group is taxed on a consolidated basis or that group relief is available, the acquiree's existing contracts will produce sufficient taxable income to enable utilisation of the loss carryforwards.

An excess of appreciated asset value over the tax bases of an entity's net assets in an amount sufficient to realise the deferred tax asset:

- an entity has invested in land that has appreciated in value. If the land were sold at its current market value, the sale would generate sufficient taxable income to utilise all tax loss carryforwards. The entity will sell the land and realise the gain if the operating loss carryforward would otherwise expire unused.

A strong earnings history exclusive of the loss that created the future deductible amount coupled with evidence indicating that the loss is not a continuing condition:

- an entity incurs operating losses that result in a carryforward for tax purposes. The loss resulted from the disposal of a subsidiary whose operations are not critical to the continuing entity and the entity's historical earnings, exclusive of the subsidiary losses, have been strong.

Conversely, there may be indicators that future taxable profits will not be available. The following are some examples of factors that may rebut the assertion that it is probable that taxable profit will be available.

History of losses in recent years (see also **4.6.3.3** below):

- an entity has incurred operating losses for financial reporting and tax purposes during recent years. The losses for financial reporting purposes exceed operating income for financial reporting purposes as measured on a cumulative basis from the most recent preceding years; or

- a currently profitable entity has a majority ownership interest in a newly formed subsidiary that has incurred operating and tax losses since its inception. The subsidiary is consolidated for financial reporting purposes. The tax jurisdiction in which the subsidiary operates prohibits it from filing a consolidated tax return (or otherwise obtaining group relief) from its parent or other group entities; or

- the entity is a start-up business or development stage enterprise or is emerging from a financial reorganisation or bankruptcy. In the early years of operation, these types of entities will frequently have a history of losses coupled with limited evidence of ability to meet budgets.

A history of operating loss or tax credit carryforwards expiring unused:

- an entity has generated tax credit carryforwards during the current year. During the past several years, tax credits that originated in prior years expired unused. There are no available tax planning strategies that would enable the entity to utilise the tax benefit of the carryforwards.

Unsettled circumstances that if unfavourably resolved would adversely affect profit levels on a continuing basis:

- during the past several years, an entity has manufactured and sold devices to the general public. The entity has discovered, through its own product testing, that the devices may malfunction under certain conditions. No malfunctions have been reported. However, management is concerned about the appropriateness of continuing to sell the product and that product generates significant revenue.

4.6.3.2   Non-recurring items

Frequently, entities will extrapolate from current profit levels to forecast future taxable profits (having due regard to anticipated growth levels etc.). When assessing the sustainability of current profit levels, it is important to make appropriate adjustments for past non-recurring items, which generally are not indicative of an entity's ability to generate taxable income in future years.

Non-recurring items that will affect the level of profitability in future accounting periods should also be considered (however, as discussed in **4.6.3** above, this does not extend to anticipating future events).

Examples of non-recurring items that should be excluded include, but are not limited to, the following:

- one-time restructuring charges;

- large litigation settlements or awards that are not expected to recur in future years;

- historical interest expense on debt that has been restructured or refinanced;

- historical fixed costs that have been reduced or eliminated; and

- severance payments relating to management changes.

Examples of items that may have an impact on the determination of future profit or loss for a number of years include, but are not limited to, the following:

- poor operating results caused by an economic downturn, government intervention or changes in regulation; and

- operating losses attributable to a change in the focus of a subsidiary or business unit.

4.6.3.3   History of recent losses

When an entity has incurred losses in recent years, additional caution should be exercised before a deferred tax asset is recognised. The Standard points out that "the existence of unused tax losses is strong evidence that future taxable profit may not be available". It goes on to say that, if there are insufficient deferred tax liabilities reversing in appropriate periods and entities, there must be "convincing other evidence" that there will be sufficient taxable profit. [IAS 12:35]

In assessing the probability that taxable profits will be available, the following should be considered:
[IAS 12:36]

- whether the entity has sufficient taxable temporary differences relating to the same tax authority and the same taxable entity, which will result in taxable amounts against which the unused tax losses or unused tax credits can be utilised before they expire;

- whether it is probable that the entity will have taxable profits before the unused tax losses or unused tax credits expire;

- whether the unused tax losses result from identifiable causes that are unlikely to recur; and

- whether tax planning opportunities are available to the entity that will create taxable profit in the period in which the unused tax losses or unused tax credits can be utilised.

The assessment as to whether an entity will have sufficient taxable profits in the future to realise a deferred tax asset is a matter requiring careful judgement based on the facts and circumstances available.

The very existence of losses calls future profitability into question and IAS 12:36(c) notes that preparers need to consider whether unused tax losses result from identifiable causes that are unlikely to recur. When the losses are expected to recur, it is unlikely that a deferred tax asset can be recognised. However, the source of the losses may have been addressed, for example, through disposal of loss-making operations, restructurings, or reductions of ongoing costs.

A history of recent losses is objectively verifiable evidence and, as a result, carries more weight than other evidence that embodies some degree of subjectivity. For this reason, whenever an entity has suffered cumulative losses in recent years, it is difficult to support the recognition of a deferred tax asset based on forecasts of future profits without a demonstrated turnaround to operating profitability. In other words, an entity that has cumulative losses will not generally be able to use forecast future profits to support a conclusion that realisation of an existing deferred tax asset is probable, unless that forecast is supported by strong evidence (which will need to be disclosed in accordance with IAS 12:82 – see **6.2** below). Examples of such evidence may include significant new contracts, an increase in the level of orders, or the disposal of an unprofitable segment.

In addition to these considerations, particular attention needs to be paid to restrictions on:

- the number of years for which the losses can be carried forward; and

- the types of profit against which the losses can be offset.

There is no specific time restriction in IAS 12 regarding the length of the 'look-forward' period which is used to determine whether taxable profits will be available. The length of the period used will depend on a number of entity-specific factors, including the entity's historical profitability, accuracy of budgetary controls and expected future activities.

The entity assesses whether any portion of the total available unused tax losses or tax credits is likely to be utilised before they expire. To the extent that it is not probable that taxable profit will be available against which the unused tax losses or unused tax credits can be utilised, the deferred tax asset is not recognised. [IAS 12:36]

4.6.4   Tax planning opportunities

Tax planning opportunities are actions that the entity can take to create or increase taxable income in a particular period before the expiry of a tax loss or tax credit carryforward. [IAS 12:30] Although such opportunities are future actions, the entity is entitled to consider them in justifying the recognition of a deferred tax asset.

Examples of tax planning opportunities include:
[IAS 12:30]

- being able to elect to have an income source taxed at an earlier point (e.g. electing to have interest income taxed on a receivable, rather than a receipts, basis);

- being able to defer to a future period the claim for certain tax deductible items (e.g. waiving a claim to first year allowances on an item of equipment, and instead taking annual allowances on the full amount in future periods);

- selling and leasing back assets that have appreciated in value, but for which the tax base has not been adjusted to reflect the appreciation; and

- selling an asset that generates non-taxable income in order to purchase another investment that generates taxable income.

In order to use a tax planning opportunity as support for the recognition of a deferred tax asset, the entity must have the ability to implement the chosen tax planning strategy. For example, a plan to take a pension holiday in order to boost taxable profit in a particular period so as to utilise tax losses that are about to expire can only be taken into account if the strategy can be controlled by the entity (e.g. it cannot be prevented by pension regulations, and is likely to be accepted by the pension fund trustees and the workforce).

The amount of the future taxable profits expected to be generated by such proposed strategies must be reduced by the cost of the strategies. The actions must be commercially viable and without significant adverse consequences – otherwise, it is unlikely that management would proceed.

4.6.5   Acquisition of tax losses at less than fair value

Example 4.6.5

Acquisition of tax losses at less than fair value

Company A acquires Company B, which is a shell entity with valuable unused tax losses. Company B does not meet the definition of a business under IFRS 3 *Business Combinations* and, therefore, the transaction is not a business combination for the purposes of that Standard.

Company A acquires Company B (and, therefore, the tax losses) for CU100,000. This is significantly lower than the tax asset that would be recognised in respect of the tax losses under IAS 12 (CU1 million). Company A expects to be able to utilise all of the available losses.

On the date of acquisition, Company A should recognise the deferred tax asset acquired at the amount paid (i.e. at CU100,000).

Subsequently, the unused tax losses in Company B are available for use against Company A's taxable profits. Accordingly, the deferred tax asset recognised at the date of acquisition should be assessed and measured in accordance with IAS 12:34 which requires that "[a] deferred tax asset shall be recognised for the carryforward of unused tax losses and unused tax credits to the extent that it is probable that future taxable profit will be available against which the unused tax losses and tax credits can be utilised".

Therefore, Company A should determine the extent to which it is probable that future taxable profits will be available against which the unused tax losses can be utilised and the deferred tax asset should be remeasured to reflect this amount. Any remeasurement should be recognised in profit or loss for the period.

In the circumstances described, if it is probable that Company A will be able to utilise all of the tax losses, the deferred tax asset should be remeasured to CU1 million with the resulting gain of CU900,000 recognised in profit or loss.

The assessment as to whether it is probable that the tax losses will be utilised should be based on the guidance provided in IAS 12:35 and IAS 12:36 (see above).

4.7   Recognition of movement in deferred tax balances

In determining how the deferred tax effects of a transaction or other event should be recognised, the underlying principle is that the accounting for such deferred tax effects should follow the accounting for the transaction or event itself. [IAS 12:57]

Deferred tax should be recognised as income or an expense and included in profit or loss for the period, except to the extent that the tax arises from: [IAS 12:58]

- a transaction or event which is recognised, in the same or a different period, outside profit or loss, either in other comprehensive income or directly in equity; or

- a business combination (see **5.1**).

For entities that have adopted the *Investment Entities* amendments (effective for annual periods beginning on or after 1 January 2014, with earlier adoption permitted – see **section 15** of **chapter A24**), IAS 12:58 is amended to clarify that the exception for business combinations does not apply to the acquisition by an investment entity, as defined in IFRS 10 *Consolidated Financial Statements*, of a subsidiary that is required to be measured at fair value through profit or loss.

Deferred tax is recognised outside profit or loss if the tax relates to items that are recognised, in the same or a different period, outside profit or loss. When the deferred tax relates to items that are recognised in other comprehensive income, the tax is also recognised in other comprehensive income (see **4.7.1**). When the deferred tax relates to items that are recognised directly in equity, the tax is also recognised in equity (see **4.7.2**). [IAS 12:61A]

4.7.1   Items recognised in other comprehensive income

Items required or permitted under IFRSs to be recognised in other comprehensive income include:

- exchange differences on the translation of the financial statements of a foreign operation under IAS 21 *The Effects of Changes in Foreign Exchange Rates*;

- the recognition of fair value movements on some financial assets (see **5.3.3** below);

- the revaluation of property, plant and equipment under IAS 16 *Property, Plant and Equipment* (see **4.7.1.1** below); and

- actuarial gains and losses relating to defined benefit pension obligations (see **5.8** below).

> Exchange differences arising on the translation of financial statements only give rise to deferred tax when the criteria in IAS 12:39 and IAS 12:44 are met, and an entity has accrued for the reversal of the temporary difference between the carrying amount of its investment (including foreign exchange gains and losses) and its tax base (see **4.4.6**).

4.7.1.1   Revaluations of property, plant and equipment

The most common example of deferred tax recognised in other comprehensive income is when an item of property, plant and equipment is revalued (see also **5.4**).

> When an entity accounts for a class of assets on a revaluation basis under IAS 16, fair value movements are generally recognised in other comprehensive income and accumulated in a revaluation reserve. While the carrying amount of the asset changes, the associated tax base may not, resulting in the creation of a, or a change in an existing, temporary difference. Under IAS 12:61A, deferred tax arising on a revaluation that is recognised in other comprehensive income is also recognised in other comprehensive income. This deferred tax is generally offset against the revaluation reserve (although such offset is not required, and the entity may choose to offset the deferred tax against another equity reserve).

While the original deferred tax arising on the revaluation is recognised in other comprehensive income, the subsequent release of that deferred tax liability due to the depreciation of the increased carrying amount is not credited in other comprehensive income, but in profit or loss, along with the depreciation expense.

This is an important principle. The deferred tax liability is initially recognised in other comprehensive income. However, because the effects of recovering the asset through use (the recognition of a depreciation expense and the generation of taxable profits) are dealt with in profit or loss, the release of the deferred tax liability (against the current tax liability arising) is also dealt with in profit or loss.

These principles are illustrated in **example 4.7.1.1.**

Example 4.7.1.1

Asset revaluation and subsequent recovery of asset – recognition of deferred tax

Company I revalues an item of property, plant and equipment from a carrying amount of CU95,000 to CU150,000. The tax base of the asset, which is not affected by the revaluation, is CU90,000. The carrying amount of the property is expected to be recovered through use. The applicable tax rate is 30 per cent. A deferred tax liability of CU1,500 (CU5,000 × 30%) has been recognised in respect of the taxable temporary difference of CU5,000 prior to the revaluation.

An additional taxable temporary difference of CU55,000 (CU150,000 – CU95,000) arises on revaluation, giving rise to an additional deferred tax liability of CU16,500 (CU55,000 × 30%). The following entries recognise the revaluation and the additional deferred tax liability.

		CU	CU
Dr	Property, plant and equipment	55,000	
Cr	Revaluation gain (other comprehensive income)		55,000
Dr	Income tax (other comprehensive income)	16,500	
Cr	Deferred tax liability		16,500

To recognise the revaluation and the deferred tax liability.

In subsequent periods, the property will be depreciated for both accounting and tax purposes, changing the temporary difference. Any movements in the deferred tax liability are recognised in profit or loss. For example, if the carrying amount of the property at the end of the next reporting period is CU130,000 and the tax base is CU85,000, there is a taxable temporary difference of CU45,000 and a deferred tax liability of CU13,500 (CU45,000 × 30%). The movement for the year is recognised as follows.

	CU	CU
Dr Deferred tax liability		
(CU1,500 + CU16,500 – CU13,500)	4,500	
Cr Income tax (profit or loss)		4,500
To recognise the movement for the year.		

IAS 16 does not specify whether an entity should transfer each year from revaluation surplus to retained earnings an amount equal to the difference between the depreciation or amortisation on a revalued asset and the depreciation or amortisation based on the historical cost of that asset. If an entity makes such a transfer, the amount transferred is net of any related deferred tax. Similar considerations apply to transfers made on the disposal of an item of property, plant or equipment. [IAS 12:64]

4.7.2   Items recognised directly in equity

Items required or permitted under IFRSs to be credited or charged directly to equity include:

- an adjustment to the opening balance of retained earnings resulting from a change in accounting policy that is accounted for retrospectively under IAS 8 or the correction of an error (see **chapter A5**);

- the initial recognition of the equity component of a compound financial instrument under IAS 32 *Financial Instruments: Presentation* (see **5.3.4**);

- when the expected tax deduction for an equity-settled share-based payment exceeds the cumulative profit or loss expense recognised in respect of that share based payment (see **5.6**); and

- when a withholding tax is charged on dividend distributions (see **4.7.2.1**).

4.7.2.1   Withholding tax

A tax jurisdiction may assess an entity with a 'withholding tax', which is paid to the tax authorities on behalf of the shareholders when the entity makes a dividend distribution. Such withholding tax is charged to equity as part of the dividends. [IAS 12:65A]

When a 'withholding tax' neither is paid on behalf of the shareholders nor gives rise to a future benefit for the entity, it should be dealt with as a higher rate of tax applied to distributed profits – see **4.5.3** above.

If an entity obtains a future benefit as a result of withholding the tax from amounts distributed (e.g. if the tax withheld is deductible against future dividend receipts), the initial payment to the tax authorities is not a 'withholding tax' as contemplated in IAS 12; in such circumstances, the initial payment to the tax authorities should be recognised as an increase in income tax expense (rather than being accounted for as part of the dividend distribution), with the future tax benefit likewise recognised as a component of tax in profit or loss. The resulting tax asset will be considered for recoverability – see **4.6** above.

Example 4.7.2.1 illustrates the appropriate treatment for two types of 'withholding tax'.

Example 4.7.2.1

Withholding tax

Scenario 1 – withholding tax as contemplated in IAS 12:65A

Company Y decides to pay dividends of CU100 to its shareholders. Local tax law requires Company Y to withhold 35 per cent of the dividends and to pay the amount withheld over to the tax authorities. The tax is paid to the tax authorities on behalf of the shareholders and does not give rise to a future benefit for Company Y.

Company Y should record the following journal entries.

		CU	CU
Dr	Retained earnings – distribution	100	
Cr	Cash		65
Cr	Payable		35

To recognise the dividend payment and related liability to pay tax on shareholders' behalf.

		CU	CU
Dr	Payable	35	
Cr	Cash		35

To recognise payment of the taxes withheld.

Scenario 2 – withholding tax with future benefit for entity paying dividends

Company Z decides to pay dividends of CU100 to its shareholders. Local tax law requires Company Z to withhold 35 per cent of the dividends and to pay the amount withheld over to the tax authorities. Company Z obtains a future tax credit equal to the amount paid to the tax authorities in connection with the dividends; the tax credit can be used to offset tax liabilities arising over the following three years.

Company Z should record the following journal entries.

	CU	CU
Dr Current tax expense	35	
Dr Retained earnings – distribution	65	
Cr Cash		65
Cr Taxes payable		35

To recognise the dividend payment and the liability to pay tax on the distribution.

	CU	CU
Dr Deferred tax asset	35	
Cr Deferred tax income		35

To recognise the future tax benefit.

	CU	CU
Dr Taxes payable	35	
Cr Cash		35

To recognise payment of the taxes withheld.

As with any other deferred tax asset, the recognition of the deferred tax is dependent on meeting the recognition criteria in IAS 12:24. If those criteria are not met, Company Z would not recognise the deferred tax asset upon payment of the tax, but rather if and when the recognition criteria are met.

IAS 12:65A addresses the treatment of withholding tax by the entity paying the withholding tax; the Standard does not address how the recipient of the dividend should account for the withholding tax. However, to the extent that withholding tax is paid entirely on behalf of the recipient, IAS 18 *Revenue* requires that the recipient should recognise the dividend income at its gross amount (i.e. before deduction of withholding tax); the tax suffered on the dividend income should be recognised by the recipient in profit or loss as part of its tax expense.

4.7.3   Uncertainty regarding the amount to be recognised outside profit or loss

When, in exceptional circumstances, an entity is unable to determine the amount of deferred tax that relates to items recognised outside profit or loss, IAS 12 allows the entity to base the amount on a reasonable pro rata allocation or some other method achieving a more appropriate allocation.

Such uncertainty can arise, for example, when:
[IAS 12:63]

*   there are graduated rates of income tax, and it is impossible to determine the rate at which a specific component of taxable profit (tax loss) has been taxed; or

- a change in the tax rate or other tax rules affects a deferred tax asset or liability relating (in whole or in part) to an item that was previously recognised outside profit or loss; or

- an entity determines that a deferred tax asset should be recognised, or should no longer be recognised in full, and the deferred tax asset relates (in whole or in part) to an item that was previously recognised outside profit or loss.

An example of how such an allocation might be made is set out in **3.2.1.3** above.

4.7.4   Reversal of deferred tax expense on reclassification from equity to profit or loss of gains and losses previously recognised in other comprehensive income

IAS 12:61A requires that current or deferred tax relating to items that are recognised, in the same or a different period, in other comprehensive income should be recognised in other comprehensive income.

In some cases, IFRSs require that gains or losses initially recognised in other comprehensive income be subsequently reclassified to profit or loss. For example:

- gains or losses arising on cash flow hedges previously recognised in other comprehensive income are reclassified from equity to profit or loss when the hedged forecast cash flows affect profit or loss (subject to the conditions in IAS 39 *Financial Instruments: Recognition and Measurement*);

- gains or losses arising on net investment hedges previously recognised in other comprehensive income are reclassified from equity to profit or loss when the net investment affects profit or loss;

- for entities that have not yet adopted IFRS 9 *Financial Instruments*, gains or losses arising on available-for-sale financial assets previously recognised in other comprehensive income are reclassified from equity to profit or loss when the asset is disposed of or is determined to be impaired; and

- on disposal or partial disposal of a foreign operation (other than a partial disposal of a subsidiary when control is retained), all or a portion of the foreign currency translation reserve is reclassified from equity to profit or loss as part of the gain or loss on disposal.

Whether such gains and losses are included in the determination of taxable profit in the period in which they are initially recognised in other comprehensive income depends on the rules in the particular tax jurisdiction.

If such gains and losses give rise to temporary differences (and, consequently, deferred tax balances) when they are recognised in other comprehensive income, when the gains and losses are subsequently reclassified to profit or loss and any current tax arising at that point is recognised in profit or loss, the deferred tax balance will be reversed. The question arises as to whether the reversal of the deferred tax balance should be recognised in other comprehensive income or in profit or loss.

The most appropriate treatment is that the reversal should be recognised in other comprehensive income because that is where the deferred tax was initially recognised.

See **example 4.7.4** for an illustration of this approach. Note that in the example there is no impact on the effective tax rate of the entity.

Example 4.7.4

Reversal of deferred tax expense on reclassification from equity to profit or loss of gains and losses previously recognised in other comprehensive income

Company Y has a portfolio of financial assets classified as available for sale in accordance with IAS 39. For financial reporting purposes, unrealised gains and losses on the assets are recognised in other comprehensive income. In accordance with IAS 12, any tax consequences are also recognised in other comprehensive income.

Under local tax laws, unrealised gains and losses on investment portfolios are not included in the determination of taxable income or loss; rather, taxable gains or losses arise only when a financial asset is disposed of. Because the movement in the value of financial assets does not affect current tax, deferred taxes should be computed in respect of the resulting temporary differences between the carrying amount of the financial assets (fair value) and their tax base.

In 20X1, there is unrealised loss on the assets of CU10 million. There is no movement in the market value of the assets during 20X2. On the last day of

20X2, Company Y sells the assets, thereby crystallising the previously recognised pre-tax loss of CU10 million.

The tax rate for 20X1 and 20X2 is 30 per cent. Company Y has net taxable income in 20X1.

The journal entries for 20X1 are as follows.

		CU'000	CU'000
Dr	Unrealised loss on investments		
	(other comprehensive income)	10,000	
Cr	Investment portfolio		10,000

To recognise the unrealised loss on the available-for-sale assets in other comprehensive income.

Dr	Deferred tax asset	3,000	
Cr	Deferred tax benefit		
	(other comprehensive income)		3,000

To recognise the tax consequences of the temporary difference resulting from the unrealised losses on the assets (CU10 million × 30 per cent – IAS 12's general recognition criteria assumed to be met).

Note – there is no impact on the effective tax rate of the entity, because both the unrealised loss and the related deferred tax are recognised outside profit or loss.

The journal entries for 20X2 are as follows.

		CU'000	CU'000
Dr	Loss on sale (profit or loss)	10,000	
Cr	Unrealised loss on investments		
	(other comprehensive income)		10,000

To recognise the reclassification from equity to profit or loss of the pre-tax loss on sale of the asset portfolio in 20X2.

		CU'000	CU'000
Dr	Current tax liability	3,000	
Dr	Deferred tax benefit		
	(other comprehensive income)	3,000	
Cr	Deferred tax asset		3,000
Dr	Current tax liability	3,000	
Cr	Current tax benefit (profit or loss)		3,000

To recognise the current tax benefit on realisation of the loss on the asset portfolio, and deferred tax expense representing utilisation of the deferred tax asset previously recognised.

4.7.5   Recognition of deferred tax arising from a business combination

When a business combination occurs, deferred tax balances can arise from a number of sources. These are described in detail in **section 5.1** below.

The amount of deferred tax arising from each of these sources is recognised and included as part of the identifiable net assets at the date of acquisition. The combined effect, therefore, affects the amount of the goodwill or bargain purchase gain arising on acquisition.

4.7.6   Revaluations for tax purposes

When an asset is revalued for tax purposes and that revaluation is related to an accounting revaluation of an earlier period, or to one that is expected to be carried out in a future period, the tax effects of both the asset revaluation and the adjustment of the tax base are recognised in other comprehensive income in the periods in which they occur. [IAS 12:65]

When an asset is revalued for tax purposes but there has not been, and is not to be, an accounting revaluation, the tax effects of the adjustment of the tax base are recognised in profit or loss. [IAS 12:65]

The most common examples of revaluations for tax, but not accounting, purposes are as follows:

- when tax authorities calculate the taxable gain on disposal of a capital asset by reference to a base cost that represents the original cost of the asset uplifted by an allowance to reflect inflation over the period of ownership or the market value of value of the asset at a specified date (see **examples 4.7.6A** and **4.7.6B** below); and

- when a group undertakes a transaction between two group entities which is internal to the group (and hence does not change group carrying amounts) but gives rise to a new tax base (see **example 4.2.5** for an illustration).

Example 4.7.6A

Tax base increased by inflation index in each period

Company J purchases an investment property for CU10,000 and accounts for it using the fair value model under IAS 40 *Investment Property* (i.e. recognising changes in the property's fair value in profit or loss and not depreciating it). The carrying amount of the property will be recovered through sale. The allowable cost for tax purposes is increased by an agreed inflation index in each period.

The tax rate for capital profits is 30 per cent and the agreed inflation increment in each period under consideration is 5 per cent and there are no changes in the fair value of the property (i.e. its carrying amount remains at CU10,000). The deferred tax consequences for the first three years are calculated as follows.

Year	Carrying amount CU	Tax base CU	Deductible temporary difference CU	Deferred tax asset CU
20X0	10,000	10,000	–	–
20X1	10,000	10,500	500	150
20X2	10,000	11,025	1,025	308

The recognition of the resultant deferred tax asset is dependent on the availability of future profits against which the capital loss can be offset.

If the deferred tax asset is recognised, the resulting credit is to profit or loss. Therefore, at the end of 20X1, the required journal entry is as follows.

		CU	CU
Dr	Deferred tax asset	150	
Cr	Income tax (profit or loss)		150

To recognise the deferred tax asset.

Example 4.7.6B

Accounting for increased allowances based on market value uplifts

Entity B operates in the extractives industry. At the beginning of 20X1, Entity B's local tax authority introduces new legislation that permits Entity B to calculate tax depreciation for certain mining assets using the market value of the assets at a specified date, rather than the cost or carrying amount of the assets. The tax depreciation calculated on the basis of the market value at the specified date is referred to as the 'starting base allowance'. The carrying amount of the assets in the financial statements of Entity B is not adjusted.

If there is insufficient profit against which the annual tax depreciation allowance can be used in any taxable period, the excess is carried forward and is available for use as a deduction against taxable profit in future periods.

How should Entity B recognise the market value uplift (i.e. the adjustment to the available tax depreciation as a result of applying the market value approach)?

Entity B should recognise the market value uplift as part of the tax base of the related mining assets so that, at the specified date, the tax base of the assets is increased to the starting base allowance.

The amount of the starting base allowance, including the market value uplift, is attributed to the related assets under the tax regime and becomes the basis for tax depreciation allowances in future periods. Therefore, the market value uplift forms part of the tax base of the related assets as defined in IAS 12:7 (i.e. "the amount that will be deductible for tax purposes against any taxable economic benefits that will flow to an entity when it recovers the carrying amount of the asset").

Because the carrying amount of the assets in the financial statements is not adjusted, a deductible temporary difference arises because the tax base of the assets is higher than their carrying amount. A deferred tax asset should be recognised to the extent that the recognition criteria in IAS 12:24 are met (see 4.4.2 above), and the corresponding credit is recognised in profit or loss in accordance with IAS 12:65.

Because the temporary difference arises when the new tax legislation is introduced, rather than on initial recognition of the mining assets, the initial recognition exception does not apply.

The conclusions above were confirmed in an IFRS Interpretations Committee agenda rejection published in the July 2012 *IFRIC Update.*

4.7.7 Changes in the carrying amount of a deferred tax asset or liability

The carrying amount of a deferred tax asset or liability may change for reasons other than a change in the temporary difference itself. Such changes might arise as a result of:

- a change in tax rates or laws; or

- reassessment of the recoverability of a deferred tax asset; or

- a change in the expected manner of recovery of an asset or the expected manner of settlement of a liability.

In such circumstances, IAS 12 requires that the change in deferred tax balances be recognised in profit or loss, except to the extent that it relates to items previously recognised outside profit or loss. [IAS 12:60]

For example, when a deferred tax amount has previously been recognised in other comprehensive income at the time of the revaluation of an asset, and the deferred tax liability subsequently changes because of a change in tax rates, the adjustment to the deferred tax liability to reflect the revised tax rates is also recognised in other comprehensive income.

The same principle applies to a change of intention. For example, when an entity has previously estimated the deferred tax liability arising on the revaluation of an owner-occupied property on the basis that it would continue to be used to generate taxable manufacturing profits, and a decision is subsequently made to dispose of the property, thus reducing the deferred tax liability, the adjustment to the deferred tax liability is also reflected in other comprehensive income.

4.7.8   Changes in the tax status of an entity or its shareholders

A change in the tax status of an entity or its shareholders may have consequences for the entity by increasing or decreasing its tax assets or liabilities. This may occur, for example, when an entity's equity shares are publicly listed for the first time, or when a controlling shareholder moves to a foreign country. As a result of such an event, the entity may be taxed differently, which may have an immediate effect on its current and deferred tax assets and liabilities. SIC-25 *Income Taxes – Changes in the Tax Status of an Entity or its Shareholders* prescribes the accounting treatment for such changes.

SIC-25 requires that the current and deferred tax consequences of a change in tax status be included in profit or loss for the period, unless those consequences relate to transactions or events that result, in the same or a different period, in a direct credit or charge to the recognised amount of equity or in amounts recognised in other comprehensive income. Those tax consequences that relate to changes in the recognised amount of equity, in the same or a different period (not included in profit or loss), should be charged or credited directly to equity. Those tax consequences that relate to amounts recognised in other comprehensive income should be recognised in other comprehensive income. [SIC-25:4]

Effectively, this means that an analysis is required of the original accounting for the transactions or events that gave rise to the current and deferred tax balances. To the extent that those transactions or events were charged or credited directly in equity (e.g. withholding tax on dividend payments), any incremental tax effects should also be charged or credited directly to equity. To the extent that those transactions or events were recognised in other comprehensive income (e.g. certain asset revaluations), any incremental tax effects should also be recognised in other comprehensive income. Thus, the aggregate amount of tax recognised outside profit or loss will be the amount that would have been recognised outside profit or loss if the new tax status had applied previously.

Example 4.7.8

Change in the tax status of an entity

Entity P has a deferred tax liability of CU1,000 arising in respect of total temporary differences of CU4,000. A CU800 temporary difference exists in

---

respect of a previous revaluation of property, plant and equipment. All other temporary differences relate to items recognised in profit or loss.

Entity P is sold into foreign ownership and, as a consequence, the tax rate increases from 25 per cent to 30 per cent. To recognise the resulting increase in the deferred tax liability, the following journal entry is recorded.

		CU	CU
Dr	Income tax (profit or loss)		
	[(30% – 25%) × (CU4,000 – CU800)]	160	
Dr	Income tax (other comprehensive income)		
	[(30% – 25%) × CU800]	40	
Cr	Deferred tax liability		200

To recognise the increase in the deferred tax liability resulting from the change in tax status.

When there is uncertainty as to the amount that was previously dealt with outside profit or loss, it may be necessary to make an allocation on a reasonable basis (see **3.2.1.3** and **4.7.3** above).

Note that SIC-25 does not permit the effect on deferred tax balances that arose at the time of a previous business combination to be dealt with as an adjustment to goodwill. The change in tax status is a post-acquisition event, and so is accounted for post-acquisition. Because the original deferred tax was not dealt with in equity or in other comprehensive income, the incremental effect is required to be dealt with in profit or loss.

If the change in tax rate is a result of an entity being acquired in a business combination, in the individual financial statements of the entity (the acquiree), the adjustments to current and deferred tax assets and liabilities will be accounted for in accordance with SIC-25, as discussed in the previous paragraphs. However, in the consolidated financial statements of the new parent (the acquirer), the accounting for the acquisition will reflect the current and deferred tax assets and liabilities measured using the revised tax rates – and, consequently, the incremental effect of the acquisition will be reflected as an adjustment to goodwill or the bargain purchase gain arising on acquisition. [IAS 12:58(b)]

The effect of a voluntary change in the tax status of an entity should be recognised when the change is approved or, if no approval is necessary, when the election is formally notified (e.g. if approval of the change is perfunctory). A change in tax status that results from a change in tax law will be recognised on the enactment date or the substantively enacted date if applicable. Substantively enacted tax rates are discussed further at **4.5.2.2** above.

5   Specific applications

5.1   Business combinations

When a business combination occurs, new or adjusted deferred tax balances can arise from the following sources:

- fair value adjustments on consolidation resulting in carrying amounts of assets or liabilities in the consolidated financial statements that differ from the carrying amounts in the acquiree's financial statements and, consequently, from their tax bases when equivalent adjustments are not recognised for tax purposes (see **5.1.1**);

- additional assets or liabilities recognised on acquisition that are not recognised in the financial statements of the acquiree (see **5.1.2**);

- additional deferred tax balances recognised on acquisition that are not recognised by the acquiree, because of the initial recognition exception (see **5.1.3**); and

- deferred tax assets not previously recognised by the acquiree because the recoverability criteria could not be met at the entity level but can be met at a group level, e.g. potential for offsetting taxable profits and losses between group entities (see **5.1.4**).

When deferred tax arises at the time of a business combination, and it has not been recognised by the acquiree prior to the acquisition, it must be recognised and taken into account in the initial accounting for the business combination. It will, therefore, affect the measurement of the goodwill or the bargain purchase gain arising on acquisition.

Reverse acquisitions (see **section 12** of **chapter A25**) occur when a business combination results in the legal subsidiary obtaining control.

Under IFRS 3 *Business Combinations*, a reverse acquisition is accounted for as a business combination in which the entity that issues securities (the legal acquirer) is identified as the acquiree for accounting purposes on the basis of the guidance in paragraphs B13 to B18 of that Standard. In such circumstances, the requirements of IFRS 3 to recognise assets and liabilities of the acquiree at fair value are applied to the assets and liabilities of the legal parent.

When accounting for a reverse acquisition, deferred tax should be recognised in the consolidated financial statements in the same way as for other business combinations. In some jurisdictions, tax law may permit the legal parent to adjust the tax values of its assets and liabilities and these amounts should be used to determine the tax base of each item for the business combination accounting. If the tax law permits an adjustment to the carrying amount of the legal subsidiary's tax values, in IFRS 3 terms these changes relate to the acquirer's assets and liabilities rather than to those of the acquiree (i.e. because the legal subsidiary is the accounting acquirer); consequently, the deferred tax impact of adjustments to the legal subsidiary's tax values should be recognised outside of the accounting for the business combination (i.e. in profit or loss or other comprehensive income, as appropriate).

In the separate financial statements of the legal parent (if prepared), deferred tax should be measured on the basis of the carrying amounts of the assets and liabilities in those financial statements.

5.1.1 Fair value adjustments

With limited exceptions, the identifiable assets, liabilities and contingent liabilities of the acquiree are recognised in the consolidated financial statements at their fair values at the acquisition date. This will often result in different carrying amounts from those recognised in the acquiree's individual financial statements. However, the tax bases of the assets and liabilities may remain unchanged.

For example, when the fair value of an asset at the date of acquisition is higher than its carrying amount in the acquiree's financial statements, and the asset is recognised at the higher amount for consolidation purposes, the tax base of the asset is unlikely to be affected. In these circumstances, a taxable temporary difference arises as a result of the acquisition. The deferred tax liability arising from the taxable temporary difference is recognised in the consolidated financial statements to reflect the future tax consequences of recovering the recognised fair value of the asset. This is illustrated in **example 5.1.4**.

5.1.2   *Additional assets or liabilities recognised on acquisition*

On acquisition, additional assets and liabilities may be identified that are not recognised in the financial statements of the acquiree. This will commonly be the case, for example, in respect of intangible assets. When such additional assets or liabilities are recognised, the deferred tax implications should also be recognised. The newly recognised assets or liabilities reflect economic benefits and outflows of the acquiree; therefore, any deferred tax should be measured at the acquiree's tax rate. These additional assets and liabilities recognised, and any related deferred tax, will be included as part of the identifiable net assets acquired. This is illustrated in **example 5.1.4**.

The recognition of goodwill may also have deferred tax implications – see **section 4.4.4** above for discussion and illustrative examples.

5.1.3   *Additional deferred tax balances recognised on acquisition*

In some circumstances, the deferred tax impact of temporary differences may not have been recognised in the acquiree's financial statements because those differences fell within one of IAS 12's recognition exceptions. For example, the differences may have arisen on the initial recognition of an asset or a liability (see **4.4.5** above) and, consequently, may not have been recognised. In these circumstances, the deferred tax impact of such temporary differences should be recognised in the consolidated financial statements even though it is not recognised in the individual financial statements of the acquiree.

These additional deferred tax balances are recognised on acquisition because, from the group's perspective, the initial recognition of the asset or liability results from a business combination and, therefore, under the rules set out at **4.4.5**, the deferred tax impact should be recognised. This is illustrated in **example 5.1.4**.

5.1.4   Deferred tax assets not previously recognised by the acquiree

In some circumstances, deferred tax assets (e.g. in respect of tax losses) may not have been recognised by the acquiree due to concerns about the recoverability of the assets in the light of anticipated levels of profitability. However, following the acquisition, in some tax jurisdictions, the losses may become available for use by other group entities, and therefore be considered recoverable. Because the asset is now recoverable from a group perspective, the deferred tax asset is recognised at the time of acquisition.

Conversely, as a result of the acquisition, some deferred tax assets previously recognised by the acquiree may no longer be available due to restrictions imposed by tax law following a change of ownership. In such cases, the deferred tax asset should not be recognised in the acquiree's statement of financial position and would, therefore, result in increased goodwill.

The example below illustrates the deferred tax effects discussed at **5.1.1** to **5.1.4**.

Example 5.1.4

Deferred tax arising on a business combination

Company K acquires 100 per cent of Company L, which holds two properties and sundry other assets. Property A (carrying amount CU100 in Company L's financial statements) and property B (carrying amount CU150 in Company L's financial statements) are, for tax and accounting purposes, depreciated over 10 years and will be recovered through use in taxable manufacturing activities. The tax rate is 30 per cent.

The following information is relevant at the date of acquisition.

- Company K pays cash consideration of CU380 for the acquisition.

- The fair values of properties A and B are measured at CU130 and CU140, respectively.

- An additional intangible asset is identified for recognition in respect of patents held by Company L; the fair value of the intangible asset is CU50 and its tax base is nil.

- Company L has other net assets with a carrying amount of CU30; the fair value of the other net assets is also CU30 and the tax base is also CU30.

- The tax bases of properties A and B are CU50 and CU150, respectively. A temporary difference arose on the acquisition of property A by Company L and, therefore, no deferred tax liability was recognised due to the initial recognition exception.

- Company L has tax losses available for offset against the future profits of any group entity amounting to CU20. It is probable that future taxable profit will be available within the group to absorb these losses. No deferred tax asset has previously been recognised by Company L in respect of these tax losses.

The goodwill arising on the acquisition of Company L is calculated as follows.

	Carrying amount in Company L's financial statements	Fair value	Tax base	Tempo-rary differ-ence	Tax rate	Deferred tax liability (asset)
Net assets of Company L	CU	CU	CU	CU	CU	CU
Property A	100	130	50	80	30%	24
Property B	150	140	150	(10)	30%	(3)
Intangible asset	–	50	–	50	30%	15
Other net assets	30	30	30	–	–	–
Tax loss c/f	–	–	–	(20)	30%	(6)
Total	280	350	230	100		30
Deferred tax arising on acquisition		(30)				
Identifiable net assets acquired		320				
Consideration		380				
Goodwill		60				

5.1.5   Deferred tax assets not previously recognised by the acquirer

Circumstances may also arise when, as a result of an acquisition, the probability of realising a pre-acquisition deferred tax asset *of the acquirer* changes so that the acquirer considers it probable that it will recover its own deferred tax asset that was not recognised prior to the business combination. For example, the acquirer may be able to utilise the benefit of its unused tax losses against the future taxable profits of the acquiree. In such circumstances, the acquirer recognises a deferred tax asset, but does not include it as part of the accounting for the business combination, and it is not taken into account in measuring the goodwill or bargain purchase gain arising in the business combination. [IAS 12:67]

5.1.6   Intangible assets recognised for accounting but not tax purposes

Depending on the tax jurisdiction and on how a business combination is structured, the carrying amounts of goodwill and intangible assets recognised under IFRS 3 may be greater than, less than, or equal to their tax bases. For example, due to differences between accounting rules and tax legislation, the amounts recognised in a business combination as separately identifiable intangible assets under IFRSs may not be separately recognised for tax reporting purposes, and may instead be included within goodwill.

In a business combination, IFRS 3 requires the recognition, separately from goodwill, of identifiable intangible assets. The local tax laws may not permit the recognition of intangible assets for tax purposes in determining the amount of tax deductible goodwill.

In such circumstances, when comparing the carrying amounts of the assets acquired to their respective tax bases in order to identify temporary differences, the intangible assets and goodwill should not be aggregated; they should be analysed separately for IAS 12 purposes. This is so even if it would otherwise appear that the tax base for goodwill corresponds to amounts recognised as intangible assets under IFRSs. This is illustrated in the following example.

Example 5.1.6

Deferred tax on intangible assets and goodwill arising on a business combination

Entity A acquires the net assets of Entity B on 15 September 20X9 in a transaction accounted for as a business combination under IFRS 3. As part of the recognition and measurement of identifiable assets and liabilities, intangible assets (customer lists) of CU15 million are identified and recognised; goodwill of CU5 million is also recognised.

For local tax reporting purposes, however, no intangible assets are recognised; instead tax deductible goodwill of CU20 million is recognised.

When comparing the carrying amounts of the assets acquired to their individual tax bases for the purpose of computing temporary differences at the date of acquisition, should the carrying amount of the customer lists and the goodwill as recognised in the consolidated financial statements be aggregated and compared with the tax base of the goodwill?

No. While it would appear that the CU15 million of additional tax deductions available for goodwill equates to the tax base of the customer lists recognised, the intangible assets and goodwill should not be aggregated, but analysed separately under IAS 12.

The result is a taxable temporary difference of CU15 million on the intangible assets for which a deferred tax liability is recognised. In addition, a deferred tax asset is recognised for the excess tax deductible goodwill (CU20 million) over the recognised goodwill (CU5 million) to the extent that it is probable that taxable profit will be available against which the deductible temporary difference can be utilised.

The deferred tax asset and liability will continue to be analysed separately over their respective lives.

5.1.7 Post-acquisition recognition of acquiree's deferred tax assets

At the date of acquisition, there may be tax losses in the acquiree available for carryforward or deductible temporary differences that do not qualify for recognition as deferred tax assets when the business combination is initially accounted for. These items may subsequently meet the criteria for recognition, and IAS 12 requires that the entity should recognise such acquired deferred tax benefits that it realises after the business combination as follows:
[IAS 12:68]

- acquired deferred tax benefits recognised within the 'measurement period' (i.e. within one year after the acquisition date) that result from new information about facts and circumstances that existed at the acquisition date reduce the amount of any goodwill related to that acquisition. If the carrying amount of that goodwill is zero, any remaining deferred tax benefits are recognised in profit or loss; and

- all other acquired deferred tax benefits realised are recognised in profit or loss (or outside profit or loss if otherwise required by IAS 12).

Example 5.1.7

Realisation of tax loss carryforward after a business combination

Company Q, with a December year end, acquires a new subsidiary, Company R, on 31 March 20X1. Company R has tax losses accumulated in previous periods giving rise to a potential deferred tax asset of CU50 million. In the initial accounting for the business combination, Company Q takes the preliminary view that these losses are not available for offset against the profits of other group entities, and does not recognise a deferred tax asset. The goodwill arising on the acquisition amounts to CU20 million.

In February 20X2 (i.e. within the 'measurement period'), upon request from Company Q, the tax authority provides its opinion that Company R's losses can be offset against certain of the profits of other group entities – the relevant profits amounting to a deferred tax asset of CU30 million at the date of acquisition. This opinion reflects the tax authority's view on how the existing tax legislation at the date of acquisition should be applied to the circumstances of Company Q and Company R at that date; accordingly, it is judged to be new information about facts and circumstances that existed at the acquisition date.

In the circumstances described, had Company Q sought advice from the tax authority at the time of the acquisition, a deferred tax asset of CU30 million could potentially have been recognised in the initial accounting for the business combination. Under IAS 12:68, because the additional information was obtained during the measurement period and it reflects facts and circumstances at the acquisition date, goodwill should be adjusted for the subsequent recognition of the deferred tax asset. However, the retrospective adjustment of goodwill is limited to the amount of the goodwill; therefore, only CU20 million is adjusted directly against goodwill in the 20X2 financial statements and the balance of CU10 million is recognised in profit or loss.

If the other group entities earn profits subsequent to the date of acquisition against which more of Company R's losses can be utilised, the effect is recognised in profit or loss.

The discussion in **example 5.1.7** reflects the requirements of IAS 12 following consequential amendments arising from IFRS 3 (as revised in 2008). Prior to those amendments, the subsequent realisation of all deferred tax assets acquired in a business combination was recognised in profit or loss with a consequential reduction in the carrying amount of goodwill to the amount that would have been recognised if the deferred tax asset had been recognised as an identifiable asset from the acquisition date, regardless of the date of realisation.

IAS 12:93 and 94 set out the transition provisions regarding the application of the revised requirements. Under those provisions, the revised IAS 12:68 applies to changes in recognised deferred tax assets occurring after the date of adoption of IFRS 3 (as revised in 2008), arising from business combinations that occurred before or after the date of adoption of IFRS 3 (as revised in 2008). This means that an acquirer does not adjust the accounting for prior business combinations for changes in previously recognised deferred tax assets outside the relevant 'measurement period'. Instead, from the date when IFRS 3 (as revised in 2008) is applied, the acquirer recognises changes in recognised deferred tax assets as an adjustment to profit or loss (or, if IAS 12 requires, outside profit or loss). Goodwill is no longer adjusted.

5.1.8   Recognition and measurement in a business combination of the potential liability arising from an uncertain tax position

Example 5.1.8

Recognition and measurement in a business combination of the potential liability arising from an uncertain tax position

Entity A acquires Entity B in a business combination. Entity B has an uncertain tax position at the acquisition date which could result in a cash outflow of CU100. Entity B estimates that at the date of acquisition the probability that an outflow will result from the uncertain tax position is 30 per cent.

For the purposes of its consolidated financial statements, at the date of acquisition of Entity B, how should Entity A account for the potential liability arising from Entity B's uncertain tax position?

Neither IAS 12 nor IFRS 3 addresses this issue specifically. In the absence of definitive guidance, Entity A should select one of the following alternatives:

• Option 1 — the potential tax liability could be recognised when the economic outflow is probable (an 'IAS 12 approach') (see **3.3.1** above); or

• Option 2 — the potential tax liability could be recognised at its fair value at the acquisition date (an 'IFRS 3 approach').

Entity A should select one of these approaches as an accounting policy choice and apply it consistently in all business combinations. The alternatives are discussed in more detail below.

Option 1 — IAS 12 approach

This option is based on the view that the uncertain tax position is outside the scope of the recognition and measurement requirements of IFRS 3 and that the potential tax liability should be accounted for in accordance with IAS 12. This view is supported by IFRS 3:IN9 which states that assets and liabilities falling within the scope of IAS 12 should be accounted for at acquisition in accordance with the recognition and measurement requirements of that Standard rather than in accordance with IFRS 3.

If Entity A selects this approach, it applies the method described at **3.3.1** both initially and for subsequent measurement.

Consequently, if Entity A selects this option as its accounting policy, it should not recognise a liability in respect of the uncertain tax position at the date of acquisition because, at that date, it is not probable (i.e. less than 50 per cent probability) that an outflow of economic resources will occur. If, subsequent to the acquisition date, it becomes probable that an outflow of resources will occur, Entity A will recognise the tax liability at its best estimate of that outflow, with the resulting charge recognised in profit or loss.

Option 2 — IFRS 3 approach

This option is based on the view that the general principles of IFRS 3 should be applied because IFRS 3 does not explicitly exclude current tax assets and liabilities from the scope of its recognition and measurement requirements. Although, as discussed under Option 1, the introduction to IFRS 3 appears to scope out all tax balances, within the body of the Standard there is no reference to excluding current tax balances — only deferred tax balances in accordance with IFRS 3:24 and 25.

IFRS 3 requires the recognition of contingent liabilities at fair value if they can be measured reliably. Under Option 2, Entity A recognises and measures the uncertain tax liability in the business combination by analogy to the treatment of contingent liabilities acquired in a business combination. The tax liability is therefore measured at its fair value at the acquisition date, which takes into account the likelihood that the tax will become payable. Thereafter, in line with the treatment of contingent liabilities under IFRS 3:56, the liability arising from the uncertain tax position should be recognised at the higher of (1) the amount initially recognised, and (2) the amount that would be recognised by analogy to IAS 37 *Provisions, Contingent Liabilities and Contingent Assets* (see **3.3.1**).

5.1.9   Tax deductible goodwill of the acquiree in a business combination

Example 5.1.9

Tax deductible goodwill of the acquiree in a business combination

Entity A acquires 100 per cent of Entity B for consideration of CU100. At the acquisition date, Entity B has:

- goodwill from a previous business combination with a tax base of CU40 in a jurisdiction with a tax rate of 20 per cent; and

- other identifiable assets and liabilities with a total fair value of CU50.

Following its acquisition by Entity A, Entity B will be entitled to continue to claim tax deductions on the previously recognised goodwill and expects to have sufficient taxable profits available to utilise those deductions as they arise. The relevant tax rate is 20 per cent.

How should the effect of the tax deductions available on the goodwill previously recognised by Entity B be treated in the consolidated financial statements of Entity A at the acquisition date?

It depends. Because goodwill represents the economic benefits arising from intangible assets that are not individually identified and separately recognised in a business combination, it may not be apparent whether the goodwill recognised on the acquisition of Entity B by Entity A arises from the same factors that gave rise to the goodwill previously recognised by Entity B. There may be circumstances when it is clear that there is no link between the previously recognised goodwill and the goodwill arising on the current business combination. There may be less common circumstances when it is clear that the goodwill recognised by Entity A is the 'same' goodwill as that previously recognised by Entity B. However, in most cases, it will not be obvious whether there is a link between the goodwill previously recognised by Entity B and the goodwill arising when Entity A acquires Entity B. In such circumstances, if the pre-existing goodwill tax deductions are to be treated as relating to the goodwill arising on the current acquisition, it must be demonstrated that the factors that gave rise to the pre-existing goodwill continue to exist and contribute to goodwill on the current acquisition.

Scenarios 1 and 2 below illustrate contrasting circumstances.

Scenario 1 – no link identified

Entity B is a holding company with two subsidiaries – one an active manufacturing entity and the other a financial services entity in 'run-off' (i.e. no longer operating other than to hold existing financial assets to their maturity). The tax deductible goodwill recognised by Entity B arose on the acquisition of the financial services entity.

In this scenario, it is evident that any goodwill arising on the acquisition of Entity B by Entity A relates to the manufacturing subsidiary. Because there is no link between the goodwill recognised by Entity A and the tax deductible goodwill previously recognised by Entity B, for the purposes of Entity A's consolidated financial statements, the tax base of CU40 does not have an associated carrying amount.

The goodwill of CU50 recognised by Entity A (i.e. consideration of CU100 less net fair value of identifiable assets and liabilities of CU50) has a tax base of CUnil, giving rise to a taxable temporary difference of CU50. No deferred tax is recognised in respect of this taxable temporary difference because it arises on the initial recognition of goodwill (see **4.4.4.1**). In addition, the goodwill previously recognised by Entity B has a tax base of CU40 and a carrying amount of CUnil, giving rise to a deductible temporary difference of CU40 which is not subject to the initial recognition exception. Consequently, subject to IAS 12's general recognition criteria, a deferred tax asset of CU8 (CU40 × 20%) is recognised in respect of Entity B's original goodwill.

At acquisition, therefore, Entity A recognises a deferred tax asset of CU8, Entity B's other identifiable assets and liabilities at their net fair value of CU50 and goodwill of CU42.

After the acquisition date, as tax deductions are claimed by Entity B in respect of the goodwill, the deferred tax asset reduces and the deferred tax expense in profit and loss offsets the current tax deduction claimed. When all available deductions have been claimed (or have expired unclaimed), no deferred tax asset will remain.

Scenario 2 – link identified

Entity B is a shell entity which acquired another entity in a transaction giving rise to tax deductible goodwill immediately before, and in anticipation of, its own acquisition by Entity A.

In this scenario, it is clear that the goodwill recognised by Entity A is substantially the same as the tax deductible goodwill previously recognised by Entity B. Consequently, the tax deductible goodwill previously recognised by Entity B gives rise to a tax base considered to relate to the goodwill recognised by Entity A.

The goodwill of CU50 recognised by Entity A therefore has a tax base of CU40, giving rise to a taxable temporary difference of CU10. No deferred tax is recognised in respect of this taxable temporary difference because it arises on the initial recognition of goodwill (see **4.4.4.1**).

At acquisition, therefore, Entity A recognises Entity B's identifiable assets and liabilities at their net fair value of CU50 and goodwill of CU50.

After the acquisition date, as tax deductions are claimed by Entity B in respect of the goodwill, a deferred tax expense will be recognised in profit or loss and a deferred tax liability will be recognised in Entity A's consolidated financial statements. The deferred tax expense offsets the current tax deductions claimed. When all available deductions have been claimed (or have expired unclaimed), a deferred tax liability of CU8 (i.e. temporary difference of CU40 not covered by the initial recognition exception at 20 per cent) will remain in place until the goodwill recognised by Entity A is either impaired or disposed of.

5.2   Eliminations of unrealised intragroup profits

When a group entity sells goods to another group entity, the seller recognises profits made on those sales in its individual financial statements. If those goods are still held in inventories by the purchaser at the end of the reporting period, the profit recognised by the seller, when viewed from the standpoint of the group as a whole, has not yet been earned, and will not be earned until the goods are eventually sold outside the group. On consolidation, the unrealised profit on closing inventories is eliminated from the group's profit, and the closing inventories of the group are recognised at cost to the group. The tax consequences to the seller (both current and deferred, if any), however, are not eliminated. If tax is charged on the results of individual entities, and not on the group, the seller will pay tax on any profits generated from the intragroup sales, even though some of those profits may be unrealised from the group's perspective.

Such consolidation adjustments may have a deferred tax impact in the consolidated financial statements. The intragroup elimination is made as a consolidation adjustment and not in the financial statements of any individual reporting entity. Therefore, the elimination will result in the creation of a temporary difference as far as the group is concerned between the carrying amount of the inventories in the consolidated financial statements and the tax base (assumed to be the carrying amount in the purchaser's individual financial statements). The deferred tax effects arising in respect of this temporary difference should be recognised in accordance with the usual principles.

The tax rate to be used when recognising the deferred tax balance arising from the elimination of unrealised profits on intragroup transactions is determined by reference to the tax jurisdiction where the temporary difference will reverse. This will generally be the tax rate in the purchaser's jurisdiction, because the deduction is available at that rate when the unrealised profit is realised from the sale to an unrelated third party. If the tax rate in the purchaser's jurisdiction differs from that in the seller's, the deferred tax recognised may not equal the tax currently payable by the seller.

In situations involving the transfer of assets intended for internal use, the deferred taxes should be amortised over the asset's expected useful life consistent with the depreciation method applied under IAS 16 *Property, Plant and Equipment*.

Example 5.2

Elimination of intragroup profits in inventories

Company P sells inventories costing CU200 to its overseas subsidiary, Company S, for CU300. Company P's tax rate is 40 per cent, Company S's is 50 per cent. At the end of the reporting period, Company S still holds the inventories.

Company P recognises a current tax liability of CU40 (CU100 × 40%) relating to the profit on sale of the inventories but does not recognise any deferred tax balances because there are no future tax consequences from Company P's point of view.

Company S is entitled to a future deduction for the CU300 paid for the inventories and this is therefore the asset's tax base from Company S's perspective. Consequently, in Company S's individual financial statements, the tax base is equal to the carrying amount and no temporary difference arises.

Company P prepares consolidated financial statements and, for financial reporting purposes, gains and losses on intragroup transactions are eliminated on consolidation. Therefore, on consolidation, the carrying amount of the inventories is reduced from CU300 to CU200 (to eliminate the unrealised profit). A CU100 deductible temporary difference arises, representing the difference between the carrying amount (CU200) and the tax base (CU300). A deferred tax asset is calculated by multiplying the temporary difference of CU100 by 50 per cent, because the deduction is available to Company S at that rate when the unrealised profit is realised outside the group on sale of the inventories by Company S. Available evidence supports a conclusion that realisation of the deferred tax asset representing the tax benefit of Company S's deductible temporary differences is probable. The deferred tax asset arising of CU50 is therefore recognised on consolidation.

The impact of this intragroup transaction on Company P's consolidated financial statements is shown below in the following journal entries.

		CU	CU
Dr	Current tax expense (CU100 × 40%)	40	
Dr	Deferred tax asset (CU100 × 50%)	50	
Cr	Current tax payable		40
Cr	Deferred tax benefit		50

To recognise the impact of the intragroup transaction.

In a subsequent period, Company S sells the inventories that it acquired from Company P to an unrelated third party for the same amount that it had previously paid Company P, i.e. CU300. The journal entry to reflect the sales and related tax consequences to be reflected in the consolidated financial statements of Company P is as follows.

		CU	CU
Dr	Cash	300	
Dr	Cost of goods sold	200	
Dr	Income tax expense	50	
Cr	Sales		300
Cr	Inventories		200
Cr	Deferred tax asset		50

To recognise the sales and related tax consequences.

5.3   Financial instruments

5.3.1   *Investments in securities – general*

Investments in securities can often give rise to significant temporary differences. In order to determine the deferred tax implications for various types of investments, it is necessary to understand the tax rules relating to those investments. Particularly, an entity should take care to understand the tax implications that arise from the recovery of the investment through dividends ('use'), sale, or a combination of the two. It is then necessary to determine how the carrying amount of the investments will be recovered.

When an entity has an investment in an equity instrument it may be appropriate to presume that the carrying amount will be recovered through sale. This will be the case if the dividends anticipated from the investment are not expected to represent a realisation of part of the carrying amount of the investment.

Sometimes it will be necessary to consider how a financial asset has been classified under IFRS 9 *Financial Instruments* (or, for entities that have not yet adopted IFRS 9, IAS 39 *Financial Instruments: Recognition and Measurement*). For example, financial assets measured at amortised cost under IFRS 9 are so classified based on the premise that the entity's business model objective is to hold those assets to collect contractual cash flows. Similarly, financial assets classified as held-to-maturity under IAS 39 are so classified based on the premise that they will not be sold prior to their maturity. When considering any tax implications, the same assumptions should be used.

5.3.2   *Financial instruments at fair value through profit or loss or classified as held for trading*

For financial instruments that are measured at fair value through profit or loss in accordance with IFRS 9 (see **chapters B2** and **B3**) or, for entities that have not yet adopted IFRS 9, that are classified as held for trading or at fair value through profit or loss in accordance with IAS 39 (see **chapters C2** and **C3**), fair value gains and losses are recognised in profit or loss. If these gains and losses are taxable, they may be taxed when they are recognised in the financial statements, or it may be that they are not reflected in tax computations until the instrument is sold or settled. When tax is assessed based on fair value movements recognised in profit or loss, there are no deferred tax implications because the gains and losses are assessed for tax in the same period in which they are recognised in profit or loss. In contrast, when gains and losses are not reflected in tax computations until the instrument is sold or settled, deferred tax consequences may arise.

5.3.3   Financial assets measured at fair value through other comprehensive income and available-for-sale financial assets

Similar issues will arise in relation to financial assets measured at fair value through other comprehensive income under IFRS 9 (see **chapters B2** and **B3**) or, for entities that have not yet adopted IFRS 9, that are classified as available for sale (AFS) under IAS 39 (see **chapters C2** and **C3**). The main difference is that the change in fair value on these assets is reported in other comprehensive income (apart from dividend income that does not clearly represent a recovery of part of the cost of the investment under IFRS 9; under IAS 39, changes in fair value recognised in other comprehensive income exclude impairment losses, exchange gains and losses, and interest and dividend income). Thus, if a deferred tax balance arises on an asset measured at fair value through other comprehensive income, or an available-for-sale asset, the deferred tax impact may also be dealt with in other comprehensive income (rather than in profit or loss) in the same manner as the deferred tax effects of revaluations of other assets.

See **4.7.4** above for a more detailed consideration of the deferred tax implications when fair value movements on available-for-sale financial assets are subsequently reclassified to profit or loss. This issue does not arise under IFRS 9 because gains and losses are not reclassified to profit or loss under that Standard.

The assessment regarding the realisation of tax benefits from unrealised losses on available-for-sale financial assets often depends on the inherent assumptions used for financial reporting purposes concerning the ultimate recovery of the carrying amount of the securities.

IAS 12:16 concludes that it is inherent in the recognition of an asset that its carrying amount will be recovered in the form of economic benefits that flow to the entity in future periods. Therefore, ordinarily, an entity should assume recovery of the carrying amount of its investments in equity instruments measured at fair value through other comprehensive income (or, under IAS 39, its available-for-sale debt securities) at their fair values at the end of each reporting period. Generally, whenever there is an unrealised holding loss, recovery at fair value would result in a capital loss deduction.

In some jurisdictions, the tax law may allow utilisation of capital losses only through offset against capital gains. In such circumstances, entities need to assess whether realisation of the loss is probable based on available evidence. For example, evidence considered might include (1) available capital loss carryback recovery of taxes paid in prior years, and (2) tax planning strategies to sell appreciated capital assets that would generate capital gain income. In these situations, available evidence should be evaluated to determine if it is probable that the entity would have sufficient capital gain income during the carryback and carryforward periods prescribed under tax law. However, in making such an assessment, the carryback and carryforward periods do not commence until the loss is realised.

5.3.4   Compound financial instruments

IAS 12 contains guidance on calculating deferred tax in relation to compound financial instruments that are accounted for under IAS 32 *Financial Instruments: Presentation*. Compound financial instruments are instruments that an entity has issued that contain both a liability and an equity component (e.g. issued convertible debt). In the case of convertible debt, the separate components are a liability component (representing borrowing with an obligation to repay), and an equity component (representing the embedded option to convert the liability into equity of the entity).

Under IAS 32, the equity and liability components of a compound instrument are accounted for separately – the proceeds of issue are allocated between the separate elements. The amount initially recognised as a liability is the present value of the cash flows discounted at a market rate for equivalent debt without the equity feature. Because the holders of the compound instrument are effectively purchasing an equity interest, the coupon on the compound instrument is almost always lower than it would be for the equivalent debt without the equity feature. Therefore, the value assigned to the debt portion of the compound instrument will be lower than the total proceeds received. For example, CU100 proceeds from the issue of a convertible bond could be allocated CU90 to debt and CU10 to equity – the carrying amount of the liability component (CU90) is less than the face value of the instrument (CU100). The detailed requirements for accounting for compound instruments are considered in **chapter B3** (or, for entities that have not yet adopted IFRS 9, in **chapter C3**).

In some jurisdictions, the tax base of the liability component on initial recognition is equal to the initial carrying amount of the sum of the liability and equity components (i.e. CU100 in the above example). If the instrument were settled at an amount equal to the carrying amount of its liability component (which is generally less than the face value and, therefore, less than the tax base), a taxable gain arises, and so a deferred tax liability arising from this taxable temporary difference is recognised. In the example cited above, if the bond were settled for CU90 (its carrying amount), a gain of CU10 would arise which could be taxable.

IAS 12's 'initial recognition exception' (see **4.4.5**) does not apply in this situation – a deferred tax liability should be recognised. This is because the temporary difference arises not from the initial recognition of the instrument, but rather from the separate recognition of the equity component. [IAS 12:23]

Because the equity component of the compound financial instrument is recognised directly in equity, the deferred tax liability arising is also recognised directly in equity. The deferred tax should be charged directly to the carrying amount of the equity component.

However, as the discount associated with the liability component of the compound financial instrument unwinds, the reduction of the associated deferred tax liability is recognised in profit or loss and not directly in equity. The recognition of the deferred tax credit in profit or loss is consistent with the recognition of the associated expense in profit or loss related to unwinding the discount on the liability component. [IAS 12:23]

In jurisdictions where any gain on settlement of the liability would not be taxable, the tax base of the liability is always equal to its carrying amount, and no temporary difference arises.

Example 5.3.4

Convertible note accounted for as a compound instrument

On 31 December 20X0, Company R issues a convertible note with a face value of CU10,000 that matures in three years. There is no interest payable during the period, but the holder has the option to convert the note into a fixed number of shares at the end of the three-year period. Had Company R

---

issued debt with no conversion rights that matured in three years, the interest rate on the bonds would have been 9 per cent.

Under IAS 32, the note is split into its liability and equity components. Using a discount rate of 9 per cent (i.e. the rate at which Company R could have issued equivalent debt with no conversion rights), the present value of the instrument is CU7,722. This is taken to be the value of the liability component, giving rise to an amount recognised directly in equity of CU2,278.

There are no tax consequences if the note is repaid at its face value, and a taxable gain arises if the note is settled for less than its face value. Therefore, the tax base of the instrument is CU10,000. The tax rate is 17.5 per cent.

If the liability were settled at its carrying amount (CU7,722), a taxable profit would arise. Thus, on the initial separation of the liability and equity components, a taxable temporary difference of CU2,278 arises. This gives rise to a deferred tax liability of CU399 (CU2,278 × 17.5%). This amount is netted against the amount recognised in respect of the equity component of the note.

The following entries are recognised at the date of issue of the convertible note.

		CU	CU
Dr	Cash	10,000	
Cr	Convertible note payable		7,722
Cr	Equity		2,278
Dr	Equity	399	
Cr	Deferred tax liability		399

To recognise the issue of the convertible note.

Each year, imputed interest on the liability will be recognised, increasing the carrying amount of the liability component and reducing the associated deferred tax liability. The reduction in the deferred tax liability is recognised in profit or loss.

The movements over the life of the convertible note can be summarised as follows.

	20X0 CU	20X1 CU	20X2 CU	20X3 CU
Liability and interest				
Opening liability		7,722	8,417	9,174
Imputed interest (9%)		695	757	826
Closing liability	7,722	8,417	9,174	10,000
Deferred tax liability				
Convertible note				
carrying amount	7,722	8,417	9,174	10,000
Tax base	10,000	10,000	10,000	10,000
Taxable temporary				
difference	2,278	1,583	826	–
Deferred tax liability				
(at 17.5%)	399	277	145	–
Deferred tax income				
(profit or loss)	–	122	132	145

5.3.5   Impact of IAS 39 hedging requirements on non-financial items

The recognition of a 'basis adjustment' for a non-financial asset or liability in accordance with IAS 39:98(b) may cause the carrying amount of the asset or liability to be different from its tax base. This may occur when the tax value ascribed to the asset or liability under the relevant tax jurisdiction is determined other than by reference to the carrying amount in the financial statements (e.g. the basis adjustment is not recognised for tax purposes at the same time as the carrying amount of the asset is adjusted for accounting purposes). Deferred tax should generally be recognised for the temporary difference arising from the difference between the carrying amount in the financial statements and the tax base.

When the different accounting and tax treatments are due to a basis adjustment, the temporary difference arises after the initial recognition of the asset or liability. Accordingly, the initial recognition exceptions in IAS 12:15 (taxable temporary differences – see **4.4.1**) and IAS 12:24 (deductible temporary differences – see **4.4.2**) do not apply and deferred tax should be recognised (subject to IAS 12's general recognition criteria).

For further information regarding deferral of hedging gains and losses into non-financial assets see **2.2.3** in **chapter B9** (or, for entities that have not yet adopted IFRS 9, see **2.2.3** in **chapter C9**).

Example 5.3.5

Cash flow hedge of forecast purchases

On 4 January 20X2, Company D has forecast purchases of 100,000 kg of cocoa on or about 31 December 20X2 from a Brazilian supplier, Company B, for a price of US$180,000. Company D's functional currency is Sterling, and Company B has a US$ functional currency. On 4 January 20X2, Company D designates the cash flow of the forecast purchase as a hedged item and enters into a currency forward contract to buy US$180,000 based on the forecast payment (100,000 kg at US$1.8 per kg). The forward contract locks in the value of the US$ amount to be paid at a rate of US$1.8:£1. At inception of the hedge, the derivative is on-market (i.e. fair value is zero). The terms of the currency forward contract and the forecast purchase match each other, and the entity designates the forward foreign exchange risk as the hedged risk.

On 31 December 20X2, the transaction occurs as expected. The fair value of the forward contract is positive £12,500 because the US dollar has continued to strengthen against Sterling. The forward contract has been fully effective in hedging the forward rate of the forecast transaction and, accordingly, all of the gain of £12,500 has been recognised in other comprehensive income.

Company D has an accounting policy of reclassifying such gains and losses and including them in the initial cost of the non-financial asset in accordance with IAS 39:98(b).

The inventories are recognised in Company D's financial statements at £100,000, being the cash payment of £112,500 (US$180,000 translated at the spot rate on 31 December 20X2), net of the gain on the forward contract of £12,500. The applicable tax rate is 30 per cent and the local tax law does not permit a reduction of the inventories for the gain or loss on the hedging instrument. Accordingly, the tax base of the inventories is £112,500. Company D should, subject to the normal recoverability criteria, recognise a deferred tax asset of £3,750 (£12,500 × 30%) in respect of the temporary difference arising from the inclusion of the hedging gains in the initial cost of the inventories. Because the £3,750 arises on the reclassification of the hedging instrument (rather than on initial recognition of the inventories), the initial recognition exception does not apply. Under local tax law, fair value gains and losses on the hedging instrument result in taxable gains and losses when they are realised. The journal entries to be recorded as at 31 December 20X2 are as follows.

		£	£
Dr	Forward contract	12,500	
Cr	Other comprehensive income		12,500

To recognise the unrealised gain on the forward contract in other comprehensive income.

		£	£
Dr	Other comprehensive income	3,750	
Cr	Deferred tax liability		3,750

To recognise the tax consequences arising from the unrealised gain on the forward contract.

Dr	Inventories	112,500	
Cr	Cash		112,500

To recognise the purchase of cocoa as inventory.

Dr	Cash	12,500	
Cr	Forward contract		12,500

To recognise the settlement of the forward contract.

Dr	Deferred tax liability	3,750	
Cr	Other comprehensive income		3,750
Dr	Income tax expense	3,750	
Cr	Current tax payable		3,750

To recognise the current tax payable on settlement of the forward contract.

Dr	Other comprehensive income	12,500	
Cr	Inventories		12,500

To recognise the gain on the forward contract as a 'basis adjustment' for the inventories.

Dr	Deferred tax asset	3,750	
Cr	Income tax expense		3,750

To recognise the deferred tax asset arising from the temporary difference on the inventories.

5.4   Properties carried at a revalued amount under IAS 16

5.4.1   Revaluation of properties

When a property is revalued under IAS 16 *Property, Plant and Equipment*, its carrying amount is increased or decreased, but there is generally no effect on the tax base of the property. As a result, deferred tax balances arise. Generally, the recognition of deferred tax arising on a revaluation is consistent with the treatment of the revaluation itself.

5.4.2   Upward revaluations

The upward revaluation of a property accounted for under IAS 16 generally gives rise to a deferred tax liability. By increasing the carrying amount of the property, the entity is acknowledging that it expects to generate returns in excess of the original carrying amount, which will lead to future taxable profits, and so tax payable.

When an upward revaluation is recognised, the deferred tax liability arising is calculated by reference to the expected manner of recovery of the property. The upward revaluation is recognised in other comprehensive income (unless it represents the reversal of a downward revaluation previously recognised in profit or loss). The deferred tax expense should, therefore, also be recognised in other comprehensive income.

Over the period of use when the temporary difference reverses, the release of the deferred tax liability will be credited to profit or loss (see **4.7.1.1** above). The deferred tax liability recognised at the date of revaluation represents a provision for the tax expected to arise on those benefits. The release of the deferred tax liability to profit or loss over the period in which those future economic benefits (i.e. taxable profits) are earned offsets the current tax expense in those years to the extent that it was anticipated at the date of the revaluation. This is illustrated in **example 5.4.2**.

Example 5.4.2

Deferred tax impact of property revaluation

An item of property, plant and equipment is acquired for CU1,000. It is depreciated for tax and accounting purposes over five years. At the end of the third year, it is revalued to CU1,200. The value of the property is expected to be recovered through use in a taxable manufacturing activity. The tax rate is 30 per cent.

	Carrying amount CU	Tax base CU	Temporary difference CU	Deferred tax liability CU	Movement for the year CU
01/01/20X1	1,000	1,000	–	–	–
31/12/20X1	800	800	–	–	–
31/12/20X2	600	600	–	–	–
31/12/20X3	1,200	400	800	240	240
31/12/20X4	600	200	400	120	(120)
31/12/20X5	–	–	–	–	(120)

The required journal entries at the end of 20X3 are as follows.

		CU	CU
Dr	Property, plant and equipment	200	
Dr	Property, plant and equipment – accumulated depreciation	600	
Cr	Gain on revaluation (other comprehensive income)		800
Dr	Income tax (other comprehensive income)	240	
Cr	Deferred tax liability		240

To recognise the required entries at the end of 20X3.

In both 20X4 and 20X5, the following entry will be recorded, to reflect the reversal of the temporary difference arising on revaluation.

	CU	CU
Dr Deferred tax liability	120	
Cr Income tax (profit or loss)		120

To recognise the tax effect of the reversal of the temporary difference arising on revaluation.

5.4.3   Downward revaluations and impairment losses

Recognition of downward revaluations and impairments of properties accounted for under IAS 16 is either in profit or loss or other comprehensive income, depending on where previous gains and losses recognised on the property have been presented. The accounting for properties under IAS 16 is discussed in further detail in **chapter A7**.

The write-down of a property for accounting purposes can give rise to a deferred tax asset, or a reduction in a deferred tax liability, depending on the tax base of the property. Any deferred tax asset arising is recognised to the extent that it is probable that sufficient taxable profit will be available in the future to allow the benefit of that deferred tax asset to be recovered.

When a property accounted for in accordance with IAS 16 has previously been revalued, and a downward valuation subsequently occurs that is recognised in other comprehensive income (i.e. to the extent that the subsequent downward valuation does not exceed the amount held in the revaluation surplus in respect of that same asset), the deferred tax effects previously recognised in other comprehensive income are reversed through other comprehensive income. If the downward revaluation exceeds the amount of revaluation surplus, the excess is recognised in profit or loss. In such circumstances, the deferred tax movement should also be split between amounts recognised in other comprehensive income and profit or loss.

Impairments are treated in the same manner as downward revaluations.

These principles are illustrated in **example 5.4.3**.

Example 5.4.3

Downward revaluation

An item of property, plant and equipment is acquired for CU1,000. It is depreciated for tax and accounting purposes over 10 years on a straight-line basis. The value of the property is expected to be recovered through use in a taxable manufacturing activity. The entity is a profitable manufacturing entity with its deferred tax assets fully recognised.

At the end of the third year (when the carrying amount is CU700), the asset is revalued to CU1,050 but no adjustment is made to its tax base. At the end of the sixth year, when the carrying amount of the asset is CU600 (i.e. CU1,050 – (3 × CU150)), it is revalued downward to CU200. The tax rate is 30 per cent.

The impact of these events is summarised as follows.

Initially, the revaluation uplift and the related deferred tax are recognised in other comprehensive income and accumulated in the revaluation reserve. Each year a transfer is made from the revaluation reserve to retained earnings equal to the depreciation of the revaluation surplus net of tax.

At the time of the downward revaluation, the balance in the revaluation reserve is CU140. This is calculated as follows.

	CU
Original revaluation uplift	350
Deferred tax thereon (CU350 × 30%)	(105)
	245
Three years' depreciation on net uplift (CU245 × 3/7)	(105)
	140

Therefore, the first CU200 of the downward revaluation is recognised as a loss in other comprehensive income, net of CU60 related tax. The remaining downward revaluation of CU200 is recognised in profit or loss (along with CU60 related tax).

The downward revaluation reduces the carrying amount below the tax base, resulting in a deferred tax asset which is recognised because the entity has forecast taxable profits.

	Carrying amount		Tax base	Temporary difference	Deferred tax liability (asset)	Move-ment for the year	Recognised in	
	Histori-cal cost	Revalua-tion uplift					Other comp. income	Profit or loss
	CU	CU	CU	CU	CU	CU	CU	CU
20X0	1,000	–	1,000	–	–	–	–	–
20X1	900	–	900	–	–	–	–	–
20X2	800	–	800	–	–	–	–	–
20X3	700	350	700	350	105	105	105	–
20X4	600	300	600	300	90	(15)	–	(15)
20X5	500	250	500	250	75	(15)	–	(15)
20X6	200	–	400	(200)	(60)	(135)	(60)	(75)
20X7	150	–	300	(150)	(45)	15	–	15
20X8	100	–	200	(100)	(30)	15	–	15
20X9	50	–	100	(50)	(15)	15	–	15
20Y0	–	–	–	–	–	15	–	15

If a decision is subsequently taken to dispose of the property, then the deferred tax implications will need to be re-examined. Because the temporary difference is calculated on the basis of management expectations as to the manner of recovery of the property, when those expectations change the deferred tax position may also change.

5.4.4   Properties to be recovered through disposal – 'clawback' of tax depreciation

It may be anticipated that the carrying amount of a revalued property will be recovered through sale (whether based on management intent or on the presumptions established in IAS 12 for non-depreciable properties and investment properties – see **4.2.6**). In such cases, the deferred tax implications are determined on the basis of the tax consequences of disposal of the property. It may be that the profit on disposal will be fully taxable, in which case the deferred tax liability arising on any revaluation of the property will be equal to the revaluation uplift multiplied by the tax rate. However, frequently, the taxation of capital gains is on a different basis (e.g. the taxable gain arising may be limited to the amount of tax depreciation previously claimed). This is often referred to as a 'claw-back'.

In such circumstances (i.e. when the disposal is not itself subject to income tax, but any deduction for tax depreciation previously claimed is taxable as a 'claw-back'), the tax base is the carrying amount less future taxable amounts. This may or may not be equal to the cost less tax depreciation to date. This point is illustrated in **example 5.4.4**.

Example 5.4.4

Property to be recovered through disposal

A building (classified as property, plant and equipment) is acquired for CU1,000 on 1 January 20X1. No deferred tax arises on initial recognition of the property, which is to be depreciated (both for tax and accounting purposes) over five years. At the end of 20X1, when its carrying amount and tax written down value is CU800, the property is remeasured to its fair value of CU1,200. At that date, it is expected that the carrying amount of the property will be recovered through disposal.

If the property were disposed of, the taxable gain arising would be limited to the amount of the tax depreciation previously claimed. The tax rate is 30 per cent.

At 31 December 20X1   Carrying amount (fair value) = CU1,200
                       Tax base = CU1,000*
                       Temporary difference = CU1,200 – CU1,000 = CU200
                       Deferred tax liability = CU200 × 30% = CU60

*   The tax base is the carrying amount of CU1,200 less future taxable amounts (i.e. the allowances that would be clawed back on disposal) of

CU200. In these circumstances, the tax base for IAS 12 is not equal to the tax written down value of CU800 (cost less accumulated tax depreciation to date).

Therefore, at the end of 20X1, a deferred tax liability of CU60 is recognised; because it relates to the revaluation of the property, the debit of CU60 is recognised in other comprehensive income.

5.5   Foreign currency translation

5.5.1   Assets or liabilities held directly

When an entity holds a foreign-currency denominated monetary asset or liability directly, retranslation at each period end results in a change in the carrying amount for accounting purposes, and a foreign exchange gain or loss that is generally recognised in profit or loss. When applicable tax law does not allow for an equivalent change in tax base, and recovery of an increased carrying amount would be taxable, a temporary difference arises on retranslation which is required to be recognised. In most circumstances, the related deferred tax is recognised in profit or loss. However, when the exchange gain or loss is itself recognised in other comprehensive income, the deferred tax is also recognised in other comprehensive income.

When the entity holds a non-monetary asset that is located overseas, the asset is recognised at its historical cost, being the original foreign currency purchase price translated at the rate on the date of purchase. When the realisation of that asset will give rise to tax consequences in the foreign country, the tax base of the asset will change as the exchange rate changes. This will give rise to a temporary difference because the recognised carrying amount of the asset does not change (see also **4.4.6.5**).

5.5.2   Consolidated financial statements

When a reporting entity incorporates the financial statements of foreign operations in its consolidated financial statements (whether by the equity method or consolidation), the deferred tax consequences will need to be evaluated. A foreign operation is defined as an entity that is a subsidiary, associate, joint arrangement or branch of a reporting entity, the activities of which are based or conducted in a country or currency other than those of the reporting entity. [IAS 21:8]

For entities that have not yet adopted IFRS 11 *Joint Arrangements* (which is effective for annual periods beginning on or after 1 January 2013 with earlier adoption permitted), the reference to a 'joint arrangement' in IAS 21:8 should be read as a reference to a 'joint venture'.

Once a foreign operation's own financial statements have been prepared in its functional currency, they must then be translated into the presentation currency of the investing entity or group, before they can be incorporated into the group's consolidated financial statements. This is dealt with in IAS 21 *The Effects of Changes in Foreign Exchange Rates* and discussed further in **chapter A19**.

The basic approach is to translate the statement of financial position using the closing rate of exchange, and income and expenses at the rates ruling on the date of transaction (or an average rate can often be used as an approximation). Exchange differences arising are recognised in other comprehensive income.

From a deferred tax perspective, this approach should not give rise to any additional temporary differences on the assets and liabilities of the foreign operation itself. This is because the carrying amounts and the tax bases of the assets and liabilities of the foreign operation are all translated using the same year-end exchange rate, and any deferred taxes will have already been recognised by the foreign operation.

Although temporary differences do not result directly from the translation of the financial statements of these foreign operations, temporary differences can still arise on their consolidation due to differences between the net investment accounted for in the consolidated financial statements (effectively the parent's share of the net assets of the operation), and the tax base of the investment itself held by the parent (see **4.4.6** above).

When a parent has a loan to a foreign subsidiary that is considered to be part of the net investment in the foreign operation, the parent will assess the likelihood of reversal of the temporary difference relating to the loan in the same manner as the temporary differences relating to the subsidiary's equity are considered. Therefore, if the parent is able to control the timing of the reversal of those temporary differences and the reversal is not expected to occur in the foreseeable future, the deferred tax would not be recognised. Conversely, if the parent has an interest-earning deposit in the subsidiary, the deferred tax arising from temporary differences would be recognised, as the exception relates to investments in subsidiaries and not to individual assets within those subsidiaries (see examples **4.4.6.1D** and **4.4.6.1E**).

5.6   Share-based payments

In some jurisdictions, entities receive tax deductions for share-based payments, although the deduction may not always equal the accounting expense, nor be in the same period as the accounting expense is recognised. For example, an entity may operate a share option scheme whereby the tax deduction occurs when the share options are exercised, and the amount is based on the entity's share price on the exercise date. [IAS 12:68A]

The difference between the tax base of the employee services received to date (being the amount accrued to date that the tax authorities will permit as a deduction in future periods), and the carrying amount for accounting purposes (i.e. nil), is a deductible temporary difference that results in a deferred tax asset. If the amount of the future tax deduction is not known at the end of the period, it should be estimated, based on information available at the end of the period. For example, if the deduction is based on the entity's share price on the exercise date (or some other future date), the measurement of the deductible temporary difference should be based on the entity's share price at the end of the period. [IAS 12:68B]

Example 5.6A

Calculation of deductible temporary difference arising from share-based payment transactions

On 1 January 20X1, Entity A grants share options to its employees that vest after three years of service. Under the tax law of the jurisdiction in which Entity A operates, a tax deduction will arise when the options are exercised and will be based on the intrinsic value of the options at that time.

At 31 December 20X2 (i.e. two years into the three-year vesting period), 100 options remain outstanding but Entity A expects that only 50 of these will be exercised; the remainder are expected either not to vest (due to employees leaving service before the end of the vesting period) or to expire unexercised (due to employees choosing not to exercise their rights under the options). The intrinsic value of each option, which is based on Entity A's share price at 31 December 20X2, is CU10 and the tax rate is 30 per cent.

Consistent with IAS 12:68B and Example 5 in the Illustrative Examples accompanying IAS 12, Entity A is required to calculate a deductible temporary difference that is based on the intrinsic value of the options at the end of the reporting period and the proportion of the service period which has elapsed.

When Entity A applies the requirements of IAS 12:68B, should the deductible temporary difference be calculated based on the total number of options outstanding at the end of the reporting period, or on the number of options expected to be exercised?

The deductible temporary difference should be calculated based on the number of options expected to be exercised. This is consistent with the requirements of IAS 12:68B, which states that "the amount the taxation authorities will permit as a deduction in future periods ... shall be estimated, based on information available at the end of the period".

In the circumstances described, Entity A should therefore calculate a deductible temporary difference of CU333 (50 options expected to be exercised × CU10 × ⅔) and should recognise a deferred tax asset of CU100 (CU333 × 30 per cent), subject to the general recognition criteria in IAS 12 for deferred tax assets.

Note that, in applying these requirements, it will generally be the case that the number of options expected to be exercised will be the same as the number expected to vest because the options will only give rise to a deductible temporary difference if they are 'in the money' and, logically, an employee would be expected to exercise an option to purchase a share for less than its market value. In addition, assumptions made about vesting of instruments for the purpose of these calculations should be consistent with expectations used when calculating the IFRS 2 expense.

If the amount of the accrued tax deduction exceeds the amount of the related cumulative remuneration expense, this indicates that the deduction relates not only to the remuneration expense but also to an equity item. Hence, in accordance with IAS 12:58, the excess of the associated current or deferred tax should be recognised directly in equity. [IAS 12:68C]

Example 5.6

Current and deferred tax arising from cash-settled share-based payments

Company A grants its employees cash-settled share appreciation rights (SARs) that vest after three years of service. The relevant tax authority of the country in which Company A is established allows a tax deduction not equal to the cash paid, but based on a different formula. To calculate the corresponding deferred tax under IAS 12:68B, Company A must estimate the amount of the tax deduction to be received in future periods by using information available at the end of the reporting period. Sometimes the amount of the estimated tax deduction measured in accordance with IAS 12:68B or ultimately received may exceed the cumulative remuneration expense recognised under IFRS 2 *Share-based Payment*.

In a cash-settled scheme of this nature, would recognition of the amount of the tax deduction in excess of the cumulative remuneration expense result in recognition, directly in equity, of the current or deferred tax arising from this excess in accordance with IAS 12:68C?

No. Although IAS 12:68C does not explicitly state that it relates only to equity-settled share-based payments, the justification given for the accounting treatment is that the excess deduction indicates that the deduction relates to an equity item as well as to the remuneration expense. In the case of cash-settled share-based payments, such awards are classified as liabilities. Therefore, there is no equity item recognised to which the deduction could relate and, accordingly, it is appropriate to recognise the entire deduction in profit or loss.

IAS 12 Appendix B contains an example of how to calculate the deferred tax asset associated with an employee share remuneration scheme.

In some cases tax deductions may be expected upon the exercise by the holder of vested share options. Because a tax deduction is expected, a deferred tax asset may have been recognised. If the holder fails to exercise the option (i.e. the share options lapse), the tax deductions cease to be expected, although the IFRS 2 expense will remain. Accordingly, there ceases to be a deductible temporary difference and the deferred tax asset should be written off to profit or loss, or to equity, consistent with the manner in which the asset was recognised (e.g. profit or loss to the extent of compensation expense, equity for any excess).

Sometimes employee share schemes are modified (e.g. from equity-settled to cash-settled). These modifications can change the accounting for the scheme (e.g. by requiring that a liability be recognised). The accounting implications of employee share schemes are considered in **chapter A16**. However, it is important to note that the modification may also affect any deferred tax balances recognised.

5.6.1   *Changes in deferred tax on share awards replaced in a business combination*

Often, as part of a business combination, the acquirer will issue equity-settled share-based payment awards to replace share options held by the employees of the acquiree. A portion of the market-based measure of the replacement awards is attributed to pre-combination services and, therefore, forms part of the consideration transferred in the business combination.

If the replacement awards are tax deductible, a deferred tax asset is recognised at the acquisition date based on the estimated tax deduction that will be received. Subsequent to the acquisition date, the acquirer's share price may change, in which case the deferred tax asset should be remeasured to reflect the anticipated tax deduction.

There are two acceptable methods of accounting for the subsequent remeasurement of the deferred tax asset related to pre-combination services. An entity should select one as an accounting policy choice to be applied consistently to all similar transactions.

Alternative 1: apply the principle established in IAS 12:68A – 68C

IAS 12:68C states that, in the context of share-based payments, "[i]f the amount of the tax deduction (or estimated future tax deduction) exceeds the amount of the related cumulative remuneration expense, this indicates that the tax deduction relates not only to remuneration expense but also to an equity item. In this situation, the excess of the associated current or deferred tax should be recognised directly in equity".

In the context of replacement awards granted as part of a business combination, the cumulative remuneration expense is comprised of the amount attributed to pre-combination services at the acquisition date (as determined in accordance with paragraph B58 of IFRS 3 *Business Combinations*) and the amount of compensation expense recognised for the replacement awards since the date of the business combination, if any. Therefore, the tax deduction related to the excess over the acquisition-date market-based value would be recognised in equity under the principle in IAS 12:68C.

Alternative 2: recognise all changes to the deferred tax assets related to pre-combination services in profit or loss

This alternative is based on the fact that Example 6 of IAS 12 does not appear to apply the principle in IAS 12:68C to distinguish whether a portion of the increase in the deferred tax asset should be recognised in equity rather than in profit or loss. The example indicates that, subsequent to the business combination, the intrinsic value of the options has increased above the market-based value of the replacement awards measured on the acquisition date. In the example, the entire change in the deferred tax asset appears to be recognised as "deferred tax income". Accordingly, based on Example 6 of IAS 12, it appears acceptable to recognise all movements in deferred tax assets related to pre-combination services in profit or loss.

Example 5.6.1 provides a numerical illustration of both of these approaches.

Example 5.6.1

Changes in tax deductions for share awards replaced in a business combination

On 1 January 20X1, Company A acquires Company B in a business combination. On the acquisition date, the employees of Company B hold fully vested share options with a market-based value of CU120. As part of the business combination, the share options held by employees of Company B are replaced by fully vested share options of Company A with a market-based value of CU120. In accordance with paragraphs B56 to B62 of IFRS 3, the market-based value of the replacement awards is determined to relate to pre-combination services and forms part of the consideration transferred to acquire Company B.

A tax deduction is available when the share options are exercised, based on the intrinsic value of the awards on the date of exercise. The tax rate applicable to Company A is 40 per cent. On the acquisition date, the intrinsic value of the awards is CU100 and, accordingly, a deferred tax asset of CU40 is recognised on that date.

On 31 December 20X1, the intrinsic value of the replacement awards has increased to CU150 such that the deferred tax asset related to the replacement awards is CU60. The increase in the deferred tax asset is recognised using either of the following two alternatives.

Alternative 1: apply the principle established in IAS 12:68A – 68C

The estimated future tax deduction of CU150 exceeds the amount of the cumulative remuneration expense of CU120 (the cumulative remuneration expense being equal to the acquisition-date market-based value because no compensation expense in respect of the replacement awards relates to the post-combination period).

Accordingly, the deferred tax asset related to the excess of CU30 is recognised in equity. Therefore, the increase of CU20 in the deferred tax asset is recognised as follows.

Increase in deferred tax asset for the year	CU20	(CU60 – CU40)
Excess recognised in equity	CU12	(CU30 × 40%)
Deferred tax income recognised in profit or loss	CU8	

> *Alternative 2: recognise all changes in the deferred tax assets related to pre-combination services in profit or loss*
>
> Under this alternative, the increase of CU20 in the deferred tax asset is recognised in profit or loss.
>
> Either of the above treatments is acceptable as an accounting policy choice to be applied consistently to all similar transactions.

5.6.2   Changes in deferred tax on share awards recognised on first-time adoption

Paragraph D2 of IFRS 1 *First-time Adoption of International Financial Reporting Standards* provides an exemption that allows entities not to apply IFRS 2 retrospectively to specified share-based payment awards on transition to IFRSs (see **section 7.2** of **chapter A3**).

Therefore, for a share option scheme awarded prior to the date of transition to IFRSs that meets the specific requirements of the exemption, an entity that recognised a remuneration expense under its previous GAAP is permitted not to restate that expense, but recognises no further expense.

The entity may be entitled to receive a tax deduction when the options are exercised based on the intrinsic value of the options at the date of exercise. IAS 12:68A to 68C require that a deferred tax asset should be recognised on all deductible temporary differences relating to share options. On the date of transition to IFRSs, the entity recognises a deferred tax asset based on the difference between the fair value of the underlying shares and the exercise price of the options. Because this is an adjustment on transition to IFRSs, it is recognised in equity.

Subsequent changes in the amount of the deferred tax asset (based on the difference between the fair value of the underlying shares on the valuation date and the exercise price of the options) should be recognised in profit or loss or in equity, depending on the expense actually recognised for the awards.

The entity should determine the 'cumulative remuneration expense' related to the estimated future tax deduction, as referred to in IAS 12:68C, by reference to the original remuneration expense recognised under previous GAAP. If the amount of the estimated future tax deduction on a subsequent reporting date is higher than the remuneration expense recognised under previous GAAP, this implies that the tax deduction relates not only to the remuneration expense but also to an equity item. In such circumstances, the changes in the deferred tax asset should be recognised partially in profit or loss (to the extent that the deferred tax asset relates to the cumulative remuneration expense recognised), with the residual recognised in equity. Similarly, if the amount of the estimated future tax deductions on a subsequent reporting date falls below the remuneration expense recognised under previous GAAP, the resulting reduction in the deferred tax asset should be recognised in equity to the extent of any amounts previously recognised in equity, with any excess recognised in profit or loss.

If no remuneration expense was recognised prior to transition to IFRSs, the 'cumulative remuneration expense' under IFRSs would be considered to be nil and all subsequent changes in the deferred tax asset would be recognised in equity. This is illustrated in **example 5.6.2** below.

Example 5.6.2

Changes in deferred tax assets for share awards recognised on first-time adoption of IFRSs

Entity A granted 100 share options with an exercise price of CU1 per share option to employees on 1 January 2001 (i.e. before the mandatory application of IFRS 2 *Share-based Payment* on 7 November 2002). The arrangement involved a five-year vesting period, following which employees have the right to exercise the options for 10 years. Entity A adopted IFRSs in 2008, with a transition date of 1 January 2007. A tax deduction is available when the share options are exercised, based on the intrinsic value of the awards at the date of exercise.

Entity A recognised a remuneration expense of CU400 for this arrangement under its previous GAAP. As permitted by IFRS 1:D2, Entity A did not apply IFRS 2 retrospectively to these share options at the date of transition to IFRSs.

On 1 January 2007, the date of transition, the fair value of Entity A's shares is CU3 per share, and all of the share options have vested and remain outstanding. Accordingly, the share options have an intrinsic value of CU2 per share (i.e. fair value of CU3 – exercise price of CU1). Assuming a tax rate of 30 per cent, on transition to IFRSs Entity A recognises a deferred tax asset of CU60 (CU2 × 100 share options × 30 per cent), with an offsetting adjustment to equity.

On 31 December 2007, Entity A's share price has increased to CU8 per share such that the share options have an intrinsic value of CU7 per share option.

The deferred tax asset relating to the share-based payment arrangement is now calculated as CU210 (i.e. CU7 × 100 share options × 30 per cent), resulting in a deferred tax credit of CU150 (i.e. deferred tax asset of CU210 at the end of the period less CU60 at the date of transition). The deferred tax credit is recognised partly in profit or loss and partly in equity as follows.

Estimated future tax deductions (CU7 × 100 share options)	CU700
Cumulative remuneration expense (previous GAAP)	CU400
Excess deduction	CU300
Deferred tax income for the period	CU150
Amount recognised directly in equity (CU300 × 30%)	CU90
Recognised in profit or loss	CU60

If, however, the cumulative remuneration expense recognised under previous GAAP had been reversed on transition to IFRSs, then the entire CU150 of tax benefit would be recognised in equity.

On 31 December 2008, Entity A's share price has decreased to CU4 per share, resulting in an intrinsic value of the options of CU3 (CU4 – CU1). Accordingly, the estimated future tax deductions are now CU300 (CU3 intrinsic value × 100 share options) and the deferred tax asset is measured at CU90 (CU300 × 30 per cent). The resulting deferred tax debit of CU120 (CU210 deferred tax asset at 31 December 2007 less deferred tax asset of CU90 at 31 December 2008) is recognised partly in profit or loss and partly in equity as follows.

Deferred tax expense for the period	CU120
Amount in excess of cumulative remuneration expense previously recognised directly in equity (CU300 × 30%)	CU90
Recognised in profit or loss	CU30

If no remuneration expense was recognised prior to transition to IFRSs, then the entire CU120 of tax expense would be recognised in equity.

5.7   Finance leases

Leasing transactions frequently give rise to deferred tax effects, but IAS 12 does not provide any specific guidance on how those effects should be accounted for.

The appropriate accounting treatment for leases is established in IAS 17 *Leases* and is discussed in detail in **chapter A17.**

If a lease is classified as a finance lease, the lessee recognises the leased asset and a corresponding lease liability in its statement of financial position; it also recognises the asset's depreciation and finance costs related to the lease liability in profit or loss.

In some jurisdictions, the tax treatment of finance leases is consistent with the accounting treatment. In other jurisdictions, however, a finance lease may be classified as an operating lease for tax purposes and tax deductions may be available only for the lease payments as they are paid (i.e. no deduction for asset depreciation or finance costs).

Sections **5.7.1** and **5.7.2** below discuss the appropriate accounting for the two most common tax treatments for finance leases.

5.7.1   *Finance lease treatment for tax and financial reporting purposes*

When the entity receives tax deductions in respect of the leased asset (depreciation allowance) and the lease liability (deduction for finance costs) in the same way as if the asset had been purchased using a loan, no special tax considerations arise. The requirements of IAS 12 are applied separately to the leased asset and the lease liability.

When the leased asset is recognised initially, if the tax base of the asset is the same as the carrying amount under IFRSs, no temporary difference arises. If the tax base ascribed to the asset is different from the carrying amount, a temporary difference arises, but no deferred tax is recognised due to the application of the initial recognition exception under IAS 12:22(c) (see **4.4.5** above). As the asset is depreciated, accounting and tax depreciation rates may differ, resulting in new deductible or taxable temporary differences for which deferred tax may be recognised in accordance with the general principles of IAS 12.

The lease liability is likely to have a tax base equal to its carrying amount because deductions are given in future for the finance cost portion of the lease payment, which is not reflected in the carrying amount of the lease liability at inception.

5.7.2   Finance lease under IAS 17 but tax deductions based on rental payments

When the lease is treated as an operating lease for tax purposes and tax deductions are received for the lease payments as they are paid (and not for depreciation or finance costs), the appropriate accounting is more complex. Given the lack of guidance in the existing literature, alternative approaches may be acceptable.

Two acceptable approaches to accounting for the deferred tax consequences in such circumstances are explained below.

Approach 1 – apply the IAS 12 requirements to the leased asset and the lease liability separately

The leased asset has a tax base of zero; the lease liability also has a tax base of zero because the lease payments are deductible in future (as lease rental payments). This gives rise to a temporary difference on initial recognition of both the leased asset and the lease liability that is not recognised due to the application of the initial recognition exception in IAS 12:22(c).

Subsequently, the temporary differences decrease as the asset is depreciated and the liability is repaid. No deferred tax is recognised on either the leased asset or the lease liability due to continued application of the initial recognition exception (assuming no new temporary differences arise).

Therefore, this approach may result in no deferred tax being recognised either initially or over the term of the lease. The impact of this may be that while the profit on the lease generally increases over time, as the interest expense decreases, the tax deductions are timed more evenly.

Approach 2 – apply the IAS 12 requirements to the leasing transaction as a whole

An alternative approach that results in the recognition of deferred tax is also seen in practice. This approach seeks to reflect the linkage between the leased asset and the lease liability and recognise deferred tax on an aggregate temporary difference basis. This method yields an effective tax rate that more closely reflects the economics of the overall lease transaction.

At inception of the lease, there is no net lease asset or liability, no tax base and, therefore, no temporary difference.

Subsequently, as depreciation on the asset (generally straight-line) initially exceeds the rate at which the debt reduces (due to lease payments made less interest recognised under the effective interest method), a net liability arises resulting in a deductible temporary difference on which a deferred tax asset should be recognised if recoverable. Assuming that the lease liability is not repaid in advance, the total discounted cash outflows should equal the total rental payments deductible for income tax purposes.

5.8   Post-retirement benefits

The accounting for defined benefit retirement benefit plans and other post-retirement benefits often gives rise to temporary differences.

5.8.1   *Temporary differences*

Tax deductions for payments into defined benefit retirement benefit plans are often allowed on a different measurement basis and in a different time period compared to the expense recognised in the financial statements under IAS 19 *Employee Benefits*. For example, the tax deduction may be available:

*   when cash contributions are paid (in some jurisdictions, the deduction is spread over a period of time); or

*   when the actual benefits are paid to individuals (this usually applies for unfunded schemes).

As a result temporary differences are likely to arise.

5.8.2   *Deferred tax asset*

A net defined benefit liability can be considered to represent the future funding the entity will be required to provide for the defined benefit scheme. If the entity will be able to claim future tax deductions for such funding, the tax base of the net defined benefit liability will be zero.

This will give rise to a deductible temporary difference. In addition, a deductible temporary difference will arise if tax deductions for contributions to a retirement benefit plan are not given in the year the contribution is paid but in later years (e.g. when the benefits are paid). In accordance with IAS 12, the entity should recognise a deferred tax asset for this temporary difference to the extent it is recoverable (see **section 4.6** above).

5.8.3   Deferred tax liability

When an entity has a net defined benefit asset in respect of a surplus in its retirement benefit plan, this represents over-funding for which tax deductions may have been received; consequently, a taxable temporary difference arises and a deferred tax liability should be recognised.

The manner of recovery of a surplus may affect the tax consequences; for example, in some jurisdictions, refunds from a retirement benefit plan may be subject to tax at a rate different from the normal income tax rate.

IFRIC 14 *IAS 19—The Limit on a Defined Benefit Asset, Minimum Funding Requirements and their Interaction* provides guidance on how to assess the recoverability of a net defined benefit asset (see **7.3** in **chapter A15** or, for entities that have not yet adopted IAS 19(2011), **7.2.1** in **appendix A3**). Application of this guidance may result in the recognition of an asset because there is legally an unconditional right to a refund. Such a refund may be taxable at a rate other than the normal income tax rate.

A net defined benefit asset may be recovered through the receipt of a taxable refund or through reduced contributions. IAS 12 requires deferred taxes to be assessed based on the expected method of recovery of the underlying asset.

IFRIC 14 states that "the economic benefit available does not depend on how the entity intends to use the surplus". Accordingly, recognition of an asset under IFRIC 14 because there is legally an unconditional right to a refund does not necessarily imply that the entity expects to recover the asset through a refund.

If it is expected that the asset will be recovered through reduced contributions, the normal income tax rate may be the most appropriate rate to be applied to the temporary difference. However, if a refund is expected, the rate applicable to refunds should be applied.

Note, however, that it would not be appropriate (in the absence of other negative factors) to argue that no deferred tax should be recognised in relation to the net defined benefit asset on the basis it may be eliminated by future market movements or other measurement factors. This is because deferred taxes are measured by reference to the carrying amount at the reporting date, not a theoretical, possible or even probable future carrying amount.

5.8.4   Allocation of tax between profit or loss and other comprehensive income

The requirements regarding the recognition of costs relating to defined benefit retirement benefit plans in profit or loss and in other comprehensive income have been changed as a result of the revised version of IAS 19 issued in June 2011 (see **chapter A15** for details of the changes made). Following the June 2011 revision, all 'remeasurements' (which include actuarial gains and losses) are required to be recognised in other comprehensive income when they arise. Prior to the June 2011 revision, entities could choose to account for actuarial gains and losses arising on such plans either in profit or loss or in other comprehensive income, and had choices regarding the timing of recognition.

IAS 12 requires that current and deferred tax should be recognised outside profit or loss if the tax relates to items that are recognised outside profit or loss (see **3.2.1** above). To the extent that gains or losses are recognised in other comprehensive income under IAS 19 (whether after or prior to adoption of the revised Standard), it is necessary to consider what amount of the current or deferred tax relates to those gains and losses. In addition, it is often not possible to determine whether contributions paid (generally the basis for tax deductions) relate to items recognised in profit or loss or items recognised in other comprehensive income. When there is no clear relationship between the expense recognised in profit or loss and the tax deductions received in the period, the current and deferred tax expense will need to be allocated between profit or loss and other comprehensive income on a reasonable basis. [IAS 12:63]

One acceptable methodology is to allocate tax deductions arising during the period first to items recognised in profit or loss, and then to allocate the remainder, if any, to the items in other comprehensive income. However, if the total tax exceeds all retirement benefit items recognised multiplied by the tax rate, that excess may be taken to profit or loss because it does not clearly relate to items reported in other comprehensive income.

Example 5.8.4

Defined benefit liability with an actuarial loss

	Defined benefit liability CU	Current tax deduction (30%) CU	Deferred tax asset (30%) CU
Brought forward	(200)		60
Profit or loss – net pension cost	(50)	15	–
Other comprehensive income – actuarial loss	(30)	6[a]	3[b]
Contribution paid / deduction received	70	21	
Carried forward	(210)		63

[a] This amount represents the remainder of the total tax deduction of CU21 in the current period after the maximum possible amount of CU15 has been allocated to amounts recognised in profit or loss.

[b] The movement between the amounts of deferred tax asset brought forward and carried forward in this case is deemed to arise on the actuarial loss because the total tax recognised in other comprehensive income is not in excess of tax on the actuarial loss (CU30 × 30% = CU9).

5.9   Decommissioning obligations

Under IAS 16 *Property, Plant and Equipment*, the cost of an item of property, plant and equipment includes the initial estimate of the costs of any decommissioning, restoration or similar obligation established under IAS 37 *Provisions, Contingent Liabilities and Contingent Assets*. The total cost of the asset is depreciated over its useful economic life unless the asset is measured under a revaluation model.

At the time of initial recognition of the asset, the carrying amount of the asset includes the estimated decommissioning cost capitalised on acquisition; however, the tax authorities may only permit tax deductions for the purchase price of the asset, with tax deductions for decommissioning costs allowed only as the decommissioning costs are paid.

IAS 12 contains no specific guidance on decommissioning obligations and there are two acceptable approaches. One approach is to apply the requirements of the Standard in the normal way to the separate asset and liability. The alternative approach views the asset and its related decommissioning liability together. Both of these methods are seen in practice.

Approach 1: view asset and liability separately

Under this approach, at initial recognition the tax base of the asset is generally its purchase price and excludes the capitalised decommissioning costs, thereby creating a taxable temporary difference. Because the temporary difference arises on the initial recognition of the asset, no deferred tax liability is recognised on acquisition in accordance with IAS 12:15. Assuming the asset is not being remeasured, if there are subsequent increases in the estimate of the decommissioning obligation, this will result in an increase in the carrying amount of the asset in accordance with IFRIC 1 *Changes in Existing Decommissioning, Restoration and Similar Liabilities*. This increases the temporary difference associated with the asset and a deferred tax liability is recognised in accordance with the general principles of IAS 12. Changes in the temporary difference giving rise to deferred tax may also arise in subsequent periods if the depreciation period differs from the period over which tax deductions are received.

Any subsequent decreases in the estimate of the decommissioning obligation would lead to a corresponding reduction in the carrying amount of the asset. If this reduces the temporary difference that existed at initial recognition, there are no deferred tax consequences.

The tax base of the decommissioning liability is the carrying amount less deductions to be received as the costs are incurred. Assuming deductions will be received when the costs are paid, the tax base of the liability is nil. Therefore, at initial recognition a deductible temporary difference exists but, similar to the asset above, no deferred tax asset is recognised because the temporary difference arises on initial recognition of the decommissioning liability.

The carrying amount of the decommissioning obligation will subsequently be increased by the unwinding of the discount, and will also be adjusted for any change in estimate of the ultimate cash outflows. An increase in the temporary difference associated with the liability will give rise to the recognition of a deferred tax asset in accordance with the general principles of IAS 12.

An increase in estimate of the decommissioning obligation will, therefore, lead to the recognition of a deferred tax liability in respect of the related asset and a deferred tax asset in respect of the decommissioning liability.

Approach 2: view asset and liability together

The other acceptable approach seen in practice is to view the asset and its related decommissioning liability in aggregate. This approach seeks to reflect the linkage between the asset and the related decommissioning liability and recognises deferred taxes on the aggregate temporary difference, rather than the two individual temporary differences. This method yields an effective tax rate that more closely reflects the economics of the asset ownership over its life.

This approach is based on the view that the decommissioning asset and the obligation are related and, therefore, should be viewed as a whole. The temporary differences related to the asset and the liability are aggregated and deferred taxes are recognised only on an overall temporary difference.

Subsequently, as the asset is depreciated and the decommissioning liability increases with the unwind of interest (using the effective interest method), a temporary difference will arise in respect of which deferred taxes should be recognised.

5.10   Hedge of net investment in a foreign operation

Entities sometimes enter into transactions to hedge their net investment in a foreign subsidiary (e.g. through the use of a foreign currency loan, or a forward contract). Under IAS 39 *Financial Instruments: Recognition and Measurement*, such a transaction may be designated as a hedge of the foreign currency exposure of a net investment in a foreign operation (see **chapter B9** or, for entities that have not yet adopted IFRS 9, see **chapter C9**). Gains and losses on the effective portion of such hedging transactions are recognised in other comprehensive income in the entity's consolidated financial statements.

If the tax base of the hedging instrument is different from its carrying amount, this creates a temporary difference and deferred tax should be recognised. This is the case regardless of whether deferred tax has been provided in respect of the parent's investment in a foreign subsidiary. To the extent that the hedge is effective, the tax consequences of establishing a deferred tax asset or liability for the hedging transaction are reported in other comprehensive income in accordance with IAS 12:61A. Recognition of amounts outside profit or loss is discussed further at **4.7.1** and **4.7.2** above.

Example 5.10

Hedge of a net investment in a foreign subsidiary

Company A (functional currency Sterling) has a wholly-owned US subsidiary, Company B (functional currency US$), which has net assets of US$120,000. Company A hedges its net investment in Company B using a US$100,000 loan. Assuming that the hedge is perfectly effective and that all the other hedge accounting requirements of IAS 39 are met, the exchange gain or loss on retranslating the loan will be recognised in other comprehensive income in Company A's consolidated financial statements. When the retranslation of the loan changes its carrying amount, but not its tax base, deferred tax on the resulting temporary difference is also recognised in other comprehensive income.

5.11   Deferred tax resulting from impairment of assets

As discussed in **chapter A10**, IAS 36 *Impairment of Assets* requires that a review for impairment be carried out if events or changes in circumstances indicate that the carrying amount of certain assets within the scope of IAS 36 may not be recoverable. An asset is considered to be impaired when its recoverable amount declines below its carrying amount. The recoverable amount of an asset is the higher of its fair value less costs of disposal (referred to as 'costs to sell' prior to the issue of IFRS 13 *Fair Value Measurement* – see **chapter A10**) and its value in use.

The calculation of the impairment loss is based on an assumption that the entity will choose to recover the carrying amount of the asset in the most beneficial way. Therefore, if the entity could earn more by selling the asset rather than by continuing to use it, it would choose to sell the asset, and vice versa.

Although an impairment loss may be measured under IAS 36 by reference to fair value less costs of disposal, rather than value in use, this does not necessarily mean that, for the purposes of measuring the related deferred tax asset or liability, management must change its expected manner of recovery in accordance with IAS 12:51A, and now use the tax base applicable to recovery through sale rather than use.

Impairment losses recognised in respect of assets carried on a historical cost basis are recognised in profit or loss; for assets carried at a revalued amount, impairment losses are treated as revaluation decreases (which may or may not lead to an expense being recognised in profit or loss).

Because an impairment loss affects the carrying amount of an asset, it affects the relationship between the asset's carrying amount and its tax base. Therefore, any deferred tax asset or liability is determined by comparing the revised carrying amount of the asset with its tax base. [IAS 36:64]

In many jurisdictions, tax deductions for assets are received at a faster rate than expense is recognised for financial reporting purposes, either because of differing depreciation methods or because different useful lives are ascribed under tax law. While this generally results in a deferred tax liability position, the recognition of an impairment loss in a reporting period may cause the carrying amount of the asset to fall below its tax base (see **example 9.1** in **chapter A10**).

In accordance with IAS 12, an entity recognises a deferred tax asset to the extent that it is probable that taxable profit will be available against which the deductible temporary difference can be utilised (see **4.6** for recognition of deferred tax assets).

5.12   Group relief

The deferred tax position of each group entity should be determined separately and the results aggregated (with some adjustments) to determine the group position. Adjustments may need to be made to reflect the deferred tax consequences of the availability of group relief altering the view of recoverability of deferred tax assets.

When losses are expected to be surrendered to another group entity that is expected to pay for the group relief then the 'deferred tax asset' may well be assessed as recoverable and recognised even though the 'asset' is actually a receipt from another group entity that recovers it from the tax authority. When losses are expected to be surrendered to another group entity but no payment is likely to be received, the entity surrendering the losses would not normally be able to assess the asset as recoverable. However, the deferred tax asset would be recognised on consolidation to the extent that the other entity is expected to utilise the losses.

When a payment is made between group entities in consideration for the transfer of tax losses, it is necessary to exercise judgement to determine the substance of the transaction (see **2.9** above).

6   Presentation and disclosure

6.1   Presentation

6.1.1   Tax expense

The tax expense or income related to profit or loss from ordinary activities should be presented as part of profit or loss in the statement(s) of profit or loss and other comprehensive income. [IAS 12:77]

IAS 12:77 has been amended by consequential amendments arising from the June 2011 amendments to IAS 1 *Presentation of Financial Statements*. The amendments reflect the new titles for the financial statements presenting profit or loss and other comprehensive income. Prior to the amendments, IAS 12:77 referred to the 'statement of comprehensive income' and IAS 12:77A (now deleted) required that when an entity presents the components of profit or loss in a separate 'income statement', the tax expense or income related to profit or loss from ordinary activities should be presented in that separate statement.

IAS 12 notes that, although IAS 21 *The Effects of Changes in Foreign Exchange Rates* requires certain exchange differences to be recognised as income or expense, that Standard does not specify where such differences should be presented in the statement of comprehensive income. Therefore, IAS 12 states that when exchange differences on deferred foreign tax liabilities or assets are recognised in the statement of comprehensive income, such differences may be classified as deferred tax expense (income) if that presentation is considered to be the most useful to financial statement users. [IAS 12:78]

An entity may incur expenses that are linked to the income tax expense, for example, fees payable to tax consultants for their tax advice (see also **2.6** above) and to accountants who assist the entity in preparing its tax returns.

Amounts paid other than to the tax authority in connection with an entity's tax expense do not represent income taxes. Therefore, such amounts should be treated as either an administrative or other expense in the entity's statement of comprehensive income depending on the format adopted, i.e. classification of expenses either by function or by nature.

When a payment is made between group entities in consideration for the transfer of tax losses, it is necessary to exercise judgement to determine the substance of the transaction (see **2.9** above).

Example 6.1.1

Presentation of payments of non-income taxes that can be claimed as an allowance against taxable profit

Entity A is required to make production-based royalty payments to Taxing Authority 1. These payments can be claimed as an allowance against taxable profit for the computation of income taxes payable to Taxing Authority 2. The production-based royalty payments do not, in themselves, meet the definition of income tax and, therefore, are outside the scope of IAS 12 (see **section 2** above), whereas the income tax payable to Taxing Authority 2 is within the scope of IAS 12.

Should the production-based royalty payments to Taxing Authority 1 be presented as a tax expense in Entity A's statement of comprehensive income?

No. The 'tax expense' line item required to be presented under paragraph 82(d) of IAS 1 is intended to require an entity to present taxes that meet the definition of income taxes under IAS 12. Because the production-based royalty payments are not income taxes, they should not be presented within that line item.

The conclusions above were confirmed in an IFRS Interpretations Committee agenda rejection published in the July 2012 *IFRIC Update*.

It is possible for an entity to designate a derivative as a cash flow hedge of the cash flow variability of a tax liability arising on the foreign exchange gain or loss on a foreign currency borrowing. Provided that such a hedge has been appropriately designated and documented, the hedge is a qualifying cash flow hedge of a non-financial liability (the tax liability) under IAS 39 *Financial Instruments: Recognition and Measurement*.

IAS 39, the Standard which prescribes the hedge accounting rules in terms of recognition and measurement, is silent on where the gains and losses on derivatives designated as hedging derivatives should be presented within profit or loss. It has become customary, and is useful to the users of the financial statements, for the hedging effects of derivatives to be presented in the statement of comprehensive income in the same line as the item that they hedge. Therefore, although the hedging gain or loss is clearly not an income tax as defined by IAS 12, an argument can be made for including the effects of the derivatives, which an entity has entered into as hedges of its tax liability, in the tax line in the statement of comprehensive income.

When an entity chooses to present derivative gains/losses relating to designated tax hedging derivatives within the tax line, this accounting policy choice should be applied consistently from period to period. Furthermore, appropriate separate disclosure in the notes of the amount attributable to hedging gains/losses should be made.

6.1.1.1   *Presentation of the release of a deferred tax liability on disposal of an asset*

Example 6.1.1.1

Presentation of the release of a deferred tax liability on disposal of an asset

Entity X owns an asset and has recognised a deferred tax liability resulting from accelerated tax depreciation on that asset.

Entity Y purchases the asset from Entity X and, as permitted by local tax law, elects to retain the tax base of the asset as it was when held by Entity X. As a result of this election, Entity X pays no tax on the disposal of the asset, but the proceeds of disposal received from Entity Y are lower than would otherwise be expected to reflect the reduced tax allowance available to Entity Y.

When Entity X derecognises the related deferred tax liability on disposal of the asset, should this reversal be presented as part of the gain or loss on disposal of the asset or as part of tax expense (tax income)?

The reversal of the deferred tax liability should be presented as part of Entity X's tax expense (tax income) because it falls within the definition of tax expense (tax income) in IAS 12:5 ("the aggregate amount included in the determination of profit or loss for the period in respect of current tax and deferred tax").

The deferred tax expense previously recognised reflected the expected tax consequences with regards to the recovery of the asset. Actual recovery of the value of the asset has been achieved with no tax payable. Therefore, from Entity X's perspective, the temporary difference has reversed and the effect of that reversal should be reflected as part of tax expense (tax income).

6.1.2   Statement of financial position

The presentation of both current and deferred tax in the statement of financial position is addressed in IAS 1 (and not in IAS 12) as follows:

- liabilities and assets for current tax should be presented in the statement of financial position; [IAS 1:54]

- deferred tax liabilities and deferred tax assets should be presented in the statement of financial position; [IAS 1:54] and

- when an entity presents current and non-current assets, and current and non-current liabilities, as separate classifications in its statement of financial position, it should not classify deferred tax assets (liabilities) as current assets (liabilities). [IAS 1:56]

Liabilities or assets arising from uncertain tax positions should be included in the statement of financial position within the amounts for current tax liabilities (or assets) and presented as current or non-current based on the general principles of IAS 1. The effect of uncertain tax positions on profit or loss or other comprehensive income (depending on the nature of the uncertain tax position) should be included in the same line item as tax expense (income).

Although uncertain tax positions are similar in nature to provisions as defined in IAS 37 *Provisions, Contingent Liabilities and Contingent Assets* (see **3.3.1**), it would be inappropriate to present the resulting liabilities with other provisions recognised under IAS 37, because they are explicitly excluded from the scope of IAS 37.

6.1.3   Offset of tax assets and liabilities

In a similar approach to that taken in IAS 1, IAS 12 takes a strong line on the extent to which tax assets and liabilities can be offset against one another to present only a net figure in the statement of financial position.

6.1.3.1   Offset of current tax assets and liabilities

An entity should offset current tax assets and current tax liabilities if, and only if, the entity:
[IAS 12:71]

- has a legally enforceable right to set off the recognised amounts; and

- intends either to settle on a net basis, or to realise the asset and settle the liability simultaneously.

The Standard explains that an entity normally has a legally enforceable right to set off current tax assets against current tax liabilities when they relate to taxes levied by the same tax authority, and that authority permits the entity to make or receive a single net payment. [IAS 12:72]

When an entity is preparing consolidated financial statements, current tax assets and liabilities arising from different group entities should not be offset unless:
[IAS 12:73]

- the entities concerned have a legally enforceable right to make or receive a single net payment; and

- the entities intend to make or receive such a net payment or to recover the asset and settle the liability simultaneously.

6.1.3.2   Offset of deferred tax assets and liabilities

An entity should offset deferred tax assets and deferred tax liabilities if, and only if:
[IAS 12:74]

- the entity has a legally enforceable right to set off current tax assets against current tax liabilities; and

- the deferred tax assets and the deferred tax liabilities relate to income taxes levied by the same tax authority on either:

    - the same taxable entity; or

    - different taxable entities which intend either to settle current tax liabilities and assets on a net basis, or to realise the assets and settle the liabilities simultaneously, in each future period in which significant amounts of deferred tax liabilities or assets are expected to be settled or recovered.

Under the above rules, deferred tax assets and liabilities arising in the same legal entity (which is also a single taxable entity) can generally be offset. However, when, for example, the taxable entity has capital losses carried forward that can only be used to reduce future capital gains, those losses can only be offset against deferred tax liabilities to the extent that recognised deferred tax liabilities arise from unrealised capital gains.

In a consolidation situation, the first condition to overcome is the requirement for the balances to be levied by the same tax authority. This effectively prohibits the offset of deferred tax assets and liabilities arising in different jurisdictions.

Even for entities operating within the same jurisdiction, except when there are formal group relief or consolidated taxation arrangements, it will be unusual for the tax authority to permit net settlement between different taxable entities.

Therefore, in preparing consolidated financial statements, the deferred tax balances of the separate entities will generally be aggregated without further setting off the deferred tax balances of one entity against those of another.

The above rules mean that, for disclosure purposes, there is no need for detailed scheduling of the timing of reversals of each temporary difference. In rare circumstances, an entity may have a legally enforceable right of set-off, and an intention to settle net, for some periods but not for others. In such situations, detailed scheduling may be required to establish reliably whether the deferred tax liability of one taxable entity will result in increased tax payments in the same period in which a deferred tax asset of another taxable entity will result in decreased payments by that second taxable entity. [IAS 12:75 & 76]

When an entity is required to offset deferred tax assets and deferred tax liabilities in its statement of financial position because it meets the conditions in IAS 12:74 (see above), the entity is not necessarily entitled to offset the related deferred tax income and deferred tax expense. IAS 12:58 requires the individual components of tax expense or tax benefit to be allocated to profit or loss for the period except to the extent that the tax arises from a transaction or event which is recognised in the same or a different period outside of profit and loss, either in other comprehensive income or directly in equity. The ability to offset the amounts in the statement of financial position does not override the requirement for the income and expense to be appropriately classified.

Example 6.1.3.2

Offsetting deferred tax income and expense

During the year, Company A revalues an item of property, plant and equipment upward by CU1,000 to CU21,000, recognising the increase in other comprehensive income. The tax base of the property, plant and equipment is CU20,000.

At the same time, Company A incurs an operating tax loss of CU800 during the period which, under the relevant tax legislation, can be carried forward indefinitely. The requirements for recognition of the deferred tax asset arising from the tax loss carried forward are satisfied. In addition, the requirements for offsetting deferred tax assets and liabilities in IAS 12:74 are met. The tax rate is 30 per cent.

Company A recognises a deferred tax liability of CU300 (CU1,000 temporary difference × 30%) and a deferred tax asset of CU240 (CU800 loss × 30%). The two amounts are set off in the statement of financial position so that a net deferred tax liability of CU60 (CU300 – CU240) is recognised. However, the deferred tax arising on the revaluation is recognised in other comprehensive income and the effect of the current year's loss is recognised in profit or loss.

6.2   Disclosure

6.2.1   Statement of comprehensive income

The major components of tax expense (income) should be disclosed separately, including:
[IAS 12:79 & 80]

- current tax expense (income);

- any adjustments recognised in the period for current tax of prior periods;

- the amount of deferred tax expense (income) relating to the origination and reversal of temporary differences;

- the amount of deferred tax expense (income) relating to changes in tax rates or the imposition of new taxes;

- the amount of the benefit arising from a previously unrecognised tax loss, tax credit or temporary difference of a prior period that is used to reduce current tax expense;

- the amount of the benefit from a previously unrecognised tax loss, tax credit or temporary difference of a prior period that is used to reduce deferred tax expense;

- deferred tax expense arising from the write-down, or reversal of a previous write-down, of a deferred tax asset in accordance with IAS 12:56; and

- the amount of tax expense (income) relating to those changes in accounting policies and errors that are included in profit or loss in accordance with IAS 8 *Accounting Policies, Changes in Accounting Estimates and Errors*, because they cannot be accounted for retrospectively.

In respect of discontinued operations, the financial statements should disclose separately the tax expense relating to:
[IAS 12:81(h)]

- the gain or loss on discontinuance; and

- the profit or loss from the ordinary activities of the discontinued operation for the period, together with the corresponding amounts for each prior period presented.

For each type of temporary difference, and each type of unused tax losses and unused tax credits, the financial statements should disclose the amount of the deferred tax income or expense recognised in profit or loss, if this is not apparent from the changes in the amounts recognised in the statement of financial position. [IAS 12:81(g)(ii)]

6.2.1.1 Reconciliation of tax expense or income

IAS 12 requires the presentation of an explanation of the relationship between the tax expense (income) and accounting profit in either or both of the following forms:
[IAS 12:81(c) & 86]

- a numerical reconciliation between tax expense (income) and the product of accounting profit multiplied by the applicable tax rate(s), disclosing also the basis on which the applicable tax rate(s) is (are) computed; or

- a numerical reconciliation between the average effective tax rate (being the tax expense (income) divided by the accounting profit) and the applicable tax rate, disclosing also the basis on which the applicable tax rate is computed.

An explanation is required of changes in the applicable tax rate(s) compared to the previous accounting period. [IAS 12:81(d)]

6.2.2 Statement of financial position

For each type of temporary difference, and each type of unused tax losses and unused tax credits, the financial statements should disclose the amount of the deferred tax assets and liabilities recognised in the statement of financial position for each period presented. The amount of deferred tax income or expense recognised in profit or loss in respect of each temporary difference must also be disclosed where it is not apparent from the changes in the amounts recognised in the statement of financial position. [IAS 12:81(g)(i)]

The following should also be disclosed:
[IAS 12:81(e) & (f)]

- the amount (and expiry date, if any) of deductible temporary differences, unused tax losses and unused tax credits for which no deferred tax asset is recognised in the statement of financial position; and

- the aggregate amount of temporary differences associated with investments in subsidiaries, branches and associates and interests in joint arrangements, for which deferred tax liabilities have not been recognised.

It would often be impracticable to compute the amount of unrecognised deferred tax liabilities arising from investments in subsidiaries, branches and associates and interests in joint arrangements, so IAS 12 requires an entity to disclose the aggregate amount of the underlying temporary differences but does not require disclosure of the deferred tax liabilities. Nevertheless, when practicable, entities are encouraged to disclose the amounts of the unrecognised deferred tax liabilities because financial statement users may find such information useful. [IAS 12:87]

> For entities that have not yet adopted IFRS 11 *Joint Arrangements* (which is effective for annual periods beginning on or after 1 January 2013 with earlier adoption permitted), the references to 'interests in joint arrangements' in IAS 12:81(f) and 87 should be read as references to 'interests in joint ventures'.

An entity should disclose the amount of a deferred tax asset and the nature of the evidence supporting its recognition, when:
[IAS 12:82]

- the utilisation of the deferred tax asset is dependent on future taxable profits in excess of the profits arising from the reversal of existing taxable temporary differences; and

- the entity has suffered a loss in either the current or preceding period in the tax jurisdiction to which the deferred tax asset relates.

When current and deferred tax assets and liabilities are measured at the tax rate applicable to undistributed profits, but the net income taxes payable will be affected if part of the retained earnings is paid out as a dividend to shareholders, the entity should disclose:
[IAS 12:82A & 87A]

- the nature of the potential income tax consequences that would result from the payment of dividends to its shareholders. This includes the important features of the income tax systems and the factors that will affect the amount of the potential income tax consequences of dividends;

- the amounts of the potential income tax consequences that are practicably determinable; and

- whether there are any potential income tax consequences that are not practicably determinable.

It is not always practicable to compute the total amount of the potential income tax consequences that would result from the payment of dividends to shareholders (e.g. when an entity has a lot of overseas subsidiaries). However, even in such circumstances, usually some consequences may be easily determinable, and these should be disclosed. IAS 12 cites the example of a consolidated group, when the parent and some of its subsidiaries may have paid income taxes at a higher rate on undistributed profits and are aware of the amount that would be refunded on the payment of future dividends to shareholders from consolidated retained earnings. In this case, the refundable amount is disclosed.

When some or all potential income tax consequences cannot be determined, the entity should disclose that there are additional potential income tax consequences not practicably determinable. In the parent's separate financial statements, the disclosure of the potential income tax consequences relates to the parent's retained earnings. [IAS 12:82A]

When current and deferred tax assets and liabilities are measured at the tax rate applicable to undistributed profits, but the net income taxes payable will be affected if part of the retained earnings is paid out as a dividend to shareholders, an entity required to provide the disclosures listed above may also be required to provide disclosures related to temporary differences associated with investments in subsidiaries, branches and associates or interests in joint arrangements. For example, an entity may be required to disclose the aggregate amount of temporary differences associated with investments in subsidiaries for which no deferred tax liabilities have been recognised. [IAS 12:81(f)] If it is impracticable to compute the amounts of unrecognised deferred tax liabilities there may be amounts of potential income tax consequences of dividends not practicably determinable related to these subsidiaries. [IAS 12:87C]

> For entities that have not yet adopted IFRS 11, the references to 'interests in joint arrangements' in IAS 12:81(f) and 87C should be read as references to 'interests in joint ventures'.

6.2.3   *Other disclosure requirements*

Other disclosure requirements include:

- the aggregate current and deferred tax relating to items that are charged or credited directly to equity; [IAS 12:81(a)]

- the amount of income tax relating to each component of other comprehensive income (revaluation surplus, foreign exchange reserve etc.); [IAS 12:81(ab)]

- the amount of income tax consequences of dividends to shareholders of the entity that were proposed or declared before the financial statements were authorised for issue, but are not recognised as a liability in the financial statements; [IAS 12:81(i)]

- if a business combination in which the entity is the acquirer causes a change in the amount recognised for its pre-acquisition deferred tax asset (under IAS 12:67 – see **5.1.5**), the amount of that change; [IAS 12:81(j)]

- if the deferred tax benefits acquired in a business combination are not recognised at the acquisition date but are recognised after the acquisition date (under IAS 12:68 – see **5.1.7**), a description of the event or change in circumstances that caused the deferred tax benefits to be recognised; [IAS 12:81(k)]

- any tax-related contingent liabilities and contingent assets in accordance with IAS 37 (e.g. from unresolved disputes with the tax authorities); [IAS 12:88] and

- when changes in tax rates or tax laws are enacted or announced after the reporting period, any significant impact on the entity's current and deferred tax assets and liabilities. [IAS 10:22(h) & IAS 12:88]

The disclosure for uncertain tax positions is governed not only by the requirements of IAS 12 but also by the requirement under IAS 1:116 to disclose key sources of estimation uncertainty when there is a significant risk of a material adjustment in carrying amounts of assets and liabilities within the next financial year (see **7.3** in **chapter A4**).

When the uncertain tax position gives rise to a contingent tax liability for which no provision is recognised (e.g. because it is not probable that a payment will be made to the tax authority), an entity must still consider the requirements of IAS 12:88, which states that "[a]n entity discloses any tax-related contingent liabilities and contingent assets in accordance with IAS 37 . . . contingent liabilities and contingent assets may arise, for example, from unresolved disputes with the taxation authorities".

A14 Revenue

Contents

1   Introduction

IAS 18 *Revenue* sets out recognition criteria for revenue, identifies the circumstances in which those criteria will be met and provides practical guidance on the application of the criteria. The Standard was most recently amended in May 2011.

2   Scope

IAS 18 is applied in accounting for revenue arising from:
[IAS 18:1]

- the sale of goods (including goods produced for sale and goods purchased for sale, such as merchandise purchased by a retailer or land and other property held for resale);

- the rendering of services; and

- the use by others of entity assets yielding interest, royalties and dividends.

IAS 18 does not deal with revenue arising from:
[IAS 18:6]

- leases (dealt with in IAS 17 *Leases* – see **chapter A17**);

- dividends arising from investments accounted for under the equity method (dealt with in IAS 28(2011) *Investments in Associates and Joint Ventures*, or, for entities that have not yet adopted IAS 28(2011), IAS 28(2003) *Investments in Associates* – see **chapter A26**);

- insurance contracts within the scope of IFRS 4 *Insurance Contracts* – see **chapter A39**;

- changes in the fair value of financial assets and financial liabilities or their disposal (dealt with in IFRS 9 *Financial Instruments* (**Volume B**), or, for entities that have not yet adopted IFRS 9, IAS 39 *Financial Instruments: Recognition and Measurement* (**Volume C**));

- changes in the value of other current assets;

- the initial recognition, and changes in the fair value, of biological assets related to agricultural activity (dealt with in IAS 41 *Agriculture* – see **chapter A38**);

- the initial recognition of agricultural produce (also dealt with in IAS 41); and

- the extraction of mineral ores (dealt with in IFRS 6 *Exploration for and Evaluation of Mineral Resources* – see **chapter A40**).

Also excluded from the scope of IAS 18 are contracts for the rendering of services that are directly related to construction contracts, e.g. those for the services of project managers and architects. These service contracts fall within the scope of IAS 11 *Construction Contracts* (see **chapter A34**). [IAS 18:4] The requirements of IFRIC 12 *Service Concession Arrangements*, which addresses the accounting by operators for public-to-private service concession arrangements, are dealt with in **chapter A35.**

> Contracts included in the scope of IFRS 4 include product warranties issued by a third party for the replacement of goods sold by a manufacturer to a customer as well as fixed fee contracts that are dependent on an uncertain future event (see **2.5** and **2.3**, respectively, in **chapter A39**). However, product warranties issued directly by a manufacturer to a customer are within the scope of IAS 18.
>
> See **8.9** in **chapter A12** for a discussion on whether warranties fall within the scope of IAS 18 or IAS 37 *Provisions, Contingent Liabilities and Contingent Assets.*

2.1   IFRIC 15 *Agreements for the Construction of Real Estate*

IFRIC 15 addresses whether an agreement is within the scope of IAS 11 or IAS 18, and when revenue from the construction of real estate should be recognised. [IFRIC 15:6]

The Interpretation applies to agreements for the construction of real estate, and to entities that undertake that construction directly or through subcontractors. [IFRIC 15:4] In addition to the construction of real estate, such agreements may include the delivery of other goods or services. [IFRIC 15:5]

> Agreements for the construction of real estate take diverse forms, in part because the underlying substance of such agreements varies. While some agreements are for the provision of construction services, others are in substance for the delivery of goods (e.g. housing units) that are not complete at the time of entering into the agreement. Thus, the percentage of completion method is appropriate for some agreements for the construction of real estate but, for others, revenue should be recognised only at the point that the constructed real estate is delivered to the customer. The Interpretation provides

guidance on how to determine which approach is appropriate in which circumstances.

IFRIC 15 is accompanied by an information note which, although not part of the Interpretation, summarises its requirements in the form of two flowcharts, reproduced as **table 2.1.1** and **table 2.1.2** below.

The detailed guidance in IFRIC 15 is written on the assumption that the entity has previously analysed the agreement for the construction of real estate and any related agreements and concluded that any other criteria for revenue recognition (discussed later in this chapter) are met. In particular, the entity must not retain continuing managerial involvement to the degree usually associated with ownership; and it must not retain effective control over the constructed real estate to an extent that would preclude recognition of some or all of the consideration as revenue. If recognition of some of the consideration as revenue is precluded, the detailed guidance in IFRIC 15 applies only to the part of the agreement for which revenue will be recognised. [IFRIC 15:7]

2.1.1   *Splitting an agreement into separately identifiable components*

It is possible that a single agreement may cover the delivery of goods or services in addition to the construction of real estate; for example, an agreement to construct real estate may also specify that property management services are to be provided.

As discussed in **section 5**, IAS 18:13 indicates that, in some circumstances, agreements may need to be split into separately identifiable components, with each such component being accounted for separately. When this is necessary, the fair value of the total consideration received or receivable for the agreement is allocated to each component. The seller then applies the requirements of IFRIC 15 to any components for the construction of real estate in order to determine whether each component is within the scope of IAS 11 or IAS 18. [IFRIC 15:8]

The segmenting criteria of IAS 11 should then be applied to any component of the agreement that is determined to be a construction contract. [IFRIC 15:8]

Table 2.1.1

[Information note accompanying IFRIC 15]

(A) – continues in **table 2.1.2** *below.*

2.1.2 Accounting for the construction of real estate

The appropriate accounting for an agreement to construct real estate (or, when an agreement is split into separately identifiable components, for a component for the construction of real estate) depends on whether the agreement (or component):

- meets the definition of a construction contract;

- is only for the rendering of services; or

- is for the sale of goods, in which case it is necessary to consider whether the criteria for recognising revenue from the sale of goods are met on a continuous basis.

Whether an agreement (or component) is within the scope of IAS 11 or IAS 18 depends on the terms of the agreement and all the surrounding facts and circumstances, and judgement will be required with respect to each agreement. [IFRIC 15:10]

Table 2.1.2

[Information note accompanying IFRIC 15]

(A) – continues from **table 2.1.1** *above.*

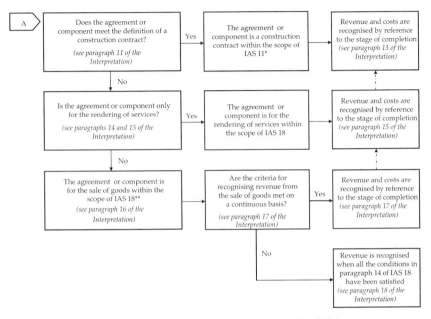

(*) The construction contract may need to be segmented in accordance with paragraph 8 of IAS 11

(**) Directly related services may need to be separated in accordance with paragraph 13 of IAS 18

2.1.2.1   *Construction contracts*

IAS 11 applies when the agreement (or component) meets the definition of a construction contract set out in IAS 11:3, namely "a contract specifically negotiated for the construction of an asset or a combination of assets ...".

IFRIC 15:11 states that an agreement for the construction of real estate will meet the definition of a construction contract when the buyer is able to:

- specify the major structural elements of the design of the real estate before construction begins; and/or

- specify major structural changes once construction is in progress, whether it exercises that ability or not.

When construction will take place on land that was already the buyer's asset before the agreement to construct real estate was envisaged, it is likely that IAS 11 will apply. This is because an owner of land will, subject to planning constraints, usually be able to decide whether to construct real estate on that land, and to specify the major structural elements of the design of any such real estate before construction.

Generally, it is likely that a buyer will be able to specify major structural changes once construction is in progress only if such a right is explicit in the agreement. But it is possible that such a right may be established by the law of a jurisdiction in which a transaction occurs.

In contrast, if buyers have only limited ability to influence the design (e.g. to select from a range of entity-specified options, or to specify only minor variations to the basic design), IFRIC 15:12 states that the agreement will be for the sale of goods and within the scope of IAS 18.

Although IFRIC 15:12 states that such an agreement will be for the sale of goods, it would seem possible in some circumstances (e.g. when construction materials will be sourced directly by the buyer) for the agreement to be for the rendering of services, as discussed at **2.1.2.2**. In any case, it is clear that the agreement will not be a construction contract.

When IAS 11 applies, the construction contract also includes any contracts or components for the rendering of services that are directly related to the construction of the real estate in accordance with IAS 11:5(a) and IAS 18:4. [IFRIC 15:11] If the outcome of the agreement (or component) can be estimated reliably, revenue is recognised by reference to the stage of completion of the contract activity in accordance with IAS 11. [IFRIC 15:13] The recognition of revenue for construction contracts is discussed in **chapter A34**.

2.1.2.2 Agreements for the rendering of services

If an agreement (or component) does not meet the definition of a construction contract, it will be within the scope of IAS 18. The Interpretation provides further guidance on how to determine whether the agreement is for the rendering of services (see below) or for the sale of goods (see **2.1.2.3**). [IFRIC 15:14]

In some cases, the entity is not required to acquire and supply construction materials because they will be sourced directly by the buyer. When this is the case, the agreement may be only an agreement for the rendering of services in accordance with IAS 18, in which case, provided that the criteria in IAS 18:20 are met, revenue will be recognised using the percentage of completion method. IAS 18:21 indicates that the requirements of IAS 11 are generally applicable to the recognition of revenue and the associated expenses for such a transaction. [IFRIC 15:15] The recognition of revenue from the provision of services is discussed in **section 7** below.

2.1.2.3   Agreements for the sale of goods

Conversely, if the entity is required to provide services together with construction materials in order to perform its contractual obligation to deliver real estate to the buyer then, assuming it does not qualify as a construction contract (see **2.1.2.1**), the agreement is for the sale of goods and the criteria set out in IAS 18:14 apply. [IFRIC 15:16]

If an agreement is determined to be for the sale of goods, the timing of revenue recognition will depend on when control and the significant risks and rewards of ownership are transferred to the buyer. IFRIC 15 envisages two possibilities, as set out below.

- The entity may transfer to the buyer control and the significant risks and rewards of ownership of the real estate in its entirety at a single time (e.g. at completion, upon or after delivery). In this case, revenue will be recognised only when all the criteria in IAS 18:14 are satisfied. [IFRIC 15:18] Those criteria are discussed in **section 6** below.

- Alternatively, the entity may transfer to the buyer control and the significant risks and rewards of ownership of the work in progress in its current state as construction progresses. In this case, if all the criteria in IAS 18:14 are met continuously as construction progresses, revenue will be recognised using the percentage of completion method. The requirements of IAS 11 are generally applicable to the recognition of revenue and the associated expenses for such a transaction. [IFRIC 15:17]

The idea that the criteria in IAS 18:14 can be met continuously as construction progresses is relatively new. In the Basis for Conclusions accompanying IFRIC 15, the IFRIC (now the IFRS Interpretations Committee) noted that agreements with 'continuous transfer' might not be encountered frequently. [IFRIC 15:BC26] When an entity adopts such accounting, specific disclosures are required, including how the entity determines which agreements meet all the criteria in IAS 18:14 continuously as construction progresses (see **2.1.3**).

The Interpretation itself does not give further guidance on how to assess whether 'continuous transfer' is present, but some further commentary is included at IE3, IE8 and IE11 in the illustrative examples accompanying IFRIC 15 (see **2.1.4**). One of the important indicators of 'continuous transfer' appears to be that, if the agreement is terminated before construction is complete, the buyer retains the work in progress and the entity has the right to be paid for the work performed to date.

When the entity is required to perform further work on real estate already delivered to the buyer, it recognises an expense in accordance with IAS 18:19 (see **6.5**), measuring the liability in accordance with IAS 37 *Provisions, Contingent Liabilities and Contingent Assets* (see **chapter A12**). When the entity is required to deliver further goods or services that are separately identifiable from the real estate already delivered to the buyer, it will already have identified the remaining goods or services as a separate component of the sale in accordance with IFRIC 15:8 (see **2.1.1**). [IFRIC 15:19]

2.1.3   Disclosures

When an entity recognises revenue using the percentage of completion method for agreements that meet all the criteria in IAS 18:14 continuously as construction progresses (see **2.1.2.3**), the following disclosures are required:
[IFRIC 15:20]

- how the entity determines which agreements meet all the criteria in IAS 18:14 continuously as construction progresses;

- the amount of revenue arising from such agreements in the period; and

- the methods used to determine the stage of completion of agreements in progress.

For any such agreements that are in progress at the reporting date, the following disclosures are also required:
[IFRIC 15:21]

- the aggregate amount of costs incurred and recognised profits (less recognised losses) to date; and

- the amount of advances received.

IFRIC 15:BC32 notes that these disclosures are similar to those required for construction contracts by IAS 11:39 and 40.

2.1.4   Illustrative examples

The following examples accompany, but are not part of, IFRIC 15.

Example 2.1.4A

Separately identifiable component for sale of land

[IFRIC 15 Illustrative example 1]

IE1   An entity buys a plot of land for the construction of commercial real estate. It designs an office block to build on the land and submits the designs to planning authorities in order to obtain building permission. The entity markets the office block to potential tenants and signs conditional lease agreements. The entity markets the office block to potential buyers and signs with one of them a conditional agreement for the sale of land and the construction of the office block. The buyer cannot put the land or the incomplete office block back to the entity. The entity receives the building permission and all agreements become unconditional. The entity is given access to the land in order to undertake the construction and then constructs the office block.

IE2   In this illustrative example, the agreement should be separated into two components: a component for the sale of land and a component for the construction of the office block. The component for the sale of land is a sale of goods within the scope of IAS 18.

IE3   Because all the major structural decisions were made by the entity and were included in the designs submitted to the planning authorities before the buyer signed the conditional agreement, it is assumed that there will be no major change in the designs after the construction has begun. Consequently, the component for the construction of the office block is not a construction contract and is within the scope of IAS 18. The facts, including that the construction takes place on land the buyer owns before construction begins and that the buyer cannot put the incomplete office block back to the entity, indicate that the entity transfers to the buyer control and the significant risks and rewards of ownership of the work in progress in its current state as construction progresses. Therefore, if all the criteria in paragraph 14 of IAS 18 are met continuously as construction progresses, the entity recognises revenue from the construction of the office block by reference to the stage of completion using the percentage of completion method.

IE4   Alternatively, assume that the construction of the office block started before the entity signed the agreement with the buyer. In that event,

---

the agreement should be separated into three components: a component for the sale of land, a component for the partially constructed office block and a component for the construction of the office block. The entity should apply the recognition criteria separately to each component. Assuming that the other facts remain unchanged, the entity recognises revenue from the component for the construction of the office block by reference to the stage of completion using the percentage of completion method as explained in paragraph IE3.

IE5   In this example, the sale of land is determined to be a separately identifiable component from the component for the construction of real estate. However, depending on facts and circumstances, the entity may conclude that such a component is not separately identifiable. For example, in some jurisdictions, a condominium is legally defined as the absolute ownership of a unit based on a legal description of the airspace the unit actually occupies, plus an undivided interest in the ownership of the common elements (that includes the land and actual building itself, all the driveways, parking, lifts, outside hallways, recreation and landscaped areas) that are owned jointly with the other condominium unit owners. In this case, the undivided interest in the ownership of the common elements does not give the buyer control and the significant risks and rewards of the land itself. Indeed, the right to the unit itself and the interest in the common elements are not separable.

Example 2.1.4B

Agreement for sale of goods

[IFRIC 15 Illustrative example 2]

IE6   An entity is developing residential real estate and starts marketing individual units (apartments) while construction is still in progress. Buyers enter into a binding sale agreement that gives them the right to acquire a specified unit when it is ready for occupation. They pay a deposit that is refundable only if the entity fails to deliver the completed unit in accordance with the contracted terms. Buyers are also required to make progress payments between the time of the initial agreement and contractual completion. The balance of the purchase price is paid only on contractual completion, when buyers obtain possession of their unit. Buyers are able to specify only minor variations to the basic design but they cannot specify or alter major structural elements of the design of their unit. In the jurisdiction, no rights to the underlying real estate asset transfer to the buyer other than through the agreement. Consequently, the construction takes place regardless of whether sale agreements exist.

IE7   In this illustrative example, the terms of the agreement and all the surrounding facts and circumstances indicate that the agreement is not a construction contract. The agreement is a forward contract that gives the buyer an asset in the form of a right to acquire, use and sell the completed real estate at a later date and an obligation to pay the purchase price in accordance with its terms. Although the buyer might be able to transfer its interest in the forward contract to another party, the entity retains control and the significant risks and rewards of ownership of the work in progress in its current state until the completed real estate is transferred. Therefore, revenue should be recognised only when all the criteria in paragraph 14 of IAS 18 are met (at completion in this example).

IE8 Alternatively, assume that, in the jurisdiction, the law requires the entity to transfer immediately to the buyer ownership of the real estate in its current state of completion and that any additional construction becomes the property of the buyer as construction progresses. The entity would need to consider all the terms of the agreement to determine whether this change in the timing of the transfer of owner-ship means that the entity transfers to the buyer control and the significant risks and rewards of ownership of the work in progress in its current state as construction progresses. For example, the fact that if the agreement is terminated before construction is complete, the buyer retains the work in progress and the entity has the right to be paid for the work performed, might indicate that control is transferred along with ownership. If it does, and if all the criteria in paragraph 14 of IAS 18 are met continuously as construction progresses, the entity recog-nises revenue by reference to the stage of completion using the percentage of completion method taking into account the stage of completion of the whole building and the agreements signed with individual buyers.

Example 2.1.4C

Continuing managerial involvement

[IFRIC 15 Illustrative example 3]

IE9 Determining whether the entity will retain neither continuing manage-rial involvement to the degree usually associated with ownership nor effective control over the constructed real estate to an extent that would preclude recognition of some or all of the consideration as revenue depends on the terms of the agreement and all the surround-ing facts and circumstances. Such a determination requires judgement. The Interpretation assumes the entity has reached the conclusion that it is appropriate to recognise revenue from the agreement and dis-cusses how to determine the appropriate pattern of revenue recogni-tion.

IE10 Agreements for the construction of real estate may include such a degree of continuing managerial involvement by the entity undertak-ing the construction that control and the significant risks and rewards of ownership are not transferred even when construction is complete and the buyer obtains possession. Examples are agreements in which the entity guarantees occupancy of the property for a specified period, or guarantees a return on the buyer's investment for a specified period. In such circumstances, recognition of revenue may be delayed or precluded altogether.

IE11   Agreements for the construction of real estate may give the buyer a right to take over the work in progress (albeit with a penalty) during construction, e.g. to engage a different entity to complete the construction. This fact, along with others, may indicate that the entity transfers to the buyer control of the work in progress in its current state as construction progresses. The entity that undertakes the construction of real estate will have access to the land and the work in progress in order to perform its contractual obligation to deliver to the buyer completed real estate. If control of the work in process is transferred continuously, that access does not necessarily imply that the entity undertaking the construction retains continuing managerial involvement with the real estate to the degree usually associated with ownership to an extent that would preclude recognition of some or all of the consideration as revenue. The entity may have control over the activities related to the performance of its contractual obligation but not over the real estate itself.

2.2   Distinguishing between the sale of goods, the rendering of services and construction contracts

Difficulties can arise in distinguishing between the sale of goods, the rendering of services and construction contracts. IAS 18 offers no guidance on how to determine whether a contract is for the supply of goods or services. Although the appropriate classification will in many cases be obvious, in some industries, such as software development, careful judgement may be required. In particular, merely because a contract requires the delivery of a customised software programme, it does not necessarily follow that the contract is a construction contract. When the software is developed entirely to customer specification, the contract is likely to be a construction contract. More complex cases may involve the modification of an already existing core product offered by a software developer and it will be necessary to exercise careful judgement in order to assess whether the specified modifications are so significant as to make the contract a construction contract or whether the contract should be regarded as, in substance, a supply of goods bundled together with more limited modification services.

The IFRIC (now the IFRS Interpretations Committee) considered the difficulty in distinguishing between the sale of goods, rendering of services and construction contracts during the development of IFRIC 15 (see **2.1**). In accordance with paragraph 11 of IAS 8 *Accounting Policies, Changes in Accounting Estimates and Errors*, the indicators identified in IFRIC 15 may be applied by analogy to other situations when the appropriate classification between these three categories is not obvious. However, because the indicators set out in IFRIC 15 were developed for real estate, it will be necessary to exercise careful judgement when considering how they might be interpreted in other contexts.

2.3   IFRIC 18 *Transfers of Assets from Customers*

IFRIC 18 aims to address divergent practice in the accounting by recipients for transfers of property, plant and equipment from 'customers'. The Interpretation concludes that when an item of property, plant and equipment transferred meets the definition of an asset from the perspective of the recipient, the recipient should recognise the asset at its fair value on the date of the transfer, with the credit recognised as revenue when the criteria in IAS 18 *Revenue* are met. IFRIC 18 does not address how a customer should account for such a transfer of property, plant and equipment.

IFRIC 18 applies to all agreements in which an entity receives from a customer an item of property, plant and equipment (or cash to construct or acquire an item of property, plant and equipment) that the entity must then use either to connect the customer to a network or to provide the customer with ongoing access to a supply of goods or services, or to do both. [IFRIC 18:5 & 6] It applies only to the accounting by the receiving entity for such transfers. [IFRIC 18:4]

In particular, in the utilities industry, an entity may receive from its customers property, plant and equipment that must be used to connect those customers to a network and provide them with ongoing access to a supply of commodities such as electricity, gas or water. [IFRIC 18:1] But the Interpretation also applies in industries other than utilities where transfers of assets from customers occur. For example, an entity outsourcing its information technology functions may transfer its existing items of property, plant and equipment to the outsourcing provider. [IFRIC 18:2]

Transfers of assets other than property, plant and equipment (e.g. intangible assets) are not within the scope of IFRIC 18. However, application by analogy in accordance with IAS 8 is not prohibited. [IFRIC 18:BC5]

IFRIC 18 refers to the entity transferring the asset as the customer. However, in some circumstances it envisages that the transferor of the asset may not be the entity that will eventually have ongoing access to the supply of goods or services and be the recipient of those goods or services. [IFRIC 18:3]

For example, a developer builds a new office building in which there is an electrical substation that is handed over to the electricity supplier when the building is completed. The electricity supplier will use the substation to distribute electricity to the future occupier of the building. For the purposes of IFRIC 18, the 'customer' making the transfer is the developer, even though the 'customer' who will use the electricity provided through the substation is the future occupier.

IFRIC 18 does not apply to agreements in which the transfer is either a government grant as defined in IAS 20 *Accounting for Government Grants and Disclosure of Government Assistance* or infrastructure used in a service concession arrangement that is within the scope of IFRIC 12. [IFRIC 18:7]

IFRIC 18 arrangements can be distinguished from service concession arrangements within the scope of IFRIC 12 because, in service concession arrangements, it is the grantor that controls the infrastructure, not the operator. Equally there is no overlap between IFRIC 18 and IAS 20 because a transfer of assets from a customer does not meet the definition of a government grant in accordance with IAS 20:3. [IFRIC 18:BC8]

IFRIC 18 addresses the following issues:

- recognition of the transferred property, plant and equipment as an asset (see **2.3.1**);
- measurement of the asset on initial recognition (see **2.3.2**);
- recognition of revenue (see **2.3.3**); and
- accounting for transfers of cash from customers (see **2.3.4**).

2.3.1   Recognition as an asset

The key question for the entity receiving the item of property, plant and equipment is whether it meets the definition of an asset under the *Conceptual Framework for Financial Reporting*. Paragraph 4:4(a) of the Conceptual Framework states that "an asset is a resource controlled by the entity as a result of past events and from which future economic benefits are expected to flow to the entity". IFRIC 18 emphasises that the entity must control the asset in order to recognise it. While, in most circumstances, the entity obtains the right of ownership of the transferred property, plant and equipment, this is not essential in determining whether an asset exists. IFRIC 18 notes that right of ownership may not of itself be sufficient to establish control. If the customer still controls the item, it will not be an asset of the receiving entity. [IFRIC 18:9]

Whether or not the entity controls the transferred property, plant and equipment is based on consideration of all relevant facts and circumstances. For example, IFRIC 18 notes that although an entity may not have discretion as to the purpose for which the item is used, when it has the ability to decide how the item is operated and maintained and when it is replaced, the entity would normally conclude that it controls the transferred item. [IFRIC 18:10]

> The draft Interpretation D24, which preceded IFRIC 18, contained a requirement to determine whether the arrangement contained a lease in accordance with IAS 17 and IFRIC 4. The IFRIC (now the IFRS Interpretations Committee) decided to simplify the proposals by removing this requirement and focusing on who controls the asset.

2.3.2   Measurement of the asset on initial recognition

When the receiving entity determines that the item of property, plant and equipment meets the definition of an asset, IFRIC 18 requires that asset to be recognised and its cost on initial recognition to be measured at its fair value in accordance with paragraph 24 of IAS 16 *Property, Plant and Equipment*. [IFRIC 18:11]

2.3.3   Recognition of revenue

IAS 18:12 states that "when goods are sold or services are rendered in exchange for dissimilar goods or services, the exchange is regarded as a transaction which generates revenue". Transactions within the scope of

IFRIC 18 are exchanges for dissimilar goods or services and, therefore, they will give rise to revenue in accordance with IAS 18. [IFRIC 18:13]

The timing of the recognition of that revenue will depend on what the entity has agreed to supply to the customer in exchange. The entity may have agreed to deliver one or more services in exchange for the transferred item of property, plant and equipment, such as connecting the customer to a network, providing the customer with ongoing access to a supply of goods or services, or both. The entity should identify the separately identifiable services included in the agreement in accordance with IAS 18:13 (see **section 5**). [IFRIC 18:14]

IFRIC 18 includes guidance based on IAS 18:13 to help identify the services to be delivered in exchange for the transferred asset. Indicators that connecting the customer to a network is a separately identifiable service and is, therefore, an event for which revenue should be recognised include:
[IFRIC 18:15]

- a service connection to a network is delivered to the customer and represents stand-alone value for that customer; and

- the fair value of the service connection to that network can be measured reliably.

> When connection to a network is a separately identifiable service, it is still necessary to consider when that service is delivered. Often, a permanent connection may be established at the outset. In such cases, revenue would be recognised at the outset, as the connection is established. Alternatively, connection may need to be delivered continuously over the period of use, in which case the connection revenue would be recognised over that period of use (or, if shorter, the useful life of the asset in accordance with IFRIC 18:20 – see below).

If the customer making the transfer of property, plant and equipment will receive ongoing access to a supply of goods or services at a lower price than would be charged without the transfer, this indicates that providing the customer with ongoing access to that supply of goods or services is a separately identifiable service. [IFRIC 18:16]

This contrasts with the scenario in which a customer making a transfer pays the same price for ongoing access to goods or services as a customer that has not made such a transfer. The features of this arrangement indicate that the obligation to provide the customer with ongoing access to a supply of goods or services arises from the terms of the entity's operating licence or other regulation rather than the agreement to transfer the property plant and equipment. [IFRIC 18:17]

If only one service is included in the agreement, the entity recognises revenue when that service is performed in accordance with IAS 18:20 (see **section 7**). If more than one separately identifiable service is provided, the fair value received or receivable is allocated between the services in accordance with IAS 18:13 (see **section 5**), and the recognition criteria of IAS 18 are then applied to each service individually. [IFRIC 18:18 & 19]

IFRIC 18 does not provide any additional guidance on how to allocate the total consideration received or receivable for the agreement. However, the Basis for Conclusions notes that relevant guidance is included in IFRIC 12:13 in respect of service concession arrangements and paragraphs 5 to 7 of IFRIC 13 *Customer Loyalty Programmes* in respect of customer loyalty programmes (see **5.5.1** below). In particular, IAS 18 does not mandate the use of any particular method of allocation.

If an ongoing service is identified as part of the agreement, the period over which revenue is recognised for that service is generally determined by the terms of the agreement with the customer. If the agreement does not specify a period, the revenue is recognised over a period no longer than the useful life of the transferred asset used to provide the ongoing service. [IFRIC 18:20]

The IFRIC (now the IFRS Interpretations Committee) justified the latter restriction on the basis that the entity can only use the transferred asset to provide ongoing access to a supply of goods or services during its useful life. Any obligation that exists after the asset is replaced does not arise from the original transfer but from the terms of the entity's operating licence or other regulation. [IFRIC 18:BC21]

2.3.4   Accounting for transfers of cash from customers

IFRIC 18 also applies to agreements in which an entity receives cash from a customer when that amount of cash must be used only to construct or acquire an item of property, plant and equipment and the entity must then use the item of property, plant and equipment either to connect the customer to a network or to provide the customer with ongoing access to a supply of goods or services, or to do both. [IFRIC 18:6]

When an entity receives such a transfer of cash from a customer, the analysis as to whether the constructed or acquired item of property, plant and equipment is an asset of the entity is performed in line with the guidance at **2.3.1** above. If the property, plant and equipment is an asset of the entity, it is recognised at cost in accordance with IAS 16. The cash received from the customer is recognised as revenue in accordance with the guidance at **2.3.3** above. [IFRIC 18:21]

2.3.5   Illustrative examples

The following examples accompany, but are not part of, IFRIC 18.

Example 2.3.5A

Electricity substation

[IFRIC 18 Illustrative example 1]

IE1   A real estate company is building a residential development in an area that is not connected to the electricity network. In order to have access to the electricity network, the real estate company is required to construct an electricity substation that is then transferred to the network company responsible for the transmission of electricity. It is assumed in this example that the network company concludes that the transferred substation meets the definition of an asset. The network company then uses the substation to connect each house of the residential development to its electricity network. In this case, it is the homeowners that will eventually use the network to access the supply of electricity, although they did not initially transfer the substation. By regulation, the network company has an obligation to provide ongoing access to the network to all users of the network at the same price, regardless of whether they transferred an asset. Therefore, users of the network that transfer an asset to the network company pay the same price for the use of the network as those that do not. Users of the network can choose to purchase their electricity from distributors other than the network company but must use the company's network to access the supply of electricity.

IE2   Alternatively, the network company could have constructed the substation and received a transfer of an amount of cash from the real estate company that had to be used only for the construction of the substation. The amount of cash transferred would not necessarily equal the entire cost of the substation. It is assumed that the substation remains an asset of the network company.

IE3   In this example, the Interpretation applies to the network company that receives the electricity substation from the real estate company. The network company recognises the substation as an item of property, plant and equipment and measures its cost on initial recognition at its fair value (or at its construction cost in the circumstances described in paragraph IE2) in accordance with IAS 16 *Property, Plant and Equipment*. The fact that users of the network that transfer an asset to the network company pay the same price for the use of the electricity network as those that do not indicates that the obligation to provide ongoing access to the network is not a separately identifiable service of the transaction. Rather, connecting the house to the network is the only service to be delivered in exchange for the substation. Therefore, the network company should recognise revenue from the exchange transaction at the fair value of the substation (or at the amount of the cash received from the real estate company in the circumstances described in paragraph IE2) when the houses are connected to the network in accordance with paragraph 20 of IAS 18 *Revenue*.

Example 2.3.5B

Connection to water main

[IFRIC 18 Illustrative example 2]

IE4   A house builder constructs a house on a redeveloped site in a major city. As part of constructing the house, the house builder installs a pipe from the house to the water main in front of the house. Because the pipe is on the house's land, the owner of the house can restrict access to the pipe. The owner is also responsible for the maintenance of the pipe. In this example, the facts indicate that the definition of an asset is not met for the water company.

IE5   Alternatively, a house builder constructs multiple houses and installs a pipe on the commonly owned or public land to connect the houses to the water main. The house builder transfers ownership of the pipe to the water company that will be responsible for its maintenance. In this example, the facts indicate that the water company controls the pipe and should recognise it.

Example 2.3.5C

Outsourcing information technology functions

[IFRIC 18 Illustrative example 3]

IE6   An entity enters into an agreement with a customer involving the outsourcing of the customer's information technology (IT) functions. As part of the agreement, the customer transfers ownership of its existing IT equipment to the entity. Initially, the entity must use the equipment to provide the service required by the outsourcing agreement. The entity is responsible for maintaining the equipment and for replacing it when the entity decides to do so. The useful life of the equipment is estimated to be three years. The outsourcing agreement requires service to be provided for ten years for a fixed price that is lower than the price the entity would have charged if the IT equipment had not been transferred.

IE7   In this example, the facts indicate that the IT equipment is an asset of the entity. Therefore, the entity should recognise the equipment and measure its cost on initial recognition at its fair value in accordance with paragraph 24 of IAS 16. The fact that the price charged for the service to be provided under the outsourcing agreement is lower than the price the entity would charge without the transfer of the IT equipment indicates that this service is a separately identifiable service included in the agreement. The facts also indicate that it is the only service to be provided in exchange for the transfer of the IT equipment. Therefore, the entity should recognise revenue arising from the exchange transaction when the service is performed, ie over the ten-year term of the outsourcing agreement.

IE8   Alternatively, assume that after the first three years, the price the entity charges under the outsourcing agreement increases to reflect the fact that it will then be replacing the equipment the customer transferred.

IE9   In this case, the reduced price for the services provided under the outsourcing agreement reflects the useful life of the transferred equipment. For this reason, the entity should recognise revenue from the exchange transaction over the first three years of the agreement.

3   Definition of revenue

IAS 18 defines revenue as the gross inflow of economic benefits during the period arising in the course of the ordinary activities of an entity when those inflows result in increases in equity, other than increases relating to contributions from equity participants. [IAS 18:7] Revenue includes such items as sales, fees, interest, dividends, royalties and rent.

The definition of revenue excludes contributions from equity participants. For example, when an entity issues warrants (options issued on the entity's own shares) for cash, the cash is credited to equity because the proceeds are received from an equity instrument. If the warrants lapse unexercised, no revenue is recognised. The fact that an equity participant no longer has an equity claim on the assets of the entity does not convert the equity contribution to revenue.

The disposal of non-current assets is a transaction that does not generate revenue. Instead, gains and losses on the disposal of non-current assets, including investments and operating assets, are reported by deducting from the proceeds on disposal the carrying amount of the asset and related selling expenses (see paragraph 34 of IAS 1 *Presentation of Financial Statements*).

However, when an entity, in the course of its ordinary activities, routinely sells items that it has held for rental to others, it transfers those assets to inventories at their carrying amount when they cease to be rented and become held for sale. Sales proceeds from such assets are recognised as revenue in accordance with IAS 18 (see paragraph 68A of IAS 16 *Property, Plant and Equipment*).

3.1 Gross or net presentation

Revenue includes only gross inflows of economic benefits that are received or receivable by the entity on its own account. The use of the word 'gross' in the definition of revenue is not intended to include amounts collected on behalf of others. For example, sales taxes collected by the entity and remitted to a customs authority will not be included as revenue. Likewise, collection agency revenue does not include the amounts actually collected on behalf of customers, but is restricted to the fee or commission relating to the collection. [IAS 18:8]

In an agency relationship, gross amounts collected by the agent on behalf of the principal are not benefits that flow to the agent and, therefore, they are not revenue. The agent's revenue is the amount of the commission. [IAS 18:8]

The following example, which is reproduced from the appendix to IAS 18, provides guidance on how to determine whether an entity is acting as a principal or as an agent.

Example 3.1A

Determining whether an entity is acting as a principal or as an agent
[IAS 18 Appendix: Example 21]

IAS 18:8 states that "in an agency relationship, the gross inflows of economic benefits include amounts collected on behalf of the principal and which do not result in increases in equity for the entity. The amounts collected on behalf of the principal are not revenue. Instead, revenue is the amount of

---

commission". Determining whether an entity is acting as a principal or as an agent requires judgement and consideration of all relevant facts and circumstances.

An entity is acting as a principal when it has exposure to the significant risks and rewards associated with the sale of goods or the rendering of services. Features that indicate that an entity is acting as a principal include:

(a)   the entity has the primary responsibility for providing the goods or services to the customer or for fulfilling the order, for example by being responsible for the acceptability of the products or services ordered or purchased by the customer;

(b)   the entity has inventory risk before or after the customer order, during shipping or on return;

(c)   the entity has latitude in establishing prices, either directly or indirectly, for example by providing additional goods or services; and

(d)   the entity bears the customer's credit risk for the amount receivable from the customer.

An entity is acting as an agent when it does not have exposure to the significant risks and rewards associated with the sale of goods or the rendering of services. One feature indicating that an entity is acting as an agent is that the amount the entity earns is predetermined, being either a fixed fee per transaction or a stated percentage of the amount billed to the customer.

The determination as to whether an entity is acting as a principal or as an agent will always depend on the specific facts and circumstances and it will generally be necessary to exercise judgement. The list of features in **example 3.1A** is not intended to be exhaustive. Moreover, in any particular scenario, some of the indicators may be judged more important than others, so it is not appropriate to apply a 'checklist' approach that would give equal weight to each.

Feature (a) above will frequently be considered a strong indicator of whether an entity is acting as a principal or as an agent. If one of the parties other than the reporting entity has the primary responsibility for providing the goods or services to the customer or for fulfilling the order (e.g. by being responsible for the acceptability of the products or services ordered or purchased by the customer), this will often indicate that the reporting entity is acting as an agent and not as a principal.

Sometimes an entity may be acting as an 'undisclosed agent', which means that the customer is not aware that the entity has agreed to act as agent for a third party. In many jurisdictions, an entity acting as an undisclosed agent has the same responsibilities to the customer as if it were a principal. When an entity acts as an undisclosed agent, it should consider whether, as a result, it has the primary responsibility for providing the goods or services to the customer or for fulfilling the order (e.g. in the event of a dispute, the customer's primary recourse would be against the entity). If so, feature (a) will be met, and it is likely that the entity should account as a principal. Such a conclusion is not typically affected by whether or not the third party supplier has indemnified the entity from loss.

Example 3.1B

Sales incentives – gross or net?

A vendor that sells its products and services through a retailer gives the retailer a cash incentive payment when a related service is sold to end customers in combination with the main product. For example, a retailer sells a warranty along with the vendor's product. The vendor's tariff schedules an additional CU10 to be received on this package. The retailer may or may not be required to follow the vendor's pricing policy. This warranty is serviced by the vendor and, therefore, the retailer's cost is zero. The retailer then remits CU8 (regardless of the actual price received from the end customer) to the vendor (or CU10 with a subsequent payment from the vendor to the retailer of CU2).

Whether the vendor should account for the incentive payment of CU2 as a reduction of revenue or as a promotion expense will depend on whether the retailer (intermediary) is acting as a principal or as an agent.

If the retailer is acting as an agent, the incentive payment to the retailer of CU2 is similar in substance to a commission and, therefore, should be treated as an expense by the vendor under IAS 18:8.

If, however, the retailer is acting as a principal, the incentive payment should be treated as a volume rebate and, accordingly, as a reduction in revenue under IAS 18:10.

Example 3.1C

Income tax withheld in a different country

Company X performs consulting services for Company C, which is in a different country from Company X. Company C withholds 20 per cent of Company X's fee as local income tax and transmits this amount to its local government on behalf of Company X. Company C pays the remaining 80 per cent balance to Company X. The countries do not have a tax treaty and Company X is not required to file a tax return in Company C's country. However, Company X may, at its option, file a tax return in Company C's country to recover taxes withheld in excess of its share of income. Company

X was fully aware that the 20 per cent income tax would be withheld in Company C's country when it agreed to perform the consulting services for Company C.

If Company X's fee is CU100 and Company C remits CU80 to Company X and CU20 to the local government, does Company X have revenue of CU100 and tax expense of CU20, or net revenue of CU80?

Company X has revenue of CU100 and income tax expense of CU20. Under Company C's local law, Company X is the primary obligor in the arrangement. The fact that the tax is paid by Company C on behalf of Company X does not affect the assessment of whether Company X is the primary obligor.

Example 3.1D

Value Added Tax (VAT) rebate

In Country C, software developers must pay 17 per cent VAT (this rate is consistent with VAT on other similar items) to the government when software is sold to distributors or end users, but 14 per cent is rebated by the government to the developer almost immediately, resulting in an effective 3 per cent VAT rate. This is well known by both the developer and the buyer, who factor it into the selling price. Even though the seller effectively pays 3 per cent, the buyer gets credit for 17 per cent if the software is resold. Assume software is sold for CU103 inclusive of VAT. This was negotiated based on selling price of CU100 plus effective VAT of CU3.

How much revenue should the seller recognise?

IAS 20 *Accounting for Government Grants and Disclosure of Government Assistance* defines a government grant as "assistance by government in the form of transfers of resources to an entity in return for past or future compliance with certain conditions relating to the operating activities of the entity". The 14 per cent VAT rebate is regarded as a government grant to encourage the software development industry. Therefore, the seller should recognise revenue of CU88 (CU103 ÷ 1.17) and government grant income of CU12 [(CU103 – CU88) × (14 ÷ 17)]. In accordance with IAS 20:29, government grants related to income may be presented separately or as 'other income'. The CU3 VAT is excluded from revenue under IAS 18:8.

Example 3.1E

Severance taxes

A government requires a mining or oil and gas producer to pay a 'severance tax' or other similar tax that is based on the value of minerals produced. The tax is payable even if the minerals are not sold.

In this case, the severance tax is an expense related to the production of the asset to be sold because the burden of the tax falls on the producer and is not dependent on sales. The producer is not considered an agent of the government for the purposes of collection of the severance tax. Therefore, the full amount of the sale should be included in revenue. This answer is appropriate even if, when the minerals are ultimately sold, the invoice shows the severance tax as a separate item.

If, on the other hand, the government levies tax only on products sold and such amounts are re-invoiced to the purchaser, the amount should be regarded as a sales tax that is excluded from revenue under IAS 18:8. In effect, the entity is acting as a collection agent for the government.

(Although revenue from the extraction of mineral ores is excluded from the scope of IAS 18, the severance tax issue is not excluded.)

Example 3.1F

Royalty payments

An entity is required by contract to pay a royalty to the government in respect of certain intangible assets. The royalty is specified as a percentage of gross proceeds from sales less costs applicable to the entity's share of production. The entity can pay the royalty in cash or in kind.

Should the royalty be netted against the entity's revenue or recognised as an operating expense?

The entity should recognise its revenue on a gross basis because it is the primary obligor in the arrangement. The royalty is recognised as an operating expense.

If the government is also a shareholder in the entity, these royalty payments should be differentiated from a distribution to shareholders in the form of a royalty.

Example 3.1G

Cash received from suppliers for 'supplementary services' (slotting fees, co-operative advertising etc.)

Company A operates a chain of supermarkets, selling food products to end consumers. Company A sells all products as a principal. To promote certain products, Company A receives cash from suppliers in respect of a variety of 'supplementary services'.

How should Company A account for the cash received in respect of supplementary services?

As a general principle, consideration received by a customer from a supplier should be presumed to be a reduction of the cost of the supplier's products and, therefore, should be accounted for by Company A as a reduction in the cost of inventories rather than as revenue. However, that presumption can be overcome in limited circumstances.

When amounts are received in respect of supplementary services, the following questions are appropriate.

- *Does the cash represent payment for goods or services supplied by Company A to the supplier that are separate and distinct from Company A's purchase of goods from the supplier?* This might arise, for example, if Company A carries out a specifically commissioned market survey on behalf of the supplier. When it is clear that such a transaction is separate from Company A's purchase of goods from the supplier, amounts received should be recognised as revenue.

- *Does the cash represent a reimbursement of costs incurred by Company A on behalf of the supplier?* For example, Company A may have incurred specific, incremental, identifiable advertising costs on behalf of the supplier. In such circumstances, the cash consideration should be accounted for as a reduction in the relevant cost (e.g. advertising) when recognised by Company A in profit or loss. Care should be exercised, however, in reaching a conclusion that costs have been incurred 'on behalf of' a supplier. Frequently, the nature of such 'co-operative' advertising arrangements is that they are primarily for the benefit of the supermarket rather than for the benefit of the supplier.

If the presumption is not overcome, the cash received should be accounted for as a reduction in the cost of the supplier's products. This will be the case, for example, if the amount paid to Company A is stated to be in return for 'prime' placement of the supplier's products in Company A's stores (these are sometimes referred to as 'slotting fees'). Slotting fees received should be treated as a reduction of the cost of inventories acquired (and, consequently, recognised as a reduction in cost of sales when the inventories are sold) in the period to which the slotting fees relate. For example, if Company A receives a slotting fee requiring it to give a supplier's product prime placement for one year, that fee received should reduce the cost of inventories purchased during that year. Frequently, the determination of the appropriate recognition period will require the exercise of judgement in the context of the specific facts and circumstances.

4   Measurement of revenue

Revenue is measured at the fair value of the consideration received or receivable. [IAS 18:9] Fair value is defined as follows:
[IAS 18:7]

- for entities applying IFRS 13, "the price that would be received to sell an asset or paid to transfer a liability in an orderly transaction between market participants at the measurement date"; and

- for entities that have not yet adopted IFRS 13, "the amount for which an asset could be exchanged, or a liability settled, between knowledgeable, willing parties in an arm's length transaction".

The application of IFRS 13's definition of fair value is discussed in detail in **chapter A6**.

4.1   Trade discounts allowed and similar items

In practice, revenue is usually determined by agreement between the entity and the buyer or user of the goods or services. Thus, the amount of revenue recognised for a transaction is net of any trade discounts or volume rebates given because these discounts and rebates are not received as consideration by the seller. [IAS 18:10]

At the meeting of the IFRIC (now the IFRS Interpretations Committee) in July 2004, IFRIC members agreed that prompt settlement discounts should be estimated at the time of sale and presented as a reduction in revenues.

Example 4.1

Cash discounts

A seller offers a cash discount for immediate or prompt payment (i.e. payment earlier than required by the normal credit terms). A sale is made for CU100 with the balance due within 90 days. If the customer pays within 10 days, the customer will receive a 2 per cent discount on the total invoice.

How should the seller account for this early payment incentive?

IAS 18:10 states that the amount of revenue arising on a transaction is the amount agreed by the buyer and seller. If the agreement between buyer and seller calls for payment within a relatively short period such as 90 days, and the environment is not hyperinflationary, a cash discount for prompt payment is not intended as a financing transaction. It is simply a way of identifying the amount agreed by the buyer and seller. It also can be viewed as a mechanism to enhance collectibility of the agreed amount. Therefore, the seller should recognise revenue net of the amount of cash discount taken. In the circumstances described, revenue is CU100 if the discount is not taken and CU98 if the discount is taken. If necessary, the seller should recognise revenue based on an estimate of the number of customers that will take the discount and 'true up' in the next reporting period for the actual number.

> This answer is consistent with the guidance in paragraph 11 of IAS 2 *Inventories*, which states that "[t]rade discounts, rebates, and other similar items are deducted in determining the costs of purchase".

Rebates and discounts are also considered in **example 3.1.1A** and **example 3.1.1B** in **chapter A11**.

4.2   Deferred consideration

In the majority of cases, the nominal amount of the consideration received or receivable will not vary materially from its fair value because most trade receivables are due within a relatively short time-frame. In the unusual circumstances when consideration is to be received outside such a short time-frame, the fair value of the consideration to be received will not be the same as the nominal amount of the consideration, due to the time value of money. Such an arrangement effectively includes a financing transaction. Therefore, to calculate the fair value of the consideration receivable, future receipts are discounted using an imputed interest rate which is the more clearly determinable of:
[IAS 18:11]

* the prevailing rate for a similar instrument of an issuer with a similar credit rating; or

* a rate of interest that discounts the nominal amount of the instrument to the current cash sales price of the goods or services.

When the second approach is taken, the resulting interest rate should be assessed for reasonableness. A rate that appears unrealistically low may indicate that the current cash sales price that would be appropriate for this particular customer has not been correctly identified.

The IFRIC (now the IFRS Interpretations Committee) considered the accounting for extended payment terms, such as six-months interest-free credit, at its meeting in July 2004. The Committee members agreed that IAS 39 *Financial Instruments: Recognition and Measurement* applies to the receivable in such circumstances, and that the effect of the time value of money should be reflected when this is material, in accordance with IAS 39:AG69 to AG82. For entities applying IFRS 9 *Financial Instruments*, this conclusion is equally applicable.

If material, the difference between the nominal amount of the consideration to be received and the discounted amount is recognised as interest revenue over the credit period, in accordance with the requirements of IAS 18 (see **section 8** below) and either IFRS 9 (see **section 4.1** of **chapter B6**) or, for entities that have not yet adopted IFRS 9, IAS 39 (see **section 4.1** of **chapter C6**).

Example 4.2A

Deferred consideration: discounting based on interest rate

An entity sells an item of equipment for CU100,000 under a financing agreement that has no stated interest rate. Annual instalments of CU20,000 are due each year for five years from the date of purchase. Thus, it is a 'zero percent' financing arrangement. The policy of not charging interest is consistent with normal industry practice.

Because industry practice is to allow deferred payment with no interest, there are no recent cash transactions from which the entity can make a reliable estimate of the cash sales price. The seller believes, however, that the buyer would be able to obtain financing from other sources at an interest rate of 10 per cent.

Step 1 Calculate the net present value of the stream of payments

Assuming no down payment, five annual instalments of CU20,000, and an interest rate of 10 per cent, the net present value of the stream of payments forming the consideration is CU75,816. Therefore, on the date of the sale, CU75,816 is recognised as revenue from the sale of goods and a related receivable is recognised.

Step 2 Calculate the amount of interest earned each period

The difference between CU100,000 and CU75,816 of CU24,184 will be recognised as interest revenue as it becomes due each year as calculated below.

	Principal amount outstanding (A) CU	Interest element of payment (Ax10% = B) CU	Principal element of payment (C-B) CU	Total payment (C) CU
End of Year 1	75,816	7,581	12,419	20,000
End of Year 2	63,397	6,340	13,660	20,000
End of Year 3	49,737	4,974	15,026	20,000
End of Year 4	34,711	3,471	16,529	20,000
End of Year 5	18,182	1,818	18,182	20,000
Total		24,184	75,816	100,000

Example 4.2B

Deferred consideration: discounting to current cash sales price

An entity sells an item of equipment for CU100,000 under a financing agreement. Annual instalments of CU20,000 are due each year for five years from the date of purchase. If the buyer had paid cash for the equipment, the sales price would have been CU80,000.

The selling entity should recognise the consideration at its fair value. Because there is a CU20,000 difference between the cash price of CU80,000 and the amount due if the equipment is paid for in instalments, the arrangement is effectively a financing transaction as well as the sale of goods. The amount of the consideration attributable to the sale of goods is the cash price of CU80,000. The remaining CU20,000 is interest revenue and is recognised as it becomes due each year using the effective interest method as illustrated below.

Step 1 Calculate the effective rate of interest

Because the cash price offered is CU80,000, it is necessary to determine the interest rate that discounts CU100,000 to CU80,000 over a 5-year period, assuming no down payment and five annual instalments of CU20,000. This interest rate is 7.93 per cent.

Step 2 Calculate the amount of interest earned each period

The difference of CU20,000 between CU100,000 and CU80,000 will be recognised as interest revenue as it becomes due each year, as calculated below.

	Principal amount outstanding	Interest element of payment	Principal element of payment	Total payment
	(A)	(Ax7.93% = B)	(C-B)	(C)
	CU	CU	CU	CU
End of Year 1	80,000	6,345	13,655	20,000
End of Year 2	66,345	5,262	14,738	20,000
End of Year 3	51,607	4,093	15,907	20,000
End of Year 4	35,700	2,831	17,169	20,000
End of Year 5	18,531	1,469	18,531	20,000
Total		20,000	80,000	100,000

4.3   Exchanges of goods or services

When goods or services are exchanged or swapped for goods or services of a similar nature and value, no revenue is recognised. [IAS 18:12] Such transactions occur in a limited number of commodity industries such as the oil or milk industries. These exchanges are generally made to help suppliers in the distribution of their products when they need a specific quantity of a commodity at a specific time in a particular location. In practice, this type of exchange of similar goods is relatively uncommon outside those industries. Another scenario in which this might apply, however, is when a wholesaler agrees that a retailer may return certain goods in exchange for others.

When goods or services are exchanged for dissimilar goods or services, a transaction that generates revenue has taken place and revenue is recognised. The revenue is measured at the fair value of the goods or services received, adjusted for any cash payments made by either the buyer or the seller. If the fair value of the goods or services received cannot be measured reliably, revenue is recognised at the fair value of the goods or services given up, adjusted for any cash payments made or received. [IAS 18:12]

When a dealer in used goods transacts with a customer and accepts other used goods in exchange, the allowance granted to the customer will typically be less than the price at which the dealer expects to resell. In effect, the customer is being charged a 'retail' price for the goods purchased but being granted only a 'wholesale' price for the goods traded in. Thus, even if the goods exchanged are similar (e.g. vehicles or CDs), their value is dissimilar because of the difference between wholesale and retail prices, and so the transaction will give rise to revenue. By contrast, when a dealer exchanges goods with a fellow dealer, both sides of the transaction are likely to be priced by reference to the 'wholesale' price. Thus, the goods will be similar in nature and value, and no revenue will be recognised.

Example 4.3A

Transport sales of oil

Company A owns and operates a pipeline to transport crude oil. Company A does not produce or distribute crude oil; it merely provides the use of its pipeline to the buyer and the seller in a contract for a usage fee. The seller and buyer independently negotiate the sales price and either the buyer or the seller pays a fee to Company A to transport the oil purchased/sold through the pipeline.

The pipeline needs to be full of oil at all times to be operational. Therefore, during initial construction of the pipeline, Company A purchases oil to fill the pipeline. Once the pipeline is operational, Company A charges a fixed fee for its transportation services and, in effect, swaps crude oil pushed into the pipeline by a seller for crude oil of the same grade and quality delivered to the customer at the exit point of the pipeline. Company A bears the risk of loss due to theft or line loss in excess of maximums allowed under the contract. Such losses are rare and normally arise as the result of a pipeline spill that is covered by insurance.

> *How should Company A recognise revenue, i.e. should it recognise revenue based on the agreed sale price for the oil or just the usage fee earned?*
>
> Company A should recognise revenue only for the fee earned for use of the pipeline.
>
> Company A's delivery of the oil from the pipeline to the ultimate customer (and replacement by equivalent product) is not regarded as a transaction that generates revenue in accordance with the requirements of IAS 18:12 (which prohibits the recognition of revenue on exchanges of goods which are 'of a similar nature and value').
>
> IAS 18 does not include any guidance on how to determine whether goods or services are of 'a similar nature or value' but, in the circumstances under consideration, it is clear that this criterion is met. In fact, the circumstances described would indicate that this is an exchange of 'identical' products.
>
> **Example 2A** in **chapter A11** addresses the appropriate classification and measurement of the pipeline fill in the circumstances described.

Example 4.3B

Transfer of inventories for an entity's own shares

Company A has produced inventories at a cost of CU80 that are normally sold to unrelated third parties at a price of CU100. Company A enters into a transaction to buy CU100 of its ordinary shares from a shareholder in return for CU100 of its inventories (priced at the retail rate).

How should Company A account for this transaction?

Company A should recognise revenue for the sale of its inventories for CU100 and treasury shares for CU100. The form of consideration should not have an impact on whether revenue is recognised. Company A would then recognise cost of sales and reduce inventories by CU80.

4.4   Barter transactions involving advertising services

SIC-31 *Revenue – Barter Transactions Involving Advertising Services* deals with the circumstances when an entity (the Seller) enters into a barter transaction to provide advertising services in exchange for receiving advertising services from its customer (the Customer). Such advertisements may be displayed on the Internet, poster sites, broadcast on television or radio, published in magazines or journals, or presented in another medium.

When the services exchanged are similar, the principles outlined at **4.3** above mean that no revenue can be recognised. When the services exchanged are dissimilar, revenue can be recognised provided that the amount of the revenue can be measured reliably. SIC-31 discusses the circumstances under which a Seller can reliably measure revenue at the fair value of advertising services received or provided in a barter transaction.

The Interpretation concludes that revenue from a barter transaction involving advertising services can never be measured reliably at the fair value of the advertising services received. [SIC-31:5]

The fair value of such barter transactions is reliably measurable only when it is supportable by reference to other transactions with knowledgeable and willing parties in an arm's length transaction. For such transactions to provide a relevant and reliable basis for support, the services involved must be similar, there must be many transactions, valuable consideration that can be reliably measured must be exchanged, and independent third parties must be involved. [SIC-31:8] The conditions set out below are designed to ensure that these characteristics are present.

Under SIC-31, a Seller can reliably measure revenue at the fair value of the advertising services it provides in a barter transaction, by reference only to non-barter transactions that:
[SIC-31:5]

- involve advertising similar to the advertising in the barter transaction;

- occur frequently;

- represent a predominant number of transactions and amount when compared to all transactions to provide advertising that is similar to the advertising in the barter transaction;

- involve cash and/or another form of consideration (such as marketable securities, non-monetary assets, and other services) that has a reliably measurable fair value; and

- do not involve the same counterparty as in the barter transaction.

4.5   Price regulation

Example 4.5

Revenue recognition in the pharmaceutical industry

The Pharmaceutical Price Regulation Scheme (PPRS) in Country A is a joint initiative between the pharmaceutical industry and the Department of Health (DH). The PPRS applies to all entities supplying branded, licensed medicines to the Public Health Service (PHS). The objectives of the PPRS are to ensure that the PHS buys medicines at reasonable prices while allowing pharmaceutical entities to earn a reasonable profit so that they are able to continue to invest in research and development activities. The PPRS operates by limiting the profits an entity can make from the supply of medicines to the PHS. The entity's return on capital employed is calculated based on the annual financial return. All excess profits earned over the prescribed limits for the current period are required to be refunded to the DH.

In the circumstances described, the pharmaceutical entities are effectively operating in a regulated market in which the prices they can charge are governed by an agreement with the DH. When the pharmaceutical entities are required to pay a refund to the DH because their profits have exceeded the allowed profits for the period, this is a reduction of the revenue already recognised and should be accounted for as such.

The appropriate accounting for government schemes to regulate the prices of pharmaceutical products should be determined based on the particular facts and circumstances of the government scheme under which the entity operates. Different types of regulations may exist in different jurisdictions; some may be in the nature of rebates or limits on profits whereas others may be in the nature of an expense.

5 Identification of the transaction

The recognition criteria specified by IAS 18 (as discussed in **sections 6** to **10** below) are usually applied separately to each transaction. To present the substance of a transaction appropriately, however, it may sometimes be necessary to apply the recognition criteria to the separately identifiable components of a single transaction. [IAS 18:13]

For example, a contract to sell software may include an element related to maintenance over a period of time. In such circumstances, it is appropriate to split the transaction into two components, a sale element and a maintenance element, and to apply the revenue recognition criteria to each component individually (see **5.1** below).

In other circumstances, several related transactions may, in substance, be part of one larger transaction when the transactions are linked in such a way that the commercial effect cannot be understood without reference to the series of transactions as a whole. For example, a seller may enter into a contract to sell goods but agree in a separate contract to repurchase the goods at a later date. In such circumstances, the revenue recognition criteria are applied to both transactions together to determine if revenue is recognised (see **5.2** below). [IAS 18:13]

5.1   Unbundling of separately identifiable components

IAS 18 does not provide any guidance on when or how to identify whether a transaction consists of separately identifiable components or how to allocate revenue to any separately identified components.

In determining the substance of a transaction, all of its aspects and implications should be identified and greater weight given to those more likely to have economic significance to the transacting parties at the time of entering into the transaction.

Generally, two or more components may have separate commercial substance and, therefore, be separately identifiable when, for example:

- one or more of the components may be seen as an 'optional extra' (i.e. the customer might reasonably choose to purchase the other components without purchasing these 'optional' components); or

- the individual components can be sourced independently of each other, thereby representing goods and/or services that can be purchased by a customer on a stand-alone basis from another supplier (i.e. the customer might reasonably buy one component from one supplier and the other component from a different, unrelated supplier).

When components are judged to be separately identifiable, it will still be necessary to consider whether it is possible to allocate revenue between them on a reliable basis, and also to consider when revenue should be recognised in respect of each component. In particular, revenue will only be recognised in respect of a separately identifiable component when all the revenue recognition criteria in IAS 18:14 (for goods) or IAS 18:20 (for services) are met (see **section 6** and **section 7**, respectively).

The fact that a seller may choose not to offer a particular component for sale by itself, but will only offer it for sale as part of a 'bundle', does not in itself preclude the component from being separately identifiable, because it is still possible that the component could be obtained on its own from a different, unrelated supplier. Conversely, the fact that a seller and customer enter into separate but simultaneous contracts for the supply of two components does not in itself prove that the components are separately identifiable, because it may be inconceivable that a customer would ever buy one without the other. Accordingly, care is always needed when assessing whether a component is separately identifiable.

Although IAS 18 does not require vendor-specific objective evidence in respect of the amount of revenue to be attributed to separately identifiable components, it is important that revenue is allocated on a reliable basis that reasonably reflects the selling prices that might be achieved in stand-alone transactions. In particular, the relative cost of components for the seller will not always be a good proxy for the price that might be achieved for each component in a sales transaction.

When selling prices are available for individual components, each separately identifiable component should be accounted for as a separate transaction in accordance with IAS 18 and the total consideration payable should be allocated to the individual components by reference to their selling prices. Often, when the 'bundled' transaction is provided at a price less than the aggregated separate selling prices of the individual components, it may be appropriate to allocate the discount or reduction to each component in proportion to its selling price. However, as noted in BC14 of IFRIC 13 *Customer Loyalty Programmes*, IAS 18 does not prescribe the use of this method, and management should use judgement in each case to select a method that will reasonably approximate the amount that the customer is paying for each component.

When separate selling prices are available only for the undelivered components, it may be appropriate to deduct these from the total transaction price to derive a selling price attributable to the delivered components (this is sometimes called the 'residual method'). However, care should be taken to ensure that revenue is not overstated in applying a similar technique when separate selling prices are available only for the delivered components (this is sometimes called the 'reverse residual method') because the 'bundled' transaction price may include a discount which will not be reflected in the normal separate selling prices of the delivered components.

In all cases, management should use judgement to ensure that the amount of revenue recognised appropriately reflects the extent to which components have been delivered to the customer. In making this judgement, consideration may be given to more detailed guidance in the most recent pronouncements of other standard-setting bodies that use a similar conceptual framework to develop accounting standards, to the extent that these do not conflict with the principles of IAS 18 (see paragraph 12 of IAS 8 *Accounting Policies, Changes in Accounting Estimates and Errors*).

5.2   Linked transactions

Although SIC-27 *Evaluating the Substance of Transactions Involving the Legal Form of a Lease* provides some guidance in the specific context of leases, IAS 18 itself provides little guidance with regards to which circumstances should cause a series of transactions to be grouped together for purposes of recognising revenue.

In assessing whether transactions should be grouped together, an entity should consider whether bundling is needed to reflect faithfully the substance of the transactions.

Factors to consider in making the assessment include, but are not limited to:

- the seller retains the risks and rewards embodied in the goods or services involved, even if legal ownership has been transferred (e.g. separate sale and repurchase agreements);

- the transactions are legally and/or economically conditional upon each other;

- the transactions were entered into at the same time with the same counterparties; and

- the individual transactions lack commercial substance when considered separately.

A typical example of transactions that may need to be grouped together for purposes of revenue recognition is a sale and subsequent repurchase when the main objective of the arrangement is to obtain financing rather than to dispose of the entity's assets. This is likely to be the case when it is clear from the outset that the seller will repurchase the asset and will pay a lender's return to the 'customer'. However, not all transactions involving a sale and subsequent repurchase will necessarily be grouped together. For example, if the repurchase price will be determined as the market value at the time of repurchase, it is possible that the significant risks and rewards of ownership may have been transferred to the customer, in which case it may still be appropriate to recognise revenue on the original sale transaction.

All relevant facts and circumstances should be considered together when assessing whether a series of transactions should be combined and accounted for as a single arrangement.

Example 7.3.3 in **chapter A17** illustrates the accounting for a linked transaction.

5.3 Sales arrangements in which the seller has partially performed its obligations

Failure to deliver one item or to perform one service specified in a sales arrangement does not necessarily preclude the immediate recognition of any revenue for that sales arrangement. IAS 18:13 notes that the revenue recognition criteria should be applied to the separately identifiable components of a single transaction. If all other recognition criteria are met, revenue can be recognised for a sales arrangement, notwithstanding the seller's remaining obligation for additional performance or delivery, as set out below.

Revenue from the sales arrangement can be recognised in full if the seller's remaining obligation is inconsequential or perfunctory. In such circumstances, costs expected to be incurred to fulfil the remaining obligation must be reliably estimable and accrued when the revenue is recognised. A remaining performance obligation is not inconsequential or perfunctory if:

- it is essential to the functionality of the delivered products or services (e.g. installation and/or training); or

- failure to complete the activities would result in the customer receiving a full or a not insignificant partial refund or the right to reject the products delivered or services performed to date.

In addition, a remaining performance obligation may not be inconsequential or perfunctory if:

- the seller does not have a demonstrated history of completing the remaining tasks in a timely manner and reliably estimating their costs;

- the cost or time to perform the remaining obligations for similar contracts historically has varied significantly from one instance to another;

- the skills or equipment required to complete the remaining activity are specialised or are not readily available in the marketplace;

- the cost of completing the obligation, or the fair value of the obligation, is more than insignificant in relation to such items as the total contract fee, gross profit and operating income;

- the period before the remaining obligation will be extinguished is lengthy; or

- the timing of payment of a portion of the sales price is coincident with completing performance of the remaining activity.

A portion of the revenue under the sales arrangement is also recognised when the seller has substantially fulfilled the terms of a separately identifiable component of the arrangement. The examples set out in the appendix to IAS 18 illustrate a number of such circumstances (see later sections of this chapter).

5.4   Up-front fees

In general, unless up-front fees are paid in exchange for products delivered or services performed and, therefore, substantial risks and rewards have been transferred to the buyer in a separate transaction as described in IAS 18:13, such fees are not recognised as revenue up front but rather deferred as unearned revenue (even if they are non-refundable). An up-front fee might not be regarded as relating to a separate transaction if, for example:

- the up-front fee is negotiated in conjunction with the pricing of other elements;

- the customer would ascribe no value to the up-front activity in the absence of the performance of the other elements of the arrangement; or

- the vendor does not sell the initial right or activities separately.

The up-front, non-refundable fees should be recognised as revenue over the life of the agreement(s) to which they relate, by reference to the goods and services supplied under the agreement(s).

In 2007, the IFRIC (now the IFRS Interpretations Committee) considered the question of up-front fees in the context of investment management fees (see the January 2007 edition of *IFRIC Update*). The IFRIC noted that IAS 18:13 states that "the recognition criteria [in IAS 18] are applied to two or more transactions together when they are linked in such a way that the commercial effect cannot be understood without reference to the series of transactions as a whole".

The IFRIC agreed that:

- fees may be recognised as revenue only to the extent that services have been provided;

- while the proportion of costs incurred in delivering services may be used to estimate the stage of completion of the transaction, incurring costs does not by itself imply that a service has been provided;

- the receipt of a non-refundable initial fee does not, in itself, give evidence that an up-front service has been provided or that the fair value of the consideration paid in respect of any up-front services is equal to the initial fee received; and

- to the extent that:

  - an initial service can be shown to have been provided to a customer,

  - the fair value of the consideration received in respect of that service can be measured reliably, and

  - the conditions for the recognition of revenue in IAS 18 have been met, up-front and ongoing fees may be recognised as revenue in line with the provision of services to the customer.

The IFRIC noted that a wide range of business models utilising initial and ongoing fees exist in different markets. The services provided and the revenue that may be recognised in each situation depend on the facts and circumstances relevant to each model.

Example 5.4A

Up-front payment by customer – lifetime membership fees in a private club

Company A owns and operates a private club. New members have an option of paying a single up-front, non-refundable lifetime membership fee rather than monthly or annual payments. That fee entitles members to most, but not all, of the club's services for the member's life. Lifetime members must pay separately for those services not covered by the lifetime membership fee.

How should revenue from the lifetime membership fee be recognised?

Revenue should be recognised rateably over the time the individual may be expected to require the services of the club. IAS 18:20 (see **section 7**) requires that revenue from a service transaction should be recognised by reference to the stage of completion of the transaction. The club member would not pay an up-front membership fee in the absence of on-going usage of the club's services. Moreover, the pricing of the lifetime membership fee and the monthly usage fee are interrelated.

Example 5.4B

Up-front payment by supplier – outsourcing arrangements

When entering into an outsourcing arrangement with a client, a service provider may make an up-front payment to the client.

How should up-front payments be treated when made to clients by service providers in the context of outsourcing arrangements?

The amount of the up-front payment and the price charged for the service provided are generally part of a global pricing agreement for that service. To the extent that the up-front payment does not correspond to an identifiable service received by the service provider from the client, or to the reimbursement by the service provider of costs necessary for the contract incurred by the client, the amount of the up-front payment should be accounted for by the service provider as a reduction of revenue.

As a result, the up-front payment would be accounted for by the service provider as an asset (rebate paid in advance) and amortised against revenue over the contract period.

5.5   IFRIC 13 *Customer Loyalty Programmes*

Entities use customer loyalty programmes to incentivise customers to buy their goods or services. Customers buying goods or services are granted customer award credits (often described as 'points') by the entity, which can be redeemed for awards such as free or discounted goods or services.

IFRIC 13 addresses the accounting by the entity that grants award credits. It applies to customer loyalty award credits that:
[IFRIC 13:3]

- entities grant to their customers as part of an IAS 18 sales transaction (a sale of goods, rendering of services, or use by the customer of entity assets); and

- the customers can redeem in future for free or discounted goods or services, subject to meeting any further qualifying conditions.

Customer loyalty programmes operate in a number of ways. Customers may not be permitted to redeem award credits until they have accumulated a specified minimum number or value. Award credits may be linked to individual purchases or groups of purchases, or to continued custom over a specified period. Entities may operate their own customer loyalty programmes or may participate in programmes operated by third parties. The awards offered may include goods or services supplied by the entity itself and/or rights to claim goods or services from a third party. [IFRIC 13:2]

> IFRIC 13 also applies when the sales transaction giving rise to award credits involves the entity receiving consideration from an intermediate party rather than directly from the customer to whom it grants the award credits. For example, credit card providers may provide services and grant award credits to credit card holders but receive consideration for doing so from vendors accepting payment by credit card. [IFRIC 13:BC4]
>
> The Interpretation is not applicable to 'money-off' vouchers that are distributed free of charge, or any other sort of promotion that is not connected to sales of an entity's goods or services. It also does not cover the accounting for the goods acquired initially or the accounting for the award credits by the customer.

IFRIC 13 requires entities to account for award credits supplied in the context of a customer loyalty programme as a separately identifiable component of the sales transaction(s) in which they are granted (applying the requirements of IAS 18:13). The fair value of the consideration received or receivable is allocated between the award credits and the other components of the sale. [IFRIC 13:5] The consideration allocated to the award credits is measured by reference to their fair value. [IFRIC 13:6]

> Prior to the application of IFRS 13 *Fair Value Measurement*, IFRIC 13 stated that the fair value of the award credits is "the amount for which the award credits could be sold separately". For entities that have adopted IFRS 13, the definition of fair value included in that Standard should be applied (see **section 4**).

Accordingly, when accounting for customer loyalty programmes, an entity is required to:

- allocate some of the consideration received or receivable from the sales transaction to the award credits and defer the recognition of that revenue; and

- recognise its share of revenue allocated to the award credits when it has fulfilled its obligations in respect of the award credits. Note that the amount and timing of revenue will typically be different depending on whether the awards are supplied by the entity itself (as principal) or by a third party (with the entity acting as an agent in respect of the award credits).

5.5.1   *Measuring the fair value of award credits*

The consideration allocated to award credits is measured by reference to their fair value.
[IFRIC 13:AG1]

- For entities applying IFRS 13, if there is not a quoted market price for an identical award credit, fair value must be measured using another valuation technique.

- For entities that have not yet adopted IFRS 13, if the fair value is not directly observable, it must be estimated.

The fair value measurement should take into account (1) the amount of the discounts or incentives that would otherwise be offered to customers who have not earned award credits from an initial sales transaction; (2) the proportion of the award credits not expected to be redeemed by customers; and (3) for entities applying IFRS 13, non-performance risk. [IFRIC 13:AG2]

> When the fair value of award credits is measured on the basis of the value of the awards for which they could be redeemed, the fair value of the award credits should take account of expected forfeitures as well as the discounts or incentives that would otherwise be offered to customers who have not earned award credits from an initial sale. [IFRIC 13:BC14A]

Example 5.5.1A

Impact of awards granted without an initial sales transaction

All visitors to Supermarket B can pick up a voucher entitling them to a reduction of CU1 off the price of Product X, irrespective of whether they make any purchases. Customers who make a purchase receive a voucher entitling them to a reduction of CU5 off the price of Product X. Only one voucher can be used for any purchase of Product X.

The CU1 vouchers are outside the scope of IFRIC 13 because they are not granted as part of a sales transaction.

In contrast, the CU5 vouchers are within the scope of IFRIC 13. Accordingly, in assessing the fair value of the CU5 vouchers for the purposes of applying that Interpretation, Supermarket B will take into account (1) the fact that customers not making a purchase could still have claimed a CU1 voucher, and (2) the number of vouchers not expected to be redeemed. Although the CU5 vouchers are not sold separately, it is clear that no customer would rationally pay more than CU4 for such a voucher because it would instead be cheaper to buy Product X using one of the free CU1 vouchers. Thus, the fair value of the CU5 vouchers will not exceed CU4, and may be lower depending on the proportion of vouchers expected to be redeemed.

If there is a range of awards that customers may choose from, the fair value of the award credits reflects the fair values of the range of available awards, weighted in proportion to the frequency with which each award is expected to be selected. [IFRIC 13:AG2]

A range of valuation techniques may be used for the purposes of measuring the fair value of awards. The Application Guidance to IFRIC 13 gives as an example the scenario in which a third party will supply the awards and the entity pays the third party for each award credit it grants; in these circumstances, the entity could measure the fair value of the award credits by reference to the amount it pays the third party, adding a reasonable profit margin. Importantly, judgement is required to select and apply the valuation technique that satisfies the requirements of IFRIC 13:6 and is most appropriate in the circumstances. [IFRIC 13:AG3]

As noted above, IFRIC 13 states that award credits should be measured "*by reference to* their fair value" (emphasis added). But it does not mandate any particular method for allocating amounts to the award credits. In particular, it does not specify whether the amount allocated to the award credits should be:
[IFRIC 13:BC14]

- equal to their fair value (irrespective of the fair values of the other components); or

- a proportion of the total consideration based on the fair value of the award credits relative to the fair values of the other components of the sale.

This is because the IFRIC (now the IFRS Interpretations Committee) decided that the Interpretation should not be more prescriptive than IAS 18, which does not specify which of these methods should be applied, or in what circumstances. Management must apply judgement in deciding to select one or other method.

The former approach involves measuring the fair value of award credits (e.g. by reference to the goods and services that may be selected, as discussed in IFRIC 13:AG2 – see above), and then allocating any residual revenue to the original sale. This is illustrated in **example 5.5.1B** below.

Example 5.5.1B

Valuing award credits by reference to goods and services that may be selected

Customers buying Product A from Company X for CU100 receive an award credit. The award credit can be used to obtain Product B free of charge, or to purchase Product C at a discounted price of CU10.

The normal selling prices of Product B and Product C are:

Product B CU5

Product C CU17

Company X estimates that 60 per cent of customers will select Product B, 30 per cent will select Product C and 10 per cent will not redeem the award credit. Company X estimates that the effect of non-performance risk is insignificant.

The fair value of the award credit may be measured as:

(60% x CU5) + (30% x [CU17 – CU10]) + (10% x CU0) = CU5.10

Accordingly, the revenue recognised in respect of Product A is CU94.90 (i.e. CU100.00 – CU5.10).

An alternative approach is to make an allocation based on relative fair values as illustrated in **example 5.5.1C** below.

Example 5.5.1C

Valuing award credits by reference to relative fair values

The facts are the same as in **example 5.5.1B**, but Company X decides to use a relative fair value approach to allocate revenue to the award credits.

The normal selling price of Product A, after taking into account discounts that are usually offered but that are not available during this promotion, is CU96.

The total revenue of CU100 is allocated between Product A and the award credit by reference to their relative fair values of CU96 and CU5.10, respectively. Accordingly:

- Revenue for Product A = CU100 x (CU96 ÷[CU96 + CU5.10]) = CU94.95

- Revenue from the award credit = CU100 x (CU5.10 ÷[CU96 + CU5.10]) = CU5.05

5.5.2   Awards supplied by the reporting entity

If the entity will supply the awards itself, it recognises the consideration allocated to award credits as revenue when award credits are redeemed and it fulfils its obligations to supply awards. The amount of revenue recognised is based on the number of award credits that have been redeemed in exchange for awards, relative to the total number expected to be redeemed. [IFRIC 13:7]

5.5.2.1   Changes in expectations

After granting award credits, the entity may revise its expectations about the proportion that will be redeemed. The change in expectations does not affect the consideration that the entity has received for supplying awards (this is fixed at the outset), but it affects the amount of revenue recognised in respect of award credits that are redeemed in the period. The change in expectations is thus accounted for as a change in estimate in the period of change and future periods, in accordance with IAS 8:36 (see **4.2** in **chapter A5**). [IFRIC 13:BC16]

Example 5.5.2.1

Awards supplied by the entity

[IFRIC 13:Illustrative example 1]

A grocery retailer operates a customer loyalty programme. It grants programme members loyalty points when they spend a specified amount on groceries. Programme members can redeem the points for further groceries. The points have no expiry date. In one period, the entity grants 100 points. Management measures the fair value of groceries for which each loyalty point can be redeemed as 1.25 currency units (CU1.25). This amount takes into account management's estimate of the discount that market participants would assume when pricing the award credits. That discount takes into account market participants' expectations of the discount that would otherwise be offered to customers who have not earned award credits from an initial sale. In addition, management estimates that market participants would expect only 80 of these points to be redeemed. Therefore, the fair value of each point is CU1, being the fair value of the award for each loyalty point granted of CU1.25 reduced to take into account points not expected to be redeemed ((80 points/100 points) × CU1.25 = CU1). Accordingly, management defers recognition of revenue of CU100. Throughout the example, management determines that non-performance risk has an immaterial effect on the measurement of its obligation under the programme.

Year 1

At the end of the first year, 40 of the points have been redeemed in exchange for groceries, i.e. half of those expected to be redeemed. The entity recognises revenue of (40 points / 80[1] points) × CU100 = CU50.

Year 2

In the second year, management revises its estimates of market participants' expectations. It now expects 90 points to be redeemed altogether.

During the second year, 41 points are redeemed, bringing the total number redeemed to 40[2]+ 41 = 81 points. The cumulative revenue that the entity recognises is (81 points / 90[3] points) × CU100 = CU90. The entity has recognised revenue of CU50 in the first year, so it recognises CU40 in the second year.

consideration for doing so. Therefore the retailer recognises revenue from the points when it sells the electrical goods.

Revenue measurement

If the retailer has collected the consideration allocated to the points on its own account, it measures its revenue as the gross CU10,000 allocated to them. It separately recognises the CU9,000 paid or payable to the airline as an expense. If the retailer has collected the consideration on behalf of the airline, i.e. as an agent for the airline, it measures its revenue as the net amount it retains on its own account. This amount of revenue is the difference between the CU10,000 consideration allocated to the points and the CU9,000 passed on to the airline.

If, at the time of the original transaction, it is made clear to the customer that a third party will be obliged to supply the awards, it is likely that the entity is collecting consideration on behalf of that third party. Conversely, if the customer believes that the entity itself is obliged to supply the awards, it is likely that the entity is collecting consideration on its own account.

5.6   Prepaid minutes cards and similar arrangements

Many entities in the telecom industry offer customers 'prepaid minutes' cards under which customers acquire prepaid cards entitling them to a fixed number of minutes. The period of redemption may be fixed or may extend indefinitely.

Other entities offer 'rollover minutes' arrangements under which customers acquire a fixed amount of minutes per month for a fixed fee. Unused minutes in a specific month can be carried forward to the next month. The arrangements either contemplate a maximum number of months over which the minutes can be rolled forward or that carryforward can be indefinite.

The question arises as to when revenue related to the prepaid minutes cards and rollover minutes should be recognised.

Under IAS 18:13, when a transaction consists of the delivery of separately identifiable components, the proceeds of the transaction are allocated to each component and recognised when the conditions for revenue recognition applicable to the specific component are satisfied.

However, IAS 18 does not provide guidance on how to achieve this result. Accordingly, an entity should establish a systematic methodology to allocate the proceeds from the sale of prepaid minutes cards (or rollover minutes) and recognise revenue associated with each minute based on this allocation method. One such allocation method is described in paragraph 7 of IFRIC 13 *Customer Loyalty Programmes*, which states that the "amount of revenue recognised shall be based on the number of award credits that have been redeemed ..., relative to the total number expected to be redeemed".

Accordingly, following the hierarchy guidance specified in IAS 8:10 to 12, to the extent that a reliable estimate can be made of the expected number of minutes to be used, a method reflecting expected utilisation, such as the one described in IFRIC 13:7, is considered preferable when determining how to recognise revenue related to prepaid minutes cards and rollover minutes.

Nonetheless, other methods (e.g. a method under which each minute is valued at the same amount and only recognised upon use by the customer or on expiry) may also be acceptable if they reflect the substance of the transaction (e.g. if the number of minutes expected to be used cannot be reliably estimated).

Note that this conclusion does not apply to arrangements under which the customers can request a cash settlement for the unused minutes, because that would be a financial liability within the scope of IFRS 9 *Financial Instruments* (or, for entities that have not yet adopted IFRS 9, IAS 39 *Financial Instruments: Recognition and Measurement*).

6   Recognition criteria – sale of goods

Revenue from the sale of goods should be recognised when all of the following criteria have been satisfied:
[IAS 18:14]

- the entity has transferred to the buyer the significant risks and rewards of ownership of the goods (see **6.1**);

- the entity retains neither continuing managerial involvement to the degree usually associated with ownership nor effective control over the goods sold (see **6.2**);

- the amount of revenue can be measured reliably (see **6.3**);

- it is probable that the economic benefits associated with the transaction will flow to the entity (see **6.4**); and

- the costs incurred or to be incurred in respect of the transaction can be measured reliably (see **6.5**).

IAS 18 offers no guidance on how to determine whether a contract is for the supply of goods or services and, in some circumstances, careful judgement may be required. In particular, merely because a contract requires items to be supplied that have not yet been manufactured, it does not necessarily follow that the contract is for manufacturing services (see the further discussion at **2.2** above).

6.1 Risks and rewards of ownership

The circumstances of the transaction must be examined to assess when a seller has transferred the significant risks and rewards of ownership to the buyer. Generally, the transfer of the risks and rewards of ownership coincides with the transfer of the legal title or the passing of possession to the buyer, as for example with most retail sales. Sometimes, however, the transfer of risks and rewards of ownership occurs at a different time from the transfer of legal title or the passing of possession. [IAS 18:15]

If significant risks of ownership are retained by the seller, the transaction is not a sale and revenue is not recognised. Such significant risks of ownership may be retained in a number of ways. Examples given by IAS 18 are: [IAS 18:16]

(a) when the seller retains an obligation for unsatisfactory performance not covered by normal warranty provisions;

(b) when the receipt of the revenue from a particular sale is contingent on the derivation of revenue by the buyer from its sale of the goods;

(c) when the goods are shipped subject to installation and the installation is a significant part of the contract which has not yet been completed by the entity; and

(d) when the buyer has the right to rescind the purchase for a reason specified in the sales contract and the seller is uncertain about the probability of return.

In addition to the examples listed above, the fact that the seller has retained the risk of physical damage, or will share in the proceeds from the onward sale of the goods, may provide evidence that significant risks and rewards of ownership have not been transferred. Similarly, when the seller has a fixed price repurchase option, or the buyer lacks economic substance outside of the transaction (e.g. it is a structured or special purpose entity set up for the purpose of the transaction), these may be further indications that a sale has not taken place.

If only an insignificant risk of ownership is retained by the seller, the transaction is a sale and revenue is recognised. For example, solely to protect the collectibility of the amount due, a seller may retain the legal title to goods. Provided that the seller has transferred the significant risks and rewards of ownership, the transaction is a sale and revenue is recognised. Similarly, an insignificant risk of ownership may be retained by the seller in a retail sale when a refund is offered if the customer is not satisfied. Revenue in such cases is recognised at the time of sale provided that the seller can reliably estimate future returns and recognises a liability and corresponding reduction in revenue for returns based on previous experience and other relevant factors. [IAS 18:17]

The examples below illustrate some common situations in which the risks and rewards of ownership have or have not been transferred.

Example 6.1A

Warranty

An entity supplies an item of machinery and gives a 3-month warranty covering the cost of any adjustments or repairs subsequent to delivery. Because of the need to suit the particular customer's environment, the product is likely to have some serious problems that will require remedy after delivery. It is not possible to estimate reliably the cost to the seller of carrying out any such adjustments or repairs. Under the terms of the sales contract, title passes from the seller to the buyer on delivery.

Revenue should be recognised when the warranty expires. The risks and rewards of ownership do not pass from the seller to the buyer until the 3-month period has expired because it is not possible to estimate reliably, and therefore accrue, any costs of repairs or adjustments under the warranty, which could be material.

Example 6.1B

CDs distributed on the basis of sale or return

A distributor of CDs sells and delivers CDs to a local shop for a fixed price. To the extent that the local shop succeeds in selling the CDs, it does so as principal; it is the primary obligor in the relationship with the end customer, and can choose how to price the CDs. If the local shop does not sell the CDs, they are returned to the distributor for a full refund or credit. It is not possible to estimate reliably at the time the CDs are delivered how many CDs will not be sold.

Revenue should be recognised by the distributor when the CDs are sold by the local shop. The risks and rewards of ownership do not pass from the distributor until the shop has sold the CDs because the receipt of revenue by the distributor is contingent on the sale of the CDs by the shop and the distributor is unable to estimate reliably how many CDs will not be sold.

Example 6.1C

Equipment sold subject to right of return

A heavy equipment manufacturer sells an item of machinery to a customer who is anticipating being awarded a particular road-building contract from the government. The sales contract gives the customer the right to return the machinery if the customer does not win the contract. There is no way to estimate reliably whether the customer will return the machinery.

Revenue should be recognised when the contract has been awarded. The risks and rewards of ownership do not pass from the seller to the buyer until the customer has been granted the road-building contract by the government. Until then, the manufacturer is exposed to the risk that the machinery may be returned, and it is not possible to estimate reliably whether the machinery will be returned.

Example 6.1D

Retail guarantee

A retail shop offers a lifetime guarantee on its products. A customer may return any item for any reason at any time and have its purchase price refunded. Based on reliable, historical data, 0.95 per cent of sales are returned under this policy.

On the basis of historical data, the shop retains only insignificant risks and rewards of ownership by offering this guarantee. Provided that the other revenue recognition criteria are met, revenue should be recognised at the time of sale for those items that are not expected to be returned (i.e. 99.05 per cent of sales) and the balance of 0.95 per cent should be recognised as a liability to cover the amounts expected to be refunded because of sales returns.

Example 6.1E

Retention of title

As a matter of policy, a manufacturer writes its sales contracts in such a way that legal title does not pass on delivery but when consideration for the goods is received. A sale is made and the related goods are delivered to a customer who is not a particular credit risk.

The risks and rewards of ownership have passed from the seller to the buyer even though title has not. Transfer of title may be an indicator that the risks and rewards of ownership have passed to the buyer, but it is not a required condition. Therefore, provided that the other revenue recognition criteria are met, revenue can be recognised if the only rights that a seller retains with the title are those enabling recovery of the goods in the event of customer default on payment.

Example 6.1F

'Trade loading' and 'channel stuffing'

Sometimes manufacturers or dealers try to enhance the apparent volume of their sales, profits, and/or market share by inducing their wholesale customers to buy more product than they can promptly resell. The result is accelerated, but not increased, volume, because the wholesalers' inventories become bloated and their future orders from the manufacturers are reduced. This practice is known as 'trade loading' or 'channel stuffing'.

Entities may induce wholesale customers to buy more product than they can promptly resell for reasons other than enhancing the appearance of their financial figures (e.g. to improve cash flows or to spread production more evenly throughout the year when sales are seasonal). If the revenue recognition criteria in IAS 18:14 for sales of goods are met, the revenue should be recognised. In many situations, however, products sold during 'channel stuffing' programmes are merely held by the wholesaler to be returned in a future accounting period when it is determined the products cannot be sold to the end user. Assuming the criteria in IAS 18:14 are met, which will require that the level of returns can be estimated reliably, revenue is recognised net of the expected returns. Therefore, management must estimate the amount of product to be returned. Historical return rates may not capture appropriately the high level of returns usually related to 'channel stuffing' programmes. If the level of returns cannot be estimated reliably, revenue should not be recognised.

Example 6.1G

Unlimited right of return

Company A distributes DVDs. Its key customers are department stores but it also sells to small shops. The sales agreements with key customers allow these customers to return any slow-moving goods, but there is no definition of 'slow-moving' in the agreements. The returns could result in replacement of the returned goods with other DVDs or return of cash. For customers other than the key customers, the sales agreement limits their returns of slow-moving goods to not more than 10 per cent of purchases. In both cases, on the basis of experience, Company A is able to make a reliable estimate of the amount of returns.

How should Company A account for its revenues from (1) key customers (whose right to return goods is unlimited), and (2) other customers (whose right of return is limited)?

A condition for recognising revenue from the sale of goods in IAS 18:14(a) is that the entity has transferred to the buyer the significant risks and rewards of ownership of the goods. In the circumstances described, both classes of customers have assumed all of the significant *rewards* of ownership of the goods, because they have an unrestricted right to resell the goods. Furthermore, because a reliable estimate of the amount of returns can be made for both classes of customers, the extent to which the buyer has assumed the significant *risks* also can be measured for both classes of customers. Therefore, revenue should be recognised on initial delivery of the goods at an amount that reflects a reduction for estimated returns.

The answer would be different for the key customers if the effect of their right to return all slow-moving goods could not be measured. In those circumstances, Company A would have retained an immeasurable risk of marketability and obsolescence. The condition in IAS 18:14(a) would not be met, and Company A would recognise revenue on a consignment basis (i.e. recognise revenue when the key customers resell the goods to third-party customers).

Example 6.1H

Customer acceptance provision

A sales contract may give the customer the unilateral right, for a specified period after delivery, to accept or reject the goods. The appropriate point for revenue recognition will depend on the probability of customer acceptance. If the seller is uncertain about the probability of acceptance, revenue recognition should not occur until the earlier of customer acceptance and expiry of the acceptance period. If the probability of customer acceptance is uncertain, the risks of ownership must be regarded as remaining with the seller.

For example, Manufacturer A produces a ball bearing for use in the manufacture of automobiles. The buyer of the ball bearing requires defects to be less than 1.0 part per million (ppm). These ball bearings are tested prior to shipment through sample analysis to ensure their quality meets the requirements of the buyer. After the sample testing is completed, it is determined that the error rate is 0.8 ppm.

Therefore, on delivery, Manufacturer A can be reasonably certain that the goods meet the specifications of the buyer and can recognise revenue. If testing was not completed or showed a probability of customer rejection, revenue would not be recognised until customer acceptance is provided.

Example 6.1I

Sale of gift certificates

Gift certificates sold by a retailer can be used by the holder to buy merchandise up to the amount indicated on the gift certificate.

Sales revenue should not be recognised for gift certificates at the time that the gift certificate is sold. Gift certificates represent prepayments of cash that can be redeemed for merchandise at a later date. Revenue is not recognised until the gift certificate is redeemed for merchandise. Instead, the retailer recognises the proceeds from gift certificates as a liability, representing the obligation to deliver merchandise at a future time.

Example 6.1J

Sale of products with a time restriction on resale or use

Company A, a manufacturer of designer clothing, ships clothing for the spring season to customers (clothing retailers) in December 20X1. Although the customers take title to the goods when they receive them, the terms of the sales prohibit the customers from displaying or selling the clothing until 15 February 20X2. The terms of the arrangement are such that payment generally is not due until the restriction is lifted.

Should revenue be recognised when the goods are delivered (20X1) or when the restriction on resale expires (20X2)?

The limitation on when the product can be sold would not, of itself, preclude revenue recognition in 20X1. IAS 18:14(a) prohibits revenue recognition until the seller has transferred to the buyer the significant risks and rewards of ownership of the goods. In the circumstances described, the timing is short compared to the life cycle of the inventories and the timing of the restriction does not affect the value of the inventories to be sold. However, if the delay were longer (e.g. until the summer season), a review of whether the significant rewards of ownership had been transferred should be performed.

6.1.1   Impact of local law

The transfer of the risks and rewards of ownership often coincides with the transfer of legal title, the timing of which can vary according to the law in the relevant jurisdiction. This does not mean that different revenue recognition criteria are applied in different jurisdictions but, rather, that the recognition criteria are met at different times in different jurisdictions. The principle is that the significant risks and rewards of ownership must have passed from the seller to the buyer. [IAS 18:Appendix]

Examples of legal requirements that can affect the transfer of risks and rewards and, therefore, the timing of revenue recognition, include:

- in some jurisdictions, title does not legally transfer until the buyer obtains physical possession of the goods; and

- a 'cooling off' period is required in property transactions (often residential property transactions) in certain jurisdictions, during which the buyer has an absolute legal right to rescind the transaction.

6.1.2   When are risks and rewards transferred?

Products may be delivered based on oral arrangements (e.g. either a telephone call from a customer or walk-in business) or on the basis of a detailed contract with specified shipping terms, with many variations in between. The judgement as to when all risks and rewards of ownership have been transferred is a determination that should consider the laws of the jurisdiction in which the sale is made, particularly if the contract does not specify shipping terms. In complex circumstances, it may be useful to obtain the advice of legal counsel regarding the rights and obligations of the parties.

The revenue recognition criteria in IAS 18 should be evaluated based on the mutually understood terms of the transaction. IAS 18 does not require a written sales agreement as a condition for revenue recognition. IAS 18 does require transfer of the significant risks and rewards of ownership of the goods from the seller to the buyer. This means that both the buyer and the seller should have a clear understanding of all terms of the transaction, including pricing, payment terms, return rights, shipping, installation and warranty rights. When there is a written sales agreement, these terms should be clearly set out. When an entity routinely provides goods or services based on oral agreements, there is an expectation that, if necessary, the entity will have clearly articulated its policies and terms of sale to its customers through brochures, store signage, notices on invoices, advertising and similar written means.

Although IAS 18 does not require a written contract as evidence of an agreement, if such a contract is being prepared and has not yet been signed, this may be evidence that agreement has not yet been reached. Great care should be taken before recognising revenue in such circumstances because the apparent absence of a contractual understanding between the parties may make it unlikely that the conditions in IAS 18:14 have been met.

Example 6.1.2A

Goods shipped FOB shipping point, but seller arranges shipping

When goods are shipped 'free on board' (FOB) shipping point, title passes to the buyer when the goods are shipped and the buyer is responsible for any loss in transit. On the other hand, when goods are shipped FOB destination, title does not pass to the buyer until delivery and the seller is responsible for any loss in transit.

Company A sells goods FOB shipping point and it is clear that title transfers to the buyer at the time of shipment. Company A's business practice is to arrange for shipping the goods to the buyer and to deal directly with the shipping company. Company A invoices the buyer for the shipping costs separately from the product. Company A's business practice is also that if there is any damage or physical loss during transit, Company A provides the buyer with replacement products at no additional cost. If the loss or damage in transit is substantial, Company A's insurance would cover all or most of the loss.

In the circumstances described, it is not appropriate for Company A to recognise revenue at the time its products have been shipped. While title has passed, Company A has retained a significant risk of ownership (i.e. responsibility for damage or loss in transit). The fact that Company A's insurance would cover a substantial loss is evidence that it has managed its risk, but Company A has still retained the risk. The criterion for recognising revenue set out in IAS 18:14(a) has not been met.

Example 6.1.2B

Goods shipped FOB destination, but shipping company assumes risk of loss

Company A sells goods 'free on board' (FOB) destination, which means that title does not pass to the buyer until delivery and Company A is responsible for any loss in transit. To protect itself from loss, Company A contracts with the shipping company for the shipping company to assume total risk of loss while the goods are in transit.

In the circumstances described, it is not appropriate for Company A to recognise revenue when the goods are shipped. While Company A has managed its risk, it has not transferred risk to the buyer. Therefore, the criterion in IAS 18:14(a) has not been met until the goods have been delivered.

Example 6.1.2C

Seller arranges for manufacturer to ship directly to buyer ('drop shipment')

A seller who arranges for direct shipping of products from a manufacturer to a buyer must first consider whether it should report revenue on a gross or net basis. This determination will depend on whether the seller is acting as a principal or an agent (see **3.1** above).

If the seller arranges to have the manufacturer ship the products directly to the buyer, and the seller is a principal rather than an agent, the seller should recognise revenue as if it had shipped the products itself. Therefore, if the terms of sale specify FOB shipping point, the seller recognises revenue when the manufacturer ships the goods. If the terms of sale specify FOB destination, the seller recognises revenue when the buyer receives the goods.

Example 6.1.2D

Written sales agreement has expired but shipments continue

An entity's normal practice is to obtain a written sales agreement signed by the buyer. The agreement has a fixed termination date and no provision for automatic extension. The seller has continued to ship products to a customer after the written agreement expires.

Should revenue be recognised?

This is essentially a legal question about the seller's and buyer's rights in the circumstances. As a result of the expiry of the agreement, it may be the case that (1) the seller has retained significant risks of ownership, (2) the amount of revenue cannot be measured reliably, or (3) it is no longer probable that amounts due from the buyer will be recovered. In any of those circumstances, IAS 18:14 would preclude revenue recognition.

Even if it is determined that revenue should be recognised in this case, a question arises as to the measurement of the revenue. If the vendor has a history of providing price or other concessions as an inducement for renewal of a sales agreement, that practice must be taken into account when measuring the revenue from the products shipped after the sales agreement has expired.

Example 6.1.2E

Vendor installation – customer acceptance

Company A sells a machine and is required to install it on the customer's premises. The sales contract requires the customer to inspect and accept or reject the installation. On the basis of Company A's experience, the probability of customer acceptance of the equipment after completion of installation is very high.

Should revenue be recognised (1) when the machine is delivered (if necessary, with recognition of a provision for estimated additional installation costs), or (2) after customer acceptance?

The appropriate timing for revenue recognition depends on whether the transaction can be unbundled into two separately identifiable components of revenue: delivery of the machine and its installation (see **5.1**). If the installation cannot be unbundled (i.e. the installation cannot be accounted for separately from the sale of the machine), then revenue should be recognised on delivery of the machine only if, among other criteria:

- it is probable that the customer will accept the machine (if relevant, see **example 6.1H**); and

- the installation process is simple in nature (e.g. the installation of a factory tested television receiver that only requires unpacking and connection of power and antennae – see **example 6.6B**).

The appendix to IAS 18 provides additional examples which illustrate the appropriate time to recognise revenue from the sale of goods. For convenience, these examples are reproduced in **6.6** below.

6.2 Continuing managerial involvement and effective control

This criterion generally goes hand-in-hand with the risks and rewards of ownership (see **6.1**). It would be unusual for an entity to retain managerial involvement to the degree usually associated with ownership or to retain effective control over goods without retaining the risks and rewards of ownership. Each situation should, however, be considered individually. It may be the case that continuing managerial involvement is not to the degree usually associated with ownership. For example, a software consultancy firm may install a software system for a client and then oversee and manage the computer department that uses the software. This outsourcing of managerial control over the computer department, which includes the newly installed software, does not necessarily prohibit revenue recognition for the provision of the software. It will be necessary to consider the terms of the agreement to determine whether the risks and rewards stemming from the software have been transferred to the client.

6.3   Reliable measurement of revenue

Until the amount of revenue to be received can be measured reliably, revenue cannot be recognised. This does not imply, however, that the consideration must have been received in all cases for revenue to be recognised. Generally, consideration will be agreed in advance and the revenue from a sale will be recognised when all of the other recognition criteria are met.

Example 6.3

Vendor installation – settlement terms

A sales contract requires payment of 90 per cent on completion of the delivery and installation of a machine, and the remaining 10 per cent at the earlier of customer acceptance or 90 days. In this particular case, the seller has determined that it is not appropriate to account for installation as a separate component.

In the circumstances described, the arrangements for customer acceptance do not affect the amount of revenue to be received, only the timing of payment. Therefore, those arrangements do not affect the timing of recognition of revenue.

Because installation is not a component of revenue to be accounted for separately, 100 per cent of the revenue should be recognised when the significant risks and rewards of ownership of the machine have been transferred to the buyer. Depending on the particular facts and circumstances, this will either be on delivery (with recognition of a provision for any estimated additional installation costs to be incurred) or on completion of installation (see **example 6.1.2E** for further guidance).

The recognition of revenue is not affected by the settlement terms unless there is uncertainty regarding the flow of the economic benefits related to the transaction to the entity.

6.4   Probability of receipt of economic benefits

Revenue cannot be recognised unless it is probable that the economic benefits or consideration associated with the transaction will flow to the entity. For example, it may not be probable that consideration will be received from a particular customer due to exchange controls in the country in which the customer operates, which limit the amount of currency that can be remitted from that country. In such cases, when it is not probable that the consideration will be received, revenue is not recognised until the consideration is received.

If revenue has been recognised and it later emerges that the related consideration will not be collectible, an expense for bad debts is recognised rather than reversing the related revenue. [IAS 18:18]

6.5 Measurement of costs incurred related to the transaction

When the costs incurred or to be incurred in a transaction cannot be measured reliably, revenue is not recognised. This criterion flows from the matching principle. Under this principle, when revenue is recognised, the related expenses are also recognised. A common example of the type of expense that should be estimated and accrued is warranty costs. If such costs cannot be estimated reliably, revenue is deferred until the amount of such expenses can be more reliably estimated or have been incurred. In these circumstances, any consideration already received from the sale of goods is recognised as a liability. [IAS 18:19]

6.6 Additional examples

The following examples of the application of the revenue recognition criteria for the sale of goods are taken from the appendix to IAS 18. Although the appendix is not part of the Standard, it provides useful application guidance. Unless stated otherwise, the examples generally assume that the amount of revenue can be measured reliably, it is probable that the economic benefits will flow to the entity, and the costs incurred or to be incurred can be measured reliably.

Example 6.6A

'Bill-and-hold' sales, in which delivery is delayed at the buyer's request, but the buyer takes title and accepts billing
[IAS 18 Appendix:Example 1]

Revenue is recognised when the buyer takes title, provided that:

- it is probable that delivery will be made;

- the item is on hand, identified and ready for delivery to the buyer at the time the sale is recognised;

- the buyer specifically acknowledges the deferred delivery instructions; and

- the usual payment terms apply.

Revenue is not recognised when there is simply an intention to acquire or manufacture the goods in time for delivery.

Example 6.6A, reproduced from the appendix to IAS 18, describes a bill-and-hold sale in which revenue would be recognised on completion of manufacture if shipping is delayed at the buyer's request. But the facts in that example are that the buyer has taken title and accepts billing. If this were not the case, so that the seller retains title and the buyer is not obligated to pay until the goods are delivered, then revenue should not be recognised until the goods are delivered. This is the case even if the order is non-cancellable.

Consistent with the revenue recognition criteria set out in **example 6.6A**:

- revenue recognition at completion of manufacture may be inappropriate if there is no fixed delivery schedule or if the delivery schedule is significantly longer than is customary in the industry; and

- revenue recognition at completion of manufacture would not be appropriate if the seller, rather than the buyer, has requested that the transaction be on a bill-and-hold basis. Also, the buyer must have a substantive business purpose for ordering the goods on a bill-and-hold basis.

Example 6.6B

Goods shipped subject to conditions
[IAS 18 Appendix:Example 2]

(a) *Installation and inspection*

Revenue is normally recognised when the buyer accepts delivery, and installation and inspection are complete. However, revenue is recognised immediately upon the buyer's acceptance of delivery when:

- the installation process is simple in nature, e.g. the installation of a factory-tested television receiver which only requires unpacking and connection of power and antennae; or

- the inspection is performed only for the purposes of final determination of contract prices, e.g. shipments of iron ore, sugar or soya beans.

(b) On approval when the buyer has negotiated a limited right of return

If there is uncertainty about the possibility of return, revenue is recognised when the shipment has been formally accepted by the buyer or the goods have been delivered and the time period for rejection has elapsed.

(c) Consignment sales under which the recipient (buyer) undertakes to sell the goods on behalf of the shipper (seller)

Revenue is recognised by the shipper when the goods are sold by the recipient to a third party.

(d) Cash on delivery sales

Revenue is recognised when delivery is made and cash is received by the seller or its agent.

Example 6.6C

Lay away sales under which the goods are delivered only when the buyer makes the final payment in a series of instalments
[IAS 18 Appendix:Example 3]

Revenue from such sales is recognised when the goods are delivered. However, when experience indicates that most such sales are consummated, revenue may be recognised when a significant deposit is received, provided that the goods are on hand, identified and ready for delivery to the buyer.

The determination as to whether a deposit is considered 'significant' is a matter requiring careful judgement based on all of the relevant facts and circumstances. Factors to consider in making this determination include, but are not limited to, the following:

- the entity's policy on lay away sales, including the amount of deposit generally required;

- the nature and amount of the goods sold;

- the history of lay away sales, including the extent to which sales are consummated; and

- the possibility of either party withdrawing from the transaction.

In any case, the final conclusion should be supported by sufficient objective evidence.

If a customer forfeits its deposit under a lay away programme, so that the seller is entitled to keep the deposit without having any further obligations, the retained deposit will satisfy the definition of revenue in IAS 18:7 at the point of forfeiture and should be presented as such. The fact that the seller has retained the deposit without having delivered any goods is an event that is part of the ordinary course of business of a lay away seller. If forfeitures are significant, it may be appropriate to disclose the amount separately.

If such forfeited deposits do not remain the property of the seller, but rather must be remitted to the government under 'escheat laws', then no revenue is recognised. As noted above, the deposit for lay away sales is normally recognised as a liability, not as revenue. However, sometimes the seller may already have recognised revenue when a 'significant' deposit was received. If that is the case, and the seller will be required to remit any forfeited deposits to the government, the seller should establish an allowance for estimated forfeitures at the time the revenue is recognised. If no such reliable estimate can be made, no revenue should be recognised.

The recognition of revenue prior to the delivery of goods will only be appropriate in situations when, in addition to the above, the criteria applicable to bill-and-hold sales are also met – for example, the seller has identified the specific goods (so they will not be sold to another party) and they are ready for delivery.

Example 6.6D

Orders when payment (or partial payment) is received in advance of delivery for goods not currently held in inventory (e.g. the goods are still to be manufactured or will be delivered directly to the customer from a third party).
[IAS 18 Appendix:Example 4]

Revenue is recognised when the goods are delivered to the buyer.

Example 6.6E

Sale and repurchase agreements (other than swap transactions), under which the seller concurrently agrees to repurchase the same goods at a later date, or when the seller has a call option to repurchase, or the buyer has a put option to require the repurchase, by the seller, of the goods.
[IAS 18 Appendix:Example 5]

For a sale and repurchase agreement on an asset other than a financial asset, the terms of the agreement need to be analysed to ascertain whether, in substance, the seller has transferred the risks and rewards of ownership to the buyer and hence revenue is recognised. When the seller has retained the risks and rewards of ownership, even though legal title has been transferred, the transaction is a financing arrangement and does not give rise to revenue. For a sale and repurchase agreement on a financial asset, IAS 39 *Financial Instruments: Recognition and Measurement* [or, when adopted, IFRS 9 *Financial Instruments*] applies.

In the circumstances described in **example 6.6E**, if the seller has an option (meaning a right but not an obligation) to buy the goods back at a fixed price for a fixed period, the seller has retained an important benefit of ownership, namely the ability to profit from the difference between the strike price of the option and the fair value of the goods at the time the option is exercised. The significance of this benefit is to be considered at the date of the transaction to determine whether to recognise revenue. If the benefits retained are significant, revenue should not be recognised until expiry of the repurchase period. On the other hand, if the seller has the right to buy the goods back at market price at the time of repurchase, and the goods are readily available in the market, then revenue is recognised at the time of delivery. The determination as to whether to recognise revenue requires the exercise of careful judgement and consideration of all relevant facts and circumstances.

Example 6.6F

Sales to intermediate parties, such as distributors, dealers or others for resale
[IAS 18 Appendix:Example 6]

Revenue from such sales is generally recognised when the risks and rewards of ownership have passed. However, when the buyer is acting, in substance, as an agent, the sale is treated as a consignment sale.

Example 6.6G

Subscriptions to publications and similar items
[IAS 18 Appendix:Example 7]

When the items involved are of similar value in each time period, revenue is recognised on a straight-line basis over the period in which the items are despatched. When the items vary in value from period to period, revenue is recognised on the basis of the sales value of the item despatched as a proportion of the total estimated sales value of all items covered by the subscription.

Example 6.6H

Instalment sales, under which consideration is receivable in instalments
[IAS 18 Appendix:Example 8]

Revenue attributable to the sales price, exclusive of interest, is recognised at the date of sale. The sale price is the present value of the consideration, determined by discounting the instalments receivable at the imputed rate of interest. The interest element is recognised as revenue as it is earned, using the effective interest method.

In some cases, because of the nature of the industry in which an entity operates, goods are sold and delivered even though collection of the sales price is not reasonably assured. Often in those cases, payment is required in periodic instalments over an extended period of time. The seller generally will retain a lien on the product sold until payment is completed. For such instalment sales, when collection of the sales price is not reasonably assured, revenue recognition is deferred. A fundamental condition for revenue recognition in IAS 18:14(d) is that it is probable that the economic benefits associated with the transaction will flow to the entity. Example 8 of the appendix presumes that collectibility is not an issue.

7   Recognition criteria – rendering of services

IAS 18 requires the use of the percentage of completion method when accounting for the rendering of services. Under the percentage of completion method, revenue is recognised as work progresses based on the percentage of work completed at the end of the reporting period. IAS 18 requires the use of this method for revenue recognition, but the recognition of related contract expenses is beyond its scope (though there is some guidance on the treatment of associated expenses in the appendix to IAS 18). The Standard refers users to IAS 11 *Construction Contracts* for further guidance on the percentage of completion method as it applies to both revenue and expenses. The requirements and guidance included in IAS 18 are set out below and a more detailed discussion of the percentage of completion method is included in **chapter A34**.

As with the supply of goods, when an uncertainty arises about the collectibility of an amount already included in revenue in relation to services, the uncollectible amount, or the amount for which recovery has ceased to be probable, is recognised as a bad debt expense, rather than as an adjustment of the amount of revenue originally recognised. [IAS 18:22]

7.1   Outcome of transaction can be estimated reliably

When the outcome of a transaction involving the rendering of services can be estimated reliably, revenue associated with the transaction is recognised by reference to the stage of completion of the transaction at the end of the reporting period (i.e. using the percentage of completion method). IAS 18 lists the following conditions for the outcome of a transaction to be estimated reliably:
[IAS 18:20]

- the amount of revenue can be measured reliably;

- it is probable that the economic benefits associated with the transaction will flow to the entity;

- the stage of completion of the transaction at the end of the reporting period can be measured reliably; and

- the costs incurred for the transaction and the costs to complete the transaction can be measured reliably.

An entity is usually able to make reliable estimates after it has agreed the following with the other parties to the transaction:
[IAS 18:23]

- each party's enforceable rights regarding the service to be provided and received by the parties;

- the consideration to be exchanged; and

- the manner and terms of settlement.

In addition, it will be necessary for an entity to have an effective internal budgeting and reporting system for it to make reliable estimates and, in subsequent periods, to compare those estimates to the actual costs incurred to date.

The Standard emphasises that the need to revise the estimates of revenue as the service is performed does not necessarily indicate that the outcome of the transaction cannot be estimated reliably. [IAS 18:23]

The stage of completion of a transaction at the end of the reporting period can be determined in a variety of ways. Progress payments and advances received from customers are, however, generally not reliable indicators of the stage of completion, because these payments are often made for reasons other than compensating for work performed. Depending on the nature of the transaction, methods for determining the stage of completion may include:
[IAS 18:24]

- surveys of work performed;

- services performed to date as a percentage of total services to be performed; or

- the proportion that costs incurred to date bear to the estimated total costs of the transaction. Only costs that reflect services performed to date are included in costs incurred to date and only costs that reflect services performed or to be performed are included in the estimated total costs of the transaction.

When services are performed by an indeterminate number of acts over a specified period of time, revenue is recognised on a straight-line basis, unless there is evidence that some other method better represents the stage of completion. For example, if a service contract relates to daily cleaning services, for practical reasons, the revenue relating to those services will be recognised on a straight-line basis as the work is performed. If one specific act is much more significant than any other acts, the recognition of revenue is postponed until the significant act is executed. [IAS 18:25]

Example 7.1A

Claims processing and billing services

Company A performs claims processing and medical billing services for health care providers. It prepares and submits claims to government agencies and insurance companies, tracks the outstanding billings, collects the amounts billed and remits payments to the health care provider. Company A's fee is 5 per cent of the amount collected. Company A has reliable, historical evidence indicating that the government agencies and insurance companies pay 85 per cent of the claims submitted with no further effort on Company A's part.

Under IAS 18:20, revenue from rendering services should be recognised by reference to the stage of completion of the transaction.

How should that principle be applied in the circumstances described? Specifically, is it acceptable for Company A to recognise as revenue its 5 per cent fee on 85 per cent of the gross billings at the time it prepares and submits the billings, or must it wait until collections occur?

The appropriate timing for recognition of revenue in such circumstances will depend on whether the amount that will be received by Company A is sufficiently predictable to be a reliable measurement. If Company A can make a reliable estimate of collections, revenue related to at least 85 per cent of the claims can be recognised. Company A should determine the pattern of revenue recognition that best reflects the stage of completion.

Similar arrangements should be analysed to ascertain whether a transaction contains multiple elements to be accounted for separately (see **5.1**). If so, revenue will be recognised separately for the different activities performed by Company A.

Example 7.1B

Membership or services when the customer is entitled to a full refund

Company A sells one-year memberships in a facility it operates. The terms state that if the customer is unhappy with the facility for any reason within 30 days of joining the facility, the customer can request a full refund of the membership fee paid upon sign up. After 30 days, the membership is non-refundable. Company A's experience is that approximately 20 per cent of its customers request a refund during the 30-day period.

When should Company A begin to recognise revenue?

If it is possible to make a reliable estimate of the level of expected refunds, Company A should begin recognising the membership fee from the date the membership contract is signed, with an appropriate reduction in the amount recognised as revenue for estimated refunds. If it is not possible to make a reliable estimate of the level of expected refunds, revenue recognition should be deferred until the 30-day money-back period elapses.

Accordingly, in the circumstances described, revenue recognition begins when the contract is signed, with a reduction in the amount recognised as revenue relating to the 20 per cent of expected refunds, if such an adjustment reflects a reliable estimate of the level of expected refunds.

Example 7.1C

Performance-based fee part way through the performance period

Company A, an investment manager, will earn a bonus of CU1 million if a managed fund's performance exceeds the performance of the S&P 500 by 20 per cent for the calendar year 20X1. Company A's financial year ends 30 June 20X1. At that time, the fund is outperforming the S&P 500 by 25 per cent.

Should Company A recognise revenue in relation to the bonus at 30 June 20X1 and, if so, CU500,000 (one half-year's worth) or CU1 million (the expected total bonus)?

IAS 18:20 states that revenue can be recognised when the amount of revenue can be measured reliably and it is probable that the economic benefits will flow to the entity. Company A will not receive any bonus unless the annual return exceeds the performance of the S&P 500 by 20 per cent. Because the markets are very volatile, it is unlikely that Company A will be able to estimate reliably at 30 June 20X1 whether the return for the year ended 31 December 20X1 will exceed the performance of the S&P 500. Consequently, no amount of the bonus can be determined reliably at 30 June 20X1 and Company A should not recognise any of the bonus at 30 June 20X1.

Example 7.1D

Accounting for 'trail commissions'

Investment Manager G engages Financial Advisor X to sell to the general public units in funds managed by G. G compensates X on a 'trail commission' basis, which means that X does not receive any cash on completion of the sale of units but instead receives an annual fee of 5 per cent of the management fee that G earns from the investors introduced by X during the period that the investors remain invested in the fund. G's management fee is calculated as a percentage of the growth in the value of the net assets in the fund.

When one of the investors introduced by X redeems its units and divests from the fund, G ceases the payment of commission to X in respect of that investor.

Should X recognise any revenue in respect of the trail commission at the time of selling units?

It is first necessary to consider whether X is required to provide additional services (e.g. of an advisory or administrative nature to G and/or the investors) subsequent to the sale of units in order to receive payment. If so, then it would not be appropriate to recognise at the outset any part of the commission that relates to subsequent additional services.

To the extent that the trail commission relates to the selling of units, this will be recognised at the outset if, and only if, all of the conditions in IAS 18:20 are met. In particular, it must be possible for the amount of the commission to be estimated reliably and it must be probable that it will be received.

In the circumstances described, it may be unlikely that X will be able to estimate reliably the amount of revenue that will be received. This is because the amount of trail commissions receivable is uncertain, and will depend both on the length of time that particular investors remain with the funds (i.e. 'churn rates') and on the growth in the value of the net assets in the fund (because the latter determines G's management fee and, consequently, the amount payable to X). In particular, X may not be able to estimate future asset growth because that would involve forecasting the future performance of the investment fund.

If X is unable to estimate revenue reliably at the outset, revenue should instead be recognised when and to the extent that it becomes reliably measurable. In practice, X may only be able to measure revenue reliably at the end of each period for which G charges management fees because only at that point will the effect of investor churn and fund performance be known. For example, if G raises management fees on a quarterly basis, X will be able to measure revenue at the end of each quarter because the amount of revenue payable to X for that quarter will then be known.

7.2   Outcome of transaction cannot be estimated reliably

When the outcome of a transaction involving the rendering of services cannot be estimated reliably, either:
[IAS 18:26 – 28]

- revenue is recognised to the extent of expenses incurred that are likely to be recovered. Thus, no profit is recognised on the transaction; or

- if it is not probable that the costs incurred will be recovered, no revenue is recognised and the costs incurred are recognised as an expense.

When the uncertainties that led to no profit being recognised on the transaction no longer exist, revenue is recognised on the percentage of completion basis.

7.3   Additional examples

The following examples of the application of the recognition criteria for the rendering of services are taken from the appendix to IAS 18. Although the appendix is not part of the Standard, it provides useful application guidance. Unless stated otherwise, the examples generally assume that the amount of revenue can be measured reliably, it is probable that the economic benefits will flow to the entity and the costs incurred or to be incurred can be measured reliably.

Example 7.3A

Installation fees
[IAS 18 Appendix:Example 10]

Installation fees are recognised as revenue by reference to the stage of completion of the installation, unless they are incidental to the sale of a product, in which case they are recognised when the goods are sold.

Example 7.3B

Servicing fees included in the price of the product
[IAS 18 Appendix:Example 11]

When the selling price of a product includes an identifiable amount for subsequent servicing (e.g. after-sales support and product enhancement on the sale of software), that amount is deferred and recognised as revenue over the period during which the service is performed. The amount deferred is that which will cover the expected costs of the services under the agreement, together with a reasonable profit on those services.

Example 7.3C

Advertising commissions
[IAS 18 Appendix:Example 12]

Media commissions are recognised when the related advertisement or commercial appears before the public. Production commissions are recognised by reference to the stage of completion of the project.

Example 7.3D

Insurance agency commissions
[IAS 18 Appendix:Example 13]

Insurance agency commissions received or receivable, which do not require the agent to render further service, are recognised as revenue by the agent on the effective commencement or renewal dates of the related policies. However, when it is probable that the agent will be required to render further services during the life of the policy, the commission, or part thereof, is deferred and recognised as revenue over the period during which the policy is in force.

Example 7.3E

Financial service fees
[IAS 18 Appendix:Example 14]

The recognition of revenue for financial service fees depends on the purposes for which the fees are assessed and the basis of accounting for any associated financial instrument. The description of fees for financial services may not be indicative of the nature and substance of the services provided.

Therefore, it is necessary to distinguish between fees that are an integral part of the effective interest rate of a financial instrument, fees that are earned as services are provided, and fees that are earned on the execution of a significant act.

(*a*) *Fees that are an integral part of the effective interest rate of a financial instrument*

Such fees are generally treated as an adjustment to the effective interest rate. However, when the financial instrument is measured at fair value with the change in fair value recognised in profit or loss, the fees are recognised as revenue when the instrument is initially recognised.

- **Origination fees received by the entity relating to the creation or acquisition of a financial asset other than one that under IAS 39 is classified as a financial asset 'at fair value through profit or loss' [or, when IFRS 9 is adopted, other than one that under IFRS 9 is measured at fair value through profit or loss].** Such fees may include compensation for activities such as evaluating the borrower's financial condition, evaluating and recording guarantees, collateral and other security arrangements, negotiating the terms of the instrument, pre-paring and processing documents and closing the transaction. These fees are an integral part of generating an involvement with the resulting financial instrument and, together with the related trans-action costs (as defined in IAS 39)*, are deferred and recognised as an adjustment to the effective interest rate.

- **Commitment fees received by the entity to originate a loan when the loan commitment is outside the scope of IAS 39 [or, when adopted, IFRS 9].** If it is probable that the entity will enter into a specific lending arrangement and the loan commitment is not within the scope of IAS 39 [or, when adopted, IFRS 9], the commitment fee received is regarded as compensation for an ongoing involvement with the acqui-sition of a financial instrument and, together with the related trans-action costs (as defined in IAS 39), is deferred and recognised as an adjustment to the effective interest rate. If the commitment expires without the entity making the loan, the fee is recognised as revenue on expiry. Loan commitments that are within the scope of IAS 39 [or, when adopted, IFRS 9] are accounted for as derivatives and measured at fair value.

- **Origination fees received on issuing financial liabilities measured at amortised cost.** These fees are an integral part of generating an involvement with a financial liability. When a financial liability is not classified as at fair value through profit or loss, the origination fees received are included, with the related transaction costs (as defined in IAS 39) incurred, in the initial carrying amount of the financial liability and recognised as an adjustment to the effective interest rate. An entity distinguishes fees and costs that are an integral part of the effective interest rate for the financial liability from origination fees and trans-action costs relating to the right to provide services, such as investment management services.

* In *Improvements to IFRSs* issued in May 2008, the IASB replaced the term 'direct costs' with 'transaction costs' as defined in IAS 39:9. This amendment removed an inconsistency for costs incurred in originating financial assets and liabilities that should be deferred and recognised as an adjustment to the underlying effective interest rate. 'Direct costs', as previously defined, did not require such costs to be incremental.

(b) *Fees earned as services are provided*

- **Fees charged for servicing a loan.** Fees charged by an entity for servicing a loan are recognised as revenue as the services are provided.

- **Commitment fees to originate a loan when the loan commitment is outside the scope of IAS 39 [or, when adopted, IFRS 9].** If it is unlikely that a specific lending arrangement will be entered into and the loan commitment is outside the scope of IAS 39 [or, when adopted, IFRS 9], the commitment fee is recognised as revenue on a time proportion basis over the commitment period. Loan commitments that are within the scope of IAS 39 [or, when adopted, IFRS 9] are accounted for as derivatives and measured at fair value.

- **Investment management fees.** Fees charged for managing invest-ments are recognised as revenue as the services are provided.

  Incremental costs that are directly attributable to securing an invest-ment management contract are recognised as an asset if they can be identified separately and measured reliably and if it is probable that they will be recovered. As in IAS 39, an incremental cost is one that would not have been incurred if the entity had not secured the investment management contract. The asset represents the entity's contractual right to benefit from providing investment management services, and is amortised as the entity recognises the related revenue. If the entity has a portfolio of investment management contracts, it may assess their recoverability on a portfolio basis.

  Some financial services contracts involve both the origination of one or more financial instruments and the provision of investment manage-ment services. An example is a long-term monthly saving contract linked to the management of a pool of equity securities. The provider of the contract distinguishes the contract cost relating to the origina-tion of the financial instrument from the costs of securing the right to provide investment management services.

(c) *Fees that are earned on the execution of a significant act*

The fees are recognised as revenue when the significant act has been completed, as in the examples below.

- **Commission on the allotment of shares to a client.** The commission is recognised as revenue when the shares have been allotted.

- **Placement fees for arranging a loan between a borrower and an investor.** The fee is recognised as revenue when the loan has been arranged.

- **Loan syndication fees.** A syndication fee received by an entity that arranges a loan and retains no part of the loan package for itself (or retains a part at the same effective interest rate for comparable risk as other participants) is compensation for the service of syndication. Such a fee is recognised as revenue when the syndication has been completed.

Example 7.3F

Admission fees
[IAS 18 Appendix:Example 15]

Revenue from artistic performances, banquets and other special events is recognised when the event takes place. When a subscription to a number of events is sold, the fee is allocated to each event on a basis that reflects the extent to which services are performed at each event.

Example 7.3G

Tuition fees
[IAS 18 Appendix:Example 16]

Revenue is recognised over the period of instruction.

Example 7.3H

Initiation, entrance and membership fees
[IAS 18 Appendix:Example 17]

Revenue recognition depends on the nature of the services provided. If the fee permits only membership, and all other services or products are paid for separately, or if there is a separate annual subscription, the fee is recognised as revenue when no significant uncertainty as to its collectibility exists. If the fee entitles the member to services or publications to be provided during the membership period, or to purchase goods or services at prices lower than those charged to non-members, it is recognised on a basis that reflects the timing, nature and value of the benefits provided.

Caution should be exercised before concluding that a fee permits only membership, particularly when goods or services are not made available to non-members at any price. In such circumstances, it will often be the case that the membership fee also provides the member with a valuable option to buy those goods and services, in which case the fee will permit more than just membership.

Example 7.3I

Franchise fees
[IAS 18 Appendix:Example 18]

Franchise fees may cover the supply of initial and subsequent services, equipment and other tangible assets, and know-how. Accordingly, franchise fees are recognised as revenue on a basis that reflects the purpose for which the fees were charged. The following methods of franchise fee recognition are appropriate:

- **Supplies of equipment and other tangible assets.** The amount, based on the fair value of the assets sold, is recognised as revenue when the items are delivered or title passes.

- **Supplies of initial and subsequent services.** Fees for the provision of continuing services, whether part of the initial fee or a separate fee, are recognised as revenue as the services are rendered. When the separate fee does not cover the cost of continuing services together with a reasonable profit, part of the initial fee, sufficient to cover the costs of continuing services and to provide a reasonable profit on those services, is deferred and recognised as revenue as the services are rendered.

  The franchise agreement may provide for the franchisor to supply equipment, inventories, or other tangible assets, at a price lower than that charged to others or a price that does not provide a reasonable profit on those sales. In these circumstances, part of the initial fee, sufficient to cover estimated costs in excess of that price and to provide a reasonable profit on those sales, is deferred and recognised over the period the goods are likely to be sold to the franchisee. The balance of an initial fee is recognised as revenue when performance of all of the initial services and other obligations required of the franchisor (such as assistance with site selection, staff training, financing and advertising) has been substantially accomplished.

  The initial services and other obligations under an area franchise agreement may depend on the number of individual outlets established in the area. In this case, the fees attributable to the initial services are recognised as revenue in proportion to the number of outlets for which the initial services have been substantially completed.

  If the initial fee is collectible over an extended period, and there is a significant uncertainty that it will be collected in full, the fee is recognised as cash instalments are received.

- **Continuing franchise fees.** Fees charged for the use of continuing rights granted by the agreement, or for other services provided during the period of the agreement, are recognised as revenue as the services are provided or the rights used.

- **Agency transactions.** Transactions may take place between the franchisor and the franchisee which, in substance, involve the franchisor acting as agent for the franchisee. For example, the franchisor may order supplies and arrange for their delivery to the franchisee at no profit. Such transactions do not give rise to revenue.

Example 7.3J

Fees from the development of customised software
[IAS 18 Appendix:Example 19]

Fees from the development of customised software are recognised as revenue by reference to the stage of completion of the development, including completion of services provided for post-delivery service support.

7.4   Milestone payments

In certain industries, entities are commonly involved in collaborative research and development activities with other entities and will often enter into arrangements that provide for milestone payments to be received either based on the passage of time or the occurrence of specific events.

Accounting for such contracts can be complex and the appropriate timing for revenue recognition will vary depending on the substance of the arrangements. In some circumstances, there may be a correlation between the timing of milestone payments and when IAS 18's revenue recognition criteria are met. However, frequently, the timing of milestone payments may be reflective of financing arrangements rather than being representative of services rendered.

When the arrangement is, in substance, a contract for the rendering of services, revenue should be recognised based on the stage of completion, regardless of the timing of receipt of milestone payments. In determining whether there is any correlation between milestone payments and the stage of completion, consideration should be given to all relevant facts and circumstances including, but not limited to, whether:

- milestone events are substantive in terms of assessing the delivery of services to the customer;

- payments received bear any relation to the costs incurred and the services rendered to date;

- any amounts received to date are repayable upon cancellation of the arrangement; and

- any fines or penalties are payable upon failure to achieve a milestone.

In addition, consideration should be given to whether any royalty, licence or similar agreement that should be accounted for as a separate component (i.e. 'unbundled') is embodied in the arrangement.

Often, there is genuine uncertainty regarding whether a particular milestone will be reached and, consequently, whether particular elements of revenue will ultimately be received (e.g. for a pharmaceutical product, a milestone may be linked to approval by the appropriate government agency). When this is the case, the amount of revenue recognised should be restricted so that amounts relating to such milestones are not recognised while their payment remains uncertain. However, if there is no uncertainty over the seller's ability to achieve a particular milestone, it will not be appropriate to restrict revenue in this way.

7.4.1   Sale of intellectual property and subsequent development services

In some industries, such as the pharmaceutical industry and some technology businesses, it is common for an entity (Company A) to sell intellectual property (IP) which it has partly developed to another entity (Company B). Company A will continue to develop the IP for Company B and, if that further development is successful, Company B will ultimately exploit the IP that it has purchased by selling products as a principal. The terms of such contracts often require Company B to pay specified amounts to Company A if and when specific 'milestones' are successfully achieved (e.g. regulatory approval being obtained) during the further development stages of the IP. In addition, such contracts often oblige Company A to continue with the development work until either it is successfully completed or both parties agree that the development work will not be successful and should be terminated.

Such contracts raise particular issues for Company A, because both the revenue and the associated costs are unknown and will depend on future outcomes that typically cannot be predicted with confidence at the outset. Often, Company A cannot know in advance whether it will successfully complete the entire contract, thus receiving all milestone payments and incurring all costs, or whether (through no fault of Company A) the development will fail at some stage, such that Company A will only receive some of the milestone payments and incur some of the costs.

Neither IAS 18 nor IAS 11 includes guidance that deals specifically with the issues that arise from such contracts. In the absence of such guidance, judgement should be used to develop and apply consistently an appropriate accounting policy that complies with the general requirements of IAS 18. The discussion below highlights an approach that may be adopted, and sets out some methods that are adopted in practice. As explained further below, it is important to note that some of these methods may be appropriate in some circumstances but not in others. Moreover, this is not a comprehensive list of possible methods and methods other than those discussed below may also be acceptable in some circumstances.

It is generally appropriate for Company A first to consider whether the contract with Company B should be unbundled between the 'initial sale' of the IP and the further development of that IP. **Section 5.1** sets out general guidance on the unbundling of contracts. If the development work to be performed by Company A could instead have been performed by another supplier, it is possible that the conditions for unbundling the 'initial sale' from the subsequent services may be met. Conversely, if only Company A is capable of providing the further development services, it is unlikely that the 'initial sale' can be unbundled.

When the contract can be unbundled, and to the extent that it is possible to measure reliably the values that should be attributed to the various components of the transaction, the total contract revenues should be apportioned between the initial sale of the IP (typically recognised on the transfer of the IP at the outset) and the subsequent provision of services (typically recognised over the period in which those services are provided). When the contract cannot be unbundled, all the contract revenues would typically be recognised over the period in which services are provided.

Company A should devise an appropriate method for recognising service revenues, which applies the principles of IAS 18 and also meets the objectives of paragraph 10 of IAS 8 *Accounting Policies, Changes in Accounting Estimates and Errors* in presenting information that is reliable in that the financial statements faithfully represent the financial position, financial performance and cash flows of the entity. Although there is no detailed IFRS guidance on this subject, there is guidance within US GAAP, which some IFRS reporters may find helpful. It can be found at 605–28 in the FASB Accounting Standards Codification Manual.

Some possible methods of accounting for such service revenues are illustrated in the example below.

Example 7.4.1

Accounting for contracts with milestone payments and uncertain outcomes

Company A and Company B enter into an agreement under which Company A will transfer to Company B all rights in respect of a drug that has been partly developed by Company A, and then will provide to Company B the service of further developing that drug. If the development process is successful, Company B will market and sell the drug after the appropriate regulatory approval is obtained. The terms of the contract are such that Company A will receive the following payments from Company B at specific 'milestone' points, if and when particular stages of the contract are completed.

	CU
On initial signing of contract	5,000
On successful completion of Stage 1 (drug developed sufficiently to submit for clinical trial)	5,000
On successful completion of Stage 2 (clinical trial successful)	1,500
On successful completion of Stage 3 (regulatory approval obtained)	1,000
Total possible revenue	12,500

Any amounts received by Company A are non-refundable provided that Company A complies with the contract terms (i.e. if a stage is unsuccessful, Company A is not required to refund any amounts already received). Company A has concluded that it is not possible to unbundle the 'initial sale' of the IP from the rest of the contract and will therefore recognise all the

---

revenues received over the period of the contract. Company A is contractually obliged to continue with the development work until either it is successfully completed or both parties agree that the development work will not be successful and should be terminated.

Company A decides that it is appropriate to apply the percentage of completion method using costs incurred as a measure of contract activity, because these are judged to be representative of the effort expended by Company A. Company A currently anticipates the costs of each stage to be as follows.

	CU
Stage 1	4,500
Stage 2	4,000
Stage 3	500
Total costs	9,000

Company A determines that all the costs of a particular stage will be incurred even if that stage is unsuccessful.

Company A concludes, therefore, that there are four possible outcomes in terms of total revenues and costs.

	Total revenue CU	Total costs CU	Total margin CU
Fail to complete Stage 1 successfully	5,000	4,500	500
Complete Stage 1, but fail to complete Stage 2 successfully	10,000	8,500	1,500
Complete Stage 2, but fail to complete Stage 3 successfully	11,500	9,000	2,500
All stages successful	12,500	9,000	3,500

This example explains and illustrates four methods that are sometimes adopted in practice, which may be considered by Company A when determining an appropriate method for recognising the revenue arising from its contract with Company B.

- **Method 1** – up-front payment recognised as revenue over whole of the contract, other milestone payments recognised in full as each becomes payable (method is appropriate in some circumstances but not others).

- **Method 2** – apply percentage of completion method on assumption that all stages will be completed successfully (method is appropriate in some circumstances but not others).

- **Method 3** – apply Method 2, but limit cumulative revenue recognised to amounts already received or reasonably certain to be received.

- **Method 4** – identify cumulative revenue for each possible outcome of the contract, select most appropriate amount (often the lowest).

Method 1

Under Method 1, any up-front payment is recognised as revenue over the whole period of the contract using an appropriate methodology that reflects the percentage of completion (see IAS 11:30). All other milestone payments are recognised as revenue in full at the point that each becomes payable as per the contract, i.e. when the milestone is judged to have been successfully achieved (see the discussion below for the conditions necessary for this method to be judged appropriate).

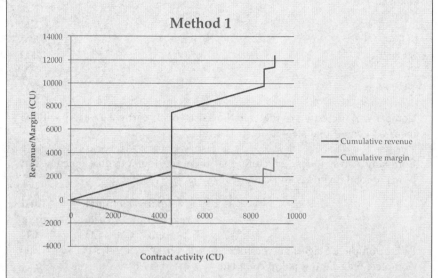

Method 1

Illustrative calculation using Company A's estimates:

	Revenue recognised	Total revenue recognised to date	Total margin recognised to date
Period from initial signing to completion of Stage 1 (costs estimated as CU4,500)	Spread CU2,500 (CU5,000*4,500/9,000)	CU2,500	CU(2,000)
On completion of Stage 1	CU5,000	CU7,500	CU3,000
Period from completion of Stage 1 to completion of Stage 2 (costs estimated as CU4,000)	Spread CU2,222 (CU5,000*4,000/9,000)	CU9,722	CU1,222
On completion of Stage 2	CU1,500	CU11,222	CU2,722
Period from completion of Stage 2 to completion of Stage 3 (costs estimated as CU500)	Spread CU278 (CU5,000*500/9,000)	CU11,500	CU2,500
On completion of Stage 3	CU1,000	CU12,500	CU3,500

This method may be judged appropriate when, for example, the initial payment broadly corresponds to the total expected contract costs, and the individual milestone payments have been set to represent an appropriate level of profit for successful completion of the preceding stage. However, in some other circumstances, this method may result in revenue being recognised in a manner that is inconsistent with the entity's contract activity, in which case it would not be judged appropriate. For example, consider a scenario in which the up-front payment and the milestone payments have each been set at a level that is intended to cover the entity's costs for the subsequent stage. In other words, the up-front payment is set to cover the costs of Stage 1, the milestone payment at the end of Stage 1 is set to cover the costs of Stage 2 etc. In such a scenario, the milestone payment at the end of Stage 1 might be best matched against the costs of Stage 2, but Method 1 will recognise the revenue from that payment in advance of the Stage 2 costs. Therefore, in some scenarios, the use of this method may not be considered appropriate because it may recognise revenues too early.

Method 1 may not be judged suitable by Company A for this particular contract, because it appears that the initial payment and milestone payments have been set at a level that is broadly intended to fund the subsequent stage's costs, rather than being reflective of contract activity to date. To illustrate, the graph indicates that almost the entire contract margin is recognised on successful completion of Stage 1, whereas a subsequent failure to complete Stage 2 successfully would result in much of the cumulative margin being reversed. Note that, on successful completion of Stage 1, Company A is obliged under the contract to continue with the development work; it is not permitted by the contract to cease contract activity at this stage.

Method 2

Under Method 2, the contract is accounted for on the assumption that it will be completely successful. The IAS 11 percentage of completion method is used to recognise the total contract revenues over the period of the contract (see the discussion below for the conditions necessary for this method to be judged appropriate).

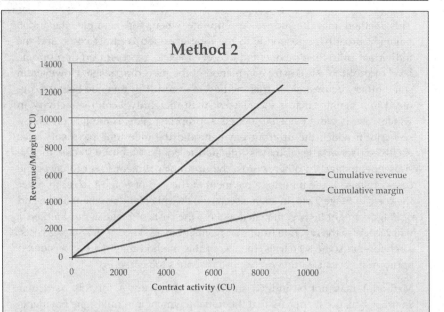

Illustrative calculation using Company A's estimates:

	Revenue recognised (cost for each stage grossed up for overall contract margin)	Total revenue recognised to date	Total margin recognised to date
Period from initial signing to completion of Stage 1	CU6,250 (CU4,500 x 12,500/9,000)	CU6,250	CU1,750
Period from completion of Stage 1 to completion of Stage 2	CU5,556 (CU4,000 x 12,500/9,000)	CU11,806	CU3,306
Period from completion of Stage 2 to completion of Stage 3	CU694 (CU500 x 12,500/9,000)	CU12,500	CU3,500

This method may be judged inappropriate in some circumstances, because it can result in the recognition of revenue that is conditional on successful completion of an uncertain future milestone, and for which there is a significant possibility of reversal in a future period. The method does not take into account the fact that some of the contract revenues are contingent on future events outside the entity's control. In some circumstances, therefore, it will be inappropriate because it would recognise revenues that are not yet reliably measurable, as required by IAS 18.

The method will be appropriate when the amount and timing of milestone payments is such that the cumulative amount of revenue recognised would always be less than the cumulative amount that has become payable under the contract (i.e. there is always a deferred revenue balance recognised in creditors during the life of the contract). This may be the case for contracts when the milestone payments are weighted in advance of contractual performance. However, for contracts in which milestone payments fall in arrears of contractual performance, this method would result in the recognition of receivables that would not be collectible unless subsequent milestones are successfully met. When such receivables are significant, and there is significant uncertainty over meeting the subsequent milestones, the associated revenue should not be recognised because it would not be reliably measurable.

Method 2 may not be judged suitable by Company A for this particular contract, because it could result in revenue being recognised that may not be reliably measurable. For example, immediately prior to completion of Stage 1, Company A would have recognised cumulative revenues of CU6,250, but CU1,250 of this would have to be reversed if Stage 1 is unsuccessful. Similarly, immediately prior to completion of Stage 2, Company A would have recognised cumulative revenues of CU11,806, but CU1,806 of this would have to be reversed if Stage 2 is unsuccessful.

Method 3

This method is a variation on Method 2, which is intended to address the potential issue relating to contingent revenues. Like Method 2, this method first calculates revenue on the basis that the contract will be completely successful and using the IAS 11 percentage of completion method to allocate the total contract revenues over the period of the contract. However, under this method, the entity will then limit the cumulative revenue recognised at any point to the amount that has already been received or is reasonably certain to become receivable at that point in time.

Method 3

Illustrative calculation using Company A's estimates:

	Revenue recognised	Total revenue recognised to date	Total margin recognised to date
Period from initial signing to costs of CU3,600*	CU5,000 (CU3,600 x 12,500/9,000)	CU5,000	CU1,400
Period from costs of CU3,600 to completion of Stage 1 (cumulative costs of CU4,500)	CUnil (cumulative revenue capped at CU5,000)	CU5,000	CU500
At completion of Stage 1	CU1,250 ((CU4,500 x 12,500/9,000) – CU5,000)	CU6,250	CU1,750
Period from completion of Stage 1 to costs of CU7,200**	CU3,750 ((CU7,200 x 12,500/9,000) – CU6,250)	CU10,000	CU2,800
Period from costs of CU7,200 to completion of Stage 2 (cumulative costs of CU8,500)	CUnil (cumulative revenue capped at CU10,000)	CU10,000	CU1,500
At completion of Stage 2	CU1,500 ((CU8,500 x 12,500/9,000 capped at CU11,500) – CU10,000)	CU11,500	CU3,000
At completion of Stage 3 (cumulative costs of CU9,000)	CU1,000 (CU12,500 – CU11,500)	CU12,500	CU3,500

*   During this period, only CU5,000 (the amount initially received) is reasonably certain. This corresponds to 40 per cent of the total contract revenue. Accordingly, it is recognised as the first 40 per cent of costs are incurred (40% x CU9,000 = CU3,600).

**   During this period, CU10,000 (the amount initially received and the first milestone payment) is reasonably certain. This corresponds to 80 per cent of the total contract revenue. Accordingly, the next tranche of revenue is recognised up to the point that 80 per cent of costs have been incurred (80% x CU9,000 = CU7,200).

This method should always result in a pattern of revenue recognition that is acceptable in accordance with IAS 18. Nevertheless, it can result in the entity reporting losses during some stages of a contract, even for a contract that will overall be profitable. In particular, whenever the 'revenue cap' comes into effect, the entity will continue to report costs incurred as an expense but will not recognise any revenues until the next milestone is achieved. (Note that it might be possible to derive a variation of this method that avoids a period of no revenues by spreading the calculated revenue for each stage over the period to the next milestone instead.)

Method 3 could be adopted by Company A for this particular contract. However, as depicted in the graph, the method will result in Company A reporting losses (reducing cumulative margin) at certain stages, namely immediately prior to successful completion of the three milestones. For that reason, Company A may wish to consider Method 4 described below.

Method 4

This method recognises that there are various different possible outcomes in terms of how much revenue will ultimately be received, depending upon which milestones are met. Under this method, the entity will assess what the cumulative revenue would be at the reporting date under the IAS 11 percentage of completion method for each possible outcome of the contract. As the contract progresses, the outcomes will narrow (i.e. when a stage is successfully completed, the number of possible outcomes decreases by one).

The following graph illustrates the possible outcomes for Company A.

Having calculated the cumulative revenue based on each of the possible outcomes, the entity then assesses which of the figures calculated should be reported, bearing in mind the requirement that revenue should only be recognised to the extent that it is reliably measurable. In many cases, it may be appropriate to recognise cumulative revenue as the lowest of the amounts calculated, because any higher amount would involve recognising revenue that may not be reliably measurable. However, in some circumstances, a higher figure may be judged reliably measurable. For example, when the lowest figure calculated is substantially below the others but the probability associated with the lowest outcome is very low, it may be possible to conclude that the next lowest figure is reliably measurable and, hence, to recognise revenue based on that amount. A consistent method should be used to determine the most appropriate amount to recognise as revenue at each reporting date throughout a contract.

The following graph illustrates the pattern of revenue recognition when Company A has recognised the lowest cumulative amount of revenue at each point throughout the contract.

Method 4 (graph 2)

The table below illustrates how Company A's calculations of revenue would be performed assuming that the contract is part way through Stage 1 at the reporting date and the costs incurred to date are CU2,300.

Possible outcomes:

	Fail to complete Stage 1	Complete Stage 1 but fail to complete Stage 2	Complete Stages 1 and 2 but fail to complete Stage 3	Complete Stage 3 – project successful.
Costs incurred to date	CU2,300	CU2,300	CU2,300	CU2,300
Total expected costs of project	CU4,500	CU8,500	CU9,000	CU9,000
% of costs incurred to date (a)	51.1%	27.1%	25.5%	25.5%
Total contracted payments (b)	CU5,000	CU10,000	CU11,500	CU12,500
Revenue at reporting date = (a)*(b)	CU2,556	CU2,706	CU2,939	CU3,194
Margin at reporting date	CU256	CU406	CU639	CU894
Anticipated profit margin	10.0%	15.0%	21.7%	28.0%

This method should result in a pattern of revenue recognition that is acceptable in accordance with IAS 18. Nevertheless, it is more complex than the others described, and entities may prefer to adopt an alternative method on grounds of simplicity.

Method 4 could be adopted by Company A for this particular contract. As depicted in the graph, it will result in Company A reporting revenues and positive margin throughout the life of the contract. But it will be more complex to apply and, consequently, Company A may prefer to adopt Method 3 as described above.

Careful judgement will be needed if, for example, most outcomes are profitable but one outcome is loss making, as to whether a loss should be recognised.

8   Recognition criteria – interest revenue

Interest revenue should be recognised using the effective interest method when:
[IAS 18:29 & 30(a)]

- it is probable that the economic benefits associated with the transaction will flow to the entity; and

- the amount of the revenue can be measured reliably.

The effective interest method is discussed in **section 4.1** of **chapter B6** (for entities applying IFRS 9) and **section 4.1** of **chapter C6** (for entities applying IAS 39).

When unpaid interest has accrued before the acquisition of an interest-bearing investment, the subsequent receipt of interest is allocated between the pre-acquisition and post-acquisition periods. [IAS 18:32] Only the post-acquisition portion is recognised as revenue. The pre-acquisition portion will offset the amount recognised at acquisition for interest receivable.

Example 8

Unpaid interest accrued before acquisition of investment

An entity purchases CU1 million face value bonds for CU1,030,000 on 1 April 20X1. The bonds pay interest at 12 per cent per annum on 31 December and 30 June each year.

The investor will receive CU60,000 as interest for the period from 1 January 20X1 to 30 June 20X1, but only CU30,000 of this should be recognised as interest revenue.

Therefore, the entries to record the acquisition of the bond and the receipt of interest at 30 June 20X1 will be as follows.

	CU'000	CU'000
Dr Investments	1,000	
Dr Debtor (interest receivable)	30	
Cr Cash		1,030
To recognise the acquisition of the bond.		

	CU'000	CU'000
Dr Cash	60	
Cr Debtor (interest receivable)		30
Cr Interest income (profit or loss)		30
To recognise the receipt of interest.		

Interest revenue is recognised only when it is probable that the economic benefits associated with the transaction will flow to the entity. However, when an uncertainty arises about the collectibility of an amount already included in revenue, the uncollectible amount, or the amount in respect of which recovery has ceased to be probable, is recognised as a bad debt expense, rather than as an adjustment of the amount of revenue originally recognised. [IAS 18:34]

9 Recognition criteria – royalty revenue

Royalty revenue should be recognised on an accrual basis in accordance with the substance of the relevant agreement when:
[IAS 18:29 & 30(b)]

- it is probable that the economic benefits associated with the trans- action will flow to the entity; and

- the amount of the revenue can be measured reliably.

Royalties accrue in accordance with the terms of the relevant agreement and are usually recognised on that basis unless, having regard to the substance of the agreement, it is more appropriate to recognise revenue on some other systematic and rational basis. [IAS 18:33]

The appendix to IAS 18 contains the following illustration of the principle of revenue recognition for royalty income.

Example 9

Licence fees and royalties
[IAS 18 Appendix: Example 20]

Fees and royalties paid for the use of an entity's assets (such as trademarks, patents, software, music copyright, record masters and motion picture films)

---

are normally recognised in accordance with the substance of the agreement. As a practical matter, this may be on a straight-line basis over the life of the agreement, e.g. when a licensee has the right to use certain technology for a specified period of time.

An assignment of rights for a fixed fee or non-refundable guarantee under a non-cancellable contract which permits the licensee to exploit those rights freely and the licensor has no remaining obligations to perform is, in substance, a sale. An example is a licensing agreement for the use of software when the licensor has no obligations subsequent to delivery. Another example is the granting of rights to exhibit a motion picture film in markets where the licensor has no control over the distributor and expects to receive no further revenues from the box office receipts. In such cases, revenue is recognised at the time of sale.

In some cases, whether or not a licence fee or royalty will be received is contingent on the occurrence of a future event. In such cases, revenue is recognised only when it is probable that the fee or royalty will be received, which is normally when the event has occurred.

Royalty revenue is recognised only when it is probable that the economic benefits associated with the transaction will flow to the entity. When an uncertainty arises about the collectibility of an amount already included in revenue, however, the uncollectible amount, or the amount in respect of which recovery has ceased to be probable, is recognised as a bad debt expense, rather than as an adjustment of the amount of revenue originally recognised. [IAS 18:34]

Royalty agreements vary, but essentially their purpose is to sell a right to use an entity's assets, such as trademarks, patents and software, for a certain period of time. The question arises as to whether, under a royalty agreement, revenue should be recognised up front when the agreement is signed or deferred and spread over the duration of the agreement.

Example 20 in the appendix to IAS 18 states that revenue under royalty agreements should be recognised in accordance with the substance of the arrangements. It further clarifies that the overriding factor in determining the accounting treatment for such arrangements should be whether the licensor has any remaining obligation to perform. The outcome of each arrangement depends on the circumstances. The discussion below describes two typical examples.

Licence to use a trademark

The sale of the right to use a trademark often requires that the licensor (seller) continue to ensure the 'quality' of the trademark. When the requirement imposes a genuine performance obligation (i.e. the licensee could realistically seek redress for non-performance), revenue recognition should be deferred and spread over the period of performance (i.e. the licence term) by the seller. If, however, the requirement is a mere formality and the seller has no remaining obligation to perform, then revenue should be recognised immediately.

Software licensing arrangement

Software licensing arrangements allow the licensee (customer) to use intellectual property. Upon delivery of the software licence, in the absence of any requirement that the licensor (seller) provide technical support, software upgrades or enhancements, a sale has occurred and revenue from the sale should be recognised in full.

If the licensor sells technical support or software upgrades together with the licence, the arrangement should be analysed as to whether it is a multiple-element arrangement, in which case revenue should be recognised separately for each of the identified components (see **5.1**).

When a royalty agreement makes provision for the payment of royalties based on the number of sales subject to a guaranteed minimum amount, careful judgement should be exercised in determining whether the guaranteed minimum amount should be recognised as revenue immediately or spread over the agreement period.

If the seller has no remaining obligation to perform (i.e. the rights and associated assets in respect of which royalties will be paid have been transferred to the customer and there are no ongoing services), the present value of the guaranteed minimum amount of royalties will be recognised immediately provided that there is no significant uncertainty that the amount will be received and the amount is non–refundable. Any additional, variable amounts that are receivable based on future sales should be recognised as revenue only when the sales giving rise to these payments occur.

10   Recognition criteria – dividend revenue

Dividend revenue should be recognised when:
[IAS 18:29 & 30(c)]

- it is probable that the economic benefits associated with the transaction will flow to the entity;

- the amount of the revenue can be measured reliably; and

- the shareholder's right to receive payment is established.

The timing of the establishment of the shareholders' right to receive payment may vary based on the laws of particular countries. In some countries, it may occur when the board of directors of an entity formally declares its intention to pay a dividend. In other countries, it may occur only after such a declaration has been approved by shareholders. In any case if, subsequent to revenue recognition but before receipt of the dividend, it becomes apparent that the investee will not be able to pay the dividend, the amount of dividend revenue previously recognised is dealt with as a bad debt expense rather than as a reversal of dividend revenue. [IAS 18:34]

10.1   Dividends on equity investments declared from pre-acquisition profits

Until it was amended in May 2008, IAS 18 required that, when dividends on equity investments are declared from pre-acquisition profits, those dividends should be deducted from the cost of the investment. Following the May 2008 amendments (effective for annual periods beginning on or after 1 January 2009), dividend revenue is recognised in profit or loss irrespective of whether it is declared from pre- or post-acquisition profits and, separately, in some cases it is necessary to consider whether the equity investment may be impaired.

10.2   Dividends in the form of equity instruments of the investee

---

Example 10.2A

Dividends in the form of equity instruments of the investee (no cash alternative)

I Limited holds an equity investment in Entity A. Entity A distributes a dividend in the form of its own equity shares to all of its ordinary shareholders on a pro rata basis. No cash alternative is offered. After the distribution, the relative shareholdings of the investors in Entity A remain unchanged.

Should I Limited recognise dividend revenue for the fair value of the shares in Entity A it receives?

No. When all ordinary shareholders are paid a share dividend on a pro rata basis, there is no change in the financial position or economic interest of any of the investors. In such circumstances, in accordance with IAS 18:29(a), the dividend is not recognised as revenue because it is not probable that there is an economic benefit associated with the transaction that will flow to the investor.

Example 10.2B

Dividends in the form of equity instruments of the investee (with a cash alternative)

I Limited holds an equity instrument in Entity A. Entity A offers all of its shareholders the right to receive a dividend in cash or in shares. I Limited subsequently elects to receive the dividend in shares.

How should I Limited recognise the dividend received?

The substance of a share dividend with a cash alternative is that of a dividend in cash with an immediate reinvestment in shares. Accordingly, at the date the dividend is authorised (i.e. the date when the shareholders' right to receive the dividend is established), I Limited should recognise the dividend as revenue, measured at the higher of the value of the shares offered and the value of the cash alternative. This reflects the fact the investor would be expected to opt for the most economically advantageous alternative.

From the date of authorisation of the dividend until the date on which I Limited elects to receive cash or shares, the estimated revenue should be adjusted to reflect changes in the fair value of the shares but it should never fall below the value of the cash alternative.

On the date that I Limited makes its final election, the revenue amount becomes fixed.

---

11   Disclosure

Entities are required to disclose the accounting policies adopted for revenue recognition, including the methods adopted to determine the stage of completion of transactions involving the rendering of services. [IAS 18:35(a)]

The following should be considered, depending on the circumstances, for disclosure in the revenue recognition accounting policy:

- if an entity has different policies for different types of revenue transactions, the policy for each material type of transaction should be disclosed;

- if sales transactions have multiple elements, such as products and services, the disclosure should include the accounting policy for each element as well as how multiple elements are determined and valued;

- changes in estimates that underlie revenue recognition, such as changes in estimated returns, should be disclosed; and

- any specific revenue transactions that are unusual because of their nature, size, or frequency of occurrence may require separate disclosure.

The amount of each significant category of revenue recognised during the period is also required to be disclosed, including revenue arising from: [IAS 18:35(b)]

- the sale of goods;

- the rendering of services;

- interest;

- royalties; and

- dividends.

The entity is also required to disclose the amount of revenue arising from exchanges of goods or services included in each significant category of revenue. [IAS 18:35(c)]

IFRIC 15 *Agreements for the Construction of Real Estate* requires certain disclosures when an entity recognises revenue using the percentage of completion method for agreements that meet all the criteria in IAS 18:14 continuously as construction progresses. These disclosures are described in **2.1.3** above.

12   Future developments

In November 2011, the IASB and the US Financial Accounting Standards Board jointly published for public comment an exposure draft (ED) ED/2011/6 *Revenue from Contracts with Customers*, being a revision of an earlier exposure draft, ED/2010/6. If adopted, the ED's proposals would supersede IAS 11 *Construction Contracts* and IAS 18 *Revenue* and related Interpretations. The core principle proposed in the ED would require an entity to recognise revenue to depict the transfer of promised goods or services to customers in an amount that reflects the consideration to which it expects to be entitled in exchange for those goods or services. To apply that principle, an entity would perform the following steps.

- **Identify the contract with a customer.** Normally each revenue transaction is a single contract, but sometimes two contracts are combined.

- **Identify the separate performance obligations in the contract.** If an entity promises to provide more than one good or service, it would account for each promised good or service as a separate performance obligation only if the good or service is distinct.

- **Determine the transaction price.** Transaction price is either the expected value or the most likely amount of consideration to which an entity expects to be entitled. This would take into account the time value of money (subject to an exemption for intervals of less than one year between performance and payment), the fair value of non-cash consideration, and consideration payable to a customer, but would not take into account collectibility.

- **Allocate the transaction price to the separate performance obligations** by reference to the stand-alone selling prices of the goods or services underlying each performance obligation, using estimation methods (which may include a residual approach in certain circumstances), when necessary.

- **Recognise revenue when (or as) the entity satisfies each performance obligation** by transferring control of the promised good or service to the customer. The ED sets out criteria to determine whether a performance obligation is satisfied over time or at a point in time.

The ED contains a great deal of detailed guidance, much of which is not reflected in IAS 11 or IAS 18. Accordingly, although for many entities the new approach will not dramatically change the amount or timing of revenue recognition, there is nevertheless likely to be some impact for many entities.

The final Standard is expected to be issued in the second half of 2013.

A15 Employee benefits

Contents

1 Introduction

In June 2011, the IASB issued a revised version of IAS 19 *Employee Benefits*, which is effective for annual periods beginning on or after 1 January 2013. IAS 19(2011) replaces the previous version of IAS 19, which was originally issued in 1998 (referred to as IAS 19(1998) and discussed in **appendix A3**). For annual periods beginning before 1 January 2013, entities may continue to apply IAS 19(1998). Alternatively, entities may choose to apply IAS 19(2011) in advance of its 2013 effective date, provided that they disclose that fact (see **section 11**).

IAS 19 sets out accounting and disclosure requirements for employee benefits. Related disclosure requirements are also set out in:

- IAS 1 *Presentation of Financial Statements*, which requires disclosure of the employee benefits expense (see **7.4.6** in **chapter A4**); and

- IAS 24 *Related Party Disclosures*, which requires disclosure of employee benefits (including share-based payments) for key management personnel (see **section 5.2** of **chapter A23**).

IAS 19 does not deal with reporting by employee benefit plans. IAS 26 *Accounting and Reporting by Retirement Benefit Plans* deals with the financial statements of pension schemes (see **chapter A41**). [IAS 19(2011):3]

1.1 Significant changes arising from IAS 19(2011)

While the headline change in the revised Standard is the elimination of the 'corridor' approach, the IASB has taken the opportunity to address a number of issues. The most significant changes are listed below. Other, more minor, changes are discussed in later sections of this chapter.

1.1.1 Full recognition of deficit (surplus) in the statement of financial position

The most significant amendment will require an entity to recognise changes in defined benefit obligations and plan assets when they occur, thus eliminating the 'corridor' approach permitted under IAS 19(1998) (discussed at **7.5** in **appendix A3**). Under IAS 19(2011), all actuarial gains and losses are recognised immediately through other comprehensive income (OCI) (the option to recognise actuarial gains and losses in profit or loss has also been removed).

Recognition of actuarial gains and losses	
IAS 19(1998) – three options	IAS 19(2011) – one required treatment
Immediately through profit or loss Immediately through OCI Deferred via the 'corridor' approach	Immediately through OCI

The IASB decided to require immediate recognition of the defined benefit deficit (surplus) on the basis that this treatment provides information that is more relevant to users of the financial statements and it improves comparability between entities by eliminating options. [IAS 19(2011):BC70 & 71] The net pension asset or liability recognised in the statement of financial position will reflect the full value of the plan deficit or surplus (subject only to the possible effect of the 'asset ceiling' – see **7.3**).

1.1.2   Interest on the net defined benefit liability (asset)

IAS 19(2011) introduces the concept of recognising net interest on the net defined benefit liability (asset) in place of the interest on the defined benefit obligation and the expected return on plan assets recognised under IAS 19(1998). Under IAS 19(2011), the net interest on the net defined benefit liability (asset) is defined as the change in the net defined benefit liability (asset) during the reporting period that arises from the passage of time; it is determined by multiplying the net defined benefit liability (asset) by the discount rate (market yield on high quality corporate bonds). Effectively, this means that the defined benefit obligation and the plan assets are multiplied by the same interest rate (see **7.4.3** for further discussion).

The interest rate specified under IAS 19(2011) is the same as that specified for the defined benefit obligation under IAS 19(2008). The effect of the changes summarised in the previous paragraph is, therefore, that income is recognised on the plan assets using that interest rate under IAS 19(2011) whereas, under IAS 19(1998), income on the plan assets is recognised based on the expected return on those assets. The expected return on plan assets recognised under

IAS 19(1998) depends on the actual investment portfolio and is typically not equal to the discount rate applied for the determination of the interest cost on the obligation. When the discount rate is lower than the expected return on plan assets (as is generally the case), application of IAS 19(2011) will reduce net profit or loss.

1.1.3   Change in presentation approach

The amendments introduce a new approach for presenting changes in defined benefit obligations and plan assets in the statement of profit or loss and other comprehensive income. Under the revised Standard:

- service cost and net interest on the net defined benefit liability (asset) are recognised in profit or loss; and

- remeasurements are recognised in OCI.

IAS 19(2011), like IAS 19(1998), does not specify in which line items within profit or loss service cost and net interest are to be presented (see **8.1.3** for further discussion).

Service cost component – recognised in profit or loss and includes current service cost, vested and unvested past service cost (together with gains and losses from curtailments) and gains or losses on settlements. The distinction between past service cost and curtailments in IAS 19(1998) is no longer necessary because both of these items are recognised immediately in profit or loss under IAS 19(2011).

Net interest component – net interest (as discussed in **1.1.2**) is recognised in profit or loss. The difference between the actual return on plan assets and the change in plan assets resulting from the passage of time is recognised in OCI as part of the remeasurement component.

Remeasurement component – recognised in OCI and comprises actuarial gains and losses on the defined benefit obligation, the difference between the actual return on plan assets and the interest on plan assets included in the net interest component, and any changes in the effect of the asset ceiling. Actuarial gains and losses

include experience adjustments and the effects of changes in actuarial assumptions. Remeasurements are never reclassified to profit or
loss but may be transferred within equity (e.g. to retained earnings).

Presentation of changes under IAS 19(2011)		
Component	Comprising	Presented in
Service cost	• Current and past service cost • Curtailments and settlements	Profit or loss
Net interest	• Interest on net surplus/deficit	Profit or loss
Remeasurement	• Actuarial gains and losses • Difference between actual return on plan assets and interest calculated on those assets • Effects of 'asset ceiling'	OCI

1.1.4   Additional disclosure requirements

IAS 19(2011) introduces more extensive disclosure requirements
relating to the characteristics, risks and amounts in the financial
statements related to defined benefit plans, as well as the effect of
defined benefit plans on the amount, timing and uncertainty of the
entity's future cash flows (see **8.2** for further discussion). The following are some of the most significant:

- a narrative description of the risks that the entity judges to be
  significant or unusual (e.g. plan assets are invested primarily in
  single class of investments where a concentration risk arises);

- actuarial gains and losses arising from changes in demographic
  assumptions separately from those arising from changes in
  financial assumptions;

- the fair value of plan assets divided into classes that distinguish
  the nature and risks of those assets and subdivided into assets
  that do and do not have a quoted market price;

- significant actuarial assumptions used to determine defined
  benefit obligations and how a reasonably possible change to the
  significant actuarial assumptions would affect the defined benefit obligation (sensitivity analysis);

- a narrative description of asset-liability matching strategies
  such as annuities or longevity swaps; and

- the expected contribution for the next annual reporting period and the weighted average duration of the defined benefit obligations.

The revised Standard also includes additional disclosure requirements regarding multi-employer defined benefit plans by requiring qualitative information about any agreed deficit or surplus allocation on wind-up of the plan, or the entity's withdrawal from the plan. If an entity accounts for a multi-employer defined benefit plan as if it were a defined contribution plan, disclosures of the level of participation in the plan and the expected contribution for the next reporting period are required (see **5.1.4** for further discussion).

1.1.5   *Classification of employee benefits*

Under IAS 19(2011), short-term employee benefits are redefined as employee benefits that are "expected to be settled wholly before twelve months after the end of the annual reporting period" and other long-term benefits as all employee benefits other than short-term employee benefits, post-employment benefits and termination benefits. Therefore, under IAS 19(2011), 'other' long-term benefits is the residual category.

Under IAS 19(1998), short-term benefits and long-term benefits are distinguished on the basis of when they are "due to be settled". The modification may result in more benefits being classified as other long-term employee benefits that will need to be measured using actuarial assumptions (see **3.1** for further discussion).

1.1.6   *Taxes payable*

IAS 19(2011) provides clarification on the treatment of taxes payable by defined benefit plans. When such taxes arise from contributions and benefits relating to service before the reporting date, they are included in the estimate of the defined benefit obligation; all other taxes are required to be deducted from the actual return on plan assets (see also **7.2.4**). [IAS 19(2011):BC121]

In contrast, IAS 19(1998) simply indicates that taxes payable by the plan are recognised as a deduction from the return on plan assets, without specifying whether this treatment applies to all taxes payable or only to those relating to plan assets.

Therefore, under IAS 19(2011), entities will need to develop actuarial assumptions about the timing and amount of taxes payable by the plan relating to service before the reporting date or imposed on benefits resulting from that service. The revised requirements could also lead to an increase in the defined benefit obligation and current service cost depending on an entity's accounting policy under IAS 19(1998).

IAS 19(2011) only addresses taxes payable by the plan itself; the IASB decided that it could not address other taxes, such as taxes that are payable by the employer, in a timely manner. It remains a matter of judgement, therefore, whether such taxes are income taxes within the scope of IAS 12 *Income Taxes*, costs of liabilities within the scope of IAS 37 *Provisions, Contingent Liabilities and Contingent Assets*, or costs of employee benefits within the scope of IAS 19. [IAS 19(2011):BC124]

1.1.7   Administration costs

IAS 19 (2011) specifies that only the costs of managing the plan assets (i.e. investment-related administration costs) should be recognised as part of the return on plan assets (and, therefore, recognised in OCI). All other administration costs are recognised when incurred in profit or loss. [IAS 19(2011):130 & BC127] (See **7.2.4.11** for further discussion.)

Under IAS 19(1998), administration costs are either included in the actuarial assumptions or deducted from the expected return on plan assets. While no further guidance was provided, it was generally considered that, based on the underlying principle that transactions should be accounted for in accordance with their substance, expenses incurred in relation to providing benefits and administering the defined benefit plan should be included in the measurement of the defined benefit obligation and that expenses incurred in relation to asset management and to the income earned on investments held by a defined benefit plan should be taken into account when determining the expected return.

1.1.8   Past service cost

Past service cost arises when an entity introduces a defined benefit plan that attributes benefits to past service or changes the benefits for past service under an existing defined benefit plan. Under IAS 19(2011), all past service cost is recognised in profit or loss when it arises. In contrast, under IAS 19(1998), when the plan imposes vesting requirements, unvested past service cost is recognised in profit or loss on a straight-line basis over the average period until the benefits become vested.

Along with the elimination of the 'corridor' approach (see **1.1.1**), this amendment also serves to remove the deferral mechanisms that are available under IAS 19(1998).

1.1.9   Risk-sharing

When revising IAS 19, the IASB has taken the opportunity to clarify certain matters with respect to risk-sharing features, such as performance targets and contributions by employees, which were not addressed in IAS 19(1998).

In particular, IAS 19(2011) addresses the treatment of defined benefit plans that include pension promises based on achieving specific performance targets. The Standard specifies that the measurement of such obligations should reflect the best estimate of the effect of the performance target or other criteria. This is consistent with the view expressed previously by the IFRIC (now the IFRS Interpretations Committee) (see the November 2007 edition of *IFRIC Update*).

IAS 19(2011) also indicates the treatment that should be applied in accounting for contributions by employees or third parties as follows:

- discretionary contributions should reduce service cost when they are paid to the plan;

- non-discretionary contributions linked to service should also reduce service cost and be attributed to periods of service as a negative benefit; and

- non-discretionary contributions required to reduce a deficit arising from losses on plan assets or actuarial losses should be recognised as part of remeasurement.

In practice, determining the reason why the employees or third party are required to contribute to the plan will require judgement (see **7.2.4.8** for further discussion).

See also **section 12** for a discussion of proposals issued in March 2013 to simplify the treatment of non-discretionary contributions linked to service.

1.1.10   Curtailments

IAS 19(2011) retains the distinction between 'curtailments' and other plan amendments – but a 'curtailment' occurs only when an entity significantly reduces the number of employees covered by a plan. The impact of this distinction under the revised Standard is limited because both types of amendments are recognised in the same manner (in profit or loss, as service cost) and at the same time (when the amendment occurs).

This represents a simplification as compared to IAS 19(1998), under which the distinction between past service cost and curtailments is more difficult to apply and has a greater significance due to the difference in treatment (mainly due to the deferred recognition of unvested past service cost) (see **7.4.2** for further discussion).

1.1.11   Settlements

The Board has clarified that settlements to be recognised in profit or loss as service cost comprise only payments of benefits that are not set out in the terms of the plan. Any payments of benefits contemplated in the terms of the plan (including options on the nature of the benefit payments) are included in the actuarial assumptions and related experience differences are recognised in OCI as remeasurements (see **7.4.2.2** for further discussion).

This is consistent with the view expressed previously by the IFRIC (now the IFRS Interpretations Committee) (see the May 2008 edition of *IFRIC Update*).

1.1.12   *Termination benefits*

While there is no fundamental change in the definition of a termination benefit, IAS 19(2011) provides additional guidance to assist in distinguishing between benefits payable in exchange for termination of employment and those payable in exchange for service. For example, if an entity makes an offer to an employee of benefits available for more than a short period, or there is more than a short period between the offer and the expected date of actual termination, this is an indication that the offer is less likely to be deemed a termination benefit.

To align the timing of recognising amounts resulting from plan amendments, curtailments, termination benefits and restructuring, IAS 19(2011) requires that:

- if a plan amendment is linked to a restructuring or termination benefit, the gain or loss should be recognised at the earlier of:

  - when the plan amendment or curtailment occurs; and

  - when the related restructuring costs or termination benefits are recognised; and

- if a termination benefit is linked to a restructuring, the termination benefit should be recognised at the earlier of:

  - when the entity can no longer withdraw an offer of the benefits; and

  - when the related restructuring costs are recognised under IAS 37.

All of these amounts are recognised at the same time if they are related to each other (see **10.2** for further discussion).

2   Objective and scope

The objective of IAS 19 is to prescribe the accounting and disclosure for employee benefits. The Standard requires an entity to recognise:
[IAS 19(2011):1]

• a liability when an employee has provided service in exchange for employee benefits to be paid in the future; and

• an expense when the entity consumes the economic benefit arising from service provided by an employee in exchange for employee benefits.

IAS 19 is required to be applied by an employer in accounting for all employee benefits, except those to which IFRS 2 *Share-based Payment* applies (see **chapter A16**). [IAS 19(2011):2] The employee benefits to which the Standard applies include those provided:
[IAS 19(2011):4]

• under formal plans or other formal agreements between an entity and individual employees, groups of employees or their representatives;

• under legislative requirements, or through industry arrangements, whereby entities are required to contribute to national, state, industry or other multi-employer plans; or

• by those informal practices that give rise to a constructive obligation. Informal practices give rise to a constructive obligation when the entity has no realistic alternative but to pay employee benefits. An example of a constructive obligation is when a change in the entity's informal practices would cause unacceptable damage to its relationship with employees.

IAS 19 defines employee benefits as all forms of consideration given by an entity in exchange for service rendered by employees or for the termination of employment. [IAS 19(2011):8] This includes:
[IAS 19(2011):6]

• benefits provided either to employees or to their dependents or beneficiaries; and

• benefits settled by payments (or the provision of goods or services) either directly to employees or to others (e.g. spouses, children or dependants, or to insurance companies).

For the purposes of IAS 19, 'employees' are considered to include directors and other management personnel, and to encompass those providing service on a full-time, part-time, permanent, casual or temporary basis. [IAS 19(2011):7]

The Standard divides the employee benefits within its scope into four categories, which are discussed in the following sections of this chapter:

- **section 3** – short-term employee benefits;

- **sections 4** to **8** – post-employment benefits;

- **section 9** – other long-term employee benefits; and

- **section 10** – termination benefits.

The following example considers whether profit-sharing benefit plans under which employees are entitled to receive a share of the 'taxable profits' of an entity should be accounted for in accordance with IAS 12 *Income Taxes* or IAS 19.

Example 2A

Statutory employee profit-sharing scheme

Entity A operates in a jurisdiction where statutory employee profit-sharing arrangements require employers to share 10 per cent of profit, calculated in accordance with applicable tax laws (subject to specific exceptions), with employees.

This statutory profit-sharing scheme falls within the scope of IAS 19. Although the arrangement calculates amounts payable to employees in accordance with applicable tax laws, it meets the definition of an employee benefit in IAS 19(2011):8 because the amounts are paid to the employees in exchange for services rendered. Therefore, the employee profit-sharing arrangement described should be accounted for in accordance with IAS 19 and not by analogy to IAS 12 *Income Taxes* or IAS 37 *Provisions, Contingent Liabilities and Contingent Assets*.

The objective of IAS 19 is to recognise compensation expense only when the employee has provided the related service. Consequently, Entity A should not recognise an asset or a liability related to future expected reversals of differences between taxable profit and accounting profit in connection with such an employee profit-sharing arrangement.

The features of statutory profit-sharing arrangements vary between jurisdictions. Features may include the following.

- the annual payment to individual employees may be limited to a specified amount, with any excess paid to the government to fund public programmes (e.g. worker education, investments);

- an entity may be permitted to apply tax losses carried forward from earlier accounting periods to reduce its profit-sharing obligation; and

- if the tax authorities adjust an entity's taxable income, the entity may be required to recalculate the profit-sharing amount for the period. If the entity made an overpayment to the employees in the previous year(s), the entity may have a right to claim a refund from the employees (even if they are no longer employed with the entity).

Even when the plans include additional features such as those described above, the substance of the arrangement remains that of a profit-sharing employee benefit to which IAS 19 applies.

This conclusion was confirmed by the IFRS Interpretations Committee in the context of IAS 19(1998) (see *IFRIC Update*, November 2010) and is not affected by the 2011 revision of IAS 19.

Example 2B

Costs of employees placed on temporary suspension

Company A temporarily suspends employees during difficult economic periods when there is a downturn in production activity. Company A and the employees enter into a temporary suspension agreement, under which:

- employees remain employed during periods of suspension on the same terms as their current employment contracts;

- during the suspension period, employees collect unemployment benefits from the State as well as a reduced salary from Company A so that the amount of cash they receive each month equates to a percentage of their current salary (i.e. Company A commits to pay employees the difference between the unemployment insurance they receive and an agreed percentage (e.g. 75 per cent) of their current salaries);

- employees are not required to physically be at work during the suspension period;

- Company A has the right to call the employees back to work as necessary during the suspension period (e.g. as production activity fluctuates); and

- employees cannot take up work elsewhere during the suspension period (i.e. they are required to stay at home unless they resign, in which case a fixed notice period is required).

The suspension of employees is expected to last for a period of between six months and two years depending on Company A's needs and the economic environment. Schemes such as these have been developed in countries where the State is reluctant to change redundancy laws in favour of employers but is willing to offer a form of subsidy by paying unemployment benefits to employees during suspension periods.

Should Company A recognise a liability for the expected cost of the suspended employees when the temporary suspension agreement is first enforced?

When the employer uses a temporary suspension arrangement of this nature in order to reduce its employment costs during periods of reduced activity, the costs of the temporary suspension should be classified as a short-term benefit similar to a paid absence (e.g. holiday or leave pay). Short-term paid absences only give rise to a liability when they are accumulating, as discussed in IAS 19(2011):13 and IAS 19(2011):18. This is not the case in the circumstances described because the employees only have a right to receive payments as suspension occurs and for as long as suspension lasts. Company A has the discretion to ask some or all of its employees to return to work at any time and revert to normal working arrangements and remuneration. Therefore, in these circumstances, the costs of suspension should be recognised over the suspension period and should not be accrued at the outset.

Note that, in the circumstances described, the payments should not be classified as termination benefits; they are paid in exchange for *suspension* of the employees' employment rather than in exchange for *termination* of the employees' employment (as would be required under the definition of termination benefits in IAS 19(2011):8 – see **section 10**).

3   Short-term employee benefits

This section addresses the distinction between benefits classified as short-term and 'other' long-term benefits under IAS 19. This classification is important for recognition and measurement but does not affect the decision on presentation of any associated liability as current or non-current in the statement of financial position (see **4.1.1.2** in **chapter A4**).

3.1   Definition

Short-term employee benefits are defined as employee benefits (other than termination benefits) that are expected to be settled wholly before 12 months after the end of the annual reporting period in which the employees render the related service. [IAS 19(2011):8] They include items such as the following, if expected to be settled wholly before 12 months after the end of the annual reporting period in which the employees render the related services:
[IAS 19(2011):9]

- wages, salaries and social security contributions;

- paid annual leave and paid sick leave;

- profit-sharing and bonuses; and

- non-monetary benefits (e.g. access to medical care, housing, cars, free or subsidised goods or services) for current employees.

Prior to the June 2011 revision of IAS 19, short-term benefits are defined as employee benefits (other than termination benefits) that are "due to be settled" within 12 months after the end of the period in which the employees render the related service. The Basis for Conclusions on IAS 19(1998) notes that the distinction between short-term and long-term employee benefits on this basis is consistent with the distinction between current and non-current liabilities under IAS 1 *Presentation of Financial Statements.* It is clear, therefore, that under IAS 19(1998) the focus is on when the employee is entitled to the benefit rather than when the benefit is expected to be settled.

In contrast, the focus in IAS 19(2011) is on the timing of the *expected* settlement. This change has been made in order to narrow the short-term benefits category (for which a simplified measurement approach is applied) to those benefits in respect of which measurement on an undiscounted basis is not materially different from the present value of the benefit. When benefits are classified on the basis of the employee's entitlement, rather than on when the benefits are expected to be settled, this is not necessarily so (see IAS 19(2011):BC18 and BC19 for further discussion).

The impact of this change is likely to be that more employee benefits will be classified as other long-term benefits, and this will result in more complex accounting (see **section 9**).

Example 3.1 illustrates this change in approach.

The changes in IAS 19(2011) mean that there is no longer consistency between the basis for classifying benefits as short- and other long-term benefits under IAS 19(2011) and the basis for presenting liabilities as current and non-current under IAS 1. The former focuses on expectations regarding the timing of settlement, whereas the latter focuses on when amounts are due to be settled, consistent with IAS 19(1998). Consequently, a benefit may be classified as an other long-term benefit under IAS 19(2011) (because employees are not expected to take all of their benefits within 12 months of the period in which the benefits are earned) but may be presented entirely as a current liability (because the employees are entitled to receive the benefits 'on demand', for example if they were to leave the entity's employment). See **4.1.1.2** in **chapter A4** for further discussion.

Example 3.1

Classification of employee benefits as short- or long-term

Employees of Company A accumulate annual leave on a pro rata basis over each calendar year. Unused annual leave can be carried forward indefinitely and must be paid up in cash when an employee leaves Company A's employment. Experience demonstrates that employees use their accumulated annual leave over a period longer than two years.

Under IAS 19(2011), the unused annual leave would not meet the definition of a short-term benefit because it is not *expected* to be settled wholly within 12 months after the end of the annual period in which the employee renders service. Consequently, it would be classified as an other long-term benefit (the residual classification) and accounted for accordingly (see **section 9**).

In contrast, under IAS 19(1998), the unused annual leave would be classified as a short-term benefit because employees are entitled to their accumulated, unused annual leave 'on demand' if they choose to leave Company A's employment. Therefore, the obligation meets the definition of a short-term employee benefit in its entirety.

The definition in IAS 19(2011) refers to classification on the basis of whether the benefit is expected to be settled 'wholly' within 12 months after the end of the annual reporting period in which the related service is rendered. Therefore, benefits that are expected to be settled over a period of time can only be classified as short-term if all of the settlements are expected to occur within that 12-month period.

While the Standard does not provide any specific guidance on the unit of account to be used in evaluating the period over which the benefit is expected to be settled (e.g. whether the assessment should be performed at the individual employee level or for the workforce as a whole), IAS 19(2011):BC20 indicates that the IASB concluded that the classification of the benefits should reflect the characteristics of the benefits, rather than the demographic or financial assumptions at a point in time. In addition, IAS 19(2011):BC21 states that the Board considered requiring an entity to classify benefits on an employee-by-employee basis, but concluded that this would not be practical and would not meet the objectives of the classification.

To illustrate, in **example 3.1**, some employees of Company A may always use their annual leave in full within 12 months after the end of the annual reporting period, but others may receive benefit later (e.g. in cash when they cease employment). The fact that some employees will receive benefit more than 12 months after the end of the annual reporting period means that all annual leave is classified as an other long-term benefit. It is not appropriate to classify the same benefit differently for individual employees or groups of employees merely because of different expectations about when they will claim it.

3.2   Change in classification of short-term benefits

An entity is required to consider whether a benefit still meets the definition of a short-term benefit if either of the following events occurs: [IAS 19(2011):10]

- the characteristics of the benefit change (e.g. a change from a non-accumulating benefit to an accumulating benefit); or

- there is a change in expectation regarding the timing of settlement that is not temporary.

An entity need not reclassify a short-term employee benefit if the entity's expectations of the timing of settlement change temporarily. [IAS 19(2011):10]

IAS 19(1998) does not specifically address the reclassification of benefits. The appropriate measurement classification for an employee benefit under IAS 19(1998) is determined when the employer and the employee enter into the contract and is not changed as time passes and the date of settlement draws nearer. The classification only changes if the nature of the benefit changes (e.g. when employees' entitlements are renegotiated).

In contrast, IAS 19(2011):10 (see above) specifically addresses the question of reclassification – which is more relevant in the context of classification based on expectations. The IASB concluded that the classification of a short-term employee benefit should be revisited if it no longer meets the definition (e.g. if the expected settlement date of a benefit classified initially as a short-term employee benefit changes subsequently to a date more than 12 months after the end of the reporting period) because the undiscounted amount of that benefit could differ materially from its present value. However, the Board also concluded that a temporary change in expectation should not trigger reclassification because such a change would not be indicative of a change in the underlying characteristics of the benefit. [IAS 19(2011):BC20(c)]

Similar concerns do not arise when a benefit previously classified as long-term subsequently meets the definition of a short-term benefit (e.g. if expectations regarding the timing of settlement change so that the benefit is now expected to be settled wholly within 12 months of the end of the period in which service is rendered). In such circumstances, the only effect of reclassification would be that the benefit would be subsequently measured at an undiscounted amount – but that would not be expected to result in a measurement that differs materially from its present value. [IAS 19(2011):BC20(c)]

3.3   Recognition and measurement of short-term employee benefits

An entity should recognise the undiscounted amount of short-term employee benefits earned by an employee in exchange for services rendered during the accounting period:
[IAS 19(2011):11]

- in the statement of financial position, as a liability (accrued expense), after deducting any amounts already paid, or as an asset (prepaid expense), if the amount already paid exceeds the undiscounted amount of the benefits, to the extent that the prepayment is recoverable (e.g. by means of a reduction in future payments or a cash refund); and

- in profit or loss, as an expense, unless another Standard requires or permits inclusion of the benefits in the cost of an asset (e.g. as part of staff costs capitalised in a self-constructed property – see **chapter A7**).

The cost of all short-term employee benefits is recognised as noted above. No actuarial assumptions are required (therefore, there are no actuarial gains or losses to address) and, due to their short-term nature, obligations are dealt with on an undiscounted basis.

When non-monetary short-term benefits are provided, the cost of providing such benefits is measured at the cost to the employer of providing the benefit and is recognised using the same principles as are applied to monetary employee benefits.

3.3.1   *Short-term paid absences*

An entity may pay employees for absence for various reasons (e.g. holidays, sickness and short-term disability, maternity or paternity leave, jury service and military service). Short-term paid absences may be classified as accumulating or non-accumulating. [IAS 19(2011):14]

Accumulating paid absences are those that can be carried forward and used in future accounting periods if the current accounting period's entitlement is not used in full. Accumulating paid absences may be further sub-divided as vesting (when employees are entitled to a cash payment for unused entitlement on leaving the entity) or non-vesting (when no such entitlement arises). [IAS 19(2011):15]

Non-accumulating paid absences cannot be carried forward, i.e. any unused entitlement is lost at the end of the current period and the employee is not entitled to a cash payment for unused entitlement on leaving the entity. This is commonly the case for sick pay (to the extent that unused past entitlement does not increase future entitlement), maternity or paternity leave, and paid absences for jury service or military service. [IAS 19(2011):18]

In applying the general requirements set out at **3.3** above to the expected cost of short-term paid absences:
[IAS 19(2011):13 & 16]

- for accumulating paid absences, the expense should be recognised when the employees render service that increases their entitlement to future paid absences, based on the additional amount that the entity expects to pay as a result of the unused entitlement accumulated at the end of the reporting period; and

- for non-accumulating paid absences, the expense should be recognised only when the absences occur. This is because employee service does not increase the amount of the benefit.

For accumulating absences, the difference between vesting and non-vesting does not affect whether an obligation exists and should be recognised, but does affect the measurement of that obligation, because there is a possibility that employees may leave before they use an accumulating non-vesting entitlement. Therefore, the expense is measured as the additional amount that the entity expects to pay, rather than the maximum amount that it could be obliged to pay. [IAS 19(2011):15]

Example 3.3.1

Measurement of obligation for short-term paid absences

Company A has 200 employees, who are each entitled to 20 working days of paid leave each year. Paid leave is first taken out of the current year's entitlement and then out of the balance brought forward from the previous year (a LIFO basis). Unused leave cannot be carried forward more than one year. Employees are not entitled to a cash payment for unused leave if they leave Company A's employment.

At 31 December 20X1, the average unused entitlement is 3 days per employee (i.e. 600 days in total). Based on past experience, Entity A expects that 175 employees will take no more than their annual entitlement in 20X2 and that the remaining 25 employees will, in total, use 70 days of the entitlement brought forward from 20X1.

The benefit described can be carried forward if the current period's entitlement is not used in full, but only for 12 months; it is therefore an 'accumulating' short-term paid absence. The accumulating paid leave is non-vesting, because employees are not entitled to a cash payment for unused leave when they leave Company A's employment (see IAS 19(2011):15).

IAS 19(2011):16 requires Company A to recognise an obligation at 31 December 20X1 for the amount it expects to pay as a result of the unused entitlement that has accumulated at the end of the period. IAS 19(2011):15 clarifies that, for non-vesting entitlements, the possibility that some employees will not take their entitlement should be reflected in that measurement.

Therefore, at 31 December 20X1, Company A recognises a liability and an expense equal to the undiscounted amount of 70 days of paid leave (i.e. the number of days of the entitlement that are expected to be taken).

IAS 19(2011):17 acknowledges that, in many cases, an entity may not need to make detailed computations to estimate that there is no material obligation for unused paid absences. For example, a sick leave obligation is likely to be material only if there is a formal or informal understanding that unused paid sick leave may be taken as paid annual leave.

3.4 Profit-sharing and bonus plans

In applying the general requirements set out at **3.3** above to the expected cost of profit-sharing and bonus plans, an entity should recognise the expected cost when, and only when:
[IAS 19(2011):19]

- it has a present legal or constructive obligation to make such payments as a result of past events; and

- a reliable estimate of the obligation can be made.

In this context, a present obligation exists when, and only when, the entity has no realistic alternative but to make the payments. [IAS 19(2011):19] The requirements therefore follow closely the general recognition criteria for provisions under IAS 37 *Provisions, Contingent Liabilities and Contingent Assets* (see **chapter A12**). Even when an entity has no legal obligation to pay a bonus, past practice of paying bonuses may give rise to a constructive obligation, if the entity has no realistic alternative but to pay the bonus. [IAS 19(2011):21]

An employee's entitlement to a profit-share may depend on the employee remaining with the entity for a specified period. In such circumstances, the plan creates a constructive obligation as employees render service that increases the amount to be paid if they remain in service until the end of that specified period. [IAS 19(2011):20]

The fact that some employees may leave without receiving payments offered under profit-sharing and bonus plans is reflected in the measurement of the obligation. It is not appropriate to defer recognition of the obligation until the employee completes the entitlement period. [IAS 19(2011):20 & 21]

Example 3.4

Profit-sharing plan

A profit-sharing plan requires Company B to pay a specified proportion of its profit before tax for the financial year to 30 June 20X1 to employees who serve throughout the calendar year 20X1. If no employees leave during the year, the total profit-sharing payments for the year will be 3 per cent of profit before tax. Company B estimates that staff turnover will reduce the payments to 2.5 per cent of profit before tax.

Although the payment is measured as a proportion of the profits for the financial year to 30 June 20X1, performance is based on an employee's service during the calendar year 20X1. Accordingly, Company B recognises a liability and an expense of 50 per cent of 2.5 per cent of the profit before tax at 30 June 20X1. A further expense of 50 per cent of 2.5 per cent should be recognised in the next period, together with a true up for any difference between the estimated amounts and the actual amounts paid.

The costs of profit-sharing and bonus plans are recognised as an expense (and not as a distribution of profit) because they result from employee service and not from a transaction with the entity's owners. [IAS 19(2011):23]

It is common practice for employees to be entitled to a bonus that is determined by reference to performance in a specific period but payable at a future date when that performance condition has been measured. Often there is a requirement for continued employment until that payment date, but the bonus is otherwise unconditional. For example, an entity with a 30 June reporting date pays a bonus in respect of each financial year to employees who have provided services during the financial year (the 'earning' period) and remain on the payroll until 30 September. The bonus pool is determined as a percentage of the entity's profits during the earning period; the additional period from 1 July to 30 September is necessary to determine the entity's profits and the bonus payable to individual employees.

The question arises as to whether the additional service condition (i.e. the requirement to remain in employment during the three-month administrative period up to 30 September) should be taken into account when considering the period over which the bonus expense is recognised.

IAS 19 is not explicit in this regard. IAS 19(2011):20 requires the obligation to be measured and recognised as an expense "as employ-ees render service that increases the amount to be paid if they remain in service until the end of the specified period", reflecting the possibility that some employees may leave without receiving bonus payments.

In the circumstances described, one interpretation of this require-ment could be that the expense should be recognised as the employ-ees render the service that increases the amount to be paid. Because the amount of the bonus does not increase after the earning period, the obligation should be measured at 30 June for the full amount expected to be paid, taking into consideration the expected forfei-tures.

Another interpretation could be that an obligation arises as employ-ees render services when they remain in service until 30 September, thereby suggesting that the period over which the bonus expense is recognised should include the three-month administrative period. This interpretation is consistent with the recognition of an expense relating to share-based payments over the vesting period in accord-ance with IFRS 2 *Share-based Payment*.

Because the wording of IAS 19 is not sufficiently clear, a case can be made for both interpretations and entities should adopt one of these approaches as an accounting policy choice.

Note that the conclusion arrived at above (i.e. that the entity can select one of two approaches as an accounting policy choice) only applies when the additional period is administrative in nature, which will only be the case if the additional period is relatively short.

If profit-sharing and bonus payments are not expected to be settled wholly before 12 months after the end of the annual reporting period in which the employees render the related service, those payments are classified as other long-term employee benefits (see **section 9**). [IAS 19(2011):24]

3.4.1   When is a reliable estimate possible?

An entity can make a reliable estimate of its legal or constructive obligation under a profit-sharing or bonus plan when, and only when: [IAS 19(2011):22]

- the formal terms of the plan contain a formula for determining the amount of the benefit; or

- the amounts to be paid are determined before the financial statements are authorised for issue; or

- past practice gives clear evidence of the amount of the constructive obligation.

3.5   Disclosure

IAS 19 does not specify any particular disclosure requirements for short-term employee benefits, but other Standards may require disclosures. For example: [IAS 19(2011):25]

- IAS 24 *Related Party Disclosures* requires disclosures about employee benefits for key management personnel; and

- IAS 1 *Presentation of Financial Statements* requires disclosure of the employee benefits expense.

4   Post-employment benefits

Post-employment benefits are defined as employee benefits (other than termination benefits and short-term employee benefits) that are payable after the completion of employment. [IAS 19(2011):8]

This definition captures retirement benefits (e.g. pensions and lump sum payments on retirement) and other post-employment benefits (e.g. post-employment life insurance and access to medical care). If an entity provides such benefits, the requirements of IAS 19 apply irrespective of whether a separate entity is established to receive contributions and to pay benefits. [IAS 19(2011):26]

4.1   Post-employment benefit plans

Post-employment benefit plans are formal or informal arrangements under which an entity provides post-employment benefits for one or more employees. [IAS 19(2011):8]

4.2   Types of post-employment benefit plans

The accounting treatment and required disclosures for a post-employment benefit plan depend upon whether it is classified as a defined contribution or a defined benefit plan. In addition to addressing defined contribution and defined benefit plans generally, the Standard also gives guidance as to how its requirements should be applied to insured benefits, multi-employer plans, group plans and state plans.

There are two main types of post-employment benefit plans:
[IAS 19(2011):8]

- **defined contribution plans** are post-employment benefit plans under which an entity pays fixed contributions into a separate entity (a fund) and will have no legal or constructive obligation to pay further contributions if the fund does not hold sufficient assets to pay all employee benefits relating to employee service in the current and prior periods; and

- **defined benefit plans** are post-employment benefit plans other than defined contribution plans.

The classification as either a defined contribution plan or a defined benefit plan depends on the economic substance of the plan as derived from its principal terms and conditions. [IAS 19(2011):27]

IAS 19 explains that, under a defined contribution plan, the amount of post-employment benefits received by an employee is determined by the amount of contributions paid to a post-employment benefit plan or to an insurance company, together with any investment returns arising from the contributions, so that actuarial risk (that benefits will be less than expected) and investment risk (that assets invested will be insufficient to meet expected benefits) fall, in substance, on the employee. [IAS 19(2011):28]

Under a defined benefit plan:
[IAS 19(2011):30]

- the entity's obligation is to provide the agreed benefits to current and former employees; and

- actuarial risk and investment risk fall, in substance, on the entity so that if actuarial or investment experience are worse than expected, the entity's obligation may be increased.

Examples of circumstances in which an entity's obligation is not limited to the amount that it agrees to contribute to a fund (and, hence, the plan is a defined benefit plan) are when the entity has a legal or constructive obligation through:
[IAS 19(2011):29]

- a plan benefit formula that is not linked solely to the amount of contributions and requires the entity to provide further contributions if assets are insufficient to meet the benefits in the plan benefit formula;

- a guarantee, either indirectly through a plan or directly, of a specified return on contributions; or

- informal practices that give rise to a constructive obligation. For example, a constructive obligation may arise when an entity has a history of increasing benefits for former employees to keep pace with inflation even where there is no legal obligation to do so.

The first bullet above was expanded when IAS 19 was revised in June 2011 to clarify that the existence of a benefit formula does not, by itself, create a defined benefit plan, but rather that there needs to be a link between the benefit formula and contributions that creates a legal or constructive obligation to contribute further amounts to meet the benefits specified by the benefit formula. This amendment is intended to address concerns regarding the classification of a plan that has a benefit formula determining the benefits to be paid if there are sufficient plan assets, but not requiring the employer to pay additional contributions if there are insufficient plan assets to pay those benefits. In such circumstances, in effect, the benefit payments are based on the lower of the benefit formula and the plan assets available. The amendments clarify that such a plan is a defined contribution plan. [IAS 19(2011):BC30] The following example illustrates this principle.

Example 4.2

Defined contribution plan with target benefits

An employer has a target benefit plan, the contributions to which are determined on the basis of each employee's age on joining the plan, projected average salary at retirement, projected mortality, and retirement age. When an employee joins the plan, a contribution percentage is computed for that employee based on relevant demographic information. Thereafter, the employer contributes that specific percentage of the employee's salary to the plan. If the employee's salary or other factors change, the employer's contribution rate will not change.

The plan is structured so that the employer's contributions accumulate in each individual employee's account. Investment gains or losses on assets in the plan accrue to the employees on a pro rata basis and are not considered in computing the employer's future contributions. If an employee's account balance at retirement or termination either exceeds or falls short of the target amount, the account balance will not be adjusted by the employer. Employees receive only the funds credited to their accounts.

This plan meets the definition of a defined contribution plan. The target benefit plan has a complex formula to compute the employer's pension contributions. However, the benefit computation is not adjusted for investment gains, losses or forfeitures on the assets contributed to the employee's individual account. As a result, the actuarial and investment risks associated with the plan effectively fall to the employee and, therefore, the plan is a defined contribution plan.

4.3   Funded and unfunded retirement plans

IAS 19 notes that retirement benefit plans can be either funded or unfunded, but it does not formally define these terms. Funded plans are taken to be those under which plan assets are held in a separate entity, usually under the supervision of an administrator. The administrator typically manages the investment of contributions and the payment of benefit entitlements to employees in accordance with the plan rules.

Although IAS 19 does not define funded and unfunded plans, it does define 'plan assets', which the Standard takes into account in measuring the surplus or deficit associated with a post-employment benefit plan. Plan assets comprise:
[IAS 19(2011):8]

- assets held by a long-term employee benefit fund; and

- qualifying insurance policies.

Assets held by a long-term employee benefit fund are assets (other than non-transferable financial instruments issued by the reporting entity) that:
[IAS 19(2011):8]

(a)   are held by an entity (a fund) that is legally separate from the reporting entity and exists solely to pay or fund employee benefits; and

(b)   are available to be used only to pay or fund employee benefits, are not available to the reporting entity's own creditors (even in bankruptcy), and cannot be returned to the reporting entity, unless either:

    (i)   the remaining assets of the fund are sufficient to meet all the related employee benefit obligations of the plan or the reporting entity; or

    (ii)   the assets are returned to the reporting entity to reimburse it for employee benefits already paid.

If these criteria are not met, it appears that the plan should be regarded as unfunded for the purposes of IAS 19. The entity should consider whether any assets underlying employee benefit plans which do not qualify as plan assets should instead appear in its own statement of financial position, because they are either held directly by the entity or, for example, by a structured or special purpose entity controlled by it, which would be consolidated in accordance with IFRS 10 *Consolidated Financial Statements* (see **chapter A24**) (or, for entities that have not yet adopted IFRS 10, SIC-12 *Consolidation – Special Purpose Entities* (see **appendix A1**)).

4.4   Insured benefits

A post-employment benefit plan that is funded by insurance premiums is treated as a defined benefit plan if the entity (either directly or indirectly through the plan) has a legal or constructive obligation either: [IAS 19(2011):46]

- to pay the employee benefits directly when they fall due; or

- to pay further amounts if the insurer does not pay all future employee benefits relating to employee service in the current or prior periods.

In the absence of such a legal or constructive obligation, the plan is treated as a defined contribution plan. [IAS 19(2011):46]

Therefore, insured plans are subject to the same distinction between accounting and funding as other plans. It should not be assumed, merely because an entity insures benefits arising under a defined benefit plan, that the plan assets are necessarily equal to the plan liabilities. IAS 19(2011):47 notes that the benefits insured by an insurance policy need not have a direct or automatic relationship with the entity's obligation for employee benefits.

If the entity retains a legal or constructive obligation, payment of the insurance premium is, in substance, an investment to meet the obligation. In such circumstances, the entity should account for its 'qualifying' insurance policies as plan assets (see **7.2.6.2**) and for other insurance policies as reimbursement rights (if the policies meet the criterion established in IAS 19(2011):116 – see **7.2.6.4**). [IAS 19(2011):48]

When an insurance policy is in the name of a specified plan participant or a group of plan participants, and the entity does not have any legal or constructive obligation to cover any loss on the policy, the entity has no obligation to pay benefits to the employees and the insurer has sole responsibility for paying the benefits. The payment of fixed premiums under such contracts is, in substance, the settlement of the employee benefit obligation, rather than an investment to meet the obligation. Consequently, the entity no longer has an asset or a liability and the entity should treat such payments as contributions to a defined contribution plan. [IAS 19(2011):49]

5   Multi-employer plans, group plans and state plans

5.1   Multi-employer plans

Multi-employer plans are defined contribution plans (other than state plans) or defined benefit plans (other than state plans) that:
[IAS 19(2011):8]

- pool the assets contributed by various entities that are not under common control; and

- use those assets to provide benefits to employees of more than one entity, on the basis that contribution and benefit levels are determined without regard to the identity of the entity that employs the employees concerned.

Multi-employer plans should be classified as defined contribution or defined benefit plans based on the criteria discussed in **section 4**, and accounted for accordingly. [IAS 19(2011):32]

The Standard cites as one example of a multi-employer defined benefit plan a plan under which:
[IAS 19(2011):35]

- the plan is financed on a pay-as-you-go basis: contributions are set at a level that is expected to be sufficient to pay the benefits falling due in the same period and future benefits earned during the current period will be paid out of future contributions; and

- employees' benefits are determined by the length of their service and the participating entities have no realistic means of withdrawing from the plan without paying a contribution for the benefits earned by employees up to the date of withdrawal. Such a plan creates actuarial risk for the entity: if the ultimate cost of benefits already earned at the end of the reporting period is more than expected, the entity will have either to increase its contributions or to persuade employees to accept a reduction in benefits. Therefore, such a plan is a defined benefit plan.

If an entity participates in a defined benefit multi-employer plan, the entity should account for its proportionate share of the defined benefit obligation, plan assets and cost associated with the plan, and provide disclosures, in the same way as for any other defined benefit plan, unless the exemption discussed at **5.1.1** below is available. [IAS 19(2011):33 & 36]

In determining when to recognise and how to measure a liability relating to the wind-up of a multi-employer defined benefit plan, or the entity's withdrawal from a multi-employer defined benefit plan, an entity should apply the requirements of IAS 37 *Provisions, Contingent Liabilities and Contingent Assets* (see **chapter A12**). [IAS 19(2011):39]

5.1.1   *Exemption for insufficient information*

The Standard acknowledges that an entity may not be able to identify its share of the underlying financial position and performance of the plan with sufficient reliability for accounting purposes. This may occur if: [IAS 19(2011):36]

- the plan exposes the participating entities to actuarial risks associated with the current and former employees of other entities, with the result that there is no consistent and reliable basis for allocating the obligations, plan assets and cost to individual entities participating in the plan; or

- the entity does not have access to sufficient information about the plan to satisfy the requirements of IAS 19.

In such circumstances (i.e. the entity participates in a multi-employer plan that is a defined benefit plan, but there is not sufficient information available to use defined-benefit accounting), the entity should: [IAS 19(2011):34]

- account for the plan as if it were a defined contribution plan; and

- make appropriate disclosures (see **5.1.4**).

The Standard emphasises that, if a participant in a defined benefit multi-employer plan:

- accounts on a defined contribution basis because it has insufficient information to apply defined-benefit accounting, but

- is party to a contractual agreement that determines how a surplus would be distributed or a deficit funded,

it should recognise the asset or liability arising from that contractual agreement, and the resulting income or expense in profit or loss. [IAS 19(2011):37] This requirement is illustrated in **example 5.1.1**, which is reproduced from the Standard.

> **Example 5.1.1**
>
> **Multi-employer plans**
>
> [Example illustrating IAS 19(2011):37]
>
> An entity participates in a multi-employer defined benefit plan that does not prepare plan valuations on an IAS 19 basis. It therefore accounts for the plan as if it were a defined contribution plan. A non-IAS 19 funding valuation shows a deficit of CU100 million in the plan. The plan has agreed under contract a schedule of contributions with the participating employers in the plan that will eliminate the deficit over the next five years. The entity's total contributions under the contract are CU8 million.
>
> *The entity recognises a liability for the contributions adjusted for the time value of money, and an equal expense in profit or loss.*

5.1.2   Group administration plans

Multi-employer plans may be differentiated from group administration plans (also known as common investment funds). Group administration plans allow participating employers to pool their assets for investment purposes, thus reducing administration and investment management costs. The claims of the different participating employers on the assets are segregated for the sole benefit of their employees and other beneficiaries of their plans, so that there is no particular accounting problem in obtaining the information relating to a particular employer. Participating employers are not exposed to the actuarial risks attaching to the obligations of the other participating employers. [IAS 19(2011):38]

Plans of this nature should be classified as either defined contribution or defined benefit in the usual manner. [IAS 19(2011):38]

5.1.3   Change from defined-contribution to defined-benefit accounting for a multi-employer plan

> **Example 5.1.3**
>
> **Change from defined-contribution to defined-benefit accounting for a multi-employer plan**
>
> Company A contributes to a multi-employer defined benefit plan. However, because the plan has never been able to provide its participants with sufficient information for them to apply the accounting requirements in IAS 19(2011):33, Company A has always accounted for the plan as if it were a defined contribution plan in accordance with the exemption in IAS 19(2011):34 (see **5.1.1** above).

At 31 December 20X1, the plan is, for the first time, able to provide the participants with sufficient information for them to apply the accounting requirements in IAS 19(2011):33.

The effect of the change from defined-contribution accounting to defined-benefit accounting should be treated as a change in estimate in accordance with IAS 8 *Accounting Policies, Changes in Accounting Estimates and Errors*, and not as a change in accounting policy.

Although Company A's accounting policy has always been to recognise its defined benefit liability (or asset), prior to being provided with the necessary information at 31 December 20X1, Company A was not in a position to do so. Company A was required to account for the plan as a defined contribution plan, with the cost of the plan measured at an amount equal to the contributions made. From 31 December 20X1, Company A has sufficient information to enable it to measure reliably the defined benefit liability (or asset) at that date, and the cost going forward. The best estimate of the liability, and not the basis of accounting for the plan, has changed and the adjustment to the carrying amount is, therefore, a change in estimate. The effect of the change in estimate should be recognised in profit or loss in the year in which the new information is obtained.

5.1.4   Disclosure

If an entity participates in a multi-employer defined benefit plan (whether accounted for as a defined benefit plan or as a defined contribution plan under the exemption discussed in **5.1.1**), the entity is required to disclose: [IAS 19(2011):148(a) – (c)]

- a description of the funding arrangements, including the method used to determine the entity's rate of contributions and any minimum funding requirements;

- a description of the extent to which the entity can be liable to the plan for other entities' obligations under the terms and conditions of the multi-employer plan; and

- a description of any agreed allocation of a deficit or surplus on:

    - wind-up of the plan; or

    - the entity's withdrawal from the plan.

If an entity participates in a multi-employer defined benefit plan, and sufficient information is available for defined-benefit accounting, the entity is also required to disclose all of the information required under IAS 19(2011):135 to 147 (see **8.2**). [IAS 19(2011):33]

If an entity participates in a multi-employer plan that is a defined benefit plan, but there is not sufficient information available to use defined-benefit accounting, the following additional disclosures are required instead of the information required under IAS 19(2011):139 to 147:
[IAS 19(2011):148(d)]

- the fact that the plan is a defined benefit plan;

- the reason why sufficient information is not available to enable the entity to account for the plan as a defined benefit plan;

- the expected contributions to the plan for the next annual reporting period;

- information about any deficit or surplus in the plan that may affect the amount of future contributions, including the basis used to determine that deficit or surplus and the implications, if any, for the entity; and

- an indication of the level of participation of the entity in the plan compared with other participating entities. Examples of measures that might provide such an indication include the entity's proportion of the total contributions to the plan or the entity's proportion of the total number of active members, retired members, and former members entitled to benefits, if that information is available.

The disclosures required in respect of multi-employer plans have been expanded in IAS 19(2011) and are intended to reflect the fact that entities participating in such plans face increased risk, in particular risks arising from actions by other participants in the plan. The new requirements to disclose qualitative information about any agreed deficit or surplus allocation upon wind-up of or withdrawal from the plan, the expected contribution for the next annual period, and the level of participation in a multi-employer plan, are designed to respond to this increased risk. [IAS 19(2011):BC245 & 246]

5.2 Group plans

A defined benefit plan that shares risks between various entities under common control (e.g. various subsidiaries within a group) is not a multi-employer plan for the purposes of IAS 19. [IAS 19(2011):40] IAS 19(2011):41 specifies the accounting requirements for such plans (referred to below as 'group plans').

Information is obtained about the group plan as a whole measured in accordance with IAS 19 on the basis of assumptions that apply to the

group plan. The amounts recognised in individual entities will vary, however, depending on the arrangements that exist for charging the net IAS 19 cost to individual group entities:
[IAS 19(2011):41]

- if there is a contractual agreement or stated policy for charging to individual group entities the net defined benefit cost for the group plan as a whole measured in accordance with IAS 19, each group entity should recognise in its separate or individual financial statements the net defined benefit cost so charged; or

- if there is no such agreement or policy, the net defined benefit cost should be recognised in the separate or individual financial statements of the group entity that is legally the sponsoring employer for the plan. Each of the other group entities should recognise, in its separate or individual financial statements, a cost equal to its contribution payable for the period.

As stated above, IAS 19(2011):41 requires that if there is a contractual agreement or stated policy for charging the IAS 19 net defined benefit cost for a group plan to individual group entities, each entity should, in its separate or individual financial statements, account for its share as a defined benefit plan (i.e. recognise a defined benefit asset or liability). The contractual agreement or stated policy must apply in respect of "the net defined benefit cost for the plan as a whole measured in accordance with [IAS 19]". The net defined benefit cost is a number calculated for financial reporting purposes that may not have a direct relationship with the payment of cash contributions.

A contractual agreement or stated policy relating to the payment of cash contributions that are based on the actuarial assumptions and methods applied to funding valuations is not sufficient because these are usually different from those used for IAS 19 purposes.

Therefore, for a group entity to meet the requirement for a contractual agreement or stated policy (i.e. in order to account for its share of the defined benefit plan), the group should establish a policy for a reasonable allocation of the IAS 19 net defined benefit cost. The allocation could be based, for example, on the proportion of contributions paid to the scheme or the proportion of pensionable payroll of each entity.

IAS 19 does not provide any guidance on how to identify the entity legally sponsoring the plan, although IAS 19(2011):BC48 clarifies that, in the absence of a contractual agreement or a stated policy, by default, the sponsoring entity will be the entity that bears the risks relating to the plan. The identity of the sponsoring employer could also be established from the plan's legal documentation, such as the plan rules. In some cases, this may not give a fair presentation; for example, the legal sponsor may be a dormant subsidiary with no substance. Such cases would be unusual but would require careful consideration.

IAS 19 emphasises that participation in a group plan is a related party transaction. [IAS 19(2011):42] Accordingly, each group entity participating in such a plan is required to disclose in its separate or individual financial statements:
[IAS 19(2011):149]

(a)   the contractual agreement or stated policy for charging the net defined benefit cost or the fact that there is no such policy;

(b)   the policy for determining the contribution to be paid by the entity;

(c)   if the entity accounts for an allocation of the net defined benefit cost in accordance with IAS 19(2011):41 (see above), all the information about the plan as a whole required by IAS 19(2011):135 to 147 (see **8.2**); and

(d)   if the entity accounts for the contribution payable for the period rather than an allocation of the net defined benefit cost, as is permitted in some circumstances under IAS 19(2011):41 (see above), the information about the plan as a whole required by IAS 19(2011):135 to 137, 139, 142 to 144, 147(a) and 147(b) (see **8.2 below**).

Entities are permitted to disclose the information about the plan as a whole required under IAS 19(2011)149:(c) and (d) by cross-reference to disclosures in another group entity's financial statements if the following conditions are met:
[IAS 19(2011):150]

•   that group entity's financial statements separately identify and disclose the information required about the plan; and

•   that group entity's financial statements are available to users of the financial statements on the same terms as the financial statements of the entity and at the same time as, or earlier than, the financial statements of the entity.

In contrast, IAS 19(1998) does not allow these disclosures to be made by way of cross-reference.

5.3   State plans

IAS 19(2011):44 explains that state plans "are established by legislation to cover all entities (or all entities in a particular category, for example, a specific industry) and are operated by national or local government or by another body (for example, an autonomous agency created specifically for this purpose) that is not subject to control or influence by the reporting entity".

The Standard notes that some plans established by an entity provide both compulsory benefits, as a substitute for benefits that would otherwise be covered under a state plan, and additional voluntary benefits. Such plans are not state plans. [IAS 19(2011):44]

State plans should be classified as defined contribution or defined benefit plans based on the criteria discussed in **section 4**. State plans are required to be accounted for in the same way as multi-employer plans (see **5.1** above). [IAS 19(2011):43]

Most commonly, state plans are defined contribution plans. For these plans, a participating employer's liability is restricted to contributions payable in a period, with the plan being funded on a pay-as-you-go basis. If the entity ceases to employ members of the state plan, it is no longer liable for further payments even if the benefits of employees for prior periods under the state plan require additional funding. In rare cases, a state plan may be considered a defined benefit plan. [IAS 19(2011):45]

6   Defined contribution plans

6.1   Basic principles

Accounting for defined contribution plans is straightforward because the reporting entity's obligation for each period is determined by the amounts to be contributed for that period. Consequently, no actuarial assumptions are required to measure the obligation or the expense and there is no possibility of any actuarial gain or loss. [IAS 19(2011):50]

An entity should recognise the contribution payable to a defined contribution plan in exchange for services rendered by an employee in an accounting period:
[IAS 19(2011):51]

- in the statement of financial position, as:

    - a liability (accrued expense), after deducting any contribution already paid, to the extent that not all of the contributions due for service before the end of the reporting period have been paid at that date; or

    - an asset (prepaid expense), if the amount already paid exceeds the contributions due for service before the end of the reporting period, to the extent that the prepayment is recoverable (e.g. by means of a reduction in future payments or a cash refund); and

- as an expense, unless another Standard requires or permits inclusion of the contribution in the cost of an asset.

If outstanding contributions to a defined contribution plan are not expected to be settled wholly within 12 months after the end of the annual reporting period in which the employees render the related service, they should be discounted using the discount rate specified by the Standard for post-employment benefit obligations (see **7.2.5**). [IAS 19(2011):52] All other defined contribution liabilities are measured on an undiscounted basis. [IAS 19(2011):50]

Under the terms of some defined contribution post-employment benefit plans, employees' entitlements to benefits are subject to their remaining in the sponsoring entity's employment for a minimum period (a vesting condition). Contributions made in respect of an employee who subsequently fails to meet this requirement revert to the entity upon the employee leaving service.

In these circumstances, the entity should recognise its contributions to the plan as an expense in the period for which they are paid because IAS 19(2011):51 requires that contributions to a defined contribution scheme should be recognised as an expense over the period of service that results in an obligation to pay those contributions to the separate entity that runs the plan, rather than over the period of service that entitles an employee to receive benefits (i.e. the vesting period).

Refunds due to the entity from the defined contribution plan should be recognised as an asset and as income when the entity becomes entitled to the refund (i.e. when the employee leaves service before meeting the vesting condition).

This conclusion, which is illustrated in **example 6.1**, is consistent with the view expressed previously by the IFRS Interpretations Committee (see the July 2011 edition of *IFRIC Update*).

Example 6.1

Defined contribution plans with vesting conditions

Entity E sponsors a defined contribution post-employment benefit plan for its 10 employees. It pays contributions of CU100 per year (CU10 per employee) to the plan.

Under the terms of the plan, employees only become entitled to post-employment benefits if they remain in Entity E's employment for a minimum of three years. Contributions made in respect of an employee who leaves before the three-year period is completed are refunded to Entity E.

Two employees leave at the start of Year 3, so that Entity E becomes entitled to a refund of CU40 (2 employees × CU10 × 2 years) in Year 3.

Entity E is obliged to pay contributions of CU10 per employee per year. It recognises an expense that is based on this obligation, without reference to the period over which the employees become entitled to the benefits. Therefore, Entity E recognises an expense in respect of contributions payable of CU100 in each of Years 1 and 2 and CU80 in Year 3. The refund of CU40 is recognised as an asset and as income in Year 3 — resulting in a net expense of CU40 in Year 3.

6.2   Disclosure

The amount recognised as an expense for defined contribution plans should be disclosed. [IAS 19(2011):53]

Additional disclosures regarding contributions to defined contribution plans for key management personnel may be required in accordance with IAS 24 *Related Party Disclosures* (see **section 5.2** of **chapter A23**). [IAS 19(2011):54]

7   Defined benefit plans

Defined benefit plans may be unfunded, or they may be wholly or partly funded by contributions by an entity, and sometimes its employees, into an entity, or fund, that is legally separate from the reporting entity and from which the employee benefits are paid. The payment of funded benefits when they fall due depends not only on the financial position and the investment performance of the fund but also on an entity's ability, and willingness, to make good any shortfall in the fund's assets. Therefore, the entity is, in substance, underwriting the actuarial and investment risks associated with the plan. Consequently, the expense recognised for a defined benefit plan is not necessarily the amount of the contribution due for the period. [IAS 19(2011):56]

7.1   Basic principles

Accounting for defined benefit plans is much more complex than accounting for defined contribution plans. It requires the use of actuarial techniques and assumptions to measure the obligation and expense, with the obligation being measured on a discounted basis. The possibility of actuarial gains and losses also arises because assumptions used very often differ from actual outcomes. [IAS 19(2011):55]

An entity should account for both its legal and its constructive obligations in relation to a defined benefit plan. A constructive obligation arises from an entity's informal practices when the entity has no realistic alternative but to pay employee benefits (e.g. when a change in the entity's informal practices would cause unacceptable damage to its relationship with employees). [IAS 19(2011):61] An example cited by IAS 19 is when the formal terms of a plan permit the employer to terminate its obligations under the plan. In practice, it would generally be very difficult for an employer to take such a course of action (without payment) so that, unless there is evidence to the contrary, it should be assumed that the employer will continue to provide benefits over the remaining working lives of employees. [IAS 19(2011):62]

Example 7.1

Employer with history of improving pension benefits retrospectively

Company O is a manufacturer with a work force whose compensation and other employee benefits are governed by a union contract established through a collective bargaining process. Company O has a history of granting improvements in pension benefits, to both retirees and active employees, during the collective bargaining process. The improvements have sometimes taken the form of fixed monetary increases in monthly benefits, lump sum payments made outside the pension plans, or formula-based cost-of-living adjustment (COLA) increases in the monthly benefit. There is no evidence of a present commitment to increase plan benefits other than Company O's history of retrospective plan amendments.

Careful judgement should be exercised in assessing whether a constructive obligation has arisen.

In the circumstances described, the employer's practice is to provide improvements only during the collective bargaining process, not during any informal process. The increases in benefits historically have been awarded in several different forms. Therefore, it does not appear that the employer has set a pattern of increases in pension benefits that can be projected reliably to give rise to a constructive obligation. However, if the practice established by an employer were that of a consistent pension-benefit enhancement as part of union negotiations that clearly established a pattern (always a COLA increase, or always fixed monetary increases), it could be concluded that a constructive obligation exists and that those additional benefits should be included in the measurement of the projected benefit obligation.

7.1.1   Accounting for defined benefit plans – four-step approach

Accounting for defined benefit plans involves four steps, as summarised in the following table. When an entity has more than one defined benefit plan, these steps should be followed separately for each material plan. [IAS 19(2011):57]

Step 1	Determining the surplus or deficit	This involves: [IAS 19(2011):57(a)] • using an actuarial technique (the projected unit credit method) to make a reliable estimate of the ultimate cost to the entity of the benefit that employees have earned in return for their service in the current and prior periods (see **7.2.2 – 7.2.4**); • discounting that benefit using an appropriate discount rate in order to determine the present value of the defined benefit obligation and the current service cost (see **7.2.5**); and • deducting the fair value of any plan assets (see **7.2.6**) from the present value of the defined benefit obligation.
Step 2	Determining the amount of the net defined benefit liability (asset)	The amount of the net defined benefit liability (asset) is the amount of the deficit or surplus determined at Step 1 adjusted for any effect of limiting a net defined benefit asset to the asset ceiling (see **7.3**).
Step 3	Determining amounts to be recognised in profit or loss	The amounts to be recognised in profit or loss are: • current service cost (see **7.4.1**); • any past service cost and gain or loss on settlement (see **7.4.2**); and • net interest on the net defined benefit liability (asset) (see **7.4.3**).

| Step 4 | Determining the remeasurements of the net defined benefit liability (asset) to be recognised in other comprehensive income | The remeasurements of the net defined benefit liability (asset) comprise (see **7.5**):
• actuarial gains and losses;
• return on plan assets, excluding amounts included in net interest on the net defined benefit liability (asset); and
• any change in the effect of the asset ceiling, excluding amounts included in net interest on the net defined benefit liability (asset). |

7.1.2   *Actuarial valuations*

IAS 19 does not specify the frequency of valuations, either for the measurement of plan assets or the determination of the present value of the defined benefit obligation. The Standard requires that an entity should determine the net defined benefit liability (asset) (see **7.2**) for a defined benefit plan with sufficient regularity that the amounts recognised in the financial statements do not differ materially from the amounts that would be determined at the end of the reporting period. [IAS 19(2011):58]

7.1.2.1   *Involvement of an actuary*

IAS 19 encourages, but does not require, an entity to involve a qualified actuary in the measurement of all material post-employment benefit obligations. [IAS 19(2011):59]

> Although IAS 19 does not require the involvement of a qualified actuary, in practice it will usually be difficult to value material defined benefit obligations without actuarial involvement.

7.1.2.2   *Date of valuation*

The Standard does not require that an actuarial valuation be carried out at the reporting date. It acknowledges that, for practical reasons, an entity may request a qualified actuary to carry out a detailed valuation of the obligation before the end of the reporting period. In such circumstances, the results of that valuation are required to be updated for any material transactions and other material changes in circumstances (including changes in market prices and interest rates) up to the end of the reporting period. [IAS 19(2011):59]

> Although many entities carry out actuarial valuations annually, at the end of the reporting period, some carry out full actuarial valuations less frequently (e.g. every three years) and update approximately to the end of each annual reporting period. Relevant factors to consider in determining the frequency of actuarial valuations may include the volatility of the economic environment and the impact of the defined benefit obligation and costs on the financial statements.
>
> Although local legislation may not require a full plan valuation every year, in order to meet the requirement of IAS 19(2011):58, it may be necessary for some aspects of the valuation to be revisited at the end of each reporting period (e.g. the fair value of plan assets and financial assumptions such as the discount rate and the rate of salary increase). Demographic assumptions, such as mortality rates and rate of employee turnover, may not require revision annually.

7.1.2.3   Interim reporting

IAS 19 does not provide any guidance as to what is expected in terms of an actuarial valuation for an interim reporting period under IAS 34 *Interim Financial Reporting*. IAS 34:B9 states that "[p]ension cost for an interim period is calculated on a year-to-date basis by using the actuarially determined pension cost rate at the end of the prior financial year, adjusted for significant market fluctuations since that time and for significant curtailments, settlements, or other significant one-time events".

> The question of remeasurement at interim reporting dates was specifically considered by the IASB when finalising IAS 19(2011). Respondents to the exposure draft preceding the revised Standard had raised concerns that the requirements for the immediate recognition of changes in the net defined benefit liability (asset) (see **7.2**) would imply that entities should remeasure the net defined benefit liability (asset) at each interim reporting date.
>
> The Board noted the requirements in IAS 34 indicating that the entity should exercise judgement in determining whether it needs to remeasure the net defined benefit liability (asset) at the end of the (interim or annual) reporting period. Because, following the June

2011 revision, entities are required to recognise remeasurements in the period in which they arise, those remeasurements are now more likely to have a material effect on the amount recognised in the financial statements than would have been the case before those amendments if an entity elected to defer recognition of actuarial gains and losses. It follows that entities previously deferring recognition of some gains and losses are now more likely to judge that remeasurement is required for interim reporting. However, the Board decided not to set out explicitly whether an entity should remeasure a net defined benefit liability (asset) at interim dates on the basis that such a change would be an exemption from the general requirements of IAS 34.

7.2   Step 1 – determining the deficit or surplus

The deficit or surplus is determined as the difference between: [IAS 19(2011):8]

- the present value of the defined benefit obligation; and

- the fair value of plan assets (if any).

Therefore, the first step involves measuring separately the defined benefit obligation and the plan assets, if any.

7.2.1   The present value of the defined benefit obligation

The present value of a defined benefit obligation is the present value, without deducting any plan assets, of expected future payments required to settle the obligation resulting from employee service in the current and prior periods. [IAS 19(2011):8]

The final cost of a defined benefit plan is influenced by many variables (e.g. final salaries, employee turnover and mortality, employee contributions and medical cost trends). [IAS 19(2011):66] The use of actuarial techniques to value an obligation and allocate it to accounting periods allows an entity to measure an obligation with sufficient reliability to justify recognition of a liability. The whole of the obligation is discounted, even if part of it is expected to be settled before 12 months after the reporting period. [IAS 19(2011):69]

Several steps are required to measure the present value of a defined benefit obligation and the associated current service cost. These steps, which are considered in the following paragraphs, are: [IAS 19(2011):66]

- to apply an actuarial valuation method (see **7.2.2**);

- to attribute benefit to the employees' periods of service (see **7.2.3**); and

- to make actuarial assumptions (see **7.2.4**).

7.2.2   *Actuarial valuation method*

Under IAS 19, an entity is required to use the projected unit credit method to determine the present value of its defined benefit obligation, the related current service cost and, when applicable, past service cost. [IAS 19(2011):67]

The projected unit credit method treats each period of service as giving rise to an additional unit of benefit entitlement and measures each unit separately to build up the final obligation. It requires an entity to attribute benefit to the current period (in order to determine current service cost) and the current and prior periods (in order to determine the present value of defined benefit obligations). An entity should attribute benefit to periods in which the obligation to provide post-employment benefits arises. That obligation arises as employees render services in return for post-employment benefits that the entity expects to pay in future reporting periods. Actuarial techniques allow an entity to measure that obligation with sufficient reliability to justify recognition of a liability. [IAS 19(2011):68 & 71]

No other valuation method is permitted under IAS 19.

The projected unit credit method referred to by IAS 19 is sometimes also called the 'accrued benefit method pro-rated on service' or the 'benefit/ years of service' method. [IAS 19(2011):68]

> The measurement of the liability should reflect the expected date of employees leaving service and should be discounted to a present value using the projected unit credit method (as illustrated in the examples below). It is not acceptable to measure the liability for vested benefits at an undiscounted amount (i.e. at the amount that would be payable if all employees left the entity at the end of the reporting period).

This conclusion was confirmed by the IFRIC (now the IFRS Interpretations Committee) in the context of IAS 19(1998) (see *IFRIC Update*, April 2002) and is not affected by the 2011 revision of IAS 19.

Example 7.2.2, which is reproduced from the Standard, provides a simple illustration of the application of the projected unit credit method.

Example 7.2.2

Projected Unit Credit Method

[Example illustrating IAS 19(2011):68]

A lump sum benefit is payable on termination of service and equal to 1 per cent of final salary for each year of service. The salary in year 1 is CU10,000 and is assumed to increase at 7 per cent (compound) each year. The discount rate used is 10 per cent per year. The following table shows how the obligation builds up for an employee who is expected to leave at the end of year 5, assuming that there are no changes in actuarial assumptions. For simplicity, this example ignores the additional adjustment needed to reflect the probability that the employee may leave the entity at an earlier or later date.

Year	1	2	3	4	5
	CU	CU	CU	CU	CU
Benefit attributed to					
– *prior years*	*0*	*131*	*262*	*393*	*524*
– *current year (1% of final salary)*	*131*	*131*	*131*	*131*	*131*
– *current and prior years*	*131*	*262*	*393*	*524*	*655*
Opening obligation	*0*	*89*	*196*	*324*	*476*
Interest at 10%	*0*	*9*	*20*	*33*	*48*
Current service cost	*89*	*98*	*108*	*119*	*131*
Closing obligation	*89*	*196*	*324*	*476*	*655*

Note:

1.   *The opening obligation is the present value of benefit attributed to prior years.*

2.   *The current service cost is the present value of benefit attributed to the current year.*

3.   *The closing obligation is the present value of benefit attributed to current and prior years.*

7.2.3   *Attributing benefit to periods of service*

When determining the present value of the defined benefit obligation, current service cost and (when applicable) past service cost, an entity should attribute benefit to periods of service using the plan's benefit formula. [IAS 19(2011):70]

An exception to the foregoing is made when an employee's service in later years will lead to a materially higher level of benefit than in earlier years, as discussed later in this section. [IAS 19(2011):70]

The following examples are included in IAS 19 to illustrate the attribution of benefit to periods of service.

Example 7.2.3A

Attributing benefit to periods of service (1)

[Examples illustrating IAS 19(2011):71]

1.   A defined benefit plan provides a lump sum benefit of CU100 payable on retirement for each year of service.

A benefit of CU100 is attributed to each year. The current service cost is the present value of CU100. The present value of the defined benefit obligation is the present value of CU100, multiplied by the number of years of service up to the end of the reporting period.

If the benefit is payable immediately when the employee leaves the entity, the current service cost and the present value of the defined benefit obligation reflect the date at which the employee is expected to leave. Thus, because of the effect of discounting, they are less than the amounts that would be determined if the employee left at the end of the reporting period.

2.   A plan provides a monthly pension of 0.2 per cent of final salary for each year of service. The pension is payable from the age of 65.

Benefit equal to the present value, at the expected retirement date, of a monthly pension of 0.2 per cent of the estimated final salary payable from the expected retirement date until the expected date of death is attributed to each year of service. The current service cost is the present value of that benefit. The present value of the defined benefit obligation is the present value of monthly pension payments of 0.2 per cent of final salary, multiplied by the number of years of service up to the end of the reporting period. The current service cost and the present value of the defined benefit obligation are discounted because pension payments begin at the age of 65.

Employee service gives rise to an obligation under a defined benefit plan even if the benefits are not vested (e.g. if they are conditional on future employment). Employee service before the vesting date gives rise to a constructive obligation because, at the end of each successive reporting period, the amount of future service that an employee will have to render before becoming entitled to the benefit is reduced. The probability that some employees may not ultimately satisfy any vesting conditions is reflected in the measurement of the defined benefit obligation. [IAS 19(2011):72]

Similarly, although some post-employment benefits (e.g. post-employment medical benefits) become payable only if a specified event occurs when an employee is no longer employed, an obligation is created when the employee renders service that will provide entitlement to the benefit if the specified event occurs. The probability that the specified event will occur affects the measurement of the obligation, but does not determine whether the obligation exists. [IAS 19(2011):72]

The following examples, which are reproduced from the Standard, illustrate the application of IAS 19(2011):72.

Example 7.2.3B

Attributing benefit to periods of service (2)

[Examples illustrating IAS 19(2011):72]

1. A plan pays a benefit of CU100 for each year of service. The benefits vest after ten years of service.

   A benefit of CU100 is attributed to each year. In each of the first ten years, the current service cost and the present value of the obligation reflect the probability that the employee may not complete ten years of service.

2. A plan pays a benefit of CU100 for each year of service, excluding service before the age of 25. The benefits vest immediately.

   No benefit is attributed to service before the age of 25 because service before that date does not lead to benefits (conditional or unconditional). A benefit of CU100 is attributed to each subsequent year.

The obligation increases until the date when further service by the employee will lead to no material amount of further benefits. Therefore, all benefit is attributed to periods ending on or before that date. Benefit is

attributed to individual accounting periods under the plan's benefit formula. However, if an employee's service in later years will lead to a materially higher level of benefit than in earlier years, an entity attributes benefit on a straight-line basis from:
[IAS 19(2011):70 & 73]

- the date when service by the employee first leads to benefits under the plan (whether or not the benefits are conditional on further service) until

- the date when further service by the employee will lead to no material amount of further benefits under the plan, other than from further salary increases.

That is because the employee's service throughout the entire period will ultimately lead to benefit at that higher level. [IAS 19(2011):73]

Example 7.2.3C

Attributing benefit to periods of service (3)

[Examples illustrating IAS 19(2011):73]

1. A plan pays a lump sum benefit of CU1,000 that vests after ten years of service. The plan provides no further benefit for subsequent service.

   A benefit of CU100 (CU1,000 divided by ten) is attributed to each of the first ten years.

   The current service cost in each of the first ten years reflects the probability that the employee may not complete ten years of service. No benefit is attributed to subsequent years.

2. A plan pays a lump sum retirement benefit of CU2,000 to all employees who are still employed at the age of 55 after twenty years of service, or who are still employed at the age of 65, regardless of their length of service.

   For employees who join before the age of 35, service first leads to benefits under the plan at the age of 35 (an employee could leave at the age of 30 and return at the age of 33, with no effect on the amount or timing of benefits). Those benefits are conditional on further service. Also, service beyond the age of 55 will lead to no material amount of further benefits. For these employees, the entity attributes benefit of 100 (2,000 divided by 20) to each year from the age of 35 to the age of 55.

   For employees who join between the ages of 35 and 45, service beyond twenty years will lead to no material amount of further benefits. For these employees, the entity attributes benefit of CU100 (CU2,000 divided by twenty) to each of the first twenty years.

> *For an employee who joins at the age of 55, service beyond ten years will lead to no material amount of further benefits. For this employee, the entity attributes benefit of CU200 (CU2,000 divided by ten) to each of the first ten years.*
>
> *For all employees, the current service cost and the present value of the obligation reflect the probability that the employee may not complete the necessary period of service.*

3. A post-employment medical plan reimburses 40 per cent of an employee's post-employment medical costs if the employee leaves after more than ten and less than twenty years of service and 50 per cent of those costs if the employee leaves after twenty or more years of service.

> *Under the plan's benefit formula, the entity attributes 4 per cent of the present value of the expected medical costs (40 per cent divided by ten) to each of the first ten years and 1 per cent (10 per cent divided by ten) to each of the second ten years. The current service cost in each year reflects the probability that the employee may not complete the necessary period of service to earn part or all of the benefits. For employees expected to leave within ten years, no benefit is attributed.*

4. A post-employment medical plan reimburses 10 per cent of an employee's post-employment medical costs if the employee leaves after more than ten and less than twenty years of service and 50 per cent of those costs if the employee leaves after twenty or more years of service.

> *Service in later years will lead to a materially higher level of benefit than in earlier years. Therefore, for employees expected to leave after twenty or more years, the entity attributes benefit on a straight-line basis under [IAS 19:71]. Service beyond twenty years will lead to no material amount of further benefits. Therefore, the benefit attributed to each of the first twenty years is 2.5 per cent of the present value of the expected medical costs (50 per cent divided by twenty).*
>
> *For employees expected to leave between ten and twenty years, the benefit attributed to each of the first ten years is 1 per cent of the present value of the expected medical costs. For these employees, no benefit is attributed to service between the end of the tenth year and the estimated date of leaving.*
>
> *For employees expected to leave within ten years, no benefit is attributed.*

When the amount of a benefit is a constant proportion of final salary for each year of service, future salary increases will affect the amount required to settle the obligation that exists for service before the end of the reporting period, but do not create an additional obligation. Therefore:
[IAS 19(2011):74]

- for the purpose of IAS 19(2011):70(b) (see above), salary increases do not lead to further benefits, even though the amount of the benefits is dependent on final salary; and

- the amount of benefit attributed to each period is a constant proportion of the salary to which the benefit is linked.

Example 7.2.3D

Attributing benefit to periods of service (4)

[Example illustrating IAS 19(2011):74]

Employees are entitled to a benefit of 3 per cent of final salary for each year of service before the age of 55.

Benefit of 3 per cent of estimated final salary is attributed to each year up to the age of 55. This is the date when further service by the employee will lead to no material amount of further benefits under the plan. No benefit is attributed to service after that age.

By completing the allocation of current service cost at the time that no further benefit accrues, this cost is allocated over a period that is shorter than the period over which an employee is expected to provide service to the employer. The reason for this, as explained in IAS 19(2011):70, is that the subsequent period of employment yields no material amount of further benefits.

7.2.3.1   Death-in-service benefits

IAS 19 does not specifically address the question of accounting for death-in-service benefits. See **9.3** for a discussion of the considerations regarding the appropriate accounting treatment for such benefits.

7.2.3.2   Career Average Revalued Earnings plans

In some jurisdictions, entities may offer to employees 'Career Average Revalued Earnings' (CARE) pension plans, also referred to as 'Pension Builder Plans'. Such plans generally provide a defined benefit pension that is determined by the employee's years of service and the average salary earned over the period of service. The plan formula is typically stated as follows:

A member shall accrue for each year of service: accrual rate x current (or average) salary*

* To maintain a pension plan's purchasing power, the salary in each year is typically revalued (either to give an adjusted current salary or to determine the adjusted average salary) in line with a specified index (e.g. price inflation) between the date of accrual and the date of retirement. The index used to revalue salaries earned in past years is typically lower than the wage increase over the period of service.

Such plans should be measured using the projected unit credit method, taking into account estimated future salary increases as required by IAS 19(2011):87(b) and IAS 19(2011):90. IAS 19(2011):70 states, in part, that:

"[i]n determining the present value of its defined benefit obligations ... an entity shall attribute benefit to periods of service under the plan's benefit formula. However, if an employee's service in later years will lead to a materially higher level of benefit than in earlier years, an entity shall attribute benefit on a straight-line basis ...".

The CARE pension plan formula described above does attribute a higher level of benefit to later years and, therefore, an entity should assess whether this is likely to be materially higher, in which case the benefits should be attributed on a straight-line basis.

7.2.4 *Actuarial assumptions*

The actuarial assumptions used for the purposes of measuring a defined benefit obligation should be unbiased and mutually compatible. [IAS 19(2011):75] Actuarial assumptions are an entity's best estimates of the variables that will determine the ultimate cost of providing post-employment benefits. [IAS 19(2011):76] They should be neither imprudent nor excessively conservative, and should reflect the economic relationships between factors such as inflation, rates of salary increase and discount rates. For example, all assumptions that depend on a particular inflation level (such as assumptions about interest rates and salary and benefit increases) in any given future period should assume the same inflation level in that period. [IAS 19(2011):77 & 78]

IAS 19(2011):76 explains that actuarial assumptions comprise:

(a)   demographic assumptions about the future characteristics of current and former employees (and their dependants) who are eligible for benefits. Demographic assumptions deal with matters such as:

(i)   mortality (see **7.2.4.1**);

(ii)   rates of employee turnover, disability and early retirement;

(iii)   the proportion of plan members with dependants who will be eligible for benefits;

(iv)   the proportion of plan members who will select each form of payment option under the plan terms; and

(v)   claim rates under medical plans; and

(b)   financial assumptions, dealing with items such as:

(i)   the discount rate (see **7.2.5** below);

(ii)   benefit levels (excluding any cost of the benefits to be met by employees), and future salary (see **7.2.4.3** below);

(iii)   in the case of medical benefits, future medical costs, including claim handling costs (i.e. the costs that will be incurred in processing and resolving claims, including legal and adjuster's fees) (see **7.2.4.4** below); and

(iv)   taxes payable by the plan on contributions relating to service before the reporting date or on benefits resulting from that service.

As part of the June 2011 revision of IAS 19, the IASB has clarified that taxes paid by the plan should be treated differently based on the nature of the amounts to which they relate. Under IAS 19(2011), estimates of taxes payable by the plan on contributions relating to service before the reporting date and on benefits resulting from that service should be included in the measurement of the defined benefit obligation; all other taxes paid by the plan are required to be deducted from the actual return on plan assets. [IAS 19(2011):BC121]

The inclusion of taxes payable in the above list means that entities will need to develop actuarial assumptions about the timing and amount of taxes payable by the plan on contributions and benefits arising from services received before the reporting date. The revised requirements could also lead to an increase in the defined benefit obligation and current service cost depending on an entity's accounting policy under IAS 19(1998).

7.2.4.1   Mortality assumptions

Mortality assumptions should be determined by reference to the entity's best estimate of the mortality of plan members both during and after employment. In order to estimate the ultimate cost of the benefit, the entity should take into consideration expected changes in mortality (e.g. by modifying standard mortality tables with estimates of mortality improvements). [IAS 19(2011):81 & 82]

This requirement was amended as part of the June 2011 revision of IAS 19 to make explicit that the mortality assumptions used to determine the defined benefit obligation are current estimates of the expected mortality rates of plan members, both during and after employment. In the Board's view, current mortality tables might need to be adjusted for expected changes in mortality (such as expected mortality improvement) to provide the best estimate of the amount that reflects the ultimate cost of settling the defined benefit obligation. [IAS 19(2011):BC142]

7.2.4.2   Financial assumptions

Financial assumptions should be based on market expectations, at the end of the reporting period, for the period over which the obligations will be settled. [IAS 19(2011):80] Discount rates and other financial assumptions should not be inflation-adjusted (i.e. 'nominal' rates should be used) unless inflation-adjusted measures (i.e. 'real' rates) are more reliable (e.g. in a hyperinflationary economy, or when benefits are index-linked and there is a deep market in index-linked bonds of the same currency and term). [IAS 19(2011):79]

7.2.4.3   Salaries and benefit levels

The measurement of the defined benefit obligation should reflect:
[IAS 19(2011):87]

- the terms of the plan regarding benefit levels, and any constructive obligation that extends those terms, at the end of the reporting period;

- any estimated future salary increases that affect the benefits payable;

- the effect of any limit on the employer's share of the cost of the future benefits;

- contributions from employees or third parties that reduce the ultimate cost to the entity of those benefits; and

- estimated future changes in the level of any state benefits that affect the benefits payable under a defined benefit plan, if, and only if, either:

  - those changes were enacted before the end of the reporting period; or

  - historical data, or other reliable evidence, indicate that those state benefits will change in some predictable manner (e.g. in line with future changes in general price levels or general salary levels).

Accordingly, actuarial assumptions should reflect only those future benefit changes that are set out in the formal terms of the plan (and any constructive obligation that extends those terms) at the end of the reporting period. This would include the effect of any obligations arising from, for example:
[IAS 19(2011):88]

- the entity's past history of increasing benefits (e.g. to mitigate the effects of inflation) when there is no indication that this practice will change in the future;

- the entity's obligation (either as required by the terms of the plan or under a constructive obligation that extends those terms) to use any surplus in the plan for the benefit of plan participants (see **7.4.2.1**); or

- benefits that vary in response to a performance target or other criteria. For example, the terms of the plan may state that it will pay reduced benefits or require additional contributions from employees if the plan assets are insufficient. The measurement of the obligation reflects the best estimate of the effect of the performance target or other criteria.

In contrast, actuarial assumptions should not reflect future benefit changes that are not set out in the formal terms of the plan (and for which there is no constructive obligation) at the end of the reporting period. Instead, when such changes to the terms of the plan are introduced, they should be reflected either (1) in past service cost (to the extent that they have a retrospective impact), or (2) in current service cost for the periods after the change (to the extent that they change benefits for service after the change). [IAS 19(2011):89]

When estimating future salary increases, account should be taken of inflation, seniority, promotion and any other relevant factors (both internal and external), such as the scarcity or surplus of potential employees with the required skills. [IAS 19(2011):90]

Some defined benefit plans limit the contributions that an entity is required to pay. The ultimate cost of the benefits takes account of the effect of a limit on contributions. The effect of a limit on the entity's contributions is determined over the shorter of (1) the estimated life of the entity, and (2) the estimated life of the plan. [IAS 19(2011):91]

Some post-employment benefits are linked to variables such as the level of state-provided retirement benefits or medical care. In such cases, the measurement of the benefits should reflect the best estimate of such variables, based on past history and other reliable evidence. [IAS 19(2011):95]

Such changes should be reflected if they were enacted before the end of the reporting period, or if past history and other reliable evidence indicate that the state benefits will change in a predictable manner (e.g. in line with general salary or price levels).

7.2.4.4   Post-employment medical benefits

When measuring post-employment medical benefits, additional assumptions are required in order to account for estimated future changes in the cost of medical services. They include general inflation and specific changes in future medical costs, level and frequency of claims, technological advances, changes in the health status of participants in the plan, and changes in the utilisation and delivery of health care. In making these assumptions, reference should be made to historical data from the entity's own records and, when necessary, external data from other entities, insurers, medical providers and other sources. It is important that such assumptions are adjusted when the population providing the historical data differs from that for which the obligation arises. For example, the level and frequency of claims may be sensitive to age, sex and current health status of those benefiting under the plan. They should also be adjusted where there is reliable evidence that historical trends will not continue. [IAS 19(2011):96 – 98]

7.2.4.5   *Pension promises based on performance targets*

Defined benefit plans may include pension promises that are based on achieving specific performance targets, such as additional pensionable earnings in the form of bonuses for achieving specified performance targets, arrangements relating to additional sponsor contributions, or additional years of deemed service. IAS 19(2011):88(c) clearly indicates that the measurement of the obligation should reflect the best estimate of the effect of the performance target or other criteria.

> This issue was not explicitly dealt with in IAS 19(1998) but had been considered by the IFRIC (now the IFRS Interpretations Committee) in the context of IAS 19(1998) – see *IFRIC Update*, January 2008. The requirements in IAS 19(2011):88(c) are consistent with the conclusion reached by the IFRIC in 2008.

7.2.4.6   *Subsequent introduction of new state cost*

> When a state introduces, in an unpredictable manner, a new significant state cost (e.g. a tax related to contributions or benefits) associated with an existing employer's defined benefit obligation, and there is no impact on the ultimate benefit to be received by employees, the change should be treated as a change in actuarial assumptions (and not as a plan amendment).
>
> IAS 19(2011):57(a)(i), IAS 19(2011):66 and IAS 19(2011):76 clearly indicate that the entity should take into account all elements that will influence the ultimate cost of providing the defined benefit. In addition, IAS 19(2011):76(b)(iv) states that actuarial assumptions include financial assumptions about "taxes payable by the plan on contributions relating to service before the reporting date or on benefits resulting from that service".
>
> More generally, IAS 19(2011):76 states that actuarial assumptions are an entity's best estimates of the variables that will determine the ultimate cost of providing post-employment benefits. When an entity does not explicitly state an assumption about such a variable, it is effectively making an assumption of zero value for that element. Any resulting differences from actual numbers are experience adjustments.

(other than those included in the actuarial assumptions used to measure the defined benefit obligation). However, IAS 19(1998) is not specific as to which costs should be included in those actuarial assumptions. IAS 19(2011) clarifies that only costs relating to the management of the plan assets should be deducted in determining the return on plan assets. Other administration costs should be recognised in profit or loss when the administration services are provided. [IAS 19(2011):BC125]

When finalising IAS 19(2011), in response to concerns raised regarding practicality, the IASB abandoned the proposal included in the exposure draft preceding the revised Standard that the present value of the defined benefit obligation should include the present value of costs relating to the administration of benefits attributable to current or past service.

The Board noted that, in some cases, a total fee is charged for both managing plan assets and other administration services. However, the Board did not consider the cost of managing plan assets would be excessively costly or difficult to estimate under these circumstances. An entity could estimate such costs by estimating the administration costs if there were no plan assets, or by observing the prices for such services in the market. [IAS 19(2011):BC125 – BC128] This explains why the Board maintained the proposal to treat administration service costs related to managing plan assets differently from other administration costs.

As discussed at **7.2.4**, IAS 19(2011) clarifies that the estimate of the defined benefit obligation includes the present value of taxes payable by the plan if they relate to service before the reporting date or are imposed on benefits resulting from that service. In addition, IAS 19(2011):130 (see **7.5** below) clarifies that other taxes should be included as a reduction to the return on plan assets. [IAS 19(2011):BC121]

7.2.5   Determination of an appropriate discount rate

The topic of the determination of an appropriate discount rate for the purpose of measuring defined benefit obligations has been the subject of much debate in recent years. In March 2013, the IASB launched a project to clarify the requirements of IAS 19, particularly around the requirement to use market yields on high quality corporate bonds or government bonds. An exposure draft is expected in the fourth quarter of 2013.

The discount rate is one of the most important assumptions utilised in measuring defined benefit obligations. The rate used should reflect the time value of money, but not credit risk specific to an entity, nor the risk that future experience may differ from assumptions, nor the actuarial or investment risk. [IAS 19(2011):84]

The Standard specifies that:
[IAS 19(2011):83]

- the rate used to discount post-employment benefit obligations (both funded and unfunded) should be determined by reference to market yields at the end of the reporting period on high quality corporate bonds;

- in countries where there is no deep market in such bonds, the market yields (at the end of the reporting period) on government bonds should be used; and

- the currency and term of the corporate bonds or government bonds should be consistent with the currency and estimated term of the post-employment benefit obligations.

IAS 19 does not provide any further guidance on the meaning of the term 'high quality corporate bonds'. In practice, the term is generally taken to refer to corporate bonds with one of the two highest ratings from a recognised rating agency in jurisdictions in which such an agency exists.

The determination as to whether a deep market for high quality corporate bonds exists is usually based on the economy in which the retirement benefit plan is located and whether the bonds are considered high quality in that economy. It is essential to look at comparisons with the government bond market and the rates for those bonds. When the market for AA- and AAA-rated bonds is narrow, judgement is required to determine whether high quality corporate bonds should be considered to exist at all in the particular economy.

In 2005, the IFRIC (now the IFRS Interpretations Committee) was asked to consider whether, in circumstances when there is no deep market in high quality corporate bonds in a country, it is appropriate to use a discount rate based on a synthetic equivalent constructed by reference to the market in another country instead of using the yield on government bonds (see *IFRIC Update*, June 2005). The IFRIC took the view that IAS 19(1998):78 (now IAS 19(2011):83) is clear that the use of such a synthetically-constructed equivalent is not appropriate, and that the yield on government bonds should be used.

However, the IFRIC observed that the reference to 'in a country' could reasonably be read as including high quality corporate bonds that are available in a regional market to which the entity has access provided that the currency of the regional market and the country are the same (e.g. the Euro).

In a volatile economic environment, the market's assessment of credit risk of entities, and therefore the yield on entities' debt, can change more quickly than assessments of credit rating. This can lead to a growing spread of yields for constituents of published indices, such as iBoxx or Bloomberg, that purport to reflect yields on entities with a specified credit rating. It might also lead to a divergence between different published indices. In such circumstances, the discount rates provided by these indices should not be used as reflecting the yield on high quality corporate bonds without challenge. It is apparent that the constituents of such indices are determined at a point in time based on the credit rating at that time. When there have been subsequent changes in market conditions these may have led to a change in the market's assessment of the credit risk of an entity, reflected in debt yields, prior to an actual credit downgrading. Or there may have been a credit downgrading, but prior to the constituent being removed from the current published index. In such circumstances, the current published index no longer reflects the yield on purely high quality corporate bonds. Therefore, an index should be adjusted so as to exclude those yields that are no longer considered to be in respect of high quality corporate bonds. In developing a methodology to adjust the particular index being used, an entity might have regard to other appropriate indices. In some circumstances, a general increase in yields may appear to affect bonds for entities in a specific industry. However, such a trend should not be taken to indicate a potential downgrading of credit rating for all entities in the industry, and, therefore, it would not be appropriate to adopt an approach that excludes all constituents of a particular industry purely because of the area of business activities. Entities should apply the approach adopted to adjust a published index consistently from one period to the next, although in a stable economic environment such a methodology may result in no adjustment.

The amount of the yield on high quality corporate bonds over time has a material effect on the measurement of pension obligations. For example, if the pension liability discussed previously in **example 7.2.2** was discounted using a rate of 5 per cent (instead of 10 per cent), the present value of the obligation would change substantially, as demonstrated below.

Year	1	2	3	4	5
	CU	CU	CU	CU	CU
Opening obligation	0	108	226	356	499
Interest at 5%	0	5	11	18	25
Current service cost	108	113	119	125	131
Closing obligation @ 5%	108	226	356	499	655
Closing obligation @ 10% (per **example 7.2.2**)	89	196	324	476	655

Comparing the results above, it becomes apparent that the longer the period remaining until retirement (i.e. the higher the number of younger active employees in a pension plan), the more dramatic the impact of changes in interest rates. For example, at the end of Year 1, the obligation discounted at 5 per cent is 20 per cent higher than that measured at 10 per cent, while that gap would narrow to about 5 per cent in Year 4. In practice, actuaries estimate that, depending on the circumstances, a decrease in the discount rate of 0.5 per cent could cause the liability to rise by up to 20 per cent, while a 2 per cent decline could increase the liability by more than 150 per cent. Fluctuations in the discount rate over time are one of the major sources of actuarial gains and losses, discussed in detail in **section 7.5** below.

Judgement should be applied in determining the discount rate at year-end, through an analysis of the various indices and possibly development of methodologies to estimate the rate.

7.2.5.1   Term of bonds and obligations

The requirement for the term of the bonds to be consistent with the term of the obligations means that the discount rate should reflect the estimated timing of the benefit payments. The Standard notes that, in practice, this may be achieved by applying a single weighted average discount rate that reflects the estimated timing and amount of benefit payments and the currency in which the benefits are to be paid. [IAS 19(2011):85]

If there is no deep market for bonds of a sufficiently long maturity date to match that of all of the obligation payments, the entity may extrapolate current market rates for a shorter period along the yield curve. [IAS 19(2011):86]

7.2.6   Plan assets

Plan assets comprise:
[IAS 19(2011):8]

* assets held by a long-term employee benefit fund (see **7.2.6.1**); and

* qualifying insurance policies (see **7.2.6.2**).

Plan assets exclude:
[IAS 19(2011):114]

* unpaid contributions due from the reporting entity to the fund; and

* any non-transferable financial instruments issued by the entity and held by the fund.

Plan assets are reduced by any liabilities of the fund that do not relate to employee benefits (e.g. trade and other payables, and liabilities resulting from derivative financial instruments). [IAS 19(2011):114]

7.2.6.1   Assets held by a long-term employee benefit fund

These are assets (other than non-transferable financial instruments issued by the reporting entity) that:
[IAS 19(2011):8]

* are held by an entity (a fund) that is legally separate from the reporting entity and exists solely to pay or fund employee benefits; and

* are available to be used only to pay or fund employee benefits, are not available to the reporting entity's own creditors (even in bank-ruptcy) and cannot be returned to the reporting entity, unless either:

  * the remaining assets of the fund are sufficient to meet all of the related employee benefit obligations of the plan or the report-ing entity; or

  * the assets are returned to the reporting entity to reimburse it for employee benefits already paid.

IAS 19 does not define the term 'non-transferable financial instruments'. In practice, financial instruments excluded under IAS 19(2011):114 are financial instruments that are issued by the reporting entity and held by a fund that cannot be transferred, sold, pledged or otherwise assigned by the fund to another party without the reporting entity's permission (i.e. the only possibility open to the fund is to hold the financial instrument to maturity).

Any funding arrangements that do not meet the criteria in IAS 19(2011):8 should not be recognised as plan assets. The entity should consider whether the assets intended to fund its pension obligations should instead be recognised as its own assets in its statement of financial position, either because they are held directly by the entity or by a structured or special purpose entity that is consolidated under IFRS 10 *Consolidated Financial Statements* (or, for entities that have not yet adopted IFRS 10, SIC-12 *Consolidation — Special Purpose Entities*).

7.2.6.2   Qualifying insurance policy

A qualifying insurance policy is an insurance policy issued by an insurer that is not a related party of the reporting entity (as defined in IAS 24 *Related Party Disclosures*), if the proceeds of the policy:
[IAS 19(2011):8]

- can be used only to pay or fund employee benefits under a defined benefit plan; and

- are not available to the reporting entity's own creditors (even in bankruptcy) and cannot be paid to the reporting entity, unless either:

  - the proceeds represent surplus assets that are not needed for the policy to meet all of the related employee benefit obligations; or

  - the proceeds are returned to the reporting entity to reimburse it for employee benefits already paid.

Example 7.2.6.2

Insurance policy issued by a related party

Company A offers its employees defined pension benefits through a pension fund. The pension fund acquires an insurance policy from Company A's subsidiary, Company B.

The insurance policy should be included as part of plan assets in Company A's financial statements (consolidated or separate) only if it meets the definition of either:

- an asset held by a long-term employee benefit fund; or

- a qualifying insurance policy.

The policy does not meet the definition of a qualifying insurance policy (see above) because it is issued by a related party. Therefore, to qualify as a plan asset, the insurance policy must meet the definition of an asset held by a long-term employee benefit fund. That definition sets out certain criteria that must be met (see **7.2.6.1**), but it automatically excludes non-transferable financial instruments issued by the reporting entity.

Consequently, in Company A's consolidated financial statements, the insurance policy cannot qualify as a plan asset unless it is a 'transferable financial instrument' (because the policy is issued by an entity within the consolidated group). An insurance policy issued by a group entity that covers the employees in a fund is often non-transferable and, consequently, will not meet the definition of a plan asset. For Company A's separate financial statements, the insurance policy is not considered to be issued by the 'reporting entity'. Accordingly, in those financial statements, the insurance policy will qualify as a plan asset if the criteria in **7.2.6.1** are met, *even if* the policy is a non-transferable financial instrument.

This conclusion was confirmed by the IFRIC (now the IFRS Interpretations Committee) in the context of IAS 19(1998) (see *IFRIC Update*, January 2008) and is not affected by the 2011 revision of IAS 19.

See **chapter A23** for guidance on whether an entity is a related party.

7.2.6.3 Measurement of plan assets

The fair value of any plan assets is deducted from the present value of the defined benefit obligation in determining the deficit or surplus. [IAS 19(2011):113]

Fair value is defined as follows:
[IAS 19(2011):8]

- for entities that have adopted IFRS 13 *Fair Value Measurement*, the price that would be received to sell an asset or paid to transfer a liability in an orderly transaction between market participants at the measurement date; and

- for entities that have not yet adopted IFRS 13, the amount for which an asset could be exchanged or a liability settled between knowledgeable, willing parties in an arm's length transaction.

For entities that have adopted IFRS 13, detailed requirements regarding the measurement of fair value are set out in that Standard (see **chapter A6**). For entities that have not yet adopted IFRS 13, IAS 19 provides no further guidance on the measurement of the fair value of plan assets, but IFRS 9 *Financial Instruments* states that the appropriate quoted market price for an asset held is usually the current bid price, i.e. the price for which the asset could be sold (see IFRS 9(2010):B5.4.4). (For entities that have not yet adopted IFRS 9, equivalent guidance is included in paragraph AG72 of IAS 39 *Financial Instruments: Recognition and Measurement*.) It follows that the bid price should generally be used when establishing the fair value of quoted plan assets.

In the absence of a market price, entities that have adopted IFRS 13 will need to refer to that Standard to determine the appropriate method to be used to evaluate the fair value of plan assets. For those entities that have not yet adopted IFRS 13, IAS 19(2011):113 indicates that one method to estimate the fair value of an asset would be to discount expected future cash flows from the asset at a rate reflecting the risk associated with the asset and its expected maturity or disposal date. If the asset does not have a maturity date, reference should be made to the settlement date of the related obligation.

When IFRS 13 is first adopted (required for annual periods beginning on or after 1 January 2013 with earlier adoption permitted), it is required to be applied prospectively and it need not be applied to comparative information provided for periods before the initial application of IFRS 13; therefore, amounts reported in prior annual periods will not be required to be restated.

When plan assets include qualifying insurance policies that exactly match the amount and timing of part or all of the benefits payable under the plan, the fair value of those insurance policies is deemed to be the present value of the related obligations (subject to any reduction required if the amounts receivable under the insurance policies are not recoverable in full). [IAS 19(2011):115]

IAS 19(2011) does not provide any guidance on how to measure the fair value of insurance policies that do not exactly match the amount and timing of the benefits payable under the plan. An entity that has adopted IFRS 13 should refer to the guidance in that Standard (see **chapter A6**). For an entity that has not yet adopted IFRS 13, various valuation techniques are available for approximating the fair value of insurance policies; the most commonly used are listed below.

- Actuarial value approach – this is typically determined as the discounted amount of future proceeds expected from the policy and is consistent with the valuation of defined benefit obligations.

- Premium value approach – this is the amount that the insurer would request at the date of the valuation to provide the benefits bought to date. This method provides a measure of the replacement cost of the insurance policy and is appropriate to use when there are underlying guarantees.

- Surrender value approach – the surrender value is represented by the amount at which an insurer is prepared to buy back the policy from the policyholder and is indicative of a realisable value rather than a bid price. (Note that IFRS 13's approach to fair value focuses on transfer rather than settlement, so such a methodology may no longer be appropriate once IFRS 13 is adopted.)

Selecting an appropriate approach will depend on each entity's circumstances and is largely a matter of judgement. It is important that the approach adopted is applied consistently from one period to the next.

Example 7.2.6.3

Measurement of qualifying insurance policies that match the benefits payable

Company A sponsors a defined benefit pension plan. Its defined benefit obligation under IAS 19 is measured at CU100. Company A buys an insurance policy from an insurance company, Company B, which will cover the entire obligation and exactly match the payments due to the employees in accordance with the benefit formula in the plan (both in amount and timing). Company B is not a related party as defined in IAS 24 *Related Party Disclosures*. It is determined that the policy represents a 'qualifying' insurance policy as defined in IAS 19(2011):8. Company B charges CU120 for the insurance policy.

What value should be attributed to the insurance policy for the purposes of measuring plan assets and, if that value is not cost, how should Company A account for the difference?

In accordance with IAS 19(2011):115, qualifying insurance policies should be reflected in plan assets at their fair value, which is defined to be the present value of the related defined benefit obligation, i.e. CU100.

In respect of the difference between this amount and the cost of the policy (CU120), either of the following treatments would generally be acceptable:

(a)   the excess of CU20 is considered a cost of the obligation being effectively assumed by Company B and is immediately recognised as an expense in profit or loss; or

(b)   Company A initially recognises the insurance policy at CU120. The policy is then immediately remeasured in line with IAS 19(2011):115. The difference of CU20 is treated as an actuarial loss and is recognised as part of remeasurements in OCI.

In some circumstances, it may be possible to determine that the difference (or a part of it) clearly relates to transaction costs. In those circumstances, the amount determined to represent transaction costs is immediately recognised as an expense in profit or loss. Any remaining difference is recognised using either treatment (a) or (b) above, based on the entity's accounting policy.

7.2.6.4   Reimbursements

When an entity is able to look to another party (e.g. an insurer) to pay part or all of the expenditure required to settle a defined benefit obligation, but the arrangement does not meet the definition of a qualifying insurance policy (see **7.2.6.2**), the reimbursement right is not a plan asset and, therefore, should not be presented as a deduction in determining the deficit or surplus. The appropriate accounting for such reimbursement rights is set out in IAS 19(2011):116. [IAS 19(2011):117 & 118]

When, and only when, it is virtually certain that another party will reimburse some or all of the expenditure required to settle a defined benefit obligation, an entity should recognise its right to reimbursement as a separate asset. The entity should measure the asset at fair value. The entity should disaggregate and recognise changes in the fair value of its right to reimbursement in the same way as for changes in the fair value of plan assets (see **7.4.3**). The components of defined benefit cost recognised in accordance with IAS 19(2011):120 may be recognised net of amounts relating to changes in the carrying amount of the right to reimbursement. [IAS 19(2011):116]

If the right to reimbursement arises under an insurance policy that exactly matches the amount and timing of part or all of the benefits payable under the plan, the fair value of the reimbursement is deemed to be the present

In the absence of statutory or contractual minimum funding requirements (see **7.3.1.3**), *a refund* is generally available to an entity only when the entity has an unconditional right to the refund: [IFRIC 14:11]

(a) during the life of the plan, without assuming that the plan liabilities must be settled in order to obtain the refund (e.g. in some jurisdictions, the entity may have a right to a refund during the life of the plan, irrespective of whether the plan liabilities are settled); or

(b) assuming the gradual settlement of the plan liabilities over time until all members have left the plan; or

(c) assuming the full settlement of the plan liabilities in a single event (i.e. as a plan wind-up).

An unconditional right to a refund can exist whatever the funding level of a plan at the end of the reporting period. [IFRIC 14:11]

If the entity's right to a refund of a surplus depends on the occurrence or non-occurrence of one or more uncertain future events not wholly within its control, the entity does not have an unconditional right and should not recognise an asset. [IFRIC 14:12]

Whether a pension surplus is 'available' will depend on a careful assessment of the legal requirements and the rules of the particular plan, often codified in a trust deed. In some jurisdictions, trustees have the ability or right to protect the interests of members, and to prevent entities from acting 'unreasonably'. Trustees or other third parties may have rights such as the ability to prevent or restrict the payment of a refund.

The circumstances in which the trustees have the ability to prevent any or all of a surplus being refunded to an entity would clearly fall within the guidance of IFRIC 14:12 as a contingent event beyond the entity's control that would prevent it from having an unconditional right to the refund and, consequently, from recognising an asset. In such circumstances, the determination of the extent to which the trustees' right of approval restricts the availability of the surplus is a matter requiring careful judgement; this would include, for example, consideration as to whether an entity could successfully challenge in court a decision by the trustees that the entity regards as unreasonable, such as refusal by the trustees to allow a refund.

IFRIC 14:BC10 clarifies that the entity's ability to improve benefits should not be taken into consideration in measuring the defined benefit obligation unless (1) the future benefit changes are set out in the formal terms of the plan, or (2) there is a constructive obligation at the end of the accounting period. However, a unilateral unlimited right of the trustees to enhance benefits would prevent an entity from having an unconditional right to a surplus even if the trustees have not yet committed to those improvements.

IFRIC 14:11(b) requires consideration of whether a refund would be available assuming the gradual settlement of pension liabilities. When considering gradual settlement, it is necessary to consider what happens at final settlement and, perhaps more importantly, when the plan is closed and members are reducing. For example, once only a limited number of employees are left in the plan, trustees may be required to wind up the plan and secure employees' benefits by purchasing matching insurance policies. IFRIC 14:14 requires an entity to "include the costs to the plan of settling the plan liabilities" and to deduct "costs of any insurance premiums that may be required to secure the liability" (see **7.3.1.2**).

7.3.1.2   Measurement of the economic benefit

The entity should measure the economic benefit available *as a refund* as the amount of the surplus at the end of the reporting period (i.e. the fair value of the plan assets less the present value of the defined benefit obligation) that the entity has a right to receive as a refund, less any associated costs (e.g. taxes other than income tax). [IFRIC 14:13]

IFRIC 14:13 refers specifically to the fair value of plan assets at the end of the reporting period. Consequently, a change of investment strategy (e.g. a move into bonds), whether determined by the entity or by the trustees, represents a potential future change in the fair value of plan assets that should not be taken into account until the investment decision is actually made and the fair value of the plan assets changes.

In measuring the amount of a refund available when the plan is wound up (under IFRIC 14:11(c) – see **7.3.1.1** above), the entity should include the costs of settling the liabilities and making the refund (e.g. professional fees and insurance costs should be deducted to the extent that they would be paid by the plan). [IFRIC 14:14]

If the refund is determined as the full amount or a proportion of the surplus, rather than a fixed amount, the amount is calculated without further adjustment for the time value of money, even if the refund is realisable only at a future date, because both the defined benefit obligation and the fair value of the plan assets are already measured on a present value basis. [IFRIC 14:15]

If there is no minimum funding requirement for contributions relating to future service, the economic benefit available as *a reduction in future contributions* is the future service cost to the entity for each period over the shorter of the expected life of the plan and the expected life of the entity. The future service cost to the entity excludes amounts that will be borne by employees. [IFRIC 14:16]

The benefit should be determined using assumptions consistent with those used to determine the defined benefit obligation and based on conditions that exist at the end of the reporting period. This means, an entity should assume:
[IFRIC 14:17]

• no change to the benefits provided by a plan in the future until the plan is amended; and

• a stable workforce, unless the entity makes a reduction in the number of employees covered by the plan. When such a reduction has been made, the assumption about the future workforce should include the reduction.

Example 7.3.1.2

Stable workforce assumption

Entity A operates a defined benefit plan with a minimum funding requirement. Under the terms of the plan, Entity A has an unconditional right to a reduction in future contributions for any excess contributions above the minimum funding requirement.

Over the next five years, Entity A expects that its workforce will decrease by approximately 20 per cent due to declining demand for its products. However, at the end of the reporting period, Entity A is not yet committed to reducing the number of employees covered by the plan.

Is it appropriate for Entity A to consider the expected decrease in its workforce when calculating the economic benefit available as a reduction in the future contributions to the defined benefit plan?

No. IFRIC 14:22 requires an entity to determine the economic benefit available as a reduction in future contributions as the present value of the

---

future service costs to the entity for each year less the estimated minimum funding contributions required in respect of the future accrual of benefits in that year (see **7.3.1.3** below).

In determining the estimated future service costs, IFRIC 14:17 requires the assumption of a stable workforce in the future unless the entity has reduced the number of employees covered by the plan by the end of the reporting period.

Contributions made to the defined benefit plan that do not provide available economic benefits are recognised as an expense in the period they are incurred.

This conclusion was confirmed by the IFRIC (now the IFRS Interpretations Committee) in the context of IAS 19(1998) (see *IFRIC Update*, November 2008) and is not affected by the 2011 revision of IAS 19.

7.3.1.3   The impact of minimum funding requirements

In many jurisdictions, entities are required, either by law or by agreement with plan managers/trustees, to provide a minimum amount or level of contributions to post-employment benefit plans over a given period, so as to improve the security of the post-employment benefit promise made to the members of such plans. Such commitments are generally referred to as minimum funding requirements.

For the purposes of IFRIC 14, minimum funding requirements are defined as any requirements to fund a post-employment or other long-term defined benefit plan. [IFRIC 14:5] Therefore, both statutory and contractual requirements are covered by the Interpretation.

If a minimum funding requirement is in place for a particular plan, IFRIC 14 distinguishes between contributions that are required to cover: [IFRIC 14:18]

(a)   any existing shortfall for past service on the minimum funding basis; and

(b)   future service.

Under (a), the minimum funding requirement relates to services already received by an entity and does not affect future contributions for future service. [IFRIC 14:19] To the extent that the contributions payable to cover an existing shortfall on a funding basis will not be available after they have been paid into the plan for a refund or reduction in future contributions, the entity should recognise a liability when the obligation to make such contributions arises. [IFRIC 14:24] In other words, if paying the contribution would give rise to an IAS 19 surplus or an increased surplus that would be irrecoverable, this is akin to an onerous contract and a liability should be recognised.

The liability recognised should reduce the net defined benefit asset or increase the net defined benefit liability so that no gain or loss is expected to result from applying IAS 19(2011):64 when the contributions are paid. [IFRIC 14:24]

For contributions that are required to cover the future accrual of benefits, if there is a minimum funding requirement for contributions relating to future service, the economic benefit available as a reduction in future contributions (and, therefore, the surplus that should be recognised as an asset) is the sum of:
[IFRIC 14:20]

(a)   any amount that reduces future minimum funding requirement contributions for future services because the entity made a prepayment (i.e. any such amount that the entity has paid before being required to do so); and

(b)   the estimated future service cost in each period less the estimated minimum funding requirement contributions that would be required for future service in those periods if there were no prepayment of those contributions as described in (a).

The estimate should:
[IFRIC 14:21]

•   take into account the effect of any existing surplus determined using the minimum funding basis (but excluding the prepayment described in the amended paragraph 20(a));

•   be based on assumptions consistent with the minimum funding basis and, for any factors not specified by that basis, on assumptions consistent with those used to determine the defined benefit obligation and with the situation that exists at the end of the reporting period as determined by IAS 19; and

•   include any changes expected as a result of the entity paying the minimum contributions when they are due; but

•   exclude the effect of expected changes in the terms and conditions of the minimum funding basis that are not substantively enacted or contractually agreed at the end of the reporting period.

If the minimum funding requirement contributions for future service exceed the future IAS 19 service cost in any given period, that excess reduces the amount of the economic benefit available as a reduction in future contributions. [IFRIC 14:22]

IFRIC 14:22 clarifies that while the amount calculated under IFRIC 14:20(b) may be negative for a given period (i.e. the estimated minimum funding requirement contribution for that period exceeds the estimated future service cost for that same period), the total amount calculated under IFRIC 14:20(b) can never be less than zero. Accordingly, the economic benefit available as a reduction in future contributions will never be less than the amount of the minimum funding prepayment, if any.

> In some jurisdictions, contribution rates are determined by law, while in others individual entities and the plan managers/trustees negotiate the appropriate level of funding. When the latter is the case, the assumptions to be used for determining the minimum funding requirement may not be clearly defined. It may be necessary to consider the overall funding objective and the basis on which the current contribution schedule was agreed to assess how contributions may be determined in the future. Contribution schedules tend to be more flexible for immature plans (i.e. plans with a high proportion of active employees) than for mature or closed plans. If future contribution levels will be revised to reflect changes in the economic circumstances of the plan (i.e. if contributions may be adjusted downwards or if entities may even take 'contribution holidays' in the event that the scheme is in surplus, an 'economic benefit in the form of reductions in future contributions' will generally be available. On the other hand, if contributions will always be higher than the IAS 19 cost, an analysis of the rules on refunds (see **7.3.1.1** above) would be required.

The following illustrative examples accompany, but are not part of, IFRIC 14.

Example 7.3.1.3A

Effect of the minimum funding requirement when there is an IAS 19 surplus and the minimum funding contributions payable are fully refundable to the entity

[Illustrative examples accompanying IFRIC 14:Example 1]

An entity has a funding level on the minimum funding requirement basis (which is measured on a different basis from that required under IAS 19) of 82 per cent in Plan A. Under the minimum funding requirements, the entity is required to increase the funding level to 95 per cent immediately. As a result, the entity has a statutory obligation at the end of the reporting period to contribute 200 to Plan A immediately. The plan rules permit a full refund of any surplus to the entity at the end of the life of the plan. The year-end valuations for Plan A are set out below.

Fair value of assets	1,200
Present value of defined benefit obligation under IAS 19	(1,100)
Surplus	100

Application of requirements

IFRIC 14:24 requires the entity to recognise a liability to the extent that the contributions payable are not fully available. Payment of the contributions of 200 will increase the IAS 19 surplus from 100 to 300. Under the rules of the plan this amount will be fully refundable to the entity with no associated costs. Therefore, no liability is recognised for the obligation to pay the contributions and the net defined benefit asset is 100.

Example 7.3.1.3B

Effect of a minimum funding requirement when there is an IAS 19 deficit and the minimum funding contributions payable would not be fully available

[Illustrative examples accompanying IFRIC 14:Example 2]

An entity has a funding level on the minimum funding requirement basis (which is measured on a different basis from that required under IAS 19) of 77 per cent in Plan B. Under the minimum funding requirements, the entity is required to increase the funding level to 100 per cent immediately. As a result, the entity has a statutory obligation at the end of the reporting period to pay additional contributions of 300 to Plan B. The plan rules permit a maximum refund of 60 per cent of the IAS 19 surplus to the entity and the entity is not permitted to reduce its contributions below a specified level which happens to equal the IAS 19 service cost. The year-end valuations for Plan B are set out below.

Fair value of assets	1,000
Present value of defined benefit obligation under IAS 19	(1,100)
Deficit	(100)

Application of requirements

The payment of 300 would change the IAS 19 deficit of 100 to a surplus of 200. Of this 200, 60 per cent (120) is refundable.

Therefore, of the contributions of 300, 100 eliminates the IAS 19 deficit and 120 (60 per cent of 200) is available as an economic benefit. The remaining 80 (40 per cent of 200) of the contributions paid is not available to the entity.

IFRIC 14:24 requires the entity to recognise a liability to the extent that the additional contributions payable are not available to it.

Therefore, the net defined benefit liability is 180, comprising the deficit of 100 plus the additional liability of 80 resulting from the requirements in paragraph 24 of IFRIC 14. No other liability is recognised in respect of the statutory obligation to pay contributions of 300.

Summary

Fair value of assets	1,000
Present value of defined benefit obligation under IAS 19	(1,100)
Deficit	(100)
Effect of the asset ceiling	(80)
Net defined benefit liability	(180)

When the contributions of 300 are paid, the net defined benefit asset will be 120.

Example 7.3.1.3C

Effect of a minimum funding requirement when the contributions payable would not be fully available and the effect on the economic benefit available as a future contribution reduction

[Illustrative examples accompanying IFRIC 14:Example 3]

An entity has a funding level on the minimum funding basis (which it measures on a different basis from that required by IAS 19) of 95 per cent in Plan C. The minimum funding requirements require the entity to pay contributions to increase the funding level to 100 per cent over the next three years. The contributions are required to make good the deficit on the minimum funding basis (shortfall) and to cover future service.

Plan C also has an IAS 19 surplus at the end of the reporting period of 50, which cannot be refunded to the entity under any circumstances.

The nominal amounts of contributions required to satisfy the minimum funding requirements in respect of the shortfall and the future service for the next three years are set out below.

Year	Total contributions for minimum funding requirement	Contributions required to make good the shortfall	Contributions required to cover future service
1	135	120	15
2	125	112	13
3	115	104	11

Application of requirements

The entity's present obligation in respect of services already received includes the contributions required to make good the shortfall but does not include the contributions required to cover future service.

The present value of the entity's obligation, assuming a discount rate of 6 per cent per year, is approximately 300, calculated as follows:

$[120/(1.06) + 112/(1.06)^2 + 104/(1.06)^3]$

When these contributions are paid into the plan, the IAS 19 surplus (ie the fair value of assets less the present value of the defined benefit obligation) would, other things being equal, increase from 50 to 350 (300 + 50).

However, the surplus is not refundable although an asset may be available as a future contribution reduction.

In accordance with IFRIC 14:20, the economic benefit available as a reduction in future contributions is the sum of:

a.   any amount that reduces future minimum funding requirement contributions for future service because the entity made a prepayment (ie paid the amount before being required to do so); and

b.   the estimated future service cost in each period in accordance with IFRIC 14:16 & 17, less the estimated minimum funding requirement contributions that would be required for future service in those periods if there were no prepayment as described in (a).

In this example there is no prepayment as described in IFRIC 14:20(a). The amounts available as a reduction in future contributions when applying IFRIC 14:20(b) are set out below.

Year	IAS 19 service cost	Minimum contributions required to cover future service	Amount available as contribution reduction
1	13	15	(2)
2	13	13	0
3	13	11	2
4+	13	9	4

Assuming a discount rate of 6 per cent, the present value of the economic benefit available as a future contribution reduction is therefore equal to:

$(2)/(1.06) + 0/(1.06)^2 + 2/(1.06)^3 + 4/(1.06)^4 \ldots = 56$

Thus in accordance with IAS 19:58(b), the present value of the economic benefit available from future contribution reductions is limited to 56.

IFRIC 14:24 requires the entity to recognise a liability to the extent that the additional contributions payable will not be fully available. Therefore, the effect of the asset ceiling is 294 (50 + 300 − 56).

The entity recognises a net defined benefit liability of 244 in the statement of financial position. No other liability is recognised in respect of the obligation to make contributions to fund the minimum funding shortfall.

Summary

Surplus	**50**
Net defined benefit asset (before consideration of the minimum funding requirement)	50
Effect of the asset ceiling	(294)
Net defined benefit liability	**(244)**

When the contributions of 300 are paid into the plan, the net defined benefit asset will become 56 (300 − 244).

Example 7.3.1.3D

Effect of a prepayment when a minimum funding requirement exceeds the expected future service charge

[Illustrative examples accompanying IFRIC 14:Example 4]

An entity is required to fund Plan D so that no deficit arises on the minimum funding basis. The entity is required to pay minimum funding requirement contributions to cover the service cost in each period determined on the minimum funding basis.

Plan D has an IAS 19 surplus of 35 at the beginning of 20X1. This example assumes that the discount rate and expected return on assets are 0 per cent, and that the plan cannot refund the surplus to the entity under any circumstances but can use the surplus for reductions of future contributions.

The minimum contributions required to cover future service are 15 for each of the next five years. The expected IAS 19 service cost is 10 in each year.

The entity makes a prepayment of 30 at the beginning of 20X1 in respect of years 20X1 and 20X2, increasing its surplus at the beginning of 20X1 to 65. That prepayment reduces the future contributions it expects to make in the following two years, as follows:

Year	IAS 19 service cost	Minimum funding requirement contribution before prepayment	Minimum funding requirement contribution after prepayment
20X1	10	15	0
20X2	10	15	0
20X3	10	15	15
20X4	10	15	15
20X5	10	15	15
Total	50	75	45

In accordance with paragraphs 20 and 22 of IFRIC 14, at the beginning of 20X1, the economic benefit available as a reduction in future contributions is the sum of:

(a)   30, being the prepayment of the minimum funding requirement contributions; and

(b)   nil. The estimated minimum funding requirement contributions required for future service would be 75 if there was no prepayment. Those contributions exceed the estimated future service cost (50); therefore the entity cannot use any part of the surplus of 35 noted in [*the second paragraph*] (see paragraph 22).

Assuming a discount rate of 0 per cent, the present value of the economic benefit available as a reduction in future contributions is equal to 30. Thus in accordance with paragraph 64 of IAS 19 the entity recognises a net defined benefit asset of 30 (because this is lower than the IAS 19 surplus of 65).

7.3.1.4   Disclosure

IFRIC 14 does not specify any additional disclosure requirements, but notes that, under paragraph 125 of IAS 1 *Presentation of Financial Statements*, entities are required to disclose information about the key sources of estimation uncertainty that have a significant risk of causing an adjustment to the carrying amount of assets and liabilities within the next financial year. Therefore, the entity should disclose information about the key sources of estimation uncertainty at the end of the reporting period that have a significant risk of causing a material adjustment to the carrying amount of the net asset or liability in the statement of financial position. This might include disclosure of any restrictions on the realisability of the surplus or disclosure of the basis used to determine the amount of the economic benefit available. [IFRIC 14:10]

7.4   Step 3 – determining amounts to be recognised in profit or loss

The amounts to be recognised in profit or loss in respect of a defined benefit plan are as follows:
[IAS 19(2011):8 & 120(a) & (b)]

- current service cost (see **7.4.1**);

- any past service cost and gain or loss on settlement (see **7.4.2**); and

- net interest on the net defined benefit liability (asset) (see **7.4.3**).

When employee costs are capitalised as part of the cost of an asset (e.g. inventories under IAS 2 *Inventories* or self-constructed property in accordance with IAS 16 *Property, Plant and Equipment*), the appropriate proportion of the components listed above is included in the employee costs capitalised. [IAS 19(2011):121]

IAS 19(2011) uses the term 'service cost' to mean the aggregate of current service cost, past service cost and any gain or loss on settlement. [IAS 19(2011):8]

7.4.1   *Current service cost*

Current service cost is the increase in the present value of the defined benefit obligation resulting from employee service in the current period. [IAS 19(2011):8]

7.4.2   *Past service cost and gain or loss on settlement*

Past service cost is the change in the present value of the defined benefit obligation for employee service in prior periods, resulting from a plan amendment (the introduction or withdrawal of, or changes to, a defined benefit plan) or a curtailment (a significant reduction by the entity in the number of employees covered by a plan). [IAS 19(2011):8 & 102]

> While the definition of past service cost distinguishes between past service cost arising from plan amendments and those arising from curtailments, this distinction has little impact on the financial statements because all past service costs are recognised in profit or loss in the period in which they occur.

Before determining past service cost, or a gain or loss on settlement, an entity should remeasure the net defined benefit liability (asset) using the current fair value of plan assets and current actuarial assumptions (including current market interest rates and other current market prices) reflecting the benefits offered under the plan before the plan amendment, curtailment or settlement. [IAS 19(2011):99]

The entity is then required to identify changes in the present value of the defined benefit obligation arising from the plan amendment, curtailment or settlement. It is not always necessary to identify each of these components separately; an entity need not distinguish between past service cost resulting from a plan amendment, past service cost resulting from a curtailment and a gain or loss on settlement if these transactions occur together. [IAS 19(2011):100] This would arise, for example, when a plan is terminated with the result that the obligation is settled and the plan ceases to exist. However, the termination of a plan is not a settlement if the plan is replaced by a new plan that offers benefits that are, in substance, the same. [IAS 19(2011):101]

In some cases, a plan amendment occurs before a settlement, such as when an entity changes the benefits under the plan and settles the amended benefits later. In such circumstances, the entity should recognise past service cost before any gain or loss on settlement. [IAS 19(2011):100]

7.4.2.1 Past service cost

An entity is required to recognise past service cost as an expense at the earlier of the following dates:
[IAS 19(2011):103]

- when the plan amendment or curtailment occurs (see below); and

- when the entity recognises related restructuring costs (see **3.9.3** in **chapter A12**) or termination benefits (see **section 10** below).

A plan amendment occurs when an entity introduces, or withdraws, a defined benefit plan or changes the benefits payable under an existing defined benefit plan. [IAS 19(2011):104]

A curtailment occurs when an entity significantly reduces the number of employees covered by a plan. A curtailment may arise from an isolated event, such as the closing of a plant, discontinuance of an operation or termination or suspension of a plan. [IAS 19(2011):104]

Under IAS 19(1998), an entity recognises curtailments resulting from a significant reduction in the number of employees covered by a plan when the entity is demonstrably committed to making the reduction. In contrast, IAS 19(2011) requires an entity to recognise a curtailment when it 'occurs'. In the Basis for Conclusions on IAS 19(2011), the IASB states as follows.

> "If a plan amendment or curtailment occurs in isolation (ie it is not triggered by a settlement, termination benefit or restructuring), determining when the plan amendment occurs requires the exercise of judgement. The timing of recognition would depend on the individual facts and circumstances and how they interact with the constructive obligation requirements in [IAS 19(2011):61 and 62 – see **7.1** above]." [IAS 19(2011):BC158]

Past service cost may be either positive (when benefits are introduced or changed so that the present value of the defined benefit obligation increases) or negative (when benefits are withdrawn or changed so that the present value of the defined benefit obligation decreases). [IAS 19(2011):106]

When an entity reduces benefits payable under an existing defined benefit plan and, at the same time, increases other benefits payable under the plan for the same employees, the entity treats the change as a single net change. [IAS 19(2011):107]

Past service cost excludes:
[IAS 19(2011):108]

- the effect of differences between actual and previously assumed salary increases on the obligation to pay benefits for service in prior years (there is no past service cost because actuarial assumptions allow for projected salaries);

- underestimates and overestimates of discretionary pension increases when an entity has a constructive obligation to grant such increases (there is no past service cost because actuarial assumptions allow for such increases);

- estimates of benefit improvements that result from actuarial gains or from the return on plan assets that have been recognised in the financial statements if the entity is obliged, by either the formal terms of a plan (or a constructive obligation that goes beyond those terms) or legislation, to use any surplus in the plan for the benefit of plan participants, even if the benefit increase has not yet been formally awarded (there is no past service cost because the resulting increase in the obligation is an actuarial loss – see **7.2.4.3**); and

- the increase in vested benefits (i.e. benefits that are not conditional on future employment – see **7.2.3**) when, in the absence of new or improved benefits, employees complete vesting requirements (there is no past service cost because the entity recognised the estimated cost of benefits as current service cost as the service was rendered).

7.4.2.2   Gains and losses on settlement

The gain or loss on a settlement is the difference between:
[IAS 19(2011):109]

- the present value of the defined benefit obligation being settled, as determined on the date of settlement; and

- the settlement price, including any plan assets transferred and any payments made directly by the entity in connection with the settlement.

An entity is required to recognise a gain or loss on the settlement of a defined benefit plan when the settlement occurs. [IAS 19(2011):110] A settlement is a transaction that eliminates all further legal or constructive obligations for part or all of the benefits provided under a defined benefit plan (other than a payment of benefits to, or on behalf of, employees that is set out in the terms of the plan and included in the actuarial assumptions). [IAS 19(2011):8] For example:
[IAS 19(2011):111]

- a one-off transfer of significant employer obligations under the plan to an insurance company through the purchase of an insurance policy is a settlement; but

- a lump sum cash payment, under the terms of the plan, to plan participants in exchange for their rights to receive specified post-employment benefits is not.

Consistent with the view expressed previously by the IFRIC (now the IFRS Interpretations Committee) (see *IFRIC Update*, May 2008), IAS 19(2011) clarifies that a settlement (for which a gain or loss is recognised in profit or loss) is a payment of benefits that is not set out in the terms of the plan (and which, therefore, could not have been considered in developing actuarial assumptions). The payment of benefits that are set out in the terms of the plan (including where there are options on the nature of the benefit payments) would be included in the actuarial assumptions and if a gain or loss arose upon payment of those benefits it would be an actuarial gain or loss, to be recognised in OCI as part of remeasurements. [IAS 19(2011):BC163]

An entity may acquire an insurance policy to fund some or all of the employee benefits relating to employee service in the current and prior periods. The acquisition of such a policy is not a settlement if the entity retains a legal or constructive obligation to pay further amounts if the insurer does not pay the employee benefits specified in the insurance policy. IAS 19's requirements regarding the recognition and measurement of reimbursement rights under insurance policies that are not plan assets are discussed at **7.2.6.4**. [IAS 19(2011):112]

Example 7.4.2.2

Settlement of defined benefit plan with an unrecognised surplus

In its statement of financial position, Entity X recognises the following amounts in respect of its defined benefit plan.

	CU
Fair value of plan assets	40
Present value of defined benefit obligation	(35)
Effect of asset ceiling	(5)
	–

No net defined benefit asset has been recognised in accordance with IAS 19(2011):64 because it was determined that no economic benefits were available in the form of refunds from the plan or reductions in future contributions to the plan.

In full settlement of its defined benefit obligation, Entity X transfers all of the plan assets to a third party and pays an additional CU10 to that third party. Entity X does not retain any legal or constructive obligation to the members of the plan.

IAS 19(2011):110 requires Entity X to recognise a gain or loss on settlement of its defined benefit plan immediately in profit or loss. The gain or loss is calculated in accordance with IAS 19(2011):109 (see above), and after remeasuring the obligation and plan assets using current actuarial assumptions and market prices. The values above include the effect of that remeasurement.

When Entity X calculates the gain or loss on settlement of its defined benefit plan to be recognised in profit or loss, what is the impact of the previously unrecognised surplus?

IAS 19(2011) does not specifically address this issue and it appears that two alternative treatments (as described below) are acceptable. Whichever of these alternatives is selected as an accounting policy by Entity X, it should be applied consistently and disclosed when the effect is material.

Alternative 1

In applying IAS 19(2011):109, the reference to 'plan assets transferred' could be read as referring to the *full* value of those assets (i.e. before the limitation imposed by the asset ceiling). If this approach is adopted, at the date of settlement Entity X should recognise the previously unrecognised surplus of CU5 as a gain in other comprehensive income (OCI).

Consequently, Entity X would recognise a settlement loss of CU15 in profit or loss (i.e. the defined benefit obligation settled of CU35 less plan assets transferred of CU40 less settlement payment of CU10).

Alternative 2

In applying IAS 19(2011):109, the reference to the 'plan assets transferred' could be read as referring to the *recognised* value of those assets (i.e. after the limitation imposed by the asset ceiling). If this approach is adopted, the asset ceiling remains in place on settlement and no gain or loss is required to be recognised in OCI.

Consequently, Entity X would recognise a settlement loss of CU10 (i.e. the defined benefit obligation settled of CU35 less recognised plan assets transferred of CU35 less settlement payment of CU10).

7.4.3   *Net interest on the net defined benefit liability (asset)*

Net interest on the net defined benefit liability (asset) is the change during the period in the net defined benefit liability (asset) that arises from the passage of time. [IAS 19(2011):8]

Net interest on the net defined benefit liability (asset) is determined by multiplying the net defined benefit liability (asset) by the discount rate specified in IAS 19(2011):83 (see **7.2.5**), both as determined at the start of the annual reporting period, taking account of any changes in the net defined benefit liability (asset) during the period as a result of contribution and benefit payments. [IAS 19(2011):123]

The net interest calculation takes account of changes in the net defined benefit liability (asset) during the period as a result of contribution and benefit payments. It does not take account of any other movements in the net defined benefit liability (asset) during the period, such as actuarial gains and losses.

IAS 19(2011) explains that net interest on the net defined benefit liability (asset) can be viewed as comprising interest income on plan assets, interest cost on the defined benefit obligation and interest on the effect of the asset ceiling. [IAS 19(2011):124]

Under IAS 19(1998), income on the plan assets and interest cost on the gross defined benefit obligation are calculated separately. The income on the plan assets is based on the expected return on those assets; this depends on the actual investment portfolio and is typically not equal to the discount rate applied for the determination of the interest cost on the obligation. In contrast, IAS 19(2011) applies the latter rate to the net defined benefit liability (asset). When that rate is lower than the expected return on plan assets (as is generally the case), application of IAS 19(2011) will decrease interest income recognised in profit or loss and, thus, reduce net profit or loss.

Under IAS 19(2011), the net interest on the net defined benefit liability (asset) is calculated taking into account the effect of the asset ceiling. Under IAS 19(1998), income on the plan assets is calculated without any restriction for effects of the asset ceiling.

Given that there has been no change in the discount rate to be used, the net interest on the net defined benefit liability will be the same as interest cost under IAS 19(1998) for unfunded plans.

Interest income on plan assets is a component of the return on plan assets, and is determined by multiplying the fair value of the plan assets by the discount rate specified in IAS 19(2011):83 (see **7.2.5**), both as determined at the start of the annual reporting period, taking account of any changes in the plan assets held during the period as a result of contributions and benefit payments. The difference between the interest income on plan assets and the return on plan assets is included in the remeasurement of the net defined benefit liability (asset). [IAS 19(2011):125]

Interest on the effect of the asset ceiling is part of the total change in the effect of the asset ceiling, and is determined by multiplying the effect of the asset ceiling by the discount rate specified in IAS 19(2011):83 (see **7.2.5**), both as determined at the start of the annual reporting period. The difference between that amount and the total change in the effect of the asset ceiling is included in the remeasurement of the net defined benefit liability (asset). [IAS 19(2011):126]

7.5   Step 4 – determining the remeasurements of the net defined benefit liability (asset) to be recognised in other comprehensive income

Remeasurements of the net defined benefit liability (asset) are required to be recognised in other comprehensive income. [IAS 19(2011):120(c)] Such remeasurements are not reclassified to profit or loss in a subsequent period. However, an entity may transfer those amounts recognised in other comprehensive income within equity. [IAS 19(2011):122]

> The IASB decided not to carry forward the requirement in IAS 19(1998) that an entity should transfer amounts recognised in other comprehensive income directly to retained earnings. IFRSs do not define the phrase 'retained earnings' and the IASB has not discussed what it should mean. Moreover, there may exist jurisdiction-specific restrictions on components of equity. Consequently, IAS 19(2011) permits an entity to transfer the cumulative remeasurements within equity, but does not impose specific requirements regarding that transfer. [IAS 19(2011):BC100]

Remeasurements of the net defined benefit liability (asset) comprise: [IAS 19(2011):8 & 127]

- actuarial gains and losses;

- the return on plan assets, excluding amounts included in net interest on the net defined benefit liability (asset) (see **7.4.3**); and

- any change in the effect of the asset ceiling, excluding amounts included in net interest on the net defined benefit liability (asset) (see **7.4.3**).

Actuarial gains and losses are decreases or increases in the present value of the defined benefit obligation because of experience adjustments (the effects of differences between the previous actuarial assumptions and what has actually occurred) and changes in actuarial assumptions. [IAS 19(2011):8] Causes of actuarial gains and losses include, for example: [IAS 19(2011):128]

- unexpectedly high or low rates of employee turnover, early retirement or mortality or of increases in salaries, benefits (if the formal or constructive terms of a plan provide for inflationary benefit increases) or medical costs;

- the effect of changes to assumptions concerning benefit payment options;

- the effect of changes in estimates of future employee turnover, early retirement or mortality or of increases in salaries, benefits (if the formal or constructive terms of a plan provide for inflationary benefit increases) or medical costs; and

- the effect of changes in the discount rate.

Actuarial gains and losses do not include changes in the present value of the defined benefit obligation because of the introduction, amendment, curtailment or settlement of the defined benefit plan, or changes to the benefits payable under the defined benefit plan. Such changes result in past service cost or gains or losses on settlement. [IAS 19(2011):129]

The return on plan assets is interest, dividends and other income derived from the plan assets, together with realised and unrealised gains or losses on the plan assets, less:
[IAS 19(2011):8 & 130]

- any costs of managing the plan assets; and

- any tax payable by the plan itself, other than tax included in the actuarial assumptions used to measure the defined benefit obligation.

Other administration costs are not deducted from the return on plan assets. [IAS 19(2011):130]

> For further discussion of administration costs, see **7.2.4.11**.

8   Presentation and disclosure for defined benefit plans

8.1   Presentation

8.1.1   Offset

An asset relating to one plan should be offset against a liability relating to another plan when, and only when, an entity:
[IAS 19(2011):131]

- has a legally enforceable right to use a surplus in one plan to settle obligations under the other plan; and

- intends either to settle the obligations on a net basis, or to realise the surplus in one plan and settle its obligation under the other plan simultaneously.

IAS 19(2011):132 notes that these offsetting criteria are similar to those established for financial instruments in IAS 32 *Financial Instruments: Presentation*.

> In practice, such offset will be available only rarely.

8.1.2 Current/non-current distinction

IAS 19 does not specify whether an entity should distinguish current and non-current portions of assets and liabilities arising from post-employment benefits. [IAS 19(2011):133]

8.1.3 Components of defined benefit cost

Under IAS 19(2011):120, an entity is required to recognise service cost and net interest on the net defined benefit liability (asset) in profit or loss. The Standard does not specify how an entity should present service cost and net interest on the net defined benefit liability (asset). The entity should determine an appropriate presentation under IAS 1 *Presentation of Financial Statements*. [IAS 19(2011):134]

> Accordingly, entities have a choice as to whether to present service cost and net interest on the net defined benefit liability (asset) separately or as a single net figure. Such a decision is an accounting policy choice, and should therefore be disclosed appropriately and applied consistently for all plans.

> Under IAS 19(1998), entities are permitted to present interest cost and expected return on plan assets as separate line items. Such a presentation does not appear appropriate under IAS 19(2011) because net interest on the net defined benefit liability (asset) is defined and is calculated as a net amount.

8.2 Disclosure

IAS 19 requires extensive disclosures in respect of defined benefit plans.

8.2.1   *General*

An entity should disclose information that:
[IAS 19(2011):135]

- explains the characteristics of its defined benefit plans and risks associated with them (see **8.2.2**);

- identifies and explains the amounts in its financial statements arising from its defined benefit plans (see **8.2.3**); and

- describes how its defined benefit plans may affect the amount, timing and uncertainty of the entity's future cash flows (see **8.2.4**).

To meet these objectives, an entity should have regard to all the following:
[IAS 19(2011):136]

- the level of detail necessary to satisfy the disclosure requirements;

- how much emphasis to place on each of the various requirements;

- how much aggregation or disaggregation to undertake; and

- whether users of financial statements need additional information to evaluate the quantitative information disclosed.

If the disclosures provided in accordance with IAS 19(2011) and other IFRSs are insufficient to meet the objectives above, additional information necessary to meet those objectives should be disclosed. For example, an entity might present an analysis of the present value of the defined benefit obligation that distinguishes the nature, characteristics and risks of the obligation. Such a disclosure could distinguish:
[IAS 19(2011):137]

- between amounts owing to active members, deferred members, and pensioners;

- between vested benefits and accrued but not vested benefits; and/or

- between conditional benefits, amounts attributable to future salary increases and other benefits.

An entity is required to assess whether all or some disclosures should be disaggregated to distinguish plans or groups of plans with materially different risks. For example, an entity might disaggregate disclosure about plans showing one or more of the following features:
[IAS 19(2011):138]

- different geographical locations;

- different characteristics such as flat salary pension plans, final salary pension plans or post-employment medical plans;

- different regulatory environments;

- different reporting segments; and/or

- different funding arrangements (e.g. wholly unfunded, wholly or partly funded).

8.2.2   Characteristics of defined benefit plans and risks associated with them

An entity should disclose:
[IAS 19(2011):139]

- information about the characteristics of its defined benefit plans, including:

  - the nature of the benefits provided by the plan (e.g. final salary defined benefit plan or contribution-based plan with guarantee);

  - a description of the regulatory framework in which the plan operates (e.g. the level of any minimum funding requirements), and any effect of the regulatory framework on the plan, such as the asset ceiling (see **7.3.1**); and

  - a description of any other entity's responsibilities for the governance of the plan, e.g. responsibilities of trustees or of board members of the plan;

- a description of the risks to which the plan exposes the entity, focused on any unusual, entity-specific or plan-specific risks, and of any significant concentrations of risk. For example, if plan assets are invested primarily in one class of investments (e.g. property), the plan may expose the entity to a concentration of property market risk; and

- a description of any plan amendments, curtailments and settlements.

8.2.3   Explanation of amounts in the financial statements

An entity should provide a reconciliation from the opening balance to the closing balance for each of the following, if applicable:
[IAS 19(2011):140]

- the net defined benefit liability (asset), showing separate reconciliations for:

- plan assets;

- the present value of the defined benefit obligation; and

- the effect of the asset ceiling; and

- any reimbursement rights. An entity should also describe the relationship between any reimbursement right and the related obligation.

Each reconciliation listed above should show each of the following, if applicable:
[IAS 19(2011):141]

- current service cost;

- interest income or expense;

- remeasurements of the net defined benefit liability (asset), showing separately:

  - the return on plan assets, excluding amounts included in interest in (b);

  - actuarial gains and losses arising from changes in demographic assumptions (see **7.2.4**);

  - actuarial gains and losses arising from changes in financial assumptions (see **7.2.4**); and

  - changes in the effect of limiting a net defined benefit asset to the asset ceiling, excluding amounts included in interest in (b). An entity should also disclose how it determined the maximum economic benefit available (i.e. whether those benefits would be in the form of refunds, reductions in future contributions or a combination of both);

- past service cost and gains and losses arising from settlements. As permitted by IAS 19(2011):100 (see **7.4.2**), past service cost and gains and losses arising from settlements need not be distinguished if they occur together;

- the effect of changes in foreign exchange rates;

- contributions to the plan, showing separately those by the employer and by plan participants;

- payments from the plan, showing separately the amount paid in respect of any settlements; and

- the effects of business combinations and disposals.

The fair value of the plan assets should be disaggregated into classes that distinguish the nature and risks of those assets, subdividing each class of plan asset into those that have a quoted market price in an active market as defined in IFRS 13 *Fair Value Measurement* (for entities that have not yet adopted IFRS 13, see paragraph B.5.4.3 of IFRS 9(2010) *Financial Instruments* or, for entities that have not yet adopted IFRS 9, see paragraph AG71 of IAS 39 *Financial Instruments: Recognition and Measurement*) and those that do not. For example, and considering the level of disclosure discussed in IAS 19(2011):136 (see **8.2.1** above), an entity might distinguish between: [IAS 19(2011):142]

- cash and cash equivalents;

- equity instruments (segregated by industry type, company size, geography etc.);

- debt instruments (segregated by type of issuer, credit quality, geography etc.);

- real estate (segregated by geography etc.);

- derivatives (segregated by type of underlying risk in the contract, e.g. interest rate contracts, foreign exchange contracts, equity contracts, credit contracts, longevity swaps etc.);

- investment funds (segregated by type of fund);

- asset-backed securities; and

- structured debt.

An entity should disclose:
[IAS 19(2011):143]

- the fair value of the entity's own transferable financial instruments held as plan assets; and

- the fair value of plan assets that are property occupied by, or other assets used by, the entity.

An entity should disclose the significant actuarial assumptions used to determine the present value of the defined benefit obligation (see **7.2.4**). Such disclosure should be in absolute terms (e.g. as an absolute percentage, and not just as a margin between different percentages and other variables). When an entity provides disclosures in total for a grouping of plans, it should provide such disclosures in the form of weighted averages or relatively narrow ranges. [IAS 19(2011):144] required to follow the requirements described in IAS 19(2011):116 to 119 for the purpose of recognising and measuring any reimbursement right. In aggregate, these requirements are discussed in **7.2** and **7.3** above (i.e. Steps 1 and 2 described for the measurement of the deficit or surplus in a defined benefit post-employment benefit plan). [IAS 19(2011):155]

As discussed at **3.1** above and at **4.1.1.2** in **chapter A4**, some obligations for other long-term employee benefits may be presented as current liabilities (based on the employees' entitlement to take their benefits within 12 months of the reporting period rather than on the expected timing of payment). In measuring such obligations, the question arises as to whether amounts should be discounted to reflect the expected timing of payment.

IAS 19(2011):155 requires that other long-term benefit obligations be measured using the same valuation methodology as defined benefit post-employment benefit obligations (except that remeasurements are required to be recognised in profit or loss). In particular, IAS 19(2011):69 specifies that "[a]n entity discounts the whole of [an other long-term] benefit obligation, even if part of the obligation is expected to be settled before twelve months after the reporting period".

Therefore, a current liability arising from other long-term employee benefits should be measured as a discounted amount.

9.1.2   Amount recognised in profit or loss

The expense recognised in profit or loss (or in the cost of an asset, when capitalisation is permitted or required) for other long-term employee benefits is the net total of:
[IAS 19(2011):156]

- service cost;

- net interest on the net defined benefit liability (asset); and

- remeasurements of the net defined benefit liability (asset).

9.1.3   Long-term disability benefit

An example of a long-term employee benefit discussed in IAS 19 is long-term disability benefit. If the amount of such a benefit is independent of years of service (i.e. the level of benefit is the same for any disabled employee regardless of years of service), no cost is recognised until an event occurs that causes a long-term disability. If the level of benefit is dependent on years of service, an obligation should be recognised as the service is rendered, based upon the probability and timing of payments expected to be made. [IAS 19(2011):157]

9.2   Disclosure

IAS 19 has no specific disclosure requirements for other long-term employment benefits, but notes that disclosures may be required under IAS 1 *Presentation of Financial Statements* (when the expense is material) or under IAS 24 *Related Party Disclosures* (if in relation to key management personnel).

In particular, the extensive disclosure requirements for post-employment benefits (discussed in **section 8.2**) do not apply to other long-term employment benefits.

9.3   Death-in-service benefits

Death-in-service benefits are employee benefits payable if an employee dies while employed by the entity. These arrangements may take various forms, including lump sum payments and widows' pensions.

Accounting for death-in-service benefits raises several issues that are not addressed in IAS 19.

The subject was discussed by the IFRIC (now the IFRS Interpretations Committee) in the context of IAS 19(1998) – see *IFRIC Update*, January 2008. The IFRIC discussions concerning death-in-service benefits focused on the appropriate manner for attributing those benefits to periods of service. The IFRIC noted the requirement in IAS 19(1998):67(b) (carried forward as IAS 19(2011):70(b)) to attribute the cost of benefits until the date when future service by the employee will lead to no material amount of future benefits under the plan, other than from salary increases.

In the case of death-in-service benefits, the IFRIC noted that:

- the expected date of death would be the date at which no material amount of further benefit would arise from the plan;

- using different mortality assumptions for a defined benefit pension plan and an associated death-in-service benefit would not comply with the requirement in IAS 19(1998):72 (carried forward as IAS 19(2011):75) to use actuarial assumptions that are mutually compatible; and

- if the conditions in IAS 19(1998):39 (carried forward as IAS 19(2011):46) were met, then accounting for death-in-service benefits on a defined contribution basis would be appropriate.

The appropriate accounting for death-in-service benefits depends on the nature of the arrangements, including:

- whether the benefits depend on the length of service or are the same irrespective of the length of service; and

- whether the benefits are provided through a post-employment benefit plan or through a stand-alone arrangement.

Although the IFRIC only considered the issue under IAS 19(1998), the paragraphs in question were not modified when IAS 19 was revised in 2011. Consequently, the discussion above remains valid.

9.3.1   Benefits related to length of service

Although IAS 19 does not specifically mention death-in-service benefits, it refers to long-term disability benefits (which may have similar features to death-in-service benefits) as an example of 'other' long-term benefits. IAS 19(2011):157 states that if the level of benefit depends on the length of service, an obligation arises when the service is rendered. Measurement of that obligation reflects the probability that payment will be required and the length of time for which payment is expected to be made. Therefore, when the level of death-in-service benefits is related to the length of service, the benefits should be attributed over the service life of the employee until the expected date of death of the employee.

If death-in-service benefits are provided as part of a defined benefit plan, an entity would recognise actuarial gains and losses arising on the death-in-service benefits as part of remeasurements of the defined benefit plan in other comprehensive income.

If death-in-service benefits related to the period of service are provided through a stand-alone plan, they would represent an other long-term employee benefit. Applying IAS 19 (2011):157 by analogy, such benefits would be attributed over the service period until the expected date of death of the employee, and actuarial gains and losses arising on such plans would be recognised in profit or loss in accordance with IAS 19(2011):156.

9.3.2   Benefits unrelated to length of service – stand-alone plans

IAS 19(2011):157 states that if the level of benefits is the same regardless of years of service (e.g. a lump sum fixed amount), the expected cost of those benefits is recognised when an event occurs that causes long-term disability. Applying IAS 19(2011):157 by analogy for death-in-service benefits that are fixed irrespective of any period of service, it would be appropriate to recognise an expense only when an employee dies.

9.3.3   Benefits unrelated to length of service – benefits provided under a defined benefit plan

The calculation of the liabilities of a defined benefit retirement benefit plan will include an assumption about employees dying before reaching normal retirement age. Such an assumption will generally result in a reduction of the liability recognised. It might, therefore, be thought imprudent to recognise that reduction without recognising the additional liabilities that will arise under the death-in-service benefit arrangements if an employee dies before normal retirement age.

The basic approach for defined benefit plans under IAS 19 is to calculate the expected obligation and attribute that benefit to periods of service. When the death-in-service benefit is a lump sum amount regardless of length of service, there is no plan benefit formula that can be used to attribute the benefit to periods of service. In the absence of such a formula, it would seem appropriate to attribute the benefit on a straight-line basis until the expected date of death of the employee, although it appears that the alternative (i.e. recognition of an expense only when an employee dies) may be justified by reference to IAS 19(2011):157.

Example 9.3.3

Measurement of incapacity benefit or death-in-service benefit based on service life

An entity operates a defined benefit post-employment benefit plan. Under the terms of the plan, the employee is entitled to a pension of 1/60th of final earnings for each year of service until retirement. If an employee becomes incapacitated or dies prior to the normal retirement date, the benefit paid (to the employee or the employee's dependant) is based on the years of employment until the date of incapacity or death, and credit is given for 50 per cent of the years from that date until the normal retirement date.

For example, an employee works for 20 years and then becomes incapacitated 10 years prior to the normal retirement date. The benefit paid is 25/60ths based on 25 years of service (the 20 years actually worked plus 50 per cent of the remaining years until the normal retirement date).

In the circumstances described, the assumptions used for attributing benefits to service periods should reflect that, for employees expected to become incapacitated or to die prior to their normal retirement date, the service period would only encompass the period until the expected incapacity or death. A consistent benefit formula should be used over the years of service to reflect the value of the benefit. The expense should be attributed to the periods of service under the benefit formula because the employee's service does not result in a materially higher level of benefit in later years than in earlier years.

In determining costs, actuaries will make assumptions about the number of employees who are expected to become incapacitated or to die prior to normal retirement date. Therefore, for the employees not expected to reach retirement age, the total expected benefit payable, including that related to credited years not actually worked (in this example, 50 per cent of the years between the date of expected incapacity or death and the normal retirement date) will be attributed to the years of expected service up to the date of expected incapacity or death.

---

10   Termination benefits

Termination benefits are defined as employee benefits provided in exchange for the termination of an employee's employment as a result of either:
[IAS 19(2011):8]

- an entity's decision to terminate an employee's employment before the normal retirement date; or

- an employee's decision to accept an offer of benefits in exchange for the termination of employment.

Termination benefits are considered a separate category of employment benefits because the event that gives rise to an obligation is the termination of employment rather than employee service. [IAS 19(2011):159]

The form of the employee benefit does not determine whether it is provided in exchange for service or in exchange for termination of the employee's employment. Termination benefits are typically lump sum payments, but sometimes also include:
[IAS 19(2011):161]

- enhancement of post-employment benefits, either indirectly through an employee benefit plan or directly; and/or

- salary until the end of a specified notice period if the employee renders no further service that provides economic benefits to the entity.

Indicators that an employee benefit is provided in exchange for services (i.e. that it is not a termination benefit) include the following:
[IAS 19(2011):162]

- the benefit is conditional on future service being provided (including benefits that increase if further service is provided); and

- the benefit is provided in accordance with the terms of an employee benefit plan.

Termination benefits differ from post-employment benefits in that an entity can avoid paying them if it does not offer them and does not terminate an employee's contract of employment. Thus, termination benefits (or redundancy payments) arise not from the rendering of service by an employee, but from the termination of that service. Consequently, they do not relate to future benefits and should be recognised as an expense immediately when the entity can no longer withdraw its offer (see **10.2** below).

Example 10A

Payments for early retirement accounted for as termination benefits

Company A is an entity that encourages employees to retire at the age of 58 years instead of the national retirement age of 65 years. The post-retirement programme in Company A's country is a state pension plan. The state sets out the conditions for an employee to receive retirement benefits before the age of 65 years. This benefit does not form part of an employee's contractual terms and conditions of employment and, each year, Company A can decide whether or not to offer early retirement to its employees. Company A is not, therefore, obligated to make such an offer. Although the retirement benefit for persons between the ages of 58 and 65 years is paid for by the government, Company A is required to fund a portion of those payments.

An employee who is offered an early retirement plan can either accept or reject the offer. The offer is normally made prior to the employee's early retirement date (this period may vary from a few months to a couple of years). If the employee does not accept the offer, he or she will continue service until normal retirement age. Early retirement plans are normally implemented to reduce the work force by a means other than compulsory redundancy. An entity may propose early retirement plans to a selected category of employees.

Under IAS 19(2011):8, termination benefits are those payable as a result of an employee's decision to accept an offer of benefits in exchange for the termination of employment. Accordingly, the arrangements described above should be accounted for as termination benefits.

Example 10B

Distinguishing between benefits provided in exchange for services and termination benefits

Entity A is an entity that encourages employees within a specified age group to reduce levels of service in advance of the national retirement age. Entity A offers bonus payments to eligible employees in exchange for a 50 per cent reduction in working hours. Employment is terminated at the end of a required service period. The bonus payments are wholly conditional on the completion of the required service period (typically one to six years).

The bonus payments described above should not be accounted for as termination benefits under IAS 19(2011). The definition of termination benefits (see above) requires that the benefits have been provided in exchange for the termination of an employee's employment, rather than in exchange for services. In distinguishing between benefits provided in exchange for services and termination benefits, it is necessary to consider:

- all the relevant facts and circumstances for each individual entity's offer of benefits;

- the indicators set out in IAS 19(2011):162 that an employee benefit is provided in exchange for services (the list is not exhaustive), i.e. if:

  - the benefit is conditional on future service being provided (including benefits that increase if further service is provided); or

  - the benefit is provided in accordance with the terms of an employee benefit plan; and

- the definitions of the employee benefit categories in IAS 19(2011).

In the circumstances described, Entity A's arrangement has attributes of both required service and termination benefits. However, Entity A's arrangement would not meet the definition of a termination benefit because, consistent with IAS 19(2011):162(a), the fact that the bonus payments are wholly conditional upon completion of employee service over a period indicates that the benefits are in exchange for that service.

This conclusion was confirmed by the IFRS Interpretations Committee (see *IFRIC Update*, January 2012).

Termination benefits do not include employee benefits resulting from termination of employment at the request of the employee without an entity's offer, or as a result of mandatory retirement requirements; those benefits are post-employment benefits. [IAS 19(2011):160]

Some termination benefits are provided in accordance with the terms of an existing employee benefit plan (e.g. by statute, employment contract or union agreement), or they may be implied as a result of the employer's past practice of providing similar benefits. Employee benefits provided in accordance with the terms of an employee benefit plan are termination benefits if they both result from an entity's decision to terminate an employee's employment and are not conditional on future service being provided. [IAS 19(2011):163]

If an entity makes an offer of benefits available for more than a short period, or there is more than a short period between the offer and the expected date of actual termination, the entity should consider whether it has established a new employee benefit plan and, therefore, whether the benefits offered under that plan are termination benefits or post-employment benefits. [IAS 19(2011):163]

10.1   Employee benefits payable irrespective of reason for employee departure

Certain employee benefits are payable irrespective of the reason for an employee's departure (subject to any vesting or minimum service requirements) but the timing of their payment is uncertain. Therefore, although such benefits may be described in some jurisdictions as termination indemnities or termination gratuities, they are post-employment benefits rather than termination benefits and should be accounted for as post-employment benefits. [IAS 19(2011):164]

Some entities provide a lower level of benefit for termination of employment at the request of the employee (in substance, a post-employment benefit) than for termination of employment at the request of the entity. In such circumstances, the difference between the benefit provided for termination of employment at the request of the employee and a higher benefit provided at the request of the entity is a termination benefit. [IAS 19(2011):160]

10.2   Timing of recognition

A liability and an expense should be recognised for termination benefits at the earlier of the following dates:
[IAS 19(2011):165]

- when the entity can no longer withdraw the offer of those benefits; and

- when the entity recognises costs for a restructuring that is within the scope of IAS 37 *Provisions, Contingent Liabilities and Contingent Assets* and involves the payment of termination benefits.

In considering the issue of the timing of recognition of termination benefits, the Board decided that the factor determining the timing of recognition is the entity's inability to withdraw the offer of termination benefit. The Board also determined that the inability to withdraw an offer is triggered by different events based on whether the termination is subject to acceptance by the employee or is imposed upon the employee.

In the first scenario (termination benefits payable as a result of an employee's decision to accept an offer of benefits in exchange for the termination of employment), the time when an entity can no longer withdraw the offer of termination benefits is the earlier of:
[IAS 19(2011):166]

- when the employee accepts the offer; and

- when a restriction (e.g. a legal, regulatory or contractual requirement or other restriction) on the entity's ability to withdraw the offer takes effect. This would be when the offer is made, if the restriction existed at the time of the offer.

In the second scenario (for termination benefits payable as a result of an entity's decision to terminate an employee's employment), the entity can no longer withdraw the offer when the entity has communicated to the affected employees a plan of termination meeting all of the following criteria:
[IAS 19(2011):167]

- actions required to complete the plan indicate that it is unlikely that significant changes to the plan will be made;

- the plan identifies the number of employees whose employment is to be terminated, their job classifications or functions and their locations (but the plan need not identify each individual employee) and the expected completion date; and

- the plan establishes the termination benefits that employees will receive in sufficient detail that employees can determine the type and amount of benefits they will receive when their employment is terminated.

Example 10.2

Termination benefits requiring regulatory approval

Entity D has offered voluntary non-statutory termination benefits to specific union employees. The identified employees have accepted the termination benefits; approval has also been obtained from the employees' union. No further acceptance procedures are required from the employees' perspective.

All non-statutory termination benefits in the jurisdiction are required to be approved by the National Employment Agency. In the circumstances under consideration, the offer of benefits was made by Entity D subject to that approval, which has not yet been obtained. At the reporting date, Entity D is not entitled to withdraw the offer, although it may be rejected by the National Employment Agency.

Should Entity D recognise the termination benefits prior to receiving regulatory approval?

Yes. In accordance with IAS 19(2011):165(a), the entity should recognise a liability and an expense for the termination benefits when it can no longer withdraw the offer of those benefits.

IAS 19(2011):166 clarifies that, for termination benefits payable as a result of an employee's decision to accept an offer of benefits in exchange for the

---

> termination of employment, the time when an entity can no longer withdraw the offer of termination benefits is the earlier of:
>
> - when the employee accepts the offer; and
>
> - when a restriction (e.g. a legal, regulatory or contractual requirement or other restriction) on the entity's ability to withdraw the offer takes effect. This would be when the offer is made, if the restriction existed at the time of the offer.
>
> In the circumstances described, the entity is committed to making the termination payments once the employees have accepted the offer. The fact that regulatory approval may not be received is not relevant in determining when the liability and expense should be recognised.

When an entity recognises termination benefits, the entity may also have to account for a plan amendment or a curtailment of other employee benefits (see **7.4.2**). [IAS 19(2011):168]

10.3   Measurement

The measurement requirements for termination benefits are determined in accordance with their nature. Accordingly, an entity should measure termination benefits as follows:
[IAS 19(2011):169]

- if the termination benefits are an enhancement to post-employment benefits, IAS 19's requirements for post-employment benefits should be applied; otherwise

- if the termination benefits are expected to be settled wholly before 12 months after the end of the annual reporting period in which the termination benefit is recognised, IAS 19's requirements for short-term employee benefits should be applied; and

- if the termination benefits are not expected to be settled wholly before 12 months after the end of the annual reporting period, IAS 19's requirements for other long-term employee benefits should be applied.

Because termination benefits are not provided in exchange for service, the requirements of IAS 19(2011):70 to 74 (see **7.2.3**) relating to the attribution of the benefit to periods of service are not relevant. [IAS 19(2011):170]

The following example is reproduced from the Standard.

Example 10.3

Recognition and measurement of termination benefits

[Example illustrating IAS 19(2011):159 – 170]

Background

As a result of a recent acquisition, an entity plans to close a factory in ten months and, at that time, terminate the employment of all of the remaining employees at the factory. Because the entity needs the expertise of the employees at the factory to complete some contracts, it announces a plan of termination as follows.

Each employee who stays and renders service until the closure of the factory will receive on the termination date a cash payment of CU30,000. Employees leaving before closure of the factory will receive CU10,000.

There are 120 employees at the factory. At the time of announcing the plan, the entity expects 20 of them to leave before closure. Therefore, the total expected cash outflows under the plan are CU3,200,000 (ie 20 × CU10,000 + 100 × CU30,000). As required by IAS 19(2011):160, the entity accounts for benefits provided in exchange for termination of employment as termination benefits and accounts for benefits provided in exchange for services as short-term employee benefits.

Termination benefits

The benefit provided in exchange for termination of employment is CU10,000. This is the amount that an entity would have to pay for terminating the employment regardless of whether the employees stay and render service until closure of the factory or they leave before closure. Even though the employees can leave before closure, the termination of all employees' employment is a result of the entity's decision to close the factory and terminate their employment (ie all employees will leave employment when the factory closes). Therefore the entity recognises a liability of CU1,200,000 (ie 120 × CU10,000) for the termination benefits provided in accordance with the employee benefit plan at the earlier of when the plan of termination is announced and when the entity recognises the restructuring costs associated with the closure of the factory.

Benefits provided in exchange for service

The incremental benefits that employees will receive if they provide services for the full ten-month period are in exchange for services provided over that period. The entity accounts for them as short-term employee benefits because the entity expects to settle them before twelve months after the end of the annual reporting period. In this example, discounting is not required, so an expense of CU200,000 (ie CU2,000,000 ÷ 10) is recognised in each month during the service period of ten months, with a corresponding increase in the carrying amount of the liability.

When termination benefits are offered as part of a restructuring and are not expected to be settled wholly before 12 months after the end of the reporting period, they will be measured differently from other non-current provisions recognised as a result of the restructuring in accordance with IAS 37. This is due to the fact that IAS 37 requires the present value of expenditures to be determined using a pre-tax discount rate that reflects current market assessments and risks specific to the liability.

In contrast, IAS 19(2011) requires all termination benefits that are not expected to be settled wholly before 12 months after the end of the reporting period to be measured as an other long-term employee benefit and, therefore, to be discounted using a discount rate determined with reference to market yields on high quality corporate bonds. If there is no deep market in such high quality corporate bonds, the market yields on government bonds should be used instead.

10.4   Disclosure

There are no specific disclosure requirements for termination benefits in IAS 19, but disclosures may be required by other Standards, for example: [IAS 19(2011):171]

- IAS 24 *Related Party Disclosures*, when termination benefits relate to key management personnel; and

- IAS 1 *Presentation of Financial Statements*, which requires disclosure of employee benefits expense.

11   Effective date and transition

IAS 19(2011) is effective for annual periods beginning on or after 1 January 2013. Earlier application is permitted. If an entity applies IAS 19(2011) for an earlier period, it is required to disclose that fact. [IAS 19(2011):172]

IAS 19(2011) is generally required to be applied retrospectively. There are two exceptions:
[IAS 19(2011):173]

- an entity need not adjust the carrying amount of assets outside the scope of the Standard for changes in employee benefit costs that were included in the carrying amount before the date of initial application.

The date of initial application is the beginning of the earliest prior period presented in the first financial statements in which the entity adopts IAS 19(2011); and

- in financial statements for periods beginning before 1 January 2014, an entity need not present comparative information for the disclosures required by IAS 19(2011):145 about the sensitivity of the defined benefit obligation (see **8.2.4**).

Therefore, for example, when IAS 19(2011) is adopted, all cumulative unrecognised actuarial gains and losses at the start of the earliest comparative period will be recognised in equity.

12   Future developments

12.1   Employee contributions

In March 2013, the IASB published an exposure draft (ED/2013/4 *Defined Benefit Plans: Employee Contributions – Proposed amendments to IAS 19*) with a view to simplifying the treatment of non-discretionary contributions to defined benefit plans linked to service (see **7.2.4.8**). The exposure draft proposed that:

- contributions from employees or third parties that are linked solely to the employee's service rendered in the same period in which they are paid may be treated as a reduction in the service cost and accounted for in that same period; and

- other contributions should be attributed to periods of service in the same way as gross benefits under the scheme.

The comment period ended on 25 July 2013. Finalised amendments are expected in the fourth quarter of 2013.

12.2   Determination of an appropriate discount rate

The issue of the determination of an appropriate discount rate for the purpose of measuring defined benefit obligations has been the subject of much debate in recent years. In March 2013, the IASB launched a project to clarify the requirements of IAS 19, particularly around the requirement to use market yields on high quality corporate bonds or government bonds. An exposure draft is expected in the fourth quarter of 2013.

A16 Share-based payment

Contents

1   Introduction

Entities often grant shares or share options to directors and employees or other parties in return for services or goods. IFRS 2 *Share-based Payment* addresses the recognition, measurement and disclosure of these transactions.

It is important to appreciate that IFRS 2 may be applicable even when the counterparty receives cash from the entity. This is because the scope of the Standard includes cash-settled share-based payment transactions, as explained in **section 2** below.

The expense recognised under IFRS 2 is unaffected by whether the award is satisfied by an issue of new shares or by shares being purchased in the market. When shares are purchased in the market, an ESOP trust may be involved. The accounting entries relating to ESOP trusts are considered at **9.4** below.

IFRS 2 was most recently amended in June 2009.

2   Scope

2.1   Definition of a share-based payment transaction

IFRS 2 should be applied to each 'share-based payment transaction' as defined in IFRS 2:Appendix A. The definition is as follows.
[IFRS 2:Appendix A]

> "A transaction in which the entity
>
> (a)   receives goods or services from the supplier of those goods or services (including an employee) in a share-based payment arrangement, or
>
> (b)   incurs an obligation to settle the transaction with the supplier in a share-based payment arrangement when another group entity receives those goods or services."

The above definition of a share-based payment transaction uses the term 'share-based payment arrangement' which is also defined in IFRS 2:Appendix A. The definition is as follows.
[IFRS 2:Appendix A]

> "An agreement between the entity (or another group entity or any share-holder of any group entity) and another party (including an employee) that entitles the other party to receive

(a)   cash or other assets of the entity for amounts that are based on the price (or value) of equity instruments (including shares or share options) of the entity or another group entity, or

(b)   equity instruments (including shares or share options) of the entity or another group entity,

provided that the specified vesting conditions, if any, are met."

A footnote to IFRS 2 notes that, for this purpose, a 'group' is defined in Appendix A of IFRS 10 *Consolidated Financial Statements* as "a parent and its subsidiaries" from the perspective of the reporting entity's ultimate parent. For entities that have not yet adopted IFRS 10, a group is instead defined in paragraph 4 of IAS 27(2008) *Consolidated and Separate Financial Statements* as "a parent and all its subsidiaries" from the perspective of the reporting entity's ultimate parent.

Cash-settled Share Appreciation Rights (SARs) are the most common example of an arrangement under which the entity acquires goods or services by incurring a liability to transfer cash or other assets for amounts based on the price (or value) of the entity's shares or other equity instruments; such arrangements are sometimes referred to as 'phantom option schemes'. Typically, these schemes put the employees in the same position as if they had been granted options, but they involve a cash payment to the employees equal to the gain that would have been made by exercising the notional options and immediately selling the shares in the market.

'Equity instrument' is defined as follows.
[IFRS 2:Appendix A]

"A contract that evidences a residual interest in the assets of an entity after deducting all of its liabilities."

This definition is consistent with paragraph 11 of IAS 32 *Financial Instruments: Presentation*.

'Equity instrument granted' is defined as follows.
[IFRS 2:Appendix A]

"The right (conditional or unconditional) to an equity instrument of the entity conferred by the entity on another party, under a share-based payment arrangement."

1256

The Standard does not include a formal definition of either goods or services, although IFRS 2:5 specifies that goods would include inventories, consumables, property, plant and equipment, intangible assets and other non-financial assets, and that equity instruments granted to employees are within the scope of the Standard. As discussed at **2.7** below, IFRS 2:2 confirms that goods or services do not have to be identifiable to be within the scope of IFRS 2.

IFRS 2 does not apply to transactions in which an entity acquires goods as part of the net assets acquired in a business combination as defined by IFRS 3 *Business Combinations* or to the contribution of a business on formation of a joint venture as defined in IFRS 11 *Joint Arrangements* (or, for entities that have not yet adopted IFRS 11, in IAS 31 *Interests in Joint Ventures*). The distinction between shares issued as remuneration and shares issued as purchase consideration is considered at **2.5** below.

2.2   Identifying share-based payment transactions

It may not always be straightforward to identify transactions falling within the scope of IFRS 2 as shown by the following examples.

Example 2.2A

Cash payment based on earnings multiple

Company N, an unlisted entity, issued instruments to its employees that entitle them to a cash payment equal to the increase in Company N's 'share price' (as defined) between the grant date and the vesting date. The terms and conditions of the instrument define the 'share price' as a specified multiple of EBITDA divided by the number of shares in issue.

Arrangements of this nature will not usually be in the scope of IFRS 2 because a specified multiple of EBITDA will not necessarily reflect the fair value of the shares; historical earnings is only one of the inputs used to determine the fair value of shares in an entity. Such arrangements will more likely fall within the scope of IAS 19 *Employee Benefits*.

Example 2.2B

Remuneration scheme based on a profit formula

Company A has a deferred bonus incentive scheme. The value of the entitlements is based on a formula derived from Company A's net profit (adjusted for specified items) and then divided by a fixed number. This entitlement vests over 3 years. The payment to the employee on vesting date, or the date that the employee chooses to receive settlement after the entitlement has vested, is funded by the cash resources of Company A.

For example: entitlement value = (operating profit × 10) ÷ CU100 million

	Year 1 CUm	Year 2 CUm	Year 3 CUm
Operating profit	3,000	3,500	4,100
	CU	CU	CU
Entitlement value	300	350	410

A participant who exercises his or her right to receive settlement for a vested entitlement will receive the difference between the current entitlement value and the grant date entitlement value in cash.

In the example, if a participant received 100 entitlements at an entitlement value of CU250, the participant would receive CU16,000 (100 × (CU410 – CU250)) at the end of Year 3.

This remuneration scheme does not fall within the scope of IFRS 2. The entitlements issued by Company A represent a bonus scheme that does not result in the issue of equity instruments or in a liability that is linked to the price of Company A's shares or other equity instruments of Company A; the scheme is an employee benefits scheme within the scope of IAS 19. The benefits payable under the scheme do not meet the definition of 'short-term employee benefits' under IAS 19(2011) because they are not expected to be settled wholly before twelve months after the end of the annual reporting period in which the related service is rendered. (For entities that have not yet adopted IAS 19(2011), the benefits payable under the scheme do not meet the definition of 'short-term employee benefits' under IAS 19(1998) because they are not due to be settled within twelve months after the end of the period in which the related service is rendered.) Therefore, the recognition and measurement requirements of IAS 19 for other long-term employee benefits should be applied.

In November 2005, the IFRIC (now the IFRS Interpretations Committee) was asked to consider the accounting treatment of employee share loan plans. Under many such plans, employee share purchases are facilitated by means of a loan from the grantor with recourse only to the shares. The IFRIC was asked whether the loan should be considered as part of a potential share-based payment, with the entire arrangement treated as an option under IFRS 2, or whether the loan should be accounted for separately as a financial asset. The IFRIC noted that when the loan is with recourse only to the shares (sometimes referred to as 'limited recourse' or 'non-recourse'), the issue of shares using the proceeds of the loan would be treated as a grant of options that are exercised when the loan is repaid. The IFRIC determined that it would not expect diversity in practice and, therefore, did not take this item onto its agenda.

Example 2.2C and **example 2.2D** below illustrate the application of this principle to a non-recourse loan. **Example 2.2E** examines the contrasting position of a full recourse loan.

Example 2.2C

Employee share loan plans

Company R grants loans to its employees that subsequently are to be used by the employees to buy shares in Company R. For the purpose of obtaining settlement of the loans, Company R only has recourse to the shares bought by the employees.

Should these loans be considered part of a share-based payment arrangement accounted for under IFRS 2 (with the entire arrangement treated as an option), or should they be accounted for as financial assets in accordance with IFRS 9 Financial Instruments *(or, for entities that have not yet adopted IFRS 9, IAS 39* Financial Instruments: Recognition and Measurement)?

The employee share loan plan should be accounted for in accordance with IFRS 2 because it falls within the scope of IFRS 2:2(c) – i.e. it results in "transactions in which the entity receives . . . services and the terms of the arrangement provide . . . the supplier of those . . . services with a choice of whether the entity settles the transaction in cash . . . or by issuing equity instruments".

Because, for the purpose of obtaining settlement of the loans, Company R only has recourse to the shares bought by the employees, Company R effectively issues share options to its employees who use the loans granted to pay for the shares. Exercise of the options would be on the date or the dates when the loan is repaid by the employee.

Example 2.2D

Non-recourse loan to purchase shares

Company L provides an interest-free loan in the amount of CU100 to one of its executives to purchase shares with a fair value of CU100 in the open market. The shares are used as collateral for the loan balance and, therefore, cannot be sold by the executive during the four-year vesting period. If the executive remains employed with Company L at the end of four years, the entire amount of the loan is forgiven and the shares are released from all restrictions. If the executive leaves Company L's employment during the vesting period, the shares are transferred to Company L and, regardless of value, are considered full payment of the loan.

Example 2.2H

Preference shares with conversion option issued as consideration for purchase of goods

Company A acquires an intellectual property intangible asset from Company X. Consideration is in the form of preference shares issued at the time of the transaction.

The issued preference shares have the following characteristics:

- entitlement to an annual non-discretionary 8 per cent dividend to perpetuity;

- the holder of the shares has the right to convert the preference shares to ordinary shares of Company A (adjusted only for capital reorganisations or capitalisation issues that affect all holders of the ordinary shares). The holder can exercise this option at any time from the date of issue of the instruments;

- entitlement to a share of net assets on liquidation after distribution to another class of preference shareholders; and

- no maturity date (i.e. will remain in existence unless converted).

Should the arrangement be accounted for in accordance with the requirements of IFRS 2, or in accordance with IAS 32 and IFRS 9 (or, for entities that have not yet adopted IFRS 9, IAS 39)?

The arrangement should be accounted for as a share-based payment transaction under IFRS 2. Company A has received goods from Company X and has, in return, provided Company X with a choice of settlement in cash (perpetual dividend stream) or equity (ordinary shares). Consequently, the transaction falls within the scope of IFRS 2:2(c).

IFRS 2:35 clarifies that if an entity has granted the counterparty the right to choose whether a share-based payment transaction is settled in cash or by the issue of equity instruments, the entity has granted a compound instrument. The instrument has:

- a liability component — Company X's right to receive a perpetual stream of 8 per cent dividends; and

- an equity component — Company X's right to convert to ordinary shares.

Each component is accounted for separately as required by IFRS 2:35:

- the liability component is measured at fair value; and

- the equity component is measured as the difference between the fair value of the intangible asset received and the fair value of the liability component, at the date when the goods or services are received.

The liability component should, in accordance with IFRS 2:30, be recognised in the statement of financial position at fair value and remeasured at the end of each accounting period, with all movements in fair value being recognised in profit or loss. The fair value of the equity component is recognised in equity, with no further remeasurement.

If Company X chooses to exercise the conversion option, at the date of conversion, the liability component is remeasured to its fair value and is transferred directly to equity as the consideration for the equity instruments issued (see IFRS 2:39).

The recognition of liability and equity components at the date of issue of the preference shares is similar to the equivalent requirements of IAS 32; however, the treatment of the liability component subsequent to the issue of the preference shares differs from the equivalent requirements of IFRS 9 (or, for entities that have not yet adopted IFRS 9, IAS 39), which would not require the liability component to be remeasured to fair value on an ongoing basis.

The application of these requirements is illustrated in **example 6.1.2** below.

2.2.1   *Awards made by shareholders*

IFRS 2:3A states that a share-based payment transaction may be settled by a shareholder (of any group entity) and still be within the scope of IFRS 2 (see also **2.3.1** below).

When a shareholder provides shares for the purposes of an employee share scheme, it will generally be clear that these benefits form part of the remuneration of the employees for their services to the entity. A charge to profit or loss will, therefore, be required in accordance with IFRS 2 for the services received.

On the other hand, a shareholder may make a gift of shares to a close relative who is coincidentally an employee of the entity. Such a gift might not form part of the remuneration of the employee but it will be necessary to look carefully at the facts of each case. For example, it would be necessary to consider whether similar benefits were given to other employees and whether the gift of shares was in any way conditional on continuing employment with the entity.

The most common instance when equity instruments are provided by a shareholder rather than the entity that has received the goods or services is within groups.

2.3   Groups

2.3.1   Parent and subsidiaries

It is often the case that employees of a subsidiary will receive part of their remuneration in the form of shares in the parent, or less commonly in shares of some other group entity. In such circumstances, IFRS 2 requires the entity that has received the benefit of the services to recognise an expense. This is so even if the equity instruments issued are those of another group entity.

The scope of the Standard includes an entity that:
[IFRS 2:3A]

- receives goods or services when another entity in the same group (or a shareholder of any group entity) has the obligation to settle the share-based payment transaction; or

- has an obligation to settle a share-based payment transaction when another entity in the same group receives the goods or services;

unless the transaction is clearly for a purpose other than payment for goods or services supplied to the entity receiving them.

Example 2.3.1

Services received in equity-settled share-based payment transaction

Company P is a publicly listed entity that applies US GAAP. Company P has a majority-owned subsidiary, Company S, which applies IFRSs. Company P issues share options in Company P's ordinary shares to certain employees of Company S.

Company S receives the benefit of the services provided by its employees. As a result, Company S should recognise the expense related to the share-based payment, regardless of whether Company S, or another group entity, issues the share options and regardless of any accounting applied by Company P under US GAAP. When Company P issues the share options, there may also be a capital contribution to be recognised by Company P and Company S (see **section 8** below).

2.3.2   Meaning of 'entity' in the context of groups

The definition of a share-based payment arrangement (see **2.1** above) refers when appropriate to an 'entity or another group entity'.

IFRS 2 is clear that an expense must be recognised by the entity that has received the benefit of the goods or services. When the parent provides the shares, the other side of this accounting entry is a credit to equity which is in the nature of a capital contribution. IFRS 2 addresses the accounting for group cash-settled share-based payment transactions in the separate or individual financial statements of the entity receiving the goods or services when the entity has no obligation to settle the share-based payment transactions. The Standard also provides guidance on the circumstances in which an arrangement is equity-settled from the perspective of the group but cash-settled from the perspective of the subsidiary (and vice versa). However, IFRS 2 does not address the effect of charges made between group entities in connection with share-based payment arrangements. The requirements of IFRS 2 for group share-based payment arrangements and some related issues not addressed by the Standard are considered in detail in **section 8**.

2.4   Transactions with owners in their capacity as owners

The requirements of IFRS 2 should not be applied to transactions with parties (e.g. employees) in their capacity as holders of equity instruments of the entity (referred to as 'owners' in IAS 1 *Presentation of Financial Statements*). For example, a rights issue may be offered to all holders of a particular class of equity. If an employee is offered the chance to participate purely because he/she is a holder of that class of equity, IFRS 2 is not applied. The requirements of IFRS 2 are only relevant for transactions in which goods or services are acquired. [IFRS 2:4]

Example 2.4

Shares purchased from employee shareholders at fair value

Company D purchases its own shares from employees (in their capacity as shareholders) for an amount that equals the fair value of those shares. This transaction would be considered a purchase of treasury shares and is not within the scope of IFRS 2. However, if Company D pays an amount in excess of fair value only to its employees, that excess would be considered a remuneration expense (see **example 4.5.2D**).

2.5   Business combinations and formation of joint ventures

IFRS 2 applies to share-based payment transactions in which an entity acquires or receives goods or services. Goods include inventories, consumables, property, plant and equipment, intangible assets and other non-financial assets. However, the IFRS is not applied to transactions in which an entity acquires goods as part of the net assets acquired in a business combination as defined by IFRS 3 *Business Combinations*, in a combination of entities or businesses under common control as described in IFRS 3:B1 to B4, or the contribution of a business on formation of a joint venture as defined by IFRS 11 *Joint Arrangements* (or, for entities that have not yet adopted IFRS 11, IAS 31 *Interests in Joint Ventures*). [IFRS 2:5]

Equity instruments issued in a business combination in exchange for control of the acquiree are not within the scope of IFRS 2. But equity instruments granted to employees of the acquiree in their capacity as employees (e.g. in return for continued services in the post-combination period) are within the scope of IFRS 2. Similarly, the cancellation, replacement or other modification of share-based payment arrangements because of a business combination or other equity restructuring are accounted for in accordance with IFRS 2. [IFRS 2:5]

When shares are issued in a business combination to previous owners of the acquiree who are also employees of the acquiree, it is necessary to determine to what extent they are purchase consideration and to what extent they are share-based payments. IFRS 3 provides guidance for determining whether equity instruments issued in a business combination are part of the consideration transferred in exchange for control of the acquiree (and, therefore, within the scope of IFRS 3) or are in return for continued service to be recognised in the post-combination period (and, therefore, within the scope of IFRS 2). This guidance is considered in **section 8.3.3** of **chapter A25**.

IFRS 3 also provides guidance on the appropriate accounting for pre-existing acquiree share-based payment awards, both vested and unvested, by an acquirer, including those that lapse, are replaced or are un-replaced (see **section 8.3.4** of **chapter A25**).

2.5.1   *Shares issued by joint ventures in exchange for contributions received*

When joint ventures are formed, they frequently issue shares in exchange for contributions from venturers. These contributions can be received in various forms (e.g. cash, assets or businesses).

When the contribution is in the form of cash and the shares are not issued as consideration for goods or services, the cash contribution is received from the venturers in their capacity as owners. It is, therefore, outside the scope of IFRS 2 for the joint venture and should be accounted for in accordance with IAS 32.

However, when a venturer contributes assets that do not comprise a business (e.g. property, plant and equipment or an intangible asset) on the formation of a joint venture, these transactions are within the scope of IFRS 2 for the joint venture because the joint venture issues shares as consideration for goods. Such transactions should be accounted for as equity-settled share-based payment transactions with non-employees.

Transactions in which a venturer contributes a business in exchange for shares in the joint venture are outside the scope of IFRS 2 and IFRS 3 for the joint venture. The selection of appropriate accounting policies for such transactions involves similar considerations to those for combinations of entities or businesses under common control which are also outside the scope of IFRS 3 (see **2.2.1** in **chapter A25**).

2.6   Financial instruments

IFRS 2 does not apply to share-based payment transactions in which the entity receives or acquires goods or services under a contract within the scope of IAS 32:8 to 10 or paragraphs 5 to 7 of IAS 39. [IFRS 2:6]

IAS 32 and IAS 39 both state that they should be applied to contracts to buy or sell a non-financial item that can be settled net in cash or by another financial instrument, or by exchanging financial instruments, as if the contracts were financial instruments (apart from contracts entered into and continuing to be held for the purpose of the receipt or delivery of a non-financial item in accordance with the entity's expected purchase, sale or usage requirements (the 'own-use' exemption)). Such contracts are considered in **chapter B1** or, for entities that have not yet adopted IFRS 9, **chapter C1**. Paragraph IFRS 2:BC28 explains that the IASB concluded that such contracts should remain within the scope of IAS 32 and IAS 39 and, therefore, excluded them from the scope of IFRS 2.

Example 2.6

Interaction with IAS 32 and IAS 39

Company C enters into a forward contract to buy 1,000 units of a commodity for consideration of 2,000 of Company C's ordinary shares. Company C can settle the contract net in cash or another financial instrument, but does not intend to do so because the commodity is being purchased for the purpose of

---

receipt in accordance with Company C's expected usage requirements; Company C does not have a past practice of settling similar contracts net in cash. Accordingly, the transaction is within the scope of IFRS 2 because it involves the issue of shares in exchange for goods.

However, if Company C had a practice of settling these contracts net, or Company C did not intend to take physical delivery of the commodity, the forward contract would be within the scope of IAS 32 and IAS 39 and, therefore, IFRS 2 would not apply.

Example 2.2H above addresses the accounting for preference shares with a conversion option that are issued as consideration for the purchase of goods.

2.7   Goods or services cannot be specifically identified

IFRS 2 applies to share-based payment transactions, whether or not the entity can identify specifically some or all of the goods or services received. [IFRS 2:2] Accordingly, the Standard applies to transactions when the identifiable consideration received (or to be received) by the entity, including cash and the fair value of identifiable non-cash consideration, appears to be less than the fair value of the equity instruments granted or the liability incurred.

In the absence of specifically identifiable goods or services, other circumstances may indicate that goods or services have been, or will be, received. In this case IFRS 2 applies. [IFRS 2:2]

If the identifiable consideration received appears to be less than the fair value of the equity instruments granted, or the liability incurred, typically this circumstance indicates that other consideration (i.e. unidentifiable goods or services) has been, or will be, received. [IFRS 2:13A]

The entity measures any identifiable goods and services in accordance with IFRS 2. Any unidentifiable goods or services received are then measured as the difference between the fair value of the share-based payment and the fair value of any identifiable goods or services received. The unidentifiable goods or services are measured at grant date although, for cash-settled arrangements, the liability is remeasured at the end of each reporting period until it is settled. [IFRS 2:13A]

IFRS 2 gives the example of a grant of shares to a charitable organisation for nil consideration as an instance when it may be difficult to demonstrate that goods or services have been, or will be, received. It notes that a similar situation might arise in transactions with other parties. [IFRS 2:IG5A]

An illustrative example that accompanies IFRS 2 deals with a situation when an entity grants shares for no consideration to parties who form a particular section of community, as a means of enhancing its corporate image. The example notes that the economic benefits might take a variety of forms such as increasing the entity's customer base, attracting and retaining employees, and improving its chances of being awarded contracts.

There may be no obvious benefits of this kind in circumstances when shares are required by law to be issued at below their market value. However, IFRS 2 should still be applied and an expense recognised. This might be viewed as 'the price of staying in business' or akin to a form of taxation.

For transactions with parties other than employees, IFRS 2 establishes a rebuttable presumption that the fair value of the goods or services received can be estimated reliably. The IASB concluded that goods or services that are unidentifiable cannot be reliably measured and so the rebuttable presumption is relevant only for identifiable goods or services. Therefore, in this case, it is necessary to derive the value of the unidentifiable goods or services received from the value of the equity instruments. [IFRS 2:BC128D]

This approach might be seen to imply that it is always necessary to consider the fair value of the equity instruments granted to see if this is greater than the fair value of the goods or services received. This is not so. IFRS 2:BC128C states that "the Board noted that it is neither necessary nor appropriate to measure the fair value of goods or services as well as the fair value of the share-based payment for every transaction in which the entity receives goods or non-employee services". In practice, it will be necessary to consider this issue only in those circumstances when the value of the goods or services received 'appears to be' less than the fair value of the equity instruments granted. For example, it would not be necessary to obtain a valuation of unquoted shares that had been issued as consideration for non-employee services unless there were indications that some other non-identifiable goods or services had also been obtained.

When the value of the shares is known because they are quoted in a market and this produces a materially different value from the value attributed to the services in accordance with IFRS 2, an additional expense may need to be recognised for unidentified goods and services. In such situations, all evidence needs to be considered carefully to understand the substance of the transaction and the reason for the apparent discrepancy. This may, in some cases, indicate that additional services were received. In other cases, the services may have been difficult to value and the conflicting evidence may prompt a reconsideration of that value. In rare cases, the arrangements may indeed relate to unidentified goods or services (e.g. because the difference represents a charitable donation).

The phrase 'the fair value of the share-based payment' refers to the value of the particular share-based payment concerned. For example, an entity might be required by legislation to issue some portion of its shares to nationals of a particular country, which may be transferred only to other nationals of that country. Such transfer restrictions may affect the fair value of the shares concerned. They may have a fair value that is less than the fair value of otherwise identical shares that do not carry the transfer restrictions. In such circumstances, if it is the restricted shares that are granted, the phrase 'the fair value of the share-based payment' in IFRS 2 refers to the fair value of the restricted shares and not to the fair value of the unrestricted shares. [IFRS 2:IG5C]

2.8   Employment taxes on share-based payments

In some jurisdictions, employment taxes may be payable which are determined by reference to the gain made by the employee on the exercise of share options.

When the amount of tax is based on the gain made by the employee (i.e. intrinsic value at exercise date), the following questions arise:

- *does the entity have a liability before the employee exercises the options?*

- *if so, how should that liability be measured at the end of each reporting period?*

Such payments of tax are outside the scope of IFRS 2 because they are not payments to the suppliers of goods or services. However, these are similar to the questions addressed in IFRS 2 for cash-settled share-based payments. A liability should, therefore, be recognised at the end of each reporting period for such tax. This is consistent with the requirements of IAS 37 *Provisions, Contingent Liabilities and Contingent Assets* as well as those of IFRS 2 because the 'obligating event' is the granting of the options by the entity rather than the exercise of the options by the employees. The liability could be measured on the same basis as required by IFRS 2, although it is acceptable to use intrinsic value at the end of the reporting period rather than fair value determined using an option pricing model, given that the liability is outside the scope of IFRS 2. Measuring the liability at fair value in accordance with IFRS 2 is nevertheless to be preferred.

Under IFRSs, staff costs generally are within the scope of IAS 19, which requires staff costs to be recognised over the period in which services are provided. Therefore, in the absence of any conflicting interpretation by the IFRS Interpretations Committee, the liability could be built up over the vesting period.

3   Classification of share-based payment transactions

Under IFRS 2, different accounting is required for different types of share-based payment transaction. Three types of transactions are identified in IFRS 2:
[IFRS 2:2]

- equity-settled share-based payment transactions;

- cash-settled share-based payment transactions; and

- transactions in which the entity receives or acquires goods or services and the terms of the arrangement provide either the entity or the supplier of those goods or services with a choice of whether the entity settles the transaction in cash (or other assets) or by issuing equity instruments.

3.1   Equity-settled share-based payment transactions

An equity-settled share-based payment transaction is defined in IFRS 2:Appendix A. The definition is as follows.
[IFRS 2:Appendix A]

> "A share-based payment transaction in which the entity

3.2.1   Conflict between IFRS 2 and IAS 32

The liability/equity distinction in IFRS 2 is drawn along different lines from the general requirements of IAS 32 (see **chapter B3** or, for entities that have not yet adopted IFRS 9 *Financial Instruments*, **chapter C3**). This is explained in the following example.

Example 3.2.1

Equity-settled or cash-settled?

Company A issues 1,000 share options to an employee with an exercise price of CU15 per share. After completion of the vesting period, the employee will receive shares with a total value equal to the intrinsic value of the options (referred to below as equity-settled SARs).

The share options should be accounted for as equity-settled because settlement will be by delivery of equity instruments.

The number of shares that could be issued under the equity-settled SARs and the value of each share issued are variable. IFRS 2:BC106 and BC108 note that, if the debt/equity requirements of IAS 32 were applied to share-based payment transactions, instruments when the number of shares issued is variable would be considered a liability. They would, therefore, be treated similarly to a cash-settled share-based payment. As a result, IFRS 2:BC110 explains that the debt/equity requirements in IAS 32, whereby some obligations to issue equity instruments are classified as liabilities, should not be applied in the IFRS on share-based payments. IFRS 2:BC107 gives a SAR settled in shares as an example of an instrument that would be accounted for differently between IAS 32 and IFRS 2.

3.3   Transactions with settlement alternatives

In certain circumstances, share-based payment transactions may provide either the entity or the counterparty with a choice as to whether settlement occurs in equity instruments or cash. The basic principle to be applied is as follows.

For share-based payment transactions in which the terms of the arrangement provide either the entity or the counterparty with the choice of whether the entity settles the transaction in cash (or other assets) or by issuing equity instruments, the transaction is, or the components of that transaction are, accounted for:
[IFRS 2:34]

- as a cash-settled share-based payment transaction if, and to the extent that, the entity has incurred a liability to settle in cash or other assets; or

- as an equity-settled share-based payment transaction if, and to the extent that, no such liability has been incurred.

IFRS 2 contains more detailed requirements concerning how to apply this principle to share-based payment transactions in which the terms of the arrangement:

- provide the counterparty with a choice of settlement (see **6.1** below); or

- provide the entity with a choice of settlement (see **6.2** below).

Contingent cash settlement provisions are considered at **6.3**. Circumstances when the terms of settlement are modified are considered at **4.5.3** (for modification of an arrangement that has been accounted for as an equity-settled share-based payment transaction) and **5.4.2** (for modification of an arrangement that has been accounted for as a cash-settled share-based payment transaction).

3.4   Equity awards settled net of tax

Sometimes the settlement of employees' equity-settled awards results in the employee receiving a reduced number of shares and a payment being made to the tax authority to settle the related tax liability. The value of the shares received is the total value of the award earned reduced by the amount of tax paid by the employer based on the employee's tax liability on the transaction. The question arises as to whether this type of settlement arrangement results in the award being considered partly cash-settled.

Whether this type of settlement arrangement should be treated as partly cash-settled or entirely equity-settled depends on whether the employer is acting as an agent for the employee in settling the employee's tax liability. The arrangement should be treated as entirely equity-settled if the employer is considered to be acting as an agent for the employee.

The assessment as to whether the entity is acting as an agent for the employee should be made on the basis of the facts and circumstances of each case. There will be circumstances when it is clear that the entity is acting as an agent (e.g. when the entity offers a broker's service to sell employees' shares and passes the cash to the tax authorities, but accepts no liability itself).

In some tax jurisdictions, the tax authority specifies situations in which the entity has a statutory duty to act as agent for its employees and remit tax on behalf of the employees.

This topic has been considered by the IFRS Interpretations Committee but no consensus emerged. The Committee identified a number of issues arising in this context for which the application of the requirements of IFRS 2 caused concern, such as separately classifying components of a single award. The Interpretations Committee has recommended to the IASB that this topic should be included in a future agenda proposal for IFRS 2.

4   Recognition and measurement: equity-settled transactions

This section discusses the appropriate accounting for equity-settled share-based payment transactions in the following sections.

Section 4.1   Recognition of equity-settled transactions

Section 4.2   Measurement of equity-settled transactions

Section 4.3   Vesting and non-vesting conditions

Section 4.4   Determining the fair value of equity instruments granted

Section 4.5   Modifications to equity-settled transactions (including cancellations and settlements)

4.1   Recognition of equity-settled transactions

The goods or services received or acquired in an equity-settled share-based payment transaction are recognised as the goods are obtained or the services are received, with a corresponding increase in equity. [IFRS 2:7]

The goods or services received in a share-based payment transaction may qualify for recognition as an asset. If not, they are recognised as an expense. [IFRS 2:8]

Services are typically consumed immediately, in which case an expense is recognised as the counterparty renders service. Goods might be consumed over a period of time or, in the case of inventories, sold at a later date, in which case an expense is recognised when the goods are consumed or sold. However, sometimes it is necessary to recognise an expense before the goods or services are consumed or sold, because they do not qualify for recognition as assets. For example, an entity might acquire goods as part of the research phase of a project to develop a new product. Although those goods have not been consumed, they might not qualify for recognition as assets under the applicable IFRS. [IFRS 2:9]

It will normally be relatively straightforward to ascertain when goods are received, but this is not necessarily so when services are involved.

The approach to be adopted in relation to the timing of recognition depends largely on the concept of vesting. IFRS 2 defines 'vest' as follows. [IFRS 2:Appendix A]

> "To become an entitlement. Under a share-based payment arrangement, a counterparty's right to receive cash, other assets, or equity instruments of the entity vests when the counterparty's entitlement is no longer conditional on the satisfaction of vesting conditions."

> As explained at IFRS 2:BC171B, a share-based payment vests when the counterparty's entitlement to it is no longer conditional on future service or performance conditions. Therefore, restrictive conditions such as non-compete provisions and transfer restrictions, which apply after the counterparty has become entitled to the share-based payment, are not vesting conditions.

If equity instruments vest immediately then, in the absence of evidence to the contrary, it is presumed that the consideration for the instruments (employee services, for example) has been received. The consideration (i.e. an expense or asset, as appropriate) should, therefore, be recognised in full, with a corresponding increase in equity. [IFRS 2:14]

If equity instruments do not vest immediately, the terms 'vesting conditions' and 'vesting period', as defined by IFRS 2, are important. Vesting conditions are defined as follows.
[IFRS 2:Appendix A]

> "The conditions that determine whether the entity receives the services that entitle the counterparty to receive cash, other assets or equity instruments of the entity, under a share-based payment arrangement. Vesting conditions are either service conditions or performance conditions. Service conditions require the counterparty to complete a specified period of service. Performance conditions require the counterparty to complete a specified period of service and specified performance targets to be met (such as a specified increase in the entity's profit over a specified period of time). A performance condition might include a market condition."

Vesting conditions are restricted to only service conditions and performance conditions. The definition clarifies that performance conditions must not only require a specified performance target to be met but also require the counterparty to complete a specified period of service. This appears to make performance conditions a sub-set of service conditions. IFRS 2:BC171A notes that "the feature that distinguishes a performance condition from a non-vesting condition is that the former has an explicit or implicit service requirement and the latter does not".

Examples of non-vesting conditions are a requirement to subscribe for shares to become entitled to be granted free 'matching shares' in certain types of share schemes and the payment of contributions to an SAYE scheme.

Under SAYE share option schemes, employees save a regular amount, usually through deduction from salary, which is applied to cover the exercise price of the options when they are exercised. Employees are free to stop contributing to the scheme and obtain a refund of contributions at any time, but forfeit their entitlement to exercise the options if they do so. IFRS 2 makes clear that the payment of contributions into an SAYE scheme is not a vesting condition; it does not meet the definition of a performance condition because it has no link to service.

Non-vesting conditions are taken into account when estimating the fair value of the equity instruments at grant date (see **4.3** below). This is the same as the treatment of a market-based vesting condition. For example, on a grant of SAYE options, an estimate should be made of the number of employees who will cease to contribute to the scheme, otherwise than through termination of their employment, before the options vest. The grant date fair value should be reduced accordingly. Failure to meet a non-vesting condition (e.g. by ceasing to contribute to an SAYE scheme) should be accounted for as a cancellation of the options so that the expense will be accelerated (see **4.5.2** below).

As part of its Annual Improvements project, the IASB has proposed to amend the definition of 'vesting conditions' by separately defining a 'service condition' and a 'performance condition' so as to make the description of each condition clearer. The proposals clarify that a performance target should relate either to the performance of the entity as a whole or to some part of the entity (e.g. a division or an individual employee). Under the proposals, a performance target is defined by reference to the entity's operations (or activities) or the price (or value) of its equity instruments. In order to constitute a performance condition, a performance target needs to have an explicit or implicit service requirement which substantially coincides with the period during which the performance target is being measured. The assessment period for the performance target may start before the service period but may not extend beyond the end of the service period. If an employee fails to complete a specified service period, this constitutes a failure to satisfy a service condition, regardless of the reason for that failure. The amendments are proposed to ensure consistent classification of conditions relating to share-based payments and to address a number of concerns raised about the current definitions (see also **section 10**).

Vesting and non-vesting conditions and their impact on the treatment of equity-settled share-based payment transactions are considered further at **4.3**.

The 'vesting period' is defined as follows.
[IFRS 2:Appendix A]

> "The period during which all the specified vesting conditions of a share-based payment arrangement are to be satisfied."

If the equity instruments granted do not vest until the counterparty completes a specified period of service, it is presumed that the service period equals the vesting period. The services are accounted for as they are rendered by the counterparty during the vesting period, with a corresponding increase in equity. [IFRS 2:15]

A simple scenario would see employees granted share options which vest only once the employees have completed a specified period of employment – say three years. In this scenario, the entity will recognise an expense over the three-year vesting period. [IFRS 2:15(a)] However, if the employees are granted share options that are conditional upon the employees working for the entity for the three financial years beyond the current one, generally, the IFRS 2 expense will be recognised over a vesting period of more than three years (specifically, three years plus the remaining months of the current year), beginning on the date of grant. This is because, in substance, the vesting is conditional on the employee continuing to render service for the remaining months of the current year, plus three subsequent years.

Example 4.1

Failure to vest as a result of termination of employment by the employer

Company A puts in place an equity-settled share-based payment arrangement covering 20 employees. The employees are required to work for three years in order for the awards to vest. During the second year, Company A makes 10 of the employees redundant. Accordingly, their awards can no longer vest.

Should Company A account for this as a cancellation or a forfeiture?

IFRS 2 does not specify whether a redundancy during the vesting period for awards, which triggers the expiry of the awards, should be treated as a cancellation (because it results from an action by the entity) or a forfeiture (because it results from failure of the employee to meet a service condition). This is an important distinction because the accounting treatment for forfeitures requires the entity to 'true up' and, as a result, reverse the IFRS 2 expense previously recognised; classification as a cancellation, on the other hand, would trigger accelerated recognition of the remaining expense.

IFRS 2:28 sets out the accounting "[i]f a grant of equity instruments is cancelled or settled". It therefore establishes the principle that the accounting treatment for a cancellation should not be affected by whether the cancellation is initiated by the employer or the employee.

IFRS 2 specifies that failure by an employee to meet a service condition (e.g. due to voluntary departure) should be treated as a forfeiture. Based on the principle introduced for the treatment of cancellations (i.e. that decisions by the entity are treated in the same way as decisions by the employee), the entity's decision to make the employee redundant should be accounted for in the same way as a voluntary departure by the employee. Consequently, the involuntary redundancy should be accounted for as a forfeiture.

However, care will be required in circumstances when the termination of an employee's contract is accompanied by a compensation package at the time of termination of employment. In such instances, relevant facts and circumstances should be considered to assess whether the severance package (or part thereof) should be treated as a modification and settlement of the original awards.

If an employee is granted share options conditional upon the achievement of a performance condition and remaining in the entity's employ until that performance condition is satisfied, and the length of the vesting period varies depending on when that performance condition is satisfied, the entity presumes that the services to be rendered by the employee as consideration for the share options will be received in the future, over the expected vesting period. The entity estimates the length of the expected vesting period at grant date, based on the most likely outcome of the performance condition. If the performance condition is a market condition (see **section 4.3** below), the estimate of the length of the expected vesting period should be consistent with the assumptions used in estimating the fair value of the options granted, and should not be subsequently revised. If the performance condition is not a market condition, the entity revises its estimate of the length of the vesting period, if necessary, if subsequent information indicates that the length of the vesting period differs from previous estimates. [IFRS 2:15(b)]

4.1.1 Adjustments after vesting date

Having recognised the goods or services received in accordance with the requirements of IFRS 2 (and a corresponding increase in equity), no subsequent adjustment should be made to equity after vesting date. For example, the amount recognised for services received from an employee is not subsequently reversed if the vested equity instruments are later forfeited or, in the case of share options, are not exercised. This requirement does not, however, preclude a transfer from one component of equity to another. [IFRS 2:23]

> For example, the expense recognised in accordance with IFRS 2 is not reversed if options vest but are not exercised because they are 'out of the money' or simply because the employee elects not to do so.

4.1.2 Presentation of increases in equity arising from equity-settled share-based payment transactions

> For equity-settled share-based payment transactions, IFRS 2:7 requires the recognition of a 'corresponding increase in equity' for goods or services received and recognised. There is nothing in IFRSs to require or prohibit the presentation of the credit entry in a separate component of equity. This is true whether the credit entry is in relation to the entity's own equity instruments or those of its parent, in which case the credit entry is in the nature of a capital contribution by the parent (as described in **example 8.2.1**).
>
> There is also nothing in IFRSs to prohibit the credit entry being recognised in retained earnings. However, local legal and regulatory requirements may need to be taken into account when determining the most appropriate treatment. In some jurisdictions, these requirements may require the credit entry to be regarded as capital and, consequently, prohibit its inclusion in retained earnings.

The position becomes more complicated when an ESOP trust is involved which is the case with some employee share schemes. For example, it may seem most appropriate to take the IFRS 2 credit entry to the 'ESOP reserve' which represents the deduction within equity for own shares held. However, the IFRS 2 credit entry based on grant date fair value is unlikely to equal the purchase price of the shares in the trust less any exercise price, so a difference will build up. These issues are addressed at **9.4** below.

4.2   Measurement of equity-settled transactions

In an equity-settled transaction, the goods or services received, and the corresponding increase in equity, should be measured at the fair value of those goods/services.

'Fair value' is defined as follows.
[IFRS 2:Appendix A]

> "The amount for which an asset could be exchanged, a liability settled, or an equity instrument granted could be exchanged, between knowledgeable, willing parties in an arm's length transaction."

IFRS 2 uses the term 'fair value' in a way that differs in some respects from the definition of fair value in IFRS 13 *Fair Value Measurement*. When applying IFRS 2, an entity should measure fair value in accordance with the guidance in IFRS 2, not IFRS 13. [IFRS 2:6A]

Market vesting conditions are taken into account when estimating the fair value of the equity instruments granted. All non-vesting conditions are similarly taken into account. However, non-market vesting conditions are not taken into account for this purpose. This is explained further at **4.3** below.

4.2.1   Transactions with employees and non-employees

For equity-settled share-based payment transactions, the goods or services received and the corresponding increase in equity are measured directly at the fair value of the goods or services received, unless that fair value cannot be estimated reliably. If it is not possible to estimate reliably the fair value of the goods or services received, the fair value of the equity instruments granted is used as a proxy. [IFRS 2:10] There is a limited exception to this requirement in rare circumstances when the entity is unable to estimate reliably the fair value of the equity instruments granted at the measurement date. This exception is considered at **4.4.8** below.

The IASB has taken the view that the fair value of the equity instruments granted should be used for transactions with employees and others providing similar services. This is because, in such transactions, "typically it is not possible to estimate reliably the fair value of the services received". The fair value of those equity instruments is measured at grant date. [IFRS 2:11 & 12]

IFRS 2 defines 'employees and others providing similar services' as follows.
[IFRS 2:Appendix A]

> "Individuals who render personal services to the entity and either (a) the individuals are regarded as employees for legal or tax purposes, (b) the individuals work for the entity under its direction in the same way as individuals who are regarded as employees for legal or tax purposes, or (c) the services rendered are similar to those rendered by employees. For example, the term encompasses all management personnel, i.e. those persons having authority and responsibility for planning, directing and controlling the activities of the entity, including non-executive directors."

Further references to employees in this chapter will include others providing similar services.

The determination as to whether an individual is 'similar to an employee' or a non-employee is a matter of careful judgement.

The following factors may indicate that the counterparty in a share-based payment transaction is an employee or is providing services similar to an employee.

- The purchasing entity is paying for the right to use certain individuals and not the actual output from the individuals (i.e. the purchasing entity has the risk of downtime).

- The individuals are under the direct supervision of the purchasing entity.

- The contract depends on the services from a specified individual.

- The purchasing entity receives substantially all of the output from the individual for a specified period of time.

- The individuals perform services that are similar to services currently provided by employees.

affect the accounting treatment described above. (The appropriate treatment of any dividends paid during the vesting period is discussed in **example 4.4.5.5** below.)

4.2.4   Shares to a monetary value

Example 4.2.4

Shares to a monetary value

On 1 January 20X5 (the grant date), an entity grants share awards to each of its employees to the value of CU1,500, conditional on them remaining in employment. If an employee remains employed with the entity until 31 December 20X7, the shares will vest and the employee will receive as many shares as are (on 31 December 20X7) worth CU1,500.

How should the entity account for this share-based payment?

The grant is an equity-settled share-based payment because the employees will receive shares. The fair value of the awards should be determined at the grant date (i.e. 1 January 20X5). Therefore, the grant date fair value of the awards is CU1,500. Although the time value of money is ignored for simplicity in this example, it should be considered in the determination of the fair value of the award. The employment condition is a service vesting condition which is reflected by adjusting the expense for changes in the number of awards that are expected to vest based on meeting this service condition.

The actual number of shares issued in settlement of the awards will vary according to the share price on the vesting date, but the total value of the awards will not change. Therefore, the expense should not be adjusted for changes in the number of shares that will be issued as a result of changes in the market value of the shares.

Therefore, the entity will recognise CU1,500 as an expense over the vesting period, subject to the employment condition, regardless of how many shares are actually issued on the vesting date.

This approach is illustrated below.

At 1 January 20X5, the market price per share is CU5. At 31 December 20X7, it is CU10. At 31 December 20X5 and 20X6, the entity expects that 95 per cent of the employees will remain employed until 31 December 20X7. Ultimately, 96 per cent of the employees remain in service at 31 December 20X7.

At the grant date, the fair value of the awards issued per employee is CU1,500.

Year	Calculation of expense: grant date fair value of awards issued × proportion expected to vest	Remuneration expense for period CU	Cumulative remuneration expense CU
1	(CU1,500 × 100 employees) × 95% expected to vest × 1/3 years	47,500	47,500
2	(CU1,500 × 100 employees) × 95% expected to vest × 2/3 years	47,500	95,000
3	(CU1,500 × 100 employees) × 96% actually vested × 3/3 years	49,000	144,000

4.2.5   Reload features

Some share options have a 'reload feature'. This entitles the employee to automatic grants of additional share options whenever he/she exercises previously granted share options and pays the exercise price in the entity's shares rather than in cash. Typically, the employee is granted a new share option, called a reload option, for each share surrendered when exercising the previous share option. The exercise price of the reload option is usually set at the market price of the shares on the date the reload option is granted. [IFRS 2:BC188]

A 'reload feature' is defined in IFRS 2 as follows.
[IFRS 2:Appendix A]

> "A feature that provides for an automatic grant of additional share options whenever the option holder exercises previously granted options using the entity's shares, rather than cash, to satisfy the exercise price."

A 'reload option' is defined as follows.
[IFRS 2:Appendix A]

> "A new share option granted when a share is used to satisfy the exercise price of a previous share option."

IFRS 2 requires that for options with a reload feature, the feature should not be taken into account when estimating the fair value of options granted at the measurement date. Instead, a reload option should be accounted for as a new option grant, if and when a reload option is subsequently granted. [IFRS 2:22]

As discussed in IFRS 2:BC189 to BC192, it may theoretically be preferable to take account of reload features when measuring the fair value of options granted. ED 2, the exposure draft that preceded IFRS

2, proposed this treatment 'when practicable'. However, in the light of comments received, the IASB decided to require the treatment set out above in all cases.

Example 4.2.5

Award with reload feature

Company M issues 100 share options to one of its directors. The total exercise price for the options is CU100. However, there is a reload feature under which the director can surrender shares to the total value of CU100 instead of paying the exercise price in cash and become entitled to a number of new share options. In this example, that number is equal to the number of shares surrendered.

If the market value of the shares on exercise is CU10, the director will surrender 10 shares worth CU100 in total to cover the exercise price on 100 options. He will then be granted 10 new options. These new options represent a new grant and are accounted for in the usual way in accordance with IFRS 2 (i.e. an expense is recognised over the applicable vesting period based on the grant date fair value of the new options).

4.2.6   Share price denominated in a foreign currency

IFRS 2 does not make reference to share-based payment transactions in which the share price is denominated in a foreign currency. An appropriate treatment for such transactions can, however, be derived from the general principles of IAS 21 *The Effects of Changes in Foreign Exchange Rates* as discussed below.

Example 4.2.6

Equity-settled share-based payment transaction with share price and option exercise price denominated in a foreign currency

Company E is a UK entity with Sterling as its functional currency. Company E is registered on the New York Stock Exchange with a current market price of US$15 per share. Company E issues 100 options to its employees with an exercise price of US$15 per share and a vesting period of three years. At the date of issue of the options, the fair value of each option is determined to be US$15 and the exchange rate is US$1.5/£1.

The share options can only be equity settled.

Given that the share price is quoted in a currency other than the functional currency of the entity, how should these arrangements be accounted for?

Summary of conditions that determine whether a counterparty receives an equity instrument granted						
	VESTING CONDITIONS			**NON-VESTING CONDITIONS**		
	Service conditions	Performance conditions				
		Performance conditions that are market conditions	Other performance conditions	Neither the entity nor the counterparty can choose whether the condition is met	Counterparty can choose whether to meet the condition	Entity can choose whether to meet the condition
Example condi-tions	Requirement to remain in service for three years	Target based on the market price of the entity's equity instruments	Target based on a successful initial public offering with a specified service requirement	Target based on a commodity index	Paying contributions towards the exercise price of a share-based payment	Continuation of the plan by the entity
Include in grant date fair value?	No	Yes	No	Yes	Yes	Yes[(a)]
Account-ing treatment if the condition is not met after the grant date and during the vesting period	Forfeiture. The entity revises the expense to reflect the best available estimate of the number of equity instruments expected to vest.	No change to accounting. The entity continues to recognise the expense over the remainder of the vesting period.	Forfeiture. The entity revises the expense to reflect the best available estimate of the number of equity instruments expected to vest.	No change to accounting. The entity continues to recognise the expense over the remainder of the vesting period.	Cancellation. The entity recognises immediately the amount of the expense that would otherwise have been recognised over the remainder of the vesting period.	Cancellation. The entity recognises immediately the amount of the expense that would otherwise have been recognised over the remainder of the vesting period.
	(para-graph 19)	(para-graph 21)	(para-graph 19)	(para-graph 21A)	(para-graph 28A)	(para-graph 28A)

(a)   In the calculation of the fair value of the share-based payment, the probability of continuation of the plan by the entity is assumed to be 100 per cent.

1291

The treatment of vesting, non-vesting and performance conditions is summarised in the following diagram and is more fully described below.

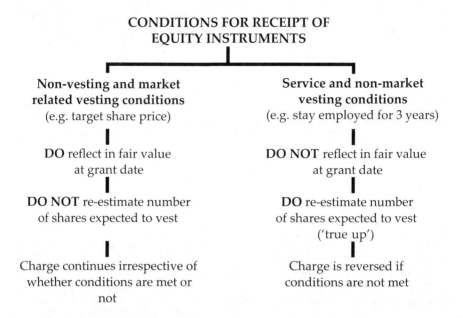

CONDITIONS FOR RECEIPT OF EQUITY INSTRUMENTS

Non-vesting and market related vesting conditions (e.g. target share price)	**Service and non-market vesting conditions** (e.g. stay employed for 3 years)
DO reflect in fair value at grant date	**DO NOT** reflect in fair value at grant date
DO NOT re-estimate number of shares expected to vest	**DO** re-estimate number of shares expected to vest ('true up')
Charge continues irrespective of whether conditions are met or not	Charge is reversed if conditions are not met

IFRS 2 distinguishes between 'market conditions' and conditions other than market conditions (referred to generally as 'non-market conditions'). A market condition is defined by IFRS 2 as follows. [IFRS 2:Appendix A]

> "A condition upon which the exercise price, vesting or exercisability of an equity instrument depends that is related to the market price of the entity's equity instruments, such as attaining a specified share price or a specified amount of intrinsic value of a share option, or achieving a specified target that is based on the market price of the entity's equity instruments relative to an index of market prices of equity instruments of other entities."

Market conditions, such as a target share price upon which vesting is conditional, are taken into account when estimating the fair value of the equity instruments granted. Therefore, for grants of equity instruments with market conditions, the entity recognises the goods or services received from a counterparty who satisfies all other vesting conditions (e.g. service conditions) irrespective of whether that market condition is satisfied. [IFRS 2:21]

Similarly, all non-vesting conditions are taken into account when estimating the fair value of the equity instruments granted. Therefore, for grants of equity instruments with non-vesting conditions, the goods or services received from a counterparty that satisfies all vesting conditions that are not market conditions (e.g. services received from an employee who remains in service for the specified period of service) are recognised, irrespective of whether those non-vesting conditions are satisfied. [IFRS 2:21A]

Vesting conditions other than market conditions are not taken into account when estimating the fair value of the shares or share options at the measurement date. Instead, those non-market vesting conditions are taken into account by adjusting the number of equity instruments included in the measurement of the transaction so that, ultimately, the amount recognised for goods or services received is based on the number of equity instruments that eventually vest. Therefore, on a cumulative basis, no amount is recognised for goods or services received if the equity instruments granted do not vest because of a failure to satisfy non-market vesting conditions. For example, this will be the case when an employee fails to complete a specified period of service. [IFRS 2:19]

To apply this requirement for non-market vesting conditions, an amount is recognised for the goods or services received during the vesting period based on the best available estimate of the number of equity instruments expected to vest. That estimate is revised if subsequent information indicates that the number of equity instruments expected to vest differs from previous estimates. On vesting date, the estimate is revised to equal the number of equity instruments that ultimately vest. [IFRS 2:20]

This approach, which is generally referred to as the 'modified grant date method', was adopted by the IASB for two primary reasons: measurement practicalities and US GAAP convergence.

Valuation models used to determine the fair value of share-based payments could be modified to incorporate non-market conditions. However, the inclusion of these conditions would increase the difficulty and reduce the reliability of the fair value measurement. Therefore, non-market conditions are not included in the grant date fair value calculation due to the practical difficulties of measuring these conditions as noted in IFRS 2:BC184.

Although IFRS 2 did not achieve complete convergence with US GAAP on the treatment of vesting conditions, the requirement to 'true up' for non-market vesting conditions is similar to US GAAP. In particular, the requirements of IFRS 2 are much closer to US GAAP than those proposed in the exposure draft that preceded the Standard, which involved including all performance and service conditions in the measurement of fair value coupled with the 'unit of service' method (see the Basis for Conclusions on IFRS 2 for further explanations).

The operation of these requirements in practice is illustrated by the examples set out in the following sections.

4.3.1   Non-market vesting condition
4.3.2   Vesting period varies with a non-market condition
4.3.3   Number of options vesting is dependent on a non-market performance condition
4.3.4   Exercise price dependent on a non-market condition
4.3.5   A market condition and a non-market condition
4.3.6   A market condition when the vesting period varies
4.3.7   Contingent issue of shares for goods or services from non-employees
4.3.8   Equity instruments vesting in instalments
4.3.9   Distinguishing market and non-market vesting conditions
4.3.10   Good leavers and bad leavers
4.3.11   Matching share awards
4.3.12   Allocation of expense when there are multiple vesting conditions
4.3.13   Effect of planned restructuring events in estimating the number of awards expected to vest
4.3.14   Conditions relating to completion of an initial public offering (IPO)
4.3.15   Pro rata vesting for good leavers

4.3.1   Non-market vesting condition

The following example, which is taken from the implementation guidance accompanying IFRS 2, illustrates the basic approach to be adopted in relation to a non-market vesting condition.

Example 4.3.1A

Non-market vesting condition

[Guidance on implementing IFRS 2:IG Example 1]

Background

An entity grants 100 share options to each of its 500 employees. Each grant is conditional upon the employee working for the entity over the next three years. The entity estimates that the fair value of each share option is CU15.

On the basis of a weighted average probability, the entity estimates that 20 per cent of employees will leave during the three-year period and therefore forfeit their rights to the share options.

Application of requirements

Scenario 1

If everything turns out exactly as expected, the entity recognises the following amounts during the vesting period, for services received as consideration for the share options.

Year	Calculation	Remuneration expense for period CU	Cumulative remuneration expense CU
1	50,000 options × 80% × CU15 × 1/3 years	200,000	200,000
2	(50,000 options × 80% × CU15 × 2/3 years) – CU200,000	200,000	400,000
3	(50,000 options × 80% × CU15 × 3/3 years) – CU400,000	200,000	600,000

Scenario 2

During year 1, 20 employees leave. The entity revises its estimate of total employee departures over the three-year period from 20 per cent (100 employees) to 15 per cent (75 employees). During year 2, a further 22 employees leave. The entity revises its estimate of total employee departures over the three-year period from 15 per cent to 12 per cent (60 employees). During year 3, a further 15 employees leave. Hence, a total of 57 employees forfeited their rights to the share options during the three-year period, and a total of 44,300 share options (443 employees × 100 options per employee) vested at the end of year 3.

Year	Calculation	Remuneration expense for period CU	Cumulative remuneration expense CU
1	50,000 options × 85% × CU15 × 1/3 years	212,500	212,500
2	(50,000 options × 88% × CU15 × 2/3 years) – CU212,500	227,500	440,000
3	(44,300 options × CU15) – CU440,000	224,500	664,500

The following example illustrates the use of probabilities when assessing non-market vesting conditions.

Example 4.3.1B

Use of probabilities to assess non-market vesting conditions

Background

Company A has issued 10 options to 10 employees (i.e. 100 options in total). The options will vest at the end of Year 2 of an employee's continued employment (i.e. the 'service period condition') and provided Company A has met a specified level of earnings-per-share (EPS) growth compared with the EPS for Year 0. However, the number of options that will vest depends on the extent of the EPS growth. Provided that an employee remains in employment, the options will vest according to the following EPS growth percentages at the end of Year 2:

- less than 4 per cent – none of the options will vest;

- between 4 per cent and 10 per cent – 50 per cent of the options will vest; and

- more than 10 per cent – all options will vest.

Therefore, if all employees remain in employment, the number of options expected eventually to vest can only be 0, 50 or 100.

Application of requirements

Scenario 1

All employees are expected to remain in employment until the end of Year 2.

The target EPS growth vesting condition is a non-market-based vesting condition. During the vesting period, an entity is required to recognise an expense (or asset, if the employee costs are capitalised as part of the cost of another asset) by determining the total number of equity instruments that are expected to vest eventually as a result of the fulfilment of non-market-based conditions (IFRS 2:19). An entity should only use probabilities when determining whether a non-market-based condition will be met – the amount recognised in accordance with IFRS 2 reflects the most likely outcome, not a weighted average of outcomes. For example, if an entity believes that there is a 90 per cent chance that a performance target will be met, the accounting for this transaction during the vesting period should reflect the target being met. The entity would recognise 100 per cent of the total expense for the reporting period (as long as all other vesting conditions are met), not 90 per cent of the total expense for the reporting period.

At the end of Year 1, Company A should estimate the most probable EPS growth figure for the end of Year 2 (using, for example, budget information or historical EPS growth) and should use this estimate to determine the number of options that will vest.

At each future reporting date, Company A should reassess expected EPS growth and 'true up' the expense accordingly. This requirement may result in greater volatility in the amount of expense recognised from year to year.

Scenario 2

Only eight employees are expected to remain until the end of Year 2.

If only 80 per cent of the employees are expected to remain employed by the entity at the end of two years, the number of options expected to vest would need to be adjusted to incorporate the impact of the service period condition (e.g. staff turnover rate should be analysed). Therefore, the actual number of options expected to vest, after the impact of the service condition and the number of employees expected to remain with the entity are taken into account, can only be one of the following:

- 0 (i.e. no options are expected to vest);

- 40 (50 per cent of 80 per cent of 100 – i.e. 50 per cent of the options are expected to vest); or

- 80 (100 per cent of 80 per cent of 100 – i.e. all options are expected to vest).

Many of the examples in the implementation guidance accompanying IFRS 2 employ percentages for determining the number of employees expected to meet a service condition. These percentages are used to estimate the number of equity instruments that will actually vest, not the probability that the employee will meet the service condition. That is, an entity expects that 80 per cent of its employees will meet the service condition, not that there is an 80 per cent chance of the service condition being met.

4.3.2   *Vesting period varies with a non-market condition*

The length of the vesting period might vary depending on when a performance condition is met. If an employee is granted share options that are conditional on the achievement of a performance condition and on remaining in employment until that performance condition is satisfied, it is presumed that the services to be rendered by the employee will be received in the future, over the expected vesting period. When this is the case, the length of the estimated vesting period at grant date is estimated based on the most likely outcome of the performance condition. [IFRS 2:15] If the performance condition is a market condition, the estimated length of the vesting period should be consistent with the assumptions used in estimating the fair value of the options granted and should not subsequently be revised. If the performance condition is a non-market condition, the initial estimate of the length of the vesting period should be revised if subsequent information indicates that the length of the vesting period differs from the previous estimate.

The following example, taken from the implementation guidance accompanying IFRS 2, illustrates the circumstances when the vesting period varies according to the achievement of a non-market condition (a specified increase in earnings).

Example 4.3.2

Grant with a performance condition, in which the length of the vesting period varies

[Guidance on implementing IFRS 2:IG Example 2]

Background

At the beginning of year 1, the entity grants 100 shares each to 500 employees, conditional upon the employees' remaining in the entity's employ during the vesting period. The shares will vest at the end of year 1 if the entity's earnings increase by more than 18 per cent; at the end of year 2 if the entity's earnings increase by more than an average of 13 per cent per year over the two-year period; and at the end of year 3 if the entity's earnings increase by more than an average of 10 per cent per year over the three-year period. The shares have a fair value of CU30 per share at the start of year 1, which equals the share price at grant date. No dividends are expected to be paid over the three-year period.

By the end of year 1, the entity's earnings have increased by 14 per cent, and 30 employees have left. The entity expects that earnings will continue to increase at a similar rate in year 2, and therefore expects that the shares will vest at the end of year 2. The entity expects, on the basis of a weighted average probability, that a further 30 employees will leave during year 2, and therefore expects that 440 employees will vest in 100 shares each at the end of year 2.

By the end of year 2, the entity's earnings have increased by only 10 per cent and therefore the shares do not vest at the end of year 2. 28 employees have left during the year. The entity expects that a further 25 employees will leave during year 3, and that the entity's earnings will increase by at least 6 per cent, thereby achieving the average of 10 per cent per year.

By the end of year 3, 23 employees have left and the entity's earnings had increased by 8 per cent, resulting in an average increase of 10.67 per cent per year. Therefore, 419 employees received 100 shares at the end of year 3.

Application of requirements

Year	Calculation	Remuneration expense for period CU	Cumulative remuneration expense CU
1	440 employees × 100 shares × CU30 × ½	660,000	660,000
2	(417 employees × 100 shares × CU30 × 2/3) – CU660,000	174,000	834,000
3	(419 employees × 100 shares × CU30 × 3/3) – CU834,000	423,000	1,257,000

Granting share options contingent on an Initial Public Offering (IPO) of an entity is another example of an award with a variable vesting period depending on a non-market vesting condition. However, no expense will be recognised unless and until the IPO is probable. This may not be the case on grant date. Therefore, in practice, the expense may sometimes be recognised over a relatively short period between the IPO becoming probable and taking place. As explained at **4.3.14** below, an IPO may be a non-vesting condition if the exercise of the options is not linked to service continuing until the IPO.

4.3.3   Number of options vesting is dependent on a non-market performance condition

A similar approach will be adopted when the number of equity instruments that might vest with each employee varies. This is illustrated in the following example which is taken from the implementation guidance accompanying IFRS 2.

Example 4.3.3

Grant with a performance condition, in which the number of equity instruments varies

[Guidance on implementing IFRS 2:IG Example 3]

Background

At the beginning of year 1, Entity A grants share options to each of its 100 employees working in the sales department. The share options will vest at the end of year 3, provided that the employees remain in the entity's employ, and provided that the volume of sales of a particular product increases by at least an average of 5 per cent per year. If the volume of sales of the product increases by an average of between 5 per cent and 10 per cent per year, each employee will receive 100 share options. If the volume of sales increases by an average of between 10 per cent and 15 per cent each year, each employee will receive 200 share options. If the volume of sales increases by an average of 15 per cent or more, each employee will receive 300 share options.

On grant date, Entity A estimates that the share options have a fair value of CU20 per option. Entity A also estimates that the volume of sales of the product will increase by an average of between 10 per cent and 15 per cent per year, and therefore expects that, for each employee who remains in service until the end of year 3, 200 share options will vest. The entity also estimates, on the basis of a weighted average probability, that 20 per cent of employees will leave before the end of year 3.

By the end of year 1, seven employees have left and the entity still expects that a total of 20 employees will leave by the end of year 3. Hence, the entity

---

1299

expects that 80 employees will remain in service for the three-year period. Product sales have increased by 12 per cent and the entity expects this rate of increase to continue over the next 2 years.

By the end of year 2, a further five employees have left, bringing the total to 12 to date. The entity now expects only three more employees will leave during year 3, and therefore expects a total of 15 employees will have left during the three-year period, and hence 85 employees are expected to remain. Product sales have increased by 18 per cent, resulting in an average of 15 per cent over the two years to date. The entity now expects that sales will average 15 per cent or more over the three-year period, and hence expects each sales employee to receive 300 share options at the end of year 3.

By the end of year 3, a further two employees have left. Hence, 14 employees have left during the three-year period, and 86 employees remain. The entity's sales have increased by an average of 16 per cent over the three years. Therefore, each of the 86 employees receives 300 share options.

Application of requirements

Year	Calculation	Remuneration expense for period CU	Cumulative remuneration expense CU
1	80 employees × 200 options × CU20 × 1/3	106,667	106,667
2	(85 employees × 300 options × CU20 × 2/3) – CU106,667	233,333	340,000
3	(86 employees × 300 options × CU20 × 3/3) – CU340,000	176,000	516,000

4.3.4   Exercise price dependent on a non-market condition

The exercise price might vary depending on whether non-market vesting conditions are satisfied. This is illustrated in the following example taken from the implementation guidance accompanying IFRS 2.

Example 4.3.4

Grant with a performance condition, in which the exercise price varies

[Guidance on implementing IFRS 2:IG Example 4]

Background

At the beginning of year 1, an entity grants to a senior executive 10,000 share options, conditional upon the executive's remaining in the entity's employ until the end of year 3. The exercise price is CU40. However, the exercise price drops to CU30 if the entity's earnings increase by at least an average of 10 per cent per year over the three-year period.

On grant date, the entity estimates that the fair value of the share options, with an exercise price of CU30, is CU16 per option. If the exercise price is CU40, the entity estimates that the share options have a fair value of CU12 per option.

During year 1, the entity's earnings increased by 12 per cent, and the entity expects that earnings will continue to increase at this rate over the next two years. The entity therefore expects that the earnings target will be achieved, and hence the share options will have an exercise price of CU30.

During year 2, the entity's earnings increased by 13 per cent, and the entity continues to expect that the earnings target will be achieved.

During year 3, the entity's earnings increased by only 3 per cent, and therefore the earnings target was not achieved. The executive completes three years' service, and therefore satisfies the service condition. Because the earnings target was not achieved, the 10,000 vested share options have an exercise price of CU40.

Application of requirements

Because the exercise price varies depending on the outcome of a performance condition that is not a market condition, the effect of that performance condition (i.e. the possibility that the exercise price might be CU40 and the possibility that the exercise price might be CU30) is not taken into account when estimating the fair value of the share options at grant date. Instead, the entity estimates the fair value of the share options at grant date under each scenario (i.e. exercise price of CU40 and exercise price of CU30) and ultimately revises the transaction amount to reflect the outcome of that performance condition, as illustrated below.

Year	Calculation	Remuneration expense for period CU	Cumulative remuneration expense CU
1	10,000 options × CU16 × 1/3	53,333	53,333
2	(10,000 options × CU16 × 2/3) – CU53,333	53,334	106,667
3	(10,000 options × CU12 × 3/3) – CU106,667	13,333	120,000

4.3.5   A market condition and a non-market condition

The following example, taken from the implementation guidance accompanying IFRS 2, illustrates the operation of the requirements of IFRS 2 for a grant of options with a market condition (a specified increase in share price) and a non-market service condition (continuing employment).

Example 4.3.5A

Grant with a market condition

[Guidance on implementing IFRS 2:IG Example 5]

Background

At the beginning of year 1, an entity grants to a senior executive 10,000 share options, conditional upon the executive remaining in the entity's employ until the end of year 3. However, the share options cannot be exercised unless the share price has increased from CU50 at the beginning of year 1 to above CU65 at the end of year 3. If the share price is above CU65 at the end of year 3, the share options can be exercised at any time during the next seven years, i.e. by the end of year 10.

The entity applies a binomial option pricing model, which takes into account the possibility that the share price will exceed CU65 at the end of year 3 (and hence the share options become exercisable) and the possibility that the share price will not exceed CU65 at the end of year 3 (and hence the options will be forfeited). It estimates the fair value of the share options with this market condition to be CU24 per option.

Application of requirements

Because paragraph 21 of IFRS 2 requires the entity to recognise the services received from a counterparty who satisfies all other vesting conditions (e.g. services received from an employee who remains in service for the specified service period), irrespective of whether that market condition is satisfied, it makes no difference whether the share price target is achieved. The possibility that the share price target might not be achieved has already been taken into account when estimating the fair value of the share options at grant date. Therefore, if the entity expects the executive to complete the three-year service period, and the executive does so, the entity recognises the following amounts in years 1, 2 and 3:

Year	Calculation	Remuneration expense for period CU	Cumulative remuneration expense CU
1	10,000 options × CU24 × 1/3	80,000	80,000
2	(10,000 options × CU24 × 2/3) – CU80,000	80,000	160,000
3	(10,000 options × CU24) – CU160,000	80,000	240,000

As noted above, these amounts are recognised irrespective of the outcome of the market condition. However, if the executive left during year 2 (or year 3), the amount recognised during year 1 (and year 2) would be reversed in year 2 (or year 3). This is because the service condition, in contrast to the market condition, was not taken into account when estimating the fair value of the share options at grant date. Instead, the service condition is taken into account by adjusting the transaction amount to be based on the number of equity instruments that ultimately vest, in accordance with paragraphs 19 and 20 of the IFRS.

Another example in which share options are granted with both market conditions and non-market conditions is set out below.

Example 4.3.5B

Share option grant with both market and non-market performance conditions

Company H issued 100 share options to certain of its employees that will vest if accumulated revenues for five years reach CU1 billion and its share price exceeds CU50 on the fifth anniversary of the grant date. The employees will have to be employed with Company H at the end of the five-year vesting period to receive the options. The share options will expire if any of these conditions has not been met at the end of the five year vesting period.

IFRS 2:21 states that the grant date fair value of a share-based payment with market-based performance conditions that has met all its other vesting conditions should be recognised, irrespective of whether that market condition is achieved. Company H determines the grant date fair value of the share-based payment excluding the non-market-based performance factor (accumulated revenues), but including the market-based performance factor (share price).

Assuming Company H determines that the fair value of the share-based payment (after taking into consideration the probability that the share price target of CU50 will be met) at the date of grant is CU20 per option, the cumulative expense recognised over the expected vesting period in the following scenarios would be:

- if all vesting conditions are met, CU2,000 [100 options × CU20];

- if all vesting conditions are met, except that the market-based performance condition of share price exceeding CU50 is not achieved, CU2,000 [100 options × CU20];

- if all vesting conditions are met, except that the non-market-based performance condition of accumulated revenues reaching CU1billion is not achieved, nil expense; and

- if all vesting conditions are met, except that employees who received half of the options leave Company H's employment prior to the vesting date, CU1,000 [50 options × CU20].

Therefore, when there are both market and non-market conditions that have to be met, an entity will still need to estimate whether non-market conditions will be satisfied even if ultimately no share options vest due to market conditions.

4.3.6   A market condition when the vesting period varies

The effect of a vesting condition may be to change the length of the vesting period. In this case, IFRS 2:15 requires the entity to presume that the services to be rendered by the employees as consideration for the equity instruments granted will be received in the future, over the expected vesting period. Hence, the entity will have to estimate the length of the expected vesting period at grant date, based on the most likely outcome of the performance condition. If the performance condition is a market condition, the estimate of the length of the expected vesting period must be consistent with the assumptions used in estimating the fair value of the share options granted and is not subsequently revised.

The following example, taken from the implementation guidance accompanying IFRS 2, illustrates the application of IFRS 2 when the vesting period varies with a market condition (a specified increase in the share price).

Example 4.3.6

Grant with a market condition, in which the length of the vesting period varies

[Guidance on implementing IFRS 2:IG Example 6]

Background

At the beginning of year 1, an entity grants 10,000 share options with a ten-year life to each of ten senior executives. The share options will vest and become exercisable immediately if and when the entity's share price increases from CU50 to CU70, provided that the executive remains in service until the share price target is achieved.

The entity applies a binomial option pricing model, which takes into account the possibility that the share price target will be achieved during the ten-year life of the options, and the possibility that the target will not be achieved. The entity estimates that the fair value of the share options at grant date is CU25 per option. From the option pricing model, the entity determines that the mode of the distribution of possible vesting dates is five years. In other words, of all the possible outcomes, the most likely outcome of the market condition is that the share price target will be achieved at the end of year 5. Therefore, the entity estimates that the expected vesting period is five years. The entity also estimates that two executives will have left by the end of year 5, and therefore expects that 80,000 share options (10,000 share options × 8 executives) will vest at the end of year 5.

Throughout years 1–4, the entity continues to estimate that a total of two executives will leave by the end of year 5. However, in total three executives leave, one in each of years 3, 4 and 5. The share price target is achieved at the end of year 6. Another executive leaves during year 6, before the share price target is achieved.

Application of requirements

Paragraph 15 of the IFRS requires the entity to recognise the services received over the expected vesting period, as estimated at grant date, and also requires the entity not to revise that estimate. Therefore, the entity recognises the services received from the executives over years 1–5. Hence, the transaction amount is ultimately based on 70,000 share options (10,000 share options × 7 executives who remain in service at the end of year 5). Although another executive left during year 6, no adjustment is made, because the executive had already completed the expected vesting period of 5 years. Therefore, the entity recognises the following amounts in years 1–5:

Year	Calculation	Remuneration expense for period CU	Cumulative remuneration expense CU
1	80,000 options × CU25 × 1/5	400,000	400,000
2	(80,000 options × CU25 × 2/5) – CU400,000	400,000	800,000
3	(80,000 options × CU25 × 3/5) – CU800,000	400,000	1,200,000
4	(80,000 options × CU25 × 4/5) – CU1,200,000	400,000	1,600,000
5	(70,000 options × CU25) – CU1,600,000	150,000	1,750,000

4.3.7   Contingent issue of shares for goods or services from non-employees

---

Example 4.3.7

Contingent issue of shares for goods or services from non-employees

Company G enters into an agreement with lawyers currently assisting in its defence of a lawsuit. If Company G is successful in winning the case, it will issue 100 of its own shares to the lawyers. If Company G is not successful, it will issue 20 of its own shares to the lawyers.

Company G expenses the amount it expects to pay to the lawyers over the service period (being the variable period to settlement of the law suit). At the end of each reporting period, Company G should make its best estimate as to whether it will win the case, as well as the most likely outcome of the period over which the case will be settled. This estimate should be revised at the end of each reporting period as long as the case is not settled.

The total expense recognised up to the date of settlement should equal the fair value of services received. This value should be calculated directly (taking into account the differential between the value of services received in winning and in losing the case – one being five times the other in this example based upon the number of shares to be delivered), unless a reliable estimate cannot be made on this basis, in which case the value should be determined indirectly by reference to the fair value of the equity instruments granted, measured at the date the entity receives the services.

4.3.8   Equity instruments vesting in instalments

Example 4.3.8

Equity instruments vesting in instalments (graded vesting)

Company A grants its employees 1,000 share options each with a fair value of CU10. The options vest pro rata over the service period (one-fourth each year). Under IFRS 2:IG11, entities are required to treat each instalment as a separate share option grant because each instalment has a different vesting period and, therefore, the grant date fair value of each instalment is likely to be different. This is because the length of the vesting period will affect, for example, the likely timing of cash flows arising from the exercise of the options.

The following table summarises how the total fair value of CU10,000 [1,000 × CU10] should be allocated to each of the four years in the vesting period. (Note that, for simplicity, it is assumed that the grant date fair value is CU10 for each tranche. In practice, as explained above, the grant date fair value might be slightly different for each tranche.)

Award	Year 1 CU	Year 2 CU	Year 3 CU	Year 4 CU
Tranche 1 [(10,000/4) × 1/1]	2,500			
Tranche 2 [(10,000/4) × 1/2]	1,250	1,250		
Tranche 3 [(10,000/4) × 1/3]	833	833	834	
Tranche 4 [(10,000)/4) × 1/4]	625	625	625	625
Total expense	5,208	2,708	1,459	625

4.3.9   Distinguishing market and non-market vesting conditions

For the majority of vesting conditions, it is straightforward to determine whether they should be viewed as market or non-market conditions. However, it is not always so straightforward to make this distinction as illustrated in the following examples.

Example 4.3.9A

Market and non-market vesting conditions (index)

Company A issues share options to certain of its employees that vest if, and when, Company A's share price growth (as a percentage) exceeds the average share price growth of Company A's 10 most significant competitors. Share price growth is calculated based on share prices only and does not factor in dividends or other factors.

IFRS 2:Appendix A defines one form of a market condition as a "condition upon which the exercise price, vesting, or exercisability of an equity instrument depends that is related to . . . achieving a specified target that is based on the market price of the entity's equity instruments relative to an index of market prices of equity instruments of other entities". IFRS 2 does not provide guidance on what constitutes an index.

While the term 'index' would appear to require a comparison of more than one entity, there clearly is no requirement that the index be a published, standard index such as the S&P 500 or FTSE 100. The following criteria should be considered in determining whether an index exists:

- the fair value at the date of grant can be reliably determined by reference to the index;

- the share prices of the entities in the index are readily available in an active market such that accurate and reliable measurements of fair value can be determined at a specific point in time; and

- a consistent and reasonable formula is used to determine the effects of the entities' performance on the performance of the index.

If these criteria are met, Company A would have a strong case for demonstrating that the vesting condition is a market condition.

Example 4.3.9B

Ranking of share price within a population

Company A issues share options to certain employees that vest if Company A's share price growth (as a percentage) ranks in the top quartile of the largest 100 entities in its market. Share price growth is calculated based on share price only and does not take account of dividends or other factors.

Should this vesting condition be considered a market condition?

It depends. The ranking within an index or group of entities may be representative of an index if it meets the criteria described in **example 4.3.9A** above – notably that the vesting condition be measured via a consistent formula based on the prices of shares in an active market. In such cases, a vesting condition based on a ranking should be considered a market condition.

Example 4.3.9C

Total shareholders' return as a market condition

Company A issues share options to certain employees, the vesting of which is subject to a Total Shareholders' Return (TSR) condition. TSR is the internal rate of return on the entity's shares calculated by assuming that:

- someone bought the share at the start of the performance period;

- any dividends received on the share had been used to buy more shares ('dividend shares') when received; and

- the shares (plus dividend shares) were sold at the end of the performance period.

For example, if no dividends were paid and the share price increased from CU100 to CU107 after one year, the TSR would be 7 per cent.

Company A's TSR condition works by comparing the entity's TSR with that of an index of the 100 largest entities in its market. For example, if Company A's TSR were to be placed in the top 30th percentile, then 90 per cent of the award would vest.

The criteria for an index described in **example 4.3.9A** above are met.

A TSR calculation includes not only changes in the entity's share price, but the effects of dividends. Nevertheless, a TSR condition should be considered a market condition because movements in the share price are the predominant factor in its calculation.

4.3.10   Good leavers and bad leavers

Vesting conditions may distinguish between 'good leavers' and 'bad leavers'. In practice, a good leaver is often defined in the terms of a share-based arrangement as an employee who leaves the entity due to injury, disability, death, redundancy or on reaching normal retirement age (see **example 4.3.10** below). A bad leaver is usually defined as any other leaver (e.g. due to resignation).

For example, an entity may grant options with a specified period of service as a vesting condition. A good leaver will be entitled to exercise all or some of the options when leaving the entity during the specified period of service. A bad leaver loses any entitlement to the award when he/she leaves during the vesting period.

Such arrangements represent share-based payment arrangements with a variable vesting period for good leavers (see **4.3.2** above). When calculating the IFRS 2 expense, the entity estimates how many good and bad leavers it expects to have. If the estimate of good leavers is material, a separate estimate should be made of the vesting period(s) for good leavers and that vesting period should be reassessed at the end of each reporting period. When accounting for all other employees (i.e. non-leavers and bad leavers), the estimate of bad leavers is used to true up the IFRS 2 expense for those failing to meet the service condition. Once the shares have vested, there is no further true up for leavers, regardless of whether they are good leavers or bad leavers. **Example 4.3.15** illustrates the accounting for pro rata vesting of shares for good leavers.

However, this guidance applies only if good and bad leavers are defined in the terms and conditions of the award. In other cases (i.e. when management or a remuneration committee determines whether an employee is a good or a bad leaver only at the time when the employee leaves employment), the particular arrangements should be considered carefully. The exercise of discretion by management may be a modification of the award and should be accounted for as such or it may affect the determination of grant date (see **example 4.4.1B** below).

Example 4.3.10

Awards exercisable on retirement

Company A grants an award that vests in five years if the employees stay in employment until the end of that period. If an employee leaves earlier

---

because of reaching the retirement age of 60, that employee will still be entitled to receive the full award at his or her retirement date.

Under this arrangement, the vesting period for those employees who, at the grant date, are more than 55 years old is shorter than the general vesting period of five years. Company A will need to determine how many employees have shorter vesting periods and recognise the grant date fair value of these awards over the applicable vesting periods. If the award is granted to an employee aged 60 or over, the award would in effect vest immediately and should be recognised as an expense in full at the grant date.

The grant date fair value of these awards may also be affected because a shorter vesting period affects the life of the options as an input to the option pricing model.

This applies even when some of the employees decide to stay and work beyond their retirement age because the employees could leave at any time after reaching the age of 60 without forfeiting the right to the award.

4.3.11   Matching share awards

Matching share awards take various forms but generally involve an arrangement under which an employee is given shares in the entity to 'match' those for which he/she subscribes. Often this is linked to a bonus payment. For example, if an employee elects to take the bonus in the form of shares to the value of the bonus, the entity makes a matching share award. The award typically has a vesting condition relating to continuing employment and/or a non-vesting condition relating to holding the purchased shares for a prescribed period.

The determination of the vesting period for a matching share award is not always straightforward. Arrangements vary with regard to whether the employee has discretion to take the bonus in cash or shares and whether the entity has discretion to provide the matching shares. When there is no discretion, the start of the vesting period for the matching share award will generally be the date when the bonus arrangements are established. However, in other cases it may be a later date. The facts and circumstances of each case should be considered carefully.

Accounting for a bonus which will be settled in a variable number of shares to the value of the bonus is considered at **4.2.4** above.

The appropriate measurement date for matching share awards is considered at **4.4.1.1** below.

4.3.12   Allocation of expense when there are multiple vesting conditions

> **Example 4.3.12**
>
> **Allocation of expense when there are multiple vesting conditions**
>
> Entity A enters into a share-based payment arrangement with certain of its employees, which contains a three-year service condition beginning on 1 January 20X1 and ending on 31 December 20X3. In addition, there is a one-year non-market performance condition assessed during the period 1 January 20X1 to 31 December 20X1.
>
> *How should Entity A recognise the share-based payment expense given that there are multiple vesting conditions with different reference periods?*
>
> Entity A should allocate the expense using a straight-line method over the service period of three years, unless there is compelling evidence that a different expense recognition pattern is appropriate.
>
> IFRS 2:15 requires that if the equity instruments do not vest until the counterparty completes a specified period of service, an entity should presume that the services to be rendered by the counterparty will be received in the future, during the vesting period. However, the Standard is silent regarding which pattern of expense allocation should be used if there are multiple vesting conditions with different reference periods.
>
> In the circumstances described, there is no evidence that employee services provided in the different periods are explicitly different. Therefore, allocation of the share-based payment expense on a straight-line basis is the most appropriate method.

4.3.13   Effect of planned restructuring event in estimating the number of awards expected to vest

> **Example 4.3.13**
>
> **Effect of planned restructuring event in estimating the number of awards expected to vest**
>
> An entity intends to restructure some of its operations. At the end of the reporting period, the costs associated with the restructuring plan do not meet the criteria for recognition of a provision under IAS 37 *Provisions, Contingent Liabilities and Contingent Assets*. However, the restructuring plan has been approved by the entity's board of directors and will be announced shortly after the end of the reporting period. The entity considers that it is probable that the restructuring will take place. As part of the restructuring plan, the entity expects to terminate the employment of some employees

who hold unvested share-based payment awards accounted for under IFRS 2. The terminations are expected to occur before the vesting date of the share-based payment awards and would result in forfeiture based on the existing terms of the share-based payment arrangement. However, the entity intends to change the terms of the arrangement to accelerate vesting of the awards held by employees terminated as a result of the restructuring plan.

At the end of the reporting period, how should the entity estimate the number of awards expected to vest?

Under IFRS 2:20, an entity recognises an expense based on the best available estimate of the number of awards expected to vest. The entity should revise this estimate if the number of instruments expected to vest changes. In the circumstances described, it is considered probable that the restructuring will take place. Therefore, at the end of the reporting period, the entity should reduce the number of awards expected to vest to reflect the forfeiture that will result when the employment of the employees is terminated under the planned restructuring. That is, the entity should reverse the expense previously recognised for the effect of awards that are no longer expected to vest because of the planned restructuring, under the terms of the arrangement in effect at the end of the reporting period.

Separately, the impact of changes to the terms of the share-based payment arrangement should only be reflected in the determination of the IFRS 2 expense on modification of the awards. Therefore, only when the terms of the arrangement have been modified (i.e. in the next reporting period) will the entity apply the requirements of IFRS 2:27 and consider these revised terms in assessing the number of awards expected to vest in accordance with IFRS 2:B43(c).

4.3.14   Conditions relating to completion of an initial public offering (IPO)

When determining the appropriate treatment of a condition related to the successful completion of an IPO, it is necessary to consider whether there is a related service condition.

One of the examples of a vesting condition in the table below IFRS 2:IG24 (see **4.3**) is the successful completion of an IPO *together with* a specified service requirement (i.e. an employee is required to be employed at the time an IPO is successfully completed). It is also clear that the successful completion of an IPO *without* any related service condition is a non-vesting condition.

If the service period is shorter than the period to the IPO, the IPO should be treated as a non-vesting condition. This would be the case if there is a service condition for a limited period (e.g. two years) and the employees are then free to leave while retaining their right to exercise the options at a later date if the IPO is achieved. In this case, any expense recognised for the options granted to employees who leave before meeting the two-year service condition will be reversed. There will be no reversal, if the IPO does not occur, in relation to the employees who are still employed at the end of the two-year service period. However, as noted above, the grant date fair value will have been adjusted to take account of the probability that the IPO will not occur.

Examples 4.3.14A to C below illustrate the appropriate accounting for share-based payment conditions involving the completion of an IPO.

Example 4.3.14A

IPO and a service condition when IPO determines vesting period

An entity grants 100 share options each to 10 of its employees. The grant is conditional on a successful IPO within the next four years, and employees working for the entity over the period until the IPO. Therefore, the vesting period is dependent on the timing of the IPO. The fair value of each share option at grant date is CU60.

At the end of Year 1, no employees have left, but the entity expects two to leave by the end of the service period. The entity believes that it is not probable that there will be a successful IPO within the next three years.

At the end of Year 2, one employee has left, and the entity expects one more employee to leave during the next year. The entity now believes that it is probable that there will be a successful IPO before the end of Year 3.

The IPO is completed successfully six months after the beginning of Year 3. Prior to the completion of the IPO, one further employee has left and the entity expects another two to leave in the final year.

During Year 4, another two employees leave as expected.

The IPO condition is a non-market performance condition because it is not related to the entity's share price and it must be met within a specified period during which the employees must remain in employment with the entity.

IFRS 2:19 requires that vesting conditions, other than market conditions, are not taken into account when estimating the fair value of the share options at the measurement date. Instead, vesting conditions are taken into account by adjusting the number of equity instruments included in the measurement of the transaction amount.

Therefore, the determination of grant date fair value excludes the probability of a successful IPO within the service period.

Year 1

The entity believes that it is not probable that there will be a successful IPO within the service period; therefore, the number of equity instruments expected to vest is zero. As a result, no accounting entries are recognised.

Year 2

Because the entity believes that it is probable that there will be a successful IPO before the end of Year 3 and eight employees are expected to be employed until the completion of the IPO, a share-based payment expense is recognised over the estimated vesting period of three years. Because no amounts were recognised in Year 1, the expense in Year 2 is recognised as follows.

		CU	CU
Dr	Share-based payment expense		
	[(CU60 × 100 × 8)/3) × 2]	32,000	
Cr	Equity		32,000

To recognise the share-based payment expense.

Year 3

Because the IPO is completed successfully six months after the beginning of Year 3 and eight employees remained employed at the time of the IPO, the final vesting period is two and a half years. Therefore, the remainder of the share-based payment expense is recognised as follows.

		CU	CU
Dr	Share-based payment expense		
	[(CU60 × 100 × 8) – CU32,000]	16,000	
Cr	Equity		16,000

To recognise the share-based payment expense.

Year 4

Because the IPO is completed successfully six months after the beginning of Year 3 and the share options are vested in full at that point, no further share-based payment expense is recognised in Year 4, regardless of whether any more employees leave.

In practice, the determination as to whether it is probable that an IPO will occur is difficult because it is dependent on factors outside the entity's control. Often it will not be possible to conclude that an IPO is probable until plans are well advanced.

Note that, in the circumstances described above, the completion of the IPO determines the required service period and so the vesting period over which the expense is spread is changed as the expectation of occurrence and timing of the IPO changes. **Example 4.3.14B** addresses the accounting if the timing of the IPO does not alter the vesting period of the share-based payments.

Example 4.3.14B

IPO and a service condition when vesting period is fixed

An entity grants 100 share options each to 10 of its employees. The grant is conditional on employees working for the entity over the next four years, and a successful IPO within that service period. Therefore, the vesting period is four years. The fair value of each share option at grant date is CU60.

At the end of Year 1, no employees have left, but the entity expects two to leave by the end of the service period. The entity believes that it is not probable that there will be a successful IPO within the next three years.

At the end of Year 2, one employee has left, and the entity expects one more employee to leave during the next year. The entity now believes that it is probable that there will be a successful IPO before the end of Year 3.

The IPO is completed successfully six months after the beginning of Year 3. Prior to completion of the IPO, another employee has left and the entity expects another two to leave in the final year.

During Year 4 another two employees leave as expected.

The IPO condition is a non-market performance condition because it is not related to the entity's share price and it must be met within a specified period during which the employees must remain in employment with the entity.

IFRS 2:19 requires that vesting conditions, other than market conditions, are not taken into account when estimating the fair value of the share options at the measurement date. Instead, vesting conditions are taken into account by adjusting the number of equity instruments included in the measurement of the transaction amount.

Therefore, the determination of grant date fair value excludes the probability of a successful IPO within the service period.

Year 1

The entity believes that it is not probable that there will be a successful IPO within the service period; therefore, the number of equity instruments expected to vest is zero. As a result, no accounting entries are recognised.

Year 2

Because the entity believes that it is probable that there will be a successful IPO before the end of Year 3 (and eight employees are expected to remain in employment to the end of Year 4), a share-based payment expense is recognised. Because no amounts were recognised in Year 1, the expense in Year 2 is recognised as follows.

	CU	CU
Dr Share-based payment expense		
[(CU60 × 100 × 8)/4] × 2]	24,000	
Cr Equity		24,000

To recognise the share-based payment expense.

Year 3

Because the IPO has been completed successfully six months after the beginning of Year 3 (and six employees are expected to remain in employment to the end of Year 4), a share-based payment expense is recognised as follows.

	CU	CU
Dr Share-based payment expense		
[(CU60 × 100 × 6)/4) × 3] – CU24,000	3,000	
Cr Equity		3,000

To recognise the share-based payment expense.

Year 4

As expected, another two employees have left; therefore, the remainder of the share-based payment expense is recognised as follows.

	CU	CU
Dr Share-based payment expense		
[(CU60 × 100 × 6) – CU27,000]	9,000	
Cr Equity		9,000

To recognise the share-based payment expense.

In practice, the determination as to whether it is probable that an IPO will occur is difficult because it is dependent on factors outside the entity's control. Often it will not be possible to conclude that an IPO is probable until plans are well advanced.

Note that, in the circumstances described above, the completion of the IPO did not alter the required service period of four years and so the vesting period over which the expense is spread was not changed. **Example 4.3.14A** addresses the accounting if the timing of the IPO determines the vesting period of the share-based payments.

Example 4.3.14C

Share-based payment conditions – IPO with no service period

An entity grants 100 share options each to 10 of its employees. The grant is conditional on the completion of a successful IPO within five years. There is no service condition attached to the awards and employees that leave the employment of the entity prior to the successful completion of the IPO will continue to be entitled to the reward if the IPO occurs within five years.

The successful IPO is a non-vesting condition because the vesting of the share options is not dependent on the entity receiving the services that entitle the employees to the reward. IFRS 2:21A requires all non-vesting conditions to be taken into account when determining the grant date fair value of the equity instruments granted. The grant date fair value of the options should, therefore, reflect the probability of a successful IPO.

Assume that on grant date the entity estimates that the share options have a fair value of CU30 per option.

Because there is no service period attached to the awards, the expense should be recognised immediately:

	CU	CU
Dr Share-based payment expense		
[CU30 × 10 × 100]	30,000	
Cr Equity		30,000

To recognise the share-based payment expense.

The above entries are not reversed if the IPO is unsuccessful.

4.3.15   Pro rata vesting for good leavers

Example 4.3.15

Pro rata vesting for good leavers

Entity A grants each of its employees 100 shares conditional solely on the employee remaining in employment with Entity A for three years. However, if an employee leaves Entity A's employment at any time during the three-year period for one of a number of reasons specified in the scheme (including, for example, termination by Entity A without cause, and invalidity), he/she will be entitled to a pro rata allocation of the 100 shares based on the number of days of service completed. (Employees entitled to such allocations are defined in the scheme as 'good leavers'.)

How should Entity A recognise the share-based payment expense for the arrangement described?

In the circumstances described, the most appropriate reflection of the service charge is achieved by allocating the share-based payment expense on a straight-line basis up to the date of vesting (i.e. the end of the three-year period).

As discussed at **4.3.10** above, arrangements of this nature represent share-based payment arrangements with a variable vesting period for good leavers (i.e. the general vesting period is three years but it will be less if the employee is a good leaver within three years). A good leaver's entitlement to receive a pro rata number of shares when he/she leaves Entity A's employment within the three-year period means that the number of shares receivable upon vesting is also variable.

IFRS 2:15 requires that an entity should account for services as they are rendered by the counterparty during the vesting period. The application of this principle to grants with a variable vesting period and a variable number of equity instruments receivable is illustrated in **example 4.3.2** and **example 4.3.3**, respectively. In both examples, the variability is addressed by making an estimate of the vesting period or number of equity instruments and revising that estimate at the end of each reporting period until vesting occurs.

In the circumstances described, the interaction between the vesting period and the number of equity instruments receivable means that a straight-line allocation of the expense for 100 shares over three years will reflect both of the sources of variability for good leavers. This is because after, say, 18 months, the cumulative expense for 100 shares and a vesting period of three years will be the same as for 50 shares and a vesting period of 18 months. As discussed at **4.3.10**, the entity's total cumulative expense will be reduced due to the estimated number of bad leavers.

This example may be distinguished from a graded vesting scheme (see **example 4.3.8**) under which awards vest in separate tranches. In contrast, here, the award vests at only one date (the earlier of three years from the grant date and the date of leaving as a good leaver).

4.4 Determining the fair value of equity instruments granted

4.4.1 Measurement date

When transactions are measured by reference to the fair value of the equity instruments granted, that fair value should be determined at the 'measurement date' which is defined in IFRS 2 as follows.
[IFRS 2:Appendix A]

"The date at which the fair value of the equity instruments granted is measured for the purposes of this IFRS. For transactions with employees and others providing similar services, the measurement date is grant date. For transactions with parties other than employees (and those providing similar services), the measurement date is the date the entity obtains the goods or the counterparty renders service."

This definition uses the term 'grant date' which is in turn defined as follows.
[IFRS 2:Appendix A]

"The date at which the entity and another party (including an employee) agree to a share-based payment arrangement, being when the entity and the counterparty have a shared understanding of the terms and conditions of the arrangement. At grant date the entity confers on the counterparty the right to cash, other assets, or equity instruments of the entity, provided the specified vesting conditions, if any, are met. If that agreement is subject to an approval process (for example, by shareholders), grant date is the date when that approval is obtained."

Example 4.4.1A

Determination of the grant date for a share-based bonus plan

On 1 January 20X1, Company A enters into an agreement with each of its executives whereby Company A will issue shares to each executive. The number of shares to be issued will vary in line with growth in revenue and profits for the year ended 31 December 20X1. Depending on audited revenue and profit growth for that year (which will be known at 31 March 20X2), Company A will issue between nil and 100 restricted shares to each employee.

The restricted shares will vest if the executive remains in Company A's employment at the end of a further three years. Therefore, the earliest an executive will be able to sell his or her restricted shares is at the end of 20X4. The board of directors has already approved the formula and no further approvals are needed.

At what date should the fair value of the shares issued be measured – 1 January 20X1 or 31 March 20X2?

IFRS 2:11 requires that the fair value of the equity instruments should be measured at the grant date, which is defined in IFRS 2:Appendix A as "the date at which the entity and another party ... agree to a share-based payment arrangement, being when the entity and the counterparty have a shared understanding of the terms and conditions of the arrangement". In the circumstances described, at 1 January 20X1 all parties understand the terms and, therefore, this should be viewed as the grant date.

An estimate of the number of shares that will vest is made at 1 January 20X1. A fair value is assigned to each share. Because the formula used to determine the number of shares that will finally be issued is considered a non-market vesting condition that should be accounted for using the 'true up' method in IFRS 2, the number of shares is adjusted at 31 March 20X2 based on the number of restricted shares actually issued to the executives. The fair value of each share should be based on its value at 1 January 20X1.

Two key factors that need to be considered when deciding on the grant date are:

- both parties need to 'agree' to a share-based payment; and

- both parties must have a shared understanding of the terms and conditions.

The word 'agree' is used in its usual sense and means that there must be both an offer and acceptance of that offer. The date of grant is when the other party accepts an offer and not when the offer is made. In some instances the agreement might be implicit (i.e. not by signing a formal contract) and this is the case for many share-based payment arrangements with employees. In these cases, the employees' agreement is evidenced by their commencing to render services. [IFRS 2:IG2]

For both parties to have agreed to the share-based payment arrangement, they must have a shared understanding of the terms and conditions of the arrangement. If some of the terms and conditions of the arrangement are agreed on one date, with the remainder of the terms and conditions agreed on a later date, then grant date is on that later date, when all of the terms and conditions have been agreed. For example, consider the situation when an entity agrees to issue share options to an employee, but the exercise price of the options will be set by a remuneration committee that meets in three months' time. The grant date is when the exercise price is set by the remuneration committee. [IFRS 2:IG3]

The scenario described in the previous paragraph differs from that described in **example 4.4.1A**. In **example 4.4.1A** the number of restricted shares to be issued, although not known, is the subject of an agreed formula which considers revenue and profit growth. In the circumstances described in the previous paragraph, the exercise price is not agreed until it is set by the remuneration committee because until then it remains subject to the committee's discretion.

Example 4.4.1B

Performance target at the discretion of the remuneration committee

Company P granted share options to its employees. The share options vest over a three-year period assuming that a specified performance target is achieved. However, under the terms of the grant, the remuneration committee has the power to vary the performance target at any time until vesting.

The terms of the agreement should be reviewed carefully to understand the limits of the remuneration committee's power. When the committee has wide discretion to vary the performance condition and is expected to use this discretion in practice, it is likely that the grant date of the options will be when they vest (i.e. when the committee exercises its discretion and the performance target is fixed). This is because there is no shared understanding of the terms of the award until that date (see below for further consideration).

However, in other cases, it will be apparent that the power to vary the performance target is intended to be used only in very rare and unusual circumstances. In such cases, it may be reasonable to assume that this term has little substance and should be ignored when accounting for the arrangement. In the event that the power is used at a later date, the amendment to the performance target should be accounted for as a modification (see **4.5** below).

When the committee's discretion is substantive, so that the grant date is not considered to occur until the options vest, this means that the grant date occurs after the employees to whom the equity instruments are granted have begun rendering services. However, IFRS 2:13 requires the entity to recognise the services when received. The guidance in IFRS 2:IG4 states that "the entity should estimate the grant date fair value of the equity instruments (e.g. by estimating the fair value of the equity instruments at the end of the reporting period)" for the purpose of recognising the services received during the period between the date of commencement of service and the grant date. Once the grant date occurs (in the example above, assuming the committee's discretion is substantive, when the options vest), the entity revises the earlier estimate so that the amounts recognised for services received in respect of the grant are ultimately based on the grant date fair value of the equity instruments.

Share-based payment arrangements take various forms. Some arrangements require explicit employee acceptance (often for legal or tax reasons). Others permit implicit acceptance evidenced by the employee rendering service.

Entities must carefully consider all the details of a share-based payment arrangement in assessing whether a requirement for explicit employee acceptance affects the determination of the grant date. Relevant considerations include, but are not limited to, whether the terms of the arrangement:

- require an employee's explicit agreement (e.g. by requiring the employee to sign the arrangement), in which case the grant date would normally be the date the employee accepts the offer by signing. However, if the offer requires shareholders' approval, the grant date would be the later of the date the shareholders approve the arrangement and the date the employee agrees to the arrangement in accordance with IFRS 2:IG4; or

- do not require an employee's explicit agreement, in which case the grant date would normally be the date the employee starts rendering services. However, if shareholders' approval is required, the grant date cannot be before the shareholders approve the arrangement.

Sometimes there is a time lapse between the date when the shareholders approve the plan and when the approval of the plan is

communicated to the employee. Normally the communication process is an administrative process and, consequently, the communication process does not defer the grant date.

The entity should also consider whether the requirement for explicit
acceptance by the employee is a substantive feature of the arrangement. In making this assessment, the entity should consider whether,
for example:

- the employee is required to accept the offer explicitly because
  acceptance of the awards triggers another event (e.g. the
  employee's liability to tax arising from the award), or whether
  acceptance is implicit by virtue of the employee providing
  services; or

- the employee has a choice between accepting the share-based
  payment award or taking the compensation in an alternative
  form (e.g. free membership of insurance scheme offered by the
  employer).

If explicit acceptance by the employee is judged not to be a substantive feature, the grant date should not be delayed until the acceptance documents have been received.

The following example applies the principles established above to a
specific situation.

Example 4.4.1C

Effect of employee acceptance conditions on grant date

In Country B, an individual is taxed in the period that share-based payments
are received. As a result, prior to issuing share-based payments to its
employees, Company X first issues an offer letter to each employee detailing
the amount of shares or share options and the exercise price. Each employee
has 30 days in which to return the offer letter to accept the options.

What is the grant date – the date of offer or the date of acceptance?

In many cases, the determination as to whether the requirement for rejection
or acceptance is explicit or implicit requires careful analysis of the facts and
circumstances. In the circumstances described, the requirement to accept is
explicit and has substance, given that the employee will be taxed immediately on the options received. While the employee understands all of the
terms and conditions, the employer does not (until acceptance) have a full

---

understanding of how many share options will be issued. Therefore, due to the explicit acceptance requirement, grant date would be the date of acceptance.

The date of grant determines the date the options should be measured, but does not affect the recognition period of the expense; that is, the option should be recognised as an expense over the service period. If the service period begins prior to the grant date (e.g. from the offer date), Company X should begin expensing the share-based payment at the date of offer at an amount that will approximate to the fair value of the share-based payment to be determined at grant date. If the period between the offer date and the grant date crosses the reporting date, the fair value should be remeasured at the reporting date. Once an employee accepts, that date would be the grant date and the fair value would be determined at that date.

4.4.1.1 *Matching share awards*

Matching share awards take various forms but generally involve an arrangement under which an employee is given shares in the entity to 'match' those for which the employee subscribes. Often this is linked to a bonus payment. For example, if an employee elects to take the bonus in the form of shares to the value of the bonus, the entity makes a matching share award. The award typically has a vesting condition relating to continuing employment and/or a non-vesting condition relating to holding the purchased shares for a prescribed period.

The determination of the measurement date for a matching share award is not always straightforward. Arrangements vary with regard to whether the employee has discretion to take the bonus in cash or shares and whether the entity has discretion to provide the matching shares. The measurement date is the grant date, which is when the entity and the employee have a shared understanding of the terms and conditions of the arrangement. When there is no discretion, the measurement date for the matching share award will generally be the date when the bonus arrangements are established. However, in other cases it may be a later date. The facts and circumstances of each case should be considered carefully.

Accounting for a bonus which will be settled in a variable number of shares to the value of the bonus is considered at **4.2.4** above.

The appropriate vesting period for matching share awards is considered at **4.3.11** above.

4.4.2   Fair value by reference to the fair value of goods or services

---

Example 4.4.2

Volume rebates

Company A purchases 1,000 computers in return for 5,000 of Company A's ordinary shares, trading at CU100 each. The seller generally sells the same computers individually for CU700 each. Company A currently trades several thousand shares a day, such that 5,000 shares would be readily convertible to cash by the seller.

How should the fair value of the computers received be determined?

When determining fair value by reference to the value of the goods or services, care should be taken to ensure that volume rebates or other discounts are considered. When the value of the goods or services received does not appear to be commensurate with the value of the equity instruments issued, the difference may be due to volume rebates. If this is the case, the amount recognised should be the fair value net of any volume rebates.

In the circumstances described, the difference between CU500,000 [5,000 × CU100] (the market value of the shares issued by Company A) and CU700,000 [1,000 × CU700] (the fair value of 1,000 computers purchased individually) may relate to a volume rebate that should be considered in the valuation. If this is the case, CU500,000 is the appropriate measure for the computers.

4.4.3   Fair value by reference to the fair value of equity instruments

When share-based payment transactions are measured by reference to the fair value of the equity instruments granted, ideally that fair value should be determined by reference to market prices. For example, in the case of an issuance of shares that must be forfeited if the employee leaves service during a three-year period, the share-based payment will be measured at the fair value of the shares at the date of grant. A share price or valuation of the entity at the date of grant would be sufficient to determine the fair value of those shares and it would not be necessary to recalculate this value unless the grant was modified.

When market prices do not exist for share options, the fair value should be determined by applying a valuation technique, usually in the form of an option pricing model. [IFRS 2:B4]

IFRS 2 does not prescribe the use of a specific valuation methodology. The overriding principle implicit in the guidance in IFRS 2:B5 is that, in the selection of the appropriate option pricing model, an entity considers factors that knowledgeable and willing market participants would consider. Generally, this will be an issue requiring careful consideration by preparers, possibly requiring the involvement of valuation experts.

It may be acceptable, and even necessary, to use different models for different schemes to reflect their particular features. It may also sometimes be appropriate to use different models for different grants under the same scheme (e.g. to change to a more complex model as amounts become more material). However, other than in the case of material error, the grant date fair value should not be adjusted, once it has been determined using a particular model, even if that model is no longer used for new grants.

Appendix B to IFRS 2 discusses measurement of the fair value of shares and share options granted, focusing on specific terms and conditions that are common features of a grant of shares or share options to employees. Examples of the types of decisions related to measurement that entities are required to make include the following.

Items to determine	Accounting decisions
Pricing model	Black-Scholes, binomial, Monte Carlo etc.
Expected life assumption/ employee behaviour	For variable exercise dates, assumptions are needed as to when employees are likely to exercise their options (e.g. in a financially optimal manner; when the option is in the money at a certain time, e.g. vesting date; when the share price hits a specified share price ('barrier'); or based on historical behaviour).
Current share price	Share price can be determined on the basis of closing price on grant date or the average price on grant date.
Expected volatility	There are various methods to calculate this amount (e.g. based on historical experience, implied volatility of traded options, volatility of comparator entities, or industry index).

Items to determine	Accounting decisions
Expected dividends	This should be the expected future dividends over the expected life of the award. This should be in line with the entity's policy, although this may be derived from historical experience or experience of competitors.
Risk-free interest rate	This should generally be the implied yield available at the date of grant on zero-coupon government issues of the country in whose currency the exercise price is expressed and of duration that is similar to the expected life of the award.

These items are addressed in more detail in the sections below.

The fair value of cash-settled share-based payments, such as share appreciation rights (SARs), should be measured by using a model similar to one used for share options. That is, future share price increases and other variables have a similar effect on the fair value of many forms of cash-settled share-based payment transactions.

4.4.4 Valuation models

Three widely accepted valuation models are generally used to value equity options: the Black-Scholes model, the binomial model and Monte Carlo model.

This section compares and contrasts the three models.

4.4.4.1 Black-Scholes

Application of the Black-Scholes model (sometimes referred to as the Black-Scholes-Merton formula) is a straightforward calculation, which requires only the six minimum inputs noted in **4.4.5** below.

The Black-Scholes approach requires a single expected life assumption as to when the option is likely to be exercised, does not allow for variable exercise dates and is not able to factor in any market-based vesting conditions.

On the issue of expected early exercise, IFRS 2:B5 states that "many employee options have long lives, are usually exercisable during the period between vesting date and the end of the options' life, and are often exercised early. These factors should be considered when estimating the grant date fair value of the options. For many entities, this might preclude the use of the Black-Scholes-Merton formula, which does not allow for the possibility of exercise before the end of the option's life and may not adequately reflect the effects of expected early exercise".

IFRS 2:B17, however, notes that this will not always be the case, stating that "the means by which the effects of expected early exercise are taken into account depends upon the type of option pricing model applied. For example, expected early exercise could be taken into account by using an estimate of the option's expected life … as an input into an option pricing model (e.g. the Black-Scholes-Merton formula). Alternatively, expected early exercise could be modelled in a binomial or similar option pricing model that uses contractual life as an input".

4.4.4.2   Binomial model

The binomial model is more complex to apply than the Black-Scholes model, but allows more factors to be taken into account (i.e. variable exercise dates and some market-based vesting conditions).

The binomial model breaks down the time to expiration into potentially a large number of time intervals or steps. A tree of share prices is initially produced working forward from the present time to expiration of the option. At each step it is assumed that the share price will move up or down by an amount calculated using the volatility assumption and the length of each time interval. The probabilities of upward and downward movements are calculated using risk-neutral probabilities derived from the size of the upward and downward steps and the risk-free rate of return. This produces a binomial distribution, or tree, of underlying share prices. The tree represents all possible paths that the share price could take during the life of the option. The effect of dividends on the share price is adjusted for in the binomial tree as they are expected to be paid during the contractual life. At the end of the tree – that is, the expiration of the option – all the terminal option payoffs for each of the final possible share prices are known as they simply equal their intrinsic values.

Next, the 'option values' at each step of the tree are calculated working back from expiration to the present. The option values at each step are used to derive the option values at the preceding step of the tree using a risk-neutral valuation. This risk-neutral valuation uses the risk-free rate of interest as a discount factor and risk-neutral probabilities of the share price moving up or down. At any point during the option's life at which exercise would be permitted, the higher of the intrinsic value (i.e. the value of the option if it were to be exercised) and the 'option value' (i.e. the value of the option if it were to be held) is taken (because a rational investor would exercise when exercising an option would give a higher value than holding on to it). In this way, the binomial model takes into account variable exercise dates. Certain adjustments to option values as a result of market-based vesting features can also be worked into the calculations at the required point in time. At the start of the tree, the option's fair value is obtained.

4.4.4.3   Monte Carlo model

A Monte Carlo model works by simulating a large number of projected random outcomes for how the share price may move in future. The relevant share price may be that of the entity and, if applicable, those of comparator entities, e.g. when there are market-based performance conditions based on relative total shareholder return.

On the basis of each simulated share price (or set of comparator entity share prices), the proportion of awards that would vest and the resultant pay-off is determined. This is then discounted back to the valuation date at the risk-free interest rate. The procedure is then repeated a large number of times to determine the expected (average) value of the award at the valuation date.

4.4.5   Basic factors affecting the valuation of share-based payments

Most employee share-based payments granted will not have an equivalent instrument traded in an active market and, therefore, when the determination of their fair values is required by IFRS 2, valuation models will need to be applied. IFRS 2 requires, at a minimum, that all valuation models consider the following six basic inputs:
[IFRS 2:B6]

- the exercise price of the option (see **4.4.5.1** below);

- the current price of the underlying shares (see **4.4.5.2** below);

- the expected life of the option (see **4.4.5.3** below);

- the expected volatility of the share price (see **4.4.5.4** below);

- the dividends expected on the shares (see **4.4.5.5** below); and

- the risk-free interest rate for the life of the option (see **4.4.5.6** below).

These variables have been widely accepted as required inputs into valuations. Therefore, it is useful first to review these basic inputs. Other factors affecting the valuation of share-based payments are addressed in **4.4.6** below.

For some of the inputs listed above, it is likely that there will be a range of reasonable expectations, e.g. for exercise behaviour of employees. If this is the case, the fair value should be calculated by weighting each amount within the range of probabilities of occurrence. [IFRS 2:B12]

4.4.5.1   Exercise price

IFRS 2 does not provide guidance on the determination of the exercise price. The exercise price should be determined from the agreement.

> It is possible for the exercise price to be variable. For example, an exercise price dependent on a non-market vesting condition is considered at **4.3.4** above.

4.4.5.2   Current share price

IFRS 2 does not provide guidance on the determination of the current share price.

The current share price should be determined in accordance with an entity's accounting policy. That policy may dictate the use of closing price or average price at the grant date. Whichever method is chosen, it should be used consistently between periods and among plans.

4.4.5.3   Expected life

There are several factors that affect the expected life of a typical non-traded share option given to employees, such as vesting features and various behavioural considerations. These factors and others are discussed in greater detail in the next section.

Some ways that the expected life of a share option may be determined are:

- by creating a binomial lattice that includes all the appropriate factors – the lattice outcomes will determine when the exercise date is most likely to occur; or

- by taking factors, such as those listed below, employee risk aversion and behaviour into consideration and estimating an expected life that is then used in, for example, a Black-Scholes model.

Factors to consider in estimating the expected exercise date of a share option include:
[IFRS 2:B18]

- the length of the vesting period, because share options typically cannot be exercised before they vest;

- historical experience related to actual lives of share options;

- the price of underlying shares (employees may tend to exercise options when the share price reaches a specified level above the exercise price);

- the expected volatility of the underlying shares (employees tend to exercise options earlier on highly volatile shares); and

- the employee's level within the organisation.

IFRS 2 suggests that different groups of employees may have homogeneous exercise behaviours and, therefore, determining the expected life for each homogeneous group may be more accurate than an expected life for all recipients of an option grant. [IFRS 2:B20] That is, one share option granted to the Chief Executive Officer may have a different value from one share option granted to a factory worker at the same time with the same term. For example, the Chief Executive Officer might have a greater understanding of when it is optimal to exercise the award and might have less restrictive cash flow constraints compared to the average worker. If the Black-Scholes model is used, IFRS 2 requires the use of the expected life of the option. Alternatively, exercise behaviours can be modelled into a binomial or similar option pricing model that uses contractual life.

4.4.5.4   *Expected volatility*

Volatility is a measure of the amount by which a share price is expected to fluctuate during a period. [IFRS 2:B22] Many of the concerns about determining the fair value of non-traded employee share options relate to determining the estimate of expected volatility over the term of the option.

Volatility may be measured by reference to the implied volatility in traded options. However, the trading of such options is quite thin and the terms tend to be much shorter than the terms of most employee share options. There is also empirical evidence that options with the same term but different strike prices have different implied volatility. This is a factor that cannot be included in the Black-Scholes model, which assumes a constant volatility.

Historical volatility is often used as a rebuttable presumption for long-term options because there is evidence that volatilities are mean-reverting. Therefore, using the long-term average historical volatility for long-term options would be sufficient if there were no reasons to assume that historical volatility would not generally be representative of future volatility. Some have suggested a blended approach utilising both implied volatility and historical volatility.

The historical volatility may be problematic for newly listed and unlisted entities. If a newly listed entity does not have sufficient historical information, it should nevertheless compute historical volatility for the longest period for which trading activity is available. It can also consider the historical volatility of similar entities following a comparable period in their lives. [IFRS 2:B26]

The unlisted entity will not have historical information to consider when estimating expected volatility. Instead, it should consider other factors, including historical or implied volatility of similar listed entities. [IFRS 2:B27 & B29]

Many factors should be considered when estimating expected volatility. For example, the estimate of volatility might first focus on implied volatilities for the terms that were available in the market and compare the implied volatility to the long-term average historical volatility for reasonableness.

In addition to implied and historical volatility, IFRS 2 suggests the following factors to be considered in estimating expected volatility: [IFRS 2:B25]

- the length of time an entity's shares have been publicly traded;

- appropriate and regular intervals for price observations; and

- other factors indicating that expected future volatility might differ from past volatility (e.g. extraordinary volatility in historical share prices).

4.4.5.5 Expected dividends

Whether expected dividends should be included in the measurement of share-based payments depends on whether the holder is entitled to dividends or dividend equivalents. For example, if employees are granted options and are entitled to dividends on the underlying shares or dividend equivalents (which might be paid in cash or applied to reduce the exercise price) between grant date and exercise date, the options granted should be valued as if no dividends will be paid on the underlying shares. That is to say, the input to the option pricing model for expected dividends should be zero. [IFRS 2:B31 & B32] If the holder of the option or share is entitled to dividends between the grant date and the exercise date, expected dividends should not be included in the fair value measurement. [IFRS 2:B33]

If the employees are not entitled to dividends or dividend equivalents during the vesting period (or, in the case of options, before exercise), the grant date valuation of the rights to shares or options should take expected dividends into account. That is to say, when the fair value of an option is estimated, expected dividends should be included in the application of the option pricing model. When the fair value of a share grant is estimated, that valuation should be reduced by the present value of dividends expected to be paid during the vesting period. [IFRS 2:B34]

IFRS 2 notes that assumptions about expected dividends should generally be based on publicly available information. An entity that does not pay dividends and has no plans to do so should assume an expected dividend yield of zero. However, a newly formed entity with no history of paying dividends might expect to begin paying dividends during the expected lives of its employee share options. Those entities could use an average of their past dividend yield (zero) and the mean dividend yield of an appropriately comparable peer group. [IFRS 2:B36]

Option pricing models usually require expected dividend yield, as input into the models. However, the models can be modified to use an expected dividend amount rather than a yield. If an entity uses the amount, it should consider its historical patterns of increases in dividends. For example, if an entity's policy has generally been to increase dividends by 3 per cent per year, its estimated option value should not assume a fixed dividend amount throughout the option's life unless there is evidence to support this. [IFRS 2:B35]

Example 4.4.5.5

Accounting for dividends paid on share options

Company B purchases its own shares in the market and holds them in an employee stock option plan (ESOP) trust (over which Company B has control) for use in settlement of an award of options to its employees. Under the terms of the award, if an employee leaves Company B within three years of the grant, the employee forfeits the share options. After three years of service, the options vest and an employee is eligible to receive shares on payment of a predetermined exercise price.

Consider the following three scenarios.

Scenario A: employees are not entitled to dividends on the shares declared prior to vesting.

Scenario B: employees are entitled to dividends in cash on the shares and any dividends declared are paid to the employees. The exercise price is unaffected by these dividends and, if the shares are forfeited, the employees retain the dividends declared and paid up to that date.

Scenario C: employees are notionally entitled to dividends, but the dividends are automatically applied to reduce the exercise price. If the shares are forfeited, the employee loses the right to dividends accrued and applied to reduce the exercise price.

- *How should dividends declared and paid on the shares be treated in measuring the share options?*

- *How should dividends be accounted for in Company B's financial statements when declared?*

IFRS 2:B32 and B34 clarify that when dividends are paid to the option holders before the exercise of the options, the value of those options is greater than the value of options for which there is no dividend entitlement prior to exercise.

Scenario A: employees not entitled to dividends declared prior to vesting

When no dividend accrues to employees, the fair value of the share options at grant date should be reduced by the present value of dividends expected to be paid during the vesting period (for example, by including the expected dividend yield in a Black-Scholes calculation).

When the share-based payment related to these options is recognised, provided that they are classified as equity-settled share-based payments, the appropriate journal entry for the shares expected to vest is as follows.

Dr   Share-based payment expense   XXX
Cr   Equity   XXX
To recognise the share-based payment expense.

Dividends accrued on the shares held by the ESOP trust are eliminated from the aggregate of dividends paid and proposed by Company B (see **section 9.2**).

Scenario B: dividends declared are paid to employees

When dividends are paid to the option holders before the exercise date of the options, the share options should be valued as if no dividends will be paid on the underlying shares during the vesting period (for example, by including an expected dividend yield of zero per cent in a Black-Scholes calculation). As a result, the grant date valuation is not reduced by the present value of the dividends expected to be paid during the vesting period.

The accounting for any dividends paid on the underlying shares will depend on whether the underlying shares are expected to vest. Provided that the share-based payment is equity-settled:

- for awards that are expected to vest, IFRS 2 treats the employees as holders of equity share options. Therefore, any dividends paid on these share options are recognised directly in equity. This is consistent with the principles of paragraph 35 of IAS 32 *Financial Instruments: Presentation* which states that "[d]istributions to holders of an equity instrument shall be debited by the entity directly to equity, net of any related income tax benefit". In addition, expensing the dividends through profit or loss as additional compensation when paid would result in double counting of an expense that has already been reflected in the grant date fair value of the award recognised under IFRS 2; and

- for awards that are not expected to vest (due to employees expected to leave during the three-year service period), employees are not treated as holders of equity share options. Any cash paid as 'dividends' on those share options represents employee remuneration in accordance with IAS 19 *Employee Benefits* and should, therefore, be recognised as an expense. The expense is measured at the amount of cash paid on these shares. Expensing these dividends through profit or loss does not result in double counting because no cumulative expense will be recognised under IFRS 2 for awards not expected to vest due to non-fulfilment of a service condition.

The appropriate journal entries are as follows.

Share-based payment expense related to the share options that are expected to vest (provided that they are considered to be an equity-settled share-based payment).

Dr	Share-based payment expense	XXX
Cr	Equity	XXX

To recognise the share-based payment expense.

Dividends paid on share options that are expected to vest.

Dr	Equity/retained earnings	XXX
Cr	Cash	XXX

To recognise the dividends paid on share options that are expected to vest.

Dividends paid on share options that are NOT expected to vest.

Dr	Employee expense	XXX
Cr	Cash	XXX

To recognise the dividends paid on share options that are not expected to vest.

If the assessment of the number of shares expected to vest changes, there will need to be an adjustment to reverse or increase the share-based payment expense as appropriate, together with an adjustment to increase or decrease the amount of dividend considered an additional employee expense.

Scenario C: dividends reduce exercise price, lost if shares forfeited

When dividends are automatically applied to reduce the exercise price, the input for dividends into the valuation of the option is the same as in Scenario B, as indicated in IFRS 2:B32.

When the share-based payment expense related to these options is recognised, provided that they are considered to be an equity-settled share-based payment, the appropriate journal entry is as follows.

Dr	Share-based payment expense	XXX
Cr	Equity	XXX

To recognise the share-based payment expense.

When the dividends are declared, the entity may make a transfer from retained earnings to another component of equity for the amount of the dividends because this represents a part of the exercise price 'paid' by the employee. This is relevant only if the credit to equity under IFRS 2 is made to a separate reserve (see **4.1.2** above).

4.4.5.6   Risk-free interest rate

The risk-free interest rate affects the price of an option in a less intuitive way than expected volatility or expected dividends. As interest rates increase, the value of a call option also increases. This is because the present value of the exercise price will decrease.

IFRS 2 states that the risk-free interest rate should be the implied yield available at the date of grant on zero-coupon government issues in whose currency the exercise price is expressed, with a remaining term equal to the expected life of the option being valued. It may be necessary to use an appropriate substitute in some circumstances. [IFRS 2:B37]

4.4.6   Other factors affecting the valuation of share-based payments

There are certain variables that affect the value of many employee share options that are not factored into the standardised Black-Scholes model. The inability to incorporate these factors directly into the Black-Scholes model limits its usefulness in estimating the fair value of the options. While the approach in IFRS 2 attempts to 'fix' this fault through adjustments to the inputs to the Black-Scholes calculation (e.g. expected life versus contractual life), many believe these adjustments are not enough. This section discusses in more detail some of these additional assumptions. However, depending upon materiality levels, the additional benefits derived from a model that involves these assumptions may not be worth the costs of preparing that model.

4.4.6.1   Performance conditions

Examples of performance conditions include the vesting of options based upon:

- the total shareholder return (TSR) of the entity, either in absolute terms or relative to a comparator group or index (market-based) (for a discussion of TSR, see **example 4.3.9C**);

- meeting a specific target share price (market-based); or

- levels of revenues (non-market-based).

As a result of those conditions, the holder of the right to an option or share may receive some or all of the vested option/shares.

As further explained in **4.3** above, IFRS 2 requires that market-based performance related vesting features be included in the determination of the fair value at the date of grant. Additionally, IFRS 2 requires the entity to estimate the vesting period at the date of grant and recognise the related expense over that period. There is no subsequent adjustment to the vesting period when the vesting period depends on a performance condition that is market-based.

Under IFRS 2, a non-market-based performance condition should not be included in the determination of the fair value at the grant date. For grants with such vesting conditions, at the end of each reporting period, the cumulative expense should equal that proportion of the charge that would have been expensed based on the multiple of the latest estimate of the number of awards that will meet that condition and the fair value of each award, i.e. it should be trued up at the end of each reporting period.

4.4.6.2 *Non-vesting conditions*

As discussed at **4.1** above, non-vesting conditions are factored into the fair value calculation. Examples of non-vesting conditions can include:

- payment of contributions into a SAYE scheme; or

- meeting a specific commodity index target.

4.4.6.3   Non-transferability

Many believe non-transferability after the vesting period does not have a material impact on the valuation of an option from the perspective of the issuer. However, because the shareholding is typically a disproportionate part of an employee's wealth, it may have a significant impact on their behaviour and, therefore, the expected life of the option. Several valuation experts have stated that the inability to transfer an employee share option does not violate option pricing model assumptions because there is no assumption about the transferability of the option in the calculation.

When estimating the fair value of an employee share option at the grant date, IFRS 2 requires the use of expected life to exercise instead of the option's contractual life to expiration to take into account the option's non-transferability. However, valuation experts agree that the use of an average expected life to exercise is not a theoretically accurate way to capture the option's non-transferability. They argue that looking only at the average expected life of the share option distribution could not capture information about that distribution. Therefore, some believe employee behaviours that result in early exercise should be explicitly modelled using a more dynamic option pricing model – such as the binomial model.

Furthermore, many valuation experts now believe that no discount is warranted for non-transferability during the vesting period. If the premise of fair value, as discussed above, is to estimate the amount that a hypothetical market participant would pay for such an option, then the estimate should incorporate employee characteristics only to the extent that they would affect the amount and timing of cash flows of the option. The only alternatives facing the employee during the vesting period are to vest or not to vest – and those two alternatives are addressed under the modified grant date approach in IFRS 2.

IFRS 2:B3 indicates that post-vesting transfer restrictions should be taken into account when estimating the fair value of the shares granted, but only to the extent that the post-vesting transfer restrictions affect the price that a knowledgeable willing market participant would pay for those shares. If the shares are actively traded in a deep and liquid market, post-vesting transfer restrictions may have little, if any, effect on the price that a knowledgeable, willing market participant would pay for those shares.

Example 4.4.6.3

Effect of post-vesting transfer restrictions when measuring fair value of equity instruments

Company A operates a share purchase plan for its employees. Company A's shares are listed and are actively traded. There are no vesting conditions; therefore, the shares vest immediately on grant date.

The plan stipulates post-vesting transfer restrictions such that employees cannot sell their shares until the end of a five-year period beginning on the grant date. The sale of those shares is legally prohibited before the end of the five-year period. Consequently, employees are required to pay the subscription price on the grant date, but they are unable to take advantage of market fluctuations during the following five years. The shares are held in a trust until the transfer restrictions expire. Dividends distributed during the restriction period are held by the trust.

In order to measure the effect of the post-vesting transfer restrictions, Company A considers a methodology that combines bank borrowings as if to acquire unrestricted shares on the market (the same number as granted in the plan) at the beginning of the five-year period and a forward to sell shares kept in the trust at the end of the five-year period. The fair value determined by such a methodology depends mainly on the interest rate applied to the borrowings. Typically, a financial markets participant (such as a bank) would be able to borrow money at a low rate such that the fair value would be less than the fair value determined on the basis of an interest rate applicable to an individual employee who does not have ready access to financial markets.

IFRS 2:Appendix A defines fair value as the "amount for which an asset could be exchanged, a liability settled, or an equity instrument granted could be exchanged, between knowledgeable, willing parties in an arm's length transaction". Based on this definition, under Company A's valuation methodology, the interest rate applied to the borrowings should be the rate applicable to the instrument. Therefore, an employee's ability to source such borrowings is not considered.

4.4.6.4   Stated exercise restrictions

Stated exercise restrictions (e.g. restrictions on exercise or sale of shares by employees) will affect the value both directly and through their impact on the behaviour of holders. The easiest way to see this is to note that employees may find themselves holding a large proportion of their wealth in the form of shares whereas, in the absence of such restrictions, they would hold a more diversified portfolio. This, in turn, will affect their behaviour and, generally (but not invariably) will cause them to exercise as early as possible so as to be out of the restricted period as fast as possible. A history of exercising options as early as possible demonstrates that the value given by the employer is less than the amount attributable to the full term of the option.

The effects of exercise restrictions will be similar to the effects of non-transferability features as discussed above. Therefore, stated exercise restrictions should be evaluated when estimating the fair value of employee share options based on their effect on the expected future cash flows from the options.

4.4.6.5   Behavioural considerations

As can be seen from the above discussion, there are many factors that affect the value of share options through their impact on employee behaviour. Behavioural considerations are critical and should be included in the valuation of share options. This is a familiar consideration in the financial markets. The entire mortgage market, for example, revolves around estimation of the behavioural influences on prepayments.

IFRS 2 requires behavioural considerations to be included in the model through an adjustment to the expected life of the option. Many believe, however, that this will generally be inadequate since the life of the option will depend on the returns for both the entity and for the market and the mechanism for this dependency will be determined by the group characteristics noted, such as risk aversion, diversification, and tax considerations. For example, as individuals grow wealthier in a rising market, the costs of poor diversification may decline and that will reduce occurrences of early exercise of the share options.

4.4.6.6   Long-term nature

The long-term nature of employee share option grants is significant and will clearly affect valuation. The Black-Scholes model uses one set of assumptions at grant date that do not change during the expected life of the options, while a binomial model can use varying assumptions at grant date depending on expected changes to the inputs during the expected life. A typical employee share option can have a contractual life of 10 years. Therefore, the use of static model inputs is not grounded in reality. Because changes in those factors over time can have a significant impact on option value, failure to model such changes over the term of the option can result in overstating or understating the fair value of an option.

Based on the results of research and discussions with valuation experts, fair value for an employee share option should incorporate at the measurement date volatility factors for discrete time periods over the term of the option, interest and dividend rates and exercise patterns over the term of the option, to correspond with historical evidence and/or current expectations, to the extent material. It is to be expected that applying a more dynamic option pricing model with changing inputs will be more difficult and, therefore, a cost benefit analysis (taking into consideration materiality) should be completed.

4.4.6.7   Effects on the capital structure of an entity

Typically, the shares underlying traded options are acquired from existing shareholders and, therefore, have no dilutive effect. [IFRS 2:B38]

Capital structure effects of non-traded options, such as dilution, can be significant and are generally anticipated by the market at the date of grant. Nevertheless, except in most unusual cases, they should have no impact on the individual employee's decision. The market's anticipation will depend, among other matters, on whether the process of share returns is the same or is altered by the dilution and the cash infusion. In many situations, the number of employee share options issued relative to the number of shares outstanding is not significant and, therefore, the effect of dilution on share price can be ignored.

IFRS 2 suggests that the issuer should consider whether the possible dilutive effect of the future exercise of options granted has an effect on the fair value of those options at grant date by an adjustment to option pricing models and factor it into the valuation. [IFRS 2:B41]

4.4.7   Example of employee share purchase plan

The following example is taken from the implementation guidance accompanying IFRS 2 and illustrates some issues about the valuation of equity instruments.

Example 4.4.7

[Guidance on implementing IFRS 2:IG Example 11]

Employee share purchase plan

Background

An entity offers all its 1,000 employees the opportunity to participate in an employee share purchase plan. The employees have two weeks to decide whether to accept the offer. Under the terms of the plan, the employees are entitled to purchase a maximum of 100 shares each. The purchase price will be 20 per cent less than the market price of the entity's shares at the date the offer is accepted and the purchase price must be paid immediately upon acceptance of the offer. All shares purchased must be held in trust for the employees, and cannot be sold for five years. The employee is not permitted to withdraw from the plan during that period. For example, if the employee ceases employment during the five-year period, the shares must nevertheless remain in the plan until the end of the five-year period. Any dividends paid during the five-year period will be held in trust for the employees until the end of the five-year period.

In total, 800 employees accept the offer and each employee purchases, on average, 80 shares, i.e. the employees purchase a total of 64,000 shares. The weighted-average market price of the shares at the purchase date is CU30 per share, and the weighted-average purchase price is CU24 per share.

Application of requirements

For transactions with employees, IFRS 2 requires the transaction amount to be measured by reference to the fair value of the equity instruments granted (IFRS 2:11). To apply this requirement, it is necessary first to determine the type of equity instrument granted to the employees. Although the plan is described as an employee share purchase plan (ESPP), some ESPPs include option features and are therefore, in effect, share option plans. For example, an ESPP might include a 'lookback feature', whereby the employee is able to purchase shares at a discount, and choose whether the discount is applied to the entity's share price at the date of grant or its share price at the date of purchase. Or an ESPP might specify the purchase price, and then allow the employees a significant period of time to decide whether to participate in the plan. Another example of an option feature is an ESPP that permits the participating employees to cancel their participation before or at the end of a specified period and obtain a refund of amounts previously paid into the plan.

However, in this example, the plan includes no option features. The discount is applied to the share price at the purchase date, and the employees are not permitted to withdraw from the plan.

Another factor to consider is the effect of post-vesting transfer restrictions, if any. Paragraph B3 of IFRS 2 states that, if shares are subject to restrictions on transfer after vesting date, that factor should be taken into account when estimating the fair value of those shares, but only to the extent that the post-vesting restrictions affect the price that a knowledgeable, willing market participant would pay for that share. For example, if the shares are actively traded in a deep and liquid market, post-vesting transfer restrictions may have little, if any, effect on the price that a knowledgeable, willing market participant would pay for those shares.

In this example, the shares are vested when purchased, but cannot be sold for five years after the date of purchase. Therefore, the entity should consider the valuation effect of the five-year post-vesting transfer restriction. This entails using a valuation technique to estimate what the price of the restricted share would have been on the purchase date in an arm's length transaction between knowledgeable, willing parties. Suppose that, in this example, the entity estimates that the fair value of each restricted share is CU28. In this case, the fair value of the equity instruments granted is CU4 per share (being the fair value of the restricted share of CU28 less the purchase price of CU24). Because 64,000 shares were purchased, the total fair value of the equity instruments granted is CU256,000.

In this example, there is no vesting period. Therefore, in accordance with paragraph 14 of IFRS 2, the entity should recognise an expense of CU256,000 immediately.

However, in some cases, the expense relating to an ESPP might not be material. IAS 8 *Accounting Policies, Changes in Accounting Estimates and Errors* states that the accounting policies in IFRSs need not be applied when the effect of applying them is immaterial (IAS 8, paragraph 8). IAS 8 also states that an omission or misstatement of an item is material if it could, individually or collectively, influence the economic decisions that users make on the basis of the financial statements. Materiality depends on the size and nature of the omission or misstatement judged in the surrounding circumstances. The size or nature of the item, or a combination of both, could be the determining factor (IAS 8:5). Therefore, in this example, the entity should consider whether the expense of CU256,000 is material.

It is unusual that the example in the implementation guidance accompanying IFRS 2 explicitly refers to the possibility that the charge might not be material. This might equally be true of most other requirements of this or other Standards. Caution should be exercised in deciding that a charge otherwise required by IFRS 2 is not material. IAS 8 provides guidance on the meaning of 'material' in the context of errors.

4.4.8   Fair value not measurable

IFRS 2 provides an exemption from fair value when the fair value of the equity instruments issued cannot be reliably measured. In these rare cases, the grant is initially measured at its intrinsic value and adjusted at the end of each reporting period for any change in intrinsic value until the options are either exercised, forfeited or lapse.

IFRS 2 defines 'intrinsic value' as follows.
[IFRS 2:Appendix A]

> "The difference between the fair value of the shares to which the counterparty has the (conditional or unconditional) right to subscribe or which it has the right to receive, and the price (if any) the counterparty is (or will be) required to pay for those shares."

For example, a share option with an exercise price of CU15 on a share with a fair value of CU20 has an intrinsic value of CU5.

When the IASB developed the exposure draft preceding IFRS 2, it concluded that there should be no exceptions to the requirement to apply a fair value measurement basis. It therefore was not necessary to include in the proposed IFRS specific requirements for share options that were difficult to value. The IASB noted that share options form part of the employee's remuneration package and that it seemed reasonable to presume that an entity's management would consider the value of the share options to satisfy itself that the package was fair and reasonable. However, after considering respondents' comments, particularly with regard to unlisted entities, the IASB reconsidered this issue.

The IASB concluded that 'in rare cases only' in which it is not possible to estimate the grant date fair value of the equity instrument granted, the alternative treatment of using intrinsic values should be permitted. [IFRS 2:BC199]

No further guidance is provided in IFRS 2 regarding the nature of the rare circumstances which would justify the use of this approach. Although unlisted entities may find it particularly difficult to apply IFRS 2, it should be remembered that even when the intrinsic value approach is used, it will still be necessary to have an estimate of the fair value of the shares at the end of each reporting period. Also, entities may be discouraged from following this route because the expense recognised using the intrinsic value approach will, in most circumstances, be higher (and more volatile) than that which would be recognised on the basis of fair value at grant date.

In the rare cases described above, the equity instruments granted are measured at their intrinsic value, initially at the date when the entity obtains the goods or the counterparty renders the services. The instrument is subsequently remeasured at intrinsic value at the end of each reporting period and at the date of final settlement, with any change in intrinsic value recognised in profit or loss. For a grant of share options, the share-based payment arrangement is finally settled when the options are exercised, are forfeited (e.g. upon cessation of employment) or lapse (e.g. at the end of the option's life). [IFRS 2:24(a)]

When this approach is used, the goods or services received should be recognised based on the number of equity instruments that ultimately vest or, when applicable, are ultimately exercised. This means that in the case of share options, the goods or services received are recognised during the vesting period in accordance IFRS 2:14 and 15 (see **4.1** above) except that the requirements of IFRS 2:15(b) concerning market conditions do not apply. The amount recognised for goods or services received during the vesting period is based on the number of share options expected to vest. That estimate is revised if subsequent information indicates that the number of options expected to vest differs from previous estimates. On vesting date, the estimate is revised to equal the number of equity instruments that ultimately vested. After vesting date, the amount recognised for goods or services received is reversed if the options are later forfeited, or lapse at the end of the option's life. [IFRS 2:24(b)]

If the intrinsic value approach is used, it is not necessary to apply IFRS 2:26 to 29, which deal with modifications to the terms and conditions on which equity instruments were granted, including cancellation and settlement (see **4.5** below). This is because any modifications to the terms and conditions on which the equity instruments were granted will be taken into account when applying the intrinsic value method described above. [IFRS 2:25]

However, if an equity instrument to which the intrinsic value method has been applied is settled and the settlement occurs during the vesting period, the settlement is accounted for as an acceleration of vesting. The amount that would otherwise have been recognised for services received over the remainder of the vesting period is, therefore, recognised immediately. In this case, any payment made on settlement is accounted for as the repurchase of equity instruments (i.e. as a deduction from equity) except to the extent that the payment exceeds the intrinsic value of the equity instruments measured at the repurchase date. Any such excess is recognised as an expense. [IFRS 2:25]

The application of the intrinsic value method is illustrated in the following example which is taken from the implementation guidance accompanying IFRS 2.

Example 4.4.8

Grant of share options that is accounted for by applying the intrinsic value method

[Guidance on implementing IFRS 2:IG Example 10]

Background

At the beginning of year 1, an entity grants 1,000 share options to 50 employees. The share options will vest at the end of year 3, provided the employees remain in service until then. The share options have a life of 10 years. The exercise price is CU60 and the entity's share price is also CU60 at the date of grant.

At the date of grant, the entity concludes that it cannot estimate reliably the fair value of the share options granted.

At the end of year 1, three employees have ceased employment and the entity estimates that a further seven employees will leave during years 2 and 3. Hence, the entity estimates that 80 per cent of the share options will vest.

Two employees leave during year 2, and the entity revises its estimate of the number of share options that it expects will vest to 86 per cent.

Two employees leave during year 3. Hence, 43,000 share options vested at the end of year 3.

The entity's share price during years 1–10, and the number of share options exercised during years 4–10, are set out below. Share options that were exercised during a particular year were all exercised at the end of that year.

Year	Share price at year-end	Number of share options exercised at year-end
1	63	0
2	65	0
3	75	0
4	88	6,000
5	100	8,000
6	90	5,000
7	96	9,000
8	105	8,000
9	108	5,000
10	115	2,000

Application of requirements

In accordance with paragraph 24 of the IFRS, the entity recognises the following amounts in years 1–10.

Year	Calculation	Expense for period CU	Cumulative expense CU
1	50,000 options × 80% × (CU63 – CU60) × 1/3 years	40,000	40,000
2	50,000 options × 86% × (CU65 – CU60) × 2/3 years – CU40,000	103,333	143,333
3	43,000 options × (CU75 – CU60) – CU143,333	501,667	645,000
4	37,000 outstanding options × (CU88 – CU75) + 6,000 exercised options × (CU88 – CU75)	559,000	1,204,000
5	29,000 outstanding options × (CU100 – CU88) + 8,000 exercised options × (CU100 – CU88)	444,000	1,648,000
6	24,000 outstanding options × (CU90 – CU100) + 5,000 exercised options × (CU90 – CU100)	(290,000)	1,358,000
7	15,000 outstanding options × (CU96 – CU90) + 9,000 exercised options × (CU96 – CU90)	144,000	1,502,000
8	7,000 outstanding options × (CU105 – CU96) + 8,000 exercised options × (CU105 – CU96)	135,000	1,637,000
9	2,000 outstanding options × (CU108 – CU105) + 5,000 exercised options × (CU108 – CU105)	21,000	1,658,000
10	2,000 exercised options × (CU115 – CU108)	14,000	1,672,000

4.5   Modifications to equity-settled transactions (including cancellations and settlements)

4.5.1   Modifications

An entity may decide to modify the terms of an existing equity instrument granted in a share-based payment transaction. For example, if there is a decline in the entity's share price an employer may decide to reduce the exercise price of options previously issued to employees, thus increasing their fair value. IFRS 2's requirements in this area are expressed in the context of transactions with employees. However, the requirements also apply to share-based payment transactions with parties other than employees that are measured by reference to the fair value of the equity instruments granted. In this case, any references to grant date are instead used to refer to the date the entity obtains the goods or the counterparty renders service. [IFRS 2:26]

As a minimum, the services received are measured at the grant date fair value, unless the instruments do not vest because of a failure to satisfy a non-market vesting condition that was specified at grant date. This applies irrespective of any modifications to the terms and conditions on which the instruments were granted (including cancellation or settlement). In addition, the effects of modifications that increase the total fair value of the share-based payment arrangement, or are otherwise beneficial to the employee, are recognised. [IFRS 2:27]

Therefore, a modification that results in a decrease in the fair value of equity instruments does not result in a reduction in the expense recognised in future periods. However, the effects of modifications that increase fair value are recognised. Appendix B of IFRS 2 provides guidance on how this requirement should be implemented. This guidance, which forms an integral part of the Standard, is summarised below.

> The transition provisions of IFRS 2 (and, for first-time adopters, the provisions of IFRS 1) do not require the Standard to be applied to awards granted before 7 November 2002. IFRS 2 does not address the modification of such awards. For such modifications, it will be necessary to recognise any incremental fair value as a result of the modification. However, this should not require the recognition of an expense for the original grant date fair value because this is not required under the transition provisions of IFRS 2 or IFRS 1.

4.5.1.1   Modification increases the fair value of the equity instruments granted

The fair value of the equity instruments granted may be increased, for example by reducing the exercise price of share options. When this happens, the incremental fair value is measured by comparing the fair value of the instrument immediately before and immediately after the modification. This incremental fair value is then included in the measurement of the amount recognised for services received.

If the modification occurs during the vesting period, the incremental fair value granted is included in the measurement of the amount recognised for services received over the period from the modification date until the date when the modified equity instruments vest. The amount based on the grant date fair value of the original equity instruments continues to be recognised over the remainder of the original vesting period.

If the modification occurs after vesting date, the incremental fair value granted is recognised immediately. If the employee is required to complete an additional period of service before becoming unconditionally entitled to the modified equity instruments, the incremental fair value granted will be recognised over the vesting period. [IFRS 2:B43(a)]

The following example, which is taken from the implementation guidance accompanying IFRS 2, illustrates the approach that should be adopted for a simple option repricing.

Example 4.5.1.1

Grant of share options that are subsequently repriced

[Guidance on implementing IFRS 2:IG Example 7]

Background

At the beginning of year 1, an entity grants 100 share options to each of its 500 employees. Each grant is conditional upon the employee remaining in service over the next three years. The entity estimates that the fair value of each option is CU15. On the basis of a weighted average probability, the entity estimates that 100 employees will leave during the three-year period and therefore forfeit their rights to the share options.

Suppose that 40 employees leave during year 1. Also suppose that by the end of year 1, the entity's share price has dropped, and the entity reprices its share options, and that the repriced share options vest at the end of year 3. The entity estimates that a further 70 employees will leave during years 2 and 3, and hence the total expected employee departures over the three-year vesting period is 110 employees. During year 2, a further 35 employees leave, and the entity estimates that a further 30 employees will leave during year 3, to bring the total expected employee departures over the three-year vesting period to 105 employees. During year 3, a total of 28 employees leave, and hence a total of 103 employees ceased employment during the vesting period. For the remaining 397 employees, the share options vested at the end of year 3.

The entity estimates that, at the date of repricing, the fair value of each of the original share options granted (ie before taking into account the repricing) is CU5 and that the fair value of each repriced share option is CU8.

Application of requirements

Paragraph 27 of the IFRS requires the entity to recognise the effects of modifications that increase the total fair value of the share-based payment arrangement or are otherwise beneficial to the employee. If the modification

---

increases the fair value of the equity instruments granted (eg by reducing the exercise price), measured immediately before and after the modification, paragraph B43(a) of Appendix B requires the entity to include the incremental fair value granted (ie the difference between the fair value of the modified equity instrument and that of the original equity instrument, both estimated as at the date of the modification) in the measurement of the amount recognised for services received as consideration for the equity instruments granted. If the modification occurs during the vesting period, the incremental fair value granted is included in the measurement of the amount recognised for services received over the period from the modification date until the date when the modified equity instruments vest, in addition to the amount based on the grant date fair value of the original equity instruments, which is recognised over the remainder of the original vesting period.

The incremental value is CU3 per share option (CU8 – CU5). This amount is recognised over the remaining two years of the vesting period, along with remuneration expense based on the original option value of CU15.

The amounts recognised in years 1–3 are as follows:

Year	Calculation	Remuneration expense for period CU	Cumulative remuneration expense CU
1	(500 – 110) employees × 100 options × CU15 × 1/3	195,000	195,000
2	(500 – 105) employees × 100 options × (CU15 × 2/3 + CU3 × 1/2) – CU195,000	259,250	454,250
3	(500 – 103) employees × 100 options × (CU15 + CU3) – CU454,250	260,350	714,600

4.5.1.2   Modification increases the number of equity instruments granted

If the modification increases the number of equity instruments granted, the fair value of the additional equity instruments granted, measured at the date of the modification, is included in the measurement of the amount recognised for services received, consistent with the requirements in **4.5.1.1** above.

For example, if the modification occurs during the vesting period, the fair value of the additional equity instruments granted is included in the amount recognised for services received over the period from the modification date until the date when the additional equity instruments vest. This is in addition to the amount based on the grant date fair value of the equity instruments originally granted which is recognised over the remainder of the original vesting period. [IFRS 2:B43(b)]

> The additional equity instruments granted as a result of the modification are, therefore, accounted for in the same way as a new grant of equity instruments on the date of the modification. The related expense is recognised over the remainder of the vesting period, in addition to the expense on the original grant.

Example 4.5.1.2

Modification increases the number of equity instruments granted

On 1 January 20X1, Company A puts in place a share-based payment arrangement under which employees will receive 10,000 shares in Company A free of charge if they stay in employment for three years. At 1 January 20X1 (the grant date), Company A's share price is CU6.

During the first half of 20X1, Company A's share price falls significantly. On 1 July 20X1, Company A modifies the scheme so that participating employees who are still employed at 31 December 20X3 will receive twice as many shares (i.e. 20,000 shares rather than 10,000 shares). On 1 July 20X1, Company A's share price is CU2.50.

At 31 December 20X1, Company A expects that shares will vest for 90 per cent of the employees (i.e. 18,000 shares are expected to vest).

Company A does not anticipate paying any dividends before 31 December 20X3 and, accordingly, the fair value of each equity instrument is determined to be Company A's share price at the grant date.

At the end of 20X1, Company A is 1/3 (12 out of 36 months) of the way through the vesting period for the original grant, and 1/5 (6 out of 30 months) of the way through the vesting period for the additional grant. Therefore, the expense for 20X1 is calculated as follows.

$(10,000 \times CU6 \times 1/3 \times 90\%) + (10,000 \times CU2.50 \times 1/5 \times 90\%) = CU22,500.$

4.5.1.3   *Vesting conditions modified in a manner that is beneficial to the employee*

The vesting conditions may be modified in a way that is beneficial to the employee. For example, the vesting period may be reduced or a performance condition might be eliminated or made less demanding. When the modification affects a market condition it is accounted for as described at **4.5.1.1** above. In all other cases, the modified vesting conditions are taken into account when applying the requirements of IFRS 2:19 to 21 (see **4.3** above). [IFRS 2:B43(c)]

The following example illustrates a modification that is beneficial to the employee as a result of the removal of a market condition.

Example 4.5.1.3A

Removal of a market condition

Company A issues 100 options each to 100 employees. The options vest if:

a)   the employees remain in employment for three years; and

b)   the share price increases to CU9 by the end of the three-year vesting period.

The share price at grant date is CU5 and the fair value of each option is CU3. It is expected that 90 of the employees will remain in Company A's employment for the three years.

In Year 1, the expense recognised is as follows.

	CU	CU
Dr Profit or loss		
[100 options × CU3 × 90 employees × 1/3]	9,000	
Cr Equity		9,000

To recognise the share-based payment expense.

At the beginning of Year 2, the market-based vesting condition (share price target) is removed. At this date, the fair value of each option with the share price target is CU2 and the fair value of each option without the share price target is CU3.50. Thus, an incremental fair value of CU1.50 per option is given to the employees. It is now expected that 92 employees will remain in Company A's employment until the end of Year 3.

In Year 2, the expense recognised is as follows.

In respect of the original scheme

	CU	CU
Dr Profit or loss		
[(100 options × CU3 × 92 employees × 2/3) –		
CU9,000]	9,400	
Cr Equity		9,400

To recognise the share-based payment expense relating to original scheme.

In respect of the modification

		CU	CU
Dr	Profit or loss	6,900	
	[100 options × CU1.50 × 92 employees × ½]		
Cr	Equity		6,900

To recognise the share-based payment expense relating to modification.

At the end of Year 3, 88 employees are still in employment. The expense recognised is as follows.

In respect of the original scheme

		CU	CU
Dr	Profit or loss		
	[(100 options × CU3 × 88 employees)		
	− CU9,000 − CU9,400]	8,000	
Cr	Equity		8,000

To recognise the share-based payment expense relating to original scheme.

In respect of the modification

		CU	CU
Dr	Profit or loss		
	[(100 options × CU1.50 × 88 employees) − CU6,900]	6,300	
Cr	Equity		6,300

To recognise the share-based payment expense relating to modification.

The following example illustrates a modification that is beneficial to the employee as a result of the removal of a non-market condition. The removal of a non-market performance condition will increase the likelihood of the instruments vesting. Overall, this will only be reflected by an increased expense in profit or loss if, and to the extent that, more instruments ultimately vest as a result of the modification.

Example 4.5.1.3B

Removal of a non-market condition

Company A issues 100 options each to 100 employees. The options vest if:

a)   the employees remain in employment for three years; and

b)   earnings per share (EPS) for Year 3 is at least CU1.

The fair value of each option is CU3. It is expected that 90 of the employees will remain in Company A's employment for the three years. At the beginning of Year 1, it is expected that the EPS condition will be met.

In Year 1, the expense recognised is as follows.

		CU	CU
Dr	Profit or loss		
	[100 options × CU3 × 90 employees × 1/3]	9,000	
Cr	Equity		9,000

To recognise the share-based payment expense.

In Year 2, because it is no longer expected that the EPS condition will be met, the expense previously recognised is reversed.

		CU	CU
Dr	Equity	9,000	
Cr	Profit or loss		9,000

To recognise the reversal of the share-based payment expense

In Year 3, the EPS condition is removed. At the end of Year 3, 88 employees are still in employment. The expense recognised is as follows (reflecting the options vesting in the absence of the now removed EPS condition).

		CU	CU
Dr	Profit or loss		
	[(100 options × CU3 × 88 employees) – nil]	26,400	
Cr	Equity		26,400

To recognise the share-based payment expense.

The effect of modifications which replace a market condition with a non-market condition is considered at **4.5.1.6** below. The effect of a modification which replaces a non-market condition with a market condition is considered at **4.5.1.7** below.

4.5.1.4   *Terms or conditions modified in a manner that is not beneficial to the employee*

The terms and conditions of the equity instruments granted may be varied in a manner that reduces the total fair value of the share-based payment arrangement, or is otherwise not beneficial to the employee. In this case, the entity continues to account for the services received as if the modification had not occurred (other than for a cancellation of some or all of the equity instruments granted which is considered at **4.5.2** below). [IFRS 2:B44]

This situation is unlikely to be common in practice because it is difficult to see why employees would consent to their agreed benefits being made less attractive. However, if this requirement did not exist it would be possible for management to reduce or eliminate the expense for 'out of the money' options because the employees might accept that they would receive no benefit anyway.

If the modification reduces the fair value of the equity instruments granted, measured immediately before and after the modification, the decrease in fair value is not taken into account. The amount recognised for services received continues to be measured based on the grant date fair value of the instrument originally granted. [IFRS 2:B44(a)]

If the modification reduces the number of equity instruments granted to an employee, the reduction is accounted for as a cancellation of that portion of the grant (see **4.5.2** below). [IFRS 2:B44(b)]

If the vesting conditions are modified in a manner that is not beneficial to the employee (e.g. by increasing the vesting period), the modified vesting conditions are not taken into account when applying the requirements of IFRS 2:19 to 21 (see **4.3** above). [IFRS 2:B44(c)]

The following example, taken from the implementation guidance accompanying IFRS 2, illustrates the application of this requirement.

Example 4.5.1.4

Grant of share options with a vesting condition that is subsequently modified

[Guidance on implementing IFRS 2:IG Example 8]

Background

At the beginning of year 1, the entity grants 1,000 share options to each member of its sales team, conditional upon the employee's remaining in the entity's employ for three years, and the team selling more than 50,000 units of a particular product over the three-year period. The fair value of the share options is CU15 per option at the date of grant.

During year 2, the entity increases the sales target to 100,000 units. By the end of year 3, the entity has sold 55,000 units, and the share options are forfeited. Twelve members of the sales team have remained in service for the three-year period.

Application of requirements

Paragraph 20 of the IFRS requires, for a performance condition that is not a market condition, the entity to recognise the services received during the vesting period based on the best available estimate of the number of equity instruments expected to vest and to revise that estimate, if necessary, if

---

subsequent information indicates that the number of equity instruments expected to vest differs from previous estimates. On vesting date, the entity revises the estimate to equal the number of equity instruments that ultimately vested. However, paragraph 27 of the IFRS requires, irrespective of any modifications to the terms and conditions on which the equity instruments were granted, or a cancellation or settlement of that grant of equity instruments, the entity to recognise, as a minimum, the services received, measured at the grant date fair value of the equity instruments granted, unless those equity instruments do not vest because of failure to satisfy a vesting condition (other than a market condition) that was specified at grant date. Furthermore, paragraph B44(c) of Appendix B specifies that, if the entity modifies the vesting conditions in a manner that is not beneficial to the employee, the entity does not take the modified vesting conditions into account when applying the requirements of paragraphs 19–21 of the IFRS.

Therefore, because the modification to the performance condition made it less likely that the share options will vest, which was not beneficial to the employee, the entity takes no account of the modified performance condition when recognising the services received. Instead, it continues to recognise the services received over the three-year period based on the original vesting conditions. Hence, the entity ultimately recognises cumulative remuneration expense of CU180,000 over the three-year period (12 employees × 1,000 options × CU15).

The same result would have occurred if, instead of modifying the performance target, the entity had increased the number of years of service required for the share options to vest from three years to ten years. Because such a modification would make it less likely that the options will vest, which would not be beneficial to the employees, the entity would take no account of the modified service condition when recognising the services received. Instead, it would recognise the services received from the twelve employees who remained in service over the original three-year vesting period.

4.5.1.5   Adjustments to preserve the rights of holders

Share options or other share-based payment arrangements may change in the case of capital changes such as bonus issues, rights issues and demergers in order to preserve the rights of the holders. For example, in the event of a one-for-one bonus issue, the number of shares in issue will double and the share price will fall by half. Therefore, to avoid the option holders being disadvantaged, it would be usual for the exercise price to be halved and the number of options to be doubled.

Such an adjustment would not result in an additional expense due to modification under IFRS 2 in the following circumstances.

- Preservation of rights in the case of a capital change is part of the scheme rules at inception. If this is the case, the adjustment is made in accordance with the original terms of the grant and there has, therefore, been no modification to the terms and conditions of the grant. This may be the case even if there is no explicit requirement in the written rules of the scheme to make the adjustment. It is important to consider whether such a requirement was implicit in the agreement and, therefore, the entity has merely acted in accordance with the original grant. For example, in some jurisdictions it may be the norm for such adjustments to be made, in which case a court might conclude that there was an implicit contract term in the absence of any evidence to the contrary.

- The option holders are treated in their capacity as equity holders, not as providers of goods or services. This is the case if an equivalent adjustment is made to all other equity or compound instruments (e.g. any convertible bonds) that would otherwise be affected at the time of the capital change and, as stated in IFRS 2:4, means that the adjustment is not subject to the requirements of IFRS 2.

If neither of these circumstances applies, or if other amendments to the terms are made that confer any additional benefit on the employees, the adjustment will be a modification and it will be necessary to compare the fair value of the rights immediately before and after the adjustment.

4.5.1.6   *Replacement of a market condition with a non-market condition*

The following example is similar to **example 4.5.1.3A** above in that a market condition has been removed, but in this case it has been replaced with a non-market condition. There will usually be an incremental fair value because an equity instrument with no market conditions attached will be more valuable than the same equity instrument with a market condition attached. However, whether that incremental fair value is charged as an expense will depend on whether the replacement non-market condition is met.

Example 4.5.1.6

Replacement of a market condition with a non-market condition

Company A issues 100 options each to 100 employees. The options vest if:

a)   the employees remain in employment for three years; and

b)   the share price increases to CU9 by the end of the three-year vesting period.

The share price at grant date is CU5 and the fair value of each option is CU3. It is expected that 90 of the employees will remain in Company A's employment for the three years.

At the beginning of Year 2, the market-based vesting condition (share price target) is removed and replaced with an earnings per share (EPS) condition such that, for the options to vest, EPS for Year 3 must be at least CU1.

At this date, the fair value of each option with the share price target is CU2 and the fair value of each option without the share price target is CU3.50. Therefore, an incremental fair value of CU1.50 per option is being given to the employees. It is now expected that 92 employees will remain in Company A's employment until the end of Year 3, and that the EPS target will be met.

At the end of Year 3, 88 employees are still in employment.

Scenario A: the EPS target is met

In Year 1, the expense recognised is as follows.

		CU	CU
Dr	Profit or loss		
	[100 options × CU3 × 90 employees × 1/3]	9,000	
Cr	Equity		9,000

To recognise the share-based payment expense.

In Year 2, the expense recognised is as follows.

In respect of the original scheme

		CU	CU
Dr	Profit or loss		
	[(100 options × CU3 × 92 employees × 2/3) –		
	CU9,000]	9,400	
Cr	Equity		9,400

To recognise the share-based payment expense in respect of original scheme.

In respect of the modification

		CU	CU
Dr	Profit or loss		
	[100 options × CU1.50 × 92 employees × ½]	6,900	
Cr	Equity		6,900

To recognise the share-based payment expense in respect of modification.

In Year 3, the expense recognised is as follows.

In respect of the original scheme

		CU	CU
Dr	Profit or loss		
	[(100 options × CU3 × 88) – CU9,000 – CU9,400]	8,000	
Cr	Equity		8,000

To recognise the share-based payment expense in respect of original scheme.

In respect of the modification

		CU	CU
Dr	Profit or loss		
	[(100 options × CU1.50 × 88) – CU6,900]	6,300	
Cr	Equity		6,300

To recognise the share-based payment expense in respect of modification.

Scenario B: the EPS target is not met

In the event that the EPS target is not met, the incremental expense in respect of the modification is reversed because the non-market condition has not been met. However, in accordance with IFRS 2:B42, Company A continues to recognise the expense in respect of the original scheme because, although the options have failed to vest, this was not because of failure to satisfy a vesting condition specified at the grant date.

Therefore, the expense recognised in Year 3 would be as follows.

In respect of the original scheme

		CU	CU
Dr	Profit or loss		
	[(100 options × CU3 × 88) – CU9,000 – CU9,400]	8,000	
Cr	Equity		8,000

To recognise the share-based payment expense in respect of original scheme.

In respect of the modification (reversal of expense previously recognised)

		CU	CU
Dr	Equity	6,900	
Cr	Profit or loss		6,900

To reverse the share-based payment expense in respect of modification.

It is possible that the modification might be structured with the intention that the fair value to the employee is the same before and after the modification. For example, this might be the case if the probability of the replacement non-market condition being met is the same as the probability of the original market condition being met. However, as illustrated in the example above, such a modification may result in an additional expense in accordance with the requirements of IFRS 2. This is a consequence of the different manner in which IFRS 2 treats market and non-market conditions.

4.5.1.7   Replacement of a non-market condition with a market condition

The following example is similar to **example 4.5.1.3B** above in that a non-market condition has been removed but in this case it has been replaced with a market condition.

Example 4.5.1.7

Replacement of a non-market condition with a market condition

Company A issues 100 options each to 100 employees. The options vest if:

a)   the employees remain in employment for three years; and

b)   earnings per share (EPS) for Year 3 is at least CU1.

The fair value of each option at grant date is CU3. It is expected that 90 of the employees will remain in Company A's employment for the three years. At the start of Year 1, it is expected that the EPS condition will be met.

In Year 1, the expense recognised is as follows.

	CU	CU
Dr Profit or loss		
[100 options × CU3 × 90 employees × 1/3]	9,000	
Cr Equity		9,000

To recognise the share-based payment expense.

At the beginning of Year 2, the EPS condition is removed and replaced with a market-based performance condition such that the share price must reach CU9 by the end of the vesting period. It is expected that 92 employees will remain in Company A's employment for the three years.

At the date of the modification, the fair value of the option with the share price target is CU2 and the fair value of the option without the share price target is CU3.50. Value to the employees is decreased but, under IFRS 2:B44, this decrease is not accounted for.

The original grant date fair value must continue to be recognised as an expense except to the extent that the shares do not vest because a service or non-market performance condition that was present at grant date is not met. The only such condition that continues to exist once the EPS condition is removed is the employment condition.

In Year 2, the expense recognised is as follows.

		CU	CU
Dr	Profit or loss		
	[100 options × CU3 × 92 employees × 2/3 – CU9,000]	9,400	
Cr	Equity		9,400

To recognise the share-based payment expense.

At the end of Year 3, 88 employees are still in employment and the share price target is not met, so the expense recognised is as follows.

		CU	CU
Dr	Profit or loss		
	[(100 options × CU3 × 88 employees)		
	- CU9,000 – CU9,400]	8,000	
Cr	Equity		8,000

To recognise the share-based payment expense.

The share-based payment expense is not reversed even though the options do not vest as a result of the market-based performance condition (the share price target). This is the case even though the effect of the market-based performance condition (i.e. reduction in fair value of the options) was not reflected in the measurement of the compensation expense as a result of IFRS 2:B44.

Replacement of a non-market performance condition with a market-based performance condition will, therefore, result in the need to recognise an expense equal to the original grant date fair value irrespective of whether the replacement market-based performance condition is met. In particular, replacement of a non-market performance condition that is not ultimately met with a market condition that is also not ultimately met will result in the need to recognise an expense that would not otherwise have been recognised. This is a consequence of the different manner in which market and non-market performance conditions are treated under IFRS 2.

4.5.1.8   *Several modifications in one*

IFRS 2:27 requires an entity to recognise the effects of modifications that increase the total fair value of the share-based payment arrangement or are otherwise beneficial to the employee in addition to the amount recognised for service received measured at the grant date fair value.

In determining the effects of modifications, IFRS 2:B42 – B44 provide the guidance set out below.

Modifications beneficial to employees:

- for those that increase the fair value of the equity instruments granted or modify a market condition, the incremental fair value granted (difference between fair value measured immediately before and after the modification) is included in the amount recognised for services received over the period from the modification date until the date when the modified equity instruments vest; and

- for those that modify the vesting conditions (other than market conditions), an adjustment is made for the number of awards expected to vest.

Modifications not beneficial to employees:

- for those that reduce the fair value of the equity instruments granted or modify a market condition, an entity continues to recognise the amount for services received based on the grant date fair value; and

- for those that modify the vesting conditions (other than market conditions), the modified vesting conditions are not taken into account and the grant date fair value is recognised over the original vesting period.

Example 4.5.1.8A

Modification by reducing both the exercise price and the vesting period

Company A awards share options to its 10 employees, which vest if the employee remains in employment for four years. The fair value of the award is CU100 (i.e. CU10 per employee). It is expected that eight employees will remain in employment until the end of Year 4.

In Year 1, the following entry is recorded.

	CU	CU
Dr Profit or loss [CU10 × 8 employees × 1/4]	20	
Cr Equity		20

To recognise the share-based payment expense.

At the beginning of the second year, Company A modifies share options by (1) reducing the exercise price, and (2) reducing the vesting period to three years.

The reduction of the exercise price increases the fair value of the award. Assume that, as a result of this modification, the fair value of the awards at the date of the modification has been increased by CU16 (i.e. CU1.6 per employee). This additional value is recognised over the period to the revised vesting date (i.e. in Years 2 and 3).

As required by IFRS 2:B43(c), a reduction in the vesting period is beneficial to the employees. The reduction in service period may affect the number of share options expected to vest and, therefore, the cumulative expense that will be recognised over the revised vesting period.

Assume that, after the modifications, it is expected that all 10 employees will complete the vesting period and the total expense recognised over three years will be CU116 (i.e. value of CU11.6 for 10 employees). At the end of Year 3, all 10 employees remain in employment.

In Year 2, the following entry is recorded.

		CU	CU
Dr	Profit or loss [(CU10 × 10 employees) × 2/3 – CU20 +(CU1.6 × 10 employees) × 1/2]	55	
Cr	Equity		55

To recognise the share-based payment expense.

In Year 3, the following entry is recorded.

		CU	CU
Dr	Profit or loss [(CU10 × 10 employees) +(CU1.6 × 10 employees) – CU20 – CU55]	41	
Cr	Equity		41

To recognise the share-based payment expense.

Example 4.5.1.8B

Modification by reducing the exercise price and increasing the vesting period

Company A awards share options to its 10 employees, which vest if the employee remains in employment for four years. The fair value of the award is CU100 (i.e. CU10 per employee). It is expected that eight employees will remain in employment until the end of year 4.

In each of Years 1 and 2, the following entry is recorded.

		CU	CU
Dr	Profit or loss [CU10 × 8 employees × 1/4]	20	
Cr	Equity		20

To recognise the share-based payment expense.

After two years, Company A modifies share options by (1) reducing the exercise price, and (2) increasing the vesting period to five years.

The reduction of the exercise price increases the fair value of the award. Assume that, as a result of this modification, the fair value of the awards has been increased by CU16 (i.e. CU1.6 per employee). This additional value is recognised over the period to the revised vesting date.

As confirmed by IFRS 2:B44(c), an increase in the vesting period is not beneficial to the employees. Accordingly, the grant date fair value (i.e. the fair value measured based on the original terms of the award) is recognised over the original vesting period of four years.

At the date of modification, it is estimated that eight employees will remain in employment until the end of Year 4 and that only five employees will stay until the end of Year 5.

- The grant date fair value is recognised over the original vesting period of four years [IFRS 2:B44(c)] for eight employees [IFRS 2:B42].

- The modification relating to the reduction of the exercise price vests over the remaining three years of the new vesting period of five years [IFRS 2:B43(a)] for five employees.

In Year 3, the following entry is recorded.

	CU	CU
Dr Profit or loss [(CU10 × 8 employees × 3/4 – CU40) + (CU1.60 × 5 employees × 1/3)]	22.67	
Cr Equity		22.67

To recognise the share-based payment expense.

By the end of Year 4, only seven employees remain (instead of the expected eight employees). It is still expected that five employees will stay until the end of Year 5.

In Year 4, the following entry is recorded.

	CU	CU
Dr Profit or loss [(CU10 × 7 employees × 4/4 – CU60) + (CU1.60 × 5 employees × 1/3)]	12.67	
Cr Equity		12.67

To recognise the share-based payment expense.

By the end of Year 5, as expected, only five employees remain.

In Year 5, the following entry is recorded.

	CU	CU
Dr Profit or loss [CU1.60 × 5 employees × 1/3]	2.66	
Cr Equity		2.66

To recognise the share-based payment expense.

The total expense over five years is CU78 (i.e. the grant date fair value of CU10 for seven employees and additional CU1.6 for five employees).

Example 4.5.1.8C

Modification by reducing the exercise price and decreasing the number of shares granted (without modification affecting the vesting period)

Company A awards 1,000 share options to one employee, which vest if the employee remains in employment for two years. The fair value of the award is CU10,000 (i.e. CU10 per share option).

In Year 1, the following entry is recorded.

	CU	CU
Dr Profit or loss [CU10 × 1,000 share options × 1/2]	5,000	
Cr Equity		5,000

To recognise the share-based payment expense.

At the beginning of the second year, Company A modifies the share option award by (1) reducing the number of granted share options from 1,000 to 800, and (2) reducing the exercise price of the share option.

The appropriate accounting depends on whether the effects of the modifications increase the total fair value of the award.

IFRS 2:B42 requires an entity to "recognise the effects of modifications that increase the total fair value of the share-based payment arrangement or are otherwise beneficial to the employee". Because, in this example, the modifications are linked, they will be considered as one modification to determine this impact (i.e. the modification in total is either beneficial or not beneficial to the counterparty). The incremental value is calculated as the change in the 'total fair value' before and after the modification.

Assume that the fair value of a share option before and after the reduction in exercise price is CU7 and CU11.

The total change in the fair value of the grant is, therefore, CU1,800 [(800 × CU11) − (1,000 × CU7)].

In Year 2, the following entry is recorded.

	CU	CU
Dr Profit or loss [(CU10 × 1,000 share options × 1/2)		
− CU5,000 + (800 × CU11) − (1,000 × CU7)]	6,800	
Cr Equity		6,800

To recognise the share-based payment expense.

The total expense over two years is CU11,800 [CU10,000 + CU1,800].

4.5.2   *Cancellations and settlements*

An entity may cancel or settle a grant of equity instruments during the vesting period. IFRS 2 includes requirements that deal with such situations. This does not cover those cases when a grant is forfeited when the vesting conditions are not satisfied which are dealt with in accordance with IFRS 2's requirements for vesting conditions (see **4.3** above).

IFRS 2:28 refers to circumstances when "a grant of equity instruments is cancelled or settled during the vesting period". Therefore, all cancellations must be dealt with in accordance with IFRS 2:28 irrespective of whether it is the entity or the counterparty that cancels the arrangements.

Similarly, if an entity or counterparty can choose whether to meet a non-vesting condition, the entity treats the failure to meet that non-vesting condition during the vesting period as a cancellation, irrespective of whether the entity or the counterparty fails to meet the non-vesting condition. [IFRS 2:28A]

> A practical example of this is when an employee stops making payments into an SAYE option scheme and, therefore, forfeits his or her entitlement under the scheme. The failure to make contributions is a failure to meet a non-vesting condition and is, therefore, accounted for as a cancellation.

The cancellation or settlement of an equity instrument is accounted for as an acceleration of vesting. The amount that would otherwise have been recognised for services received over the remainder of the vesting period is, therefore, recognised immediately. [IFRS 2:28(a)]

Any payment made to the employee on cancellation or settlement is accounted for as a repurchase of an equity interest (i.e. as a deduction from equity) except to the extent that the payment exceeds the fair value of the equity instrument granted, measured at the repurchase date. Any such excess is recognised as an expense. [IFRS 2:28(b)]

If the share-based payment arrangement included liability components, the fair value of the liability at the date of cancellation or settlement should be remeasured. Any payment made to settle the liability component is accounted for as an extinguishment of the liability.

> IFRS 2:28(a) requires that an "entity shall account for the cancellation or settlement as an acceleration of vesting, and shall therefore recognise immediately the amount that otherwise *would have been* recognised for services received over the remainder of the vesting period" (emphasis added). The Standard does not specify whether the

amount that 'would have been' recognised refers to the compensation expense that would have been recognised if all of the awards outstanding at the settlement date had vested, or whether it should take into account the entity's estimate of the number of awards that would have vested if the settlement had not occurred.

In the absence of clear guidance on the issue, an entity may adopt either alternative as an accounting policy choice. The accounting policy adopted should be disclosed and applied consistently.

Regardless of the treatment adopted as an accounting policy, entities will need to consider whether additional compensation expense should be recognised under IFRS 2:28(b) by comparing the settlement payment to the fair value of the awards measured at the settlement date. Although not explicitly stated in IFRS 2:28(b), the settlement payment should be compared to the settlement date fair value of the number of awards used to determine 'the amount that would have been recognised over the remaining vesting period' (i.e. in a manner consistent with the choice of accounting policy described above). **Example 4.5.2A** illustrates the alternative accounting policies.

Example 4.5.2A

Meaning of 'would have been' as used in IFRS 2:28

At the beginning of 20X0, Entity A granted 100 equity-settled share-based awards to each of 120 employees. The number of awards depends on whether specified profit thresholds are met at the end of the second year. The awards vest if the employees remain in Entity A's employment for two years. At the grant date, Entity A estimates that 80 employees will complete the required two-year service period and that 90 per cent of the awards held by those employees will vest (based on the profits estimated for Years 1 and 2 at the grant date); therefore, 7,200 awards (i.e. 90 awards for 80 employees) are expected to vest.

At the beginning of 20X1, Entity A settles all 12,000 awards in cash (all employees remained in Entity A's employment at that date).

At the date of settlement, consistent with estimates made at the grant date, Entity A estimates that if the awards had remained in place until the contractual vesting date, 80 employees would have completed the required two-year service period and 90 per cent of the awards held by those employees would have vested.

The fair value of each award on the grant date was CU10 and on the settlement date was CU6.

How should Entity A determine the amount that 'would have been' recognised over the remaining vesting period as required by IFRS 2:28(a)?

The various alternatives for Entity A as explained above are illustrated below.

Scenario 1: settlement amount for each award outstanding is lower than the fair value of the award at the settlement date

Assume that Entity A settles each award for cash of CU5.

Accounting policy to recognise expense that would have been recognised if all of the awards outstanding at the settlement date had vested

- Compensation expense recognised in 20X0 is CU36,000 [(7,200 × CU10)/2].

- Compensation expense recognised upon settlement under IFRS 2:28(a) is CU84,000 [(12,000 × CU10) − CU36,000 compensation expense recognised in prior period].

- Additional compensation expense recognised upon settlement under IFRS 2:28(b) is nil because the payment made on settlement (CU5 × 12,000) is lower than the fair value of the awards measured at the settlement date (CU6 × 12,000).

- Total compensation expense is CU120,000.

Accounting policy to recognise expense taking into account the estimate of the number of awards that would have vested had settlement not occurred

- Compensation expense recognised in 20X0 is CU36,000 [(7,200 × CU10)/2].

- Compensation expense recognised upon settlement under IFRS 2:28(a) is CU36,000 [(7,200 × CU10) − CU36,000 compensation expense recognised in prior period].

- Additional compensation expense recognised upon settlement under IFRS 2:28(b) is CU16,800, representing the excess of the payment made on settlement (CU5 × 12,000) over the fair value of the awards measured at the settlement date (CU6 × 7,200).

- Total compensation expense is CU88,800.

Scenario 2: settlement amount for each award outstanding is greater than the fair value of the awards at the settlement date

Assume that Entity A settles each award for cash of CU7.

Accounting policy to recognise expense that would have been recognised if all of the awards outstanding at the settlement date had vested

- Compensation expense recognised in 20X0 is CU36,000 [(7,200 × CU10)/2].

- Compensation expense recognised upon settlement under IFRS 2:28(a) is CU84,000 [(12,000 × CU10) – CU36,000 compensation expense recognised in prior period].

- Additional compensation expense recognised upon settlement under IFRS 2:28(b) is CU12,000, representing the excess of the payment made on settlement (CU7 × 12,000) over the fair value of the awards measured at the settlement date (CU6 × 12,000).

- Total compensation expense is CU132,000.

Accounting policy to recognise expense taking into account the estimate of the number of awards that would have vested had settlement not occurred

- Compensation expense recognised in 20X0 is CU36,000 [(7,200 × CU10)/2].

- Compensation expense recognised upon settlement under IFRS 2:28(a) is CU36,000 [(7,200 × CU10) – CU36,000 compensation expense recognised in prior period].

- Additional compensation expense recognised upon settlement under IFRS 2:28(b) is CU40,800, representing the excess of the payment made on settlement (CU7 × 12,000) over the fair value of the awards measured at the settlement date (CU6 × 7,200).

- Total compensation expense is CU112,800.

IFRS 2 also deals with the situation when new equity instruments may be granted to an employee in connection with the cancellation of existing equity instruments. If new equity instruments are granted and they are identified, on the date when they are granted, as replacement equity instruments for the cancelled equity instruments, this is accounted for as a modification of the original equity instruments (see **4.5.1** above). The incremental fair value granted is the difference between the fair value of the replacement equity instruments and the net fair value of the cancelled equity instruments at the date the replacement equity instruments are granted. The net fair value of the cancelled equity instruments is their fair value, immediately before the cancellation, less the amount of any payment made to the employee that is accounted for as deduction from equity in accordance with IFRS 2:28(b). [IFRS 2:28(c)]

If the entity does not identify new equity instruments granted as replacement equity instruments for those cancelled, the new equity instruments are accounted for as a new grant.

The Standard appears to imply a free choice as to whether an entity decides to identify replacement instruments. As illustrated in **example 4.5.2B** below, it will often be attractive to identify the new options as replacements because this will avoid accelerating the expense recognised for the original options. However, it would not give a fair presentation to characterise equity instruments as replacements when they were clearly unrelated to the cancelled instruments.

The determination as to whether the issue of new options is a replacement of cancelled options requires careful assessment of the facts and circumstances surrounding such transactions. IFRS 2 does not provide specific guidance in this area. Factors that may indicate that a new issue of options is a replacement of cancelled options include:

- the new share options are with the same participants as the cancelled options;

- the new share options are issued at a fair value that is broadly consistent with the fair value of the cancelled options determined either at their original grant date (indicating a repricing) or the cancellation date (indicating a replacement);

- the transactions to issue and cancel the options are part of the same arrangement;

- the cancellation of the options would not have occurred unless the new options were issued; and

- the cancellation of the options does not make commercial sense without the issue of the new options (and vice-versa).

If vested equity instruments are repurchased from employees, the payment made is accounted for as a deduction from equity, except to the extent that the payment exceeds the fair value of the repurchased instruments, measured at the repurchase date. Any such excess is recognised as an expense. [IFRS 2:29]

These requirements are illustrated by the following example.

Example 4.5.2B

Replacement of share options

Company O issued options with a four-year vesting period to employees in 20X3. The options had an exercise price of CU10 per share and the aggregate

---

fair value of the options determined at the grant date was CU100,000. In 20X5, Company O cancelled those options and issued new options with an exercise price of CU3 per share.

The aggregate fair value of the new share options at the grant date is CU75,000, while the aggregate fair value of the cancelled options at that date is CU20,000.

If the new issue of options is considered a replacement of the cancelled options

Company O accounts for the transaction in the same way as for a modification. Therefore, Company O will continue to expense the portion of the CU100,000 not yet recognised over the original vesting period. Additionally, Company O will expense the incremental fair value of the new instruments over the old instruments determined at the date of modification (in this example, CU55,000 [CU75,000 – CU20,000]) over the remaining vesting period. Therefore, a total of CU155,000 is expensed related to these options.

If the new issue of options is not considered a replacement of the cancelled share options

The remaining portion of the original fair value of CU100,000 is expensed immediately and the fair value of the new issue is recognised over its vesting period. Therefore, a total of CU175,000 is expensed related to these options, much of the expense in earlier periods.

The following example considers the situation when the replacement options are issued by a different entity in a group.

Example 4.5.2C

Issue of new options as a replacement of cancelled options

Company S is a publicly listed subsidiary of Company P which is also publicly listed. Company P decides to de-list Company S by purchasing all of its outstanding shares from existing shareholders at an amount determined to be fair value. As part of the transaction, all outstanding share options in Company S are cancelled. In return, Company P issues share options in Company P to the same employees of Company S whose share options in Company S were cancelled. The fair value of the new share options determined at the grant date approximates the fair value of the replaced options determined at the cancellation date. In addition, the vesting terms and option lives of the new share options are adjusted to ensure consistency with the cancelled options.

In the circumstances described, even though the share options are in a different entity that has a different risk profile from Company S, the intention is to replace value held by the employees. Therefore, the transaction should be considered a replacement of equity instruments and accounted for in accordance with IFRS 2:28(c).

The following example considers the settlement in cash of a fully vested equity-settled share-based payment.

Example 4.5.2D

Settlement in cash of a fully vested equity-settled share-based payment

On 1 January 20X5, Company A issued 100 share options with an exercise price of CU15 per option to certain of its employees. The options vest if the employees remain employed by Company A for four years. The share options can only be settled by delivery of Company A's equity instruments and, therefore, they are classified as equity-settled share-based payments. At the grant date, the fair value of the instruments was determined to be CU5 per option.

As at 31 December 20X8, Company A had recognised a cumulative expense of CU500 [(CU5 × 100) × 4/4 years] because all options had vested. On that date, Company A decided to settle the fully vested equity-settled share-based payments in cash to the value of the share options (rather than settling by delivery of equity instruments). The fair value of the share options as at 31 December 20X8 is CU2,400. Therefore, Company A will pay the employees CU2,400 in cash.

In accordance with IFRS 2:29, a cash payment made to settle a fully vested equity-settled share-based payment should be accounted for as a repurchase of equity instruments. Accordingly, the payment made to the employees is accounted for as a deduction from equity, except to the extent that the payment exceeds the fair value of the instruments repurchased, measured at the repurchase date. Any such excess should be recognised as an additional remuneration expense.

Therefore, the cash settlement of CU2,400 is accounted for as a reduction in equity. If the payment made to the employees had been greater than CU2,400 (the fair value of the original awards at settlement date), Company A would have recognised the excess in profit or loss as an additional remuneration expense.

4.5.3   Changes to method of settlement of equity-settled transactions

IFRS 2 contains specific requirements for modifications to the terms and conditions on which equity instruments are granted (see above). It also deals with circumstances when there is choice between cash settlement and equity settlement (see **3.3** above).

4.5.3.1   Addition of a cash alternative

An entity may decide, during the vesting period for an equity-settled transaction, to add an employee option to choose a cash alternative. From the date of such a modification, the transaction should be accounted for as a compound instrument as outlined at **6.1** below. This approach is illustrated in the following example which is taken from the implementation guidance accompanying IFRS 2.

Example 4.5.3.1A

Grant of shares, with a cash alternative subsequently added

[Guidance on implementing IFRS 2:IG Example 9]

Background

At the beginning of year 1, the entity grants 10,000 shares with a fair value of CU33 per share to a senior executive, conditional upon the completion of three years' service. By the end of year 2, the share price has dropped to CU25 per share. At that date, the entity adds a cash alternative to the grant, whereby the executive can choose whether to receive 10,000 shares or cash equal to the value of 10,000 shares on vesting date. The share price is CU22 on vesting date.

Application of requirements

Paragraph 27 of the IFRS requires, irrespective of any modifications to the terms and conditions on which the equity instruments were granted, or a cancellation or settlement of that grant of equity instruments, the entity to recognise, as a minimum, the services received measured at the grant date fair value of the equity instruments granted, unless those equity instruments do not vest because of failure to satisfy a vesting condition (other than a market condition) that was specified at grant date. Therefore, the entity recognises the services received over the three-year period, based on the grant date fair value of the shares.

Furthermore, the addition of the cash alternative at the end of year 2 creates an obligation to settle in cash. In accordance with the requirements for cash-settled share-based payment transactions (paragraphs 30–33 of the IFRS), the entity recognises the liability to settle in cash at the modification date, based on the fair value of the shares at the modification date and the extent to which the specified services have been received. Furthermore, the entity remeasures the fair value of the liability at the end of each reporting

---

period and at the date of settlement, with any changes in fair value recognised in profit or loss for the period. Therefore, the entity recognises the following amounts:

Year	Calculation	Expense CU	Equity CU	Liability CU
1	Remuneration expense for year: 10,000 shares × CU33 × 1/3	110,000	110,000	
2	Remuneration expense for year: (10,000 shares × CU33 × 2/3) – CU110,000	110,000	110,000	
	Reclassify equity to liabilities: 10,000 shares × CU25 × 2/3		(166,667)	166,667
3	Remuneration expense for year: (10,000 shares × CU33 × 3/3) – CU220,000	110,000	26,667*	83,333*
	Adjust liability to closing fair value: (CU166,667 + CU83,333) – (CU22 × 10,000 shares)	(30,000)		(30,000)
	Total	300,000	80,000	220,000

*   Allocated between liabilities and equity, to bring in the final third of the liability based on the fair value of the shares as at the date of the modification.

The following example is based on similar facts to the one above but assumes that the share price has increased rather than decreased by the end of Year 2.

Example 4.5.3.1B

Equity-settled share-based payment when a cash alternative is subsequently offered

At the beginning of Year 1, an entity grants 10,000 shares with a fair value of CU33 per share to a senior executive, conditional on the completion of three years of service. By the end of Year 2, the share price has increased to CU50 per share. At that date, the entity adds a cash alternative to the grant, whereby the executive can choose whether to receive 10,000 shares, or take the cash equivalent to the value of the 10,000 shares on the vesting date. This cash alternative has the same value as the shares. The share price decreased to CU45 at the end of Year 3.

IFRS 2:27 requires an entity to "recognise, as a minimum, services received measured at the grant date fair value of the equity instruments granted, unless those equity instruments do not vest because of failure to satisfy a vesting condition (other than a market condition) that was specified at grant date". In addition, the entity must recognise in profit or loss the effects of modifications that increase the total fair value of the share-based payment arrangement.

Because the modification to the share-based payment to add a cash alternative does not increase the total fair value of the share-based payment arrangement at the date of the modification, the entity continues to recognise an IFRS 2 expense for the services received during the three-year period, based on the grant date fair value of the shares.

However, the addition of the cash alternative at the end of Year 2 creates an obligation to settle in cash. In accordance with the requirements for cash-settled share-based payment transactions (IFRS 2:30 to 33), the entity recognises the liability to settle in cash at the modification date. In a manner consistent with **example 4.5.3.1A** above, the liability is measured at the value of the shares on the date of modification, pro-rated for the effect of the service vesting condition. This effect of the modification is recognised in equity and not in profit or loss. Thereafter, the cost of the original equity grant is recognised in profit or loss. The increase in the liability for the remaining service period, which is based on the modification-date value, is recognised in equity. Subsequent remeasurement of the liability to fair value at each reporting date and at the date of settlement is recognised in profit or loss.

Year	Calculation	Expense CU	Equity CU	Liability CU
1	Remuneration expense for year: 10,000 shares × CU33 × 1/3	110,000	110,000	
2	Remuneration expense for year: (10,000 shares × CU33 × 2/3) – CU110,000	110,000	110,000	
	Reclassify equity to liabilities: 10,000 shares × CU50 × 2/3		(333,333)	333,333
3	Remuneration expense for year: (10,000 shares × CU33 × 3/3) – CU220,000	110,000	110,000	
	Final third of liability at modification value: (10,000 shares × CU50 × 3/3) – CU333,333		(166,667)	166,667
	Remeasurement of liability: (10,000 shares × CU45 ×3/3) – CU500,000	(50,000)		(50,000)
	Total	280,000	(170,000)	450,000

In the entry in Year 2, therefore, the value of the cash modification is recognised in equity and not in profit or loss. In Year 3, the cost of the original equity grant is recognised in profit or loss, along with the remeasurement in the liability value to CU450,000 at the end of the year. The remaining unvested portion of the fair value of the liability at the modification date, which is CU166,667 [(10,000 shares × CU50 × 3/3) – CU333,333], is recognised in equity.

4.5.3.2 Change from equity-settled to cash-settled

The following example considers a change in the terms whereby options that were originally to be equity-settled will be cash-settled.

Example 4.5.3.2

Modification from an equity-settled to a cash-settled share-based payment arrangement during the vesting period

On 1 January 20X3, Company A issued 100 share options to certain employees, with a strike price of CU15 per option. The options vest if the employees remain in Company A's employment after four years. The share options can only be settled by delivery of Company A's equity instruments and, therefore, they are classified as equity-settled share-based payments. Company A determined the fair value of the instruments to be CU5 per option.

At 31 December 20X4, Company A had recognised a cumulative expense of CU250 [(CU5 × 100) × 2/4 years], because it expected all of the options to vest. On 1 January 20X5, Company A modified the options so that they could only be settled in cash. Therefore, upon settlement, Company A will pay the employees in cash the amount equal to the intrinsic value on the settlement date. On the date of modification, the fair value of each share option is determined to be CU8.

IFRS 2:B43, which contains guidance on the application of IFRS 2:27, states, in part, that "if the modification increases the fair value of the equity instruments granted ..., measured immediately before and after the modification, the entity shall include the incremental fair value granted in the measurement of the amount recognised for services received as consideration for the equity instruments granted". IFRS 2:B43 further clarifies that the "incremental fair value granted is the difference between the fair value of the modified equity instrument and that of the original equity instrument, both estimated as at the date of the modification".

Therefore, the fair value of the share options is reclassified from equity to liability to the extent to which specified services have been received, i.e. CU400 (CU800 × 2/4) as follows.

		CU	CU
Dr	Equity	400	
Cr	Liability		400

To recognise the reclassification from equity to liability.

This results in a cumulative debit within equity of CU150, comprising the debit of CU400 arising on the modification less the credit of CU250 which arose under the equity-settled arrangements prior to the modification date (IFRS 2:BC267 and BC268).

5   Recognition and measurement: cash-settled transactions

This section discusses the appropriate accounting for cash-settled share-based payment transactions in the following sections.

Section 5.1   Recognition of cash-settled transactions

Section 5.2   Measurement of cash-settled transactions

Section 5.3   Vesting conditions

Section 5.4   Modifications to cash-settled share-based payments

5.1   Recognition of cash-settled transactions

As indicated in **2.1** above, IFRS 2 applies to transactions in which the entity acquires goods or services by incurring a liability to transfer cash or other assets for amounts based on the price (or value) of the shares or other equity instruments of the entity or of another group entity.

> The most common examples of such arrangements are cash-settled Share Appreciation Rights (SARs) which are also sometimes referred to as 'phantom option schemes' (see **2.1**).

For cash-settled share-based payment transactions, the goods or services acquired and the liability incurred are measured at the fair value of the liability. Until the liability is settled, the liability is remeasured at fair value at the end of each reporting period (and the settlement date). Any changes in fair value are recognised in profit or loss for the period. [IFRS 2:30]

IFRS 2 uses the term 'fair value' in a way that differs in some respects from the definition of fair value in IFRS 13 *Fair Value Measurement*. When applying IFRS 2, an entity should measure fair value in accordance with the guidance in IFRS 2, not IFRS 13. [IFRS 2:6A]

The effect of vesting conditions on the fair value measurement is discussed at **5.3** below.

> For cash-settled share-based payment transactions, under IFRS 2:30, the goods or services acquired and the liability incurred are measured at the fair value of the liability. Until the liability is settled, the liability is remeasured at fair value at the end of each reporting period (and at the settlement date) and any changes in fair value are recognised in profit or loss for the period.
>
> However, if the amount recognised for the goods or services received was capitalised as part of the carrying amount of an asset recognised in the entity's statement of financial position, the carrying amount of that asset can be adjusted for the effects of the liability remeasurement during the period that is the shorter of:
>
> - the period during which costs are eligible for capitalisation in accordance with whichever Standard is applicable to the asset in question (e.g. IAS 2 for inventories, IAS 16 for property, plant and equipment etc.); and

- the vesting period.

Subsequent to the capitalisation period, the carrying amount of that asset is not adjusted for any further remeasurement of the liability and any subsequent changes in the fair value of the liability are recognised in profit or loss.

The services received and the liability to pay for those services are recognised as the employees render service. For example, some SARs vest immediately and the employees are not, therefore, required to complete a specified period of service to become entitled to the cash payment. In the absence of evidence to the contrary, it should be presumed that the services rendered by the employees in exchange for the SARs have been received. In this case, the expense for the services received and the liability to pay for them should be recognised immediately. But if the rights do not vest until the employees have completed a specified period of service, the services received and the liability to pay for them should be recognised as the employees render service during the period. [IFRS 2:32]

5.1.1   Presentation of liability

The following example considers the presentation and disclosure of the liability for cash-settled SARs.

Example 5.1.1

Presentation of SARs in the statement of financial position

Company C issues 12 cash-settled share appreciation rights (SARs) to certain of its employees. The SARs vest over a three-year period. At the end of the vesting period, Company C expects that three of the SARs will be exercised within one year and the remaining nine SARs will be exercised after one year.

Company C should consider whether the liability should be presented separately in the statement of financial position, and whether it should be presented as current or non-current.

IFRS 2 does not require separate presentation of the carrying amount of liabilities relating to share-based payments in the statement of financial position, but requires this information to be disclosed in the financial statements. Liabilities arising from share-based payments are financial liabilities, although they are excluded from the scope of IAS 32 *Financial Instruments: Presentation* and IAS 39 *Financial Instruments: Recognition and Measurement*.

Therefore, an entity should consider whether share-based payment liabilities should be grouped with other financial liabilities in the statement of financial position. IAS 1:29 requires each material class of similar items to be presented separately in the financial statements. Items of a dissimilar nature or function are presented separately unless they are immaterial. IAS 1:30 explains that if a line item is not individually material, it is aggregated with other items either on the face of the financial statements or in the notes. Share-based payment liabilities are likely to be different from other financial liabilities in nature and function.

IAS 1:60 requires separate presentation in the statement of financial position for current and non-current liabilities. Based on the above facts, because all of the SARs can be exercised within the next year, these liabilities should be presented as current liabilities in Year 3. If Company C determines that presentation on a liquidity basis is more relevant, the current portion of the liability should be disclosed in accordance with IAS 1:61.

5.2 Measurement of cash-settled transactions

The liability is measured, initially and at the end of each reporting period until settled, at the fair value of the SARs by applying an option pricing model, taking into account the terms and conditions upon which the rights were granted and the extent to which the employees have rendered service to date. The use of option pricing models is considered in **section 4.4**.

A simpler approach would have been to base the liability on the intrinsic value of the SARs at the end of the reporting period (i.e. the difference between the fair value of the shares and the exercise price, if any). It can be argued that the additional cost and effort of using an option pricing model is not justified given that the cumulative expense is always trued up to the actual cash payment. However, the IASB rejected this approach and concluded that measuring SARs at intrinsic value would be inconsistent with the fair value measurement basis applied in the rest of the IFRS.

The following example, which is taken from the implementation guidance accompanying IFRS 2, illustrates the application of these requirements.

Example 5.2

Cash-settled share appreciation rights

[Guidance on implementing IFRS 2:IG Example 12]

Background

An entity grants 100 cash share appreciation rights (SARs) to each of its 500 employees, on condition that the employees remain in its employ for the next three years.

During year 1, 35 employees leave. The entity estimates that a further 60 will leave during years 2 and 3. During year 2, 40 employees leave and the entity estimates that a further 25 will leave during year 3. During year 3, 22 employees leave. At the end of year 3, 150 employees exercise their SARs, another 140 employees exercise their SARs at the end of year 4 and the remaining 113 employees exercise their SARs at the end of year 5.

The entity estimates the fair value of the SARs at the end of each year in which a liability exists as shown below. At the end of year 3, all SARs held by the remaining employees vest. The intrinsic values of the SARs at the date of exercise (which equal the cash paid out) at the end of years 3, 4 and 5 are also shown below.

Year	Fair value	Intrinsic value
1	CU14.40	
2	CU15.50	
3	CU18.20	CU15.00
4	CU21.40	CU20.00
5		CU25.00

Application of requirements

Year	Calculation	Expense CU	Liability CU
1	(500 – 95) employees × 100 SARs × CU14.40 × 1/3	194,400	194,400
2	(500 – 100) employees × 100 SARs × CU15.50 × 2/3 – CU194,400	218,933	413,333
3	(500 – 97 – 150) employees × 100 SARs × CU18.20 – CU413,333	47,127	460,460
	+ 150 employees × 100 SARs × CU15.00	225,000	
	Total	272,127	
4	(253 – 140) employees × 100 SARs × CU21.40 – CU460,460	(218,640)	241,820
	+ 140 employees × 100 SARs × CU20.00	280,000	
	Total	61,360	
5	CU0 – CU241,820	(241,820)	0
	+ 113 employees × 100 SARs × CU25.00	282,500	
	Total	40,680	
	Total	787,500	

Note that remeasurement of the liability is not recognised as one amount immediately. Instead this amount is spread over the remaining vesting period of the liability.

5.2.1 Share price denominated in a foreign currency

Example 5.2.1

Cash-settled share-based payment arrangement with share price and option exercise price denominated in a foreign currency

Company E is a UK entity with Sterling as its functional currency. Company E is registered on the New York Stock Exchange with a current market price of US$15 per share. Company E issues 100 options to its employees with an exercise price of US$15 per share and a vesting period of three years. The share options can only be cash settled.

For cash-settled share options, the liability recognised would be considered a US dollar denominated liability and would need to be remeasured at the end of each reporting period (the remeasurement would include the effect of changes in the foreign exchange rate).

This issue is considered at **4.2.6** in relation to equity-settled share-based payments.

5.3   Vesting conditions

An issue that arises is whether vesting conditions should be considered in determining the fair value of cash-settled share-based payments. The requirements of IFRS 2 are not clear in this regard.

IFRS 2:30 requires that the liability incurred from a cash-settled share-based payment transaction should be measured at the fair value of the liability. There is no discussion in IFRS 2 regarding whether the fair value of the liability for a cash-settled share-based payment should include the effects of vesting conditions.

The definition of fair value is "[t]he amount for which an asset could be exchanged, a liability settled, or an equity instrument granted could be exchanged, between knowledgeable, willing parties in an arm's length transaction". [IFRS 2:Appendix A] From this perspective, the fair value measurement should include all terms and conditions, including all vesting conditions.

However, non-market vesting conditions are excluded from the grant date fair value of equity-settled share-based payments because the 'true up' model is applied to those transactions. As noted in IFRS 2:19, the exclusion of non-market vesting conditions from the measurement of equity-settled share-based payments has the effect of creating a measurement that is not a true fair value measurement. Similar statements are not made regarding the measurement of cash-settled share-based payments.

Example 5.2 above (which is taken from the implementation guidance accompanying IFRS 2) provides an illustration of the accounting for one form of cash-settled share-based payments (share appreciate rights, or SARs). In this illustration, employees must remain in the entity's employment for the next three years for their SARs to vest. The illustration does not include the effects of this vesting condition in determining the fair value of the SARs at the end of each reporting period, but bases the total liability on the best estimate of the number of SARs that will vest.

While **example 5.2** excludes one type of non-market vesting condition (remaining in the employment of an entity for a specified period of time), it is not clear whether the implication of this exclusion should extend to other non-market vesting conditions, such as achieving a target revenue.

Given the lack of clarity regarding how vesting conditions should be reflected in the fair value measurement, it appears that there are two acceptable approaches; an entity should measure the liability arising from a cash-settled share-based payment on one of the following bases:

- at true fair value (i.e. the fair value measurement of the liability reflects all vesting and non-vesting conditions, including service and non-market performance conditions); or

- by analogy to the measurement of equity-settled share-based payments (i.e. the fair value measurement of the liability reflects market and non-vesting conditions only. Service and non-market performance conditions are taken into account by adjusting the number of rights to receive cash that are expected to vest).

An entity should choose one of the two approaches as an accounting policy and apply this policy consistently. Whichever approach is adopted, until the liability is settled, an entity should remeasure the fair value of the liability at the end of each reporting period and at the date of settlement with any changes in fair value recognised in profit or loss for that period.

5.4   Modifications to cash-settled share-based payments

IFRS 2 does not make specific reference to the treatment of modifications to cash-settled share-based payment arrangements.

5.4.1   Modifications, cancellations and settlements

A modification of a cash-settled share-based payment transaction such as a share appreciation right (SAR) is accounted for as the exchange of the original award for a new award. However, because cash-settled share-based payment transactions are remeasured based on their fair value at each reporting date, no special guidance is necessary in accounting for a modification of a cash-settled award that remains a cash-settled award after the modification. The requirements of IFRS 2:33 apply to the measurement of cash-settled share-based payment transactions (i.e. the liability is measured at the fair value of the SARs multiplied by the proportion of the vesting period which has been completed). Any increase or decrease in the value of the liability would be recognised immediately in profit or loss or, when the relevant criteria are met, included in the cost of an asset (e.g. when a payment to employees relates to the construction of property, plant and equipment). The application of this treatment to two possible modifications of SARs is illustrated in **examples 5.4.1A** and **5.4.1B** below.

Example 5.4.1A

Reduction of the vesting period of a cash-settled share-based payment transaction

100 cash-settled SARs are granted on 1 January 20X0 with a fair value of CU10 each. The terms of the award require the employee to provide service for four years in order to earn the award. At the end of the second year of service (20X1), the employer modifies the terms of the award to require only three years of service from the employee to earn the award. The fair value of each SAR at each reporting date is as follows:

31 December 20X0	CU12
31 December 20X1	CU20
31 December 20X2	CU15

The following journal entries reflect the accounting for the award at each period end (assuming there are no expected forfeitures).

At 31 December 20X0

		CU	CU
Dr	Profit or loss [CU12 × 100 awards × 1 year/4 years of service required]	300	
Cr	Liability		300

To recognise the share-based payment expense and associated liability.

At 31 December 20X1

		CU	CU
Dr	Profit or loss [(CU20 × 100 awards × 2 years/3 years of service required) = CU1,333 − CU300 previously recognised]	1,033	
Cr	Liability		1,033

To recognise the share-based payment expense and remeasurement of associated liability.

At 31 December 20X2

		CU	CU
Dr	Profit or loss [(CU15 × 100 awards × 3 years/3 years of service required) = CU1,500 − CU1,333 previously recognised]	167	
Cr	Liability		167

To recognise the share-based payment expense and remeasurement of associated liability.

Example 5.4.1B

Cancellation of a cash-settled share-based payment transaction

100 cash-settled SARs are granted on 1 January 20X0 with a fair value of CU10 each. The terms of the award require the employee to provide service for four years in order to earn the award. At the end of the second year of service (20X1), the employer cancels the award without issuing any replacement award or cash. The fair value of each SAR at each reporting date is as follows.

31 December 20X0	CU12
31 December 20X1	CU5

The following journal entries reflect the accounting for the award at each period end (assuming there are no expected forfeitures).

At 31 December 20X0

		CU	CU
Dr	Profit or loss [CU12 × 100 awards × 1 year/4 years of service required]	300	
Cr	Liability		300

To recognise the share-based payment expense and associated liability.

At 31 December 20X1

		CU	CU
Dr	Liability	300	
Cr	Profit or loss		300

To recognise the reversal of the share-based payment expense and associated liability.

Because, in this example, the award is cancelled without issuing anything in return, the value of the liability at 31 December 20X1 should be adjusted to CUnil. Therefore, all prior share-based payment expense recognised should be reversed.

5.4.2   Changes to methods of settlement of cash-settled transactions

IFRS 2 does not specify how to account for a modification of a share-based payment arrangement from cash-settled to equity-settled; the guidance in IFRS 2 deals only with modifications to the terms and conditions of equity-settlement arrangements.

The principles of IFRS 2 are generally consistent with those of US GAAP, namely FASB Accounting Standards Codification (ASC) Topic 718, *Stock Compensation* (previously SFAS 123R *Share-based Payment*). In particular, modifications to the terms and conditions of equity-settled share-based payments are generally treated consistently under IFRS 2 and ASC 718. ASC 718 also specifies how to account for a modification to a share-based payment arrangement that results in a change in its classification from being cash-settled to equity-settled, and it is appropriate for such modifications to be accounted for in the same way under IFRS 2.

The guidance in ASC 718 requires the existing cash-settled liability to be reclassified to equity at the date of modification. The cash-settled share-based payment expense recognised up to the date of modification is not adjusted and the expense recognised from the date of modification over the remainder of the vesting period is determined based on the fair value of the reclassified equity award at the date of the modification. In other words, the modification is accounted for as if the liability existing at the date of modification is effectively settled with an equity award with the same fair value.

Example 5.4.2

Modification from cash-settled to equity-settled

On 1 January 20X3, Company A issues 100 share options to some of its employees with a strike price of CU15 per option. The share options vest if the employee remains in Company A's employment after four years. The share options can only be cash-settled. Company A has determined that the fair value of the instruments at the date of grant is CU5 per option.

At 31 December 20X4, the fair value of the cash-settled share-based payment is CU6 per option. To date, Company A has recognised a cumulative share-based payment expense of CU300 [(CU6 × 100) × 2/4 years] because Company A expects all of the options to vest. On 1 January 20X5, Company A modifies the options such that they can only be settled by delivery of Company A's equity instruments (one share option entitles the employee to one ordinary share of Company A, and there is no change to the strike price of CU15). No other terms or vesting conditions of the share-based payment arrangement are amended.

Applying the requirements of ASC 718, at the date of modification (1 January 20X5), Company A is required to derecognise the existing cash-settled liability because the liability has effectively been settled by the issue of an equity instrument. The existing cash-settled liability is, therefore, reclassified to equity. The cash-settled compensation cost recognised to date is not adjusted, except for subsequent 'true up' if vesting conditions are not met. The compensation cost to be recognised over the remaining vesting period is based on the fair value of the equity instrument at the time of the modification. Therefore, the cumulative compensation cost recognised for the share-based payment arrangement will reflect fair value for the equity award at 1 January 20X5.

In this example, the fair value at modification is CU6 per option. The cost to be recognised in each of 20X5 and 20X6 (Years 3 and 4 of the award), provided that all awards vest, will be CU150:

20X5: [(CU6 × 100) × 3/4 years] – CU 300   CU150
20X6: [(CU6 × 100) × 4/4 years] – CU 450   CU150

5.4.3   Repricing of cash-settled transactions

Example 5.4.3

Repricing of cash-settled transactions

Company T issues cash-settled share appreciation rights (SARs) to employees with a fair value of CU100 on 1 January 20X6. The SARs vest over a period of four years. At 31 December 20X6, the fair value of the SARs is CU120 and, therefore, Company T has a liability of CU30 [CU120 × 1/4]. On 1 January 20X7, Company T reprices the SARs so that the fair value of the award is now CU280. The modification affects no other terms or conditions of the SARs, and does not change the number of SARs expected to vest.

The repricing increases the value of the SARs and, therefore, the incremental value should be recognised over the vesting period. Because one quarter of the vesting period is complete, the liability should be increased to CU70 — requiring the immediate recognition of CU40 [(CU280 × 1/4) – CU30] of remuneration expense. Therefore, if the fair value did not change in the

> remaining three years, CU70 [(CU280 – CU70) × 1/3)] would be recognised in profit or loss in each of the remaining three years.

6 Recognition and measurement: transactions with settlement alternatives

For share-based payment transactions in which the terms of the arrangement provide either the entity or the counterparty with the choice of whether the entity settles the transaction in cash (or other assets) or by issuing equity instruments, the transaction, or the components of that transaction, are accounted for:
[IFRS 2:34]

- as a cash-settled share-based payment transaction if, and to the extent that, the entity has incurred a liability to settle in cash or other assets; or

- as an equity-settled share-based payment transaction if, and to the extent that, no such liability has been incurred.

IFRS 2 contains more detailed requirements concerning how to apply this principle to share-based payment transactions in which the terms of the arrangement:

- provide the counterparty with a choice of settlement (see **6.1** below); and

- provide the entity with a choice of settlement (see **6.2** below).

Contingent cash settlement provisions are considered at **6.3**. Circumstances when there is a modification to the terms of settlement are considered at **4.5.3** (for modification of an arrangement that has been accounted for as an equity-settled share-based payment transaction) and **5.4.2** (for modification of an arrangement that has been accounted for as a cash-settled share-based payment transaction).

References to cash, in the remainder of this section, also include other assets.

6.1 Counterparty's choice

If the counterparty has the choice as to whether an entity settles a share-based payment transaction in cash or with equity instruments, the entity has granted a compound financial instrument, similar to convertible debt. The instrument has:

- a debt component – the counterparty's right to demand cash; and

- an equity component – the counterparty's option to receive equity instruments rather than cash.

Each component is accounted for separately, in a manner similar to the equivalent requirements of IAS 32 *Financial Instruments: Presentation*, as described below.

The following example illustrates the need to consider the substance of the arrangement when the cash alternative is provided through a separate agreement.

Example 6.1

Counterparty choice in settlement of a share-based payment

Company A grants share options to its employees that vest over a three-year period. These share options can only be settled by the issue of Company A's shares at the end of the vesting period. In a separate legal agreement entered into at the same time as the grant of the share options, Company A issues a put option to its employees that can (at the option of the employee) require Company A to settle the share options in cash, based on the intrinsic value of the options at the settlement date. The put option is only exercisable between the vesting date and the expiration of the options.

The two contracts (share options and written put option) should be linked and the transaction accounted for as a share-based payment with a cash alternative.

The substance of this arrangement is the issue of an equity instrument to employees with a cash alternative. Therefore, the accounting should be the same whether the transaction is consummated through one or more contracts. As a result, Company A should measure the liability component at fair value first, and then measure the equity component at fair value, taking into account the fact that the employee must forfeit the right to receive cash in order to receive the equity instrument (see IFRS 2:37). Because the fair value of the equity component in this example would be nil (see **6.1.1** below), the transaction is accounted for in the same way as a cash-settled share-based payment up to the date of exercise.

6.1.1   Measurement

For transactions with parties other than employees, the fair value of goods or services is measured directly (if that is possible with sufficient reliability – see **4.2.1** and **4.4.8** above). For such transactions, the equity component is measured as the difference between the fair value of the goods or services received and the fair value of the debt component, at the date when goods or services are received. [IFRS 2:35] This is the basic approach that is adopted for compound instruments that are accounted for under IAS 32 (see **section 3** of **chapter B3** or, for entities that have not yet adopted IFRS 9 *Financial Instruments*, **section 3** of **chapter C3**).

For other transactions, including those with employees, the fair value of the compound financial instrument is measured at the measurement date, taking into account the terms and conditions on which the rights to cash or equity instruments were granted. [IFRS 2:36] To do this, the debt component is measured first and then the equity component is measured. The fact that the counterparty must forfeit the right to receive cash to receive the equity instrument should be taken into account. The fair value of the compound financial instrument is the sum of the fair values of the two components. [IFRS 2:37]

Under IAS 32:32, the carrying amount of the equity instruments is determined by deducting the fair value of the financial liability from the fair value of the compound financial instrument as a whole. This is straightforward when the fair value of the combined instrument is reliably known (e.g. when it is the proceeds of an issue for cash). However, IFRS 2:BC260 explains that, when this is not the case, it will be necessary to estimate the fair value of the compound instrument itself. The IASB therefore concluded, as stated above, that the compound instrument should be measured first by valuing the liability component (i.e. the cash alternative) and then valuing the equity component and adding the two components together.

Entities will often structure share-based payment transactions in which the counterparty has the choice of settlement in such a way that the fair value of one settlement alternative is the same as the other. For example, the counterparty might have the choice of receiving share options or cash-settled share appreciation rights. In such cases, the fair value of the equity component is zero and, consequently, the fair value of the compound financial instrument is the same as the fair value of the debt component. [IFRS 2:37]

IFRS 2 notes that, conversely, if the fair values of the settlement alternatives differ, the fair value of the equity component will usually be greater than zero. In such circumstances, the fair value of the compound financial instrument will be greater than the fair value of the debt component.

IFRS 2:BC259 explains that the fair value of the compound financial instrument will usually exceed both:

- the individual fair value of the cash alternative – because of the possibility that the shares or share options may be more valuable than the cash alternative; and

- that of the shares or options – because of the possibility that the cash alternative may be more valuable than the shares or options.

But, as explained above, in many practical situations the fair value of the settlement alternatives will be the same and there will be no equity component.

Example 6.1.1

Share-based payment with settlement alternatives – measurement and recognition

On 1 January 20X1, an entity enters into an agreement with 10 employees whereby the employees receive a bonus payment of CU300 if they complete a 3-year service period.

On completion of the 3-year service period, the employees can choose between the following settlement alternatives:

- Alternative A – receive the full amount of CU300 in cash; or

- Alternative B – receive CU150 in cash and the remaining 50 per cent of the reward in the form of shares that are, on 31 December 20X3, worth CU150 (say 500 shares).

Employees that opt for settlement Alternative B will, in addition to the original 500 shares, receive a further 500 shares (i.e. 'matching shares') upon completion of an additional 2-year service period (i.e. they have to be employed until 31 December 20X5). Employees that leave employment during the additional 2-year service period forfeit the matching shares and the original 500 shares awarded (i.e. they lose the first award even if the initial 3-year service period was completed).

The award can be summarised as follows:

- cash of CU300 at the end of Year 3; or

- cash of CU150 at the end of Year 3, plus shares worth CU300 as at 31 December 20X3 (original award of shares worth CU150 plus the matching shares worth CU150) with all shares subject to remaining in employment until the end of Year 5.

In accordance with IFRS 2:35, an entity that has granted a counterparty the right to choose whether a share-based payment transaction is settled in cash or by issuing equity instruments has granted a compound financial instrument which includes a debt component (the right to demand settlement in cash) and an equity component (the right to demand settlement in equity instruments).

The fair value of the compound financial instrument is measured at the grant date (1 January 20X1) taking into account the terms and conditions under which the rights to cash or equity instruments are granted. To arrive at this measurement, the fair value of the debt component should be measured first and then the fair value of the equity component should be measured, adjusting for the fact that the counterparty must forfeit the right to receive cash to receive the equity instrument. The fair value of the compound instrument is the sum of the fair values of the two components. [IFRS 2:37]

In this example, it is assumed for simplicity that the fair value of the debt component is CU300 and the fair value of the equity component is CU150.

In the three years to 31 December 20X3, expenses of CU300 and CU90 (CU150 × 3/5) are recognised on the debt and equity components, respectively.

If the employees choose Alternative B (i.e. they take settlement of part of the share-based arrangement in shares at 31 December 20X3), the portion of the liability settled in shares at that date (CU150) will be reclassified to equity.

If the employees opt for Alternative A (i.e. cash settlement at 31 December 20X3), the scheme has vested and the total grant date fair value of the compound financial instrument should, therefore, be recognised. As a result, the unrecognised portion of the equity component (CU150 × 2/5 = CU60) will be recognised as a share-based payment expense at 31 December 20X3.

6.1.2   Subsequent accounting

Once the debt and equity components have been separately identified and measured, the goods or services received in respect of each component are accounted for separately. For the debt component, the goods or services received, and a corresponding liability, are recognised in accordance with the requirements applying to cash-settled transactions (see **section 5**). For the equity component, if any, the goods or services received are recognised as the counterparty supplies goods or renders services in accordance with the requirements for equity-settled transactions (see **section 4**). [IFRS 2:38]

At the date of settlement, the liability is remeasured at its fair value. If equity instruments are issued in settlement rather than cash, the liability is transferred direct to equity as the consideration for the equity instruments issued. [IFRS 2:39]

If settlement is in cash rather than equity instruments, the payment made is applied to settle the liability in full. Any equity component previously recognised remains in equity. By electing to receive cash settlement, the counterparty forfeited the right to receive equity instruments. But this does not preclude a transfer from one component of equity to another. [IFRS 2:40]

The application of these requirements is illustrated by the following example which is taken from the implementation guidance accompanying IFRS 2. It illustrates the circumstances in which the cash alternative is less favourable than the equity-settled alternative and so the equity component is not zero.

Example 6.1.2

Subsequent accounting when counter-party has choice of settlement

[Guidance on implementing IFRS 2:IG Example 13]

Background

An entity grants to an employee the right to choose either 1,000 phantom shares (i.e. a right to a cash payment equal to the value of 1,000 shares) or 1,200 shares. The grant is conditional upon the completion of three years' service. If the employee chooses the share alternative, the shares must be held for three years after vesting date.

At grant date, the entity's share price is CU50 per share. At the end of years 1, 2 and 3, the share price is CU52, CU55 and CU60, respectively. The entity does not expect to pay dividends in the next three years. After taking into account the effects of the post-vesting transfer restrictions, the entity estimates that the grant date fair value of the share alternative is CU48 per share.

At the end of year 3, the employee chooses:

Scenario 1: The cash alternative

Scenario 2: The equity alternative

Application of requirements

The fair value of the equity alternative is CU57,600 (1,200 shares × CU48). The fair value of the cash alternative is CU50,000 (1,000 phantom shares × CU50). Therefore, the fair value of the equity component of the compound instrument is CU7,600 (CU57,600 − CU50,000).

The entity recognises the following amounts:

Year		Expense CU	Equity CU	Liability CU
1	Liability component: (1,000 × CU52 × 1/3)	17,333		**17,333**
	Equity component: (CU7,600 × 1/3)	2,533	2,533	
2	Liability component: (1,000 × CU55 × 2/3) – CU17,333	19,333		19,333
	Equity component: (CU7,600 × 1/3)	2,533	2,533	
3	Liability component: (1,000 × CU60) – CU36,666	23,334		23,334
	Equity component: (CU7,600 × 1/3)	2,534	2,534	
End Year 3	Scenario 1: cash of CU60,000 paid			(60,000)
	Scenario 1 totals	67,600	7,600	0
	Scenario 2: 1,200 shares issued		60,000	(60,000)
	Scenario 2 totals	67,600	67,600	0

6.2   Entity's choice

The terms of a share-based payment transaction may provide an entity with the choice as to whether to settle in cash or by issuing equity instruments. In this case, it is necessary to determine whether the entity has a present obligation to settle in cash and to account for the transaction accordingly. IFRS 2 states that the entity has a present obligation to settle in cash if:
[IFRS 2:41]

- the choice of settlement in equity instruments has no commercial substance, for example because the entity is legally prohibited from issuing shares; or

- the entity has a past practice or stated policy of settling in cash; or

- the entity generally settles in cash whenever the counterparty asks for cash settlement.

When the entity has a present obligation to settle in cash, the transaction is accounted for as a cash-settled transaction (see **section 5**). [IFRS 2:42]

If no such obligation exists, the transaction is accounted for in accordance with IFRS 2's requirements for equity-settled transactions (see **section 4**).

The application of these classification requirements is illustrated in the following example.

Example 6.2

Classification of an employee share option plan in which the entity has the choice of settlement

Company A, a listed entity, grants its employees options to acquire ordinary shares in Company A. Company A's shares trade in an active market. The exercise of the options is conditional upon the achievement of certain performance conditions during the vesting period. In addition, the holders of the options have to be employed within the group headed by Company A or can be retired, if they retire at the normal retirement age.

Employees can exercise the options over a period of 5 years. Following the exercise of an option, the employee is required to sell the shares obtained immediately. Company A has first right to purchase these shares at a price equal to the market price at the moment employees exercise the underlying options. If Company A chooses not to purchase the shares, there are no constraints on how the employees dispose of the shares, or to whom. There is no enforcement mechanism by Company A.

Company A has the legal right to buy its own shares in the market, and has sufficient authorised capital to issue new shares to deliver the required number of shares to the employees upon exercise.

The share option scheme is a new arrangement, and there have been no other arrangements in the past when the entity has had a choice of cash or equity settlement; therefore, there is no evidence regarding past practice of settlement in cash. The share option scheme has been approved by the shareholders without objection, and no indication was provided as to what course of action Company A would take when the exercise date is reached (i.e. whether Company A would seek to acquire the shares based on its pre-emptive right or choose not to do so).

Company A represents that it will act in its own interest every time it has the right to buy back shares, and that it does not believe any situation exists which would force it to buy back the shares given to the employees under the scheme.

Under applicable regulatory rules, employees cannot exercise their rights during a 'closed period'. Therefore, employees will not be able to sell shares in a closed period.

When employees exercise the options granted by Company A, they are obliged to sell the shares on the date of exercise. Company A has first right to purchase these shares. In substance, this right to repurchase shares immediately gives Company A an option to settle the share-based payment transaction in cash. Therefore, IFRS 2:41 to 43 apply.

IFRS 2:41 requires an entity that has a choice of settlement to determine whether it has a present obligation to settle the share-based payment transaction in cash. The entity has a present obligation to settle in cash if the choice of settlement in equity instruments has no commercial substance (e.g. because the entity is legally prohibited from issuing shares), or the entity has a past practice or a stated policy of settling in cash, or generally settles in cash whenever the counterparty asks for cash settlement.

If an entity with a choice of settlement has no present obligation to settle the transaction in cash, IFRS 2:43 requires that "the entity shall account for the transaction in accordance with the requirements applying to equity-settled share-based payment transactions, in paragraphs 10 – 29".

The management of Company A considers all relevant facts and circumstances to determine whether there are any factors that could create an obligation to deliver cash and concludes that there are no situations in which the entity would have a legal obligation, or has created a constructive obligation, to repurchase the shares and thereby deliver cash.

In particular:

- there is an active market in which the shares could be sold;

- from a legal perspective, Company A has sufficient authorised share capital in order to be able to issue new shares;

- current shareholders raised no objection to the scheme in the general shareholders' meeting and the entity did not raise an expectation of a particular action;

- no restrictions on trading in a closed period apply as exercise is prohibited in this period; and

- there is no stated policy or constructive obligation created by past practice.

Therefore, this scheme should be accounted for as an equity-settled share-based payment arrangement.

However, it remains the responsibility of management to consider all facts and circumstances affecting the entity to determine whether there are any other circumstances in which the company would have an obligation to repurchase the shares, resulting in a different conclusion.

On settlement of an arrangement that is accounted for as equity-settled (i.e. because there is no obligation to settle in cash): [IFRS 2:43]

- if the entity elects to settle in cash, the cash payment is accounted for as the repurchase of an equity interest. It is, therefore, treated as a deduction from equity except as described below; and

- if the entity elects to settle by issuing equity instruments, no further accounting is required except as noted below and except for a transfer from one component of equity to another component of equity, if necessary.

> These requirements are not consistent with the requirements of IAS 32 for other circumstances in which the entity has a choice of settlement. IAS 32 requires such arrangements to be classified wholly as a liability (if the contract is a derivative contract) or as a compound instrument (if the contract is a non-derivative contract). The IASB decided to retain this difference pending the outcome of its longer-term project on the distinction between liabilities and equity. [IFRS 2:BC266]

If the entity elects for the settlement alternative with the higher fair value, as at the date of settlement, the entity should recognise an additional expense for the excess value given. That is:
[IFRS 2:43]

- the difference between the cash paid and the fair value of the equity instruments that would have been issued; or

- the difference between the fair value of the equity instruments issued and the amount of cash that would otherwise have been paid.

> Thus, an additional expense is recognised when an entity elects to use the settlement alternative with the higher fair value. But this does not mean that the expense recognised will be the same as it would have been if the method of settlement assumed at the outset was the same as the actual method of settlement. For example, consider the case of share appreciation rights when the cash-settled and equity-settled alternatives have the same fair value because the cash payment is equal to the gain that would arise on exercise of the options. If these were assumed to be cash-settled from the outset, the cumulative expense recognised would be based on the actual cash payment made (i.e. intrinsic value on exercise). If these were assumed to be equity-settled from the outset, the cumulative expense recognised would be based on fair value at grant date (which would usually be lower).

> If the entity concluded, at the outset, that there was no obligation to settle in cash but it subsequently did so, the expense recognised would be based on fair value at grant date and would not be

adjusted to the amount of the cash payment made. The IASB considered and rejected the argument that an additional expense should be recognised in these circumstances as described in IFRS 2:BC267.

If the entity has the choice of settlement, it may, therefore, appear advantageous to conclude that there is no obligation to settle in cash and to account for the arrangements as equity-settled. When the entity has no past practice or stated policy of settling in cash, there is nothing in the Standard to prevent this. But an entity that tried to exploit this could do so only for a limited time because it might, in due course, establish a practice of settling in cash.

6.3 Contingent cash settlement provisions

IFRS 2 does not address specifically the treatment of provisions under which share-based payment transactions are settled in cash on the occurrence of a contingent event which is in the control of neither the entity nor the counterparty.

Example 6.3

Contingently cash-settled share-based payment whose contingent event is not within the control of the entity

An entity enters into an equity-settled share option arrangement. The terms of the arrangement stipulate that, if a change of control occurs before the end of the plan's exercise period, the entity will be required to repurchase the outstanding share options, as well as any shares already issued under the plan, at fair value.

A change of control normally requires shareholder approval. The shareholders of an entity are generally not considered to be a part of the entity because they act as investors and not on behalf of the entity. When a shareholder is faced with a decision to sell his or her shares, he/she makes that decision as an investor and not as part of the entity even if he/she is also a director or employee of the entity.

Therefore, a change of control by way of an Initial Public Offering or in some other manner should be regarded as an event that is not within the control of the entity because it is within the control of the shareholders (acting in their capacity as investors). Consequently, such share-based payment transactions should not be considered to provide the entity with a choice of settlement; they are not share-based payments with a cash alternative for either the employee or the employer.

---

7   Disclosure

Paragraphs 44 to 52 of IFRS 2 set out detailed disclosure requirements for share-based payments. The main requirements are summarised below. Additional information should be disclosed if the detailed information required to be disclosed by the IFRS does not satisfy the principles in IFRS 2:44, 46 and 50 (see **7.1, 7.2** and **7.3** below). [IFRS 2:52]

When separate financial statements are presented for a parent, these disclosures will be required for both the parent's separate financial statements and for the consolidated financial statements of the group. Some of the disclosures (e.g. regarding the nature of the schemes and the option pricing models used) will be common to both and need not be repeated. However, some details (e.g. regarding the numerical details of the number of options outstanding) will have to be disclosed separately for the parent as well as for the group.

Paragraph 8 of IAS 8 *Accounting Policies, Changes in Accounting Estimates and Errors* states that accounting policies set out in IFRSs do not need to be applied when the effect is not material. IAS 1:31 states that an entity need not provide a specific disclosure required by an IFRS if the information is not material. Both quantitative and qualitative factors should be assessed to determine materiality of share-based payment transactions. This applies not only to recognition and measurement but also to disclosures in the financial statements.

In addition to the IFRS 2 disclosure requirements, however, there may be local legal or regulatory requirements (e.g. in company law or listing rules). Such local requirements may apply irrespective of materiality, or different materiality considerations may be relevant (e.g. whether the arrangements are material to an individual director).

When no IFRS 2 disclosures are provided on the basis of materiality, but the existence of share-based payment arrangements is disclosed in other parts of the annual report, the potential implications should be considered. Users of the financial statements may interpret the inconsistency as an error. To avoid such a misunderstanding, it may be useful to include an explanation that the IFRS 2 disclosures have been omitted because the amounts involved are not material.

7.1   Nature and extent of share-based payments

An entity should disclose information that enables users of the financial statements to understand the nature and extent of share-based payment arrangements that existed during the period. [IFRS 2:44] To give effect to this principle, IFRS 2 specifies that at least the following should be disclosed:
[IFRS 2:45]

- a description of each type of share-based payment arrangement that existed at any time during the period, including the general terms and conditions of each arrangement such as:

  - the vesting requirements;

  - the maximum term of options granted; and

  - the method of settlement (e.g. whether in cash or equity).

  An entity with substantially similar types of share-based payment arrangements may aggregate this information, unless separate disclosure of each arrangement is necessary to satisfy the principle in IFRS 2:44;

- the number and weighted average exercise prices of share options for each of the following groups of options:

  - outstanding at the beginning of the period;

  - granted during the period;

  - forfeited during the period;

  - exercised during the period;

  - expired during the period;

  - outstanding at the end of the period; and

  - exercisable at the end of the period;

- for share options exercised during the period, the weighted average share price at the date of exercise. If options were exercised on a regular basis throughout the period, the weighted average share price during the period may instead be disclosed; and

- for share options outstanding at the end of the period, the range of exercise prices and weighted average contractual life. If the range of exercise prices is wide, the outstanding options should be divided into ranges that are meaningful for assessing the number and timing of additional shares that may be issued and the cash that may be received upon exercise of those options.

As explained at **8.5.1** below, a parent may grant rights to its equity instruments to the employees of its subsidiaries which are conditional upon the completion of continuing service with the group, rather than a specified subsidiary, for a specified period. In accordance with IFRS 2:B59 and B61, each subsidiary will recognise an expense for the period of service of the employee with that subsidiary and may also need to 'true up' for the outcome of any non-market vesting conditions. The question arises as to whether the disclosure requirements described above apply only in relation to the current employees of a subsidiary or extend to former employees who are now employed elsewhere in the group.

When deciding on the appropriate disclosures, regard should be had to the principle in IFRS 2:44 that the information should enable users of the financial statements to understand the nature and extent of share-based payment arrangements that existed during the period. Therefore, disclosures should, at a minimum, deal with options held by employees of the entity during the financial year. The table of options required by IFRS 2:45(b) should include a line or column to adjust for the numbers for employees transferring in or out of the entity. On this basis, the number of options outstanding at the end of the period will include only current employees; employees who have transferred to another subsidiary will be included in that subsidiary's disclosures.

A subsidiary may remain exposed to adjustments to the expense recognised for former employees when there are non-market vesting conditions. This may require disclosure, in some cases, if the effect is, or is expected to be, material.

7.2   How fair value is determined

An entity should disclose information that enables users of the financial statements to understand how the fair value of the goods or services received, or the fair value of the equity instruments granted, during the period was determined. [IFRS 2:46]

To give effect to this principle, IFRS 2 specifies that at least the following should be disclosed if the entity has measured the fair value of goods and services received indirectly, by reference to the fair value of the equity instruments granted:
[IFRS 2:47]

- for share options granted during the period, the weighted average fair value of those options at the measurement date and information on how the fair value was measured, including:

- the option pricing model used and the inputs to that model, including the weighted average share price, exercise price, expected volatility, option life, expected dividends, the risk-free interest rate and any other inputs to the model, including the method used and the assumptions made to incorporate the effects of expected early exercise;

- how expected volatility was determined, including an explanation of the extent to which it was based on historical volatility; and

- whether and how any other features of the option grant were incorporated into the measurement of fair value, such as a market condition;

- for other equity instruments granted during the period (i.e. other than share options) the number and weighted average fair value of those equity instruments at the measurement date, and information on how that fair value was determined, including:

  - if the fair value was not measured on the basis of observable market price, how it was determined;

  - whether and how expected dividends were incorporated into the measurement of fair value; and

  - whether and how any other features of the equity instruments granted were incorporated into the measurement of fair value; and

- for share-based payment arrangements that were modified during the period:

  - an explanation of those modifications;

  - the incremental fair value granted as a result of those modifications; and

  - information on how the incremental fair value was measured.

If the entity has measured directly the fair value of goods or services received during the period, disclosure is required of how that fair value was determined (e.g. whether fair value was measured at a market price for those goods or services). [IFRS 2:48]

The presumption in IFRS 2:13 is that, in the case of transactions with parties other than employees, the fair value of the goods or services received can be estimated reliably (see **4.2.1**). If that presumption has been rebutted, that fact should be disclosed together with an explanation of why the presumption was rebutted. [IFRS 2:49]

7.3   Effect of share-based payment transactions on profit or loss and financial position

An entity should disclose information that enables users of the financial statements to understand the effect of share-based payment transactions on its profit or loss for the period and on its financial position. [IFRS 2:50] To give effect to this principle, IFRS 2 specifies that at least the following should be disclosed:
[IFRS 2:51]

- the total expense recognised for the period arising from share-based payment transactions in which the goods or services received did not qualify for recognition as assets and hence were recognised immediately as an expense, including separate disclosure of that portion of the total expense that arises from transactions accounted for as equity-settled share-based payment transactions; and

- for liabilities arising from share-based payment transactions:

    - the total carrying amount at the end of the period; and

    - the total intrinsic value at the end of the period of liabilities for which the counterparty's right to cash or other assets had vested by the end of the period (e.g. vested share appreciation rights).

7.4   Illustrative disclosures

Illustrative disclosures for share-based payment transactions are included in the implementation guidance accompanying IFRS 2 (IFRS 2:IG23) and in Deloitte's IFRS model financial statements, available on *www.iasplus. com*.

8   Accounting by entities within groups

As explained at **2.3** above, it is often the case that employees of a subsidiary will receive part of their remuneration in the form of shares in the parent, or less commonly in some other group entity. When this is the case, IFRS 2 requires the entity that has received the benefit of the services to recognise the expense. This is so even if the equity instruments issued are those of another entity within the group.

IFRS 2 also specifies the accounting for group cash-settled share-based payment transactions in the separate or individual financial statements of the entity receiving the goods or services when the entity has no obligation to settle the share-based payment transactions (see **8.3.4** below).

This section also deals with some related issues, such as intragroup recharges, which are not addressed in IFRSs.

The requirements of IFRS 2 concerning share-based payment transactions among group entities focus on transactions with employees. They also apply to similar transactions with suppliers of goods or services other than employees. [IFRS 2:B46]

For share-based payment transactions among group entities, in its separate or individual financial statements, the entity receiving the goods or services measures the goods or services received as either an equity-settled or a cash-settled share-based payment transaction by assessing:

- the nature of the awards granted; and

- its own rights and obligations.

The amount recognised by the entity receiving the goods or services may differ from the amount recognised by the consolidated group or by another group entity settling the share-based payment transaction. [IFRS 2:43A]

The entity receiving the goods or services measures them as equity-settled share-based payment transactions when:

- the awards granted are its own equity instruments; or

- the entity has no obligation to settle the share-based payment transaction.

The entity subsequently remeasures such an equity-settled share-based payment transaction only for changes in non-market vesting conditions. In all other circumstances, the entity receiving the goods or services measures them as a cash-settled share-based payment transaction. [IFRS 2:43B]

The entity settling a share-based payment transaction, when another entity in the group receives the goods or services, recognises the transaction as an equity-settled share-based payment transaction only if it is settled in the entity's own equity instruments. Otherwise, the transaction is recognised as a cash-settled share-based payment transaction. [IFRS 2:43C]

Some group transactions involve repayment arrangements that require one group entity to pay another group entity for the provision of the share-based payments to the suppliers of goods or services. In such cases, the entity that receives the goods or services accounts for the share-based payment transaction in accordance with IFRS 2:43B regardless of any intragroup repayment arrangements.

> The classification of common forms of share-based payment arrangement in consolidated, parent and subsidiary financial statements is summarised below.

Entity receiving goods or services	Entity with obligation to settle	Settled in	Classification		
			Parent's separate financial statements	Subsidiary's individual financial statements	Consolidated financial statements
Subsidiary	Subsidiary	Subsidiary's equity	N/A (see **8.1**)	Equity (see **8.1**)	Equity
Subsidiary	Subsidiary	Cash	N/A (see **8.3.2**)	Cash (see **8.3.2**)	Cash
Subsidiary	Subsidiary	Parent's equity	N/A (see **8.3.3**)	Cash (see **8.2.2**)	Equity
Subsidiary	Parent	Subsidiary's equity	Cash (see **8.1**)	Equity (see **8.1**)	Equity
Subsidiary	Parent	Parent's equity	Equity (see **8.3.1**)	Equity (see **8.2.1**)	Equity
Subsidiary	Parent	Cash	Cash (see **8.3.4**)	Equity (see **8.3.4**)	Cash

8.1   Share-based payment arrangements involving an entity's own equity instruments

IFRS 2 addresses whether the following transactions involving an entity's own equity instruments should be accounted for as equity-settled or cash-settled under the requirements of IFRS 2:
[IFRS 2:B48]

- an entity grants to its employees rights to equity instruments of the entity (e.g. share options) and either chooses or is required (either by contract or necessity) to buy equity instruments (i.e. treasury shares) from another party, to satisfy its obligation to its employees; and

- an entity's employees are granted rights to equity instruments of the entity (e.g. share options), either by the entity itself or by its shareholders, and the shareholders of the entity provide the equity instruments needed.

Share-based payment transactions in which an entity receives services as consideration for its own equity instruments are accounted for as equity-settled. IFRS 2 confirms that this applies regardless of whether the entity

chooses or is required to buy those equity instruments from another party to satisfy its obligations to its employees. This also applies regardless of whether:
[IFRS 2:B49]

- the employee's rights to the entity's equity instruments were granted by the entity itself or by its shareholders; or

- the share-based payment arrangement was settled by the entity or by its shareholders.

These requirements are straightforward and simply remove any doubt that such transactions should be accounted for as equity-settled even though the entity may not itself issue or transfer any equity instruments as part of the transaction.

If the shareholder has an obligation to settle the transaction with its investee's employees, it provides equity instruments of its investee rather than its own. Therefore, if the investee is in the same group as the shareholder, the shareholder measures its obligation in accordance with the requirements applicable to cash-settled share-based payment transactions in the shareholder's separate financial statements and those applicable to equity-settled share-based payment transactions in the shareholder's consolidated financial statements. [IFRS 2:B50]

If the shareholder has no such obligation, it has no accounting entries to make as it is not party to the transaction.

8.2 Share-based payment arrangements involving equity instruments of the parent – accounting in the subsidiary's financial statements

Another issue addressed by IFRS 2 concerns share-based payment arrangements that involve two or more entities within the same group and relate to an equity instrument of another group entity. For example, the employees of a subsidiary may be granted rights to equity instruments of its parent as consideration for the services they provide to the subsidiary. [IFRS 2:B51]

IFRS 2 addresses the following share-based payment arrangements: [IFRS 2:B52]

- a parent grants rights to its equity instruments direct to the employees of its subsidiary so that the parent (and not the subsidiary) has the obligation to provide the employees of the subsidiary with the equity instruments needed (addressed at **8.2.1** below); and

- a subsidiary grants rights to equity instruments of its parent to its employees so that the subsidiary (and not the parent) has the obligation to provide its employees with the equity instruments needed (addressed at **8.2.2** below).

IFRS 2 assumes that it is clear whether the parent or the subsidiary granted the rights to equity instruments and prescribes a different accounting treatment in each case. It may not, in practice, be clear which entity in a group granted the rights to the employees. Often this is done by mutual agreement between the subsidiary and the parent. The application of IFRS 2 in these circumstances is considered at **8.2.3** below.

IFRS 2 does not address the appropriate accounting for any intragroup payments that may be made in the scenarios described (which is considered at **8.4** below). However, the Standard does state that classification of the share-based arrangement is not affected by the existence (or otherwise) of payment arrangements between a subsidiary and parent.

8.2.1 Parent grants rights to its equity instruments to employees of its subsidiary

When a parent grants rights to its equity instruments to employees of its subsidiary, the subsidiary does not have an obligation to provide its parent's equity instruments to its employees. The arrangement is accounted for as equity-settled in the consolidated financial statements. The subsidiary should, in its own separate financial statements, measure the services received from its employees in accordance with the requirements of IFRS 2 applicable to equity-settled share-based payment transactions. There will be a corresponding increase recognised in equity as a capital contribution from the parent. [IFRS 2:B53]

This requirement is straightforward to apply. The expense recognised in the consolidated financial statements is 'pushed down' into the accounts of the relevant subsidiaries that receive the services of the employees.

Example 8.2.1

Parent grants rights to its equity instruments to employees of its subsidiary

Parent P grants each of Subsidiary S's 100 employees 30 shares in Parent P, subject to the conditions that they remain in employment for three years and that Subsidiary S meets a specified profit target. The fair value on grant date is CU5 per share. Assume that at the outset, and at the end of Years 1 and 2, it is expected that the profit target will be met and that no employees leave. Subsidiary S is not required to reimburse Parent P for the shares granted to its employees.

At the end of Year 3, the profit target is met.

Accounting by Subsidiary S

In each of Years 1 to 3, Subsidiary S will recognise an IFRS 2 expense in profit or loss, and a corresponding entry in equity, which reflects the capital contribution it receives from Parent P.

		CU	CU
Dr	Profit or loss [CU5 × 30 × 100 / 3 years]	5,000	
Cr	Equity (capital contribution)		5,000

To recognise the share-based payment expense.

Because Subsidiary S has no obligation to reimburse Parent P for the share-based payment, no further accounting entries are required when the shares are transferred to the employees by Parent P.

There is no requirement in IFRSs to credit the capital contribution to a separate component of equity. Therefore, it may be credited to retained earnings if this is permitted in the legal jurisdiction in which Subsidiary S operates (see general discussion of this issue at **4.1.2** above).

The accounting in the separate financial statements of the parent is addressed in **example 8.3.1A**.

8.2.2 Subsidiary grants rights to equity instruments of its parent to its employees

When the subsidiary grants rights to equity instruments of its parent to employees, the subsidiary accounts for the transaction with its employees as cash-settled. This requirement applies irrespective of how the subsidiary obtains the equity instruments to satisfy the obligations to its employees. [IFRS 2:B55]

The practical implications of accounting for arrangements as cash-settled in the subsidiary while they are equity-settled from the perspective of the group are considered further at **8.7** below.

> IFRS 2 does not address the accounting required in the subsidiary when it has recognised a liability for a cash-settled share-based payment arrangement but subsequently makes no cash payment because the parent provides the shares without any right to reimbursement. IFRS 2 addresses transactions with settlement alternatives (see **section 3.3** above) but this guidance does not apply to the circumstances under consideration because the guidance envisages only the grantor of the rights or the counterparty having the choice whereas, in this case, the choice lies with a third party (i.e. the parent). If the parent satisfies the subsidiary's obligation, the liability will be removed from the statement of financial position of the subsidiary with the credit recognised in equity as a capital contribution from the parent. The expense recognised in respect of the services received is not reversed (see **example 8.3.3** below).

8.2.3   Determining which entity has granted the rights

> To apply the requirements of IFRS 2 set out at **8.2.1** and **8.2.2** above, it will be necessary to determine which entity in the group granted the rights to the employees and thereby assumed the obligation to settle the transaction with the employees. This will require a careful assessment of the particular facts and circumstances. The factors to be considered include, but are not limited to:
>
> - the contractual terms of the share scheme;
>
> - any formal documentation provided to the employees that are granted the rights;
>
> - any other communications provided to employees;
>
> - whether the scheme is specific to one subsidiary or covers a number of subsidiaries within a group; and
>
> - any other aspects of the arrangements, whether formally documented or not.

8.3   Accounting in the parent's separate financial statements

IFRS 2 states that when a parent grants rights to its equity instruments to the employees of its subsidiary, the parent does have an obligation to settle the transaction with the subsidiary's employees by providing the parent's own equity instruments. Therefore, the parent measures its obligation in accordance with the requirements applicable to equity-settled share-based payment transactions. [IFRS 2:B54]

IFRS 2 offers no further guidance on application of the requirement to account for such transactions in the parent's separate financial statements.

The illustrative example accompanying IFRIC D17 (the exposure draft upon which IFRIC 11 *IFRS 2 – Group and Treasury Share Transactions* was based) did, however, include entries in the separate financial statements of the parent. The illustrative example accompanying D17 dealt with the case when the parent has granted the rights so that the arrangement is equity-settled for both the group and the subsidiary but it is possible to apply the same principles in other cases (see **8.3.1** to **8.3.3** below).

8.3.1   *Equity-settled for the group and the subsidiary*

The illustrative example accompanying IFRIC D17 suggested that the parent should recognise an entry each year to debit the cost of investment in subsidiary and credit equity with an amount equal to the expense recognised in the subsidiary in accordance with IFRS 2. This was not explained in the Basis for Conclusions which accompanied IFRIC D17 but the rationale was that the parent had made a capital contribution to the subsidiary (assuming the subsidiary had not paid fair value as reimbursement to the parent) by taking on the cost of remunerating the subsidiary's employees that the subsidiary would otherwise have had to bear, and had also granted an equity instrument in accepting the obligation to those employees. This is consistent with the credit to equity recognised in the subsidiary.

Increasing the cost of investment in a subsidiary may, in rare cases, give rise to impairment issues and this should be considered when appropriate.

Example 8.3.1A

Equity-settled for the group and the subsidiary (1)

The facts are the same as in **example 8.2.1** above.

Accounting by Parent P

In each of Years 1 to 3, Parent P would recognise the enhancement to its investment in Subsidiary S, and a corresponding entry in equity which reflects the capital contribution being made to Subsidiary S and the equity instruments being granted to Subsidiary S's employees.

		CU	CU
Dr	Cost of investment	5,000	
Cr	Equity		5,000

To recognise the grant of equity instruments to employees of subsidiary.

Additional entries will be required when Parent P transfers the shares to the employees. These entries will depend on whether Parent P issues new shares or utilises shares purchased in the market and held as treasury shares. The entries may also be affected by the involvement of an employee share trust (see **8.6** below).

In the same way that the subsidiary will 'true up' the IFRS 2 expense to reflect changes in non-market vesting conditions, so will the parent 'true up' its contributions to the subsidiary. This will usually result in symmetrical accounting for the capital contribution between the parent and subsidiary.

Example 8.3.1B

Equity-settled for the group and the subsidiary (2)

The facts are the same as in **example 8.2.1** above except that at the end of Year 3 the profit target is not met.

Accounting by Parent P

In each of Years 1 and 2, Parent P will recognise an enhancement to its investment in Subsidiary S, and a corresponding entry in equity, which reflect the capital contribution being made to Subsidiary S and the equity instruments being granted to Subsidiary S's employees.

		CU	CU
Dr	Cost of investment	5,000	
Cr	Equity		5,000

To recognise the grant of equity instruments to employees of subsidiary.

At the end of Year 3, the profit target is not met, so Parent P must 'true up' the amounts recognised to reflect the non-market vesting condition not being met.

		CU	CU
Dr	Equity	10,000	
Cr	Cost of investment		10,000

To recognise the true up in respect of equity instruments granted to employees of subsidiary.

This true up in Parent P mirrors the accounting entries in Subsidiary S.

8.3.2   Cash-settled for the group and the subsidiary

A scheme will only be accounted for as cash-settled both by the group and by the subsidiary when the subsidiary itself has the obligation to transfer cash or other assets (other than equity instruments of the group) to its employees. (Historically, this approach might also have been applied by a subsidiary that was not yet applying IFRS 2 as amended in July 2009 whose parent had the obligation to transfer cash or other assets (other than equity instruments of the group) to that subsidiary's employees. IFRS 2 now makes clear that such a subsidiary should regard the arrangement as equity-settled – see **8.3.4** below.)

No accounting is required by the parent when the subsidiary has the obligation to its employees and makes a cash payment to satisfy the obligation. When the subsidiary has the obligation to make a cash payment to its employees but the parent settles the obligation on behalf of the subsidiary, the amount of the cash payment is accounted for as a capital contribution, increasing the cost of investment in the subsidiary in the parent's separate financial statements and increasing equity in the subsidiary's financial statements.

When the parent has the obligation to make a cash payment to the employees of its subsidiary, the parent recognises the amount of the cash payment as a capital contribution, increasing the cost of investment in its subsidiary. The subsidiary accounts for such a scheme as equity-settled. Such arrangements are considered further at **8.3.4** below.

8.3.3   Equity-settled for the group but cash-settled for the subsidiary

---

Example 8.3.3

Equity-settled for the group but cash-settled for the subsidiary

Subsidiary S has entered into a share-based payment arrangement with its employees under which Subsidiary S has the obligation to deliver shares of Parent P to its employees. Subsequently, Parent P provides the shares to the employees to satisfy Subsidiary S's obligation. Parent P has no right to reimbursement from Subsidiary S.

How should Subsidiary S and Parent P account for the original share-based payment arrangement and its subsequent settlement by Parent P?

Accounting by Subsidiary S

IFRS 2:B55 requires that arrangements should be accounted for as cash-settled by the subsidiary if it is the subsidiary that has granted rights to employees over its parent's equity instruments, irrespective of how the subsidiary obtains the equity instruments to satisfy its obligation to its employees. Therefore, in the circumstances described, Subsidiary S initially recognises a liability for its obligation, which is measured in accordance with the requirements of IFRS 2 regarding cash-settled transactions.

When the parent subsequently provides shares to the subsidiary's employees for no consideration, the subsidiary should recognise the credit arising from the derecognition of the liability directly in equity as a capital contribution received from the parent. The expense recognised in respect of the services received is not reversed.

Accounting by Parent P

Parent P does not account for the share-based payment arrangement prior to settling the subsidiary's obligation because it is not party to the share-based payment arrangement.

When Parent P provides the shares to the subsidiary's employees for no consideration, it should recognise a capital contribution to Subsidiary S in its separate financial statements. There are two acceptable views regarding the value at which that capital contribution should be recognised:

- the equity-settled amount recognised in the consolidated financial statements; or

- the cash-settled amount recognised in the subsidiary's financial statements.

Recognition at the equity-settled amount recognised in the consolidated financial statements is based on the argument that when the parent has not made a cash payment to settle the share-based payment award but has

---

issued its own equity instruments to satisfy the obligation, the credit to equity in the parent's separate financial statements should be the same as the equivalent credit in the consolidated financial statements because they relate to the same equity instrument.

However, recognition of a capital contribution for the same amount as the cash-settled amount recognised in the subsidiary's financial statements is more logical and consistent with the fact that, under IFRS 2, the parent has no obligation. Although the group has an obligation that will be settled by the issuance of equity instruments, the parent creates an equity instrument of its own at the entity level only when it provides the shares to the subsidiary's employees. From the parent's perspective, the equity instruments are issued to settle the cash-settled liability of the subsidiary on its behalf and, therefore, measurement of that capital contribution for the same amount is reasonable.

The parent should select one of the approaches as its accounting policy and apply it consistently.

Practical application of these principles is considered further at **8.7** below.

8.3.4   Cash-settled for the group but equity-settled for the subsidiary

An entity may receive goods or services from its suppliers (including employees) under share-based payment arrangements that are cash-settled when the entity itself does not have any obligation to make the required payments to its suppliers. For example, a parent (not the entity itself) may have an obligation to make the required cash payments to the employees of the entity and:
[IFRS 2:B56]

- the employees of the entity will receive cash payments that are linked to the price of its own equity instruments; or

- the employees of the entity will receive cash payments that are linked to the price of its parent's equity instruments.

In this case, the subsidiary does not have an obligation to settle the transaction with its employees. Therefore, the subsidiary accounts for the transaction as equity-settled and recognises a corresponding increase in equity as a contribution from its parent. The subsidiary remeasures the cost of the transaction subsequently for any changes resulting from non-market vesting conditions not being met. This differs from the measurement of the transaction as cash-settled in the consolidated financial statements of the group. [IFRS 2:B57]

The parent has an obligation to settle the transaction with the employees and the consideration is cash. The parent and the consolidated group measure the obligation in accordance with the requirements of IFRS 2 applicable to cash-settled share-based payment transactions. [IFRS 2:B58]

IFRS 2 does not address the treatment of the debit entry arising from recognition and remeasurement of the obligation in the parent's separate financial statements. However, it will be debited to the cost of investment in the subsidiary as a capital contribution. The amount of this contribution will be a different amount from the capital contribution recognised in the subsidiary in accordance with IFRS 2:B57. In some cases, it may be necessary to consider whether the investment in the subsidiary is impaired.

8.4   Intragroup recharges

IFRS 2 does not address the appropriate accounting for intragroup recharges, except to say that intragroup payment arrangements should not affect the accounting for the underlying share-based payment arrangement.

Although the appropriate accounting for intragroup recharges is not addressed in IFRS 2, an illustrative example accompanying IFRIC D17 (the exposure draft upon which IFRIC 11 was based) indicated that if the parent levies an intragroup recharge on the subsidiary, the amount of that recharge is offset against the capital contribution arising for the share-based payment in the individual and separate financial statements of the subsidiary and in any separate financial statements of the parent. The example also indicated that if the amount of the recharge exceeds the capital contribution, that excess is accounted for as a distribution from the subsidiary to the parent. Thus, in effect, IFRIC D17 proposed to account for any difference between share-based payment expense and reimbursement as a transaction with shareholders (i.e. a capital contribution or distribution).

The same logic applies irrespective of whether an arrangement is an equity-settled or cash-settled share-based payment arrangement in the parent's separate financial statements and the consolidated financial statements.

Some complexities may arise if the timing of the intragroup recharges is different from the recognition of the expense under IFRS 2. For example, it is possible that the recharge might be levied only when the options are exercised by the employees. Some of these issues are considered in detail in **examples 8.4A** to **8.4D** below.

These examples distinguish between circumstances in which a right to reimbursement exists at the inception of the share-based payment arrangement and circumstances in which no such right exists at that time. A right to reimbursement may exist in the absence of a written contract. For example, it may exist if it is the clear intention of the parties, when the share-based payment arrangement is established, that reimbursement will occur and the basis for calculating the amount of that reimbursement is also agreed at that time.

When the recharge made exceeds the expense recognised in accordance with IFRS 2, as will typically be the case if the recharge is based on the intrinsic value on exercise of the options, the excess will be accounted for as a distribution by the subsidiary. Consequently, it will not be recognised as an expense in the subsidiary's financial statements, but will be recognised as a distribution received (dividend income) in the parent's separate financial statements. This is illustrated in **example 8.4D**.

The fact that the excess recharge will be accounted for as a distribution does not necessarily mean that it will be a distribution as a matter of law. The position may vary according to the legal jurisdiction. Legal advice should be sought when necessary.

There is no specific requirement in IFRSs to present intragroup recharges for share-based payments in this way, but the net approach illustrated in IFRIC D17 appears reasonable and has been used as the basis for **examples 8.4A** and **8.4C** below when the parent has a right to reimbursement. Nevertheless, other approaches may also be acceptable, provided that they do not result in a misstatement of the amount of share-based payment expense recognised.

For example, an entity may elect to account separately for services received (as a capital contribution) and for payments made (as a distribution), without offsetting the two. Moreover, when the amount payable to the parent is conditional on share awards vesting, a reimbursement obligation might be measured at fair value. Whatever the approach adopted, careful judgement should be applied to ensure that the accounting properly reflects the substance of the arrangement.

Example 8.4A

Reimbursement over the term of the arrangement

A parent, Company P, grants 30 of its shares to each of 100 employees of its subsidiary, Company S, on condition that the employees remain employed by Company S for three years. Assume that at the outset, and at the end of Years 1 and 2, it is expected that all of the employees will remain employed for all three years. At the end of Year 3, none of the employees has left. The fair value of the shares on grant date is CU5 per share.

Company S agrees to reimburse Company P over the term of the arrangement for 75 per cent of the final expense recognised by Company S. Over that period, Company S expects to recognise an expense totalling CU15,000 and, therefore, expects the total reimbursement to be CU11,250 (CU15,000 × 75 per cent). Company S therefore reimburses Company P CU3,750 (CU11,250 × 1/3) each year.

The following illustrates one of several acceptable approaches (as discussed above) to accounting for recharges of share-based payment costs.

Accounting by Company S

In each of Years 1 to 3, Company S recognises an IFRS 2 expense in profit or loss, the cash paid to Company P, and the balance of the capital contribution it has received from Company P.

		CU	CU
Dr	Profit or loss	5,000	
Cr	Cash		3,750
Cr	Equity (capital contribution)		1,250

To recognise the share-based payment expense and partial reimbursement to parent.

Accounting by Company P

In each of Years 1 to 3, Company P recognises an increase in equity for the instruments being granted, the cash reimbursed by Company S, and the balance of the capital contribution it has made to Company S.

		CU	CU
Dr	Cost of investment	1,250	
Dr	Cash	3,750	
Cr	Equity		5,000

To recognise the grant of equity instruments to employees of subsidiary less partial reimbursement from subsidiary.

Example 8.4B

Reimbursement (if any) at the end of the arrangement when initially there exists no right to reimbursement

The facts are as in **example 8.4A**, except that, before vesting, there exists no right to reimbursement. At the end of the arrangement (i.e. when the shares vest), Company S agrees to pay Company P 75 per cent of the final expense recognised by Company S.

The following illustrates one of several acceptable approaches (as discussed at **8.4** above) to accounting for recharges of share-based payment costs.

Accounting by Company S

In each of Years 1 to 3, Company S recognises the IFRS 2 expense in profit or loss and a capital contribution from Company P.

		CU	CU
Dr	Profit or loss	5,000	
Cr	Equity (capital contribution)		5,000

To recognise the share-based payment expense.

At the end of Year 3, all the shares vest and Company S pays Company P CU11,250. The payment is treated as a distribution to Company P.

		CU	CU
Dr	Equity (distribution)	11,250	
Cr	Cash		11,250

To recognise the distribution to parent.

Accounting by Company P

In each of Years 1 to 3, Company P recognises an increase in equity for the instruments being granted and the capital contribution made to Company S.

		CU	CU
Dr	Cost of investment	5,000	
Cr	Equity		5,000

To recognise the grant of equity instruments to employees of subsidiary.

At the end of Year 3, all the shares vest and Company S pays Company P CU11,250. The payment is recognised as dividend income in profit or loss by Company P and is accounted for in accordance with IAS 18 *Revenue*.

		CU	CU
Dr	Cash	11,250	
Cr	Dividend income (profit or loss)		11,250

To recognise the distribution from subsidiary.

If the increased cost of investment and reduction in the value of Company S from the payment of a dividend result in the carrying amount of Company P's investment in Company S no longer being supportable, Company P should also recognise an impairment loss in respect of the cost of its investment in Company S.

Example 8.4C

Reimbursement at the end of the arrangement when there is a right to reimbursement

The facts are as in **example 8.4A**, except that, on grant date, Company S and Company P enter into a binding agreement under which Company S will reimburse Company P 75 per cent of the final expense recognised by Company S. The payment is made at the end of the arrangement (i.e. when the shares vest).

The following illustrates one of several acceptable approaches (as discussed at **8.4** above) for accounting for recharges of share-based payment costs.

Accounting by Company S

In each of Years 1 to 3, Company S recognises the IFRS 2 expense in profit or loss, a payable due to Company P for 75 per cent of this amount, and a capital contribution from Company P for the balance.

		CU	CU
Dr	Profit or loss	5,000	
Cr	Intragroup payables		3,750
Cr	Equity (capital contribution)		1,250

To recognise the share-based payment expense and accrual of partial reimbursement to parent.

At the end of Year 3, all the shares vest and Company S pays Company P CU11,250, settling the liability previously recognised.

		CU	CU
Dr	Intragroup payables	11,250	
Cr	Cash		11,250

To recognise the settlement of reimbursement to parent.

Accounting by Company P

In each of Years 1 to 3, Company P recognises an increase in equity for the instruments being granted and a receivable from Company S and the balance of the capital contribution it has made to Company S.

		CU	CU
Dr	Intragroup receivables	3,750	
Dr	Cost of investment	1,250	
Cr	Equity		5,000

To recognise the grant of equity instruments to employees of subsidiary less accrual of partial reimbursement from subsidiary.

At the end of Year 3, all the shares vest and Company S pays Company P CU11,250.

		CU	CU
Dr	Cash	11,250	
Cr	Intragroup receivables		11,250

To recognise the settlement of reimbursement by subsidiary.

For simplicity, this example assumes that any effect of discounting would not be material. When reimbursement balances are very large, consideration should be given to whether discounting is necessary.

A common situation is that reimbursement is based on the intrinsic value on vesting (or on actual exercise in the case of options). This will often result in a reimbursement that exceeds the grant date fair value recognised under IFRS 2. The excess of the amount of the reimbursement over the IFRS 2 expense will be accounted for as a distribution by the subsidiary. This is illustrated in the following example.

Example 8.4D

Reimbursement at the end of the arrangement equal to the intrinsic value at that date when initially there is no right to reimbursement

The facts are as in **example 8.4A**, except that Company S pays Company P at the end of the arrangement an amount equal to the intrinsic value of the shares at that date. This amount is CU25,000.

For simplicity, it has been assumed that there is no entitlement to the reimbursement and that it is, therefore, accounted for only when made. Otherwise it would be necessary for Company S to estimate the amount of the accrued reimbursement to be recognised at the end of each reporting period.

The following illustrates one of several acceptable approaches (as discussed at **8.4** above) for accounting for recharges of share-based payment costs.

Accounting by Company S

In each of Years 1 to 3, Company S recognises the IFRS 2 expense in profit or loss and a capital contribution from Company P.

		CU	CU
Dr	Profit or loss	5,000	
Cr	Equity (capital contribution)		5,000

To recognise the share-based payment expense.

At the end of Year 3, all the shares vest and Company S pays Company P CU25,000. The payment is treated as a distribution by Company P.

		CU	CU
Dr	Equity (distribution)	25,000	
Cr	Cash		25,000

To recognise the distribution to parent.

Accounting by Company P

In each of Years 1 to 3, Company P recognises an increase in equity for the instruments being granted and the capital contribution made to Company S.

		CU	CU
Dr	Cost of investment	5,000	
Cr	Equity		5,000

To recognise the grant of equity instruments to employees of subsidiary.

At the end of Year 3, all the shares vest and Company S pays Company P CU25,000. The payment is treated as dividend income by Company P, and is accounted for in accordance with IAS 18.

		CU	CU
Dr	Cash	25,000	
Cr	Profit or loss (dividend income)		25,000

To recognise the distribution from subsidiary.

If the increased cost of investment and reduction in the value of Company S from the payment of a dividend result in the carrying amount of Company P's investment in Company S no longer being supportable, Company P should also recognise an impairment loss in respect of the cost of its investment in Company S.

8.5   Transfers of employees between group entities

8.5.1   Transfers of employees between group entities: parent has obligation

A parent may grant rights to its equity instruments to the employees of its subsidiaries that are conditional upon the completion of continuing service with the group (rather than a specified subsidiary) for a specified period. An employee may, therefore, transfer employment from one subsidiary to another during the specified vesting period without the employee's rights under the arrangements being affected. If the subsidiaries have no obligation to settle the share-based payment transaction with their employees, they account for it as an equity-settled transaction. When this is the case, each subsidiary measures the services received from its employee by reference to the fair value of the equity instruments at the date when the rights were originally granted by the parent and the proportion of the vesting period served by the employee with that subsidiary. [IFRS 2:B59]

Such an employee, after transferring between group entities, may fail to satisfy a vesting condition (e.g. the employee may leave the group before completing the required period of service) other than a market condition. In this case, because the vesting condition is service to the group, each subsidiary adjusts the amount previously recognised in respect of the services received from the employee in accordance with IFRS 2:19. Consequently, if the rights to equity instruments do not vest because of a failure to meet a vesting condition (other than a market condition), no amount is recognised on a cumulative basis for the services received from that employee in the financial statements of both subsidiaries. [IFRS 2:B61]

> This requirement for all affected entities to 'true up' at vesting date means that a subsidiary may need to make adjustments to its share-based payment expense several years after an employee has transferred elsewhere within the group.

8.5.2   Transfers of employees between group entities: subsidiary has obligation

If the subsidiary has an obligation to settle the transaction with its employees in its parent's equity instruments, it accounts for the transaction as cash-settled. IFRS 2 requires that each subsidiary measures the services received on the basis of grant date fair value of the equity instruments for the proportion of the vesting period the employee served with each subsidiary. In addition, each subsidiary recognises any change in the fair value of the equity instruments during the employee's service period with each subsidiary. [IFRS 2:B60]

> IFRS 2:B61 deals with failure to meet vesting conditions and appears to refer back to IFRS 2:B60 because it begins with the words 'such employees'. However, the requirements of IFRS 2:19 regarding the treatment of vesting conditions may not be relevant to cash-settled arrangements (see **5.3** above). In practice, any failure to meet a non-market vesting condition will be reflected in the remeasurement of the liability and accounted for in accordance with IFRS 2:B60 so there is no need to apply IFRS 2:B61.

In each case it will be necessary to consider which entity or entities in the group have the obligation to settle with the employee and recognise their liabilities accordingly. This will depend on the particular terms of the scheme. Each subsidiary will recognise an expense in relation to the period of service with that subsidiary in accordance with IFRS 2:B60. When one subsidiary assumes the cumulative liability for past service provided to other subsidiaries, the assumption of this liability at the date of transfer will be debited to equity as it is a form of distribution. The other subsidiaries should credit the release of their liability to equity as a capital contribution (i.e. the expense previously recognised for the service previously provided by the employee is not reversed merely because the liability will be settled by another party).

8.6   Effect of the use of ESOP trusts

ESOP trusts may potentially be accounted for in two different ways depending on the circumstances (see **section 9** below). When the assets and liabilities of the trust are recognised as those of the sponsoring entity, any obligations of the trust will be regarded as obligations of the sponsoring entity.

The analysis will be different when the trust is regarded as a subsidiary. In such circumstances, the rights and obligations of the trust will be reflected in its own individual financial statements, rather than those of the sponsoring entity.

It will be necessary to apply the requirements of IFRS 2:B46 to B61 and the other guidance in this section to the particular facts of each case. In particular, the guidance at **8.2.3** above will be relevant to determining which entity has granted the rights and, therefore, has the obligation to employees.

The analysis might be further complicated when in practice three entities are involved in the arrangement. The third entity might be a fellow subsidiary or intermediate parent which grants the options and delivers the shares to the employees (either directly or via an ESOP trust).

8.7   Subsidiary purchases parent's shares

To settle its obligation to employees, the subsidiary will often need to acquire its parent's shares either in the market or directly from the parent.

Example 8.7

Subsidiary purchases parent's shares to settle cash-settled obligation to employees

A subsidiary has an obligation under a share-based payment arrangement to deliver its parent's shares to its employees. To settle its obligation to its employees, the subsidiary will need to acquire its parent's shares either in the market or directly from the parent.

In accordance with IFRS 2:43B, the subsidiary accounts for this as a cash-settled share-based payment arrangement.

The accounting by the subsidiary depends upon (1) whether it purchases the shares at the vesting date or at an earlier date, and (2) if it purchases the shares before the vesting date, whether the subsidiary applies IFRS 9 *Financial Instruments* or IAS 39 *Financial Instruments: Recognition and Measurement* in accounting for its financial instruments.

Subsidiary purchases shares at the vesting date

When the subsidiary purchases the required shares in the market at the vesting date, the price paid for the shares (less any exercise price paid by the employees) is usually the same as the liability already recognised, so that no gain or loss arises on settlement. The subsidiary is not required to recognise any movements in equity arising from the arrangements because it has not issued any equity instruments and it has not received any capital contribution from its parent.

When the parent issues the required shares to the subsidiary at the vesting date at market price, from the subsidiary's perspective this is no different from purchasing shares in the market, and the treatment described in the previous paragraph is appropriate. The parent should recognise an issue of shares for full consideration in the usual manner.

When the parent issues the required shares to the subsidiary at the vesting date for no consideration, or for consideration lower than market price, the difference between the consideration paid and market value represents a capital contribution from the parent to the subsidiary and does not result in any change to the expense recognised under IFRS 2.

Subsidiary purchases shares prior to the vesting date and applies IFRS 9

If a subsidiary purchases and holds shares in its parent, they are recognised and measured as financial assets in the individual financial statements of the

---

subsidiary even though they are treated as treasury shares in the consolidated financial statements of the parent. Under IFRS 9, the shares will either be classified as at fair value through profit or loss (FVTPL) (which is the default category) or designated as at fair value through other comprehensive income (FVTOCI).

Under either classification, the carrying amount of the shares at the vesting date (less any exercise price paid by the employees) is usually the same as the liability already recognised, so that no gain or loss will arise on settlement (when assets are designated as at FVTOCI under IFRS 9, the cumulative gains or losses accumulated in other comprehensive income are not reclassified to profit or loss on disposal).

Subsidiary purchases shares prior to the vesting date and applies IAS 39

Under IAS 39 (for entities that have not yet adopted IFRS 9), in the subsidiary's financial statements, the shares are either classified as available for sale (AFS) (which is the default category) or designated as at FVTPL if the relevant requirements of IAS 39 are met.

Under IAS 39, one of the circumstances in which an asset may be designated as at FVTPL is when the designation results in more relevant information because it eliminates or significantly reduces a measurement or recognition inconsistency (sometimes referred to as 'an accounting mismatch') that would otherwise arise from measuring the assets or liabilities, or recognising the gains and losses on them, on different bases. The determination as to whether designation as at FVTPL eliminates or significantly reduces an accounting mismatch should be based on a careful analysis of the specific facts and circumstances in each case.

When shares are classified as at FVTPL, the carrying amount of the shares at the vesting date (less any exercise price paid by the employees) is usually the same as the liability already recognised, so that no gain or loss arises on settlement.

When the shares are classified as AFS, although the carrying amount of the shares at the vesting date (less any exercise price paid by the employees) is usually the same as the liability already recognised, a gain or loss may arise on settlement because the cumulative gains or losses previously recognised in other comprehensive income are reclassified to profit or loss on disposal (i.e. when the shares are delivered to employees). The shares cannot be designated as a hedging instrument in a hedge of the share-based payment obligation.

8.7.1 Hedge accounting under IAS 39

Although 'economic hedges' can be achieved for some share-based arrangements, as described at **8.7** above, IAS 39 sets out detailed rules on hedge accounting, including which items can be hedged and which instruments can qualify as hedging instruments.

Under IAS 39, it is not possible to apply hedge accounting to an equity-settled share-based payment arrangement because that Standard prohibits own equity as a hedged item.

Although a liability recognised under a cash-settled share-based payment arrangement can qualify as a hedged item, it is important to note that the subsidiary cannot designate shares in its parent (whether held directly or via an employee share trust) as a hedging instrument. Instead of purchasing the shares of the parent before the vesting date, a subsidiary might consider purchasing options over its parent's shares and designating them as a hedging instrument in hedging the forecast employee expense. However, it will still need to meet the detailed requirements of IAS 39 in order to achieve hedge accounting, including those relating to effectiveness.

9   Employee share ownership plans (ESOPs)

9.1   Background

ESOP trusts, created by a sponsoring entity for employees, are designed to facilitate employee shareholding and are often used as vehicles for distributing shares to employees under remuneration schemes. The detailed structures of individual trusts are many and varied, as are the reasons for establishing them.

Reasons for establishing ESOPs include the following (although it should be noted that some of these are not permitted in some jurisdictions):

- to fund a matching programme for a sponsor's defined contribution plan or other employee benefits;

- to raise new capital or to create a marketplace for existing shares;

- to replace lost benefits from the termination of other employee benefit plans or to provide benefits under post-retirement plans (particularly medical benefits);

- to be part of the financing package in leveraged buy-outs;

- to provide tax-advantaged means for owners to terminate ownership;

- to be part of a long-term programme to restructure the equity section of a sponsor's statement of financial position; and

- to defend the entity against a hostile takeover.

ESOPs can be leveraged or non-leveraged. In a leveraged ESOP, the plan borrows money to purchase shares, usually guaranteed by the sponsor.

9.2   Accounting requirements

The IFRIC (now the IFRS Interpretations Committee) was asked by the IASB to consider whether the scope exclusion in SIC-12 *Consolidation – Special Purpose Entities* (see **appendix A1**) for equity compensation plans should be removed when IFRS 2 became effective. Prior to IFRS 2 becoming effective, these plans were within the scope of IAS 19 *Employee Benefits*, although the Standard did not specify any recognition and measurement requirements for such benefits. Once IFRS 2 became effective, IAS 19 no longer applied to equity compensation plans. Also, IFRS 2 amended IAS 32 *Financial Instruments: Presentation* so that its requirement to deduct treasury shares from equity also applies to shares purchased, sold, issued or cancelled in connection with employee share option plans, employee share purchase plans and all other share-based payment arrangements.

The IFRIC concluded that, to ensure consistency with IFRS 2 and IAS 32, the scope of SIC-12 should be amended to remove the scope exclusion for equity compensation plans. This proposal was approved and issued in final form in November 2004. The amendment was effective for annual periods beginning on or after 1 January 2005 (i.e. the same as IFRS 2). The Press Release issued by the IASB on publication of the amendment commented that, as a consequence of the amendment "an entity that controls an employee benefit trust (or similar entity) set up for the purposes of a share-based payment arrangement will be required to consolidate that trust".

These considerations were not revisited in the development of IFRS 10 *Consolidated Financial Statements* and that Standard includes no scope exemption for ESOP trusts. Accordingly, entities that have adopted IFRS 10 will need to consider whether an ESOP trust is controlled under the definition of that term in IFRS 10:7 (see **section 5** of **chapter A24**).

When considering the amendment to SIC-12 to remove the exemption for equity compensation plans, the IFRIC noted that there were further issues about such arrangements that might be considered. These included the question of whether the arrangements should be accounted for by consolidation or by inclusion in the separate financial statements of the sponsoring entity. However, this matter is not on the IFRS Interpretations Committee's current agenda and, in the absence of further clarification from the Committee, it is reasonable to assume that, at least in some circumstances, accounting for trust assets and liabilities may be required only in the consolidated financial statements (see also the discussion below and at **4.6** in **chapter A29** – or, for entities that have not yet adopted IFRS 10, at **3.3.2** in **appendix A1**).

Trusts created by a sponsoring entity for employees are designed to facilitate employee shareholdings and often used as vehicles for distributing shares to employees under remuneration schemes. The sponsoring entity must consolidate a trust if the sponsoring entity has control over it. As noted above, the primary criteria for determining whether the entity has control over an employee share trust are set out in IFRS 10 (or, for entities that have not yet adopted IFRS 10, in IAS 27(2008) *Consolidated and Separate Financial Statements* and SIC-12). In addition to those factors, the following indicators may also provide evidence of control over the trust. However, no one factor, or the absence of one factor, is a determinant of control, or absence of control, without a complete analysis of all the relevant facts and circumstances.

Indicators of control may include:

- the trust is designed to serve the purposes of the sponsoring entity – that is, to compensate the sponsoring entity's employees;

- the sponsoring entity appoints trustees to the trust;

- trustees usually act on advice from the sponsoring entity, e.g. letters of wishes indicating how funds of the trust might be allocated;

- the assets of the trust can be recaptured by the sponsoring entity or its creditors (e.g. in a bankruptcy situation);

- the liabilities of the trust are guaranteed by the sponsoring entity;

- the assets of the trust revert to the sponsoring entity if shares do not vest;

- the sponsoring entity determines the level of future funding to the trust;

- the sponsoring entity has a practice of buying shares from the trust (instead of requiring the trust to sell the shares on the market to be able to pay an employee who wishes to exercise his/her right);

- the sponsoring entity determines the allocation of shares to employees;

- the sponsoring entity provides guarantees (or other contracts) to protect the trust from liquidity risks;

- at the end of the life of the trust, any surplus in the trust is to be paid to the entity, and any shortfall owing to the entity will constitute a loss by it (or the subsidiaries);

- if the trust makes any profit during a year (with its portfolio), this profit is ceded to the sponsoring entity; and

- the sponsoring entity guarantees a minimum value of the shares.

When a sponsoring entity has control, the assets, liabilities and treasury shares should be recognised in the consolidated financial statements, and:

- consideration paid or received for the purchase or sale of the entity's own shares in a trust should be shown as separate amounts in the statement of changes in equity;

- no gain or loss should be recognised in profit or loss on purchase, sale, issue or cancellation of the entity's own shares;

- finance costs and any administration expenses should be recognised as they accrue and not as funding payments are made to the trust; and

- any dividend income on the entity's own shares should be excluded in determining profit before tax and deducted from the aggregate of dividends paid and proposed.

Sufficient information should be disclosed in the financial statements of the sponsoring entity to enable readers to understand the significance of the trust in the context of the sponsoring entity.

9.3   Identification of sponsoring entity

As explained at **9.2** above, in some cases it will be appropriate to account for the assets and liabilities of an employee share trust in the separate financial statement of the sponsoring entity. However, it is not always straightforward to determine which entity within a group is the sponsoring entity.

If an employee share trust is set up to hold shares that will be used to settle share awards granted by a particular entity, it is likely that the entity that has the obligation to the employees will be the sponsoring entity of the trust because that is the entity that needs to acquire the shares to meet its obligations. **Section 8.2.3** above provides guidance on the factors to consider in determining which entity has this obligation.

When a parent makes a share award to the employees of its subsidiary, the parent has the obligation to settle the share award. When this is the case, it is unlikely to be appropriate to treat the subsidiary as the sponsoring employer of a trust set up to hold shares to settle the share awards because, as discussed at **4.6** in **chapter A29** (or, for entities that have not yet adopted IFRS 10, at **3.3.2** in **appendix A1**), this would result in recognition of the shares as an asset on the statement of financial position but there would be no corresponding obligation to settle the share awards. However, each situation will require judgement based on the particular facts.

9.4   Presentation of movements in equity relating to ESOP trust

This section considers the accounting entries that may be required within equity in the consolidated financial statements when an entity's own shares are held by an ESOP trust that is consolidated by the entity. From the perspective of the consolidated financial statements (and entity-only financial statements when a 'look-through' approach is applied (see **4.6** in **chapter A29** or, for entities that have not yet adopted IFRS 10, **3.3.2** in **appendix A1**)), such shares are 'treasury shares' and are deducted from equity in accordance with IAS 32:33. IAS 32:34 states that the amount of treasury shares held should be disclosed separately either in the statement of financial position or in the notes. This can be done either by presenting treasury shares as a separate component of equity or by including the deduction from equity within another component of equity, for example within retained earnings (disclosed by way of note). It may be clearer to present a separate component of equity when the amount is material.

Example 9.4

Presentation of movements in equity relating to ESOP trusts

For the purposes of the following illustration, it is assumed that a separate ESOP reserve is maintained.

When shares are purchased in the market by an ESOP trust, they will initially be recognised as a debit to the ESOP reserve for the price paid. For example, suppose that the price paid is CU1,000.

	CU	CU
Dr ESOP reserve	1,000	
Cr Cash		1,000

To recognise the acquisition of shares for cash.

Exercise price is lower than price paid by the ESOP

If options are subsequently granted over those shares with an exercise price of CU800, the following entry will generally be required when the share options are exercised.

	CU	CU
Dr Cash	800	
Dr Equity	200	
Cr ESOP reserve		1,000

To remove balance from ESOP reserve when options are exercised.

This is because it is illogical to leave a balance on the ESOP reserve which relates to shares that are no longer held. The difference between the price paid by the ESOP to purchase the shares initially and the amount received when the shares are reissued upon exercise of the options must be recognised in equity and retained earnings may be an appropriate caption.

Exercise price is higher than price paid by the ESOP

If options are subsequently granted over those shares with an exercise price of CU1,300, the following entry will generally be required when the share options are exercised.

		CU	CU
Dr	Cash	1,300	
Cr	ESOP reserve		1,000
Cr	Equity		300

To remove balance from ESOP reserve when options are exercised.

Any excess of the amount received upon exercise of the options over the price paid by the ESOP to purchase the shares initially is accounted for directly in equity, for example in retained earnings or another part of equity specified by local law and regulations.

Note that this example does not deal with the accounting entries in equity that may be required by IFRS 2. These are discussed at **4.1.2** above. They will generally involve a credit to equity equal to the expense recognised. Whether this credit is recognised in retained earnings or as a separate reserve will depend on the entity's accounting policy.

When recognising the IFRS 2 expense, it may be tempting to recognise the credit entry in the ESOP reserve when one exists and the options are to be satisfied by using the shares held by the trust. However, in practice, this does not generally make sense. The credit entry is based on the fair value at grant date and is unlikely to coincide with the difference between the purchase price of the shares by the trust and the option exercise price (if any). Therefore, recognising the credit entry in the ESOP reserve would likely result in an ESOP reserve balance that is not meaningful because it represents neither the cost of treasury shares held by the trust nor the value of the IFRS 2 expense. In an ESOP arrangement, it is, therefore, generally preferable for the credit entry arising from IFRS 2 and the effects of any purchase of own shares through the ESOP trust to be considered separately.

9.5   Accounting for share awards settled via an employee trust

---

Example 9.5

Accounting for share awards settled via an employee trust

A trust is created by a sponsoring entity, Company P, which is a listed entity. The trust is designed to facilitate shareholding by employees and is used to distribute shares in Company P to its employees under its share-based payment arrangements.

The trust may be funded in a number of ways and may also obtain shares in Company P in a number of ways. For example, the trust may receive a loan from Company P with which it may either subscribe for new shares in Company P or purchase shares in Company P in the market. Alternatively, the trust may finance subscription for, or purchase of, shares in Company P by raising a third-party loan guaranteed by Company P.

The trust purchases 100 shares in Company P for CU10,000. At the same time, Company P grants 100 shares to 10 of its employees under a share-based payment arrangement; the principal terms of the arrangement are that each employee will be granted 10 shares conditional on completing three years of service. At the end of the three-year vesting period, the employees can elect to either receive the shares or to receive cash equal to the fair value of the shares at that time. When an employee exercises the option to receive cash, the trust may either sell the shares in Company P or it may obtain funding in order to settle Company P's share-based payment arrangement with the employees on Company P's behalf.

How should Company P and the trust account for this arrangement in their separate financial statements?

(This example does not consider the accounting for the transaction to finance the purchase of the shares.)

Company P

In Company P's separate financial statements, the substance is a share-based payment arrangement for employees with a cash alternative (i.e. the entity has granted a compound financial instrument).

IFRS 2 will be applied in the usual way to determine the expense to be recognised in Company P's profit or loss; the fact that a trust has been established to facilitate settlement of Company P's commitment does not alter the accounting under IFRS 2.

The fair value of the liability component of the compound instrument should be determined first, and then the equity component should be measured at fair value, taking into account the fact that the employee must forfeit the right to receive cash in order to receive the equity instrument (see IFRS 2:37).

In this scenario, the value of the equity component would be nil and, as a consequence, the transaction would be accounted for in the same way as a cash-settled share-based payment up to the date of exercise (see also **example 6.1**).

Depending on the nature of the trust, it may be appropriate for Company P to account for its investment in the trust as a subsidiary or to adopt a 'look-through' approach (i.e. accounting for the trust as, in substance, an extension of itself). For further guidance, see the discussion at **4.6** in **chapter A29** or, for entities that have not yet adopted IFRS 10, at **3.3.2** in **appendix A1**.

Trust

The shares in Company P are recognised as an asset (as noted above, financing of this acquisition is ignored in this example).

The trust does not recognise a liability in respect of the share-based payment arrangement because it is not the employing entity and does not receive the benefit of the employee services and it does not have the obligation to the employees (i.e. the trust settles the award on Company P's behalf).

10   Future developments

In May 2012, the IASB issued an exposure draft (ED/2012/1 *Annual Improvements to IFRSs 2010–2012 Cycle*) proposing changes to a number of Standards as part of its Annual Improvements project. Amendments are proposed for IFRS 2 to amend the definition of 'vesting conditions' by separately defining a 'service condition' and a 'performance condition' to make the description of each condition clearer (see **4.1** above). The proposals clarify that:

- a performance target should relate either to the performance of the entity as a whole or to some part of the entity (e.g. a division or an individual employee);

- a performance target is defined by reference to the entity's operations (or activities) or the price (or value) of its equity instruments;

- in order to constitute a performance condition, a performance target needs to have an explicit or implicit service requirement which substantially coincides with the period during which the performance target is being measured. The assessment period for the performance target may start before the service period but may not extend beyond the end of the service period; and

- if an employee fails to complete a specified service period, this constitutes a failure to satisfy a service condition, regardless of the reason for that failure.

The amendments are proposed to ensure consistent classification of conditions of share-based payments and to address a number of concerns raised about the current definitions including:

- the correlation between an employee's responsibility and a performance target;

- whether a share market index target would meet the definition of a performance condition or a non-vesting condition;

- whether a performance target that refers to a longer period than the required service period may constitute a performance condition; and

- whether the employee's failure to complete a required service period is considered to be a failure to satisfy a service condition.

Finalised amendments are expected in the fourth quarter of 2013.